Learning Python

FOURTH EDITION

Learning Python

Mark Lutz

O'REILLY®

Beijing · Cambridge · Farnham · Köln · Sebastopol · Tokyo

Learning Python, Fourth Edition
by Mark Lutz

Published by O'Reilly Media, Inc., 1005 Gravenstein Highway North, Sebastopol, CA 95472.

O'Reilly books may be purchased for educational, business, or sales promotional use. Online editions are also available for most titles (*http://my.safaribooksonline.com*). For more information, contact our corporate/institutional sales department: (800) 998-9938 or *corporate@oreilly.com*.

Editor: Julie Steele	**Indexer:** John Bickelhaupt	
Production Editor: Sumita Mukherji	**Cover Designer:** Karen Montgomery	
Copyeditor: Rachel Head	**Interior Designer:** David Futato	
Production Services: Newgen North America	**Illustrator:** Robert Romano	

March 1999:	First Edition.
December 2003:	Second Edition.
October 2007:	Third Edition.
September 2009:	Fourth Edition.

Revision History for the First Edition:

See *http://oreilly.com/catalog/errata.csp?isbn=9780596158064* for release details.

ISBN: 978-0-596-15806-4

[QGT]   [2011-11-04]

1320345638

To Vera.
You are my life.

Table of Contents

Part III. Statements and Syntax

Part V. Modules

Part VI. Classes and OOP

29. Operator Overloading

Part VII.   Exceptions and Tools

Part VIII. Advanced Topics

Preface

This book provides an introduction to the Python programming language. *Python* is a popular open source programming language used for both standalone programs and scripting applications in a wide variety of domains. It is free, portable, powerful, and remarkably easy and fun to use. Programmers from every corner of the software industry have found Python's focus on developer productivity and software quality to be a strategic advantage in projects both large and small.

Whether you are new to programming or are a professional developer, this book's goal is to bring you quickly up to speed on the fundamentals of the core Python language. After reading this book, you will know enough about Python to apply it in whatever application domains you choose to explore.

By design, this book is a tutorial that focuses on the *core Python language* itself, rather than specific applications of it. As such, it's intended to serve as the first in a two-volume set:

- *Learning Python*, this book, teaches Python itself.
- *Programming Python*, among others, shows what you can do with Python after you've learned it.

That is, applications-focused books such as *Programming Python* pick up where this book leaves off, exploring Python's role in common domains such as the Web, graphical user interfaces (GUIs), and databases. In addition, the book *Python Pocket Reference* provides additional reference materials not included here, and it is designed to supplement this book.

Because of this book's foundations focus, though, it is able to present Python fundamentals with more depth than many programmers see when first learning the language. And because it's based upon a three-day Python training class with quizzes and exercises throughout, this book serves as a self-paced introduction to the language.

About This Fourth Edition

This fourth edition of this book has changed in three ways. This edition:

- Covers both Python 3.0 and Python 2.6—it emphasizes 3.0, but notes differences in 2.6
- Includes a set of new chapters mainly targeted at advanced core-language topics
- Reorganizes some existing material and expands it with new examples for clarity

As I write this edition in 2009, Python comes in two flavors—version 3.0 is an emerging and incompatible mutation of the language, and 2.6 retains backward compatibility with the vast body of existing Python code. Although Python 3 is viewed as the future of Python, Python 2 is still widely used and will be supported in parallel with Python 3 for years to come. While 3.0 is largely the same language, it runs almost no code written for prior releases (the mutation of `print` from statement to function alone, aesthetically sound as it may be, breaks nearly every Python program ever written).

This split presents a bit of a dilemma for both programmers and book authors. While it would be easier for a book to pretend that Python 2 never existed and cover 3 only, this would not address the needs of the large Python user base that exists today. A vast amount of existing code was written for Python 2, and it won't be going away any time soon. And while newcomers to the language can focus on Python 3, anyone who must use code written in the past needs to keep one foot in the Python 2 world today. Since it may be years before all third-party libraries and extensions are ported to Python 3, this fork might not be entirely temporary.

Coverage for Both 3.0 and 2.6

To address this dichotomy and to meet the needs of all potential readers, this edition of this book has been updated to cover *both* Python 3.0 and Python 2.6 (and later releases in the 3.X and 2.X lines). It's intended for programmers using Python 2, programmers using Python 3, and programmers stuck somewhere between the two.

That is, you can use this book to learn either Python line. Although the focus here is on 3.0 primarily, 2.6 differences and tools are also noted along the way for programmers using older code. While the two versions are largely the same, they diverge in some important ways, and I'll point these out along the way.

For instance, I'll use 3.0 `print` calls in most examples, but will describe the 2.6 `print` statement, too, so you can make sense of earlier code. I'll also freely introduce new features, such as the `nonlocal` statement in 3.0 and the string `format` method in 2.6 and 3.0, and will point out when such extensions are not present in older Pythons.

If you are learning Python for the first time and don't need to use any legacy code, I encourage you to begin with Python 3.0; it cleans up some longstanding warts in the language, while retaining all the original core ideas and adding some nice new tools.

Many popular Python libraries and tools will likely be available for Python 3.0 by the time you read these words, especially given the file I/O performance improvements expected in the upcoming 3.1 release. If you are using a system based on Python 2.X, however, you'll find that this book addresses your concerns, too, and will help you migrate to 3.0 in the future.

By proxy, this edition addresses other Python version 2 and 3 releases as well, though some older version 2.X code may not be able to run all the examples here. Although class decorators are available in both Python 2.6 and 3.0, for example, you cannot use them in an older Python 2.X that did not yet have this feature. See Tables P-1 and P-2 later in this Preface for summaries of 2.6 and 3.0 changes.

Shortly before going to press, this book was also augmented with notes about prominent extensions in the upcoming Python 3.1 release—comma separators and automatic field numbering in string `format` method calls, multiple context manager syntax in `with` statements, new methods for numbers, and so on. Because Python 3.1 was targeted primarily at optimization, this book applies directly to this new release as well. In fact, because Python 3.1 supersedes 3.0, and because the latest Python is usually the best Python to fetch and use anyhow, in this book the term "Python 3.0" generally refers to the language variations introduced by Python 3.0 but that are present in the entire 3.X line.

New Chapters

Although the main purpose of this edition is to update the examples and material from the preceding edition for 3.0 and 2.6, I've also added five new chapters to address new topics and add context:

- Chapter 27 is a new class tutorial, using a more realistic example to explore the basics of Python object-oriented programming (OOP).
- Chapter 36 provides details on Unicode and byte strings and outlines string and file differences between 3.0 and 2.6.
- Chapter 37 collects managed attribute tools such as properties and provides new coverage of descriptors.
- Chapter 38 presents function and class decorators and works through comprehensive examples.
- Chapter 39 covers metaclasses and compares and contrasts them with decorators.

The first of these chapters provides a gradual, step-by-step tutorial for using classes and OOP in Python. It's based upon a live demonstration I have been using in recent years in the training classes I teach, but has been honed here for use in a book. The chapter is designed to show OOP in a more realistic context than earlier examples and to illustrate how class concepts come together into larger, working programs. I hope it works as well here as it has in live classes.

The last four of these new chapters are collected in a new final part of the book, "Advanced Topics." Although these are technically core language topics, not every Python programmer needs to delve into the details of Unicode text or metaclasses. Because of this, these four chapters have been separated out into this new part, and are officially *optional reading*. The details of Unicode and binary data strings, for example, have been moved to this final part because most programmers use simple ASCII strings and don't need to know about these topics. Similarly, decorators and metaclasses are specialist topics that are usually of more interest to API builders than application programmers.

If you do use such tools, though, or use code that does, these new advanced topic chapters should help you master the basics. In addition, these chapters' examples include case studies that tie core language concepts together, and they are more substantial than those in most of the rest of the book. Because this new part is optional reading, it has end-of-chapter quizzes but no end-of-part exercises.

Changes to Existing Material

In addition, some material from the prior edition has been *reorganized*, or supplemented with *new examples*. Multiple inheritance, for instance, gets a new case study example that lists class trees in Chapter 30; new examples for generators that manually implement map and zip are provided in Chapter 20; static and class methods are illustrated by new code in Chapter 31; package relative imports are captured in action in Chapter 23; and the __contains__, __bool__, and __index__ operator overloading methods are illustrated by example now as well in Chapter 29, along with the new overloading protocols for slicing and comparison.

This edition also incorporates some reorganization for clarity. For instance, to accommodate new material and topics, and to avoid chapter topic overload, five prior chapters have been split into two each here. The result is new standalone chapters on operator overloading, scopes and arguments, exception statement details, and comprehension and iteration topics. Some reordering has been done within the existing chapters as well, to improve topic flow.

This edition also tries to minimize forward references with some reordering, though Python 3.0's changes make this impossible in some cases: to understand printing and the string format method, you now must know keyword arguments for functions; to understand dictionary key lists and key tests, you must now know iteration; to use exec to run code, you need to be able to use file objects; and so on. A linear reading still probably makes the most sense, but some topics may require nonlinear jumps and random lookups.

All told, there have been hundreds of changes in this edition. The next section's tables alone document 27 additions and 57 changes in Python. In fact, it's fair to say that this edition is somewhat more advanced, because Python is somewhat more advanced. As for Python 3.0 itself, though, you're probably better off discovering most of this book's changes for yourself, rather than reading about them further in this Preface.

Specific Language Extensions in 2.6 and 3.0

In general, Python 3.0 is a *cleaner* language, but it is also in some ways a more *sophisticated* language. In fact, some of its changes seem to assume you must already know Python in order to learn Python! The prior section outlined some of the more prominent circular knowledge dependencies in 3.0; as a random example, the rationale for wrapping dictionary views in a `list` call is incredibly subtle and requires substantial fore-knowledge. Besides teaching Python fundamentals, this book serves to help bridge this knowledge gap.

Table P-1 lists the most prominent new language features covered in this edition, along with the primary chapters in which they appear.

Table P-1. Extensions in Python 2.6 and 3.0

Extension	Covered in chapter(s)
The `print` function in 3.0	11
The `nonlocal x,y` statement in 3.0	17
The `str.format` method in 2.6 and 3.0	7
String types in 3.0: `str` for Unicode text, `bytes` for binary data	7, 36
Text and binary file distinctions in 3.0	9, 36
Class decorators in 2.6 and 3.0: `@private('age')`	31, 38
New iterators in 3.0: `range`, `map`, `zip`	14, 20
Dictionary views in 3.0: `D.keys`, `D.values`, `D.items`	8, 14
Division operators in 3.0: remainders, `/` and `//`	5
Set literals in 3.0: `{a, b, c}`	5
Set comprehensions in 3.0: `{x**2 for x in seq}`	4, 5, 14, 20
Dictionary comprehensions in 3.0: `{x: x**2 for x in seq}`	4, 8, 14, 20
Binary digit-string support in 2.6 and 3.0: `0b0101`, `bin(I)`	5
The fraction number type in 2.6 and 3.0: `Fraction(1, 3)`	5
Function annotations in 3.0: `def f(a:99, b:str)->int`	19
Keyword-only arguments in 3.0: `def f(a, *b, c, **d)`	18, 20
Extended sequence unpacking in 3.0: `a, *b = seq`	11, 13
Relative import syntax for packages enabled in 3.0: `from .`	23
Context managers enabled in 2.6 and 3.0: `with/as`	33, 35
Exception syntax changes in 3.0: `raise`, `except/as`, superclass	33, 34

Extension	Covered in chapter(s)
Exception chaining in 3.0: `raise e2 from e1`	33
Reserved word changes in 2.6 and 3.0	11
New-style class cutover in 3.0	31
Property decorators in 2.6 and 3.0: `@property`	37
Descriptor use in 2.6 and 3.0	31, 38
Metaclass use in 2.6 and 3.0	31, 39
Abstract base classes support in 2.6 and 3.0	28

Specific Language Removals in 3.0

In addition to extensions, a number of language tools have been removed in 3.0 in an effort to clean up its design. Table P-2 summarizes the changes that impact this book, covered in various chapters of this edition. Many of the removals listed in Table P-2 have direct replacements, some of which are also available in 2.6 to support future migration to 3.0.

Table P-2. Removals in Python 3.0 that impact this book

Removed	Replacement	Covered in chapter(s)
`reload(M)`	`imp.reload(M)` (or exec)	3, 22
`apply(f, ps, ks)`	`f(*ps, **ks)`	18
`` `X` ``	`repr(X)`	5
`X <> Y`	`X != Y`	5
`long`	`int`	5
`9999L`	`9999`	5
`D.has_key(K)`	`K in D` (or `D.get(key) != None`)	8
`raw_input`	`input`	3, 10
old `input`	`eval(input())`	3
`xrange`	`range`	14
`file`	`open` (and io module classes)	9
`X.next`	`X.__next__`, called by `next(X)`	14, 20, 29
`X.__getslice__`	`X.__getitem__` passed a slice object	7, 29
`X.__setslice__`	`X.__setitem__` passed a slice object	7, 29
`reduce`	`functools.reduce` (or loop code)	14, 19
`execfile(filename)`	`exec(open(filename).read())`	3
`exec open(filename)`	`exec(open(filename).read())`	3
`0777`	`0o777`	5
`print x, y`	`print(x, y)`	11

Removed	Replacement	Covered in chapter(s)
`print >> F, x, y`	`print(x, y, file=F)`	11
`print x, y,`	`print(x, y, end=' ')`	11
`u'ccc'`	`'ccc'`	7, 36
`'bbb'` for byte strings	`b'bbb'`	7, 9, 36
`raise E, V`	`raise E(V)`	32, 33, 34
`except E, X:`	`except E as X:`	32, 33, 34
`def f((a, b)):`	`def f(x): (a, b) = x`	11, 18, 20
`file.xreadlines`	`for line in file:` (or `X=iter(file)`)	13, 14
`D.keys()`, etc. as lists	`list(D.keys())` (dictionary views)	8, 14
`map()`, `range()`, etc. as lists	`list(map())`, `list(range())` (built-ins)	14
`map(None, ...)`	`zip` (or manual code to pad results)	13, 20
`X=D.keys(); X.sort()`	`sorted(D)` (or `list(D.keys())`)	4, 8, 14
`cmp(x, y)`	`(x > y) - (x < y)`	29
`X.__cmp__(y)`	`__lt__`, `__gt__`, `__eq__`, etc.	29
`X.__nonzero__`	`X.__bool__`	29
`X.__hex__`, `X.__oct__`	`X.__index__`	29
Sort comparison functions	Use `key=transform` or `reverse=True`	8
Dictionary `<, >, <=, >=`	Compare `sorted(D.items())` (or loop code)	8, 9
`types.ListType`	`list` (`types` is for nonbuilt-in names only)	9
`__metaclass__ = M`	`class C(metaclass=M):`	28, 31, 39
`__builtin__`	`builtins` (renamed)	17
`Tkinter`	`tkinter` (renamed)	18, 19, 24, 29, 30
`sys.exc_type, exc_value`	`sys.exc_info()[0], [1]`	34, 35
`function.func_code`	`function.__code__`	19, 38
`__getattr__` run by built-ins	Redefine `__X__` methods in wrapper classes	30, 37, 38
`-t, -tt` command-line switches	Inconsistent tabs/spaces use is always an error	10, 12
`from ... *`, within a function	May only appear at the top level of a file	22
`import mod`, in same package	`from . import mod`, package-relative form	23
`class MyException:`	`class MyException(Exception):`	34
`exceptions` module	Built-in scope, library manual	34
`thread, Queue` modules	`_thread, queue` (both renamed)	17
`anydbm` module	`dbm` (renamed)	27
`cPickle` module	`_pickle` (renamed, used automatically)	9
`os.popen2/3/4`	`subprocess.Popen` (`os.popen` retained)	14
String-based exceptions	Class-based exceptions (also required in 2.6)	32, 33, 34

Removed	Replacement	Covered in chapter(s)
String module functions	String object methods	7
Unbound methods	Functions (`staticmethod` to call via instance)	30, 31
Mixed type comparisons, sorts	Nonnumeric mixed type comparisons are errors	5, 9

There are additional changes in Python 3.0 that are not listed in this table, simply because they don't affect this book. Changes in the standard library, for instance, might have a larger impact on applications-focused books like *Programming Python* than they do here; although most standard library functionality is still present, Python 3.0 takes further liberties with renaming modules, grouping them into packages, and so on. For a more comprehensive list of changes in 3.0, see the "What's New in Python 3.0" document in Python's standard manual set.

If you are migrating from Python 2.X to Python 3.X, be sure to also see the *2to3* automatic code conversion script that is available with Python 3.0. It can't translate everything, but it does a reasonable job of converting the majority of 2.X code to run under 3.X. As I write this, a new *3to2* back-conversion project is also underway to translate Python 3.X code to run in 2.X environments. Either tool may prove useful if you must maintain code for both Python lines; see the Web for details.

Because this fourth edition is mostly a fairly straightforward update for 3.0 with a handful of new chapters, and because it's only been two years since the prior edition was published, the rest of this Preface is taken from the prior edition with only minor updating.

About The Third Edition

In the four years between the publication of the second and third editions of this book there were substantial changes in Python itself, and in the topics I presented in Python training sessions. The third edition reflected these changes, and also incorporated a handful of structural changes.

The Third Edition's Python Language Changes

On the language front, the third edition was thoroughly updated to reflect Python 2.5 and all changes to the language since the publication of the second edition in late 2003. (The second edition was based largely on Python 2.2, with some 2.3 features grafted on at the end of the project.) In addition, discussions of anticipated changes in the upcoming Python 3.0 release were incorporated where appropriate. Here are some of the major language topics for which new or expanded coverage was provided (chapter numbers here have been updated to reflect the fourth edition):

- The new `B if A else C` conditional expression (Chapter 19)
- `with/as` context managers (Chapter 33)
- `try/except/finally` unification (Chapter 33)
- Relative import syntax (Chapter 23)
- Generator expressions (Chapter 20)
- New generator function features (Chapter 20)
- Function decorators (Chapter 31)
- The set object type (Chapter 5)
- New built-in functions: `sorted`, `sum`, `any`, `all`, `enumerate` (Chapters 13 and 14)
- The decimal fixed-precision object type (Chapter 5)
- Files, list comprehensions, and iterators (Chapters 14 and 20)
- New development tools: Eclipse, `distutils`, `unittest` and `doctest`, IDLE enhancements, Shedskin, and so on (Chapters 2 and 35)

Smaller language changes (for instance, the widespread use of `True` and `False`; the new `sys.exc_info` for fetching exception details; and the demise of string-based exceptions, string methods, and the `apply` and `reduce` built-ins) are discussed throughout the book. The third edition also expanded coverage of some of the features that were new in the second edition, including three-limit slices and the arbitrary arguments call syntax that subsumed `apply`.

The Third Edition's Python Training Changes

Besides such language changes, the third edition was augmented with new topics and examples presented in my Python training sessions. Changes included (chapter numbers again updated to reflect those in the fourth edition):

- A new chapter introducing built-in types (Chapter 4)
- A new chapter introducing statement syntax (Chapter 10)
- A new full chapter on dynamic typing, with enhanced coverage (Chapter 6)
- An expanded OOP introduction (Chapter 25)
- New examples for files, scopes, statement nesting, classes, exceptions, and more

Many additions and changes were made with Python beginners in mind, and some topics were moved to appear at the places where they proved simplest to digest in training classes. List comprehensions and iterators, for example, now make their initial appearance in conjunction with the `for` loop statement, instead of later with functional tools.

Coverage of many original core language topics also was substantially expanded in the third edition, with new discussions and examples added. Because this text has become something of a de facto standard resource for learning the core Python language, the presentation was made more complete and augmented with new use cases throughout.

In addition, a new set of Python tips and tricks, gleaned from 10 years of teaching classes and 15 years of using Python for real work, was incorporated, and the exercises were updated and expanded to reflect current Python best practices, new language features, and common beginners' mistakes witnessed firsthand in classes. Overall, the core language coverage was expanded.

The Third Edition's Structural Changes

Because the material was more complete, it was split into bite-sized chunks. The core language material was organized into many multichapter parts to make it easier to tackle. Types and statements, for instance, are now two top-level parts, with one chapter for each major type and statement topic. Exercises and "gotchas" (common mistakes) were also moved from chapter ends to part ends, appearing at the end of the last chapter in each part.

In the third edition, I also augmented the end-of-part exercises with end-of-chapter summaries and end-of-chapter quizzes to help you review chapters as you complete them. Each chapter concludes with a set of questions to help you review and test your understanding of the chapter's material. Unlike the end-of-part exercises, whose solutions are presented in Appendix B, the solutions to the end-of-chapter quizzes appear immediately after the questions; I encourage you to look at the solutions even if you're sure you've answered the questions correctly because the answers are a sort of review in themselves.

Despite all the new topics, the book is still oriented toward Python newcomers and is designed to be a first Python text for programmers. Because it is largely based on time-tested training experience and materials, it can still serve as a self-paced introductory Python class.

The Third Edition's Scope Changes

As of its third edition, this book is intended as a tutorial on the core Python language, and nothing else. It's about learning the language in an in-depth fashion, before applying it in application-level programming. The presentation here is bottom-up and gradual, but it provides a complete look at the entire language, in isolation from its application roles.

For some, "learning Python" involves spending an hour or two going through a tutorial on the Web. This works for already advanced programmers, up to a point; Python is, after all, relatively simple in comparison to other languages. The problem with this fast-track approach is that its practitioners eventually stumble onto unusual cases and get stuck—variables change out from under them, mutable default arguments mutate inexplicably, and so on. The goal here is instead to provide a solid grounding in Python fundamentals, so that even the unusual cases will make sense when they crop up.

This scope is deliberate. By restricting our gaze to language fundamentals, we can investigate them here in more satisfying depth. Other texts, described ahead, pick up where this book leaves off and provide a more complete look at application-level topics and additional reference materials. The purpose of the book you are reading now is solely to teach Python itself so that you can apply it to whatever domain you happen to work in.

About This Book

This section underscores some important points about this book in general, regardless of its edition number. No book addresses every possible audience, so it's important to understand a book's goals up front.

This Book's Prerequisites

There are no absolute prerequisites to speak of, really. Both true beginners and crusty programming veterans have used this book successfully. If you are motivated to learn Python, this text will probably work for you. In general, though, I have found that any exposure to programming or scripting before this book can be helpful, even if not required for every reader.

This book is designed to be an introductory-level Python text for programmers.* It may not be an ideal text for someone who has never touched a computer before (for instance, we're not going to spend any time exploring what a computer is), but I haven't made many assumptions about your programming background or education.

On the other hand, I won't insult readers by assuming they are "dummies," either, whatever that means—it's easy to do useful things in Python, and this book will show you how. The text occasionally contrasts Python with languages such as C, C++, Java, and Pascal, but you can safely ignore these comparisons if you haven't used such languages in the past.

This Book's Scope and Other Books

Although this book covers all the essentials of the Python language, I've kept its scope narrow in the interests of speed and size. To keep things simple, this book focuses on core concepts, uses small and self-contained examples to illustrate points, and

---

* And by "programmers," I mean anyone who has written a single line of code in any programming or scripting language in the past. If this doesn't include you, you will probably find this book useful anyhow, but be aware that it will spend more time teaching Python than programming fundamentals.

sometimes omits the small details that are readily available in reference manuals. Because of that, this book is probably best described as an introduction and a stepping-stone to more advanced and complete texts.

For example, we won't talk much about Python/C integration—a complex topic that is nevertheless central to many Python-based systems. We also won't talk much about Python's history or development processes. And popular Python applications such as GUIs, system tools, and network scripting get only a short glance, if they are mentioned at all. Naturally, this scope misses some of the big picture.

By and large, Python is about raising the quality bar a few notches in the scripting world. Some of its ideas require more context than can be provided here, and I'd be remiss if I didn't recommend further study after you finish this book. I hope that most readers of this book will eventually go on to gain a more complete understanding of application-level programming from other texts.

Because of its beginner's focus, *Learning Python* is designed to be naturally complemented by O'Reilly's other Python books. For instance, *Programming Python*, another book I authored, provides larger and more complete examples, along with tutorials on application programming techniques, and was explicitly designed to be a follow-up text to the one you are reading now. Roughly, the current editions of *Learning Python* and *Programming Python* reflect the two halves of their author's training materials—the core language, and application programming. In addition, O'Reilly's *Python Pocket Reference* serves as a quick reference supplement for looking up some of the finer details skipped here.

Other follow-up books can also provide references, additional examples, or details about using Python in specific domains such as the Web and GUIs. For instance, O'Reilly's *Python in a Nutshell* and Sams's *Python Essential Reference* serve as useful references, and O'Reilly's *Python Cookbook* offers a library of self-contained examples for people already familiar with application programming techniques. Because reading books is such a subjective experience, I encourage you to browse on your own to find advanced texts that suit your needs. Regardless of which books you choose, though, keep in mind that the rest of the Python story requires studying examples that are more realistic than there is space for here.

Having said that, I think you'll find this book to be a good first text on Python, despite its limited scope (and perhaps because of it). You'll learn everything you need to get started writing useful standalone Python programs and scripts. By the time you've finished this book, you will have learned not only the language itself, but also how to apply it well to your day-to-day tasks. And you'll be equipped to tackle more advanced topics and examples as they come your way.

This Book's Style and Structure

This book is based on training materials developed for a three-day hands-on Python course. You'll find quizzes at the end of each chapter, and exercises at the end of the last chapter of each part. Solutions to chapter quizzes appear in the chapters themselves, and solutions to part exercises show up in Appendix B. The quizzes are designed to review material, while the exercises are designed to get you coding right away and are usually one of the highlights of the course.

I strongly recommend working through the quizzes and exercises along the way, not only to gain Python programming experience, but also because some of the exercises raise issues not covered elsewhere in the book. The solutions in the chapters and in Appendix B should help you if you get stuck (and you are encouraged to peek at the answers as much and as often as you like).

The overall structure of this book is also derived from class materials. Because this text is designed to introduce language basics quickly, I've organized the presentation by major language features, not examples. We'll take a bottom-up approach here: from built-in object types, to statements, to program units, and so on. Each chapter is fairly self-contained, but later chapters draw upon ideas introduced in earlier ones (e.g., by the time we get to classes, I'll assume you know how to write functions), so a linear reading makes the most sense for most readers.

In general terms, this book presents the Python language in a linear fashion. It is organized with one part per major language feature—types, functions, and so forth—and most of the examples are small and self-contained (some might also call the examples in this text artificial, but they illustrate the points it aims to make). More specifically, here is what you will find:

Part I, *Getting Started*

> We begin with a general overview of Python that answers commonly asked initial questions—why people use the language, what it's useful for, and so on. The first chapter introduces the major ideas underlying the technology to give you some background context. Then the technical material of the book begins, as we explore the ways that both we and Python run programs. The goal of this part of the book is to give you just enough information to be able to follow along with later examples and exercises.

Part II, *Types and Operations*

> Next, we begin our tour of the Python language, studying Python's major built-in object types in depth: numbers, lists, dictionaries, and so on. You can get a lot done in Python with these tools alone. This is the most substantial part of the book because we lay groundwork here for later chapters. We'll also look at dynamic typing and its references—keys to using Python well—in this part.

Part III, *Statements and Syntax*

The next part moves on to introduce Python's *statements*—the code you type to create and process objects in Python. It also presents Python's general syntax model. Although this part focuses on syntax, it also introduces some related tools, such as the PyDoc system, and explores coding alternatives.

Part IV, *Functions*

This part begins our look at Python's higher-level program structure tools. *Functions* turn out to be a simple way to package code for reuse and avoid code redundancy. In this part, we will explore Python's scoping rules, argument-passing techniques, and more.

Part V, *Modules*

Python *modules* let you organize statements and functions into larger components, and this part illustrates how to create, use, and reload modules. We'll also look at some more advanced topics here, such as module packages, module reloading, and the __name__ variable.

Part VI, *Classes and OOP*

Here, we explore Python's object-oriented programming tool, the *class*—an optional but powerful way to structure code for customization and reuse. As you'll see, classes mostly reuse ideas we will have covered by this point in the book, and OOP in Python is mostly about looking up names in linked objects. As you'll also see, OOP is optional in Python, but it can shave development time substantially, especially for long-term strategic project development.

Part VII, *Exceptions and Tools*

We conclude the language fundamentals coverage in this text with a look at Python's exception handling model and statements, plus a brief overview of development tools that will become more useful when you start writing larger programs (debugging and testing tools, for instance). Although exceptions are a fairly lightweight tool, this part appears after the discussion of classes because exceptions should now all be classes.

Part VIII, *Advanced Topics* (new in the fourth edition)

In the final part, we explore some advanced topics. Here, we study Unicode and byte strings, managed attribute tools like properties and descriptors, function and class decorators, and metaclasses. These chapters are all optional reading, because not all programmers need to understand the subjects they address. On the other hand, readers who must process internationalized text or binary data, or are responsible for developing APIs for other programmers to use, should find something of interest in this part.

Part IX, *Appendixes*

The book wraps up with a pair of appendixes that give platform-specific tips for using Python on various computers (Appendix A) and provide solutions to the end-of-part exercises (Appendix B). Solutions to end-of-chapter quizzes appear in the chapters themselves.

Note that the index and table of contents can be used to hunt for details, but there are no reference appendixes in this book (this book is a tutorial, not a reference). As mentioned earlier, you can consult *Python Pocket Reference*, as well as other books, and the free Python reference manuals maintained at *http://www.python.org* for syntax and built-in tool details.

Book Updates

Improvements happen (and so do mis^H^H^H typos). Updates, supplements, and corrections for this book will be maintained (or referenced) on the Web at one of the following sites:

http://www.oreilly.com/catalog/9780596158064 (O'Reilly's web page for the book)
http://www.rmi.net/~lutz (the author's site)
http://www.rmi.net/~lutz/about-lp.html (the author's web page for the book)

The last of these three URLs points to a web page for this book where I will post updates, but be sure to search the Web if this link becomes invalid. If I could become more clairvoyant, I would, but the Web changes faster than printed books.

About the Programs in This Book

This fourth edition of this book, and all the program examples in it, is based on Python version 3.0. In addition, most of its examples run under Python 2.6, as described in the text, and notes for Python 2.6 readers are mixed in along the way.

Because this text focuses on the core language, however, you can be fairly sure that most of what it has to say won't change very much in future releases of Python. Most of this book applies to earlier Python versions, too, except when it does not; naturally, if you try using extensions added after the release you've got, all bets are off.

As a rule of thumb, the latest Python is the best Python. Because this book focuses on the core language, most of it also applies to Jython, the Java-based Python language implementation, as well as other Python implementations described in Chapter 2.

Source code for the book's examples, as well as exercise solutions, can be fetched from the book's website at *http://www.oreilly.com/catalog/9780596158064/*. So, how do you run the examples? We'll study startup details in Chapter 3, so please stay tuned for information on this front.

Using Code Examples

This book is here to help you get your job done. In general, you may use the code in this book in your programs and documentation. You do not need to contact us for permission unless you're reproducing a significant portion of the code. For example, writing a program that uses several chunks of code from this book does not require permission. Selling or distributing a CD-ROM of examples from O'Reilly books *does* require permission. Answering a question by citing this book and quoting example code does not require permission. Incorporating a significant amount of example code from this book into your product's documentation *does* require permission.

We appreciate, but do not require, attribution. An attribution usually includes the title, author, publisher, and ISBN. For example: "*Learning Python*, Fourth Edition, by Mark Lutz. Copyright 2009 Mark Lutz, 978-0-596-15806-4."

If you feel your use of code examples falls outside fair use or the permission given above, feel free to contact us at *permissions@oreilly.com*.

Font Conventions

This book uses the following typographical conventions:

Italic
> Used for email addresses, URLs, filenames, pathnames, and emphasizing new terms when they are first introduced

`Constant width`
> Used for the contents of files and the output from commands, and to designate modules, methods, statements, and commands

`Constant width bold`
> Used in code sections to show commands or text that would be typed by the user, and, occasionally, to highlight portions of code

`Constant width italic`
> Used for replaceables and some comments in code sections

`<Constant width>`
> Indicates a syntactic unit that should be replaced with real code

Indicates a tip, suggestion, or general note relating to the nearby text.

Indicates a warning or caution relating to the nearby text.

Notes specific to this book: In this book's examples, the % character at the start of a system command line stands for the system's prompt, whatever that may be on your machine (e.g., `C:\Python30>` in a DOS window). Don't type the % character (or the system prompt it sometimes stands for) yourself.

Similarly, in interpreter interaction listings, do not type the `>>>` and `...` characters shown at the start of lines—these are prompts that Python displays. Type just the text after these prompts. To help you remember this, user inputs are shown in bold font in this book.

Also, you normally don't need to type text that starts with a # in listings; as you'll learn, these are comments, not executable code.

Safari® Books Online

Safari Books Online is an on-demand digital library that lets you easily search over 7,500 technology and creative reference books and videos to find the answers you need quickly.

With a subscription, you can read any page and watch any video from our library online. Read books on your cell phone and mobile devices. Access new titles before they are available for print, and get exclusive access to manuscripts in development and post feedback for the authors. Copy and paste code samples, organize your favorites, download chapters, bookmark key sections, create notes, print out pages, and benefit from tons of other time-saving features.

O'Reilly Media has uploaded this book to the Safari Books Online service. To have full digital access to this book and others on similar topics from O'Reilly and other publishers, sign up for free at *http://my.safaribooksonline.com*.

How to Contact Us

Please address comments and questions concerning this book to the publisher:

O'Reilly Media, Inc.
1005 Gravenstein Highway North
Sebastopol, CA 95472
800-998-9938 (in the United States or Canada)
707-829-0515 (international or local)
707-829-0104 (fax)

We will also maintain a web page for this book, where we list errata, examples, and any additional information. You can access this page at:

http://www.oreilly.com/catalog/9780596158064/

To comment or ask technical questions about this book, send email to:

> bookquestions@oreilly.com

For more information about our books, conferences, Resource Centers, and the O'Reilly Network, see our website at:

> http://www.oreilly.com

For book updates, be sure to also see the other links mentioned earlier in this Preface.

Acknowledgments

As I write this fourth edition of this book in 2009, I can't help but be in a sort of "mission accomplished" state of mind. I have now been using and promoting Python for 17 years, and have been teaching it for 12 years. Despite the passage of time and events, I am still constantly amazed at how successful Python has been over the years. It has grown in ways that most of us could not possibly have imagined in 1992. So, at the risk of sounding like a hopelessly self-absorbed author, you'll have to pardon a few words of reminiscing, congratulations, and thanks here.

It's been the proverbial long and winding road. Looking back today, when I first discovered Python in 1992, I had no idea what an impact it would have on the next 17 years of my life. Two years after writing the first edition of *Programming Python* in 1995, I began traveling around the country and the world teaching Python to beginners and experts. Since finishing the first edition of *Learning Python* in 1999, I've been an independent Python trainer and writer, thanks largely to Python's exponential growth in popularity.

As I write these words in mid-2009, I have written 12 Python books (4 editions of 3). I have also been teaching Python for more than a decade; have taught some 225 Python training sessions in the U.S., Europe, Canada, and Mexico; and have met over 3,000 students along the way. Besides racking up frequent flyer miles, these classes helped me refine this text as well as my other Python books. Over the years, teaching honed the books, and vice versa. In fact, the book you're reading is derived almost entirely from my classes.

Because of this, I'd like to thank all the students who have participated in my courses during the last 12 years. Along with changes in Python itself, your feedback played a huge role in shaping this text. (There's nothing quite as instructive as watching 3,000 students repeat the same beginner's mistakes!) This edition owes its changes primarily to classes held after 2003, though every class held since 1997 has in some way helped refine this book. I'd especially like to single out clients who hosted classes in Dublin, Mexico City, Barcelona, London, Edmonton, and Puerto Rico; better perks would be hard to imagine.

I'd also like to express my gratitude to everyone who played a part in producing this book. To the editors who worked on this project: Julie Steele on this edition, Tatiana

Apandi on the prior edition, and many others on earlier editions. To Doug Hellmann and Jesse Noller for taking part in the technical review of this book. And to O'Reilly for giving me a chance to work on those 12 book projects—it's been net fun (and only feels a little like the movie *Groundhog Day*).

I want to thank my original coauthor David Ascher as well for his work on the first two editions of this book. David contributed the "Outer Layers" part in prior editions, which we unfortunately had to trim to make room for new core language materials in the third edition. To compensate, I added a handful of more advanced programs as a self-study final exercise in the third edition, and added both new advanced examples and a new complete part for advanced topics in the fourth edition. Also see the prior notes in this Preface about follow-up application-level texts you may want to consult once you've learned the fundamentals here.

For creating such an enjoyable and useful language, I owe additional thanks to Guido van Rossum and the rest of the Python community. Like most open source systems, Python is the product of many heroic efforts. After 17 years of programming Python, I still find it to be seriously fun. It's been my privilege to watch Python grow from a new kid on the scripting languages block to a widely used tool, deployed in some fashion by almost every organization writing software. That has been an exciting endeavor to be a part of, and I'd like to thank and congratulate the entire Python community for a job well done.

I also want to thank my original editor at O'Reilly, the late Frank Willison. This book was largely Frank's idea, and it reflects the contagious vision he had. In looking back, Frank had a profound impact on both my own career and that of Python itself. It is not an exaggeration to say that Frank was responsible for much of the fun and success of Python when it was new. We still miss him.

Finally, a few personal notes of thanks. To OQO for the best toys so far (while they lasted). To the late Carl Sagan for inspiring an 18-year-old kid from Wisconsin. To my Mom, for courage. And to all the large corporations I've come across over the years, for reminding me how lucky I have been to be self-employed for the last decade!

To my children, Mike, Sammy, and Roxy, for whatever futures you will choose to make. You were children when I began with Python, and you seem to have somehow grown up along the way; I'm proud of you. Life may compel us down paths all our own, but there will always be a path home.

And most of all, to Vera, my best friend, my girlfriend, and my wife. The best day of my life was the day I finally found you. I don't know what the next 50 years hold, but I do know that I want to spend all of them holding you.

—Mark Lutz
Sarasota, Florida
July 2009

## PART I

Getting Started

## CHAPTER 1

A Python Q&A Session

If you've bought this book, you may already know what Python is and why it's an important tool to learn. If you don't, you probably won't be sold on Python until you've learned the language by reading the rest of this book and have done a project or two. But before we jump into details, the first few pages of this book will briefly introduce some of the main reasons behind Python's popularity. To begin sculpting a definition of Python, this chapter takes the form of a question-and-answer session, which poses some of the most common questions asked by beginners.

Why Do People Use Python?

Because there are many programming languages available today, this is the usual first question of newcomers. Given that there are roughly 1 million Python users out there at the moment, there really is no way to answer this question with complete accuracy; the choice of development tools is sometimes based on unique constraints or personal preference.

But after teaching Python to roughly 225 groups and over 3,000 students during the last 12 years, some common themes have emerged. The primary factors cited by Python users seem to be these:

Software quality
> For many, Python's focus on readability, coherence, and software quality in general sets it apart from other tools in the scripting world. Python code is designed to be readable, and hence reusable and maintainable—much more so than traditional scripting languages. The uniformity of Python code makes it easy to understand, even if you did not write it. In addition, Python has deep support for more advanced software reuse mechanisms, such as object-oriented programming (OOP).

Developer productivity
> Python boosts developer productivity many times beyond compiled or statically typed languages such as C, C++, and Java. Python code is typically one-third to one-fifth the size of equivalent C++ or Java code. That means there is less to type,

less to debug, and less to maintain after the fact. Python programs also run immediately, without the lengthy compile and link steps required by some other tools, further boosting programmer speed.

Program portability

Most Python programs run unchanged on all major computer platforms. Porting Python code between Linux and Windows, for example, is usually just a matter of copying a script's code between machines. Moreover, Python offers multiple options for coding portable graphical user interfaces, database access programs, web-based systems, and more. Even operating system interfaces, including program launches and directory processing, are as portable in Python as they can possibly be.

Support libraries

Python comes with a large collection of prebuilt and portable functionality, known as the *standard library*. This library supports an array of application-level programming tasks, from text pattern matching to network scripting. In addition, Python can be extended with both homegrown libraries and a vast collection of third-party application support software. Python's third-party domain offers tools for website construction, numeric programming, serial port access, game development, and much more. The NumPy extension, for instance, has been described as a free and more powerful equivalent to the Matlab numeric programming system.

Component integration

Python scripts can easily communicate with other parts of an application, using a variety of integration mechanisms. Such integrations allow Python to be used as a product customization and extension tool. Today, Python code can invoke C and C++ libraries, can be called from C and C++ programs, can integrate with Java and .NET components, can communicate over frameworks such as COM, can interface with devices over serial ports, and can interact over networks with interfaces like SOAP, XML-RPC, and CORBA. It is not a standalone tool.

Enjoyment

Because of Python's ease of use and built-in toolset, it can make the act of programming more pleasure than chore. Although this may be an intangible benefit, its effect on productivity is an important asset.

Of these factors, the first two (quality and productivity) are probably the most compelling benefits to most Python users.

Software Quality

By design, Python implements a deliberately simple and readable syntax and a highly coherent programming model. As a slogan at a recent Python conference attests, the net result is that Python seems to "fit your brain"—that is, features of the language interact in consistent and limited ways and follow naturally from a small set of core concepts. This makes the language easier to learn, understand, and remember. In practice, Python programmers do not need to constantly refer to manuals when reading or writing code; it's a consistently designed system that many find yields surprisingly regular-looking code.

By philosophy, Python adopts a somewhat minimalist approach. This means that although there are usually multiple ways to accomplish a coding task, there is usually just one obvious way, a few less obvious alternatives, and a small set of coherent interactions everywhere in the language. Moreover, Python doesn't make arbitrary decisions for you; when interactions are ambiguous, explicit intervention is preferred over "magic." In the Python way of thinking, explicit is better than implicit, and simple is better than complex.*

Beyond such design themes, Python includes tools such as modules and OOP that naturally promote code reusability. And because Python is focused on quality, so too, naturally, are Python programmers.

Developer Productivity

During the great Internet boom of the mid-to-late 1990s, it was difficult to find enough programmers to implement software projects; developers were asked to implement systems as fast as the Internet evolved. Today, in an era of layoffs and economic recession, the picture has shifted. Programming staffs are often now asked to accomplish the same tasks with even fewer people.

In both of these scenarios, Python has shined as a tool that allows programmers to get more done with less effort. It is deliberately optimized for *speed of development*—its simple syntax, dynamic typing, lack of compile steps, and built-in toolset allow programmers to develop programs in a fraction of the time needed when using some other tools. The net effect is that Python typically boosts developer productivity many times beyond the levels supported by traditional languages. That's good news in both boom and bust times, and everywhere the software industry goes in between.

Is Python a "Scripting Language"?

Python is a general-purpose programming language that is often applied in scripting roles. It is commonly defined as an *object-oriented scripting language*—a definition that blends support for OOP with an overall orientation toward scripting roles. In fact, people often use the word "script" instead of "program" to describe a Python code file. In this book, the terms "script" and "program" are used interchangeably, with a slight

---

* For a more complete look at the Python philosophy, type the command `import this` at any Python interactive prompt (you'll see how in Chapter 2). This invokes an "Easter egg" hidden in Python—a collection of design principles underlying Python. The acronym EIBTI is now fashionable jargon for the "explicit is better than implicit" rule.

preference for "script" to describe a simpler top-level file and "program" to refer to a more sophisticated multifile application.

Because the term "scripting language" has so many different meanings to different observers, some would prefer that it not be applied to Python at all. In fact, people tend to make three very different associations, some of which are more useful than others, when they hear Python labeled as such:

Shell tools

Sometimes when people hear Python described as a scripting language, they think it means that Python is a tool for coding operating-system-oriented scripts. Such programs are often launched from console command lines and perform tasks such as processing text files and launching other programs.

Python programs can and do serve such roles, but this is just one of dozens of common Python application domains. It is not just a better shell-script language.

Control language

To others, scripting refers to a "glue" layer used to control and direct (i.e., script) other application components. Python programs are indeed often deployed in the context of larger applications. For instance, to test hardware devices, Python programs may call out to components that give low-level access to a device. Similarly, programs may run bits of Python code at strategic points to support end-user product customization without the need to ship and recompile the entire system's source code.

Python's simplicity makes it a naturally flexible control tool. Technically, though, this is also just a common Python role; many (perhaps most) Python programmers code standalone scripts without ever using or knowing about any integrated components. It is not just a control language.

Ease of use

Probably the best way to think of the term "scripting language" is that it refers to a simple language used for quickly coding tasks. This is especially true when the term is applied to Python, which allows much faster program development than compiled languages like C++. Its rapid development cycle fosters an exploratory, incremental mode of programming that has to be experienced to be appreciated.

Don't be fooled, though—Python is not just for simple tasks. Rather, it makes tasks simple by its ease of use and flexibility. Python has a simple feature set, but it allows programs to scale up in sophistication as needed. Because of that, it is commonly used for quick tactical tasks and longer-term strategic development.

So, is Python a scripting language or not? It depends on whom you ask. In general, the term "scripting" is probably best used to describe the rapid and flexible mode of development that Python supports, rather than a particular application domain.

OK, but What's the Downside?

After using it for 17 years and teaching it for 12, the only downside to Python I've found is that, as currently implemented, its execution speed may not always be as fast as that of compiled languages such as C and C++.

We'll talk about implementation concepts in detail later in this book. In short, the standard implementations of Python today compile (i.e., translate) source code statements to an intermediate format known as *byte code* and then interpret the byte code. Byte code provides portability, as it is a platform-independent format. However, because Python is not compiled all the way down to binary machine code (e.g., instructions for an Intel chip), some programs will run more slowly in Python than in a fully compiled language like C.

Whether you will ever *care* about the execution speed difference depends on what kinds of programs you write. Python has been optimized numerous times, and Python code runs fast enough by itself in most application domains. Furthermore, whenever you do something "real" in a Python script, like processing a file or constructing a graphical user interface (GUI), your program will actually run at C speed, since such tasks are immediately dispatched to compiled C code inside the Python interpreter. More fundamentally, Python's speed-of-development gain is often far more important than any speed-of-execution loss, especially given modern computer speeds.

Even at today's CPU speeds, though, there still are some domains that do require optimal execution speeds. Numeric programming and animation, for example, often need at least their core number-crunching components to run at C speed (or better). If you work in such a domain, you can still use Python—simply split off the parts of the application that require optimal speed into *compiled extensions*, and link those into your system for use in Python scripts.

We won't talk about extensions much in this text, but this is really just an instance of the Python-as-control-language role we discussed earlier. A prime example of this dual language strategy is the *NumPy* numeric programming extension for Python; by combining compiled and optimized numeric extension libraries with the Python language, NumPy turns Python into a numeric programming tool that is efficient and easy to use. You may never need to code such extensions in your own Python work, but they provide a powerful optimization mechanism if you ever do.

Who Uses Python Today?

At this writing, the best estimate anyone can seem to make of the size of the Python user base is that there are roughly 1 million Python users around the world today (plus or minus a few). This estimate is based on various statistics, like download rates and developer surveys. Because Python is open source, a more exact count is difficult—there are no license registrations to tally. Moreover, Python is automatically included

Higher-level toolkits such as *PythonCard* and *Dabo* are built on top of base APIs such as wxPython and tkinter. With the proper library, you can also use GUI support in other toolkits in Python, such as *Qt* with PyQt, *GTK* with PyGTK, *MFC* with PyWin32, *.NET* with IronPython, and *Swing* with Jython (the Java version of Python, described in Chapter 2) or JPype. For applications that run in web browsers or have simple interface requirements, both Jython and Python web frameworks and server-side CGI scripts, described in the next section, provide additional user interface options.

Internet Scripting

Python comes with standard Internet modules that allow Python programs to perform a wide variety of networking tasks, in client and server modes. Scripts can communicate over sockets; extract form information sent to server-side CGI scripts; transfer files by FTP; parse, generate, and analyze XML files; send, receive, compose, and parse email; fetch web pages by URLs; parse the HTML and XML of fetched web pages; communicate over XML-RPC, SOAP, and Telnet; and more. Python's libraries make these tasks remarkably simple.

In addition, a large collection of third-party tools are available on the Web for doing Internet programming in Python. For instance, the *HTMLGen* system generates HTML files from Python class-based descriptions, the *mod_python* package runs Python efficiently within the Apache web server and supports server-side templating with its Python Server Pages, and the Jython system provides for seamless Python/Java integration and supports coding of server-side applets that run on clients.

In addition, full-blown web development framework packages for Python, such as *Django*, *TurboGears*, *web2py*, *Pylons*, *Zope*, and *WebWare*, support quick construction of full-featured and production-quality websites with Python. Many of these include features such as object-relational mappers, a Model/View/Controller architecture, server-side scripting and templating, and AJAX support, to provide complete and enterprise-level web development solutions.

Component Integration

We discussed the component integration role earlier when describing Python as a control language. Python's ability to be extended by and embedded in C and C++ systems makes it useful as a flexible glue language for scripting the behavior of other systems and components. For instance, integrating a C library into Python enables Python to test and launch the library's components, and embedding Python in a product enables onsite customizations to be coded without having to recompile the entire product (or ship its source code at all).

Tools such as the *SWIG* and *SIP* code generators can automate much of the work needed to link compiled components into Python for use in scripts, and the *Cython* system allows coders to mix Python and C-like code. Larger frameworks, such as Python's COM support on Windows, the Jython Java-based implementation, the IronPython .NET-based implementation, and various CORBA toolkits for Python, provide alternative ways to script components. On Windows, for example, Python scripts can use frameworks to script Word and Excel.

Database Programming

For traditional database demands, there are Python interfaces to all commonly used relational database systems—Sybase, Oracle, Informix, ODBC, MySQL, PostgreSQL, SQLite, and more. The Python world has also defined a *portable database API* for accessing SQL database systems from Python scripts, which looks the same on a variety of underlying database systems. For instance, because the vendor interfaces implement the portable API, a script written to work with the free MySQL system will work largely unchanged on other systems (such as Oracle); all you have to do is replace the underlying vendor interface.

Python's standard `pickle` module provides a simple *object persistence* system—it allows programs to easily save and restore entire Python objects to files and file-like objects. On the Web, you'll also find a third-party open source system named *ZODB* that provides a complete object-oriented database system for Python scripts, and others (such as *SQLObject* and *SQLAlchemy*) that map relational tables onto Python's class model. Furthermore, as of Python 2.5, the in-process *SQLite* embedded SQL database engine is a standard part of Python itself.

Rapid Prototyping

To Python programs, components written in Python and C look the same. Because of this, it's possible to prototype systems in Python initially, and then move selected components to a compiled language such as C or C++ for delivery. Unlike some prototyping tools, Python doesn't require a complete rewrite once the prototype has solidified. Parts of the system that don't require the efficiency of a language such as C++ can remain coded in Python for ease of maintenance and use.

Numeric and Scientific Programming

The *NumPy* numeric programming extension for Python mentioned earlier includes such advanced tools as an array object, interfaces to standard mathematical libraries, and much more. By integrating Python with numeric routines coded in a compiled language for speed, NumPy turns Python into a sophisticated yet easy-to-use numeric programming tool that can often replace existing code written in traditional compiled languages such as FORTRAN or C++. Additional numeric tools for Python support animation, 3D visualization, parallel processing, and so on. The popular *SciPy* and *ScientificPython* extensions, for example, provide additional libraries of scientific programming tools and use NumPy code.

Gaming, Images, Serial Ports, XML, Robots, and More

Python is commonly applied in more domains than can be mentioned here. For example, you can do:

- Game programming and multimedia in Python with the *pygame* system
- Serial port communication on Windows, Linux, and more with the *PySerial* extension
- Image processing with *PIL*, *PyOpenGL*, *Blender*, *Maya*, and others
- Robot control programming with the *PyRo* toolkit
- XML parsing with the `xml` library package, the `xmlrpclib` module, and third-party extensions
- Artificial intelligence programming with neural network simulators and expert system shells
- Natural language analysis with the *NLTK* package

You can even play solitaire with the *PySol* program. You'll find support for many such fields at the PyPI websites, and via web searches (search Google or *http://www.python .org* for links).

Many of these specific domains are largely just instances of Python's component integration role in action again. Adding it as a frontend to libraries of components written in a compiled language such as C makes Python useful for scripting in a wide variety of domains. As a general-purpose language that supports integration, Python is widely applicable.

How Is Python Supported?

As a popular open source system, Python enjoys a large and active development community that responds to issues and develops enhancements with a speed that many commercial software developers would find remarkable (if not downright shocking). Python developers coordinate work online with a source-control system. Changes follow a formal *PEP* (Python Enhancement Proposal) protocol and must be accompanied by extensions to Python's extensive regression testing system. In fact, modifying Python today is roughly as involved as changing commercial software—a far cry from Python's early days, when an email to its creator would suffice, but a good thing given its current large user base.

The *PSF* (Python Software Foundation), a formal nonprofit group, organizes conferences and deals with intellectual property issues. Numerous Python conferences are held around the world; O'Reilly's OSCON and the PSF's PyCon are the largest. The former of these addresses multiple open source projects, and the latter is a Python-only event that has experienced strong growth in recent years. Attendance at PyCon 2008 nearly *doubled* from the prior year, growing from 586 attendees in 2007 to over 1,000 in 2008. This was on the heels of a 40% attendance increase in 2007, from 410 in 2006. PyCon 2009 had 943 attendees, a slight decrease from 2008, but a still very strong showing during a global recession.

What Are Python's Technical Strengths?

Naturally, this is a developer's question. If you don't already have a programming background, the language in the next few sections may be a bit baffling—don't worry, we'll explore all of these terms in more detail as we proceed through this book. For developers, though, here is a quick introduction to some of Python's top technical features.

It's Object-Oriented

Python is an object-oriented language, from the ground up. Its class model supports advanced notions such as polymorphism, operator overloading, and multiple inheritance; yet, in the context of Python's simple syntax and typing, OOP is remarkably easy to apply. In fact, if you don't understand these terms, you'll find they are much easier to learn with Python than with just about any other OOP language available.

Besides serving as a powerful code structuring and reuse device, Python's OOP nature makes it ideal as a scripting tool for object-oriented systems languages such as C++ and Java. For example, with the appropriate glue code, Python programs can subclass (specialize) classes implemented in C++, Java, and C#.

Of equal significance, OOP is an *option* in Python; you can go far without having to become an object guru all at once. Much like C++, Python supports both procedural and object-oriented programming modes. Its object-oriented tools can be applied if and when constraints allow. This is especially useful in tactical development modes, which preclude design phases.

It's Free

Python is completely free to use and distribute. As with other open source software, such as Tcl, Perl, Linux, and Apache, you can fetch the entire Python system's source code for free on the Internet. There are no restrictions on copying it, embedding it in your systems, or shipping it with your products. In fact, you can even sell Python's source code, if you are so inclined.

But don't get the wrong idea: "free" doesn't mean "unsupported." On the contrary, the Python online community responds to user queries with a speed that most commercial software help desks would do well to try to emulate. Moreover, because Python comes with complete source code, it empowers developers, leading to the creation of a large team of implementation experts. Although studying or changing a programming language's implementation isn't everyone's idea of fun, it's comforting to know that you can do so if you need to. You're not dependent on the whims of a commercial vendor; the ultimate documentation source is at your disposal.

As mentioned earlier, Python development is performed by a community that largely coordinates its efforts over the Internet. It consists of Python's creator—*Guido van Rossum*, the officially anointed Benevolent Dictator for Life (BDFL) of Python—plus a supporting cast of thousands. Language changes must follow a formal enhancement procedure and be scrutinized by both other developers and the BDFL. Happily, this tends to make Python more conservative with changes than some other languages.

It's Portable

The standard implementation of Python is written in portable ANSI C, and it compiles and runs on virtually every major platform currently in use. For example, Python programs run today on everything from PDAs to supercomputers. As a partial list, Python is available on:

- Linux and Unix systems
- Microsoft Windows and DOS (all modern flavors)
- Mac OS (both OS X and Classic)
- BeOS, OS/2, VMS, and QNX
- Real-time systems such as VxWorks
- Cray supercomputers and IBM mainframes
- PDAs running Palm OS, PocketPC, and Linux
- Cell phones running Symbian OS and Windows Mobile
- Gaming consoles and iPods
- And more

Like the language interpreter itself, the standard library modules that ship with Python are implemented to be as portable across platform boundaries as possible. Further, Python programs are automatically compiled to portable byte code, which runs the same on any platform with a compatible version of Python installed (more on this in the next chapter).

What that means is that Python programs using the core language and standard libraries run the same on Linux, Windows, and most other systems with a Python interpreter. Most Python ports also contain platform-specific extensions (e.g., COM support on Windows), but the core Python language and libraries work the same everywhere. As mentioned earlier, Python also includes an interface to the Tk GUI toolkit called tkinter (Tkinter in 2.6), which allows Python programs to implement full-featured graphical user interfaces that run on all major GUI platforms without program changes.

It's Powerful

From a features perspective, Python is something of a hybrid. Its toolset places it between traditional scripting languages (such as Tcl, Scheme, and Perl) and systems development languages (such as C, C++, and Java). Python provides all the simplicity and ease of use of a scripting language, along with more advanced software-engineering tools typically found in compiled languages. Unlike some scripting languages, this combination makes Python useful for large-scale development projects. As a preview, here are some of the main things you'll find in Python's toolbox:

Dynamic typing
Python keeps track of the kinds of objects your program uses when it runs; it doesn't require complicated type and size declarations in your code. In fact, as you'll see in Chapter 6, there is no such thing as a type or variable declaration anywhere in Python. Because Python code does not constrain data types, it is also usually automatically applicable to a whole range of objects.

Automatic memory management
Python automatically allocates objects and reclaims ("garbage collects") them when they are no longer used, and most can grow and shrink on demand. As you'll learn, Python keeps track of low-level memory details so you don't have to.

Programming-in-the-large support
For building larger systems, Python includes tools such as modules, classes, and exceptions. These tools allow you to organize systems into components, use OOP to reuse and customize code, and handle events and errors gracefully.

Built-in object types
Python provides commonly used data structures such as lists, dictionaries, and strings as intrinsic parts of the language; as you'll see, they're both flexible and easy to use. For instance, built-in objects can grow and shrink on demand, can be arbitrarily nested to represent complex information, and more.

Built-in tools
To process all those object types, Python comes with powerful and standard operations, including concatenation (joining collections), slicing (extracting sections), sorting, mapping, and more.

Library utilities

For more specific tasks, Python also comes with a large collection of precoded library tools that support everything from regular expression matching to networking. Once you learn the language itself, Python's library tools are where much of the application-level action occurs.

Third-party utilities

Because Python is open source, developers are encouraged to contribute precoded tools that support tasks beyond those supported by its built-ins; on the Web, you'll find free support for COM, imaging, CORBA ORBs, XML, database access, and much more.

Despite the array of tools in Python, it retains a remarkably simple syntax and design. The result is a powerful programming tool with all the usability of a scripting language.

It's Mixable

Python programs can easily be "glued" to components written in other languages in a variety of ways. For example, Python's C API lets C programs call and be called by Python programs flexibly. That means you can add functionality to the Python system as needed, and use Python programs within other environments or systems.

Mixing Python with libraries coded in languages such as C or C++, for instance, makes it an easy-to-use frontend language and customization tool. As mentioned earlier, this also makes Python good at rapid prototyping; systems may be implemented in Python first, to leverage its speed of development, and later moved to C for delivery, one piece at a time, according to performance demands.

It's Easy to Use

To run a Python program, you simply type it and run it. There are no intermediate compile and link steps, like there are for languages such as C or C++. Python executes programs immediately, which makes for an interactive programming experience and rapid turnaround after program changes—in many cases, you can witness the effect of a program change as fast as you can type it.

Of course, development cycle turnaround is only one aspect of Python's ease of use. It also provides a deliberately simple syntax and powerful built-in tools. In fact, some have gone so far as to call Python "executable pseudocode." Because it eliminates much of the complexity in other tools, Python programs are simpler, smaller, and more flexible than equivalent programs in languages like C, C++, and Java.

It's Easy to Learn

This brings us to a key point of this book: compared to other programming languages, the core Python language is remarkably easy to learn. In fact, you can expect to be coding significant Python programs in a matter of days (or perhaps in just hours, if you're already an experienced programmer). That's good news for professional developers seeking to learn the language to use on the job, as well as for end users of systems that expose a Python layer for customization or control.

Today, many systems rely on the fact that end users can quickly learn enough Python to tailor their Python customizations' code onsite, with little or no support. Although Python does have advanced programming tools, its core language will still seem simple to beginners and gurus alike.

It's Named After Monty Python

OK, this isn't quite a technical strength, but it does seem to be a surprisingly well-kept secret that I wish to expose up front. Despite all the reptile icons in the Python world, the truth is that Python creator Guido van Rossum named it after the BBC comedy series *Monty Python's Flying Circus*. He is a big fan of Monty Python, as are many software developers (indeed, there seems to almost be a symmetry between the two fields).

This legacy inevitably adds a humorous quality to Python code examples. For instance, the traditional "foo" and "bar" for generic variable names become "spam" and "eggs" in the Python world. The occasional "Brian," "ni," and "shrubbery" likewise owe their appearances to this namesake. It even impacts the Python community at large: talks at Python conferences are regularly billed as "The Spanish Inquisition."

All of this is, of course, very funny if you are familiar with the show, but less so otherwise. You don't need to be familiar with the series to make sense of examples that borrow references to Monty Python (including many you will see in this book), but at least you now know their root.

How Does Python Stack Up to Language X?

Finally, to place it in the context of what you may already know, people sometimes compare Python to languages such as Perl, Tcl, and Java. We talked about performance earlier, so here we'll focus on functionality. While other languages are also useful tools to know and use, many people find that Python:

- Is more powerful than Tcl. Python's support for "programming in the large" makes it applicable to the development of larger systems.

- Has a cleaner syntax and simpler design than Perl, which makes it more readable and maintainable and helps reduce program bugs.

- Is simpler and easier to use than Java. Python is a scripting language, but Java inherits much of the complexity and syntax of systems languages such as C++.

- Is simpler and easier to use than C++, but it doesn't often compete with C++; as a scripting language, Python typically serves different roles.

- Is both more powerful and more cross-platform than Visual Basic. Its open source nature also means it is not controlled by a single company.

- Is more readable and general-purpose than PHP. Python is sometimes used to construct websites, but it's also widely used in nearly every other computer domain, from robotics to movie animation.

- Is more mature and has a more readable syntax than Ruby. Unlike Ruby and Java, OOP is an option in Python—Python does not impose OOP on users or projects to which it may not apply.

- Has the dynamic flavor of languages like SmallTalk and Lisp, but also has a simple, traditional syntax accessible to developers as well as end users of customizable systems.

Especially for programs that do more than scan text files, and that might have to be read in the future by others (or by you!), many people find that Python fits the bill better than any other scripting or programming language available today. Furthermore, unless your application requires peak performance, Python is often a viable alternative to systems development languages such as C, C++, and Java: Python code will be much less difficult to write, debug, and maintain.

Of course, your author has been a card-carrying Python evangelist since 1992, so take these comments as you may. They do, however, reflect the common experience of many developers who have taken time to explore what Python has to offer.

Chapter Summary

And that concludes the hype portion of this book. In this chapter, we've explored some of the reasons that people pick Python for their programming tasks. We've also seen how it is applied and looked at a representative sample of who is using it today. My goal is to teach Python, though, not to sell it. The best way to judge a language is to see it in action, so the rest of this book focuses entirely on the language details we've glossed over here.

The next two chapters begin our technical introduction to the language. In them, we'll explore ways to run Python programs, peek at Python's byte code execution model, and introduce the basics of module files for saving code. The goal will be to give you just enough information to run the examples and exercises in the rest of the book. You won't really start programming per se until Chapter 4, but make sure you have a handle on the startup details before moving on.

Test Your Knowledge: Quiz

In this edition of the book, we will be closing each chapter with a quick pop quiz about the material presented therein to help you review the key concepts. The answers for these quizzes appear immediately after the questions, and you are encouraged to read the answers once you've taken a crack at the questions yourself. In addition to these end-of-chapter quizzes, you'll find lab exercises at the end of each part of the book, designed to help you start coding Python on your own. For now, here's your first test. Good luck!

1. What are the six main reasons that people choose to use Python?
2. Name four notable companies or organizations using Python today.
3. Why might you *not* want to use Python in an application?
4. What can you do with Python?
5. What's the significance of the Python `import this` statement?
6. Why does "spam" show up in so many Python examples in books and on the Web?
7. What is your favorite color?

Test Your Knowledge: Answers

How did you do? Here are the answers I came up with, though there may be multiple solutions to some quiz questions. Again, even if you're sure you got a question right, I encourage you to look at these answers for additional context. See the chapter's text for more details if any of these responses don't make sense to you.

1. Software quality, developer productivity, program portability, support libraries, component integration, and simple enjoyment. Of these, the quality and productivity themes seem to be the main reasons that people choose to use Python.
2. Google, Industrial Light & Magic, EVE Online, Jet Propulsion Labs, Maya, ESRI, and many more. Almost every organization doing software development uses Python in some fashion, whether for long-term strategic product development or for short-term tactical tasks such as testing and system administration.
3. Python's downside is performance: it won't run as quickly as fully compiled languages like C and C++. On the other hand, it's quick enough for most applications, and typical Python code runs at close to C speed anyhow because it invokes

linked-in C code in the interpreter. If speed is critical, compiled extensions are available for number-crunching parts of an application.

4. You can use Python for nearly anything you can do with a computer, from website development and gaming to robotics and spacecraft control.

5. `import this` triggers an Easter egg inside Python that displays some of the design philosophies underlying the language. You'll learn how to run this statement in the next chapter.

6. "Spam" is a reference from a famous Monty Python skit in which people trying to order food in a cafeteria are drowned out by a chorus of Vikings singing about spam. Oh, and it's also a common variable name in Python scripts....

7. Blue. No, yellow!

Python Is Engineering, Not Art

When Python first emerged on the software scene in the early 1990s, it spawned what is now something of a classic conflict between its proponents and those of another popular scripting language, Perl. Personally, I think the debate is tired and unwarranted today—developers are smart enough to draw their own conclusions. Still, this is one of the most common topics I'm asked about on the training road, so it seems fitting to say a few words about it here.

The short story is this: *you can do everything in Python that you can in Perl, but you can read your code after you do it*. That's it—their domains largely overlap, but Python is more focused on producing readable code. For many, the enhanced readability of Python translates to better code reusability and maintainability, making Python a better choice for programs that will not be written once and thrown away. Perl code is easy to write, but difficult to read. Given that most software has a lifespan much longer than its initial creation, many see Python as a more effective tool.

The somewhat longer story reflects the backgrounds of the designers of the two languages and underscores some of the main reasons people choose to use Python. Python's creator is a mathematician by training; as such, he produced a language with a high degree of uniformity—its syntax and toolset are remarkably coherent. Moreover, like math, Python's design is orthogonal—most of the language follows from a small set of core concepts. For instance, once one grasps Python's flavor of polymorphism, the rest is largely just details.

By contrast, the creator of the Perl language is a linguist, and its design reflects this heritage. There are many ways to accomplish the same tasks in Perl, and language constructs interact in context-sensitive and sometimes quite subtle ways—much like natural language. As the well-known Perl motto states, "There's more than one way to do it." Given this design, both the Perl language and its user community have historically encouraged freedom of expression when writing code. One person's Perl code can be radically different from another's. In fact, writing unique, tricky code is often a source of pride among Perl users.

But as anyone who has done any substantial code maintenance should be able to attest, *freedom of expression is great for art, but lousy for engineering.* In engineering, we need a minimal feature set and predictability. In engineering, freedom of expression can lead to maintenance nightmares. As more than one Perl user has confided to me, the result of too much freedom is often code that is much easier to rewrite from scratch than to modify.

Consider this: when people create a painting or a sculpture, they do so for themselves for purely aesthetic purposes. The possibility of someone else having to change that painting or sculpture later does not enter into it. This is a critical difference between art and engineering. When people write software, they are not writing it for themselves. In fact, they are not even writing primarily for the computer. Rather, good programmers know that code is written for the next human being who has to read it in order to maintain or reuse it. If that person cannot understand the code, it's all but useless in a realistic development scenario.

This is where many people find that Python most clearly differentiates itself from scripting languages like Perl. Because Python's syntax model almost forces users to write readable code, Python programs lend themselves more directly to the full software development cycle. And because Python emphasizes ideas such as limited interactions, code uniformity and regularity, and feature consistency, it more directly fosters code that can be used long after it is first written.

In the long run, Python's focus on code quality in itself boosts programmer productivity, as well as programmer satisfaction. Python programmers can be creative, too, of course, and as we'll see, the language does offer multiple solutions for some tasks. At its core, though, Python encourages good engineering in ways that other scripting languages often do not.

At least, that's the common consensus among many people who have adopted Python. You should always judge such claims for yourself, of course, by learning what Python has to offer. To help you get started, let's move on to the next chapter.

CHAPTER 2

How Python Runs Programs

This chapter and the next take a quick look at program execution—how you launch code, and how Python runs it. In this chapter, we'll study the Python interpreter. Chapter 3 will then show you how to get your own programs up and running.

Startup details are inherently platform-specific, and some of the material in these two chapters may not apply to the platform you work on, so you should feel free to skip parts not relevant to your intended use. Likewise, more advanced readers who have used similar tools in the past and prefer to get to the meat of the language quickly may want to file some of this chapter away as "for future reference." For the rest of you, let's learn how to run some code.

Introducing the Python Interpreter

So far, I've mostly been talking about Python as a programming language. But, as currently implemented, it's also a software package called an *interpreter*. An interpreter is a kind of program that executes other programs. When you write a Python program, the Python interpreter reads your program and carries out the instructions it contains. In effect, the interpreter is a layer of software logic between your code and the computer hardware on your machine.

When the Python package is installed on your machine, it generates a number of components—minimally, an interpreter and a support library. Depending on how you use it, the Python interpreter may take the form of an executable program, or a set of libraries linked into another program. Depending on which flavor of Python you run, the interpreter itself may be implemented as a C program, a set of Java classes, or something else. Whatever form it takes, the Python code you write must always be run by this interpreter. And to enable that, you must install a Python interpreter on your computer.

Python installation details vary by platform and are covered in more depth in Appendix A. In short:

- Windows users fetch and run a self-installing executable file that puts Python on their machines. Simply double-click and say Yes or Next at all prompts.

- Linux and Mac OS X users probably already have a usable Python preinstalled on their computers—it's a standard component on these platforms today.

- Some Linux and Mac OS X users (and most Unix users) compile Python from its full source code distribution package.

- Linux users can also find RPM files, and Mac OS X users can find various Mac-specific installation packages.

- Other platforms have installation techniques relevant to those platforms. For instance, Python is available on cell phones, game consoles, and iPods, but installation details vary widely.

Python itself may be fetched from the downloads page on the website, *http://www .python.org*. It may also be found through various other distribution channels. Keep in mind that you should always check to see whether Python is already present before installing it. If you're working on Windows, you'll usually find Python in the Start menu, as captured in Figure 2-1 (these menu options are discussed in the next chapter). On Unix and Linux, Python probably lives in your */usr* directory tree.

Because installation details are so platform-specific, we'll finesse the rest of this story here. For more details on the installation process, consult Appendix A. For the purposes of this chapter and the next, I'll assume that you've got Python ready to go.

Program Execution

What it means to write and run a Python script depends on whether you look at these tasks as a programmer, or as a Python interpreter. Both views offer important perspectives on Python programming.

The Programmer's View

In its simplest form, a Python program is just a text file containing Python statements. For example, the following file, named *script0.py*, is one of the simplest Python scripts I could dream up, but it passes for a fully functional Python program:

```
print('hello world')
print(2 ** 100)
```

This file contains two Python `print` statements, which simply print a string (the text in quotes) and a numeric expression result (2 to the power 100) to the output stream. Don't worry about the syntax of this code yet—for this chapter, we're interested only in getting it to run. I'll explain the `print` statement, and why you can raise 2 to the power 100 in Python without overflowing, in the next parts of this book.

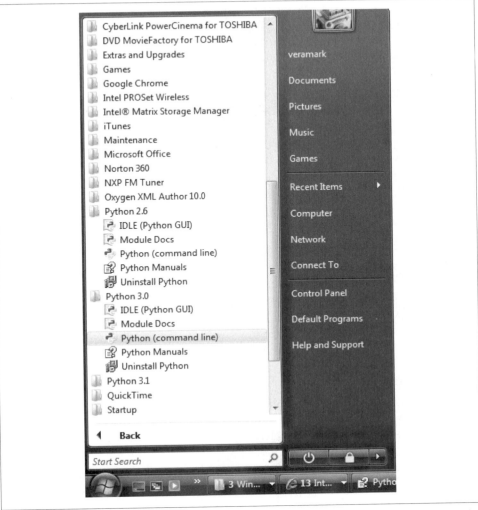

Figure 2-1. When installed on Windows, this is how Python shows up in your Start button menu. This can vary a bit from release to release, but IDLE starts a development GUI, and Python starts a simple interactive session. Also here are the standard manuals and the PyDoc documentation engine (Module Docs).

You can create such a file of statements with any text editor you like. By convention, Python program files are given names that end in *.py*; technically, this naming scheme is required only for files that are "imported," as shown later in this book, but most Python files have *.py* names for consistency.

After you've typed these statements into a text file, you must tell Python to *execute* the file—which simply means to run all the statements in the file from top to bottom, one after another. As you'll see in the next chapter, you can launch Python program files by shell command lines, by clicking their icons, from within IDEs, and with other standard techniques. If all goes well, when you execute the file, you'll see the results of the two `print` statements show up somewhere on your computer—by default, usually in the same window you were in when you ran the program:

```
hello world
1267650600228229401496703205376
```

For example, here's what happened when I ran this script from a DOS command line on a Windows laptop (typically called a Command Prompt window, found in the Accessories program menu), to make sure it didn't have any silly typos:

```
C:\temp> python script0.py
hello world
1267650600228229401496703205376
```

We've just run a Python script that prints a string and a number. We probably won't win any programming awards with this code, but it's enough to capture the basics of program execution.

Python's View

The brief description in the prior section is fairly standard for scripting languages, and it's usually all that most Python programmers need to know. You type code into text files, and you run those files through the interpreter. Under the hood, though, a bit more happens when you tell Python to "go." Although knowledge of Python internals is not strictly required for Python programming, a basic understanding of the runtime structure of Python can help you grasp the bigger picture of program execution.

When you instruct Python to run your script, there are a few steps that Python carries out before your code actually starts crunching away. Specifically, it's first compiled to something called "byte code" and then routed to something called a "virtual machine."

Byte code compilation

Internally, and almost completely hidden from you, when you execute a program Python first compiles your *source code* (the statements in your file) into a format known as *byte code*. Compilation is simply a translation step, and byte code is a lower-level, platform-independent representation of your source code. Roughly, Python translates each of your source statements into a group of byte code instructions by decomposing them into individual steps. This byte code translation is performed to speed execution—byte code can be run much more quickly than the original source code statements in your text file.

You'll notice that the prior paragraph said that this is *almost* completely hidden from you. If the Python process has write access on your machine, it will store the byte code of your programs in files that end with a *.pyc* extension (".pyc" means compiled ".py" source). You will see these files show up on your computer after you've run a few programs alongside the corresponding source code files (that is, in the same directories).

Python saves byte code like this as a startup speed optimization. The next time you run your program, Python will load the *.pyc* files and skip the compilation step, as long as you haven't changed your source code since the byte code was last saved. Python automatically checks the timestamps of source and byte code files to know when it must recompile—if you resave your source code, byte code is automatically re-created the next time your program is run. Imports also check to see if the file must be recompiled because it was created by a different Python version, using a "magic" number in the byte-code file itself.

If Python cannot write the byte code files to your machine, your program still works—the byte code is generated in memory and simply discarded on program exit.* However, because *.pyc* files speed startup time, you'll want to make sure they are written for larger programs. Byte code files are also one way to ship Python programs—Python is happy to run a program if all it can find are *.pyc* files, even if the original *.py* source files are absent. (See "Frozen Binaries" on page 32 for another shipping option.)

The Python Virtual Machine (PVM)

Once your program has been compiled to byte code (or the byte code has been loaded from existing *.pyc* files), it is shipped off for execution to something generally known as the Python Virtual Machine (PVM, for the more acronym-inclined among you). The PVM sounds more impressive than it is; really, it's not a separate program, and it need not be installed by itself. In fact, the PVM is just a big loop that iterates through your byte code instructions, one by one, to carry out their operations. The PVM is the run-time engine of Python; it's always present as part of the Python system, and it's the component that truly runs your scripts. Technically, it's just the last step of what is called the "Python interpreter."

Figure 2-2 illustrates the runtime structure described here. Keep in mind that all of this complexity is deliberately hidden from Python programmers. Byte code compilation is automatic, and the PVM is just part of the Python system that you have installed on your machine. Again, programmers simply code and run files of statements.

Performance implications

Readers with a background in fully compiled languages such as C and C++ might notice a few differences in the Python model. For one thing, there is usually no build or "make" step in Python work: code runs immediately after it is written. For another, Python byte

---

* And, strictly speaking, byte code is saved only for files that are imported, not for the top-level file of a program. We'll explore imports in Chapter 3, and again in Part V. Byte code is also never saved for code typed at the interactive prompt, which is described in Chapter 3.

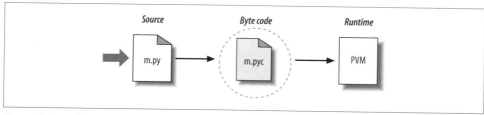

Figure 2-2. Python's traditional runtime execution model: source code you type is translated to byte code, which is then run by the Python Virtual Machine. Your code is automatically compiled, but then it is interpreted.

code is not binary machine code (e.g., instructions for an Intel chip). Byte code is a Python-specific representation.

This is why some Python code may not run as fast as C or C++ code, as described in Chapter 1—the PVM loop, not the CPU chip, still must interpret the byte code, and byte code instructions require more work than CPU instructions. On the other hand, unlike in classic interpreters, there is still an internal compile step—Python does not need to reanalyze and reparse each source statement repeatedly. The net effect is that pure Python code runs at speeds somewhere between those of a traditional compiled language and a traditional interpreted language. See Chapter 1 for more on Python performance tradeoffs.

Development implications

Another ramification of Python's execution model is that there is really no distinction between the development and execution environments. That is, the systems that compile and execute your source code are really one and the same. This similarity may have a bit more significance to readers with a background in traditional compiled languages, but in Python, the compiler is always present at runtime and is part of the system that runs programs.

This makes for a much more rapid development cycle. There is no need to precompile and link before execution may begin; simply type and run the code. This also adds a much more dynamic flavor to the language—it is possible, and often very convenient, for Python programs to construct and execute other Python programs at runtime. The **eval** and **exec** built-ins, for instance, accept and run strings containing Python program code. This structure is also why Python lends itself to product customization—because Python code can be changed on the fly, users can modify the Python parts of a system onsite without needing to have or compile the entire system's code.

At a more fundamental level, keep in mind that all we really have in Python is *runtime*—there is no initial compile-time phase at all, and everything happens as the program is running. This even includes operations such as the creation of functions and classes and the linkage of modules. Such events occur before execution in more static languages, but happen as programs execute in Python. As we'll see, the net effect makes for a much more dynamic programming experience than that to which some readers may be accustomed.

Execution Model Variations

Before moving on, I should point out that the internal execution flow described in the prior section reflects the standard implementation of Python today but is not really a requirement of the Python language itself. Because of that, the execution model is prone to changing with time. In fact, there are already a few systems that modify the picture in Figure 2-2 somewhat. Let's take a few moments to explore the most prominent of these variations.

Python Implementation Alternatives

Really, as this book is being written, there are three primary implementations of the Python language—*CPython*, *Jython*, and *IronPython*—along with a handful of secondary implementations such as *Stackless Python*. In brief, CPython is the standard implementation; all the others have very specific purposes and roles. All implement the same Python language but execute programs in different ways.

CPython

The original, and standard, implementation of Python is usually called CPython, when you want to contrast it with the other two. Its name comes from the fact that it is coded in portable ANSI C language code. This is the Python that you fetch from *http://www .python.org*, get with the ActivePython distribution, and have automatically on most Linux and Mac OS X machines. If you've found a preinstalled version of Python on your machine, it's probably CPython, unless your company is using Python in very specialized ways.

Unless you want to script Java or .NET applications with Python, you probably want to use the standard CPython system. Because it is the reference implementation of the language, it tends to run the fastest, be the most complete, and be more robust than the alternative systems. Figure 2-2 reflects CPython's runtime architecture.

Jython

The Jython system (originally known as JPython) is an alternative implementation of the Python language, targeted for integration with the Java programming language. Jython consists of Java classes that compile Python source code to Java byte code and then route the resulting byte code to the Java Virtual Machine (JVM). Programmers still code Python statements in *.py* text files as usual; the Jython system essentially just replaces the rightmost two bubbles in Figure 2-2 with Java-based equivalents.

Jython's goal is to allow Python code to script Java applications, much as CPython allows Python to script C and C++ components. Its integration with Java is remarkably seamless. Because Python code is translated to Java byte code, it looks and feels like a true Java program at runtime. Jython scripts can serve as web applets and servlets, build Java-based GUIs, and so on. Moreover, Jython includes integration support that allows Python code to import and use Java classes as though they were coded in Python. Because Jython is slower and less robust than CPython, though, it is usually seen as a tool of interest primarily to Java developers looking for a scripting language to be a frontend to Java code.

IronPython

A third implementation of Python, and newer than both CPython and Jython, IronPython is designed to allow Python programs to integrate with applications coded to work with Microsoft's .NET Framework for Windows, as well as the Mono open source equivalent for Linux. .NET and its C# programming language runtime system are designed to be a language-neutral object communication layer, in the spirit of Microsoft's earlier COM model. IronPython allows Python programs to act as both client and server components, accessible from other .NET languages.

By implementation, IronPython is very much like Jython (and, in fact, was developed by the same creator)—it replaces the last two bubbles in Figure 2-2 with equivalents for execution in the .NET environment. Also, like Jython, IronPython has a special focus—it is primarily of interest to developers integrating Python with .NET components. Because it is being developed by Microsoft, though, IronPython might also be able to leverage some important optimization tools for better performance. IronPython's scope is still evolving as I write this; for more details, consult the Python online resources or search the Web.[†]

Execution Optimization Tools

CPython, Jython, and IronPython all implement the Python language in similar ways: by compiling source code to byte code and executing the byte code on an appropriate virtual machine. Still other systems, including the Psyco just-in-time compiler and the Shedskin C++ translator, instead attempt to optimize the basic execution model. These systems are not required knowledge at this point in your Python career, but a quick look at their place in the execution model might help demystify the model in general.

[†] Jython and IronPython are completely independent implementations of Python that compile Python source for different runtime architectures. It is also possible to access Java and .NET software from standard CPython programs: JPype and Python for .NET systems, for example, allow CPython code to call out to Java and .NET components.

The Psyco just-in-time compiler

The Psyco system is not another Python implementation, but rather a component that extends the byte code execution model to make programs run faster. In terms of Figure 2-2, Psyco is an enhancement to the PVM that collects and uses type information while the program runs to translate portions of the program's byte code all the way down to real binary machine code for faster execution. Psyco accomplishes this translation without requiring changes to the code or a separate compilation step during development.

Roughly, while your program runs, Psyco collects information about the kinds of objects being passed around; that information can be used to generate highly efficient machine code tailored for those object types. Once generated, the machine code then replaces the corresponding part of the original byte code to speed your program's overall execution. The net effect is that, with Psyco, your program becomes much quicker over time and as it is running. In ideal cases, some Python code may become as fast as compiled C code under Psyco.

Because this translation from byte code happens at program runtime, Psyco is generally known as a *just-in-time* (JIT) compiler. Psyco is actually a bit different from the JIT compilers some readers may have seen for the Java language, though. Really, Psyco is a *specializing JIT compiler*—it generates machine code tailored to the data types that your program actually uses. For example, if a part of your program uses different data types at different times, Psyco may generate a different version of machine code to support each different type combination.

Psyco has been shown to speed Python code dramatically. According to its web page, Psyco provides "2x to 100x speed-ups, typically 4x, with an unmodified Python interpreter and unmodified source code, just a dynamically loadable C extension module." Of equal significance, the largest speedups are realized for algorithmic code written in pure Python—exactly the sort of code you might normally migrate to C to optimize. With Psyco, such migrations become even less important.

Psyco is not yet a standard part of Python; you will have to fetch and install it separately. It is also still something of a research project, so you'll have to track its evolution online. In fact, at this writing, although Psyco can still be fetched and installed by itself, it appears that much of the system may eventually be absorbed into the newer "PyPy" project—an attempt to reimplement Python's PVM in Python code, to better support optimizations like Psyco.

Perhaps the largest downside of Psyco is that it currently only generates machine code for Intel x86 architecture chips, though this includes Windows and Linux boxes and recent Macs. For more details on the Psyco extension, and other JIT efforts that may arise, consult *http://www.python.org*; you can also check out Psyco's home page, which currently resides at *http://psyco.sourceforge.net*.

The Shedskin C++ translator

Shedskin is an emerging system that takes a different approach to Python program execution—it attempts to translate Python source code to C++ code, which your computer's C++ compiler then compiles to machine code. As such, it represents a platform-neutral approach to running Python code. Shedskin is still somewhat experimental as I write these words, and it limits Python programs to an implicit statically typed constraint that is technically not normal Python, so we won't go into further detail here. Initial results, though, show that it has the potential to outperform both standard Python and the Psyco extension in terms of execution speed, and it is a promising project. Search the Web for details on the project's current status.

Frozen Binaries

Sometimes when people ask for a "real" Python compiler, what they're really seeking is simply a way to generate standalone binary executables from their Python programs. This is more a packaging and shipping idea than an execution-flow concept, but it's somewhat related. With the help of third-party tools that you can fetch off the Web, it is possible to turn your Python programs into true executables, known as *frozen binaries* in the Python world.

Frozen binaries bundle together the byte code of your program files, along with the PVM (interpreter) and any Python support files your program needs, into a single package. There are some variations on this theme, but the end result can be a single binary executable program (e.g., an *.exe* file on Windows) that can easily be shipped to customers. In Figure 2-2, it is as though the byte code and PVM are merged into a single component—a frozen binary file.

Today, three primary systems are capable of generating frozen binaries: *py2exe* (for Windows), *PyInstaller* (which is similar to py2exe but also works on Linux and Unix and is capable of generating self-installing binaries), and *freeze* (the original). You may have to fetch these tools separately from Python itself, but they are available free of charge. They are also constantly evolving, so consult *http://www.python.org* or your favorite web search engine for more on these tools. To give you an idea of the scope of these systems, py2exe can freeze standalone programs that use the tkinter, PMW, wxPython, and PyGTK GUI libraries; programs that use the *pygame* game programming toolkit; win32com client programs; and more.

Frozen binaries are not the same as the output of a true compiler—they run byte code through a virtual machine. Hence, apart from a possible startup improvement, frozen binaries run at the same speed as the original source files. Frozen binaries are not small (they contain a PVM), but by current standards they are not unusually large either. Because Python is embedded in the frozen binary, though, it does not have to be installed on the receiving end to run your program. Moreover, because your code is embedded in the frozen binary, it is more effectively hidden from recipients.

This single file-packaging scheme is especially appealing to developers of commercial software. For instance, a Python-coded user interface program based on the tkinter toolkit can be frozen into an executable file and shipped as a self-contained program on a CD or on the Web. End users do not need to install (or even have to know about) Python to run the shipped program.

Other Execution Options

Still other schemes for running Python programs have more focused goals:

- The *Stackless Python* system is a standard CPython implementation variant that does not save state on the C language call stack. This makes Python more easy to port to small stack architectures, provides efficient multiprocessing options, and fosters novel programming structures such as coroutines.

- The *Cython* system (based on work done by the *Pyrex* project) is a hybrid language that combines Python code with the ability to call C functions and use C type declarations for variables, parameters, and class attributes. Cython code can be compiled to C code that uses the Python/C API, which may then be compiled completely. Though not completely compatible with standard Python, Cython can be useful both for wrapping external C libraries and for coding efficient C extensions for Python.

For more details on these systems, search the Web for recent links.

Future Possibilities?

Finally, note that the runtime execution model sketched here is really an artifact of the current implementation of Python, not of the language itself. For instance, it's not impossible that a full, traditional compiler for translating Python source code to machine code may appear during the shelf life of this book (although one has not in nearly two decades!). New byte code formats and implementation variants may also be adopted in the future. For instance:

- The *Parrot* project aims to provide a common byte code format, virtual machine, and optimization techniques for a variety of programming languages (see *http://www.python.org*). Python's own PVM runs Python code more efficiently than Parrot, but it's unclear how Parrot will evolve.

- The *PyPy* project is an attempt to reimplement the PVM in Python itself to enable new implementation techniques. Its goal is to produce a fast and flexible implementation of Python.

- The Google-sponsored *Unladen Swallow* project aims to make standard Python faster by a factor of at least 5, and fast enough to replace the C language in many contexts. It is an optimization branch of CPython, intended to be fully compatible and significantly faster. This project also hopes to remove the Python multithreading Global Interpreter Lock (GIL), which prevents pure Python threads from truly overlapping in time. This is currently an emerging project being developed as open source by Google engineers; it is initially targeting Python 2.6, though 3.0 may acquire its changes too. Search Google for up-to-date details.

Although such future implementation schemes may alter the runtime structure of Python somewhat, it seems likely that the byte code compiler will still be the standard for some time to come. The portability and runtime flexibility of byte code are important features of many Python systems. Moreover, adding type constraint declarations to support static compilation would break the flexibility, conciseness, simplicity, and overall spirit of Python coding. Due to Python's highly dynamic nature, any future implementation will likely retain many artifacts of the current PVM.

Chapter Summary

This chapter introduced the execution model of Python (how Python runs your programs) and explored some common variations on that model (just-in-time compilers and the like). Although you don't really need to come to grips with Python internals to write Python scripts, a passing acquaintance with this chapter's topics will help you truly understand how your programs run once you start coding them. In the next chapter, you'll start actually running some code of your own. First, though, here's the usual chapter quiz.

Test Your Knowledge: Quiz

1. What is the Python interpreter?
2. What is source code?
3. What is byte code?
4. What is the PVM?
5. Name two variations on Python's standard execution model.
6. How are CPython, Jython, and IronPython different?

Test Your Knowledge: Answers

1. The Python interpreter is a program that runs the Python programs you write.
2. Source code is the statements you write for your program—it consists of text in text files that normally end with a *.py* extension.
3. Byte code is the lower-level form of your program after Python compiles it. Python automatically stores byte code in files with a *.pyc* extension.

4. The PVM is the Python Virtual Machine—the runtime engine of Python that interprets your compiled byte code.

5. Psyco, Shedskin, and frozen binaries are all variations on the execution model.

6. CPython is the standard implementation of the language. Jython and IronPython implement Python programs for use in Java and .NET environments, respectively; they are alternative compilers for Python.

## CHAPTER 3

How You Run Programs

OK, it's time to start running some code. Now that you have a handle on program execution, you're finally ready to start some real Python programming. At this point, I'll assume that you have Python installed on your computer; if not, see the prior chapter and Appendix A for installation and configuration hints.

There are a variety of ways to tell Python to execute the code you type. This chapter discusses all the program launching techniques in common use today. Along the way, you'll learn how to type code *interactively* and how to save it in *files* to be run with system command lines, icon clicks, module imports and reloads, **exec** calls, menu options in GUIs such as IDLE, and more.

If you just want to find out how to run a Python program quickly, you may be tempted to read the parts of this chapter that pertain only to your platform and move on to Chapter 4. But don't skip the material on module imports, as that's essential to understanding Python's program architecture. I also encourage you to at least skim the sections on IDLE and other IDEs, so you'll know what tools are available for when you start developing more sophisticated Python programs.

The Interactive Prompt

Perhaps the simplest way to run Python programs is to type them at Python's interactive command line, sometimes called the *interactive prompt*. There are a variety of ways to start this command line: in an IDE, from a system console, and so on. Assuming the interpreter is installed as an executable program on your system, the most platform-neutral way to start an interactive interpreter session is usually just to type **python** at your operating system's prompt, without any arguments. For example:

```
% python
Python 3.0.1 (r301:69561, Feb 13 2009, 20:04:18) [MSC v.1500 32 bit (Intel)] ...
Type "help", "copyright", "credits" or "license" for more information.
>>>
```

Typing the word "python" at your system shell prompt like this begins an interactive Python session; the "%" character at the start of this listing stands for a generic system prompt in this book—it's not input that you type yourself. The notion of a system shell prompt is generic, but exactly how you access it varies by platform:

- On Windows, you can type **python** in a DOS console window (a.k.a. the Command Prompt, usually found in the Accessories section of the Start→Programs menu) or in the Start→Run... dialog box.

- On Unix, Linux, and Mac OS X, you might type this command in a shell or terminal window (e.g., in an *xterm* or console running a shell such as *ksh* or *csh*).

- Other systems may use similar or platform-specific devices. On handheld devices, for example, you generally click the Python icon in the home or application window to launch an interactive session.

If you have not set your shell's PATH environment variable to include Python's install directory, you may need to replace the word "python" with the full path to the Python executable on your machine. On Unix, Linux, and similar, **/usr/local/bin/python** or **/usr/bin/python** will often suffice. On Windows, try typing **C:\Python30\python** (for version 3.0):

```
C:\misc> c:\python30\python
Python 3.0.1 (r301:69561, Feb 13 2009, 20:04:18) [MSC v.1500 32 bit (Intel)] ...
Type "help", "copyright", "credits" or "license" for more information.
>>>
```

Alternatively, you can run a change-directory command to go to Python's install directory before typing "python"—try the **cd c:\python30** command on Windows, for example:

```
C:\misc> cd C:\Python30
C:\Python30> python
Python 3.0.1 (r301:69561, Feb 13 2009, 20:04:18) [MSC v.1500 32 bit (Intel)] ...
Type "help", "copyright", "credits" or "license" for more information.
>>>
```

On Windows, besides typing **python** in a shell window, you can also begin similar interactive sessions by starting IDLE's main window (discussed later) or by selecting the "Python (command line)" menu option from the Start button menu for Python, as shown in Figure 2-1 back in Chapter 2. Both spawn a Python interactive prompt with equivalent functionality; typing a shell command isn't necessary.

Running Code Interactively

However it's started, the Python interactive session begins by printing two lines of informational text (which I'll omit from most of this book's examples to save space), then prompts for input with >>> when it's waiting for you to type a new Python statement or expression. When working interactively, the results of your code are displayed after the >>> lines after you press the Enter key.

For instance, here are the results of two Python `print` statements (`print` is really a function call in Python 3.0, but not in 2.6, so the parentheses here are required in 3.0 only):

```
% python
>>> print('Hello world!')
Hello world!
>>> print(2 ** 8)
256
```

Again, you don't need to worry about the details of the `print` statements shown here yet; we'll start digging into syntax in the next chapter. In short, they print a Python string and an integer, as shown by the output lines that appear after each >>> input line (2 ** 8 means 2 raised to the power 8 in Python).

When coding interactively like this, you can type as many Python commands as you like; each is run immediately after it's entered. Moreover, because the interactive session automatically prints the results of expressions you type, you don't usually need to say "print" explicitly at this prompt:

```
>>> lumberjack = 'okay'
>>> lumberjack
'okay'
>>> 2 ** 8
256
>>>                      <== Use Ctrl-D (on Unix) or Ctrl-Z (on Windows) to exit
%
```

Here, the first line saves a value by assigning it to a variable, and the last two lines typed are expressions (`lumberjack` and 2 ** 8)—their results are displayed automatically. To exit an interactive session like this one and return to your system shell prompt, type Ctrl-D on Unix-like machines; on MS-DOS and Windows systems, type Ctrl-Z to exit. In the IDLE GUI discussed later, either type Ctrl-D or simply close the window.

Now, we didn't do much in this session's code—just typed some Python `print` and assignment statements, along with a few expressions, which we'll study in detail later. The main thing to notice is that the interpreter executes the code entered on each line immediately, when the Enter key is pressed.

For example, when we typed the first print statement at the >>> prompt, the output (a Python string) was echoed back right away. There was no need to create a source-code file, and no need to run the code through a compiler and linker first, as you'd normally do when using a language such as C or C++. As you'll see in later chapters, you can also run multiline statements at the interactive prompt; such a statement runs immediately after you've entered all of its lines and pressed Enter twice to add a blank line.

Why the Interactive Prompt?

The interactive prompt runs code and echoes results as you go, but it doesn't save your code in a file. Although this means you won't do the bulk of your coding in interactive sessions, the interactive prompt turns out to be a great place to both *experiment* with the language and *test* program files on the fly.

Experimenting

Because code is executed immediately, the interactive prompt is a perfect place to experiment with the language and will be used often in this book to demonstrate smaller examples. In fact, this is the first rule of thumb to remember: if you're ever in doubt about how a piece of Python code works, fire up the interactive command line and try it out to see what happens.

For instance, suppose you're reading a Python program's code and you come across an expression like 'Spam!' * 8 whose meaning you don't understand. At this point, you can spend 10 minutes wading through manuals and books to try to figure out what the code does, or you can simply run it interactively:

```
>>> 'Spam!' * 8                              <== Learning by trying
'Spam!Spam!Spam!Spam!Spam!Spam!Spam!Spam!'
```

The immediate feedback you receive at the interactive prompt is often the quickest way to deduce what a piece of code does. Here, it's clear that it does string repetition: in Python * means multiply for numbers, but repeat for strings—it's like concatenating a string to itself repeatedly (more on strings in Chapter 4).

Chances are good that you won't break anything by experimenting this way—at least, not yet. To do real damage, like deleting files and running shell commands, you must really try, by importing modules explicitly (you also need to know more about Python's system interfaces in general before you will become that dangerous!). Straight Python code is almost always safe to run.

For instance, watch what happens when you make a mistake at the interactive prompt:

```
>>> X                                              <== Making mistakes
Traceback (most recent call last):
  File "<stdin>", line 1, in <module>
NameError: name 'X' is not defined
```

In Python, using a variable before it has been assigned a value is always an error (otherwise, if names were filled in with defaults, some errors might go undetected). We'll learn more about that later; the important point here is that you don't crash Python or your computer when you make a mistake this way. Instead, you get a meaningful error message pointing out the mistake and the line of code that made it, and you can continue on in your session or script. In fact, once you get comfortable with Python, its error messages may often provide as much debugging support as you'll need (you'll read more on debugging in the sidebar "Debugging Python Code" on page 69).

Testing

Besides serving as a tool for experimenting while you're learning the language, the interactive interpreter is also an ideal place to test code you've written in files. You can import your module files interactively and run tests on the tools they define by typing calls at the interactive prompt.

For instance, the following tests a function in a precoded module that ships with Python in its standard library (it prints the name of the directory you're currently working in), but you can do the same once you start writing module files of your own:

```
>>> import os
>>> os.getcwd()                                    <== Testing on the fly
'c:\\Python30'
```

More generally, the interactive prompt is a place to test program components, regardless of their source—you can import and test functions and classes in your Python files, type calls to linked-in C functions, exercise Java classes under Jython, and more. Partly because of its interactive nature, Python supports an experimental and exploratory programming style you'll find convenient when getting started.

Using the Interactive Prompt

Although the interactive prompt is simple to use, there are a few tips that beginners should keep in mind. I'm including lists of common mistakes like this in this chapter for reference, but they might also spare you from a few headaches if you read them up front:

- **Type Python commands only**. First of all, remember that you can only type Python code at the Python prompt, not system commands. There are ways to run system commands from within Python code (e.g., with `os.system`), but they are not as direct as simply typing the commands themselves.

- **print statements are required only in files**. Because the interactive interpreter automatically prints the results of expressions, you do not need to type complete print statements interactively. This is a nice feature, but it tends to confuse users when they move on to writing code in files: within a code file, you must use print statements to see your output because expression results are not automatically echoed. Remember, you must say print in files, but not interactively.

- **Don't indent at the interactive prompt (yet)**. When typing Python programs, either interactively or into a text file, be sure to start all your unnested statements in column 1 (that is, all the way to the left). If you don't, Python may print a "SyntaxError" message, because blank space to the left of your code is taken to be indentation that groups nested statements. Until Chapter 10, all statements you write will be unnested, so this includes everything for now. This seems to be a recurring confusion in introductory Python classes. Remember, a leading space generates an error message.

- **Watch out for prompt changes for compound statements**. We won't meet *compound* (multiline) statements until Chapter 4, and not in earnest until Chapter 10, but as a preview, you should know that when typing lines 2 and beyond of a compound statement interactively, the prompt may change. In the simple shell window interface, the interactive prompt changes to ... instead of >>> for lines 2 and beyond; in the IDLE interface, lines after the first are automatically indented.

  You'll see why this matters in Chapter 10. For now, if you happen to come across a ... prompt or a blank line when entering your code, it probably means that you've somehow confused interactive Python into thinking you're typing a multiline statement. Try hitting the Enter key or a Ctrl-C combination to get back to the main prompt. The >>> and ... prompt strings can also be changed (they are available in the built-in module sys), but I'll assume they have not been in the book's example listings.

- **Terminate compound statements at the interactive prompt with a blank line**. At the interactive prompt, inserting a blank line (by hitting the Enter key at the start of a line) is necessary to tell interactive Python that you're done typing the multiline statement. That is, you must press Enter twice to make a compound statement run. By contrast, blank lines are not required in files and are simply ignored if present. If you don't press Enter twice at the end of a compound statement when working interactively, you'll appear to be stuck in a limbo state, because the interactive interpreter will do nothing at all—it's waiting for you to press Enter again!

- **The interactive prompt runs one statement at a time**. At the interactive prompt, you must run one statement to completion before typing another. This is natural for simple statements, because pressing the Enter key runs the statement entered. For compound statements, though, remember that you must submit a blank line to terminate the statement and make it run before you can type the next statement.

Entering multiline statements

At the risk of repeating myself, I received emails from readers who'd gotten burned by the last two points as I was updating this chapter, so it probably merits emphasis. I'll introduce multiline (a.k.a. compound) statements in the next chapter, and we'll explore their syntax more formally later in this book. Because their behavior differs slightly in files and at the interactive prompt, though, two cautions are in order here.

First, be sure to terminate multiline compound statements like `for` loops and `if` tests at the interactive prompt with a blank line. *You must press the Enter key twice*, to terminate the whole multiline statement and then make it run. For example (pun not intended...):

```
>>> for x in 'spam':
...     print(x)            <== Press Enter twice here to make this loop run
...
```

You don't need the blank line after compound statements in a script file, though; this is required *only* at the interactive prompt. In a file, blank lines are not required and are simply ignored when present; at the interactive prompt, they terminate multiline statements.

Also bear in mind that the interactive prompt runs just *one statement at a time*: you must press Enter twice to run a loop or other multiline statement before you can type the next statement:

```
>>> for x in 'spam':
...     print(x)            <== Need to press Enter twice before a new statement
... print('done')
  File "<stdin>", line 3
    print('done')
        ^
SyntaxError: invalid syntax
```

This means you can't cut and paste multiple lines of code into the interactive prompt, unless the code includes blank lines after each compound statement. Such code is better run in a file—the next section's topic.

System Command Lines and Files

Although the interactive prompt is great for experimenting and testing, it has one big disadvantage: programs you type there go away as soon as the Python interpreter executes them. Because the code you type interactively is never stored in a file, you can't run it again without retyping it from scratch. Cut-and-paste and command recall can help some here, but not much, especially when you start writing larger programs. To cut and paste code from an interactive session, you would have to edit out Python prompts, program outputs, and so on—not exactly a modern software development methodology!

To save programs permanently, you need to write your code in files, which are usually known as *modules*. Modules are simply text files containing Python statements. Once coded, you can ask the Python interpreter to execute the statements in such a file any number of times, and in a variety of ways—by system command lines, by file icon clicks, by options in the IDLE user interface, and more. Regardless of how it is run, Python executes all the code in a module file from top to bottom each time you run the file.

Terminology in this domain can vary somewhat. For instance, module files are often referred to as *programs* in Python—that is, a program is considered to be a series of precoded statements stored in a file for repeated execution. Module files that are run directly are also sometimes called *scripts*—an informal term usually meaning a top-level program file. Some reserve the term "module" for a file imported from another file. (More on the meaning of "top-level" and imports in a few moments.)

Whatever you call them, the next few sections explore ways to run code typed into module files. In this section, you'll learn how to run files in the most basic way: by listing their names in a `python` command line entered at your computer's system prompt. Though it might seem primitive to some, for many programmers a system shell command-line window, together with a text editor window, constitutes as much of an integrated development environment as they will ever need.

A First Script

Let's get started. Open your favorite text editor (e.g., *vi*, Notepad, or the IDLE editor), and type the following statements into a new text file named *script1.py*:

```
# A first Python script
import sys                    # Load a library module
print(sys.platform)
print(2 ** 100)               # Raise 2 to a power
x = 'Spam!'
print(x * 8)                  # String repetition
```

This file is our first official Python script (not counting the two-liner in Chapter 2). You shouldn't worry too much about this file's code, but as a brief description, this file:

- Imports a Python module (libraries of additional tools), to fetch the name of the platform
- Runs three `print` function calls, to display the script's results
- Uses a variable named x, created when it's assigned, to hold onto a string object
- Applies various object operations that we'll begin studying in the next chapter

The `sys.platform` here is just a string that identifies the kind of computer you're working on; it lives in a standard Python module called `sys`, which you must import to load (again, more on imports later).

For color, I've also added some formal Python *comments* here—the text after the # characters. Comments can show up on lines by themselves, or to the right of code on a line. The text after a # is simply ignored as a human-readable comment and is not considered part of the statement's syntax. If you're copying this code, you can ignore the comments as well. In this book, we usually use a different formatting style to make comments more visually distinctive, but they'll appear as normal text in your code.

Again, don't focus on the syntax of the code in this file for now; we'll learn about all of it later. The main point to notice is that you've typed this code into a file, rather than at the interactive prompt. In the process, you've coded a fully functional Python script.

Notice that the module file is called *script1.py*. As for all top-level files, it could also be called simply *script*, but files of code you want to *import* into a client have to end with a *.py* suffix. We'll study imports later in this chapter. Because you may want to import them in the future, it's a good idea to use *.py* suffixes for most Python files that you code. Also, some text editors detect Python files by their *.py* suffix; if the suffix is not present, you may not get features like syntax colorization and automatic indentation.

Running Files with Command Lines

Once you've saved this text file, you can ask Python to run it by listing its full filename as the first argument to a `python` command, typed at the system shell prompt:

```
% python script1.py
win32
1267650600228229401496703205376
Spam!Spam!Spam!Spam!Spam!Spam!Spam!Spam!
```

Again, you can type such a system shell command in whatever your system provides for command-line entry—a Windows Command Prompt window, an xterm window, or similar. Remember to replace "python" with a full directory path, as before, if your PATH setting is not configured.

If all works as planned, this shell command makes Python run the code in this file line by line, and you will see the output of the script's three `print` statements—the name of the underlying platform, 2 raised to the power 100, and the result of the same string repetition expression we saw earlier (again, more on the last two of these in Chapter 4).

If all didn't work as planned, you'll get an error message—make sure you've entered the code in your file exactly as shown, and try again. We'll talk about debugging options in the sidebar "Debugging Python Code" on page 69, but at this point in the book your best bet is probably rote imitation.

Because this scheme uses shell command lines to start Python programs, all the usual shell syntax applies. For instance, you can route the output of a Python script to a file to save it for later use or inspection by using special shell syntax:

```
% python script1.py > saveit.txt
```

In this case, the three output lines shown in the prior run are stored in the file *saveit.txt* instead of being printed. This is generally known as *stream redirection*; it works for input and output text and is available on Windows and Unix-like systems. It also has little to do with Python (Python simply supports it), so we will skip further details on shell redirection syntax here.

If you are working on a Windows platform, this example works the same, but the system prompt is normally different:

```
C:\Python30> python script1.py
win32
1267650600228229401496703205376
Spam! Spam! Spam! Spam! Spam! Spam! Spam! Spam!
```

As usual, be sure to type the full path to Python if you haven't set your PATH environment variable to include this path or run a change-directory command to go to the path:

```
D:\temp> C:\python30\python script1.py
win32
1267650600228229401496703205376
Spam! Spam! Spam! Spam! Spam! Spam! Spam! Spam!
```

On all recent versions of Windows, you can also type just the name of your script, and omit the name of Python itself. Because newer Windows systems use the Windows Registry to find a program with which to run a file, you don't need to name "python" on the command line explicitly to run a *.py* file. The prior command, for example, could be simplified to this on most Windows machines:

```
D:\temp> script1.py
```

Finally, remember to give the full path to your script file if it lives in a different directory from the one in which you are working. For example, the following system command line, run from *D:\other*, assumes Python is in your system path but runs a file located elsewhere:

```
D:\other> python c:\code\otherscript.py
```

If your PATH doesn't include Python's directory, and neither Python nor your script file is in the directory you're working in, use full paths for both:

```
D:\other> C:\Python30\python c:\code\otherscript.py
```

Using Command Lines and Files

Running program files from system command lines is also a fairly straightforward launch option, especially if you are familiar with command lines in general from prior work. For newcomers, though, here are a few pointers about common beginner traps that might help you avoid some frustration:

- **Beware of automatic extensions on Windows**. If you use the Notepad program to code program files on Windows, be careful to pick the type All Files when it comes time to save your file, and give the file a *.py* suffix explicitly. Otherwise, Notepad will save your file with a *.txt* extension (e.g., as *script1.py.txt*), making it difficult to run in some launching schemes.

  Worse, Windows hides file extensions by default, so unless you have changed your view options you may not even notice that you've coded a text file and not a Python file. The file's icon may give this away—if it doesn't have a snake on it, you may have trouble. Uncolored code in IDLE and files that open to edit instead of run when clicked are other symptoms of this problem.

  Microsoft Word similarly adds a *.doc* extension by default; much worse, it adds formatting characters that are not legal Python syntax. As a rule of thumb, always pick All Files when saving under Windows, or use a more programmer-friendly text editor such as IDLE. IDLE does not even add a *.py* suffix automatically—a feature programmers tend to like, but users do not.

- **Use file extensions and directory paths at system prompts, but not for imports**. Don't forget to type the full name of your file in system command lines— that is, use `python script1.py` rather than `python script1`. By contrast, Python's `import` statements, which we'll meet later in this chapter, omit both the *.py* file suffix and the directory path (e.g., `import script1`). This may seem trivial, but confusing these two is a common mistake.

  At the system prompt, you are in a system shell, not Python, so Python's module file search rules do not apply. Because of that, you must include both the *.py* extension and, if necessary, the full directory path leading to the file you wish to run. For instance, to run a file that resides in a different directory from the one in which you are working, you would typically list its full path (e.g., `python d:\tests\spam.py`). Within Python code, however, you can just say `import spam` and rely on the Python module search path to locate your file, as described later.

- **Use `print` statements in files**. Yes, we've already been over this, but it is such a common mistake that it's worth repeating at least once here. Unlike in interactive coding, you generally must use `print` statements to see output from program files. If you don't see any output, make sure you've said "print" in your file. Again, though, `print` statements are *not* required in an interactive session, since Python automatically echoes expression results; `print`s don't hurt here, but are superfluous extra typing.

Unix Executable Scripts (#!)

If you are going to use Python on a Unix, Linux, or Unix-like system, you can also turn files of Python code into executable programs, much as you would for programs coded in a shell language such as *csh* or *ksh*. Such files are usually called *executable scripts*. In simple terms, Unix-style executable scripts are just normal text files containing Python statements, but with two special properties:

- **Their first line is special**. Scripts usually start with a line that begins with the characters #! (often called "hash bang"), followed by the path to the Python interpreter on your machine.

- **They usually have executable privileges**. Script files are usually marked as executable to tell the operating system that they may be run as top-level programs. On Unix systems, a command such as `chmod +x file.py` usually does the trick.

Let's look at an example for Unix-like systems. Use your text editor again to create a file of Python code called *brian*:

```
#!/usr/local/bin/python
print('The Bright Side ' + 'of Life...')        # + means concatenate for strings
```

The special line at the top of the file tells the system where the Python interpreter lives. Technically, the first line is a Python comment. As mentioned earlier, all comments in Python programs start with a # and span to the end of the line; they are a place to insert extra information for human readers of your code. But when a comment such as the first line in this file appears, it's special because the operating system uses it to find an interpreter for running the program code in the rest of the file.

Also, note that this file is called simply *brian*, without the *.py* suffix used for the module file earlier. Adding a *.py* to the name wouldn't hurt (and might help you remember that this is a Python program file), but because you don't plan on letting other modules import the code in this file, the name of the file is irrelevant. If you give the file executable privileges with a `chmod +x brian` shell command, you can run it from the operating system shell as though it were a binary program:

```
% brian
The Bright Side of Life...
```

A note for Windows users: the method described here is a Unix trick, and it may not work on your platform. Not to worry; just use the basic command-line technique explored earlier. List the file's name on an explicit `python` command line:[*]

---

[*] As we discussed when exploring command lines, modern Windows versions also let you type just the name of a *.py* file at the system command line—they use the Registry to determine that the file should be opened with Python (e.g., typing **brian.py** is equivalent to typing **python brian.py**). This command-line mode is similar in spirit to the Unix #!, though it is system-wide on Windows, not per-file. Note that some *programs* may actually interpret and use a first #! line on Windows much like on Unix, but the DOS system shell on Windows simply ignores it.

```
C:\misc> python brian
The Bright Side of Life...
```

In this case, you don't need the special #! comment at the top (although Python just ignores it if it's present), and the file doesn't need to be given executable privileges. In fact, if you want to run files portably between Unix and Microsoft Windows, your life will probably be simpler if you always use the basic command-line approach, not Unix-style scripts, to launch programs.

The Unix env Lookup Trick

On some Unix systems, you can avoid hardcoding the path to the Python interpreter by writing the special first-line comment like this:

```
#!/usr/bin/env python
...script goes here...
```

When coded this way, the *env* program locates the Python interpreter according to your system search path settings (i.e., in most Unix shells, by looking in all the directories listed in the PATH environment variable). This scheme can be more portable, as you don't need to hardcode a Python install path in the first line of all your scripts.

Provided you have access to *env* everywhere, your scripts will run no matter where Python lives on your system—you need only change the PATH environment variable settings across platforms, not in the first line in all your scripts. Of course, this assumes that *env* lives in the same place everywhere (on some machines, it may be in */sbin*, */bin*, or elsewhere); if not, all portability bets are off!

Clicking File Icons

On Windows, the Registry makes opening files with icon clicks easy. Python automatically registers itself to be the program that opens Python program files when they are clicked. Because of that, it is possible to launch the Python programs you write by simply clicking (or double-clicking) on their file icons with your mouse cursor.

On non-Windows systems, you will probably be able to perform a similar trick, but the icons, file explorer, navigation schemes, and more may differ slightly. On some Unix systems, for instance, you may need to register the *.py* extension with your file explorer GUI, make your script executable using the #! trick discussed in the previous section, or associate the file MIME type with an application or command by editing files, installing programs, or using other tools. See your file explorer's documentation for more details if clicks do not work correctly right off the bat.

Clicking Icons on Windows

To illustrate, let's keep using the script we wrote earlier, *script1.py*, repeated here to minimize page flipping:

```
# A first Python script
import sys                              # Load a library module
print(sys.platform)
print(2 ** 100)                         # Raise 2 to a power
x = 'Spam!'
print(x * 8)                            # String repetition
```

As we've seen, you can always run this file from a system command line:

```
C:\misc> c:\python30\python script1.py
win32
1267650600228229401496703205376
Spam!Spam!Spam!Spam!Spam!Spam!Spam!Spam!
```

However, icon clicks allow you to run the file without any typing at all. If you find this file's icon—for instance, by selecting Computer (or My Computer in XP) in your Start menu and working your way down on the C drive on Windows—you will get the file explorer picture captured in Figure 3-1 (Windows Vista is being used here). Python source files show up with white backgrounds on Windows, and byte code files show up with black backgrounds. You will normally want to click (or otherwise run) the source code file, in order to pick up your most recent changes. To launch the file here, simply click on the icon for *script1.py*.

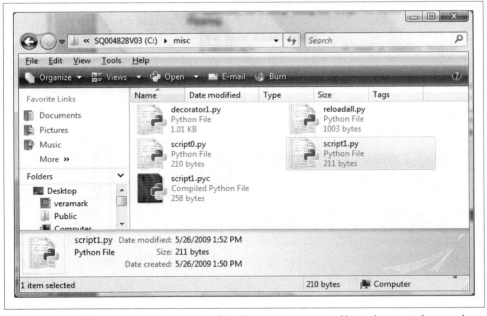

Figure 3-1. On Windows, Python program files show up as icons in file explorer windows and can automatically be run with a double-click of the mouse (though you might not see printed output or error messages this way).

The input Trick

Unfortunately, on Windows, the result of clicking on a file icon may not be incredibly satisfying. In fact, as it is, this example script generates a perplexing "flash" when clicked—not exactly the sort of feedback that budding Python programmers usually hope for! This is not a bug, but has to do with the way the Windows version of Python handles printed output.

By default, Python generates a pop-up black DOS console window to serve as a clicked file's input and output. If a script just prints and exits, well, it just prints and exits—the console window appears, and text is printed there, but the console window closes and disappears on program exit. Unless you are very fast, or your machine is very slow, you won't get to see your output at all. Although this is normal behavior, it's probably not what you had in mind.

Luckily, it's easy to work around this. If you need your script's output to stick around when you launch it with an icon click, simply put a call to the built-in `input` function at the very bottom of the script (`raw_input` in 2.6: see the note ahead). For example:

```
# A first Python script
import sys                 # Load a library module
print(sys.platform)
print(2 ** 100)            # Raise 2 to a power
x = 'Spam!'
print(x * 8)              # String repetition
input()                  # <== ADDED
```

In general, `input` reads the next line of standard input, waiting if there is none yet available. The net effect in this context will be to pause the script, thereby keeping the output window shown in Figure 3-2 open until you press the Enter key.

Figure 3-2. When you click a program's icon on Windows, you will be able to see its printed output if you include an input call at the very end of the script. But you only need to do so in this context!

Now that I've shown you this trick, keep in mind that it is usually only required for Windows, and then only if your script prints text and exits and only if you will launch the script by clicking its file icon. You should add this call to the bottom of your top-level files if and only if all of these three conditions apply. There is no reason to add this call in any other contexts (unless you're unreasonably fond of pressing your computer's Enter key!).† That may sound obvious, but it's another common mistake in live classes.

Before we move ahead, note that the `input` call applied here is the input counterpart of using the `print` statement for outputs. It is the simplest way to read user input, and it is more general than this example implies. For instance, `input`:

- Optionally accepts a string that will be printed as a prompt (e.g., `input('Press Enter to exit')`)
- Returns to your script a line of text read as a string (e.g., `nextinput = input()`)
- Supports input stream redirections at the system shell level (e.g., `python spam.py < input.txt`), just as the `print` statement does for output

We'll use `input` in more advanced ways later in this text; for instance, Chapter 10 will apply it in an interactive loop.

 Version skew note: If you are working in Python 2.6 or earlier, use `raw_input()` instead of `input()` in this code. The former was renamed to the latter in Python 3.0. Technically, 2.6 has an `input` too, but it also *evaluates* strings as though they are program code typed into a script, and so will not work in this context (an empty string is an error). Python 3.0's `input` (and 2.6's `raw_input`) simply returns the entered text as a string, unevaluated. To simulate 2.6's `input` in 3.0, use `eval(input())`.

Other Icon-Click Limitations

Even with the `input` trick, clicking file icons is not without its perils. You also may not get to see Python error messages. If your script generates an error, the error message text is written to the pop-up console window—which then immediately disappears! Worse, adding an `input` call to your file will not help this time because your script will likely abort long before it reaches this call. In other words, you won't be able to tell what went wrong.

---

† It is also possible to completely suppress the pop-up DOS console window for clicked files on Windows. Files whose names end in a *.pyw* extension will display only windows constructed by your script, not the default DOS console window. *.pyw* files are simply *.py* source files that have this special operational behavior on Windows. They are mostly used for Python-coded user interfaces that build windows of their own, often in conjunction with various techniques for saving printed output and errors to files.

Because of these limitations, it is probably best to view icon clicks as a way to launch programs after they have been debugged or have been instrumented to write their output to a file. Especially when starting out, use other techniques—such as system command lines and IDLE (discussed further in the section "The IDLE User Interface" on page 60)—so that you can see generated error messages and view your normal output without resorting to coding tricks. When we discuss exceptions later in this book, you'll also learn that it is possible to intercept and recover from errors so that they do not terminate your programs. Watch for the discussion of the `try` statement later in this book for an alternative way to keep the console window from closing on errors.

Module Imports and Reloads

So far, I've been talking about "importing modules" without really explaining what this term means. We'll study modules and larger program architecture in depth in Part V, but because imports are also a way to launch programs, this section will introduce enough module basics to get you started.

In simple terms, every file of Python source code whose name ends in a *.py* extension is a module. Other files can access the items a module defines by *importing* that module; `import` operations essentially load another file and grant access to that file's contents. The contents of a module are made available to the outside world through its attributes (a term I'll define in the next section).

This module-based services model turns out to be the core idea behind program architecture in Python. Larger programs usually take the form of multiple module files, which import tools from other module files. One of the modules is designated as the main or *top-level* file, and this is the one launched to start the entire program.

We'll delve into such architectural issues in more detail later in this book. This chapter is mostly interested in the fact that import operations *run* the code in a file that is being loaded as a final step. Because of this, importing a file is yet another way to launch it.

For instance, if you start an interactive session (from a system command line, from the Start menu, from IDLE, or otherwise), you can run the *script1.py* file you created earlier with a simple import (be sure to delete the `input` line you added in the prior section first, or you'll need to press Enter for no reason):

```
C:\misc> c:\python30\python
>>> import script1
win32
1267650600228229401496703205376
Spam!Spam!Spam!Spam!Spam!Spam!Spam!Spam!
```

This works, but only once per session (really, process) by default. After the first import, later imports do nothing, even if you change and save the module's source file again in another window:

```
>>> import script1
>>> import script1
```

This is by design; imports are too expensive an operation to repeat more than once per file, per program run. As you'll learn in Chapter 21, imports must find files, compile them to byte code, and run the code.

If you really want to force Python to run the file again in the same session without stopping and restarting the session, you need to instead call the `reload` function available in the `imp` standard library module (this function is also a simple built-in in Python 2.6, but not in 3.0):

```
>>> from imp import reload              # Must load from module in 3.0
>>> reload(script1)
win32
65536
Spam!Spam!Spam!Spam!Spam!Spam!Spam!Spam!
<module 'script1' from 'script1.py'>
>>>
```

The `from` statement here simply copies a name out of a module (more on this soon). The `reload` function itself loads and runs the current version of your file's code, picking up changes if you've changed and saved it in another window.

This allows you to edit and pick up new code on the fly within the current Python interactive session. In this session, for example, the second `print` statement in *script1.py* was changed in another window to print `2 ** 16` between the time of the first `import` and the `reload` call.

The `reload` function expects the name of an already loaded module object, so you have to have successfully imported a module once before you reload it. Notice that `reload` also expects parentheses around the module object name, whereas `import` does not. `reload` is a function that is *called*, and `import` is a statement.

That's why you must pass the module name to `reload` as an argument in parentheses, and that's why you get back an extra output line when reloading. The last output line is just the display representation of the `reload` call's return value, a Python module object. We'll learn more about using functions in general in Chapter 16.

Version skew note: Python 3.0 moved the `reload` built-in function to the `imp` standard library module. It still reloads files as before, but you must import it in order to use it. In 3.0, run an `import imp` and use `imp.reload(M)`, or run a `from imp import reload` and use `reload(M)`, as shown here. We'll discuss `import` and `from` statements in the next section, and more formally later in this book.

If you are working in Python 2.6 (or 2.X in general), `reload` is available as a built-in function, so no import is required. In Python 2.6, `reload` is available in *both* forms—built-in and module function—to aid the transition to 3.0. In other words, reloading is still available in 3.0, but an extra line of code is required to fetch the `reload` call.

The move in 3.0 was likely motivated in part by some well-known issues involving `reload` and `from` statements that we'll encounter in the next section. In short, names loaded with a `from` are not directly updated by a `reload`, but names accessed with an `import` statement are. If your names don't seem to change after a `reload`, try using `import` and *module.attribute* name references instead.

The Grander Module Story: Attributes

Imports and reloads provide a natural program launch option because import operations execute files as a last step. In the broader scheme of things, though, modules serve the role of *libraries* of tools, as you'll learn in Part V. More generally, a module is mostly just a package of variable names, known as a *namespace*. The names within that package are called *attributes*—an attribute is simply a variable name that is attached to a specific object (like a module).

In typical use, importers gain access to all the names assigned at the top level of a module's file. These names are usually assigned to tools exported by the module—functions, classes, variables, and so on—that are intended to be used in other files and other programs. Externally, a module file's names can be fetched with two Python statements, `import` and `from`, as well as the `reload` call.

To illustrate, use a text editor to create a one-line Python module file called *myfile.py* with the following contents:

```
title = "The Meaning of Life"
```

This may be one of the world's simplest Python modules (it contains a single assignment statement), but it's enough to illustrate the point. When this file is imported, its code is run to generate the module's attribute. The assignment statement creates a module attribute named `title`.

You can access this module's `title` attribute in other components in two different ways. First, you can load the module as a whole with an `import` statement, and then *qualify* the module name with the attribute name to fetch it:

```
% python                      # Start Python
>>> import myfile             # Run file; load module as a whole
>>> print(myfile.title)       # Use its attribute names: '.' to qualify
The Meaning of Life
```

In general, the dot expression syntax *object.attribute* lets you fetch any attribute attached to any object, and this is a very common operation in Python code. Here, we've used it to access the string variable `title` inside the module `myfile`—in other words, `myfile.title`.

Alternatively, you can fetch (really, copy) names out of a module with `from` statements:

```
% python                      # Start Python
>>> from myfile import title  # Run file; copy its names
>>> print(title)              # Use name directly: no need to qualify
The Meaning of Life
```

As you'll see in more detail later, `from` is just like an `import`, with an extra assignment to names in the importing component. Technically, `from` copies a module's *attributes*, such that they become simple *variables* in the recipient—thus, you can simply refer to the imported string this time as `title` (a variable) instead of `myfile.title` (an attribute reference).‡

Whether you use `import` or `from` to invoke an import operation, the statements in the module file *myfile.py* are executed, and the importing component (here, the interactive prompt) gains access to names assigned at the top level of the file. There's only one such name in this simple example—the variable `title`, assigned to a string—but the concept will be more useful when you start defining objects such as functions and classes in your modules: such objects become reusable software components that can be accessed by name from one or more client modules.

In practice, module files usually define more than one name to be used in and outside the files. Here's an example that defines three:

```
a = 'dead'                    # Define three attributes
b = 'parrot'                  # Exported to other files
c = 'sketch'
print(a, b, c)                # Also used in this file
```

This file, *threenames.py*, assigns three variables, and so generates three attributes for the outside world. It also uses its own three variables in a `print` statement, as we see when we run this as a top-level file:

---

‡ Notice that `import` and `from` both list the name of the module file as simply *myfile* without its *.py* suffix. As you'll learn in Part V, when Python looks for the actual file, it knows to include the suffix in its search procedure. Again, you must include the `.py` suffix in system shell command lines, but not in `import` statements.

```
% python threenames.py
dead parrot sketch
```

All of this file's code runs as usual the first time it is imported elsewhere (by either an `import` or `from`). Clients of this file that use `import` get a module with attributes, while clients that use `from` get copies of the file's names:

```
% python
>>> import threenames              # Grab the whole module
dead parrot sketch
>>>
>>> threenames.b, threenames.c
('parrot', 'sketch')
>>>
>>> from threenames import a, b, c      # Copy multiple names
>>> b, c
('parrot', 'sketch')
```

The results here are printed in parentheses because they are really *tuples* (a kind of object covered in the next part of this book); you can safely ignore them for now.

Once you start coding modules with multiple names like this, the built-in `dir` function starts to come in handy—you can use it to fetch a list of the names available inside a module. The following returns a Python list of strings (we'll start studying lists in the next chapter):

```
>>> dir(threenames)
['__builtins__', '__doc__', '__file__', '__name__', '__package__', 'a', 'b', 'c']
```

I ran this on Python 3.0 and 2.6; older Pythons may return fewer names. When the `dir` function is called with the name of an imported module passed in parentheses like this, it returns all the attributes inside that module. Some of the names it returns are names you get "for free": names with leading and trailing double underscores are built-in names that are always predefined by Python and that have special meaning to the interpreter. The variables our code defined by assignment—a, b, and c—show up last in the `dir` result.

Modules and namespaces

Module imports are a way to run files of code, but, as we'll discuss later in the book, modules are also the largest program structure in Python programs.

In general, Python programs are composed of multiple module files, linked together by `import` statements. Each module file is a self-contained package of variables—that is, a namespace. One module file cannot see the names defined in another file unless it explicitly imports that other file, so modules serve to minimize name collisions in your code—because each file is a self-contained namespace, the names in one file cannot clash with those in another, even if they are spelled the same way.

In fact, as you'll see, modules are one of a handful of ways that Python goes to great lengths to package your variables into compartments to avoid name clashes. We'll discuss modules and other namespace constructs (including classes and function scopes) further later in the book. For now, modules will come in handy as a way to run your code many times without having to retype it.

 import versus from: I should point out that the from statement in a sense defeats the namespace partitioning purpose of modules—because the from copies variables from one file to another, it can cause same-named variables in the importing file to be overwritten (and won't warn you if it does). This essentially collapses namespaces together, at least in terms of the copied variables.

Because of this, some recommend using import instead of from. I won't go that far, though; not only does from involve less typing, but its purported problem is rarely an issue in practice. Besides, this is something *you* control by listing the variables you want in the from; as long as you understand that they'll be assigned values, this is no more dangerous than coding assignment statements—another feature you'll probably want to use!

import and reload Usage Notes

For some reason, once people find out about running files using import and reload, many tend to focus on this alone and forget about other launch options that always run the current version of the code (e.g., icon clicks, IDLE menu options, and system command lines). This approach can quickly lead to confusion, though—you need to remember when you've imported to know if you can reload, you need to remember to use parentheses when you call reload (only), and you need to remember to use reload in the first place to get the current version of your code to run. Moreover, reloads aren't transitive—reloading a module reloads that module only, not any modules it may import—so you sometimes have to reload multiple files.

Because of these complications (and others we'll explore later, including the reload/ from issue mentioned in a prior note in this chapter), it's generally a good idea to avoid the temptation to launch by imports and reloads for now. The IDLE Run→Run Module menu option described in the next section, for example, provides a simpler and less error-prone way to run your files, and always runs the current version of your code. System shell command lines offer similar benefits. You don't need to use reload if you use these techniques.

In addition, you may run into trouble if you use modules in unusual ways at this point in the book. For instance, if you want to import a module file that is stored in a directory other than the one you're working in, you'll have to skip ahead to Chapter 21 and learn about the *module search path*.

For now, if you must import, try to keep all your files in the directory you are working in to avoid complications.§

That said, imports and reloads have proven to be a popular testing technique in Python classes, and you may prefer using this approach too. As usual, though, if you find yourself running into a wall, stop running into a wall!

Using exec to Run Module Files

In fact, there are more ways to run code stored in module files than have yet been exposed here. For instance, the exec(open('module.py').read()) built-in function call is another way to launch files from the interactive prompt without having to import and later reload. Each exec runs the current version of the file, without requiring later reloads (*script1.py* is as we left it after a reload in the prior section):

```
C:\misc> c:\python30\python
>>> exec(open('script1.py').read())
win32
65536
Spam! Spam! Spam! Spam! Spam! Spam! Spam! Spam!

...change script1.py in a text edit window...

>>> exec(open('script1.py').read())
win32
4294967296
Spam! Spam! Spam! Spam! Spam! Spam! Spam! Spam!
```

The exec call has an effect similar to an import, but it doesn't technically import the module—by default, each time you call exec this way it runs the file anew, as though you had pasted it in at the place where exec is called. Because of that, exec does not require module reloads after file changes—it skips the normal module import logic.

On the downside, because it works as if pasting code into the place where it is called, exec, like the from statement mentioned earlier, has the potential to silently overwrite variables you may currently be using. For example, our *script1.py* assigns to a variable named x. If that name is also being used in the place where exec is called, the name's value is replaced:

```
>>> x = 999
>>> exec(open('script1.py').read())     # Code run in this namespace by default
...same output...
>>> x                                   # Its assignments can overwrite names here
'Spam!'
```

§ If you're burning with curiosity, the short story is that Python searches for imported modules in every directory listed in sys.path—a Python list of directory name strings in the sys module, which is initialized from a PYTHONPATH environment variable, plus a set of standard directories. If you want to import from a directory other than the one you are working in, that directory must generally be listed in your PYTHONPATH setting. For more details, see Chapter 21.

By contrast, the basic `import` statement runs the file only once per process, and it makes the file a separate module namespace so that its assignments will not change variables in your scope. The price you pay for the namespace partitioning of modules is the need to reload after changes.

> *Version skew note*: Python 2.6 also includes an `execfile('module.py')` built-in function, in addition to allowing the form `exec(open('module.py'))`, which both automatically read the file's content. Both of these are equivalent to the `exec(open('module.py').read())` form, which is more complex but runs in both 2.6 and 3.0.
>
> Unfortunately, neither of these two simpler 2.6 forms is available in 3.0, which means you must understand both files and their read methods to fully understand this technique today (alas, this seems to be a case of aesthetics trouncing practicality in 3.0). In fact, the `exec` form in 3.0 involves so much typing that the best advice may simply be not to do it—it's usually best to launch files by typing system shell command lines or by using the IDLE menu options described in the next section. For more on the file interfaces used by the 3.0 `exec` form, see Chapter 9.

The IDLE User Interface

So far, we've seen how to run Python code with the interactive prompt, system command lines, icon clicks, and module imports and `exec` calls. If you're looking for something a bit more visual, IDLE provides a graphical user interface for doing Python development, and it's a standard and free part of the Python system. It is usually referred to as an *integrated development environment* (IDE), because it binds together various development tasks into a single view.‖

In short, IDLE is a GUI that lets you edit, run, browse, and debug Python programs, all from a single interface. Moreover, because IDLE is a Python program that uses the *tkinter* GUI toolkit (known as Tkinter in 2.6), it runs portably on most Python platforms, including Microsoft Windows, X Windows (for Linux, Unix, and Unix-like platforms), and the Mac OS (both Classic and OS X). For many, IDLE represents an easy-to-use alternative to typing command lines, and a less problem-prone alternative to clicking on icons.

IDLE Basics

Let's jump right into an example. IDLE is easy to start under Windows—it has an entry in the Start button menu for Python (see Figure 2-1, shown previously), and it can also be selected by right-clicking on a Python program icon. On some Unix-like systems,

---

‖ IDLE is officially a corruption of IDE, but it's really named in honor of Monty Python member Eric Idle.

you may need to launch IDLE's top-level script from a command line, or by clicking on the icon for the *idle.pyw* or *idle.py* file located in the *idlelib* subdirectory of Python's *Lib* directory. On Windows, IDLE is a Python script that currently lives in *C:\Python30\Lib\idlelib* (or *C:\Python26\Lib\idlelib* in Python 2.6).#

Figure 3-3 shows the scene after starting IDLE on Windows. The Python shell window that opens initially is the main window, which runs an interactive session (notice the >>> prompt). This works like all interactive sessions—code you type here is run immediately after you type it—and serves as a testing tool.

Figure 3-3. The main Python shell window of the IDLE development GUI, shown here running on Windows. Use the File menu to begin (New Window) or change (Open...) a source file; use the text edit window's Run menu to run the code in that window (Run Module).

#IDLE is a Python program that uses the standard library's tkinter GUI toolkit (a.k.a. Tkinter in Python 2.6) to build the IDLE GUI. This makes IDLE portable, but it also means that you'll need to have tkinter support in your Python to use IDLE. The Windows version of Python has this by default, but some Linux and Unix users may need to install the appropriate tkinter support (a `yum tkinter` command may suffice on some Linux distributions, but see the installation hints in Appendix A for details). Mac OS X may have everything you need preinstalled, too; look for an `idle` command or script on your machine.

IDLE uses familiar menus with keyboard shortcuts for most of its operations. To make (or edit) a source code file under IDLE, open a text edit window: in the main window, select the File pull-down menu, and pick New Window (or Open... to open a text edit window displaying an existing file for editing).

Although it may not show up fully in this book's graphics, IDLE uses syntax-directed *colorization* for the code typed in both the main window and all text edit windows—keywords are one color, literals are another, and so on. This helps give you a better picture of the components in your code (and can even help you spot mistakes—run-on strings are all one color, for example).

To run a file of code that you are editing in IDLE, select the file's text edit window, open that window's Run pull-down menu, and choose the Run Module option listed there (or use the equivalent keyboard shortcut, given in the menu). Python will let you know that you need to save your file first if you've changed it since it was opened or last saved and forgot to save your changes—a common mistake when you're knee deep in coding.

When run this way, the output of your script and any error messages it may generate show up back in the main interactive window (the Python shell window). In Figure 3-3, for example, the three lines after the "RESTART" line near the middle of the window reflect an execution of our *script1.py* file opened in a separate edit window. The "RESTART" message tells us that the user-code process was restarted to run the edited script and serves to separate script output (it does not appear if IDLE is started without a user-code subprocess—more on this mode in a moment).

IDLE hint of the day: If you want to repeat prior commands in IDLE's main interactive window, you can use the Alt-P key combination to scroll backward through the command history, and Alt-N to scroll forward (on some Macs, try Ctrl-P and Ctrl-N instead). Your prior commands will be recalled and displayed, and may be edited and rerun. You can also recall commands by positioning the cursor on them, or use cut-and-paste operations, but these techniques tend to involve more work. Outside IDLE, you may be able to recall commands in an interactive session with the arrow keys on Windows.

Using IDLE

IDLE is free, easy to use, portable, and automatically available on most platforms. I generally recommend it to Python newcomers because it sugarcoats some of the details and does not assume prior experience with system command lines. However, it is somewhat limited compared to more advanced commercial IDEs. To help you avoid some common pitfalls, here is a list of issues that IDLE beginners should bear in mind:

- **You must add ".py" explicitly when saving your files**. I mentioned this when talking about files in general, but it's a common IDLE stumbling block, especially

---

for Windows users. IDLE does not automatically add a *.py* extension to filenames when files are saved. Be careful to type the *.py* extension yourself when saving a file for the first time. If you don't, while you will be able to run your file from IDLE (and system command lines), you will not be able to import it either interactively or from other modules.

- **Run scripts by selecting Run→Run Module in text edit windows, not by interactive imports and reloads**. Earlier in this chapter, we saw that it's possible to run a file by importing it interactively. However, this scheme can grow complex because it requires you to manually reload files after changes. By contrast, using the Run→Run Module menu option in IDLE always runs the most current version of your file, just like running it using a system shell command line. IDLE also prompts you to save your file first, if needed (another common mistake outside IDLE).

- **You need to reload only modules being tested interactively**. Like system shell command lines, IDLE's Run→Run Module menu option always runs the current version of both the top-level file and any modules it imports. Because of this, Run→Run Module eliminates common confusions surrounding imports. You only need to reload modules that you are importing and testing interactively in IDLE. If you choose to use the import and reload technique instead of Run→Run Module, remember that you can use the Alt-P/Alt-N key combinations to recall prior commands.

- **You can customize IDLE**. To change the text fonts and colors in IDLE, select the Configure option in the Options menu of any IDLE window. You can also customize key combination actions, indentation settings, and more; see IDLE's Help pull-down menu for more hints.

- **There is currently no clear-screen option in IDLE**. This seems to be a frequent request (perhaps because it's an option available in similar IDEs), and it might be added eventually. Today, though, there is no way to clear the interactive window's text. If you want the window's text to go away, you can either press and hold the Enter key, or type a Python loop to print a series of blank lines (nobody really uses the latter technique, of course, but it sounds more high-tech than pressing the Enter key!).

- **tkinter GUI and threaded programs may not work well with IDLE**. Because IDLE is a Python/tkinter program, it can hang if you use it to run certain types of advanced Python/tkinter programs. This has become less of an issue in more recent versions of IDLE that run user code in one process and the IDLE GUI itself in another, but some programs (especially those that use multithreading) might still hang the GUI. Your code may not exhibit such problems, but as a rule of thumb, it's always safe to use IDLE to edit GUI programs but launch them using other options, such as icon clicks or system command lines. When in doubt, if your code fails in IDLE, try it outside the GUI.

- **If connection errors arise, try starting IDLE in single-process mode**. Because IDLE requires communication between its separate user and GUI processes, it can sometimes have trouble starting up on certain platforms (notably, it fails to start occasionally on some Windows machines, due to firewall software that blocks connections). If you run into such connection errors, it's always possible to start IDLE with a system command line that forces it to run in single-process mode without a user-code subprocess and therefore avoids communication issues: its -n command-line flag forces this mode. On Windows, for example, start a Command Prompt window and run the system command line `idle.py -n` from within the directory *C:\Python30\Lib\idlelib* (`cd` there first if needed).

- **Beware of some IDLE usability features**. IDLE does much to make life easier for beginners, but some of its tricks won't apply outside the IDLE GUI. For instance, IDLE runs your scripts in its own interactive namespace, so variables in your code show up automatically in the IDLE interactive session—you don't always need to run `import` commands to access names at the top level of files you've already run. This can be handy, but it can also be confusing, because outside the IDLE environment names must always be imported from files to be used.

  IDLE also automatically changes both to the directory of a file just run and adds its directory to the module import search path—a handy feature that allows you to import files there without search path settings, but also something that won't work the same when you run files outside IDLE. It's OK to use such features, but don't forget that they are IDLE behavior, not Python behavior.

Advanced IDLE Tools

Besides the basic edit and run functions, IDLE provides more advanced features, including a point-and-click program debugger and an object browser. The IDLE debugger is enabled via the Debug menu and the object browser via the File menu. The browser allows you to navigate through the module search path to files and objects in files; clicking on a file or object opens the corresponding source in a text edit window.

IDLE debugging is initiated by selecting the Debug→Debugger menu option in the main window and then starting your script by selecting the Run→Run Module option in the text edit window; once the debugger is enabled, you can set breakpoints in your code that stop its execution by right-clicking on lines in the text edit windows, show variable values, and so on. You can also watch program execution when debugging—the current line of code is noted as you step through your code.

For simpler debugging operations, you can also right-click with your mouse on the text of an error message to quickly jump to the line of code where the error occurred—a trick that makes it simple and fast to repair and run again. In addition, IDLE's text editor offers a large collection of programmer-friendly tools, including automatic indentation, advanced text and file search operations, and more. Because IDLE uses intuitive GUI interactions, you should experiment with the system live to get a feel for its other tools.

Other IDEs

Because IDLE is free, portable, and a standard part of Python, it's a nice first development tool to become familiar with if you want to use an IDE at all. Again, I recommend that you use IDLE for this book's exercises if you're just starting out, unless you are already familiar with and prefer a command-line-based development mode. There are, however, a handful of alternative IDEs for Python developers, some of which are substantially more powerful and robust than IDLE. Here are some of the most commonly used IDEs:

Eclipse and PyDev

Eclipse is an advanced open source IDE GUI. Originally developed as a Java IDE, Eclipse also supports Python development when you install the PyDev (or a similar) plug-in. Eclipse is a popular and powerful option for Python development, and it goes well beyond IDLE's feature set. It includes support for code completion, syntax highlighting, syntax analysis, refactoring, debugging, and more. Its downsides are that it is a large system to install and may require shareware extensions for some features (this may vary over time). Still, when you are ready to graduate from IDLE, the Eclipse/PyDev combination is worth your attention.

Komodo

A full-featured development environment GUI for Python (and other languages), Komodo includes standard syntax-coloring, text-editing, debugging, and other features. In addition, Komodo offers many advanced features that IDLE does not, including project files, source-control integration, regular-expression debugging, and a drag-and-drop GUI builder that generates Python/tkinter code to implement the GUIs you design interactively. At this writing, Komodo is not free; it is available at *http://www.activestate.com*.

NetBeans IDE for Python

NetBeans is a powerful open-source development environment GUI with support for many advanced features for Python developers: code completion, automatic indentation and code colorization, editor hints, code folding, refactoring, debugging, code coverage and testing, projects, and more. It may be used to develop both CPython and Jython code. Like Eclipse, NetBeans requires installation steps beyond those of the included IDLE GUI, but it is seen by many as more than worth the effort. Search the Web for the latest information and links.

PythonWin

PythonWin is a free Windows-only IDE for Python that ships as part of ActiveState's ActivePython distribution (and may also be fetched separately from *http://www.python.org* resources). It is roughly like IDLE, with a handful of useful Windows-specific extensions added; for example, PythonWin has support for

COM objects. Today, IDLE is probably more advanced than PythonWin (for instance, IDLE's dual-process architecture often prevents it from hanging). However, PythonWin still offers tools for Windows developers that IDLE does not. See *http://www.activestate.com* for more information.

Others

There are roughly half a dozen other widely used IDEs that I'm aware of (including the commercial *Wing IDE* and *PythonCard*) but do not have space to do justice to here, and more will probably appear over time. In fact, almost every programmer-friendly text editor has some sort of support for Python development these days, whether it be preinstalled or fetched separately. Emacs and Vim, for instance, have substantial Python support.

I won't try to document all such options here; for more information, see the resources available at *http://www.python.org* or search the Web for "Python IDE." You might also try running a web search for "Python editors"—today, this leads you to a wiki page that maintains information about many IDE and text-editor options for Python programming.

Other Launch Options

At this point, we've seen how to run code typed interactively, and how to launch code saved in files in a variety of ways—system command lines, imports and execs, GUIs like IDLE, and more. That covers most of the cases you'll see in this book. There are additional ways to run Python code, though, most of which have special or narrow roles. The next few sections take a quick look at some of these.

Embedding Calls

In some specialized domains, Python code may be run automatically by an enclosing system. In such cases, we say that the Python programs are *embedded* in (i.e., run by) another program. The Python code itself may be entered into a text file, stored in a database, fetched from an HTML page, parsed from an XML document, and so on. But from an operational perspective, another system—not you—may tell Python to run the code you've created.

Such an embedded execution mode is commonly used to support end-user customization—a game program, for instance, might allow for play modifications by running user-accessible embedded Python code at strategic points in time. Users can modify this type of system by providing or changing Python code. Because Python code is interpreted, there is no need to recompile the entire system to incorporate the change (see Chapter 2 for more on how Python code is run).

In this mode, the enclosing system that runs your code might be written in C, C++, or even Java when the Jython system is used. As an example, it's possible to create and run strings of Python code from a C program by calling functions in the Python runtime API (a set of services exported by the libraries created when Python is compiled on your machine):

```
#include <Python.h>
...
Py_Initialize();                                    // This is C, not Python
PyRun_SimpleString("x = 'brave ' + 'sir robin'");   // But it runs Python code
```

In this C code snippet, a program coded in the C language embeds the Python interpreter by linking in its libraries, and passes it a Python assignment statement string to run. C programs may also gain access to Python modules and objects and process or execute them using other Python API tools.

This book isn't about Python/C integration, but you should be aware that, depending on how your organization plans to use Python, you may or may not be the one who actually starts the Python programs you create. Regardless, you can usually still use the interactive and file-based launching techniques described here to test code in isolation from those enclosing systems that may eventually use it.*

Frozen Binary Executables

Frozen binary executables, described in Chapter 2, are packages that combine your program's byte code and the Python interpreter into a single executable program. This approach enables Python programs to be launched in the same ways that you would launch any other executable program (icon clicks, command lines, etc.). While this option works well for delivery of products, it is not really intended for use during program development; you normally freeze just before shipping (after development is finished). See the prior chapter for more on this option.

Text Editor Launch Options

As mentioned previously, although they're not full-blown IDE GUIs, most programmer-friendly text editors have support for editing, and possibly running, Python programs. Such support may be built in or fetchable on the Web. For instance, if you are familiar with the Emacs text editor, you can do all your Python editing and launching from inside that text editor. See the text editor resources page at *http://www.python .org/editors* for more details, or search the Web for the phrase "Python editors."

---

* See *Programming Python* (O'Reilly) for more details on embedding Python in C/C++. The embedding API can call Python functions directly, load modules, and more. Also, note that the Jython system allows Java programs to invoke Python code using a Java-based API (a Python interpreter class).

Still Other Launch Options

Depending on your platform, there may be additional ways that you can start Python programs. For instance, on some Macintosh systems you may be able to drag Python program file icons onto the Python interpreter icon to make them execute, and on Windows you can always start Python scripts with the Run... option in the Start menu. Additionally, the Python standard library has utilities that allow Python programs to be started by other Python programs in separate processes (e.g., `os.popen`, `os.system`), and Python scripts might also be spawned in larger contexts like the Web (for instance, a web page might invoke a script on a server); however, these are beyond the scope of the present chapter.

Future Possibilities?

This chapter reflects current practice, but much of the material is both platform- and time-specific. Indeed, many of the execution and launch details presented arose during the shelf life of this book's various editions. As with program execution options, it's not impossible that new program launch options may arise over time.

New operating systems, and new versions of existing systems, may also provide execution techniques beyond those outlined here. In general, because Python keeps pace with such changes, you should be able to launch Python programs in whatever way makes sense for the machines you use, both now and in the future—be that by drawing on tablet PCs or PDAs, grabbing icons in a virtual reality, or shouting a script's name over your coworkers' conversations.

Implementation changes may also impact launch schemes somewhat (e.g., a full compiler could produce normal executables that are launched much like frozen binaries today). If I knew what the future truly held, though, I would probably be talking to a stockbroker instead of writing these words!

Which Option Should I Use?

With all these options, one question naturally arises: which one is best for me? In general, you should give the IDLE interface a try if you are just getting started with Python. It provides a user-friendly GUI environment and hides some of the underlying configuration details. It also comes with a platform-neutral text editor for coding your scripts, and it's a standard and free part of the Python system.

If, on the other hand, you are an experienced programmer, you might be more comfortable with simply the text editor of your choice in one window, and another window for launching the programs you edit via system command lines and icon clicks (in fact, this is how I develop Python programs, but I have a Unix-biased past). Because the choice of development environments is very subjective, I can't offer much more in the way of universal guidelines; in general, whatever environment you like to use will be the best for you to use.

Debugging Python Code

Naturally, none of my readers or students ever have bugs in their code (*insert smiley here*), but for less fortunate friends of yours who may, here's a quick look at the strategies commonly used by real-world Python programmers to debug code:

- **Do nothing**. By this, I don't mean that Python programmers don't debug their code—but when you make a mistake in a Python program, you get a very useful and readable error message (you'll get to see some soon, if you haven't already). If you already know Python, and especially for your own code, this is often enough—read the error message, and go fix the tagged line and file. For many, this *is* debugging in Python. It may not always be ideal for larger system you didn't write, though.

- **Insert print statements**. Probably the main way that Python programmers debug their code (and the way that I debug Python code) is to insert `print` statements and run again. Because Python runs immediately after changes, this is usually the quickest way to get more information than error messages provide. The `print` statements don't have to be sophisticated—a simple "I am here" or display of variable values is usually enough to provide the context you need. Just remember to delete or comment out (i.e., add a # before) the debugging `print`s before you ship your code!

- **Use IDE GUI debuggers**. For larger systems you didn't write, and for beginners who want to trace code in more detail, most Python development GUIs have some sort of point-and-click debugging support. IDLE has a debugger too, but it doesn't appear to be used very often in practice—perhaps because it has no command line, or perhaps because adding `print` statements is usually quicker than setting up a GUI debugging session. To learn more, see IDLE's Help, or simply try it on your own; its basic interface is described in the section "Advanced IDLE Tools" on page 64. Other IDEs, such as Eclipse, NetBeans, Komodo, and Wing IDE, offer advanced point-and-click debuggers as well; see their documentation if you use them.

- **Use the pdb command-line debugger**. For ultimate control, Python comes with a source-code debugger named *pdb*, available as a module in Python's standard library. In pdb, you type commands to step line by line, display variables, set and clear breakpoints, continue to a breakpoint or error, and so on. pdb can be launched interactively by importing it, or as a top-level script. Either way, because you can type commands to control the session, it provides a powerful debugging tool. pdb also includes a postmortem function you can run after an exception occurs, to get information from the time of the error. See the Python library manual and Chapter 35 for more details on pdb.

- **Other options**. For more specific debugging requirements, you can find additional tools in the open source domain, including support for multithreaded programs, embedded code, and process attachment. The *Winpdb* system, for example, is a

---

standalone debugger with advanced debugging support and cross-platform GUI and console interfaces.

These options will become more important as we start writing larger scripts. Probably the best news on the debugging front, though, is that errors are detected and reported in Python, rather than passing silently or crashing the system altogether. In fact, errors themselves are a well-defined mechanism known as *exceptions*, which you can catch and process (more on exceptions in Part VII). Making mistakes is never fun, of course, but speaking as someone who recalls when debugging meant getting out a hex calculator and poring over piles of memory dump printouts, Python's debugging support makes errors much less painful than they might otherwise be.

Chapter Summary

In this chapter, we've looked at common ways to launch Python programs: by running code typed interactively, and by running code stored in files with system command lines, file-icon clicks, module imports, exec calls, and IDE GUIs such as IDLE. We've covered a lot of pragmatic startup territory here. This chapter's goal was to equip you with enough information to enable you to start writing some code, which you'll do in the next part of the book. There, we will start exploring the Python language itself, beginning with its core data types.

First, though, take the usual chapter quiz to exercise what you've learned here. Because this is the last chapter in this part of the book, it's followed with a set of more complete exercises that test your mastery of this entire part's topics. For help with the latter set of problems, or just for a refresher, be sure to turn to Appendix B after you've given the exercises a try.

Test Your Knowledge: Quiz

1. How can you start an interactive interpreter session?
2. Where do you type a system command line to launch a script file?
3. Name four or more ways to run the code saved in a script file.
4. Name two pitfalls related to clicking file icons on Windows.
5. Why might you need to reload a module?
6. How do you run a script from within IDLE?
7. Name two pitfalls related to using IDLE.
8. What is a namespace, and how does it relate to module files?

Test Your Knowledge: Answers

1. You can start an interactive session on Windows by clicking your Start button, picking the All Programs option, clicking the Python entry, and selecting the "Python (command line)" menu option. You can also achieve the same effect on Windows and other platforms by typing **python** as a system command line in your system's console window (a Command Prompt window on Windows). Another alternative is to launch IDLE, as its main Python shell window is an interactive session. If you have not set your system's PATH variable to find Python, you may need to **cd** to where Python is installed, or type its full directory path instead of just **python** (e.g., **C:\Python30\python** on Windows).

2. You type system command lines in whatever your platform provides as a system console: a Command Prompt window on Windows; an xterm or terminal window on Unix, Linux, and Mac OS X; and so on.

3. Code in a script (really, module) file can be run with system command lines, file icon clicks, imports and reloads, the **exec** built-in function, and IDE GUI selections such as IDLE's Run→Run Module menu option. On Unix, they can also be run as executables with the #! trick, and some platforms support more specialized launching techniques (e.g., drag-and-drop). In addition, some text editors have unique ways to run Python code, some Python programs are provided as standalone "frozen binary" executables, and some systems use Python code in embedded mode, where it is run automatically by an enclosing program written in a language like C, C++, or Java. The latter technique is usually done to provide a user customization layer.

4. Scripts that print and then exit cause the output file to disappear immediately, before you can view the output (which is why the **input** trick comes in handy); error messages generated by your script also appear in an output window that closes before you can examine its contents (which is one reason that system command lines and IDEs such as IDLE are better for most development).

5. Python only imports (loads) a module once per process, by default, so if you've changed its source code and want to run the new version without stopping and restarting Python, you'll have to reload it. You must import a module at least once before you can reload it. Running files of code from a system shell command line, via an icon click, or via an IDE such as IDLE generally makes this a nonissue, as those launch schemes usually run the current version of the source code file each time.

6. Within the text edit window of the file you wish to run, select the window's Run→Run Module menu option. This runs the window's source code as a top-level script file and displays its output back in the interactive Python shell window.

7. IDLE can still be hung by some types of programs—especially GUI programs that perform multithreading (an advanced technique beyond this book's scope). Also, IDLE has some usability features that can burn you once you leave the IDLE GUI:

a script's variables are automatically imported to the interactive scope in IDLE, for instance, but not by Python in general.

8. A namespace is just a package of variables (i.e., names). It takes the form of an object with attributes in Python. Each module file is automatically a namespace— that is, a package of variables reflecting the assignments made at the top level of the file. Namespaces help avoid name collisions in Python programs: because each module file is a self-contained namespace, files must explicitly import other files in order to use their names.

Test Your Knowledge: Part I Exercises

It's time to start doing a little coding on your own. This first exercise session is fairly simple, but a few of these questions hint at topics to come in later chapters. Be sure to check "Part I, Getting Started" on page 1103 in the solutions appendix (Appendix B) for the answers; the exercises and their solutions sometimes contain supplemental information not discussed in the main text, so you should take a peek at the solutions even if you manage to answer all the questions on your own.

1. *Interaction.* Using a system command line, IDLE, or another method, start the Python interactive command line (>>> prompt), and type the expression "Hello World!" (including the quotes). The string should be echoed back to you. The purpose of this exercise is to get your environment configured to run Python. In some scenarios, you may need to first run a cd shell command, type the full path to the Python executable, or add its path to your PATH environment variable. If desired, you can set PATH in your *.cshrc* or *.kshrc* file to make Python permanently available on Unix systems; on Windows, use a *setup.bat*, *autoexec.bat*, or the environment variable GUI. See Appendix A for help with environment variable settings.

2. *Programs.* With the text editor of your choice, write a simple module file containing the single statement print('Hello module world!') and store it as *module1.py*. Now, run this file by using any launch option you like: running it in IDLE, clicking on its file icon, passing it to the Python interpreter on the system shell's command line (e.g., python module1.py), built-in exec calls, imports and reloads, and so on. In fact, experiment by running your file with as many of the launch techniques discussed in this chapter as you can. Which technique seems easiest? (There is no right answer to this, of course.)

3. *Modules.* Start the Python interactive command line (>>> prompt) and import the module you wrote in exercise 2. Try moving the file to a different directory and importing it again from its original directory (i.e., run Python in the original directory when you import). What happens? (Hint: is there still a *module1.pyc* byte code file in the original directory?)

4. *Scripts.* If your platform supports it, add the `#!` line to the top of your *module1.py* module file, give the file executable privileges, and run it directly as an executable. What does the first line need to contain? `#!` usually only has meaning on Unix, Linux, and Unix-like platforms such as Mac OS X; if you're working on Windows, instead try running your file by listing just its name in a DOS console window without the word "python" before it (this works on recent versions of Windows), or via the Start→Run... dialog box.

5. *Errors and debugging.* Experiment with typing mathematical expressions and assignments at the Python interactive command line. Along the way, type the expressions `2 ** 500` and `1 / 0`, and reference an undefined variable name as we did in this chapter. What happens?

   You may not know it yet, but when you make a mistake, you're doing exception processing (a topic we'll explore in depth in Part VII). As you'll learn there, you are technically triggering what's known as the *default exception handler*—logic that prints a standard error message. If you do not catch an error, the default handler does and prints the standard error message in response.

   Exceptions are also bound up with the notion of *debugging* in Python. When you're first starting out, Python's default error messages on exceptions will probably provide as much error-handling support as you need—they give the cause of the error, as well as showing the lines in your code that were active when the error occurred. For more about debugging, see the sidebar "Debugging Python Code" on page 69.

6. *Breaks and cycles.* At the Python command line, type:

   ```
   L = [1, 2]          # Make a 2-item list
   L.append(L)         # Append L as a single item to itself
   L                   # Print L
   ```

   What happens? In all recent versions of Python, you'll see a strange output that we'll describe in the solutions appendix, and which will make more sense when we study references in the next part of the book. If you're using a Python version older than 1.5.1, a Ctrl-C key combination will probably help on most platforms. Why do you think your version of Python responds the way it does for this code?

    If you do have a Python older than Release 1.5.1 (a hopefully rare scenario today!), make sure your machine can stop a program with a Ctrl-C key combination of some sort before running this test, or you may be waiting a long time.

7. *Documentation.* Spend at least 17 minutes browsing the Python library and language manuals before moving on to get a feel for the available tools in the standard library and the structure of the documentation set. It takes at least this long to become familiar with the locations of major topics in the manual set; once you've

done this, it's easy to find what you need. You can find this manual via the Python Start button entry on Windows, in the Python Docs option on the Help pull-down menu in IDLE, or online at *http://www.python.org/doc*. I'll also have a few more words to say about the manuals and other documentation sources available (including PyDoc and the `help` function) in Chapter 15. If you still have time, go explore the Python website, as well as its PyPI third-party extension repository. Especially check out the Python.org documentation and search pages; they can be crucial resources.

## PART II

Types and Operations

## CHAPTER 4

Introducing Python Object Types

This chapter begins our tour of the Python language. In an informal sense, in Python, we do things with stuff. "Things" take the form of operations like addition and concatenation, and "stuff" refers to the objects on which we perform those operations. In this part of the book, our focus is on that stuff, and the things our programs can do with it.

Somewhat more formally, in Python, data takes the form of *objects*—either built-in objects that Python provides, or objects we create using Python or external language tools such as C extension libraries. Although we'll firm up this definition later, objects are essentially just pieces of memory, with values and sets of associated operations.

Because objects are the most fundamental notion in Python programming, we'll start this chapter with a survey of Python's built-in object types.

By way of introduction, however, let's first establish a clear picture of how this chapter fits into the overall Python picture. From a more concrete perspective, Python programs can be decomposed into modules, statements, expressions, and objects, as follows:

1. Programs are composed of modules.
2. Modules contain statements.
3. Statements contain expressions.
4. *Expressions create and process objects.*

The discussion of modules in Chapter 3 introduced the highest level of this hierarchy. This part's chapters begin at the bottom, exploring both built-in objects and the expressions you can code to use them.

Why Use Built-in Types?

If you've used lower-level languages such as C or C++, you know that much of your work centers on implementing *objects*—also known as *data structures*—to represent the components in your application's domain. You need to lay out memory structures, manage memory allocation, implement search and access routines, and so on. These chores are about as tedious (and error-prone) as they sound, and they usually distract from your program's real goals.

In typical Python programs, most of this grunt work goes away. Because Python provides powerful object types as an intrinsic part of the language, there's usually no need to code object implementations before you start solving problems. In fact, unless you have a need for special processing that built-in types don't provide, you're almost always better off using a built-in object instead of implementing your own. Here are some reasons why:

- **Built-in objects make programs easy to write**. For simple tasks, built-in types are often all you need to represent the structure of problem domains. Because you get powerful tools such as collections (lists) and search tables (dictionaries) for free, you can use them immediately. You can get a lot of work done with Python's built-in object types alone.

- **Built-in objects are components of extensions**. For more complex tasks, you may need to provide your own objects using Python classes or C language interfaces. But as you'll see in later parts of this book, objects implemented manually are often built on top of built-in types such as lists and dictionaries. For instance, a stack data structure may be implemented as a class that manages or customizes a built-in list.

- **Built-in objects are often more efficient than custom data structures**. Python's built-in types employ already optimized data structure algorithms that are implemented in C for speed. Although you can write similar object types on your own, you'll usually be hard-pressed to get the level of performance built-in object types provide.

- **Built-in objects are a standard part of the language**. In some ways, Python borrows both from languages that rely on built-in tools (e.g., LISP) and languages that rely on the programmer to provide tool implementations or frameworks of their own (e.g., C++). Although you can implement unique object types in Python, you don't need to do so just to get started. Moreover, because Python's built-ins are standard, they're always the same; proprietary frameworks, on the other hand, tend to differ from site to site.

In other words, not only do built-in object types make programming easier, but they're also more powerful and efficient than most of what can be created from scratch. Regardless of whether you implement new object types, built-in objects form the core of every Python program.

Python's Core Data Types

Table 4-1 previews Python's built-in object types and some of the syntax used to code their *literals*—that is, the expressions that generate these objects.* Some of these types will probably seem familiar if you've used other languages; for instance, numbers and strings represent numeric and textual values, respectively, and files provide an interface for processing files stored on your computer.

Table 4-1. Built-in objects preview

Object type	Example literals/creation
Numbers	1234, 3.1415, 3+4j, Decimal, Fraction
Strings	'spam', "guido's", b'a\x01c'
Lists	[1, [2, 'three'], 4]
Dictionaries	{'food': 'spam', 'taste': 'yum'}
Tuples	(1, 'spam', 4, 'U')
Files	myfile = open('eggs', 'r')
Sets	set('abc'), {'a', 'b', 'c'}
Other core types	Booleans, types, None
Program unit types	Functions, modules, classes (Part IV, Part V, Part VI)
Implementation-related types	Compiled code, stack tracebacks (Part IV, Part VII)

Table 4-1 isn't really complete, because *everything* we process in Python programs is a kind of object. For instance, when we perform text pattern matching in Python, we create pattern objects, and when we perform network scripting, we use socket objects. These other kinds of objects are generally created by importing and using modules and have behavior all their own.

As we'll see in later parts of the book, *program units* such as functions, modules, and classes are objects in Python too—they are created with statements and expressions such as `def`, `class`, `import`, and `lambda` and may be passed around scripts freely, stored within other objects, and so on. Python also provides a set of *implementation-related* types such as compiled code objects, which are generally of interest to tool builders more than application developers; these are also discussed in later parts of this text.

We usually call the other object types in Table 4-1 *core* data types, though, because they are effectively built into the Python language—that is, there is specific expression syntax for generating most of them. For instance, when you run the following code:

```
>>> 'spam'
```

---

* In this book, the term *literal* simply means an expression whose syntax generates an object—sometimes also called a *constant*. Note that the term "constant" does not imply objects or variables that can never be changed (i.e., this term is unrelated to C++'s `const` or Python's "immutable"—a topic explored in the section "Immutability" on page 84).

you are, technically speaking, running a literal expression that generates and returns a new string object. There is specific Python language syntax to make this object. Similarly, an expression wrapped in square brackets makes a list, one in curly braces makes a dictionary, and so on. Even though, as we'll see, there are no type declarations in Python, the syntax of the expressions you run determines the types of objects you create and use. In fact, object-generation expressions like those in Table 4-1 are generally where types originate in the Python language.

Just as importantly, once you create an object, you bind its operation set for all time—you can perform only string operations on a string and list operations on a list. As you'll learn, Python is *dynamically typed* (it keeps track of types for you automatically instead of requiring declaration code), but it is also *strongly typed* (you can perform on an object only operations that are valid for its type).

Functionally, the object types in Table 4-1 are more general and powerful than what you may be accustomed to. For instance, you'll find that lists and dictionaries alone are powerful data representation tools that obviate most of the work you do to support collections and searching in lower-level languages. In short, lists provide ordered collections of other objects, while dictionaries store objects by key; both lists and dictionaries may be nested, can grow and shrink on demand, and may contain objects of any type.

We'll study each of the object types in Table 4-1 in detail in upcoming chapters. Before digging into the details, though, let's begin by taking a quick look at Python's core objects in action. The rest of this chapter provides a preview of the operations we'll explore in more depth in the chapters that follow. Don't expect to find the full story here—the goal of this chapter is just to whet your appetite and introduce some key ideas. Still, the best way to get started is to get started, so let's jump right into some real code.

Numbers

If you've done any programming or scripting in the past, some of the object types in Table 4-1 will probably seem familiar. Even if you haven't, numbers are fairly straightforward. Python's core objects set includes the usual suspects: integers (numbers without a fractional part), floating-point numbers (roughly, numbers with a decimal point in them), and more exotic numeric types (complex numbers with imaginary parts, fixed-precision decimals, rational fractions with numerator and denominator, and full-featured sets).

Although it offers some fancier options, Python's basic number types are, well, basic. Numbers in Python support the normal mathematical operations. For instance, the plus sign (+) performs addition, a star (*) is used for multiplication, and two stars (**) are used for exponentiation:

```
>>> 123 + 222          # Integer addition
345
>>> 1.5 * 4            # Floating-point multiplication
6.0
>>> 2 ** 100           # 2 to the power 100
1267650600228229401496703205376
```

Notice the last result here: Python 3.0's integer type automatically provides extra precision for large numbers like this when needed (in 2.6, a separate long integer type handles numbers too large for the normal integer type in similar ways). You can, for instance, compute 2 to the power 1,000,000 as an integer in Python, but you probably shouldn't try to print the result—with more than 300,000 digits, you may be waiting awhile!

```
>>> len(str(2 ** 1000000))    # How many digits in a really BIG number?
301030
```

Once you start experimenting with floating-point numbers, you're likely to stumble across something that may look a bit odd on first glance:

```
>>> 3.1415 * 2                # repr: as code
6.2830000000000004
>>> print(3.1415 * 2)         # str: user-friendly
6.283
```

The first result isn't a bug; it's a display issue. It turns out that there are two ways to print every object: with full precision (as in the first result shown here), and in a user-friendly form (as in the second). Formally, the first form is known as an object's as-code `repr`, and the second is its user-friendly `str`. The difference can matter when we step up to using classes; for now, if something looks odd, try showing it with a `print` built-in call statement.

Besides expressions, there are a handful of useful numeric modules that ship with Python—*modules* are just packages of additional tools that we import to use:

```
>>> import math
>>> math.pi
3.1415926535897931
>>> math.sqrt(85)
9.2195444572928871
```

The `math` module contains more advanced numeric tools as functions, while the `random` module performs random number generation and random selections (here, from a Python list, introduced later in this chapter):

```
>>> import random
>>> random.random()
0.59268735266273953
>>> random.choice([1, 2, 3, 4])
1
```

Python also includes more exotic numeric objects—such as complex, fixed-precision, and rational numbers, as well as sets and Booleans—and the third-party open source extension domain has even more (e.g., matrixes and vectors). We'll defer discussion of these types until later in the book.

So far, we've been using Python much like a simple calculator; to do better justice to its built-in types, let's move on to explore strings.

Strings

Strings are used to record textual information as well as arbitrary collections of bytes. They are our first example of what we call a *sequence* in Python—that is, a positionally ordered collection of other objects. Sequences maintain a left-to-right order among the items they contain: their items are stored and fetched by their relative position. Strictly speaking, strings are sequences of one-character strings; other types of sequences include lists and tuples, covered later.

Sequence Operations

As sequences, strings support operations that assume a positional ordering among items. For example, if we have a four-character string, we can verify its length with the built-in len function and fetch its components with *indexing* expressions:

```
>>> S = 'Spam'
>>> len(S)              # Length
4
>>> S[0]                # The first item in S, indexing by zero-based position
'S'
>>> S[1]                # The second item from the left
'p'
```

In Python, indexes are coded as offsets from the front, and so start from 0: the first item is at index 0, the second is at index 1, and so on.

Notice how we assign the string to a *variable* named S here. We'll go into detail on how this works later (especially in Chapter 6), but Python variables never need to be declared ahead of time. A variable is created when you assign it a value, may be assigned any type of object, and is replaced with its value when it shows up in an expression. It must also have been previously assigned by the time you use its value. For the purposes of this chapter, it's enough to know that we need to assign an object to a variable in order to save it for later use.

In Python, we can also index backward, from the end—positive indexes count from the left, and negative indexes count back from the right:

```
>>> S[-1]               # The last item from the end in S
'm'
>>> S[-2]               # The second to last item from the end
'a'
```

Formally, a negative index is simply added to the string's size, so the following two operations are equivalent (though the first is easier to code and less easy to get wrong):

```
>>> S[-1]          # The last item in S
'm'
>>> S[len(S)-1]    # Negative indexing, the hard way
'm'
```

Notice that we can use an arbitrary expression in the square brackets, not just a hard-coded number literal—anywhere that Python expects a value, we can use a literal, a variable, or any expression. Python's syntax is completely general this way.

In addition to simple positional indexing, sequences also support a more general form of indexing known as *slicing*, which is a way to extract an entire section (slice) in a single step. For example:

```
>>> S              # A 4-character string
'Spam'
>>> S[1:3]         # Slice of S from offsets 1 through 2 (not 3)
'pa'
```

Probably the easiest way to think of slices is that they are a way to extract an entire *column* from a string in a single step. Their general form, X[I:J], means "give me everything in X from offset I up to but not including offset J." The result is returned in a new object. The second of the preceding operations, for instance, gives us all the characters in string S from offsets 1 through 2 (that is, 3 – 1) as a new string. The effect is to slice or "parse out" the two characters in the middle.

In a slice, the left bound defaults to zero, and the right bound defaults to the length of the sequence being sliced. This leads to some common usage variations:

```
>>> S[1:]          # Everything past the first (1:len(S))
'pam'
>>> S              # S itself hasn't changed
'Spam'
>>> S[0:3]         # Everything but the last
'Spa'
>>> S[:3]          # Same as S[0:3]
'Spa'
>>> S[:-1]         # Everything but the last again, but simpler (0:-1)
'Spa'
>>> S[:]           # All of S as a top-level copy (0:len(S))
'Spam'
```

Note how negative offsets can be used to give bounds for slices, too, and how the last operation effectively copies the entire string. As you'll learn later, there is no reason to copy a string, but this form can be useful for sequences like lists.

Finally, as sequences, strings also support *concatenation* with the plus sign (joining two strings into a new string) and *repetition* (making a new string by repeating another):

```
>>> S
'Spam'
>>> S + 'xyz'      # Concatenation
```

```
'Spamxyz'
>>> S                          # S is unchanged
'Spam'
>>> S * 8                      # Repetition
'SpamSpamSpamSpamSpamSpamSpamSpam'
```

Notice that the plus sign (+) means different things for different objects: addition for numbers, and concatenation for strings. This is a general property of Python that we'll call *polymorphism* later in the book—in sum, the meaning of an operation depends on the objects being operated on. As you'll see when we study dynamic typing, this polymorphism property accounts for much of the conciseness and flexibility of Python code. Because types aren't constrained, a Python-coded operation can normally work on many different types of objects automatically, as long as they support a compatible interface (like the + operation here). This turns out to be a huge idea in Python; you'll learn more about it later on our tour.

Immutability

Notice that in the prior examples, we were not changing the original string with any of the operations we ran on it. Every string operation is defined to produce a new string as its result, because strings are *immutable* in Python—they cannot be changed in-place after they are created. For example, you can't change a string by assigning to one of its positions, but you can always build a new one and assign it to the same name. Because Python cleans up old objects as you go (as you'll see later), this isn't as inefficient as it may sound:

```
>>> S
'Spam'
>>> S[0] = 'z'                 # Immutable objects cannot be changed
...error text omitted...
TypeError: 'str' object does not support item assignment

>>> S = 'z' + S[1:]            # But we can run expressions to make new objects
>>> S
'zpam'
```

Every object in Python is classified as either immutable (unchangeable) or not. In terms of the core types, numbers, strings, and tuples are immutable; lists and dictionaries are not (they can be changed in-place freely). Among other things, immutability can be used to guarantee that an object remains constant throughout your program.

Type-Specific Methods

Every string operation we've studied so far is really a sequence operation—that is, these operations will work on other sequences in Python as well, including lists and tuples. In addition to generic sequence operations, though, strings also have operations all their own, available as *methods*—functions attached to the object, which are triggered with a call expression.

For example, the string `find` method is the basic substring search operation (it returns the offset of the passed-in substring, or −1 if it is not present), and the string `replace` method performs global searches and replacements:

```
>>> S.find('pa')              # Find the offset of a substring
1
>>> S
'Spam'
>>> S.replace('pa', 'XYZ')    # Replace occurrences of a substring with another
'SXYZm'
>>> S
'Spam'
```

Again, despite the names of these string methods, we are not changing the original strings here, but creating new strings as the results—because strings are immutable, we have to do it this way. String methods are the first line of text-processing tools in Python. Other methods split a string into substrings on a delimiter (handy as a simple form of parsing), perform case conversions, test the content of the string (digits, letters, and so on), and strip whitespace characters off the ends of the string:

```
>>> line = 'aaa,bbb,ccccc,dd'
>>> line.split(',')           # Split on a delimiter into a list of substrings
['aaa', 'bbb', 'ccccc', 'dd']
>>> S = 'spam'
>>> S.upper()                 # Upper- and lowercase conversions
'SPAM'

>>> S.isalpha()               # Content tests: isalpha, isdigit, etc.
True

>>> line = 'aaa,bbb,ccccc,dd\n'
>>> line = line.rstrip()      # Remove whitespace characters on the right side
>>> line
'aaa,bbb,ccccc,dd'
```

Strings also support an advanced substitution operation known as *formatting*, available as both an expression (the original) and a string method call (new in 2.6 and 3.0):

```
>>> '%s, eggs, and %s' % ('spam', 'SPAM!')       # Formatting expression (all)
'spam, eggs, and SPAM!'

>>> '{0}, eggs, and {1}'.format('spam', 'SPAM!')  # Formatting method (2.6, 3.0)
'spam, eggs, and SPAM!'
```

One note here: although sequence operations are generic, methods are not—although some types share some method names, string method operations generally work only on strings, and nothing else. As a rule of thumb, Python's toolset is layered: generic operations that span multiple types show up as built-in functions or expressions (e.g., `len(X)`, `X[0]`), but type-specific operations are method calls (e.g., `aString.upper()`). Finding the tools you need among all these categories will become more natural as you use Python more, but the next section gives a few tips you can use right now.

Getting Help

The methods introduced in the prior section are a representative, but small, sample of what is available for string objects. In general, this book is not exhaustive in its look at object methods. For more details, you can always call the built-in `dir` function, which returns a list of all the attributes available for a given object. Because methods are function attributes, they will show up in this list. Assuming S is still the string, here are its attributes on Python 3.0 (Python 2.6 varies slightly):

```
>>> dir(S)
['__add__', '__class__', '__contains__', '__delattr__', '__doc__', '__eq__',
'__format__', '__ge__', '__getattribute__', '__getitem__', '__getnewargs__',
'__gt__', '__hash__', '__init__', '__iter__', '__le__', '__len__', '__lt__',
'__mod__', '__mul__', '__ne__', '__new__', '__reduce__', '__reduce_ex__',
'__repr__', '__rmod__', '__rmul__', '__setattr__', '__sizeof__', '__str__',
'__subclasshook__', '_formatter_field_name_split', '_formatter_parser',
'capitalize', 'center', 'count', 'encode', 'endswith', 'expandtabs', 'find',
'format', 'index', 'isalnum','isalpha', 'isdecimal', 'isdigit', 'isidentifier',
'islower', 'isnumeric', 'isprintable', 'isspace', 'istitle', 'isupper', 'join',
'ljust', 'lower', 'lstrip', 'maketrans', 'partition', 'replace', 'rfind',
'rindex', 'rjust', 'rpartition', 'rsplit', 'rstrip', 'split', 'splitlines',
'startswith', 'strip', 'swapcase', 'title', 'translate', 'upper', 'zfill']
```

You probably won't care about the names with underscores in this list until later in the book, when we study operator overloading in classes—they represent the implementation of the string object and are available to support customization. In general, leading and trailing double underscores is the naming pattern Python uses for implementation details. The names without the underscores in this list are the callable methods on string objects.

The `dir` function simply gives the methods' names. To ask what they do, you can pass them to the `help` function:

```
>>> help(S.replace)
Help on built-in function replace:

replace(...)
    S.replace (old, new[, count]) -> str

    Return a copy of S with all occurrences of substring
    old replaced by new.  If the optional argument count is
    given, only the first count occurrences are replaced.
```

`help` is one of a handful of interfaces to a system of code that ships with Python known as *PyDoc*—a tool for extracting documentation from objects. Later in the book, you'll see that PyDoc can also render its reports in HTML format.

You can also ask for help on an entire string (e.g., `help(S)`), but you may get more help than you want to see—i.e., information about every string method. It's generally better to ask about a specific method.

For more details, you can also consult Python's standard library reference manual or commercially published reference books, but `dir` and `help` are the first line of documentation in Python.

Other Ways to Code Strings

So far, we've looked at the string object's sequence operations and type-specific methods. Python also provides a variety of ways for us to code strings, which we'll explore in greater depth later. For instance, special characters can be represented as backslash escape sequences:

```
>>> S = 'A\nB\tC'          # \n is end-of-line, \t is tab
>>> len(S)                 # Each stands for just one character
5

>>> ord('\n')              # \n is a byte with the binary value 10 in ASCII
10

>>> S = 'A\0B\0C'          # \0, a binary zero byte, does not terminate string
>>> len(S)
5
```

Python allows strings to be enclosed in single or double quote characters (they mean the same thing). It also allows multiline string literals enclosed in triple quotes (single or double)—when this form is used, all the lines are concatenated together, and end-of-line characters are added where line breaks appear. This is a minor syntactic convenience, but it's useful for embedding things like HTML and XML code in a Python script:

```
>>> msg = """ aaaaaaaaaaaaa
bbb'''bbbbbbbbbb""bbbbbbb'bbbb
cccccccccccccc"""
>>> msg
'\naaaaaaaaaaaaa\nbbb\'\'\'bbbbbbbbbb""bbbbbbb\'bbbb\ncccccccccccccc'
```

Python also supports a *raw* string literal that turns off the backslash escape mechanism (such string literals start with the letter r), as well as *Unicode* string support that supports internationalization. In 3.0, the basic `str` string type handles Unicode too (which makes sense, given that ASCII text is a simple kind of Unicode), and a `bytes` type represents raw byte strings; in 2.6, Unicode is a separate type, and `str` handles both 8-bit strings and binary data. Files are also changed in 3.0 to return and accept `str` for text and `bytes` for binary data. We'll meet all these special string forms in later chapters.

Pattern Matching

One point worth noting before we move on is that none of the string object's methods support pattern-based text processing. Text pattern matching is an advanced tool outside this book's scope, but readers with backgrounds in other scripting languages may be interested to know that to do pattern matching in Python, we import a module called re. This module has analogous calls for searching, splitting, and replacement, but because we can use patterns to specify substrings, we can be much more general:

```
>>> import re
>>> match = re.match('Hello[ \t]*(.*)world', 'Hello    Python world')
>>> match.group(1)
'Python '
```

This example searches for a substring that begins with the word "Hello," followed by zero or more tabs or spaces, followed by arbitrary characters to be saved as a matched group, terminated by the word "world." If such a substring is found, portions of the substring matched by parts of the pattern enclosed in parentheses are available as groups. The following pattern, for example, picks out three groups separated by slashes:

```
>>> match = re.match('/(.*)/(.*)/(.*)', '/usr/home/lumberjack')
>>> match.groups()
('usr', 'home', 'lumberjack')
```

Pattern matching is a fairly advanced text-processing tool by itself, but there is also support in Python for even more advanced text and language processing, including XML parsing and natural language analysis. I've already said enough about strings for this tutorial, though, so let's move on to the next type.

Lists

The Python list object is the most general sequence provided by the language. Lists are positionally ordered collections of arbitrarily typed objects, and they have no fixed size. They are also mutable—unlike strings, lists can be modified in-place by assignment to offsets as well as a variety of list method calls.

Sequence Operations

Because they are sequences, lists support all the sequence operations we discussed for strings; the only difference is that the results are usually lists instead of strings. For instance, given a three-item list:

```
>>> L = [123, 'spam', 1.23]          # A list of three different-type objects
>>> len(L)                            # Number of items in the list
3
```

we can index, slice, and so on, just as for strings:

```
>>> L[0]                              # Indexing by position
123

>>> L[:-1]                            # Slicing a list returns a new list
[123, 'spam']

>>> L + [4, 5, 6]                     # Concatenation makes a new list too
[123, 'spam', 1.23, 4, 5, 6]
```

```
>>> L                              # We're not changing the original list
[123, 'spam', 1.23]
```

Type-Specific Operations

Python's lists are related to arrays in other languages, but they tend to be more powerful. For one thing, they have no fixed type constraint—the list we just looked at, for example, contains three objects of completely different types (an integer, a string, and a floating-point number). Further, lists have no fixed size. That is, they can grow and shrink on demand, in response to list-specific operations:

```
>>> L.append('NI')                 # Growing: add object at end of list
>>> L
[123, 'spam', 1.23, 'NI']

>>> L.pop(2)                       # Shrinking: delete an item in the middle
1.23

>>> L                              # "del L[2]" deletes from a list too
[123, 'spam', 'NI']
```

Here, the list append method expands the list's size and inserts an item at the end; the pop method (or an equivalent del statement) then removes an item at a given offset, causing the list to shrink. Other list methods insert an item at an arbitrary position (insert), remove a given item by value (remove), and so on. Because lists are mutable, most list methods also change the list object in-place, instead of creating a new one:

```
>>> M = ['bb', 'aa', 'cc']
>>> M.sort()
>>> M
['aa', 'bb', 'cc']
>>> M.reverse()
>>> M
['cc', 'bb', 'aa']
```

The list sort method here, for example, orders the list in ascending fashion by default, and reverse reverses it—in both cases, the methods modify the list directly.

Bounds Checking

Although lists have no fixed size, Python still doesn't allow us to reference items that are not present. Indexing off the end of a list is always a mistake, but so is assigning off the end:

```
>>> L
[123, 'spam', 'NI']

>>> L[99]
...error text omitted...
IndexError: list index out of range
```

```
>>> L[99] = 1
...error text omitted...
IndexError: list assignment index out of range
```

This is intentional, as it's usually an error to try to assign off the end of a list (and a particularly nasty one in the C language, which doesn't do as much error checking as Python). Rather than silently growing the list in response, Python reports an error. To grow a list, we call list methods such as append instead.

Nesting

One nice feature of Python's core data types is that they support arbitrary nesting—we can nest them in any combination, and as deeply as we like (for example, we can have a list that contains a dictionary, which contains another list, and so on). One immediate application of this feature is to represent matrixes, or "multidimensional arrays" in Python. A list with nested lists will do the job for basic applications:

```
>>> M = [[1, 2, 3],        # A 3 x 3 matrix, as nested lists
         [4, 5, 6],        # Code can span lines if bracketed
         [7, 8, 9]]
>>> M
[[1, 2, 3], [4, 5, 6], [7, 8, 9]]
```

Here, we've coded a list that contains three other lists. The effect is to represent a 3 × 3 matrix of numbers. Such a structure can be accessed in a variety of ways:

```
>>> M[1]                   # Get row 2
[4, 5, 6]

>>> M[1][2]                # Get row 2, then get item 3 within the row
6
```

The first operation here fetches the entire second row, and the second grabs the third item within that row. Stringing together index operations takes us deeper and deeper into our nested-object structure.†

Comprehensions

In addition to sequence operations and list methods, Python includes a more advanced operation known as a *list comprehension expression*, which turns out to be a powerful way to process structures like our matrix. Suppose, for instance, that we need to extract the second column of our sample matrix. It's easy to grab rows by simple indexing

---

† This matrix structure works for small-scale tasks, but for more serious number crunching you will probably want to use one of the numeric extensions to Python, such as the open source *NumPy* system. Such tools can store and process large matrixes much more efficiently than our nested list structure. NumPy has been said to turn Python into the equivalent of a free and more powerful version of the Matlab system, and organizations such as NASA, Los Alamos, and JPMorgan Chase use this tool for scientific and financial tasks. Search the Web for more details.

because the matrix is stored by rows, but it's almost as easy to get a column with a list comprehension:

```
>>> col2 = [row[1] for row in M]          # Collect the items in column 2
>>> col2
[2, 5, 8]

>>> M                                     # The matrix is unchanged
[[1, 2, 3], [4, 5, 6], [7, 8, 9]]
```

List comprehensions derive from set notation; they are a way to build a new list by running an expression on each item in a sequence, one at a time, from left to right. List comprehensions are coded in square brackets (to tip you off to the fact that they make a list) and are composed of an expression and a looping construct that share a variable name (row, here). The preceding list comprehension means basically what it says: "Give me row[1] for each row in matrix M, in a new list." The result is a new list containing column 2 of the matrix.

List comprehensions can be more complex in practice:

```
>>> [row[1] + 1 for row in M]             # Add 1 to each item in column 2
[3, 6, 9]

>>> [row[1] for row in M if row[1] % 2 == 0]   # Filter out odd items
[2, 8]
```

The first operation here, for instance, adds 1 to each item as it is collected, and the second uses an if clause to filter odd numbers out of the result using the % modulus expression (remainder of division). List comprehensions make new lists of results, but they can be used to iterate over any iterable object. Here, for instance, we use list comprehensions to step over a hardcoded list of coordinates and a string:

```
>>> diag = [M[i][i] for i in [0, 1, 2]]   # Collect a diagonal from matrix
>>> diag
[1, 5, 9]

>>> doubles = [c * 2 for c in 'spam']     # Repeat characters in a string
>>> doubles
['ss', 'pp', 'aa', 'mm']
```

List comprehensions, and relatives like the map and filter built-in functions, are a bit too involved for me to say more about them here. The main point of this brief introduction is to illustrate that Python includes both simple and advanced tools in its arsenal. List comprehensions are an optional feature, but they tend to be handy in practice and often provide a substantial processing speed advantage. They also work on any type that is a sequence in Python, as well as some types that are not. You'll hear much more about them later in this book.

As a preview, though, you'll find that in recent Pythons, comprehension syntax in parentheses can also be used to create *generators* that produce results on demand (the sum built-in, for instance, sums items in a sequence):

```
>>> G = (sum(row) for row in M)          # Create a generator of row sums
>>> next(G)                              # iter(G) not required here
6
>>> next(G)                              # Run the iteration protocol
15
```

The map built-in can do similar work, by generating the results of running items through a function. Wrapping it in `list` forces it to return all its values in Python 3.0:

```
>>> list(map(sum, M))                    # Map sum over items in M
[6, 15, 24]
```

In Python 3.0, comprehension syntax can also be used to create *sets* and *dictionaries*:

```
>>> {sum(row) for row in M}              # Create a set of row sums
{24, 6, 15}

>>> {i : sum(M[i]) for i in range(3)}    # Creates key/value table of row sums
{0: 6, 1: 15, 2: 24}
```

In fact, lists, sets, and dictionaries can all be built with comprehensions in 3.0:

```
>>> [ord(x) for x in 'spaam']            # List of character ordinals
[115, 112, 97, 97, 109]
>>> {ord(x) for x in 'spaam'}            # Sets remove duplicates
{112, 97, 115, 109}
>>> {x: ord(x) for x in 'spaam'}         # Dictionary keys are unique
{'a': 97, 'p': 112, 's': 115, 'm': 109}
```

To understand objects like generators, sets, and dictionaries, though, we must move ahead.

Dictionaries

Python dictionaries are something completely different (Monty Python reference intended)—they are not sequences at all, but are instead known as *mappings*. Mappings are also collections of other objects, but they store objects by key instead of by relative position. In fact, mappings don't maintain any reliable left-to-right order; they simply map keys to associated values. Dictionaries, the only mapping type in Python's core objects set, are also mutable: they may be changed in-place and can grow and shrink on demand, like lists.

Mapping Operations

When written as literals, dictionaries are coded in curly braces and consist of a series of "key: value" pairs. Dictionaries are useful anytime we need to associate a set of values with keys—to describe the properties of something, for instance. As an example, consider the following three-item dictionary (with keys "food," "quantity," and "color"):

```
>>> D = {'food': 'Spam', 'quantity': 4, 'color': 'pink'}
```

We can index this dictionary by key to fetch and change the keys' associated values. The dictionary index operation uses the same syntax as that used for sequences, but the item in the square brackets is a key, not a relative position:

```
>>> D['food']              # Fetch value of key 'food'
'Spam'

>>> D['quantity'] += 1     # Add 1 to 'quantity' value
>>> D
{'food': 'Spam', 'color': 'pink', 'quantity': 5}
```

Although the curly-braces literal form does see use, it is perhaps more common to see dictionaries built up in different ways. The following code, for example, starts with an empty dictionary and fills it out one key at a time. Unlike out-of-bounds assignments in lists, which are forbidden, assignments to new dictionary keys create those keys:

```
>>> D = {}
>>> D['name'] = 'Bob'      # Create keys by assignment
>>> D['job']  = 'dev'
>>> D['age']  = 40

>>> D
{'age': 40, 'job': 'dev', 'name': 'Bob'}

>>> print(D['name'])
Bob
```

Here, we're effectively using dictionary keys as field names in a record that describes someone. In other applications, dictionaries can also be used to replace searching operations—indexing a dictionary by key is often the fastest way to code a search in Python. As we'll learn later, dictionaries may also be made by passing keyword arguments to the type name: dict(name='Bob', job='dev', age=40) makes the same dictionary.

Nesting Revisited

In the prior example, we used a dictionary to describe a hypothetical person, with three keys. Suppose, though, that the information is more complex. Perhaps we need to record a first name and a last name, along with multiple job titles. This leads to another application of Python's object nesting in action. The following dictionary, coded all at once as a literal, captures more structured information:

```
>>> rec = {'name': {'first': 'Bob', 'last': 'Smith'},
           'job':  ['dev', 'mgr'],
           'age':  40.5}
```

Here, we again have a three-key dictionary at the top (keys "name," "job," and "age"), but the values have become more complex: a nested dictionary for the name to support multiple parts, and a nested list for the job to support multiple roles and future expansion. We can access the components of this structure much as we did for our matrix earlier, but this time some of our indexes are dictionary keys, not list offsets:

```
>>> rec['name']                          # 'name' is a nested dictionary
{'last': 'Smith', 'first': 'Bob'}

>>> rec['name']['last']                   # Index the nested dictionary
'Smith'

>>> rec['job']                            # 'job' is a nested list
['dev', 'mgr']
>>> rec['job'][-1]                        # Index the nested list
'mgr'

>>> rec['job'].append('janitor')          # Expand Bob's job description in-place
>>> rec
{'age': 40.5, 'job': ['dev', 'mgr', 'janitor'], 'name': {'last': 'Smith',
'first': 'Bob'}}
```

Notice how the last operation here expands the nested job list—because the job list is a separate piece of memory from the dictionary that contains it, it can grow and shrink freely (object memory layout will be discussed further later in this book).

The real reason for showing you this example is to demonstrate the *flexibility* of Python's core data types. As you can see, nesting allows us to build up complex information structures directly and easily. Building a similar structure in a low-level language like C would be tedious and require much more code: we would have to lay out and declare structures and arrays, fill out values, link everything together, and so on. In Python, this is all automatic—running the expression creates the entire nested object structure for us. In fact, this is one of the main benefits of scripting languages like Python.

Just as importantly, in a lower-level language we would have to be careful to clean up all of the object's space when we no longer need it. In Python, when we lose the last reference to the object—by assigning its variable to something else, for example—all of the memory space occupied by that object's structure is automatically cleaned up for us:

```
>>> rec = 0                               # Now the object's space is reclaimed
```

Technically speaking, Python has a feature known as *garbage collection* that cleans up unused memory as your program runs and frees you from having to manage such details in your code. In Python, the space is reclaimed immediately, as soon as the last reference to an object is removed. We'll study how this works later in this book; for now, it's enough to know that you can use objects freely, without worrying about creating their space or cleaning up as you go.‡

---

‡ Keep in mind that the rec record we just created really could be a database record, when we employ Python's *object persistence* system—an easy way to store native Python objects in files or access-by-key databases. We won't go into details here, but watch for discussion of Python's pickle and shelve modules later in this book.

Sorting Keys: for Loops

As mappings, as we've already seen, dictionaries only support accessing items by key. However, they also support type-specific operations with method calls that are useful in a variety of common use cases.

As mentioned earlier, because dictionaries are not sequences, they don't maintain any dependable left-to-right order. This means that if we make a dictionary and print it back, its keys may come back in a different order than that in which we typed them:

```
>>> D = {'a': 1, 'b': 2, 'c': 3}
>>> D
{'a': 1, 'c': 3, 'b': 2}
```

What do we do, though, if we do need to impose an ordering on a dictionary's items? One common solution is to grab a list of keys with the dictionary **keys** method, sort that with the list **sort** method, and then step through the result with a Python **for** loop (be sure to press the Enter key twice after coding the **for** loop below—as explained in Chapter 3, an empty line means "go" at the interactive prompt, and the prompt changes to "..." on some interfaces):

```
>>> Ks = list(D.keys())          # Unordered keys list
>>> Ks                           # A list in 2.6, "view" in 3.0: use list()
['a', 'c', 'b']

>>> Ks.sort()                    # Sorted keys list
>>> Ks
['a', 'b', 'c']

>>> for key in Ks:               # Iterate though sorted keys
        print(key, '=>', D[key]) # <== press Enter twice here

a => 1
b => 2
c => 3
```

This is a three-step process, although, as we'll see in later chapters, in recent versions of Python it can be done in one step with the newer **sorted** built-in function. The **sorted** call returns the result and sorts a variety of object types, in this case sorting dictionary keys automatically:

```
>>> D
{'a': 1, 'c': 3, 'b': 2}

>>> for key in sorted(D):
        print(key, '=>', D[key])

a => 1
b => 2
c => 3
```

Besides showcasing dictionaries, this use case serves to introduce the Python **for** loop. The **for** loop is a simple and efficient way to step through all the items in a sequence and run a block of code for each item in turn. A user-defined loop variable (key, here) is used to reference the current item each time through. The net effect in our example is to print the unordered dictionary's keys and values, in sorted-key order.

The for loop, and its more general cousin the while loop, are the main ways we code repetitive tasks as statements in our scripts. Really, though, the for loop (like its relative the list comprehension, which we met earlier) is a sequence operation. It works on any object that is a sequence and, like the list comprehension, even on some things that are not. Here, for example, it is stepping across the characters in a string, printing the uppercase version of each as it goes:

```
>>> for c in 'spam':
        print(c.upper())

S
P
A
M
```

Python's while loop is a more general sort of looping tool, not limited to stepping across sequences:

```
>>> x = 4
>>> while x > 0:
        print('spam!' * x)
        x -= 1

spam!spam!spam!spam!
spam!spam!spam!
spam!spam!
spam!
```

We'll discuss looping statements, syntax, and tools in depth later in the book.

Iteration and Optimization

If the last section's for loop looks like the list comprehension expression introduced earlier, it should: both are really general iteration tools. In fact, both will work on any object that follows the *iteration protocol*—a pervasive idea in Python that essentially means a physically stored sequence in memory, or an object that generates one item at a time in the context of an iteration operation. An object falls into the latter category if it responds to the iter built-in with an object that advances in response to next. The *generator* comprehension expression we saw earlier is such an object.

I'll have more to say about the iteration protocol later in this book. For now, keep in mind that every Python tool that scans an object from left to right uses the iteration protocol. This is why the sorted call used in the prior section works on the dictionary directly—we don't have to call the keys method to get a sequence because dictionaries are iterable objects, with a next that returns successive keys.

This also means that any list comprehension expression, such as this one, which computes the squares of a list of numbers:

```
>>> squares = [x ** 2 for x in [1, 2, 3, 4, 5]]
>>> squares
[1, 4, 9, 16, 25]
```

can always be coded as an equivalent for loop that builds the result list manually by appending as it goes:

```
>>> squares = []
>>> for x in [1, 2, 3, 4, 5]:        # This is what a list comprehension does
        squares.append(x ** 2)       # Both run the iteration protocol internally

>>> squares
[1, 4, 9, 16, 25]
```

The list comprehension, though, and related functional programming tools like map and filter, will generally run faster than a for loop today (perhaps even twice as fast)—a property that could matter in your programs for large data sets. Having said that, though, I should point out that performance measures are tricky business in Python because it optimizes so much, and performance can vary from release to release.

A major rule of thumb in Python is to code for simplicity and readability first and worry about performance later, after your program is working, and after you've proved that there is a genuine performance concern. More often than not, your code will be quick enough as it is. If you do need to tweak code for performance, though, Python includes tools to help you out, including the time and timeit modules and the profile module. You'll find more on these later in this book, and in the Python manuals.

Missing Keys: if Tests

One other note about dictionaries before we move on. Although we can assign to a new key to expand a dictionary, fetching a nonexistent key is still a mistake:

```
>>> D
{'a': 1, 'c': 3, 'b': 2}

>>> D['e'] = 99              # Assigning new keys grows dictionaries
>>> D
{'a': 1, 'c': 3, 'b': 2, 'e': 99}

>>> D['f']                   # Referencing a nonexistent key is an error
...error text omitted...
KeyError: 'f'
```

This is what we want—it's usually a programming error to fetch something that isn't really there. But in some generic programs, we can't always know what keys will be present when we write our code. How do we handle such cases and avoid errors? One trick is to test ahead of time. The dictionary in membership expression allows us to query the existence of a key and branch on the result with a Python `if` statement (as with the `for`, be sure to press Enter twice to run the `if` interactively here):

```
>>> 'f' in D
False

>>> if not 'f' in D:
        print('missing')

missing
```

I'll have much more to say about the `if` statement and statement syntax in general later in this book, but the form we're using here is straightforward: it consists of the word `if`, followed by an expression that is interpreted as a true or false result, followed by a block of code to run if the test is true. In its full form, the `if` statement can also have an `else` clause for a default case, and one or more `elif` (else if) clauses for other tests. It's the main selection tool in Python, and it's the way we code logic in our scripts.

Still, there are other ways to create dictionaries and avoid accessing nonexistent keys: the `get` method (a conditional index with a default); the Python 2.X `has_key` method (which is no longer available in 3.0); the `try` statement (a tool we'll first meet in Chapter 10 that catches and recovers from exceptions altogether); and the `if`/`else` expression (essentially, an `if` statement squeezed onto a single line). Here are a few examples:

```
>>> value = D.get('x', 0)                    # Index but with a default
>>> value
0
>>> value = D['x'] if 'x' in D else 0        # if/else expression form
>>> value
0
```

We'll save the details on such alternatives until a later chapter. For now, let's move on to tuples.

Tuples

The tuple object (pronounced "toople" or "tuhple," depending on who you ask) is roughly like a list that cannot be changed—tuples are sequences, like lists, but they are immutable, like strings. Syntactically, they are coded in parentheses instead of square brackets, and they support arbitrary types, arbitrary nesting, and the usual sequence operations:

```
>>> T = (1, 2, 3, 4)          # A 4-item tuple
>>> len(T)                    # Length
4

>> T + (5, 6)                 # Concatenation
(1, 2, 3, 4, 5, 6)

>>> T[0]                      # Indexing, slicing, and more
1
```

Tuples also have two type-specific callable methods in Python 3.0, but not nearly as many as lists:

```
>>> T.index(4)              # Tuple methods: 4 appears at offset 3
3
>>> T.count(4)              # 4 appears once
1
```

The primary distinction for tuples is that they cannot be changed once created. That is, they are immutable sequences:

```
>>> T[0] = 2                # Tuples are immutable
...error text omitted...
TypeError: 'tuple' object does not support item assignment
```

Like lists and dictionaries, tuples support mixed types and nesting, but they don't grow and shrink because they are immutable:

```
>>> T = ('spam', 3.0, [11, 22, 33])
>>> T[1]
3.0
>>> T[2][1]
22
>>> T.append(4)
AttributeError: 'tuple' object has no attribute 'append'
```

Why Tuples?

So, why have a type that is like a list, but supports fewer operations? Frankly, tuples are not generally used as often as lists in practice, but their immutability is the whole point. If you pass a collection of objects around your program as a list, it can be changed anywhere; if you use a tuple, it cannot. That is, tuples provide a sort of integrity constraint that is convenient in programs larger than those we'll write here. We'll talk more about tuples later in the book. For now, though, let's jump ahead to our last major core type: the file.

Files

File objects are Python code's main interface to external files on your computer. Files are a core type, but they're something of an oddball—there is no specific literal syntax for creating them. Rather, to create a file object, you call the built-in open function, passing in an external filename and a processing mode as strings. For example, to create a text output file, you would pass in its name and the 'w' processing mode string to write data:

```
>>> f = open('data.txt', 'w')    # Make a new file in output mode
>>> f.write('Hello\n')           # Write strings of bytes to it
6
>>> f.write('world\n')           # Returns number of bytes written in Python 3.0
6
>>> f.close()                    # Close to flush output buffers to disk
```

This creates a file in the current directory and writes text to it (the filename can be a full directory path if you need to access a file elsewhere on your computer). To read back what you just wrote, reopen the file in `'r'` processing mode, for reading text input—this is the default if you omit the mode in the call. Then read the file's content into a string, and display it. A file's contents are always a string in your script, regardless of the type of data the file contains:

```
>>> f = open('data.txt')          # 'r' is the default processing mode
>>> text = f.read()               # Read entire file into a string
>>> text
'Hello\nworld\n'

>>> print(text)                   # print interprets control characters
Hello
world

>>> text.split()                  # File content is always a string
['Hello', 'world']
```

Other file object methods support additional features we don't have time to cover here. For instance, file objects provide more ways of reading and writing (read accepts an optional byte size, readline reads one line at a time, and so on), as well as other tools (seek moves to a new file position). As we'll see later, though, the best way to read a file today is to *not read it at all*—files provide an *iterator* that automatically reads line by line in for loops and other contexts.

We'll meet the full set of file methods later in this book, but if you want a quick preview now, run a dir call on any open file and a help on any of the method names that come back:

```
>>> dir(f)
[ ...many names omitted...
'buffer', 'close', 'closed', 'encoding', 'errors', 'fileno', 'flush', 'isatty',
'line_buffering', 'mode', 'name', 'newlines', 'read', 'readable', 'readline',
'readlines', 'seek', 'seekable', 'tell', 'truncate', 'writable', 'write',
'writelines']

>>>help(f.seek)
...try it and see...
```

Later in the book, we'll also see that files in Python 3.0 draw a sharp distinction between text and binary data. *Text files* represent content as strings and perform Unicode encoding and decoding automatically, while *binary files* represent content as a special bytes string type and allow you to access file content unaltered (the following partial example assumes there is already a binary file in your current directory):

```
>>> data = open('data.bin', 'rb').read()    # Open binary file
>>> data                                     # bytes string holds binary data
b'\x00\x00\x00\x07spam\x00\x08'
>>> data[4:8]
b'spam'
```

Although you won't generally need to care about this distinction if you deal only with ASCII text, Python 3.0's strings and files are an asset if you deal with internationalized applications or byte-oriented data.

Other File-Like Tools

The open function is the workhorse for most file processing you will do in Python. For more advanced tasks, though, Python comes with additional file-like tools: pipes, FIFOs, sockets, keyed-access files, persistent object shelves, descriptor-based files, relational and object-oriented database interfaces, and more. Descriptor files, for instance, support file locking and other low-level tools, and sockets provide an interface for networking and interprocess communication. We won't cover many of these topics in this book, but you'll find them useful once you start programming Python in earnest.

Other Core Types

Beyond the core types we've seen so far, there are others that may or may not qualify for membership in the set, depending on how broadly it is defined. *Sets*, for example, are a recent addition to the language that are neither mappings nor sequences; rather, they are unordered collections of unique and immutable objects. Sets are created by calling the built-in set function or using new set literals and expressions in 3.0, and they support the usual mathematical set operations (the choice of new {...} syntax for set literals in 3.0 makes sense, since sets are much like the keys of a valueless dictionary):

```
>>> X = set('spam')                    # Make a set out of a sequence in 2.6 and 3.0
>>> Y = {'h', 'a', 'm'}                # Make a set with new 3.0 set literals
>>> X, Y
({'a', 'p', 's', 'm'}, {'a', 'h', 'm'})

>>> X & Y                              # Intersection
{'a', 'm'}

>>> X | Y                              # Union
{'a', 'p', 's', 'h', 'm'}

>>> X - Y                              # Difference
{'p', 's'}

>>> {x ** 2 for x in [1, 2, 3, 4]}     # Set comprehensions in 3.0
{16, 1, 4, 9}
```

In addition, Python recently grew a few new numeric types: *decimal* numbers (fixed-precision floating-point numbers) and *fraction* numbers (rational numbers with both a numerator and a denominator). Both can be used to work around the limitations and inherent inaccuracies of floating-point math:

```
>>> 1 / 3                              # Floating-point (use .0 in Python 2.6)
0.33333333333333331
>>> (2/3) + (1/2)
```

```
1.1666666666666665

>>> import decimal                        # Decimals: fixed precision
>>> d = decimal.Decimal('3.141')
>>> d + 1
Decimal('4.141')

>>> decimal.getcontext().prec = 2
>>> decimal.Decimal('1.00') / decimal.Decimal('3.00')
Decimal('0.33')

>>> from fractions import Fraction        # Fractions: numerator+denominator
>>> f = Fraction(2, 3)
>>> f + 1
Fraction(5, 3)
>>> f + Fraction(1, 2)
Fraction(7, 6)
```

Python also comes with *Booleans* (with predefined `True` and `False` objects that are essentially just the integers 1 and 0 with custom display logic), and it has long supported a special placeholder object called `None` commonly used to initialize names and objects:

```
>>> 1 > 2, 1 < 2                          # Booleans
(False, True)
>>> bool('spam')
True

>>> X = None                             # None placeholder
>>> print(X)
None
>>> L = [None] * 100                      # Initialize a list of 100 Nones
>>> L
[None, None, None, None, None, None, None, None, None, None, None, None,
 None, None, None, None, None, None, None, None, ...a list of 100 Nones...]
```

How to Break Your Code's Flexibility

I'll have more to say about all of Python's object types later, but one merits special treatment here. The *type* object, returned by the `type` built-in function, is an object that gives the type of another object; its result differs slightly in 3.0, because types have merged with classes completely (something we'll explore in the context of "new-style" classes in Part VI). Assuming L is still the list of the prior section:

```
# In Python 2.6:

>>> type(L)                               # Types: type of L is list type object
<type 'list'>
>>> type(type(L))                         # Even types are objects
<type 'type'>

# In Python 3.0:

>>> type(L)                               # 3.0: types are classes, and vice versa
<class 'list'>
```

```
>>> type(type(L))                    # See Chapter 31 for more on class types
<class 'type'>
```

Besides allowing you to explore your objects interactively, the practical application of this is that it allows code to check the types of the objects it processes. In fact, there are at least three ways to do so in a Python script:

```
>>> if type(L) == type([]):          # Type testing, if you must...
        print('yes')

yes
>>> if type(L) == list:              # Using the type name
        print('yes')

yes
>>> if isinstance(L, list):          # Object-oriented tests
        print('yes')

yes
```

Now that I've shown you all these ways to do type testing, however, I am required by law to tell you that doing so is almost always the wrong thing to do in a Python program (and often a sign of an ex-C programmer first starting to use Python!). The reason why won't become completely clear until later in the book, when we start writing larger code units such as functions, but it's a (perhaps *the*) core Python concept. By checking for specific types in your code, you effectively break its flexibility—you limit it to working on just one type. Without such tests, your code may be able to work on a whole range of types.

This is related to the idea of polymorphism mentioned earlier, and it stems from Python's lack of type declarations. As you'll learn, in Python, we code to object *interfaces* (operations supported), not to types. Not caring about specific types means that code is automatically applicable to many of them—any object with a compatible interface will work, regardless of its specific type. Although type checking is supported—and even required, in some rare cases—you'll see that it's not usually the "Pythonic" way of thinking. In fact, you'll find that polymorphism is probably the key idea behind using Python well.

User-Defined Classes

We'll study *object-oriented programming* in Python—an optional but powerful feature of the language that cuts development time by supporting programming by customization—in depth later in this book. In abstract terms, though, classes define new types of objects that extend the core set, so they merit a passing glance here. Say, for example, that you wish to have a type of object that models employees. Although there is no such specific core type in Python, the following user-defined class might fit the bill:

```
>>> class Worker:
        def __init__(self, name, pay):    # Initialize when created
            self.name = name              # self is the new object
```

```
        self.pay  = pay
    def lastName(self):
        return self.name.split()[-1]          # Split string on blanks
    def giveRaise(self, percent):
        self.pay *= (1.0 + percent)           # Update pay in-place
```

This class defines a new kind of object that will have name and pay attributes (sometimes called *state information*), as well as two bits of behavior coded as functions (normally called *methods*). Calling the class like a function generates instances of our new type, and the class's methods automatically receive the instance being processed by a given method call (in the self argument):

```
>>> bob = Worker('Bob Smith', 50000)          # Make two instances
>>> sue = Worker('Sue Jones', 60000)          # Each has name and pay attrs
>>> bob.lastName()                            # Call method: bob is self
'Smith'
>>> sue.lastName()                            # sue is the self subject
'Jones'
>>> sue.giveRaise(.10)                        # Updates sue's pay
>>> sue.pay
66000.0
```

The implied "self" object is why we call this an object-oriented model: there is always an implied subject in functions within a class. In a sense, though, the class-based type simply builds on and uses core types—a user-defined Worker object here, for example, is just a collection of a string and a number (name and pay, respectively), plus functions for processing those two built-in objects.

The larger story of classes is that their inheritance mechanism supports software hierarchies that lend themselves to customization by extension. We extend software by writing new classes, not by changing what already works. You should also know that classes are an optional feature of Python, and simpler built-in types such as lists and dictionaries are often better tools than user-coded classes. This is all well beyond the bounds of our introductory object-type tutorial, though, so consider this just a preview; for full disclosure on user-defined types coded with classes, you'll have to read on to Part VI.

And Everything Else

As mentioned earlier, everything you can process in a Python script is a type of object, so our object type tour is necessarily incomplete. However, even though everything in Python is an "object," only those types of objects we've met so far are considered part of Python's core type set. Other types in Python either are objects related to program execution (like functions, modules, classes, and compiled code), which we will study later, or are implemented by imported module functions, not language syntax. The latter of these also tend to have application-specific roles—text patterns, database interfaces, network connections, and so on.

Moreover, keep in mind that the objects we've met here are objects, but not necessarily *object-oriented*—a concept that usually requires inheritance and the Python `class` statement, which we'll meet again later in this book. Still, Python's core objects are the workhorses of almost every Python script you're likely to meet, and they usually are the basis of larger noncore types.

Chapter Summary

And that's a wrap for our concise data type tour. This chapter has offered a brief introduction to Python's core object types and the sorts of operations we can apply to them. We've studied generic operations that work on many object types (sequence operations such as indexing and slicing, for example), as well as type-specific operations available as method calls (for instance, string splits and list appends). We've also defined some key terms, such as immutability, sequences, and polymorphism.

Along the way, we've seen that Python's core object types are more flexible and powerful than what is available in lower-level languages such as C. For instance, Python's lists and dictionaries obviate most of the work you do to support collections and searching in lower-level languages. Lists are ordered collections of other objects, and dictionaries are collections of other objects that are indexed by key instead of by position. Both dictionaries and lists may be nested, can grow and shrink on demand, and may contain objects of any type. Moreover, their space is automatically cleaned up as you go.

I've skipped most of the details here in order to provide a quick tour, so you shouldn't expect all of this chapter to have made sense yet. In the next few chapters, we'll start to dig deeper, filling in details of Python's core object types that were omitted here so you can gain a more complete understanding. We'll start off in the next chapter with an in-depth look at Python numbers. First, though, another quiz to review.

Test Your Knowledge: Quiz

We'll explore the concepts introduced in this chapter in more detail in upcoming chapters, so we'll just cover the big ideas here:

1. Name four of Python's core data types.
2. Why are they called "core" data types?
3. What does "immutable" mean, and which three of Python's core types are considered immutable?
4. What does "sequence" mean, and which three types fall into that category?

5. What does "mapping" mean, and which core type is a mapping?

6. What is "polymorphism," and why should you care?

Test Your Knowledge: Answers

1. Numbers, strings, lists, dictionaries, tuples, files, and sets are generally considered to be the core object (data) types. Types, None, and Booleans are sometimes classified this way as well. There are multiple number types (integer, floating point, complex, fraction, and decimal) and multiple string types (simple strings and Unicode strings in Python 2.X, and text strings and byte strings in Python 3.X).

2. They are known as "core" types because they are part of the Python language itself and are always available; to create other objects, you generally must call functions in imported modules. Most of the core types have specific syntax for generating the objects: 'spam', for example, is an expression that makes a string and determines the set of operations that can be applied to it. Because of this, core types are hardwired into Python's syntax. In contrast, you must call the built-in open function to create a file object.

3. An "immutable" object is an object that cannot be changed after it is created. Numbers, strings, and tuples in Python fall into this category. While you cannot change an immutable object in-place, you can always make a new one by running an expression.

4. A "sequence" is a positionally ordered collection of objects. Strings, lists, and tuples are all sequences in Python. They share common sequence operations, such as indexing, concatenation, and slicing, but also have type-specific method calls.

5. The term "mapping" denotes an object that maps keys to associated values. Python's dictionary is the only mapping type in the core type set. Mappings do not maintain any left-to-right positional ordering; they support access to data stored by key, plus type-specific method calls.

6. "Polymorphism" means that the meaning of an operation (like a +) depends on the objects being operated on. This turns out to be a key idea (perhaps *the* key idea) behind using Python well—not constraining code to specific types makes that code automatically applicable to many types.

## CHAPTER 5

Numeric Types

This chapter begins our in-depth tour of the Python language. In Python, data takes the form of *objects*—either built-in objects that Python provides, or objects we create using Python tools and other languages such as C. In fact, objects are the basis of every Python program you will ever write. Because they are the most fundamental notion in Python programming, objects are also our first focus in this book.

In the preceding chapter, we took a quick pass over Python's core object types. Although essential terms were introduced in that chapter, we avoided covering too many specifics in the interest of space. Here, we'll begin a more careful second look at data type concepts, to fill in details we glossed over earlier. Let's get started by exploring our first data type category: Python's numeric types.

Numeric Type Basics

Most of Python's number types are fairly typical and will probably seem familiar if you've used almost any other programming language in the past. They can be used to keep track of your bank balance, the distance to Mars, the number of visitors to your website, and just about any other numeric quantity.

In Python, numbers are not really a single object type, but a category of similar types. Python supports the usual numeric types (integers and floating points), as well as literals for creating numbers and expressions for processing them. In addition, Python provides more advanced numeric programming support and objects for more advanced work. A complete inventory of Python's numeric toolbox includes:

- Integers and floating-point numbers
- Complex numbers
- Fixed-precision decimal numbers

- Rational fraction numbers
- Sets
- Booleans
- Unlimited integer precision
- A variety of numeric built-ins and modules

This chapter starts with basic numbers and fundamentals, then moves on to explore the other tools in this list. Before we jump into code, though, the next few sections get us started with a brief overview of how we write and process numbers in our scripts.

Numeric Literals

Among its basic types, Python provides *integers* (positive and negative whole numbers) and *floating-point* numbers (numbers with a fractional part, sometimes called "floats" for economy). Python also allows us to write integers using hexadecimal, octal, and binary literals; offers a complex number type; and allows integers to have unlimited precision (they can grow to have as many digits as your memory space allows). Table 5-1 shows what Python's numeric types look like when written out in a program, as literals.

Table 5-1. Basic numeric literals

Literal	Interpretation
1234, -24, 0, 99999999999999	Integers (unlimited size)
1.23, 1., 3.14e-10, 4E210, 4.0e+210	Floating-point numbers
0177, 0x9ff, 0b101010	Octal, hex, and binary literals in 2.6
0o177, 0x9ff, 0b101010	Octal, hex, and binary literals in 3.0
3+4j, 3.0+4.0j, 3J	Complex number literals

In general, Python's numeric type literals are straightforward to write, but a few coding concepts are worth highlighting here:

Integer and floating-point literals

Integers are written as strings of decimal digits. Floating-point numbers have a decimal point and/or an optional signed exponent introduced by an e or E and followed by an optional sign. If you write a number with a decimal point or exponent, Python makes it a floating-point object and uses floating-point (not integer) math when the object is used in an expression. Floating-point numbers are implemented as C "doubles," and therefore get as much precision as the C compiler used to build the Python interpreter gives to doubles.

Integers in Python 2.6: normal and long

In Python 2.6 there are two integer types, normal (32 bits) and long (unlimited precision), and an integer may end in an l or L to force it to become a long integer. Because integers are automatically converted to long integers when their values overflow 32 bits, you never need to type the letter L yourself—Python automatically converts up to long integer when extra precision is needed.

Integers in Python 3.0: a single type

In Python 3.0, the normal and long integer types have been merged—there is only integer, which automatically supports the unlimited precision of Python 2.6's separate long integer type. Because of this, integers can no longer be coded with a trailing l or L, and integers never print with this character either. Apart from this, most programs are unaffected by this change, unless they do type testing that checks for 2.6 long integers.

Hexadecimal, octal, and binary literals

Integers may be coded in decimal (base 10), hexadecimal (base 16), octal (base 8), or binary (base 2). Hexadecimals start with a leading 0x or 0X, followed by a string of hexadecimal digits (0–9 and A–F). Hex digits may be coded in lower- or uppercase. Octal literals start with a leading 0o or 0O (zero and lower- or uppercase letter "o"), followed by a string of digits (0–7). In 2.6 and earlier, octal literals can also be coded with just a leading 0, but not in 3.0 (this original octal form is too easily confused with decimal, and is replaced by the new 0o format). Binary literals, new in 2.6 and 3.0, begin with a leading 0b or 0B, followed by binary digits (0–1).

Note that all of these literals produce integer objects in program code; they are just alternative syntaxes for specifying values. The built-in calls hex(I), oct(I), and bin(I) convert an integer to its representation string in these three bases, and int(str, base) converts a runtime string to an integer per a given base.

Complex numbers

Python complex literals are written as *realpart+imaginarypart*, where the *imaginarypart* is terminated with a j or J. The *realpart* is technically optional, so the *imaginarypart* may appear on its own. Internally, complex numbers are implemented as pairs of floating-point numbers, but all numeric operations perform complex math when applied to complex numbers. Complex numbers may also be created with the complex(*real, imag*) built-in call.

Coding other numeric types

As we'll see later in this chapter, there are additional, more advanced number types not included in Table 5-1. Some of these are created by calling functions in imported modules (e.g., decimals and fractions), and others have literal syntax all their own (e.g., sets).

Built-in Numeric Tools

Besides the built-in number literals shown in Table 5-1, Python provides a set of tools for processing number objects:

Expression operators
  +, -, *, /, >>, **, &, etc.

Built-in mathematical functions
  pow, abs, round, int, hex, bin, etc.

Utility modules
  random, math, etc.

We'll meet all of these as we go along.

Although numbers are primarily processed with expressions, built-ins, and modules, they also have a handful of type-specific *methods* today, which we'll meet in this chapter as well. Floating-point numbers, for example, have an `as_integer_ratio` method that is useful for the fraction number type, and an `is_integer` method to test if the number is an integer. Integers have various attributes, including a new `bit_length` method in the upcoming Python 3.1 release that gives the number of bits necessary to represent the object's value. Moreover, as part collection and part number, *sets* also support both methods and expressions.

Since expressions are the most essential tool for most number types, though, let's turn to them next.

Python Expression Operators

Perhaps the most fundamental tool that processes numbers is the *expression*: a combination of numbers (or other objects) and operators that computes a value when executed by Python. In Python, expressions are written using the usual mathematical notation and operator symbols. For instance, to add two numbers X and Y you would say X + Y, which tells Python to apply the + operator to the values named by X and Y. The result of the expression is the sum of X and Y, another number object.

Table 5-2 lists all the operator expressions available in Python. Many are self-explanatory; for instance, the usual mathematical operators (+, -, *, /, and so on) are supported. A few will be familiar if you've used other languages in the past: % computes a division remainder, << performs a bitwise left-shift, & computes a bitwise AND result, and so on. Others are more Python-specific, and not all are numeric in nature: for example, the `is` operator tests object identity (i.e., address in memory, a strict form of equality), and `lambda` creates unnamed functions.

Table 5-2. Python expression operators and precedence

Operators	Description
`yield x`	Generator function send protocol
`lambda args: expression`	Anonymous function generation
`x if y else z`	Ternary selection (x is evaluated only if y is true)
`x or y`	Logical OR (y is evaluated only if x is false)
`x and y`	Logical AND (y is evaluated only if x is true)
`not x`	Logical negation
`x in y, x not in y`	Membership (iterables, sets)
`x is y, x is not y`	Object identity tests
`x < y, x <= y, x > y, x >= y`	Magnitude comparison, set subset and superset;
`x == y, x != y`	Value equality operators
`x | y`	Bitwise OR, set union
`x ^ y`	Bitwise XOR, set symmetric difference
`x & y`	Bitwise AND, set intersection
`x << y, x >> y`	Shift x left or right by y bits
`x + y`	Addition, concatenation;
`x - y`	Subtraction, set difference
`x * y`	Multiplication, repetition;
`x % y`	Remainder, format;
`x / y, x // y`	Division: true and floor
`-x, +x`	Negation, identity
`~x`	Bitwise NOT (inversion)
`x ** y`	Power (exponentiation)
`x[i]`	Indexing (sequence, mapping, others)
`x[i:j:k]`	Slicing
`x(...)`	Call (function, method, class, other callable)
`x.attr`	Attribute reference
`(...)`	Tuple, expression, generator expression
`[...]`	List, list comprehension
`{...}`	Dictionary, set, set and dictionary comprehensions

Since this book addresses both Python 2.6 and 3.0, here are some notes about version differences and recent additions related to the operators in Table 5-2:

- In Python 2.6, value inequality can be written as either X != Y or X <> Y. In Python 3.0, the latter of these options is removed because it is redundant. In either version, best practice is to use X != Y for all value inequality tests.

- In Python 2.6, a backquotes expression `X` works the same as repr(X) and converts objects to display strings. Due to its obscurity, this expression is removed in Python 3.0; use the more readable str and repr built-in functions, described in "Numeric Display Formats" on page 117.

- The X // Y floor division expression always truncates fractional remainders in both Python 2.6 and 3.0. The X / Y expression performs true division in 3.0 (retaining remainders) and classic division in 2.6 (truncating for integers). See "Division: Classic, Floor, and True" on page 119.

- The syntax [...] is used for both list literals and list comprehension expressions. The latter of these performs an implied loop and collects expression results in a new list. See Chapters 4, 14, and 20 for examples.

- The syntax (...) is used for tuples and expressions, as well as generator expressions—a form of list comprehension that produces results on demand, instead of building a result list. See Chapters 4 and 20 for examples. The parentheses may sometimes be omitted in all three constructs.

- The syntax {...} is used for dictionary literals, and in Python 3.0 for set literals and both dictionary and set comprehensions. See the set coverage in this chapter and Chapters 4, 8, 14, and 20 for examples.

- The yield and ternary if/else selection expressions are available in Python 2.5 and later. The former returns send(...) arguments in generators; the latter is shorthand for a multiline if statement. yield requires parentheses if not alone on the right side of an assignment statement.

- Comparison operators may be chained: X < Y < Z produces the same result as X < Y and Y < Z. See "Comparisons: Normal and Chained" on page 118 for details.

- In recent Pythons, the slice expression X[I:J:K] is equivalent to indexing with a slice object: X[slice(I, J, K)].

- In Python 2.X, magnitude comparisons of mixed types—converting numbers to a common type, and ordering other mixed types according to the type name—are allowed. In Python 3.0, nonnumeric mixed-type magnitude comparisons are not allowed and raise exceptions; this includes sorts by proxy.

- Magnitude comparisons for dictionaries are also no longer supported in Python 3.0 (though equality tests are); comparing sorted(dict.items()) is one possible replacement.

We'll see most of the operators in Table 5-2 in action later; first, though, we need to take a quick look at the ways these operators may be combined in expressions.

Mixed operators follow operator precedence

As in most languages, in Python, more complex expressions are coded by stringing together the operator expressions in Table 5-2. For instance, the sum of two multiplications might be written as a mix of variables and operators:

```
A * B + C * D
```

So, how does Python know which operation to perform first? The answer to this question lies in *operator precedence*. When you write an expression with more than one operator, Python groups its parts according to what are called *precedence rules*, and this grouping determines the order in which the expression's parts are computed. Table 5-2 is ordered by operator precedence:

- Operators lower in the table have higher precedence, and so bind more tightly in mixed expressions.
- Operators in the same row in Table 5-2 generally group from left to right when combined (except for exponentiation, which groups right to left, and comparisons, which chain left to right).

For example, if you write X + Y * Z, Python evaluates the multiplication first (Y * Z), then adds that result to X because * has higher precedence (is lower in the table) than +. Similarly, in this section's original example, both multiplications (A * B and C * D) will happen before their results are added.

Parentheses group subexpressions

You can forget about precedence completely if you're careful to group parts of expressions with parentheses. When you enclose subexpressions in parentheses, you override Python's precedence rules; Python always evaluates expressions in parentheses first before using their results in the enclosing expressions.

For instance, instead of coding X + Y * Z, you could write one of the following to force Python to evaluate the expression in the desired order:

```
(X + Y) * Z
X + (Y * Z)
```

In the first case, + is applied to X and Y first, because this subexpression is wrapped in parentheses. In the second case, the * is performed first (just as if there were no parentheses at all). Generally speaking, adding parentheses in large expressions is a good idea—it not only forces the evaluation order you want, but also aids readability.

Mixed types are converted up

Besides mixing operators in expressions, you can also mix numeric types. For instance, you can add an integer to a floating-point number:

```
40 + 3.14
```

But this leads to another question: what type is the result—integer or floating-point? The answer is simple, especially if you've used almost any other language before: in mixed-type numeric expressions, Python first converts operands *up* to the type of the most complicated operand, and then performs the math on same-type operands. This behavior is similar to type conversions in the C language.

Python ranks the complexity of numeric types like so: integers are simpler than floating-point numbers, which are simpler than complex numbers. So, when an integer is mixed with a floating point, as in the preceding example, the integer is converted up to a floating-point value first, and floating-point math yields the floating-point result. Similarly, any mixed-type expression where one operand is a complex number results in the other operand being converted up to a complex number, and the expression yields a complex result. (In Python 2.6, normal integers are also converted to long integers whenever their values are too large to fit in a normal integer; in 3.0, integers subsume longs entirely.)

You can force the issue by calling built-in functions to convert types manually:

```
>>> int(3.1415)        # Truncates float to integer
3
>>> float(3)           # Converts integer to float
3.0
```

However, you won't usually need to do this: because Python automatically converts up to the more complex type within an expression, the results are normally what you want.

Also, keep in mind that all these mixed-type conversions apply only when mixing *numeric* types (e.g., an integer and a floating-point) in an expression, including those using numeric and comparison operators. In general, Python does not convert across any other type boundaries automatically. Adding a string to an integer, for example, results in an error, unless you manually convert one or the other; watch for an example when we meet strings in Chapter 7.

 In Python 2.6, nonnumeric mixed types can be compared, but no conversions are performed (mixed types compare according to a fixed but arbitrary rule). In 3.0, nonnumeric mixed-type comparisons are not allowed and raise exceptions.

Preview: Operator overloading and polymorphism

Although we're focusing on built-in numbers right now, all Python operators may be overloaded (i.e., implemented) by Python classes and C extension types to work on objects you create. For instance, you'll see later that objects coded with classes may be added or concatenated with + expressions, indexed with [i] expressions, and so on.

Furthermore, Python itself automatically overloads some operators, such that they perform different actions depending on the type of built-in objects being processed.

For example, the + operator performs addition when applied to numbers but performs concatenation when applied to sequence objects such as strings and lists. In fact, + can mean anything at all when applied to objects you define with classes.

As we saw in the prior chapter, this property is usually called *polymorphism*—a term indicating that the meaning of an operation depends on the type of the objects being operated on. We'll revisit this concept when we explore functions in Chapter 16, because it becomes a much more obvious feature in that context.

Numbers in Action

On to the code! Probably the best way to understand numeric objects and expressions is to see them in action, so let's start up the interactive command line and try some basic but illustrative operations (see Chapter 3 for pointers if you need help starting an interactive session).

Variables and Basic Expressions

First of all, let's exercise some basic math. In the following interaction, we first assign two *variables* (a and b) to integers so we can use them later in a larger expression. Variables are simply names—created by you or Python—that are used to keep track of information in your program. We'll say more about this in the next chapter, but in Python:

- Variables are created when they are first assigned values.
- Variables are replaced with their values when used in expressions.
- Variables must be assigned before they can be used in expressions.
- Variables refer to objects and are never declared ahead of time.

In other words, these assignments cause the variables a and b to spring into existence automatically:

```
% python
>>> a = 3          # Name created
>>> b = 4
```

I've also used a *comment* here. Recall that in Python code, text after a # mark and continuing to the end of the line is considered to be a comment and is ignored. Comments are a way to write human-readable documentation for your code. Because code you type interactively is temporary, you won't normally write comments in this context, but I've added them to some of this book's examples to help explain the code.* In the next part of the book, we'll meet a related feature—documentation strings—that attaches the text of your comments to objects.

---

* If you're working along, you don't need to type any of the comment text from the # through to the end of the line; comments are simply ignored by Python and not required parts of the statements we're running.

Now, let's use our new integer objects in some expressions. At this point, the values of a and b are still 3 and 4, respectively. Variables like these are replaced with their values whenever they're used inside an expression, and the expression results are echoed back immediately when working interactively:

```
>>> a + 1, a - 1          # Addition (3 + 1), subtraction (3 - 1)
(4, 2)
>>> b * 3, b / 2          # Multiplication (4 * 3), division (4 / 2)
(12, 2.0)
>>> a % 2, b ** 2         # Modulus (remainder), power (4 ** 2)
(1, 16)
>>> 2 + 4.0, 2.0 ** b     # Mixed-type conversions
(6.0, 16.0)
```

Technically, the results being echoed back here are *tuples* of two values because the lines typed at the prompt contain two expressions separated by commas; that's why the results are displayed in parentheses (more on tuples later). Note that the expressions work because the variables a and b within them have been assigned values. If you use a different variable that has never been assigned, Python reports an error rather than filling in some default value:

```
>>> c * 2
Traceback (most recent call last):
  File "<stdin>", line 1, in ?
NameError: name 'c' is not defined
```

You don't need to predeclare variables in Python, but they must have been assigned at least once before you can use them. In practice, this means you have to initialize counters to zero before you can add to them, initialize lists to an empty list before you can append to them, and so on.

Here are two slightly larger expressions to illustrate operator grouping and more about conversions:

```
>>> b / 2 + a            # Same as ((4 / 2) + 3)
5.0
>>> print(b / (2.0 + a)) # Same as (4 / (2.0 + 3))
0.8
```

In the first expression, there are no parentheses, so Python automatically groups the components according to its precedence rules—because / is lower in Table 5-2 than +, it binds more tightly and so is evaluated first. The result is as if the expression had been organized with parentheses as shown in the comment to the right of the code.

Also, notice that all the numbers are integers in the first expression. Because of that, Python 2.6 performs integer division and addition and will give a result of 5, whereas Python 3.0 performs true division with remainders and gives the result shown. If you want integer division in 3.0, code this as b // 2 + a (more on division in a moment).

In the second expression, parentheses are added around the + part to force Python to evaluate it first (i.e., before the /). We also made one of the operands floating-point by adding a decimal point: 2.0. Because of the mixed types, Python converts the integer referenced by a to a floating-point value (3.0) before performing the +. If all the numbers in this expression were integers, integer division (4 / 5) would yield the truncated integer 0 in Python 2.6 but the floating-point 0.8 in Python 3.0 (again, stay tuned for division details).

Numeric Display Formats

Notice that we used a print operation in the last of the preceding examples. Without the print, you'll see something that may look a bit odd at first glance:

```
>>> b / (2.0 + a)          # Auto echo output: more digits
0.80000000000000004

>>> print(b / (2.0 + a))   # print rounds off digits
0.8
```

The full story behind this odd result has to do with the limitations of floating-point hardware and its inability to exactly represent some values in a limited number of bits. Because computer architecture is well beyond this book's scope, though, we'll finesse this by saying that all of the digits in the first output are really there in your computer's floating-point hardware—it's just that you're not accustomed to seeing them. In fact, this is really just a display issue—the interactive prompt's automatic result echo shows more digits than the print statement. If you don't want to see all the digits, use print; as the sidebar "str and repr Display Formats" on page 118 will explain, you'll get a user-friendly display.

Note, however, that not all values have so many digits to display:

```
>>> 1 / 2.0
0.5
```

and that there are more ways to display the bits of a number inside your computer than using print and automatic echoes:

```
>>> num = 1 / 3.0
>>> num                       # Echoes
0.33333333333333331
>>> print(num)                # print rounds
0.333333333333

>>> '%e' % num                # String formatting expression
'3.333333e-001'
>>> '%4.2f' % num             # Alternative floating-point format
'0.33'
>>> '{0:4.2f}'.format(num)    # String formatting method (Python 2.6 and 3.0)
'0.33'
```

The last three of these expressions employ *string formatting*, a tool that allows for format flexibility, which we will explore in the upcoming chapter on strings (Chapter 7). Its results are strings that are typically printed to displays or reports.

---

str and repr Display Formats

Technically, the difference between default interactive echoes and `print` corresponds to the difference between the built-in `repr` and `str` functions:

```
>>> num = 1 / 3
>>> repr(num)                    # Used by echoes: as-code form
'0.33333333333333331'
>>> str(num)                     # Used by print: user-friendly form
'0.333333333333'
```

Both of these convert arbitrary objects to their string representations: `repr` (and the default interactive echo) produces results that look as though they were code; `str` (and the `print` operation) converts to a typically more user-friendly format if available. Some objects have both—a `str` for general use, and a `repr` with extra details. This notion will resurface when we study both strings and operator overloading in classes, and you'll find more on these built-ins in general later in the book.

Besides providing print strings for arbitrary objects, the `str` built-in is also the name of the string data type and may be called with an encoding name to decode a Unicode string from a byte string. We'll study the latter advanced role in Chapter 36 of this book.

Comparisons: Normal and Chained

So far, we've been dealing with standard numeric operations (addition and multiplication), but numbers can also be compared. Normal comparisons work for numbers exactly as you'd expect—they compare the relative magnitudes of their operands and return a Boolean result (which we would normally test in a larger statement):

```
>>> 1 < 2                        # Less than
True
>>> 2.0 >= 1                     # Greater than or equal: mixed-type 1 converted to 1.0
True
>>> 2.0 == 2.0                   # Equal value
True
>>> 2.0 != 2.0                   # Not equal value
False
```

Notice again how mixed types are allowed in numeric expressions (only); in the second test here, Python compares values in terms of the more complex type, float.

Interestingly, Python also allows us to *chain* multiple comparisons together to perform range tests. Chained comparisons are a sort of shorthand for larger Boolean expressions. In short, Python lets us string together magnitude comparison tests to code chained comparisons such as range tests. The expression (A < B < C), for instance, tests whether B is between A and C; it is equivalent to the Boolean test (A < B and B < C) but is easier on the eyes (and the keyboard). For example, assume the following assignments:

```
>>> X = 2
>>> Y = 4
>>> Z = 6
```

The following two expressions have identical effects, but the first is shorter to type, and it may run slightly faster since Python needs to evaluate Y only once:

```
>>> X < Y < Z                    # Chained comparisons: range tests
True
>>> X < Y and Y < Z
True
```

The same equivalence holds for false results, and arbitrary chain lengths are allowed:

```
>>> X < Y > Z
False
>>> X < Y and Y > Z
False

>>> 1 < 2 < 3.0 < 4
True
>>> 1 > 2 > 3.0 > 4
False
```

You can use other comparisons in chained tests, but the resulting expressions can become nonintuitive unless you evaluate them the way Python does. The following, for instance, is false just because 1 is not equal to 2:

```
>>> 1 == 2 < 3        # Same as: 1 == 2 and 2 < 3
False                 # Not same as: False < 3 (which means 0 < 3, which is true)
```

Python does not compare the `1 == 2 False` result to 3—this would technically mean the same as `0 < 3`, which would be `True` (as we'll see later in this chapter, `True` and `False` are just customized 1 and 0).

Division: Classic, Floor, and True

You've seen how division works in the previous sections, so you should know that it behaves slightly differently in Python 3.0 and 2.6. In fact, there are actually three flavors of division, and two different division operators, one of which changes in 3.0:

X / Y

> *Classic* and *true* division. In Python 2.6 and earlier, this operator performs *classic* division, truncating results for integers and keeping remainders for floating-point numbers. In Python 3.0, it performs *true* division, always keeping remainders regardless of types.

X // Y

> *Floor* division. Added in Python 2.2 and available in both Python 2.6 and 3.0, this operator always truncates fractional remainders down to their floor, regardless of types.

True division was added to address the fact that the results of the original classic division model are dependent on operand types, and so can be difficult to anticipate in a dynamically typed language like Python. Classic division was removed in 3.0 because of this constraint—the / and // operators implement true and floor division in 3.0.

In sum:

- *In 3.0*, the / now always performs *true* division, returning a float result that includes any remainder, regardless of operand types. The // performs *floor* division, which truncates the remainder and returns an integer for integer operands or a float if any operand is a float.
- *In 2.6*, the / does *classic* division, performing truncating integer division if both operands are integers and float division (keeping remainders) otherwise. The // does *floor* division and works as it does in 3.0, performing truncating division for integers and floor division for floats.

Here are the two operators at work in 3.0 and 2.6:

```
C:\misc> C:\Python30\python
>>>
>>> 10 / 4              # Differs in 3.0: keeps remainder
2.5
>>> 10 // 4             # Same in 3.0: truncates remainder
2
>>> 10 / 4.0            # Same in 3.0: keeps remainder
2.5
>>> 10 // 4.0           # Same in 3.0: truncates to floor
2.0

C:\misc> C:\Python26\python
>>>
>>> 10 / 4
2
>>> 10 // 4
2
>>> 10 / 4.0
2.5
>>> 10 // 4.0
2.0
```

Notice that the data type of the result for // is still dependent on the operand types in 3.0: if either is a float, the result is a float; otherwise, it is an integer. Although this may seem similar to the type-dependent behavior of / in 2.X that motivated its change in 3.0, the type of the return value is much less critical than differences in the return value itself. Moreover, because // was provided in part as a backward-compatibility tool for programs that rely on truncating integer division (and this is more common than you might expect), it must return integers for integers.

Supporting either Python

Although / behavior differs in 2.6 and 3.0, you can still support both versions in your code. If your programs depend on truncating integer division, use // in both 2.6 and 3.0. If your programs require floating-point results with remainders for integers, use float to guarantee that one operand is a float around a / when run in 2.6:

```
X = Y // Z        # Always truncates, always an int result for ints in 2.6 and 3.0

X = Y / float(Z)   # Guarantees float division with remainder in either 2.6 or 3.0
```

Alternatively, you can enable 3.0 / division in 2.6 with a __future__ import, rather than forcing it with float conversions:

```
C:\misc> C:\Python26\python
>>> from __future__ import division        # Enable 3.0 "/" behavior
>>> 10 / 4
2.5
>>> 10 // 4
2
```

Floor versus truncation

One subtlety: the // operator is generally referred to as *truncating* division, but it's more accurate to refer to it as *floor* division—it truncates the result down to its floor, which means the closest whole number below the true result. The net effect is to round down, not strictly truncate, and this matters for negatives. You can see the difference for yourself with the Python math module (modules must be imported before you can use their contents; more on this later):

```
>>> import math
>>> math.floor(2.5)
2
>>> math.floor(-2.5)
-3
>>> math.trunc(2.5)
2
>>> math.trunc(-2.5)
-2
```

When running division operators, you only really truncate for positive results, since truncation is the same as floor; for negatives, it's a floor result (really, they are both floor, but floor is the same as truncation for positives). Here's the case for 3.0:

```
C:\misc> c:\python30\python
>>> 5 / 2, 5 / -2
(2.5, -2.5)

>>> 5 // 2, 5 // -2        # Truncates to floor: rounds to first lower integer
(2, -3)                    # 2.5 becomes 2, -2.5 becomes -3

>>> 5 / 2.0, 5 / -2.0
(2.5, -2.5)
```

```
>>> 5 // 2.0, 5 // -2.0        # Ditto for floats, though result is float too
(2.0, -3.0)
```

The 2.6 case is similar, but / results differ again:

```
C:\misc> c:\python26\python
>>> 5 / 2, 5 / -2              # Differs in 3.0
(2, -3)

>>> 5 // 2, 5 // -2            # This and the rest are the same in 2.6 and 3.0
(2, -3)

>>> 5 / 2.0, 5 / -2.0
(2.5, -2.5)

>>> 5 // 2.0, 5 // -2.0
(2.0, -3.0)
```

If you really want truncation regardless of sign, you can always run a float division result through math.trunc, regardless of Python version (also see the round built-in for related functionality):

```
C:\misc> c:\python30\python
>>> import math
>>> 5 / -2                     # Keep remainder
-2.5
>>> 5 // -2                    # Floor below result
-3
>>> math.trunc(5 / -2)         # Truncate instead of floor
-2

C:\misc> c:\python26\python
>>> import math
>>> 5 / float(-2)             # Remainder in 2.6
-2.5
>>> 5 / -2, 5 // -2           # Floor in 2.6
(-3, -3)
>>> math.trunc(5 / float(-2)) # Truncate in 2.6
-2
```

Why does truncation matter?

If you are using 3.0, here is the short story on division operators for reference:

```
>>> (5 / 2), (5 / 2.0), (5 / -2.0), (5 / -2)      # 3.0 true division
(2.5, 2.5, -2.5, -2.5)

>>> (5 // 2), (5 // 2.0), (5 // -2.0), (5 // -2)   # 3.0 floor division
(2, 2.0, -3.0, -3)

>>> (9 / 3), (9.0 / 3), (9 // 3), (9 // 3.0)       # Both
(3.0, 3.0, 3, 3.0)
```

For 2.6 readers, division works as follows:

```
>>> (5 / 2), (5 / 2.0), (5 / -2.0), (5 / -2)      # 2.6 classic division
(2, 2.5, -2.5, -3)
```

```
>>> (5 // 2), (5 // 2.0), (5 // -2.0), (5 // -2)    # 2.6 floor division (same)
(2, 2.0, -3.0, -3)

>>> (9 / 3), (9.0 / 3), (9 // 3), (9 // 3.0)        # Both
(3, 3.0, 3, 3.0)
```

Although results have yet to come in, it's possible that the nontruncating behavior of / in 3.0 may break a significant number of programs. Perhaps because of a C language legacy, many programmers rely on division truncation for integers and will have to learn to use // in such contexts instead. Watch for a simple prime number while loop example in Chapter 13, and a corresponding exercise at the end of Part IV that illustrates the sort of code that may be impacted by this / change. Also stay tuned for more on the special from command used in this section; it's discussed further in Chapter 24.

Integer Precision

Division may differ slightly across Python releases, but it's still fairly standard. Here's something a bit more exotic. As mentioned earlier, Python 3.0 integers support unlimited size:

```
>>> 999999999999999999999999999999 + 1
1000000000000000000000000000000
```

Python 2.6 has a separate type for long integers, but it automatically converts any number too large to store in a normal integer to this type. Hence, you don't need to code any special syntax to use longs, and the only way you can tell that you're using 2.6 longs is that they print with a trailing "L":

```
>>> 999999999999999999999999999999 + 1
1000000000000000000000000000000L
```

Unlimited-precision integers are a convenient built-in tool. For instance, you can use them to count the U.S. national debt in pennies in Python directly (if you are so inclined, and have enough memory on your computer for this year's budget!). They are also why we were able to raise 2 to such large powers in the examples in Chapter 3. Here are the 3.0 and 2.6 cases:

```
>>> 2 ** 200
1606938044258990275541962092341162602522202993782792835301376
```

```
>>> 2 ** 200
1606938044258990275541962092341162602522202993782792835301376L
```

Because Python must do extra work to support their extended precision, integer math is usually substantially slower than normal when numbers grow large. However, if you need the precision, the fact that it's built in for you to use will likely outweigh its performance penalty.

Complex Numbers

Although less widely used than the types we've been exploring thus far, complex numbers are a distinct core object type in Python. If you know what they are, you know why they are useful; if not, consider this section optional reading.

Complex numbers are represented as two floating-point numbers—the real and imaginary parts—and are coded by adding a j or J suffix to the imaginary part. We can also write complex numbers with a nonzero real part by adding the two parts with a +. For example, the complex number with a real part of 2 and an imaginary part of -3 is written 2 + -3j. Here are some examples of complex math at work:

```
>>> 1j * 1J
(-1+0j)
>>> 2 + 1j * 3
(2+3j)
>>> (2 + 1j) * 3
(6+3j)
```

Complex numbers also allow us to extract their parts as attributes, support all the usual mathematical expressions, and may be processed with tools in the standard cmath module (the complex version of the standard math module). Complex numbers typically find roles in engineering-oriented programs. Because they are advanced tools, check Python's language reference manual for additional details.

Hexadecimal, Octal, and Binary Notation

As described earlier in this chapter, Python integers can be coded in hexadecimal, octal, and binary notation, in addition to the normal base 10 decimal coding. The coding rules were laid out at the start of this chapter; let's look at some live examples here.

Keep in mind that these literals are simply an alternative syntax for specifying the value of an integer object. For example, the following literals coded in Python 3.0 or 2.6 produce normal integers with the specified values in all three bases:

```
>>> 0o1, 0o20, 0o377        # Octal literals
(1, 16, 255)
>>> 0x01, 0x10, 0xFF        # Hex literals
(1, 16, 255)
>>> 0b1, 0b10000, 0b11111111    # Binary literals
(1, 16, 255)
```

Here, the octal value 0o377, the hex value 0xFF, and the binary value 0b11111111 are all decimal 255. Python prints in decimal (base 10) by default but provides built-in functions that allow you to convert integers to other bases' digit strings:

```
>>> oct(64), hex(64), bin(64)
('0o100', '0x40', '0b1000000')
```

The oct function converts decimal to octal, hex to hexadecimal, and bin to binary. To go the other way, the built-in int function converts a string of digits to an integer, and an optional second argument lets you specify the numeric base:

```
>>> int('64'), int('100', 8), int('40', 16), int('1000000', 2)
(64, 64, 64, 64)
```

```
>>> int('0x40', 16), int('0b1000000', 2)      # Literals okay too
(64, 64)
```

The eval function, which you'll meet later in this book, treats strings as though they were Python code. Therefore, it has a similar effect (but usually runs more slowly—it actually compiles and runs the string as a piece of a program, and it assumes you can trust the source of the string being run; a clever user might be able to submit a string that deletes files on your machine!):

```
>>> eval('64'), eval('0o100'), eval('0x40'), eval('0b1000000')
(64, 64, 64, 64)
```

Finally, you can also convert integers to octal and hexadecimal strings with *string formatting* method calls and expressions:

```
>>> '{0:o}, {1:x}, {2:b}'.format(64, 64, 64)
'100, 40, 1000000'
```

```
>>> '%o, %x, %X' % (64, 255, 255)
'100, ff, FF'
```

String formatting is covered in more detail in Chapter 7.

Two notes before moving on. First, Python 2.6 users should remember that you can code octals with simply a leading zero, the original octal format in Python:

```
>>> 0o1, 0o20, 0o377      # New octal format in 2.6 (same as 3.0)
(1, 16, 255)
>>> 01, 020, 0377         # Old octal literals in 2.6 (and earlier)
(1, 16, 255)
```

In 3.0, the syntax in the second of these examples generates an error. Even though it's not an error in 2.6, be careful not to begin a string of digits with a leading zero unless you really mean to code an octal value. Python 2.6 will treat it as base 8, which may not work as you'd expect—010 is always decimal 8 in 2.6, not decimal 10 (despite what you may or may not think!). This, along with symmetry with the hex and binary forms, is why the octal format was changed in 3.0—you must use 0o010 in 3.0, and probably should in 2.6.

Secondly, note that these literals can produce arbitrarily long integers. The following, for instance, creates an integer with hex notation and then displays it first in decimal and then in octal and binary with converters (run in 2.6 here to reveal the long precision):

```
>>> X = 0xFFFFFFFFFFFFFFFFFFFFFFFFFFFFFFFF
>>> X
5192296858534827628530496329220095L
```

```
>>> oct(X)
'01777777777777777777777777777777777777777L'
>>> bin(X)
'0b1111111111111111111111111111111111111111111111111111111111111 ...and so on...
```

Speaking of binary digits, the next section shows tools for processing individual bits.

Bitwise Operations

Besides the normal numeric operations (addition, subtraction, and so on), Python supports most of the numeric expressions available in the C language. This includes operators that treat integers as strings of binary bits. For instance, here it is at work performing bitwise shift and Boolean operations:

```
>>> x = 1                # 0001
>>> x << 2               # Shift left 2 bits: 0100
4
>>> x | 2                # Bitwise OR: 0011
3
>>> x & 1                # Bitwise AND: 0001
1
```

In the first expression, a binary 1 (in base 2, 0001) is shifted left two slots to create a binary 4 (0100). The last two operations perform a binary OR (0001|0010 = 0011) and a binary AND (0001&0001 = 0001). Such bit-masking operations allow us to encode multiple flags and other values within a single integer.

This is one area where the binary and hexadecimal number support in Python 2.6 and 3.0 become especially useful—they allow us to code and inspect numbers by bit-strings:

```
>>> X = 0b0001           # Binary literals
>>> X << 2               # Shift left
4
>>> bin(X << 2)          # Binary digits string
'0b100'

>>> bin(X | 0b010)       # Bitwise OR
'0b11'
>>> bin(X & 0b1)         # Bitwise AND
'0b1'

>>> X = 0xFF             # Hex literals
>>> bin(X)
'0b11111111'
>>> X ^ 0b10101010       # Bitwise XOR
85
>>> bin(X ^ 0b10101010)
'0b1010101'

>>> int('1010101', 2)    # String to int per base
85
>>> hex(85)              # Hex digit string
'0x55'
```

We won't go into much more detail on "bit-twiddling" here. It's supported if you need it, and it comes in handy if your Python code must deal with things like network packets or packed binary data produced by a C program. Be aware, though, that bitwise operations are often not as important in a high-level language such as Python as they are in a low-level language such as C. As a rule of thumb, if you find yourself wanting to flip bits in Python, you should think about which language you're really coding. In general, there are often better ways to encode information in Python than bit strings.

 In the upcoming Python 3.1 release, the integer bit_length method also allows you to query the number of bits required to represent a number's value in binary. The same effect can often be achieved by subtracting 2 from the length of the bin string using the len built-in function we met in Chapter 4, though it may be less efficient:

```
>>> X = 99
>>> bin(X), X.bit_length()
('0b1100011', 7)
>>> bin(256), (256).bit_length()
('0b100000000', 9)
>>> len(bin(256)) - 2
9
```

Other Built-in Numeric Tools

In addition to its core object types, Python also provides both built-in functions and standard library modules for numeric processing. The pow and abs built-in functions, for instance, compute powers and absolute values, respectively. Here are some examples of the built-in math module (which contains most of the tools in the C language's math library) and a few built-in functions at work:

```
>>> import math
>>> math.pi, math.e                          # Common constants
(3.1415926535897931, 2.7182818284590451)

>>> math.sin(2 * math.pi / 180)              # Sine, tangent, cosine
0.034899496702500969

>>> math.sqrt(144), math.sqrt(2)             # Square root
(12.0, 1.4142135623730951)

>>> pow(2, 4), 2 ** 4                         # Exponentiation (power)
(16, 16)

>>> abs(-42.0), sum((1, 2, 3, 4))            # Absolute value, summation
(42.0, 10)

>>> min(3, 1, 2, 4), max(3, 1, 2, 4)         # Minimum, maximum
(1, 4)
```

The sum function shown here works on a sequence of numbers, and min and max accept either a sequence or individual arguments. There are a variety of ways to drop the decimal digits of floating-point numbers. We met truncation and floor earlier; we can also round, both numerically and for display purposes:

```
>>> math.floor(2.567), math.floor(-2.567)      # Floor (next-lower integer)
(2, -3)

>>> math.trunc(2.567), math.trunc(-2.567)      # Truncate (drop decimal digits)
(2, -2)

>>> int(2.567), int(-2.567)                    # Truncate (integer conversion)
(2, -2)

>>> round(2.567), round(2.467), round(2.567, 2)   # Round (Python 3.0 version)
(3, 2, 2.5699999999999998)

>>> '%.1f' % 2.567, '{0:.2f}'.format(2.567)    # Round for display (Chapter 7)
('2.6', '2.57')
```

As we saw earlier, the last of these produces strings that we would usually print and supports a variety of formatting options. As also described earlier, the second to last test here will output (3, 2, 2.57) if we wrap it in a `print` call to request a more user-friendly display. The last two lines still differ, though—round rounds a floating-point number but still yields a floating-point number in memory, whereas string formatting produces a string and doesn't yield a modified number:

```
>>> (1 / 3), round(1 / 3, 2), ('%.2f' % (1 / 3))
(0.33333333333333331, 0.33000000000000002, '0.33')
```

Interestingly, there are three ways to compute *square roots* in Python: using a module function, an expression, or a built-in function (if you're interested in performance, we will revisit these in an exercise and its solution at the end of Part IV, to see which runs quicker):

```
>>> import math
>>> math.sqrt(144)          # Module
12.0
>>> 144 ** .5               # Expression
12.0
>>> pow(144, .5)            # Built-in
12.0

>>> math.sqrt(1234567890)   # Larger numbers
35136.418286444619
>>> 1234567890 ** .5
35136.418286444619
>>> pow(1234567890, .5)
35136.418286444619
```

Notice that standard library modules such as `math` must be imported, but built-in functions such as `abs` and `round` are always available without imports. In other words, modules are external components, but built-in functions live in an implied namespace that Python automatically searches to find names used in your program. This namespace corresponds to the module called `builtins` in Python 3.0 (`__builtin__` in 2.6). There is much more about name resolution in the function and module parts of this book; for now, when you hear "module," think "import."

The standard library `random` module must be imported as well. This module provides tools for picking a random floating-point number between 0 and 1, selecting a random integer between two numbers, choosing an item at random from a sequence, and more:

```
>>> import random
>>> random.random()
0.44694718823781876
>>> random.random()
0.28970426439292829

>>> random.randint(1, 10)
5
>>> random.randint(1, 10)
4

>>> random.choice(['Life of Brian', 'Holy Grail', 'Meaning of Life'])
'Life of Brian'
>>> random.choice(['Life of Brian', 'Holy Grail', 'Meaning of Life'])
'Holy Grail'
```

The `random` module can be useful for shuffling cards in games, picking images at random in a slideshow GUI, performing statistical simulations, and much more. For more details, see Python's library manual.

Other Numeric Types

So far in this chapter, we've been using Python's core numeric types—integer, floating point, and complex. These will suffice for most of the number crunching that most programmers will ever need to do. Python comes with a handful of more exotic numeric types, though, that merit a quick look here.

Decimal Type

Python 2.4 introduced a new core numeric type: the decimal object, formally known as `Decimal`. Syntactically, decimals are created by calling a function within an imported module, rather than running a literal expression. Functionally, decimals are like floating-point numbers, but they have a fixed number of decimal points. Hence, decimals are *fixed-precision* floating-point values.

For example, with decimals, we can have a floating-point value that always retains just two decimal digits. Furthermore, we can specify how to round or truncate the extra decimal digits beyond the object's cutoff. Although it generally incurs a small performance penalty compared to the normal floating-point type, the decimal type is well suited to representing fixed-precision quantities like sums of money and can help you achieve better numeric accuracy.

The basics

The last point merits elaboration. As you may or may not already know, floating-point math is less than exact, because of the limited space used to store values. For example, the following should yield zero, but it does not. The result is close to zero, but there are not enough bits to be precise here:

```
>>> 0.1 + 0.1 + 0.1 - 0.3
5.5511151231257827e-17
```

Printing the result to produce the user-friendly display format doesn't completely help either, because the hardware related to floating-point math is inherently limited in terms of accuracy:

```
>>> print(0.1 + 0.1 + 0.1 - 0.3)
5.55111512313e-17
```

However, with decimals, the result can be dead-on:

```
>>> from decimal import Decimal
>>> Decimal('0.1') + Decimal('0.1') + Decimal('0.1') - Decimal('0.3')
Decimal('0.0')
```

As shown here, we can make decimal objects by calling the Decimal constructor function in the decimal module and passing in strings that have the desired number of decimal digits for the resulting object (we can use the str function to convert floating-point values to strings if needed). When decimals of different precision are mixed in expressions, Python converts up to the largest number of decimal digits automatically:

```
>>> Decimal('0.1') + Decimal('0.10') + Decimal('0.10') - Decimal('0.30')
Decimal('0.00')
```

 In Python 3.1 (to be released after this book's publication), it's also possible to create a decimal object from a floating-point object, with a call of the form decimal.Decimal.from_float(1.25). The conversion is exact but can sometimes yield a large number of digits.

Setting precision globally

Other tools in the decimal module can be used to set the precision of all decimal numbers, set up error handling, and more. For instance, a context object in this module allows for specifying precision (number of decimal digits) and rounding modes (down, ceiling, etc.). The precision is applied globally for all decimals created in the calling thread:

```
>>> import decimal
>>> decimal.Decimal(1) / decimal.Decimal(7)
Decimal('0.1428571428571428571428571429')

>>> decimal.getcontext().prec = 4
>>> decimal.Decimal(1) / decimal.Decimal(7)
Decimal('0.1429')
```

This is especially useful for monetary applications, where cents are represented as two decimal digits. Decimals are essentially an alternative to manual rounding and string formatting in this context:

```
>>> 1999 + 1.33
2000.3299999999999
>>>
>>> decimal.getcontext().prec = 2
>>> pay = decimal.Decimal(str(1999 + 1.33))
>>> pay
Decimal('2000.33')
```

Decimal context manager

In Python 2.6 and 3.0 (and later), it's also possible to reset precision temporarily by using the `with` context manager statement. The precision is reset to its original value on statement exit:

```
C:\misc> C:\Python30\python
>>> import decimal
>>> decimal.Decimal('1.00') / decimal.Decimal('3.00')
Decimal('0.3333333333333333333333333333')
>>>
>>> with decimal.localcontext() as ctx:
...     ctx.prec = 2
...     decimal.Decimal('1.00') / decimal.Decimal('3.00')
...
Decimal('0.33')
>>>
>>> decimal.Decimal('1.00') / decimal.Decimal('3.00')
Decimal('0.3333333333333333333333333333')
```

Though useful, this statement requires much more background knowledge than you've obtained at this point; watch for coverage of the `with` statement in Chapter 33.

Because use of the decimal type is still relatively rare in practice, I'll defer to Python's standard library manuals and interactive help for more details. And because decimals address some of the same floating-point accuracy issues as the fraction type, let's move on to the next section to see how the two compare.

Fraction Type

Python 2.6 and 3.0 debut a new numeric type, `Fraction`, which implements a *rational number* object. It essentially keeps both a numerator and a denominator explicitly, so as to avoid some of the inaccuracies and limitations of floating-point math.

The basics

`Fraction` is a sort of cousin to the existing `Decimal` fixed-precision type described in the prior section, as both can be used to control numerical accuracy by fixing decimal digits and specifying rounding or truncation policies. It's also used in similar ways—like

Decimal, Fraction resides in a module; import its constructor and pass in a numerator and a denominator to make one. The following interaction shows how:

```
>>> from fractions import Fraction
>>> x = Fraction(1, 3)          # Numerator, denominator
>>> y = Fraction(4, 6)          # Simplified to 2, 3 by gcd

>>> x
Fraction(1, 3)
>>> y
Fraction(2, 3)
>>> print(y)
2/3
```

Once created, Fractions can be used in mathematical expressions as usual:

```
>>> x + y
Fraction(1, 1)
>>> x - y                       # Results are exact: numerator, denominator
Fraction(-1, 3)
>>> x * y
Fraction(2, 9)
```

Fraction objects can also be created from floating-point number strings, much like decimals:

```
>>> Fraction('.25')
Fraction(1, 4)
>>> Fraction('1.25')
Fraction(5, 4)
>>>
>>> Fraction('.25') + Fraction('1.25')
Fraction(3, 2)
```

Numeric accuracy

Notice that this is different from floating-point-type math, which is constrained by the underlying limitations of floating-point hardware. To compare, here are the same operations run with floating-point objects, and notes on their limited accuracy:

```
>>> a = 1 / 3.0                 # Only as accurate as floating-point hardware
>>> b = 4 / 6.0                 # Can lose precision over calculations
>>> a
0.33333333333333331
>>> b
0.66666666666666663

>>> a + b
1.0
>>> a - b
-0.33333333333333331
>>> a * b
0.22222222222222221
```

This floating-point limitation is especially apparent for values that cannot be represented accurately given their limited number of bits in memory. Both Fraction and

Decimal provide ways to get exact results, albeit at the cost of some speed. For instance, in the following example (repeated from the prior section), floating-point numbers do not accurately give the zero answer expected, but both of the other types do:

```
>>> 0.1 + 0.1 + 0.1 - 0.3                 # This should be zero (close, but not exact)
5.5511151231257827e-17

>>> from fractions import Fraction
>>> Fraction(1, 10) + Fraction(1, 10) + Fraction(1, 10) - Fraction(3, 10)
Fraction(0, 1)

>>> from decimal import Decimal
>>> Decimal('0.1') + Decimal('0.1') + Decimal('0.1') - Decimal('0.3')
Decimal('0.0')
```

Moreover, fractions and decimals both allow more intuitive and accurate results than floating points sometimes can, in different ways (by using rational representation and by limiting precision):

```
>>> 1 / 3                                 # Use 3.0 in Python 2.6 for true "/"
0.33333333333333331

>>> Fraction(1, 3)                        # Numeric accuracy
Fraction(1, 3)

>>> import decimal
>>> decimal.getcontext().prec = 2
>>> decimal.Decimal(1) / decimal.Decimal(3)
Decimal('0.33')
```

In fact, fractions both retain accuracy and automatically simplify results. Continuing the preceding interaction:

```
>>> (1 / 3) + (6 / 12)                    # Use ".0" in Python 2.6 for true "/"
0.83333333333333326

>>> Fraction(6, 12)                       # Automatically simplified
Fraction(1, 2)

>>> Fraction(1, 3) + Fraction(6, 12)
Fraction(5, 6)

>>> decimal.Decimal(str(1/3)) + decimal.Decimal(str(6/12))
Decimal('0.83')

>>> 1000.0 / 1234567890
8.1000000737100011e-07
>>> Fraction(1000, 1234567890)
Fraction(100, 123456789)
```

Conversions and mixed types

To support fraction conversions, floating-point objects now have a method that yields their numerator and denominator ratio, fractions have a `from_float` method, and float accepts a Fraction as an argument. Trace through the following interaction to see how this pans out (the * in the second test is special syntax that expands a tuple into individual arguments; more on this when we study function argument passing in Chapter 18):

```
>>> (2.5).as_integer_ratio()          # float object method
(5, 2)

>>> f = 2.5
>>> z = Fraction(*f.as_integer_ratio())   # Convert float -> fraction: two args
>>> z                                  # Same as Fraction(5, 2)
Fraction(5, 2)

>>> x                                  # x from prior interaction
Fraction(1, 3)
>>> x + z
Fraction(17, 6)                        # 5/2 + 1/3 = 15/6 + 2/6

>>> float(x)                           # Convert fraction -> float
0.33333333333333331
>>> float(z)
2.5
>>> float(x + z)
2.8333333333333335
>>> 17 / 6
2.8333333333333335

>>> Fraction.from_float(1.75)          # Convert float -> fraction: other way
Fraction(7, 4)
>>> Fraction(*(1.75).as_integer_ratio())
Fraction(7, 4)
```

Finally, some type mixing is allowed in expressions, though Fraction must sometimes be manually propagated to retain accuracy. Study the following interaction to see how this works:

```
>>> x
Fraction(1, 3)
>>> x + 2                              # Fraction + int -> Fraction
Fraction(7, 3)
>>> x + 2.0                            # Fraction + float -> float
2.3333333333333335
>>> x + (1./3)                         # Fraction + float -> float
0.66666666666666663

>>> x + (4./3)
1.6666666666666665
>>> x + Fraction(4, 3)                 # Fraction + Fraction -> Fraction
Fraction(5, 3)
```

Caveat: although you can convert from floating-point to fraction, in some cases there is an unavoidable precision loss when you do so, because the number is inaccurate in its original floating-point form. When needed, you can simplify such results by limiting the maximum denominator value:

```
>>> 4.0 / 3
1.3333333333333333
>>> (4.0 / 3).as_integer_ratio()          # Precision loss from float
(6004799503160661, 4503599627370496)

>>> x
Fraction(1, 3)
>>> a = x + Fraction(*(4.0 / 3).as_integer_ratio())
>>> a
Fraction(22517998136852479, 13510798882111488)

>>> 22517998136852479 / 13510798882111488.     # 5 / 3 (or close to it!)
1.6666666666666667

>>> a.limit_denominator(10)                # Simplify to closest fraction
Fraction(5, 3)
```

For more details on the Fraction type, experiment further on your own and consult the Python 2.6 and 3.0 library manuals and other documentation.

Sets

Python 2.4 also introduced a new collection type, the *set*—an unordered collection of unique and immutable objects that supports operations corresponding to mathematical set theory. By definition, an item appears only once in a set, no matter how many times it is added. As such, sets have a variety of applications, especially in numeric and database-focused work.

Because sets are collections of other objects, they share some behavior with objects such as lists and dictionaries that are outside the scope of this chapter. For example, sets are iterable, can grow and shrink on demand, and may contain a variety of object types. As we'll see, a set acts much like the keys of a valueless dictionary, but it supports extra operations.

However, because sets are unordered and do not map keys to values, they are neither sequence nor mapping types; they are a type category unto themselves. Moreover, because sets are fundamentally mathematical in nature (and for many readers, may seem more academic and be used much less often than more pervasive objects like dictionaries), we'll explore the basic utility of Python's set objects here.

Set basics in Python 2.6

There are a few ways to make sets today, depending on whether you are using Python 2.6 or 3.0. Since this book covers both, let's begin with the 2.6 case, which also is available (and sometimes still required) in 3.0; we'll refine this for 3.0 extensions in a moment. To make a set object, pass in a sequence or other iterable object to the built-in set function:

```
>>> x = set('abcde')
>>> y = set('bdxyz')
```

You get back a set object, which contains all the items in the object passed in (notice that sets do not have a positional ordering, and so are not sequences):

```
>>> x
set(['a', 'c', 'b', 'e', 'd'])                    # 2.6 display format
```

Sets made this way support the common mathematical set operations with *expression* operators. Note that we can't perform these expressions on plain sequences—we must create sets from them in order to apply these tools:

```
>>> 'e' in x                                      # Membership
True

>>> x - y                                         # Difference
set(['a', 'c', 'e'])

>>> x | y                                         # Union
set(['a', 'c', 'b', 'e', 'd', 'y', 'x', 'z'])

>>> x & y                                         # Intersection
set(['b', 'd'])

>>> x ^ y                                         # Symmetric difference (XOR)
set(['a', 'c', 'e', 'y', 'x', 'z'])

>>> x > y, x < y                                  # Superset, subset
(False, False)
```

In addition to expressions, the set object provides *methods* that correspond to these operations and more, and that support set changes—the set add method inserts one item, update is an in-place union, and remove deletes an item by value (run a dir call on any set instance or the set type name to see all the available methods). Assuming x and y are still as they were in the prior interaction:

```
>>> z = x.intersection(y)                         # Same as x & y
>>> z
set(['b', 'd'])
>>> z.add('SPAM')                                 # Insert one item
>>> z
set(['b', 'd', 'SPAM'])
>>> z.update(set(['X', 'Y']))                     # Merge: in-place union
>>> z
set(['Y', 'X', 'b', 'd', 'SPAM'])
>>> z.remove('b')                                 # Delete one item
>>> z
set(['Y', 'X', 'd', 'SPAM'])
```

As *iterable* containers, sets can also be used in operations such as len, for loops, and list comprehensions. Because they are unordered, though, they don't support sequence operations like indexing and slicing:

```
>>> for item in set('abc'): print(item * 3)
...
aaa
```

```
ccc
bbb
```

Finally, although the set expressions shown earlier generally require two sets, their method-based counterparts can often work with *any iterable type* as well:

```
>>> S = set([1, 2, 3])

>>> S | set([3, 4])              # Expressions require both to be sets
set([1, 2, 3, 4])
>>> S | [3, 4]
TypeError: unsupported operand type(s) for |: 'set' and 'list'

>>> S.union([3, 4])             # But their methods allow any iterable
set([1, 2, 3, 4])
>>> S.intersection((1, 3, 5))
set([1, 3])
>>> S.issubset(range(-5, 5))
True
```

For more details on set operations, see Python's library reference manual or a reference book. Although set operations can be coded manually in Python with other types, like lists and dictionaries (and often were in the past), Python's built-in sets use efficient algorithms and implementation techniques to provide quick and standard operation.

Set literals in Python 3.0

If you think sets are "cool," they recently became noticeably cooler. In Python 3.0 we can still use the **set** built-in to make set objects, but 3.0 also adds a new set literal form, using the curly braces formerly reserved for dictionaries. In 3.0, the following are equivalent:

```
set([1, 2, 3, 4])               # Built-in call
{1, 2, 3, 4}                    # 3.0 set literals
```

This syntax makes sense, given that sets are essentially like *valueless dictionaries*—because a set's items are unordered, unique, and immutable, the items behave much like a dictionary's keys. This operational similarity is even more striking given that dictionary key lists in 3.0 are *view* objects, which support set-like behavior such as intersections and unions (see Chapter 8 for more on dictionary view objects).

In fact, regardless of how a set is made, 3.0 displays it using the new literal format. The **set** built-in is still required in 3.0 to create empty sets and to build sets from existing iterable objects (short of using set comprehensions, discussed later in this chapter), but the new literal is convenient for initializing sets of known structure:

```
C:\Misc> c:\python30\python
>>> set([1, 2, 3, 4])           # Built-in: same as in 2.6
{1, 2, 3, 4}
>>> set('spam')                 # Add all items in an iterable
{'a', 'p', 's', 'm'}

>>> {1, 2, 3, 4}                # Set literals: new in 3.0
```

```
{1, 2, 3, 4}
>>> S = {'s', 'p', 'a', 'm'}
>>> S.add('alot')
>>> S
{'a', 'p', 's', 'm', 'alot'}
```

All the set processing operations discussed in the prior section work the same in 3.0, but the result sets print differently:

```
>>> S1 = {1, 2, 3, 4}
>>> S1 & {1, 3}                    # Intersection
{1, 3}
>>> {1, 5, 3, 6} | S1              # Union
{1, 2, 3, 4, 5, 6}
>>> S1 - {1, 3, 4}                 # Difference
{2}
>>> S1 > {1, 3}                    # Superset
True
```

Note that {} is still a dictionary in Python. *Empty* sets must be created with the set built-in, and print the same way:

```
>>> S1 - {1, 2, 3, 4}             # Empty sets print differently
set()
>>> type({})                      # Because {} is an empty dictionary
<class 'dict'>

>>> S = set()                     # Initialize an empty set
>>> S.add(1.23)
>>> S
{1.23}
```

As in Python 2.6, sets created with 3.0 literals support the same methods, some of which allow general iterable operands that expressions do not:

```
>>> {1, 2, 3} | {3, 4}
{1, 2, 3, 4}
>>> {1, 2, 3} | [3, 4]
TypeError: unsupported operand type(s) for |: 'set' and 'list'

>>> {1, 2, 3}.union([3, 4])
{1, 2, 3, 4}
>>> {1, 2, 3}.union({3, 4})
{1, 2, 3, 4}
>>> {1, 2, 3}.union(set([3, 4]))
{1, 2, 3, 4}

>>> {1, 2, 3}.intersection((1, 3, 5))
{1, 3}
>>> {1, 2, 3}.issubset(range(-5, 5))
True
```

Immutable constraints and frozen sets

Sets are powerful and flexible objects, but they do have one constraint in both 3.0 and 2.6 that you should keep in mind—largely because of their implementation, sets can

---

only contain immutable (a.k.a "hashable") object types. Hence, lists and dictionaries cannot be embedded in sets, but tuples can if you need to store compound values. Tuples compare by their full values when used in set operations:

```
>>> S
{1.23}
>>> S.add([1, 2, 3])                # Only immutable objects work in a set
TypeError: unhashable type: 'list'
>>> S.add({'a':1})
TypeError: unhashable type: 'dict'
>>> S.add((1, 2, 3))
>>> S                               # No list or dict, but tuple okay
{1.23, (1, 2, 3)}

>>> S | {(4, 5, 6), (1, 2, 3)}      # Union: same as S.union(...)
{1.23, (4, 5, 6), (1, 2, 3)}
>>> (1, 2, 3) in S                  # Membership: by complete values
True
>>> (1, 4, 3) in S
False
```

Tuples in a set, for instance, might be used to represent dates, records, IP addresses, and so on (more on tuples later in this part of the book). Sets themselves are mutable too, and so cannot be nested in other sets directly; if you need to store a set inside another set, the `frozenset` built-in call works just like `set` but creates an immutable set that cannot change and thus can be embedded in other sets.

Set comprehensions in Python 3.0

In addition to literals, 3.0 introduces a set comprehension construct; it is similar in form to the list comprehension we previewed in Chapter 4, but is coded in curly braces instead of square brackets and run to make a set instead of a list. Set comprehensions run a loop and collect the result of an expression on each iteration; a loop variable gives access to the current iteration value for use in the collection expression. The result is a new set created by running the code, with all the normal set behavior:

```
>>> {x ** 2 for x in [1, 2, 3, 4]}      # 3.0 set comprehension
{16, 1, 4, 9}
```

In this expression, the loop is coded on the right, and the collection expression is coded on the left (`x ** 2`). As for list comprehensions, we get back pretty much what this expression says: "Give me a new set containing X squared, for every X in a list." Comprehensions can also iterate across other kinds of objects, such as strings (the first of the following examples illustrates the comprehension-based way to make a set from an existing iterable):

```
>>> {x for x in 'spam'}                 # Same as: set('spam')
{'a', 'p', 's', 'm'}

>>> {c * 4 for c in 'spam'}             # Set of collected expression results
{'ssss', 'aaaa', 'pppp', 'mmmm'}
>>> {c * 4 for c in 'spamham'}
```

```
{'ssss', 'aaaa', 'hhhh', 'pppp', 'mmmm'}

>>> S = {c * 4 for c in 'spam'}
>>> S | {'mmmm', 'xxxx'}
{'ssss', 'aaaa', 'pppp', 'mmmm', 'xxxx'}
>>> S & {'mmmm', 'xxxx'}
{'mmmm'}
```

Because the rest of the comprehensions story relies upon underlying concepts we're not yet prepared to address, we'll postpone further details until later in this book. In Chapter 8, we'll meet a first cousin in 3.0, the dictionary comprehension, and I'll have much more to say about all comprehensions (list, set, dictionary, and generator) later, especially in Chapters 14 and 20. As we'll learn later, all comprehensions, including sets, support additional syntax not shown here, including nested loops and if tests, which can be difficult to understand until you've had a chance to study larger statements.

Why sets?

Set operations have a variety of common uses, some more practical than mathematical. For example, because items are stored only once in a set, sets can be used to filter duplicates out of other collections. Simply convert the collection to a set, and then convert it back again (because sets are iterable, they work in the list call here):

```
>>> L = [1, 2, 1, 3, 2, 4, 5]
>>> set(L)
{1, 2, 3, 4, 5}
>>> L = list(set(L))              # Remove duplicates
>>> L
[1, 2, 3, 4, 5]
```

Sets can also be used to keep track of where you've already been when traversing a graph or other cyclic structure. For example, the transitive module reloader and inheritance tree lister examples we'll study in Chapters 24 and 30, respectively, must keep track of items visited to avoid loops. Although recording states visited as keys in a dictionary is efficient, sets offer an alternative that's essentially equivalent (and may be more or less intuitive, depending on who you ask).

Finally, sets are also convenient when dealing with large data sets (database query results, for example)—the intersection of two sets contains objects in common to both categories, and the union contains all items in either set. To illustrate, here's a somewhat more realistic example of set operations at work, applied to lists of people in a hypothetical company, using 3.0 set literals (use set in 2.6):

```
>>> engineers = {'bob', 'sue', 'ann', 'vic'}
>>> managers  = {'tom', 'sue'}

>>> 'bob' in engineers            # Is bob an engineer?
True

>>> engineers & managers          # Who is both engineer and manager?
```

```
{'sue'}

>>> engineers | managers                    # All people in either category
{'vic', 'sue', 'tom', 'bob', 'ann'}

>>> engineers - managers                     # Engineers who are not managers
{'vic', 'bob', 'ann'}

>>> managers - engineers                     # Managers who are not engineers
{'tom'}

>>> engineers > managers                     # Are all managers engineers? (superset)
False

>>> {'bob', 'sue'} < engineers               # Are both engineers? (subset)
True

>>> (managers | engineers) > managers        # All people is a superset of managers
True

>>> managers ^ engineers                     # Who is in one but not both?
{'vic', 'bob', 'ann', 'tom'}

>>> (managers | engineers) - (managers ^ engineers)    # Intersection!
{'sue'}
```

You can find more details on set operations in the Python library manual and some mathematical and relational database theory texts. Also stay tuned for Chapter 8's revival of some of the set operations we've seen here, in the context of dictionary view objects in Python 3.0.

Booleans

Some argue that the Python Boolean type, bool, is numeric in nature because its two values, True and False, are just customized versions of the integers 1 and 0 that print themselves differently. Although that's all most programmers need to know, let's explore this type in a bit more detail.

More formally, Python today has an explicit Boolean data type called bool, with the values True and False available as new preassigned built-in names. Internally, the names True and False are instances of bool, which is in turn just a subclass (in the object-oriented sense) of the built-in integer type int. True and False behave exactly like the integers 1 and 0, except that they have customized printing logic—they print themselves as the words True and False, instead of the digits 1 and 0. bool accomplishes this by redefining str and repr string formats for its two objects.

Because of this customization, the output of Boolean expressions typed at the interactive prompt prints as the words True and False instead of the older and less obvious 1 and 0. In addition, Booleans make truth values more explicit. For instance, an infinite loop can now be coded as while True: instead of the less intuitive while 1:. Similarly, flags can be initialized more clearly with `flag = False`. We'll discuss these statements further in Part III.

Again, though, for all other practical purposes, you can treat `True` and `False` as though they are predefined variables set to integer 1 and 0. Most programmers used to preassign `True` and `False` to 1 and 0 anyway; the `bool` type simply makes this standard. Its implementation can lead to curious results, though. Because `True` is just the integer 1 with a custom display format, `True + 4` yields 5 in Python:

```
>>> type(True)
<class 'bool'>
>>> isinstance(True, int)
True
>>> True == 1               # Same value
True
>>> True is 1               # But different object: see the next chapter
False
>>> True or False           # Same as: 1 or 0
True
>>> True + 4                # (Hmmm)
5
```

Since you probably won't come across an expression like the last of these in real Python code, you can safely ignore its deeper metaphysical implications....

We'll revisit Booleans in Chapter 9 (to define Python's notion of truth) and again in Chapter 12 (to see how Boolean operators like and and or work).

Numeric Extensions

Finally, although Python core numeric types offer plenty of power for most applications, there is a large library of third-party open source extensions available to address more focused needs. Because numeric programming is a popular domain for Python, you'll find a wealth of advanced tools.

For example, if you need to do serious number crunching, an optional extension for Python called *NumPy* (Numeric Python) provides advanced numeric programming tools, such as a matrix data type, vector processing, and sophisticated computation libraries. Hardcore scientific programming groups at places like Los Alamos and NASA use Python with NumPy to implement the sorts of tasks they previously coded in C++, FORTRAN, or Matlab. The combination of Python and NumPy is often compared to a free, more flexible version of Matlab—you get NumPy's performance, plus the Python language and its libraries.

Because it's so advanced, we won't talk further about NumPy in this book. You can find additional support for advanced numeric programming in Python, including graphics and plotting tools, statistics libraries, and the popular *SciPy* package at Python's PyPI site, or by searching the Web. Also note that NumPy is currently an optional extension; it doesn't come with Python and must be installed separately.

Chapter Summary

This chapter has taken a tour of Python's numeric object types and the operations we can apply to them. Along the way, we met the standard integer and floating-point types, as well as some more exotic and less commonly used types such as complex numbers, fractions, and sets. We also explored Python's expression syntax, type conversions, bitwise operations, and various literal forms for coding numbers in scripts.

Later in this part of the book, I'll fill in some details about the next object type, the string. In the next chapter, however, we'll take some time to explore the mechanics of variable assignment in more detail than we have here. This turns out to be perhaps the most fundamental idea in Python, so make sure you check out the next chapter before moving on. First, though, it's time to take the usual chapter quiz.

Test Your Knowledge: Quiz

1. What is the value of the expression 2 * (3 + 4) in Python?
2. What is the value of the expression 2 * 3 + 4 in Python?
3. What is the value of the expression 2 + 3 * 4 in Python?
4. What tools can you use to find a number's square root, as well as its square?
5. What is the type of the result of the expression 1 + 2.0 + 3?
6. How can you truncate and round a floating-point number?
7. How can you convert an integer to a floating-point number?
8. How would you display an integer in octal, hexadecimal, or binary notation?
9. How might you convert an octal, hexadecimal, or binary string to a plain integer?

Test Your Knowledge: Answers

1. The value will be 14, the result of 2 * 7, because the parentheses force the addition to happen before the multiplication.
2. The value will be 10, the result of 6 + 4. Python's operator precedence rules are applied in the absence of parentheses, and multiplication has higher precedence than (i.e., happens before) addition, per Table 5-2.
3. This expression yields 14, the result of 2 + 12, for the same precedence reasons as in the prior question.
4. Functions for obtaining the square root, as well as *pi*, tangents, and more, are available in the imported math module. To find a number's square root, import math and call math.sqrt(N). To get a number's square, use either the exponent

expression X ** 2 or the built-in function pow(X, 2). Either of these last two can also compute the square root when given a power of 0.5 (e.g., X ** .5).

5. The result will be a floating-point number: the integers are converted up to floating point, the most complex type in the expression, and floating-point math is used to evaluate it.

6. The int(N) and math.trunc(N) functions truncate, and the round(N, *digits*) function rounds. We can also compute the floor with math.floor(N) and round for display with string formatting operations.

7. The float(I) function converts an integer to a floating point; mixing an integer with a floating point within an expression will result in a conversion as well. In some sense, Python 3.0 / division converts too—it always returns a floating-point result that includes the remainder, even if both operands are integers.

8. The oct(I) and hex(I) built-in functions return the octal and hexadecimal string forms for an integer. The bin(I) call also returns a number's binary digits string in Python 2.6 and 3.0. The % string formatting expression and format string method also provide targets for some such conversions.

9. The int(S, *base*) function can be used to convert from octal and hexadecimal strings to normal integers (pass in 8, 16, or 2 for the base). The eval(S) function can be used for this purpose too, but it's more expensive to run and can have security issues. Note that integers are always stored in binary in computer memory; these are just display string format conversions.

## CHAPTER 6

The Dynamic Typing Interlude

In the prior chapter, we began exploring Python's core object types in depth with a look at Python numbers. We'll resume our object type tour in the next chapter, but before we move on, it's important that you get a handle on what may be the most fundamental idea in Python programming and is certainly the basis of much of both the conciseness and flexibility of the Python language—dynamic typing, and the polymorphism it yields.

As you'll see here and later in this book, in Python, we do not declare the specific types of the objects our scripts use. In fact, programs should not even care about specific types; in exchange, they are naturally applicable in more contexts than we can sometimes even plan ahead for. Because dynamic typing is the root of this flexibility, let's take a brief look at the model here.

The Case of the Missing Declaration Statements

If you have a background in compiled or statically typed languages like C, C++, or Java, you might find yourself a bit perplexed at this point in the book. So far, we've been using variables without declaring their existence or their types, and it somehow works. When we type a = 3 in an interactive session or program file, for instance, how does Python know that a should stand for an integer? For that matter, how does Python know what a is at all?

Once you start asking such questions, you've crossed over into the domain of Python's *dynamic typing* model. In Python, types are determined automatically at runtime, not in response to declarations in your code. This means that you never declare variables ahead of time (a concept that is perhaps simpler to grasp if you keep in mind that it all boils down to variables, objects, and the links between them).

Variables, Objects, and References

As you've seen in many of the examples used so far in this book, when you run an assignment statement such as a = 3 in Python, it works even if you've never told Python to use the name a as a variable, or that a should stand for an integer-type object. In the Python language, this all pans out in a very natural way, as follows:

Variable creation
>   A variable (i.e., name), like a, is created when your code first assigns it a value. Future assignments change the value of the already created name. Technically, Python detects some names before your code runs, but you can think of it as though initial assignments make variables.

Variable types
>   A variable never has any type information or constraints associated with it. The notion of type lives with objects, not names. Variables are generic in nature; they always simply refer to a particular object at a particular point in time.

Variable use
>   When a variable appears in an expression, it is immediately replaced with the object that it currently refers to, whatever that may be. Further, all variables must be explicitly assigned before they can be used; referencing unassigned variables results in errors.

In sum, variables are created when assigned, can reference any type of object, and must be assigned before they are referenced. This means that you never need to declare names used by your script, but you must initialize names before you can update them; counters, for example, must be initialized to zero before you can add to them.

This dynamic typing model is strikingly different from the typing model of traditional languages. When you are first starting out, the model is usually easier to understand if you keep clear the distinction between names and objects. For example, when we say this:

```
>>> a = 3
```

at least conceptually, Python will perform three distinct steps to carry out the request. These steps reflect the operation of all assignments in the Python language:

1. Create an object to represent the value 3.
2. Create the variable a, if it does not yet exist.
3. Link the variable a to the new object 3.

The net result will be a structure inside Python that resembles Figure 6-1. As sketched, variables and objects are stored in different parts of memory and are associated by links (the link is shown as a pointer in the figure). Variables always link to objects and never to other variables, but larger objects may link to other objects (for instance, a list object has links to the objects it contains).

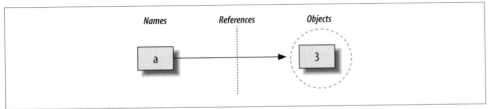

Figure 6-1. Names and objects after running the assignment a = 3. Variable a becomes a reference to the object 3. Internally, the variable is really a pointer to the object's memory space created by running the literal expression 3.

These links from variables to objects are called *references* in Python—that is, a reference is a kind of association, implemented as a pointer in memory.* Whenever the variables are later used (i.e., referenced), Python automatically follows the variable-to-object links. This is all simpler than the terminology may imply. In concrete terms:

- *Variables* are entries in a system table, with spaces for links to objects.
- *Objects* are pieces of allocated memory, with enough space to represent the values for which they stand.
- *References* are automatically followed pointers from variables to objects.

At least conceptually, each time you generate a new value in your script by running an expression, Python creates a new object (i.e., a chunk of memory) to represent that value. Internally, as an optimization, Python caches and reuses certain kinds of unchangeable objects, such as small integers and strings (each 0 is not really a new piece of memory—more on this caching behavior later). But, from a logical perspective, it works as though each expression's result value is a distinct object and each object is a distinct piece of memory.

Technically speaking, objects have more structure than just enough space to represent their values. Each object also has two standard header fields: a *type designator* used to mark the type of the object, and a *reference counter* used to determine when it's OK to reclaim the object. To understand how these two header fields factor into the model, we need to move on.

Types Live with Objects, Not Variables

To see how object types come into play, watch what happens if we assign a variable multiple times:

---

* Readers with a background in C may find Python references similar to C pointers (memory addresses). In fact, references are implemented as pointers, and they often serve the same roles, especially with objects that can be changed in-place (more on this later). However, because references are always automatically dereferenced when used, you can never actually do anything useful with a reference itself; this is a feature that eliminates a vast category of C bugs. You can think of Python references as C "void*" pointers, which are automatically followed whenever used.

```
>>> a = 3          # It's an integer
>>> a = 'spam'     # Now it's a string
>>> a = 1.23       # Now it's a floating point
```

This isn't typical Python code, but it does work—a starts out as an integer, then becomes a string, and finally becomes a floating-point number. This example tends to look especially odd to ex-C programmers, as it appears as though the *type* of a changes from integer to string when we say a = 'spam'.

However, that's not really what's happening. In Python, things work more simply. Names have no types; as stated earlier, types live with objects, not names. In the preceding listing, we've simply changed a to reference different objects. Because variables have no type, we haven't actually changed the type of the variable a; we've simply made the variable reference a different type of object. In fact, again, all we can ever say about a variable in Python is that it references a particular object at a particular point in time.

Objects, on the other hand, know what type they are—each object contains a header field that tags the object with its type. The integer object 3, for example, will contain the value 3, plus a designator that tells Python that the object is an integer (strictly speaking, a pointer to an object called int, the name of the integer type). The type designator of the 'spam' string object points to the string type (called str) instead. Because objects know their types, variables don't have to.

To recap, types are associated with objects in Python, not with variables. In typical code, a given variable usually will reference just one kind of object. Because this isn't a requirement, though, you'll find that Python code tends to be much more flexible than you may be accustomed to—if you use Python well, your code might work on many types automatically.

I mentioned that objects have two header fields, a type designator and a reference counter. To understand the latter of these, we need to move on and take a brief look at what happens at the end of an object's life.

Objects Are Garbage-Collected

In the prior section's listings, we assigned the variable a to different types of objects in each assignment. But when we reassign a variable, what happens to the value it was previously referencing? For example, after the following statements, what happens to the object 3?

```
>>> a = 3
>>> a = 'spam'
```

The answer is that in Python, whenever a name is assigned to a new object, the space held by the prior object is reclaimed (if it is not referenced by any other name or object). This automatic reclamation of objects' space is known as *garbage collection*.

To illustrate, consider the following example, which sets the name x to a different object on each assignment:

```
>>> x = 42
>>> x = 'shrubbery'       # Reclaim 42 now (unless referenced elsewhere)
>>> x = 3.1415            # Reclaim 'shrubbery' now
>>> x = [1, 2, 3]         # Reclaim 3.1415 now
```

First, notice that x is set to a different type of object each time. Again, though this is not really the case, the effect is as though the type of x is changing over time. Remember, in Python types live with objects, not names. Because names are just generic references to objects, this sort of code works naturally.

Second, notice that references to objects are discarded along the way. Each time x is assigned to a new object, Python reclaims the prior object's space. For instance, when it is assigned the string 'shrubbery', the object 42 is immediately reclaimed (assuming it is not referenced anywhere else)—that is, the object's space is automatically thrown back into the free space pool, to be reused for a future object.

Internally, Python accomplishes this feat by keeping a counter in every object that keeps track of the number of references currently pointing to that object. As soon as (and exactly when) this counter drops to zero, the object's memory space is automatically reclaimed. In the preceding listing, we're assuming that each time x is assigned to a new object, the prior object's reference counter drops to zero, causing it to be reclaimed.

The most immediately tangible benefit of garbage collection is that it means you can use objects liberally without ever needing to free up space in your script. Python will clean up unused space for you as your program runs. In practice, this eliminates a substantial amount of bookkeeping code required in lower-level languages such as C and C++.

Technically speaking, Python's garbage collection is based mainly upon *reference counters*, as described here; however, it also has a component that detects and reclaims objects with *cyclic references* in time. This component can be disabled if you're sure that your code doesn't create cycles, but it is enabled by default.

Because references are implemented as pointers, it's possible for an object to reference itself, or reference another object that does. For example, exercise 3 at the end of Part I and its solution in Appendix B show how to create a cycle by embedding a reference to a list within itself. The same phenomenon can occur for assignments to attributes of objects created from user-defined classes. Though relatively rare, because the reference counts for such objects never drop to zero, they must be treated specially.

For more details on Python's cycle detector, see the documentation for the gc module in Python's library manual. Also note that this description of Python's garbage collector applies to the standard CPython only; Jython and IronPython may use different schemes, though the net effect in all is similar—unused space is reclaimed for you automatically.

Shared References

So far, we've seen what happens as a single variable is assigned references to objects. Now let's introduce another variable into our interaction and watch what happens to its names and objects:

```
>>> a = 3
>>> b = a
```

Typing these two statements generates the scene captured in Figure 6-2. The second line causes Python to create the variable b; the variable a is being used and not assigned here, so it is replaced with the object it references (3), and b is made to reference that object. The net effect is that the variables a and b wind up referencing the same object (that is, pointing to the same chunk of memory). This scenario, with multiple names referencing the same object, is called a *shared reference* in Python.

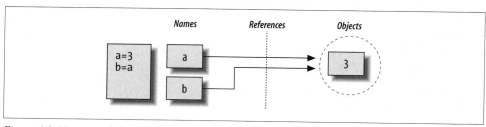

Figure 6-2. Names and objects after next running the assignment b = a. Variable b becomes a reference to the object 3. Internally, the variable is really a pointer to the object's memory space created by running the literal expression 3.

Next, suppose we extend the session with one more statement:

```
>>> a = 3
>>> b = a
>>> a = 'spam'
```

As with all Python assignments, this statement simply makes a new object to represent the string value 'spam' and sets a to reference this new object. It does not, however, change the value of b; b still references the original object, the integer 3. The resulting reference structure is shown in Figure 6-3.

The same sort of thing would happen if we changed b to 'spam' instead—the assignment would change only b, not a. This behavior also occurs if there are no type differences at all. For example, consider these three statements:

```
>>> a = 3
>>> b = a
>>> a = a + 2
```

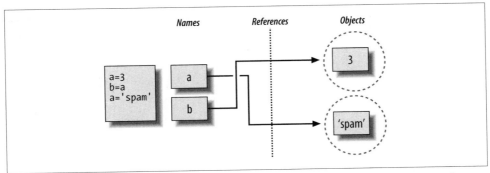

Figure 6-3. Names and objects after finally running the assignment a = 'spam'. Variable a references the new object (i.e., piece of memory) created by running the literal expression 'spam', but variable b still refers to the original object 3. Because this assignment is not an in-place change to the object 3, it changes only variable a, not b.

In this sequence, the same events transpire. Python makes the variable a reference the object 3 and makes b reference the same object as a, as in Figure 6-2; as before, the last assignment then sets a to a completely different object (in this case, the integer 5, which is the result of the + expression). It does not change b as a side effect. In fact, there is no way to ever overwrite the value of the object 3—as introduced in Chapter 4, integers are immutable and thus can never be changed in-place.

One way to think of this is that, unlike in some languages, in Python variables are always pointers to objects, not labels of changeable memory areas: setting a variable to a new value does not alter the original object, but rather causes the variable to reference an entirely different object. The net effect is that assignment to a variable can impact only the single variable being assigned. When mutable objects and in-place changes enter the equation, though, the picture changes somewhat; to see how, let's move on.

Shared References and In-Place Changes

As you'll see later in this part's chapters, there are objects and operations that perform in-place object changes. For instance, an assignment to an offset in a list actually changes the list object itself in-place, rather than generating a brand new list object. For objects that support such in-place changes, you need to be more aware of shared references, since a change from one name may impact others.

To further illustrate, let's take another look at the list objects introduced in Chapter 4. Recall that lists, which do support in-place assignments to positions, are simply collections of other objects, coded in square brackets:

```
>>> L1 = [2, 3, 4]
>>> L2 = L1
```

L1 here is a list containing the objects 2, 3, and 4. Items inside a list are accessed by their positions, so L1[0] refers to object 2, the first item in the list L1. Of course, lists are also objects in their own right, just like integers and strings. After running the two prior assignments, L1 and L2 reference the same object, just like a and b in the prior example (see Figure 6-2). Now say that, as before, we extend this interaction to say the following:

```
>>> L1 = 24
```

This assignment simply sets L1 is to a different object; L2 still references the original list. If we change this statement's syntax slightly, however, it has a radically different effect:

```
>>> L1 = [2, 3, 4]          # A mutable object
>>> L2 = L1                 # Make a reference to the same object
>>> L1[0] = 24              # An in-place change

>>> L1                      # L1 is different
[24, 3, 4]
>>> L2                      # But so is L2!
[24, 3, 4]
```

Really, we haven't changed L1 itself here; we've changed a component of the *object* that L1 references. This sort of change overwrites part of the list object in-place. Because the list object is shared by (referenced from) other variables, though, an in-place change like this doesn't only affect L1—that is, you must be aware that when you make such changes, they can impact other parts of your program. In this example, the effect shows up in L2 as well because it references the same object as L1. Again, we haven't actually changed L2, either, but its value will appear different because it has been overwritten.

This behavior is usually what you want, but you should be aware of how it works, so that it's expected. It's also just the default: if you don't want such behavior, you can request that Python *copy* objects instead of making references. There are a variety of ways to copy a list, including using the built-in list function and the standard library copy module. Perhaps the most common way is to slice from start to finish (see Chapters 4 and 7 for more on slicing):

```
>>> L1 = [2, 3, 4]
>>> L2 = L1[:]              # Make a copy of L1
>>> L1[0] = 24

>>> L1
[24, 3, 4]
>>> L2                      # L2 is not changed
[2, 3, 4]
```

Here, the change made through L1 is not reflected in L2 because L2 references a copy of the object L1 references; that is, the two variables point to different pieces of memory.

Note that this slicing technique won't work on the other major mutable core types, dictionaries and sets, because they are not sequences—to copy a dictionary or set, instead use their X.copy() method call. Also, note that the standard library copy module has a call for copying any object type generically, as well as a call for copying nested object structures (a dictionary with nested lists, for example):

```
import copy
X = copy.copy(Y)            # Make top-level "shallow" copy of any object Y
X = copy.deepcopy(Y)        # Make deep copy of any object Y: copy all nested parts
```

We'll explore lists and dictionaries in more depth, and revisit the concept of shared references and copies, in Chapters 8 and 9. For now, keep in mind that objects that can be changed in-place (that is, mutable objects) are always open to these kinds of effects. In Python, this includes lists, dictionaries, and some objects defined with class statements. If this is not the desired behavior, you can simply copy your objects as needed.

Shared References and Equality

In the interest of full disclosure, I should point out that the garbage-collection behavior described earlier in this chapter may be more conceptual than literal for certain types. Consider these statements:

```
>>> x = 42
>>> x = 'shrubbery'      # Reclaim 42 now?
```

Because Python caches and reuses small integers and small strings, as mentioned earlier, the object 42 here is probably not literally reclaimed; instead, it will likely remain in a system table to be reused the next time you generate a 42 in your code. Most kinds of objects, though, are reclaimed immediately when they are no longer referenced; for those that are not, the caching mechanism is irrelevant to your code.

For instance, because of Python's reference model, there are two different ways to check for equality in a Python program. Let's create a shared reference to demonstrate:

```
>>> L = [1, 2, 3]
>>> M = L                # M and L reference the same object
>>> L == M               # Same value
True
>>> L is M               # Same object
True
```

The first technique here, the == operator, tests whether the two referenced objects have the same values; this is the method almost always used for equality checks in Python. The second method, the is operator, instead tests for object identity—it returns True only if both names point to the exact same object, so it is a much stronger form of equality testing.

Really, is simply compares the pointers that implement references, and it serves as a way to detect shared references in your code if needed. It returns False if the names point to equivalent but different objects, as is the case when we run two different literal expressions:

```
>>> L = [1, 2, 3]
>>> M = [1, 2, 3]        # M and L reference different objects
>>> L == M               # Same values
True
>>> L is M               # Different objects
False
```

Now, watch what happens when we perform the same operations on small numbers:

```
>>> X = 42
>>> Y = 42               # Should be two different objects
>>> X == Y
True
>>> X is Y               # Same object anyhow: caching at work!
True
```

In this interaction, X and Y should be == (same value), but not is (same object) because we ran two different literal expressions. Because small integers and strings are cached and reused, though, is tells us they reference the same single object.

In fact, if you really want to look under the hood, you can always ask Python how many references there are to an object: the getrefcount function in the standard sys module returns the object's reference count. When I ask about the integer object 1 in the IDLE GUI, for instance, it reports 837 reuses of this same object (most of which are in IDLE's system code, not mine):

```
>>> import sys
>>> sys.getrefcount(1)    # 837 pointers to this shared piece of memory
837
```

This object caching and reuse is irrelevant to your code (unless you run the is check!). Because you cannot change numbers or strings in-place, it doesn't matter how many references there are to the same object. Still, this behavior reflects one of the many ways Python optimizes its model for execution speed.

Dynamic Typing Is Everywhere

Of course, you don't really need to draw name/object diagrams with circles and arrows to use Python. When you're starting out, though, it sometimes helps you understand unusual cases if you can trace their reference structures. If a mutable object changes out from under you when passed around your program, for example, chances are you are witnessing some of this chapter's subject matter firsthand.

Moreover, even if dynamic typing seems a little abstract at this point, you probably will care about it eventually. Because *everything* seems to work by assignment and references in Python, a basic understanding of this model is useful in many different contexts. As you'll see, it works the same in assignment statements, function arguments, for loop variables, module imports, class attributes, and more. The good news is that there is just one assignment model in Python; once you get a handle on dynamic typing, you'll find that it works the same everywhere in the language.

At the most practical level, dynamic typing means there is less code for you to write. Just as importantly, though, dynamic typing is also the root of Python's *polymorphism*, a concept we introduced in Chapter 4 and will revisit again later in this book. Because we do not constrain types in Python code, it is highly flexible. As you'll see, when used well, dynamic typing and the polymorphism it provides produce code that automatically adapts to new requirements as your systems evolve.

Chapter Summary

This chapter took a deeper look at Python's dynamic typing model—that is, the way that Python keeps track of object types for us automatically, rather than requiring us to code declaration statements in our scripts. Along the way, we learned how variables and objects are associated by references in Python; we also explored the idea of garbage collection, learned how shared references to objects can affect multiple variables, and saw how references impact the notion of equality in Python.

Because there is just one assignment model in Python, and because assignment pops up everywhere in the language, it's important that you have a handle on the model before moving on. The following quiz should help you review some of this chapter's ideas. After that, we'll resume our object tour in the next chapter, with strings.

Test Your Knowledge: Quiz

1. Consider the following three statements. Do they change the value printed for A?

    ```
    A = "spam"
    B = A
    B = "shrubbery"
    ```

2. Consider these three statements. Do they change the printed value of A?

    ```
    A = ["spam"]
    B = A
    B[0] = "shrubbery"
    ```

3. How about these—is A changed now?

    ```
    A = ["spam"]
    B = A[:]
    B[0] = "shrubbery"
    ```

Test Your Knowledge: Answers

1. No: A still prints as `"spam"`. When B is assigned to the string `"shrubbery"`, all that happens is that the variable B is reset to point to the new string object. A and B initially share (i.e., reference/point to) the same single string object `"spam"`, but two names are never linked together in Python. Thus, setting B to a different object has no effect on A. The same would be true if the last statement here was `B = B + 'shrubbery'`, by the way—the concatenation would make a new object for its result, which would then be assigned to B only. We can never overwrite a string (or number, or tuple) in-place, because strings are immutable.

2. Yes: A now prints as `["shrubbery"]`. Technically, we haven't really changed either A or B; instead, we've changed part of the object they both reference (point to) by overwriting that object in-place through the variable B. Because A references the same object as B, the update is reflected in A as well.

3. No: A still prints as `["spam"]`. The in-place assignment through B has no effect this time because the slice expression made a copy of the list object before it was assigned to B. After the second assignment statement, there are two different list objects that have the same value (in Python, we say they are `==`, but not `is`). The third statement changes the value of the list object pointed to by B, but not that pointed to by A.

## CHAPTER 7

Strings

The next major type on our built-in object tour is the Python *string*—an ordered collection of characters used to store and represent text-based information. We looked briefly at strings in Chapter 4. Here, we will revisit them in more depth, filling in some of the details we skipped then.

From a functional perspective, strings can be used to represent just about anything that can be encoded as text: symbols and words (e.g., your name), contents of text files loaded into memory, Internet addresses, Python programs, and so on. They can also be used to hold the absolute binary values of bytes, and multibyte Unicode text used in internationalized programs.

You may have used strings in other languages, too. Python's strings serve the same role as character arrays in languages such as C, but they are a somewhat higher-level tool than arrays. Unlike in C, in Python, strings come with a powerful set of processing tools. Also unlike languages such as C, Python has no distinct type for individual characters; instead, you just use one-character strings.

Strictly speaking, Python strings are categorized as immutable sequences, meaning that the characters they contain have a left-to-right positional order and that they cannot be changed in-place. In fact, strings are the first representative of the larger class of objects called *sequences* that we will study here. Pay special attention to the sequence operations introduced in this chapter, because they will work the same on other sequence types we'll explore later, such as lists and tuples.

Table 7-1 previews common string literals and operations we will discuss in this chapter. Empty strings are written as a pair of quotation marks (single or double) with nothing in between, and there are a variety of ways to code strings. For processing, strings support *expression* operations such as concatenation (combining strings), slicing (extracting sections), indexing (fetching by offset), and so on. Besides expressions, Python also provides a set of string *methods* that implement common string-specific tasks, as well as *modules* for more advanced text-processing tasks such as pattern matching. We'll explore all of these later in the chapter.

Table 7-1. Common string literals and operations

Operation	Interpretation
S = ''	Empty string
S = "spam's"	Double quotes, same as single
S = 's\np\ta\x00m'	Escape sequences
S = """...""""	Triple-quoted block strings
S = r'\temp\spam'	Raw strings
S = b'spam'	Byte strings in 3.0 (Chapter 36)
S = u'spam'	Unicode strings in 2.6 only (Chapter 36)
S1 + S2	Concatenate, repeat
S * 3	
S[i]	Index, slice, length
S[i:j]	
len(S)	
"a %s parrot" % kind	String formatting expression
"a {0} parrot".format(kind)	String formatting method in 2.6 and 3.0
S.find('pa')	String method calls: search,
S.rstrip()	remove whitespace,
S.replace('pa', 'xx')	replacement,
S.split(',')	split on delimiter,
S.isdigit()	content test,
S.lower()	case conversion,
S.endswith('spam')	end test,
'spam'.join(strlist)	delimiter join,
S.encode('latin-1')	Unicode encoding, etc.
for x in S: print(x)	Iteration, membership
'spam' in S	
[c * 2 for c in S]	
map(ord, S)	

Beyond the core set of string tools in Table 7-1, Python also supports more advanced pattern-based string processing with the standard library's **re** (regular expression) module, introduced in Chapter 4, and even higher-level text processing tools such as XML parsers, discussed briefly in Chapter 36. This book's scope, though, is focused on the fundamentals represented by Table 7-1.

To cover the basics, this chapter begins with an overview of string literal forms and string expressions, then moves on to look at more advanced tools such as string methods and formatting. Python comes with many string tools, and we won't look at them all here; the complete story is chronicled in the Python library manual. Our goal here is to explore enough commonly used tools to give you a representative sample; methods we won't see in action here, for example, are largely analogous to those we will.

Content note: Technically speaking, this chapter tells only part of the string story in Python—the part most programmers need to know. It presents the basic `str` string type, which handles ASCII text and works the same regardless of which version of Python you use. That is, this chapter intentionally limits its scope to the string processing essentials that are used in most Python scripts.

From a more formal perspective, ASCII is a simple form of Unicode text. Python addresses the distinction between text and binary data by including distinct object types:

- In Python 3.0 there are three string types: `str` is used for Unicode text (ASCII or otherwise), `bytes` is used for binary data (including encoded text), and `bytearray` is a mutable variant of `bytes`.

- In Python 2.6, `unicode` strings represent wide Unicode text, and `str` strings handle both 8-bit text and binary data.

The `bytearray` type is also available as a back-port in 2.6, but not earlier, and it's not as closely bound to binary data as it is in 3.0. Because most programmers don't need to dig into the details of Unicode encodings or binary data formats, though, I've moved all such details to the Advanced Topics part of this book, in Chapter 36.

If you do need to deal with more advanced string concepts such as alternative character sets or packed binary data and files, see Chapter 36 after reading the material here. For now, we'll focus on the basic string type and its operations. As you'll find, the basics we'll study here also apply directly to the more advanced string types in Python's toolset.

String Literals

By and large, strings are fairly easy to use in Python. Perhaps the most complicated thing about them is that there are so many ways to write them in your code:

- Single quotes: `'spa"m'`
- Double quotes: `"spa'm"`
- Triple quotes: `'''... spam ...''', """... spam ..."""`
- Escape sequences: `"s\tp\na\0m"`
- Raw strings: `r"C:\new\test.spm"`

- Byte strings in 3.0 (see Chapter 36): `b'sp\x01am'`
- Unicode strings in 2.6 only (see Chapter 36): `u'eggs\u0020spam'`

The single- and double-quoted forms are by far the most common; the others serve specialized roles, and we're postponing discussion of the last two advanced forms until Chapter 36. Let's take a quick look at all the other options in turn.

Single- and Double-Quoted Strings Are the Same

Around Python strings, single and double quote characters are interchangeable. That is, string literals can be written enclosed in either two single or two double quotes—the two forms work the same and return the same type of object. For example, the following two strings are identical, once coded:

```
>>> 'shrubbery', "shrubbery"
('shrubbery', 'shrubbery')
```

The reason for supporting both is that it allows you to embed a quote character of the other variety inside a string without escaping it with a backslash. You may embed a single quote character in a string enclosed in double quote characters, and vice versa:

```
>>> 'knight"s', "knight's"
('knight"s', "knight's")
```

Incidentally, Python automatically concatenates adjacent string literals in any expression, although it is almost as simple to add a + operator between them to invoke concatenation explicitly (as we'll see in Chapter 12, wrapping this form in parentheses also allows it to span multiple lines):

```
>>> title = "Meaning " 'of' " Life"        # Implicit concatenation
>>> title
'Meaning of Life'
```

Notice that adding commas between these strings would result in a tuple, not a string. Also notice in all of these outputs that Python prefers to print strings in single quotes, unless they embed one. You can also embed quotes by escaping them with backslashes:

```
>>> 'knight\'s', "knight\"s"
("knight's", 'knight"s')
```

To understand why, you need to know how escapes work in general.

Escape Sequences Represent Special Bytes

The last example embedded a quote inside a string by preceding it with a backslash. This is representative of a general pattern in strings: backslashes are used to introduce special byte codings known as *escape sequences*.

Escape sequences let us embed byte codes in strings that cannot easily be typed on a keyboard. The character \, and one or more characters following it in the string literal, are replaced with a single character in the resulting string object, which has the binary value specified by the escape sequence. For example, here is a five-character string that embeds a newline and a tab:

```
>>> s = 'a\nb\tc'
```

The two characters \n stand for a single character—the byte containing the binary value of the newline character in your character set (usually, ASCII code 10). Similarly, the sequence \t is replaced with the tab character. The way this string looks when printed depends on how you print it. The interactive echo shows the special characters as escapes, but print interprets them instead:

```
>>> s
'a\nb\tc'
>>> print(s)
a
b       c
```

To be completely sure how many bytes are in this string, use the built-in len function—it returns the actual number of bytes in a string, regardless of how it is displayed:

```
>>> len(s)
5
```

This string is five bytes long: it contains an ASCII *a* byte, a newline byte, an ASCII *b* byte, and so on. Note that the original backslash characters are not really stored with the string in memory; they are used to tell Python to store special byte values in the string. For coding such special bytes, Python recognizes a full set of escape code sequences, listed in Table 7-2.

Table 7-2. String backslash characters

Escape	Meaning
\newline	Ignored (continuation line)
\\	Backslash (stores one \)
\'	Single quote (stores ')
\"	Double quote (stores ")
\a	Bell
\b	Backspace
\f	Formfeed
\n	Newline (linefeed)
\r	Carriage return
\t	Horizontal tab
\v	Vertical tab
\xhh	Character with hex value hh (at most 2 digits)
\ooo	Character with octal value ooo (up to 3 digits)
\0	Null: binary 0 character (doesn't end string)

Escape	Meaning
\N{ id }	Unicode database ID
\uhhhh	Unicode 16-bit hex
\Uhhhhhhhh	Unicode 32-bit hex[a]
\other	Not an escape (keeps both \ and *other*)

[a] The \Uhhhh... escape sequence takes exactly eight hexadecimal digits (*h*); both \u and \U can be used only in Unicode string literals.

Some escape sequences allow you to embed absolute binary values into the bytes of a string. For instance, here's a five-character string that embeds two binary zero bytes (coded as octal escapes of one digit):

```
>>> s = 'a\0b\0c'
>>> s
'a\x00b\x00c'
>>> len(s)
5
```

In Python, the zero (null) byte does not terminate a string the way it typically does in C. Instead, Python keeps both the string's length and text in memory. In fact, no character terminates a string in Python. Here's a string that is all absolute binary escape codes—a binary 1 and 2 (coded in octal), followed by a binary 3 (coded in hexadecimal):

```
>>> s = '\001\002\x03'
>>> s
'\x01\x02\x03'
>>> len(s)
3
```

Notice that Python displays nonprintable characters in hex, regardless of how they were specified. You can freely combine absolute value escapes and the more symbolic escape types in Table 7-2. The following string contains the characters "spam", a tab and newline, and an absolute zero value byte coded in hex:

```
>>> S = "s\tp\na\x00m"
>>> S
's\tp\na\x00m'
>>> len(S)
7
>>> print(S)
s       p
a m
```

This becomes more important to know when you process binary data files in Python. Because their contents are represented as strings in your scripts, it's OK to process binary files that contain any sorts of binary byte values (more on files in Chapter 9).*

---

* If you need to care about binary data files, the chief distinction is that you open them in binary mode (using open mode flags with a b, such as 'rb', 'wb', and so on). In Python 3.0, binary file content is a **bytes** string, with an interface similar to that of normal strings; in 2.6, such content is a normal **str** string. See also the standard **struct** module introduced in Chapter 9, which can parse binary data loaded from a file, and the extended coverage of binary files and byte strings in Chapter 36.

Finally, as the last entry in Table 7-2 implies, if Python does not recognize the character after a \ as being a valid escape code, it simply keeps the backslash in the resulting string:

```
>>> x = "C:\py\code"          # Keeps \ literally
>>> x
'C:\\py\\code'
>>> len(x)
10
```

Unless you're able to commit all of Table 7-2 to memory, though, you probably shouldn't rely on this behavior.[†] To code literal backslashes explicitly such that they are retained in your strings, double them up (\\ is an escape for one \) or use raw strings; the next section shows how.

Raw Strings Suppress Escapes

As we've seen, escape sequences are handy for embedding special byte codes within strings. Sometimes, though, the special treatment of backslashes for introducing escapes can lead to trouble. It's surprisingly common, for instance, to see Python newcomers in classes trying to open a file with a filename argument that looks something like this:

```
myfile = open('C:\new\text.dat', 'w')
```

thinking that they will open a file called *text.dat* in the directory *C:\new*. The problem here is that \n is taken to stand for a newline character, and \t is replaced with a tab. In effect, the call tries to open a file named *C:(newline)ew(tab)ext.dat*, with usually less than stellar results.

This is just the sort of thing that raw strings are useful for. If the letter **r** (uppercase or lowercase) appears just before the opening quote of a string, it turns off the escape mechanism. The result is that Python retains your backslashes literally, exactly as you type them. Therefore, to fix the filename problem, just remember to add the letter **r** on Windows:

```
myfile = open(r'C:\new\text.dat', 'w')
```

Alternatively, because two backslashes are really an escape sequence for one backslash, you can keep your backslashes by simply doubling them up:

```
myfile = open('C:\\new\\text.dat', 'w')
```

In fact, Python itself sometimes uses this doubling scheme when it prints strings with embedded backslashes:

```
>>> path = r'C:\new\text.dat'
>>> path                      # Show as Python code
'C:\\new\\text.dat'
>>> print(path)               # User-friendly format
```

---

† In classes, I've met people who have indeed committed most or all of this table to memory; I'd probably think that was really sick, but for the fact that I'm a member of the set, too.

```
C:\new\text.dat
>>> len(path)                      # String length
15
```

As with numeric representation, the default format at the interactive prompt prints results as if they were code, and therefore escapes backslashes in the output. The `print` statement provides a more user-friendly format that shows that there is actually only one backslash in each spot. To verify this is the case, you can check the result of the built-in `len` function, which returns the number of bytes in the string, independent of display formats. If you count the characters in the `print(path)` output, you'll see that there really is just 1 character per backslash, for a total of 15.

Besides directory paths on Windows, raw strings are also commonly used for regular expressions (text pattern matching, supported with the `re` module introduced in Chapter 4). Also note that Python scripts can usually use *forward* slashes in directory paths on Windows and Unix because Python tries to interpret paths portably (i.e., `'C:/new/text.dat'` works when opening files, too). Raw strings are useful if you code paths using native Windows backslashes, though.

Despite its role, even a raw string cannot end in a single backslash, because the backslash escapes the following quote character—you still must escape the surrounding quote character to embed it in the string. That is, `r"...\"` is not a valid string literal—a raw string cannot end in an odd number of backslashes. If you need to end a raw string with a single backslash, you can use two and slice off the second (`r'1\nb\tc\\'[:-1]`), tack one on manually (`r'1\nb\tc' + '\\'`), or skip the raw string syntax and just double up the backslashes in a normal string (`'1\\nb\\tc\\'`). All three of these forms create the same eight-character string containing three backslashes.

Triple Quotes Code Multiline Block Strings

So far, you've seen single quotes, double quotes, escapes, and raw strings in action. Python also has a triple-quoted string literal format, sometimes called a *block string*, that is a syntactic convenience for coding multiline text data. This form begins with three quotes (of either the single or double variety), is followed by any number of lines of text, and is closed with the same triple-quote sequence that opened it. Single and double quotes embedded in the string's text may be, but do not have to be, escaped—the string does not end until Python sees three unescaped quotes of the same kind used to start the literal. For example:

```
>>> mantra = """Always look
...   on the bright
... side of life."""
>>>
>>> mantra
'Always look\n on the bright\nside of life.'
```

This string spans three lines (in some interfaces, the interactive prompt changes to ... on continuation lines; IDLE simply drops down one line). Python collects all the triple-quoted text into a single multiline string, with embedded newline characters (\n) at the places where your code has line breaks. Notice that, as in the literal, the second line in the result has a leading space, but the third does not—what you type is truly what you get. To see the string with the newlines interpreted, print it instead of echoing:

```
>>> print(mantra)
Always look
 on the bright
side of life.
```

Triple-quoted strings are useful any time you need multiline text in your program; for example, to embed multiline error messages or HTML or XML code in your source code files. You can embed such blocks directly in your scripts without resorting to external text files or explicit concatenation and newline characters.

Triple-quoted strings are also commonly used for documentation strings, which are string literals that are taken as comments when they appear at specific points in your file (more on these later in the book). These don't have to be triple-quoted blocks, but they usually are to allow for multiline comments.

Finally, triple-quoted strings are also sometimes used as a "horribly hackish" way to temporarily disable lines of code during development (OK, it's not really too horrible, and it's actually a fairly common practice). If you wish to turn off a few lines of code and run your script again, simply put three quotes above and below them, like this:

```
X = 1
"""
import os                          # Disable this code temporarily
print(os.getcwd())
"""
Y = 2
```

I said this was hackish because Python really does make a string out of the lines of code disabled this way, but this is probably not significant in terms of performance. For large sections of code, it's also easier than manually adding hash marks before each line and later removing them. This is especially true if you are using a text editor that does not have support for editing Python code specifically. In Python, practicality often beats aesthetics.

Strings in Action

Once you've created a string with the literal expressions we just met, you will almost certainly want to do things with it. This section and the next two demonstrate string expressions, methods, and formatting—the first line of text-processing tools in the Python language.

Basic Operations

Let's begin by interacting with the Python interpreter to illustrate the basic string operations listed earlier in Table 7-1. Strings can be concatenated using the + operator and repeated using the * operator:

```
% python
>>> len('abc')              # Length: number of items
3
>>> 'abc' + 'def'           # Concatenation: a new string
'abcdef'
>>> 'Ni!' * 4               # Repetition: like "Ni!" + "Ni!" + ...
'Ni!Ni!Ni!Ni!'
```

Formally, adding two string objects creates a new string object, with the contents of its operands joined. Repetition is like adding a string to itself a number of times. In both cases, Python lets you create arbitrarily sized strings; there's no need to predeclare anything in Python, including the sizes of data structures.‡ The len built-in function returns the length of a string (or any other object with a length).

Repetition may seem a bit obscure at first, but it comes in handy in a surprising number of contexts. For example, to print a line of 80 dashes, you can count up to 80, or let Python count for you:

```
>>> print('------- ...more... ---')    # 80 dashes, the hard way
>>> print('-' * 80)                     # 80 dashes, the easy way
```

Notice that operator overloading is at work here already: we're using the same + and * operators that perform addition and multiplication when using numbers. Python does the correct operation because it knows the types of the objects being added and multiplied. But be careful: the rules aren't quite as liberal as you might expect. For instance, Python doesn't allow you to mix numbers and strings in + expressions: 'abc'+9 raises an error instead of automatically converting 9 to a string.

As shown in the last row in Table 7-1, you can also iterate over strings in loops using for statements and test membership for both characters and substrings with the in expression operator, which is essentially a search. For substrings, in is much like the str.find() method covered later in this chapter, but it returns a Boolean result instead of the substring's position:

```
>>> myjob = "hacker"
>>> for c in myjob: print(c, end=' ')   # Step through items
...
```

---

‡ Unlike with C character arrays, you don't need to allocate or manage storage arrays when using Python strings; you can simply create string objects as needed and let Python manage the underlying memory space. As discussed in Chapter 6, Python reclaims unused objects' memory space automatically, using a reference-count garbage-collection strategy. Each object keeps track of the number of names, data structures, etc., that reference it; when the count reaches zero, Python frees the object's space. This scheme means Python doesn't have to stop and scan all the memory to find unused space to free (an additional garbage component also collects cyclic objects).

```
h a c k e r
>>> "k" in myjob              # Found
True
>>> "z" in myjob              # Not found
False
>>> 'spam' in 'abcspamdef'    # Substring search, no position returned
True
```

The for loop assigns a variable to successive items in a sequence (here, a string) and executes one or more statements for each item. In effect, the variable c becomes a cursor stepping across the string here. We will discuss iteration tools like these and others listed in Table 7-1 in more detail later in this book (especially in Chapters 14 and 20).

Indexing and Slicing

Because strings are defined as ordered collections of characters, we can access their components by position. In Python, characters in a string are fetched by *indexing*— providing the numeric offset of the desired component in square brackets after the string. You get back the one-character string at the specified position.

As in the C language, Python offsets start at 0 and end at one less than the length of the string. Unlike C, however, Python also lets you fetch items from sequences such as strings using *negative* offsets. Technically, a negative offset is added to the length of a string to derive a positive offset. You can also think of negative offsets as counting backward from the end. The following interaction demonstrates:

```
>>> S = 'spam'
>>> S[0], S[-2]               # Indexing from front or end
('s', 'a')
>>> S[1:3], S[1:], S[:-1]     # Slicing: extract a section
('pa', 'pam', 'spa')
```

The first line defines a four-character string and assigns it the name S. The next line indexes it in two ways: S[0] fetches the item at offset 0 from the left (the one-character string 's'), and S[-2] gets the item at offset 2 back from the end (or equivalently, at offset (4 + (−2)) from the front). Offsets and slices map to cells as shown in Figure 7-1.§

The last line in the preceding example demonstrates *slicing*, a generalized form of indexing that returns an entire *section*, not a single item. Probably the best way to think of slicing is that it is a type of *parsing* (analyzing structure), especially when applied to strings—it allows us to extract an entire section (substring) in a single step. Slices can be used to extract columns of data, chop off leading and trailing text, and more. In fact, we'll explore slicing in the context of text parsing later in this chapter.

The basics of slicing are straightforward. When you index a sequence object such as a string on a pair of offsets separated by a colon, Python returns a new object containing

§ More mathematically minded readers (and students in my classes) sometimes detect a small asymmetry here: the leftmost item is at offset 0, but the rightmost is at offset −1. Alas, there is no such thing as a distinct −0 value in Python.

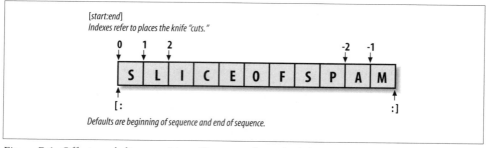

Figure 7-1. Offsets and slices: positive offsets start from the left end (offset 0 is the first item), and negatives count back from the right end (offset –1 is the last item). Either kind of offset can be used to give positions in indexing and slicing operations.

the contiguous section identified by the offset pair. The left offset is taken to be the lower bound (*inclusive*), and the right is the upper bound (*noninclusive*). That is, Python fetches all items from the lower bound up to but not including the upper bound, and returns a new object containing the fetched items. If omitted, the left and right bounds default to 0 and the length of the object you are slicing, respectively.

For instance, in the example we just saw, S[1:3] extracts the items at offsets 1 and 2: it grabs the second and third items, and stops before the fourth item at offset 3. Next, S[1:] gets *all items beyond the first*—the upper bound, which is not specified, defaults to the length of the string. Finally, S[:-1] fetches *all but the last item*—the lower bound defaults to 0, and –1 refers to the last item, noninclusive.

This may seem confusing at first glance, but indexing and slicing are simple and powerful tools to use, once you get the knack. Remember, if you're unsure about the effects of a slice, try it out interactively. In the next chapter, you'll see that it's even possible to change an entire section of another object in one step by assigning to a slice (though not for immutables like strings). Here's a summary of the details for reference:

- *Indexing* (S[i]) fetches components at offsets:
  - The first item is at offset 0.
  - Negative indexes mean to count backward from the end or right.
  - S[0] fetches the first item.
  - S[-2] fetches the second item from the end (like S[len(S)-2]).
- *Slicing* (S[i:j]) extracts contiguous sections of sequences:
  - The upper bound is noninclusive.
  - Slice boundaries default to 0 and the sequence length, if omitted.
  - S[1:3] fetches items at offsets 1 up to but not including 3.
  - S[1:] fetches items at offset 1 through the end (the sequence length).

— S[:3] fetches items at offset 0 up to but not including 3.

— S[:-1] fetches items at offset 0 up to but not including the last item.

— S[:] fetches items at offsets 0 through the end—this effectively performs a top-level copy of S.

The last item listed here turns out to be a very common trick: it makes a full top-level *copy* of a sequence object—an object with the same value, but a distinct piece of memory (you'll find more on copies in Chapter 9). This isn't very useful for immutable objects like strings, but it comes in handy for objects that may be changed in-place, such as lists.

In the next chapter, you'll see that the syntax used to index by offset (square brackets) is used to index dictionaries by key as well; the operations look the same but have different interpretations.

Extended slicing: the third limit and slice objects

In Python 2.3 and later, slice expressions have support for an optional third index, used as a *step* (sometimes called a *stride*). The step is added to the index of each item extracted. The full-blown form of a slice is now X[I:J:K], which means "extract all the items in X, from offset I through J–1, by K." The third limit, K, defaults to 1, which is why normally all items in a slice are extracted from left to right. If you specify an explicit value, however, you can use the third limit to skip items or to reverse their order.

For instance, X[1:10:2] will fetch *every other item* in X from offsets 1–9; that is, it will collect the items at offsets 1, 3, 5, 7, and 9. As usual, the first and second limits default to 0 and the length of the sequence, respectively, so X[::2] gets every other item from the beginning to the end of the sequence:

```
>>> S = 'abcdefghijklmnop'
>>> S[1:10:2]
'bdfhj'
>>> S[::2]
'acegikmo'
```

You can also use a negative stride. For example, the slicing expression "hello"[::-1] returns the new string "olleh"—the first two bounds default to 0 and the length of the sequence, as before, and a stride of –1 indicates that the slice should go from right to left instead of the usual left to right. The effect, therefore, is to *reverse* the sequence:

```
>>> S = 'hello'
>>> S[::-1]
'olleh'
```

With a negative stride, the meanings of the first two bounds are essentially reversed. That is, the slice S[5:1:-1] fetches the items from 2 to 5, in reverse order (the result contains items from offsets 5, 4, 3, and 2):

```
>>> S = 'abcedfg'
>>> S[5:1:-1]
'fdec'
```

Skipping and reversing like this are the most common use cases for three-limit slices, but see Python's standard library manual for more details (or run a few experiments interactively). We'll revisit three-limit slices again later in this book, in conjunction with the `for` loop statement.

Later in the book, we'll also learn that slicing is equivalent to indexing with a *slice object*, a finding of importance to class writers seeking to support both operations:

```
>>> 'spam'[1:3]                        # Slicing syntax
'pa'
>>> 'spam'[slice(1, 3)]                # Slice objects
'pa'
>>> 'spam'[::-1]
'maps'
>>> 'spam'[slice(None, None, -1)]
'maps'
```

Why You Will Care: Slices

Throughout this book, I will include common use case sidebars (such as this one) to give you a peek at how some of the language features being introduced are typically used in real programs. Because you won't be able to make much sense of real use cases until you've seen more of the Python picture, these sidebars necessarily contain many references to topics not introduced yet; at most, you should consider them previews of ways that you may find these abstract language concepts useful for common programming tasks.

For instance, you'll see later that the argument words listed on a system command line used to launch a Python program are made available in the `argv` attribute of the built-in `sys` module:

```
# File echo.py
import sys
print(sys.argv)

% python echo.py -a -b -c
['echo.py', '-a', '-b', '-c']
```

Usually, you're only interested in inspecting the arguments that follow the program name. This leads to a very typical application of slices: a single slice expression can be used to return all but the first item of a list. Here, `sys.argv[1:]` returns the desired list, `['-a', '-b', '-c']`. You can then process this list without having to accommodate the program name at the front.

Slices are also often used to clean up lines read from input files. If you know that a line will have an end-of-line character at the end (a \n newline marker), you can get rid of it with a single expression such as `line[:-1]`, which extracts all but the last character in the line (the lower limit defaults to 0). In both cases, slices do the job of logic that must be explicit in a lower-level language.

Note that calling the `line.rstrip` method is often preferred for stripping newline characters because this call leaves the line intact if it has no newline character at the end—a common case for files created with some text-editing tools. Slicing works if you're sure the line is properly terminated.

String Conversion Tools

One of Python's design mottos is that it refuses the temptation to guess. As a prime example, you cannot add a number and a string together in Python, even if the string looks like a number (i.e., is all digits):

```
>>> "42" + 1
TypeError: cannot concatenate 'str' and 'int' objects
```

This is by design: because + can mean both addition and concatenation, the choice of conversion would be ambiguous. So, Python treats this as an error. In Python, magic is generally omitted if it will make your life more complex.

What to do, then, if your script obtains a number as a text string from a file or user interface? The trick is that you need to employ conversion tools before you can treat a string like a number, or vice versa. For instance:

```
>>> int("42"), str(42)        # Convert from/to string
(42, '42')
>>> repr(42)                  # Convert to as-code string
'42'
```

The int function converts a string to a number, and the `str` function converts a number to its string representation (essentially, what it looks like when printed). The `repr` function (and the older backquotes expression, removed in Python 3.0) also converts an object to its string representation, but returns the object as a string of code that can be rerun to recreate the object. For strings, the result has quotes around it if displayed with a `print` statement:

```
>>> print(str('spam'), repr('spam'))
('spam', "'spam'")
```

See the sidebar "str and repr Display Formats" on page 118 for more on this topic. Of these, int and str are the generally prescribed conversion techniques.

Now, although you can't mix strings and number types around operators such as +, you can manually convert operands before that operation if needed:

```
>>> S = "42"
>>> I = 1
>>> S + I
TypeError: cannot concatenate 'str' and 'int' objects

>>> int(S) + I              # Force addition
43
```

```
>>> S + str(I)                 # Force concatenation
'421'
```

Similar built-in functions handle floating-point number conversions to and from strings:

```
>>> str(3.1415), float("1.5")
('3.1415', 1.5)

>>> text = "1.234E-10"
>>> float(text)
1.2340000000000001e-010
```

Later, we'll further study the built-in eval function; it runs a string containing Python expression code and so can convert a string to any kind of object. The functions int and float convert only to numbers, but this restriction means they are usually faster (and more secure, because they do not accept arbitrary expression code). As we saw briefly in Chapter 5, the string formatting expression also provides a way to convert numbers to strings. We'll discuss formatting further later in this chapter.

Character code conversions

On the subject of conversions, it is also possible to convert a single character to its underlying ASCII integer code by passing it to the built-in ord function—this returns the actual binary value of the corresponding byte in memory. The chr function performs the inverse operation, taking an ASCII integer code and converting it to the corresponding character:

```
>>> ord('s')
115
>>> chr(115)
's'
```

You can use a loop to apply these functions to all characters in a string. These tools can also be used to perform a sort of string-based math. To advance to the next character, for example, convert and do the math in integer:

```
>>> S = '5'
>>> S = chr(ord(S) + 1)
>>> S
'6'
>>> S = chr(ord(S) + 1)
>>> S
'7'
```

At least for single-character strings, this provides an alternative to using the built-in int function to convert from string to integer:

```
>>> int('5')
5
>>> ord('5') - ord('0')
5
```

Such conversions can be used in conjunction with looping statements, introduced in Chapter 4 and covered in depth in the next part of this book, to convert a string of binary digits to their corresponding integer values. Each time through the loop, multiply the current value by 2 and add the next digit's integer value:

```
>>> B = '1101'                # Convert binary digits to integer with ord
>>> I = 0
>>> while B != '':
...        I = I * 2 + (ord(B[0]) - ord('0'))
...        B = B[1:]
...
>>> I
13
```

A left-shift operation (I << 1) would have the same effect as multiplying by 2 here. We'll leave this change as a suggested exercise, though, both because we haven't studied loops in detail yet and because the int and bin built-ins we met in Chapter 5 handle binary conversion tasks for us in Python 2.6 and 3.0:

```
>>> int('1101', 2)            # Convert binary to integer: built-in
13
>>> bin(13)                   # Convert integer to binary
'0b1101'
```

Given enough time, Python tends to automate most common tasks!

Changing Strings

Remember the term "immutable sequence"? The *immutable* part means that you can't change a string in-place (e.g., by assigning to an index):

```
>>> S = 'spam'
>>> S[0] = "x"
Raises an error!
```

So, how do you modify text information in Python? To change a string, you need to build and assign a new string using tools such as concatenation and slicing, and then, if desired, assign the result back to the string's original name:

```
>>> S = S + 'SPAM!'           # To change a string, make a new one
>>> S
'spamSPAM!'
>>> S = S[:4] + 'Burger' + S[-1]
>>> S
'spamBurger!'
```

The first example adds a substring at the end of S, by concatenation (really, it makes a new string and assigns it back to S, but you can think of this as "changing" the original string). The second example replaces four characters with six by slicing, indexing, and concatenating. As you'll see in the next section, you can achieve similar effects with string method calls like replace:

```
>>> S = 'splot'
>>> S = S.replace('pl', 'pamal')
>>> S
'spamalot'
```

Like every operation that yields a new string value, string methods generate new string objects. If you want to retain those objects, you can assign them to variable names. Generating a new string object for each string change is not as inefficient as it may sound—remember, as discussed in the preceding chapter, Python automatically garbage collects (reclaims the space of) old unused string objects as you go, so newer objects reuse the space held by prior values. Python is usually more efficient than you might expect.

Finally, it's also possible to build up new text values with string formatting expressions. Both of the following substitute objects into a string, in a sense converting the objects to strings and changing the original string according to a format specification:

```
>>> 'That is %d %s bird!' % (1, 'dead')        # Format expression
That is 1 dead bird!
>>> 'That is {0} {1} bird!'.format(1, 'dead')  # Format method in 2.6 and 3.0
'That is 1 dead bird!'
```

Despite the substitution metaphor, though, the result of formatting is a new string object, not a modified one. We'll study formatting later in this chapter; as we'll find, formatting turns out to be more general and useful than this example implies. Because the second of the preceding calls is provided as a method, though, let's get a handle on string method calls before we explore formatting further.

 As we'll see in Chapter 36, Python 3.0 and 2.6 introduce a new string type known as bytearray, which *is* mutable and so may be changed in place. bytearray objects aren't really strings; they're sequences of small, 8-bit integers. However, they support most of the same operations as normal strings and print as ASCII characters when displayed. As such, they provide another option for large amounts of text that must be changed frequently. In Chapter 36 we'll also see that ord and chr handle Unicode characters, too, which might not be stored in single bytes.

String Methods

In addition to expression operators, strings provide a set of *methods* that implement more sophisticated text-processing tasks. Methods are simply functions that are associated with particular objects. Technically, they are attributes attached to objects that happen to reference callable functions. In Python, expressions and built-in functions may work across a range of types, but methods are generally *specific to object types*— string methods, for example, work only on string objects. The method sets of some types intersect in Python 3.0 (e.g., many types have a count method), but they are still more type-specific than other tools.

In finer-grained detail, functions are packages of code, and method calls combine two operations at once (an attribute fetch and a call):

Attribute fetches
> An expression of the form *object.attribute* means "fetch the value of *attribute* in *object*."

Call expressions
> An expression of the form *function(arguments)* means "invoke the code of *function*, passing zero or more comma-separated *argument* objects to it, and return *function*'s result value."

Putting these two together allows us to call a method of an object. The method call expression *object.method(arguments)* is evaluated from left to right—Python will first fetch the *method* of the *object* and then call it, passing in the *arguments*. If the method computes a result, it will come back as the result of the entire method-call expression.

As you'll see throughout this part of the book, most objects have callable methods, and all are accessed using this same method-call syntax. To call an object method, as you'll see in the following sections, you have to go through an existing object.

Table 7-3 summarizes the methods and call patterns for built-in string objects in Python 3.0; these change frequently, so be sure to check Python's standard library manual for the most up-to-date list, or run a `help` call on any string interactively. Python 2.6's string methods vary slightly; it includes a `decode`, for example, because of its different handling of Unicode data (something we'll discuss in Chapter 36). In this table, `S` is a string object, and optional arguments are enclosed in square brackets. String methods in this table implement higher-level operations such as splitting and joining, case conversions, content tests, and substring searches and replacements.

Table 7-3. String method calls in Python 3.0

`S.capitalize()`	`S.ljust(width [, fill])`
`S.center(width [, fill])`	`S.lower()`
`S.count(sub [, start [, end]])`	`S.lstrip([chars])`
`S.encode([encoding [,errors]])`	`S.maketrans(x[, y[, z]])`
`S.endswith(suffix [, start [, end]])`	`S.partition(sep)`
`S.expandtabs([tabsize])`	`S.replace(old, new [, count])`
`S.find(sub [, start [, end]])`	`S.rfind(sub [,start [,end]])`
`S.format(fmtstr, *args, **kwargs)`	`S.rindex(sub [, start [, end]])`
`S.index(sub [, start [, end]])`	`S.rjust(width [, fill])`
`S.isalnum()`	`S.rpartition(sep)`
`S.isalpha()`	`S.rsplit([sep[, maxsplit]])`
`S.isdecimal()`	`S.rstrip([chars])`
`S.isdigit()`	`S.split([sep [,maxsplit]])`

```
S.isidentifier()                    S.splitlines([keepends])

S.islower()                         S.startswith(prefix [, start [, end]])

S.isnumeric()                       S.strip([chars])

S.isprintable()                     S.swapcase()

S.isspace()                         S.title()

S.istitle()                         S.translate(map)

S.isupper()                         S.upper()

S.join(iterable)                    S.zfill(width)
```

As you can see, there are quite a few string methods, and we don't have space to cover them all; see Python's library manual or reference texts for all the fine points. To help you get started, though, let's work through some code that demonstrates some of the most commonly used methods in action, and illustrates Python text-processing basics along the way.

String Method Examples: Changing Strings

As we've seen, because strings are immutable, they cannot be changed in-place directly. To make a new text value from an existing string, you construct a new string with operations such as slicing and concatenation. For example, to replace two characters in the middle of a string, you can use code like this:

```
>>> S = 'spammy'
>>> S = S[:3] + 'xx' + S[5:]
>>> S
'spaxxy'
```

But, if you're really just out to replace a substring, you can use the string `replace` method instead:

```
>>> S = 'spammy'
>>> S = S.replace('mm', 'xx')
>>> S
'spaxxy'
```

The `replace` method is more general than this code implies. It takes as arguments the original substring (of any length) and the string (of any length) to replace it with, and performs a global search and replace:

```
>>> 'aa$bb$cc$dd'.replace('$', 'SPAM')
'aaSPAMbbSPAMccSPAMdd'
```

In such a role, `replace` can be used as a tool to implement template replacements (e.g., in form letters). Notice that this time we simply printed the result, instead of assigning it to a name—you need to assign results to names only if you want to retain them for later use.

If you need to replace one fixed-size string that can occur at any offset, you can do a replacement again, or search for the substring with the string `find` method and then slice:

```
>>> S = 'xxxxSPAMxxxxSPAMxxxx'
>>> where = S.find('SPAM')          # Search for position
>>> where                            # Occurs at offset 4
4
>>> S = S[:where] + 'EGGS' + S[(where+4):]
>>> S
'xxxxEGGSxxxxSPAMxxxx'
```

The `find` method returns the offset where the substring appears (by default, searching from the front), or -1 if it is not found. As we saw earlier, it's a substring search operation just like the `in` expression, but `find` returns the position of a located substring.

Another option is to use `replace` with a third argument to limit it to a single substitution:

```
>>> S = 'xxxxSPAMxxxxSPAMxxxx'
>>> S.replace('SPAM', 'EGGS')       # Replace all
'xxxxEGGSxxxxEGGSxxxx'

>>> S.replace('SPAM', 'EGGS', 1)    # Replace one
'xxxxEGGSxxxxSPAMxxxx'
```

Notice that `replace` returns a new string object each time. Because strings are immutable, methods never really change the subject strings in-place, even if they are called "replace"!

The fact that concatenation operations and the `replace` method generate new string objects each time they are run is actually a potential downside of using them to change strings. If you have to apply many changes to a very large string, you might be able to improve your script's performance by converting the string to an object that does support in-place changes:

```
>>> S = 'spammy'
>>> L = list(S)
>>> L
['s', 'p', 'a', 'm', 'm', 'y']
```

The built-in `list` function (or an object construction call) builds a new list out of the items in any sequence—in this case, "exploding" the characters of a string into a list. Once the string is in this form, you can make multiple changes to it without generating a new copy for each change:

```
>>> L[3] = 'x'                       # Works for lists, not strings
>>> L[4] = 'x'
>>> L
['s', 'p', 'a', 'x', 'x', 'y']
```

If, after your changes, you need to convert back to a string (e.g., to write to a file), use the string `join` method to "implode" the list back into a string:

```
>>> S = ''.join(L)
>>> S
'spaxxy'
```

The `join` method may look a bit backward at first sight. Because it is a method of strings (not of lists), it is called through the desired delimiter. `join` puts the strings in a list (or other iterable) together, with the delimiter between list items; in this case, it uses an empty string delimiter to convert from a list back to a string. More generally, any string delimiter and iterable of strings will do:

```
>>> 'SPAM'.join(['eggs', 'sausage', 'ham', 'toast'])
'eggsSPAMsausageSPAMhamSPAMtoast'
```

In fact, joining substrings all at once this way often runs much faster than concatenating them individually. Be sure to also see the earlier note about the mutable `bytearray` string in Python 3.0 and 2.6, described fully in Chapter 36; because it may be changed in place, it offers an alternative to this `list`/`join` combination for some kinds of text that must be changed often.

String Method Examples: Parsing Text

Another common role for string methods is as a simple form of text *parsing*—that is, analyzing structure and extracting substrings. To extract substrings at fixed offsets, we can employ slicing techniques:

```
>>> line = 'aaa bbb ccc'
>>> col1 = line[0:3]
>>> col3 = line[8:]
>>> col1
'aaa'
>>> col3
'ccc'
```

Here, the columns of data appear at fixed offsets and so may be sliced out of the original string. This technique passes for parsing, as long as the components of your data have fixed positions. If instead some sort of delimiter separates the data, you can pull out its components by splitting. This will work even if the data may show up at arbitrary positions within the string:

```
>>> line = 'aaa bbb  ccc'
>>> cols = line.split()
>>> cols
['aaa', 'bbb', 'ccc']
```

The string `split` method chops up a string into a list of substrings, around a delimiter string. We didn't pass a delimiter in the prior example, so it defaults to whitespace—the string is split at groups of one or more spaces, tabs, and newlines, and we get back a list of the resulting substrings. In other applications, more tangible delimiters may separate the data. This example splits (and hence parses) the string at commas, a separator common in data returned by some database tools:

```
>>> line = 'bob,hacker,40'
>>> line.split(',')
['bob', 'hacker', '40']
```

Delimiters can be longer than a single character, too:

```
>>> line = "i'mSPAMaSPAMlumberjack"
>>> line.split("SPAM")
["i'm", 'a', 'lumberjack']
```

Although there are limits to the parsing potential of slicing and splitting, both run very fast and can handle basic text-extraction chores.

Other Common String Methods in Action

Other string methods have more focused roles—for example, to strip off whitespace at the end of a line of text, perform case conversions, test content, and test for a substring at the end or front:

```
>>> line = "The knights who say Ni!\n"
>>> line.rstrip()
'The knights who say Ni!'
>>> line.upper()
'THE KNIGHTS WHO SAY NI!\n'
>>> line.isalpha()
False
>>> line.endswith('Ni!\n')
True
>>> line.startswith('The')
True
```

Alternative techniques can also sometimes be used to achieve the same results as string methods—the in membership operator can be used to test for the presence of a substring, for instance, and length and slicing operations can be used to mimic endswith:

```
>>> line
'The knights who say Ni!\n'

>>> line.find('Ni') != -1          # Search via method call or expression
True
>>> 'Ni' in line
True

>>> sub = 'Ni!\n'
>>> line.endswith(sub)             # End test via method call or slice
True
>>> line[-len(sub):] == sub
True
```

See also the format string formatting method described later in this chapter; it provides more advanced substitution tools that combine many operations in a single step.

Again, because there are so many methods available for strings, we won't look at every one here. You'll see some additional string examples later in this book, but for more details you can also turn to the Python library manual and other documentation sources, or simply experiment interactively on your own. You can also check the help(S.*method*) results for a *method* of any string object S for more hints.

Note that none of the string methods accepts *patterns*—for pattern-based text processing, you must use the Python re standard library module, an advanced tool that was introduced in Chapter 4 but is mostly outside the scope of this text (one further example appears at the end of Chapter 36). Because of this limitation, though, string methods may sometimes run more quickly than the re module's tools.

The Original string Module (Gone in 3.0)

The history of Python's string methods is somewhat convoluted. For roughly the first decade of its existence, Python provided a standard library module called string that contained functions that largely mirrored the current set of string object methods. In response to user requests, in Python 2.0 these functions were made available as methods of string objects. Because so many people had written so much code that relied on the original string module, however, it was retained for backward compatibility.

Today, you should use *only string methods*, not the original string module. In fact, the original module-call forms of today's string methods have been removed completely from Python in Release 3.0. However, because you may still see the module in use in older Python code, a brief look is in order here.

The upshot of this legacy is that in Python 2.6, there technically are still two ways to invoke advanced string operations: by calling object methods, or by calling string module functions and passing in the objects as arguments. For instance, given a variable X assigned to a string object, calling an object method:

    X.*method*(*arguments*)

is usually equivalent to calling the same operation through the string module (provided that you have already imported the module):

    string.*method*(X, *arguments*)

Here's an example of the method scheme in action:

```
>>> S = 'a+b+c+'
>>> x = S.replace('+', 'spam')
>>> x
'aspambspamcspam'
```

To access the same operation through the string module in Python 2.6, you need to import the module (at least once in your process) and pass in the object:

```
>>> import string
>>> y = string.replace(S, '+', 'spam')
>>> y
'aspambspamcspam'
```

Because the module approach was the standard for so long, and because strings are such a central component of most programs, you might see both call patterns in Python 2.X code you come across.

Again, though, today you should always use method calls instead of the older module calls. There are good reasons for this, besides the fact that the module calls have gone away in Release 3.0. For one thing, the module call scheme requires you to import the `string` module (methods do not require imports). For another, the module makes calls a few characters longer to type (when you load the module with `import`, that is, not using `from`). And, finally, the module runs more slowly than methods (the module maps most calls back to the methods and so incurs an extra call along the way).

The original `string` module itself, without its string method equivalents, is retained in Python 3.0 because it contains additional tools, including predefined string constants and a template object system (a relatively obscure tool omitted here—see the Python library manual for details on template objects). Unless you really want to have to change your 2.6 code to use 3.0, though, you should consider the basic string operation calls in it to be just ghosts from the past.

String Formatting Expressions

Although you can get a lot done with the string methods and sequence operations we've already met, Python also provides a more advanced way to combine string processing tasks—*string formatting* allows us to perform multiple type-specific substitutions on a string in a single step. It's never strictly required, but it can be convenient, especially when formatting text to be displayed to a program's users. Due to the wealth of new ideas in the Python world, string formatting is available in two flavors in Python today:

String formatting expressions
> The original technique, available since Python's inception; this is based upon the C language's "printf" model and is used in much existing code.

String formatting method calls
> A newer technique added in Python 2.6 and 3.0; this is more unique to Python and largely overlaps with string formatting expression functionality.

Since the method call flavor is new, there is some chance that one or the other of these may become deprecated over time. The expressions are more likely to be deprecated in later Python releases, though this should depend on the future practice of real Python programmers. As they are largely just variations on a theme, though, either technique is valid to use today. Since string formatting expressions are the original in this department, let's start with them.

Python defines the `%` binary operator to work on strings (you may recall that this is also the remainder of division, or modulus, operator for numbers). When applied to strings, the `%` operator provides a simple way to format values as strings according to a format definition. In short, the % operator provides a compact way to code multiple string substitutions all at once, instead of building and concatenating parts individually.

To format strings:

1. On the left of the % operator, provide a format string containing one or more embedded conversion targets, each of which starts with a % (e.g., %d).

2. On the right of the % operator, provide the object (or objects, embedded in a tuple) that you want Python to insert into the format string on the left in place of the conversion target (or targets).

For instance, in the formatting example we saw earlier in this chapter, the integer 1 replaces the %d in the format string on the left, and the string 'dead' replaces the %s. The result is a new string that reflects these two substitutions:

```
>>> 'That is %d %s bird!' % (1, 'dead')          # Format expression
That is 1 dead bird!
```

Technically speaking, string formatting expressions are usually optional—you can generally do similar work with multiple concatenations and conversions. However, formatting allows us to combine many steps into a single operation. It's powerful enough to warrant a few more examples:

```
>>> exclamation = "Ni"
>>> "The knights who say %s!" % exclamation
'The knights who say Ni!'

>>> "%d %s %d you" % (1, 'spam', 4)
'1 spam 4 you'

>>> "%s -- %s -- %s" % (42, 3.14159, [1, 2, 3])
'42 -- 3.14159 -- [1, 2, 3]'
```

The first example here plugs the string "Ni" into the target on the left, replacing the %s marker. In the second example, three values are inserted into the target string. Note that when you're inserting more than one value, you need to group the values on the right in parentheses (i.e., put them in a tuple). The % formatting expression operator expects either a single item or a tuple of one or more items on its right side.

The third example again inserts three values—an integer, a floating-point object, and a list object—but notice that all of the targets on the left are %s, which stands for conversion to string. As every type of object can be converted to a string (the one used when printing), every object type works with the %s conversion code. Because of this, unless you will be doing some special formatting, %s is often the only code you need to remember for the formatting expression.

Again, keep in mind that formatting always makes a new string, rather than changing the string on the left; because strings are immutable, it must work this way. As before, assign the result to a variable name if you need to retain it.

Advanced String Formatting Expressions

For more advanced type-specific formatting, you can use any of the conversion type codes listed in Table 7-4 in formatting expressions; they appear after the % character in substitution targets. C programmers will recognize most of these because Python string formatting supports all the usual C `printf` format codes (but returns the result, instead of displaying it, like `printf`). Some of the format codes in the table provide alternative ways to format the same type; for instance, %e, %f, and %g provide alternative ways to format floating-point numbers.

Table 7-4. String formatting type codes

Code	Meaning
s	String (or any object's `str(X)` string)
r	s, but uses `repr`, not `str`
c	Character
d	Decimal (integer)
i	Integer
u	Same as d (obsolete: no longer unsigned)
o	Octal integer
x	Hex integer
X	x, but prints uppercase
e	Floating-point exponent, lowercase
E	Same as e, but prints uppercase
f	Floating-point decimal
F	Floating-point decimal
g	Floating-point e or f
G	Floating-point E or F
%	Literal %

In fact, conversion targets in the format string on the expression's left side support a variety of conversion operations with a fairly sophisticated syntax all their own. The general structure of conversion targets looks like this:

```
%[(name)][flags][width][.precision]typecode
```

The character type codes in Table 7-4 show up at the end of the target string. Between the % and the character code, you can do any of the following: provide a dictionary key; list flags that specify things like left justification (-), numeric sign (+), and zero fills (0); give a total minimum field width and the number of digits after a decimal point; and more. Both *width* and *precision* can also be coded as a * to specify that they should take their values from the next item in the input values.

Formatting target syntax is documented in full in the Python standard manuals, but to demonstrate common usage, let's look at a few examples. This one formats integers by default, and then in a six-character field with left justification and zero padding:

```
>>> x = 1234
>>> res = "integers: ...%d...%-6d...%06d" % (x, x, x)
>>> res
'integers: ...1234...1234  ...001234'
```

The %e, %f, and %g formats display floating-point numbers in different ways, as the following interaction demonstrates (%E is the same as %e but the exponent is uppercase):

```
>>> x = 1.23456789
>>> x
1.2345678899999999

>>> '%e | %f | %g' % (x, x, x)
'1.234568e+00 | 1.234568 | 1.23457'

>>> '%E' % x
'1.234568E+00'
```

For floating-point numbers, you can achieve a variety of additional formatting effects by specifying left justification, zero padding, numeric signs, field width, and digits after the decimal point. For simpler tasks, you might get by with simply converting to strings with a format expression or the str built-in function shown earlier:

```
>>> '%-6.2f | %05.2f | %+06.1f' % (x, x, x)
'1.23   | 01.23 | +001.2'

>>> "%s" % x, str(x)
('1.23456789', '1.23456789')
```

When sizes are not known until runtime, you can have the width and precision computed by specifying them with a * in the format string to force their values to be taken from the next item in the inputs to the right of the % operator—the 4 in the tuple here gives precision:

```
>>> '%f, %.2f, %.*f' % (1/3.0, 1/3.0, 4, 1/3.0)
'0.333333, 0.33, 0.3333'
```

If you're interested in this feature, experiment with some of these examples and operations on your own for more information.

Dictionary-Based String Formatting Expressions

String formatting also allows conversion targets on the left to refer to the keys in a dictionary on the right and fetch the corresponding values. I haven't told you much about dictionaries yet, so here's an example that demonstrates the basics:

```
>>> "%(n)d %(x)s" % {"n":1, "x":"spam"}
'1 spam'
```

Here, the (n) and (x) in the format string refer to keys in the dictionary literal on the right and fetch their associated values. Programs that generate text such as HTML or XML often use this technique—you can build up a dictionary of values and substitute them all at once with a single formatting expression that uses key-based references:

```
>>> reply = """                        # Template with substitution targets
Greetings...
Hello %(name)s!
Your age squared is %(age)s
"""
>>> values = {'name': 'Bob', 'age': 40}   # Build up values to substitute
>>> print(reply % values)                 # Perform substitutions

Greetings...
Hello Bob!
Your age squared is 40
```

This trick is also used in conjunction with the `vars` built-in function, which returns a dictionary containing all the variables that exist in the place it is called:

```
>>> food = 'spam'
>>> age = 40
>>> vars()
{'food': 'spam', 'age': 40, ...many more... }
```

When used on the right of a format operation, this allows the format string to refer to variables by name (i.e., by dictionary key):

```
>>> "%(age)d %(food)s" % vars()
'40 spam'
```

We'll study dictionaries in more depth in Chapter 8. See also Chapter 5 for examples that convert to hexadecimal and octal number strings with the `%x` and `%o` formatting target codes.

String Formatting Method Calls

As mentioned earlier, Python 2.6 and 3.0 introduced a new way to format strings that is seen by some as a bit more Python-specific. Unlike formatting expressions, formatting method calls are not closely based upon the C language's "printf" model, and they are more verbose and explicit in intent. On the other hand, the new technique still relies on some "printf" concepts, such as type codes and formatting specifications. Moreover, it largely overlaps with (and sometimes requires a bit more code than) formatting expressions, and it can be just as complex in advanced roles. Because of this, there is no best-use recommendation between expressions and method calls today, so most programmers would be well served by a cursory understanding of both schemes.

The Basics

In short, the new string object's `format` method in 2.6 and 3.0 (and later) uses the subject string as a template and takes any number of arguments that represent values to be substituted according to the template. Within the subject string, curly braces designate substitution targets and arguments to be inserted either by position (e.g., `{1}`) or keyword (e.g., `{food}`). As we'll learn when we study argument passing in depth in Chapter 18, arguments to functions and methods may be passed by position or keyword name, and Python's ability to collect arbitrarily many positional and keyword arguments allows for such general method call patterns. In Python 2.6 and 3.0, for example:

```
>>> template = '{0}, {1} and {2}'                          # By position
>>> template.format('spam', 'ham', 'eggs')
'spam, ham and eggs'

>>> template = '{motto}, {pork} and {food}'                # By keyword
>>> template.format(motto='spam', pork='ham', food='eggs')
'spam, ham and eggs'

>>> template = '{motto}, {0} and {food}'                   # By both
>>> template.format('ham', motto='spam', food='eggs')
'spam, ham and eggs'
```

Naturally, the string can also be a literal that creates a temporary string, and arbitrary object types can be substituted:

```
>>> '{motto}, {0} and {food}'.format(42, motto=3.14, food=[1, 2])
'3.14, 42 and [1, 2]'
```

Just as with the `%` expression and other string methods, `format` creates and returns a new string object, which can be printed immediately or saved for further work (recall that strings are immutable, so `format` really *must* make a new object). String formatting is not just for display:

```
>>> X = '{motto}, {0} and {food}'.format(42, motto=3.14, food=[1, 2])
>>> X
'3.14, 42 and [1, 2]'

>>> X.split(' and ')
['3.14, 42', '[1, 2]']

>>> Y = X.replace('and', 'but under no circumstances')
>>> Y
'3.14, 42 but under no circumstances [1, 2]'
```

Adding Keys, Attributes, and Offsets

Like % formatting expressions, format calls can become more complex to support more advanced usage. For instance, format strings can name object attributes and dictionary keys—as in normal Python syntax, square brackets name dictionary keys and dots denote object attributes of an item referenced by position or keyword. The first of the following examples indexes a dictionary on the key "spam" and then fetches the attribute "platform" from the already imported sys module object. The second does the same, but names the objects by keyword instead of position:

```
>>> import sys

>>> 'My {1[spam]} runs {0.platform}'.format(sys, {'spam': 'laptop'})
'My laptop runs win32'

>>> 'My {config[spam]} runs {sys.platform}'.format(sys=sys,
                                      config={'spam': 'laptop'})
'My laptop runs win32'
```

Square brackets in format strings can name list (and other sequence) offsets to perform indexing, too, but only single positive offsets work syntactically within format strings, so this feature is not as general as you might think. As with % expressions, to name negative offsets or slices, or to use arbitrary expression results in general, you must run expressions outside the format string itself (note the use of *parts here to unpack a tuple's items into individual arguments, as we did on Page 132 when studying fractions; more on this in Chapter 18):

```
>>> somelist = list('SPAM')
>>> somelist
['S', 'P', 'A', 'M']

>>> 'first={0[0]}, third={0[2]}'.format(somelist)
'first=S, third=A'

>>> 'first={0}, last={1}'.format(somelist[0], somelist[-1])   # [-1] fails in fmt
'first=S, last=M'

>>> parts = somelist[0], somelist[-1], somelist[1:3]          # [1:3] fails in fmt
>>> 'first={0}, last={1}, middle={2}'.format(*parts)
"first=S, last=M, middle=['P', 'A']"
```

Adding Specific Formatting

Another similarity with % expressions is that more specific layouts can be achieved by adding extra syntax in the format string. For the formatting method, we use a colon after the substitution target's identification, followed by a format specifier that can name the field size, justification, and a specific type code. Here's the formal structure of what can appear as a substitution target in a format string:

```
{fieldname!conversionflag:formatspec}
```

In this substitution target syntax:

- *fieldname* is a number or keyword naming an argument, followed by optional ".name" attribute or "[index]" component references.
- *conversionflag* can be r, s, or a to call repr, str, or ascii built-in functions on the value, respectively.

- *formatspec* specifies how the value should be presented, including details such as field width, alignment, padding, decimal precision, and so on, and ends with an optional data type code.

The *formatspec* component after the colon character is formally described as follows (brackets denote optional components and are not coded literally):

```
[[fill]align][sign][#][0][width][.precision][typecode]
```

align may be <, >, =, or ^, for left alignment, right alignment, padding after a sign character, or centered alignment, respectively. The *formatspec* also contains nested {} format strings with field names only, to take values from the arguments list dynamically (much like the * in formatting expressions).

See Python's library manual for more on substitution syntax and a list of the available type codes—they almost completely overlap with those used in % expressions and listed previously in Table 7-4, but the format method also allows a "b" type code used to display integers in binary format (it's equivalent to using the bin built-in call), allows a "%" type code to display percentages, and uses only "d" for base-10 integers (not "i" or "u").

As an example, in the following {0:10} means the first positional argument in a field 10 characters wide, {1:<10} means the second positional argument left-justified in a 10-character-wide field, and {0.platform:>10} means the platform attribute of the first argument right-justified in a 10-character-wide field (note the use of dict() to make a dictionary from keyword arguments, introduced in Chapter 4 and covered in Chapter 8):

```
>>> '{0:10} = {1:10}'.format('spam', 123.4567)
'spam       =    123.457'

>>> '{0:>10} = {1:<10}'.format('spam', 123.4567)
'      spam = 123.457   '

>>> '{0.platform:>10} = {1[item]:<10}'.format(sys, dict(item='laptop'))
'     win32 = laptop    '
```

Floating-point numbers support the same type codes and formatting specificity in formatting method calls as in % expressions. For instance, in the following {2:g} means the third argument formatted by default according to the "g" floating-point representation, {1:.2f} designates the "f" floating-point format with just 2 decimal digits, and {2:06.2f} adds a field with a width of 6 characters and zero padding on the left:

```
>>> '{0:e}, {1:.3e}, {2:g}'.format(3.14159, 3.14159, 3.14159)
'3.141590e+00, 3.142e+00, 3.14159'

>>> '{0:f}, {1:.2f}, {2:06.2f}'.format(3.14159, 3.14159, 3.14159)
'3.141590, 3.14, 003.14'
```

Hex, octal, and binary formats are supported by the `format` method as well. In fact, string formatting is an alternative to some of the built-in functions that format integers to a given base:

```
>>> '{0:X}, {1:o}, {2:b}'.format(255, 255, 255)     # Hex, octal, binary
'FF, 377, 11111111'

>>> bin(255), int('11111111', 2), 0b11111111        # Other to/from binary
('0b11111111', 255, 255)

>>> hex(255), int('FF', 16), 0xFF                    # Other to/from hex
('0xff', 255, 255)

>>> oct(255), int('377', 8), 0o377, 0377            # Other to/from octal
('0377', 255, 255, 255)                             # 0377 works in 2.6, not 3.0!
```

Formatting parameters can either be hardcoded in format strings or taken from the arguments list dynamically by nested format syntax, much like the star syntax in formatting expressions:

```
>>> '{0:.2f}'.format(1 / 3.0)                       # Parameters hardcoded
'0.33'
>>> '%.2f' % (1 / 3.0)
'0.33'

>>> '{0:.{1}f}'.format(1 / 3.0, 4)                  # Take value from arguments
'0.3333'
>>> '%.*f' % (4, 1 / 3.0)                           # Ditto for expression
'0.3333'
```

Finally, Python 2.6 and 3.0 also provide a new built-in `format` function, which can be used to format a single item. It's a more concise alternative to the string `format` method, and is roughly similar to formatting a single item with the % formatting expression:

```
>>> '{0:.2f}'.format(1.2345)                        # String method
'1.23'
>>> format(1.2345, '.2f')                           # Built-in function
'1.23'
>>> '%.2f' % 1.2345                                 # Expression
'1.23'
```

Technically, the `format` built-in runs the subject object's `__format__` method, which the `str.format` method does internally for each formatted item. It's still more verbose than the original % expression's equivalent, though—which leads us to the next section.

Comparison to the % Formatting Expression

If you study the prior sections closely, you'll probably notice that at least for positional references and dictionary keys, the string `format` method looks very much like the % formatting expression, especially in advanced use with type codes and extra formatting syntax. In fact, in common use cases formatting expressions may be easier to code than formatting method calls, especially when using the generic %s print-string substitution target:

```
print('%s=%s' % ('spam', 42))          # 2.X+ format expression

print('{0}={1}'.format('spam', 42))     # 3.0 (and 2.6) format method
```

As we'll see in a moment, though, more complex formatting tends to be a draw in terms of complexity (difficult tasks are generally difficult, regardless of approach), and some see the formatting method as largely redundant.

On the other hand, the formatting method also offers a few potential advantages. For example, the original % expression can't handle keywords, attribute references, and binary type codes, although dictionary key references in % format strings can often achieve similar goals. To see how the two techniques overlap, compare the following % expressions to the equivalent format method calls shown earlier:

```
# The basics: with % instead of format()

>>> template = '%s, %s, %s'
>>> template % ('spam', 'ham', 'eggs')                    # By position
    'spam, ham, eggs'

>>> template = '%(motto)s, %(pork)s and %(food)s'
>>> template % dict(motto='spam', pork='ham', food='eggs')   # By key
'spam, ham and eggs'

>>> '%s, %s and %s' % (3.14, 42, [1, 2])                   # Arbitrary types
'3.14, 42 and [1, 2]'


# Adding keys, attributes, and offsets

>>> 'My %(spam)s runs %(platform)s' % {'spam': 'laptop', 'platform': sys.platform}
'My laptop runs win32'

>>> 'My %(spam)s runs %(platform)s' % dict(spam='laptop', platform=sys.platform)
'My laptop runs win32'

>>> somelist = list('SPAM')
>>> parts = somelist[0], somelist[-1], somelist[1:3]
>>> 'first=%s, last=%s, middle=%s' % parts
"first=S, last=M, middle=['P', 'A']"
```

When more complex formatting is applied the two techniques approach parity in terms of complexity, although if you compare the following with the format method call equivalents listed earlier you'll again find that the % expressions tend to be a bit simpler and more concise:

```
# Adding specific formatting

>>> '%-10s = %10s' % ('spam', 123.4567)
'spam       =    123.4567'
```

```
>>> '%10s = %-10s' % ('spam', 123.4567)
'      spam = 123.4567  '

>>> '%(plat)10s = %(item)-10s' % dict(plat=sys.platform, item='laptop')
'     win32 = laptop    '
```

```
# Floating-point numbers
```

```
>>> '%e, %.3e, %g' % (3.14159, 3.14159, 3.14159)
'3.141590e+00, 3.142e+00, 3.14159'

>>> '%f, %.2f, %06.2f' % (3.14159, 3.14159, 3.14159)
'3.141590, 3.14, 003.14'
```

```
# Hex and octal, but not binary
```

```
>>> '%x, %o' % (255, 255)
'ff, 377'
```

The format method has a handful of advanced features that the % expression does not, but even more involved formatting still seems to be essentially a draw in terms of complexity. For instance, the following shows the same result generated with both techniques, with field sizes and justifications and various argument reference methods:

```
# Hardcoded references in both
```

```
>>> import sys
```

```
>>> 'My {1[spam]:<8} runs {0.platform:>8}'.format(sys, {'spam': 'laptop'})
'My laptop   runs    win32'
```

```
>>> 'My %(spam)-8s runs %(plat)8s' % dict(spam='laptop', plat=sys.platform)
'My laptop   runs    win32'
```

In practice, programs are less likely to hardcode references like this than to execute code that builds up a set of substitution data ahead of time (to collect data to substitute into an HTML template all at once, for instance). When we account for common practice in examples like this, the comparison between the format method and the % expression is even more direct (as we'll see in Chapter 18, the **data in the method call here is special syntax that unpacks a dictionary of keys and values into individual "name=value" keyword arguments so they can be referenced by name in the format string):

```
# Building data ahead of time in both
```

```
>>> data = dict(platform=sys.platform, spam='laptop')
```

```
>>> 'My {spam:<8} runs {platform:>8}'.format(**data)
'My laptop   runs    win32'
```

```
>>> 'My %(spam)-8s runs %(platform)8s' % data
'My laptop   runs    win32'
```

As usual, the Python community will have to decide whether % expressions, `format` method calls, or a toolset with both techniques proves better over time. Experiment with these techniques on your own to get a feel for what they offer, and be sure to see the Python 2.6 and 3.0 library manuals for more details.

String format method enhancements in Python 3.1: The upcoming 3.1 release (in alpha form as this chapter was being written) will add a thousand-separator syntax for numbers, which inserts commas between three-digit groups. Add a comma before the type code to make this work, as follows:

```
>>> '{0:d}'.format(999999999999)
'999999999999'

>>> '{0:,d}'.format(999999999999)
'999,999,999,999'
```

Python 3.1 also assigns relative numbers to substitution targets automatically if they are not included explicitly, though using this extension may negate one of the main benefits of the formatting method, as the next section describes:

```
>>> '{:,d}'.format(999999999999)
'999,999,999,999'

>>> '{:,d} {:,d}'.format(9999999, 8888888)
'9,999,999 8,888,888'

>>> '{:,.2f}'.format(296999.2567)
'296,999.26'
```

This book doesn't cover 3.1 officially, so you should take this as a preview. Python 3.1 will also address a major performance issue in 3.0 related to the speed of file input/output operations, which made 3.0 impractical for many types of programs. See the 3.1 release notes for more details. See also the *formats.py* comma-insertion and money-formatting function examples in Chapter 24 for a manual solution that can be imported and used prior to Python 3.1.

Why the New Format Method?

Now that I've gone to such lengths to compare and contrast the two formatting techniques, I need to explain why you might want to consider using the `format` method variant at times. In short, although the formatting method can sometimes require more code, it also:

- Has a few extra features not found in the % expression
- Can make substitution value references more explicit
- Trades an operator for an arguably more mnemonic method name
- Does not support different syntax for single and multiple substitution value cases

Although both techniques are available today and the formatting expression is still widely used, the `format` method might eventually subsume it. But because the choice is currently still yours to make, let's briefly expand on some of the differences before moving on.

Extra features

The method call supports a few extras that the expression does not, such as binary type codes and (coming in Python 3.1) thousands groupings. In addition, the method call supports key and attribute references directly. As we've seen, though, the formatting expression can usually achieve the same effects in other ways:

```
>>> '{0:b}'.format((2 ** 16) -1)
'1111111111111111'

>>> '%b' % ((2 ** 16) -1)
ValueError: unsupported format character 'b' (0x62) at index 1

>>> bin((2 ** 16) -1)
'0b1111111111111111'

>>> '%s' % bin((2 ** 16) -1)[2:]
'1111111111111111'
```

See also the prior examples that compare dictionary-based formatting in the % expression to key and attribute references in the `format` method; especially in common practice, the two seem largely variations on a theme.

Explicit value references

One use case where the `format` method is at least debatably clearer is when there are many values to be substituted into the format string. The *lister.py* classes example we'll meet in Chapter 30, for example, substitutes six items into a single string, and in this case the method's `{i}` position labels seem easier to read than the expression's `%s`:

```
'\n%s<Class %s, address %s:\n%s%s%s>\n' % (...)          # Expression

'\n{0}<Class {1}, address {2}:\n{3}{4}{5}>\n'.format(...)   # Method
```

On the other hand, using dictionary keys in % expressions can mitigate much of this difference. This is also something of a worst-case scenario for formatting complexity, and not very common in practice; more typical use cases seem largely a tossup. Moreover, in Python 3.1 (still in alpha release form as I write these words), numbering substitution values will become optional, thereby subverting this purported benefit altogether:

```
C:\misc> C:\Python31\python
>>> 'The {0} side {1} {2}'.format('bright', 'of', 'life')
'The bright side of life'
>>>
>>> 'The {} side {} {}'.format('bright', 'of', 'life')      # Python 3.1+
'The bright side of life'
```

```
>>>
>>> 'The %s side %s %s' % ('bright', 'of', 'life')
'The bright side of life'
```

Using 3.1's automatic relative numbering like this seems to negate a large part of the method's advantage. Compare the effect on floating-point formatting, for example—the formatting expression is still more concise, and still seems less cluttered:

```
C:\misc> C:\Python31\python
>>> '{0:f}, {1:.2f}, {2:05.2f}'.format(3.14159, 3.14159, 3.14159)
'3.141590, 3.14, 03.14'
>>>
>>> '{:f}, {:.2f}, {:06.2f}'.format(3.14159, 3.14159, 3.14159)
'3.141590, 3.14, 003.14'
>>>
>>> '%f, %.2f, %06.2f' % (3.14159, 3.14159, 3.14159)
'3.141590, 3.14, 003.14'
```

Method names and general arguments

Given this 3.1 auto-numbering change, the only clearly remaining potential advantages of the formatting method are that it replaces the % operator with a more mnemonic `format` method name and does not distinguish between single and multiple substitution values. The former may make the method appear simpler to beginners at first glance ("format" may be easier to parse than multiple "%" characters), though this is too subjective to call.

The latter difference might be more significant—with the format expression, a single value can be given by itself, but multiple values must be enclosed in a tuple:

```
>>> '%.2f' % 1.2345
'1.23'
>>> '%.2f %s' % (1.2345, 99)
'1.23 99'
```

Technically, the formatting expression accepts either a single substitution value, or a tuple of one or more items. In fact, because a single item can be given *either* by itself or within a tuple, a tuple to be formatted must be provided as nested tuples:

```
>>> '%s' % 1.23
'1.23'
>>> '%s' % (1.23,)
'1.23'
>>> '%s' % ((1.23,),)
'(1.23,)'
```

The formatting method, on the other hand, tightens this up by accepting general function arguments in both cases:

```
>>> '{0:.2f}'.format(1.2345)
'1.23'
>>> '{0:.2f} {1}'.format(1.2345, 99)
'1.23 99'
```

```
>>> '{0}'.format(1.23)
'1.23'
>>> '{0}'.format((1.23,))
'(1.23,)'
```

Consequently, it might be less confusing to beginners and cause fewer programming mistakes. This is still a fairly minor issue, though—if you always enclose values in a tuple and ignore the nontupled option, the expression is essentially the same as the method call here. Moreover, the method incurs an extra price in inflated code size to achieve its limited flexibility. Given that the expression has been used extensively throughout Python's history, it's not clear that this point justifies breaking existing code for a new tool that is so similar, as the next section argues.

Possible future deprecation?

As mentioned earlier, there is some risk that Python developers may deprecate the % expression in favor of the `format` method in the future. In fact, there is a note to this effect in Python 3.0's manuals.

This has not yet occurred, of course, and both formatting techniques are fully available and reasonable to use in Python 2.6 and 3.0 (the versions of Python this book covers). Both techniques are supported in the upcoming Python 3.1 release as well, so deprecation of either seems unlikely for the foreseeable future. Moreover, because formatting expressions are used extensively in almost all existing Python code written to date, most programmers will benefit from being familiar with both techniques for many years to come.

If this deprecation ever does occur, though, you may need to recode all your % expressions as `format` methods, and translate those that appear in this book, in order to use a newer Python release. At the risk of editorializing here, I hope that such a change will be based upon the future common practice of actual Python programmers, not the whims of a handful of core developers—particularly given that the window for Python 3.0's many incompatible changes is now closed. Frankly, this deprecation would seem like trading one complicated thing for another complicated thing—one that is largely equivalent to the tool it would replace! If you care about migrating to future Python releases, though, be sure to watch for developments on this front over time.

General Type Categories

Now that we've explored the first of Python's collection objects, the string, let's pause to define a few general type concepts that will apply to most of the types we look at from here on. With regard to built-in types, it turns out that operations work the same for all the types in the same category, so we'll only need to define most of these ideas once. We've only examined numbers and strings so far, but because they are representative of two of the three major type categories in Python, you already know more about several other types than you might think.

Types Share Operation Sets by Categories

As you've learned, strings are immutable sequences: they cannot be changed in-place (the *immutable* part), and they are positionally ordered collections that are accessed by offset (the *sequence* part). Now, it so happens that all the sequences we'll study in this part of the book respond to the same sequence operations shown in this chapter at work on strings—concatenation, indexing, iteration, and so on. More formally, there are three major type (and operation) categories in Python:

Numbers (integer, floating-point, decimal, fraction, others)
> Support addition, multiplication, etc.

Sequences (strings, lists, tuples)
> Support indexing, slicing, concatenation, etc.

Mappings (dictionaries)
> Support indexing by key, etc.

Sets are something of a category unto themselves (they don't map keys to values and are not positionally ordered sequences), and we haven't yet explored mappings on our in-depth tour (dictionaries are discussed in the next chapter). However, many of the other types we will encounter will be similar to numbers and strings. For example, for any sequence objects X and Y:

- X + Y makes a new sequence object with the contents of both operands.
- X * N makes a new sequence object with N copies of the sequence operand X.

In other words, these operations work the same way on any kind of sequence, including strings, lists, tuples, and some user-defined object types. The only difference is that the new result object you get back is of the same type as the operands X and Y—if you concatenate lists, you get back a new list, not a string. Indexing, slicing, and other sequence operations work the same on all sequences, too; the type of the objects being processed tells Python which flavor of the task to perform.

Mutable Types Can Be Changed In-Place

The immutable classification is an important constraint to be aware of, yet it tends to trip up new users. If an object type is immutable, you cannot change its value in-place; Python raises an error if you try. Instead, you must run code to make a new object containing the new value. The major core types in Python break down as follows:

Immutables (numbers, strings, tuples, frozensets)
> None of the object types in the immutable category support in-place changes, though we can always run expressions to make new objects and assign their results to variables as needed.

Mutables (lists, dictionaries, sets, bytearray)

> Conversely, the mutable types can always be changed in-place with operations that do not create new objects. Although such objects can be copied, in-place changes support direct modification.

Generally, immutable types give some degree of integrity by guaranteeing that an object won't be changed by another part of a program. For a refresher on why this matters, see the discussion of shared object references in Chapter 6. To see how lists, dictionaries, and tuples participate in type categories, we need to move ahead to the next chapter.

Chapter Summary

In this chapter, we took an in-depth tour of the string object type. We learned about coding string literals, and we explored string operations, including sequence expressions, string method calls, and string formatting with both expressions and method calls. Along the way, we studied a variety of concepts in depth, such as slicing, method call syntax, and triple-quoted block strings. We also defined some core ideas common to a variety of types: sequences, for example, share an entire set of operations.

In the next chapter, we'll continue our types tour with a look at the most general object collections in Python—lists and dictionaries. As you'll find, much of what you've learned here will apply to those types as well. And as mentioned earlier, in the final part of this book we'll return to Python's string model to flesh out the details of Unicode text and binary data, which are of interest to some, but not all, Python programmers. Before moving on, though, here's another chapter quiz to review the material covered here.

Test Your Knowledge: Quiz

1. Can the string `find` method be used to search a list?
2. Can a string slice expression be used on a list?
3. How would you convert a character to its ASCII integer code? How would you convert the other way, from an integer to a character?
4. How might you go about changing a string in Python?
5. Given a string S with the value `"s,pa,m"`, name two ways to extract the two characters in the middle.
6. How many characters are there in the string `"a\nb\x1f\000d"`?
7. Why might you use the `string` module instead of string method calls?

Test Your Knowledge: Answers

1. No, because methods are always type-specific; that is, they only work on a single data type. Expressions like X+Y and built-in functions like len(X) are generic, though, and may work on a variety of types. In this case, for instance, the in membership expression has a similar effect as the string find, but it can be used to search both strings and lists. In Python 3.0, there is some attempt to group methods by categories (for example, the mutable sequence types list and bytearray have similar method sets), but methods are still more type-specific than other operation sets.

2. Yes. Unlike methods, expressions are generic and apply to many types. In this case, the slice expression is really a sequence operation—it works on any type of sequence object, including strings, lists, and tuples. The only difference is that when you slice a list, you get back a new list.

3. The built-in ord(S) function converts from a one-character string to an integer character code; chr(I) converts from the integer code back to a string.

4. Strings cannot be changed; they are immutable. However, you can achieve a similar effect by creating a new string—by concatenating, slicing, running formatting expressions, or using a method call like replace—and then assigning the result back to the original variable name.

5. You can slice the string using S[2:4], or split on the comma and index the string using S.split(',')[1]. Try these interactively to see for yourself.

6. Six. The string "a\nb\x1f\000d" contains the bytes a, newline (\n), b, binary 31 (a hex escape \x1f), binary 0 (an octal escape \000), and d. Pass the string to the built-in len function to verify this, and print each of its character's ord results to see the actual byte values. See Table 7-2 for more details.

7. You should never use the string module instead of string object method calls today—it's deprecated, and its calls are removed completely in Python 3.0. The only reason for using the string module at all is for its other tools, such as predefined constants. You might also see it appear in what is now very old and dusty Python code.

## CHAPTER 8

Lists and Dictionaries

This chapter presents the list and dictionary object types, both of which are collections of other objects. These two types are the main workhorses in almost all Python scripts. As you'll see, both types are remarkably flexible: they can be changed in-place, can grow and shrink on demand, and may contain and be nested in any other kind of object. By leveraging these types, you can build up and process arbitrarily rich information structures in your scripts.

Lists

The next stop on our built-in object tour is the Python *list*. Lists are Python's most flexible ordered collection object type. Unlike strings, lists can contain any sort of object: numbers, strings, and even other lists. Also, unlike strings, lists may be changed in-place by assignment to offsets and slices, list method calls, deletion statements, and more—they are *mutable* objects.

Python lists do the work of most of the collection data structures you might have to implement manually in lower-level languages such as C. Here is a quick look at their main properties. Python lists are:

Ordered collections of arbitrary objects

From a functional view, lists are just places to collect other objects so you can treat them as groups. Lists also maintain a left-to-right positional ordering among the items they contain (i.e., they are sequences).

Accessed by offset

Just as with strings, you can fetch a component object out of a list by indexing the list on the object's offset. Because items in lists are ordered by their positions, you can also do tasks such as slicing and concatenation.

Variable-length, heterogeneous, and arbitrarily nestable

Unlike strings, lists can grow and shrink in-place (their lengths can vary), and they can contain any sort of object, not just one-character strings (they're heterogeneous). Because lists can contain other complex objects, they also support arbitrary nesting; you can create lists of lists of lists, and so on.

Of the category "mutable sequence"

In terms of our type category qualifiers, lists are mutable (i.e., can be changed in-place) and can respond to all the sequence operations used with strings, such as indexing, slicing, and concatenation. In fact, sequence operations work the same on lists as they do on strings; the only difference is that sequence operations such as concatenation and slicing return new lists instead of new strings when applied to lists. Because lists are mutable, however, they also support other operations that strings don't (such as deletion and index assignment operations, which change the lists in-place).

Arrays of object references

Technically, Python lists contain zero or more references to other objects. Lists might remind you of arrays of pointers (addresses) if you have a background in some other languages. Fetching an item from a Python list is about as fast as indexing a C array; in fact, lists really are arrays inside the standard Python interpreter, not linked structures. As we learned in Chapter 6, though, Python always follows a reference to an object whenever the reference is used, so your program deals only with objects. Whenever you assign an object to a data structure component or variable name, Python always stores a reference to that same object, not a copy of it (unless you request a copy explicitly).

Table 8-1 summarizes common and representative list object operations. As usual, for the full story see the Python standard library manual, or run a `help(list)` or `dir(list)` call interactively for a complete list of list methods—you can pass in a real list, or the word `list`, which is the name of the list data type.

Table 8-1. Common list literals and operations

Operation	Interpretation
L = []	An empty list
L = [0, 1, 2, 3]	Four items: indexes 0..3
L = ['abc', ['def', 'ghi']]	Nested sublists
L = list('spam')	Lists of an iterable's items, list of successive integers
L = list(range(-4, 4))	
L[i]	Index, index of index, slice, length
L[i][j]	
L[i:j]	
len(L)	

Operation	Interpretation
`L1 + L2`	Concatenate, repeat
`L * 3`	
`for x in L: print(x)`	Iteration, membership
`3 in L`	
`L.append(4)`	Methods: growing
`L.extend([5,6,7])`	
`L.insert(I, X)`	
`L.index(1)`	Methods: searching
`L.count(X)`	
`L.sort()`	Methods: sorting, reversing, etc.
`L.reverse()`	
`del L[k]`	Methods, statement: shrinking
`del L[i:j]`	
`L.pop()`	
`L.remove(2)`	
`L[i:j] = []`	
`L[i] = 1`	Index assignment, slice assignment
`L[i:j] = [4,5,6]`	
`L = [x**2 for x in range(5)]`	List comprehensions and maps (Chapters 14, 20)
`list(map(ord, 'spam'))`	

When written down as a literal expression, a list is coded as a series of objects (really, expressions that return objects) in square brackets, separated by commas. For instance, the second row in Table 8-1 assigns the variable L to a four-item list. A nested list is coded as a nested square-bracketed series (row 3), and the empty list is just a square-bracket pair with nothing inside (row 1).[*]

Many of the operations in Table 8-1 should look familiar, as they are the same sequence operations we put to work on strings—indexing, concatenation, iteration, and so on. Lists also respond to list-specific method calls (which provide utilities such as sorting, reversing, adding items to the end, etc.), as well as in-place change operations (deleting items, assignment to indexes and slices, and so forth). Lists have these tools for change operations because they are a mutable object type.

---

[*] In practice, you won't see many lists written out like this in list-processing programs. It's more common to see code that processes lists constructed dynamically (at runtime). In fact, although it's important to master literal syntax, most data structures in Python are built by running program code at runtime.

Lists in Action

Perhaps the best way to understand lists is to see them at work. Let's once again turn to some simple interpreter interactions to illustrate the operations in Table 8-1.

Basic List Operations

Because they are sequences, lists support many of the same operations as strings. For example, lists respond to the + and * operators much like strings—they mean concatenation and repetition here too, except that the result is a new list, not a string:

```
% python
>>> len([1, 2, 3])                    # Length
3
>>> [1, 2, 3] + [4, 5, 6]             # Concatenation
[1, 2, 3, 4, 5, 6]
>>> ['Ni!'] * 4                        # Repetition
['Ni!', 'Ni!', 'Ni!', 'Ni!']
```

Although the + operator works the same for lists and strings, it's important to know that it expects the same sort of sequence on both sides—otherwise, you get a type error when the code runs. For instance, you cannot concatenate a list and a string unless you first convert the list to a string (using tools such as `str` or `%` formatting) or convert the string to a list (the `list` built-in function does the trick):

```
>>> str([1, 2]) + "34"                # Same as "[1, 2]" + "34"
'[1, 2]34'
>>> [1, 2] + list("34")               # Same as [1, 2] + ["3", "4"]
[1, 2, '3', '4']
```

List Iteration and Comprehensions

More generally, lists respond to all the sequence operations we used on strings in the prior chapter, including iteration tools:

```
>>> 3 in [1, 2, 3]                    # Membership
True
>>> for x in [1, 2, 3]:
...     print(x, end=' ')             # Iteration
...
1 2 3
```

We will talk more formally about `for` iteration and the `range` built-ins in Chapter 13, because they are related to statement syntax. In short, `for` loops step through items in any sequence from left to right, executing one or more statements for each item.

The last items in Table 8-1, list comprehensions and `map` calls, are covered in more detail in Chapter 14 and expanded on in Chapter 20. Their basic operation is straightforward, though—as introduced in Chapter 4, list comprehensions are a way to build a new list by applying an expression to each item in a sequence, and are close relatives to `for` loops:

```
>>> res = [c * 4 for c in 'SPAM']        # List comprehensions
>>> res
['SSSS', 'PPPP', 'AAAA', 'MMMM']
```

This expression is functionally equivalent to a `for` loop that builds up a list of results manually, but as we'll learn in later chapters, list comprehensions are simpler to code and faster to run today:

```
>>> res = []
>>> for c in 'SPAM':                      # List comprehension equivalent
...     res.append(c * 4)
...
>>> res
['SSSS', 'PPPP', 'AAAA', 'MMMM']
```

As also introduced in Chapter 4, the `map` built-in function does similar work, but applies a function to items in a sequence and collects all the results in a new list:

```
>>> list(map(abs, [-1, -2, 0, 1, 2]))     # map function across sequence
[1, 2, 0, 1, 2]
```

Because we're not quite ready for the full iteration story, we'll postpone further details for now, but watch for a similar comprehension expression for dictionaries later in this chapter.

Indexing, Slicing, and Matrixes

Because lists are sequences, indexing and slicing work the same way for lists as they do for strings. However, the result of indexing a list is whatever type of object lives at the offset you specify, while slicing a list always returns a new list:

```
>>> L = ['spam', 'Spam', 'SPAM!']
>>> L[2]                                   # Offsets start at zero
'SPAM!'
>>> L[-2]                                  # Negative: count from the right
'Spam'
>>> L[1:]                                  # Slicing fetches sections
['Spam', 'SPAM!']
```

One note here: because you can nest lists and other object types within lists, you will sometimes need to string together index operations to go deeper into a data structure. For example, one of the simplest ways to represent matrixes (multidimensional arrays) in Python is as lists with nested sublists. Here's a basic 3 × 3 two-dimensional list-based array:

```
>>> matrix = [[1, 2, 3], [4, 5, 6], [7, 8, 9]]
```

With one index, you get an entire row (really, a nested sublist), and with two, you get an item within the row:

```
>>> matrix[1]
[4, 5, 6]
>>> matrix[1][1]
5
>>> matrix[2][0]
7
>>> matrix = [[1, 2, 3],
...           [4, 5, 6],
...           [7, 8, 9]]
>>> matrix[1][1]
5
```

Notice in the preceding interaction that lists can naturally span multiple lines if you want them to because they are contained by a pair of brackets (more on syntax in the next part of the book). Later in this chapter, you'll also see a dictionary-based matrix representation. For high-powered numeric work, the NumPy extension mentioned in Chapter 5 provides other ways to handle matrixes.

Changing Lists In-Place

Because lists are mutable, they support operations that change a list object *in-place*. That is, the operations in this section all modify the list object directly, without requiring that you make a new copy, as you had to for strings. Because Python deals only in object references, this distinction between changing an object in-place and creating a new object matters—as discussed in Chapter 6, if you change an object in-place, you might impact more than one reference to it at the same time.

Index and slice assignments

When using a list, you can change its contents by assigning to either a particular item (offset) or an entire section (slice):

```
>>> L = ['spam', 'Spam', 'SPAM!']
>>> L[1] = 'eggs'                      # Index assignment
>>> L
['spam', 'eggs', 'SPAM!']
>>> L[0:2] = ['eat', 'more']           # Slice assignment: delete+insert
>>> L                                  # Replaces items 0,1
['eat', 'more', 'SPAM!']
```

Both index and slice assignments are in-place changes—they modify the subject list directly, rather than generating a new list object for the result. Index assignment in Python works much as it does in C and most other languages: Python replaces the object reference at the designated offset with a new one.

Slice assignment, the last operation in the preceding example, replaces an entire section of a list in a single step. Because it can be a bit complex, it is perhaps best thought of as a combination of two steps:

1. *Deletion.* The slice you specify to the left of the = is deleted.

2. *Insertion.* The new items contained in the object to the right of the = are inserted into the list on the left, at the place where the old slice was deleted.[†]

This isn't what really happens, but it tends to help clarify why the number of items inserted doesn't have to match the number of items deleted. For instance, given a list L that has the value [1,2,3], the assignment L[1:2]=[4,5] sets L to the list [1,4,5,3]. Python first deletes the 2 (a one-item slice), then inserts the 4 and 5 where the deleted 2 used to be. This also explains why L[1:2]=[] is really a deletion operation—Python deletes the slice (the item at offset 1), and then inserts nothing.

In effect, slice assignment replaces an entire section, or "column," all at once. Because the length of the sequence being assigned does not have to match the length of the slice being assigned to, slice assignment can be used to replace (by overwriting), expand (by inserting), or shrink (by deleting) the subject list. It's a powerful operation, but frankly, one that you may not see very often in practice. There are usually more straightforward ways to replace, insert, and delete (concatenation and the insert, pop, and remove list methods, for example), which Python programmers tend to prefer in practice.

List method calls

Like strings, Python list objects also support type-specific method calls, many of which change the subject list in-place:

```
>>> L.append('please')          # Append method call: add item at end
>>> L
['eat', 'more', 'SPAM!', 'please']
>>> L.sort()                    # Sort list items ('S' < 'e')
>>> L
['SPAM!', 'eat', 'more', 'please']
```

Methods were introduced in Chapter 7. In brief, they are functions (really, attributes that reference functions) that are associated with particular objects. Methods provide type-specific tools; the list methods presented here, for instance, are generally available only for lists.

Perhaps the most commonly used list method is append, which simply tacks a single item (object reference) onto the end of the list. Unlike concatenation, append expects you to pass in a single object, not a list. The effect of L.append(X) is similar to L+[X], but while the former changes L in-place, the latter makes a new list.[‡]

Another commonly seen method, sort, orders a list in-place; it uses Python standard comparison tests (here, string comparisons), and by default sorts in ascending order.

---

† This description needs elaboration when the value and the slice being assigned overlap: L[2:5]=L[3:6], for instance, works fine because the value to be inserted is fetched before the deletion happens on the left.

‡ Unlike + concatenation, append doesn't have to generate new objects, so it's usually faster. You can also mimic append with clever slice assignments: L[len(L):]=[X] is like L.append(X), and L[:0]=[X] is like appending at the front of a list. Both delete an empty slice and insert X, changing L in-place quickly, like append.

You can modify sort behavior by passing in *keyword arguments*—a special "name=value" syntax in function calls that specifies passing by name and is often used for giving configuration options. In sorts, the `key` argument gives a one-argument function that returns the value to be used in sorting, and the `reverse` argument allows sorts to be made in descending instead of ascending order:

```
>>> L = ['abc', 'ABD', 'aBe']
>>> L.sort()                              # Sort with mixed case
>>> L
['ABD', 'aBe', 'abc']
>>> L = ['abc', 'ABD', 'aBe']
>>> L.sort(key=str.lower)                 # Normalize to lowercase
>>> L
['abc', 'ABD', 'aBe']
>>>
>>> L = ['abc', 'ABD', 'aBe']
>>> L.sort(key=str.lower, reverse=True)   # Change sort order
>>> L
['aBe', 'ABD', 'abc']
```

The sort `key` argument might also be useful when sorting lists of dictionaries, to pick out a sort key by indexing each dictionary. We'll study dictionaries later in this chapter, and you'll learn more about keyword function arguments in Part IV.

Comparison and sorts in 3.0: In Python 2.6 and earlier, comparisons of differently typed objects (e.g., a string and a list) work—the language defines a fixed ordering among different types, which is deterministic, if not aesthetically pleasing. That is, the ordering is based on the names of the types involved: all integers are less than all strings, for example, because `"int"` is less than `"str"`. Comparisons never automatically convert types, except when comparing numeric type objects.

In Python 3.0, this has changed: comparison of mixed types raises an exception instead of falling back on the fixed cross-type ordering. Because sorting uses comparisons internally, this means that `[1, 2, 'spam'].sort()` succeeds in Python 2.X but will raise an exception in Python 3.0 and later.

Python 3.0 also no longer supports passing in an arbitrary *comparison function* to sorts, to implement different orderings. The suggested workaround is to use the key=*func* keyword argument to code value transformations during the sort, and use the `reverse=True` keyword argument to change the sort order to descending. These were the typical uses of comparison functions in the past.

One warning here: beware that `append` and `sort` change the associated list object in-place, but don't return the list as a result (technically, they both return a value called `None`). If you say something like `L=L.append(X)`, you won't get the modified value of `L` (in fact, you'll lose the reference to the list altogether!). When you use attributes such as `append` and `sort`, objects are changed as a side effect, so there's no reason to reassign.

Partly because of such constraints, sorting is also available in recent Pythons as a built-in function, which sorts any collection (not just lists) and returns a new list for the result (instead of in-place changes):

```
>>> L = ['abc', 'ABD', 'aBe']
>>> sorted(L, key=str.lower, reverse=True)          # Sorting built-in
['aBe', 'ABD', 'abc']

>>> L = ['abc', 'ABD', 'aBe']
>>> sorted([x.lower() for x in L], reverse=True)    # Pretransform items: differs!
['abe', 'abd', 'abc']
```

Notice the last example here—we can convert to lowercase prior to the sort with a list comprehension, but the result does not contain the original list's values as it does with the key argument. The latter is applied temporarily during the sort, instead of changing the values to be sorted. As we move along, we'll see contexts in which the sorted built-in can sometimes be more useful than the sort method.

Like strings, lists have other methods that perform other specialized operations. For instance, reverse reverses the list in-place, and the extend and pop methods insert multiple items at the end of and delete an item from the end of the list, respectively. There is also a reversed built-in function that works much like sorted, but it must be wrapped in a list call because it's an iterator (more on iterators later):

```
>>> L = [1, 2]
>>> L.extend([3,4,5])          # Add many items at end
>>> L
[1, 2, 3, 4, 5]
>>> L.pop()                    # Delete and return last item
5
>>> L
[1, 2, 3, 4]
>>> L.reverse()                # In-place reversal method
>>> L
[4, 3, 2, 1]
>>> list(reversed(L))          # Reversal built-in with a result
[1, 2, 3, 4]
```

In some types of programs, the list pop method used here is often used in conjunction with append to implement a quick last-in-first-out (LIFO) *stack* structure. The end of the list serves as the top of the stack:

```
>>> L = []
>>> L.append(1)                # Push onto stack
>>> L.append(2)
>>> L
[1, 2]
>>> L.pop()                    # Pop off stack
2
>>> L
[1]
```

The pop method also accepts an optional offset of the item to be deleted and returned (the default is the last item). Other list methods remove an item by value (remove), insert an item at an offset (insert), search for an item's offset (index), and more:

```
>>> L = ['spam', 'eggs', 'ham']
>>> L.index('eggs')              # Index of an object
1
>>> L.insert(1, 'toast')         # Insert at position
>>> L
['spam', 'toast', 'eggs', 'ham']
>>> L.remove('eggs')             # Delete by value
>>> L
['spam', 'toast', 'ham']
>>> L.pop(1)                     # Delete by position
'toast'
>>> L
['spam', 'ham']
```

See other documentation sources or experiment with these calls interactively on your own to learn more about list methods.

Other common list operations

Because lists are mutable, you can use the del statement to delete an item or section in-place:

```
>>> L
['SPAM!', 'eat', 'more', 'please']
>>> del L[0]                     # Delete one item
>>> L
['eat', 'more', 'please']
>>> del L[1:]                    # Delete an entire section
>>> L                            # Same as L[1:] = []
['eat']
```

Because slice assignment is a deletion plus an insertion, you can also delete a section of a list by assigning an empty list to a slice (L[i:j]=[]); Python deletes the slice named on the left, and then inserts nothing. Assigning an empty list to an index, on the other hand, just stores a reference to the empty list in the specified slot, rather than deleting it:

```
>>> L = ['Already', 'got', 'one']
>>> L[1:] = []
>>> L
['Already']
>>> L[0] = []
>>> L
[[]]
```

Although all the operations just discussed are typical, there are additional list methods and operations not illustrated here (including methods for inserting and searching). For a comprehensive and up-to-date list of type tools, you should always consult

Python's manuals, Python's `dir` and `help` functions (which we first met in Chapter 4), or one of the reference texts mentioned in the Preface.

I'd also like to remind you one more time that all the in-place change operations discussed here work only for mutable objects: they won't work on strings (or tuples, discussed in Chapter 9), no matter how hard you try. Mutability is an inherent property of each object type.

Dictionaries

Apart from lists, *dictionaries* are perhaps the most flexible built-in data type in Python. If you think of lists as ordered collections of objects, you can think of dictionaries as unordered collections; the chief distinction is that in dictionaries, items are stored and fetched by *key*, instead of by positional offset.

Being a built-in type, dictionaries can replace many of the searching algorithms and data structures you might have to implement manually in lower-level languages— indexing a dictionary is a very fast search operation. Dictionaries also sometimes do the work of records and symbol tables used in other languages, can represent sparse (mostly empty) data structures, and much more. Here's a rundown of their main properties. Python dictionaries are:

Accessed by key, not offset
> Dictionaries are sometimes called *associative arrays* or *hashes*. They associate a set of values with keys, so you can fetch an item out of a dictionary using the key under which you originally stored it. You use the same indexing operation to get components in a dictionary as you do in a list, but the index takes the form of a key, not a relative offset.

Unordered collections of arbitrary objects
> Unlike in a list, items stored in a dictionary aren't kept in any particular order; in fact, Python randomizes their left-to-right order to provide quick lookup. Keys provide the symbolic (not physical) locations of items in a dictionary.

Variable-length, heterogeneous, and arbitrarily nestable
> Like lists, dictionaries can grow and shrink in-place (without new copies being made), they can contain objects of any type, and they support nesting to any depth (they can contain lists, other dictionaries, and so on).

Of the category "mutable mapping"
> Dictionaries can be changed in-place by assigning to indexes (they are mutable), but they don't support the sequence operations that work on strings and lists. Because dictionaries are unordered collections, operations that depend on a fixed positional order (e.g., concatenation, slicing) don't make sense. Instead, dictionaries are the only built-in representatives of the mapping type category (objects that map keys to values).

Tables of object references (hash tables)

If lists are arrays of object references that support access by position, dictionaries are unordered tables of object references that support access by key. Internally, dictionaries are implemented as hash tables (data structures that support very fast retrieval), which start small and grow on demand. Moreover, Python employs optimized hashing algorithms to find keys, so retrieval is quick. Like lists, dictionaries store object references (not copies).

Table 8-2 summarizes some of the most common and representative dictionary operations (again, see the library manual or run a `dir(dict)` or `help(dict)` call for a complete list—dict is the name of the type). When coded as a literal expression, a dictionary is written as a series of *key:value* pairs, separated by commas, enclosed in curly braces.§ An empty dictionary is an empty set of braces, and dictionaries can be nested by writing one as a value inside another dictionary, or within a list or tuple.

Table 8-2. Common dictionary literals and operations

Operation	Interpretation
`D = {}`	Empty dictionary
`D = {'spam': 2, 'eggs': 3}`	Two-item dictionary
`D = {'food': {'ham': 1, 'egg': 2}}`	Nesting
`D = dict(name='Bob', age=40)`	Alternative construction techniques:
`D = dict(zip(keyslist, valslist))`	keywords, zipped pairs, key lists
`D = dict.fromkeys(['a', 'b'])`	
`D['eggs']`	Indexing by key
`D['food']['ham']`	
`'eggs' in D`	Membership: key present test
`D.keys()`	Methods: keys,
`D.values()`	values,
`D.items()`	keys+values,
`D.copy()`	copies,
`D.get(key, default)`	defaults,
`D.update(D2)`	merge,
`D.pop(key)`	delete, etc.
`len(D)`	Length: number of stored entries
`D[key] = 42`	Adding/changing keys

§ As with lists, you won't often see dictionaries constructed using literals. Lists and dictionaries are grown in different ways, though. As you'll see in the next section, dictionaries are typically built up by assigning to new keys at runtime; this approach fails for lists (lists are commonly grown with append instead).

Operation	Interpretation
`del D[key]`	Deleting entries by key
`list(D.keys())`	Dictionary views (Python 3.0)
`D1.keys() & D2.keys()`	
`D = {x: x*2 for x in range(10)}`	Dictionary comprehensions (Python 3.0)

Dictionaries in Action

As Table 8-2 suggests, dictionaries are indexed by key, and nested dictionary entries are referenced by a series of indexes (keys in square brackets). When Python creates a dictionary, it stores its items in any left-to-right order it chooses; to fetch a value back, you supply the key with which it is associated, not its relative position. Let's go back to the interpreter to get a feel for some of the dictionary operations in Table 8-2.

Basic Dictionary Operations

In normal operation, you create dictionaries with literals and store and access items by key with indexing:

```
% python
>>> D = {'spam': 2, 'ham': 1, 'eggs': 3}    # Make a dictionary
>>> D['spam']                               # Fetch a value by key
2
>>> D                                       # Order is scrambled
{'eggs': 3, 'ham': 1, 'spam': 2}
```

Here, the dictionary is assigned to the variable D; the value of the key 'spam' is the integer 2, and so on. We use the same square bracket syntax to index dictionaries by key as we did to index lists by offset, but here it means access by key, not by position.

Notice the end of this example: the left-to-right order of keys in a dictionary will almost always be different from what you originally typed. This is on purpose: to implement fast key lookup (a.k.a. hashing), keys need to be reordered in memory. That's why operations that assume a fixed left-to-right order (e.g., slicing, concatenation) do not apply to dictionaries; you can fetch values only by key, not by position.

The built-in len function works on dictionaries, too; it returns the number of items stored in the dictionary or, equivalently, the length of its keys list. The dictionary in membership operator allows you to test for key existence, and the keys method returns all the keys in the dictionary. The latter of these can be useful for processing dictionaries sequentially, but you shouldn't depend on the order of the keys list. Because the keys result can be used as a normal list, however, it can always be sorted if order matters (more on sorting and dictionaries later):

```
>>> len(D)                      # Number of entries in dictionary
3
>>> 'ham' in D                  # Key membership test alternative
```

```
True
>>> list(D.keys())                    # Create a new list of my keys
['eggs', 'ham', 'spam']
```

Notice the second expression in this listing. As mentioned earlier, the `in` membership test used for strings and lists also works on dictionaries—it checks whether a key is stored in the dictionary. Technically, this works because dictionaries define *iterators* that step through their keys lists. Other types provide iterators that reflect their common uses; files, for example, have iterators that read line by line. We'll discuss iterators in Chapters 14 and 20.

Also note the syntax of the last example in this listing. We have to enclose it in a `list` call in Python 3.0 for similar reasons—`keys` in 3.0 returns an iterator, instead of a physical list. The `list` call forces it to produce all its values at once so we can print them. In 2.6, `keys` builds and returns an actual list, so the `list` call isn't needed to display results. More on this later in this chapter.

 The order of keys in a dictionary is arbitrary and can change from release to release, so don't be alarmed if your dictionaries print in a different order than shown here. In fact, the order has changed for me too—I'm running all these examples with Python 3.0, but their keys had a different order in an earlier edition when displayed. You shouldn't depend on dictionary key ordering, in either programs or books!

Changing Dictionaries In-Place

Let's continue with our interactive session. Dictionaries, like lists, are mutable, so you can change, expand, and shrink them in-place without making new dictionaries: simply assign a value to a key to change or create an entry. The `del` statement works here, too; it deletes the entry associated with the key specified as an index. Notice also the nesting of a list inside a dictionary in this example (the value of the key `'ham'`). All collection data types in Python can nest inside each other arbitrarily:

```
>>> D
{'eggs': 3, 'ham': 1, 'spam': 2}

>>> D['ham'] = ['grill', 'bake', 'fry']              # Change entry
>>> D
{'eggs': 3, 'ham': ['grill', 'bake', 'fry'], 'spam': 2}

>>> del D['eggs']                                    # Delete entry
>>> D
{'ham': ['grill', 'bake', 'fry'], 'spam': 2}

>>> D['brunch'] = 'Bacon'                            # Add new entry
>>> D
{'brunch': 'Bacon', 'ham': ['grill', 'bake', 'fry'], 'spam': 2}
```

As with lists, assigning to an existing index in a dictionary changes its associated value. Unlike with lists, however, whenever you assign a *new* dictionary key (one that hasn't been assigned before) you create a new entry in the dictionary, as was done in the previous example for the key 'brunch'. This doesn't work for lists because Python considers an offset beyond the end of a list out of bounds and throws an error. To expand a list, you need to use tools such as the append method or slice assignment instead.

More Dictionary Methods

Dictionary methods provide a variety of tools. For instance, the dictionary values and items methods return the dictionary's values and (*key,value*) pair tuples, respectively (as with keys, wrap them in a list call in Python 3.0 to collect their values for display):

```
>>> D = {'spam': 2, 'ham': 1, 'eggs': 3}
>>> list(D.values())
[3, 1, 2]
>>> list(D.items())
[('eggs', 3), ('ham', 1), ('spam', 2)]
```

Such lists are useful in loops that need to step through dictionary entries one by one. Fetching a nonexistent key is normally an error, but the get method returns a default value (None, or a passed-in default) if the key doesn't exist. It's an easy way to fill in a default for a key that isn't present and avoid a missing-key error:

```
>>> D.get('spam')                    # A key that is there
2
>>> print(D.get('toast'))            # A key that is missing
None
>>> D.get('toast', 88)
88
```

The update method provides something similar to concatenation for dictionaries, though it has nothing to do with left-to-right ordering (again, there is no such thing in dictionaries). It merges the keys and values of one dictionary into another, blindly overwriting values of the same key:

```
>>> D
{'eggs': 3, 'ham': 1, 'spam': 2}
>>> D2 = {'toast':4, 'muffin':5}
>>> D.update(D2)
>>> D
{'toast': 4, 'muffin': 5, 'eggs': 3, 'ham': 1, 'spam': 2}
```

Finally, the dictionary pop method deletes a key from a dictionary and returns the value it had. It's similar to the list pop method, but it takes a key instead of an optional position:

```
# pop a dictionary by key
>>> D
{'toast': 4, 'muffin': 5, 'eggs': 3, 'ham': 1, 'spam': 2}
>>> D.pop('muffin')
```

```
5
>>> D.pop('toast')                              # Delete and return from a key
4
>>> D
{'eggs': 3, 'ham': 1, 'spam': 2}

# pop a list by position
>>> L = ['aa', 'bb', 'cc', 'dd']
>>> L.pop()                                     # Delete and return from the end
'dd'
>>> L
['aa', 'bb', 'cc']
>>> L.pop(1)                                    # Delete from a specific position
'bb'
>>> L
['aa', 'cc']
```

Dictionaries also provide a copy method; we'll discuss this in Chapter 9, as it's a way to avoid the potential side effects of shared references to the same dictionary. In fact, dictionaries come with many more methods than those listed in Table 8-2; see the Python library manual or other documentation sources for a comprehensive list.

A Languages Table

Let's look at a more realistic dictionary example. The following example creates a table that maps programming language names (the keys) to their creators (the values). You fetch creator names by indexing on language names:

```
>>> table = {'Python': 'Guido van Rossum',
...          'Perl':   'Larry Wall',
...          'Tcl':    'John Ousterhout' }
>>>
>>> language = 'Python'
>>> creator  = table[language]
>>> creator
'Guido van Rossum'

>>> for lang in table:                          # Same as: for lang in table.keys()
...     print(lang, '\t', table[lang])
...
Tcl      John Ousterhout
Python   Guido van Rossum
Perl     Larry Wall
```

The last command uses a for loop, which we haven't covered in detail yet. If you aren't familiar with for loops, this command simply iterates through each key in the table and prints a tab-separated list of keys and their values. We'll learn more about for loops in Chapter 13.

Dictionaries aren't sequences like lists and strings, but if you need to step through the items in a dictionary, it's easy—calling the dictionary keys method returns all stored keys, which you can iterate through with a `for`. If needed, you can index from key to value inside the `for` loop, as was done in this code.

In fact, Python also lets you step through a dictionary's keys list without actually calling the `keys` method in most `for` loops. For any dictionary D, saying `for key in D:` works the same as saying the complete `for key in D.keys():`. This is really just another instance of the iterators mentioned earlier, which allow the `in` membership operator to work on dictionaries as well (more on iterators later in this book).

Dictionary Usage Notes

Dictionaries are fairly straightforward tools once you get the hang of them, but here are a few additional pointers and reminders you should be aware of when using them:

- **Sequence operations don't work**. Dictionaries are mappings, not sequences; because there's no notion of ordering among their items, things like concatenation (an ordered joining) and slicing (extracting a contiguous section) simply don't apply. In fact, Python raises an error when your code runs if you try to do such things.

- **Assigning to new indexes adds entries**. Keys can be created when you write a dictionary literal (in which case they are embedded in the literal itself), or when you assign values to new keys of an existing dictionary object. The end result is the same.

- **Keys need not always be strings**. Our examples so far have used strings as keys, but any other *immutable* objects (i.e., not lists) work just as well. For instance, you can use integers as keys, which makes the dictionary look much like a list (when indexing, at least). Tuples are sometimes used as dictionary keys too, allowing for compound key values. Class instance objects (discussed in Part VI) can also be used as keys, as long as they have the proper protocol methods; roughly, they need to tell Python that their values are hashable and won't change, as otherwise they would be useless as fixed keys.

Using dictionaries to simulate flexible lists

The last point in the prior list is important enough to demonstrate with a few examples. When you use lists, it is illegal to assign to an offset that is off the end of the list:

```
>>> L = []
>>> L[99] = 'spam'
Traceback (most recent call last):
  File "<stdin>", line 1, in ?
IndexError: list assignment index out of range
```

Although you can use repetition to preallocate as big a list as you'll need (e.g., `[0]*100`), you can also do something that looks similar with dictionaries that does not require such space allocations. By using integer keys, dictionaries can emulate lists that seem to grow on offset assignment:

```
>>> D = {}
>>> D[99] = 'spam'
>>> D[99]
'spam'
>>> D
{99: 'spam'}
```

Here, it looks as if D is a 100-item list, but it's really a dictionary with a single entry; the value of the key 99 is the string 'spam'. You can access this structure with offsets much like a list, but you don't have to allocate space for all the positions you might ever need to assign values to in the future. When used like this, dictionaries are like more flexible equivalents of lists.

Using dictionaries for sparse data structures

In a similar way, dictionary keys are also commonly leveraged to implement *sparse* data structures—for example, multidimensional arrays where only a few positions have values stored in them:

```
>>> Matrix = {}
>>> Matrix[(2, 3, 4)] = 88
>>> Matrix[(7, 8, 9)] = 99
>>>
>>> X = 2; Y = 3; Z = 4          # ; separates statements
>>> Matrix[(X, Y, Z)]
88
>>> Matrix
{(2, 3, 4): 88, (7, 8, 9): 99}
```

Here, we've used a dictionary to represent a three-dimensional array that is empty except for the two positions (2,3,4) and (7,8,9). The keys are *tuples* that record the coordinates of nonempty slots. Rather than allocating a large and mostly empty three-dimensional matrix to hold these values, we can use a simple two-item dictionary. In this scheme, accessing an empty slot triggers a nonexistent key exception, as these slots are not physically stored:

```
>>> Matrix[(2,3,6)]
Traceback (most recent call last):
  File "<stdin>", line 1, in ?
KeyError: (2, 3, 6)
```

Avoiding missing-key errors

Errors for nonexistent key fetches are common in sparse matrixes, but you probably won't want them to shut down your program. There are at least three ways to fill in a default value instead of getting such an error message—you can test for keys ahead of time in if statements, use a try statement to catch and recover from the exception explicitly, or simply use the dictionary get method shown earlier to provide a default for keys that do not exist:

```
>>> if (2,3,6) in Matrix:          # Check for key before fetch
...     print(Matrix[(2,3,6)])     # See Chapter 12 for if/else
```

```
... else:
...     print(0)
...
0
>>> try:
...     print(Matrix[(2,3,6)])          # Try to index
... except KeyError:                    # Catch and recover
...     print(0)                        # See Chapter 33 for try/except
...
0
>>> Matrix.get((2,3,4), 0)              # Exists; fetch and return
88
>>> Matrix.get((2,3,6), 0)             # Doesn't exist; use default arg
0
```

Of these, the `get` method is the most concise in terms of coding requirements; we'll study the `if` and `try` statements in more detail later in this book.

Using dictionaries as "records"

As you can see, dictionaries can play many roles in Python. In general, they can replace search data structures (because indexing by key is a search operation) and can represent many types of structured information. For example, dictionaries are one of many ways to describe the properties of an item in your program's domain; that is, they can serve the same role as "records" or "structs" in other languages.

The following, for example, fills out a dictionary by assigning to new keys over time:

```
>>> rec = {}
>>> rec['name'] = 'mel'
>>> rec['age']  = 45
>>> rec['job']  = 'trainer/writer'
>>>
>>> print(rec['name'])
mel
```

Especially when nested, Python's built-in data types allow us to easily represent structured information. This example again uses a dictionary to capture object properties, but it codes it all at once (rather than assigning to each key separately) and nests a list and a dictionary to represent structured property values:

```
>>> mel = {'name': 'Mark',
...        'jobs': ['trainer', 'writer'],
...        'web':  'www.rmi.net/~lutz',
...        'home': {'state': 'CO', 'zip':80513}}
```

To fetch components of nested objects, simply string together indexing operations:

```
>>> mel['name']
'Mark'
>>> mel['jobs']
['trainer', 'writer']
>>> mel['jobs'][1]
'writer'
```

```
>>> mel['home']['zip']
80513
```

Although we'll learn in Part VI that classes (which group both data and logic) can be better in this record role, dictionaries are an easy-to-use tool for simpler requirements.

Why You Will Care: Dictionary Interfaces

Dictionaries aren't just a convenient way to store information by key in your programs—some Python extensions also present interfaces that look like and work the same as dictionaries. For instance, Python's interface to DBM access-by-key files looks much like a dictionary that must be opened. Strings are stored and fetched using key indexes:

```
import dbm
file = dbm.open("filename")     # Link to file
file['key'] = 'data'            # Store data by key
data = file['key']              # Fetch data by key
```

In Chapter 27, you'll see that you can store entire Python objects this way, too, if you replace dbm in the preceding code with shelve (shelves are access-by-key databases of persistent Python objects). For Internet work, Python's CGI script support also presents a dictionary-like interface. A call to cgi.FieldStorage yields a dictionary-like object with one entry per input field on the client's web page:

```
import cgi
form = cgi.FieldStorage()          # Parse form data
if 'name' in form:
    showReply('Hello, ' + form['name'].value)
```

All of these, like dictionaries, are instances of mappings. Once you learn dictionary interfaces, you'll find that they apply to a variety of built-in tools in Python.

Other Ways to Make Dictionaries

Finally, note that because dictionaries are so useful, more ways to build them have emerged over time. In Python 2.3 and later, for example, the last two calls to the dict constructor (really, type name) shown here have the same effect as the literal and key-assignment forms above them:

```
{'name': 'mel', 'age': 45}                    # Traditional literal expression

D = {}                                        # Assign by keys dynamically
D['name'] = 'mel'
D['age']  = 45

dict(name='mel', age=45)                      # dict keyword argument form

dict([('name', 'mel'), ('age', 45)])          # dict key/value tuples form
```

All four of these forms create the same two-key dictionary, but they are useful in differing circumstances:

- The first is handy if you can spell out the entire dictionary ahead of time.
- The second is of use if you need to create the dictionary one field at a time on the fly.
- The third involves less typing than the first, but it requires all keys to be strings.
- The last is useful if you need to build up keys and values as sequences at runtime.

We met keyword arguments earlier when sorting; the third form illustrated in this code listing has become especially popular in Python code today, since it has less syntax (and hence there is less opportunity for mistakes). As suggested previously in Table 8-2, the last form in the listing is also commonly used in conjunction with the `zip` function, to combine separate lists of keys and values obtained dynamically at runtime (parsed out of a data file's columns, for instance). More on this option in the next section.

Provided all the key's values are the same initially, you can also create a dictionary with this special form—simply pass in a list of keys and an initial value for all of the values (the default is `None`):

```
>>> dict.fromkeys(['a', 'b'], 0)
{'a': 0, 'b': 0}
```

Although you could get by with just literals and key assignments at this point in your Python career, you'll probably find uses for all of these dictionary-creation forms as you start applying them in realistic, flexible, and dynamic Python programs.

The listings in this section document the various ways to create dictionaries in both Python 2.6 and 3.0. However, there is yet another way to create dictionaries, available only in Python 3.0 (and later): the *dictionary comprehension* expression. To see how this last form looks, we need to move on to the next section.

Dictionary Changes in Python 3.0

This chapter has so far focused on dictionary basics that span releases, but the dictionary's functionality has mutated in Python 3.0. If you are using Python 2.X code, you may come across some dictionary tools that either behave differently or are missing altogether in 3.0. Moreover, 3.0 coders have access to additional dictionary tools not available in 2.X. Specifically, dictionaries in 3.0:

- Support a new dictionary comprehension expression, a close cousin to list and set comprehensions
- Return iterable views instead of lists for the methods `D.keys`, `D.values`, and `D.items`
- Require new coding styles for scanning by sorted keys, because of the prior point
- No longer support relative magnitude comparisons directly—compare manually instead
- No longer have the `D.has_key` method—the `in` membership test is used instead

Let's take a look at what's new in 3.0 dictionaries.

Dictionary comprehensions

As mentioned at the end of the prior section, dictionaries in 3.0 can also be created with dictionary comprehensions. Like the set comprehensions we met in Chapter 5, dictionary comprehensions are available only in 3.0 (not in 2.6). Like the longstanding list comprehensions we met briefly in Chapter 4 and earlier in this chapter, they run an implied loop, collecting the key/value results of expressions on each iteration and using them to fill out a new dictionary. A loop variable allows the comprehension to use loop iteration values along the way.

For example, a standard way to initialize a dictionary dynamically in both 2.6 and 3.0 is to zip together its keys and values and pass the result to the `dict` call. As we'll learn in more detail in Chapter 13, the `zip` function is a way to construct a dictionary from key and value lists in a single call. If you cannot predict the set of keys and values in your code, you can always build them up as lists and zip them together:

```
>>> list(zip(['a', 'b', 'c'], [1, 2, 3]))      # Zip together keys and values
[('a', 1), ('b', 2), ('c', 3)]

>>> D = dict(zip(['a', 'b', 'c'], [1, 2, 3]))     # Make a dict from zip result
>>> D
{'a': 1, 'c': 3, 'b': 2}
```

In Python 3.0, you can achieve the same effect with a dictionary comprehension expression. The following builds a new dictionary with a key/value pair for every such pair in the `zip` result (it reads almost the same in Python, but with a bit more formality):

```
C:\misc> c:\python30\python              # Use a dict comprehension

>>> D = {k: v for (k, v) in zip(['a', 'b', 'c'], [1, 2, 3])}
>>> D
{'a': 1, 'c': 3, 'b': 2}
```

Comprehensions actually require more code in this case, but they are also more general than this example implies—we can use them to map a single stream of values to dictionaries as well, and keys can be computed with expressions just like values:

```
>>> D = {x: x ** 2 for x in [1, 2, 3, 4]}      # Or: range(1, 5)
>>> D
{1: 1, 2: 4, 3: 9, 4: 16}

>>> D = {c: c * 4 for c in 'SPAM'}             # Loop over any iterable
>>> D
{'A': 'AAAA', 'P': 'PPPP', 'S': 'SSSS', 'M': 'MMMM'}

>>> D = {c.lower(): c + '!' for c in ['SPAM', 'EGGS', 'HAM']}
>>> D
{'eggs': 'EGGS!', 'ham': 'HAM!', 'spam': 'SPAM!'}
```

Dictionary comprehensions are also useful for initializing dictionaries from keys lists, in much the same way as the `fromkeys` method we met at the end of the preceding section:

```
>>> D = dict.fromkeys(['a', 'b', 'c'], 0)          # Initialize dict from keys
>>> D
{'a': 0, 'c': 0, 'b': 0}

>>> D = {k:0 for k in ['a', 'b', 'c']}             # Same, but with a comprehension
>>> D
{'a': 0, 'c': 0, 'b': 0}

>>> D = dict.fromkeys('spam')                       # Other iterators, default value
>>> D
{'a': None, 'p': None, 's': None, 'm': None}

>>> D = {k: None for k in 'spam'}
>>> D
{'a': None, 'p': None, 's': None, 'm': None}
```

Like related tools, dictionary comprehensions support additional syntax not shown here, including nested loops and `if` clauses. Unfortunately, to truly understand dictionary comprehensions, we need to also know more about iteration statements and concepts in Python, and we don't yet have enough information to address that story well. We'll learn much more about all flavors of comprehensions (list, set, and dictionary) in Chapters 14 and 20, so we'll defer further details until later. We'll also study the `zip` built-in we used in this section in more detail in Chapter 13, when we explore `for` loops.

Dictionary views

In 3.0 the dictionary `keys`, `values`, and `items` methods all return *view objects*, whereas in 2.6 they return actual result lists. View objects are *iterables*, which simply means objects that generate result items one at a time, instead of producing the result list all at once in memory. Besides being iterable, dictionary views also retain the original order of dictionary components, reflect future changes to the dictionary, and may support set operations. On the other hand, they are not lists, and they do not support operations like indexing or the list `sort` method; nor do they display their items when printed.

We'll discuss the notion of iterables more formally in Chapter 14, but for our purposes here it's enough to know that we have to run the results of these three methods through the `list` built-in if we want to apply list operations or display their values:

```
>>> D = dict(a=1, b=2, c=3)
>>> D
{'a': 1, 'c': 3, 'b': 2}

>>> K = D.keys()                        # Makes a view object in 3.0, not a list
>>> K
<dict_keys object at 0x026D83C0>
>>> list(K)                             # Force a real list in 3.0 if needed
['a', 'c', 'b']

>>> V = D.values()                      # Ditto for values and items views
>>> V
<dict_values object at 0x026D8260>
```

```
>>> list(V)
[1, 3, 2]

>>> list(D.items())
[('a', 1), ('c', 3), ('b', 2)]

>>> K[0]                              # List operations fail unless converted
TypeError: 'dict_keys' object does not support indexing
>>> list(K)[0]
'a'
```

Apart from when displaying results at the interactive prompt, you will probably rarely even notice this change, because looping constructs in Python automatically force iterable objects to produce one result on each iteration:

```
>>> for k in D.keys(): print(k)     # Iterators used automatically in loops
...
a
c
b
```

In addition, 3.0 dictionaries still have iterators themselves, which return successive keys—as in 2.6, it's still often not necessary to call keys directly:

```
>>> for key in D: print(key)        # Still no need to call keys() to iterate
...
a
c
b
```

Unlike 2.X's list results, though, dictionary views in 3.0 are not carved in stone when created—they *dynamically reflect future changes* made to the dictionary after the view object has been created:

```
>>> D = {'a':1, 'b':2, 'c':3}
>>> D
{'a': 1, 'c': 3, 'b': 2}

>>> K = D.keys()
>>> V = D.values()
>>> list(K)                         # Views maintain same order as dictionary
['a', 'c', 'b']
>>> list(V)
[1, 3, 2]

>>> del D['b']                      # Change the dictionary in-place
>>> D
{'a': 1, 'c': 3}

>>> list(K)                         # Reflected in any current view objects
['a', 'c']
>>> list(V)                         # Not true in 2.X!
[1, 3]
```

Dictionary views and sets

Also unlike 2.X's list results, 3.0's view objects returned by the keys method are *set-like* and support common set operations such as intersection and union; values views are not, since they aren't unique, but items results are if their (*key, value*) pairs are unique and hashable. Given that sets behave much like valueless dictionaries (and are even coded in curly braces like dictionaries in 3.0), this is a logical symmetry. Like dictionary keys, set items are unordered, unique, and immutable.

Here is what keys lists look like when used in set operations. In set operations, views may be mixed with other views, sets, and dictionaries (dictionaries are treated the same as their keys views in this context):

```
>>> K | {'x': 4}                    # Keys (and some items) views are set-like
{'a', 'x', 'c'}

>>> V & {'x': 4}
TypeError: unsupported operand type(s) for &: 'dict_values' and 'dict'
>>> V & {'x': 4}.values()
TypeError: unsupported operand type(s) for &: 'dict_values' and 'dict_values'

>>> D = {'a':1, 'b':2, 'c':3}
>>> D.keys() & D.keys()             # Intersect keys views
{'a', 'c', 'b'}
>>> D.keys() & {'b'}                # Intersect keys and set
{'b'}
>>> D.keys() & {'b': 1}             # Intersect keys and dict
{'b'}
>>> D.keys() | {'b', 'c', 'd'}      # Union keys and set
{'a', 'c', 'b', 'd'}
```

Dictionary items views are set-like too if they are hashable—that is, if they contain only immutable objects:

```
>>> D = {'a': 1}
>>> list(D.items())                 # Items set-like if hashable
[('a', 1)]
>>> D.items() | D.keys()            # Union view and view
{('a', 1), 'a'}
>>> D.items() | D                   # dict treated same as its keys
{('a', 1), 'a'}

>>> D.items() | {('c', 3), ('d', 4)}        # Set of key/value pairs
{('a', 1), ('d', 4), ('c', 3)}
>>> dict(D.items() | {('c', 3), ('d', 4)})  # dict accepts iterable sets too
{'a': 1, 'c': 3, 'd': 4}
```

For more details on set operations in general, see Chapter 5. Now, let's look at three other quick coding notes for 3.0 dictionaries.

Sorting dictionary keys

First of all, because **keys** does not return a list, the traditional coding pattern for scanning a dictionary by sorted keys in 2.X won't work in 3.0. You must either convert to a list manually or use the **sorted** call introduced in Chapter 4 and earlier in this chapter on either a **keys** view or the dictionary itself:

```
>>> D = {'a':1, 'b':2, 'c':3}
>>> D
{'a': 1, 'c': 3, 'b': 2}

>>> Ks = D.keys()                          # Sorting a view object doesn't work!
>>> Ks.sort()
AttributeError: 'dict_keys' object has no attribute 'sort'

>>> Ks = list(Ks)                          # Force it to be a list and then sort
>>> Ks.sort()
>>> for k in Ks: print(k, D[k])
...
a 1
b 2
c 3

>>> D
{'a': 1, 'c': 3, 'b': 2}
>>> Ks = D.keys()                          # Or you can use sorted() on the keys
>>> for k in sorted(Ks): print(k, D[k])    # sorted() accepts any iterable
...                                        # sorted() returns its result
a 1
b 2
c 3

>>> D
{'a': 1, 'c': 3, 'b': 2}                    # Better yet, sort the dict directly
>>> for k in sorted(D): print(k, D[k])      # dict iterators return keys
...
a 1
b 2
c 3
```

Dictionary magnitude comparisons no longer work

Secondly, while in Python 2.6 dictionaries may be compared for relative magnitude directly with <, >, and so on, in Python 3.0 this no longer works. However, it can be simulated by comparing sorted keys lists manually:

```
sorted(D1.items()) < sorted(D2.items())     # Like 2.6 D1 < D2
```

Dictionary equality tests still work in 3.0, though. Since we'll revisit this in the next chapter in the context of comparisons at large, we'll defer further details here.

The has_key method is dead: long live in!

Finally, the widely used dictionary has_key key presence test method is gone in 3.0. Instead, use the in membership expression, or a get with a default test (of these, in is generally preferred):

```
>>> D
{'a': 1, 'c': 3, 'b': 2}

>>> D.has_key('c')                                      # 2.X only: True/False
AttributeError: 'dict' object has no attribute 'has_key'

>>> 'c' in D
True
>>> 'x' in D
False
>>> if 'c' in D: print('present', D['c'])               # Preferred in 3.0
...
present 3

>>> print(D.get('c'))
3
>>> print(D.get('x'))
None
>>> if D.get('c') != None: print('present', D['c'])     # Another option
...
present 3
```

If you work in 2.6 and care about 3.0 compatibility, note that the first two changes (comprehensions and views) can only be coded in 3.0, but the last three (sorted, manual comparisons, and in) can be coded in 2.6 today to ease 3.0 migration in the future.

Chapter Summary

In this chapter, we explored the list and dictionary types—probably the two most common, flexible, and powerful collection types you will see and use in Python code. We learned that the list type supports positionally ordered collections of arbitrary objects, and that it may be freely nested and grown and shrunk on demand. The dictionary type is similar, but it stores items by key instead of by position and does not maintain any reliable left-to-right order among its items. Both lists and dictionaries are mutable, and so support a variety of in-place change operations not available for strings: for example, lists can be grown by append calls, and dictionaries by assignment to new keys.

In the next chapter, we will wrap up our in-depth core object type tour by looking at tuples and files. After that, we'll move on to statements that code the logic that processes our objects, taking us another step toward writing complete programs. Before we tackle those topics, though, here are some chapter quiz questions to review.

Test Your Knowledge: Quiz

1. Name two ways to build a list containing five integer zeros.
2. Name two ways to build a dictionary with two keys, `'a'` and `'b'`, each having an associated value of `0`.
3. Name four operations that change a list object in-place.
4. Name four operations that change a dictionary object in-place.

Test Your Knowledge: Answers

1. A literal expression like `[0, 0, 0, 0, 0]` and a repetition expression like `[0] * 5` will each create a list of five zeros. In practice, you might also build one up with a loop that starts with an empty list and appends `0` to it in each iteration:

   `L.append(0)`. A list comprehension (`[0 for i in range(5)]`) could work here, too, but this is more work than you need to do.

2. A literal expression such as `{'a': 0, 'b': 0}` or a series of assignments like `D = {}`, `D['a'] = 0`, and `D['b'] = 0` would create the desired dictionary. You can also use the newer and simpler-to-code `dict(a=0, b=0)` keyword form, or the more flexible `dict([('a', 0), ('b', 0)])` key/value sequences form. Or, because all the values are the same, you can use the special form `dict.fromkeys('ab', 0)`. In 3.0, you can also use a dictionary comprehension: `{k:0 for k in 'ab'}`.

3. The `append` and `extend` methods grow a list in-place, the `sort` and `reverse` methods order and reverse lists, the `insert` method inserts an item at an offset, the `remove` and `pop` methods delete from a list by value and by position, the `del` statement deletes an item or slice, and index and slice assignment statements replace an item or entire section. Pick any four of these for the quiz.

4. Dictionaries are primarily changed by assignment to a new or existing key, which creates or changes the key's entry in the table. Also, the `del` statement deletes a key's entry, the dictionary `update` method merges one dictionary into another in-place, and `D.pop(key)` removes a key and returns the value it had. Dictionaries also have other, more exotic in-place change methods not listed in this chapter, such as `setdefault`; see reference sources for more details.

## CHAPTER 9

Tuples, Files, and Everything Else

This chapter rounds out our in-depth look at the core object types in Python by exploring the *tuple*, a collection of other objects that cannot be changed, and the *file*, an interface to external files on your computer. As you'll see, the tuple is a relatively simple object that largely performs operations you've already learned about for strings and lists. The file object is a commonly used and full-featured tool for processing files; the basic overview of files here is supplemented by larger examples in later chapters.

This chapter also concludes this part of the book by looking at properties common to all the core object types we've met—the notions of equality, comparisons, object copies, and so on. We'll also briefly explore other object types in the Python toolbox; as you'll see, although we've covered all the primary built-in types, the object story in Python is broader than I've implied thus far. Finally, we'll close this part of the book by taking a look at a set of common object type pitfalls and exploring some exercises that will allow you to experiment with the ideas you've learned.

Tuples

The last collection type in our survey is the Python tuple. Tuples construct simple groups of objects. They work exactly like lists, except that tuples can't be changed in-place (they're immutable) and are usually written as a series of items in parentheses, not square brackets. Although they don't support as many methods, tuples share most of their properties with lists. Here's a quick look at the basics. Tuples are:

Ordered collections of arbitrary objects
> Like strings and lists, tuples are positionally ordered collections of objects (i.e., they maintain a left-to-right order among their contents); like lists, they can embed any kind of object.

Accessed by offset
> Like strings and lists, items in a tuple are accessed by offset (not by key); they support all the offset-based access operations, such as indexing and slicing.

Of the category "immutable sequence"

Like strings and lists, tuples are sequences; they support many of the same operations. However, like strings, tuples are immutable; they don't support any of the in-place change operations applied to lists.

Fixed-length, heterogeneous, and arbitrarily nestable

Because tuples are immutable, you cannot change the size of a tuple without making a copy. On the other hand, tuples can hold any type of object, including other compound objects (e.g., lists, dictionaries, other tuples), and so support arbitrary nesting.

Arrays of object references

Like lists, tuples are best thought of as object reference arrays; tuples store access points to other objects (references), and indexing a tuple is relatively quick.

Table 9-1 highlights common tuple operations. A tuple is written as a series of objects (technically, expressions that generate objects), separated by commas and normally enclosed in parentheses. An empty tuple is just a parentheses pair with nothing inside.

Table 9-1. Common tuple literals and operations

Operation	Interpretation
()	An empty tuple
T = (0,)	A one-item tuple (not an expression)
T = (0, 'Ni', 1.2, 3)	A four-item tuple
T = 0, 'Ni', 1.2, 3	Another four-item tuple (same as prior line)
T = ('abc', ('def', 'ghi'))	Nested tuples
T = tuple('spam')	Tuple of items in an iterable
T[i]	Index, index of index, slice, length
T[i][j]	
T[i:j]	
len(T)	
T1 + T2	Concatenate, repeat
T * 3	
for x in T: print(x)	Iteration, membership
'spam' in T	
[x ** 2 for x in T]	
T.index('Ni')	Methods in 2.6 and 3.0: search, count
T.count('Ni')	

Tuples in Action

As usual, let's start an interactive session to explore tuples at work. Notice in Table 9-1 that tuples do not have all the methods that lists have (e.g., an append call won't work here). They do, however, support the usual sequence operations that we saw for both strings and lists:

```
>>> (1, 2) + (3, 4)          # Concatenation
(1, 2, 3, 4)

>>> (1, 2) * 4               # Repetition
(1, 2, 1, 2, 1, 2, 1, 2)

>>> T = (1, 2, 3, 4)         # Indexing, slicing
>>> T[0], T[1:3]
(1, (2, 3))
```

Tuple syntax peculiarities: Commas and parentheses

The second and fourth entries in Table 9-1 merit a bit more explanation. Because parentheses can also enclose expressions (see Chapter 5), you need to do something special to tell Python when a single object in parentheses is a tuple object and not a simple expression. If you really want a single-item tuple, simply add a trailing comma after the single item, before the closing parenthesis:

```
>>> x = (40)           # An integer!
>>> x
40
>>> y = (40,)          # A tuple containing an integer
>>> y
(40,)
```

As a special case, Python also allows you to omit the opening and closing parentheses for a tuple in contexts where it isn't syntactically ambiguous to do so. For instance, the fourth line of Table 9-1 simply lists four items separated by commas. In the context of an assignment statement, Python recognizes this as a tuple, even though it doesn't have parentheses.

Now, some people will tell you to always use parentheses in your tuples, and some will tell you to never use parentheses in tuples (and still others have lives, and won't tell you what to do with your tuples!). The only significant places where the parentheses are *required* are when a tuple is passed as a literal in a function call (where parentheses matter), and when one is listed in a Python 2.X print statement (where commas are significant).

For beginners, the best advice is that it's probably easier to use the parentheses than it is to figure out when they are optional. Many programmers (myself included) also find that parentheses tend to aid script readability by making the tuples more explicit, but your mileage may vary.

Conversions, methods, and immutability

Apart from literal syntax differences, tuple operations (the middle rows in Table 9-1) are identical to string and list operations. The only differences worth noting are that the +, *, and slicing operations return new *tuples* when applied to tuples, and that tuples don't provide the same methods you saw for strings, lists, and dictionaries. If you want to sort a tuple, for example, you'll usually have to either first convert it to a list to gain access to a sorting method call and make it a mutable object, or use the newer `sorted` built-in that accepts any sequence object (and more):

```
>>> T = ('cc', 'aa', 'dd', 'bb')
>>> tmp = list(T)                    # Make a list from a tuple's items
>>> tmp.sort()                       # Sort the list
>>> tmp
['aa', 'bb', 'cc', 'dd']
>>> T = tuple(tmp)                   # Make a tuple from the list's items
>>> T
('aa', 'bb', 'cc', 'dd')

>>> sorted(T)                        # Or use the sorted built-in
['aa', 'bb', 'cc', 'dd']
```

Here, the `list` and `tuple` built-in functions are used to convert the object to a list and then back to a tuple; really, both calls make new objects, but the net effect is like a conversion.

List comprehensions can also be used to convert tuples. The following, for example, makes a list from a tuple, adding 20 to each item along the way:

```
>>> T = (1, 2, 3, 4, 5)
>>> L = [x + 20 for x in T]
>>> L
[21, 22, 23, 24, 25]
```

List comprehensions are really sequence operations—they always build new lists, but they may be used to iterate over any sequence objects, including tuples, strings, and other lists. As we'll see later in the book, they even work on some things that are not physically stored sequences—any iterable objects will do, including files, which are automatically read line by line.

Although tuples don't have the same methods as lists and strings, they do have two of their own as of Python 2.6 and 3.0—`index` and `count` works as they do for lists, but they are defined for tuple objects:

```
>>> T = (1, 2, 3, 2, 4, 2)           # Tuple methods in 2.6 and 3.0
>>> T.index(2)                       # Offset of first appearance of 2
1
>>> T.index(2, 2)                    # Offset of appearance after offset 2
3
>>> T.count(2)                       # How many 2s are there?
3
```

Prior to 2.6 and 3.0, tuples have no methods at all—this was an old Python convention for immutable types, which was violated years ago on grounds of practicality with strings, and more recently with both numbers and tuples.

Also, note that the rule about tuple *immutability* applies only to the top level of the tuple itself, not to its contents. A list inside a tuple, for instance, can be changed as usual:

```
>>> T = (1, [2, 3], 4)
>>> T[1] = 'spam'                  # This fails: can't change tuple itself
TypeError: object doesn't support item assignment

>>> T[1][0] = 'spam'               # This works: can change mutables inside
>>> T
(1, ['spam', 3], 4)
```

For most programs, this one-level-deep immutability is sufficient for common tuple roles. Which, coincidentally, brings us to the next section.

Why Lists and Tuples?

This seems to be the first question that always comes up when teaching beginners about tuples: why do we need tuples if we have lists? Some of the reasoning may be historic; Python's creator is a mathematician by training, and he has been quoted as seeing a tuple as a simple association of objects and a list as a data structure that changes over time. In fact, this use of the word "tuple" derives from mathematics, as does its frequent use for a row in a relational database table.

The best answer, however, seems to be that the immutability of tuples provides some *integrity*—you can be sure a tuple won't be changed through another reference elsewhere in a program, but there's no such guarantee for lists. Tuples, therefore, serve a similar role to "constant" declarations in other languages, though the notion of constantness is associated with objects in Python, not variables.

Tuples can also be used in places that lists cannot—for example, as dictionary keys (see the sparse matrix example in Chapter 8). Some built-in operations may also require or imply tuples, not lists, though such operations have often been generalized in recent years. As a rule of thumb, lists are the tool of choice for ordered collections that might need to change; tuples can handle the other cases of fixed associations.

Files

You may already be familiar with the notion of files, which are named storage compartments on your computer that are managed by your operating system. The last major built-in object type that we'll examine on our object types tour provides a way to access those files inside Python programs.

In short, the built-in open function creates a Python file object, which serves as a link to a file residing on your machine. After calling open, you can transfer strings of data to and from the associated external file by calling the returned file object's methods.

Compared to the types you've seen so far, file objects are somewhat unusual. They're not numbers, sequences, or mappings, and they don't respond to expression operators; they export only methods for common file-processing tasks. Most file methods are concerned with performing input from and output to the external file associated with a file object, but other file methods allow us to seek to a new position in the file, flush output buffers, and so on. Table 9-2 summarizes common file operations.

Table 9-2. Common file operations

Operation	Interpretation
output = open(r'C:\spam', 'w')	Create output file ('w' means write)
input = open('data', 'r')	Create input file ('r' means read)
input = open('data')	Same as prior line ('r' is the default)
aString = input.read()	Read entire file into a single string
aString = input.read(N)	Read up to next N characters (or bytes) into a string
aString = input.readline()	Read next line (including \n newline) into a string
aList = input.readlines()	Read entire file into list of line strings (with \n)
output.write(aString)	Write a string of characters (or bytes) into file
output.writelines(aList)	Write all line strings in a list into file
output.close()	Manual close (done for you when file is collected)
output.flush()	Flush output buffer to disk without closing
anyFile.seek(N)	Change file position to offset N for next operation
for line in open('data'): *use line*	File iterators read line by line
open('f.txt', encoding='latin-1')	Python 3.0 Unicode text files (str strings)
open('f.bin', 'rb')	Python 3.0 binary bytes files (bytes strings)

Opening Files

To open a file, a program calls the built-in open function, with the external filename first, followed by a processing *mode*. The mode is typically the string 'r' to open for text input (the default), 'w' to create and open for text output, or 'a' to open for appending text to the end. The processing mode argument can specify additional options:

• Adding a b to the mode string allows for *binary* data (end-of-line translations and 3.0 Unicode encodings are turned off).

- Adding a + opens the file for *both* input and output (i.e., you can both read and write to the same file object, often in conjunction with seek operations to reposition in the file).

Both arguments to `open` must be Python strings, and an optional third argument can be used to control output buffering—passing a zero means that output is unbuffered (it is transferred to the external file immediately on a write method call). The external filename argument may include a platform-specific and absolute or relative directory path prefix; without a directory path, the file is assumed to exist in the current working directory (i.e., where the script runs). We'll cover file fundamentals and explore some basic examples here, but we won't go into all file-processing mode options; as usual, consult the Python library manual for additional details.

Using Files

Once you make a file object with `open`, you can call its methods to read from or write to the associated external file. In all cases, file text takes the form of strings in Python programs; reading a file returns its text in strings, and text is passed to the write methods as strings. Reading and writing methods come in multiple flavors; Table 9-2 lists the most common. Here are a few fundamental usage notes:

File iterators are best for reading lines
>Though the reading and writing methods in the table are common, keep in mind that probably the best way to read lines from a text file today is to not read the file at all—as we'll see in Chapter 14, files also have an *iterator* that automatically reads one line at a time in a `for` loop, list comprehension, or other iteration context.

Content is strings, not objects
>Notice in Table 9-2 that data read from a file always comes back to your script as a string, so you'll have to convert it to a different type of Python object if a string is not what you need. Similarly, unlike with the `print` operation, Python does not add any formatting and does not convert objects to strings automatically when you write data to a file—you must send an already formatted string. Because of this, the tools we have already met to convert objects to and from strings (e.g., `int`, `float`, `str`, and the string formatting expression and method) come in handy when dealing with files. Python also includes advanced standard library tools for handling generic object storage (such as the `pickle` module) and for dealing with packed binary data in files (such as the `struct` module). We'll see both of these at work later in this chapter.

`close` *is usually optional*
>Calling the file `close` method terminates your connection to the external file. As discussed in Chapter 6, in Python an object's memory space is automatically reclaimed as soon as the object is no longer referenced anywhere in the program. When file objects are reclaimed, Python also automatically closes the files if they are still open (this also happens when a program shuts down). This means you

don't always need to manually close your files, especially in simple scripts that don't run for long. On the other hand, including manual `close` calls can't hurt and is usually a good idea in larger systems. Also, strictly speaking, this auto-close-on-collection feature of files is not part of the language definition, and it may change over time. Consequently, manually issuing file `close` method calls is a good habit to form. (For an alternative way to guarantee automatic file closes, also see this section's later discussion of the file object's *context manager*, used with the new `with`/`as` statement in Python 2.6 and 3.0.)

Files are buffered and seekable.

The prior paragraph's notes about closing files are important, because closing both frees up operating system resources and flushes output buffers. By default, output files are always buffered, which means that text you write may not be transferred from memory to disk immediately—closing a file, or running its `flush` method, forces the buffered data to disk. You can avoid buffering with extra `open` arguments, but it may impede performance. Python files are also random-access on a byte offset basis—their `seek` method allows your scripts to jump around to read and write at specific locations.

Files in Action

Let's work through a simple example that demonstrates file-processing basics. The following code begins by opening a new text file for output, writing two lines (strings terminated with a newline marker, `\n`), and closing the file. Later, the example opens the same file again in input mode and reads the lines back one at a time with `readline`. Notice that the third `readline` call returns an empty string; this is how Python file methods tell you that you've reached the end of the file (empty lines in the file come back as strings containing just a newline character, not as empty strings). Here's the complete interaction:

```
>>> myfile = open('myfile.txt', 'w')        # Open for text output: create/empty
>>> myfile.write('hello text file\n')        # Write a line of text: string
16
>>> myfile.write('goodbye text file\n')
18
>>> myfile.close()                           # Flush output buffers to disk

>>> myfile = open('myfile.txt')              # Open for text input: 'r' is default
>>> myfile.readline()                        # Read the lines back
'hello text file\n'
>>> myfile.readline()
'goodbye text file\n'
>>> myfile.readline()                        # Empty string: end of file
''
```

Notice that file `write` calls return the number of characters written in Python 3.0; in 2.6 they don't, so you won't see these numbers echoed interactively. This example writes each line of text, including its end-of-line terminator, `\n`, as a string; write methods don't add the end-of-line character for us, so we must include it to properly terminate our lines (otherwise the next write will simply extend the current line in the file).

If you want to display the file's content with end-of-line characters interpreted, read the entire file into a string *all at once* with the file object's **read** method and print it:

```
>>> open('myfile.txt').read()          # Read all at once into string
'hello text file\ngoodbye text file\n'

>>> print(open('myfile.txt').read())    # User-friendly display
hello text file
goodbye text file
```

And if you want to scan a text file line by line, *file iterators* are often your best option:

```
>>> for line in open('myfile.txt'):     # Use file iterators, not reads
...     print(line, end='')
...
hello text file
goodbye text file
```

When coded this way, the temporary file object created by **open** will automatically read and return one line on each loop iteration. This form is usually easiest to code, good on memory use, and may be faster than some other options (depending on many variables, of course). Since we haven't reached statements or iterators yet, though, you'll have to wait until Chapter 14 for a more complete explanation of this code.

Text and binary files in Python 3.0

Strictly speaking, the example in the prior section uses text files. In both Python 3.0 and 2.6, file type is determined by the second argument to **open**, the mode string—an included "b" means binary. Python has always supported both text and binary files, but in Python 3.0 there is a sharper distinction between the two:

- *Text files* represent content as normal **str** strings, perform Unicode encoding and decoding automatically, and perform end-of-line translation by default.
- *Binary files* represent content as a special **bytes** string type and allow programs to access file content unaltered.

In contrast, Python 2.6 text files handle both 8-bit text and binary data, and a special string type and file interface (**unicode** strings and **codecs.open**) handles Unicode text. The differences in Python 3.0 stem from the fact that simple and Unicode text have been merged in the normal string type—which makes sense, given that all text is Unicode, including ASCII and other 8-bit encodings.

Because most programmers deal only with ASCII text, they can get by with the basic text file interface used in the prior example, and normal strings. All strings are technically Unicode in 3.0, but ASCII users will not generally notice. In fact, files and strings work the same in 3.0 and 2.6 if your script's scope is limited to such simple forms of text.

If you need to handle internationalized applications or byte-oriented data, though, the distinction in 3.0 impacts your code (usually for the better). In general, you must use **bytes** strings for binary files, and normal **str** strings for text files. Moreover, because text files implement Unicode encodings, you cannot open a binary data file in text mode—decoding its content to Unicode text will likely fail.

Let's look at an example. When you read a binary data file you get back a **bytes** object—a sequence of small integers that represent absolute byte values (which may or may not correspond to characters), which looks and feels almost exactly like a normal string:

```
>>> data = open('data.bin', 'rb').read()    # Open binary file: rb=read binary
>>> data                                      # bytes string holds binary data
b'\x00\x00\x00\x07spam\x00\x08'
>>> data[4:8]                                 # Act like strings
b'spam'
>>> data[4:8][0]                              # But really are small 8-bit integers
115
>>> bin(data[4:8][0])                         # Python 3.0 bin() function
'0b1110011'
```

In addition, binary files do not perform any end-of-line translation on data; text files by default map all forms to and from \n when written and read and implement Unicode encodings on transfers. Since Unicode and binary data is of marginal interest to many Python programmers, we'll postpone the full story until Chapter 36. For now, let's move on to some more substantial file examples.

Storing and parsing Python objects in files

Our next example writes a variety of Python objects into a text file on multiple lines. Notice that it must convert objects to strings using conversion tools. Again, file data is always strings in our scripts, and write methods do not do any automatic to-string formatting for us (for space, I'm omitting byte-count return values from **write** methods from here on):

```
>>> X, Y, Z = 43, 44, 45                      # Native Python objects
>>> S = 'Spam'                                # Must be strings to store in file
>>> D = {'a': 1, 'b': 2}
>>> L = [1, 2, 3]
>>>
>>> F = open('datafile.txt', 'w')             # Create output file
>>> F.write(S + '\n')                         # Terminate lines with \n
>>> F.write('%s,%s,%s\n' % (X, Y, Z))         # Convert numbers to strings
>>> F.write(str(L) + '$' + str(D) + '\n')     # Convert and separate with $
>>> F.close()
```

Once we have created our file, we can inspect its contents by opening it and reading it into a string (a single operation). Notice that the interactive echo gives the exact byte contents, while the **print** operation interprets embedded end-of-line characters to render a more user-friendly display:

```
>>> chars = open('datafile.txt').read()       # Raw string display
>>> chars
```

```
"Spam\n43,44,45\n[1, 2, 3]${'a': 1, 'b': 2}\n"
>>> print(chars)                                    # User-friendly display
Spam
43,44,45
[1, 2, 3]${'a': 1, 'b': 2}
```

We now have to use other conversion tools to translate from the strings in the text file to real Python objects. As Python never converts strings to numbers (or other types of objects) automatically, this is required if we need to gain access to normal object tools like indexing, addition, and so on:

```
>>> F = open('datafile.txt')            # Open again
>>> line = F.readline()                 # Read one line
>>> line
'Spam\n'
>>> line.rstrip()                       # Remove end-of-line
'Spam'
```

For this first line, we used the string `rstrip` method to get rid of the trailing end-of-line character; a `line[:-1]` slice would work, too, but only if we can be sure all lines end in the `\n` character (the last line in a file sometimes does not).

So far, we've read the line containing the string. Now let's grab the next line, which contains numbers, and parse out (that is, extract) the objects on that line:

```
>>> line = F.readline()                 # Next line from file
>>> line                                # It's a string here
'43,44,45\n'
>>> parts = line.split(',')             # Split (parse) on commas
>>> parts
['43', '44', '45\n']
```

We used the string `split` method here to chop up the line on its comma delimiters; the result is a list of substrings containing the individual numbers. We still must convert from strings to integers, though, if we wish to perform math on these:

```
>>> int(parts[1])                       # Convert from string to int
44
>>> numbers = [int(P) for P in parts]   # Convert all in list at once
>>> numbers
[43, 44, 45]
```

As we have learned, `int` translates a string of digits into an integer object, and the list comprehension expression introduced in Chapter 4 can apply the call to each item in our list all at once (you'll find more on list comprehensions later in this book). Notice that we didn't have to run `rstrip` to delete the `\n` at the end of the last part; `int` and some other converters quietly ignore whitespace around digits.

Finally, to convert the stored list and dictionary in the third line of the file, we can run them through `eval`, a built-in function that treats a string as a piece of executable program code (technically, a string containing a Python expression):

```
>>> line = F.readline()
>>> line
```

```
"[1, 2, 3]${'a': 1, 'b': 2}\n"
>>> parts = line.split('$')            # Split (parse) on $
>>> parts
['[1, 2, 3]', "{'a': 1, 'b': 2}\n"]
>>> eval(parts[0])                      # Convert to any object type
[1, 2, 3]
>>> objects = [eval(P) for P in parts]  # Do same for all in list
>>> objects
[[1, 2, 3], {'a': 1, 'b': 2}]
```

Because the end result of all this parsing and converting is a list of normal Python objects instead of strings, we can now apply list and dictionary operations to them in our script.

Storing native Python objects with pickle

Using eval to convert from strings to objects, as demonstrated in the preceding code, is a powerful tool. In fact, sometimes it's *too* powerful. eval will happily run any Python expression—even one that might delete all the files on your computer, given the necessary permissions! If you really want to store native Python objects, but you can't trust the source of the data in the file, Python's standard library pickle module is ideal.

The pickle module is an advanced tool that allows us to store almost any Python object in a file directly, with no to- or from-string conversion requirement on our part. It's like a super-general data formatting and parsing utility. To store a dictionary in a file, for instance, we pickle it directly:

```
>>> D = {'a': 1, 'b': 2}
>>> F = open('datafile.pkl', 'wb')
>>> import pickle
>>> pickle.dump(D, F)                   # Pickle any object to file
>>> F.close()
```

Then, to get the dictionary back later, we simply use pickle again to re-create it:

```
>>> F = open('datafile.pkl', 'rb')
>>> E = pickle.load(F)                  # Load any object from file
>>> E
{'a': 1, 'b': 2}
```

We get back an equivalent dictionary object, with no manual splitting or converting required. The pickle module performs what is known as *object serialization*—converting objects to and from strings of bytes—but requires very little work on our part. In fact, pickle internally translates our dictionary to a string form, though it's not much to look at (and may vary if we pickle in other data protocol modes):

```
>>> open('datafile.pkl', 'rb').read()   # Format is prone to change!
b'\x80\x03}q\x00(X\x01\x00\x00\x00aq\x01K\x01X\x01\x00\x00\x00bq\x02K\x02u.'
```

Because pickle can reconstruct the object from this format, we don't have to deal with that ourselves. For more on the pickle module, see the Python standard library manual, or import pickle and pass it to help interactively. While you're exploring, also take a look at the shelve module. shelve is a tool that uses pickle to store Python objects in an access-by-key filesystem, which is beyond our scope here (though you will get to see an example of `shelve` in action in Chapter 27, and other `pickle` examples in Chapters 30 and 36).

 Note that I opened the file used to store the pickled object in *binary mode*; binary mode is always required in Python 3.0, because the pickler creates and uses a `bytes` string object, and these objects imply binary-mode files (text-mode files imply `str` strings in 3.0). In earlier Pythons it's OK to use text-mode files for protocol 0 (the default, which creates ASCII text), as long as text mode is used consistently; higher protocols require binary-mode files. Python 3.0's default protocol is 3 (binary), but it creates `bytes` even for protocol 0. See Chapter 36, Python's library manual, or reference books for more details on this.

Python 2.6 also has a `cPickle` module, which is an optimized version of `pickle` that can be imported directly for speed. Python 3.0 renames this module `_pickle` and uses it automatically in `pickle`—scripts simply import `pickle` and let Python optimize itself.

Storing and parsing packed binary data in files

One other file-related note before we move on: some advanced applications also need to deal with packed binary data, created perhaps by a C language program. Python's standard library includes a tool to help in this domain—the **struct** module knows how to both compose and parse packed binary data. In a sense, this is another data-conversion tool that interprets strings in files as binary data.

To create a packed binary data file, for example, open it in `'wb'` (write binary) mode, and pass `struct` a format string and some Python objects. The format string used here means pack as a 4-byte integer, a 4-character string, and a 2-byte integer, all in big-endian form (other format codes handle padding bytes, floating-point numbers, and more):

```
>>> F = open('data.bin', 'wb')              # Open binary output file
>>> import struct
>>> data = struct.pack('>i4sh', 7, 'spam', 8)    # Make packed binary data
>>> data
b'\x00\x00\x00\x07spam\x00\x08'
>>> F.write(data)                           # Write byte string
>>> F.close()
```

Python creates a binary `bytes` data string, which we write out to the file normally—this one consists mostly of nonprintable characters printed in hexadecimal escapes, and is the same binary file we met earlier. To parse the values out to normal Python objects, we simply read the string back and unpack it using the same format string. Python extracts the values into normal Python objects—integers and a string:

```
>>> F = open('data.bin', 'rb')
>>> data = F.read()                         # Get packed binary data
>>> data
b'\x00\x00\x00\x07spam\x00\x08'
```

```
>>> values = struct.unpack('>i4sh', data)       # Convert to Python objects
>>> values
(7, b'spam', 8)
```

Binary data files are advanced and somewhat low-level tools that we won't cover in more detail here; for more help, see Chapter 36, consult the Python library manual, or import `struct` and pass it to the `help` function interactively. Also note that the binary file-processing modes `'wb'` and `'rb'` can be used to process a simpler binary file such as an image or audio file as a whole without having to unpack its contents.

File context managers

You'll also want to watch for Chapter 33's discussion of the file's *context manager* support, new in Python 3.0 and 2.6. Though more a feature of exception processing than files themselves, it allows us to wrap file-processing code in a logic layer that ensures that the file will be closed automatically on exit, instead of relying on the auto-close on garbage collection:

```
with open(r'C:\misc\data.txt') as myfile:       # See Chapter 33 for details
    for line in myfile:
        ...use line here...
```

The `try/finally` statement we'll look at in Chapter 33 can provide similar functionality, but at some cost in extra code—three extra lines, to be precise (though we can often avoid both options and let Python close files for us automatically):

```
myfile = open(r'C:\misc\data.txt')
try:
    for line in myfile:
        ...use line here...
finally:
    myfile.close()
```

Since both these options require more information than we have yet obtained, we'll postpone details until later in this book.

Other File Tools

There are additional, more advanced file methods shown in Table 9-2, and even more that are not in the table. For instance, as mentioned earlier, **seek** resets your current position in a file (the next read or write happens at that position), **flush** forces buffered output to be written out to disk (by default, files are always buffered), and so on.

The Python standard library manual and the reference books described in the Preface provide complete lists of file methods; for a quick look, run a `dir` or `help` call interactively, passing in an open file object (in Python 2.6 but not 3.0, you can pass in the name `file` instead). For more file-processing examples, watch for the sidebar "Why You Will Care: File Scanners" on page 342. It sketches common file-scanning loop code patterns with statements we have not covered enough yet to use here.

Also, note that although the open function and the file objects it returns are your main interface to external files in a Python script, there are additional file-like tools in the Python toolset. Also available, to name a few, are:

Standard streams
Preopened file objects in the sys module, such as sys.stdout (see "Print Operations" on page 299)

Descriptor files in the os module
Integer file handles that support lower-level tools such as file locking

Sockets, pipes, and FIFOs
File-like objects used to synchronize processes or communicate over networks

Access-by-key files known as "shelves"
Used to store unaltered Python objects directly, by key (used in Chapter 27)

Shell command streams
Tools such as os.popen and subprocess.Popen that support spawning shell commands and reading and writing to their standard streams

The third-party open source domain offers even more file-like tools, including support for communicating with serial ports in the *PySerial* extension and interactive programs in the *pexpect* system. See more advanced Python texts and the Web at large for additional information on file-like tools.

 Version skew note: In Python 2.5 and earlier, the built-in name open is essentially a synonym for the name file, and files may technically be opened by calling either open or file (though open is generally preferred for opening). In Python 3.0, the name file is no longer available, because of its redundancy with open.

Python 2.6 users may also use the name file as the file object type, in order to customize files with object-oriented programming (described later in this book). In Python 3.0, files have changed radically. The classes used to implement file objects live in the standard library module io. See this module's documentation or code for the classes it makes available for customization, and run a type(F) call on open files F for hints.

Type Categories Revisited

Now that we've seen all of Python's core built-in types in action, let's wrap up our object types tour by reviewing some of the properties they share. Table 9-3 classifies all the major types we've seen so far according to the type categories introduced earlier. Here are some points to remember:

- Objects share operations according to their category; for instance, strings, lists, and tuples all share sequence operations such as concatenation, length, and indexing.

- Only mutable objects (lists, dictionaries, and sets) may be changed in-place; you cannot change numbers, strings, or tuples in-place.

- Files export only methods, so mutability doesn't really apply to them—their state may be changed when they are processed, but this isn't quite the same as Python core type mutability constraints.

- "Numbers" in Table 9-3 includes all number types: integer (and the distinct long integer in 2.6), floating-point, complex, decimal, and fraction.

- "Strings" in Table 9-3 includes `str`, as well as `bytes` in 3.0 and `unicode` in 2.6; the `bytearray` string type in 3.0 is mutable.

- Sets are something like the keys of a valueless dictionary, but they don't map to values and are not ordered, so sets are neither a mapping nor a sequence type; `frozenset` is an immutable variant of `set`.

- In addition to type category operations, as of Python 2.6 and 3.0 all the types in Table 9-3 have callable methods, which are generally specific to their type.

Table 9-3. Object classifications

Object type	Category	Mutable?
Numbers (all)	Numeric	No
Strings	Sequence	No
Lists	Sequence	Yes
Dictionaries	Mapping	Yes
Tuples	Sequence	No
Files	Extension	N/A
Sets	Set	Yes
`frozenset`	Set	No
`bytearray` (3.0)	Sequence	Yes

Why You Will Care: Operator Overloading

In Part VI of this book, we'll see that objects we implement with classes can pick and choose from these categories arbitrarily. For instance, if we want to provide a new kind of specialized sequence object that is consistent with built-in sequences, we can code a class that overloads things like indexing and concatenation:

```
class MySequence:
    def __getitem__(self, index):
        # Called on self[index], others
    def __add__(self, other):
        # Called on self + other
```

and so on. We can also make the new object mutable or not by selectively implementing methods called for in-place change operations (e.g., __setitem__ is called on self[index]=value assignments). Although it's beyond this book's scope, it's also possible to implement new objects in an external language like C as C extension types. For these, we fill in C function pointer slots to choose between number, sequence, and mapping operation sets.

Object Flexibility

This part of the book introduced a number of compound object types (collections with components). In general:

- Lists, dictionaries, and tuples can hold any kind of object.
- Lists, dictionaries, and tuples can be arbitrarily nested.
- Lists and dictionaries can dynamically grow and shrink.

Because they support arbitrary structures, Python's compound object types are good at representing complex information in programs. For example, values in dictionaries may be lists, which may contain tuples, which may contain dictionaries, and so on. The nesting can be as deep as needed to model the data to be processed.

Let's look at an example of nesting. The following interaction defines a tree of nested compound sequence objects, shown in Figure 9-1. To access its components, you may include as many index operations as required. Python evaluates the indexes from left to right, and fetches a reference to a more deeply nested object at each step. Figure 9-1 may be a pathologically complicated data structure, but it illustrates the syntax used to access nested objects in general:

```
>>> L = ['abc', [(1, 2), ([3], 4)], 5]
>>> L[1]
[(1, 2), ([3], 4)]
>>> L[1][1]
([3], 4)
>>> L[1][1][0]
[3]
>>> L[1][1][0][0]
3
```

References Versus Copies

Chapter 6 mentioned that assignments always store references to objects, not copies of those objects. In practice, this is usually what you want. Because assignments can generate multiple references to the same object, though, it's important to be aware that changing a mutable object in-place may affect other references to the same object

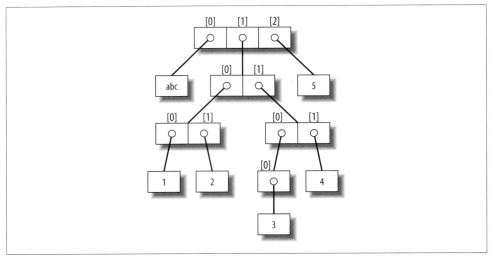

Figure 9-1. A nested object tree with the offsets of its components, created by running the literal expression ['abc', [(1, 2), ([3], 4)], 5]. Syntactically nested objects are internally represented as references (i.e., pointers) to separate pieces of memory.

elsewhere in your program. If you don't want such behavior, you'll need to tell Python to copy the object explicitly.

We studied this phenomenon in Chapter 6, but it can become more subtle when larger objects come into play. For instance, the following example creates a list assigned to X, and another list assigned to L that embeds a reference back to list X. It also creates a dictionary D that contains another reference back to list X:

```
>>> X = [1, 2, 3]
>>> L = ['a', X, 'b']        # Embed references to X's object
>>> D = {'x':X, 'y':2}
```

At this point, there are three references to the first list created: from the name X, from inside the list assigned to L, and from inside the dictionary assigned to D. The situation is illustrated in Figure 9-2.

Because lists are mutable, changing the shared list object from any of the three references also changes what the other two reference:

```
>>> X[1] = 'surprise'        # Changes all three references!
>>> L
['a', [1, 'surprise', 3], 'b']
>>> D
{'x': [1, 'surprise', 3], 'y': 2}
```

References are a higher-level analog of pointers in other languages. Although you can't grab hold of the reference itself, it's possible to store the same reference in more than one place (variables, lists, and so on). This is a feature—you can pass a large object

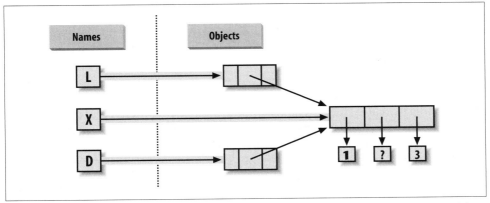

Figure 9-2. Shared object references: because the list referenced by variable X is also referenced from within the objects referenced by L and D, changing the shared list from X makes it look different from L and D, too.

around a program without generating expensive copies of it along the way. If you really do want copies, however, you can request them:

- Slice expressions with empty limits (L[:]) copy sequences.
- The dictionary and set copy method (X.copy()) copies a dictionary or set.
- Some built-in functions, such as list, make copies (list(L)).
- The copy standard library module makes full copies.

For example, say you have a list and a dictionary, and you don't want their values to be changed through other variables:

```
>>> L = [1,2,3]
>>> D = {'a':1, 'b':2}
```

To prevent this, simply assign copies to the other variables, not references to the same objects:

```
>>> A = L[:]          # Instead of A = L (or list(L))
>>> B = D.copy()      # Instead of B = D (ditto for sets)
```

This way, changes made from the other variables will change the copies, not the originals:

```
>>> A[1] = 'Ni'
>>> B['c'] = 'spam'
>>>
>>> L, D
([1, 2, 3], {'a': 1, 'b': 2})
>>> A, B
([1, 'Ni', 3], {'a': 1, 'c': 'spam', 'b': 2})
```

In terms of our original example, you can avoid the reference side effects by slicing the original list instead of simply naming it:

```
>>> X = [1, 2, 3]
>>> L = ['a', X[:], 'b']          # Embed copies of X's object
>>> D = {'x':X[:], 'y':2}
```

This changes the picture in Figure 9-2—L and D will now point to different lists than X. The net effect is that changes made through X will impact only X, not L and D; similarly, changes to L or D will not impact X.

One final note on copies: empty-limit slices and the dictionary copy method only make *top-level* copies; that is, they do not copy nested data structures, if any are present. If you need a complete, fully independent copy of a deeply nested data structure, use the standard copy module: include an `import copy` statement and say X = `copy.deep copy(Y)` to fully copy an arbitrarily nested object Y. This call recursively traverses objects to copy all their parts. This is a much more rare case, though (which is why you have to say more to make it go). References are usually what you will want; when they are not, slices and copy methods are usually as much copying as you'll need to do.

Comparisons, Equality, and Truth

All Python objects also respond to comparisons: tests for equality, relative magnitude, and so on. Python comparisons always inspect all parts of compound objects until a result can be determined. In fact, when nested objects are present, Python automatically traverses data structures to apply comparisons *recursively* from left to right, and as deeply as needed. The first difference found along the way determines the comparison result.

For instance, a comparison of list objects compares all their components automatically:

```
>>> L1 = [1, ('a', 3)]
>>> L2 = [1, ('a', 3)]           # Same value, unique objects
>>> L1 == L2, L1 is L2           # Equivalent? Same object?
(True, False)
```

Here, L1 and L2 are assigned lists that are equivalent but distinct objects. Because of the nature of Python references (studied in Chapter 6), there are two ways to test for equality:

- **The == operator tests value equivalence**. Python performs an equivalence test, comparing all nested objects recursively.

- **The is operator tests object identity**. Python tests whether the two are really the same object (i.e., live at the same address in memory).

In the preceding example, L1 and L2 pass the == test (they have equivalent values because all their components are equivalent) but fail the is check (they reference two different objects, and hence two different pieces of memory). Notice what happens for short strings, though:

```
>>> S1 = 'spam'
>>> S2 = 'spam'
```

```
>>> S1 == S2, S1 is S2
(True, True)
```

Here, we should again have two distinct objects that happen to have the same value: == should be true, and `is` should be false. But because Python internally caches and reuses some strings as an optimization, there really is just a single string `'spam'` in memory, shared by S1 and S2; hence, the `is` identity test reports a true result. To trigger the normal behavior, we need to use longer strings:

```
>>> S1 = 'a longer string'
>>> S2 = 'a longer string'
>>> S1 == S2, S1 is S2
(True, False)
```

Of course, because strings are immutable, the object caching mechanism is irrelevant to your code—strings can't be changed in-place, regardless of how many variables refer to them. If identity tests seem confusing, see Chapter 6 for a refresher on object reference concepts.

As a rule of thumb, the == operator is what you will want to use for almost all equality checks; `is` is reserved for highly specialized roles. We'll see cases where these operators are put to use later in the book.

Relative magnitude comparisons are also applied recursively to nested data structures:

```
>>> L1 = [1, ('a', 3)]
>>> L2 = [1, ('a', 2)]
>>> L1 < L2, L1 == L2, L1 > L2          # Less, equal, greater: tuple of results
(False, False, True)
```

Here, L1 is greater than L2 because the nested 3 is greater than 2. The result of the last line is really a tuple of three objects—the results of the three expressions typed (an example of a tuple without its enclosing parentheses).

In general, Python compares types as follows:

- Numbers are compared by relative magnitude.
- Strings are compared lexicographically, character by character (`"abc" < "ac"`).
- Lists and tuples are compared by comparing each component from left to right.
- Dictionaries compare as equal if their sorted (*key, value*) lists are equal. Relative magnitude comparisons are not supported for dictionaries in Python 3.0, but they work in 2.6 and earlier as though comparing sorted (*key, value*) lists.
- Nonnumeric mixed-type comparisons (e.g., `1 < 'spam'`) are errors in Python 3.0. They are allowed in Python 2.6, but use a fixed but arbitrary ordering rule. By proxy, this also applies to sorts, which use comparisons internally: nonnumeric mixed-type collections cannot be sorted in 3.0.

In general, comparisons of structured objects proceed as though you had written the objects as literals and compared all their parts one at a time from left to right. In later chapters, we'll see other object types that can change the way they get compared.

Python 3.0 Dictionary Comparisons

The second to last point in the preceding section merits illustration. In Python 2.6 and earlier, dictionaries support magnitude comparisons, as though you were comparing sorted key/value lists:

```
C:\misc> c:\python26\python
>>> D1 = {'a':1, 'b':2}
>>> D2 = {'a':1, 'b':3}
>>> D1 == D2
False
>>> D1 < D2
True
```

In Python 3.0, magnitude comparisons for dictionaries are removed because they incur too much overhead when equality is desired (equality uses an optimized scheme in 3.0 that doesn't literally compare sorted key/value lists). The alternative in 3.0 is to either write loops to compare values by key or compare the sorted key/value lists manually—the items dictionary methods and sorted built-in suffice:

```
C:\misc> c:\python30\python
>>> D1 = {'a':1, 'b':2}
>>> D2 = {'a':1, 'b':3}
>>> D1 == D2
False
>>> D1 < D2
TypeError: unorderable types: dict() < dict()

>>> list(D1.items())
[('a', 1), ('b', 2)]
>>> sorted(D1.items())
[('a', 1), ('b', 2)]

>>> sorted(D1.items()) < sorted(D2.items())
True
>>> sorted(D1.items()) > sorted(D2.items())
False
```

In practice, most programs requiring this behavior will develop more efficient ways to compare data in dictionaries than either this workaround or the original behavior in Python 2.6.

The Meaning of True and False in Python

Notice that the test results returned in the last two examples represent true and false values. They print as the words True and False, but now that we're using logical tests like these in earnest, I should be a bit more formal about what these names really mean.

In Python, as in most programming languages, an integer 0 represents false, and an integer 1 represents true. In addition, though, Python recognizes any empty data structure as false and any nonempty data structure as true. More generally, the notions of

---

true and false are intrinsic properties of every object in Python—each object is either true or false, as follows:

- Numbers are true if nonzero.
- Other objects are true if nonempty.

Table 9-4 gives examples of true and false objects in Python.

Table 9-4. Example object truth values

Object	Value
"spam"	True
""	False
[]	False
{}	False
1	True
0.0	False
None	False

As one application, because objects are true or false themselves, it's common to see Python programmers code tests like if X:, which, assuming X is a string, is the same as if X != '':. In other words, you can test the object itself, instead of comparing it to an empty object. (More on if statements in Part III.)

The None object

As shown in the last item in Table 9-4, Python also provides a special object called None, which is always considered to be false. None was introduced in Chapter 4; it is the only value of a special data type in Python and typically serves as an empty placeholder (much like a NULL pointer in C).

For example, recall that for lists you cannot assign to an offset unless that offset already exists (the list does not magically grow if you make an out-of-bounds assignment). To preallocate a 100-item list such that you can add to any of the 100 offsets, you can fill it with None objects:

```
>>> L = [None] * 100
>>>
>>> L
[None, None, None, None, None, None, None, ... ]
```

This doesn't limit the size of the list (it can still grow and shrink later), but simply presets an initial size to allow for future index assignments. You could initialize a list with zeros the same way, of course, but best practice dictates using None if the list's contents are not yet known.

Keep in mind that None does not mean "undefined." That is, None is something, not nothing (despite its name!)—it is a real object and piece of memory, given a built-in name by Python. Watch for other uses of this special object later in the book; it is also the default return value of functions, as we'll see in Part IV.

The bool type

Also keep in mind that the Python Boolean type bool, introduced in Chapter 5, simply augments the notions of true and false in Python. As we learned in Chapter 5, the built-in words True and False are just customized versions of the integers 1 and 0—it's as if these two words have been preassigned to 1 and 0 everywhere in Python. Because of the way this new type is implemented, this is really just a minor extension to the notions of true and false already described, designed to make truth values more explicit:

- When used explicitly in truth test code, the words True and False are equivalent to 1 and 0, but they make the programmer's intent clearer.

- Results of Boolean tests run interactively print as the words True and False, instead of as 1 and 0, to make the type of result clearer.

You are not required to use only Boolean types in logical statements such as if; all objects are still inherently true or false, and all the Boolean concepts mentioned in this chapter still work as described if you use other types. Python also provides a bool built-in function that can be used to test the Boolean value of an object (i.e., whether it is True—that is, nonzero or nonempty):

```
>>> bool(1)
True
>>> bool('spam')
True
>>> bool({})
False
```

In practice, though, you'll rarely notice the Boolean type produced by logic tests, because Boolean results are used automatically by if statements and other selection tools. We'll explore Booleans further when we study logical statements in Chapter 12.

Python's Type Hierarchies

Figure 9-3 summarizes all the built-in object types available in Python and their relationships. We've looked at the most prominent of these; most of the other kinds of objects in Figure 9-3 correspond to program units (e.g., functions and modules) or exposed interpreter internals (e.g., stack frames and compiled code).

The main point to notice here is that *everything* in a Python system is an object type and may be processed by your Python programs. For instance, you can pass a class to a function, assign it to a variable, stuff it in a list or dictionary, and so on.

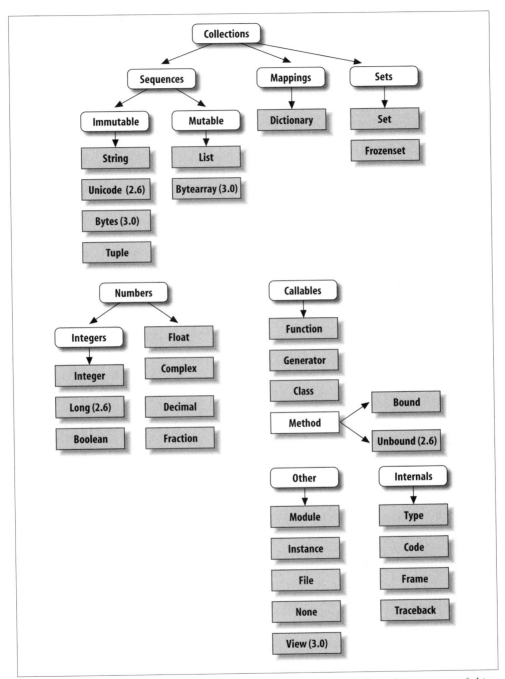

Figure 9-3. Python's major built-in object types, organized by categories. Everything is a type of object in Python, even the type of an object!

Type Objects

In fact, even types themselves are an object type in Python: the type of an object is an object of type type (say that three times fast!). Seriously, a call to the built-in function type(X) returns the type object of object X. The practical application of this is that type objects can be used for manual type comparisons in Python if statements. However, for reasons introduced in Chapter 4, manual type testing is usually not the right thing to do in Python, since it limits your code's flexibility.

One note on type names: as of Python 2.2, each core type has a new built-in name added to support type customization through object-oriented subclassing: dict, list, str, tuple, int, float, complex, bytes, type, set, and more (in Python 2.6 but not 3.0, file is also a type name and a synonym for open). Calls to these names are really object constructor calls, not simply conversion functions, though you can treat them as simple functions for basic usage.

In addition, the types standard library module in Python 3.0 provides additional type names for types that are not available as built-ins (e.g., the type of a function; in Python 2.6 but not 3.0, this module also includes synonyms for built-in type names), and it is possible to do type tests with the isinstance function. For example, all of the following type tests are true:

```
type([1]) == type([])        # Type of another list
type([1]) == list            # List type name
isinstance([1], list)        # List or customization thereof

import types                 # types has names for other types
def f(): pass
type(f) == types.FunctionType
```

Because types can be subclassed in Python today, the isinstance technique is generally recommended. See Chapter 31 for more on subclassing built-in types in Python 2.2 and later.

Also in Chapter 31, we will explore how type(X) and type-testing in general apply to instances of user-defined *classes*. In short, in Python 3.0 and for new-style classes in Python 2.6, the type of a class instance is the class from which the instance was made. For classic classes in Python 2.6 and earlier, all class instances are of the type "instance," and we must compare instance __class__ attributes to compare their types meaningfully. Since we're not ready for classes yet, we'll postpone the rest of this story until Chapter 31.

Other Types in Python

Besides the core objects studied in this part of the book, and the program-unit objects such as functions, modules, and classes that we'll meet later, a typical Python installation has dozens of additional object types available as linked-in C extensions or

Python classes—regular expression objects, DBM files, GUI widgets, network sockets, and so on.

The main difference between these extra tools and the built-in types we've seen so far is that the built-ins provide special language creation syntax for their objects (e.g., 4 for an integer, [1,2] for a list, the open function for files, and def and lambda for functions). Other tools are generally made available in standard library modules that you must first import to use. For instance, to make a regular expression object, you import re and call re.compile(). See Python's library reference for a comprehensive guide to all the tools available to Python programs.

Built-in Type Gotchas

That's the end of our look at core data types. We'll wrap up this part of the book with a discussion of common problems that seem to bite new users (and the occasional expert), along with their solutions. Some of this is a review of ideas we've already covered, but these issues are important enough to warn about again here.

Assignment Creates References, Not Copies

Because this is such a central concept, I'll mention it again: you need to understand what's going on with shared references in your program. For instance, in the following example, the list object assigned to the name L is referenced from L and from inside the list assigned to the name M. Changing L in-place changes what M references, too:

```
>>> L = [1, 2, 3]
>>> M = ['X', L, 'Y']          # Embed a reference to L
>>> M
['X', [1, 2, 3], 'Y']

>>> L[1] = 0                   # Changes M too
>>> M
['X', [1, 0, 3], 'Y']
```

This effect usually becomes important only in larger programs, and shared references are often exactly what you want. If they're not, you can avoid sharing objects by copying them explicitly. For lists, you can always make a top-level copy by using an empty-limits slice:

```
>>> L = [1, 2, 3]
>>> M = ['X', L[:], 'Y']       # Embed a copy of L
>>> L[1] = 0                   # Changes only L, not M
>>> L
[1, 0, 3]
>>> M
['X', [1, 2, 3], 'Y']
```

Remember, slice limits default to 0 and the length of the sequence being sliced; if both are omitted, the slice extracts every item in the sequence and so makes a top-level copy (a new, unshared object).

Repetition Adds One Level Deep

Repeating a sequence is like adding it to itself a number of times. However, when mutable sequences are nested, the effect might not always be what you expect. For instance, in the following example X is assigned to L repeated four times, whereas Y is assigned to a list *containing* L repeated four times:

```
>>> L = [4, 5, 6]
>>> X = L * 4                    # Like [4, 5, 6] + [4, 5, 6] + ...
>>> Y = [L] * 4                  # [L] + [L] + ... = [L, L,...]

>>> X
[4, 5, 6, 4, 5, 6, 4, 5, 6, 4, 5, 6]
>>> Y
[[4, 5, 6], [4, 5, 6], [4, 5, 6], [4, 5, 6]]
```

Because L was nested in the second repetition, Y winds up embedding references back to the original list assigned to L, and so is open to the same sorts of side effects noted in the last section:

```
>>> L[1] = 0                     # Impacts Y but not X
>>> X
[4, 5, 6, 4, 5, 6, 4, 5, 6, 4, 5, 6]
>>> Y
[[4, 0, 6], [4, 0, 6], [4, 0, 6], [4, 0, 6]]
```

The same solutions to this problem apply here as in the previous section, as this is really just another way to create the shared mutable object reference case. If you remember that repetition, concatenation, and slicing copy only the top level of their operand objects, these sorts of cases make much more sense.

Beware of Cyclic Data Structures

We actually encountered this concept in a prior exercise: if a collection object contains a reference to itself, it's called a *cyclic object*. Python prints a [...] whenever it detects a cycle in the object, rather than getting stuck in an infinite loop:

```
>>> L = ['grail']                # Append reference to same object
>>> L.append(L)                  # Generates cycle in object: [...]
>>> L
['grail', [...]]
```

Besides understanding that the three dots in square brackets represent a cycle in the object, this case is worth knowing about because it can lead to gotchas—cyclic structures may cause code of your own to fall into unexpected loops if you don't anticipate them. For instance, some programs keep a list or dictionary of already visited items and check it to determine whether they're in a cycle. See the solutions to the "Test Your Knowledge: Part I Exercises" in Appendix B for more on this problem, and check out the *reloadall.py* program in Chapter 24 for a solution.

Don't use cyclic references unless you really need to. There are good reasons to create cycles, but unless you have code that knows how to handle them, you probably won't want to make your objects reference themselves very often in practice.

Immutable Types Can't Be Changed In-Place

You can't change an immutable object in-place. Instead, you construct a new object with slicing, concatenation, and so on, and assign it back to the original reference, if needed:

```
T = (1, 2, 3)

T[2] = 4                # Error!

T = T[:2] + (4,)        # OK: (1, 2, 4)
```

That might seem like extra coding work, but the upside is that the previous gotchas can't happen when you're using immutable objects such as tuples and strings; because they can't be changed in-place, they are not open to the sorts of side effects that lists are.

Chapter Summary

This chapter explored the last two major core object types—the tuple and the file. We learned that tuples support all the usual sequence operations, have just a few methods, and do not allow any in-place changes because they are immutable. We also learned that files are returned by the built-in open function and provide methods for reading and writing data. We explored how to translate Python objects to and from strings for storing in files, and we looked at the pickle and struct modules for advanced roles (object serialization and binary data). Finally, we wrapped up by reviewing some properties common to all object types (e.g., shared references) and went through a list of common mistakes ("gotchas") in the object type domain.

In the next part, we'll shift gears, turning to the topic of statement syntax in Python—we'll explore all of Python's basic procedural statements in the chapters that follow. The next chapter kicks off that part of the book with an introduction to Python's general syntax model, which is applicable to all statement types. Before moving on, though, take the chapter quiz, and then work through the end-of-part lab exercises to review type concepts. Statements largely just create and process objects, so make sure you've mastered this domain by working through all the exercises before reading on.

Test Your Knowledge: Quiz

1. How can you determine how large a tuple is? Why is this tool located where it is?

2. Write an expression that changes the first item in a tuple. (4, 5, 6) should become (1, 5, 6) in the process.

3. What is the default for the processing mode argument in a file open call?

4. What module might you use to store Python objects in a file without converting them to strings yourself?

5. How might you go about copying all parts of a nested structure at once?

6. When does Python consider an object true?

7. What is your quest?

Test Your Knowledge: Answers

1. The built-in len function returns the length (number of contained items) for any container object in Python, including tuples. It is a built-in function instead of a type method because it applies to many different types of objects. In general, built-in functions and expressions may span many object types; methods are specific to a single object type, though some may be available on more than one type (index, for example, works on lists and tuples).

2. Because they are immutable, you can't really change tuples in-place, but you can generate a new tuple with the desired value. Given T = (4, 5, 6), you can change the first item by making a new tuple from its parts by slicing and concatenating: T = (1,) + T[1:]. (Recall that single-item tuples require a trailing comma.) You could also convert the tuple to a list, change it in-place, and convert it back to a tuple, but this is more expensive and is rarely required in practice—simply use a list if you know that the object will require in-place changes.

3. The default for the processing mode argument in a file open call is 'r', for reading text input. For input text files, simply pass in the external file's name.

4. The pickle module can be used to store Python objects in a file without explicitly converting them to strings. The struct module is related, but it assumes the data is to be in packed binary format in the file.

5. Import the copy module, and call copy.deepcopy(X) if you need to copy all parts of a nested structure X. This is also rarely seen in practice; references are usually the desired behavior, and shallow copies (e.g., aList[:], aDict.copy()) usually suffice for most copies.

6. An object is considered true if it is either a nonzero number or a nonempty collection object. The built-in words `True` and `False` are essentially predefined to have the same meanings as integer `1` and `0`, respectively.

7. Acceptable answers include "To learn Python," "To move on to the next part of the book," or "To seek the Holy Grail."

Test Your Knowledge: Part II Exercises

This session asks you to get your feet wet with built-in object fundamentals. As before, a few new ideas may pop up along the way, so be sure to flip to the answers in Appendix B when you're done (or when you're not, if necessary). If you have limited time, I suggest starting with exercises 10 and 11 (the most practical of the bunch), and then working from first to last as time allows. This is all fundamental material, though, so try to do as many of these as you can.

1. *The basics.* Experiment interactively with the common type operations found in the various operation tables in this part of the book. To get started, bring up the Python interactive interpreter, type each of the following expressions, and try to explain what's happening in each case. Note that the semicolon in some of these is being used as a statement separator, to squeeze multiple statements onto a single line: for example, X=1;X assigns and then prints a variable (more on statement syntax in the next part of the book). Also remember that a comma between expressions usually builds a tuple, even if there are no enclosing parentheses: X,Y,Z is a three-item tuple, which Python prints back to you in parentheses.

```
2 ** 16
2 / 5, 2 / 5.0

"spam" + "eggs"
S = "ham"
"eggs " + S
S * 5
S[:0]
"green %s and %s" % ("eggs", S)
'green {0} and {1}'.format('eggs', S)

('x',)[0]
('x', 'y')[1]

L = [1,2,3] + [4,5,6]
L, L[:], L[:0], L[-2], L[-2:]
([1,2,3] + [4,5,6])[2:4]
[L[2], L[3]]
L.reverse(); L
L.sort(); L
L.index(4)

{'a':1, 'b':2}['b']
D = {'x':1, 'y':2, 'z':3}
```

```
D['w'] = 0
D['x'] + D['w']
D[(1,2,3)] = 4
list(D.keys()), list(D.values()), (1,2,3) in D
```

```
[[]], ["",[],(),{},None]
```

2. *Indexing and slicing.* At the interactive prompt, define a list named L that contains four strings or numbers (e.g., L=[0,1,2,3]). Then, experiment with some boundary cases; you may not ever see these cases in real programs, but they are intended to make you think about the underlying model, and some may be useful in less artificial forms:

  a. What happens when you try to index out of bounds (e.g., L[4])?

  b. What about slicing out of bounds (e.g., L[-1000:100])?

  c. Finally, how does Python handle it if you try to extract a sequence in reverse, with the lower bound greater than the higher bound (e.g., L[3:1])? Hint: try assigning to this slice (L[3:1]=['?']), and see where the value is put. Do you think this may be the same phenomenon you saw when slicing out of bounds?

3. *Indexing, slicing, and del.* Define another list L with four items, and assign an empty list to one of its offsets (e.g., L[2]=[]). What happens? Then, assign an empty list to a slice (L[2:3]=[]). What happens now? Recall that slice assignment deletes the slice and inserts the new value where it used to be.

  The del statement deletes offsets, keys, attributes, and names. Use it on your list to delete an item (e.g., del L[0]). What happens if you delete an entire slice (del L[1:])? What happens when you assign a nonsequence to a slice (L[1:2]=1)?

4. *Tuple assignment.* Type the following lines:

```
>>> X = 'spam'
>>> Y = 'eggs'
>>> X, Y = Y, X
```

  What do you think is happening to X and Y when you type this sequence?

5. *Dictionary keys.* Consider the following code fragments:

```
>>> D = {}
>>> D[1] = 'a'
>>> D[2] = 'b'
```

  You've learned that dictionaries aren't accessed by offsets, so what's going on here? Does the following shed any light on the subject? (Hint: strings, integers, and tuples share which type category?)

```
>>> D[(1, 2, 3)] = 'c'
>>> D
{1: 'a', 2: 'b', (1, 2, 3): 'c'}
```

6. *Dictionary indexing*. Create a dictionary named `D` with three entries, for keys `'a'`, `'b'`, and `'c'`. What happens if you try to index a nonexistent key (`D['d']`)? What does Python do if you try to assign to a nonexistent key `'d'` (e.g., `D['d']='spam'`)? How does this compare to out-of-bounds assignments and references for lists? Does this sound like the rule for variable names?

7. *Generic operations*. Run interactive tests to answer the following questions:

   a. What happens when you try to use the `+` operator on different/mixed types (e.g., string + list, list + tuple)?

   b. Does `+` work when one of the operands is a dictionary?

   c. Does the `append` method work for both lists and strings? How about using the `keys` method on lists? (Hint: what does `append` assume about its subject object?)

   d. Finally, what type of object do you get back when you slice or concatenate two lists or two strings?

8. *String indexing*. Define a string `S` of four characters: `S = "spam"`. Then type the following expression: `S[0][0][0][0][0]`. Any clue as to what's happening this time? (Hint: recall that a string is a collection of characters, but Python characters are one-character strings.) Does this indexing expression still work if you apply it to a list such as `['s', 'p', 'a', 'm']`? Why?

9. *Immutable types*. Define a string `S` of four characters again: `S = "spam"`. Write an assignment that changes the string to `"slam"`, using only slicing and concatenation. Could you perform the same operation using just indexing and concatenation? How about index assignment?

10. *Nesting*. Write a data structure that represents your personal information: name (first, middle, last), age, job, address, email address, and phone number. You may build the data structure with any combination of built-in object types you like (lists, tuples, dictionaries, strings, numbers). Then, access the individual components of your data structures by indexing. Do some structures make more sense than others for this object?

11. *Files*. Write a script that creates a new output file called *myfile.txt* and writes the string `"Hello file world!"` into it. Then write another script that opens *myfile.txt* and reads and prints its contents. Run your two scripts from the system command line. Does the new file show up in the directory where you ran your scripts? What if you add a different directory path to the filename passed to `open`? Note: file `write` methods do not add newline characters to your strings; add an explicit `\n` at the end of the string if you want to fully terminate the line in the file.

## PART III

Statements and Syntax

## CHAPTER 10

Introducing Python Statements

Now that you're familiar with Python's core built-in object types, this chapter begins our exploration of its fundamental statement forms. As in the previous part, we'll begin here with a general introduction to statement syntax, and we'll follow up with more details about specific statements in the next few chapters.

In simple terms, *statements* are the things you write to tell Python what your programs should do. If programs "do things with stuff," statements are the way you specify what sort of things a program does. Python is a procedural, statement-based language; by combining statements, you specify a procedure that Python performs to satisfy a program's goals.

Python Program Structure Revisited

Another way to understand the role of statements is to revisit the concept hierarchy introduced in Chapter 4, which talked about built-in objects and the expressions used to manipulate them. This chapter climbs the hierarchy to the next level:

1. Programs are composed of modules.
2. Modules contain statements.
3. *Statements contain expressions.*
4. Expressions create and process objects.

At its core, Python syntax is composed of statements and expressions. Expressions process objects and are embedded in statements. Statements code the larger *logic* of a program's operation—they use and direct expressions to process the objects we studied in the preceding chapters. Moreover, statements are where objects spring into existence (e.g., in expressions within assignment statements), and some statements create entirely new kinds of objects (functions, classes, and so on). Statements always exist in modules, which themselves are managed with statements.

Python's Statements

Table 10-1 summarizes Python's statement set. This part of the book deals with entries in the table from the top through `break` and `continue`. You've informally been introduced to a few of the statements in Table 10-1 already; this part of the book will fill in details that were skipped earlier, introduce the rest of Python's procedural statement set, and cover the overall syntax model. Statements lower in Table 10-1 that have to do with larger program units—functions, classes, modules, and exceptions—lead to larger programming ideas, so they will each have a section of their own. More focused statements (like `del`, which deletes various components) are covered elsewhere in the book, or in Python's standard manuals.

Table 10-1. Python 3.0 statements

Statement	Role	Example
Assignment	Creating references	`a, *b = 'good', 'bad', 'ugly'`
Calls and other expressions	Running functions	`log.write("spam, ham")`
`print` calls	Printing objects	`print('The Killer', joke)`
`if/elif/else`	Selecting actions	`if "python" in text:` `print(text)`
`for/else`	Sequence iteration	`for x in mylist:` `print(x)`
`while/else`	General loops	`while X > Y:` `print('hello')`
`pass`	Empty placeholder	`while True:` `pass`
`break`	Loop exit	`while True:` `if exittest(): break`
`continue`	Loop continue	`while True:` `if skiptest(): continue`
`def`	Functions and methods	`def f(a, b, c=1, *d):` `print(a+b+c+d[0])`
`return`	Functions results	`def f(a, b, c=1, *d):` `return a+b+c+d[0]`
`yield`	Generator functions	`def gen(n):` `for i in n: yield i*2`

`global`	Namespaces	`x = 'old'`
		`def function():`
		    `global x, y; x = 'new'`

`nonlocal`	Namespaces (3.0+)	`def outer():`
		    `x = 'old'`
		    `def function():`
		        `nonlocal x; x = 'new'`

`import`	Module access	`import sys`
`from`	Attribute access	`from sys import stdin`

`class`	Building objects	`class Subclass(Superclass):`
		    `staticData = []`
		    `def method(self): pass`

Statement	Role	Example

try/except/finally	Catching exceptions	<pre>try:
		    action()
		except:
		    print('action error')</pre>

raise	Triggering exceptions	`raise EndSearch(location)`
assert	Debugging checks	`assert X > Y, 'X too small'`

with/as	Context managers (2.6+)	<pre>with open('data') as myfile:
		    process(myfile)</pre>

del	Deleting references	<pre>del data[k]
		del data[i:j]
		del obj.attr
		del variable</pre>

Table 10-1 reflects the statement forms in Python 3.0—units of code that each have a specific syntax and purpose. Here are a few fine points about its content:

- Assignment statements come in a variety of syntax flavors, described in Chapter 11: basic, sequence, augmented, and more.
- `print` is technically neither a reserved word nor a statement in 3.0, but a built-in function call; because it will nearly always be run as an expression statement, though (that is, on a line by itself), it's generally thought of as a statement type. We'll study print operations in Chapter 11 the next chapter.
- `yield` is actually an expression instead of a statement too, as of 2.5; like `print`, it's typically used in a line by itself and so is included in this table, but scripts occasionally assign or otherwise use its result, as we'll see in Chapter 20. As an expression, `yield` is also a reserved word, unlike `print`.

Most of this table applies to Python 2.6, too, except where it doesn't—if you are using Python 2.6 or older, here are a few notes for your Python, too:

- In 2.6, `nonlocal` is not available; as we'll see in Chapter 17, there are alternative ways to achieve this statement's writeable state-retention effect.
- In 2.6, `print` is a statement instead of a built-in function call, with specific syntax covered in Chapter 11.
- In 2.6, the 3.0 `exec` code execution built-in function is a statement, with specific syntax; since it supports enclosing parentheses, though, you can generally use its 3.0 call form in 2.6 code.
- In 2.5, the `try/except` and `try/finally` statements were merged: the two were formerly separate statements, but we can now say both `except` and `finally` in the same `try` statement.
- In 2.5, `with/as` is an optional extension, and it is not available unless you explicitly turn it on by running the statement `from __future__ import with_statement` (see Chapter 33).

A Tale of Two ifs

Before we delve into the details of any of the concrete statements in Table 10-1, I want to begin our look at Python statement syntax by showing you what you are *not* going to type in Python code so you can compare and contrast it with other syntax models you might have seen in the past.

Consider the following `if` statement, coded in a C-like language:

```
if (x > y) {
    x = 1;
    y = 2;
}
```

This might be a statement in C, C++, Java, JavaScript, or Perl. Now, look at the equivalent statement in the Python language:

```
if x > y:
    x = 1
    y = 2
```

The first thing that may pop out at you is that the equivalent Python statement is less, well, cluttered—that is, there are fewer syntactic components. This is by design; as a scripting language, one of Python's goals is to make programmers' lives easier by requiring less typing.

More specifically, when you compare the two syntax models, you'll notice that Python adds one new thing to the mix, and that three items that are present in the C-like language are not present in Python code.

What Python Adds

The one new syntax component in Python is the colon character (`:`). All Python *compound statements* (i.e., statements that have statements nested inside them) follow the same general pattern of a header line terminated in a colon, followed by a nested block of code usually indented underneath the header line, like this:

```
Header line:
    Nested statement block
```

The colon is required, and omitting it is probably the most common coding mistake among new Python programmers—it's certainly one I've witnessed thousands of times in Python training classes. In fact, if you are new to Python, you'll almost certainly forget the colon character very soon. Most Python-friendly editors make this mistake easy to spot, and including it eventually becomes an unconscious habit (so much so that you may start typing colons in your C++ code, too, generating many entertaining error messages from your C++ compiler!).

What Python Removes

Although Python requires the extra colon character, there are three things programmers in C-like languages must include that you don't generally have to in Python.

Parentheses are optional

The first of these is the set of parentheses around the tests at the top of the statement:

```
if (x < y)
```

The parentheses here are required by the syntax of many C-like languages. In Python, though, they are not—we simply omit the parentheses, and the statement works the same way:

```
if x < y
```

Technically speaking, because every expression can be enclosed in parentheses, including them will not hurt in this Python code, and they are not treated as an error if present. *But don't do that*: you'll be wearing out your keyboard needlessly, and broadcasting to the world that you're an ex-C programmer still learning Python (I was once, too). The Python way is to simply omit the parentheses in these kinds of statements altogether.

End of line is end of statement

The second and more significant syntax component you won't find in Python code is the semicolon. You don't need to terminate statements with semicolons in Python the way you do in C-like languages:

```
x = 1;
```

In Python, the general rule is that the end of a line automatically terminates the statement that appears on that line. In other words, you can leave off the semicolons, and it works the same way:

```
x = 1
```

There are some ways to work around this rule, as you'll see in a moment. But, in general, you write one statement per line for the vast majority of Python code, and no semicolon is required.

Here, too, if you are pining for your C programming days (if such a state is possible...) you can continue to use semicolons at the end of each statement—the language lets you get away with them if they are present. *But don't do that either* (really!); again, doing so tells the world that you're still a C programmer who hasn't quite made the switch to Python coding. The Pythonic style is to leave off the semicolons altogether.

End of indentation is end of block

The third and final syntax component that Python removes, and the one that may seem the most unusual to soon-to-be-ex-C programmers (until they've used it for 10 minutes and realize it's actually a feature), is that you do not type anything explicit in your code to syntactically mark the beginning and end of a nested block of code. You don't need to include `begin`/`end`, `then`/`endif`, or braces around the nested block, as you do in C-like languages:

```
if (x > y) {
    x = 1;
    y = 2;
}
```

Instead, in Python, we consistently indent all the statements in a given single nested block the same distance to the right, and Python uses the statements' physical indentation to determine where the block starts and stops:

```
if x > y:
    x = 1
    y = 2
```

By *indentation*, I mean the blank whitespace all the way to the left of the two nested statements here. Python doesn't care how you indent (you may use either spaces or tabs), or how much you indent (you may use any number of spaces or tabs). In fact, the indentation of one nested block can be totally different from that of another. The syntax rule is only that for a given single nested block, all of its statements must be indented the same distance to the right. If this is not the case, you will get a syntax error, and your code will not run until you repair its indentation to be consistent.

Why Indentation Syntax?

The indentation rule may seem unusual at first glance to programmers accustomed to C-like languages, but it is a deliberate feature of Python, and it's one of the main ways that Python almost forces programmers to produce uniform, regular, and readable code. It essentially means that you must line up your code vertically, in columns, according to its logical structure. The net effect is to make your code more consistent and readable (unlike much of the code written in C-like languages).

To put that more strongly, aligning your code according to its logical structure is a major part of making it readable, and thus reusable and maintainable, by yourself and others. In fact, even if you never use Python after reading this book, you should get into the habit of aligning your code for readability in any block-structured language. Python forces the issue by making this a part of its syntax, but it's an important thing to do in any programming language, and it has a huge impact on the usefulness of your code.

Your experience may vary, but when I was still doing development on a full-time basis, I was mostly paid to work on large old C++ programs that had been worked on by many programmers over the years. Almost invariably, each programmer had his or her own style for indenting code. For example, I'd often be asked to change a `while` loop coded in the C++ language that began like this:

```
while (x > 0) {
```

Before we even get into indentation, there are three or four ways that programmers can arrange these braces in a C-like language, and organizations often have political debates and write standards manuals to address the options (which seems more than a little off-topic for the problem to be solved by programming). Ignoring that, here's the scenario I often encountered in C++ code. The first person who worked on the code indented the loop four spaces:

```
while (x > 0) {
    --------;
    --------;
```

That person eventually moved on to management, only to be replaced by someone who liked to indent further to the right:

```
while (x > 0) {
    --------;
    --------;
            --------;
            --------;
```

That person later moved on to other opportunities, and someone else picked up the code who liked to indent less:

```
while (x > 0) {
    --------;
    --------;
            --------;
            --------;
  --------;
  --------;
  }
```

And so on. Eventually, the block is terminated by a closing brace (}), which of course makes this "block-structured code" (he says, sarcastically). In any block-structured language, Python or otherwise, if nested blocks are not indented consistently, they become very difficult for the reader to interpret, change, or reuse, because the code no longer visually reflects its logical meaning. Readability matters, and indentation is a major component of readability.

Here is another example that may have burned you in the past if you've done much programming in a C-like language. Consider the following statement in C:

```
if (x)
    if (y)
        statement1;
else
    statement2;
```

Which if does the else here go with? Surprisingly, the else is paired with the nested if statement (if (y)), even though it looks visually as though it is associated with the outer if (x). This is a classic pitfall in the C language, and it can lead to the reader completely misinterpreting the code and changing it incorrectly in ways that might not be uncovered until the Mars rover crashes into a giant rock!

This cannot happen in Python—because indentation is significant, the way the code looks is the way it will work. Consider an equivalent Python statement:

```
if x:
    if y:
        statement1
else:
    statement2
```

In this example, the if that the else lines up with vertically is the one it is associated with logically (the outer if x). In a sense, Python is a WYSIWYG language—what you see is what you get because the way code looks is the way it runs, regardless of who coded it.

If this still isn't enough to underscore the benefits of Python's syntax, here's another anecdote. Early in my career, I worked at a successful company that developed systems software in the C language, where consistent indentation is not required. Even so, when we checked our code into source control at the end of the day, this company ran an automated script that analyzed the indentation used in the code. If the script noticed that we'd indented our code inconsistently, we received an automated email about it the next morning—and so did our managers!

The point is that even when a language doesn't require it, good programmers know that consistent use of indentation has a huge impact on code readability and quality. The fact that Python promotes this to the level of syntax is seen by most as a feature of the language.

Also keep in mind that nearly every programmer-friendly text editor has built-in support for Python's syntax model. In the IDLE Python GUI, for example, lines of code are automatically indented when you are typing a nested block; pressing the Backspace key backs up one level of indentation, and you can customize how far to the right IDLE indents statements in a nested block. There is no universal standard on this: four spaces or one tab per level is common, but it's up to you to decide how and how much you wish to indent. Indent further to the right for further nested blocks, and less to close the prior block.

As a rule of thumb, you probably shouldn't mix tabs and spaces in the same block in Python, unless you do so consistently; use tabs or spaces in a given block, but not both (in fact, Python 3.0 now issues an error for inconsistent use of tabs and spaces, as we'll see in Chapter 12). But you probably shouldn't mix tabs or spaces in indentation in *any* structured language—such code can cause major readability issues if the next programmer has his or her editor set to display tabs differently than yours. C-like languages might let coders get away with this, but they shouldn't: the result can be a mangled mess.

I can't stress enough that regardless of which language you code in, you should be indenting consistently for readability. In fact, if you weren't taught to do this earlier in your career, your teachers did you a disservice. Most programmers—especially those who must read others' code—consider it a major asset that Python elevates this to the level of syntax. Moreover, generating tabs instead of braces is no more difficult in practice for tools that must output Python code. In general, if you do what you should be doing in a C-like language anyhow, but get rid of the braces, your code will satisfy Python's syntax rules.

A Few Special Cases

As mentioned previously, in Python's syntax model:

- The end of a line terminates the statement on that line (without semicolons).
- Nested statements are blocked and associated by their physical indentation (without braces).

Those rules cover almost all Python code you'll write or see in practice. However, Python also provides some special-purpose rules that allow customization of both statements and nested statement blocks.

Statement rule special cases

Although statements normally appear one per line, it is possible to squeeze more than one statement onto a single line in Python by separating them with semicolons:

```
a = 1; b = 2; print(a + b)        # Three statements on one line
```

This is the only place in Python where semicolons are required: as *statement separators*. This only works, though, if the statements thus combined are not themselves compound statements. In other words, you can chain together only simple statements, like assignments, `print`s, and function calls. Compound statements must still appear on lines of their own (otherwise, you could squeeze an entire program onto one line, which probably would not make you very popular among your coworkers!).

The other special rule for statements is essentially the inverse: you can make a single statement span across multiple lines. To make this work, you simply have to enclose part of your statement in a bracketed pair—parentheses (()), square brackets ([]), or curly braces ({}). Any code enclosed in these constructs can cross multiple lines: your statement doesn't end until Python reaches the line containing the closing part of the pair. For instance, to continue a list literal:

```
mlist = [111,
         222,
         333]
```

Because the code is enclosed in a square brackets pair, Python simply drops down to the next line until it encounters the closing bracket. The curly braces surrounding dictionaries (as well as set literals and dictionary and set comprehensions in 3.0) allow them to span lines this way too, and parentheses handle tuples, function calls, and expressions. The indentation of the continuation lines does not matter, though common sense dictates that the lines should be aligned somehow for readability.

Parentheses are the catchall device—because any expression can be wrapped up in them, simply inserting a left parenthesis allows you to drop down to the next line and continue your statement:

```
X = (A + B +
     C + D)
```

This technique works with compound statements, too, by the way. Anywhere you need to code a large expression, simply wrap it in parentheses to continue it on the next line:

```
if (A == 1 and
    B == 2 and
    C == 3):
        print('spam' * 3)
```

An older rule also allows for continuation lines when the prior line ends in a backslash:

```
X = A + B + \                    # An error-prone alternative
    C + D
```

This alternative technique is dated, though, and is frowned on today because it's difficult to notice and maintain the backslashes, and it's fairly brittle—there can be no spaces after the backslash, and omitting it can have unexpected effects if the next line is mistaken to be a new statement. It's also another throwback to the C language, where it is commonly used in "#define" macros; again, when in Pythonland, do as Pythonistas do, not as C programmers do.

Block rule special case

As mentioned previously, statements in a nested block of code are normally associated by being indented the same amount to the right. As one special case here, the body of a compound statement can instead appear on the same line as the header in Python, after the colon:

```
if x > y: print(x)
```

This allows us to code single-line if statements, single-line loops, and so on. Here again, though, this will work only if the body of the compound statement itself does not contain any compound statements. That is, only simple statements—assignments, prints, function calls, and the like—are allowed after the colon. Larger statements must still appear on lines by themselves. Extra parts of compound statements (such as the else part of an if, which we'll meet later) must also be on separate lines of their own. The body can consist of multiple simple statements separated by semicolons, but this tends to be frowned upon.

In general, even though it's not always required, if you keep all your statements on individual lines and always indent your nested blocks, your code will be easier to read and change in the future. Moreover, some code profiling and coverage tools may not be able to distinguish between multiple statements squeezed onto a single line or the header and body of a one-line compound statement. It is almost always to your advantage to keep things simple in Python.

To see a prime and common exception to one of these rules in action, however (the use of a single-line `if` statement to break out of a loop), let's move on to the next section and write some real code.

A Quick Example: Interactive Loops

We'll see all these syntax rules in action when we tour Python's specific compound statements in the next few chapters, but they work the same everywhere in the Python language. To get started, let's work through a brief, realistic example that demonstrates the way that statement syntax and statement nesting come together in practice, and introduces a few statements along the way.

A Simple Interactive Loop

Suppose you're asked to write a Python program that interacts with a user in a console window. Maybe you're accepting inputs to send to a database, or reading numbers to be used in a calculation. Regardless of the purpose, you need to code a loop that reads one or more inputs from a user typing on a keyboard, and prints back a result for each. In other words, you need to write a classic read/evaluate/print loop program.

In Python, typical boilerplate code for such an interactive loop might look like this:

```
while True:
    reply = input('Enter text:')
    if reply == 'stop': break
    print(reply.upper())
```

This code makes use of a few new ideas:

- The code leverages the Python `while` loop, Python's most general looping statement. We'll study the `while` statement in more detail later, but in short, it consists of the word `while`, followed by an expression that is interpreted as a true or false result, followed by a nested block of code that is repeated while the test at the top is true (the word `True` here is considered always true).

- The `input` built-in function we met earlier in the book is used here for general console input—it prints its optional argument string as a prompt and returns the user's typed reply as a string.

- A single-line `if` statement that makes use of the special rule for nested blocks also appears here: the body of the `if` appears on the header line after the colon instead of being indented on a new line underneath it. This would work either way, but as it's coded, we've saved an extra line.

- Finally, the Python break statement is used to exit the loop immediately—it simply jumps out of the loop statement altogether, and the program continues after the loop. Without this exit statement, the while would loop forever, as its test is always true.

In effect, this combination of statements essentially means "read a line from the user and print it in uppercase until the user enters the word 'stop.'" There are other ways to code such a loop, but the form used here is very common in Python code.

Notice that all three lines nested under the while header line are indented the same amount—because they line up vertically in a column this way, they are the block of code that is associated with the while test and repeated. Either the end of the source file or a lesser-indented statement will terminate the loop body block.

When run, here is the sort of interaction we get from this code:

```
Enter text:spam
SPAM
Enter text:42
42
Enter text:stop
```

 Version skew note: This example is coded for Python 3.0. If you are working in Python 2.6 or earlier, the code works the same, but you should use raw_input instead of input, and you can omit the outer parentheses in print statements. In 3.0 the former was renamed, and the latter is a built-in function instead of a statement (more on prints in the next chapter).

Doing Math on User Inputs

Our script works, but now suppose that instead of converting a text string to uppercase, we want to do some math with numeric input—squaring it, for example, perhaps in some misguided effort to discourage users who happen to be obsessed with youth. We might try statements like these to achieve the desired effect:

```
>>> reply = '20'
>>> reply ** 2
...error text omitted...
TypeError: unsupported operand type(s) for ** or pow(): 'str' and 'int'
```

This won't quite work in our script, though, because (as discussed in the prior part of the book) Python won't convert object types in expressions unless they are all numeric, and input from a user is always returned to our script as a string. We cannot raise a string of digits to a power unless we convert it manually to an integer:

```
>>> int(reply) ** 2
400
```

Armed with this information, we can now recode our loop to perform the necessary math. Type the following in a file to test it:

```
while True:
    reply = input('Enter text:')
    if reply == 'stop': break
    print(int(reply) ** 2)
print('Bye')
```

This script uses a single-line if statement to exit on "stop" as before, but it also converts inputs to perform the required math. This version also adds an exit message at the bottom. Because the print statement in the last line is not indented as much as the nested block of code, it is not considered part of the loop body and will run only once, after the loop is exited:

```
Enter text:2
4
Enter text:40
1600
Enter text:stop
Bye
```

One note here: I'm assuming that this code is stored in and run from a script file. If you are entering this code interactively, be sure to include a blank line (i.e., press Enter twice) before the final print statement, to terminate the loop. The final print doesn't quite make sense in interactive mode, though (you'll have to code it after interacting with the loop!).

Handling Errors by Testing Inputs

So far so good, but notice what happens when the input is invalid:

```
Enter text:xxx
...error text omitted...
ValueError: invalid literal for int() with base 10: 'xxx'
```

The built-in int function raises an exception here in the face of a mistake. If we want our script to be robust, we can check the string's content ahead of time with the string object's isdigit method:

```
>>> S = '123'
>>> T = 'xxx'
>>> S.isdigit(), T.isdigit()
(True, False)
```

This also gives us an excuse to further nest the statements in our example. The following new version of our interactive script uses a full-blown if statement to work around the exception on errors:

```
while True:
    reply = input('Enter text:')
```

```
        if reply == 'stop':
            break
        elif not reply.isdigit():
            print('Bad!' * 8)
        else:
            print(int(reply) ** 2)
    print('Bye')
```

We'll study the `if` statement in more detail in Chapter 12, but it's a fairly lightweight tool for coding logic in scripts. In its full form, it consists of the word `if` followed by a test and an associated block of code, one or more optional `elif` ("else if") tests and code blocks, and an optional `else` part, with an associated block of code at the bottom to serve as a default. Python runs the block of code associated with the first test that is true, working from top to bottom, or the `else` part if all tests are false.

The `if`, `elif`, and `else` parts in the preceding example are associated as part of the same statement because they all line up vertically (i.e., share the same level of indentation). The `if` statement spans from the word `if` to the start of the `print` statement on the last line of the script. In turn, the entire `if` block is part of the `while` loop because all of it is indented under the loop's header line. Statement nesting is natural once you get the hang of it.

When we run our new script, its code catches errors before they occur and prints an (arguably silly) error message to demonstrate:

```
Enter text:5
25
Enter text:xyz
Bad!Bad!Bad!Bad!Bad!Bad!Bad!Bad!
Enter text:10
100
Enter text:stop
```

Handling Errors with try Statements

The preceding solution works, but as you'll see later in the book, the most general way to handle errors in Python is to catch and recover from them completely using the Python `try` statement. We'll explore this statement in depth in Part VII of this book, but as a preview, using a `try` here can lead to code that some would claim is simpler than the prior version:

```
while True:
    reply = input('Enter text:')
    if reply == 'stop': break
    try:
        num = int(reply)
    except:
        print('Bad!' * 8)
    else:
        print(int(reply) ** 2)
print('Bye')
```

This version works exactly like the previous one, but we've replaced the explicit error check with code that assumes the conversion will work and wraps it up in an exception handler for cases when it doesn't. This `try` statement is composed of the word `try`, followed by the main block of code (the action we are trying to run), followed by an `except` part that gives the exception handler code and an `else` part to be run if no exception is raised in the `try` part. Python first runs the `try` part, then runs either the `except` part (if an exception occurs) or the `else` part (if no exception occurs).

In terms of statement nesting, because the words `try`, `except`, and `else` are all indented to the same level, they are all considered part of the same single `try` statement. Notice that the `else` part is associated with the `try` here, not the `if`. As we've seen, `else` can appear in `if` statements in Python, but it can also appear in `try` statements and loops—its indentation tells you what statement it is a part of. In this case, the `try` statement spans from the word `try` through the code indented under the word `else`, because the `else` is indented to the same level as `try`. The `if` statement in this code is a one-liner and ends after the `break`.

Again, we'll come back to the `try` statement later in this book. For now, be aware that because `try` can be used to intercept any error, it reduces the amount of error-checking code you have to write, and it's a very general approach to dealing with unusual cases. If we wanted to support input of floating-point numbers instead of just integers, for example, using `try` would be much easier than manual error testing—we could simply run a `float` call and catch its exceptions, instead of trying to analyze all possible floating-point syntax.

Nesting Code Three Levels Deep

Let's look at one last mutation of our script. Nesting can take us even further if we need it to—we could, for example, branch to one of a set of alternatives based on the relative magnitude of a valid input:

```python
while True:
    reply = input('Enter text:')
    if reply == 'stop':
        break
    elif not reply.isdigit():
        print('Bad!' * 8)
    else:
        num = int(reply)
        if num < 20:
            print('low')
        else:
            print(num ** 2)
print('Bye')
```

This version includes an `if` statement nested in the `else` clause of another `if` statement, which is in turn nested in the `while` loop. When code is conditional, or repeated like this, we simply indent it further to the right. The net effect is like that of the prior versions, but we'll now print "low" for numbers less than 20:

```
Enter text:19
low
Enter text:20
400
Enter text:spam
Bad!Bad!Bad!Bad!Bad!Bad!Bad!Bad!
Enter text:stop
Bye
```

Chapter Summary

That concludes our quick look at Python statement syntax. This chapter introduced the general rules for coding statements and blocks of code. As you've learned, in Python we normally code one statement per line and indent all the statements in a nested block the same amount (indentation is part of Python's syntax). However, we also looked at a few exceptions to these rules, including continuation lines and single-line tests and loops. Finally, we put these ideas to work in an interactive script that demonstrated a handful of statements and showed statement syntax in action.

In the next chapter, we'll start to dig deeper by going over each of Python's basic procedural statements in depth. As you'll see, though, all statements follow the same general rules introduced here.

Test Your Knowledge: Quiz

1. What three things are required in a C-like language but omitted in Python?
2. How is a statement normally terminated in Python?
3. How are the statements in a nested block of code normally associated in Python?
4. How can you make a single statement span multiple lines?
5. How can you code a compound statement on a single line?
6. Is there any valid reason to type a semicolon at the end of a statement in Python?
7. What is a `try` statement for?
8. What is the most common coding mistake among Python beginners?

Test Your Knowledge: Answers

1. C-like languages require parentheses around the tests in some statements, semicolons at the end of each statement, and braces around a nested block of code.

2. The end of a line terminates the statement that appears on that line. Alternatively, if more than one statement appears on the same line, they can be terminated with semicolons; similarly, if a statement spans many lines, you must terminate it by closing a bracketed syntactic pair.

3. The statements in a nested block are all indented the same number of tabs or spaces.

4. A statement can be made to span many lines by enclosing part of it in parentheses, square brackets, or curly braces; the statement ends when Python sees a line that contains the closing part of the pair.

5. The body of a compound statement can be moved to the header line after the colon, but only if the body consists of only noncompound statements.

6. Only when you need to squeeze more than one statement onto a single line of code. Even then, this only works if all the statements are noncompound, and it's discouraged because it can lead to code that is difficult to read.

7. The **try** statement is used to catch and recover from exceptions (errors) in a Python script. It's usually an alternative to manually checking for errors in your code.

8. Forgetting to type the colon character at the end of the header line in a compound statement is the most common beginner's mistake. If you haven't made it yet, you probably will soon!

Assignments, Expressions, and Prints

Now that we've had a quick introduction to Python statement syntax, this chapter begins our in-depth tour of specific Python statements. We'll begin with the basics: assignment statements, expression statements, and print operations. We've already seen all of these in action, but here we'll fill in important details we've skipped so far. Although they're fairly simple, as you'll see, there are optional variations for each of these statement types that will come in handy once you begin writing real Python programs.

Assignment Statements

We've been using the Python assignment statement for a while to assign objects to names. In its basic form, you write the *target* of an assignment on the left of an equals sign, and the *object* to be assigned on the right. The target on the left may be a name or object component, and the object on the right can be an arbitrary expression that computes an object. For the most part, assignments are straightforward, but here are a few properties to keep in mind:

- **Assignments create object references**. As discussed in Chapter 6, Python assignments store references to objects in names or data structure components. They always create references to objects instead of copying the objects. Because of that, Python variables are more like pointers than data storage areas.

- **Names are created when first assigned**. Python creates a variable name the first time you assign it a value (i.e., an object reference), so there's no need to predeclare names ahead of time. Some (but not all) data structure slots are created when assigned, too (e.g., dictionary entries, some object attributes). Once assigned, a name is replaced with the value it references whenever it appears in an expression.

- **Names must be assigned before being referenced**. It's an error to use a name to which you haven't yet assigned a value. Python raises an exception if you try, rather than returning some sort of ambiguous default value; if it returned a default instead, it would be more difficult for you to spot typos in your code.

- **Some operations perform assignments implicitly**. In this section we're concerned with the = statement, but assignment occurs in many contexts in Python. For instance, we'll see later that module imports, function and class definitions, for loop variables, and function arguments are all implicit assignments. Because assignment works the same everywhere it pops up, all these contexts simply bind names to object references at runtime.

Assignment Statement Forms

Although assignment is a general and pervasive concept in Python, we are primarily interested in assignment *statements* in this chapter. Table 11-1 illustrates the different assignment statement forms in Python.

Table 11-1. Assignment statement forms

Operation	Interpretation
spam = 'Spam'	Basic form
spam, ham = 'yum', 'YUM'	Tuple assignment (positional)
[spam, ham] = ['yum', 'YUM']	List assignment (positional)
a, b, c, d = 'spam'	Sequence assignment, generalized
a, *b = 'spam'	Extended sequence unpacking (Python 3.0)
spam = ham = 'lunch'	Multiple-target assignment
spams += 42	Augmented assignment (equivalent to spams = spams + 42)

The first form in Table 11-1 is by far the most common: binding a name (or data structure component) to a single object. In fact, you could get all your work done with this basic form alone. The other table entries represent special forms that are all optional, but that programmers often find convenient in practice:

Tuple- and list-unpacking assignments

   The second and third forms in the table are related. When you code a tuple or list on the left side of the =, Python pairs objects on the right side with targets on the left by position and assigns them from left to right. For example, in the second line of Table 11-1, the name spam is assigned the string 'yum', and the name ham is bound to the string 'YUM'. In this case Python internally makes a tuple of the items on the right, which is why this is called tuple-unpacking assignment.

Sequence assignments

   In recent versions of Python, tuple and list assignments have been generalized into instances of what we now call *sequence assignment*—any sequence of names can be assigned to any sequence of values, and Python assigns the items one at a time by position. We can even mix and match the types of the sequences involved. The fourth line in Table 11-1, for example, pairs a tuple of names with a string of characters: a is assigned 's', b is assigned 'p', and so on.

Extended sequence unpacking

In Python 3.0, a new form of sequence assignment allows us to be more flexible in how we select portions of a sequence to assign. The fifth line in Table 11-1, for example, matches a with the first character in the string on the right and b with the rest: a is assigned 's', and b is assigned 'pam'. This provides a simpler alternative to assigning the results of manual slicing operations.

Multiple-target assignments

The sixth line in Table 11-1 shows the multiple-target form of assignment. In this form, Python assigns a reference to the same object (the object farthest to the right) to all the targets on the left. In the table, the names spam and ham are both assigned references to the same string object, 'lunch'. The effect is the same as if we had coded ham = 'lunch' followed by spam = ham, as ham evaluates to the original string object (i.e., not a separate copy of that object).

Augmented assignments

The last line in Table 11-1 is an example of *augmented assignment*—a shorthand that combines an expression and an assignment in a concise way. Saying spam += 42, for example, has the same effect as spam = spam + 42, but the augmented form requires less typing and is generally quicker to run. In addition, if the subject is mutable and supports the operation, an augmented assignment may run even quicker by choosing an in-place update operation instead of an object copy. There is one augmented assignment statement for every binary expression operator in Python.

Sequence Assignments

We've already used basic assignments in this book. Here are a few simple examples of sequence-unpacking assignments in action:

```
% python
>>> nudge = 1
>>> wink  = 2
>>> A, B = nudge, wink        # Tuple assignment
>>> A, B                       # Like A = nudge; B = wink
(1, 2)
>>> [C, D] = [nudge, wink]    # List assignment
>>> C, D
(1, 2)
```

Notice that we really are coding two tuples in the third line in this interaction—we've just omitted their enclosing parentheses. Python pairs the values in the tuple on the right side of the assignment operator with the variables in the tuple on the left side and assigns the values one at a time.

Tuple assignment leads to a common coding trick in Python that was introduced in a solution to the exercises at the end of Part II. Because Python creates a temporary tuple that saves the original values of the variables on the right while the statement runs, unpacking assignments are also a way to *swap* two variables' values without creating a temporary variable of your own—the tuple on the right remembers the prior values of the variables automatically:

```
>>> nudge = 1
>>> wink  = 2
>>> nudge, wink = wink, nudge      # Tuples: swaps values
>>> nudge, wink                    # Like T = nudge; nudge = wink; wink = T
(2, 1)
```

In fact, the original tuple and list assignment forms in Python have been generalized to accept any type of sequence on the right as long as it is of the same length as the sequence on the left. You can assign a tuple of values to a list of variables, a string of characters to a tuple of variables, and so on. In all cases, Python assigns items in the sequence on the right to variables in the sequence on the left by position, from left to right:

```
>>> [a, b, c] = (1, 2, 3)          # Assign tuple of values to list of names
>>> a, c
(1, 3)
>>> (a, b, c) = "ABC"              # Assign string of characters to tuple
>>> a, c
('A', 'C')
```

Technically speaking, sequence assignment actually supports any *iterable* object on the right, not just any sequence. This is a more general concept that we will explore in Chapters 14 and 20.

Advanced sequence assignment patterns

Although we can mix and match sequence types around the = symbol, we must have the *same number* of items on the right as we have variables on the left, or we'll get an error. Python 3.0 allows us to be more general with extended unpacking syntax, described in the next section. But normally, and always in Python 2.X, the number of items in the assignment target and subject must match:

```
>>> string = 'SPAM'
>>> a, b, c, d = string                   # Same number on both sides
>>> a, d
('S', 'M')

>>> a, b, c = string                      # Error if not
...error text omitted...
ValueError: too many values to unpack
```

To be more general, we can slice. There are a variety of ways to employ slicing to make this last case work:

```
>>> a, b, c = string[0], string[1], string[2:]   # Index and slice
>>> a, b, c
('S', 'P', 'AM')

>>> a, b, c = list(string[:2]) + [string[2:]]    # Slice and concatenate
>>> a, b, c
```

```
('S', 'P', 'AM')

>>> a, b = string[:2]                                      # Same, but simpler
>>> c = string[2:]
>>> a, b, c
('S', 'P', 'AM')

>>> (a, b), c = string[:2], string[2:]                     # Nested sequences
>>> a, b, c
('S', 'P', 'AM')
```

As the last example in this interaction demonstrates, we can even assign *nested* sequences, and Python unpacks their parts according to their shape, as expected. In this case, we are assigning a tuple of two items, where the first item is a nested sequence (a string), exactly as though we had coded it this way:

```
>>> ((a, b), c) = ('SP', 'AM')                             # Paired by shape and position
>>> a, b, c
('S', 'P', 'AM')
```

Python pairs the first string on the right ('SP') with the first tuple on the left ((a, b)) and assigns one character at a time, before assigning the entire second string ('AM') to the variable c all at once. In this event, the sequence-nesting shape of the object on the left must match that of the object on the right. Nested sequence assignment like this is somewhat advanced, and rare to see, but it can be convenient for picking out the parts of data structures with known shapes.

For example, we'll see in Chapter 13 that this technique also works in for loops, because loop items are assigned to the target given in the loop header:

```
for (a, b, c) in [(1, 2, 3), (4, 5, 6)]: ...               # Simple tuple assignment

for ((a, b), c) in [((1, 2), 3), ((4, 5), 6)]: ...         # Nested tuple assignment
```

In a note in Chapter 18, we'll also see that this nested tuple (really, sequence) unpacking assignment form works for function argument lists in Python 2.6 (though not in 3.0), because function arguments are passed by assignment as well:

```
def f(((a, b), c)):                      # For arguments too in Python 2.6, but not 3.0
f(((1, 2), 3))
```

Sequence-unpacking assignments also give rise to another common coding idiom in Python—assigning an integer series to a set of variables:

```
>>> red, green, blue = range(3)
>>> red, blue
(0, 2)
```

This initializes the three names to the integer codes 0, 1, and 2, respectively (it's Python's equivalent of the *enumerated* data types you may have seen in other languages). To make sense of this, you need to know that the range built-in function generates a list of successive integers:

```
>>> range(3)                        # Use list(range(3)) in Python 3.0
[0, 1, 2]
```

Because range is commonly used in for loops, we'll say more about it in Chapter 13.

Another place you may see a tuple assignment at work is for splitting a sequence into its front and the rest in loops like this:

```
>>> L = [1, 2, 3, 4]
>>> while L:
...     front, L = L[0], L[1:]      # See next section for 3.0 alternative
...     print(front, L)
...
1 [2, 3, 4]
2 [3, 4]
3 [4]
4 []
```

The tuple assignment in the loop here could be coded as the following two lines instead, but it's often more convenient to string them together:

```
...     front = L[0]
...     L = L[1:]
```

Notice that this code is using the list as a sort of stack data structure, which can often also be achieved with the append and pop methods of list objects; here, front = L.pop(0) would have much the same effect as the tuple assignment statement, but it would be an in-place change. We'll learn more about while loops, and other (often better) ways to step through a sequence with for loops, in Chapter 13.

Extended Sequence Unpacking in Python 3.0

The prior section demonstrated how to use manual slicing to make sequence assignments more general. In Python 3.0 (but not 2.6), sequence assignment has been generalized to make this easier. In short, a single *starred name*, *X, can be used in the assignment target in order to specify a more general matching against the sequence—the starred name is assigned a list, which collects all items in the sequence not assigned to other names. This is especially handy for common coding patterns such as splitting a sequence into its "front" and "rest", as in the preceding section's last example.

Extended unpacking in action

Let's look at an example. As we've seen, sequence assignments normally require exactly as many names in the target on the left as there are items in the subject on the right. We get an error if the lengths disagree (unless we manually sliced on the right, as shown in the prior section):

```
C:\misc> c:\python30\python
>>> seq = [1, 2, 3, 4]
>>> a, b, c, d = seq
>>> print(a, b, c, d)
1 2 3 4
```

```
>>> a, b = seq
ValueError: too many values to unpack
```

In Python 3.0, though, we can use a single starred name in the target to match more generally. In the following continuation of our interactive session, a matches the first item in the sequence, and b matches the rest:

```
>>> a, *b = seq
>>> a
1
>>> b
[2, 3, 4]
```

When a starred name is used, the number of items in the target on the left need not match the length of the subject sequence. In fact, the starred name can appear anywhere in the target. For instance, in the next interaction b matches the last item in the sequence, and a matches everything before the last:

```
>>> *a, b = seq
>>> a
[1, 2, 3]
>>> b
4
```

When the starred name appears in the middle, it collects everything between the other names listed. Thus, in the following interaction a and c are assigned the first and last items, and b gets everything in between them:

```
>>> a, *b, c = seq
>>> a
1
>>> b
[2, 3]
>>> c
4
```

More generally, wherever the starred name shows up, it will be assigned a list that collects every unassigned name at that position:

```
>>> a, b, *c = seq
>>> a
1
>>> b
2
>>> c
[3, 4]
```

Naturally, like normal sequence assignment, extended sequence unpacking syntax works for any sequence types, not just lists. Here it is unpacking characters in a string:

```
>>> a, *b = 'spam'
>>> a, b
('s', ['p', 'a', 'm'])

>>> a, *b, c = 'spam'
```

```
>>> a, b, c
('s', ['p', 'a'], 'm')
```

This is similar in spirit to slicing, but not exactly the same—a sequence unpacking assignment always returns a *list* for multiple matched items, whereas slicing returns a sequence of the same type as the object sliced:

```
>>> S = 'spam'

>>> S[0], S[1:]        # Slices are type-specific, * assignment always returns a list
('s', 'pam')

>>> S[0], S[1:3], S[3]
('s', 'pa', 'm')
```

Given this extension in 3.0, as long as we're processing a list the last example of the prior section becomes even simpler, since we don't have to manually slice to get the first and rest of the items:

```
>>> L = [1, 2, 3, 4]
>>> while L:
...       front, *L = L                 # Get first, rest without slicing
...       print(front, L)
...
1 [2, 3, 4]
2 [3, 4]
3 [4]
4 []
```

Boundary cases

Although extended sequence unpacking is flexible, some boundary cases are worth noting. First, the starred name may match just a single item, but is always assigned a list:

```
>>> seq
[1, 2, 3, 4]

>>> a, b, c, *d = seq
>>> print(a, b, c, d)
1 2 3 [4]
```

Second, if there is nothing left to match the starred name, it is assigned an empty list, regardless of where it appears. In the following, a, b, c, and d have matched every item in the sequence, but Python assigns e an empty list instead of treating this as an error case:

```
>>> a, b, c, d, *e = seq
>>> print(a, b, c, d, e)
1 2 3 4 []

>>> a, b, *e, c, d = seq
>>> print(a, b, c, d, e)
1 2 3 4 []
```

Finally, errors can still be triggered if there is more than one starred name, if there are too few values and no star (as before), and if the starred name is not itself coded inside a sequence:

```
>>> a, *b, c, *d = seq
SyntaxError: two starred expressions in assignment

>>> a, b = seq
ValueError: too many values to unpack

>>> *a = seq
SyntaxError: starred assignment target must be in a list or tuple

>>> *a, = seq
>>> a
[1, 2, 3, 4]
```

A useful convenience

Keep in mind that extended sequence unpacking assignment is just a convenience. We can usually achieve the same effects with explicit indexing and slicing (and in fact must in Python 2.X), but extended unpacking is simpler to code. The common "first, rest" splitting coding pattern, for example, can be coded either way, but slicing involves extra work:

```
>>> seq
[1, 2, 3, 4]

>>> a, *b = seq                    # First, rest
>>> a, b
(1, [2, 3, 4])

>>> a, b = seq[0], seq[1:]         # First, rest: traditional
>>> a, b
(1, [2, 3, 4])
```

The also common "rest, last" splitting pattern can similarly be coded either way, but the new extended unpacking syntax requires noticeably fewer keystrokes:

```
>>> *a, b = seq                    # Rest, last
>>> a, b
([1, 2, 3], 4)

>>> a, b = seq[:-1], seq[-1]       # Rest, last: traditional
>>> a, b
([1, 2, 3], 4)
```

Because it is not only simpler but, arguably, more natural, extended sequence unpacking syntax will likely become widespread in Python code over time.

Application to for loops

Because the loop variable in the for loop statement can be any assignment target, extended sequence assignment works here too. We met the for loop iteration tool briefly in Part II and will study it formally in Chapter 13. In Python 3.0, extended assignments may show up after the word for, where a simple variable name is more commonly used:

```
for (a, *b, c) in [(1, 2, 3, 4), (5, 6, 7, 8)]:
    ...
```

When used in this context, on each iteration Python simply assigns the next tuple of values to the tuple of names. On the first loop, for example, it's as if we'd run the following assignment statement:

```
a, *b, c = (1, 2, 3, 4)                              # b gets [2, 3]
```

The names a, b, and c can be used within the loop's code to reference the extracted components. In fact, this is really not a special case at all, but just an instance of general assignment at work. As we saw earlier in this chapter, we can do the same thing with simple tuple assignment in both Python 2.X and 3.X:

```
for (a, b, c) in [(1, 2, 3), (4, 5, 6)]:             # a, b, c = (1, 2, 3), ...
```

And we can always emulate 3.0's extended assignment behavior in 2.6 by manually slicing:

```
for all in [(1, 2, 3, 4), (5, 6, 7, 8)]:
    a, b, c = all[0], all[1:3], all[3]
```

Since we haven't learned enough to get more detailed about the syntax of for loops, we'll return to this topic in Chapter 13.

Multiple-Target Assignments

A multiple-target assignment simply assigns all the given names to the object all the way to the right. The following, for example, assigns the three variables a, b, and c to the string 'spam':

```
>>> a = b = c = 'spam'
>>> a, b, c
('spam', 'spam', 'spam')
```

This form is equivalent to (but easier to code than) these three assignments:

```
>>> c = 'spam'
>>> b = c
>>> a = b
```

Multiple-target assignment and shared references

Keep in mind that there is just one object here, shared by all three variables (they all wind up pointing to the same object in memory). This behavior is fine for immutable types—for example, when initializing a set of counters to zero (recall that variables

---

must be assigned before they can be used in Python, so you must initialize counters to zero before you can start adding to them):

```
>>> a = b = 0
>>> b = b + 1
>>> a, b
(0, 1)
```

Here, changing b only changes b because numbers do not support in-place changes. As long as the object assigned is immutable, it's irrelevant if more than one name references it.

As usual, though, we have to be more cautious when initializing variables to an empty mutable object such as a list or dictionary:

```
>>> a = b = []
>>> b.append(42)
>>> a, b
([42], [42])
```

This time, because a and b reference the same object, appending to it in-place through b will impact what we see through a as well. This is really just another example of the shared reference phenomenon we first met in Chapter 6. To avoid the issue, initialize mutable objects in separate statements instead, so that each creates a distinct empty object by running a distinct literal expression:

```
>>> a = []
>>> b = []
>>> b.append(42)
>>> a, b
([], [42])
```

Augmented Assignments

Beginning with Python 2.0, the set of additional assignment statement formats listed in Table 11-2 became available. Known as *augmented assignments*, and borrowed from the C language, these formats are mostly just shorthand. They imply the combination of a binary expression and an assignment. For instance, the following two formats are now roughly equivalent:

```
X = X + Y            # Traditional form
X += Y               # Newer augmented form
```

Table 11-2. Augmented assignment statements

X += Y	X &= Y	X -= Y	X |= Y
X *= Y	X ^= Y	X /= Y	X >>= Y
X %= Y	X <<= Y	X **= Y	X //= Y

Augmented assignment works on any type that supports the implied binary expression. For example, here are two ways to add 1 to a name:

```
>>> x = 1
>>> x = x + 1                    # Traditional
>>> x
2
>>> x += 1                       # Augmented
>>> x
3
```

When applied to a string, the augmented form performs concatenation instead. Thus, the second line here is equivalent to typing the longer S = S + "SPAM":

```
>>> S = "spam"
>>> S += "SPAM"                  # Implied concatenation
>>> S
'spamSPAM'
```

As shown in Table 11-2, there are analogous augmented assignment forms for every Python binary expression operator (i.e., each operator with values on the left and right side). For instance, X *= Y multiplies and assigns, X >>= Y shifts right and assigns, and so on. X //= Y (for floor division) was added in version 2.2.

Augmented assignments have three advantages:[*]

- There's less for you to type. Need I say more?
- The left side only has to be evaluated once. In X += Y, X may be a complicated object expression. In the augmented form, it only has to be evaluated once. However, in the long form, X = X + Y, X appears twice and must be run twice. Because of this, augmented assignments usually run faster.
- The optimal technique is automatically chosen. That is, for objects that support in-place changes, the augmented forms automatically perform in-place change operations instead of slower copies.

The last point here requires a bit more explanation. For augmented assignments, in-place operations may be applied for mutable objects as an optimization. Recall that lists can be extended in a variety of ways. To add a single item to the end of a list, we can concatenate or call append:

```
>>> L = [1, 2]
>>> L = L + [3]                  # Concatenate: slower
>>> L
[1, 2, 3]
>>> L.append(4)                  # Faster, but in-place
>>> L
[1, 2, 3, 4]
```

---

[*] C/C++ programmers take note: although Python now supports statements like X += Y, it still does not have C's auto-increment/decrement operators (e.g., X++, --X). These don't quite map to the Python object model because Python has no notion of in-place changes to immutable objects like numbers.

And to add a set of items to the end, we can either concatenate again or call the list extend method:[†]

```
>>> L = L + [5, 6]          # Concatenate: slower
>>> L
[1, 2, 3, 4, 5, 6]
>>> L.extend([7, 8])        # Faster, but in-place
>>> L
[1, 2, 3, 4, 5, 6, 7, 8]
```

In both cases, concatenation is less prone to the side effects of shared object references but will generally run slower than the in-place equivalent. Concatenation operations must create a new object, copy in the list on the left, and then copy in the list on the right. By contrast, in-place method calls simply add items at the end of a memory block.

When we use augmented assignment to extend a list, we can forget these details—for example, Python automatically calls the quicker extend method instead of using the slower concatenation operation implied by +:

```
>>> L += [9, 10]            # Mapped to L.extend([9, 10])
>>> L
[1, 2, 3, 4, 5, 6, 7, 8, 9, 10]
```

Augmented assignment and shared references

This behavior is usually what we want, but notice that it implies that the += is an in-place change for lists; thus, it is not exactly like + concatenation, which always makes a new object. As for all shared reference cases, this difference might matter if other names reference the object being changed:

```
>>> L = [1, 2]
>>> M = L                   # L and M reference the same object
>>> L = L + [3, 4]          # Concatenation makes a new object
>>> L, M                    # Changes L but not M
([1, 2, 3, 4], [1, 2])

>>> L = [1, 2]
>>> M = L
>>> L += [3, 4]             # But += really means extend
>>> L, M                    # M sees the in-place change too!
([1, 2, 3, 4], [1, 2, 3, 4])
```

This only matters for mutables like lists and dictionaries, and it is a fairly obscure case (at least, until it impacts your code!). As always, make copies of your mutable objects if you need to break the shared reference structure.

---

† As suggested in Chapter 6, we can also use slice assignment (e.g., L[len(L):] = [11,12,13]), but this works roughly the same as the simpler list extend method.

Variable Name Rules

Now that we've explored assignment statements, it's time to get more formal about the use of variable names. In Python, names come into existence when you assign values to them, but there are a few rules to follow when picking names for things in your programs:

Syntax: (underscore or letter) + (any number of letters, digits, or underscores)
> Variable names must start with an underscore or letter, which can be followed by any number of letters, digits, or underscores. _spam, spam, and Spam_1 are legal names, but 1_Spam, spam$, and @#! are not.

Case matters: SPAM is not the same as spam
> Python always pays attention to case in programs, both in names you create and in reserved words. For instance, the names X and x refer to two different variables. For portability, case also matters in the names of imported module files, even on platforms where the filesystems are case-insensitive.

Reserved words are off-limits
> Names you define cannot be the same as words that mean special things in the Python language. For instance, if you try to use a variable name like class, Python will raise a syntax error, but klass and Class work fine. Table 11-3 lists the words that are currently reserved (and hence off-limits for names of your own) in Python.

Table 11-3. Python 3.0 reserved words

False	class	finally	is	return
None	continue	for	lambda	try
True	def	from	nonlocal	while
and	del	global	not	with
as	elif	if	or	yield
assert	else	import	pass	
break	except	in	raise	

Table 11-3 is specific to Python 3.0. In Python 2.6, the set of reserved words differs slightly:

- print is a reserved word, because printing is a statement, not a built-in (more on this later in this chapter).
- exec is a reserved word, because it is a statement, not a built-in function.
- nonlocal is not a reserved word because this statement is not available.

In older Pythons the story is also more or less the same, with a few variations:

- `with` and `as` were not reserved until 2.6, when context managers were officially enabled.
- `yield` was not reserved until Python 2.3, when generator functions were enabled.
- `yield` morphed from statement to expression in 2.5, but it's still a reserved word, not a built-in function.

As you can see, most of Python's reserved words are all lowercase. They are also all truly reserved—unlike names in the built-in scope that you will meet in the next part of this book, you cannot redefine reserved words by assignment (e.g., `and = 1` results in a syntax error).[‡]

Besides being of mixed case, the first three entries in Table 11-3, `True`, `False`, and `None`, are somewhat unusual in meaning—they also appear in the built-in scope of Python described in Chapter 17, and they are technically names assigned to objects. They are truly reserved in all other senses, though, and cannot be used for any other purpose in your script other than that of the objects they represent. All the other reserved words are hardwired into Python's syntax and can appear only in the specific contexts for which they are intended.

Furthermore, because module names in `import` statements become variables in your scripts, variable name constraints extend to your *module filenames* too. For instance, you can code files called *and.py* and *my-code.py* and run them as top-level scripts, but you cannot import them: their names without the ".py" extension become *variables* in your code and so must follow all the variable rules just outlined. Reserved words are off-limits, and dashes won't work, though underscores will. We'll revisit this idea in Part V of this book.

Python's Deprecation Protocol

It is interesting to note how reserved word changes are gradually phased into the language. When a new feature might break existing code, Python normally makes it an option and begins issuing "deprecation" warnings one or more releases before the feature is officially enabled. The idea is that you should have ample time to notice the warnings and update your code before migrating to the new release. This is not true for major new releases like 3.0 (which breaks existing code freely), but it is generally true in other cases.

For example, `yield` was an optional extension in Python 2.2, but is a standard keyword as of 2.3. It is used in conjunction with generator functions. This was one of a small handful of instances where Python broke with backward compatibility. Still, `yield` was phased in over time: it began generating deprecation warnings in 2.2 and was not enabled until 2.3.

[‡] In the Jython Java-based implementation of Python, though, user-defined variable names can sometimes be the same as Python reserved words. See Chapter 2 for an overview of the Jython system.

Similarly, in Python 2.6, the words `with` and `as` become new reserved words for use in context managers (a newer form of exception handling). These two words are not reserved in 2.5, unless the context manager feature is turned on manually with a `from__future__`import (discussed later in this book). When used in 2.5, `with` and `as` generate warnings about the upcoming change—except in the version of IDLE in Python 2.5, which appears to have enabled this feature for you (that is, using these words as variable names does generate errors in 2.5, but only in its version of the IDLE GUI).

Naming conventions

Besides these rules, there is also a set of naming *conventions*—rules that are not required but are followed in normal practice. For instance, because names with two leading and trailing underscores (e.g., `__name__`) generally have special meaning to the Python interpreter, you should avoid this pattern for your own names. Here is a list of the conventions Python follows:

- Names that begin with a single underscore (`_X`) are not imported by a `from module import *` statement (described in Chapter 22).

- Names that have two leading and trailing underscores (`__X__`) are system-defined names that have special meaning to the interpreter.

- Names that begin with two underscores and do not end with two more (`__X`) are localized ("mangled") to enclosing classes (see the discussion of pseudoprivate attributes in Chapter 30).

- The name that is just a single underscore (`_`) retains the result of the last expression when working interactively.

In addition to these Python interpreter conventions, there are various other conventions that Python programmers usually follow. For instance, later in the book we'll see that class names commonly start with an uppercase letter and module names with a lowercase letter, and that the name `self`, though not reserved, usually has a special role in classes. In Chapter 17 we'll also study another, larger category of names known as the *built-ins*, which are predefined but not reserved (and so can be reassigned: `open = 42` works, though sometimes you might wish it didn't!).

Names have no type, but objects do

This is mostly review, but remember that it's crucial to keep Python's distinction between names and objects clear. As described in Chapter 6, objects have a type (e.g., integer, list) and may be mutable or not. Names (a.k.a. variables), on the other hand, are always just references to objects; they have no notion of mutability and have no associated type information, apart from the type of the object they happen to reference at a given point in time.

Thus, it's OK to assign the same name to different kinds of objects at different times:

```
>>> x = 0          # x bound to an integer object
>>> x = "Hello"    # Now it's a string
>>> x = [1, 2, 3]  # And now it's a list
```

In later examples, you'll see that this generic nature of names can be a decided advantage in Python programming. In Chapter 17, you'll also learn that names also live in something called a *scope*, which defines where they can be used; the place where you assign a name determines where it is visible.[§]

 For additional naming suggestions, see the discussion of naming conventions in Python's semi-official style guide, known as *PEP 8*. This guide is available at *http://www.python.org/dev/peps/pep-0008*, or via a web search for "Python PEP 8." Technically, this document formalizes coding standards for Python library code.

Though useful, the usual caveats about coding standards apply here. For one thing, PEP 8 comes with more detail than you are probably ready for at this point in the book. And frankly, it has become more complex, rigid, and subjective than it needs to be—some of its suggestions are not at all universally accepted or followed by Python programmers doing real work. Moreover, some of the most prominent companies using Python today have adopted coding standards of their own that differ.

PEP 8 does codify useful rule-of-thumb Python knowledge, though, and it's a great read for Python beginners, as long as you take its recommendations as guidelines, not gospel.

Expression Statements

In Python, you can use an expression as a statement, too—that is, on a line by itself. But because the result of the expression won't be saved, it usually makes sense to do so only if the expression does something useful as a side effect. Expressions are commonly used as statements in two situations:

For calls to functions and methods

> Some functions and methods do lots of work without returning a value. Such functions are sometimes called *procedures* in other languages. Because they don't return values that you might be interested in retaining, you can call these functions with expression statements.

[§] If you've used a more restrictive language like C++, you may be interested to know that there is no notion of C++'s const declaration in Python; certain objects may be *immutable*, but names can always be assigned. Python also has ways to hide names in classes and modules, but they're not the same as C++'s declarations (if hiding attributes matters to you, see the coverage of _X module names in Chapter 24, __X class names in Chapter 30, and the Private and Public class decorators example in Chapter 38).

For printing values at the interactive prompt

Python echoes back the results of expressions typed at the interactive command line. Technically, these are expression statements, too; they serve as a shorthand for typing `print` statements.

Table 11-4 lists some common expression statement forms in Python. Calls to functions and methods are coded with zero or more argument objects (really, expressions that evaluate to objects) in parentheses, after the function/method name.

Table 11-4. Common Python expression statements

Operation	Interpretation
`spam(eggs, ham)`	Function calls
`spam.ham(eggs)`	Method calls
`spam`	Printing variables in the interactive interpreter
`print(a, b, c, sep='')`	Printing operations in Python 3.0
`yield x ** 2`	Yielding expression statements

The last two entries in Table 11-4 are somewhat special cases—as we'll see later in this chapter, printing in Python 3.0 is a function call usually coded on a line by itself, and the `yield` operation in generator functions (discussed in Chapter 20) is often coded as a statement as well. Both are really just instances of expression statements.

For instance, though you normally run a `print` call on a line by itself as an expression statement, it returns a value like any other function call (its return value is `None`, the default return value for functions that don't return anything meaningful):

```
>>> x = print('spam')      # print is a function call expression in 3.0
spam
>>> print(x)               # But it is coded as an expression statement
None
```

Also keep in mind that although expressions can appear as statements in Python, statements cannot be used as expressions. For example, Python doesn't allow you to embed assignment statements (=) in other expressions. The rationale for this is that it avoids common coding mistakes; you can't accidentally change a variable by typing = when you really mean to use the == equality test. You'll see how to code around this when you meet the Python `while` loop in Chapter 13.

Expression Statements and In-Place Changes

This brings up a mistake that is common in Python work. Expression statements are often used to run list methods that change a list in-place:

```
>>> L = [1, 2]
>>> L.append(3)            # Append is an in-place change
>>> L
[1, 2, 3]
```

However, it's not unusual for Python newcomers to code such an operation as an assignment statement instead, intending to assign L to the larger list:

```
>>> L = L.append(4)        # But append returns None, not L
>>> print(L)               # So we lose our list!
None
```

This doesn't quite work, though. Calling an in-place change operation such as `append`, `sort`, or `reverse` on a list always changes the list in-place, but these methods do not return the list they have changed; instead, they return the `None` object. Thus, if you assign such an operation's result back to the variable name, you effectively lose the list (and it is probably garbage collected in the process!).

The moral of the story is, don't do this. We'll revisit this phenomenon in the section "Common Coding Gotchas" on page 389 at the end of this part of the book because it can also appear in the context of some looping statements we'll meet in later chapters.

Print Operations

In Python, `print` prints things—it's simply a programmer-friendly interface to the standard output stream.

Technically, printing converts one or more objects to their textual representations, adds some minor formatting, and sends the resulting text to either standard output or another file-like stream. In a bit more detail, `print` is strongly bound up with the notions of files and streams in Python:

File object methods
> In Chapter 9, we learned about file object methods that write text (e.g., `file.write(str)`). Printing operations are similar, but more focused—whereas file write methods write strings to arbitrary files, `print` writes objects to the `stdout` stream by default, with some automatic formatting added. Unlike with file methods, there is no need to convert objects to strings when using print operations.

Standard output stream
> The standard output stream (often known as `stdout`) is simply a default place to send a program's text output. Along with the standard input and error streams, it's one of three data connections created when your script starts. The standard output stream is usually mapped to the window where you started your Python program, unless it's been redirected to a file or pipe in your operating system's shell.
>
> Because the standard output stream is available in Python as the `stdout` file object in the built-in `sys` module (i.e., `sys.stdout`), it's possible to emulate `print` with file write method calls. However, `print` is noticeably easier to use and makes it easy to print text to other files and streams.

Printing is also one of the most visible places where Python 3.0 and 2.6 have diverged. In fact, this divergence is usually the first reason that most 2.X code won't run unchanged under 3.X. Specifically, the way you code print operations depends on which version of Python you use:

- In Python 3.X, printing is a *built-in function*, with keyword arguments for special modes.
- In Python 2.X, printing is a *statement* with specific syntax all its own.

Because this book covers both 3.0 and 2.6, we will look at each form in turn here. If you are fortunate enough to be able to work with code written for just one version of Python, feel free to pick the section that is relevant to you; however, as your circumstances may change, it probably won't hurt to be familiar with both cases.

The Python 3.0 print Function

Strictly speaking, printing is not a separate statement form in 3.0. Instead, it is simply an instance of the *expression statement* we studied in the preceding section.

The `print` built-in function is normally called on a line of its own, because it doesn't return any value we care about (technically, it returns `None`). Because it is a normal function, though, printing in 3.0 uses *standard function-call syntax*, rather than a special statement form. Because it provides special operation modes with keyword arguments, this form is both more general and supports future enhancements better.

By comparison, Python 2.6 `print` statements have somewhat ad-hoc syntax to support extensions such as end-of-line suppression and target files. Further, the 2.6 statement does not support separator specification at all; in 2.6, you wind up building strings ahead of time more often than you do in 3.0.

Call format

Syntactically, calls to the 3.0 `print` function have the following form:

```
print([object, ...][, sep=' '][, end='\n'][, file=sys.stdout])
```

In this formal notation, items in square brackets are optional and may be omitted in a given call, and values after = give argument defaults. In English, this built-in function prints the textual representation of one or more `object`s separated by the string `sep` and followed by the string `end` to the stream `file`.

The `sep`, `end`, and `file` parts, if present, must be given as *keyword arguments*—that is, you must use a special "name=value" syntax to pass the arguments by name instead of position. Keyword arguments are covered in depth in Chapter 18, but they're straightforward to use. The keyword arguments sent to this call may appear in any left-to-right order following the objects to be printed, and they control the `print` operation:

- **sep** is a string inserted between each object's text, which defaults to a single space if not passed; passing an empty string suppresses separators altogether.
- **end** is a string added at the end of the printed text, which defaults to a \n newline character if not passed. Passing an empty string avoids dropping down to the next output line at the end of the printed text—the next **print** will keep adding to the end of the current output line.
- **file** specifies the file, standard stream, or other file-like object to which the text will be sent; it defaults to the **sys.stdout** standard output stream if not passed. Any object with a file-like **write(string)** method may be passed, but real files should be already opened for output.

The textual representation of each **object** to be printed is obtained by passing the object to the **str** built-in call; as we've seen, this built-in returns a "user friendly" display string for any object.|| With no arguments at all, the **print** function simply prints a newline character to the standard output stream, which usually displays a blank line.

The 3.0 print function in action

Printing in 3.0 is probably simpler than some of its details may imply. To illustrate, let's run some quick examples. The following prints a variety of object types to the default standard output stream, with the default separator and end-of-line formatting added (these are the defaults because they are the most common use case):

```
C:\misc> c:\python30\python
>>>
>>> print()                          # Display a blank line

>>> x = 'spam'
>>> y = 99
>>> z = ['eggs']
>>>
>>> print(x, y, z)                   # Print 3 objects per defaults
spam 99 ['eggs']
```

There's no need to convert objects to strings here, as would be required for file write methods. By default, **print** calls add a space between the objects printed. To suppress this, send an empty string to the **sep** keyword argument, or send an alternative separator of your choosing:

```
>>> print(x, y, z, sep='')           # Suppress separator
spam99['eggs']
>>>
>>> print(x, y, z, sep=', ')         # Custom separator
spam, 99, ['eggs']
```

|| Technically, printing uses the equivalent of str in the internal implementation of Python, but the effect is the same. Besides this to-string conversion role, str is also the name of the string data type and can be used to decode Unicode strings from raw bytes with an extra encoding argument, as we'll learn in Chapter 36; this latter role is an advanced usage that we can safely ignore here.

Also by default, `print` adds an end-of-line character to terminate the output line. You can suppress this and avoid the line break altogether by passing an empty string to the end keyword argument, or you can pass a different terminator of your own (include a \n character to break the line manually):

```
>>> print(x, y, z, end='')            # Suppress line break
spam 99 ['eggs']>>>
>>>
>>> print(x, y, z, end=''); print(x, y, z)   # Two prints, same output line
spam 99 ['eggs']spam 99 ['eggs']
>>> print(x, y, z, end='...\n')        # Custom line end
spam 99 ['eggs']...
>>>
```

You can also combine keyword arguments to specify both separators and end-of-line strings—they may appear in any order but must appear after all the objects being printed:

```
>>> print(x, y, z, sep='...', end='!\n')   # Multiple keywords
spam...99...['eggs']!
>>> print(x, y, z, end='!\n', sep='...')   # Order doesn't matter
spam...99...['eggs']!
```

Here is how the `file` keyword argument is used—it directs the printed text to an open output file or other compatible object for the duration of the single `print` (this is really a form of stream redirection, a topic we will revisit later in this section):

```
>>> print(x, y, z, sep='...', file=open('data.txt', 'w'))   # Print to a file
>>> print(x, y, z)                      # Back to stdout
spam 99 ['eggs']
>>> print(open('data.txt').read())      # Display file text
spam...99...['eggs']
```

Finally, keep in mind that the separator and end-of-line options provided by print operations are just conveniences. If you need to display more specific formatting, don't print this way, Instead, build up a more complex string ahead of time or within the `print` itself using the string tools we met in Chapter 7, and print the string all at once:

```
>>> text = '%s: %-.4f, %05d' % ('Result', 3.14159, 42)
>>> print(text)
Result: 3.1416, 00042
>>> print('%s: %-.4f, %05d' % ('Result', 3.14159, 42))
Result: 3.1416, 00042
```

As we'll see in the next section, almost everything we've just seen about the 3.0 `print` function also applies directly to 2.6 `print` statements—which makes sense, given that the function was intended to both emulate and improve upon 2.6 printing support.

The Python 2.6 print Statement

As mentioned earlier, printing in Python 2.6 uses a statement with unique and specific syntax, rather than a built-in function. In practice, though, 2.6 printing is mostly a variation on a theme; with the exception of separator strings (which are supported in

3.0 but not 2.6), everything we can do with the 3.0 `print` function has a direct translation to the 2.6 `print` statement.

Statement forms

Table 11-5 lists the `print` statement's forms in Python 2.6 and gives their Python 3.0 `print` function equivalents for reference. Notice that the *comma* is significant in `print` statements—it separates objects to be printed, and a trailing comma suppresses the end-of-line character normally added at the end of the printed text (not to be confused with tuple syntax!). The `>>` syntax, normally used as a bitwise right-shift operation, is used here as well, to specify a target output stream other than the `sys.stdout` default.

Table 11-5. Python 2.6 print statement forms

Python 2.6 statement	Python 3.0 equivalent	Interpretation
`print x, y`	`print(x, y)`	Print objects' textual forms to `sys.stdout`; add a space between the items and an end-of-line at the end
`print x, y,`	`print(x, y, end='')`	Same, but don't add end-of-line at end of text
`print >> afile, x, y`	`print(x, y, file=afile)`	Send text to `afile.write`, not to `sys.stdout.write`

The 2.6 print statement in action

Although the 2.6 `print` statement has more unique syntax than the 3.0 function, it's similarly easy to use. Let's turn to some basic examples again. By default, the 2.6 `print` statement adds a space between the items separated by commas and adds a line break at the end of the current output line:

```
C:\misc> c:\python26\python
>>>
>>> x = 'a'
>>> y = 'b'
>>> print x, y
a b
```

This formatting is just a default; you can choose to use it or not. To suppress the line break so you can add more text to the current line later, end your `print` statement with a comma, as shown in the second line of Table 11-5 (the following is two statements on one line, separated by a semicolon):

```
>>> print x, y,; print x, y
a b a b
```

To suppress the space between items, again, don't print this way. Instead, build up an output string using the string concatenation and formatting tools covered in Chapter 7, and print the string all at once:

```
>>> print x + y
ab
>>> print '%s...%s' % (x, y)
a...b
```

As you can see, apart from their special syntax for usage modes, 2.6 `print` statements are roughly as simple to use as 3.0's function. The next section uncovers the way that files are specified in 2.6 `print`s.

Print Stream Redirection

In both Python 3.0 and 2.6, printing sends text to the standard output stream by default. However, it's often useful to send it elsewhere—to a text file, for example, to save results for later use or testing purposes. Although such redirection can be accomplished in system shells outside Python itself, it turns out to be just as easy to redirect a script's streams from within the script.

The Python "hello world" program

Let's start off with the usual (and largely pointless) language benchmark—the "hello world" program. To print a "hello world" message in Python, simply print the string per your version's print operation:

```
>>> print('hello world')          # Print a string object in 3.0
hello world
```

```
>>> print 'hello world'           # Print a string object in 2.6
hello world
```

Because expression results are echoed on the interactive command line, you often don't even need to use a `print` statement there—simply type the expressions you'd like to have printed, and their results are echoed back:

```
>>> 'hello world'                 # Interactive echoes
'hello world'
```

This code isn't exactly an earth-shattering piece of software mastery, but it serves to illustrate printing behavior. Really, the `print` operation is just an ergonomic feature of Python—it provides a simple interface to the `sys.stdout` object, with a bit of default formatting. In fact, if you enjoy working harder than you must, you can also code print operations this way:

```
>>> import sys                    # Printing the hard way
>>> sys.stdout.write('hello world\n')
hello world
```

This code explicitly calls the `write` method of `sys.stdout`—an attribute preset when Python starts up to an open file object connected to the output stream. The `print` operation hides most of those details, providing a simple tool for simple printing tasks.

Manual stream redirection

So, why did I just show you the hard way to print? The `sys.stdout` print equivalent turns out to be the basis of a common technique in Python. In general, `print` and `sys.stdout` are directly related as follows. This statement:

```
print(X, Y)                          # Or, in 2.6: print X, Y
```

is equivalent to the longer:

```
import sys
sys.stdout.write(str(X) + ' ' + str(Y) + '\n')
```

which manually performs a string conversion with `str`, adds a separator and newline with +, and calls the output stream's `write` method. Which would you rather code? (He says, hoping to underscore the programmer-friendly nature of prints....)

Obviously, the long form isn't all that useful for printing by itself. However, it is useful to know that this is exactly what `print` operations do because it is possible to *reassign* `sys.stdout` to something different from the standard output stream. In other words, this equivalence provides a way of making your `print` operations send their text to other places. For example:

```
import sys
sys.stdout = open('log.txt', 'a')        # Redirects prints to a file
...
print(x, y, x)                           # Shows up in log.txt
```

Here, we reset `sys.stdout` to a manually opened file named *log.txt*, located in the script's working directory and opened in append mode (so we add to its current content). After the reset, every `print` operation anywhere in the program will write its text to the end of the file *log.txt* instead of to the original output stream. The `print` operations are happy to keep calling `sys.stdout`'s `write` method, no matter what `sys.stdout` happens to refer to. Because there is just one `sys` module in your process, assigning `sys.stdout` this way will redirect every `print` anywhere in your program.

In fact, as this chapter's upcoming sidebar about `print` and `stdout` will explain, you can even reset `sys.stdout` to an object that isn't a file at all, as long as it has the expected interface: a method named `write` to receive the printed text string argument. When that object is a *class*, printed text can be routed and processed arbitrarily per a `write` method you code yourself.

This trick of resetting the output stream is primarily useful for programs originally coded with `print` statements. If you know that output should go to a file to begin with, you can always call file write methods instead. To redirect the output of a `print`-based program, though, resetting `sys.stdout` provides a convenient alternative to changing every `print` statement or using system shell-based redirection syntax.

Automatic stream redirection

This technique of redirecting printed text by assigning `sys.stdout` is commonly used in practice. One potential problem with the last section's code, though, is that there is no direct way to restore the original output stream should you need to switch back after printing to a file. Because `sys.stdout` is just a normal file object, you can always save it and restore it if needed:#

```
C:\misc> c:\python30\python
>>> import sys
>>> temp = sys.stdout                       # Save for restoring later
>>> sys.stdout = open('log.txt', 'a')       # Redirect prints to a file
>>> print('spam')                           # Prints go to file, not here
>>> print(1, 2, 3)
>>> sys.stdout.close()                      # Flush output to disk
>>> sys.stdout = temp                       # Restore original stream

>>> print('back here')                      # Prints show up here again
back here
>>> print(open('log.txt').read())           # Result of earlier prints
spam
1 2 3
```

As you can see, though, manual saving and restoring of the original output stream like this involves quite a bit of extra work. Because this crops up fairly often, a `print` extension is available to make it unnecessary.

In 3.0, the `file` keyword allows a single `print` call to send its text to a file's `write` method, without actually resetting `sys.stdout`. Because the redirection is temporary, normal `print` calls keep printing to the original output stream. In 2.6, a `print` statement that begins with a `>>` followed by an output file object (or other compatible object) has the same effect. For example, the following again sends printed text to a file named *log.txt*:

```
log = open('log.txt', 'a')          # 3.0
print(x, y, z, file=log)            # Print to a file-like object
print(a, b, c)                      # Print to original stdout

log = open('log.txt', 'a')          # 2.6
print >> log, x, y, z               # Print to a file-like object
print a, b, c                       # Print to original stdout
```

These redirected forms of `print` are handy if you need to print to *both* files and the standard output stream in the same program. If you use these forms, however, be sure

---

#In both 2.6 and 3.0 you may also be able to use the __stdout__ attribute in the sys module, which refers to the original value sys.stdout had at program startup time. You still need to restore sys.stdout to sys.__stdout__ to go back to this original stream value, though. See the sys module documentation for more details.

to give them a file object (or an object that has the same `write` method as a file object), not a file's name string. Here is the technique in action:

```
C:\misc> c:\python30\python
>>> log = open('log.txt', 'w')
>>> print(1, 2, 3, file=log)            # 2.6: print >> log, 1, 2, 3
>>> print(4, 5, 6, file=log)
>>> log.close()
>>> print(7, 8, 9)                      # 2.6: print 7, 8, 9
7 8 9
>>> print(open('log.txt').read())
1 2 3
4 5 6
```

These extended forms of `print` are also commonly used to print error messages to the standard error stream, available to your script as the preopened file object `sys.stderr`. You can either use its file `write` methods and format the output manually, or print with redirection syntax:

```
>>> import sys
>>> sys.stderr.write(('Bad!' * 8) + '\n')
Bad!Bad!Bad!Bad!Bad!Bad!Bad!Bad!

>>> print('Bad!' * 8, file=sys.stderr)       # 2.6: print >> sys.stderr, 'Bad!' * 8
Bad!Bad!Bad!Bad!Bad!Bad!Bad!Bad!
```

Now that you know all about print redirections, the equivalence between printing and file `write` methods should be fairly obvious. The following interaction prints both ways in 3.0, then redirects the output to an external file to verify that the same text is printed:

```
>>> X = 1; Y = 2
>>> print(X, Y)                                      # Print: the easy way
1 2
>>> import sys                                        # Print: the hard way
>>> sys.stdout.write(str(X) + ' ' + str(Y) + '\n')
1 2
4
>>> print(X, Y, file=open('temp1', 'w'))             # Redirect text to file

>>> open('temp2', 'w').write(str(X) + ' ' + str(Y) + '\n')   # Send to file manually
4
>>> print(open('temp1', 'rb').read())                # Binary mode for bytes
b'1 2\r\n'
>>> print(open('temp2', 'rb').read())
b'1 2\r\n'
```

As you can see, unless you happen to enjoy typing, print operations are usually the best option for displaying text. For another example of the equivalence between prints and file writes, watch for a 3.0 print function emulation example in Chapter 18; it uses this code pattern to provide a general 3.0 `print` function equivalent for use in Python 2.6.

Version-Neutral Printing

Finally, if you cannot restrict your work to Python 3.0 but still want your prints to be compatible with 3.0, you have some options. For one, you can code 2.6 `print` statements and let 3.0's `2to3` conversion script translate them to 3.0 function calls automatically. See the Python 3.0 documentation for more details about this script; it attempts to translate 2.X code to run under 3.0.

Alternatively, you can code 3.0 `print` function calls in your 2.6 code, by enabling the function call variant with a statement like the following:

```
from __future__ import print_function
```

This statement changes 2.6 to support 3.0's `print` functions exactly. This way, you can use 3.0 print features and won't have to change your prints if you later migrate to 3.0.

Also keep in mind that simple prints, like those in the first row of Table 11-5, work in *either* version of Python—because any expression may be enclosed in parentheses, we can always pretend to be calling a 3.0 `print` function in 2.6 by adding outer parentheses. The only downside to this is that it makes a tuple out of your printed objects if there are more than one—they will print with extra enclosing parentheses. In 3.0, for example, any number of objects may be listed in the call's parentheses:

```
C:\misc> c:\python30\python
>>> print('spam')                    # 3.0 print function call syntax
spam
>>> print('spam', 'ham', 'eggs')     # These are mutiple argments
spam ham eggs
```

The first of these works the same in 2.6, but the second generates a tuple in the output:

```
C:\misc> c:\python26\python
>>> print('spam')                    # 2.6 print statement, enclosing parens
spam
>>> print('spam', 'ham', 'eggs')     # This is really a tuple object!
('spam', 'ham', 'eggs')
```

To be truly portable, you can format the print string as a single object, using the string formatting expression or method call, or other string tools that we studied in Chapter 7:

```
>>> print('%s %s %s' % ('spam', 'ham', 'eggs'))
spam ham eggs
>>> print('{0} {1} {2}'.format('spam', 'ham', 'eggs'))
spam ham eggs
```

Of course, if you can use 3.0 exclusively you can forget such mappings entirely, but many Python programmers will at least encounter, if not write, 2.X code and systems for some time to come.

I use Python 3.0 `print` function calls throughout this book. I'll usually warn you that the results may have extra enclosing parentheses in 2.6 because multiple items are a tuple, but I sometimes don't, so please consider this note a blanket warning—if you see extra parentheses in your printed text in 2.6, either drop the parentheses in your `print` statements, recode your prints using the version-neutral scheme outlined here, or learn to love superfluous text.

Why You Will Care: print and stdout

The equivalence between the `print` operation and writing to `sys.stdout` is important. It makes it possible to reassign `sys.stdout` to any user-defined object that provides the same `write` method as files. Because the `print` statement just sends text to the `sys.stdout.write` method, you can capture printed text in your programs by assigning `sys.stdout` to an object whose `write` method processes the text in arbitrary ways.

For instance, you can send printed text to a GUI window, or tee it off to multiple destinations, by defining an object with a `write` method that does the required routing. You'll see an example of this trick when we study classes in Part VI of this book, but abstractly, it looks like this:

```
class FileFaker:
    def write(self, string):
        # Do something with printed text in string

import sys
sys.stdout = FileFaker()
print(someObjects)                  # Sends to class write method
```

This works because `print` is what we will call in the next part of this book a *polymorphic* operation—it doesn't care what `sys.stdout` is, only that it has a method (i.e., interface) called `write`. This redirection to objects is made even simpler with the `file` keyword argument in 3.0 and the `>>` extended form of `print` in 2.6, because we don't need to reset `sys.stdout` explicitly—normal prints will still be routed to the `stdout` stream:

```
myobj = FileFaker()                  # 3.0: Redirect to object for one print
print(someObjects, file=myobj)       # Does not reset sys.stdout

myobj = FileFaker()                  # 2.6: same effect
print >> myobj, someObjects          # Does not reset sys.stdout
```

Python's built-in `input` function reads from the `sys.stdin` file, so you can intercept read requests in a similar way, using classes that implement file-like `read` methods instead. See the `input` and `while` loop example in Chapter 10 for more background on this.

Notice that because printed text goes to the `stdout` stream, it's the way to print HTML in CGI scripts used on the Web. It also enables you to redirect Python script input and output at the operating system's shell command line, as usual:

```
python script.py < inputfile > outputfile
python script.py | filterProgram
```

Python's print operation redirection tools are essentially pure-Python alternatives to these shell syntax forms.

Chapter Summary

In this chapter, we began our in-depth look at Python statements by exploring assignments, expressions, and print operations. Although these are generally simple to use, they have some alternative forms that, while optional, are often convenient in practice: augmented assignment statements and the redirection form of `print` operations, for example, allow us to avoid some manual coding work. Along the way, we also studied the syntax of variable names, stream redirection techniques, and a variety of common mistakes to avoid, such as assigning the result of an `append` method call back to a variable.

In the next chapter, we'll continue our statement tour by filling in details about the `if` statement, Python's main selection tool; there, we'll also revisit Python's syntax model in more depth and look at the behavior of Boolean expressions. Before we move on, though, the end-of-chapter quiz will test your knowledge of what you've learned here.

Test Your Knowledge: Quiz

1. Name three ways that you can assign three variables to the same value.
2. Why might you need to care when assigning three variables to a mutable object?
3. What's wrong with saying L = L.sort()?
4. How might you use the `print` operation to send text to an external file?

Test Your Knowledge: Answers

1. You can use multiple-target assignments (A = B = C = 0), sequence assignment (A, B, C = 0, 0, 0), or multiple assignment statements on three separate lines (A = 0, B = 0, and C = 0). With the latter technique, as introduced in Chapter 10, you can also string the three separate statements together on the same line by separating them with semicolons (A = 0; B = 0; C = 0).

2. If you assign them this way:

```
A = B = C = []
```

all three names reference the same object, so changing it in-place from one (e.g., `A.append(99)`) will affect the others. This is true only for in-place changes to mutable objects like lists and dictionaries; for immutable objects such as numbers and strings, this issue is irrelevant.

3. The list `sort` method is like `append` in that it makes an in-place change to the subject list—it returns `None`, not the list it changes. The assignment back to L sets L to `None`, not to the sorted list. As we'll see later in this part of the book, a newer built-in function, `sorted`, sorts any sequence and returns a new list with the sorting result; because this is not an in-place change, its result can be meaningfully assigned to a name.

4. To print to a file for a single `print` operation, you can use 3.0's `print(X, file=F)` call form, use 2.6's extended `print >> file, X` statement form, or assign `sys.stdout` to a manually opened file before the `print` and restore the original after. You can also redirect all of a program's printed text to a file with special syntax in the system shell, but this is outside Python's scope.

if Tests and Syntax Rules

This chapter presents the Python `if` statement, which is the main statement used for selecting from alternative actions based on test results. Because this is our first in-depth look at *compound statements*—statements that embed other statements—we will also explore the general concepts behind the Python statement syntax model here in more detail than we did in the introduction in Chapter 10. Because the `if` statement introduces the notion of tests, this chapter will also deal with Boolean expressions and fill in some details on truth tests in general.

if Statements

In simple terms, the Python `if` statement selects actions to perform. It's the primary selection tool in Python and represents much of the *logic* a Python program possesses. It's also our first compound statement. Like all compound Python statements, the `if` statement may contain other statements, including other `if`s. In fact, Python lets you combine statements in a program sequentially (so that they execute one after another), and in an arbitrarily nested fashion (so that they execute only under certain conditions).

General Format

The Python `if` statement is typical of `if` statements in most procedural languages. It takes the form of an `if` test, followed by one or more optional `elif` ("else if") tests and a final optional `else` block. The tests and the `else` part each have an associated block of nested statements, indented under a header line. When the `if` statement runs, Python executes the block of code associated with the first test that evaluates to true, or the `else` block if all tests prove false. The general form of an `if` statement looks like this:

```
if <test1>:            # if test
    <statements1>      # Associated block
elif <test2>:          # Optional elifs
    <statements2>
else:                  # Optional else
    <statements3>
```

Basic Examples

To demonstrate, let's look at a few simple examples of the `if` statement at work. All parts are optional, except the initial `if` test and its associated statements. Thus, in the simplest case, the other parts are omitted:

```
>>> if 1:
...     print('true')
...
true
```

Notice how the prompt changes to `...` for continuation lines when typing interactively in the basic interface used here; in IDLE, you'll simply drop down to an indented line instead (hit Backspace to back up). A blank line (which you can get by pressing Enter twice) terminates and runs the entire statement. Remember that `1` is Boolean true, so this statement's test always succeeds. To handle a false result, code the `else`:

```
>>> if not 1:
...     print('true')
... else:
...     print('false')
...
false
```

Multiway Branching

Now here's an example of a more complex `if` statement, with all its optional parts present:

```
>>> x = 'killer rabbit'
>>> if x == 'roger':
...     print("how's jessica?")
... elif x == 'bugs':
...     print("what's up doc?")
... else:
...     print('Run away! Run away!')
...
Run away! Run away!
```

This multiline statement extends from the `if` line through the `else` block. When it's run, Python executes the statements nested under the first test that is true, or the `else` part if all tests are false (in this example, they are). In practice, both the `elif` and `else` parts may be omitted, and there may be more than one statement nested in each section. Note that the words `if`, `elif`, and `else` are associated by the fact that they line up vertically, with the same indentation.

If you've used languages like C or Pascal, you might be interested to know that there is no `switch` or `case` statement in Python that selects an action based on a variable's value. Instead, *multiway branching* is coded either as a series of `if`/`elif` tests, as in the prior example, or by indexing dictionaries or searching lists. Because dictionaries and lists can be built at runtime, they're sometimes more flexible than hardcoded `if` logic:

```
>>> choice = 'ham'
>>> print({'spam': 1.25,            # A dictionary-based 'switch'
...        'ham':  1.99,            # Use has_key or get for default
...        'eggs': 0.99,
...        'bacon': 1.10}[choice])
1.99
```

Although it may take a few moments for this to sink in the first time you see it, this dictionary is a multiway branch—indexing on the key `choice` branches to one of a set of values, much like a `switch` in C. An almost equivalent but more verbose Python `if` statement might look like this:

```
>>> if choice == 'spam':
...     print(1.25)
... elif choice == 'ham':
...     print(1.99)
... elif choice == 'eggs':
...     print(0.99)
... elif choice == 'bacon':
...     print(1.10)
... else:
...     print('Bad choice')
...
1.99
```

Notice the `else` clause on the `if` here to handle the default case when no key matches. As we saw in Chapter 8, dictionary defaults can be coded with `in` expressions, `get` method calls, or exception catching. All of the same techniques can be used here to code a default action in a dictionary-based multiway branch. Here's the `get` scheme at work with defaults:

```
>>> branch = {'spam': 1.25,
...           'ham':  1.99,
...           'eggs': 0.99}

>>> print(branch.get('spam', 'Bad choice'))
1.25
>>> print(branch.get('bacon', 'Bad choice'))
Bad choice
```

An `in` membership test in an `if` statement can have the same default effect:

```
>>> choice = 'bacon'
>>> if choice in branch:
...     print(branch[choice])
... else:
...     print('Bad choice')
...
Bad choice
```

Dictionaries are good for associating values with keys, but what about the more complicated actions you can code in the statement blocks associated with `if` statements? In Part IV, you'll learn that dictionaries can also contain *functions* to represent more complex branch actions and implement general jump tables. Such functions appear as dictionary values, may be coded as function names or `lambda`s, and are called by adding parentheses to trigger their actions; stay tuned for more on this topic in Chapter 19.

Although dictionary-based multiway branching is useful in programs that deal with more dynamic data, most programmers will probably find that coding an `if` statement is the most straightforward way to perform multiway branching. As a rule of thumb in coding, when in doubt, err on the side of simplicity and readability; it's the "Pythonic" way.

Python Syntax Rules

I introduced Python's syntax model in Chapter 10. Now that we're stepping up to larger statements like the `if`, this section reviews and expands on the syntax ideas introduced earlier. In general, Python has a simple, statement-based syntax. However, there are a few properties you need to know about:

- **Statements execute one after another, until you say otherwise**. Python normally runs statements in a file or nested block in order from first to last, but statements like `if` (and, as you'll see, loops) cause the interpreter to jump around in your code. Because Python's path through a program is called the *control flow*, statements such as `if` that affect it are often called *control-flow statements*.

- **Block and statement boundaries are detected automatically**. As we've seen, there are no braces or "begin/end" delimiters around blocks of code in Python; instead, Python uses the indentation of statements under a header to group the statements in a nested block. Similarly, Python statements are not normally terminated with semicolons; rather, the end of a line usually marks the end of the statement coded on that line.

- **Compound statements = header + ":" + indented statements**. All compound statements in Python follow the same pattern: a header line terminated with a colon, followed by one or more nested statements, usually indented under the header. The indented statements are called a *block* (or sometimes, a suite). In the `if` statement, the `elif` and `else` clauses are part of the `if`, but they are also header lines with nested blocks of their own.

- **Blank lines, spaces, and comments are usually ignored**. Blank lines are ignored in files (but not at the interactive prompt, when they terminate compound statements). Spaces inside statements and expressions are almost always ignored (except in string literals, and when used for indentation). Comments are always ignored: they start with a # character (not inside a string literal) and extend to the end of the current line.

- **Docstrings are ignored but are saved and displayed by tools**. Python supports an additional comment form called documentation strings (*docstrings* for short), which, unlike # comments, are retained at runtime for inspection. Docstrings are simply strings that show up at the top of program files and some statements. Python ignores their contents, but they are automatically attached to objects at runtime and may be displayed with documentation tools. Docstrings are part of Python's larger documentation strategy and are covered in the last chapter in this part of the book.

As you've seen, there are no variable type declarations in Python; this fact alone makes for a much simpler language syntax than what you may be used to. However, for most new users the lack of the braces and semicolons used to mark blocks and statements in many other languages seems to be the most novel syntactic feature of Python, so let's explore what this means in more detail.

Block Delimiters: Indentation Rules

Python detects block boundaries automatically, by line *indentation*—that is, the empty space to the left of your code. All statements indented the same distance to the right belong to the same block of code. In other words, the statements within a block line up vertically, as in a column. The block ends when the end of the file or a lesser-indented line is encountered, and more deeply nested blocks are simply indented further to the right than the statements in the enclosing block.

For instance, Figure 12-1 demonstrates the block structure of the following code:

```
x = 1
if x:
    y = 2
    if y:
        print('block2')
    print('block1')
print('block0')
```

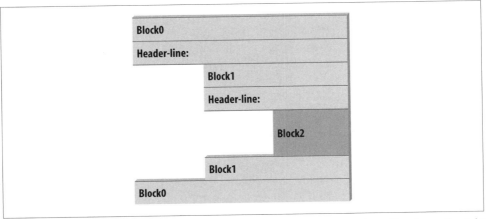

Figure 12-1. Nested blocks of code: a nested block starts with a statement indented further to the right and ends with either a statement that is indented less, or the end of the file.

This code contains three blocks: the first (the top-level code of the file) is not indented at all, the second (within the outer `if` statement) is indented four spaces, and the third (the `print` statement under the nested `if`) is indented eight spaces.

In general, top-level (unnested) code must start in column 1. Nested blocks can start in any column; indentation may consist of any number of spaces and tabs, as long as it's the same for all the statements in a given single block. That is, Python doesn't care *how* you indent your code; it only cares that it's done consistently. Four spaces or one tab per indentation level are common conventions, but there is no absolute standard in the Python world.

Indenting code is quite natural in practice. For example, the following (arguably silly) code snippet demonstrates common indentation errors in Python code:

```
      x = 'SPAM'                          # Error: first line indented
  if 'rubbery' in 'shrubbery':
      print(x * 8)
          x += 'NI'                       # Error: unexpected indentation
          if x.endswith('NI'):
                  x *= 2
              print(x)                    # Error: inconsistent indentation
```

The properly indented version of this code looks like the following—even for an artificial example like this, proper indentation makes the code's intent much more apparent:

```
  x = 'SPAM'
  if 'rubbery' in 'shrubbery':
      print(x * 8)
      x += 'NI'
      if x.endswith('NI'):
          x *= 2
          print(x)                        # Prints "SPAMNISPAMNI"
```

It's important to know that the only major place in Python where whitespace matters is where it's used to the left of your code, for indentation; in most other contexts, space can be coded or not. However, indentation is really part of Python syntax, not just a stylistic suggestion: all the statements within any given single block must be indented to the same level, or Python reports a syntax error. This is intentional—because you don't need to explicitly mark the start and end of a nested block of code, some of the syntactic clutter found in other languages is unnecessary in Python.

As described in Chapter 10, making indentation part of the syntax model also enforces consistency, a crucial component of readability in structured programming languages like Python. Python's syntax is sometimes described as "what you see is what you get"—the indentation of each line of code unambiguously tells readers what it is associated with. This uniform and consistent appearance makes Python code easier to maintain and reuse.

Indentation is more natural than the details might imply, and it makes your code reflect its logical structure. Consistently indented code always satisfies Python's rules. Moreover, most text editors (including IDLE) make it easy to follow Python's indentation model by automatically indenting code as you type it.

Avoid mixing tabs and spaces: New error checking in 3.0

One rule of thumb: although you can use spaces or tabs to indent, it's usually not a good idea to mix the two within a block—use one or the other. Technically, tabs count for enough spaces to move the current column number up to a multiple of 8, and your code will work if you mix tabs and spaces consistently. However, such code can be difficult to change. Worse, mixing tabs and spaces makes your code difficult to read— tabs may look very different in the next programmer's editor than they do in yours.

In fact, Python 3.0 now issues an error, for these very reasons, when a script mixes tabs and spaces for indentation inconsistently within a block (that is, in a way that makes it dependent on a tab's equivalent in spaces). Python 2.6 allows such scripts to run, but it has a -t command-line flag that will warn you about inconsistent tab usage and a -tt flag that will issue errors for such code (you can use these switches in a command line like `python -t main.py` in a system shell window). Python 3.0's error case is equivalent to 2.6's -tt switch.

Statement Delimiters: Lines and Continuations

A statement in Python normally ends at the end of the line on which it appears. When a statement is too long to fit on a single line, though, a few special rules may be used to make it span multiple lines:

- **Statements may span multiple lines if you're continuing an open syntactic pair**. Python lets you continue typing a statement on the next line if you're coding something enclosed in a (), {}, or [] pair. For instance, expressions in parentheses and dictionary and list literals can span any number of lines; your statement doesn't end until the Python interpreter reaches the line on which you type the closing part of the pair (a), }, or]). Continuation lines (lines 2 and beyond of the statement) can start at any indentation level you like, but you should try to make them align vertically for readability if possible. This open pairs rule also covers set and dictionary comprehensions in Python 3.0.

- **Statements may span multiple lines if they end in a backslash**. This is a somewhat outdated feature, but if a statement needs to span multiple lines, you can also add a backslash (a \ not embedded in a string literal or comment) at the end of the prior line to indicate you're continuing on the next line. Because you can also continue by adding parentheses around most constructs, backslashes are almost never used. This approach is error-prone: accidentally forgetting a \ usually generates a syntax error and might even cause the next line to be silently mistaken to be a new statement, with unexpected results.

- **Special rules for string literals**. As we learned in Chapter 7, triple-quoted string blocks are designed to span multiple lines normally. We also learned in Chapter 7 that adjacent string literals are implicitly concatenated; when used in conjunction with the open pairs rule mentioned earlier, wrapping this construct in parentheses allows it to span multiple lines.

- **Other rules**. There are a few other points to mention with regard to statement delimiters. Although uncommon, you can terminate a statement with a semicolon—this convention is sometimes used to squeeze more than one simple (noncompound) statement onto a single line. Also, comments and blank lines can appear anywhere in a file; comments (which begin with a # character) terminate at the end of the line on which they appear.

A Few Special Cases

Here's what a continuation line looks like using the open syntactic pairs rule. Delimited constructs, such as lists in square brackets, can span across any number of lines:

```
L = ["Good",
     "Bad",
     "Ugly"]                      # Open pairs may span lines
```

This also works for anything in parentheses (expressions, function arguments, function headers, tuples, and generator expressions), as well as anything in curly braces (dictionaries and, in 3.0, set literals and set and dictionary comprehensions). Some of these are tools we'll study in later chapters, but this rule naturally covers most constructs that span lines in practice.

If you like using backslashes to continue lines, you can, but it's not common practice in Python:

```
if a == b and c == d and  \
   d == e and f == g:
   print('olde')                  # Backslashes allow continuations...
```

Because any expression can be enclosed in parentheses, you can usually use the open pairs technique instead if you need your code to span multiple lines—simply wrap a part of your statement in parentheses:

```
if (a == b and c == d and
    d == e and e == f):
    print('new')                  # But parentheses usually do too
```

In fact, backslashes are frowned on, because they're too easy to not notice and too easy to omit altogether. In the following, x is assigned 10 with the backslash, as intended; if the backslash is accidentally omitted, though, x is assigned 6 instead, and no error is reported (the +4 is a valid expression statement by itself).

In a real program with a more complex assignment, this could be the source of a very nasty bug:[*]

```
x = 1 + 2 + 3 \              # Omitting the \ makes this very different
+4
```

As another special case, Python allows you to write more than one noncompound statement (i.e., statements without nested statements) on the same line, separated by semicolons. Some coders use this form to save program file real estate, but it usually makes for more readable code if you stick to one statement per line for most of your work:

```
x = 1; y = 2; print(x)      # More than one simple statement
```

As we learned in Chapter 7, triple-quoted string literals span lines too. In addition, if two string literals appear next to each other, they are concatenated as if a + had been added between them—when used in conjunction with the open pairs rule, wrapping in parentheses allows this form to span multiple lines. For example, the first of the following inserts newline characters at line breaks and assigns S to `'\naaaa\nbbbb\ncccc'`, and the second implicitly concatenates and assigns S to `'aaaabbbbcccc'`; comments are ignored in the second form, but included in the string in the first:

```
S = """
aaaa
bbbb
cccc"""

S = ('aaaa'
     'bbbb'                  # Comments here are ignored
     'cccc')
```

Finally, Python lets you move a compound statement's body up to the header line, provided the body is just a simple (noncompound) statement. You'll most often see this used for simple `if` statements with a single test and action:

```
if 1: print('hello')        # Simple statement on header line
```

You can combine some of these special cases to write code that is difficult to read, but I don't recommend it; as a rule of thumb, try to keep each statement on a line of its own, and indent all but the simplest of blocks. Six months down the road, you'll be happy you did.

---

[*] Frankly, it's surprising that this wasn't removed in Python 3.0, given some of its other changes! (See Table P-2 of the Preface for a list of 3.0 removals; some seem fairly innocuous in comparison with the dangers inherent in backslash continuations.) Then again, this book's goal is Python instruction, not populist outrage, so the best advice I can give is simply: don't do this.

Truth Tests

The notions of comparison, equality, and truth values were introduced in Chapter 9. Because the `if` statement is the first statement we've looked at that actually uses test results, we'll expand on some of these ideas here. In particular, Python's Boolean operators are a bit different from their counterparts in languages like C. In Python:

- Any nonzero number or nonempty object is true.
- Zero numbers, empty objects, and the special object `None` are considered false.
- Comparisons and equality tests are applied recursively to data structures.
- Comparisons and equality tests return `True` or `False` (custom versions of `1` and `0`).
- Boolean **and** and **or** operators return a true or false operand object.

In short, Boolean operators are used to combine the results of other tests. There are three Boolean expression operators in Python:

`X and Y`
> Is true if both `X` and `Y` are true

`X or Y`
> Is true if either `X` or `Y` is true

`not X`
> Is true if `X` is false (the expression returns `True` or `False`)

Here, `X` and `Y` may be any truth value, or any expression that returns a truth value (e.g., an equality test, range comparison, and so on). Boolean operators are typed out as words in Python (instead of C's `&&`, `||`, and `!`). Also, Boolean **and** and **or** operators return a true or false *object* in Python, not the values `True` or `False`. Let's look at a few examples to see how this works:

```
>>> 2 < 3, 3 < 2        # Less-than: return True or False (1 or 0)
(True, False)
```

Magnitude comparisons such as these return `True` or `False` as their truth results, which, as we learned in Chapters 5 and 9, are really just custom versions of the integers `1` and `0` (they print themselves differently but are otherwise the same).

On the other hand, the **and** and **or** operators always return an object—either the object on the left side of the operator or the object on the right. If we test their results in `if` or other statements, they will be as expected (remember, every object is inherently true or false), but we won't get back a simple `True` or `False`.

For or tests, Python evaluates the operand objects from left to right and returns the first one that is true. Moreover, Python stops at the first true operand it finds. This is usually called *short-circuit evaluation*, as determining a result short-circuits (terminates) the rest of the expression:

```
>>> 2 or 3, 3 or 2      # Return left operand if true
(2, 3)                  # Else, return right operand (true or false)
>>> [] or 3
3
>>> [] or {}
{}
```

In the first line of the preceding example, both operands (2 and 3) are true (i.e., are nonzero), so Python always stops and returns the one on the left. In the other two tests, the left operand is false (an empty object), so Python simply evaluates and returns the object on the right (which may happen to have either a true or a false value when tested).

and operations also stop as soon as the result is known; however, in this case Python evaluates the operands from left to right and stops at the first *false* object:

```
>>> 2 and 3, 3 and 2    # Return left operand if false
(3, 2)                  # Else, return right operand (true or false)
>>> [] and {}
[]
>>> 3 and []
[]
```

Here, both operands are true in the first line, so Python evaluates both sides and returns the object on the right. In the second test, the left operand is false ([]), so Python stops and returns it as the test result. In the last test, the left side is true (3), so Python evaluates and returns the object on the right (which happens to be a false []).

The end result of all this is the same as in C and most other languages—you get a value that is logically true or false if tested in an if or while. However, in Python Booleans return either the left or the right object, not a simple integer flag.

This behavior of and and or may seem esoteric at first glance, but see this chapter's sidebar "Why You Will Care: Booleans" on page 325 for examples of how it is sometimes used to advantage in coding by Python programmers. The next section also shows a common way to leverage this behavior, and its replacement in more recent versions of Python.

The if/else Ternary Expression

One common role for the prior section's Boolean operators is to code an expression that runs the same as an if statement. Consider the following statement, which sets A to either Y or Z, based on the truth value of X:

```
if X:
    A = Y
else:
    A = Z
```

Sometimes, though, the items involved in such a statement are so simple that it seems like overkill to spread them across four lines. At other times, we may want to nest such a construct in a larger statement instead of assigning its result to a variable. For these reasons (and, frankly, because the C language has a similar tool†), Python 2.5 introduced a new expression format that allows us to say the same thing in one expression:

```
A = Y if X else Z
```

This expression has the exact same effect as the preceding four-line `if` statement, but it's simpler to code. As in the statement equivalent, Python runs expression Y only if X turns out to be true, and runs expression Z only if X turns out to be false. That is, it *short-circuits*, just like the Boolean operators described in the prior section. Here are some examples of it in action:

```
>>> A = 't' if 'spam' else 'f'        # Nonempty is true
>>> A
't'
>>> A = 't' if '' else 'f'
>>> A
'f'
```

Prior to Python 2.5 (and after 2.5, if you insist), the same effect can often be achieved by a careful combination of the `and` and `or` operators, because they return either the object on the left side or the object on the right:

```
A = ((X and Y) or Z)
```

This works, but there is a catch—you have to be able to assume that Y will be Boolean true. If that is the case, the effect is the same: the `and` runs first and returns Y if X is true; if it's not, the `or` simply returns Z. In other words, we get "if X then Y else Z."

This `and/or` combination also seems to require a "moment of great clarity" to understand the first time you see it, and it's no longer required as of 2.5—use the equivalent and more robust and mnemonic Y `if` X `else` Z instead if you need this as an expression, or use a full `if` statement if the parts are nontrivial.

As a side note, using the following expression in Python is similar because the `bool` function will translate X into the equivalent of integer 1 or 0, which can then be used to pick true and false values from a list:

```
A = [Z, Y][bool(X)]
```

---

† In fact, Python's X `if` Y `else` Z has a slightly different order than C's Y ? X : Z. This was reportedly done in response to analysis of common use patterns in Python code. According to rumor, this order was also chosen in part to discourage ex-C programmers from overusing it! Remember, simple is better than complex, in Python and elsewhere.

For example:

```
>>> ['f', 't'][bool('')]
'f'
>>> ['f', 't'][bool('spam')]
't'
```

However, this isn't exactly the same, because Python will not short-circuit—it will always run both Z and Y, regardless of the value of X. Because of such complexities, you're better off using the simpler and more easily understood if/else expression as of Python 2.5 and later. Again, though, you should use even that sparingly, and only if its parts are all fairly simple; otherwise, you're better off coding the full if statement form to make changes easier in the future. Your coworkers will be happy you did.

Still, you may see the and/or version in code written prior to 2.5 (and in code written by C programmers who haven't quite let go of their dark coding pasts...).

Why You Will Care: Booleans

One common way to use the somewhat unusual behavior of Python Boolean operators is to select from a set of objects with an or. A statement such as this:

```
X = A or B or C or None
```

sets X to the first nonempty (that is, true) object among A, B, and C, or to None if all of them are empty. This works because the or operator returns one of its two objects, and it turns out to be a fairly common coding paradigm in Python: to select a nonempty object from among a fixed-size set, simply string them together in an or expression. In simpler form, this is also commonly used to designate a default—the following sets X to A if A is true (or nonempty), and to default otherwise:

```
X = A or default
```

It's also important to understand short-circuit evaluation because expressions on the right of a Boolean operator might call functions that perform substantial or important work, or have side effects that won't happen if the short-circuit rule takes effect:

```
if f1() or f2(): ...
```

Here, if f1 returns a true (or nonempty) value, Python will never run f2. To guarantee that both functions will be run, call them before the or:

```
tmp1, tmp2 = f1(), f2()
if tmp1 or tmp2: ...
```

You've already seen another application of this behavior in this chapter: because of the way Booleans work, the expression ((A and B) or C) can be used to emulate an if/else statement—almost (see this chapter's discussion of this form for details).

We met additional Boolean use cases in prior chapters. As we saw in Chapter 9, because all objects are inherently true or false, it's common and easier in Python to test an object directly (if X:) than to compare it to an empty value (if X != '':). For a string, the two tests are equivalent. As we also saw in Chapter 5, the preset Booleans values True and False are the same as the integers 1 and 0 and are useful for initializing variables

---

(X = False), for loop tests (while True:), and for displaying results at the interactive prompt.

Also watch for the discussion of operator overloading in Part VI: when we define new object types with classes, we can specify their Boolean nature with either the __bool__ or __len__ methods (__bool__ is named __nonzero__ in 2.6). The latter of these is tried if the former is absent and designates false by returning a length of zero—an empty object is considered false.

Chapter Summary

In this chapter, we studied the Python if statement. Additionally, because this was our first compound and logical statement, we reviewed Python's general syntax rules and explored the operation of truth tests in more depth than we were able to previously. Along the way, we also looked at how to code multiway branching in Python and learned about the if/else expression introduced in Python 2.5.

The next chapter continues our look at procedural statements by expanding on the while and for loops. There, we'll learn about alternative ways to code loops in Python, some of which may be better than others. Before that, though, here is the usual chapter quiz.

Test Your Knowledge: Quiz

1. How might you code a multiway branch in Python?
2. How can you code an if/else statement as an expression in Python?
3. How can you make a single statement span many lines?
4. What do the words True and False mean?

Test Your Knowledge: Answers

1. An if statement with multiple elif clauses is often the most straightforward way to code a multiway branch, though not necessarily the most concise. Dictionary indexing can often achieve the same result, especially if the dictionary contains callable functions coded with def statements or lambda expressions.
2. In Python 2.5 and later, the expression form Y if X else Z returns Y if X is true, or Z otherwise; it's the same as a four-line if statement. The and/or combination (((X and Y) or Z)) can work the same way, but it's more obscure and requires that the Y part be true.

3. Wrap up the statement in an open syntactic pair ((), [], or {}), and it can span as many lines as you like; the statement ends when Python sees the closing (right) half of the pair, and lines 2 and beyond of the statement can begin at any indentation level.

4. `True` and `False` are just custom versions of the integers 1 and 0, respectively: they always stand for Boolean true and false values in Python. They're available for use in truth tests and variable initialization and are printed for expression results at the interactive prompt.

while and for Loops

This chapter concludes our tour of Python procedural statements by presenting the language's two main *looping* constructs—statements that repeat an action over and over. The first of these, the while statement, provides a way to code general loops. The second, the for statement, is designed for stepping through the items in a sequence object and running a block of code for each.

We've seen both of these informally already, but we'll fill in additional usage details here. While we're at it, we'll also study a few less prominent statements used within loops, such as break and continue, and cover some built-ins commonly used with loops, such as range, zip, and map.

Although the while and for statements covered here are the primary syntax provided for coding repeated actions, there are additional looping operations and concepts in Python. Because of that, the iteration story is continued in the next chapter, where we'll explore the related ideas of Python's *iteration protocol* (used by the for loop) and *list comprehensions* (a close cousin to the for loop). Later chapters explore even more exotic iteration tools such as *generators*, filter, and reduce. For now, though, let's keep things simple.

while Loops

Python's while statement is the most general iteration construct in the language. In simple terms, it repeatedly executes a block of (normally indented) statements as long as a test at the top keeps evaluating to a true value. It is called a "loop" because control keeps looping back to the start of the statement until the test becomes false. When the test becomes false, control passes to the statement that follows the while block. The net effect is that the loop's body is executed repeatedly while the test at the top is true; if the test is false to begin with, the body never runs.

General Format

In its most complex form, the `while` statement consists of a header line with a test expression, a body of one or more indented statements, and an optional `else` part that is executed if control exits the loop without a `break` statement being encountered. Python keeps evaluating the test at the top and executing the statements nested in the loop body until the test returns a false value:

```
while <test>:              # Loop test
    <statements1>          # Loop body
else:                      # Optional else
    <statements2>          # Run if didn't exit loop with break
```

Examples

To illustrate, let's look at a few simple `while` loops in action. The first, which consists of a `print` statement nested in a `while` loop, just prints a message forever. Recall that `True` is just a custom version of the integer 1 and always stands for a Boolean true value; because the test is always true, Python keeps executing the body forever, or until you stop its execution. This sort of behavior is usually called an *infinite loop*:

```
>>> while True:
...     print('Type Ctrl-C to stop me!')
```

The next example keeps slicing off the first character of a string until the string is empty and hence false. It's typical to test an object directly like this instead of using the more verbose equivalent (`while x != '':`). Later in this chapter, we'll see other ways to step more directly through the items in a string with a `for` loop.

```
>>> x = 'spam'
>>> while x:                        # While x is not empty
...     print(x, end=' ')
...     x = x[1:]                   # Strip first character off x
...
spam pam am m
```

Note the `end=' '` keyword argument used here to place all outputs on the same line separated by a space; see Chapter 11 if you've forgotten why this works as it does. The following code counts from the value of a up to, but not including, b. We'll see an easier way to do this with a Python `for` loop and the built-in `range` function later:

```
>>> a=0; b=10
>>> while a < b:                    # One way to code counter loops
...     print(a, end=' ')
...     a += 1                      # Or, a = a + 1
...
0 1 2 3 4 5 6 7 8 9
```

Finally, notice that Python doesn't have what some languages call a "do until" loop statement. However, we can simulate one with a test and `break` at the bottom of the loop body:

```
while True:
    ...loop body...
    if exitTest(): break
```

To fully understand how this structure works, we need to move on to the next section and learn more about the `break` statement.

break, continue, pass, and the Loop else

Now that we've seen a few Python loops in action, it's time to take a look at two simple statements that have a purpose only when nested inside loops—the `break` and continue statements. While we're looking at oddballs, we will also study the loop `else` clause here, because it is intertwined with `break`, and Python's empty placeholder statement, the `pass` (which is not tied to loops per se, but falls into the general category of simple one-word statements). In Python:

`break`
> Jumps out of the closest enclosing loop (past the entire loop statement)

`continue`
> Jumps to the top of the closest enclosing loop (to the loop's header line)

`pass`
> Does nothing at all: it's an empty statement placeholder

`Loop else block`
> Runs if and only if the loop is exited normally (i.e., without hitting a `break`)

General Loop Format

Factoring in `break` and `continue` statements, the general format of the `while` loop looks like this:

```
while <test1>:
    <statements1>
    if <test2>: break        # Exit loop now, skip else
    if <test3>: continue     # Go to top of loop now, to test1
else:
    <statements2>            # Run if we didn't hit a 'break'
```

`break` and `continue` statements can appear anywhere inside the `while` (or `for`) loop's body, but they are usually coded further nested in an `if` test to take action in response to some condition.

Let's turn to a few simple examples to see how these statements come together in practice.

pass

Simple things first: the **pass** statement is a no-operation placeholder that is used when the syntax requires a statement, but you have nothing useful to say. It is often used to code an empty body for a compound statement. For instance, if you want to code an infinite loop that does nothing each time through, do it with a **pass**:

```
while True: pass          # Type Ctrl-C to stop me!
```

Because the body is just an empty statement, Python gets stuck in this loop. **pass** is roughly to statements as **None** is to objects—an explicit nothing. Notice that here the **while** loop's body is on the same line as the header, after the colon; as with **if** statements, this only works if the body isn't a compound statement.

This example does nothing forever. It probably isn't the most useful Python program ever written (unless you want to warm up your laptop computer on a cold winter's day!); frankly, though, I couldn't think of a better **pass** example at this point in the book.

We'll see other places where **pass** makes more sense later—for instance, to ignore exceptions caught by **try** statements, and to define empty **class** objects with attributes that behave like "structs" and "records" in other languages. A **pass** is also sometime coded to mean "to be filled in later," to stub out the bodies of functions temporarily:

```
def func1():
    pass                  # Add real code here later

def func2():
    pass
```

We can't leave the body empty without getting a syntax error, so we say **pass** instead.

 Version skew note: Python 3.0 (but not 2.6) allows *ellipses* coded as ... (literally, three consecutive dots) to appear any place an expression can. Because ellipses do nothing by themselves, this can serve as an alternative to the **pass** statement, especially for code to be filled in later—a sort of Python "TBD":

```
def func1():
    ...                   # Alternative to pass

def func2():
    ...

func1()                   # Does nothing if called
```

Ellipses can also appear on the same line as a statement header and may be used to initialize variable names if no specific type is required:

```
def func1(): ...          # Works on same line too
def func2(): ...

>>> X = ...               # Alternative to None
```

```
>>> X
Ellipsis
```

This notation is new in Python 3.0 (and goes well beyond the original intent of ... in slicing extensions), so time will tell if it becomes widespread enough to challenge pass and None in these roles.

continue

The continue statement causes an immediate jump to the top of a loop. It also sometimes lets you avoid statement nesting. The next example uses continue to skip odd numbers. This code prints all even numbers less than 10 and greater than or equal to 0. Remember, 0 means false and % is the remainder of division operator, so this loop counts down to 0, skipping numbers that aren't multiples of 2 (it prints 8 6 4 2 0):

```
x = 10
while x:
    x = x-1                    # Or, x -= 1
    if x % 2 != 0: continue    # Odd? -- skip print
    print(x, end=' ')
```

Because continue jumps to the top of the loop, you don't need to nest the print statement inside an if test; the print is only reached if the continue is not run. If this sounds similar to a "goto" in other languages, it should. Python has no "goto" statement, but because continue lets you jump about in a program, many of the warnings about readability and maintainability you may have heard about goto apply. continue should probably be used sparingly, especially when you're first getting started with Python. For instance, the last example might be clearer if the print were nested under the if:

```
x = 10
while x:
    x = x-1
    if x % 2 == 0:             # Even? -- print
        print(x, end=' ')
```

break

The break statement causes an immediate exit from a loop. Because the code that follows it in the loop is not executed if the break is reached, you can also sometimes avoid nesting by including a break. For example, here is a simple interactive loop (a variant of a larger example we studied in Chapter 10) that inputs data with input (known as raw_input in Python 2.6) and exits when the user enters "stop" for the name request:

```
>>> while True:
...     name = input('Enter name:')
...     if name == 'stop': break
...     age  = input('Enter age: ')
...     print('Hello', name, '=>', int(age) ** 2)
...
Enter name:mel
Enter age: 40
```

```
Hello mel => 1600
Enter name:bob
Enter age: 30
Hello bob => 900
Enter name:stop
```

Notice how this code converts the age input to an integer with int before raising it to the second power; as you'll recall, this is necessary because input returns user input as a string. In Chapter 35, you'll see that input also raises an exception at end-of-file (e.g., if the user types Ctrl-Z or Ctrl-D); if this matters, wrap input in try statements.

Loop else

When combined with the loop else clause, the break statement can often eliminate the need for the search status flags used in other languages. For instance, the following piece of code determines whether a positive integer y is prime by searching for factors greater than 1:

```
x = y // 2                          # For some y > 1
while x > 1:
    if y % x == 0:                  # Remainder
        print(y, 'has factor', x)
        break                       # Skip else
    x -= 1
else:                               # Normal exit
    print(y, 'is prime')
```

Rather than setting a flag to be tested when the loop is exited, it inserts a break where a factor is found. This way, the loop else clause can assume that it will be executed only if no factor is found; if you don't hit the break, the number is prime.

The loop else clause is also run if the body of the loop is never executed, as you don't run a break in that event either; in a while loop, this happens if the test in the header is false to begin with. Thus, in the preceding example you still get the "is prime" message if x is initially less than or equal to 1 (for instance, if y is 2).

 This example determines primes, but only informally so. Numbers less than 2 are not considered prime by the strict mathematical definition. To be really picky, this code also fails for negative numbers and succeeds for floating-point numbers with no decimal digits. Also note that its code must use // instead of / in Python 3.0 because of the migration of / to "true division," as described in Chapter 5 (we need the initial division to truncate remainders, not retain them!). If you want to experiment with this code, be sure to see the exercise at the end of Part IV, which wraps it in a function for reuse.

More on the loop else

Because the loop `else` clause is unique to Python, it tends to perplex some newcomers. In general terms, the loop `else` provides explicit syntax for a common coding scenario—it is a coding structure that lets us catch the "other" way out of a loop, without setting and checking flags or conditions.

Suppose, for instance, that we are writing a loop to search a list for a value, and we need to know whether the value was found after we exit the loop. We might code such a task this way (this code is intentionally abstract and incomplete; x is a sequence and match() is a tester function to be defined):

```
found = False
while x and not found:
    if match(x[0]):                 # Value at front?
        print('Ni')
        found = True
    else:
        x = x[1:]                   # Slice off front and repeat
if not found:
    print('not found')
```

Here, we initialize, set, and later test a flag to determine whether the search succeeded or not. This is valid Python code, and it does work; however, this is exactly the sort of structure that the loop `else` clause is there to handle. Here's an `else` equivalent:

```
while x:                            # Exit when x empty
    if match(x[0]):
        print('Ni')
        break                       # Exit, go around else
    x = x[1:]
else:
    print('Not found')              # Only here if exhausted x
```

This version is more concise. The flag is gone, and we've replaced the `if` test at the loop end with an `else` (lined up vertically with the word `while`). Because the `break` inside the main part of the `while` exits the loop and goes around the `else`, this serves as a more structured way to catch the search-failure case.

Some readers might have noticed that the prior example's `else` clause could be replaced with a test for an empty x after the loop (e.g., `if not x:`). Although that's true in this example, the `else` provides explicit syntax for this coding pattern (it's more obviously a search-failure clause here), and such an explicit empty test may not apply in some cases. The loop `else` becomes even more useful when used in conjunction with the `for` loop—the topic of the next section—because sequence iteration is not under your control.

for Loops

The for loop is a generic sequence iterator in Python: it can step through the items in any ordered sequence object. The for statement works on strings, lists, tuples, other built-in iterables, and new objects that we'll see how to create later with classes. We met it in brief when studying sequence object types; let's expand on its usage more formally here.

General Format

The Python for loop begins with a header line that specifies an assignment target (or targets), along with the object you want to step through. The header is followed by a block of (normally indented) statements that you want to repeat:

```
for <target> in <object>:          # Assign object items to target
    <statements>                    # Repeated loop body: use target
else:
    <statements>                    # If we didn't hit a 'break'
```

When Python runs a for loop, it assigns the items in the sequence object to the target one by one and executes the loop body for each. The loop body typically uses the assignment target to refer to the current item in the sequence as though it were a cursor stepping through the sequence.

The name used as the assignment target in a for header line is usually a (possibly new) variable in the scope where the for statement is coded. There's not much special about it; it can even be changed inside the loop's body, but it will automatically be set to the next item in the sequence when control returns to the top of the loop again. After the loop this variable normally still refers to the last item visited, which is the last item in the sequence unless the loop exits with a break statement.

The for statement also supports an optional else block, which works exactly as it does in a while loop—it's executed if the loop exits without running into a break statement (i.e., if all items in the sequence have been visited). The break and continue statements introduced earlier also work the same in a for loop as they do in a while. The for loop's complete format can be described this way:

```
for <target> in <object>:          # Assign object items to target
    <statements>
    if <test>: break                # Exit loop now, skip else
    if <test>: continue             # Go to top of loop now
else:
    <statements>                    # If we didn't hit a 'break'
```

Examples

Let's type a few for loops interactively now, so you can see how they are used in practice.

Basic usage

As mentioned earlier, a for loop can step across any kind of sequence object. In our first example, for instance, we'll assign the name x to each of the three items in a list in turn, from left to right, and the print statement will be executed for each. Inside the print statement (the loop body), the name x refers to the current item in the list:

```
>>> for x in ["spam", "eggs", "ham"]:
...     print(x, end=' ')
...
spam eggs ham
```

The next two examples compute the sum and product of all the items in a list. Later in this chapter and later in the book we'll meet tools that apply operations such as + and * to items in a list automatically, but it's usually just as easy to use a for:

```
>>> sum = 0
>>> for x in [1, 2, 3, 4]:
...     sum = sum + x
...
>>> sum
10
>>> prod = 1
>>> for item in [1, 2, 3, 4]: prod *= item
...
>>> prod
24
```

Other data types

Any sequence works in a `for`, as it's a generic tool. For example, `for` loops work on strings and tuples:

```
>>> S = "lumberjack"
>>> T = ("and", "I'm", "okay")

>>> for x in S: print(x, end=' ')        # Iterate over a string
...
l u m b e r j a c k

>>> for x in T: print(x, end=' ')        # Iterate over a tuple
...
and I'm okay
```

In fact, as we'll in the next chapter when we explore the notion of "iterables," `for` loops can even work on some objects that are not sequences—files and dictionaries work, too!

Tuple assignment in for loops

If you're iterating through a sequence of tuples, the loop target itself can actually be a *tuple* of targets. This is just another case of the tuple-unpacking assignment we studied in Chapter 11 at work. Remember, the `for` loop assigns items in the sequence object to the target, and assignment works the same everywhere:

```
>>> T = [(1, 2), (3, 4), (5, 6)]
>>> for (a, b) in T:              # Tuple assignment at work
...     print(a, b)
...
...
1 2
3 4
5 6
```

Here, the first time through the loop is like writing (a,b) = (1,2), the second time is like writing (a,b) = (3,4), and so on. The net effect is to automatically unpack the current tuple on each iteration.

This form is commonly used in conjunction with the `zip` call we'll meet later in this chapter to implement parallel traversals. It also makes regular appearances in conjunction with SQL databases in Python, where query result tables are returned as sequences

---

of sequences like the list used here—the outer list is the database table, the nested tuples are the rows within the table, and tuple assignment extracts columns.

Tuples in `for` loops also come in handy to iterate through *both* keys and values in dictionaries using the `items` method, rather than looping through the keys and indexing to fetch the values manually:

```
>>> D = {'a': 1, 'b': 2, 'c': 3}
>>> for key in D:
...     print(key, '=>', D[key])          # Use dict keys iterator and index
...
a => 1
c => 3
b => 2

>>> list(D.items())
[('a', 1), ('c', 3), ('b', 2)]

>>> for (key, value) in D.items():
...     print(key, '=>', value)           # Iterate over both keys and values
...
a => 1
c => 3
b => 2
```

It's important to note that tuple assignment in `for` loops isn't a special case; any assignment target works syntactically after the word `for`. Although we can always assign manually within the loop to unpack:

```
>>> T
[(1, 2), (3, 4), (5, 6)]

>>> for both in T:
...     a, b = both                        # Manual assignment equivalent
...     print(a, b)
...
1 2
3 4
5 6
```

Tuples in the loop header save us an extra step when iterating through sequences of sequences. As suggested in Chapter 11, even *nested* structures may be automatically unpacked this way in a `for`:

```
>>> ((a, b), c) = ((1, 2), 3)             # Nested sequences work too
>>> a, b, c
(1, 2, 3)

>>> for ((a, b), c) in [((1, 2), 3), ((4, 5), 6)]: print(a, b, c)
...
1 2 3
4 5 6
```

But this is no special case—the for loop simply runs the sort of assignment we ran just before it, on each iteration. Any nested sequence structure may be unpacked this way, just because *sequence assignment* is so generic:

```
>>> for ((a, b), c) in [([1, 2], 3), ['XY', 6]]: print(a, b, c)
...
1 2 3
X Y 6
```

Python 3.0 extended sequence assignment in for loops

In fact, because the loop variable in a for loop can really be any assignment target, we can also use Python 3.0's extended sequence-unpacking assignment syntax here to extract items and sections of sequences within sequences. Really, this isn't a special case either, but simply a new assignment form in 3.0 (as discussed in Chapter 11); because it works in assignment statements, it automatically works in for loops.

Consider the tuple assignment form introduced in the prior section. A tuple of values is assigned to a tuple of names on each iteration, exactly like a simple assignment statement:

```
>>> a, b, c = (1, 2, 3)                         # Tuple assignment
>>> a, b, c
(1, 2, 3)

>>> for (a, b, c) in [(1, 2, 3), (4, 5, 6)]:    # Used in for loop
...     print(a, b, c)
...
...
1 2 3
4 5 6
```

In Python 3.0, because a sequence can be assigned to a more general set of names with a starred name to collect multiple items, we can use the same syntax to extract parts of nested sequences in the for loop:

```
>>> a, *b, c = (1, 2, 3, 4)                     # Extended seq assignment
>>> a, b, c
(1, [2, 3], 4)

>>> for (a, *b, c) in [(1, 2, 3, 4), (5, 6, 7, 8)]:
...     print(a, b, c)
...
1 [2, 3] 4
5 [6, 7] 8
```

In practice, this approach might be used to pick out multiple columns from rows of data represented as nested sequences. In Python 2.X starred names aren't allowed, but you can achieve similar effects by slicing. The only difference is that slicing returns a type-specific result, whereas starred names always are assigned lists:

```
>>> for all in [(1, 2, 3, 4), (5, 6, 7, 8)]:    # Manual slicing in 2.6
...     a, b, c = all[0], all[1:3], all[3]
...     print(a, b, c)
```

```
...
1 (2, 3) 4
5 (6, 7) 8
```

See Chapter 11 for more on this assignment form.

Nested for loops

Now let's look at a `for` loop that's a bit more sophisticated than those we've seen so far. The next example illustrates statement nesting and the loop `else` clause in a `for`. Given a list of objects (`items`) and a list of keys (`tests`), this code searches for each key in the objects list and reports on the search's outcome:

```
>>> items = ["aaa", 111, (4, 5), 2.01]   # A set of objects
>>> tests = [(4, 5), 3.14]                # Keys to search for
>>>
>>> for key in tests:                     # For all keys
...       for item in items:              # For all items
...           if item == key:             # Check for match
...               print(key, "was found")
...               break
...       else:
...           print(key, "not found!")
...
(4, 5) was found
3.14 not found!
```

Because the nested `if` runs a `break` when a match is found, the loop `else` clause can assume that if it is reached, the search has failed. Notice the nesting here. When this code runs, there are two loops going at the same time: the outer loop scans the keys list, and the inner loop scans the items list for each key. The nesting of the loop `else` clause is critical; it's indented to the same level as the header line of the inner `for` loop, so it's associated with the inner loop, not the `if` or the outer `for`.

Note that this example is easier to code if we employ the `in` operator to test membership. Because `in` implicitly scans an object looking for a match (at least logically), it replaces the inner loop:

```
>>> for key in tests:                     # For all keys
...       if key in items:                # Let Python check for a match
...           print(key, "was found")
...       else:
...           print(key, "not found!")
...
(4, 5) was found
3.14 not found!
```

In general, it's a good idea to let Python do as much of the work as possible (as in this solution) for the sake of brevity and performance.

The next example performs a typical data-structure task with a `for`—collecting common items in two sequences (strings). It's roughly a simple set intersection routine; after the loop runs, `res` refers to a list that contains all the items found in `seq1` and `seq2`:

```
>>> seq1 = "spam"
>>> seq2 = "scam"
>>>
>>> res = []                            # Start empty
>>> for x in seq1:                      # Scan first sequence
...     if x in seq2:                   # Common item?
...         res.append(x)               # Add to result end
...
>>> res
['s', 'a', 'm']
```

Unfortunately, this code is equipped to work only on two specific variables: seq1 and seq2. It would be nice if this loop could somehow be generalized into a tool you could use more than once. As you'll see, that simple idea leads us to *functions*, the topic of the next part of the book.

Why You Will Care: File Scanners

In general, loops come in handy anywhere you need to repeat an operation or process something more than once. Because files contain multiple characters and lines, they are one of the more typical use cases for loops. To load a file's contents into a string all at once, you simply call the file object's **read** method:

```
file = open('test.txt', 'r')    # Read contents into a string
print(file.read())
```

But to load a file in smaller pieces, it's common to code either a while loop with breaks on end-of-file, or a for loop. To read by characters, either of the following codings will suffice:

```
file = open('test.txt')
while True:
    char = file.read(1)         # Read by character
    if not char: break
    print(char)

for char in open('test.txt').read():
    print(char)
```

The for loop here also processes each character, but it loads the file into memory all at once (and assumes it fits!). To read by lines or blocks instead, you can use while loop code like this:

```
file = open('test.txt')
while True:
    line = file.readline()      # Read line by line
    if not line: break
    print(line, end='')         # Line already has a \n

file = open('test.txt', 'rb')
while True:
    chunk = file.read(10)       # Read byte chunks: up to 10 bytes
    if not chunk: break
    print(chunk)
```

You typically read binary data in blocks. To read text files line by line, though, the for loop tends to be easiest to code and the quickest to run:

```
for line in open('test.txt').readlines():
    print(line, end='')

for line in open('test.txt'):        # Use iterators: best text input mode
    print(line, end='')
```

The file readlines method loads a file all at once into a line-string list, and the last example here relies on file *iterators* to automatically read one line on each loop iteration (iterators are covered in detail in Chapter 14). See the library manual for more on the calls used here. The last example here is generally the best option for text files—besides its simplicity, it works for arbitrarily large files and doesn't load the entire file into memory all at once. The iterator version may be the quickest, but I/O performance is less clear-cut in Python 3.0.

In some 2.X Python code, you may also see the name open replaced with file and the file object's older xreadlines method used to achieve the same effect as the file's automatic line iterator (it's like readlines but doesn't load the file into memory all at once). Both file and xreadlines are removed in Python 3.0, because they are redundant; you shouldn't use them in 2.6 either, but they may pop up in older code and resources. Watch for more on reading files in Chapter 36; as we'll see there, text and binary files have slightly different semantics in 3.0.

Loop Coding Techniques

The for loop subsumes most counter-style loops. It's generally simpler to code and quicker to run than a while, so it's the first tool you should reach for whenever you need to step through a sequence. But there are also situations where you will need to iterate in more specialized ways. For example, what if you need to visit every second or third item in a list, or change the list along the way? How about traversing more than one sequence in parallel, in the same for loop?

You can always code such unique iterations with a while loop and manual indexing, but Python provides two built-ins that allow you to specialize the iteration in a for:

- The built-in range function produces a series of successively higher integers, which can be used as indexes in a for.
- The built-in zip function returns a series of parallel-item tuples, which can be used to traverse multiple sequences in a for.

Because for loops typically run quicker than while-based counter loops, it's to your advantage to use tools like these that allow you to use for when possible. Let's look at each of these built-ins in turn.

Counter Loops: while and range

The `range` function is really a general tool that can be used in a variety of contexts. Although it's used most often to generate indexes in a `for`, you can use it anywhere you need a list of integers. In Python 3.0, `range` is an *iterator* that generates items on demand, so we need to wrap it in a `list` call to display its results all at once (more on iterators in Chapter 14):

```
>>> list(range(5)), list(range(2, 5)), list(range(0, 10, 2))
([0, 1, 2, 3, 4], [2, 3, 4], [0, 2, 4, 6, 8])
```

With one argument, `range` generates a list of integers from zero up to but not including the argument's value. If you pass in two arguments, the first is taken as the lower bound. An optional third argument can give a *step*; if it is used, Python adds the step to each successive integer in the result (the step defaults to 1). Ranges can also be nonpositive and nonascending, if you want them to be:

```
>>> list(range(-5, 5))
[-5, -4, -3, -2, -1, 0, 1, 2, 3, 4]

>>> list(range(5, -5, -1))
[5, 4, 3, 2, 1, 0, -1, -2, -3, -4]
```

Although such `range` results may be useful all by themselves, they tend to come in most handy within `for` loops. For one thing, they provide a simple way to repeat an action a specific number of times. To print three lines, for example, use a `range` to generate the appropriate number of integers; `for` loops force results from `range` automatically in 3.0, so we don't need `list` here:

```
>>> for i in range(3):
...     print(i, 'Pythons')
...
0 Pythons
1 Pythons
2 Pythons
```

`range` is also commonly used to iterate over a sequence indirectly. The easiest and fastest way to step through a sequence exhaustively is always with a simple `for`, as Python handles most of the details for you:

```
>>> X = 'spam'
>>> for item in X: print(item, end=' ')        # Simple iteration
...
s p a m
```

Internally, the `for` loop handles the details of the iteration automatically when used this way. If you really need to take over the indexing logic explicitly, you can do it with a `while` loop:

```
>>> i = 0
>>> while i < len(X):                           # while loop iteration
...     print(X[i], end=' ')
...     i += 1
```

```
...
s p a m
```

You can also do manual indexing with a `for`, though, if you use `range` to generate a list
of indexes to iterate through. It's a multistep process, but it's sufficient to generate
offsets, rather than the items at those offsets:

```
>>> X
'spam'
>>> len(X)                                  # Length of string
4
>>> list(range(len(X)))                     # All legal offsets into X
[0, 1, 2, 3]
>>>
>>> for i in range(len(X)): print(X[i], end=' ')   # Manual for indexing
...
s p a m
```

Note that because this example is stepping over a list of *offsets* into X, not the actual
items of X, we need to index back into X within the loop to fetch each item.

Nonexhaustive Traversals: range and Slices

The last example in the prior section works, but it's not the fastest option. It's also
more work than we need to do. Unless you have a special indexing requirement, you're
always better off using the simple `for` loop form in Python—as a general rule, use `for`
instead of `while` whenever possible, and don't use `range` calls in `for` loops except as a
last resort. This simpler solution is better:

```
>>> for item in X: print(item)             # Simple iteration
...
```

However, the coding pattern used in the prior example does allow us to do more specialized sorts of traversals. For instance, we can skip items as we go:

```
>>> S = 'abcdefghijk'
>>> list(range(0, len(S), 2))
[0, 2, 4, 6, 8, 10]

>>> for i in range(0, len(S), 2): print(S[i], end=' ')
...
a c e g i k
```

Here, we visit every *second* item in the string S by stepping over the generated `range`
list. To visit every third item, change the third `range` argument to be 3, and so on. In
effect, using `range` this way lets you skip items in loops while still retaining the simplicity
of the `for` loop construct.

Still, this is probably not the ideal best-practice technique in Python today. If you really
want to skip items in a sequence, the extended three-limit form of the *slice expression*, presented in Chapter 7, provides a simpler route to the same goal. To visit every
second character in S, for example, slice with a stride of 2:

```
>>> S = 'abcdefghijk'
>>> for c in S[::2]: print(c, end=' ')
...
a c e g i k
```

The result is the same, but substantially easier for you to write and for others to read. The only real advantage to using range here instead is that it does not copy the string and does not create a list in 3.0; for very large strings, it may save memory.

Changing Lists: range

Another common place where you may use the range and for combination is in loops that change a list as it is being traversed. Suppose, for example, that you need to add 1 to every item in a list. You can try this with a simple for loop, but the result probably won't be exactly what you want:

```
>>> L = [1, 2, 3, 4, 5]

>>> for x in L:
...     x += 1
...
>>> L
[1, 2, 3, 4, 5]
>>> x
6
```

This doesn't quite work—it changes the loop variable x, not the list L. The reason is somewhat subtle. Each time through the loop, x refers to the next integer already pulled out of the list. In the first iteration, for example, x is integer 1. In the next iteration, the loop body sets x to a different object, integer 2, but it does not update the list where 1 originally came from.

To really change the list as we march across it, we need to use indexes so we can assign an updated value to each position as we go. The range/len combination can produce the required indexes for us:

```
>>> L = [1, 2, 3, 4, 5]

>>> for i in range(len(L)):     # Add one to each item in L
...     L[i] += 1               # Or L[i] = L[i] + 1
...
>>> L
[2, 3, 4, 5, 6]
```

When coded this way, the list is changed as we proceed through the loop. There is no way to do the same with a simple for x in L:-style loop, because such a loop iterates through actual items, not list positions. But what about the equivalent while loop? Such a loop requires a bit more work on our part, and likely runs more slowly:

```
>>> i = 0
>>> while i < len(L):
...     L[i] += 1
```

```
...      i += 1
...
>>> L
[3, 4, 5, 6, 7]
```

Here again, though, the `range` solution may not be ideal either. A list comprehension expression of the form:

```
[x+1 for x in L]
```

would do similar work, albeit without changing the original list in-place (we could assign the expression's new list object result back to L, but this would not update any other references to the original list). Because this is such a central looping concept, we'll save a complete exploration of list comprehensions for the next chapter.

Parallel Traversals: zip and map

As we've seen, the `range` built-in allows us to traverse sequences with `for` in a nonexhaustive fashion. In the same spirit, the built-in `zip` function allows us to use `for` loops to visit multiple sequences *in parallel*. In basic operation, `zip` takes one or more sequences as arguments and returns a series of tuples that pair up parallel items taken from those sequences. For example, suppose we're working with two lists:

```
>>> L1 = [1,2,3,4]
>>> L2 = [5,6,7,8]
```

To combine the items in these lists, we can use `zip` to create a list of tuple pairs (like `range`, `zip` is an iterable object in 3.0, so we must wrap it in a `list` call to display all its results at once—more on iterators in the next chapter):

```
>>> zip(L1, L2)
<zip object at 0x026523C8>
>>> list(zip(L1, L2))            # list() required in 3.0, not 2.6
[(1, 5), (2, 6), (3, 7), (4, 8)]
```

Such a result may be useful in other contexts as well, but when wedded with the `for` loop, it supports parallel iterations:

```
>>> for (x, y) in zip(L1, L2):
...      print(x, y, '--', x+y)
...
1 5 -- 6
2 6 -- 8
3 7 -- 10
4 8 -- 12
```

Here, we step over the result of the `zip` call—that is, the pairs of items pulled from the two lists. Notice that this `for` loop again uses the tuple assignment form we met earlier to unpack each tuple in the `zip` result. The first time through, it's as though we ran the assignment statement (x, y) = (1, 5).

It turns out, though, that in Python 2.2 and later you can skip the `for` loop altogether and simply pass the zipped keys/values lists to the built-in `dict` constructor call:

```
>>> keys = ['spam', 'eggs', 'toast']
>>> vals = [1, 3, 5]

>>> D3 = dict(zip(keys, vals))
>>> D3
{'toast': 5, 'eggs': 3, 'spam': 1}
```

The built-in name `dict` is really a type name in Python (you'll learn more about type names, and subclassing them, in Chapter 31). Calling it achieves something like a list-to-dictionary conversion, but it's really an object construction request. In the next chapter we'll explore a related but richer concept, the *list comprehension*, which builds lists in a single expression; we'll also revisit 3.0 *dictionary comprehensions*, an alternative to the `dict` call for zipped key/value pairs.

Generating Both Offsets and Items: enumerate

Earlier, we discussed using `range` to generate the offsets of items in a string, rather than the items at those offsets. In some programs, though, we need both: the item to use, plus an offset as we go. Traditionally, this was coded with a simple `for` loop that also kept a counter of the current offset:

```
>>> S = 'spam'
>>> offset = 0
>>> for item in S:
...     print(item, 'appears at offset', offset)
...     offset += 1
...
s appears at offset 0
p appears at offset 1
a appears at offset 2
m appears at offset 3
```

This works, but in recent Python releases a new built-in named `enumerate` does the job for us:

```
>>> S = 'spam'
>>> for (offset, item) in enumerate(S):
...     print(item, 'appears at offset', offset)
...
s appears at offset 0
p appears at offset 1
a appears at offset 2
m appears at offset 3
```

The `enumerate` function returns a *generator object*—a kind of object that supports the iteration protocol that we will study in the next chapter and will discuss in more detail in the next part of the book. In short, it has a __next__ method called by the `next` built-in function, which returns an (*index, value*) tuple each time through the loop. We can unpack these tuples with tuple assignment in the `for` loop (much like using `zip`):

```
>>> E = enumerate(S)
>>> E
<enumerate object at 0x02765AA8>
>>> next(E)
(0, 's')
>>> next(E)
(1, 'p')
>>> next(E)
(2, 'a')
```

As usual, we don't normally see this machinery because iteration contexts—including list comprehensions, the subject of Chapter 14—run the iteration protocol automatically:

```
>>> [c * i for (i, c) in enumerate(S)]
['', 'p', 'aa', 'mmm']
```

To fully understand iteration concepts like enumerate, zip, and list comprehensions, we need to move on to the next chapter for a more formal dissection.

Chapter Summary

In this chapter, we explored Python's looping statements as well as some concepts related to looping in Python. We looked at the while and for loop statements in depth, and we learned about their associated else clauses. We also studied the break and continue statements, which have meaning only inside loops, and met several built-in tools commonly used in for loops, including range, zip, map, and enumerate (although their roles as iterators in Python 3.0 won't be fully uncovered until the next chapter).

In the next chapter, we continue the iteration story by discussing list comprehensions and the iteration protocol in Python—concepts strongly related to for loops. There, we'll also explain some of the subtleties of iterable tools we met here, such as range and zip. As always, though, before moving on let's exercise what you've picked up here with a quiz.

Test Your Knowledge: Quiz

1. What are the main functional differences between a while and a for?
2. What's the difference between break and continue?
3. When is a loop's else clause executed?
4. How can you code a counter-based loop in Python?
5. What can a range be used for in a for loop?

Test Your Knowledge: Answers

1. The `while` loop is a general looping statement, but the `for` is designed to iterate across items in a sequence (really, iterable). Although the `while` can imitate the `for` with counter loops, it takes more code and might run slower.

2. The `break` statement exits a loop immediately (you wind up below the entire `while` or `for` loop statement), and `continue` jumps back to the top of the loop (you wind up positioned just before the test in `while` or the next item fetch in `for`).

3. The `else` clause in a `while` or `for` loop will be run once as the loop is exiting, if the loop exits normally (without running into a `break` statement). A `break` exits the loop immediately, skipping the `else` part on the way out (if there is one).

4. Counter loops can be coded with a `while` statement that keeps track of the index manually, or with a `for` loop that uses the `range` built-in function to generate successive integer offsets. Neither is the preferred way to work in Python, if you need to simply step across all the items in a sequence. Instead, use a simple `for` loop instead, without `range` or counters, whenever possible; it will be easier to code and usually quicker to run.

5. The `range` built-in can be used in a `for` to implement a fixed number of repetitions, to scan by offsets instead of items at offsets, to skip successive items as you go, and to change a list while stepping across it. None of these roles requires `range`, and most have alternatives—scanning actual items, three-limit slices, and list comprehensions are often better solutions today (despite the natural inclinations of ex-C programmers to want to count things!).

## CHAPTER 14

Iterations and Comprehensions, Part 1

In the prior chapter we met Python's two looping statements, while and for. Although they can handle most repetitive tasks programs need to perform, the need to iterate over sequences is so common and pervasive that Python provides additional tools to make it simpler and more efficient. This chapter begins our exploration of these tools. Specifically, it presents the related concepts of Python's *iteration protocol*—a method-call model used by the for loop—and fills in some details on *list comprehensions*—a close cousin to the for loop that applies an expression to items in an iterable.

Because both of these tools are related to both the for loop and functions, we'll take a two-pass approach to covering them in this book: this chapter introduces the basics in the context of looping tools, serving as something of continuation of the prior chapter, and a later chapter (Chapter 20) revisits them in the context of function-based tools. In this chapter, we'll also sample additional iteration tools in Python and touch on the new iterators available in Python 3.0.

One note up front: some of the concepts presented in these chapters may seem advanced at first glance. With practice, though, you'll find that these tools are useful and powerful. Although never strictly required, because they've become commonplace in Python code, a basic understanding can also help if you must read programs written by others.

Iterators: A First Look

In the preceding chapter, I mentioned that the for loop can work on any sequence type in Python, including lists, tuples, and strings, like this:

```
>>> for x in [1, 2, 3, 4]: print(x ** 2, end=' ')
...
1 4 9 16

>>> for x in (1, 2, 3, 4): print(x ** 3, end=' ')
...
1 8 27 64
```

```
>>> for x in 'spam': print(x * 2, end=' ')
...
ss pp aa mm
```

Actually, the for loop turns out to be even more generic than this—it works on any *iterable object*. In fact, this is true of all iteration tools that scan objects from left to right in Python, including for loops, the list comprehensions we'll study in this chapter, in membership tests, the map built-in function, and more.

The concept of "iterable objects" is relatively recent in Python, but it has come to permeate the language's design. It's essentially a generalization of the notion of sequences—an object is considered *iterable* if it is either a physically stored sequence or an object that produces one result at a time in the context of an iteration tool like a for loop. In a sense, iterable objects include both physical sequences and *virtual sequences* computed on demand.*

The Iteration Protocol: File Iterators

One of the easiest ways to understand what this means is to look at how it works with a built-in type such as the file. Recall from Chapter 9 that open file objects have a method called readline, which reads one line of text from a file at a time—each time we call the readline method, we advance to the next line. At the end of the file, an empty string is returned, which we can detect to break out of the loop:

```
>>> f = open('script1.py')        # Read a 4-line script file in this directory
>>> f.readline()                  # readline loads one line on each call
'import sys\n'
>>> f.readline()
'print(sys.path)\n'
>>> f.readline()
'x = 2\n'
>>> f.readline()
'print(2 ** 33)\n'
>>> f.readline()                  # Returns empty string at end-of-file
''
```

However, files also have a method named __next__ that has a nearly identical effect—it returns the next line from a file each time it is called. The only noticeable difference is that __next__ raises a built-in StopIteration exception at end-of-file instead of returning an empty string:

```
>>> f = open('script1.py')        # __next__ loads one line on each call too
>>> f.__next__()                  # But raises an exception at end-of-file
'import sys\n'
>>> f.__next__()
'print(sys.path)\n'
```

---

* Terminology in this topic tends to be a bit loose. This text uses the terms "iterable" and "iterator" interchangeably to refer to an object that supports iteration in general. Sometimes the term "iterable" refers to an object that supports iter and "iterator" refers to an object return by iter that supports next(I), but that convention is not universal in either the Python world or this book.

```
>>> f.__next__()
'x = 2\n'
>>> f.__next__()
'print(2 ** 33)\n'
>>> f.__next__()
Traceback (most recent call last):
...more exception text omitted...
StopIteration
```

This interface is exactly what we call the *iteration protocol* in Python. Any object with a __next__ method to advance to a next result, which raises StopIteration at the end of the series of results, is considered iterable in Python. Any such object may also be stepped through with a for loop or other iteration tool, because all iteration tools normally work internally by calling __next__ on each iteration and catching the StopIteration exception to determine when to exit.

The net effect of this magic is that, as mentioned in Chapter 9, the best way to read a text file line by line today is to *not read it at all*—instead, allow the for loop to automatically call __next__ to advance to the next line on each iteration. The file object's iterator will do the work of automatically loading lines as you go. The following, for example, reads a file line by line, printing the uppercase version of each line along the way, without ever explicitly reading from the file at all:

```
>>> for line in open('script1.py'):       # Use file iterators to read by lines
...     print(line.upper(), end='')        # Calls __next__, catches StopIteration
...
IMPORT SYS
PRINT(SYS.PATH)
X = 2
PRINT(2 ** 33)
```

Notice that the print uses end='' here to suppress adding a \n, because line strings already have one (without this, our output would be double-spaced). This is considered the best way to read text files line by line today, for three reasons: it's the simplest to code, might be the quickest to run, and is the best in terms of memory usage. The older, original way to achieve the same effect with a for loop is to call the file readlines method to load the file's content into memory as a list of line strings:

```
>>> for line in open('script1.py').readlines():
...     print(line.upper(), end='')
...
IMPORT SYS
PRINT(SYS.PATH)
X = 2
PRINT(2 ** 33)
```

This readlines technique still works, but it is not considered the best practice today and performs poorly in terms of memory usage. In fact, because this version really does load the entire file into memory all at once, it will not even work for files too big to fit into the memory space available on your computer. By contrast, because it reads one line at a time, the iterator-based version is immune to such memory-explosion issues.

The iterator version might run quicker too, though this can vary per release (Python 3.0 made this advantage less clear-cut by rewriting I/O libraries to support Unicode text and be less system-dependent).

As mentioned in the prior chapter's sidebar, "Why You Will Care: File Scanners" on page 342, it's also possible to read a file line by line with a while loop:

```
>>> f = open('script1.py')
>>> while True:
...     line = f.readline()
...     if not line: break
...     print(line.upper(), end='')
...
...same output...
```

However, this may run slower than the iterator-based for loop version, because iterators run at C language speed inside Python, whereas the while loop version runs Python byte code through the Python virtual machine. Any time we trade Python code for C code, speed tends to increase. This is not an absolute truth, though, especially in Python 3.0; we'll see timing techniques later in this book for measuring the relative speed of alternatives like these.

Manual Iteration: iter and next

To support manual iteration code (with less typing), Python 3.0 also provides a built-in function, next, that automatically calls an object's __next__ method. Given an iterable object X, the call next(X) is the same as X.__next__(), but noticeably simpler. With files, for instance, either form may be used:

```
>>> f = open('script1.py')
>>> f.__next__()                    # Call iteration method directly
'import sys\n'
>>> f.__next__()
'print(sys.path)\n'

>>> f = open('script1.py')
>>> next(f)                         # next built-in calls __next__
'import sys\n'
>>> next(f)
'print(sys.path)\n'
```

Technically, there is one more piece to the iteration protocol. When the for loop begins, it obtains an iterator from the iterable object by passing it to the iter built-in function; the object returned by iter has the required next method. This becomes obvious if we look at how for loops internally process built-in sequence types such as lists:

```
>>> L = [1, 2, 3]
>>> I = iter(L)                     # Obtain an iterator object
>>> I.__next__()                    # Call next to advance to next item
1
>>> I.__next__()
2
```

```
>>> I.__next__()
3
>>> I.__next__()
Traceback (most recent call last):
...more omitted...
StopIteration
```

This initial step is not required for files, because a file object is its own iterator. That is, files have their own __next__ method and so do not need to return a different object that does:

```
>>> f = open('script1.py')
>>> iter(f) is f
True
>>> f.__next__()
'import sys\n'
```

Lists, and many other built-in objects, are not their own iterators because they support multiple open iterations. For such objects, we must call iter to start iterating:

```
>>> L = [1, 2, 3]
>>> iter(L) is L
False
>>> L.__next__()
AttributeError: 'list' object has no attribute '__next__'

>>> I = iter(L)
>>> I.__next__()
1
>>> next(I)                      # Same as I.__next__()
2
```

Although Python iteration tools call these functions automatically, we can use them to apply the iteration protocol *manually*, too. The following interaction demonstrates the equivalence between automatic and manual iteration:[†]

```
>>> L = [1, 2, 3]
>>>
>>> for X in L:                   # Automatic iteration
...     print(X ** 2, end=' ')    # Obtains iter, calls __next__, catches exceptions
...
...
1 4 9

>>> I = iter(L)                   # Manual iteration: what for loops usually do
```

---

† Technically speaking, the for loop calls the internal equivalent of I.__next__, instead of the next(I) used here. There is rarely any difference between the two, but as we'll see in the next section, there are some built-in objects in 3.0 (such as os.popen results) that support the former and not the latter, but may be still be iterated across in for loops. Your manual iterations can generally use either call scheme. If you care for the full story, in 3.0 os.popen results have been reimplemented with the subprocess module and a wrapper class, whose __getattr__ method is no longer called in 3.0 for implicit __next__ fetches made by the next built-in, but is called for explicit fetches by name—a 3.0 change issue we'll confront in Chapters 37 and 38, which apparently burns some standard library code too! Also in 3.0, the related 2.6 calls os.popen2/3/4 are no longer available; use subprocess.Popen with appropriate arguments instead (see the Python 3.0 library manual for the new required code).

Now that you have a better understanding of this protocol, you should be able to see how it explains why the enumerate tool introduced in the prior chapter works the way it does:

```
>>> E = enumerate('spam')          # enumerate is an iterable too
>>> E
<enumerate object at 0x0253F508>
>>> I = iter(E)
>>> next(I)                        # Generate results with iteration protocol
(0, 's')
>>> next(I)                        # Or use list to force generation to run
(1, 'p')
>>> list(enumerate('spam'))
[(0, 's'), (1, 'p'), (2, 'a'), (3, 'm')]
```

We don't normally see this machinery because for loops run it for us automatically to step through results. In fact, everything that scans left-to-right in Python employs the iteration protocol in the same way—including the topic of the next section.

List Comprehensions: A First Look

Now that we've seen how the iteration protocol works, let's turn to a very common use case. Together with for loops, list comprehensions are one of the most prominent contexts in which the iteration protocol is applied.

In the previous chapter, we learned how to use range to change a list as we step across it:

```
>>> L = [1, 2, 3, 4, 5]

>>> for i in range(len(L)):
...     L[i] += 10
...
>>> L
[11, 12, 13, 14, 15]
```

This works, but as I mentioned there, it may not be the optimal "best-practice" approach in Python. Today, the list comprehension expression makes many such prior use cases obsolete. Here, for example, we can replace the loop with a single expression that produces the desired result list:

```
>>> L = [x + 10 for x in L]
>>> L
[21, 22, 23, 24, 25]
```

The net result is the same, but it requires less coding on our part and is likely to run substantially faster. The list comprehension isn't exactly the same as the for loop statement version because it makes a *new* list object (which might matter if there are multiple references to the original list), but it's close enough for most applications and is a common and convenient enough approach to merit a closer look here.

List Comprehension Basics

We met the list comprehension briefly in Chapter 4. Syntactically, its syntax is derived from a construct in set theory notation that applies an operation to each item in a set, but you don't have to know set theory to use this tool. In Python, most people find that a list comprehension simply looks like a backward `for` loop.

To get a handle on the syntax, let's dissect the prior section's example in more detail:

```
>>> L = [x + 10 for x in L]
```

List comprehensions are written in square brackets because they are ultimately a way to construct a new list. They begin with an arbitrary expression that we make up, which uses a loop variable that we make up (`x + 10`). That is followed by what you should now recognize as the header of a `for` loop, which names the loop variable, and an iterable object (`for x in L`).

To run the expression, Python executes an iteration across `L` inside the interpreter, assigning `x` to each item in turn, and collects the results of running the items through the expression on the left side. The result list we get back is exactly what the list comprehension says—a new list containing `x + 10`, for every `x` in `L`.

Technically speaking, list comprehensions are never really required because we can always build up a list of expression results manually with `for` loops that append results as we go:

```
>>> res = []
>>> for x in L:
...     res.append(x + 10)
...
>>> res
[21, 22, 23, 24, 25]
```

In fact, this is exactly what the list comprehension does internally.

However, list comprehensions are more concise to write, and because this code pattern of building up result lists is so common in Python work, they turn out to be very handy in many contexts. Moreover, list comprehensions can run much faster than manual `for` loop statements (often roughly twice as fast) because their iterations are performed at C language speed inside the interpreter, rather than with manual Python code; especially for larger data sets, there is a major performance advantage to using them.

Using List Comprehensions on Files

Let's work through another common use case for list comprehensions to explore them in more detail. Recall that the file object has a `readlines` method that loads the file into a list of line strings all at once:

```
>>> f = open('script1.py')
>>> lines = f.readlines()
```

```
>>> lines
['import sys\n', 'print(sys.path)\n', 'x = 2\n', 'print(2 ** 33)\n']
```

This works, but the lines in the result all include the newline character (\n) at the end. For many programs, the newline character gets in the way—we have to be careful to avoid double-spacing when printing, and so on. It would be nice if we could get rid of these newlines all at once, wouldn't it?

Any time we start thinking about performing an operation on each item in a sequence, we're in the realm of list comprehensions. For example, assuming the variable lines is as it was in the prior interaction, the following code does the job by running each line in the list through the string rstrip method to remove whitespace on the right side (a line[:-1] slice would work, too, but only if we can be sure all lines are properly terminated):

```
>>> lines = [line.rstrip() for line in lines]
>>> lines
['import sys', 'print(sys.path)', 'x = 2', 'print(2 ** 33)']
```

This works as planned. Because list comprehensions are an iteration context just like for loop statements, though, we don't even have to open the file ahead of time. If we open it inside the expression, the list comprehension will automatically use the iteration protocol we met earlier in this chapter. That is, it will read one line from the file at a time by calling the file's next method, run the line through the rstrip expression, and add it to the result list. Again, we get what we ask for—the rstrip result of a line, for every line in the file:

```
>>> lines = [line.rstrip() for line in open('script1.py')]
>>> lines
['import sys', 'print(sys.path)', 'x = 2', 'print(2 ** 33)']
```

This expression does a lot implicitly, but we're getting a lot of work for free here—Python scans the file and builds a list of operation results automatically. It's also an efficient way to code this operation: because most of this work is done inside the Python interpreter, it is likely much faster than an equivalent for statement. Again, especially for large files, the speed advantages of list comprehensions can be significant.

Besides their efficiency, list comprehensions are also remarkably expressive. In our example, we can run any string operation on a file's lines as we iterate. Here's the list comprehension equivalent to the file iterator uppercase example we met earlier, along with a few others (the method chaining in the second of these examples works because string methods return a new string, to which we can apply another string method):

```
>>> [line.upper() for line in open('script1.py')]
['IMPORT SYS\n', 'PRINT(SYS.PATH)\n', 'X = 2\n', 'PRINT(2 ** 33)\n']

>>> [line.rstrip().upper() for line in open('script1.py')]
['IMPORT SYS', 'PRINT(SYS.PATH)', 'X = 2', 'PRINT(2 ** 33)']

>>> [line.split() for line in open('script1.py')]
[['import', 'sys'], ['print(sys.path)'], ['x', '=', '2'], ['print(2', '**','33)']]
```

```
>>> [line.replace(' ', '!') for line in open('script1.py')]
['import!sys\n', 'print(sys.path)\n', 'x!=!2\n', 'print(2!**!33)\n']

>>> [('sys' in line, line[0]) for line in open('script1.py')]
[(True, 'i'), (True, 'p'), (False, 'x'), (False, 'p')]
```

Extended List Comprehension Syntax

In fact, list comprehensions can be even more advanced in practice. As one particularly useful extension, the for loop nested in the expression can have an associated if clause to filter out of the result items for which the test is not true.

For example, suppose we want to repeat the prior section's file-scanning example, but we need to collect only lines that begin with the letter *p* (perhaps the first character on each line is an action code of some sort). Adding an if filter clause to our expression does the trick:

```
>>> lines = [line.rstrip() for line in open('script1.py') if line[0] == 'p']
>>> lines
['print(sys.path)', 'print(2 ** 33)']
```

Here, the if clause checks each line read from the file to see whether its first character is *p*; if not, the line is omitted from the result list. This is a fairly big expression, but it's easy to understand if we translate it to its simple for loop statement equivalent. In general, we can always translate a list comprehension to a for statement by appending as we go and further indenting each successive part:

```
>>> res = []
>>> for line in open('script1.py'):
...     if line[0] == 'p':
...         res.append(line.rstrip())
...
>>> res
['print(sys.path)', 'print(2 ** 33)']
```

This for statement equivalent works, but it takes up four lines instead of one and probably runs substantially slower.

List comprehensions can become even more complex if we need them to—for instance, they may contain nested loops, coded as a series of for clauses. In fact, their full syntax allows for any number of for clauses, each of which can have an optional associated if clause (we'll be more formal about their syntax in Chapter 20).

For example, the following builds a list of the concatenation of x + y for every x in one string and every y in another. It effectively collects the permutation of the characters in two strings:

```
>>> [x + y for x in 'abc' for y in 'lmn']
['al', 'am', 'an', 'bl', 'bm', 'bn', 'cl', 'cm', 'cn']
```

Again, one way to understand this expression is to convert it to statement form by indenting its parts. The following is an equivalent, but likely slower, alternative way to achieve the same effect:

```
>>> res = []
>>> for x in 'abc':
...     for y in 'lmn':
...         res.append(x + y)
...
>>> res
['al', 'am', 'an', 'bl', 'bm', 'bn', 'cl', 'cm', 'cn']
```

Beyond this complexity level, though, list comprehension expressions can often become too compact for their own good. In general, they are intended for simple types of iterations; for more involved work, a simpler for statement structure will probably be easier to understand and modify in the future. As usual in programming, if something is difficult for you to understand, it's probably not a good idea.

We'll revisit list comprehensions in Chapter 20, in the context of functional programming tools; as we'll see, they turn out to be just as related to functions as they are to looping statements.

Other Iteration Contexts

Later in the book, we'll see that user-defined classes can implement the iteration protocol too. Because of this, it's sometimes important to know which built-in tools make use of it—any tool that employs the iteration protocol will automatically work on any built-in type or user-defined class that provides it.

So far, I've been demonstrating iterators in the context of the for loop statement, because this part of the book is focused on statements. Keep in mind, though, that every tool that scans from left to right across objects uses the iteration protocol. This includes the for loops we've seen:

```
>>> for line in open('script1.py'):       # Use file iterators
...     print(line.upper(), end='')
...
IMPORT SYS
PRINT(SYS.PATH)
X = 2
PRINT(2 ** 33)
```

However, list comprehensions, the in membership test, the map built-in function, and other built-ins such as the sorted and zip calls also leverage the iteration protocol. When applied to a file, all of these use the file object's iterator automatically to scan line by line:

```
>>> uppers = [line.upper() for line in open('script1.py')]
>>> uppers
['IMPORT SYS\n', 'PRINT(SYS.PATH)\n', 'X = 2\n', 'PRINT(2 ** 33)\n']
```

```
>>> map(str.upper, open('script1.py'))        # map is an iterable in 3.0
<map object at 0x02660710>

>>> list( map(str.upper, open('script1.py')) )
['IMPORT SYS\n', 'PRINT(SYS.PATH)\n', 'X = 2\n', 'PRINT(2 ** 33)\n']

>>> 'y = 2\n' in open('script1.py')
False
>>> 'x = 2\n' in open('script1.py')
True
```

We introduced the map call used here in the preceding chapter; it's a built-in that applies a function call to each item in the passed-in iterable object. map is similar to a list comprehension but is more limited because it requires a function instead of an arbitrary expression. It also *returns* an iterable object itself in Python 3.0, so we must wrap it in a list call to force it to give us all its values at once; more on this change later in this chapter. Because map, like the list comprehension, is related to both for loops and functions, we'll also explore both again in Chapters 19 and 20.

Python includes various additional built-ins that process iterables, too: sorted sorts items in an iterable, zip combines items from iterables, enumerate pairs items in an iterable with relative positions, filter selects items for which a function is true, and reduce runs pairs of items in an iterable through a function. All of these accept iterables, and zip, enumerate, and filter also return an iterable in Python 3.0, like map. Here they are in action running the file's iterator automatically to scan line by line:

```
>>> sorted(open('script1.py'))
['import sys\n', 'print(2 ** 33)\n', 'print(sys.path)\n', 'x = 2\n']

>>> list(zip(open('script1.py'), open('script1.py')))
[('import sys\n', 'import sys\n'), ('print(sys.path)\n', 'print(sys.path)\n'),
('x = 2\n', 'x = 2\n'), ('print(2 ** 33)\n', 'print(2 ** 33)\n')]

>>> list(enumerate(open('script1.py')))
[(0, 'import sys\n'), (1, 'print(sys.path)\n'), (2, 'x = 2\n'),
(3, 'print(2 ** 33)\n')]

>>> list(filter(bool, open('script1.py')))
['import sys\n', 'print(sys.path)\n', 'x = 2\n', 'print(2 ** 33)\n']

>>> import functools, operator
>>> functools.reduce(operator.add, open('script1.py'))
'import sys\nprint(sys.path)\nx = 2\nprint(2 ** 33)\n'
```

All of these are iteration tools, but they have unique roles. We met zip and enumerate in the prior chapter; filter and reduce are in Chapter 19's functional programming domain, so we'll defer details for now.

We first saw the sorted function used here at work in Chapter 4, and we used it for dictionaries in Chapter 8. sorted is a built-in that employs the iteration protocol—it's like the original list sort method, but it returns the new sorted list as a result and runs on any iterable object. Notice that, unlike `map` and others, `sorted` returns an actual *list* in Python 3.0 instead of an iterable.

Other built-in functions support the iteration protocol as well (but frankly, are harder to cast in interesting examples related to files). For example, the `sum` call computes the sum of all the numbers in any iterable; the `any` and `all` built-ins return `True` if any or all items in an iterable are `True`, respectively; and `max` and `min` return the largest and smallest item in an iterable, respectively. Like `reduce`, all of the tools in the following examples accept any iterable as an argument and use the iteration protocol to scan it, but return a single result:

```
>>> sum([3, 2, 4, 1, 5, 0])            # sum expects numbers only
15
>>> any(['spam', '', 'ni'])
True
>>> all(['spam', '', 'ni'])
False
>>> max([3, 2, 5, 1, 4])
5
>>> min([3, 2, 5, 1, 4])
1
```

Strictly speaking, the `max` and `min` functions can be applied to files as well—they automatically use the iteration protocol to scan the file and pick out the lines with the highest and lowest string values, respectively (though I'll leave valid use cases to your imagination):

```
>>> max(open('script1.py'))            # Line with max/min string value
'x = 2\n'
>>> min(open('script1.py'))
'import sys\n'
```

Interestingly, the iteration protocol is even more pervasive in Python today than the examples so far have demonstrated—*everything* in Python's built-in toolset that scans an object from left to right is defined to use the iteration protocol on the subject object. This even includes more esoteric tools such as the `list` and `tuple` built-in functions (which build new objects from iterables), the string `join` method (which puts a substring between strings contained in an iterable), and even sequence assignments. Consequently, all of these will also work on an open file and automatically read one line at a time:

```
>>> list(open('script1.py'))
['import sys\n', 'print(sys.path)\n', 'x = 2\n', 'print(2 ** 33)\n']

>>> tuple(open('script1.py'))
('import sys\n', 'print(sys.path)\n', 'x = 2\n', 'print(2 ** 33)\n')

>>> '&&'.join(open('script1.py'))
'import sys\n&&print(sys.path)\n&&x = 2\n&&print(2 ** 33)\n'

>>> a, b, c, d = open('script1.py')
>>> a, d
```

```
('import sys\n', 'print(2 ** 33)\n')

>>> a, *b = open('script1.py')          # 3.0 extended form
>>> a, b
('import sys\n', ['print(sys.path)\n', 'x = 2\n', 'print(2 ** 33)\n'])
```

Earlier, we saw that the built-in `dict` call accepts an iterable `zip` result, too. For that matter, so does the `set` call, as well as the new *set* and *dictionary comprehension expressions* in Python 3.0, which we met in Chapters 4, 5, and 8:

```
>>> set(open('script1.py'))
{'print(sys.path)\n', 'x = 2\n', 'print(2 ** 33)\n', 'import sys\n'}

>>> {line for line in open('script1.py')}
{'print(sys.path)\n', 'x = 2\n', 'print(2 ** 33)\n', 'import sys\n'}

>>> {ix: line for ix, line in enumerate(open('script1.py'))}
{0: 'import sys\n', 1: 'print(sys.path)\n', 2: 'x = 2\n', 3: 'print(2 ** 33)\n'}
```

In fact, both set and dictionary comprehensions support the extended syntax of list comprehensions we met earlier in this chapter, including `if` tests:

```
>>> {line for line in open('script1.py') if line[0] == 'p'}
{'print(sys.path)\n', 'print(2 ** 33)\n'}

>>> {ix: line for (ix, line) in enumerate(open('script1.py')) if line[0] == 'p'}
{1: 'print(sys.path)\n', 3: 'print(2 ** 33)\n'}
```

Like the list comprehension, both of these scan the file line by line and pick out lines that begin with the letter "p." They also happen to build sets and dictionaries in the end, but we get a lot of work "for free" by combining file iteration and comprehension syntax.

There's one last iteration context that's worth mentioning, although it's a bit of a preview: in Chapter 18, we'll learn that a special `*arg` form can be used in function calls to unpack a collection of values into individual arguments. As you can probably predict by now, this accepts any iterable, too, including files (see Chapter 18 for more details on the call syntax):

```
>>> def f(a, b, c, d): print(a, b, c, d, sep='&')
...
>>> f(1, 2, 3, 4)
1&2&3&4
>>> f(*[1, 2, 3, 4])              # Unpacks into arguments
1&2&3&4

>>> f(*open('script1.py'))       # Iterates by lines too!
import sys
&print(sys.path)
&x = 2
&print(2 ** 33)
```

In fact, because this argument-unpacking syntax in calls accepts iterables, it's also possible to use the `zip` built-in to *unzip* zipped tuples, by making prior or nested `zip` results arguments for another `zip` call (warning: you probably shouldn't read the following example if you plan to operate heavy machinery anytime soon!):

```
>>> X = (1, 2)
>>> Y = (3, 4)
>>>
>>> list(zip(X, Y))          # Zip tuples: returns an iterable
[(1, 3), (2, 4)]
>>>
>>> A, B = zip(*zip(X, Y))    # Unzip a zip!
>>> A
(1, 2)
>>> B
(3, 4)
```

Still other tools in Python, such as the range built-in and dictionary view objects, return iterables instead of processing them. To see how these have been absorbed into the iteration protocol in Python 3.0 as well, we need to move on to the next section.

New Iterables in Python 3.0

One of the fundamental changes in Python 3.0 is that it has a stronger emphasis on iterators than 2.X. In addition to the iterators associated with built-in types such as files and dictionaries, the dictionary methods keys, values, and items return iterable objects in Python 3.0, as do the built-in functions range, map, zip, and filter. As shown in the prior section, the last three of these functions both return iterators and process them. All of these tools produce results on demand in Python 3.0, instead of constructing result lists as they do in 2.6.

Although this saves memory space, it can impact your coding styles in some contexts. In various places in this book so far, for example, we've had to wrap up various function and method call results in a list(...) call in order to force them to produce all their results at once:

```
>>> zip('abc', 'xyz')            # An iterable in Python 3.0 (a list in 2.6)
<zip object at 0x02E66710>

>>> list(zip('abc', 'xyz'))       # Force list of results in 3.0 to display
[('a', 'x'), ('b', 'y'), ('c', 'z')]
```

This isn't required in 2.6, because functions like zip return lists of results. In 3.0, though, they return iterable objects, producing results on demand. This means extra typing is required to display the results at the interactive prompt (and possibly in some other contexts), but it's an asset in larger programs—delayed evaluation like this conserves memory and avoids pauses while large result lists are computed. Let's take a quick look at some of the new 3.0 iterables in action.

The range Iterator

We studied the `range` built-in's basic behavior in the prior chapter. In 3.0, it returns an iterator that generates numbers in the range on demand, instead of building the result list in memory. This subsumes the older 2.X `xrange` (see the upcoming version skew note), and you must use `list(range(...))` to force an actual range list if one is needed (e.g., to display results):

```
C:\\misc> c:\python30\python
>>> R = range(10)                # range returns an iterator, not a list
>>> R
range(0, 10)

>>> I = iter(R)                  # Make an iterator from the range
>>> next(I)                      # Advance to next result
0                                # What happens in for loops, comprehensions, etc.
>>> next(I)
1
>>> next(I)
2

>>> list(range(10))              # To force a list if required
[0, 1, 2, 3, 4, 5, 6, 7, 8, 9]
```

Unlike the list returned by this call in 2.X, `range` objects in 3.0 support only iteration, indexing, and the `len` function. They do not support any other sequence operations (use `list(...)` if you require more list tools):

```
>>> len(R)                       # range also does len and indexing, but no others
10
>>> R[0]
0
>>> R[-1]
9

>>> next(I)                      # Continue taking from iterator, where left off
3
>>> I.__next__()                 # .next() becomes .__next__(), but use new next()
4
```

Version skew note: Python 2.X also has a built-in called `xrange`, which is like `range` but produces items on demand instead of building a list of results in memory all at once. Since this is exactly what the new iterator-based `range` does in Python 3.0, `xrange` is no longer available in 3.0—it has been subsumed. You may still see it in 2.X code, though, especially since `range` builds result lists there and so is not as efficient in its memory usage. As noted in a sidebar in the prior chapter, the `file.xread lines()` method used to minimize memory use in 2.X has been dropped in Python 3.0 for similar reasons, in favor of file iterators.

The map, zip, and filter Iterators

Like `range`, the `map`, `zip`, and `filter` built-ins also become iterators in 3.0 to conserve space, rather than producing a result list all at once in memory. All three not only process iterables, as in 2.X, but also return iterable results in 3.0. Unlike `range`, though, they are their own iterators—after you step through their results once, they are exhausted. In other words, you can't have multiple iterators on their results that maintain different positions in those results.

Here is the case for the `map` built-in we met in the prior chapter. As with other iterators, you can force a list with `list(...)` if you really need one, but the default behavior can save substantial space in memory for large result sets:

```
>>> M = map(abs, (-1, 0, 1))          # map returns an iterator, not a list
>>> M
<map object at 0x0276B890>
>>> next(M)                           # Use iterator manually: exhausts results
1                                     # These do not support len() or indexing
>>> next(M)
0
>>> next(M)
1
>>> next(M)
StopIteration

>>> for x in M: print(x)              # map iterator is now empty: one pass only
...

>>> M = map(abs, (-1, 0, 1))          # Make a new iterator to scan again
>>> for x in M: print(x)              # Iteration contexts auto call next()
...
1
0
1
>>> list(map(abs, (-1, 0, 1)))        # Can force a real list if needed
[1, 0, 1]
```

The `zip` built-in, introduced in the prior chapter, returns iterators that work the same way:

```
>>> Z = zip((1, 2, 3), (10, 20, 30))  # zip is the same: a one-pass iterator
>>> Z
<zip object at 0x02770EE0>

>>> list(Z)
[(1, 10), (2, 20), (3, 30)]

>>> for pair in Z: print(pair)        # Exhausted after one pass
...

>>> Z = zip((1, 2, 3), (10, 20, 30))
>>> for pair in Z: print(pair)        # Iterator used automatically or manually
...
(1, 10)
```

```
(2, 20)
(3, 30)
>>> Z = zip((1, 2, 3), (10, 20, 30))
>>> next(Z)
(1, 10)
>>> next(Z)
(2, 20)
```

The `filter` built-in, which we'll study in the next part of this book, is also analogous. It returns items in an iterable for which a passed-in function returns `True` (as we've learned, in Python `True` includes nonempty objects):

```
>>> filter(bool, ['spam', '', 'ni'])
<filter object at 0x0269C6D0>
>>> list(filter(bool, ['spam', '', 'ni']))
['spam', 'ni']
```

Like most of the tools discussed in this section, `filter` both accepts an iterable to process and returns an iterable to generate results in 3.0.

Multiple Versus Single Iterators

It's interesting to see how the `range` object differs from the built-ins described in this section—it supports `len` and indexing, it is not its own iterator (you make one with `iter` when iterating manually), and it supports multiple iterators over its result that remember their positions independently:

```
>>> R = range(3)                          # range allows multiple iterators
>>> next(R)
TypeError: range object is not an iterator

>>> I1 = iter(R)
>>> next(I1)
0
>>> next(I1)
1
>>> I2 = iter(R)                          # Two iterators on one range
>>> next(I2)
0
>>> next(I1)                              # I1 is at a different spot than I2
2
```

By contrast, `zip`, `map`, and `filter` do not support multiple active iterators on the same result:

```
>>> Z = zip((1, 2, 3), (10, 11, 12))
>>> I1 = iter(Z)
>>> I2 = iter(Z)                          # Two iterators on one zip
>>> next(I1)
(1, 10)
>>> next(I1)
(2, 11)
>>> next(I2)                              # I2 is at same spot as I1!
```

```
(3, 12)
>>> M = map(abs, (-1, 0, 1))                    # Ditto for map (and filter)
>>> I1 = iter(M); I2 = iter(M)
>>> print(next(I1), next(I1), next(I1))
1 0 1
>>> next(I2)
StopIteration

>>> R = range(3)                                # But range allows many iterators
>>> I1, I2 = iter(R), iter(R)
>>> [next(I1), next(I1), next(I1)]
[0 1 2]
>>> next(I2)
0
```

When we code our own iterable objects with classes later in the book (Chapter 29), we'll see that multiple iterators are usually supported by returning new objects for the iter call; a single iterator generally means an object returns itself. In Chapter 20, we'll also find that *generator functions and expressions* behave like map and zip instead of range in this regard, supporting a single active iteration. In that chapter, we'll see some subtle implications of one-shot iterators in loops that attempt to scan multiple times.

Dictionary View Iterators

As we saw briefly in Chapter 8, in Python 3.0 the dictionary keys, values, and items methods return iterable *view* objects that generate result items one at a time, instead of producing result lists all at once in memory. View items maintain the same physical ordering as that of the dictionary and reflect changes made to the underlying dictionary. Now that we know more about iterators, here's the rest of the story:

```
>>> D = dict(a=1, b=2, c=3)
>>> D
{'a': 1, 'c': 3, 'b': 2}

>>> K = D.keys()                                # A view object in 3.0, not a list
>>> K
<dict_keys object at 0x026D83C0>

>>> next(K)                                     # Views are not iterators themselves
TypeError: dict_keys object is not an iterator

>>> I = iter(K)                                 # Views have an iterator,
>>> next(I)                                     # which can be used manually
'a'                                             # but does not support len(), index
>>> next(I)
'c'

>>> for k in D.keys(): print(k, end=' ')        # All iteration contexts use auto
...
a c b
```

As for all iterators, you can always force a 3.0 dictionary view to build a real list by passing it to the `list` built-in. However, this usually isn't required except to display results interactively or to apply list operations like indexing:

```
>>> K = D.keys()
>>> list(K)                          # Can still force a real list if needed
['a', 'c', 'b']

>>> V = D.values()                   # Ditto for values() and items() views
>>> V
<dict_values object at 0x026D8260>
>>> list(V)
[1, 3, 2]

>>> list(D.items())
[('a', 1), ('c', 3), ('b', 2)]

>>> for (k, v) in D.items(): print(k, v, end=' ')
...
a 1 c 3 b 2
```

In addition, 3.0 dictionaries still have iterators themselves, which return successive keys. Thus, it's not often necessary to call keys directly in this context:

```
>>> D                                # Dictionaries still have own iterator
{'a': 1, 'c': 3, 'b': 2}             # Returns next key on each iteration
>>> I = iter(D)
>>> next(I)
'a'
>>> next(I)
'c'

>>> for key in D: print(key, end=' ')    # Still no need to call keys() to iterate
...                                       # But keys is an iterator in 3.0 too!
a c b
```

Finally, remember again that because keys no longer returns a list, the traditional coding pattern for scanning a dictionary by sorted keys won't work in 3.0. Instead, convert keys views first with a `list` call, or use the `sorted` call on either a keys view or the dictionary itself, as follows:

```
>>> D
{'a': 1, 'c': 3, 'b': 2}
>>> for k in sorted(D.keys()): print(k, D[k], end=' ')
...
a 1 b 2 c 3

>>> D
{'a': 1, 'c': 3, 'b': 2}
>>> for k in sorted(D): print(k, D[k], end=' ')      # Best practice key sorting
...
a 1 b 2 c 3
```

Other Iterator Topics

We'll learn more about both list comprehensions and iterators in Chapter 20, in conjunction with functions, and again in Chapter 29 when we study classes. As you'll see later:

- User-defined functions can be turned into iterable *generator functions*, with `yield` statements.

- List comprehensions morph into iterable *generator expressions* when coded in parentheses.

- User-defined classes are made iterable with `__iter__` or `__getitem__` *operator overloading.*

In particular, user-defined iterators defined with classes allow arbitrary objects and operations to be used in any of the iteration contexts we've met here.

Chapter Summary

In this chapter, we explored concepts related to looping in Python. We took our first substantial look at the *iteration protocol* in Python—a way for nonsequence objects to take part in iteration loops—and at *list comprehensions*. As we saw, a list comprehension is an expression similar to a `for` loop that applies another expression to all the items in any iterable object. Along the way, we also saw other built-in iteration tools at work and studied recent iteration additions in Python 3.0.

This wraps up our tour of specific procedural statements and related tools. The next chapter closes out this part of the book by discussing documentation options for Python code; documentation is also part of the general syntax model, and it's an important component of well-written programs. In the next chapter, we'll also dig into a set of exercises for this part of the book before we turn our attention to larger structures such as functions. As usual, though, let's first exercise what we've learned here with a quiz.

Test Your Knowledge: Quiz

1. How are `for` loops and iterators related?
2. How are `for` loops and list comprehensions related?
3. Name four iteration contexts in the Python language.
4. What is the best way to read line by line from a text file today?
5. What sort of weapons would you expect to see employed by the Spanish Inquisition?

Test Your Knowledge: Answers

1. The `for` loop uses the *iteration protocol* to step through items in the object across which it is iterating. It calls the object's `__next__` method (run by the `next` built-in) on each iteration and catches the `StopIteration` exception to determine when to stop looping. Any object that supports this model works in a `for` loop and in other iteration contexts.

2. Both are iteration tools. List comprehensions are a concise and efficient way to perform a common `for` loop task: collecting the results of applying an expression to all items in an iterable object. It's always possible to translate a list comprehension to a `for` loop, and part of the list comprehension expression looks like the header of a `for` loop syntactically.

3. Iteration contexts in Python include the `for` loop; list comprehensions; the `map` built-in function; the `in` membership test expression; and the built-in functions `sorted`, `sum`, `any`, and `all`. This category also includes the `list` and `tuple` built-ins, string `join` methods, and sequence assignments, all of which use the iteration protocol (the `__next__` method) to step across iterable objects one item at a time.

4. The best way to read lines from a text file today is to not read it explicitly at all: instead, open the file within an iteration context such as a `for` loop or list comprehension, and let the iteration tool automatically scan one line at a time by running the file's `next` method on each iteration. This approach is generally best in terms of coding simplicity, execution speed, and memory space requirements.

5. I'll accept any of the following as correct answers: fear, intimidation, nice red uniforms, a comfy chair, and soft pillows.

## CHAPTER 15

The Documentation Interlude

This part of the book concludes with a look at techniques and tools used for documenting Python code. Although Python code is designed to be readable, a few well-placed human-readable comments can do much to help others understand the workings of your programs. Python includes syntax and tools to make documentation easier.

Although this is something of a tools-related concept, the topic is presented here partly because it involves Python's syntax model, and partly as a resource for readers struggling to understand Python's toolset. For the latter purpose, I'll expand here on documentation pointers first given in Chapter 4. As usual, in addition to the chapter quiz this concluding chapter ends with some warnings about common pitfalls and a set of exercises for this part of the text.

Python Documentation Sources

By this point in the book, you're probably starting to realize that Python comes with an amazing amount of prebuilt functionality—built-in functions and exceptions, predefined object attributes and methods, standard library modules, and more. And we've really only scratched the surface of each of these categories.

One of the first questions that bewildered beginners often ask is: how do I find information on all the built-in tools? This section provides hints on the various documentation sources available in Python. It also presents *documentation strings* (docstrings) and the *PyDoc* system that makes use of them. These topics are somewhat peripheral to the core language itself, but they become essential knowledge as soon as your code reaches the level of the examples and exercises in this part of the book.

As summarized in Table 15-1, there are a variety of places to look for information on Python, with generally increasing verbosity. Because documentation is such a crucial tool in practical programming, we'll explore each of these categories in the sections that follow.

Table 15-1. Python documentation sources

Form	Role
# comments	In-file documentation
The `dir` function	Lists of attributes available in objects
Docstrings: `__doc__`	In-file documentation attached to objects
PyDoc: The `help` function	Interactive help for objects
PyDoc: HTML reports	Module documentation in a browser
The standard manual set	Official language and library descriptions
Web resources	Online tutorials, examples, and so on
Published books	Commercially available reference texts

Comments

Hash-mark comments are the most basic way to document your code. Python simply ignores all the text following a # (as long as it's not inside a string literal), so you can follow this character with words and descriptions meaningful to programmers. Such comments are accessible only in your source files, though; to code comments that are more widely available, you'll need to use docstrings.

In fact, current best practice generally dictates that docstrings are best for larger functional documentation (e.g., "my file does this"), and # comments are best limited to smaller code documentation (e.g., "this strange expression does that"). More on docstrings in a moment.

The dir Function

The built-in `dir` function is an easy way to grab a list of all the attributes available inside an object (i.e., its methods and simpler data items). It can be called on any object that has attributes. For example, to find out what's available in the standard library's `sys` module, import it and pass it to `dir` (these results are from Python 3.0; they might vary slightly on 2.6):

```
>>> import sys
>>> dir(sys)
['__displayhook__', '__doc__', '__excepthook__', '__name__', '__package__',
'__stderr__', '__stdin__', '__stdout__', '_clear_type_cache', '_current_frames',
'_getframe', 'api_version', 'argv', 'builtin_module_names', 'byteorder',
'call_tracing', 'callstats', 'copyright', 'displayhook', 'dllhandle',
'dont_write_bytecode', 'exc_info', 'excepthook', 'exec_prefix', 'executable',
'exit', 'flags', 'float_info', 'getcheckinterval', 'getdefaultencoding',
...more names omitted...]
```

Only some of the many names are displayed here; run these statements on your machine to see the full list.

To find out what attributes are provided in built-in object types, run `dir` on a literal (or existing instance) of the desired type. For example, to see list and string attributes, you can pass empty objects:

```
>>> dir([])
['__add__', '__class__', '__contains__', ...more...
'append', 'count', 'extend', 'index', 'insert', 'pop', 'remove',
'reverse', 'sort']

>>> dir('')
['__add__', '__class__', '__contains__', ...more...
'capitalize', 'center', 'count', 'encode', 'endswith', 'expandtabs',
'find', 'format', 'index', 'isalnum', 'isalpha', 'isdecimal',
'isdigit', 'isidentifier', 'islower', 'isnumeric', 'isprintable',
'isspace', 'istitle', 'isupper', 'join', 'ljust', 'lower', 'lstrip', '
maketrans', 'partition', 'replace', 'rfind', 'rindex', 'rjust',
...more names omitted...]
```

`dir` results for any built-in type include a set of attributes that are related to the implementation of that type (technically, operator overloading methods); they all begin and end with double underscores to make them distinct, and you can safely ignore them at this point in the book.

Incidentally, you can achieve the same effect by passing a type name to `dir` instead of a literal:

```
>>> dir(str) == dir('')          # Same result as prior example
True
>>> dir(list) == dir([])
True
```

This works because names like `str` and `list` that were once type converter functions are actually names of types in Python today; calling one of these invokes its constructor to generate an instance of that type. I'll have more to say about constructors and operator overloading methods when we discuss classes in Part VI.

The `dir` function serves as a sort of memory-jogger—it provides a list of attribute names, but it does not tell you anything about what those names mean. For such extra information, we need to move on to the next documentation source.

Docstrings: __doc__

Besides # comments, Python supports documentation that is automatically attached to objects and retained at runtime for inspection. Syntactically, such comments are coded as strings at the tops of module files and function and class statements, before any other executable code (# comments are OK before them). Python automatically stuffs the strings, known as *docstrings*, into the __doc__ attributes of the corresponding objects.

User-defined docstrings

For example, consider the following file, *docstrings.py*. Its docstrings appear at the beginning of the file and at the start of a function and a class within it. Here, I've used triple-quoted block strings for multiline comments in the file and the function, but any sort of string will work. We haven't studied the `def` or `class` statements in detail yet, so ignore everything about them except the strings at their tops:

```
"""
Module documentation
Words Go Here
"""

spam = 40

def square(x):
    """
    function documentation
    can we have your liver then?
    """
    return x ** 2          # square

class Employee:
    "class documentation"
    pass

print(square(4))
print(square.__doc__)
```

The whole point of this documentation protocol is that your comments are retained for inspection in `__doc__` attributes after the file is imported. Thus, to display the docstrings associated with the module and its objects, we simply import the file and print their `__doc__` attributes, where Python has saved the text:

```
>>> import docstrings
16

    function documentation
    can we have your liver then?

>>> print(docstrings.__doc__)

Module documentation
Words Go Here

>>> print(docstrings.square.__doc__)

    function documentation
    can we have your liver then?

>>> print(docstrings.Employee.__doc__)
    class documentation
```

Note that you will generally want to use `print` to print docstrings; otherwise, you'll get a single string with embedded newline characters.

You can also attach docstrings to *methods* of classes (covered in Part VI), but because these are just `def` statements nested in `class` statements, they're not a special case. To fetch the docstring of a method function inside a class within a module, you would simply extend the path to go through the class: `module.class.method.__doc__` (we'll see an example of method docstrings in Chapter 28).

Docstring standards

There is no broad standard about what should go into the text of a docstring (although some companies have internal standards). There have been various markup language and template proposals (e.g., HTML or XML), but they don't seem to have caught on in the Python world. And frankly, convincing Python programmers to document their code using handcoded HTML is probably not going to happen in our lifetimes!

Documentation tends to have a low priority amongst programmers in general. Usually, if you get any comments in a file at all, you count yourself lucky. I strongly encourage you to document your code liberally, though—it really is an important part of well-written programs. The point here is that there is presently no standard on the structure of docstrings; if you want to use them, anything goes today.

Built-in docstrings

As it turns out, built-in modules and objects in Python use similar techniques to attach documentation above and beyond the attribute lists returned by `dir`. For example, to see an actual human-readable description of a built-in module, import it and print its `__doc__` string:

```
>>> import sys
>>> print(sys.__doc__)
This module provides access to some objects used or maintained by the
interpreter and to functions that interact strongly with the interpreter.

Dynamic objects:

argv -- command line arguments; argv[0] is the script pathname if known
path -- module search path; path[0] is the script directory, else ''
modules -- dictionary of loaded modules
...more text omitted...
```

Functions, classes, and methods within built-in modules have attached descriptions in their `__doc__` attributes as well:

```
>>> print(sys.getrefcount.__doc__)
getrefcount(object) -> integer

Return the reference count of object.  The count returned is generally
one higher than you might expect, because it includes the (temporary)
...more text omitted...
```

You can also read about built-in functions via their docstrings:

```
>>> print(int.__doc__)
int(x[, base]) -> integer

Convert a string or number to an integer, if possible.  A floating
point argument will be truncated towards zero (this does not include a
...more text omitted...

>>> print(map.__doc__)
map(func, *iterables) --> map object

Make an iterator that computes the function using arguments from
each of the iterables.  Stops when the shortest iterable is exhausted.
```

You can get a wealth of information about built-in tools by inspecting their docstrings this way, but you don't have to—the `help` function, the topic of the next section, does this automatically for you.

PyDoc: The help Function

The docstring technique proved to be so useful that Python now ships with a tool that makes docstrings even easier to display. The standard *PyDoc* tool is Python code that knows how to extract docstrings and associated structural information and format them into nicely arranged reports of various types. Additional tools for extracting and formatting docstrings are available in the open source domain (including tools that may support structured text—search the Web for pointers), but Python ships with PyDoc in its standard library.

There are a variety of ways to launch PyDoc, including command-line script options (see the Python library manual for details). Perhaps the two most prominent PyDoc interfaces are the built-in `help` function and the PyDoc GUI/HTML interface. The `help` function invokes PyDoc to generate a simple textual report (which looks much like a "manpage" on Unix-like systems):

```
>>> import sys
>>> help(sys.getrefcount)
Help on built-in function getrefcount in module sys:

getrefcount(...)
    getrefcount(object) -> integer

    Return the reference count of object.  The count returned is generally
    one higher than you might expect, because it includes the (temporary)
    ...more omitted...
```

Note that you do not have to import `sys` in order to call `help`, but you do have to import `sys` to get help on `sys`; it expects an object reference to be passed in. For larger objects such as modules and classes, the `help` display is broken down into multiple sections, a few of which are shown here. Run this interactively to see the full report:

```
>>> help(sys)
Help on built-in module sys:

NAME
    sys

FILE
    (built-in)

MODULE DOCS
    http://docs.python.org/library/sys

DESCRIPTION
    This module provides access to some objects used or maintained by the
    interpreter and to functions that interact strongly with the interpreter.
    ...more omitted...

FUNCTIONS
    __displayhook__ = displayhook(...)
        displayhook(object) -> None

        Print an object to sys.stdout and also save it in builtins.
        ...more omitted...

DATA
    __stderr__ = <io.TextIOWrapper object at 0x0236E950>
    __stdin__ = <io.TextIOWrapper object at 0x02366550>
    __stdout__ = <io.TextIOWrapper object at 0x02366E30>
    ...more omitted...
```

Some of the information in this report is docstrings, and some of it (e.g., function call
patterns) is structural information that PyDoc gleans automatically by inspecting objects' internals, when available. You can also use help on built-in functions, methods,
and types. To get help for a built-in type, use the type name (e.g., dict for dictionary,
str for string, list for list). You'll get a large display that describes all the methods
available for that type:

```
>>> help(dict)
Help on class dict in module builtins:

class dict(object)
 |  dict() -> new empty dictionary.
 |  dict(mapping) -> new dictionary initialized from a mapping object's
 ...more omitted...

>>> help(str.replace)
Help on method_descriptor:

replace(...)
    S.replace (old, new[, count]) -> str

    Return a copy of S with all occurrences of substring
    ...more omitted...

>>> help(ord)
```

```
Help on built-in function ord in module builtins:

ord(...)
    ord(c) -> integer

    Return the integer ordinal of a one-character string.
```

Finally, the help function works just as well on your modules as it does on built-ins. Here it is reporting on the *docstrings.py* file we coded earlier. Again, some of this is docstrings, and some is information automatically extracted by inspecting objects' structures:

```
>>> import docstrings
>>> help(docstrings.square)
Help on function square in module docstrings:

square(x)
    function documentation
    can we have your liver then?

>>> help(docstrings.Employee)
Help on class Employee in module docstrings:

class Employee(builtins.object)
 |  class documentation
 |
 |  Data descriptors defined here:
...more omitted...

>>> help(docstrings)
Help on module docstrings:

NAME
    docstrings

FILE
    c:\misc\docstrings.py

DESCRIPTION
    Module documentation
    Words Go Here

CLASSES
    builtins.object
        Employee

    class Employee(builtins.object)
     |  class documentation
     |
     |  Data descriptors defined here:
    ...more omitted...

FUNCTIONS
    square(x)
        function documentation
```

```
        can we have your liver then?

    DATA
        spam = 40
```

PyDoc: HTML Reports

The `help` function is nice for grabbing documentation when working interactively. For a more grandiose display, however, PyDoc also provides a GUI interface (a simple but portable Python/tkinter script) and can render its report in HTML page format, viewable in any web browser. In this mode, PyDoc can run locally or as a remote server in client/server mode; reports contain automatically created hyperlinks that allow you to click your way through the documentation of related components in your application.

To start PyDoc in this mode, you generally first launch the search engine GUI captured in Figure 15-1. You can start this either by selecting the "Module Docs" item in Python's Start button menu on Windows, or by launching the *pydoc.py* script in Python's standard library directory: *Lib* on Windows (run `pydoc.py` with a `-g` command-line argument). Enter the name of a module you're interested in, and press the Enter key; PyDoc will march down your module import search path (`sys.path`) looking for references to the requested module.

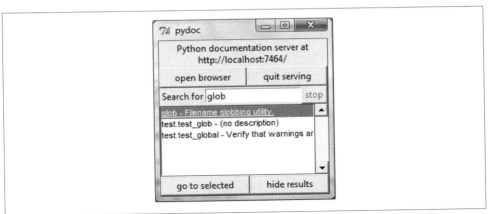

Figure 15-1. The Pydoc top-level search engine GUI: type the name of a module you want documentation for, press Enter, select the module, and then press "go to selected" (or omit the module name and press "open browser" to see all available modules).

Once you've found a promising entry, select it and click "go to selected." PyDoc will spawn a web browser on your machine to display the report rendered in HTML format. Figure 15-2 shows the information PyDoc displays for the built-in `glob` module.

Notice the hyperlinks in the Modules section of this page—you can click these to jump to the PyDoc pages for related (imported) modules. For larger pages, PyDoc also generates hyperlinks to sections within the page.

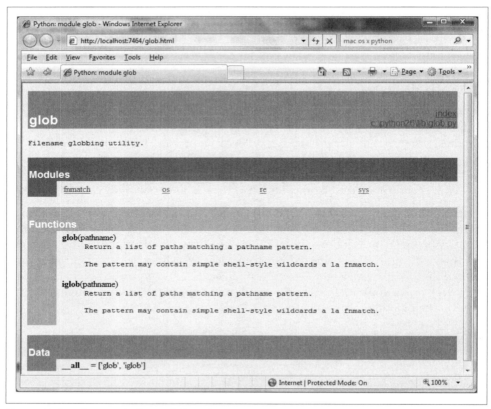

Figure 15-2. When you find a module in the Figure 15-1 GUI (such as this built-in standard library module) and press "go to selected," the module's documentation is rendered in HTML and displayed in a web browser window like this one.

Like the `help` function interface, the GUI interface works on user-defined modules as well as built-ins. Figure 15-3 shows the page generated for our *docstrings.py* module file.

PyDoc can be customized and launched in various ways we won't cover here; see its entry in Python's standard library manual for more details. The main thing to take away from this section is that PyDoc essentially gives you implementation reports "for free"—if you are good about using docstrings in your files, PyDoc does all the work of collecting and formatting them for display. PyDoc only helps for objects like functions and modules, but it provides an easy way to access a middle level of documentation for such tools—its reports are more useful than raw attribute lists, and less exhaustive than the standard manuals.

Cool PyDoc trick of the day: If you leave the module name empty in the top input field of the window in Figure 15-1 and press the "open browser" button, PyDoc will produce a web page containing a hyperlink to every module you can possibly import on your computer. This includes Python standard library modules, modules of third-party

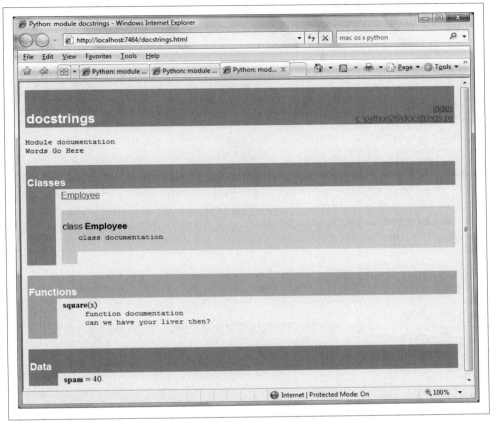

Figure 15-3. PyDoc can serve up documentation pages for both built-in and user-coded modules. Here is the page for a user-defined module, showing all its documentation strings (docstrings) extracted from the source file.

extensions you may have installed, user-defined modules on your import search path, and even statically or dynamically linked-in C-coded modules. Such information is hard to come by otherwise without writing code that inspects a set of module sources.

PyDoc can also be run to save the HTML documentation for a module in a file for later viewing or printing; see its documentation for pointers. Also, note that PyDoc might not work well if run on scripts that read from standard input—PyDoc imports the target module to inspect its contents, and there may be no connection for standard input text when it is run in GUI mode. Modules that can be imported without immediate input requirements will always work under PyDoc, though.

The Standard Manual Set

For the complete and most up-to-date description of the language and its toolset, Python's standard manuals stand ready to serve. Python's manuals ship in HTML and other formats, and they are installed with the Python system on Windows—they are available in your Start button's menu for Python, and they can also be opened from the Help menu within IDLE. You can also fetch the manual set separately from *http://www.python.org* in a variety of formats, or read them online at that site (follow the Documentation link). On Windows, the manuals are a compiled help file to support searches, and the online versions at the Python website include a web-based search page.

When opened, the Windows format of the manuals displays a root page like that in Figure 15-4. The two most important entries here are most likely the Library Reference (which documents built-in types, functions, exceptions, and standard library modules) and the Language Reference (which provides a formal description of language-level details). The tutorial listed on this page also provides a brief introduction for newcomers.

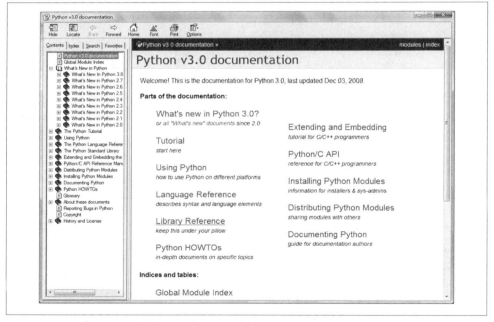

Figure 15-4. Python's standard manual set, available online at http://www.python.org, from IDLE's Help menu, and in the Windows Start button menu. It's a searchable help file on Windows, and there is a search engine for the online version. Of these, the Library Reference is the one you'll want to use most of the time.

Web Resources

At the official Python website (*http://www.python.org*), you'll find links to various Python resources, some of which cover special topics or domains. Click the Documentation link to access an online tutorial and the Beginners Guide to Python. The site also lists non-English Python resources.

You will find numerous Python wikis, blogs, websites, and a host of other resources on the Web today. To sample the online community, try searching for a term like "Python programming" in Google.

Published Books

As a final resource, you can choose from a large collection of reference books for Python. Bear in mind that books tend to lag behind the cutting edge of Python changes, partly because of the work involved in writing, and partly because of the natural delays built into the publishing cycle. Usually, by the time a book comes out, it's three or more months behind the current Python state. Unlike standard manuals, books are also generally not free.

Still, for many, the convenience and quality of a professionally published text is worth the cost. Moreover, Python changes so slowly that books are usually still relevant years after they are published, especially if their authors post updates on the Web. See the Preface for pointers to other Python books.

Common Coding Gotchas

Before the programming exercises for this part of the book, let's run through some of the most common mistakes beginners make when coding Python statements and programs. Many of these are warnings I've thrown out earlier in this part of the book, collected here for ease of reference. You'll learn to avoid these pitfalls once you've gained a bit of Python coding experience, but a few words now might help you avoid falling into some of these traps initially:

- **Don't forget the colons**. Always remember to type a : at the end of compound statement headers (the first line of an if, while, for, etc.). You'll probably forget at first (I did, and so have most of my 3,000 Python students over the years), but you can take some comfort from the fact that it will soon become an unconscious habit.
- **Start in column 1**. Be sure to start top-level (unnested) code in column 1. That includes unnested code typed into module files, as well as unnested code typed at the interactive prompt.

- **Blank lines matter at the interactive prompt**. Blank lines in compound statements are always ignored in module files, but when you're typing code at the interactive prompt, they end the statement. In other words, blank lines tell the interactive command line that you've finished a compound statement; if you want to continue, don't hit the Enter key at the `...` prompt (or in IDLE) until you're really done.

- **Indent consistently**. Avoid mixing tabs and spaces in the indentation of a block, unless you know what your text editor does with tabs. Otherwise, what you see in your editor may not be what Python sees when it counts tabs as a number of spaces. This is true in any block-structured language, not just Python—if the next programmer has her tabs set differently, she will not understand the structure of your code. It's safer to use all tabs or all spaces for each block.

- **Don't code C in Python**. A reminder for C/C++ programmers: you don't need to type parentheses around tests in `if` and `while` headers (e.g., `if (X==1):`). You can, if you like (any expression can be enclosed in parentheses), but they are fully superfluous in this context. Also, do not terminate all your statements with semicolons; it's technically legal to do this in Python as well, but it's totally useless unless you're placing more than one statement on a single line (the end of a line normally terminates a statement). And remember, don't embed assignment statements in `while` loop tests, and don't use {} around blocks (indent your nested code blocks consistently instead).

- **Use simple `for` loops instead of `while` or `range`**. Another reminder: a simple `for` loop (e.g., `for x in seq:`) is almost always simpler to code and quicker to run than a `while`- or `range`-based counter loop. Because Python handles indexing internally for a simple `for`, it can sometimes be twice as fast as the equivalent `while`. Avoid the temptation to count things in Python!

- **Beware of mutables in assignments**. I mentioned this in Chapter 11: you need to be careful about using mutables in a multiple-target assignment (`a = b = []`), as well as in an augmented assignment (`a += [1, 2]`). In both cases, in-place changes may impact other variables. See Chapter 11 for details.

- **Don't expect results from functions that change objects in-place**. We encountered this one earlier, too: in-place change operations like the `list.append` and `list.sort` methods introduced in Chapter 8 do not return values (other than `None`), so you should call them without assigning the result. It's not uncommon for beginners to say something like `mylist = mylist.append(X)` to try to get the result of an `append`, but what this actually does is assign `mylist` to `None`, not to the modified list (in fact, you'll lose your reference to the list altogether).

  A more devious example of this pops up in Python 2.X code when trying to step through dictionary items in a sorted fashion. It's fairly common to see code like `for k in D.keys().sort():`. This almost works—the `keys` method builds a keys list, and the `sort` method orders it—but because the `sort` method returns `None`, the loop fails because it is ultimately a loop over `None` (a nonsequence). This fails even sooner in Python 3.0, because dictionary keys are views, not lists! To code this correctly, either use the newer **sorted** built-in function, which returns the sorted list, or split the method calls out to statements: Ks = list(D.keys()), then Ks.sort(), and finally, for k in Ks:. This, by the way, is one case where you'll still want to call the **keys** method explicitly for looping, instead of relying on the dictionary iterators—iterators do not sort.

- **Always use parentheses to call a function**. You must add parentheses after a function name to call it, whether it takes arguments or not (e.g., use function(), not function). In Part IV, we'll see that functions are simply objects that have a special operation—a call that you trigger with the parentheses.

  In classes, this problem seems to occur most often with files; it's common to see beginners type file.close to close a file, rather than file.close(). Because it's legal to reference a function without calling it, the first version with no parentheses succeeds silently, but it does not close the file!

- **Don't use extensions or paths in imports and reloads**. Omit directory paths and file suffixes in import statements (e.g., say import mod, not import mod.py). (We discussed module basics in Chapter 3 and will continue studying modules in Part V.) Because modules may have other suffixes besides *.py* (*.pyc*, for instance), hardcoding a particular suffix is not only illegal syntax, but doesn't make sense. Any platform-specific directory path syntax comes from module search path settings, not the import statement.

Chapter Summary

This chapter took us on a tour of program documentation—both documentation we write ourselves for our own programs, and documentation available for built-in tools. We met docstrings, explored the online and manual resources for Python reference, and learned how PyDoc's help function and web page interface provide extra sources of documentation. Because this is the last chapter in this part of the book, we also reviewed common coding mistakes to help you avoid them.

In the next part of this book, we'll start applying what we already know to larger program constructs: functions. Before moving on, however, be sure to work through the set of lab exercises for this part of the book that appear at the end of this chapter. And even before that, let's run through this chapter's quiz.

Test Your Knowledge: Quiz

1. When should you use documentation strings instead of hash-mark comments?
2. Name three ways you can view documentation strings.

3. How can you obtain a list of the available attributes in an object?

4. How can you get a list of all available modules on your computer?

5. Which Python book should you purchase after this one?

Test Your Knowledge: Answers

1. Documentation strings (docstrings) are considered best for larger, functional documentation, describing the use of modules, functions, classes, and methods in your code. Hash-mark comments are today best limited to micro-documentation about arcane expressions or statements. This is partly because docstrings are easier to find in a source file, but also because they can be extracted and displayed by the PyDoc system.

2. You can see docstrings by printing an object's __doc__ attribute, by passing it to PyDoc's help function, and by selecting modules in PyDoc's GUI search engine in client/server mode. Additionally, PyDoc can be run to save a module's documentation in an HTML file for later viewing or printing.

3. The built-in dir(X) function returns a list of all the attributes attached to any object.

4. Run the PyDoc GUI interface, leave the module name blank, and select "open browser"; this opens a web page containing a link to every module available to your programs.

5. Mine, of course. (Seriously, the Preface lists a few recommended follow-up books, both for reference and for application tutorials.)

Test Your Knowledge: Part III Exercises

Now that you know how to code basic program logic, the following exercises will ask you to implement some simple tasks with statements. Most of the work is in exercise 4, which lets you explore coding alternatives. There are always many ways to arrange statements, and part of learning Python is learning which arrangements work better than others.

See Part III in Appendix B for the solutions.

1. *Coding basic loops.*
    a. Write a for loop that prints the ASCII code of each character in a string named S. Use the built-in function ord(character) to convert each character to an ASCII integer. (Test it interactively to see how it works.)

    b. Next, change your loop to compute the sum of the ASCII codes of all the characters in a string.

c. Finally, modify your code again to return a new list that contains the ASCII codes of each character in the string. Does the expression `map(ord, S)` have a similar effect? (Hint: see Chapter 14.)

2. *Backslash characters.* What happens on your machine when you type the following code interactively?

```
for i in range(50):
    print('hello %d\n\a' % i)
```

Beware that if it's run outside of the IDLE interface this example may beep at you, so you may not want to run it in a crowded lab. IDLE prints odd characters instead of beeping (see the backslash escape characters in Table 7-2).

3. *Sorting dictionaries.* In Chapter 8, we saw that dictionaries are unordered collections. Write a `for` loop that prints a dictionary's items in sorted (ascending) order. (Hint: use the dictionary `keys` and list `sort` methods, or the newer `sorted` built-in function.)

4. *Program logic alternatives.* Consider the following code, which uses a `while` loop and `found` flag to search a list of powers of 2 for the value of 2 raised to the fifth power (32). It's stored in a module file called *power.py*.

```
L = [1, 2, 4, 8, 16, 32, 64]
X = 5

found = False
i = 0
while not found and i < len(L):
    if 2 ** X == L[i]:
        found = True
    else:
        i = i+1

if found:
    print('at index', i)
else:
    print(X, 'not found')

C:\book\tests> python power.py
at index 5
```

As is, the example doesn't follow normal Python coding techniques. Follow the steps outlined here to improve it (for all the transformations, you may either type your code interactively or store it in a script file run from the system command line—using a file makes this exercise much easier):

a. First, rewrite this code with a `while` loop `else` clause to eliminate the `found` flag and final `if` statement.

b. Next, rewrite the example to use a `for` loop with an `else` clause, to eliminate the explicit list-indexing logic. (Hint: to get the index of an item, use the list `index` method—`L.index(X)` returns the offset of the first X in list L.)

c. Next, remove the loop completely by rewriting the example with a simple `in` operator membership expression. (See Chapter 8 for more details, or type this to test: `2 in [1,2,3]`.)

d. Finally, use a `for` loop and the list `append` method to generate the powers-of-2 list (L) instead of hardcoding a list literal.

Deeper thoughts:

e. Do you think it would improve performance to move the `2 ** X` expression outside the loops? How would you code that?

f. As we saw in exercise 1, Python includes a `map(function, list)` tool that can generate a powers-of-2 list, too: `map(lambda x: 2 ** x, range(7))`. Try typing this code interactively; we'll meet `lambda` more formally in Chapter 19.

## PART IV

Functions

## CHAPTER 16

Function Basics

In Part III, we looked at basic procedural statements in Python. Here, we'll move on to explore a set of additional statements that we can use to create functions of our own.

In simple terms, a *function* is a device that groups a set of statements so they can be run more than once in a program. Functions also can compute a result value and let us specify parameters that serve as function inputs, which may differ each time the code is run. Coding an operation as a function makes it a generally useful tool, which we can use in a variety of contexts.

More fundamentally, functions are the alternative to programming by cutting and pasting—rather than having multiple redundant copies of an operation's code, we can factor it into a single function. In so doing, we reduce our future work radically: if the operation must be changed later, we only have one copy to update, not many.

Functions are the most basic program structure Python provides for maximizing *code reuse* and minimizing *code redundancy*. As we'll see, functions are also a design tool that lets us split complex systems into manageable parts. Table 16-1 summarizes the primary function-related tools we'll study in this part of the book.

Table 16-1. Function-related statements and expressions

Statement	Examples
Calls	`myfunc('spam', 'eggs', meat=ham)`
def, return	`def adder(a, b=1, *c):` `    return a + b + c[0]`
global	`def changer():` `    global x; x = 'new'`
nonlocal	`def changer():` `    nonlocal x; x = 'new'`
yield	`def squares(x):` `    for i in range(x): yield i ** 2`
lambda	`funcs = [lambda x: x**2, lambda x: x*3]`

Why Use Functions?

Before we get into the details, let's establish a clear picture of what functions are all about. Functions are a nearly universal program-structuring device. You may have come across them before in other languages, where they may have been called *subroutines* or *procedures*. As a brief introduction, functions serve two primary development roles:

Maximizing code reuse and minimizing redundancy

As in most programming languages, Python functions are the simplest way to package logic you may wish to use in more than one place and more than one time. Up until now, all the code we've been writing has run immediately. Functions allow us to group and generalize code to be used arbitrarily many times later. Because they allow us to code an operation in a single place and use it in many places, Python functions are the most basic *factoring* tool in the language: they allow us to reduce code redundancy in our programs, and thereby reduce maintenance effort.

Procedural decomposition

Functions also provide a tool for splitting systems into pieces that have well-defined roles. For instance, to make a pizza from scratch, you would start by mixing the dough, rolling it out, adding toppings, baking it, and so on. If you were programming a pizza-making robot, functions would help you divide the overall "make pizza" task into chunks—one function for each subtask in the process. It's easier to implement the smaller tasks in isolation than it is to implement the entire process at once. In general, functions are about *procedure*—how to do something, rather than what you're doing it to. We'll see why this distinction matters in Part VI, when we start making new object with classes.

In this part of the book, we'll explore the tools used to code functions in Python: function basics, scope rules, and argument passing, along with a few related concepts such as generators and functional tools. Because its importance begins to become more apparent at this level of coding, we'll also revisit the notion of polymorphism introduced earlier in the book. As you'll see, functions don't imply much new syntax, but they do lead us to some bigger programming ideas.

Coding Functions

Although it wasn't made very formal, we've already used some functions in earlier chapters. For instance, to make a file object, we called the built-in open function; similarly, we used the len built-in function to ask for the number of items in a collection object.

In this chapter, we will explore how to write *new* functions in Python. Functions we write behave the same way as the built-ins we've already seen: they are called in expressions, are passed values, and return results. But writing new functions requires the application of a few additional ideas that haven't yet been introduced. Moreover, functions behave very differently in Python than they do in compiled languages like C. Here is a brief introduction to the main concepts behind Python functions, all of which we will study in this part of the book:

- **def is executable code**. Python functions are written with a new statement, the def. Unlike functions in compiled languages such as C, def is an executable statement—your function does not exist until Python reaches and runs the def. In fact, it's legal (and even occasionally useful) to nest def statements inside if statements, while loops, and even other defs. In typical operation, def statements are coded in module files and are naturally run to generate functions when a module file is first imported.

- **def creates an object and assigns it to a name**. When Python reaches and runs a def statement, it generates a new function object and assigns it to the function's name. As with all assignments, the function name becomes a reference to the function object. There's nothing magic about the name of a function—as you'll see, the function object can be assigned to other names, stored in a list, and so on. Function objects may also have arbitrary user-defined *attributes* attached to them to record data.

- **lambda creates an object but returns it as a result**. Functions may also be created with the lambda expression, a feature that allows us to in-line function definitions in places where a def statement won't work syntactically (this is a more advanced concept that we'll defer until Chapter 19).

- **return sends a result object back to the caller**. When a function is called, the caller stops until the function finishes its work and returns control to the caller. Functions that compute a value send it back to the caller with a return statement; the returned value becomes the result of the function call.

- **yield sends a result object back to the caller, but remembers where it left off**. Functions known as *generators* may also use the yield statement to send back a value and suspend their state such that they may be resumed later, to produce a series of results over time. This is another advanced topic covered later in this part of the book.

- **global declares module-level variables that are to be assigned**. By default, all names assigned in a function are local to that function and exist only while the function runs. To assign a name in the enclosing module, functions need to list it in a global statement. More generally, names are always looked up in *scopes*—places where variables are stored—and assignments bind names to scopes.

- **nonlocal declares enclosing function variables that are to be assigned**. Similarly, the nonlocal statement added in Python 3.0 allows a function to assign a name that exists in the scope of a syntactically enclosing def statement. This allows enclosing functions to serve as a place to retain *state*—information remembered when a function is called—without using shared global names.

- **Arguments are passed by assignment (object reference)**. In Python, arguments are passed to functions by assignment (which, as we've learned, means by object reference). As you'll see, in Python's model the caller and function share objects by references, but there is no name aliasing. Changing an argument name within a function does not also change the corresponding name in the caller, but changing passed-in mutable objects can change objects shared by the caller.

- **Arguments, return values, and variables are not declared**. As with everything in Python, there are no type constraints on functions. In fact, nothing about a function needs to be declared ahead of time: you can pass in arguments of any type, return any kind of object, and so on. As one consequence, a single function can often be applied to a variety of object types—any objects that sport a compatible *interface* (methods and expressions) will do, regardless of their specific types.

If some of the preceding words didn't sink in, don't worry—we'll explore all of these concepts with real code in this part of the book. Let's get started by expanding on some of these ideas and looking at a few examples.

def Statements

The def statement creates a function object and assigns it to a name. Its general format is as follows:

```
def <name>(arg1, arg2,... argN):
    <statements>
```

As with all compound Python statements, def consists of a header line followed by a block of statements, usually indented (or a simple statement after the colon). The statement block becomes the function's *body*—that is, the code Python executes each time the function is called.

The def header line specifies a function *name* that is assigned the function object, along with a list of zero or more *arguments* (sometimes called *parameters*) in parentheses. The argument names in the header are assigned to the objects passed in parentheses at the point of call.

Function bodies often contain a return statement:

```
def <name>(arg1, arg2,... argN):
    ...
    return <value>
```

The Python return statement can show up anywhere in a function body; it ends the function call and sends a result back to the caller. The return statement consists of an object expression that gives the function's result. The return statement is optional; if it's not present, the function exits when the control flow falls off the end of the function body. Technically, a function without a `return` statement returns the `None` object automatically, but this return value is usually ignored.

Functions may also contain `yield` statements, which are designed to produce a series of values over time, but we'll defer discussion of these until we survey generator topics in Chapter 20.

def Executes at Runtime

The Python `def` is a true executable statement: when it runs, it creates a new function object and assigns it to a name. (Remember, all we have in Python is *runtime*; there is no such thing as a separate compile time.) Because it's a statement, a `def` can appear anywhere a statement can—even nested in other statements. For instance, although `def`s normally are run when the module enclosing them is imported, it's also completely legal to nest a function `def` inside an `if` statement to select between alternative definitions:

```
if test:
    def func():           # Define func this way
        ...
else:
    def func():           # Or else this way
        ...
...
func()                    # Call the version selected and built
```

One way to understand this code is to realize that the `def` is much like an = statement: it simply assigns a name at runtime. Unlike in compiled languages such as C, Python functions do not need to be fully defined before the program runs. More generally, `def`s are not evaluated until they are reached and run, and the code *inside* `def`s is not evaluated until the functions are later called.

Because function definition happens at runtime, there's nothing special about the function name. What's important is the object to which it refers:

```
othername = func          # Assign function object
othername()               # Call func again
```

Here, the function was assigned to a different name and called through the new name. Like everything else in Python, functions are just *objects*; they are recorded explicitly in memory at program execution time. In fact, besides calls, functions allow arbitrary *attributes* to be attached to record information for later use:

```
def func(): ...           # Create function object
func()                    # Call object
func.attr = value         # Attach attributes
```

A First Example: Definitions and Calls

Apart from such runtime concepts (which tend to seem most unique to programmers with backgrounds in traditional compiled languages), Python functions are straightforward to use. Let's code a first real example to demonstrate the basics. As you'll see, there are two sides to the function picture: a *definition* (the def that creates a function) and a *call* (an expression that tells Python to run the function's body).

Definition

Here's a definition typed interactively that defines a function called times, which returns the product of its two arguments:

```
>>> def times(x, y):        # Create and assign function
...     return x * y        # Body executed when called
...
```

When Python reaches and runs this def, it creates a new function object that packages the function's code and assigns the object to the name times. Typically, such a statement is coded in a module file and runs when the enclosing file is imported; for something this small, though, the interactive prompt suffices.

Calls

After the def has run, you can call (run) the function in your program by adding parentheses after the function's name. The parentheses may optionally contain one or more object arguments, to be passed (assigned) to the names in the function's header:

```
>>> times(2, 4)             # Arguments in parentheses
8
```

This expression passes two arguments to times. As mentioned previously, arguments are passed by assignment, so in this case the name x in the function header is assigned the value 2, y is assigned the value 4, and the function's body is run. For this function, the body is just a return statement that sends back the result as the value of the call expression. The returned object was printed here interactively (as in most languages, 2 * 4 is 8 in Python), but if we needed to use it later we could instead assign it to a variable. For example:

```
>>> x = times(3.14, 4)      # Save the result object
>>> x
12.56
```

Now, watch what happens when the function is called a third time, with very different kinds of objects passed in:

```
>>> times('Ni', 4)          # Functions are "typeless"
'NiNiNiNi'
```

This time, our function means something completely different (Monty Python reference again intended). In this third call, a string and an integer are passed to x and y, instead of two numbers. Recall that * works on both numbers and sequences; because we never declare the types of variables, arguments, or return values in Python, we can use times to either *multiply* numbers or *repeat* sequences.

In other words, what our times function means and does depends on what we pass into it. This is a core idea in Python (and perhaps the key to using the language well), which we'll explore in the next section.

Polymorphism in Python

As we just saw, the very meaning of the expression x * y in our simple times function depends completely upon the kinds of objects that x and y are—thus, the same function can perform multiplication in one instance and repetition in another. Python leaves it up to the *objects* to do something reasonable for the syntax. Really, * is just a dispatch mechanism that routes control to the objects being processed.

This sort of type-dependent behavior is known as *polymorphism*, a term we first met in Chapter 4 that essentially means that the meaning of an operation depends on the objects being operated upon. Because it's a dynamically typed language, polymorphism runs rampant in Python. In fact, every operation is a polymorphic operation in Python: printing, indexing, the * operator, and much more.

This is deliberate, and it accounts for much of the language's conciseness and flexibility. A single function, for instance, can generally be applied to a whole category of object types automatically. As long as those objects support the expected interface (a.k.a. protocol), the function can process them. That is, if the objects passed into a function have the expected methods and expression operators, they are plug-and-play compatible with the function's logic.

Even in our simple times function, this means that *any* two objects that support a * will work, no matter what they may be, and no matter when they are coded. This function will work on two numbers (performing multiplication), or a string and a number (performing repetition), or any other combination of objects supporting the expected interface—even class-based objects we have not even coded yet.

Moreover, if the objects passed in do *not* support this expected interface, Python will detect the error when the * expression is run and raise an exception automatically. It's therefore pointless to code error checking ourselves. In fact, doing so would limit our function's utility, as it would be restricted to work only on objects whose types we test for.

This turns out to be a crucial philosophical difference between Python and statically typed languages like C++ and Java: in Python, your code is *not supposed to care* about specific data types. If it does, it will be limited to working on just the types you antici-pated when you wrote it, and it will not support other compatible object types that may be coded in the future. Although it is possible to test for types with tools like the type built-in function, doing so breaks your code's flexibility. By and large, we code to object *interfaces* in Python, not data types.

Of course, this polymorphic model of programming means we have to test our code to detect errors, rather than providing type declarations a compiler can use to detect some types of errors for us ahead of time. In exchange for an initial bit of testing, though, we radically reduce the amount of code we have to write and radically increase our code's flexibility. As you'll learn, it's a net win in practice.

A Second Example: Intersecting Sequences

Let's look at a second function example that does something a bit more useful than multiplying arguments and further illustrates function basics.

In Chapter 13, we coded a for loop that collected items held in common in two strings. We noted there that the code wasn't as useful as it could be because it was set up to work only on specific variables and could not be rerun later. Of course, we could copy the code and paste it into each place where it needs to be run, but this solution is neither good nor general—we'd still have to edit each copy to support different sequence names, and changing the algorithm would then require changing multiple copies.

Definition

By now, you can probably guess that the solution to this dilemma is to package the for loop inside a function. Doing so offers a number of advantages:

- Putting the code in a function makes it a tool that you can run as many times as you like.
- Because callers can pass in arbitrary arguments, functions are general enough to work on any two sequences (or other iterables) you wish to intersect.
- When the logic is packaged in a function, you only have to change code in one place if you ever need to change the way the intersection works.
- Coding the function in a module file means it can be imported and reused by any program run on your machine.

In effect, wrapping the code in a function makes it a general intersection utility:

```
def intersect(seq1, seq2):
    res = []                    # Start empty
    for x in seq1:              # Scan seq1
        if x in seq2:           # Common item?
            res.append(x)       # Add to end
    return res
```

The transformation from the simple code of Chapter 13 to this function is straightforward; we've just nested the original logic under a def header and made the objects on which it operates passed-in parameter names. Because this function computes a result, we've also added a `return` statement to send a result object back to the caller.

Calls

Before you can call a function, you have to make it. To do this, run its `def` statement, either by typing it interactively or by coding it in a module file and importing the file. Once you've run the `def`, you can call the function by passing any two sequence objects in parentheses:

```
>>> s1 = "SPAM"
>>> s2 = "SCAM"
>>> intersect(s1, s2)          # Strings
['S', 'A', 'M']
```

Here, we've passed in two strings, and we get back a list containing the characters in common. The algorithm the function uses is simple: "for every item in the first argument, if that item is also in the second argument, append the item to the result." It's a little shorter to say that in Python than in English, but it works out the same.

To be fair, our intersect function is fairly slow (it executes nested loops), isn't really mathematical intersection (there may be duplicates in the result), and isn't required at all (as we've seen, Python's set data type provides a built-in intersection operation). Indeed, the function could be replaced with a single list comprehension expression, as it exhibits the classic loop collector code pattern:

```
>>> [x for x in s1 if x in s2]
['S', 'A', 'M']
```

As a function basics example, though, it does the job—this single piece of code can apply to an entire range of object types, as the next section explains.

Polymorphism Revisited

Like all functions in Python, `intersect` is polymorphic. That is, it works on arbitrary types, as long as they support the expected object interface:

```
>>> x = intersect([1, 2, 3], (1, 4))     # Mixed types
>>> x                                      # Saved result object
[1]
```

This time, we passed in different types of objects to our function—a list and a tuple (mixed types)—and it still picked out the common items. Because you don't have to specify the types of arguments ahead of time, the `intersect` function happily iterates through any kind of sequence objects you send it, as long as they support the expected interfaces.

For `intersect`, this means that the first argument has to support the `for` loop, and the second has to support the `in` membership test. Any two such objects will work, regardless of their specific types—that includes physically stored sequences like strings and lists; all the iterable objects we met in Chapter 14, including files and dictionaries; and even any class-based objects we code that apply operator overloading techniques (we'll discuss these later in the book).*

Here again, if we pass in objects that do not support these interfaces (e.g., numbers), Python will automatically detect the mismatch and raise an exception for us—which is exactly what we want, and the best we could do on our own if we coded explicit type tests. By not coding type tests and allowing Python to detect the mismatches for us, we both reduce the amount of code we need to write and increase our code's flexibility.

Local Variables

Probably the most interesting part of this example is its names. It turns out that the variable `res` inside `intersect` is what in Python is called a *local variable*—a name that is visible only to code inside the function `def` and that exists only while the function runs. In fact, because all names *assigned* in any way inside a function are classified as local variables by default, nearly all the names in `intersect` are local variables:

- `res` is obviously assigned, so it is a local variable.
- Arguments are passed by assignment, so `seq1` and `seq2` are, too.
- The `for` loop assigns items to a variable, so the name `x` is also local.

All these local variables appear when the function is called and disappear when the function exits—the `return` statement at the end of `intersect` sends back the result *object*, but the *name* `res` goes away. To fully explore the notion of locals, though, we need to move on to Chapter 17.

Chapter Summary

This chapter introduced the core ideas behind function definition—the syntax and operation of the `def` and `return` statements, the behavior of function call expressions, and the notion and benefits of polymorphism in Python functions. As we saw, a `def` statement is executable code that creates a function object at runtime; when the function is later called, objects are passed into it by assignment (recall that assignment means object reference in Python, which, as we learned in Chapter 6, really means pointer internally), and computed values are sent back by `return`. We also began

---

* This code will always work if we intersect files' contents obtained with `file.readlines()`. It may not work to intersect lines in open input files directly, though, depending on the file object's implementation of the `in` operator or general iteration. Files must generally be rewound (e.g., with a `file.seek(0)` or another `open`) after they have been read to end-of-file once. As we'll see in Chapter 29 when we study operator overloading, classes implement the `in` operator either by providing the specific `__contains__` method or by supporting the general iteration protocol with the `__iter__` or older `__getitem__` methods; if coded, classes can define what iteration means for their data.

exploring the concepts of local variables and scopes in this chapter, but we'll save all the details on those topics for Chapter 17. First, though, a quick quiz.

Test Your Knowledge: Quiz

1. What is the point of coding functions?
2. At what time does Python create a function?
3. What does a function return if it has no `return` statement in it?
4. When does the code nested inside the function definition statement run?
5. What's wrong with checking the types of objects passed into a function?

Test Your Knowledge: Answers

1. Functions are the most basic way of avoiding code *redundancy* in Python—factoring code into functions means that we have only one copy of an operation's code to update in the future. Functions are also the basic unit of code *reuse* in Python—wrapping code in functions makes it a reusable tool, callable in a variety of programs. Finally, functions allow us to divide a complex system into manageable parts, each of which may be developed individually.

2. A function is created when Python reaches and runs the `def` statement; this statement creates a function object and assigns it the function's name. This normally happens when the enclosing module file is imported by another module (recall that imports run the code in a file from top to bottom, including any `def`s), but it can also occur when a `def` is typed interactively or nested in other statements, such as `if`s.

3. A function returns the `None` object by default if the control flow falls off the end of the function body without running into a `return` statement. Such functions are usually called with expression statements, as assigning their `None` results to variables is generally pointless.

4. The function body (the code nested inside the function definition statement) is run when the function is later called with a call expression. The body runs anew each time the function is called.

5. Checking the types of objects passed into a function effectively breaks the function's flexibility, constraining the function to work on specific types only. Without such checks, the function would likely be able to process an entire range of object types—any objects that support the interface expected by the function will work. (The term *interface* means the set of methods and expression operators the function's code runs.)

## CHAPTER 17

Scopes

Chapter 16 introduced basic function definitions and calls. As we saw, Python's basic function model is simple to use, but even simple function examples quickly led us to questions about the meaning of variables in our code. This chapter moves on to present the details behind Python's *scopes*—the places where variables are defined and looked up. As we'll see, the place where a name is assigned in our code is crucial to determining what the name means. We'll also find that scope usage can have a major impact on program maintenance effort; overuse of globals, for example, is a generally bad thing.

Python Scope Basics

Now that you're ready to start writing your own functions, we need to get more formal about what names mean in Python. When you use a name in a program, Python creates, changes, or looks up the name in what is known as a *namespace*—a place where names live. When we talk about the search for a name's value in relation to code, the term *scope* refers to a namespace: that is, the location of a name's assignment in your code determines the scope of the name's visibility to your code.

Just about everything related to names, including scope classification, happens at assignment time in Python. As we've seen, names in Python spring into existence when they are first assigned values, and they must be assigned before they are used. Because names are not declared ahead of time, Python uses the location of the assignment of a name to associate it with (i.e., *bind* it to) a particular namespace. In other words, the place where you assign a name in your source code determines the namespace it will live in, and hence its scope of visibility.

Besides packaging code, functions add an extra namespace layer to your programs— by default, all names assigned inside a function are associated with that function's namespace, and no other. This means that:

- Names defined inside a `def` can only be seen by the code within that `def`. You cannot even refer to such names from outside the function.

- Names defined inside a `def` do not clash with variables outside the `def`, even if the same names are used elsewhere. A name X assigned outside a given `def` (i.e., in a different `def` or at the top level of a module file) is a completely different variable from a name X assigned inside that `def`.

In all cases, the scope of a variable (where it can be used) is always determined by where it is assigned in your source code and has nothing to do with which functions call which. In fact, as we'll learn in this chapter, variables may be assigned in three different places, corresponding to three different scopes:

- If a variable is assigned inside a `def`, it is *local* to that function.
- If a variable is assigned in an enclosing `def`, it is *nonlocal* to nested functions.
- If a variable is assigned outside all `def`s, it is *global* to the entire file.

We call this *lexical scoping* because variable scopes are determined entirely by the locations of the variables in the source code of your program files, not by function calls.

For example, in the following module file, the X = 99 assignment creates a *global* variable named X (visible everywhere in this file), but the X = 88 assignment creates a *local* variable X (visible only within the `def` statement):

```
X = 99

def func():
    X = 88
```

Even though both variables are named X, their scopes make them different. The net effect is that function scopes help to avoid name clashes in your programs and help to make functions more self-contained program units.

Scope Rules

Before we started writing functions, all the code we wrote was at the top level of a module (i.e., not nested in a `def`), so the names we used either lived in the module itself or were built-ins predefined by Python (e.g., `open`). Functions provide nested namespaces (scopes) that localize the names they use, such that names inside a function won't clash with those outside it (in a module or another function). Again, functions define a *local scope*, and modules define a *global scope*. The two scopes are related as follows:

- **The enclosing module is a global scope**. Each module is a global scope—that is, a namespace in which variables created (assigned) at the top level of the module file live. Global variables become attributes of a module object to the outside world but can be used as simple variables within a module file.
- **The global scope spans a single file only**. Don't be fooled by the word "global" here—names at the top level of a file are only global to code within that single file. There is really no notion of a single, all-encompassing global file-based scope in

Python. Instead, names are partitioned into modules, and you must always import a module explicitly if you want to be able to use the names its file defines. When you hear "global" in Python, think "module."

- **Each call to a function creates a new local scope**. Every time you call a function, you create a new local scope—that is, a namespace in which the names created inside that function will usually live. You can think of each `def` statement (and `lambda` expression) as defining a new local scope, but because Python allows functions to call themselves to loop (an advanced technique known as *recursion*), the local scope in fact technically corresponds to a function call—in other words, each call creates a new local namespace. Recursion is useful when processing structures whose shapes can't be predicted ahead of time.

- **Assigned names are local unless declared global or nonlocal**. By default, all the names assigned inside a function definition are put in the local scope (the namespace associated with the function call). If you need to assign a name that lives at the top level of the module enclosing the function, you can do so by declaring it in a `global` statement inside the function. If you need to assign a name that lives in an enclosing `def`, as of Python 3.0 you can do so by declaring it in a `nonlocal` statement.

- **All other names are enclosing function locals, globals, or built-ins**. Names not assigned a value in the function definition are assumed to be enclosing scope locals (in an enclosing `def`), globals (in the enclosing module's namespace), or built-ins (in the predefined `__builtin__` module Python provides).

There are a few subtleties to note here. First, keep in mind that code typed at the *interactive command prompt* follows these same rules. You may not know it yet, but code run interactively is really entered into a built-in module called `__main__`; this module works just like a module file, but results are echoed as you go. Because of this, interactively created names live in a module, too, and thus follow the normal scope rules: they are global to the interactive session. You'll learn more about modules in the next part of this book.

Also note that *any type of assignment* within a function classifies a name as local. This includes = statements, module names in `import`, function names in `def`, function argument names, and so on. If you assign a name in any way within a `def`, it will become a local to that function.

Conversely, *in-place changes* to objects do not classify names as locals; only actual name assignments do. For instance, if the name L is assigned to a list at the top level of a module, a statement L = X within a function will classify L as a local, but L.append(X) will not. In the latter case, we are changing the list object that L references, not L itself— L is found in the global scope as usual, and Python happily modifies it without requiring a `global` (or `nonlocal`) declaration. As usual, it helps to keep the distinction between names and objects clear: changing an object is not an assignment to a name.

Name Resolution: The LEGB Rule

If the prior section sounds confusing, it really boils down to three simple rules. With a `def` statement:

- Name references search at most four scopes: local, then enclosing functions (if any), then global, then built-in.

- Name assignments create or change local names by default.

- `global` and `nonlocal` declarations map assigned names to enclosing module and function scopes.

In other words, all names assigned inside a function `def` statement (or a `lambda`, an expression we'll meet later) are locals by default. Functions can freely use names assigned in syntactically enclosing functions and the global scope, but they must declare such nonlocals and globals in order to change them.

Python's name-resolution scheme is sometimes called the *LEGB rule*, after the scope names:

- When you use an unqualified name inside a function, Python searches up to four scopes—the local (*L*) scope, then the local scopes of any enclosing (*E*) `def`s and `lambda`s, then the global (*G*) scope, and then the built-in (*B*) scope—and stops at the first place the name is found. If the name is not found during this search, Python reports an error. As we learned in Chapter 6, names must be assigned before they can be used.

- When you assign a name in a function (instead of just referring to it in an expression), Python always creates or changes the name in the local scope, unless it's declared to be global or nonlocal in that function.

- When you assign a name outside any function (i.e., at the top level of a module file, or at the interactive prompt), the local scope is the same as the global scope—the module's namespace.

Figure 17-1 illustrates Python's four scopes. Note that the second scope lookup layer, *E*—the scopes of enclosing `def`s or `lambda`s—can technically correspond to more than one lookup layer. This case only comes into play when you nest functions within functions, and it is addressed by the `nonlocal` statement.[*]

Also keep in mind that these rules apply only to simple *variable* names (e.g., `spam`). In Parts V and VI, we'll see that qualified *attribute* names (e.g., `object.spam`) live in particular objects and follow a completely different set of lookup rules than those

---

[*] The scope lookup rule was called the "LGB rule" in the first edition of this book. The enclosing `def` "E" layer was added later in Python to obviate the task of passing in enclosing scope names explicitly with default arguments—a topic usually of marginal interest to Python beginners that we'll defer until later in this chapter. Since this scope is addressed by the `nonlocal` statement in Python 3.0, I suppose the lookup rule might now be better named "LNGB," but backward compatibility matters in books, too!

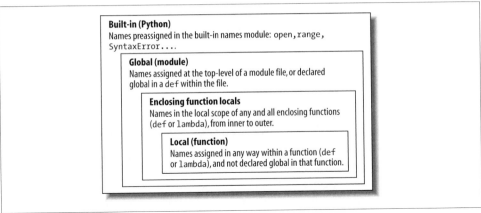

Figure 17-1. The LEGB scope lookup rule. When a variable is referenced, Python searches for it in this order: in the local scope, in any enclosing functions' local scopes, in the global scope, and finally in the built-in scope. The first occurrence wins. The place in your code where a variable is assigned usually determines its scope. In Python 3, nonlocal declarations can also force names to be mapped to enclosing function scopes, whether assigned or not.

covered here. References to attribute names following periods (.) search one or more *objects*, not scopes, and may invoke something called "inheritance"; more on this in Part VI of this book.

Scope Example

Let's look at a larger example that demonstrates scope ideas. Suppose we wrote the following code in a module file:

```
# Global scope
X = 99              # X and func assigned in module: global

def func(Y):        # Y and Z assigned in function: locals
    # Local scope
    Z = X + Y       # X is a global
    return Z

func(1)             # func in module: result=100
```

This module and the function it contains use a number of names to do their business. Using Python's scope rules, we can classify the names as follows:

Global names: X, func

X is global because it's assigned at the top level of the module file; it can be referenced inside the function without being declared global. func is global for the same reason; the def statement assigns a function object to the name func at the top level of the module.

Local names: Y, Z

> Y and Z are local to the function (and exist only while the function runs) because they are both assigned values in the function definition: Z by virtue of the = statement, and Y because arguments are always passed by assignment.

The whole point behind this name-segregation scheme is that local variables serve as temporary names that you need only while a function is running. For instance, in the preceding example, the argument Y and the addition result Z exist only inside the function; these names don't interfere with the enclosing module's namespace (or any other function, for that matter).

The local/global distinction also makes functions easier to understand, as most of the names a function uses appear in the function itself, not at some arbitrary place in a module. Also, because you can be sure that local names will not be changed by some remote function in your program, they tend to make programs easier to debug and modify.

The Built-in Scope

We've been talking about the built-in scope in the abstract, but it's a bit simpler than you may think. Really, the built-in scope is just a built-in module called `builtins`, but you have to import `builtins` to query built-ins because the name `builtins` is not itself built-in....

No, I'm serious! The built-in scope is implemented as a standard library module named `builtins`, but that name itself is not placed in the built-in scope, so you have to import it in order to inspect it. Once you do, you can run a `dir` call to see which names are predefined. In Python 3.0:

```
>>> import builtins
>>> dir(builtins)
['ArithmeticError', 'AssertionError', 'AttributeError', 'BaseException',
'BufferError', 'BytesWarning', 'DeprecationWarning', 'EOFError', 'Ellipsis',
    ...many more names omitted...
'print', 'property', 'quit', 'range', 'repr', 'reversed', 'round', 'set',
'setattr', 'slice', 'sorted', 'staticmethod', 'str', 'sum', 'super', 'tuple',
'type', 'vars', 'zip']
```

The names in this list constitute the built-in scope in Python; roughly the first half are built-in exceptions, and the second half are built-in functions. Also in this list are the special names None, True, and False, though they are treated as reserved words. Because Python automatically searches this module last in its LEGB lookup, you get all the names in this list "for free;" that is, you can use them without importing any modules. Thus, there are really two ways to refer to a built-in function—by taking advantage of the LEGB rule, or by manually importing the `builtins` module:

```
>>> zip                          # The normal way
<class 'zip'>
```

```
>>> import builtins                    # The hard way
>>> builtins.zip
<class 'zip'>
```

The second of these approaches is sometimes useful in advanced work. The careful reader might also notice that because the LEGB lookup procedure takes the first occurrence of a name that it finds, names in the local scope may override variables of the same name in both the global and built-in scopes, and global names may override built-ins. A function can, for instance, create a local variable called open by assigning to it:

```
def hider():
    open = 'spam'              # Local variable, hides built-in
    ...
    open('data.txt')           # This won't open a file now in this scope!
```

However, this will hide the built-in function called open that lives in the built-in (outer) scope. It's also usually a bug, and a nasty one at that, because Python will not issue a warning message about it (there are times in advanced programming where you may really want to replace a built-in name by redefining it in your code). Functions can similarly hide global variables of the same name with locals:

```
X = 88                         # Global X

def func():
    X = 99                     # Local X: hides global

func()
print(X)                       # Prints 88: unchanged
```

Here, the assignment within the function creates a local X that is a completely different variable from the global X in the module outside the function. Because of this, there is no way to change a name outside a function without adding a global (or nonlocal) declaration to the def, as described in the next section.[†]

> *Version skew note*: Actually, the tongue twisting gets a bit worse. The Python 3.0 builtins module used here is named __builtin__ in Python 2.6. And just for fun, the name __builtins__ (with the "s") is preset in most global scopes, including the interactive session, to reference the module known as builtins (a.k.a. __builtin__ in 2.6).
>
> That is, after importing builtins, __builtins__ is builtins is True in 3.0, and __builtins__ is __builtin__ is True in 2.6. The net effect is that we can inspect the built-in scope by simply running dir(__builtins__) with no import in both 3.0 and 2.6, but we are advised to use builtins for real work in 3.0. Who said documenting this stuff was easy?

---

† There is technically one more scope in Python: loop variables in comprehension and generator expressions are local to the expression itself in 3.X (in 2.X, they are local in generators but not in list comprehensions). This is a special and obscure case that rarely impacts real code, and differs from for-loop statements which never localize their variables.

> ## Breaking the Universe in Python 2.6
>
> Here's another thing you can do in Python that you probably shouldn't—because the names True and False in 2.6 are just variables in the built-in scope and are not reserved, it's possible to reassign them with a statement like True = False. Don't worry, you won't actually break the logical consistency of the universe in so doing! This statement merely redefines the word True for the single scope in which it appears. All other scopes still find the originals in the built-in scope.
>
> For more fun, though, in Python 2.6 you could say __builtin__.True = False, to reset True to False for the entire Python process. Alas, this type of assignment has been disallowed in Python 3.0, because True and False are treated as actual reserved words, just like None. In 2.6, though, it sends IDLE into a strange panic state that resets the user code process.
>
> This technique can be useful, however, both to illustrate the underlying namespace model and for tool writers who must change built-ins such as open to customized functions. Also, note that third-party tools such as PyChecker will warn about common programming mistakes, including accidental assignment to built-in names (this is known as "shadowing" a built-in in PyChecker).

The global Statement

The global statement and its nonlocal cousin are the only things that are remotely like declaration statements in Python. They are not type or size declarations, though; they are *namespace declarations*. The global statement tells Python that a function plans to change one or more global names—i.e., names that live in the enclosing module's scope (namespace).

We've talked about global in passing already. Here's a summary:

- Global names are variables assigned at the top level of the enclosing module file.
- Global names must be declared only if they are assigned within a function.
- Global names may be referenced within a function without being declared.

In other words, global allows us to change names that live outside a def at the top level of a module file. As we'll see later, the nonlocal statement is almost identical but applies to names in the enclosing def's local scope, rather than names in the enclosing module.

The global statement consists of the keyword global, followed by one or more names separated by commas. All the listed names will be mapped to the enclosing module's scope when assigned or referenced within the function body. For instance:

```
X = 88                    # Global X

def func():
    global X
    X = 99                # Global X: outside def
```

```
    func()
    print(X)                                # Prints 99
```

We've added a `global` declaration to the example here, such that the X inside the `def` now refers to the X outside the `def`; they are the same variable this time. Here is a slightly more involved example of `global` at work:

```
    y, z = 1, 2                             # Global variables in module
    def all_global():
        global x                            # Declare globals assigned
        x = y + z                           # No need to declare y, z: LEGB rule
```

Here, x, y, and z are all globals inside the function `all_global`. y and z are global because they aren't assigned in the function; x is global because it was listed in a `global` statement to map it to the module's scope explicitly. Without the `global` here, x would be considered local by virtue of the assignment.

Notice that y and z are not declared global; Python's LEGB lookup rule finds them in the module automatically. Also, notice that x might not exist in the enclosing module before the function runs; in this case, the assignment in the function creates x in the module.

Minimize Global Variables

By default, names assigned in functions are locals, so if you want to change names outside functions you have to write extra code (e.g., `global` statements). This is by design—as is common in Python, you have to say more to do the potentially "wrong" thing. Although there are times when globals are useful, variables assigned in a `def` are local by default because that is normally the best policy. Changing globals can lead to well-known software engineering problems: because the variables' values are dependent on the order of calls to arbitrarily distant functions, programs can become difficult to debug.

Consider this module file, for example:

```
    X = 99
    def func1():
        global X
        X = 88

    def func2():
        global X
        X = 77
```

Now, imagine that it is your job to modify or reuse this module file. What will the value of X be here? Really, that question has no meaning unless it's qualified with a point of reference in time—the value of X is timing-dependent, as it depends on which function was called last (something we can't tell from this file alone).

The net effect is that to understand this code, you have to trace the flow of control through the *entire program*. And, if you need to reuse or modify the code, you have to keep the entire program in your head all at once. In this case, you can't really use one of these functions without bringing along the other. They are dependent on (that is, *coupled* with) the global variable. This is the problem with globals—they generally make code more difficult to understand and use than code consisting of self-contained functions that rely on locals.

On the other hand, short of using object-oriented programming and classes, global variables are probably the most straightforward way to retain shared state information (information that a function needs to remember for use the next time it is called) in Python—local variables disappear when the function returns, but globals do not. Other techniques, such as default mutable arguments and enclosing function scopes, can achieve this, too, but they are more complex than pushing values out to the global scope for retention.

Some programs designate a single module to collect globals; as long as this is expected, it is not as harmful. In addition, programs that use multithreading to do parallel processing in Python commonly depend on global variables—they become shared memory between functions running in parallel threads, and so act as a communication device.‡

For now, though, especially if you are relatively new to programming, avoid the temptation to use globals whenever you can—try to communicate with passed-in arguments and return values instead. Six months from now, both you and your coworkers will be happy you did.

Minimize Cross-File Changes

Here's another scope-related issue: although we *can* change variables in another file directly, we usually shouldn't. Module files were introduced in Chapter 3 and are covered in more depth in the next part of this book. To illustrate their relationship to scopes, consider these two module files:

```
# first.py
X = 99                       # This code doesn't know about second.py

# second.py
import first
print(first.X)               # Okay: references a name in another file
first.X = 88                 # But changing it can be too subtle and implicit
```

---

‡ *Multithreading* runs function calls in parallel with the rest of the program and is supported by Python's standard library modules _thread, threading, and queue (thread, threading, and Queue in Python 2.6). Because all threaded functions run in the same process, global scopes often serve as shared memory between them. Threading is commonly used for long-running tasks in GUIs, to implement nonblocking operations in general and to leverage CPU capacity. It is also beyond this book's scope; see the Python library manual, as well as the follow-up texts listed in the Preface (such as O'Reilly's *Programming Python*), for more details.

The first defines a variable X, which the second prints and then changes by assignment. Notice that we must import the first module into the second file to get to its variable at all—as we've learned, each module is a self-contained namespace (package of variables), and we must import one module to see inside it from another. That's the main point about modules: by segregating variables on a per-file basis, they avoid name collisions across files.

Really, though, in terms of this chapter's topic, the global scope of a module file *becomes* the attribute namespace of the module object once it is imported—importers automatically have access to all of the file's global variables, because a file's global scope morphs into an object's attribute namespace when it is imported.

After importing the first module, the second module prints its variable and then assigns it a new value. Referencing the module's variable to print it is fine—this is how modules are linked together into a larger system normally. The problem with the assignment, however, is that it is far too implicit: whoever's charged with maintaining or reusing the first module probably has no clue that some arbitrarily far-removed module on the import chain can change X out from under him at runtime. In fact, the second module may be in a completely different directory, and so difficult to notice at all.

Although such cross-file variable changes are always possible in Python, they are usually much more subtle than you will want. Again, this sets up too strong a *coupling* between the two files—because they are both dependent on the value of the variable X, it's difficult to understand or reuse one file without the other. Such implicit cross-file dependencies can lead to inflexible code at best, and outright bugs at worst.

Here again, the best prescription is generally to not do this—the best way to communicate across file boundaries is to call functions, passing in arguments and getting back return values. In this specific case, we would probably be better off coding an *accessor function* to manage the change:

```
# first.py
X = 99

def setX(new):
    global X
    X = new

# second.py
import first
first.setX(88)
```

This requires more code and may seem like a trivial change, but it makes a huge difference in terms of readability and maintainability—when a person reading the first module by itself sees a function, that person will know that it is a point of *interface* and will expect the change to the X. In other words, it removes the element of surprise that is rarely a good thing in software projects. Although we cannot prevent cross-file changes from happening, common sense dictates that they should be minimized unless widely accepted across the program.

Other Ways to Access Globals

Interestingly, because global-scope variables morph into the attributes of a loaded module object, we can emulate the global statement by importing the enclosing module and assigning to its attributes, as in the following example module file. Code in this file imports the enclosing module, first by name, and then by indexing the sys.modules loaded modules table (more on this table in Chapter 21):

```
# thismod.py

var = 99                              # Global variable == module attribute

def local():
    var = 0                           # Change local var

def glob1():
    global var                        # Declare global (normal)
    var += 1                          # Change global var

def glob2():
    var = 0                           # Change local var
    import thismod                    # Import myself
    thismod.var += 1                  # Change global var

def glob3():
    var = 0                           # Change local var
    import sys                        # Import system table
    glob = sys.modules['thismod']     # Get module object (or use __name__)
    glob.var += 1                     # Change global var

def test():
    print(var)
    local(); glob1(); glob2(); glob3()
    print(var)
```

When run, this adds 3 to the global variable (only the first function does not impact it):

```
>>> import thismod
>>> thismod.test()
99
102
>>> thismod.var
102
```

This works, and it illustrates the equivalence of globals to module attributes, but it's much more work than using the global statement to make your intentions explicit.

As we've seen, global allows us to change names in a module outside a function. It has a cousin named nonlocal that can be used to change names in enclosing functions, too, but to understand how that can be useful, we first need to explore enclosing functions in general.

Scopes and Nested Functions

So far, I've omitted one part of Python's scope rules on purpose, because it's relatively rare to encounter it in practice. However, it's time to take a deeper look at the letter *E* in the LEGB lookup rule. The *E* layer is fairly new (it was added in Python 2.2); it takes the form of the local scopes of any and all enclosing function defs. Enclosing scopes are sometimes also called *statically nested scopes*. Really, the nesting is a lexical one—nested scopes correspond to physically and syntactically nested code structures in your program's source code.

Nested Scope Details

With the addition of nested function scopes, variable lookup rules become slightly more complex. Within a function:

- A reference (X) looks for the name X first in the current local scope (function); then in the local scopes of any lexically enclosing functions in your source code, from inner to outer; then in the current global scope (the module file); and finally in the built-in scope (the module `builtins`). `global` declarations make the search begin in the global (module file) scope instead.

- An assignment (X = value) creates or changes the name X in the current local scope, by default. If X is declared *global* within the function, the assignment creates or changes the name X in the enclosing module's scope instead. If, on the other hand, X is declared *nonlocal* within the function, the assignment changes the name X in the closest enclosing function's local scope.

Notice that the `global` declaration still maps variables to the enclosing module. When nested functions are present, variables in enclosing functions may be referenced, but they require `nonlocal` declarations to be changed.

Nested Scope Examples

To clarify the prior section's points, let's illustrate with some real code. Here is what an enclosing function scope looks like:

```
X = 99                    # Global scope name: not used

def f1():
    X = 88                # Enclosing def local
    def f2():
        print(X)          # Reference made in nested def
    f2()

f1()                      # Prints 88: enclosing def local
```

First off, this is legal Python code: the def is simply an executable statement, which can appear anywhere any other statement can—including nested in another def. Here, the nested `def` runs while a call to the function `f1` is running; it generates a function and assigns it to the name `f2`, a local variable within `f1`'s local scope. In a sense, `f2` is a temporary function that lives only during the execution of (and is visible only to code in) the enclosing `f1`.

But notice what happens inside `f2`: when it prints the variable `X`, it refers to the `X` that lives in the enclosing `f1` function's local scope. Because functions can access names in all physically enclosing `def` statements, the `X` in `f2` is automatically mapped to the `X` in `f1`, by the LEGB lookup rule.

This enclosing scope lookup works even if the enclosing function has already returned. For example, the following code defines a function that makes and returns another function:

```
def f1():
    X = 88
    def f2():
        print(X)        # Remembers X in enclosing def scope
    return f2           # Return f2 but don't call it

action = f1()           # Make, return function
action()                # Call it now: prints 88
```

In this code, the call to `action` is really running the function we named `f2` when `f1` ran. `f2` remembers the enclosing scope's `X` in `f1`, even though `f1` is no longer active.

Factory functions

Depending on whom you ask, this sort of behavior is also sometimes called a *closure* or *factory* function. These terms refer to a function object that remembers values in enclosing scopes regardless of whether those scopes are still present in memory. Although classes (described in Part VI of this book) are usually best at remembering state because they make it explicit with attribute assignments, such functions provide an alternative.

For instance, factory functions are sometimes used by programs that need to generate event handlers on the fly in response to conditions at runtime (e.g., user inputs that cannot be anticipated). Look at the following function, for example:

```
>>> def maker(N):
...     def action(X):              # Make and return action
...         return X ** N           # action retains N from enclosing scope
...     return action
...
```

This defines an outer function that simply generates and returns a nested function, without calling it. If we call the outer function:

```
>>> f = maker(2)                    # Pass 2 to N
>>> f
<function action at 0x014720B0>
```

what we get back is a reference to the generated nested function—the one created by running the nested def. If we now call what we got back from the outer function:

```
>>> f(3)                          # Pass 3 to X, N remembers 2: 3 ** 2
9
>>> f(4)                          # 4 ** 2
16
```

it invokes the nested function—the one called action within maker. The most unusual part of this is that the nested function remembers integer 2, the value of the variable N in maker, even though maker has returned and exited by the time we call action. In effect, N from the enclosing local scope is retained as state information attached to action, and we get back its argument squared.

If we now call the outer function again, we get back a new nested function with different state information attached. That is, we get the argument cubed instead of squared, but the original still squares as before:

```
>>> g = maker(3)                  # g remembers 3, f remembers 2
>>> g(3)                          # 3 ** 3
27
>>> f(3)                          # 3 ** 2
9
```

This works because each call to a factory function like this gets its own set of state information. In our case, the function we assign to name g remembers 3, and f remembers 2, because each has its own state information retained by the variable N in maker.

This is an advanced technique that you're unlikely to see very often in most code, except among programmers with backgrounds in functional programming languages. On the other hand, enclosing scopes are often employed by lambda function-creation expressions (discussed later in this chapter)—because they are expressions, they are almost always nested within a def. Moreover, function nesting is commonly used for *decorators* (explored in Chapter 38)—in some cases, it's the most reasonable coding pattern.

As a general rule, *classes* are better at "memory" like this because they make the state retention explicit in attributes. Short of using classes, though, globals, enclosing scope references like these, and default arguments are the main ways that Python functions can retain state information. To see how they compete, Chapter 18 provides complete coverage of defaults, but the next section gives enough of an introduction to get us started.

Retaining enclosing scopes' state with defaults

In earlier versions of Python, the sort of code in the prior section failed because nested defs did not do anything about scopes—a reference to a variable within f2 would search only the local (f2), then global (the code outside f1), and then built-in scopes. Because it skipped the scopes of enclosing functions, an error would result. To work around this, programmers typically used *default argument values* to pass in and remember the objects in an enclosing scope:

```
def f1():
    x = 88
    def f2(x=x):                    # Remember enclosing scope X with defaults
        print(x)
    f2()

f1()                                # Prints 88
```

This code works in all Python releases, and you'll still see this pattern in some existing Python code. In short, the syntax arg = val in a def header means that the argument arg will default to the value val if no real value is passed to arg in a call.

In the modified f2 here, the x=x means that the argument x will default to the value of x in the enclosing scope—because the second x is evaluated before Python steps into the nested def, it still refers to the x in f1. In effect, the default remembers what x was in f1 (i.e., the object 88).

That's fairly complex, and it depends entirely on the timing of default value evaluations. In fact, the nested scope lookup rule was added to Python to make defaults unnecessary for this role—today, Python automatically remembers any values required in the enclosing scope for use in nested defs.

Of course, the best prescription for most code is simply to avoid nesting defs within defs, as it will make your programs much simpler. The following is an equivalent of the prior example that banishes the notion of nesting. Notice the forward reference in this code—it's OK to call a function defined after the function that calls it, as long as the second def runs before the first function is actually called. Code inside a def is never evaluated until the function is actually called:

```
>>> def f1():
...     x = 88                      # Pass x along instead of nesting
...     f2(x)                       # Forward reference okay
...
>>> def f2(x):
...     print(x)
...
>>> f1()
88
```

If you avoid nesting this way, you can almost forget about the nested scopes concept in Python, unless you need to code in the factory function style discussed earlier—at least, for def statements. lambdas, which almost naturally appear nested in defs, often rely on nested scopes, as the next section explains.

Nested scopes and lambdas

While they're rarely used in practice for defs themselves, you are more likely to care about nested function scopes when you start coding lambda expressions. We won't cover lambda in depth until Chapter 19, but in short, it's an expression that generates a new function to be called later, much like a def statement. Because it's an expression, though, it can be used in places that def cannot, such as within list and dictionary literals.

Like a def, a lambda expression introduces a new local scope for the function it creates. Thanks to the enclosing scopes lookup layer, lambdas can see all the variables that live in the functions in which they are coded. Thus, the following code works, but only because the nested scope rules are applied:

```
def func():
    x = 4
    action = (lambda n: x ** n)          # x remembered from enclosing def
    return action

x = func()
print(x(2))                              # Prints 16, 4 ** 2
```

Prior to the introduction of nested function scopes, programmers used defaults to pass values from an enclosing scope into lambdas, just as for defs. For instance, the following works on all Python releases:

```
def func():
    x = 4
    action = (lambda n, x=x: x ** n)     # Pass x in manually
    return action
```

Because lambdas are expressions, they naturally (and even normally) nest inside enclosing defs. Hence, they are perhaps the biggest beneficiaries of the addition of enclosing function scopes in the lookup rules; in most cases, it is no longer necessary to pass values into lambdas with defaults.

Scopes versus defaults with loop variables

There is one notable exception to the rule I just gave: if a lambda or def defined within a function is nested inside a loop, and the nested function references an enclosing scope variable that is changed by that loop, all functions generated within the loop will have the same value—the value the referenced variable had in the last loop iteration.

For instance, the following attempts to build up a list of functions that each remember the current variable i from the enclosing scope:

```
>>> def makeActions():
...     acts = []
...     for i in range(5):                    # Tries to remember each i
...         acts.append(lambda x: i ** x)     # All remember same last i!
...     return acts
...
>>> acts = makeActions()
>>> acts[0]
<function <lambda> at 0x012B16B0>
```

This doesn't quite work, though—because the enclosing scope variable is looked up when the nested functions are later *called*, they all effectively remember the same value (the value the loop variable had on the *last* loop iteration). That is, we get back 4 to the power of 2 for each function in the list, because i is the same in all of them:

```
>>> acts[0](2)                        # All are 4 ** 2, value of last i
16
>>> acts[2](2)                        # This should be 2 ** 2
16
>>> acts[4](2)                        # This should be 4 ** 2
16
```

This is the one case where we still have to explicitly retain enclosing scope values with default arguments, rather than enclosing scope references. That is, to make this sort of code work, we must pass in the *current* value of the enclosing scope's variable with a default. Because defaults are evaluated when the nested function is *created* (not when it's later *called*), each remembers its own value for i:

```
>>> def makeActions():
...     acts = []
...     for i in range(5):              # Use defaults instead
...         acts.append(lambda x, i=i: i ** x)   # Remember current i
...     return acts
...
>>> acts = makeActions()
>>> acts[0](2)                          # 0 ** 2
0
>>> acts[2](2)                          # 2 ** 2
4
>>> acts[4](2)                          # 4 ** 2
16
```

This is a fairly obscure case, but it can come up in practice, especially in code that generates callback handler functions for a number of widgets in a GUI (e.g., button-press handlers). We'll talk more about defaults in Chapter 18 and lambdas in Chapter 19, so you may want to return and review this section later.§

Arbitrary scope nesting

Before ending this discussion, I should note that scopes may nest arbitrarily, but only enclosing function def statements (not classes, described in Part VI) are searched:

```
>>> def f1():
...     x = 99
...     def f2():
...         def f3():
...             print(x)              # Found in f1's local scope!
...         f3()
```

---

§ In the section "Function Gotchas" on page 520 at the end of this part of the book, we'll also see that there is an issue with using mutable objects like lists and dictionaries for default arguments (e.g., def f(a=[]))— because defaults are implemented as single objects attached to functions, mutable defaults retain state from call to call, rather then being initialized anew on each call. Depending on whom you ask, this is either considered a feature that supports state retention, or a strange wart on the language. More on this at the end of Chapter 20.

```
...    f2()
...
>>> f1()
99
```

Python will search the local scopes of *all* enclosing `def`s, from inner to outer, after the referencing function's local scope and before the module's global scope or built-ins. However, this sort of code is even less likely to pop up in practice. In Python, we say *flat is better than nested*—except in very limited contexts, your life (and the lives of your coworkers) will generally be better if you minimize nested function definitions.

The nonlocal Statement

In the prior section we explored the way that nested functions can *reference* variables in an enclosing function's scope, even if that function has already returned. It turns out that, as of Python 3.0, we can also *change* such enclosing scope variables, as long as we declare them in `nonlocal` statements. With this statement, nested `def`s can have both read and write access to names in enclosing functions.

The `nonlocal` statement is a close cousin to `global`, covered earlier. Like `global`, `nonlocal` declares that a name will be changed in an enclosing scope. Unlike `global`, though, `nonlocal` applies to a name in an enclosing function's scope, not the global module scope outside all `def`s. Also unlike `global`, `nonlocal` names must already exist in the enclosing function's scope when declared—they can exist only in enclosing functions and cannot be created by a first assignment in a nested `def`.

In other words, `nonlocal` both allows assignment to names in enclosing function scopes and limits scope lookups for such names to enclosing `def`s. The net effect is a more direct and reliable implementation of changeable state information, for programs that do not desire or need classes with attributes.

nonlocal Basics

Python 3.0 introduces a new `nonlocal` statement, which has meaning only inside a function:

```
def func():
    nonlocal name1, name2, ...
```

This statement allows a nested function to change one or more names defined in a syntactically enclosing function's scope. In Python 2.X (including 2.6), when one function `def` is nested in another, the nested function can reference any of the names defined by assignment in the enclosing `def`'s scope, but it cannot change them. In 3.0, declaring the enclosing scopes' names in a `nonlocal` statement enables nested functions to assign and thus change such names as well.

This provides a way for enclosing functions to provide *writeable* state information, remembered when the nested function is later called. Allowing the state to change makes it more useful to the nested function (imagine a counter in the enclosing scope, for instance). In 2.X, programmers usually achieve similar goals by using classes or other schemes. Because nested functions have become a more common coding pattern for state retention, though, nonlocal makes it more generally applicable.

Besides allowing names in enclosing defs to be changed, the nonlocal statement also forces the issue for references—just like the global statement, nonlocal causes searches for the names listed in the statement to begin in the enclosing defs' scopes, not in the local scope of the declaring function. That is, nonlocal also means "skip my local scope entirely."

In fact, the names listed in a nonlocal *must* have been previously defined in an enclosing def when the nonlocal is reached, or an error is raised. The net effect is much like global: global means the names reside in the enclosing module, and nonlocal means they reside in an enclosing def. nonlocal is even more strict, though—scope search is restricted to *only* enclosing defs. That is, nonlocal names can appear only in enclosing defs, not in the module's global scope or built-in scopes outside the defs.

The addition of nonlocal does not alter name reference scope rules in general; they still work as before, per the "LEGB" rule described earlier. The nonlocal statement mostly serves to allow names in enclosing scopes to be changed rather than just referenced. However, global and nonlocal statements do both restrict the lookup rules somewhat, when coded in a function:

- global makes scope lookup begin in the enclosing module's scope and allows names there to be assigned. Scope lookup continues on to the built-in scope if the name does not exist in the module, but assignments to global names always create or change them in the module's scope.

- nonlocal restricts scope lookup to just enclosing defs, requires that the names already exist there, and allows them to be assigned. Scope lookup does not continue on to the global or built-in scopes.

In Python 2.6, references to enclosing def scope names are allowed, but not assignment. However, you can still use classes with explicit attributes to achieve the same changeable state information effect as nonlocals (and you may be better off doing so in some contexts); globals and function attributes can sometimes accomplish similar goals as well. More on this in a moment; first, let's turn to some working code to make this more concrete.

nonlocal in Action

On to some examples, all run in 3.0. References to enclosing def scopes work as they do in 2.6. In the following, tester builds and returns the function nested, to be called later, and the state reference in nested maps the local scope of tester using the normal scope lookup rules:

```
C:\\misc>c:\python30\python

>>> def tester(start):
...     state = start          # Referencing nonlocals works normally
...     def nested(label):
...         print(label, state) # Remembers state in enclosing scope
...     return nested
...
>>> F = tester(0)
>>> F('spam')
spam 0
>>> F('ham')
ham 0
```

Changing a name in an enclosing def's scope is not allowed by default, though; this is the normal case in 2.6 as well:

```
>>> def tester(start):
...     state = start
...     def nested(label):
...         print(label, state)
...         state += 1          # Cannot change by default (or in 2.6)
...     return nested
...
>>> F = tester(0)
>>> F('spam')
UnboundLocalError: local variable 'state' referenced before assignment
```

Using nonlocal for changes

Now, under 3.0, if we declare state in the tester scope as nonlocal within nested, we get to change it inside the nested function, too. This works even though tester has returned and exited by the time we call the returned nested function through the name F:

```
>>> def tester(start):
...     state = start          # Each call gets its own state
...     def nested(label):
...         nonlocal state      # Remembers state in enclosing scope
...         print(label, state)
...         state += 1          # Allowed to change it if nonlocal
...     return nested
...
>>> F = tester(0)
>>> F('spam')                   # Increments state on each call
spam 0
>>> F('ham')
ham 1
>>> F('eggs')
eggs 2
```

As usual with enclosing scope references, we can call the tester factory function multiple times to get multiple copies of its state in memory. The state object in the enclosing scope is essentially attached to the nested function object returned; each call makes a new, distinct state object, such that updating one function's state won't impact the other. The following continues the prior listing's interaction:

```
>>> G = tester(42)             # Make a new tester that starts at 42
>>> G('spam')
spam 42

>>> G('eggs')                  # My state information updated to 43
eggs 43

>>> F('bacon')                 # But F's is where it left off: at 3
bacon 3                        # Each call has different state information
```

Boundary cases

There are a few things to watch out for. First, unlike the global statement, nonlocal names really *must* have previously been assigned in an enclosing def's scope when a nonlocal is evaluated, or else you'll get an error—you cannot create them dynamically by assigning them anew in the enclosing scope:

```
>>> def tester(start):
...     def nested(label):
...         nonlocal state        # Nonlocals must already exist in enclosing def!
...         state = 0
...         print(label, state)
...     return nested
...
SyntaxError: no binding for nonlocal 'state' found

>>> def tester(start):
...     def nested(label):
...         global state          # Globals don't have to exist yet when declared
...         state = 0             # This creates the name in the module now
...         print(label, state)
...     return nested
...
>>> F = tester(0)
>>> F('abc')
abc 0
>>> state
0
```

Second, nonlocal restricts the scope lookup to just enclosing defs; nonlocals are not looked up in the enclosing module's global scope or the built-in scope outside all defs, even if they are already there:

```
>>> spam = 99
>>> def tester():
...     def nested():
...         nonlocal spam         # Must be in a def, not the module!
...         print('Current=', spam)
...         spam += 1
...     return nested
...
SyntaxError: no binding for nonlocal 'spam' found
```

These restrictions make sense once you realize that Python would not otherwise generally know which enclosing scope to create a brand new name in. In the prior listing, should spam be assigned in tester, or the module outside? Because this is ambiguous, Python must resolve nonlocals at function *creation* time, not function *call* time.

Why nonlocal?

Given the extra complexity of nested functions, you might wonder what the fuss is about. Although it's difficult to see in our small examples, state information becomes crucial in many programs. There are a variety of ways to "remember" information across function and method calls in Python. While there are tradeoffs for all, nonlocal does improve this story for enclosing scope references—the nonlocal statement allows multiple copies of changeable state to be retained in memory and addresses simple state-retention needs where classes may not be warranted.

As we saw in the prior section, the following code allows state to be retained and modified in an enclosing scope. Each call to tester creates a little self-contained *package of changeable information*, whose names do not clash with any other part of the program:

```
def tester(start):
    state = start          # Each call gets its own state
    def nested(label):
        nonlocal state     # Remembers state in enclosing scope
        print(label, state)
        state += 1         # Allowed to change it if nonlocal
    return nested

F = tester(0)
F('spam')
```

Unfortunately, this code only works in Python 3.0. If you are using Python 2.6, other options are available, depending on your goals. The next three sections present some alternatives.

Shared state with globals

One usual prescription for achieving the nonlocal effect in 2.6 and earlier is to simply move the state out to the *global scope* (the enclosing module):

```
>>> def tester(start):
...     global state            # Move it out to the module to change it
...     state = start           # global allows changes in module scope
...     def nested(label):
...         global state
...         print(label, state)
...         state += 1
...     return nested
...
>>> F = tester(0)
>>> F('spam')                    # Each call increments shared global state
```

```
spam 0
>>> F('eggs')
eggs 1
```

This works in this case, but it requires `global` declarations in both functions and is prone to name collisions in the global scope (what if "state" is already being used?). A worse, and more subtle, problem is that it only allows for a *single shared copy* of the state information in the module scope—if we call `tester` again, we'll wind up resetting the module's `state` variable, such that prior calls will see their `state` overwritten:

```
>>> G = tester(42)              # Resets state's single copy in global scope
>>> G('toast')
toast 42

>>> G('bacon')
bacon 43

>>> F('ham')                    # Oops -- my counter has been overwritten!
ham 44
```

As shown earlier, when using `nonlocal` instead of `global`, each call to `tester` remembers its own unique copy of the `state` object.

State with classes (preview)

The other prescription for changeable state information in 2.6 and earlier is to use *classes with attributes* to make state information access more explicit than the implicit magic of scope lookup rules. As an added benefit, each instance of a class gets a fresh copy of the state information, as a natural byproduct of Python's object model.

We haven't explored classes in detail yet, but as a brief preview, here is a reformulation of the `tester`/`nested` functions used earlier as a class—state is recorded in objects explicitly as they are created. To make sense of this code, you need to know that a `def` within a `class` like this works exactly like a `def` outside of a `class`, except that the function's `self` argument automatically receives the implied subject of the call (an instance object created by calling the class itself):

```
>>> class tester:                       # Class-based alternative (see Part VI)
...     def __init__(self, start):      # On object construction,
...         self.state = start          # save state explicitly in new object
...     def nested(self, label):
...         print(label, self.state)    # Reference state explicitly
...         self.state += 1             # Changes are always allowed
...
>>> F = tester(0)                       # Create instance, invoke __init__
>>> F.nested('spam')                    # F is passed to self
spam 0
>>> F.nested('ham')
ham 1

>>> G = tester(42)                      # Each instance gets new copy of state
>>> G.nested('toast')                   # Changing one does not impact others
toast 42
```

```
>>> G.nested('bacon')
bacon 43

>>> F.nested('eggs')                    # F's state is where it left off
eggs 2
>>> F.state                             # State may be accessed outside class
3
```

With just slightly more magic, which we'll delve into later in this book, we could also make our class look like a callable function using operator overloading. __call__ intercepts direct calls on an instance, so we don't need to call a named method:

```
>>> class tester:
...     def __init__(self, start):
...         self.state = start
...     def __call__(self, label):      # Intercept direct instance calls
...         print(label, self.state)    # So .nested() not required
...         self.state += 1
...
>>> H = tester(99)
>>> H('juice')                          # Invokes __call__
juice 99
>>> H('pancakes')
pancakes 100
```

Don't sweat the details in this code too much at this point in the book; we'll explore classes in depth in Part VI and will look at specific operator overloading tools like __call__ in Chapter 29, so you may wish to file this code away for future reference. The point here is that classes can make state information more obvious, by leveraging explicit attribute assignment instead of scope lookups.

While using classes for state information is generally a good rule of thumb to follow, they might be overkill in cases like this, where state is a single counter. Such trivial state cases are more common than you might think; in such contexts, nested defs are sometimes more lightweight than coding classes, especially if you're not familiar with OOP yet. Moreover, there are some scenarios in which nested defs may actually work better than classes (see the description of *method decorators* in Chapter 38 for an example that is far beyond this chapter's scope).

State with function attributes

As a final state-retention option, we can also sometimes achieve the same effect as nonlocals with *function attributes*—user-defined names attached to functions directly. Here's a final version of our example based on this technique—it replaces a nonlocal with an attribute attached to the nested function. Although this scheme may not be as intuitive to some, it also allows the state variable to be accessed *outside* the nested function (with nonlocals, we can only see state variables within the nested def):

```
>>> def tester(start):
...     def nested(label):
...         print(label, nested.state)  # nested is in enclosing scope
...         nested.state += 1           # Change attr, not nested itself
```

```
...        nested.state = start              # Initial state after func defined
...        return nested
...
>>> F = tester(0)
>>> F('spam')                               # F is a 'nested' with state attached
spam 0
>>> F('ham')
ham 1
>>> F.state                                 # Can access state outside functions too
2
>>>
>>> G = tester(42)                          # G has own state, doesn't overwrite F's
>>> G('eggs')
eggs 42
>>> F('ham')
ham 2
```

This code relies on the fact that the function name nested is a local variable in the
tester scope enclosing nested; as such, it can be referenced freely inside nested. This
code also relies on the fact that changing an object in-place is not an assignment to a
name; when it increments nested.state, it is changing part of the object nested references, not the name nested itself. Because we're not really assigning a name in the
enclosing scope, no nonlocal is needed.

As you can see, globals, nonlocals, classes, and function attributes all offer
state-retention options. Globals only support shared data, classes require a basic
knowledge of OOP, and both classes and function attributes allow state to be accessed
outside the nested function itself. As usual, the best tool for your program depends
upon your program's goals.‖

Chapter Summary

In this chapter, we studied one of two key concepts related to functions: *scopes* (how
variables are looked up when they are used). As we learned, variables are considered
local to the function definitions in which they are assigned, unless they are specifically
declared to be global or nonlocal. We also studied some more advanced scope concepts
here, including nested function scopes and function attributes. Finally, we looked at
some general design ideas, such as the need to avoid globals and cross-file changes.

In the next chapter, we're going to continue our function tour with the second key
function-related concept: argument passing. As we'll find, arguments are passed into
a function by assignment, but Python also provides tools that allow functions to be

---

‖ Function attributes are supported in both Python 2.6 and 3.X. We'll explore them further in Chapter 19, and
revisit all the state options introduced here in Chapter 38 in a more realistic context. Also note that it's possible
to change a mutable object in the enclosing scope in 2.X and 3.X without declaring its name nonlocal (e.g,
state=[start] in tester, state[0]+=1 in nested), though it's perhaps more obscure than either function
attributes or 3.X's nonlocal.

flexible in how items are passed. Before we move on, let's take this chapter's quiz to review the scope concepts we've covered here.

Test Your Knowledge: Quiz

1. What is the output of the following code, and why?

   ```
   >>> X = 'Spam'
   >>> def func():
   ...     print(X)
   ...
   >>> func()
   ```

2. What is the output of this code, and why?

   ```
   >>> X = 'Spam'
   >>> def func():
   ...     X = 'NI!'
   ...
   >>> func()
   >>> print(X)
   ```

3. What does this code print, and why?

   ```
   >>> X = 'Spam'
   >>> def func():
   ...     X = 'NI'
   ...     print(X)
   ...
   >>> func()
   >>> print(X)
   ```

4. What output does this code produce? Why?

   ```
   >>> X = 'Spam'
   >>> def func():
   ...     global X
   ...     X = 'NI'
   ...
   >>> func()
   >>> print(X)
   ```

5. What about this code—what's the output, and why?

   ```
   >>> X = 'Spam'
   >>> def func():
   ...     X = 'NI'
   ...     def nested():
   ...         print(X)
   ...     nested()
   ...
   >>> func()
   >>> X
   ```

6. How about this example: what is its output in Python 3.0, and why?

```
>>> def func():
...     X = 'NI'
...     def nested():
...         nonlocal X
...         X = 'Spam'
...     nested()
...     print(X)
...
>>> func()
```

7. Name three or more ways to retain state information in a Python function.

Test Your Knowledge: Answers

1. The output here is `'Spam'`, because the function references a global variable in the enclosing module (because it is not assigned in the function, it is considered global).

2. The output here is `'Spam'` again because assigning the variable inside the function makes it a local and effectively hides the global of the same name. The `print` statement finds the variable unchanged in the global (module) scope.

3. It prints `'NI'` on one line and `'Spam'` on another, because the reference to the variable within the function finds the assigned local and the reference in the `print` statement finds the global.

4. This time it just prints `'NI'` because the global declaration forces the variable assigned inside the function to refer to the variable in the enclosing global scope.

5. The output in this case is again `'NI'` on one line and `'Spam'` on another, because the `print` statement in the nested function finds the name in the enclosing function's local scope, and the `print` at the end finds the variable in the global scope.

6. This example prints `'Spam'`, because the `nonlocal` statement (available in Python 3.0 but not 2.6) means that the assignment to `X` inside the nested function changes `X` in the enclosing function's local scope. Without this statement, this assignment would classify `X` as local to the nested function, making it a different variable; the code would then print `'NI'` instead.

7. Although the values of local variables go away when a function returns, you can make a Python function retain state information by using shared global variables, enclosing function scope references within nested functions, or using default argument values. Function attributes can sometimes allow state to be attached to the function itself, instead of looked up in scopes. Another alternative, using OOP with classes, sometimes supports state retention better than any of the scope-based techniques because it makes it explicit with attribute assignments; we'll explore this option in Part VI.

## CHAPTER 18

Arguments

Chapter 17 explored the details behind Python's *scopes*—the places where variables are defined and looked up. As we learned, the place where a name is defined in our code determines much of its meaning. This chapter continues the function story by studying the concepts in Python *argument passing*—the way that objects are sent to functions as inputs. As we'll see, arguments (a.k.a. parameters) are assigned to names in a function, but they have more to do with object references than with variable scopes. We'll also find that Python provides extra tools, such as keywords, defaults, and arbitrary argument collectors, that allow for wide flexibility in the way arguments are sent to a function.

Argument-Passing Basics

Earlier in this part of the book, I noted that arguments are passed by *assignment*. This has a few ramifications that aren't always obvious to beginners, which I'll expand on in this section. Here is a rundown of the key points in passing arguments to functions:

- **Arguments are passed by automatically assigning objects to local variable names**. Function arguments—references to (possibly) shared objects sent by the caller—are just another instance of Python assignment at work. Because references are implemented as pointers, all arguments are, in effect, passed by pointer. Objects passed as arguments are never automatically copied.

- **Assigning to argument names inside a function does not affect the caller**. Argument names in the function header become new, local names when the function runs, in the scope of the function. There is no aliasing between function argument names and variable names in the scope of the caller.

- **Changing a mutable object argument in a function may impact the caller**. On the other hand, as arguments are simply assigned to passed-in objects, functions can change passed-in mutable objects in place, and the results may affect the caller. Mutable arguments can be input and output for functions.

For more details on *references*, see Chapter 6; everything we learned there also applies to function arguments, though the assignment to argument names is automatic and implicit.

Python's pass-by-assignment scheme isn't quite the same as C++'s reference parameters option, but it turns out to be very similar to the C language's argument-passing model in practice:

- **Immutable arguments are effectively passed "by value."** Objects such as integers and strings are passed by object reference instead of by copying, but because you can't change immutable objects in-place anyhow, the effect is much like making a copy.

- **Mutable arguments are effectively passed "by pointer."** Objects such as lists and dictionaries are also passed by object reference, which is similar to the way C passes arrays as pointers—mutable objects can be changed in-place in the function, much like C arrays.

Of course, if you've never used C, Python's argument-passing mode will seem simpler still—it involves just the assignment of objects to names, and it works the same whether the objects are mutable or not.

Arguments and Shared References

To illustrate argument-passing properties at work, consider the following code:

```
>>> def f(a):            # a is assigned to (references) passed object
...     a = 99           # Changes local variable a only
...
>>> b = 88
>>> f(b)                 # a and b both reference same 88 initially
>>> print(b)             # b is not changed
88
```

In this example the variable a is assigned the object 88 at the moment the function is called with f(b), but a lives only within the called function. Changing a inside the function has no effect on the place where the function is called; it simply resets the local variable a to a completely different object.

That's what is meant by a lack of name *aliasing*—assignment to an argument name inside a function (e.g., a=99) does not magically change a variable like b in the scope of the function call. Argument names may share passed objects initially (they are essentially pointers to those objects), but only temporarily, when the function is first called. As soon as an argument name is reassigned, this relationship ends.

At least, that's the case for assignment to argument *names* themselves. When arguments are passed *mutable* objects like lists and dictionaries, we also need to be aware that in-place changes to such *objects* may live on after a function exits, and hence impact callers. Here's an example that demonstrates this behavior:

```
>>> def changer(a, b):        # Arguments assigned references to objects
...     a = 2                  # Changes local name's value only
...     b[0] = 'spam'          # Changes shared object in-place
...
>>> X = 1
>>> L = [1, 2]                 # Caller
>>> changer(X, L)             # Pass immutable and mutable objects
>>> X, L                       # X is unchanged, L is different!
(1, ['spam', 2])
```

In this code, the changer function assigns values to argument a itself, and to a component of the object referenced by argument b. These two assignments within the function are only slightly different in syntax but have radically different results:

- Because a is a local variable name in the function's scope, the first assignment has no effect on the caller—it simply changes the local variable a to reference a completely different object, and does not change the binding of the name X in the caller's scope. This is the same as in the prior example.

- Argument b is a local variable name, too, but it is passed a mutable object (the list that L references in the caller's scope). As the second assignment is an in-place object change, the result of the assignment to b[0] in the function impacts the value of L after the function returns.

Really, the second assignment statement in changer doesn't change b—it changes part of the object that b currently references. This in-place change impacts the caller only because the changed object outlives the function call. The name L hasn't changed either—it still references the same, changed object—but it seems as though L differs after the call because the value it references has been modified within the function.

Figure 18-1 illustrates the name/object bindings that exist immediately after the function has been called, and before its code has run.

If this example is still confusing, it may help to notice that the effect of the automatic assignments of the passed-in arguments is the same as running a series of simple assignment statements. In terms of the first argument, the assignment has no effect on the caller:

```
>>> X = 1
>>> a = X                      # They share the same object
>>> a = 2                      # Resets 'a' only, 'X' is still 1
>>> print(X)
1
```

The assignment through the second argument does affect a variable at the call, though, because it is an in-place object change:

```
>>> L = [1, 2]
>>> b = L                      # They share the same object
>>> b[0] = 'spam'             # In-place change: 'L' sees the change too
>>> print(L)
['spam', 2]
```

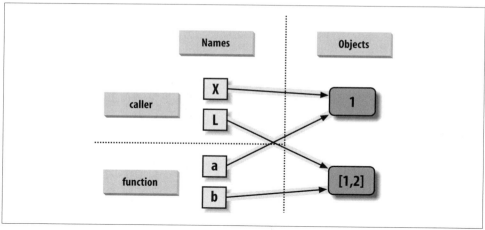

Figure 18-1. References: arguments. Because arguments are passed by assignment, argument names in the function may share objects with variables in the scope of the call. Hence, in-place changes to mutable arguments in a function can impact the caller. Here, a and b in the function initially reference the objects referenced by variables X and L when the function is first called. Changing the list through variable b makes L appear different after the call returns.

If you recall our discussions about shared mutable objects in Chapters 6 and 9, you'll recognize the phenomenon at work: changing a mutable object in-place can impact other references to that object. Here, the effect is to make one of the arguments work like both an input and an *output* of the function.

Avoiding Mutable Argument Changes

This behavior of in-place changes to mutable arguments isn't a bug—it's simply the way argument passing works in Python. Arguments are passed to functions by reference (a.k.a. pointer) by default because that is what we normally want. It means we can pass large objects around our programs without making multiple copies along the way, and we can easily update these objects as we go. In fact, as we'll see in Part VI, Python's class model *depends* upon changing a passed-in "self" argument in-place, to update object state.

If we don't want in-place changes within functions to impact objects we pass to them, though, we can simply make explicit copies of mutable objects, as we learned in Chapter 6. For function arguments, we can always copy the list at the point of call:

```
L = [1, 2]
changer(X, L[:])        # Pass a copy, so our 'L' does not change
```

We can also copy within the function itself, if we never want to change passed-in objects, regardless of how the function is called:

```
def changer(a, b):
    b = b[:]            # Copy input list so we don't impact caller
```

```
        a = 2
        b[0] = 'spam'          # Changes our list copy only
```

Both of these copying schemes don't stop the function from changing the object—they just prevent those changes from impacting the caller. To really prevent changes, we can always convert to immutable objects to force the issue. Tuples, for example, throw an exception when changes are attempted:

```
        L = [1, 2]
        changer(X, tuple(L))     # Pass a tuple, so changes are errors
```

This scheme uses the built-in `tuple` function, which builds a new tuple out of all the items in a sequence (really, any iterable). It's also something of an extreme—because it forces the function to be written to never change passed-in arguments, this solution might impose more limitations on the function than it should, and so should generally be avoided (you never know when changing arguments might come in handy for other calls in the future). Using this technique will also make the function lose the ability to call any list-specific methods on the argument, including methods that do not change the object in-place.

The main point to remember here is that functions might update mutable objects like lists and dictionaries passed into them. This isn't necessarily a problem if it's expected, and often serves useful purposes. Moreover, functions that change passed-in mutable objects in place are probably designed and intended to do so—the change is likely part of a well-defined API that you shouldn't violate by making copies.

However, you do have to be aware of this property—if objects change out from under you unexpectedly, check whether a called function might be responsible, and make copies when objects are passed if needed.

Simulating Output Parameters

We've already discussed the `return` statement and used it in a few examples. Here's another way to use this statement: because `return` can send back any sort of object, it can return *multiple values* by packaging them in a tuple or other collection type. In fact, although Python doesn't support what some languages label "call-by-reference" argument passing, we can usually simulate it by returning tuples and assigning the results back to the original argument names in the caller:

```
>>> def multiple(x, y):
...     x = 2               # Changes local names only
...     y = [3, 4]
...     return x, y         # Return new values in a tuple
...
>>> X = 1
>>> L = [1, 2]
>>> X, L = multiple(X, L)   # Assign results to caller's names
>>> X, L
(2, [3, 4])
```

It looks like the code is returning two values here, but it's really just one—a two-item tuple with the optional surrounding parentheses omitted. After the call returns, we can use tuple assignment to unpack the parts of the returned tuple. (If you've forgotten why this works, flip back to "Tuples" on page 227 in Chapter 4, Chapter 9, and "Assignment Statements" on page 281 in Chapter 11.) The net effect of this coding pattern is to simulate the output parameters of other languages by explicit assignments. X and L change after the call, but only because the code said so.

Unpacking arguments in Python 2.X: The preceding example unpacks a tuple returned by the function with tuple assignment. In Python 2.6, it's also possible to automatically unpack tuples in arguments passed to a function. In 2.6, a function defined by this header:

```
def f((a, (b, c))):
```

can be called with tuples that match the expected structure: `f((1, (2, 3)))` assigns a, b, and c to 1, 2, and 3, respectively. Naturally, the passed tuple can also be an object created before the call (`f(T)`). This def syntax is no longer supported in Python 3.0. Instead, code this function as:

```
def f(T): (a, (b, c)) = T
```

to unpack in an explicit assignment statement. This explicit form works in both 3.0 and 2.6. Argument unpacking is an obscure and rarely used feature in Python 2.X. Moreover, a function header in 2.6 supports only the tuple form of sequence assignment; more general sequence assignments (e.g., `def f((a, [b, c])):`) fail on syntax errors in 2.6 as well and require the explicit assignment form.

Tuple unpacking argument syntax is also disallowed by 3.0 in lambda function argument lists: see the sidebar "Why You Will Care: List Comprehensions and map" on page 493 for an example. Somewhat asymmetrically, tuple unpacking assignment is still automatic in 3.0 for loops targets, though; see Chapter 13 for examples.

Special Argument-Matching Modes

As we've just seen, arguments are always passed by *assignment* in Python; names in the def header are assigned to passed-in objects. On top of this model, though, Python provides additional tools that alter the way the argument objects in a call are *matched* with argument names in the header prior to assignment. These tools are all optional, but they allow us to write functions that support more flexible calling patterns, and you may encounter some libraries that require them.

By default, arguments are matched by position, from left to right, and you must pass exactly as many arguments as there are argument names in the function header. However, you can also specify matching by name, default values, and collectors for extra arguments.

The Basics

Before we go into the syntactic details, I want to stress that these special modes are optional and only have to do with matching objects to names; the underlying passing mechanism after the matching takes place is still assignment. In fact, some of these tools are intended more for people writing libraries than for application developers. But because you may stumble across these modes even if you don't code them yourself, here's a synopsis of the available tools:

Positionals: matched from left to right
    The normal case, which we've mostly been using so far, is to match passed argument values to argument names in a function header by position, from left to right.

Keywords: matched by argument name
    Alternatively, callers can specify which argument in the function is to receive a value by using the argument's name in the call, with the `name=value` syntax.

Defaults: specify values for arguments that aren't passed
    Functions themselves can specify default values for arguments to receive if the call passes too few values, again using the `name=value` syntax.

Varargs collecting: collect arbitrarily many positional or keyword arguments
    Functions can use special arguments preceded with one or two * characters to collect an arbitrary number of extra arguments (this feature is often referred to as *varargs*, after the varargs feature in the C language, which also supports variable-length argument lists).

Varargs unpacking: pass arbitrarily many positional or keyword arguments
    Callers can also use the * syntax to unpack argument collections into discrete, separate arguments. This is the inverse of a * in a function header—in the header it means collect arbitrarily many arguments, while in the call it means pass arbitrarily many arguments.

Keyword-only arguments: arguments that must be passed by name
    In Python 3.0 (but not 2.6), functions can also specify arguments that must be passed by name with keyword arguments, not by position. Such arguments are typically used to define configuration options in addition to actual arguments.

Matching Syntax

Table 18-1 summarizes the syntax that invokes the special argument-matching modes.

Table 18-1. Function argument-matching forms

Syntax	Location	Interpretation
func(value)	Caller	Normal argument: matched by position
func(name=value)	Caller	Keyword argument: matched by name
func(*sequence)	Caller	Pass all objects in sequence as individual positional arguments
func(**dict)	Caller	Pass all key/value pairs in dict as individual keyword arguments
def func(name)	Function	Normal argument: matches any passed value by position or name
def func(name=value)	Function	Default argument value, if not passed in the call
def func(*name)	Function	Matches and collects remaining positional arguments in a tuple
def func(**name)	Function	Matches and collects remaining keyword arguments in a dictionary
def func(*args, name)	Function	Arguments that must be passed by keyword only in calls (3.0)
def func(*, name=value)		

These special matching modes break down into function calls and definitions as follows:

- In a *function call* (the first four rows of the table), simple values are matched by position, but using the name=value form tells Python to match by name to arguments instead; these are called *keyword arguments*. Using a *sequence or **dict in a call allows us to package up arbitrarily many positional or keyword objects in sequences and dictionaries, respectively, and unpack them as separate, individual arguments when they are passed to the function.

- In a *function header* (the rest of the table), a simple name is matched by position or name depending on how the caller passes it, but the name=value form specifies a *default value*. The *name form collects any extra unmatched positional arguments in a tuple, and the **name form collects extra keyword arguments in a dictionary. In Python 3.0 and later, any normal or defaulted argument names following a *name or a bare * are *keyword-only* arguments and must be passed by keyword in calls.

Of these, keyword arguments and defaults are probably the most commonly used in Python code. We've informally used both of these earlier in this book:

- We've already used *keywords* to specify options to the 3.0 print function, but they are more general—keywords allow us to label any argument with its name, to make calls more informational.

- We met *defaults* earlier, too, as a way to pass in values from the enclosing function's scope, but they are also more general—they allow us to make any argument optional, providing its default value in a function definition.

As we'll see, the combination of defaults in a function header and keywords in a call further allows us to pick and choose which defaults to override.

In short, special argument-matching modes let you be fairly liberal about how many arguments must be passed to a function. If a function specifies defaults, they are used if you pass *too few* arguments. If a function uses the * variable argument list forms, you can pass *too many* arguments; the * names collect the extra arguments in data structures for processing in the function.

The Gritty Details

If you choose to use and combine the special argument-matching modes, Python will ask you to follow these ordering rules:

- In a function *call*, arguments must appear in this order: any positional arguments (`value`), followed by a combination of any keyword arguments (`name=value`) and the `*sequence` form, followed by the `**dict` form.
- In a function *header*, arguments must appear in this order: any normal arguments (`name`), followed by any default arguments (`name=value`), followed by the `*name` (or `*` in 3.0) form if present, followed by any `name` or `name=value` keyword-only arguments (in 3.0), followed by the `**name` form.

In both the call and header, the `**arg` form must appear last if present. If you mix arguments in any other order, you will get a syntax error because the combinations can be ambiguous. The steps that Python internally carries out to match arguments before assignment can roughly be described as follows:

1. Assign nonkeyword arguments by position.
2. Assign keyword arguments by matching names.
3. Assign extra nonkeyword arguments to `*name` tuple.
4. Assign extra keyword arguments to `**name` dictionary.
5. Assign default values to unassigned arguments in header.

After this, Python checks to make sure each argument is passed just one value; if not, an error is raised. When all matching is complete, Python assigns argument names to the objects passed to them.

The actual matching algorithm Python uses is a bit more complex (it must also account for keyword-only arguments in 3.0, for instance), so we'll defer to Python's standard language manual for a more exact description. It's not required reading, but tracing Python's matching algorithm may help you to understand some convoluted cases, especially when modes are mixed.

 In Python 3.0, argument names in a function header can also have *an-notation* values, specified as `name:value` (or `name:value=default` when defaults are present). This is simply additional syntax for arguments and does not augment or change the argument-ordering rules described here. The function itself can also have an annotation value, given as `def f()->value`. See the discussion of function annotation in Chapter 19 for more details.

Keyword and Default Examples

This is all simpler in code than the preceding descriptions may imply. If you don't use any special matching syntax, Python matches names by position from left to right, like most other languages. For instance, if you define a function that requires three arguments, you must call it with three arguments:

```
>>> def f(a, b, c): print(a, b, c)
...
```

Here, we pass them by position—a is matched to 1, b is matched to 2, and so on (this works the same in Python 3.0 and 2.6, but extra tuple parentheses are displayed in 2.6 because we're using 3.0 `print` calls):

```
>>> f(1, 2, 3)
1 2 3
```

Keywords

In Python, though, you can be more specific about what goes where when you call a function. Keyword arguments allow us to match by *name*, instead of by position:

```
>>> f(c=3, b=2, a=1)
1 2 3
```

The c=3 in this call, for example, means send 3 to the argument named c. More formally, Python matches the name c in the call to the argument named c in the function definition's header, and then passes the value 3 to that argument. The net effect of this call is the same as that of the prior call, but notice that the left-to-right order of the arguments no longer matters when keywords are used because arguments are matched by name, not by position. It's even possible to combine positional and keyword arguments in a single call. In this case, all positionals are matched first from left to right in the header, before keywords are matched by name:

```
>>> f(1, c=3, b=2)
1 2 3
```

When most people see this the first time, they wonder why one would use such a tool. Keywords typically have two roles in Python. First, they make your calls a bit more self-documenting (assuming that you use better argument names than a, b, and c). For example, a call of this form:

```
func(name='Bob', age=40, job='dev')
```

is much more meaningful than a call with three naked values separated by commas— the keywords serve as labels for the data in the call. The second major use of keywords occurs in conjunction with defaults, which we turn to next.

Defaults

We talked about defaults in brief earlier, when discussing nested function scopes. In short, defaults allow us to make selected function arguments optional; if not passed a value, the argument is assigned its default before the function runs. For example, here is a function that requires one argument and defaults two:

```
>>> def f(a, b=2, c=3): print(a, b, c)
...
```

When we call this function, we must provide a value for a, either by position or by keyword; however, providing values for b and c is optional. If we don't pass values to b and c, they default to 2 and 3, respectively:

```
>>> f(1)
1 2 3
>>> f(a=1)
1 2 3
```

If we pass two values, only c gets its default, and with three values, no defaults are used:

```
>>> f(1, 4)
1 4 3
>>> f(1, 4, 5)
1 4 5
```

Finally, here is how the keyword and default features interact. Because they subvert the normal left-to-right positional mapping, keywords allow us to essentially skip over arguments with defaults:

```
>>> f(1, c=6)
1 2 6
```

Here, a gets 1 by position, c gets 6 by keyword, and b, in between, defaults to 2.

Be careful not to confuse the special name=value syntax in a function header and a function call; in the call it means a match-by-name keyword argument, while in the header it specifies a default for an optional argument. In both cases, this is not an assignment statement (despite its appearance); it is special syntax for these two contexts, which modifies the default argument-matching mechanics.

Combining keywords and defaults

Here is a slightly larger example that demonstrates keywords and defaults in action. In the following, the caller must always pass at least two arguments (to match spam and eggs), but the other two are optional. If they are omitted, Python assigns toast and ham to the defaults specified in the header:

```
def func(spam, eggs, toast=0, ham=0):    # First 2 required
    print((spam, eggs, toast, ham))

func(1, 2)                               # Output: (1, 2, 0, 0)
func(1, ham=1, eggs=0)                   # Output: (1, 0, 0, 1)
func(spam=1, eggs=0)                     # Output: (1, 0, 0, 0)
func(toast=1, eggs=2, spam=3)            # Output: (3, 2, 1, 0)
func(1, 2, 3, 4)                         # Output: (1, 2, 3, 4)
```

Notice again that when keyword arguments are used in the call, the order in which the arguments are listed doesn't matter; Python matches by name, not by position. The caller must supply values for spam and eggs, but they can be matched by position or by name. Again, keep in mind that the form name=value means different things in the call and the def: a keyword in the call and a default in the header.

Arbitrary Arguments Examples

The last two matching extensions, * and **, are designed to support functions that take any number of arguments. Both can appear in either the function definition or a function call, and they have related purposes in the two locations.

Collecting arguments

The first use, in the function definition, collects unmatched *positional* arguments into a tuple:

```
>>> def f(*args): print(args)
...
```

When this function is called, Python collects all the positional arguments into a new tuple and assigns the variable args to that tuple. Because it is a normal tuple object, it can be indexed, stepped through with a for loop, and so on:

```
>>> f()
()
>>> f(1)
(1,)
>>> f(1, 2, 3, 4)
(1, 2, 3, 4)
```

The ** feature is similar, but it only works for *keyword* arguments—it collects them into a new dictionary, which can then be processed with normal dictionary tools. In a sense, the ** form allows you to convert from keywords to dictionaries, which you can then step through with keys calls, dictionary iterators, and the like:

```
>>> def f(**args): print(args)
...
>>> f()
{}
>>> f(a=1, b=2)
{'a': 1, 'b': 2}
```

Finally, function headers can combine normal arguments, the *, and the ** to imple-ment wildly flexible call signatures. For instance, in the following, 1 is passed to a by position, 2 and 3 are collected into the pargs positional tuple, and x and y wind up in the kargs keyword dictionary:

```
>>> def f(a, *pargs, **kargs): print(a, pargs, kargs)
...
>>> f(1, 2, 3, x=1, y=2)
1 (2, 3) {'y': 2, 'x': 1}
```

In fact, these features can be combined in even more complex ways that may seem ambiguous at first glance—an idea we will revisit later in this chapter. First, though, let's see what happens when * and ** are coded in function calls instead of definitions.

Unpacking arguments

In recent Python releases, we can use the * syntax when we call a function, too. In this context, its meaning is the inverse of its meaning in the function definition—it unpacks a collection of arguments, rather than building a collection of arguments. For example, we can pass four arguments to a function in a tuple and let Python unpack them into individual arguments:

```
>>> def func(a, b, c, d): print(a, b, c, d)
...
>>> args = (1, 2)
>>> args += (3, 4)
>>> func(*args)
1 2 3 4
```

Similarly, the ** syntax in a function call unpacks a dictionary of key/value pairs into separate keyword arguments:

```
>>> args = {'a': 1, 'b': 2, 'c': 3}
>>> args['d'] = 4
>>> func(**args)
1 2 3 4
```

Again, we can combine normal, positional, and keyword arguments in the call in very flexible ways:

```
>>> func(*(1, 2), **{'d': 4, 'c': 4})
1 2 4 4

>>> func(1, *(2, 3), **{'d': 4})
1 2 3 4

>>> func(1, c=3, *(2,), **{'d': 4})
```

```
1 2 3 4

>>> func(1, *(2, 3), d=4)
1 2 3 4

>>> func(1, *(2,), c=3, **{'d':4})
1 2 3 4
```

This sort of code is convenient when you cannot predict the number of arguments that
will be passed to a function when you write your script; you can build up a collection
of arguments at runtime instead and call the function generically this way. Again, don't
confuse the */** syntax in the function header and the function call—in the header it
collects any number of arguments, while in the call it unpacks any number of
arguments.

> As we saw in Chapter 14, the *pargs form in a call is an *iteration con-
> text*, so technically it accepts any iterable object, not just tuples or other
> sequences as shown in the examples here. For instance, a file object
> works after the *, and unpacks its lines into individual arguments (e.g.,
> func(*open('fname'))).
>
> This generality is supported in both Python 3.0 and 2.6, but it holds true
> only for *calls*—a *pargs in a call allows any iterable, but the same form
> in a def header always bundles extra arguments into a *tuple*. This header
> behavior is similar in spirit and syntax to the * in Python 3.0 extended
> sequence unpacking assignment forms we met in Chapter 11 (e.g., x,
> *y = z), though that feature always creates lists, not tuples.

Applying functions generically

The prior section's examples may seem obtuse, but they are used more often than you
might expect. Some programs need to call arbitrary functions in a generic fashion,
without knowing their names or arguments ahead of time. In fact, the real power of
the special "varargs" call syntax is that you don't need to know how many arguments
a function call requires before you write a script. For example, you can use if logic to
select from a set of functions and argument lists, and call any of them generically:

```
if <test>:
    action, args = func1, (1,)              # Call func1 with 1 arg in this case
else:
    action, args = func2, (1, 2, 3)         # Call func2 with 3 args here
...
action(*args)                               # Dispatch generically
```

More generally, this varargs call syntax is useful any time you cannot predict the arguments list. If your user selects an arbitrary function via a user interface, for instance,
you may be unable to hardcode a function call when writing your script. To work
around this, simply build up the arguments list with sequence operations, and call it
with starred names to unpack the arguments:

```
>>> args = (2,3)
>>> args += (4,)
>>> args
(2, 3, 4)
>>> func(*args)
```

Because the arguments list is passed in as a tuple here, the program can build it at runtime. This technique also comes in handy for functions that test or time other functions. For instance, in the following code we support any function with any arguments by passing along whatever arguments were sent in:

```
def tracer(func, *pargs, **kargs):          # Accept arbitrary arguments
    print('calling:', func.__name__)
    return func(*pargs, **kargs)            # Pass along arbitrary arguments

def func(a, b, c, d):
    return a + b + c + d

print(tracer(func, 1, 2, c=3, d=4))
```

When this code is run, arguments are collected by the tracer and then *propagated* with varargs call syntax:

```
calling: func
10
```

We'll see larger examples of such roles later in this book; see especially the sequence timing example in Chapter 20 and the various decorator tools we will code in Chapter 38.

The defunct apply built-in (Python 2.6)

Prior to Python 3.0, the effect of the `*args` and `**args` varargs call syntax could be achieved with a built-in function named `apply`. This original technique has been removed in 3.0 because it is now redundant (3.0 cleans up many such dusty tools that have been subsumed over the years). It's still available in Python 2.6, though, and you may come across it in older 2.X code.

In short, the following are equivalent prior to Python 3.0:

```
func(*pargs, **kargs)           # Newer call syntax: func(*sequence, **dict)

apply(func, pargs, kargs)       # Defunct built-in: apply(func, sequence, dict)
```

For example, consider the following function, which accepts any number of positional or keyword arguments:

```
>>> def echo(*args, **kwargs): print(args, kwargs)
...
>>> echo(1, 2, a=3, b=4)
(1, 2) {'a': 3, 'b': 4}
```

In Python 2.6, we can call it generically with `apply`, or with the call syntax that is now required in 3.0:

```
>>> pargs = (1, 2)
>>> kargs = {'a':3, 'b':4}

>>> apply(echo, pargs, kargs)
(1, 2) {'a': 3, 'b': 4}

>>> echo(*pargs, **kargs)
(1, 2) {'a': 3, 'b': 4}
```

The unpacking call syntax form is newer than the `apply` function, is preferred in general, and is required in 3.0. Apart from its symmetry with the *pargs and **kargs collector forms in `def` headers, and the fact that it requires fewer keystrokes overall, the newer call syntax also allows us to pass along additional arguments without having to manually extend argument sequences or dictionaries:

```
>>> echo(0, c=5, *pargs, **kargs)       # Normal, keyword, *sequence, **dictionary
(0, 1, 2) {'a': 3, 'c': 5, 'b': 4}
```

That is, the call syntax form is *more general*. Since it's required in 3.0, you should now disavow all knowledge of `apply` (unless, of course, it appears in 2.X code you must use or maintain...).

Python 3.0 Keyword-Only Arguments

Python 3.0 generalizes the ordering rules in function headers to allow us to specify *keyword-only arguments*—arguments that must be passed by keyword only and will never be filled in by a positional argument. This is useful if we want a function to both process any number of arguments and accept possibly optional configuration options.

Syntactically, keyword-only arguments are coded as named arguments that appear after *args in the arguments list. All such arguments must be passed using keyword syntax in the call. For example, in the following, a may be passed by name or position, b collects any extra positional arguments, and c must be passed by keyword only:

```
>>> def kwonly(a, *b, c):
...     print(a, b, c)
...
>>> kwonly(1, 2, c=3)
1 (2,) 3
>>> kwonly(a=1, c=3)
1 () 3
>>> kwonly(1, 2, 3)
TypeError: kwonly() needs keyword-only argument c
```

We can also use a * character by itself in the arguments list to indicate that a function does not accept a variable-length argument list but still expects all arguments following the * to be passed as keywords. In the next function, a may be passed by position or name again, but b and c must be keywords, and no extra positionals are allowed:

```
>>> def kwonly(a, *, b, c):
...     print(a, b, c)
...
>>> kwonly(1, c=3, b=2)
1 2 3
>>> kwonly(c=3, b=2, a=1)
1 2 3
>>> kwonly(1, 2, 3)
TypeError: kwonly() takes exactly 1 positional argument (3 given)
>>> kwonly(1)
TypeError: kwonly() needs keyword-only argument b
```

You can still use defaults for keyword-only arguments, even though they appear after the * in the function header. In the following code, a may be passed by name or position, and b and c are optional but must be passed by keyword if used:

```
>>> def kwonly(a, *, b='spam', c='ham'):
...     print(a, b, c)
...
>>> kwonly(1)
1 spam ham
>>> kwonly(1, c=3)
1 spam 3
>>> kwonly(a=1)
1 spam ham
>>> kwonly(c=3, b=2, a=1)
1 2 3
>>> kwonly(1, 2)
TypeError: kwonly() takes exactly 1 positional argument (2 given)
```

In fact, keyword-only arguments with defaults are optional, but those without defaults effectively become required keywords for the function:

```
>>> def kwonly(a, *, b, c='spam'):
...     print(a, b, c)
...
>>> kwonly(1, b='eggs')
1 eggs spam
>>> kwonly(1, c='eggs')
TypeError: kwonly() needs keyword-only argument b
>>> kwonly(1, 2)
TypeError: kwonly() takes exactly 1 positional argument (2 given)

>>> def kwonly(a, *, b=1, c, d=2):
...     print(a, b, c, d)
...
>>> kwonly(3, c=4)
3 1 4 2
>>> kwonly(3, c=4, b=5)
3 5 4 2
>>> kwonly(3)
TypeError: kwonly() needs keyword-only argument c
>>> kwonly(1, 2, 3)
TypeError: kwonly() takes exactly 1 positional argument (3 given)
```

Ordering rules

Finally, note that keyword-only arguments must be specified after a single star, not two—named arguments cannot appear after the **args arbitrary keywords form, and a ** can't appear by itself in the arguments list. Both attempts generate a syntax error:

```
>>> def kwonly(a, **pargs, b, c):
SyntaxError: invalid syntax
>>> def kwonly(a, **, b, c):
SyntaxError: invalid syntax
```

This means that in a function *header*, keyword-only arguments must be coded before the **args arbitrary keywords form and after the *args arbitrary positional form, when both are present. Whenever an argument name appears before *args, it is a possibly default positional argument, not keyword-only:

```
>>> def f(a, *b, **d, c=6): print(a, b, c, d)      # Keyword-only before **!
SyntaxError: invalid syntax

>>> def f(a, *b, c=6, **d): print(a, b, c, d)      # Collect args in header
...
>>> f(1, 2, 3, x=4, y=5)                           # Default used
1 (2, 3) 6 {'y': 5, 'x': 4}

>>> f(1, 2, 3, x=4, y=5, c=7)                      # Override default
1 (2, 3) 7 {'y': 5, 'x': 4}

>>> f(1, 2, 3, c=7, x=4, y=5)                      # Anywhere in keywords
1 (2, 3) 7 {'y': 5, 'x': 4}

>>> def f(a, c=6, *b, **d): print(a, b, c, d)      # c is not keyword-only!
...
>>> f(1, 2, 3, x=4)
1 (3,) 2 {'x': 4}
```

In fact, similar ordering rules hold true in function *calls*: when keyword-only arguments are passed, they must appear before a **args form. The keyword-only argument can be coded either before or after the *args, though, and may be included in **args:

```
>>> def f(a, *b, c=6, **d): print(a, b, c, d)      # KW-only between * and **
...
>>> f(1, *(2, 3), **dict(x=4, y=5))                # Unpack args at call
1 (2, 3) 6 {'y': 5, 'x': 4}

>>> f(1, *(2, 3), **dict(x=4, y=5), c=7)           # Keywords before **args!
SyntaxError: invalid syntax

>>> f(1, *(2, 3), c=7, **dict(x=4, y=5))           # Override default
1 (2, 3) 7 {'y': 5, 'x': 4}

>>> f(1, c=7, *(2, 3), **dict(x=4, y=5))           # After or before *
1 (2, 3) 7 {'y': 5, 'x': 4}

>>> f(1, *(2, 3), **dict(x=4, y=5, c=7))           # Keyword-only in **
1 (2, 3) 7 {'y': 5, 'x': 4}
```

Trace through these cases on your own, in conjunction with the general argument-ordering rules described formally earlier. They may appear to be worst cases in the artificial examples here, but they can come up in real practice, especially for people who write libraries and tools for other Python programmers to use.

Why keyword-only arguments?

So why care about keyword-only arguments? In short, they make it easier to allow a function to accept both any number of positional arguments to be processed, and configuration options passed as keywords. While their use is optional, without keyword-only arguments extra work may be required to provide defaults for such options and to verify that no superfluous keywords were passed.

Imagine a function that processes a set of passed-in objects and allows a tracing flag to be passed:

```
process(X, Y, Z)            # use flag's default
process(X, Y, notify=True)  # override flag default
```

Without keyword-only arguments we have to use both *args and **args and manually inspect the keywords, but with keyword-only arguments less code is required. The following guarantees that no positional argument will be incorrectly matched against notify and requires that it be a keyword if passed:

```
def process(*args, notify=False): ...
```

Since we're going to see a more realistic example of this later in this chapter, in "Emulating the Python 3.0 print Function" on page 459, I'll postpone the rest of this story until then. For an additional example of keyword-only arguments in action, see the iteration options timing case study in Chapter 20. And for additional function definition enhancements in Python 3.0, stay tuned for the discussion of function annotation syntax in Chapter 19.

The min Wakeup Call!

Time for something more realistic. To make this chapter's concepts more concrete, let's work through an exercise that demonstrates a practical application of argument-matching tools.

Suppose you want to code a function that is able to compute the minimum value from an arbitrary set of arguments and an arbitrary set of object data types. That is, the function should accept zero or more arguments, as many as you wish to pass. Moreover, the function should work for all kinds of Python object types: numbers, strings, lists, lists of dictionaries, files, and even None.

The first requirement provides a natural example of how the * feature can be put to good use—we can collect arguments into a tuple and step over each of them in turn with a simple for loop. The second part of the problem definition is easy: because every object type supports comparisons, we don't have to specialize the function per type (an application of polymorphism); we can simply compare objects blindly and let Python worry about what sort of comparison to perform.

Full Credit

The following file shows three ways to code this operation, at least one of which was suggested by a student in one of my courses:

- The first function fetches the first argument (args is a tuple) and traverses the rest by slicing off the first (there's no point in comparing an object to itself, especially if it might be a large structure).
- The second version lets Python pick off the first and rest of the arguments automatically, and so avoids an index and slice.
- The third converts from a tuple to a list with the built-in list call and employs the list sort method.

The sort method is coded in C, so it can be quicker than the other approaches at times, but the linear scans of the first two techniques will make them faster most of the time.* The file *mins.py* contains the code for all three solutions:

```
def min1(*args):
    res = args[0]
    for arg in args[1:]:
        if arg < res:
            res = arg
    return res

def min2(first, *rest):
    for arg in rest:
        if arg < first:
            first = arg
    return first

def min3(*args):
    tmp = list(args)          # Or, in Python 2.4+: return sorted(args)[0]
    tmp.sort()
    return tmp[0]

print(min1(3,4,1,2))
```

---

* Actually, this is fairly complicated. The Python sort routine is coded in C and uses a highly optimized algorithm that attempts to take advantage of partial ordering in the items to be sorted. It's named "timsort" after Tim Peters, its creator, and in its documentation it claims to have "supernatural performance" at times (pretty good, for a sort!). Still, sorting is an inherently exponential operation (it must chop up the sequence and put it back together many times), and the other versions simply perform one linear left-to-right scan. The net effect is that sorting is quicker if the arguments are partially ordered, but is likely to be slower otherwise. Even so, Python performance can change over time, and the fact that sorting is implemented in the C language can help greatly; for an exact analysis, you should time the alternatives with the time or timeit modules we'll meet in Chapter 20.

```
print(min2("bb", "aa"))
print(min3([2,2], [1,1], [3,3]))
```

All three solutions produce the same result when the file is run. Try typing a few calls interactively to experiment with these on your own:

```
% python mins.py
1
aa
[1, 1]
```

Notice that none of these three variants tests for the case where no arguments are passed in. They could, but there's no point in doing so here—in all three solutions, Python will automatically raise an exception if no arguments are passed in. The first variant raises an exception when we try to fetch item 0, the second when Python detects an argument list mismatch, and the third when we try to return item 0 at the end.

This is exactly what we want to happen—because these functions support any data type, there is no valid sentinel value that we could pass back to designate an error. There are exceptions to this rule (e.g., if you have to run expensive actions before you reach the error), but in general it's better to assume that arguments will work in your functions' code and let Python raise errors for you when they do not.

Bonus Points

You can get bonus points here for changing these functions to compute the *maximum*, rather than minimum, values. This one's easy: the first two versions only require changing < to >, and the third simply requires that we return tmp[-1] instead of tmp[0]. For an extra point, be sure to set the function name to "max" as well (though this part is strictly optional).

It's also possible to generalize a single function to compute either a minimum *or* a maximum value, by evaluating comparison expression strings with a tool like the eval built-in function (see the library manual) or passing in an arbitrary comparison function. The file *minmax.py* shows how to implement the latter scheme:

```
def minmax(test, *args):
    res = args[0]
    for arg in args[1:]:
        if test(arg, res):
            res = arg
    return res

def lessthan(x, y): return x < y          # See also: lambda
def grtrthan(x, y): return x > y

print(minmax(lessthan, 4, 2, 1, 5, 6, 3))  # Self-test code
print(minmax(grtrthan, 4, 2, 1, 5, 6, 3))

% python minmax.py
```

Functions are another kind of object that can be passed into a function like this one. To make this a `max` (or other) function, for example, we could simply pass in the right sort of `test` function. This may seem like extra work, but the main point of generalizing functions this way (instead of cutting and pasting to change just a single character) is that we'll only have one version to change in the future, not two.

The Punch Line...

Of course, all this was just a coding exercise. There's really no reason to code `min` or `max` functions, because both are built-ins in Python! We met them briefly in Chapter 5 in conjunction with numeric tools, and again in Chapter 14 when exploring iteration contexts. The built-in versions work almost exactly like ours, but they're coded in C for optimal speed and accept either a single iterable or multiple arguments. Still, though it's superfluous in this context, the general coding pattern we used here might be useful in other scenarios.

Generalized Set Functions

Let's look at a more useful example of special argument-matching modes at work. At the end of Chapter 16, we wrote a function that returned the intersection of two sequences (it picked out items that appeared in both). Here is a version that intersects an arbitrary number of sequences (one or more) by using the varargs matching form `*args` to collect all the passed-in arguments. Because the arguments come in as a tuple, we can process them in a simple `for` loop. Just for fun, we'll code a `union` function that also accepts an arbitrary number of arguments to collect items that appear in any of the operands:

```
def intersect(*args):
    res = []
    for x in args[0]:                   # Scan first sequence
        for other in args[1:]:          # For all other args
            if x not in other: break    # Item in each one?
        else:                           # No: break out of loop
            res.append(x)               # Yes: add items to end
    return res

def union(*args):
    res = []
    for seq in args:                    # For all args
        for x in seq:                   # For all nodes
            if not x in res:
                res.append(x)           # Add new items to result
    return res
```

Because these are tools worth reusing (and they're too big to retype interactively), we'll store the functions in a module file called *inter2.py* (if you've forgotten how modules and imports work, see the introduction in Chapter 3, or stay tuned for in-depth coverage in Part V). In both functions, the arguments passed in at the call come in as the `args` tuple. As in the original `intersect`, both work on any kind of sequence. Here, they are processing strings, mixed types, and more than two sequences:

```
% python
>>> from inter2 import intersect, union
>>> s1, s2, s3 = "SPAM", "SCAM", "SLAM"

>>> intersect(s1, s2), union(s1, s2)            # Two operands
(['S', 'A', 'M'], ['S', 'P', 'A', 'M', 'C'])

>>> intersect([1,2,3], (1,4))                   # Mixed types
[1]

>>> intersect(s1, s2, s3)                       # Three operands
['S', 'A', 'M']

>>> union(s1, s2, s3)
['S', 'P', 'A', 'M', 'C', 'L']
```

 I should note that because Python now has a *set object type* (described in Chapter 5), none of the set-processing examples in this book are strictly required anymore; they are included only as demonstrations of coding techniques. Because it's constantly improving, Python has an uncanny way of conspiring to make my book examples obsolete over time!

Emulating the Python 3.0 print Function

To round out the chapter, let's look at one last example of argument matching at work. The code you'll see here is intended for use in Python 2.6 or earlier (it works in 3.0, too, but is pointless there): it uses both the `*args` arbitrary positional tuple and the `**args` arbitrary keyword-arguments dictionary to simulate most of what the Python 3.0 `print` function does.

As we learned in Chapter 11, this isn't actually required, because 2.6 programmers can always enable the 3.0 `print` function with an import of this form:

```
from __future__ import print_function
```

To demonstrate argument matching in general, though, the following file, *print30.py*, does the same job in a small amount of reusable code:

```
"""
Emulate most of the 3.0 print function for use in 2.X
call signature: print30(*args, sep=' ', end='\n', file=None)
"""
import sys

def print30(*args, **kargs):
    sep  = kargs.get('sep', ' ')                # Keyword arg defaults
    end  = kargs.get('end', '\n')
    file = kargs.get('file', sys.stdout)
    output = ''
    first  = True
    for arg in args:
        output += ('' if first else sep) + str(arg)
        first = False
    file.write(output + end)
```

To test it, import this into another file or the interactive prompt, and use it like the 3.0
print function. Here is a test script, *testprint30.py* (notice that the function must be
called "print30", because "print" is a reserved word in 2.6):

```
from print30 import print30
print30(1, 2, 3)
print30(1, 2, 3, sep='')                # Suppress separator
print30(1, 2, 3, sep='...')
print30(1, [2], (3,), sep='...')        # Various object types

print30(4, 5, 6, sep='', end='')        # Suppress newline
print30(7, 8, 9)
print30()                               # Add newline (or blank line)

import sys
print30(1, 2, 3, sep='??', end='.\n', file=sys.stderr)     # Redirect to file
```

When run under 2.6, we get the same results as 3.0's print function:

```
C:\misc> c:\python26\python testprint30.py
1 2 3
123
1...2...3
1...[2]...(3,)
4567 8 9

1??2??3.
```

Although pointless in 3.0, the results are the same when run there. As usual, the generality of Python's design allows us to prototype or develop concepts in the Python
language itself. In this case, argument-matching tools are as flexible in Python code as
they are in Python's internal implementation.

Using Keyword-Only Arguments

It's interesting to notice that this example could be coded with Python 3.0 keyword-only arguments, described earlier in this chapter, to automatically validate configuration arguments:

```
# Use keyword-only args

def print30(*args, sep=' ', end='\n', file=sys.stdout):
    output = ''
    first  = True
    for arg in args:
        output += ('' if first else sep) + str(arg)
        first = False
    file.write(output + end)
```

This version works the same as the original, and it's a prime example of how keyword-only arguments come in handy. The original version assumes that all positional arguments are to be printed, and all keywords are for options only. That's almost sufficient, but any extra keyword arguments are silently ignored. A call like the following, for instance, will generate an exception with the keyword-only form:

```
>>> print30(99, name='bob')
TypeError: print30() got an unexpected keyword argument 'name'
```

but will silently ignore the name argument in the original version. To detect superfluous keywords manually, we could use dict.pop() to delete fetched entries, and check if the dictionary is not empty. Here is an equivalent to the keyword-only version:

```
# Use keyword args deletion with defaults

def print30(*args, **kargs):
    sep  = kargs.pop('sep', ' ')
    end  = kargs.pop('end', '\n')
    file = kargs.pop('file', sys.stdout)
    if kargs: raise TypeError('extra keywords: %s' % kargs)
    output = ''
    first  = True
    for arg in args:
        output += ('' if first else sep) + str(arg)
        first = False
    file.write(output + end)
```

This works as before, but it now catches extraneous keyword arguments, too:

```
>>> print30(99, name='bob')
TypeError: extra keywords: {'name': 'bob'}
```

This version of the function runs under Python 2.6, but it requires four more lines of code than the keyword-only version. Unfortunately, the extra code is required in this case—the keyword-only version only works on 3.0, which negates most of the reason that I wrote this example in the first place (a 3.0 emulator that only works on 3.0 isn't incredibly useful!). In programs written to run on 3.0, though, keyword-only arguments can simplify a specific category of functions that accept both arguments and options. For another example of 3.0 keyword-only arguments, be sure to see the upcoming iteration timing case study in Chapter 20.

Why You Will Care: Keyword Arguments

As you can probably tell, advanced argument-matching modes can be complex. They are also entirely optional; you can get by with just simple positional matching, and it's probably a good idea to do so when you're starting out. However, because some Python tools make use of them, some general knowledge of these modes is important.

For example, keyword arguments play an important role in `tkinter`, the de facto standard GUI API for Python (this module's name is `Tkinter` in Python 2.6). We touch on `tkinter` only briefly at various points in this book, but in terms of its call patterns, keyword arguments set configuration options when GUI components are built. For instance, a call of the form:

```
from tkinter import *
widget = Button(text="Press me", command=someFunction)
```

creates a new button and specifies its text and callback function, using the `text` and `command` keyword arguments. Since the number of configuration options for a widget can be large, keyword arguments let you pick and choose which to apply. Without them, you might have to either list all the possible options by position or hope for a judicious positional argument defaults protocol that would handle every possible option arrangement.

Many built-in functions in Python expect us to use keywords for usage-mode options as well, which may or may not have defaults. As we learned in Chapter 8, for instance, the `sorted` built-in:

```
sorted(iterable, key=None, reverse=False)
```

expects us to pass an iterable object to be sorted, but also allows us to pass in optional keyword arguments to specify a dictionary sort key and a reversal flag, which default to `None` and `False`, respectively. Since we normally don't use these options, they may be omitted to use defaults.

Chapter Summary

In this chapter, we studied the second of two key concepts related to functions: *arguments* (how objects are passed into a function). As we learned, arguments are passed into a function by assignment, which means by object reference, which really means

---

by pointer. We also studied some more advanced extensions, including default and keyword arguments, tools for using arbitrarily many arguments, and keyword-only arguments in 3.0. Finally, we saw how mutable arguments can exhibit the same behavior as other shared references to objects—unless the object is explicitly copied when it's sent in, changing a passed-in mutable in a function can impact the caller.

The next chapter continues our look at functions by exploring some more advanced function-related ideas: function annotations, `lambda`s, and functional tools such as `map` and `filter`. Many of these concepts stem from the fact that functions are normal objects in Python, and so support some advanced and very flexible processing modes. Before diving into those topics, however, take this chapter's quiz to review the argument ideas we've studied here.

Test Your Knowledge: Quiz

1. What is the output of the following code, and why?

   ```
   >>> def func(a, b=4, c=5):
   ...     print(a, b, c)
   ...
   >>> func(1, 2)
   ```

2. What is the output of this code, and why?

   ```
   >>> def func(a, b, c=5):
   ...     print(a, b, c)
   ...
   >>> func(1, c=3, b=2)
   ```

3. How about this code: what is its output, and why?

   ```
   >>> def func(a, *pargs):
   ...     print(a, pargs)
   ...
   >>> func(1, 2, 3)
   ```

4. What does this code print, and why?

   ```
   >>> def func(a, **kargs):
   ...     print(a, kargs)
   ...
   >>> func(a=1, c=3, b=2)
   ```

5. One last time: what is the output of this code, and why?

   ```
   >>> def func(a, b, c=3, d=4): print(a, b, c, d)
   ...
   >>> func(1, *(5,6))
   ```

6. Name three or more ways that functions can communicate results to a caller.

Test Your Knowledge: Answers

1. The output here is '1 2 5', because 1 and 2 are passed to a and b by position, and c is omitted in the call and defaults to 5.

2. The output this time is '1 2 3': 1 is passed to a by position, and b and c are passed 2 and 3 by name (the left-to-right order doesn't matter when keyword arguments are used like this).

3. This code prints '1 (2, 3)', because 1 is passed to a and the *pargs collects the remaining positional arguments into a new tuple object. We can step through the extra positional arguments tuple with any iteration tool (e.g., for arg in pargs: ...).

4. This time the code prints '1 {'c': 3, 'b': 2}', because 1 is passed to a by name and the **kargs collects the remaining keyword arguments into a dictionary. We could step through the extra keyword arguments dictionary by key with any iteration tool (e.g., for key in kargs: ...).

5. The output here is '1 5 6 4': 1 matches a by position, 5 and 6 match b and c by *name positionals (6 overrides c's default), and d defaults to 4 because it was not passed a value.

6. Functions can send back results with return statements, by changing passed-in mutable arguments, and by setting global variables. Globals are generally frowned upon (except for very special cases, like multithreaded programs) because they can make code more difficult to understand and use. return statements are usually best, but changing mutables is fine, if expected. Functions may also communicate with system devices such as files and sockets, but these are beyond our scope here.

## CHAPTER 19

Advanced Function Topics

This chapter introduces a collection of more advanced function-related topics: recursive functions, function attributes and annotations, the `lambda` expression, and functional programming tools such as `map` and `filter`. These are all somewhat advanced tools that, depending on your job description, you may not encounter on a regular basis. Because of their roles in some domains, though, a basic understanding can be useful; `lambda`s, for instance, are regular customers in GUIs.

Part of the art of using functions lies in the interfaces between them, so we will also explore some general function design principles here. The next chapter continues this advanced theme with an exploration of generator functions and expressions and a revival of list comprehensions in the context of the functional tools we will study here.

Function Design Concepts

Now that we've had a chance to study function basics in Python, let's begin this chapter with a few words of context. When you start using functions in earnest, you're faced with choices about how to glue components together—for instance, how to decompose a task into purposeful functions (known as *cohesion*), how your functions should communicate (called *coupling*), and so on. You also need to take into account concepts such as the size of your functions, because they directly impact code usability. Some of this falls into the category of structured analysis and design, but it applies to Python code as to any other.

We introduced some ideas related to function and module coupling in the Chapter 17 when studying scopes, but here is a review of a few general guidelines for function beginners:

- **Coupling: use arguments for inputs and return for outputs**. Generally, you should strive to make a function independent of things outside of it. Arguments and `return` statements are often the best ways to isolate external dependencies to a small number of well-known places in your code.

- **Coupling: use global variables only when truly necessary**. Global variables (i.e., names in the enclosing module) are usually a poor way for functions to communicate. They can create dependencies and timing issues that make programs difficult to debug and change.

- **Coupling: don't change mutable arguments unless the caller expects it**. Functions can change parts of passed-in mutable objects, but (as with global variables) this creates lots of coupling between the caller and callee, which can make a function too specific and brittle.

- **Cohesion: each function should have a single, unified purpose**. When designed well, each of your functions should do one thing—something you can summarize in a simple declarative sentence. If that sentence is very broad (e.g., "this function implements my whole program"), or contains lots of conjunctions (e.g., "this function gives employee raises *and* submits a pizza order"), you might want to think about splitting it into separate and simpler functions. Otherwise, there is no way to reuse the code behind the steps mixed together in the function.

- **Size: each function should be relatively small**. This naturally follows from the preceding goal, but if your functions start spanning multiple pages on your display, it's probably time to split them. Especially given that Python code is so concise to begin with, a long or deeply nested function is often a symptom of design problems. Keep it simple, and keep it short.

- **Coupling: avoid changing variables in another module file directly**. We introduced this concept in Chapter 17, and we'll revisit it in the next part of the book when we focus on modules. For reference, though, remember that changing variables across file boundaries sets up a coupling between modules similar to how global variables couple functions—the modules become difficult to understand and reuse. Use accessor functions whenever possible, instead of direct assignment statements.

Figure 19-1 summarizes the ways functions can talk to the outside world; inputs may come from items on the left side, and results may be sent out in any of the forms on the right. Good function designers prefer to use only arguments for inputs and `return` statements for outputs, whenever possible.

Of course, there are plenty of exceptions to the preceding design rules, including some related to Python's OOP support. As you'll see in Part VI, Python classes *depend* on changing a passed-in mutable object—class functions set attributes of an automatically passed-in argument called `self` to change per-object state information (e.g., `self.name='bob'`). Moreover, if classes are not used, global variables are often the most straightforward way for functions in modules to retain state between calls. Side effects are dangerous only if they're unexpected.

In general though, you should strive to minimize external dependencies in functions and other program components. The more *self-contained* a function is, the easier it will be to understand, reuse, and modify.

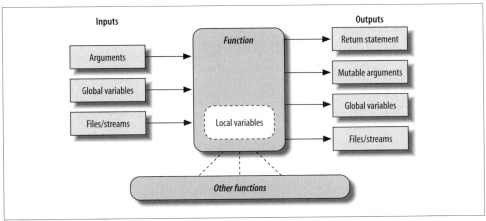

Figure 19-1. Function execution environment. Functions may obtain input and produce output in a variety of ways, though functions are usually easier to understand and maintain if you use arguments for input and return statements and anticipated mutable argument changes for output. In Python 3, outputs may also take the form of declared nonlocal names that exist in an enclosing function scope.

Recursive Functions

While discussing scope rules near the start of Chapter 17, we briefly noted that Python supports *recursive functions*—functions that call themselves either directly or indirectly in order to loop. Recursion is a somewhat advanced topic, and it's relatively rare to see in Python. Still, it's a useful technique to know about, as it allows programs to traverse structures that have arbitrary and unpredictable shapes. Recursion is even an alternative for simple loops and iterations, though not necessarily the simplest or most efficient one.

Summation with Recursion

Let's look at some examples. To sum a list (or other sequence) of numbers, we can either use the built-in sum function or write a more custom version of our own. Here's what a custom summing function might look like when coded with recursion:

```
>>> def mysum(L):
...     if not L:
...         return 0
...     else:
...         return L[0] + mysum(L[1:])        # Call myself

>>> mysum([1, 2, 3, 4, 5])
15
```

At each level, this function calls itself recursively to compute the sum of the rest of the list, which is later added to the item at the front. The recursive loop ends and zero is returned when the list becomes empty. When using recursion like this, each open level of call to the function has its own copy of the function's local scope on the runtime call stack—here, that means L is different in each level.

If this is difficult to understand (and it often is for new programmers), try adding a print of L to the function and run it again, to trace the current list at each call level:

```
>>> def mysum(L):
...     print(L)                           # Trace recursive levels
...     if not L:                          # L shorter at each level
...         return 0
...     else:
...         return L[0] + mysum(L[1:])
...
>>> mysum([1, 2, 3, 4, 5])
[1, 2, 3, 4, 5]
[2, 3, 4, 5]
[3, 4, 5]
[4, 5]
[5]
[]
15
```

As you can see, the list to be summed grows smaller at each recursive level, until it becomes empty—the termination of the recursive loop. The sum is computed as the recursive calls unwind.

Coding Alternatives

Interestingly, we can also use Python's if/else ternary expression (described in Chapter 12) to save some code real-estate here. We can also generalize for any summable type (which is easier if we assume at least one item in the input, as we did in Chapter 18's minimum value example) and use Python 3.0's extended sequence assignment to make the first/rest unpacking simpler (as covered in Chapter 11):

```
def mysum(L):
    return 0 if not L else L[0] + mysum(L[1:])          # Use ternary expression

def mysum(L):
    return L[0] if len(L) == 1 else L[0] + mysum(L[1:])  # Any type, assume one

def mysum(L):
    first, *rest = L
    return first if not rest else first + mysum(rest)    # Use 3.0 ext seq assign
```

The latter two of these fail for empty lists but allow for sequences of any object type that supports +, not just numbers:

```
>>> mysum([1])                              # mysum([]) fails in last 2
1
>>> mysum([1, 2, 3, 4, 5])
15
>>> mysum(('s', 'p', 'a', 'm'))             # But various types now work
'spam'
```

```
>>> mysum(['spam', 'ham', 'eggs'])
'spamhameggs'
```

If you study these three variants, you'll find that the latter two also work on a single string argument (e.g., mysum ('spam')), because strings are sequences of one-character strings; the third variant works on arbitrary iterables, including open input files, but the others do not because they index; and the function header def mysum(first, * rest), although similar to the third variant, wouldn't work at all, because it expects individual arguments, not a single iterable.

Keep in mind that recursion can be direct, as in the examples so far, or *indirect*, as in the following (a function that calls another function, which calls back to its caller). The net effect is the same, though there are two function calls at each level instead of one:

```
>>> def mysum(L):
...         if not L: return 0
...         return nonempty(L)              # Call a function that calls me
...
>>> def nonempty(L):
...         return L[0] + mysum(L[1:])      # Indirectly recursive
...
>>> mysum([1.1, 2.2, 3.3, 4.4])
11.0
```

Loop Statements Versus Recursion

Though recursion works for summing in the prior sections' examples, it's probably overkill in this context. In fact, recursion is not used nearly as often in Python as in more esoteric languages like Prolog or Lisp, because Python emphasizes simpler procedural statements like loops, which are usually more natural. The while, for example, often makes things a bit more concrete, and it doesn't require that a function be defined to allow recursive calls:

```
>>> L = [1, 2, 3, 4, 5]
>>> sum = 0
>>> while L:
...         sum += L[0]
...         L = L[1:]
...
>>> sum
15
```

Better yet, for loops iterate for us automatically, making recursion largely extraneous in most cases (and, in all likelihood, less efficient in terms of memory space and execution time):

```
>>> L = [1, 2, 3, 4, 5]
>>> sum = 0
>>> for x in L: sum += x
...
>>> sum
15
```

With looping statements, we don't require a fresh copy of a local scope on the call stack for each iteration, and we avoid the speed costs associated with function calls in general. (Stay tuned for Chapter 20's timer case study for ways to compare the execution times of alternatives like these.)

Handling Arbitrary Structures

On the other hand, recursion (or equivalent explicit stack-based algorithms, which we'll finesse here) can be required to traverse arbitrarily shaped structures. As a simple example of recursion's role in this context, consider the task of computing the sum of all the numbers in a nested sublists structure like this:

```
[1, [2, [3, 4], 5], 6, [7, 8]]          # Arbitrarily nested sublists
```

Simple looping statements won't work here because this not a linear iteration. Nested looping statements do not suffice either, because the sublists may be nested to arbitrary depth and in an arbitrary shape. Instead, the following code accommodates such general nesting by using recursion to visit sublists along the way:

```
def sumtree(L):
    tot = 0
    for x in L:                          # For each item at this level
        if not isinstance(x, list):
            tot += x                     # Add numbers directly
        else:
            tot += sumtree(x)            # Recur for sublists
    return tot

L = [1, [2, [3, 4], 5], 6, [7, 8]]       # Arbitrary nesting
print(sumtree(L))                        # Prints 36


# Pathological cases

print(sumtree([1, [2, [3, [4, [5]]]]]))  # Prints 15 (right-heavy)

print(sumtree([[[[[1], 2], 3], 4], 5]))  # Prints 15 (left-heavy)
```

Trace through the test cases at the bottom of this script to see how recursion traverses their nested lists. Although this example is artificial, it is representative of a larger class of programs; inheritance trees and module import chains, for example, can exhibit similarly general structures. In fact, we will use recursion again in such roles in more realistic examples later in this book:

- In Chapter 24's *reloadall.py*, to traverse import chains
- In Chapter 28's *classtree.py*, to traverse class inheritance trees
- In Chapter 30's *lister.py*, to traverse class inheritance trees again

Although you should generally prefer looping statements to recursion for linear iterations on the grounds of simplicity and efficiency, we'll find that recursion is essential in scenarios like those in these later examples.

Moreover, you sometimes need to be aware of the potential of *unintended* recursion in your programs. As you'll also see later in the book, some operator overloading methods in classes such as __setattr__ and __getattribute__ have the potential to recursively loop if used incorrectly. Recursion is a powerful tool, but it tends to be best when expected!

Function Objects: Attributes and Annotations

Python functions are more flexible than you might think. As we've seen in this part of the book, functions in Python are much more than code-generation specifications for a compiler—Python functions are full-blown *objects*, stored in pieces of memory all their own. As such, they can be freely passed around a program and called indirectly. They also support operations that have little to do with calls at all—attribute storage and annotation.

Indirect Function Calls

Because Python functions are objects, you can write programs that process them generically. Function objects may be assigned to other names, passed to other functions, embedded in data structures, returned from one function to another, and more, as if they were simple numbers or strings. Function objects also happen to support a special operation: they can be called by listing arguments in parentheses after a function expression. Still, functions belong to the same general category as other objects.

We've seen some of these generic use cases for functions in earlier examples, but a quick review helps to underscore the object model. For example, there's really nothing special about the name used in a def statement: it's just a variable assigned in the current scope, as if it had appeared on the left of an = sign. After a def runs, the function name is simply a reference to an object—you can *reassign* that object to other names freely and call it through any reference:

```
>>> def echo(message):            # Name echo assigned to function object
...     print(message)
...
>>> echo('Direct call')           # Call object through original name
Direct call

>>> x = echo                      # Now x references the function too
>>> x('Indirect call!')           # Call object through name by adding ()
Indirect call!
```

Because arguments are passed by assigning objects, it's just as easy to *pass* functions to other functions as arguments. The callee may then call the passed-in function just by adding arguments in parentheses:

```
>>> def indirect(func, arg):
...     func(arg)                      # Call the passed-in object by adding ()
...
>>> indirect(echo, 'Argument call!')   # Pass the function to another function
Argument call!
```

You can even stuff function objects into data structures, as though they were integers or strings. The following, for example, *embeds* the function twice in a list of tuples, as a sort of actions table. Because Python compound types like these can contain any sort of object, there's no special case here, either:

```
>>> schedule = [ (echo, 'Spam!'), (echo, 'Ham!') ]
>>> for (func, arg) in schedule:
...     func(arg)                      # Call functions embedded in containers
...
Spam!
Ham!
```

This code simply steps through the schedule list, calling the echo function with one argument each time through (notice the tuple-unpacking assignment in the for loop header, introduced in Chapter 13). As we saw in Chapter 17's examples, functions can also be created and *returned* for use elsewhere:

```
>>> def make(label):                   # Make a function but don't call it
...     def echo(message):
...         print(label + ':' + message)
...     return echo
...
>>> F = make('Spam')                   # Label in enclosing scope is retained
>>> F('Ham!')                          # Call the function that make returned
Spam:Ham!
>>> F('Eggs!')
Spam:Eggs!
```

Python's universal object model and lack of type declarations make for an incredibly flexible programming language.

Function Introspection

Because they are objects, we can also process functions with normal object tools. In fact, functions are more flexible than you might expect. For instance, once we make a function, we can call it as usual:

```
>>> def func(a):
...     b = 'spam'
...     return b * a
...
>>> func(8)
'spamspamspamspamspamspamspamspam'
```

But the call expression is just one operation defined to work on function objects. We can also inspect their attributes generically (the following is run in Python 3.0, but 2.6 results are similar):

```
>>> func.__name__
'func'
>>> dir(func)
['__annotations__', '__call__', '__class__', '__closure__', '__code__',
...more omitted...
'__repr__', '__setattr__', '__sizeof__', '__str__', '__subclasshook__']
```

Introspection tools allow us to explore implementation details too—functions have attached *code objects*, for example, which provide details on aspects such as the functions' local variables and arguments:

```
>>> func.__code__
<code object func at 0x0257C9B0, file "<stdin>", line 1>

>>> dir(func.__code__)
['__class__', '__delattr__', '__doc__', '__eq__', '__format__', '__ge__',
...more omitted...
'co_argcount', 'co_cellvars', 'co_code', 'co_consts', 'co_filename',
'co_firstlineno', 'co_flags', 'co_freevars', 'co_kwonlyargcount', 'co_lnotab',
'co_name', 'co_names', 'co_nlocals', 'co_stacksize', 'co_varnames']

>>> func.__code__.co_varnames
('a', 'b')
>>> func.__code__.co_argcount
1
```

Tool writers can make use of such information to manage functions (in fact, we will too in Chapter 38, to implement validation of function arguments in decorators).

Function Attributes

Function objects are not limited to the system-defined attributes listed in the prior section, though. As we learned in Chapter 17, it's possible to attach arbitrary user-defined attributes to them as well:

```
>>> func
<function func at 0x0257C738>
>>> func.count = 0
>>> func.count += 1
>>> func.count
1
>>> func.handles = 'Button-Press'
>>> func.handles
'Button-Press'
>>> dir(func)
['__annotations__', '__call__', '__class__', '__closure__', '__code__',
...more omitted...
'__str__', '__subclasshook__', 'count', 'handles']
```

As we saw in that chapter, such attributes can be used to attach *state information* to function objects directly, instead of using other techniques such as globals, nonlocals, and classes. Unlike nonlocals, such attributes are accessible anywhere the function itself is. In a sense, this is also a way to emulate "static locals" in other languages—variables whose names are local to a function, but whose values are retained after a function exits. Attributes are related to objects instead of scopes, but the net effect is similar.

Function Annotations in 3.0

In Python 3.0 (but not 2.6), it's also possible to attach *annotation information*— arbitrary user-defined data about a function's arguments and result—to a function object. Python provides special syntax for specifying annotations, but it doesn't do anything with them itself; annotations are completely optional, and when present are simply attached to the function object's __annotations__ attribute for use by other tools.

We met Python 3.0's keyword-only arguments in the prior chapter; annotations generalize function header syntax further. Consider the following nonannotated function, which is coded with three arguments and returns a result:

```
>>> def func(a, b, c):
...     return a + b + c
...
>>> func(1, 2, 3)
6
```

Syntactically, function annotations are coded in def header lines, as arbitrary expressions associated with arguments and return values. For arguments, they appear after a colon immediately following the argument's name; for return values, they are written after a -> following the arguments list. This code, for example, annotates all three of the prior function's arguments, as well as its return value:

```
>>> def func(a: 'spam', b: (1, 10), c: float) -> int:
...     return a + b + c
...
>>> func(1, 2, 3)
6
```

Calls to an annotated function work as usual, but when annotations are present Python collects them in a *dictionary* and attaches it to the function object itself. Argument names become keys, the return value annotation is stored under key "return" if coded, and the values of annotation keys are assigned to the results of the annotation expressions:

```
>>> func.__annotations__
{'a': 'spam', 'c': <class 'float'>, 'b': (1, 10), 'return': <class 'int'>}
```

Because they are just Python objects attached to a Python object, annotations are straightforward to process. The following annotates just two of three arguments and steps through the attached annotations generically:

```
>>> def func(a: 'spam', b, c: 99):
...     return a + b + c
...
>>> func(1, 2, 3)
6
>>> func.__annotations__
{'a': 'spam', 'c': 99}

>>> for arg in func.__annotations__:
...     print(arg, '=>', func.__annotations__[arg])
...
a => spam
c => 99
```

There are two fine points to note here. First, you can still use *defaults* for arguments if you code annotations—the annotation (and its : character) appear before the default (and its = character). In the following, for example, a: 'spam' = 4 means that argument a defaults to 4 and is annotated with the string 'spam':

```
>>> def func(a: 'spam' = 4, b: (1, 10) = 5, c: float = 6) -> int:
...     return a + b + c
...
>>> func(1, 2, 3)
6
>>> func()                      # 4 + 5 + 6  (all defaults)
15
>>> func(1, c=10)               # 1 + 5 + 10  (keywords work normally)
16
>>> func.__annotations__
{'a': 'spam', 'c': <class 'float'>, 'b': (1, 10), 'return': <class 'int'>}
```

Second, note that the *blank spaces* in the prior example are all optional—you can use spaces between components in function headers or not, but omitting them might degrade your code's readability to some observers:

```
>>> def func(a:'spam'=4, b:(1,10)=5, c:float=6)->int:
...     return a + b + c
...
>>> func(1, 2)                  # 1 + 2 + 6
9
>>> func.__annotations__
{'a': 'spam', 'c': <class 'float'>, 'b': (1, 10), 'return': <class 'int'>}
```

Annotations are a new feature in 3.0, and some of their potential uses remain to be uncovered. It's easy to imagine annotations being used to specify constraints for argument types or values, though, and larger APIs might use this feature as a way to register function interface information. In fact, we'll see a potential application in Chapter 38, where we'll look at annotations as an alternative to *function decorator arguments* (a more general concept in which information is coded outside the function header and so is not limited to a single role). Like Python itself, annotation is a tool whose roles are shaped by your imagination.

Finally, note that annotations work only in `def` statements, not `lambda` expressions, because `lambda`'s syntax already limits the utility of the functions it defines. Coincidentally, this brings us to our next topic.

Anonymous Functions: lambda

Besides the `def` statement, Python also provides an expression form that generates function objects. Because of its similarity to a tool in the Lisp language, it's called `lambda`.* Like `def`, this expression creates a function to be called later, but it returns the function instead of assigning it to a name. This is why `lambda`s are sometimes known as *anonymous* (i.e., unnamed) functions. In practice, they are often used as a way to inline a function definition, or to defer execution of a piece of code.

lambda Basics

The `lambda`'s general form is the keyword `lambda`, followed by one or more arguments (exactly like the arguments list you enclose in parentheses in a `def` header), followed by an expression after a colon:

```
lambda argument1, argument2,... argumentN :expression using arguments
```

Function objects returned by running `lambda` expressions work exactly the same as those created and assigned by `def`s, but there are a few differences that make `lambda`s useful in specialized roles:

- **lambda is an expression, not a statement**. Because of this, a `lambda` can appear in places a `def` is not allowed by Python's syntax—inside a list literal or a function call's arguments, for example. As an expression, `lambda` returns a value (a new function) that can optionally be assigned a name. In contrast, the `def` statement always assigns the new function to the name in the header, instead of returning it as a result.

- **lambda's body is a single expression, not a block of statements**. The `lambda`'s body is similar to what you'd put in a `def` body's `return` statement; you simply type the result as a naked expression, instead of explicitly returning it. Because it is limited to an expression, a `lambda` is less general than a `def`—you can only squeeze so much logic into a `lambda` body without using statements such as `if`. This is by design, to limit program nesting: `lambda` is designed for coding simple functions, and `def` handles larger tasks.

---

* The `lambda` tends to intimidate people more than it should. This reaction seems to stem from the name "lambda" itself—a name that comes from the Lisp language, which got it from lambda calculus, which is a form of symbolic logic. In Python, though, it's really just a keyword that introduces the expression syntactically. Obscure mathematical heritage aside, `lambda` is simpler to use than you may think.

Apart from those distinctions, `def`s and `lambda`s do the same sort of work. For instance, we've seen how to make a function with a `def` statement:

```
>>> def func(x, y, z): return x + y + z
...
>>> func(2, 3, 4)
9
```

But you can achieve the same effect with a `lambda` expression by explicitly assigning its result to a name through which you can later call the function:

```
>>> f = lambda x, y, z: x + y + z
>>> f(2, 3, 4)
9
```

Here, `f` is assigned the function object the `lambda` expression creates; this is how `def` works, too, but its assignment is automatic.

Defaults work on `lambda` arguments, just like in a `def`:

```
>>> x = (lambda a="fee", b="fie", c="foe": a + b + c)
>>> x("wee")
'weefiefoe'
```

The code in a `lambda` body also follows the same scope lookup rules as code inside a `def`. `lambda` expressions introduce a local scope much like a nested `def`, which automatically sees names in enclosing functions, the module, and the built-in scope (via the LEGB rule):

```
>>> def knights():
...     title = 'Sir'
...     action = (lambda x: title + ' ' + x)     # Title in enclosing def
...     return action                            # Return a function
...
>>> act = knights()
>>> act('robin')
'Sir robin'
```

In this example, prior to Release 2.2, the value for the name `title` would typically have been passed in as a default argument value instead; flip back to the scopes coverage in Chapter 17 if you've forgotten why.

Why Use lambda?

Generally speaking, `lambda`s come in handy as a sort of function shorthand that allows you to embed a function's definition within the code that uses it. They are entirely optional (you can always use `def`s instead), but they tend to be simpler coding constructs in scenarios where you just need to embed small bits of executable code.

For instance, we'll see later that callback handlers are frequently coded as inline `lambda` expressions embedded directly in a registration call's arguments list, instead of being defined with a `def` elsewhere in a file and referenced by name (see the sidebar "Why You Will Care: Callbacks" on page 481 for an example).

`lambda`s are also commonly used to code *jump tables*, which are lists or dictionaries of actions to be performed on demand. For example:

```
L = [lambda x: x ** 2,          # Inline function definition
     lambda x: x ** 3,
     lambda x: x ** 4]          # A list of 3 callable functions

for f in L:
    print(f(2))                 # Prints 4, 8, 16

print(L[0](3))                  # Prints 9
```

The `lambda` expression is most useful as a shorthand for `def`, when you need to stuff small pieces of executable code into places where statements are illegal syntactically. This code snippet, for example, builds up a list of three functions by embedding `lambda` expressions inside a list literal; a `def` won't work inside a list literal like this because it is a statement, not an expression. The equivalent `def` coding would require temporary function names and function definitions outside the context of intended use:

```
def f1(x): return x ** 2
def f2(x): return x ** 3        # Define named functions
def f3(x): return x ** 4

L = [f1, f2, f3]                # Reference by name

for f in L:
    print(f(2))                 # Prints 4, 8, 16

print(L[0](3))                  # Prints 9
```

In fact, you can do the same sort of thing with dictionaries and other data structures in Python to build up more general sorts of action tables. Here's another example to illustrate, at the interactive prompt:

```
>>> key = 'got'
>>> {'already': (lambda: 2 + 2),
...  'got':     (lambda: 2 * 4),
...  'one':     (lambda: 2 ** 6)}[key]()
8
```

Here, when Python makes the temporary dictionary, each of the nested `lambda`s generates and leaves behind a function to be called later. Indexing by key fetches one of those functions, and parentheses force the fetched function to be called. When coded this way, a dictionary becomes a more general multiway branching tool than what I could show you in Chapter 12's coverage of `if` statements.

To make this work without `lambda`, you'd need to instead code three `def` statements somewhere else in your file, outside the dictionary in which the functions are to be used, and reference the functions by name:

```
>>> def f1(): return 2 + 2
...
>>> def f2(): return 2 * 4
...
```

```
>>> def f3(): return 2 ** 6
...
>>> key = 'one'
>>> {'already': f1, 'got': f2, 'one': f3}[key]()
64
```

This works, too, but your defs may be arbitrarily far away in your file, even if they are just little bits of code. The *code proximity* that lambdas provide is especially useful for functions that will only be used in a single context—if the three functions here are not useful anywhere else, it makes sense to embed their definitions within the dictionary as lambdas. Moreover, the def form requires you to make up names for these little functions that may clash with other names in this file (perhaps unlikely, but always possible).

lambdas also come in handy in function-call argument lists as a way to inline temporary function definitions not used anywhere else in your program; we'll see some examples of such other uses later in this chapter, when we study map.

How (Not) to Obfuscate Your Python Code

The fact that the body of a lambda has to be a single expression (not a series of statements) would seem to place severe limits on how much logic you can pack into a lambda. If you know what you're doing, though, you can code most statements in Python as expression-based equivalents.

For example, if you want to print from the body of a lambda function, simply say print(X) in Python 3.X (where this becomes a call expression instead of a statement), but say sys.stdout.write(str(x)+'\n') in either Python 2.X or 3.X to make sure it's an expression portably (recall from Chapter 11 that this is what print really does). Similarly, to nest logic in a lambda, you can use the if/else ternary expression introduced in Chapter 12, or the equivalent but trickier and/or combination also described there. As you learned earlier, the following statement:

```
if a:
    b
else:
    c
```

can be emulated by either of these roughly equivalent expressions:

```
b if a else c
((a and b) or c)
```

Because expressions like these can be placed inside a lambda, they may be used to implement selection logic within a lambda function:

```
>>> lower = (lambda x, y: x if x < y else y)
>>> lower('bb', 'aa')
'aa'
>>> lower('aa', 'bb')
'aa'
```

Furthermore, if you need to perform loops within a lambda, you can also embed things like map calls and list comprehension expressions (tools we met in earlier chapters and will revisit in this and the next chapter):

```
>>> import sys
>>> showall = lambda x: list(map(sys.stdout.write, x))        # Use list in 3.0

>>> t = showall(['spam\n', 'toast\n', 'eggs\n'])
spam
toast
eggs

>>> showall = lambda x: [sys.stdout.write(line) for line in x]

>>> t = showall(('bright\n', 'side\n', 'of\n', 'life\n'))
bright
side
of
life
```

Now that I've shown you these tricks, I am required by law to ask you to please only use them as a last resort. Without due care, they can lead to unreadable (a.k.a. *obfuscated*) Python code. In general, simple is better than complex, explicit is better than implicit, and full statements are better than arcane expressions. That's why lambda is limited to expressions. If you have larger logic to code, use def; lambda is for small pieces of inline code. On the other hand, you may find these techniques useful in moderation.

Nested lambdas and Scopes

lambdas are the main beneficiaries of nested function scope lookup (the E in the LEGB scope rule we studied in Chapter 17). In the following, for example, the lambda appears inside a def—the typical case—and so can access the value that the name x had in the enclosing function's scope at the time that the enclosing function was called:

```
>>> def action(x):
...      return (lambda y: x + y)        # Make and return function, remember x
...
>>> act = action(99)
>>> act
<function <lambda> at 0x00A16A88>
>>> act(2)                               # Call what action returned
101
```

What wasn't illustrated in the prior discussion of nested function scopes is that a lambda also has access to the names in any enclosing lambda. This case is somewhat obscure, but imagine if we recoded the prior def with a lambda:

```
>>> action = (lambda x: (lambda y: x + y))
>>> act = action(99)
>>> act(3)
102
```

```
>>> ((lambda x: (lambda y: x + y))(99))(4)
103
```

Here, the nested `lambda` structure makes a function that makes a function when called. In both cases, the nested `lambda`'s code has access to the variable `x` in the enclosing `lambda`. This works, but it's fairly convoluted code; in the interest of readability, nested `lambda`s are generally best avoided.

Why You Will Care: Callbacks

Another very common application of `lambda` is to define inline callback functions for Python's `tkinter` GUI API (this module is named `Tkinter` in Python 2.6). For example, the following creates a button that prints a message on the console when pressed, assuming `tkinter` is available on your computer (it is by default on Windows and other OSs):

```
import sys
from tkinter import Button, mainloop      # Tkinter in 2.6
x = Button(
        text ='Press me',
        command=(lambda:sys.stdout.write('Spam\n')))
x.pack()
mainloop()
```

Here, the callback handler is registered by passing a function generated with a `lambda` to the `command` keyword argument. The advantage of `lambda` over `def` here is that the code that handles a button press is right here, embedded in the button-creation call.

In effect, the `lambda` *defers* execution of the handler until the event occurs: the `write` call happens on button presses, not when the button is created.

Because the nested function scope rules apply to `lambda`s as well, they are also easier to use as callback handlers, as of Python 2.2—they automatically see names in the functions in which they are coded and no longer require passed-in defaults in most cases. This is especially handy for accessing the special `self` instance argument that is a local variable in enclosing class method functions (more on classes in Part VI):

```
class MyGui:
    def makewidgets(self):
        Button(command=(lambda: self.onPress("spam")))
    def onPress(self, message):
        ...use message...
```

In prior releases, even `self` had to be passed in to a `lambda` with defaults.

Mapping Functions over Sequences: map

One of the more common things programs do with lists and other sequences is apply an operation to each item and collect the results. For instance, updating all the counters in a list can be done easily with a `for` loop:

```
>>> counters = [1, 2, 3, 4]
>>>
>>> updated = []
>>> for x in counters:
...     updated.append(x + 10)            # Add 10 to each item
...
>>> updated
[11, 12, 13, 14]
```

But because this is such a common operation, Python actually provides a built-in that does most of the work for you. The map function applies a passed-in function to each item in an iterable object and returns a list containing all the function call results. For example:

```
>>> def inc(x): return x + 10            # Function to be run
...
>>> list(map(inc, counters))             # Collect results
[11, 12, 13, 14]
```

We met map briefly in Chapters 13 and 14, as a way to apply a built-in function to items in an iterable. Here, we make better use of it by passing in a user-defined function to be applied to each item in the list—map calls inc on each list item and collects all the return values into a new list. Remember that map is an iterable in Python 3.0, so a list call is used to force it to produce all its results for display here; this isn't necessary in 2.6.

Because map expects a function to be passed in, it also happens to be one of the places where lambda commonly appears:

```
>>> list(map((lambda x: x + 3), counters))     # Function expression
[4, 5, 6, 7]
```

Here, the function adds 3 to each item in the counters list; as this little function isn't needed elsewhere, it was written inline as a lambda. Because such uses of map are equivalent to for loops, with a little extra code you can always code a general mapping utility yourself:

```
>>> def mymap(func, seq):
...     res = []
...     for x in seq: res.append(func(x))
...     return res
```

Assuming the function inc is still as it was when it was shown previously, we can map it across a sequence with the built-in or our equivalent:

```
>>> list(map(inc, [1, 2, 3]))            # Built-in is an iterator
[11, 12, 13]
>>> mymap(inc, [1, 2, 3])                # Ours builds a list (see generators)
[11, 12, 13]
```

However, as map is a built-in, it's always available, always works the same way, and has some performance benefits (as we'll prove in the next chapter, it's usually faster than a manually coded for loop). Moreover, map can be used in more advanced ways than shown here. For instance, given multiple sequence arguments, it sends items taken from sequences in parallel as distinct arguments to the function:

```
>>> pow(3, 4)                               # 3**4
81
>>> list(map(pow, [1, 2, 3], [2, 3, 4]))    # 1**2, 2**3, 3**4
[1, 8, 81]
```

With multiple sequences, `map` expects an N-argument function for N sequences. Here, the `pow` function takes two arguments on each call—one from each sequence passed to `map`. It's not much extra work to simulate this multiple-sequence generality in code, too, but we'll postpone doing so until later in the next chapter, after we've met some additional iteration tools.

The `map` call is similar to the list comprehension expressions we studied in Chapter 14 and will meet again in the next chapter, but `map` applies a *function* call to each item instead of an arbitrary *expression*. Because of this limitation, it is a somewhat less general tool. However, in some cases `map` may be faster to run than a list comprehension (e.g., when mapping a built-in function), and it may also require less coding.

Functional Programming Tools: filter and reduce

The `map` function is the simplest representative of a class of Python built-ins used for *functional programming*—tools that apply functions to sequences and other iterables. Its relatives filter out items based on a test function (`filter`) and apply functions to pairs of items and running results (`reduce`). Because they return iterables, `range` and `filter` both require `list` calls to display all their results in 3.0. For example, the following `filter` call picks out items in a sequence that are greater than zero:

```
>>> list(range(-5, 5))                          # An iterator in 3.0
[-5, -4, -3, -2, -1, 0, 1, 2, 3, 4]

>>> list(filter((lambda x: x > 0), range(-5, 5)))   # An iterator in 3.0
[1, 2, 3, 4]
```

Items in the sequence or iterable for which the function returns a true result are added to the result list. Like `map`, this function is roughly equivalent to a `for` loop, but it is built-in and fast:

```
>>> res = []
>>> for x in range(-5, 5):
...        if x > 0:
...            res.append(x)
...
>>> res
[1, 2, 3, 4]
```

`reduce`, which is a simple built-in function in 2.6 but lives in the `functools` module in 3.0, is more complex. It accepts an iterator to process, but it's not an iterator itself—it returns a single result. Here are two **reduce** calls that compute the sum and product of the items in a list:

```
>>> from functools import reduce        # Import in 3.0, not in 2.6

>>> reduce((lambda x, y: x + y), [1, 2, 3, 4])
10
>>> reduce((lambda x, y: x * y), [1, 2, 3, 4])
24
```

At each step, **reduce** passes the current sum or product, along with the next item from the list, to the passed-in `lambda` function. By default, the first item in the sequence initializes the starting value. To illustrate, here's the `for` loop equivalent to the first of these calls, with the addition hardcoded inside the loop:

```
>>> L = [1,2,3,4]
>>> res = L[0]
>>> for x in L[1:]:
...     res = res + x
...
>>> res
10
```

Coding your own version of **reduce** is actually fairly straightforward. The following function emulates most of the built-in's behavior and helps demystify its operation in general:

```
>>> def myreduce(function, sequence):
...     tally = sequence[0]
...     for next in sequence[1:]:
...         tally = function(tally, next)
...     return tally
...
>>> myreduce((lambda x, y: x + y), [1, 2, 3, 4, 5])
15
>>> myreduce((lambda x, y: x * y), [1, 2, 3, 4, 5])
120
```

The built-in **reduce** also allows an optional third argument placed before the items in the sequence to serve as a default result when the sequence is empty, but we'll leave this extension as a suggested exercise.

If this coding technique has sparked your interest, you might also be interested in the standard library `operator` module, which provides functions that correspond to built-in expressions and so comes in handy for some uses of functional tools (see Python's library manual for more details on this module):

```
>>> import operator, functools
>>> functools.reduce(operator.add, [2, 4, 6])        # Function-based +
12
>>> functools.reduce((lambda x, y: x + y), [2, 4, 6])
12
```

Together with `map`, `filter` and `reduce` support powerful functional programming techniques. Some observers might also extend the functional programming toolset in Python to include `lambda`, discussed earlier, as well as list comprehensions—a topic we will return to in the next chapter.

Chapter Summary

This chapter took us on a tour of advanced function-related concepts: recursive functions; function annotations; `lambda` expression functions; functional tools such as `map`, `filter`, and `reduce`; and general function design ideas. The next chapter continues the advanced topics motif with a look at generators and a reprisal of iterators and list comprehensions—tools that are just as related to functional programming as to looping statements. Before you move on, though, make sure you've mastered the concepts covered here by working through this chapter's quiz.

Test Your Knowledge: Quiz

1. How are `lambda` expressions and `def` statements related?
2. What's the point of using `lambda`?
3. Compare and contrast `map`, `filter`, and `reduce`.
4. What are function annotations, and how are they used?
5. What are recursive functions, and how are they used?
6. What are some general design guidelines for coding functions?

Test Your Knowledge: Answers

1. Both `lambda` and `def` create function objects to be called later. Because `lambda` is an expression, though, it returns a function object instead of assigning it to a name, and it can be used to nest a function definition in places where a `def` will not work syntactically. A `lambda` only allows for a single implicit return value expression, though; because it does not support a block of statements, it is not ideal for larger functions.

2. `lambda`s allow us to "inline" small units of executable code, defer its execution, and provide it with state in the form of default arguments and enclosing scope variables. Using a `lambda` is never required; you can always code a `def` instead and reference the function by name. `lambda`s come in handy, though, to embed small pieces of deferred code that are unlikely to be used elsewhere in a program. They commonly appear in callback-based program such as GUIs, and they have a natural affinity with function tools like `map` and `filter` that expect a processing function.

3. These three built-in functions all apply another function to items in a sequence (iterable) object and collect results. map passes each item to the function and collects all results, filter collects items for which the function returns a True value, and reduce computes a single value by applying the function to an accumulator and successive items. Unlike the other two, reduce is available in the functools module in 3.0, not the built-in scope.

4. Function annotations, available in 3.0 and later, are syntactic embellishments of a function's arguments and result, which are collected into a dictionary assigned to the function's __annotations__ attribute. Python places no semantic meaning on these annotations, but simply packages them for potential use by other tools.

5. Recursive functions call themselves either directly or indirectly in order to loop. They may be used to traverse arbitrarily shaped structures, but they can also be used for iteration in general (though the latter role is often more simply and efficiently coded with looping statements).

6. Functions should generally be small, as self-contained as possible, have a single unified purpose, and communicate with other components through input arguments and return values. They may use mutable arguments to communicate results too if changes are expected, and some types of programs imply other communication mechanisms.

## CHAPTER 20

Iterations and Comprehensions, Part 2

This chapter continues the advanced function topics theme, with a reprisal of the comprehension and iteration concepts introduced in Chapter 14. Because list comprehensions are as much related to the prior chapter's functional tools (e.g., `map` and `filter`) as they are to `for` loops, we'll revisit them in this context here. We'll also take a second look at iterators in order to study generator functions and their generator expression relatives—user-defined ways to produce results on demand.

Iteration in Python also encompasses user-defined classes, but we'll defer that final part of this story until Part VI, when we study operator overloading. As this is the last pass we'll make over built-in iteration tools, though, we will summarize the various tools we've met thus far, and time the relative performance of some of them. Finally, because this is the last chapter in the part of the book, we'll close with the usual sets of "gotchas" and exercises to help you start coding the ideas you've read about.

List Comprehensions Revisited: Functional Tools

In the prior chapter, we studied functional programming tools like `map` and `filter`, which map operations over sequences and collect results. Because this is such a common task in Python coding, Python eventually sprouted a new expression—the *list comprehension*—that is even more flexible than the tools we just studied. In short, list comprehensions apply an arbitrary *expression* to items in an iterable, rather than applying a function. As such, they can be more general tools.

We met list comprehensions in Chapter 14, in conjunction with looping statements. Because they're also related to functional programming tools like the `map` and `filter` calls, though, we'll resurrect the topic here for one last look. Technically, this feature is not tied to functions—as we'll see, list comprehensions can be a more general tool than `map` and `filter`—but it is sometimes best understood by analogy to function-based alternatives.

List Comprehensions Versus map

Let's work through an example that demonstrates the basics. As we saw in Chapter 7, Python's built-in ord function returns the ASCII integer code of a single character (the chr built-in is the converse—it returns the character for an ASCII integer code):

```
>>> ord('s')
115
```

Now, suppose we wish to collect the ASCII codes of *all* characters in an entire string. Perhaps the most straightforward approach is to use a simple for loop and append the results to a list:

```
>>> res = []
>>> for x in 'spam':
...     res.append(ord(x))
...
>>> res
[115, 112, 97, 109]
```

Now that we know about map, though, we can achieve similar results with a single function call without having to manage list construction in the code:

```
>>> res = list(map(ord, 'spam'))      # Apply function to sequence
>>> res
[115, 112, 97, 109]
```

However, we can get the same results from a list comprehension expression—while map maps a *function* over a sequence, list comprehensions map an *expression* over a sequence:

```
>>> res = [ord(x) for x in 'spam']     # Apply expression to sequence
>>> res
[115, 112, 97, 109]
```

List comprehensions collect the results of applying an arbitrary expression to a sequence of values and return them in a new list. Syntactically, list comprehensions are enclosed in square brackets (to remind you that they construct lists). In their simple form, within the brackets you code an expression that names a variable followed by what looks like a for loop header that names the same variable. Python then collects the expression's results for each iteration of the implied loop.

The effect of the preceding example is similar to that of the manual for loop and the map call. List comprehensions become more convenient, though, when we wish to apply an arbitrary expression to a sequence:

```
>>> [x ** 2 for x in range(10)]
[0, 1, 4, 9, 16, 25, 36, 49, 64, 81]
```

Here, we've collected the squares of the numbers 0 through 9 (we're just letting the interactive prompt print the resulting list; assign it to a variable if you need to retain it). To do similar work with a map call, we would probably need to invent a little function to implement the square operation. Because we won't need this function elsewhere,

---

we'd typically (but not necessarily) code it inline, with a `lambda`, instead of using a `def` statement elsewhere:

```
>>> list(map((lambda x: x ** 2), range(10)))
[0, 1, 4, 9, 16, 25, 36, 49, 64, 81]
```

This does the same job, and it's only a few keystrokes longer than the equivalent list comprehension. It's also only marginally more complex (at least, once you understand the `lambda`). For more advanced kinds of expressions, though, list comprehensions will often require considerably less typing. The next section shows why.

Adding Tests and Nested Loops: filter

List comprehensions are even more general than shown so far. For instance, as we learned in Chapter 14, you can code an `if` clause after the `for` to add selection logic. List comprehensions with `if` clauses can be thought of as analogous to the `filter` built-in discussed in the prior chapter—they skip sequence items for which the `if` clause is not true.

To demonstrate, here are both schemes picking up even numbers from 0 to 4; like the `map` list comprehension alternative of the prior section, the `filter` version here must invent a little `lambda` function for the test expression. For comparison, the equivalent `for` loop is shown here as well:

```
>>> [x for x in range(5) if x % 2 == 0]
[0, 2, 4]

>>> list(filter((lambda x: x % 2 == 0), range(5)))
[0, 2, 4]

>>> res = []
>>> for x in range(5):
...     if x % 2 == 0:
...         res.append(x)
...
>>> res
[0, 2, 4]
```

All of these use the modulus (remainder of division) operator, %, to detect even numbers: if there is no remainder after dividing a number by 2, it must be even. The `filter` call here is not much longer than the list comprehension either. However, we can combine an `if` clause and an arbitrary expression in our list comprehension, to give it the effect of a `filter` *and* a `map`, in a single expression:

```
>>> [x ** 2 for x in range(10) if x % 2 == 0]
[0, 4, 16, 36, 64]
```

This time, we collect the squares of the even numbers from 0 through 9: the `for` loop skips numbers for which the attached `if` clause on the right is false, and the expression on the left computes the squares. The equivalent `map` call would require a lot more work on our part—we would have to combine `filter` selections with `map` iteration, making for a noticeably more complex expression:

```
>>> list( map((lambda x: x**2), filter((lambda x: x % 2 == 0), range(10))) )
[0, 4, 16, 36, 64]
```

In fact, list comprehensions are more general still. You can code any number of nested `for` loops in a list comprehension, and each may have an optional associated `if` test. The general structure of list comprehensions looks like this:

```
[ expression for target1 in iterable1 [if condition1]
             for target2 in iterable2 [if condition2] ...
             for targetN in iterableN [if conditionN] ]
```

When `for` clauses are nested within a list comprehension, they work like equivalent nested `for` loop statements. For example, the following:

```
>>> res = [x + y for x in [0, 1, 2] for y in [100, 200, 300]]
>>> res
[100, 200, 300, 101, 201, 301, 102, 202, 302]
```

has the same effect as this substantially more verbose equivalent:

```
>>> res = []
>>> for x in [0, 1, 2]:
...     for y in [100, 200, 300]:
...         res.append(x + y)
...
>>> res
[100, 200, 300, 101, 201, 301, 102, 202, 302]
```

Although list comprehensions construct lists, remember that they can iterate over any sequence or other iterable type. Here's a similar bit of code that traverses strings instead of lists of numbers, and so collects concatenation results:

```
>>> [x + y for x in 'spam' for y in 'SPAM']
['sS', 'sP', 'sA', 'sM', 'pS', 'pP', 'pA', 'pM',
 'aS', 'aP', 'aA', 'aM', 'mS', 'mP', 'mA', 'mM']
```

Finally, here is a much more complex list comprehension that illustrates the effect of attached `if` selections on nested `for` clauses:

```
>>> [(x, y) for x in range(5) if x % 2 == 0 for y in range(5) if y % 2 == 1]
[(0, 1), (0, 3), (2, 1), (2, 3), (4, 1), (4, 3)]
```

This expression permutes even numbers from 0 through 4 with odd numbers from 0 through 4. The `if` clauses filter out items in each sequence iteration. Here is the equivalent statement-based code:

```
>>> res = []
>>> for x in range(5):
...     if x % 2 == 0:
...         for y in range(5):
...             if y % 2 == 1:
...                 res.append((x, y))
...
```

```
>>> res
[(0, 1), (0, 3), (2, 1), (2, 3), (4, 1), (4, 3)]
```

Recall that if you're confused about what a complex list comprehension does, you can always nest the list comprehension's `for` and `if` clauses inside each other (indenting successively further to the right) to derive the equivalent statements. The result is longer, but perhaps clearer.

The `map` and `filter` equivalent would be wildly complex and deeply nested, so I won't even try showing it here. I'll leave its coding as an exercise for Zen masters, ex-Lisp programmers, and the criminally insane....

List Comprehensions and Matrixes

Not all list comprehensions are so artificial, of course. Let's look at one more application to stretch a few synapses. One basic way to code matrixes (a.k.a. multidimensional arrays) in Python is with nested list structures. The following, for example, defines two 3 × 3 matrixes as lists of nested lists:

```
>>> M = [[1, 2, 3],
...      [4, 5, 6],
...      [7, 8, 9]]

>>> N = [[2, 2, 2],
...      [3, 3, 3],
...      [4, 4, 4]]
```

Given this structure, we can always index rows, and columns within rows, using normal index operations:

```
>>> M[1]
[4, 5, 6]

>>> M[1][2]
6
```

List comprehensions are powerful tools for processing such structures, though, because they automatically scan rows and columns for us. For instance, although this structure stores the matrix by rows, to collect the second column we can simply iterate across the rows and pull out the desired column, or iterate through positions in the rows and index as we go:

```
>>> [row[1] for row in M]
[2, 5, 8]

>>> [M[row][1] for row in (0, 1, 2)]
[2, 5, 8]
```

Given positions, we can also easily perform tasks such as pulling out a diagonal. The following expression uses `range` to generate the list of offsets and then indexes with the row and column the same, picking out `M[0][0]`, then `M[1][1]`, and so on (we assume the matrix has the same number of rows and columns):

```
>>> [M[i][i] for i in range(len(M))]
[1, 5, 9]
```

Finally, with a bit of creativity, we can also use list comprehensions to combine multiple matrixes. The following first builds a flat list that contains the result of multiplying the matrixes pairwise, and then builds a nested list structure having the same values by nesting list comprehensions:

```
>>> [M[row][col] * N[row][col] for row in range(3) for col in range(3)]
[2, 4, 6, 12, 15, 18, 28, 32, 36]

>>> [[M[row][col] * N[row][col] for col in range(3)] for row in range(3)]
[[2, 4, 6], [12, 15, 18], [28, 32, 36]]
```

This last expression works because the row iteration is an outer loop: for each row, it runs the nested column iteration to build up one row of the result matrix. It's equivalent to this statement-based code:

```
>>> res = []
>>> for row in range(3):
...     tmp = []
...     for col in range(3):
...         tmp.append(M[row][col] * N[row][col])
...     res.append(tmp)
...
>>> res
[[2, 4, 6], [12, 15, 18], [28, 32, 36]]
```

Compared to these statements, the list comprehension version requires only one line of code, will probably run substantially faster for large matrixes, and just might make your head explode! Which brings us to the next section.

Comprehending List Comprehensions

With such generality, list comprehensions can quickly become, well, incomprehensible, especially when nested. Consequently, my advice is typically to use simple for loops when getting started with Python, and map or comprehensions in isolated cases where they are easy to apply. The "keep it simple" rule applies here, as always: code conciseness is a much less important goal than code readability.

However, in this case, there is currently a substantial performance advantage to the extra complexity: based on tests run under Python today, map calls are roughly twice as fast as equivalent for loops, and list comprehensions are usually slightly faster than map calls.* This speed difference is generally due to the fact that map and list

---

* These performance generalizations can depend on call patterns, as well as changes and optimizations in Python itself. Recent Python releases have sped up the simple for loop statement, for example. Usually, though, list comprehensions are still substantially faster than for loops and even faster than map (though map can still win for built-in functions). To time these alternatives yourself, see the standard library's time module's time.clock and time.time calls, the newer timeit module added in Release 2.4, or this chapter's upcoming section "Timing Iteration Alternatives" on page 511.

comprehensions run at C language speed inside the interpreter, which is much faster than stepping through Python for loop code within the PVM.

Because for loops make logic more explicit, I recommend them in general on the grounds of simplicity. However, map and list comprehensions are worth knowing and using for simpler kinds of iterations, and if your application's speed is an important consideration. In addition, because map and list comprehensions are both expressions, they can show up syntactically in places that for loop statements cannot, such as in the bodies of lambda functions, within list and dictionary literals, and more. Still, you should try to keep your map calls and list comprehensions simple; for more complex tasks, use full statements instead.

Why You Will Care: List Comprehensions and map

Here's a more realistic example of list comprehensions and map in action (we solved this problem with list comprehensions in Chapter 14, but we'll revive it here to add map-based alternatives). Recall that the file readlines method returns lines with \n end-of-line characters at the ends:

```
>>> open('myfile').readlines()
['aaa\n', 'bbb\n', 'ccc\n']
```

If you don't want the end-of-line characters, you can slice them off all the lines in a single step with a list comprehension or a map call (map results are iterables in Python 3.0, so we must run them through list to see all their results at once):

```
>>> [line.rstrip() for line in open('myfile').readlines()]
['aaa', 'bbb', 'ccc']

>>> [line.rstrip() for line in open('myfile')]
['aaa', 'bbb', 'ccc']

>>> list(map((lambda line: line.rstrip()), open('myfile')))
['aaa', 'bbb', 'ccc']
```

The last two of these make use of *file iterators* (which essentially means that you don't need a method call to grab all the lines in iteration contexts such as these). The map call is slightly longer than the list comprehension, but neither has to manage result list construction explicitly.

A list comprehension can also be used as a sort of column projection operation. Python's standard SQL database API returns query results as a list of tuples much like the following—the list is the table, tuples are rows, and items in tuples are column values:

```
listoftuple = [('bob', 35, 'mgr'), ('mel', 40, 'dev')]
```

A for loop could pick up all the values from a selected column manually, but map and list comprehensions can do it in a single step, and faster:

```
>>> [age for (name, age, job) in listoftuple]
[35, 40]

>>> list(map((lambda row: row[1]), listoftuple))
[35, 40]
```

The first of these makes use of *tuple assignment* to unpack row tuples in the list, and the second uses indexing. In Python 2.6 (but not in 3.0—see the note on 2.6 argument unpacking in Chapter 18), map can use tuple unpacking on its argument, too:

```
# 2.6 only
>>> list(map((lambda (name, age, job): age), listoftuple))
[35, 40]
```

See other books and resources for more on Python's database API.

Beside the distinction between running functions versus expressions, the biggest difference between map and list comprehensions in Python 3.0 is that map is an *iterator*, generating results on demand; to achieve the same memory economy, list comprehensions must be coded as generator expressions (one of the topics of this chapter).

Iterators Revisited: Generators

Python today supports procrastination much more than it did in the past—it provides tools that produce results only when needed, instead of all at once. In particular, two language constructs delay result creation whenever possible:

- *Generator functions* are coded as normal def statements but use yield statements to return results one at a time, suspending and resuming their state between each.

- *Generator expressions* are similar to the list comprehensions of the prior section, but they return an object that produces results on demand instead of building a result list.

Because neither constructs a result list all at once, they save memory space and allow computation time to be split across result requests. As we'll see, both of these ultimately perform their delayed-results magic by implementing the *iteration protocol* we studied in Chapter 14.

Generator Functions: yield Versus return

In this part of the book, we've learned about coding normal functions that receive input parameters and send back a single result immediately. It is also possible, however, to write functions that may send back a value and later be resumed, picking up where they left off. Such functions are known as *generator functions* because they generate a sequence of values over time.

Generator functions are like normal functions in most respects, and in fact are coded with normal def statements. However, when created, they are automatically made to implement the iteration protocol so that they can appear in iteration contexts. We studied iterators in Chapter 14; here, we'll revisit them to see how they relate to generators.

State suspension

Unlike normal functions that return a value and exit, generator functions automatically suspend and resume their execution and state around the point of value generation. Because of that, they are often a useful alternative to both computing an entire series of values up front and manually saving and restoring state in classes. Because the state that generator functions retain when they are suspended includes their entire local scope, their local variables retain information and make it available when the functions are resumed.

The chief code difference between generator and normal functions is that a generator *yields* a value, rather than *returning* one—the `yield` statement suspends the function and sends a value back to the caller, but retains enough state to enable the function to resume from where it left off. When resumed, the function continues execution immediately after the last `yield` run. From the function's perspective, this allows its code to produce a series of values over time, rather than computing them all at once and sending them back in something like a list.

Iteration protocol integration

To truly understand generator functions, you need to know that they are closely bound up with the notion of the iteration protocol in Python. As we've seen, iterable objects define a `__next__` method, which either returns the next item in the iteration, or raises the special `StopIteration` exception to end the iteration. An object's iterator is fetched with the `iter` built-in function.

Python `for` loops, and all other iteration contexts, use this iteration protocol to step through a sequence or value generator, if the protocol is supported; if not, iteration falls back on repeatedly indexing sequences instead.

To support this protocol, functions containing a `yield` statement are compiled specially as *generators*. When called, they return a generator object that supports the iteration interface with an automatically created method named `__next__` to resume execution. Generator functions may also have a `return` statement that, along with falling off the end of the `def` block, simply terminates the generation of values—technically, by raising a `StopIteration` exception after any normal function exit actions. From the caller's perspective, the generator's `__next__` method resumes the function and runs until either the next `yield` result is returned or a `StopIteration` is raised.

The net effect is that generator functions, coded as `def` statements containing `yield` statements, are automatically made to support the iteration protocol and thus may be used in any iteration context to produce results over time and on demand.

As noted in Chapter 14, in Python 2.6 and earlier, iterable objects define a method named next instead of __next__. This includes the generator objects we are using here. In 3.0 this method is renamed to __next__. The next built-in function is provided as a convenience and portability tool: next(I) is the same as I.__next__() in 3.0 and I.next() in 2.6. Prior to 2.6, programs simply call I.next() instead to iterate manually.

Generator functions in action

To illustrate generator basics, let's turn to some code. The following code defines a generator function that can be used to generate the squares of a series of numbers over time:

```
>>> def gensquares(N):
...     for i in range(N):
...         yield i ** 2        # Resume here later
...
```

This function yields a value, and so returns to its caller, each time through the loop; when it is resumed, its prior state is restored and control picks up again immediately after the yield statement. For example, when it's used in the body of a for loop, control returns to the function after its yield statement each time through the loop:

```
>>> for i in gensquares(5):     # Resume the function
...     print(i, end=' : ')     # Print last yielded value
...
0 : 1 : 4 : 9 : 16 :
>>>
```

To end the generation of values, functions either use a return statement with no value or simply allow control to fall off the end of the function body.

If you want to see what is going on inside the for, call the generator function directly:

```
>>> x = gensquares(4)
>>> x
<generator object at 0x0086C378>
```

You get back a generator object that supports the iteration protocol we met in Chapter 14—the generator object has a __next__ method that starts the function, or resumes it from where it last yielded a value, and raises a StopIteration exception when the end of the series of values is reached. For convenience, the next(X) built-in calls an object's X.__next__() method for us:

```
>>> next(x)                     # Same as x.__next__() in 3.0
0
>>> next(x)                     # Use x.next() or next() in 2.6
1
>>> next(x)
4
>>> next(x)
9
>>> next(x)
```

```
Traceback (most recent call last):
...more text omitted...
StopIteration
```

As we learned in Chapter 14, for loops (and other iteration contexts) work with generators in the same way—by calling the __next__ method repeatedly, until an exception is caught. If the object to be iterated over does not support this protocol, for loops instead use the indexing protocol to iterate.

Note that in this example, we could also simply build the list of yielded values all at once:

```
>>> def buildsquares(n):
...     res = []
...     for i in range(n): res.append(i ** 2)
...     return res
...
>>> for x in buildsquares(5): print(x, end=' : ')
...
0 : 1 : 4 : 9 : 16 :
```

For that matter, we could use any of the for loop, map, or list comprehension techniques:

```
>>> for x in [n ** 2 for n in range(5)]:
...     print(x, end=' : ')
...
0 : 1 : 4 : 9 : 16 :

>>> for x in map((lambda n: n ** 2), range(5)):
...     print(x, end=' : ')
...
0 : 1 : 4 : 9 : 16 :
```

However, generators can be better in terms of both memory use and performance. They allow functions to avoid doing all the work up front, which is especially useful when the result lists are large or when it takes a lot of computation to produce each value. Generators distribute the time required to produce the series of values among loop iterations.

Moreover, for more advanced uses, generators can provide a simpler alternative to manually saving the state between iterations in class objects—with generators, variables accessible in the function's scopes are saved and restored automatically.[†] We'll discuss class-based iterators in more detail in Part VI.

[†] Interestingly, generator functions are also something of a "poor man's" *multithreading* device—they interleave a function's work with that of its caller, by dividing its operation into steps run between yields. Generators are not threads, though: the program is explicitly directed to and from the function within a single thread of control. In one sense, threading is more general (producers can run truly independently and post results to a queue), but generators may be simpler to code. See the second footnote in Chapter 17 for a brief introduction to Python multithreading tools. Note that because control is routed explicitly at yield and next calls, generators are also not *backtracking*, but are more strongly related to *coroutines*—formal concepts that are both beyond this chapter's scope.

Extended generator function protocol: send versus next

In Python 2.5, a send method was added to the generator function protocol. The send method advances to the next item in the series of results, just like __next__, but also provides a way for the caller to communicate with the generator, to affect its operation.

Technically, yield is now an expression form that returns the item passed to send, not a statement (though it can be called either way—as yield X, or A = (yield X)). The expression must be enclosed in parentheses unless it's the only item on the right side of the assignment statement. For example, X = yield Y is OK, as is X = (yield Y) + 42.

When this extra protocol is used, values are sent into a generator G by calling G.send(*value*). The generator's code is then resumed, and the yield expression in the generator returns the value passed to send. If the regular G.__next__() method (or its next(G) equivalent) is called to advance, the yield simply returns None. For example:

```
>>> def gen():
...     for i in range(10):
...         X = yield i
...         print(X)
...
>>> G = gen()
>>> next(G)                   # Must call next() first, to start generator
0
>>> G.send(77)                # Advance, and send value to yield expression
77
1
>>> G.send(88)
88
2
>>> next(G)                   # next() and X.__next__() send None
None
3
```

The send method can be used, for example, to code a generator that its caller can terminate by sending a termination code, or redirect by passing a new position. In addition, generators in 2.5 also support a throw(*type*) method to raise an exception inside the generator at the latest yield, and a close method that raises a special Generator Exit exception inside the generator to terminate the iteration. These are advanced features that we won't delve into in more detail here; see reference texts and Python's standard manuals for more information.

Note that while Python 3.0 provides a next(X) convenience built-in that calls the X.__next__() method of an object, other generator methods, like send, must be called as methods of generator objects directly (e.g., G.send(X)). This makes sense if you realize that these extra methods are implemented on built-in generator objects only, whereas the __next__ method applies to all iterable objects (both built-in types and user-defined classes).

Generator Expressions: Iterators Meet Comprehensions

In all recent versions of Python, the notions of iterators and list comprehensions are combined in a new feature of the language, *generator expressions*. Syntactically, generator expressions are just like normal list comprehensions, but they are enclosed in parentheses instead of square brackets:

```
>>> [x ** 2 for x in range(4)]          # List comprehension: build a list
[0, 1, 4, 9]

>>> (x ** 2 for x in range(4))          # Generator expression: make an iterable
<generator object at 0x011DC648>
```

In fact, at least on a function basis, coding a list comprehension is essentially the same as wrapping a generator expression in a `list` built-in call to force it to produce all its results in a list at once:

```
>>> list(x ** 2 for x in range(4))      # List comprehension equivalence
[0, 1, 4, 9]
```

Operationally, however, generator expressions are very different—instead of building the result list in memory, they return a generator object, which in turn supports the *iteration protocol* to yield one piece of the result list at a time in any iteration context:

```
>>> G = (x ** 2 for x in range(4))
>>> next(G)
0
>>> next(G)
1
>>> next(G)
4
>>> next(G)
9
>>> next(G)

Traceback (most recent call last):
...more text omitted...
StopIteration
```

We don't typically see the `next` iterator machinery under the hood of a generator expression like this because `for` loops trigger it for us automatically:

```
>>> for num in (x ** 2 for x in range(4)):
...     print('%s, %s' % (num, num / 2.0))
...
0, 0.0
1, 0.5
4, 2.0
9, 4.5
```

As we've already learned, every iteration context does this, including the `sum`, `map`, and `sorted` built-in functions; list comprehensions; and other iteration contexts we learned about in Chapter 14, such as the `any`, `all`, and `list` built-in functions.

Notice that the parentheses are not required around a generator expression if they are the sole item enclosed in other parentheses, like those of a function call. Extra parentheses are required, however, in the second call to sorted:

```
>>> sum(x ** 2 for x in range(4))
14

>>> sorted(x ** 2 for x in range(4))
[0, 1, 4, 9]

>>> sorted((x ** 2 for x in range(4)), reverse=True)
[9, 4, 1, 0]

>>> import math
>>> list( map(math.sqrt, (x ** 2 for x in range(4))) )
[0.0, 1.0, 2.0, 3.0]
```

Generator expressions are primarily a memory-space optimization—they do not require the entire result list to be constructed all at once, as the square-bracketed list comprehension does. They may also run slightly slower in practice, so they are probably best used only for very large result sets. A more authoritative statement about performance, though, will have to await the timing script we'll code later in this chapter.

Generator Functions Versus Generator Expressions

Interestingly, the same iteration can often be coded with either a generator function or a generator expression. The following *generator expression*, for example, repeats each character in a string four times:

```
>>> G = (c * 4 for c in 'SPAM')     # Generator expression
>>> list(G)                          # Force generator to produce all results
['SSSS', 'PPPP', 'AAAA', 'MMMM']
```

The equivalent *generator function* requires slightly more code, but as a multistatement function it will be able to code more logic and use more state information if needed:

```
>>> def timesfour(S):                # Generator function
...     for c in S:
...         yield c * 4
...
>>> G = timesfour('spam')
>>> list(G)                          # Iterate automatically
['ssss', 'pppp', 'aaaa', 'mmmm']
```

Both expressions and functions support both automatic and manual iteration—the prior list call iterates automatically, and the following iterate manually:

```
>>> G = (c * 4 for c in 'SPAM')
>>> I = iter(G)                      # Iterate manually
>>> next(I)
'SSSS'
>>> next(I)
'PPPP'
```

```
>>> G = timesfour('spam')
>>> I = iter(G)
>>> next(I)
'ssss'
>>> next(I)
'pppp'
```

Notice that we make new generators here to iterate again—as explained in the next section, generators are one-shot iterators.

Generators Are Single-Iterator Objects

Both generator functions and generator expressions are their own iterators and thus support just *one active iteration*—unlike some built-in types, you can't have multiple iterators of either positioned at different locations in the set of results. For example, using the prior section's generator expression, a generator's iterator is the generator itself (in fact, calling `iter` on a generator is a no-op):

```
>>> G = (c * 4 for c in 'SPAM')
>>> iter(G) is G                        # My iterator is myself: G has __next__
True
```

If you iterate over the results stream manually with multiple iterators, they will all point to the same position:

```
>>> G = (c * 4 for c in 'SPAM')         # Make a new generator
>>> I1 = iter(G)                        # Iterate manually
>>> next(I1)
'SSSS'
>>> next(I1)
'PPPP'
>>> I2 = iter(G)                        # Second iterator at same position!
>>> next(I2)
'AAAA'
```

Moreover, once any iteration runs to completion, all are exhausted—we have to make a new generator to start again:

```
>>> list(I1)                            # Collect the rest of I1's items
['MMMM']
>>> next(I2)                            # Other iterators exhausted too
StopIteration

>>> I3 = iter(G)                        # Ditto for new iterators
>>> next(I3)
StopIteration

>>> I3 = iter(c * 4 for c in 'SPAM')    # New generator to start over
>>> next(I3)
'SSSS'
```

The same holds true for generator functions—the following def statement-based equivalent supports just one active iterator and is exhausted after one pass:

```
>>> def timesfour(S):
...     for c in S:
...         yield c * 4
...
>>> G = timesfour('spam')          # Generator functions work the same way
>>> iter(G) is G
True
>>> I1, I2 = iter(G), iter(G)
>>> next(I1)
'ssss'
>>> next(I1)
'pppp'
>>> next(I2)                       # I2 at same position as I1
'aaaa'
```

This is different from the behavior of some built-in types, which support multiple iterators and passes and reflect their in-place changes in active iterators:

```
>>> L = [1, 2, 3, 4]
>>> I1, I2 = iter(L), iter(L)
>>> next(I1)
1
>>> next(I1)
2
>>> next(I2)                       # Lists support multiple iterators
1
>>> del L[2:]                      # Changes reflected in iterators
>>> next(I1)
StopIteration
```

When we begin coding class-based iterators in Part VI, we'll see that it's up to us to decide how many iterations we wish to support for our objects, if any.

Emulating zip and map with Iteration Tools

To demonstrate the power of iteration tools in action, let's turn to some more advanced use case examples. Once you know about list comprehensions, generators, and other iteration tools, it turns out that emulating many of Python's functional built-ins is both straightforward and instructive.

For example, we've already seen how the built-in zip and map functions combine iterables and project functions across them, respectively. With multiple sequence arguments, map projects the function across items taken from each sequence in much the same way that zip pairs them up:

```
>>> S1 = 'abc'
>>> S2 = 'xyz123'
>>> list(zip(S1, S2))              # zip pairs items from iterables
[('a', 'x'), ('b', 'y'), ('c', 'z')]
```

```
# zip pairs items, truncates at shortest

>>> list(zip([-2, -1, 0, 1, 2]))          # Single sequence: 1-ary tuples
[(-2,), (-1,), (0,), (1,), (2,)]

>>> list(zip([1, 2, 3], [2, 3, 4, 5]))    # N sequences: N-ary tuples
[(1, 2), (2, 3), (3, 4)]

# map passes paired itenms to a function, truncates

>>> list(map(abs, [-2, -1, 0, 1, 2]))     # Single sequence: 1-ary function
[2, 1, 0, 1, 2]

>>> list(map(pow, [1, 2, 3], [2, 3, 4, 5]))   # N sequences: N-ary function
[1, 8, 81]
```

Though they're being used for different purposes, if you study these examples long enough, you might notice a relationship between `zip` results and mapped function arguments that our next example can exploit.

Coding your own map(func, ...)

Although the `map` and `zip` built-ins are fast and convenient, it's always possible to emulate them in code of our own. In the preceding chapter, for example, we saw a function that emulated the `map` built-in for a single sequence argument. It doesn't take much more work to allow for multiple sequences, as the built-in does:

```
# map(func, seqs...) workalike with zip

def mymap(func, *seqs):
    res = []
    for args in zip(*seqs):
        res.append(func(*args))
    return res

print(mymap(abs, [-2, -1, 0, 1, 2]))
print(mymap(pow, [1, 2, 3], [2, 3, 4, 5]))
```

This version relies heavily upon the special `*args` argument-passing syntax—it collects multiple sequence (really, iterable) arguments, unpacks them as `zip` arguments to combine, and then unpacks the paired `zip` results as arguments to the passed-in function. That is, we're using the fact that the zipping is essentially a nested operation in mapping. The test code at the bottom applies this to both one and two sequences to produce this output (the same we would get with the built-in `map`):

```
[2, 1, 0, 1, 2]
[1, 8, 81]
```

Really, though, the prior version exhibits the classic *list comprehension pattern*, building a list of operation results within a `for` loop. We can code our map more concisely as an equivalent one-line list comprehension:

```
# Using a list comprehension

def mymap(func, *seqs):
    return [func(*args) for args in zip(*seqs)]

print(mymap(abs, [-2, -1, 0, 1, 2]))
print(mymap(pow, [1, 2, 3], [2, 3, 4, 5]))
```

When this is run the result is the same as before, but the code is more concise and might run faster (more on performance in the section "Timing Iteration Alternatives" on page 511). Both of the preceding `mymap` versions build result lists all at once, though, and this can waste memory for larger lists. Now that we know about *generator functions and expressions*, it's simple to recode both these alternatives to produce results on demand instead:

```
# Using generators: yield and (...)

def mymap(func, *seqs):
    res = []
    for args in zip(*seqs):
        yield func(*args)

def mymap(func, *seqs):
    return (func(*args) for args in zip(*seqs))
```

These versions produce the same results but return generators designed to support the iteration protocol—the first yields one result at a time, and the second returns a generator expression's result to do the same. They produce the same results if we wrap them in `list` calls to force them to produce their values all at once:

```
print(list(mymap(abs, [-2, -1, 0, 1, 2])))
print(list(mymap(pow, [1, 2, 3], [2, 3, 4, 5])))
```

No work is really done here until the `list` calls force the generators to run, by activating the iteration protocol. The generators returned by these functions themselves, as well as that returned by the Python 3.0 flavor of the `zip` built-in they use, produce results only on demand.

Coding your own zip(...) and map(None, ...)

Of course, much of the magic in the examples shown so far lies in their use of the `zip` built-in to pair arguments from multiple sequences. You'll also note that our `map` workalikes are really emulating the behavior of the Python 3.0 `map`—they truncate at the length of the shortest sequence, and they do not support the notion of padding results when lengths differ, as `map` does in Python 2.X with a `None` argument:

```
C:\misc> c:\python26\python
>>> map(None, [1, 2, 3], [2, 3, 4, 5])
[(1, 2), (2, 3), (3, 4), (None, 5)]
>>> map(None, 'abc', 'xyz123')
[('a', 'x'), ('b', 'y'), ('c', 'z'), (None, '1'), (None, '2'), (None, '3')]
```

Using iteration tools, we can code workalikes that emulate both truncating `zip` and 2.6's padding `map`—these turn out to be nearly the same in code:

```
# zip(seqs...) and 2.6 map(None, seqs...) workalikes

def myzip(*seqs):
    seqs = [list(S) for S in seqs]
    res  = []
    while all(seqs):
        res.append(tuple(S.pop(0) for S in seqs))
    return res

def mymapPad(*seqs, pad=None):
    seqs = [list(S) for S in seqs]
    res  = []
    while any(seqs):
        res.append(tuple((S.pop(0) if S else pad) for S in seqs))
    return res

S1, S2 = 'abc', 'xyz123'
print(myzip(S1, S2))
print(mymapPad(S1, S2))
print(mymapPad(S1, S2, pad=99))
```

Both of the functions coded here work on any type of iterable object, because they run their arguments through the `list` built-in to force result generation (e.g., files would work as arguments, in addition to sequences like strings). Notice the use of the `all` and `any` built-ins here—these return `True` if all and any items in an iterable are `True` (or equivalently, nonempty), respectively. These built-ins are used to stop looping when any or all of the listified arguments become empty after deletions.

Also note the use of the Python 3.0 *keyword-only* argument, `pad`; unlike the 2.6 `map`, our version will allow any pad object to be specified (if you're using 2.6, use a `**kargs` form to support this option instead; see Chapter 18 for details). When these functions are run, the following results are printed—a `zip`, and two padding `map`s:

```
[('a', 'x'), ('b', 'y'), ('c', 'z')]
[('a', 'x'), ('b', 'y'), ('c', 'z'), (None, '1'), (None, '2'), (None, '3')]
[('a', 'x'), ('b', 'y'), ('c', 'z'), (99, '1'), (99, '2'), (99, '3')]
```

These functions aren't amenable to list comprehension translation because their loops are too specific. As before, though, while our `zip` and `map` workalikes currently build and return result lists, it's just as easy to turn them into *generators* with `yield` so that they each return one piece of their result set at a time. The results are the same as before, but we need to use `list` again to force the generators to yield their values for display:

```
# Using generators: yield

def myzip(*seqs):
    seqs = [list(S) for S in seqs]
    while all(seqs):
        yield tuple(S.pop(0) for S in seqs)
```

```
def mymapPad(*seqs, pad=None):
    seqs = [list(S) for S in seqs]
    while any(seqs):
        yield tuple((S.pop(0) if S else pad) for S in seqs)

S1, S2 = 'abc', 'xyz123'
print(list(myzip(S1, S2)))
print(list(mymapPad(S1, S2)))
print(list(mymapPad(S1, S2, pad=99)))
```

Finally, here's an alternative implementation of our `zip` and `map` emulators—rather than deleting arguments from lists with the `pop` method, the following versions do their job by calculating the minimum and maximum *argument lengths*. Armed with these lengths, it's easy to code nested list comprehensions to step through argument index ranges:

```
# Alternate implementation with lengths

def myzip(*seqs):
    minlen = min(len(S) for S in seqs)
    return [tuple(S[i] for S in seqs) for i in range(minlen)]

def mymapPad(*seqs, pad=None):
    maxlen = max(len(S) for S in seqs)
    index  = range(maxlen)
    return [tuple((S[i] if len(S) > i else pad) for S in seqs) for i in index]

S1, S2 = 'abc', 'xyz123'
print(myzip(S1, S2))
print(mymapPad(S1, S2))
print(mymapPad(S1, S2, pad=99))
```

Because these use `len` and indexing, they assume that arguments are sequences or similar, not arbitrary iterables. The outer comprehensions here step through argument index ranges, and the inner comprehensions (passed to `tuple`) step through the passed-in sequences to pull out arguments in parallel. When they're run, the results are as before.

Most strikingly, generators and iterators seem to run rampant in this example. The arguments passed to `min` and `max` are generator expressions, which run to completion before the nested comprehensions begin iterating. Moreover, the nested list comprehensions employ two levels of delayed evaluation—the Python 3.0 `range` built-in is an iterable, as is the generator expression argument to `tuple`.

In fact, no results are produced here until the square brackets of the list comprehensions request values to place in the result list—they force the comprehensions and generators to run. To turn these functions themselves into generators instead of list builders, use parentheses instead of square brackets again. Here's the case for our `zip`:

```
# Using generators: (...)

def myzip(*seqs):
    minlen = min(len(S) for S in seqs)
```

```
    return (tuple(S[i] for S in seqs) for i in range(minlen))

print(list(myzip(S1, S2)))
```

In this case, it takes a `list` call to activate the generators and iterators to produce their results. Experiment with these on your own for more details. Developing further coding alternatives is left as a suggested exercise (see also the sidebar "Why You Will Care: One-Shot Iterations" for investigation of one such option).

Why You Will Care: One-Shot Iterations

In Chapter 14, we saw how some built-ins (like `map`) support only a single traversal and are empty after it occurs, and I promised to show you an example of how that can become subtle but important in practice. Now that we've studied a few more iteration topics, I can make good on this promise. Consider the following clever alternative coding for this chapter's `zip` emulation examples, adapted from one in Python's manuals:

```
def myzip(*args):
    iters = map(iter, args)
    while iters:
        res = [next(i) for i in iters]
        yield tuple(res)
```

Because this code uses `iter` and `next`, it works on any type of iterable. Note that there is no reason to catch the `StopIteration` raised by the `next(it)` inside the comprehension here when any one of the arguments' iterators is exhausted—allowing it to pass ends this generator function and has the same effect that a `return` statement would. The `while iters:` suffices to loop if at least one argument is passed, and avoids an infinite loop otherwise (the list comprehension would always return an empty list).

This code works fine in Python 2.6 as is:

```
>>> list(myzip('abc', 'lmnop'))
[('a', 'l'), ('b', 'm'), ('c', 'n')]
```

But it falls into an infinite loop and fails in Python 3.0, because the 3.0 `map` returns a one-shot iterable object instead of a list as in 2.6. In 3.0, as soon as we've run the list comprehension inside the loop once, `iters` will be empty (and `res` will be `[]`) forever. To make this work in 3.0, we need to use the `list` built-in function to create an object that can support multiple iterations:

```
def myzip(*args):
    iters = list(map(iter, args))
    ...rest as is...
```

Run this on your own to trace its operation. The lesson here: wrapping `map` calls in `list` calls in 3.0 is not just for display!

Value Generation in Built-in Types and Classes

Finally, although we've focused on coding value generators ourselves in this section, don't forget that many built-in types behave in similar ways—as we saw in Chapter 14, for example, dictionaries have iterators that produce keys on each iteration:

```
>>> D = {'a':1, 'b':2, 'c':3}
>>> x = iter(D)
>>> next(x)
'a'
>>> next(x)
'c'
```

Like the values produced by handcoded generators, dictionary keys may be iterated over both manually and with automatic iteration tools including **for** loops, map calls, list comprehensions, and the many other contexts we met in Chapter 14:

```
>>> for key in D:
...     print(key, D[key])
...
a 1
c 3
b 2
```

As we've also seen, for file iterators, Python simply loads lines from the file on demand:

```
>>> for line in open('temp.txt'):
...     print(line, end='')
...
Tis but
a flesh wound.
```

While built-in type iterators are bound to a specific type of value generation, the concept is similar to generators we code with expressions and functions. Iteration contexts like **for** loops accept any iterable, whether user-defined or built-in.

Although beyond the scope of this chapter, it is also possible to implement arbitrary user-defined generator objects with *classes* that conform to the iteration protocol. Such classes define a special __iter__ method run by the iter built-in function that returns an object having a __next__ method run by the next built-in function (a __getitem__ indexing method is also available as a fallback option for iteration).

The instance objects created from such a class are considered iterable and may be used in **for** loops and all other iteration contexts. With classes, though, we have access to richer logic and data structuring options than other generator constructs can offer.

The iterator story won't really be complete until we've seen how it maps to classes, too. For now, we'll have to settle for postponing its conclusion until we study class-based iterators in Chapter 29.

3.0 Comprehension Syntax Summary

We've been focusing on list comprehensions and generators in this chapter, but keep in mind that there are two other comprehension expression forms: set and dictionary comprehensions are also available as of Python 3.0. We met these briefly in Chapters 5 and 8, but with our new knowledge of comprehensions and generators, you should now be able to grasp these 3.0 extensions in full:

- For *sets*, the new literal form {1, 3, 2} is equivalent to set([1, 3, 2]), and the new set comprehension syntax {f(x) for x in S if P(x)} is like the generator expression set(f(x) for x in S if P(x)), where f(x) is an arbitrary expression.

- For *dictionaries*, the new dictionary comprehension syntax {key: val for (key, val) in zip(keys, vals)} works like the form dict(zip(keys, vals)), and {x: f(x) for x in items} is like the generator expression dict((x, f(x)) for x in items).

Here's a summary of all the comprehension alternatives in 3.0. The last two are new and are not available in 2.6:

```
>>> [x * x for x in range(10)]          # List comprehension: builds list
[0, 1, 4, 9, 16, 25, 36, 49, 64, 81]    # like list(generator expr)

>>> (x * x for x in range(10))          # Generator expression: produces items
<generator object at 0x009E7328>        # Parens are often optional

>>> {x * x for x in range(10)}          # Set comprehension, new in 3.0
{0, 1, 4, 81, 64, 9, 16, 49, 25, 36}    # {x, y} is a set in 3.0 too

>>> {x: x * x for x in range(10)}       # Dictionary comprehension, new in 3.0
{0: 0, 1: 1, 2: 4, 3: 9, 4: 16, 5: 25, 6: 36, 7: 49, 8: 64, 9: 81}
```

Comprehending Set and Dictionary Comprehensions

In a sense, set and dictionary comprehensions are just syntactic sugar for passing generator expressions to the type names. Because both accept any iterable, a generator works well here:

```
>>> {x * x for x in range(10)}          # Comprehension
{0, 1, 4, 81, 64, 9, 16, 49, 25, 36}
>>> set(x * x for x in range(10))       # Generator and type name
{0, 1, 4, 81, 64, 9, 16, 49, 25, 36}

>>> {x: x * x for x in range(10)}
{0: 0, 1: 1, 2: 4, 3: 9, 4: 16, 5: 25, 6: 36, 7: 49, 8: 64, 9: 81}
>>> dict((x, x * x) for x in range(10))
{0: 0, 1: 1, 2: 4, 3: 9, 4: 16, 5: 25, 6: 36, 7: 49, 8: 64, 9: 81}
```

As for list comprehensions, though, we can always build the result objects with manual code, too. Here are statement-based equivalents of the last two comprehensions:

```
>>> res = set()
>>> for x in range(10):                           # Set comprehension equivalent
...     res.add(x * x)
...
>>> res
{0, 1, 4, 81, 64, 9, 16, 49, 25, 36}

>>> res = {}
>>> for x in range(10):                           # Dict comprehension equivalent
...     res[x] = x * x
...
>>> res
{0: 0, 1: 1, 2: 4, 3: 9, 4: 16, 5: 25, 6: 36, 7: 49, 8: 64, 9: 81}
```

Notice that although both forms accept iterators, they have no notion of generating results on demand—both forms build objects all at once. If you mean to produce keys and values upon request, a generator expression is more appropriate:

```
>>> G = ((x, x * x) for x in range(10))
>>> next(G)
(0, 0)
>>> next(G)
(1, 1)
```

Extended Comprehension Syntax for Sets and Dictionaries

Like list comprehensions and generator expressions, both set and dictionary comprehensions support nested associated if clauses to filter items out of the result—the following collect squares of even items (i.e., items having no remainder for division by 2) in a range:

```
>>> [x * x for x in range(10) if x % 2 == 0]      # Lists are ordered
[0, 4, 16, 36, 64]
>>> {x * x for x in range(10) if x % 2 == 0}      # But sets are not
{0, 16, 4, 64, 36}
>>> {x: x * x for x in range(10) if x % 2 == 0}   # Neither are dict keys
{0: 0, 8: 64, 2: 4, 4: 16, 6: 36}
```

Nested for loops work as well, though the unordered and no-duplicates nature of both types of objects can make the results a bit less straightforward to decipher:

```
>>> [x + y for x in [1, 2, 3] for y in [4, 5, 6]]  # Lists keep duplicates
[5, 6, 7, 6, 7, 8, 7, 8, 9]
>>> {x + y for x in [1, 2, 3] for y in [4, 5, 6]}  # But sets do not
{8, 9, 5, 6, 7}
>>> {x: y for x in [1, 2, 3] for y in [4, 5, 6]}   # Neither do dict keys
{1: 6, 2: 6, 3: 6}
```

Like list comprehensions, the set and dictionary varieties can also iterate over any type of iterator—lists, strings, files, ranges, and anything else that supports the iteration protocol:

```
>>> {x + y for x in 'ab' for y in 'cd'}
{'bd', 'ac', 'ad', 'bc'}
```

```
>>> {x + y: (ord(x), ord(y)) for x in 'ab' for y in 'cd'}
{'bd': (98, 100), 'ac': (97, 99), 'ad': (97, 100), 'bc': (98, 99)}

>>> {k * 2 for k in ['spam', 'ham', 'sausage'] if k[0] == 's'}
{'sausagesausage', 'spamspam'}

>>> {k.upper(): k * 2 for k in ['spam', 'ham', 'sausage'] if k[0] == 's'}
{'SAUSAGE': 'sausagesausage', 'SPAM': 'spamspam'}
```

For more details, experiment with these tools on your own. They may or may not have a performance advantage over the generator or `for` loop alternatives, but we would have to time their performance explicitly to be sure—which seems a natural segue to the next section.

Timing Iteration Alternatives

We've met quite a few iteration alternatives in this book. To summarize, let's work through a larger case study that pulls together some of the things we've learned about iteration and functions.

I've mentioned a few times that list comprehensions have a speed performance advantage over `for` loop statements, and that `map` performance can be better or worse depending on call patterns. The generator expressions of the prior sections tend to be slightly slower than list comprehensions, though they minimize memory space requirements.

All that's true today, but relative performance can vary over time because Python's internals are constantly being changed and optimized. If you want to verify their performance for yourself, you need to time these alternatives on your own computer and your own version of Python.

Timing Module

Luckily, Python makes it easy to time code. To see how the iteration options stack up, let's start with a simple but general timer utility function coded in a module file, so it can be used in a variety of programs:

```
# File mytimer.py

import time
reps = 1000
repslist = range(reps)

def timer(func, *pargs, **kargs):
    start = time.clock()
    for i in repslist:
        ret = func(*pargs, **kargs)
    elapsed = time.clock() - start
    return (elapsed, ret)
```

Operationally, this module times calls to any function with any positional and keyword arguments by fetching the start time, calling the function a fixed number of times, and subtracting the start time from the stop time. Points to notice:

- Python's `time` module gives access to the current time, with precision that varies per platform. On Windows, this call is claimed to give microsecond granularity and so is very accurate.

- The `range` call is hoisted out of the timing loop, so its construction cost is not charged to the timed function in Python 2.6. In 3.0 `range` is an iterator, so this step isn't required (but doesn't hurt).

- The `reps` count is a global that importers can change if needed: `mytimer.reps = N`.

When complete, the total elapsed time for all calls is returned in a tuple, along with the timed function's final return value so callers can verify its operation.

From a larger perspective, because this function is coded in a module file, it becomes a generally useful tool anywhere we wish to import it. You'll learn more about modules and imports in the next part of this book—simply import the module and call the function to use this file's timer (and see Chapter 3's coverage of module attributes if you need a refresher).

Timing Script

To time iteration tool speed, run the following script—it uses the timer module we wrote to time the relative speeds of the list construction techniques we've studied:

```python
# File timeseqs.py

import sys, mytimer                            # Import timer function
reps = 10000
repslist = range(reps)                         # Hoist range out in 2.6

def forLoop():
    res = []
    for x in repslist:
        res.append(abs(x))
    return res

def listComp():
    return [abs(x) for x in repslist]

def mapCall():
    return list(map(abs, repslist))            # Use list in 3.0 only

def genExpr():
    return list(abs(x) for x in repslist)      # list forces results

def genFunc():
    def gen():
        for x in repslist:
```

```
            yield abs(x)
        return list(gen())

print(sys.version)
for test in (forLoop, listComp, mapCall, genExpr, genFunc):
    elapsed, result = mytimer.timer(test)
    print ('-' * 33)
    print ('%-9s: %.5f => [%s...%s]' %
           (test.__name__, elapsed, result[0], result[-1]))
```

This script tests five alternative ways to build lists of results and, as shown, executes on the order of 10 million steps for each—that is, each of the five tests builds a list of 10,000 items 1,000 times.

Notice how we have to run the generator expression and function results through the built-in `list` call to force them to yield all of their values; if we did not, we would just produce generators that never do any real work. In Python 3.0 (only) we must do the same for the `map` result, since it is now an iterable object as well. Also notice how the code at the bottom steps through a tuple of five function objects and prints the `__name__` of each: as we've seen, this is a built-in attribute that gives a function's name.[‡]

Timing Results

When the script of the prior section is run under Python 3.0, I get these results on my Windows Vista laptop—`map` is slightly faster than list comprehensions, both are quicker than `for` loops, and generator expressions and functions place in the middle:

```
C:\misc> c:\python30\python timeseqs.py
3.0.1 (r301:69561, Feb 13 2009, 20:04:18) [MSC v.1500 32 bit (Intel)]
---------------------------------
forLoop  : 2.64441 => [0...9999]
---------------------------------
listComp : 1.60110 => [0...9999]
---------------------------------
mapCall  : 1.41977 => [0...9999]
---------------------------------
genExpr  : 2.21758 => [0...9999]
---------------------------------
genFunc  : 2.18696 => [0...9999]
```

If you study this code and its output long enough, you'll notice that generator expressions run slower than list comprehensions. Although wrapping a generator expression in a `list` call makes it functionally equivalent to a square-bracketed list comprehension, the internal implementations of the two expressions appear to differ (though we're also effectively timing the `list` call for the generator test):

```
return [abs(x) for x in range(size)]       # 1.6 seconds
return list(abs(x) for x in range(size))   # 2.2 seconds: differs internally
```

[‡] Also note how we must pass functions in to the timer manually here. In Chapters 38 and 39 we'll see decorator-based timer alternatives with which timed functions are called normally.

Interestingly, when I ran this on Windows XP with Python 2.5 for the prior edition of this book, the results were relatively similar—list comprehensions were nearly twice as fast as equivalent for loop statements, and map was slightly quicker than list comprehensions when mapping a built-in function such as abs (absolute value). I didn't test generator functions then, and the output format wasn't quite as grandiose:

```
2.5 (r25:51908, Sep 19 2006, 09:52:17) [MSC v.1310 32 bit (Intel)]
forStatement        => 6.10899996758
listComprehension   => 3.51499986649
mapFunction         => 2.73399996758
generatorExpression => 4.11600017548
```

The fact that the actual 2.5 test times listed here are over two times as slow as the output I showed earlier is likely due to my using a quicker laptop for the more recent test, not due to improvements in Python 3.0. In fact, all the 2.6 results for this script are slightly quicker than 3.0 on this same machine if the list call is removed from the map test to avoid creating the results list twice (try this on your own to verify).

Watch what happens, though, if we change this script to perform a real operation on each iteration, such as addition, instead of calling a trivial built-in function like abs (the omitted parts of the following are the same as before):

```
# File timeseqs.py
...
...
def forLoop():
    res = []
    for x in repslist:
        res.append(x + 10)
    return res

def listComp():
    return [x + 10 for x in repslist]

def mapCall():
    return list(map((lambda x: x + 10), repslist))     # list in 3.0 only

def genExpr():
    return list(x + 10 for x in repslist)               # list in 2.6 + 3.0

def genFunc():
    def gen():
        for x in repslist:
            yield x + 10
    return list(gen())
...
...
```

Now the need to call a user-defined function for the map call makes it slower than the for loop statements, despite the fact that the looping statements version is larger in terms of code. On Python 3.0:

```
C:\misc> c:\python30\python timeseqs.py
3.0.1 (r301:69561, Feb 13 2009, 20:04:18) [MSC v.1500 32 bit (Intel)]
```

```
---------------------------------
forLoop  : 2.60754 => [10...10009]
---------------------------------
listComp : 1.57585 => [10...10009]
---------------------------------
mapCall  : 3.10276 => [10...10009]
---------------------------------
genExpr  : 1.96482 => [10...10009]
---------------------------------
genFunc  : 1.95340 => [10...10009]
```

The Python 2.5 results on a slower machine were again relatively similar in the prior edition, but twice as slow due to test machine differences:

```
2.5 (r25:51908, Sep 19 2006, 09:52:17) [MSC v.1310 32 bit (Intel)]
forStatement          => 5.25699996948
listComprehension     => 2.68400001526
mapFunction           => 5.96900010109
generatorExpression   => 3.37400007248
```

Because the interpreter optimizes so much internally, performance analysis of Python code like this is a very tricky affair. It's virtually impossible to guess which method will perform the best—the best you can do is time your own code, on your computer, with your version of Python. In this case, all we should say for certain is that on this Python, using a user-defined function in `map` calls can slow performance by at least a factor of 2, and that list comprehensions run quickest for this test.

As I've mentioned before, however, performance should not be your primary concern when writing Python code—the first thing you should do to optimize Python code is to not optimize Python code! Write for *readability and simplicity* first, then optimize later, if and only if needed. It could very well be that any of the five alternatives is quick enough for the data sets your program needs to process; if so, program clarity should be the chief goal.

Timing Module Alternatives

The timing module of the prior section works, but it's a bit primitive on multiple fronts:

- It always uses the `time.clock` call to time code. While that option is best on Windows, the `time.time` call may provide better resolution on some Unix platforms.
- Adjusting the number of repetitions requires changing module-level globals—a less than ideal arrangement if the `timer` function is being used and shared by multiple importers.
- As is, the timer works by running the test function a large number of times. To account for random system load fluctuations, it might be better to select the *best* time among all the tests, instead of the *total* time.

The following alternative implements a more sophisticated timer module that addresses all three points by selecting a timer call based on platform, allowing the repeat count to be passed in as a keyword argument named _reps, and providing a best-of-N alternative timing function:

```
# File mytimer.py (2.6 and 3.0)

"""
timer(spam, 1, 2, a=3, b=4, _reps=1000) calls and times spam(1, 2, a=3)
_reps times, and returns total time for all runs, with final result;

best(spam, 1, 2, a=3, b=4, _reps=50) runs best-of-N timer to filter out
any system load variation, and returns best time among _reps tests
"""

import time, sys
if sys.platform[:3] == 'win':
    timefunc = time.clock            # Use time.clock on Windows
else:
    timefunc = time.time             # Better resolution on some Unix platforms

def trace(*args): pass               # Or: print args

def timer(func, *pargs, **kargs):
    _reps = kargs.pop('_reps', 1000) # Passed-in or default reps
    trace(func, pargs, kargs, _reps)
    repslist = range(_reps)          # Hoist range out for 2.6 lists
    start = timefunc()
    for i in repslist:
        ret = func(*pargs, **kargs)
    elapsed = timefunc() - start
    return (elapsed, ret)

def best(func, *pargs, **kargs):
    _reps = kargs.pop('_reps', 50)
    best = 2 ** 32
    for i in range(_reps):
        (time, ret) = timer(func, *pargs, _reps=1, **kargs)
        if time < best: best = time
    return (best, ret)
```

This module's docstring at the top of the file describes its intended usage. It uses dictionary **pop** operations to remove the _reps argument from arguments intended for the test function and provide it with a default, and it traces arguments during development if you change its **trace** function to **print**. To test with this new timer module on either Python 3.0 or 2.6, change the timing script as follows (the omitted code in the test functions of this version use the x + 1 operation for each test, as coded in the prior section):

```
# File timeseqs.py

import sys, mytimer
reps = 10000
repslist = range(reps)

def forLoop(): ...
```

```
def listComp(): ...

def mapCall(): ...

def genExpr(): ...

def genFunc(): ...

print(sys.version)
for tester in (mytimer.timer, mytimer.best):
    print('<%s>' % tester.__name__)
    for test in (forLoop, listComp, mapCall, genExpr, genFunc):
        elapsed, result = tester(test)
        print ('-' * 35)
        print ('%-9s: %.5f => [%s...%s]' %
               (test.__name__, elapsed, result[0], result[-1]))
```

When run under Python 3.0, the timing results are essentially the same as before, and relatively the same for both the total-of-N and best-of-N timing techniques—running tests many times seems to do as good a job filtering out system load fluctuations as taking the best case, but the best-of-N scheme may be better when testing a long-running function. The results on my machine are as follows:

```
C:\misc> c:\python30\python timeseqs.py
3.0.1 (r301:69561, Feb 13 2009, 20:04:18) [MSC v.1500 32 bit (Intel)]
<timer>
-----------------------------------
forLoop  : 2.35371 => [10...10009]
-----------------------------------
listComp : 1.29640 => [10...10009]
-----------------------------------
mapCall  : 3.16556 => [10...10009]
-----------------------------------
genExpr  : 1.97440 => [10...10009]
-----------------------------------
genFunc  : 1.95072 => [10...10009]
<best>
-----------------------------------
forLoop  : 0.00193 => [10...10009]
-----------------------------------
listComp : 0.00124 => [10...10009]
-----------------------------------
mapCall  : 0.00268 => [10...10009]
-----------------------------------
genExpr  : 0.00164 => [10...10009]
-----------------------------------
genFunc  : 0.00165 => [10...10009]
```

The times reported by the best-of-N timer here are small, of course, but they might become significant if your program iterates many times over large data sets. At least in terms of relative performance, list comprehensions appear best in most cases; map is only slightly better when built-ins are applied.

Using keyword-only arguments in 3.0

We can also make use of Python 3.0 *keyword-only arguments* here to simplify the timer module's code. As we learned in Chapter 19, keyword-only arguments are ideal for configuration options such as our functions' _reps argument. They must be coded after a * and before a ** in the function header, and in a function call they must be passed by keyword and appear before the ** if used. Here's a keyword-only-based alternative to the prior module. Though simpler, it compiles and runs under Python 3.X only, not 2.6:

```
# File mytimer.py (3.X only)

"""
Use 3.0 keyword-only default arguments, instead of ** and dict pops.
No need to hoist range() out of test in 3.0: a generator, not a list
"""

import time, sys
trace = lambda *args: None   # or print
timefunc = time.clock if sys.platform == 'win32' else time.time

def timer(func, *pargs, _reps=1000, **kargs):
    trace(func, pargs, kargs, _reps)
    start = timefunc()
    for i in range(_reps):
        ret = func(*pargs, **kargs)
    elapsed = timefunc() - start
    return (elapsed, ret)

def best(func, *pargs, _reps=50, **kargs):
    best = 2 ** 32
    for i in range(_reps):
        (time, ret) = timer(func, *pargs, _reps=1, **kargs)
        if time < best: best = time
    return (best, ret)
```

This version is used the same way as and produces results identical to the prior version, not counting negligible test time differences from run to run:

```
C:\misc> c:\python30\python timeseqs.py
...same results as before...
```

In fact, for variety we can also test this version of the module from the interactive prompt, completely independent of the sequence timer script—it's a general-purpose tool:

```
C:\misc> c:\python30\python
>>> from mytimer import timer, best
>>>
>>> def power(X, Y): return X ** Y          # Test function
...
>>> timer(power, 2, 32)                      # Total time, last result
(0.002625403507987747, 4294967296)
>>> timer(power, 2, 32, _reps=1000000)       # Override defult reps
```

```
(1.1822605247314932, 4294967296)
>>> timer(power, 2, 100000)[0]            # 2 ** 100,000 tot time @1,000 reps
2.2496919999608878

>>> best(power, 2, 32)                    # Best time, last result
(5.58730229727189e-06, 4294967296)
>>> best(power, 2, 100000)[0]             # 2 ** 100,000 best time
0.0019937589833460834
>>> best(power, 2, 100000, _reps=500)[0]  # Override default reps
0.0019845399345541637
```

For trivial functions like the one tested in this interactive session, the costs of the timer's code are probably as significant as those of the timed function, so you should not take timer results too absolutely (we are timing more than just X ** Y here). The timer's results can help you judge relative speeds of coding alternatives, though, and may be more meaningful for longer-running operations like the following—calculating 2 to the power one million takes an order of magnitude (power of 10) longer than the preceding 2**100,000:

```
>>> timer(power, 2, 1000000, _reps=1)[0]   # 2 ** 1,000,000: total time
0.088112804839710179
>>> timer(power, 2, 1000000, _reps=10)[0]
0.40922470593329763

>>> best(power, 2, 1000000, _reps=1)[0]    # 2 ** 1,000,000: best time
0.086550036387279761
>>> best(power, 2, 1000000, _reps=10)[0]   # 10 is sometimes as good as 50
0.029616752967200455
>>> best(power, 2, 1000000, _reps=50)[0]   # Best resolution
0.029486918030102061
```

Again, although the times measured here are small, the differences can be significant in programs that compute powers often.

See Chapter 19 for more on keyword-only arguments in 3.0; they can simplify code for configurable tools like this one but are not backward compatible with 2.X Pythons. If you want to compare 2.X and 3.X speed, for example, or support programmers using either Python line, the prior version is likely a better choice. If you're using Python 2.6, the above session runs the same with the prior version of the timer module.

Other Suggestions

For more insight, try modifying the repetition counts used by these modules, or explore the alternative timeit module in Python's standard library, which automates timing of code, supports command-line usage modes, and finesses some platform-specific issues. Python's manuals document its use.

You might also want to look at the profile standard library module for a complete source code profiler tool—we'll learn more about it in Chapter 35 in the context of development tools for large projects. In general, you should profile code to isolate bottlenecks before recoding and timing alternatives as we've done here.

It might be useful to experiment with the new `str.format` method in Python 2.6 and 3.0 instead of the `%` formatting expression (which could potentially be deprecated in the future!), by changing the timing script's formatted `print` lines as follows:

```
print('<%s>' % tester.__name__)            # From expression

print('<{0}>'.format(tester.__name__))     # To method call

    print ('%-9s: %.5f => [%s...%s]' %
           (test.__name__, elapsed, result[0], result[-1]))

    print('{0:<9}: {1:.5f} => [{2}...{3}]'.format(
           test.__name__, elapsed, result[0], result[-1]))
```

You can judge the difference between these techniques yourself.

You might try modifying or emulating the timing script to measure the speed of the 3.0 *set and dictionary comprehensions* shown in this chapter, and their for loop equivalents. Using them is less common in Python programs than building lists of results, so we'll leave this task in the suggested exercise column (and please, no wagering...).

Finally, keep the timing module we wrote here filed away for future reference—we'll repurpose it to measure performance of alternative numeric square root operations in an exercise at the end of this chapter. If you're interested in pursuing this topic further, we'll also experiment with techniques for timing dictionary comprehensions versus for loops interactively.§

Function Gotchas

Now that we've reached the end of the function story, let's review some common pitfalls. Functions have some jagged edges that you might not expect. They're all obscure, and a few have started to fall away from the language completely in recent releases, but most have been known to trip up new users.

Local Names Are Detected Statically

As you know, Python classifies names assigned in a function as *locals* by default; they live in the function's scope and exist only while the function is running. What you may not realize is that Python detects locals statically, when it compiles the def's code, rather than by noticing assignments as they happen at runtime. This leads to one of the most common oddities posted on the Python newsgroup by beginners.

---

§ For more fun, apply a simple user-defined function like `def f(I): return(I)` in all five iteration techniques timed. The results are similar to using a built-in function like `abs`: among the five iteration techniques, `map` is fastest today if all five call a function, built-in or not, but slowest when the others do not. That is, `map` appears to be slower simply because it requires function calls, and function calls are relatively slow in general. Since `map` can't avoid calling functions, it can lose by association.

Normally, a name that isn't assigned in a function is looked up in the enclosing module:

```
>>> X = 99

>>> def selector():        # X used but not assigned
...     print(X)           # X found in global scope
...
>>> selector()
99
```

Here, the X in the function resolves to the X in the module. But watch what happens if you add an assignment to X after the reference:

```
>>> def selector():
...     print(X)           # Does not yet exist!
...     X = 88             # X classified as a local name (everywhere)
...                        # Can also happen for "import X", "def X"...
>>> selector()
UnboundLocalError: local variable 'X' referenced before assignment
```

You get the name usage error shown here, but the reason is subtle. Python reads and compiles this code when it's typed interactively or imported from a module. While compiling, Python sees the assignment to X and decides that X will be a local name everywhere in the function. But when the function is actually run, because the assignment hasn't yet happened when the print executes, Python says you're using an undefined name. According to its name rules, it should say this; the local X is used before being assigned. In fact, any assignment in a function body makes a name local. Imports, =, nested defs, nested classes, and so on are all susceptible to this behavior.

The problem occurs because assigned names are treated as locals everywhere in a function, not just after the statements where they're assigned. The previous example is ambiguous: was the intention to print the global X and create a local X, or is this a real programming error? Because Python treats X as a local everywhere, it's seen as an error; if you mean to print the global X, you need to declare it in a global statement:

```
>>> def selector():
...     global X           # Force X to be global (everywhere)
...     print(X)
...     X = 88
...
>>> selector()
99
```

Remember, though, that this means the assignment also changes the global X, not a local X. Within a function, you can't use both local and global versions of the same simple name. If you really meant to print the global and then set a local of the same name, you'd need to import the enclosing module and use module attribute notation to get to the global version:

```
>>> X = 99
>>> def selector():
...     import __main__           # Import enclosing module
...     print(__main__.X)         # Qualify to get to global version of name
...     X = 88                    # Unqualified X classified as local
```

```
...        print(X)                         # Prints local version of name
...
>>> selector()
99
88
```

Qualification (the .X part) fetches a value from a namespace object. The interactive namespace is a module called __main__, so __main__.X reaches the global version of X. If that isn't clear, check out Chapter 17.

In recent versions Python has improved on this story somewhat by issuing for this case the more specific "unbound local" error message shown in the example listing (it used to simply raise a generic name error); this gotcha is still present in general, though.

Defaults and Mutable Objects

Default argument values are evaluated and saved when a def statement is run, not when the resulting function is called. Internally, Python saves one object per default argument attached to the function itself.

That's usually what you want—because defaults are evaluated at def time, it lets you save values from the enclosing scope, if needed. But because a default retains an object between calls, you have to be careful about changing mutable defaults. For instance, the following function uses an empty list as a default value, and then changes it in-place each time the function is called:

```
>>> def saver(x=[]):              # Saves away a list object
...        x.append(1)            # Changes same object each time!
...        print(x)
...
>>> saver([2])                    # Default not used
[2, 1]
>>> saver()                       # Default used
[1]
>>> saver()                       # Grows on each call!
[1, 1]
>>> saver()
[1, 1, 1]
```

Some see this behavior as a feature—because mutable default arguments retain their state between function calls, they can serve some of the same roles as *static* local function variables in the C language. In a sense, they work sort of like global variables, but their names are local to the functions and so will not clash with names elsewhere in a program.

To most observers, though, this seems like a gotcha, especially the first time they run into it. There are better ways to retain state between calls in Python (e.g., using classes, which will be discussed in Part VI).

Moreover, mutable defaults are tricky to remember (and to understand at all). They depend upon the timing of default object construction. In the prior example, there is just one list object for the default value—the one created when the def is executed. You don't get a new list every time the function is called, so the list grows with each new append; it is not reset to empty on each call.

If that's not the behavior you want, simply make a copy of the default at the start of the function body, or move the default value expression into the function body. As long as the value resides in code that's actually executed each time the function runs, you'll get a new object each time through:

```
>>> def saver(x=None):
...     if x is None:          # No argument passed?
...         x = []             # Run code to make a new list
...     x.append(1)            # Changes new list object
...     print(x)
...
>>> saver([2])
[2, 1]
>>> saver()                    # Doesn't grow here
[1]
>>> saver()
[1]
```

By the way, the if statement in this example could *almost* be replaced by the assignment x = x or [], which takes advantage of the fact that Python's or returns one of its operand objects: if no argument was passed, x would default to None, so the or would return the new empty list on the right.

However, this isn't exactly the same. If an empty list were passed in, the or expression would cause the function to extend and return a newly created list, rather than extending and returning the passed-in list like the if version. (The expression becomes [] or [], which evaluates to the new empty list on the right; see the section "Truth Tests" on page 322 if you don't recall why). Real program requirements may call for either behavior.

Today, another way to achieve the effect of mutable defaults in a possibly less confusing way is to use the *function attributes* we discussed in Chapter 19:

```
>>> def saver():
...     saver.x.append(1)
...     print(saver.x)
...
>>> saver.x = []
>>> saver()
[1]
>>> saver()
[1, 1]
>>> saver()
[1, 1, 1]
```

The function name is global to the function itself, but it need not be declared because it isn't changed directly within the function. This isn't used in exactly the same way, but when coded like this, the attachment of an object to the function is much more explicit (and arguably less magical).

Functions Without returns

In Python functions, `return` (and `yield`) statements are optional. When a function doesn't return a value explicitly, the function exits when control falls off the end of the function body. Technically, all functions return a value; if you don't provide a `return` statement, your function returns the `None` object automatically:

```
>>> def proc(x):
...     print(x)                    # No return is a None return
...
>>> x = proc('testing 123...')
testing 123...
>>> print(x)
None
```

Functions such as this without a `return` are Python's equivalent of what are called "procedures" in some languages. They're usually invoked as statements, and the `None` results are ignored, as they do their business without computing a useful result.

This is worth knowing, because Python won't tell you if you try to use the result of a function that doesn't return one. For instance, assigning the result of a list `append` method won't raise an error, but you'll get back `None`, not the modified list:

```
>>> list = [1, 2, 3]
>>> list = list.append(4)          # append is a "procedure"
>>> print(list)                    # append changes list in-place
None
```

As mentioned in "Common Coding Gotchas" on page 389 in Chapter 15, such functions do their business as a side effect and are usually designed to be run as statements, not expressions.

Enclosing Scope Loop Variables

We described this gotcha in Chapter 17's discussion of enclosing function scopes, but as a reminder, be careful about relying on enclosing function scope lookup for variables that are changed by enclosing loops—all such references will remember the value of the *last* loop iteration. Use defaults to save loop variable values instead (see Chapter 17 for more details on this topic).

Chapter Summary

This chapter wrapped up our coverage of built-in comprehension and iteration tools. It explored list comprehensions in the context of functional tools and presented generator functions and expressions as additional iteration protocol tools. As a finale, we also measured the performance of iteration alternatives, and we closed with a review of common function-related mistakes to help you avoid pitfalls.

This concludes the functions part of this book. In the next part, we will study *modules*—the topmost organizational structure in Python, and the structure in which our functions always live. After that, we will explore classes, tools that are largely packages of functions with special first arguments. As we'll see, user-defined classes can implement objects that tap into the iteration protocol, just like the generators and iterables we met here. Everything we have learned in this part of the book will apply when functions pop up later in the context of class methods.

Before moving on to modules, though, be sure to work through this chapter's quiz and the exercises for this part of the book, to practice what we've learned about functions here.

Test Your Knowledge: Quiz

1. What is the difference between enclosing a list comprehension in square brackets and parentheses?
2. How are generators and iterators related?
3. How can you tell if a function is a generator function?
4. What does a `yield` statement do?
5. How are `map` calls and list comprehensions related? Compare and contrast the two.

Test Your Knowledge: Answers

1. List comprehensions in square brackets produce the result list all at once in memory. When they are enclosed in parentheses instead, they are actually generator expressions—they have a similar meaning but do not produce the result list all at once. Instead, generator expressions return a generator object, which yields one item in the result at a time when used in an iteration context.
2. Generators are objects that support the iteration protocol—they have a `__next__` method that repeatedly advances to the next item in a series of results and raises an exception at the end of the series. In Python, we can code generator functions with `def`, generator expressions with parenthesized list comprehensions, and generator objects with classes that define a special method named `__iter__` (discussed later in the book).
3. A generator function has a `yield` statement somewhere in its code. Generator functions are otherwise identical to normal functions syntactically, but they are compiled specially by Python so as to return an iterable object when called.

4. When present, this statement makes Python compile the function specially as a generator; when called, the function returns a generator object that supports the iteration protocol. When the yield statement is run, it sends a result back to the caller and suspends the function's state; the function can then be resumed after the last yield statement, in response to a next built-in or __next__ method call issued by the caller. Generator functions may also have a return statement, which terminates the generator.

5. The map call is similar to a list comprehension—both build a new list by collecting the results of applying an operation to each item in a sequence or other iterable, one item at a time. The main difference is that map applies a function call to each item, and list comprehensions apply arbitrary expressions. Because of this, list comprehensions are more general; they can apply a function call expression like map, but map requires a function to apply other kinds of expressions. List comprehensions also support extended syntax such as nested for loops and if clauses that subsume the filter built-in.

Test Your Knowledge: Part IV Exercises

In these exercises, you're going to start coding more sophisticated programs. Be sure to check the solutions in "Part IV, Functions" on page 1113 in Appendix B, and be sure to start writing your code in module files. You won't want to retype these exercises from scratch if you make a mistake.

1. *The basics.* At the Python interactive prompt, write a function that prints its single argument to the screen and call it interactively, passing a variety of object types: string, integer, list, dictionary. Then, try calling it without passing any argument. What happens? What happens when you pass two arguments?

2. *Arguments.* Write a function called adder in a Python module file. The function should accept two arguments and return the sum (or concatenation) of the two. Then, add code at the bottom of the file to call the adder function with a variety of object types (two strings, two lists, two floating points), and run this file as a script from the system command line. Do you have to print the call statement results to see results on your screen?

3. *varargs.* Generalize the adder function you wrote in the last exercise to compute the sum of an arbitrary number of arguments, and change the calls to pass more or fewer than two arguments. What type is the return value sum? (Hints: a slice such as S[:0] returns an empty sequence of the same type as S, and the type built-in function can test types; but see the manually coded min examples in Chapter 18 for a simpler approach.) What happens if you pass in arguments of different types? What about passing in dictionaries?

4. *Keywords.* Change the `adder` function from exercise 2 to accept and sum/concatenate three arguments: `def adder(good, bad, ugly)`. Now, provide default values for each argument, and experiment with calling the function interactively. Try passing one, two, three, and four arguments. Then, try passing keyword arguments. Does the call `adder(ugly=1, good=2)` work? Why? Finally, generalize the new `adder` to accept and sum/concatenate an arbitrary number of keyword arguments. This is similar to what you did in exercise 3, but you'll need to iterate over a dictionary, not a tuple. (Hint: the `dict.keys` method returns a list you can step through with a `for` or `while`, but be sure to wrap it in a `list` call to index it in 3.0!)

5. Write a function called `copyDict(dict)` that copies its dictionary argument. It should return a new dictionary containing all the items in its argument. Use the dictionary `keys` method to iterate (or, in Python 2.2, step over a dictionary's keys without calling `keys`). Copying sequences is easy (`X[:]` makes a top-level copy); does this work for dictionaries, too?

6. Write a function called `addDict(dict1, dict2)` that computes the union of two dictionaries. It should return a new dictionary containing all the items in both its arguments (which are assumed to be dictionaries). If the same key appears in both arguments, feel free to pick a value from either. Test your function by writing it in a file and running the file as a script. What happens if you pass lists instead of dictionaries? How could you generalize your function to handle this case, too? (Hint: see the `type` built-in function used earlier.) Does the order of the arguments passed in matter?

7. *More argument-matching examples.* First, define the following six functions (either interactively or in a module file that can be imported):

```
def f1(a, b): print(a, b)        # Normal args
def f2(a, *b): print(a, b)       # Positional varargs

def f3(a, **b): print(a, b)      # Keyword varargs

def f4(a, *b, **c): print(a, b, c)   # Mixed modes

def f5(a, b=2, c=3): print(a, b, c)  # Defaults

def f6(a, b=2, *c): print(a, b, c)   # Defaults and positional varargs
```

Now, test the following calls interactively, and try to explain each result; in some cases, you'll probably need to fall back on the matching algorithm shown in Chapter 18. Do you think mixing matching modes is a good idea in general? Can you think of cases where it would be useful?

```
>>> f1(1, 2)
>>> f1(b=2, a=1)

>>> f2(1, 2, 3)
>>> f3(1, x=2, y=3)
>>> f4(1, 2, 3, x=2, y=3)
```

```
>>> f5(1)
>>> f5(1, 4)

>>> f6(1)
>>> f6(1, 3, 4)
```

8. *Primes revisited.* Recall the following code snippet from Chapter 13, which simplistically determines whether a positive integer is prime:

```
x = y // 2                        # For some y > 1
while x > 1:
    if y % x == 0:                # Remainder
        print(y, 'has factor', x)
        break                     # Skip else
    x -= 1
else:                             # Normal exit
    print(y, 'is prime')
```

Package this code as a reusable function in a module file (y should be a passed-in argument), and add some calls to the function at the bottom of your file. While you're at it, experiment with replacing the first line's // operator with / to see how true division changes the / operator in Python 3.0 and breaks this code (refer back to Chapter 5 if you need a refresher). What can you do about negatives, and the values 0 and 1? How about speeding this up? Your outputs should look something like this:

```
13 is prime
13.0 is prime
15 has factor 5
15.0 has factor 5.0
```

9. *List comprehensions.* Write code to build a new list containing the square roots of all the numbers in this list: [2, 4, 9, 16, 25]. Code this as a for loop first, then as a map call, and finally as a list comprehension. Use the sqrt function in the built-in math module to do the calculation (i.e., import math and say math.sqrt(x)). Of the three, which approach do you like best?

10. *Timing tools.* In Chapter 5, we saw three ways to compute square roots: math.sqrt(X), X ** .5, and pow(X, .5). If your programs run a lot these, their relative performance might become important. To see which is quickest, repurpose the *timerseqs.py* script we wrote in this chapter to time each of these three tools. Use the *mytimer.py* timer module with the best function (you can use either the 3.0-ony keyword-only variant, or the 2.6/3.0 version). You might also want to repackage the testing code in this script for better reusability—by passing a test functions tuple to a general tester function, for example (for this exercise a copy-and-modify approach is fine). Which of the three square root tools seems to run fastest on your machine and Python in general? Finally, how might you go about interactively timing the speed of dictionary comprehensions versus for loops?

## PART V

Modules

## CHAPTER 21

Modules: The Big Picture

This chapter begins our in-depth look at the Python *module*, the highest-level program organization unit, which packages program code and data for reuse. In concrete terms, modules usually correspond to Python program files (or extensions coded in external languages such as C, Java, or C#). Each file is a module, and modules import other modules to use the names they define. Modules are processed with two statements and one important function:

import
> Lets a client (importer) fetch a module as a whole

from
> Allows clients to fetch particular names from a module

imp.reload
> Provides a way to reload a module's code without stopping Python

Chapter 3 introduced module fundamentals, and we've been using them ever since. This part of the book begins by expanding on core module concepts, then moves on to explore more advanced module usage. This first chapter offers a general look at the role of modules in overall program structure. In the following chapters, we'll dig into the coding details behind the theory.

Along the way, we'll flesh out module details omitted so far: you'll learn about reloads, the __name__ and __all__ attributes, package imports, relative import syntax, and so on. Because modules and classes are really just glorified namespaces, we'll formalize namespace concepts here as well.

Why Use Modules?

In short, modules provide an easy way to organize components into a system by serving as self-contained packages of variables known as *namespaces*. All the names defined at the top level of a module file become attributes of the imported module object. As we saw in the last part of this book, imports give access to names in a module's global scope. That is, the module file's global scope morphs into the module object's attribute namespace when it is imported. Ultimately, Python's modules allow us to link individual files into a larger program system.

More specifically, from an abstract perspective, modules have at least three roles:

Code reuse
> As discussed in Chapter 3, modules let you save code in files permanently. Unlike code you type at the Python interactive prompt, which goes away when you exit Python, code in module files is persistent—it can be reloaded and rerun as many times as needed. More to the point, modules are a place to define names, known as *attributes*, which may be referenced by multiple external clients.

System namespace partitioning
> Modules are also the highest-level program organization unit in Python. Fundamentally, they are just packages of names. Modules seal up names into self-contained packages, which helps avoid name clashes—you can never see a name in another file, unless you explicitly import that file. In fact, everything "lives" in a module—code you execute and objects you create are always implicitly enclosed in modules. Because of that, modules are natural tools for grouping system components.

Implementing shared services or data
> From an operational perspective, modules also come in handy for implementing components that are shared across a system and hence require only a single copy. For instance, if you need to provide a global object that's used by more than one function or file, you can code it in a module that can then be imported by many clients.

For you to truly understand the role of modules in a Python system, though, we need to digress for a moment and explore the general structure of a Python program.

Python Program Architecture

So far in this book, I've sugarcoated some of the complexity in my descriptions of Python programs. In practice, programs usually involve more than just one file; for all but the simplest scripts, your programs will take the form of multifile systems. And even if you can get by with coding a single file yourself, you will almost certainly wind up using external files that someone else has already written.

This section introduces the general architecture of Python programs—the way you divide a program into a collection of source files (a.k.a. modules) and link the parts into a whole. Along the way, we'll also explore the central concepts of Python modules, imports, and object attributes.

How to Structure a Program

Generally, a Python program consists of multiple text files containing Python *statements*. The program is structured as one main, *top-level* file, along with zero or more supplemental files known as *modules* in Python.

In Python, the top-level (a.k.a. script) file contains the main flow of control of your program—this is the file you run to launch your application. The module files are libraries of tools used to collect components used by the top-level file (and possibly elsewhere). Top-level files use tools defined in module files, and modules use tools defined in other modules.

Module files generally don't do anything when run directly; rather, they define tools intended for use in other files. In Python, a file *imports* a module to gain access to the tools it defines, which are known as its *attributes* (i.e., variable names attached to objects such as functions). Ultimately, we import modules and access their attributes to use their tools.

Imports and Attributes

Let's make this a bit more concrete. Figure 21-1 sketches the structure of a Python program composed of three files: *a.py*, *b.py*, and *c.py*. The file *a.py* is chosen to be the top-level file; it will be a simple text file of statements, which is executed from top to bottom when launched. The files *b.py* and *c.py* are modules; they are simple text files of statements as well, but they are not usually launched directly. Instead, as explained previously, modules are normally imported by other files that wish to use the tools they define.

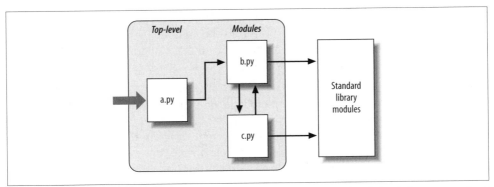

Figure 21-1. Program architecture in Python. A program is a system of modules. It has one top-level script file (launched to run the program), and multiple module files (imported libraries of tools). Scripts and modules are both text files containing Python statements, though the statements in modules usually just create objects to be used later. Python's standard library provides a collection of precoded modules.

For instance, suppose the file *b.py* in Figure 21-1 defines a function called `spam`, for external use. As we learned when studying functions in Part IV, *b.py* will contain a Python `def` statement to generate the function, which can later be run by passing zero or more values in parentheses after the function's name:

```
def spam(text):
    print(text, 'spam')
```

Now, suppose *a.py* wants to use `spam`. To this end, it might contain Python statements such as the following:

```
import b
b.spam('gumby')
```

The first of these, a Python `import` statement, gives the file *a.py* access to everything defined by top-level code in the file *b.py*. It roughly means "load the file *b.py* (unless it's already loaded), and give me access to all its attributes through the name b." `import` (and, as you'll see later, `from`) statements execute and load other files at runtime.

In Python, cross-file module linking is not resolved until such `import` statements are executed at runtime; their net effect is to assign module names—simple variables—to loaded module objects. In fact, the module name used in an `import` statement serves two purposes: it identifies the external file to be loaded, but it also becomes a variable assigned to the loaded module. Objects defined by a module are also created at runtime, as the `import` is executing: `import` literally runs statements in the target file one at a time to create its contents.

The second of the statements in *a.py* calls the function `spam` defined in the module b, using object attribute notation. The code `b.spam` means "fetch the value of the name `spam` that lives within the object b." This happens to be a callable function in our example, so we pass a string in parentheses (`'gumby'`). If you actually type these files, save them, and run *a.py*, the words "gumby spam" will be printed.

You'll see the `object.attribute` notation used throughout Python scripts—most objects have useful attributes that are fetched with the "." operator. Some are callable things like functions, and others are simple data values that give object properties (e.g., a person's name).

The notion of importing is also completely general throughout Python. Any file can import tools from any other file. For instance, the file *a.py* may import *b.py* to call its function, but *b.py* might also import *c.py* to leverage different tools defined there. Import chains can go as deep as you like: in this example, the module a can import b, which can import c, which can import b again, and so on.

Besides serving as the highest organizational structure, modules (and module packages, described in Chapter 23) are also the highest level of *code reuse* in Python. Coding components in module files makes them useful in your original program, and in any other programs you may write. For instance, if after coding the program in Figure 21-1 we discover that the function `b.spam` is a general-purpose tool, we can reuse it in a completely different program; all we have to do is import the file *b.py* again from the other program's files.

Standard Library Modules

Notice the rightmost portion of Figure 21-1. Some of the modules that your programs will import are provided by Python itself and are not files you will code.

Python automatically comes with a large collection of utility modules known as the *standard library*. This collection, roughly 200 modules large at last count, contains platform-independent support for common programming tasks: operating system interfaces, object persistence, text pattern matching, network and Internet scripting, GUI construction, and much more. None of these tools are part of the Python language itself, but you can use them by importing the appropriate modules on any standard Python installation. Because they are standard library modules, you can also be reasonably sure that they will be available and will work portably on most platforms on which you will run Python.

You will see a few of the standard library modules in action in this book's examples, but for a complete look you should browse the standard Python library reference manual, available either with your Python installation (via IDLE or the Python Start button menu on Windows) or online at *http://www.python.org*.

Because there are so many modules, this is really the only way to get a feel for what tools are available. You can also find tutorials on Python library tools in commercial books that cover application-level programming, such as O'Reilly's *Programming Python*, but the manuals are free, viewable in any web browser (they ship in HTML format), and updated each time Python is rereleased.

How Imports Work

The prior section talked about importing modules without really explaining what happens when you do so. Because imports are at the heart of program structure in Python, this section goes into more detail on the import operation to make this process less abstract.

Some C programmers like to compare the Python module import operation to a C `#include`, but they really shouldn't—in Python, imports are not just textual insertions of one file into another. They are really runtime operations that perform three distinct steps the first time a program imports a given file:

1. *Find* the module's file.
2. *Compile* it to byte code (if needed).
3. *Run* the module's code to build the objects it defines.

To better understand module imports, we'll explore these steps in turn. Bear in mind that all three of these steps are carried out only the *first time* a module is imported during a program's execution; later imports of the same module bypass all of these steps and simply fetch the already loaded module object in memory. Technically, Python does this by storing loaded modules in a table named `sys.modules` and checking there at the start of an import operation. If the module is not present, a three-step process begins.

1. Find It

First, Python must locate the module file referenced by an `import` statement. Notice that the `import` statement in the prior section's example names the file without a *.py* suffix and without its directory path: it just says `import b`, instead of something like `import c:\dir1\b.py`. In fact, you can only list a simple name; path and suffix details are omitted on purpose and Python uses a standard *module search path* to locate the module file corresponding to an `import` statement.[*] Because this is the main part of the import operation that programmers must know about, we'll return to this topic in a moment.

2. Compile It (Maybe)

After finding a source code file that matches an `import` statement by traversing the module search path, Python next compiles it to byte code, if necessary. (We discussed byte code in Chapter 2.)

Python checks the file timestamps and, if the byte code file is older than the source file (i.e., if you've changed the source), automatically regenerates the byte code when the program is run. If, on the other hand, it finds a *.pyc* byte code file that is not older than the corresponding *.py* source file, it skips the source-to–byte code compile step. In addition, if Python finds only a byte code file on the search path and no source, it simply loads the byte code directly (this means you can ship a program as just byte code files and avoid sending source). In other words, the compile step is bypassed if possible to speed program startup. As noted in Chapter 2, imports also recreate byte code if its "magic" Python version number does not match.

Notice that compilation happens when a file is being imported. Because of this, you will not usually see a *.pyc* byte code file for the top-level file of your program, unless it is also imported elsewhere—only imported files leave behind *.pyc* files on your

---

[*] It's actually syntactically illegal to include path and suffix details in a standard `import`. *Package imports*, which we'll discuss in Chapter 23, allow `import` statements to include part of the directory path leading to a file as a set of period-separated names; however, package imports still rely on the normal module search path to locate the leftmost directory in a package path (i.e., they are relative to a directory in the search path). They also cannot make use of any platform-specific directory syntax in the `import` statements; such syntax only works on the search path. Also, note that module file search path issues are not as relevant when you run *frozen executables* (discussed in Chapter 2); they typically embed byte code in the binary image.

machine. The byte code of top-level files is used internally and discarded; byte code of imported files is saved in files to speed future imports.

Top-level files are often designed to be executed directly and not imported at all. Later, we'll see that it is possible to design a file that serves both as the top-level code of a program and as a module of tools to be imported. Such a file may be both executed and imported, and thus does generate a *.pyc*. To learn how this works, watch for the discussion of the special __name__ attribute and __main__ in Chapter 24.

3. Run It

The final step of an import operation executes the byte code of the module. All statements in the file are executed in turn, from top to bottom, and any assignments made to names during this step generate attributes of the resulting module object. This execution step therefore generates all the tools that the module's code defines. For instance, def statements in a file are run at import time to create functions and assign attributes within the module to those functions. The functions can then be called later in the program by the file's importers.

Because this last import step actually runs the file's code, if any top-level code in a module file does real work, you'll see its results at import time. For example, top-level print statements in a module show output when the file is imported. Function def statements simply define objects for later use.

As you can see, import operations involve quite a bit of work—they search for files, possibly run a compiler, and run Python code. Because of this, any given module is imported only *once* per process by default. Future imports skip all three import steps and reuse the already loaded module in memory. If you need to import a file again after it has already been loaded (for example, to support end-user customization), you have to force the issue with an imp.reload call—a tool we'll meet in the next chapter.[†]

The Module Search Path

As mentioned earlier, the part of the import procedure that is most important to programmers is usually the first—locating the file to be imported (the "find it" part). Because you may need to tell Python where to look to find files to import, you need to know how to tap into its search path in order to extend it.

[†] As described earlier, Python keeps already imported modules in the built-in sys.modules dictionary so it can keep track of what's been loaded. In fact, if you want to see which modules are loaded, you can import sys and print list(sys.modules.keys()). More on other uses for this internal table in Chapter 24.

In many cases, you can rely on the automatic nature of the module import search path and won't need to configure this path at all. If you want to be able to import files across directory boundaries, though, you will need to know how the search path works in order to customize it. Roughly, Python's module search path is composed of the concatenation of these major components, some of which are preset for you and some of which you can tailor to tell Python where to look:

1. The home directory of the program
2. PYTHONPATH directories (if set)
3. Standard library directories
4. The contents of any *.pth* files (if present)

Ultimately, the concatenation of these four components becomes sys.path, a list of directory name strings that I'll expand upon later in this section. The first and third elements of the search path are defined automatically. Because Python searches the concatenation of these components from first to last, though, the second and fourth elements can be used to extend the path to include your own source code directories. Here is how Python uses each of these path components:

Home directory
> Python first looks for the imported file in the home directory. The meaning of this entry depends on how you are running the code. When you're running a program, this entry is the directory containing your program's top-level script file. When you're working interactively, this entry is the directory in which you are working (i.e., the current working directory).
>
> Because this directory is always searched first, if a program is located entirely in a single directory, all of its imports will work automatically with no path configuration required. On the other hand, because this directory is searched first, its files will also override modules of the same name in directories elsewhere on the path; be careful not to accidentally hide library modules this way if you need them in your program.

PYTHONPATH *directories*
> Next, Python searches all directories listed in your PYTHONPATH environment variable setting, from left to right (assuming you have set this at all). In brief, PYTHONPATH is simply set to a list of user-defined and platform-specific names of directories that contain Python code files. You can add all the directories from which you wish to be able to import, and Python will extend the module search path to include all the directories your PYTHONPATH lists.
>
> Because Python searches the home directory first, this setting is only important when importing files across directory boundaries—that is, if you need to import a file that is stored in a different directory from the file that imports it. You'll probably want to set your PYTHONPATH variable once you start writing substantial programs, but when you're first starting out, as long as you save all your module files in the

directory in which you're working (i.e., the home directory, described earlier) your imports will work without you needing to worry about this setting at all.

Standard library directories

Next, Python automatically searches the directories where the standard library modules are installed on your machine. Because these are always searched, they normally do not need to be added to your PYTHONPATH or included in path files (discussed next).

.pth path file directories

Finally, a lesser-used feature of Python allows users to add directories to the module search path by simply listing them, one per line, in a text file whose name ends with a *.pth* suffix (for "path"). These path configuration files are a somewhat advanced installation-related feature; we won't cover them fully here, but they provide an alternative to PYTHONPATH settings.

In short, text files of directory names dropped in an appropriate directory can serve roughly the same role as the PYTHONPATH environment variable setting. For instance, if you're running Windows and Python 3.0, a file named *myconfig.pth* may be placed at the top level of the Python install directory (*C:\Python30*) or in the *site-packages* subdirectory of the standard library there (*C:\Python30\Lib\site-packages*) to extend the module search path. On Unix-like systems, this file might be located in *usr/local/lib/python3.0/site-packages* or */usr/local/lib/site-python* instead.

When present, Python will add the directories listed on each line of the file, from first to last, near the end of the module search path list. In fact, Python will collect the directory names in all the path files it finds and will filter out any duplicates and nonexistent directories. Because they are files rather than shell settings, path files can apply to all users of an installation, instead of just one user or shell. Moreover, for some users text files may be simpler to code than environment settings.

This feature is more sophisticated than I've described here. For more details consult the Python library manual, and especially its documentation for the standard library module site—this module allows the locations of Python libraries and path files to be configured, and its documentation describes the expected locations of path files in general. I recommend that beginners use PYTHONPATH or perhaps a single *.pth* file, and then only if you must import across directories. Path files are used more often by third-party libraries, which commonly install a path file in Python's *site-packages* directory so that user settings are not required (Python's distutils install system, described in an upcoming sidebar, automates many install steps).

Configuring the Search Path

The net effect of all of this is that both the PYTHONPATH and path file components of the search path allow you to tailor the places where imports look for files. The way you set environment variables and where you store path files varies per platform. For instance, on Windows, you might use your Control Panel's System icon to set PYTHONPATH to a list of directories separated by semicolons, like this:

```
c:\pycode\utilities;d:\pycode\package1
```

Or you might instead create a text file called *C:\Python30\pydirs.pth*, which looks like this:

```
c:\pycode\utilities
d:\pycode\package1
```

These settings are analogous on other platforms, but the details can vary too widely for us to cover in this chapter. See Appendix A for pointers on extending your module search path with PYTHONPATH or *.pth* files on various platforms.

Search Path Variations

This description of the module search path is accurate, but generic; the exact configuration of the search path is prone to changing across platforms and Python releases. Depending on your platform, additional directories may automatically be added to the module search path as well.

For instance, Python may add an entry for the *current working directory*—the directory from which you launched your program—in the search path after the PYTHONPATH directories, and before the standard library entries. When you're launching from a command line, the current working directory may not be the same as the home directory of your top-level file (i.e., the directory where your program file resides). Because the current working directory can vary each time your program runs, you normally shouldn't depend on its value for import purposes. See Chapter 3 for more on launching programs from command lines.‡

To see how your Python configures the module search path on your platform, you can always inspect sys.path—the topic of the next section.

The sys.path List

If you want to see how the module search path is truly configured on your machine, you can always inspect the path as Python knows it by printing the built-in sys.path list (that is, the path attribute of the standard library module sys). This list of directory name strings is the actual search path within Python; on imports, Python searches each directory in this list from left to right.

---

‡ See also Chapter 23's discussion of the new *relative import syntax* in Python 3.0; this modifies the search path for from statements in files inside packages when "." characters are used (e.g., from . import string). By default, a package's own directory is not automatically searched by imports in Python 3.0, unless relative imports are used by files in the package itself.

Really, `sys.path` *is* the module search path. Python configures it at program startup, automatically merging the home directory of the top-level file (or an empty string to designate the current working directory), any `PYTHONPATH` directories, the contents of any *.pth* file paths you've created, and the standard library directories. The result is a list of directory name strings that Python searches on each import of a new file.

Python exposes this list for two good reasons. First, it provides a way to verify the search path settings you've made—if you don't see your settings somewhere in this list, you need to recheck your work. For example, here is what my module search path looks like on Windows under Python 3.0, with my `PYTHONPATH` set to `C:\users` and a *C:\Python30\mypath.pth* path file that lists `C:\users\mark`. The empty string at the front means current directory and my two settings are merged in (the rest are standard library directories and files):

```
>>> import sys
>>> sys.path
['', 'C:\\users', 'C:\\Windows\\system32\\python30.zip', 'c:\\Python30\\DLLs',
 'c:\\Python30\\lib', 'c:\\Python30\\lib\\plat-win', 'c:\\Python30',
 'C:\\Users\\Mark', 'c:\\Python30\\lib\\site-packages']
```

Second, if you know what you're doing, this list provides a way for scripts to tailor their search paths manually. As you'll see later in this part of the book, by modifying the `sys.path` list, you can modify the search path for all future imports. Such changes only last for the duration of the script, however; `PYTHONPATH` and *.pth* files offer more permanent ways to modify the path.§

Module File Selection

Keep in mind that filename suffixes (e.g., *.py*) are intentionally omitted from `import` statements. Python chooses the first file it can find on the search path that matches the imported name. For example, an `import` statement of the form `import b` might load:

- A source code file named *b.py*
- A byte code file named *b.pyc*
- A directory named *b*, for package imports (described in Chapter 23)
- A compiled extension module, usually coded in C or C++ and dynamically linked when imported (e.g., *b.so* on Linux, or *b.dll* or *b.pyd* on Cygwin and Windows)
- A compiled built-in module coded in C and statically linked into Python
- A ZIP file component that is automatically extracted when imported
- An in-memory image, for frozen executables

---

§ Some programs really need to change `sys.path`, though. Scripts that run on web servers, for example, often run as the user "nobody" to limit machine access. Because such scripts cannot usually depend on "nobody" to have set `PYTHONPATH` in any particular way, they often set `sys.path` manually to include required source directories, prior to running any `import` statements. A `sys.path.append(dirname)` will often suffice.

- A Java class, in the Jython version of Python
- A .NET component, in the IronPython version of Python

C extensions, Jython, and package imports all extend imports beyond simple files. To importers, though, differences in the loaded file type are completely transparent, both when importing and when fetching module attributes. Saying `import b` gets whatever module b is, according to your module search path, and `b.attr` fetches an item in the module, be it a Python variable or a linked-in C function. Some standard modules we will use in this book are actually coded in C, not Python; because of this transparency, their clients don't have to care.

If you have both a *b.py* and a *b.so* in different directories, Python will always load the one found in the first (leftmost) directory of your module search path during the left-to-right search of `sys.path`. But what happens if it finds both a *b.py* and a *b.so* in the *same* directory? In this case, Python follows a standard picking order, though this order is not guaranteed to stay the same over time. In general, you should not depend on which type of file Python will choose within a given directory—make your module names distinct, or configure your module search path to make your module selection preferences more obvious.

Advanced Module Selection Concepts

Normally, imports work as described in this section—they find and load files on your machine. However, it is possible to redefine much of what an import operation does in Python, using what are known as *import hooks*. These hooks can be used to make imports do various useful things, such as loading files from archives, performing decryption, and so on.

In fact, Python itself makes use of these hooks to enable files to be directly imported from ZIP archives: archived files are automatically extracted at import time when a *.zip* file is selected from the module import search path. One of the standard library directories in the earlier `sys.path` display, for example, is a *.zip* file today. For more details, see the Python standard library manual's description of the built-in `__import__` function, the customizable tool that `import` statements actually run.

Python also supports the notion of *.pyo* optimized byte code files, created and run with the `-O` Python command-line flag; because these run only slightly faster than normal *.pyc* files (typically 5 percent faster), however, they are infrequently used. The Psyco system (see Chapter 2) provides more substantial speedups.

Third-Party Software: distutils

This chapter's description of module search path settings is targeted mainly at user-defined source code that you write on your own. Third-party extensions for Python typically use the `distutils` tools in the standard library to automatically install themselves, so no path configuration is required to use their code.

Systems that use `distutils` generally come with a *setup.py* script, which is run to install them; this script imports and uses `distutils` modules to place such systems in a directory that is automatically part of the module search path (usually in the *Lib\site-packages* subdirectory of the Python install tree, wherever that resides on the target machine).

For more details on distributing and installing with `distutils`, see the Python standard manual set; its use is beyond the scope of this book (for instance, it also provides ways to automatically compile C-coded extensions on the target machine). Also check out the emerging third-party open source *eggs* system, which adds dependency checking for installed Python software.

Chapter Summary

In this chapter, we covered the basics of modules, attributes, and imports and explored the operation of `import` statements. We learned that imports find the designated file on the module search path, compile it to byte code, and execute all of its statements to generate its contents. We also learned how to configure the search path to be able to import from directories other than the home directory and the standard library directories, primarily with `PYTHONPATH` settings.

As this chapter demonstrated, the import operation and modules are at the heart of program architecture in Python. Larger programs are divided into multiple files, which are linked together at runtime by imports. Imports in turn use the module search path to locate files, and modules define attributes for external use.

Of course, the whole point of imports and modules is to provide a structure to your program, which divides its logic into self-contained software components. Code in one module is isolated from code in another; in fact, no file can ever see the names defined in another, unless explicit `import` statements are run. Because of this, modules minimize name collisions between different parts of your program.

You'll see what this all means in terms of actual statements and code in the next chapter. Before we move on, though, let's run through the chapter quiz.

Test Your Knowledge: Quiz

1. How does a module source code file become a module object?
2. Why might you have to set your `PYTHONPATH` environment variable?
3. Name the four major components of the module import search path.
4. Name four file types that Python might load in response to an import operation.
5. What is a namespace, and what does a module's namespace contain?

Test Your Knowledge: Answers

1. A module's source code file automatically becomes a module object when that module is imported. Technically, the module's source code is run during the import, one statement at a time, and all the names assigned in the process become attributes of the module object.

2. You only need to set PYTHONPATH to import from directories other than the one in which you are working (i.e., the current directory when working interactively, or the directory containing your top-level file).

3. The four major components of the module import search path are the top-level script's home directory (the directory containing it), all directories listed in the PYTHONPATH environment variable, the standard library directories, and all directories listed in *.pth* path files located in standard places. Of these, programmers can customize PYTHONPATH and *.pth* files.

4. Python might load a source code (*.py*) file, a byte code (*.pyc*) file, a C extension module (e.g., a *.so* file on Linux or a *.dll* or *.pyd* file on Windows), or a directory of the same name for package imports. Imports may also load more exotic things such as ZIP file components, Java classes under the Jython version of Python, .NET components under IronPython, and statically linked C extensions that have no files present at all. With import hooks, imports can load anything.

5. A namespace is a self-contained package of variables, which are known as the *attributes* of the namespace object. A module's namespace contains all the names assigned by code at the top level of the module file (i.e., not nested in def or class statements). Technically, a module's global scope morphs into the module object's attributes namespace. A module's namespace may also be altered by assignments from other files that import it, though this is frowned upon (see Chapter 17 for more on this issue).

## CHAPTER 22

Module Coding Basics

Now that we've looked at the larger ideas behind modules, let's turn to a simple example of modules in action. Python modules are easy to *create*; they're just files of Python program code created with a text editor. You don't need to write special syntax to tell Python you're making a module; almost any text file will do. Because Python handles all the details of finding and loading modules, modules are also easy to *use*; clients simply import a module, or specific names a module defines, and use the objects they reference.

Module Creation

To define a module, simply use your text editor to type some Python code into a text file, and save it with a ".py" extension; any such file is automatically considered a Python module. All the names assigned at the top level of the module become its *attributes* (names associated with the module object) and are exported for clients to use.

For instance, if you type the following def into a file called *module1.py* and import it, you create a module object with one attribute—the name `printer`, which happens to be a reference to a function object:

```
def printer(x):                    # Module attribute
    print(x)
```

Before we go on, I should say a few more words about module filenames. You can call modules just about anything you like, but module filenames should end in a *.py* suffix if you plan to import them. The *.py* is technically optional for top-level files that will be run but not imported, but adding it in all cases makes your files' types more obvious and allows you to import any of your files in the future.

Because module names become variable names inside a Python program (without the *.py*), they should also follow the normal variable name rules outlined in Chapter 11. For instance, you can create a module file named *if.py*, but you cannot import it because `if` is a reserved word—when you try to run `import if`, you'll get a syntax error. In fact, both the names of module files and the names of directories used in package imports (discussed in the next chapter) must conform to the rules for variable names presented in Chapter 11; they may, for instance, contain only letters, digits, and underscores. Package directories also cannot contain platform-specific syntax such as spaces in their names.

When a module is imported, Python maps the internal module name to an external filename by adding a directory path from the module search path to the front, and a *.py* or other extension at the end. For instance, a module named M ultimately maps to some external file *<directory>\M.<extension>* that contains the module's code.

As mentioned in the preceding chapter, it is also possible to create a Python module by writing code in an external language such as C or C++ (or Java, in the Jython implementation of the language). Such modules are called *extension modules*, and they are generally used to wrap up external libraries for use in Python scripts. When imported by Python code, extension modules look and feel the same as modules coded as Python source code files—they are accessed with import statements, and they provide functions and objects as module attributes. Extension modules are beyond the scope of this book; see Python's standard manuals or advanced texts such as *Programming Python* for more details.

Module Usage

Clients can use the simple module file we just wrote by running an import or from statement. Both statements find, compile, and run a module file's code, if it hasn't yet been loaded. The chief difference is that import fetches the module as a whole, so you must qualify to fetch its names; in contrast, from fetches (or copies) specific names out of the module.

Let's see what this means in terms of code. All of the following examples wind up calling the printer function defined in the prior section's *module1.py* module file, but in different ways.

The import Statement

In the first example, the name module1 serves two different purposes—it identifies an external file to be loaded, and it becomes a variable in the script, which references the module object after the file is loaded:

```
>>> import module1                          # Get module as a whole
>>> module1.printer('Hello world!')         # Qualify to get names
Hello world!
```

Because import gives a name that refers to the whole module object, we must go through the module name to fetch its attributes (e.g., module1.printer).

The from Statement

By contrast, because `from` also copies names from one file over to another scope, it allows us to use the copied names directly in the script without going through the module (e.g., `printer`):

```
>>> from module1 import printer        # Copy out one variable
>>> printer('Hello world!')            # No need to qualify name
Hello world!
```

This has the same effect as the prior example, but because the imported name is copied into the scope where the `from` statement appears, using that name in the script requires less typing: we can use it directly instead of naming the enclosing module.

As you'll see in more detail later, the `from` statement is really just a minor extension to the `import` statement—it imports the module file as usual, but adds an extra step that copies one or more names out of the file.

The from * Statement

Finally, the next example uses a special form of `from`: when we use a *, we get copies of *all* the names assigned at the top level of the referenced module. Here again, we can then use the copied name `printer` in our script without going through the module name:

```
>>> from module1 import *              # Copy out all variables
>>> printer('Hello world!')
Hello world!
```

Technically, both `import` and `from` statements invoke the same import operation; the `from *` form simply adds an extra step that copies all the names in the module into the importing scope. It essentially collapses one module's namespace into another; again, the net effect is less typing for us.

And that's it—modules really are simple to use. To give you a better understanding of what really happens when you define and use modules, though, let's move on to look at some of their properties in more detail.

In Python 3.0, the `from ...*` statement form described here can be used *only* at the top level of a module file, not within a function. Python 2.6 allows it to be used within a function, but issues a warning. It's extremely rare to see this statement used inside a function in practice; when present, it makes it impossible for Python to detect variables statically, before the function runs.

Imports Happen Only Once

One of the most common questions people seem to ask when they start using modules is, "Why won't my imports keep working?" They often report that the first import works fine, but later imports during an interactive session (or program run) seem to have no effect. In fact, they're not supposed to. This section explains why.

Modules are loaded and run on the first `import` or `from`, and only the first. This is on purpose—because importing is an expensive operation, by default Python does it just once per file, per process. Later import operations simply fetch the already loaded module object.

As one consequence, because top-level code in a module file is usually executed only once, you can use it to initialize variables. Consider the file *simple.py*, for example:

```
print('hello')
spam = 1                        # Initialize variable
```

In this example, the `print` and `=` statements run the first time the module is imported, and the variable `spam` is initialized at import time:

```
% python
>>> import simple              # First import: loads and runs file's code
hello
>>> simple.spam                # Assignment makes an attribute
1
```

Second and later imports don't rerun the module's code; they just fetch the already created module object from Python's internal modules table. Thus, the variable `spam` is not reinitialized:

```
>>> simple.spam = 2            # Change attribute in module
>>> import simple              # Just fetches already loaded module
>>> simple.spam                # Code wasn't rerun: attribute unchanged
2
```

Of course, sometimes you really want a module's code to be rerun on a subsequent import. We'll see how to do this with Python's `reload` function later in this chapter.

import and from Are Assignments

Just like `def`, `import` and `from` are executable statements, not compile-time declarations. They may be nested in `if` tests, appear in function `defs`, and so on, and they are not resolved or run until Python reaches them while executing your program. In other words, imported modules and names are not available until their associated `import` or `from` statements run. Also, like `def`, `import` and `from` are implicit assignments:

- `import` assigns an entire module object to a single name.
- `from` assigns one or more names to objects of the same names in another module.

All the things we've already discussed about assignment apply to module access, too. For instance, names copied with a `from` become references to shared objects; as with function arguments, reassigning a fetched name has no effect on the module from which it was copied, but changing a fetched *mutable object* can change it in the module from which it was imported. To illustrate, consider the following file, *small.py*:

```
x = 1
y = [1, 2]

% python
>>> from small import x, y          # Copy two names out
>>> x = 42                          # Changes local x only
>>> y[0] = 42                       # Changes shared mutable in-place
```

Here, `x` is not a shared mutable object, but `y` is. The name `y` in the importer and the importee reference the same list object, so changing it from one place changes it in the other:

```
>>> import small                    # Get module name (from doesn't)
>>> small.x                         # Small's x is not my x
1
>>> small.y                         # But we share a changed mutable
[42, 2]
```

For a graphical picture of what `from` assignments do with references, flip back to Figure 18-1 (function argument passing), and mentally replace "caller" and "function" with "imported" and "importer." The effect is the same, except that here we're dealing with names in modules, not functions. Assignment works the same everywhere in Python.

Cross-File Name Changes

Recall from the preceding example that the assignment to `x` in the interactive session changed the name `x` in that scope only, not the `x` in the file—there is no link from a name copied with `from` back to the file it came from. To really change a global name in another file, you must use `import`:

```
% python
>>> from small import x, y          # Copy two names out
>>> x = 42                          # Changes my x only

>>> import small                    # Get module name
>>> small.x = 42                    # Changes x in other module
```

This phenomenon was introduced in Chapter 17. Because changing variables in other modules like this is a common source of confusion (and often a bad design choice), we'll revisit this technique again later in this part of the book. Note that the change to `y[0]` in the prior session is different; it changes an object, not a name.

import and from Equivalence

Notice in the prior example that we have to execute an `import` statement after the `from` to access the `small` module name at all. `from` only copies names from one module to another; it does not assign the module name itself. At least conceptually, a `from` statement like this one:

```
from module import name1, name2     # Copy these two names out (only)
```

is equivalent to this statement sequence:

```
import module                # Fetch the module object
name1 = module.name1         # Copy names out by assignment
name2 = module.name2
del module                   # Get rid of the module name
```

Like all assignments, the `from` statement creates new variables in the importer, which initially refer to objects of the same names in the imported file. Only the names are copied out, though, not the module itself. When we use the `from *` form of this statement (`from module import *`), the equivalence is the same, but all the top-level names in the module are copied over to the importing scope this way.

Notice that the first step of the `from` runs a normal `import` operation. Because of this, the `from` always imports the entire module into memory if it has not yet been imported, regardless of how many names it copies out of the file. There is no way to load just part of a module file (e.g., just one function), but because modules are byte code in Python instead of machine code, the performance implications are generally negligible.

Potential Pitfalls of the from Statement

Because the `from` statement makes the location of a variable more implicit and obscure (`name` is less meaningful to the reader than `module.name`), some Python users recommend using `import` instead of `from` most of the time. I'm not sure this advice is warranted, though; `from` is commonly and widely used, without too many dire consequences. In practice, in realistic programs, it's often convenient not to have to type a module's name every time you wish to use one of its tools. This is especially true for large modules that provide many attributes—the standard library's `tkinter` GUI module, for example.

It is true that the `from` statement has the potential to corrupt namespaces, at least in principle—if you use it to import variables that happen to have the same names as existing variables in your scope, your variables will be silently overwritten. This problem doesn't occur with the simple `import` statement because you must always go through a module's name to get to its contents (`module.attr` will not clash with a variable named `attr` in your scope). As long as you understand and expect that this can happen when using `from`, though, this isn't a major concern in practice, especially if you list the imported names explicitly (e.g., `from module import x, y, z`).

On the other hand, the `from` statement has more serious issues when used in conjunction with the `reload` call, as imported names might reference prior versions of objects.

Moreover, the `from module import *` form really can corrupt namespaces and make names difficult to understand, especially when applied to more than one file—in this case, there is no way to tell which module a name came from, short of searching the external source files. In effect, the `from *` form collapses one namespace into another, and so defeats the namespace partitioning feature of modules. We will explore these issues in more detail in the section "Module Gotchas" on page 601 at the end of this part of the book (see Chapter 24).

Probably the best real-world advice here is to generally prefer `import` to `from` for simple modules, to explicitly list the variables you want in most `from` statements, and to limit the `from *` form to just one import per file. That way, any undefined names can be assumed to live in the module referenced with the `from *`. Some care is required when using the `from` statement, but armed with a little knowledge, most programmers find it to be a convenient way to access modules.

When import is required

The only time you really must use `import` instead of `from` is when you must use the same name defined in two different modules. For example, if two files define the same name differently:

```
# M.py

def func():
    ...do something...
```

```
# N.py

def func():
    ...do something else...
```

and you must use both versions of the name in your program, the `from` statement will fail—you can only have one assignment to the name in your scope:

```
# O.py

from M import func
from N import func      # This overwites the one we got from M
func()                  # Calls N.func only
```

An `import` will work here, though, because including the name of the enclosing module makes the two names unique:

```
# O.py

import M, N             # Get the whole modules, not their names
M.func()                # We can call both names now
N.func()                # The module names make them unique
```

This case is unusual enough that you're unlikely to encounter it very often in practice. If you do, though, `import` allows you to avoid the name collision.

Module Namespaces

Modules are probably best understood as simply packages of names—i.e., places to define names you want to make visible to the rest of a system. Technically, modules usually correspond to files, and Python creates a module object to contain all the names assigned in a module file. But in simple terms, modules are just namespaces (places where names are created), and the names that live in a module are called its *attributes*. We'll explore how all this works in this section.

Files Generate Namespaces

So, how do files morph into namespaces? The short story is that every name that is assigned a value at the top level of a module file (i.e., not nested in a function or class body) becomes an attribute of that module.

For instance, given an assignment statement such as X = 1 at the top level of a module file *M.py*, the name X becomes an attribute of M, which we can refer to from outside the module as M.X. The name X also becomes a global variable to other code inside *M.py*, but we need to explain the notion of module loading and scopes a bit more formally to understand why:

- **Module statements run on the first import**. The first time a module is imported anywhere in a system, Python creates an empty module object and executes the statements in the module file one after another, from the top of the file to the bottom.

- **Top-level assignments create module attributes**. During an import, statements at the top level of the file not nested in a def or class that assign names (e.g., =, def) create attributes of the module object; assigned names are stored in the module's namespace.

- **Module namespaces can be accessed via the attribute __dict__ or dir(M)**. Module namespaces created by imports are dictionaries; they may be accessed through the built-in __dict__ attribute associated with module objects and may be inspected with the dir function. The dir function is roughly equivalent to the sorted keys list of an object's __dict__ attribute, but it includes inherited names for classes, may not be complete, and is prone to changing from release to release.

- **Modules are a single scope (local is global)**. As we saw in Chapter 17, names at the top level of a module follow the same reference/assignment rules as names in a function, but the local and global scopes are the same (more formally, they follow the LEGB scope rule we met in Chapter 17, but without the L and E lookup layers). But, in modules, the module *scope* becomes an attribute dictionary of a module *object* after the module has been loaded. Unlike with functions (where the local namespace exists only while the function runs), a module file's scope becomes a module object's attribute namespace and lives on after the import.

Here's a demonstration of these ideas. Suppose we create the following module file in a text editor and call it *module2.py*:

```
print('starting to load...')
import sys
name = 42

def func(): pass

class klass: pass

print('done loading.')
```

The first time this module is imported (or run as a program), Python executes its statements from top to bottom. Some statements create names in the module's namespace as a side effect, but others do actual work while the import is going on. For instance, the two `print` statements in this file execute at import time:

```
>>> import module2
starting to load...
done loading.
```

Once the module is loaded, its scope becomes an attribute namespace in the module object we get back from `import`. We can then access attributes in this namespace by qualifying them with the name of the enclosing module:

```
>>> module2.sys
<module 'sys' (built-in)>

>>> module2.name
42

>>> module2.func
<function func at 0x026D3BB8>

>>> module2.klass
<class 'module2.klass'>
```

Here, `sys`, `name`, `func`, and `klass` were all assigned while the module's statements were being run, so they are attributes after the import. We'll talk about classes in Part VI, but notice the `sys` attribute—`import` statements really *assign* module objects to names, and any type of assignment to a name at the top level of a file generates a module attribute.

Internally, module namespaces are stored as dictionary objects. These are just normal dictionary objects with the usual methods. We can access a module's namespace dictionary through the module's `__dict__` attribute (remember to wrap this in a `list` call in Python 3.0—it's a view object):

```
>>> list(module2.__dict__.keys())
['name', '__builtins__', '__file__', '__package__', 'sys', 'klass', 'func',
'__name__', '__doc__']
```

The names we assigned in the module file become dictionary keys internally, so most of the names here reflect top-level assignments in our file. However, Python also adds some names in the module's namespace for us; for instance, __file__ gives the name of the file the module was loaded from, and __name__ gives its name as known to importers (without the *.py* extension and directory path).

Attribute Name Qualification

Now that you're becoming more familiar with modules, we should look at the notion of name *qualification* (fetching attributes) in more depth. In Python, you can access the attributes of any object that has attributes using the qualification syntax `object.attribute`.

Qualification is really an expression that returns the value assigned to an attribute name associated with an object. For example, the expression `module2.sys` in the previous example fetches the value assigned to `sys` in `module2`. Similarly, if we have a built-in list object `L`, `L.append` returns the `append` method object associated with that list.

So, what does attribute qualification do to the scope rules we studied in Chapter 17? Nothing, really: it's an independent concept. When you use qualification to access names, you give Python an explicit object from which to fetch the specified names. The LEGB rule applies only to bare, unqualified names. Here are the rules:

Simple variables
    `X` means search for the name `X` in the current scopes (following the LEGB rule).

Qualification
    `X.Y` means find `X` in the current scopes, then search for the attribute `Y` in the object `X` (not in scopes).

Qualification paths
    `X.Y.Z` means look up the name `Y` in the object `X`, then look up `Z` in the object `X.Y`.

Generality
    Qualification works on all objects with attributes: modules, classes, C extension types, etc.

In Part VI, we'll see that qualification means a bit more for classes (it's also the place where something called *inheritance* happens), but in general, the rules outlined here apply to all names in Python.

Imports Versus Scopes

As we've learned, it is never possible to access names defined in another module file without first importing that file. That is, you never automatically get to see names in another file, regardless of the structure of imports or function calls in your program. A variable's meaning is always determined by the locations of assignments in your source code, and attributes are always requested of an object explicitly.

For example, consider the following two simple modules. The first, *moda.py*, defines a variable X global to code in its file only, along with a function that changes the global X in this file:

```
X = 88              # My X: global to this file only
def f():
    global X        # Change this file's X
    X = 99          # Cannot see names in other modules
```

The second module, *modb.py*, defines its own global variable X and imports and calls the function in the first module:

```
X = 11              # My X: global to this file only

import moda         # Gain access to names in moda
moda.f()            # Sets moda.X, not this file's X
print(X, moda.X)
```

When run, `moda.f` changes the X in `moda`, not the X in `modb`. The global scope for `moda.f` is always the file enclosing it, regardless of which module it is ultimately called from:

```
% python modb.py
11 99
```

In other words, import operations never give upward visibility to code in imported files—an imported file cannot see names in the importing file. More formally:

- Functions can never see names in other functions, unless they are physically enclosing.
- Module code can never see names in other modules, unless they are explicitly imported.

Such behavior is part of the *lexical scoping* notion—in Python, the scopes surrounding a piece of code are completely determined by the code's physical position in your file. Scopes are never influenced by function calls or module imports.[*]

Namespace Nesting

In some sense, although imports do not nest namespaces upward, they do nest downward. Using attribute qualification paths, it's possible to descend into arbitrarily nested modules and access their attributes. For example, consider the next three files. *mod3.py* defines a single global name and attribute by assignment:

```
X = 3
```

mod2.py in turn defines its own X, then imports mod3 and uses qualification to access the imported module's attribute:

---

[*] Some languages act differently and provide for *dynamic scoping*, where scopes really may depend on runtime calls. This tends to make code trickier, though, because the meaning of a variable can differ over time.

```
X = 2
import mod3

print(X, end=' ')            # My global X
print(mod3.X)                # mod3's X
```

mod1.py also defines its own X, then imports mod2, and fetches attributes in both the first and second files:

```
X = 1
import mod2

print(X, end=' ')            # My global X
print(mod2.X, end=' ')       # mod2's X
print(mod2.mod3.X)           # Nested mod3's X
```

Really, when mod1 imports mod2 here, it sets up a two-level namespace nesting. By using the path of names mod2.mod3.X, it can descend into mod3, which is nested in the imported mod2. The net effect is that mod1 can see the Xs in all three files, and hence has access to all three global scopes:

```
% python mod1.py
2 3
1 2 3
```

The reverse, however, is not true: mod3 cannot see names in mod2, and mod2 cannot see names in mod1. This example may be easier to grasp if you don't think in terms of namespaces and scopes, but instead focus on the objects involved. Within mod1, mod2 is just a name that refers to an object with attributes, some of which may refer to other objects with attributes (import is an assignment). For paths like mod2.mod3.X, Python simply evaluates from left to right, fetching attributes from objects along the way.

Note that mod1 can say import mod2, and then mod2.mod3.X, but it cannot say import mod2.mod3—this syntax invokes something called package (directory) imports, described in the next chapter. Package imports also create module namespace nesting, but their import statements are taken to reflect directory trees, not simple import chains.

Reloading Modules

As we've seen, a module's code is run only once per process by default. To force a module's code to be reloaded and rerun, you need to ask Python to do so explicitly by calling the reload built-in function. In this section, we'll explore how to use reloads to make your systems more dynamic. In a nutshell:

- Imports (via both import and from statements) load and run a module's code only the first time the module is imported in a process.

- Later imports use the already loaded module object without reloading or rerunning the file's code.

- The `reload` function forces an already loaded module's code to be reloaded and rerun. Assignments in the file's new code change the existing module object in-place.

Why all the fuss about reloading modules? The `reload` function allows parts of a program to be changed without stopping the whole program. With `reload`, therefore, the effects of changes in components can be observed immediately. Reloading doesn't help in every situation, but where it does, it makes for a much shorter development cycle. For instance, imagine a database program that must connect to a server on startup; because program changes or customizations can be tested immediately after reloads, you need to connect only once while debugging. Long-running servers can update themselves this way, too.

Because Python is interpreted (more or less), it already gets rid of the compile/link steps you need to go through to get a C program to run: modules are loaded dynamically when imported by a running program. Reloading offers a further performance advantage by allowing you to also change parts of running programs without stopping. Note that `reload` currently only works on modules written in Python; compiled extension modules coded in a language such as C can be dynamically loaded at runtime, too, but they can't be reloaded.

 Version skew note: In Python 2.6, `reload` is available as a built-in function. In Python 3.0, it has been moved to the `imp` standard library module—it's known as `imp.reload` in 3.0. This simply means that an extra `import` or `from` statement is required to load this tool (in 3.0 only). Readers using 2.6 can ignore these imports in this book's examples, or use them anyhow—2.6 also has a `reload` in its `imp` module to ease migration to 3.0. Reloading works the same regardless of its packaging.

reload Basics

Unlike `import` and `from`:

- `reload` is a function in Python, not a statement.
- `reload` is passed an existing module object, not a name.
- `reload` lives in a module in Python 3.0 and must be imported itself.

Because `reload` expects an object, a module must have been previously imported successfully before you can reload it (if the import was unsuccessful, due to a syntax or other error, you may need to repeat it before you can reload the module). Furthermore, the syntax of `import` statements and `reload` calls differs: reloads require parentheses, but imports do not. Reloading looks like this:

```
import module                    # Initial import
...use module.attributes...
...                              # Now, go change the module file
...
```

```
from imp import reload          # Get reload itself (in 3.0)
reload(module)                  # Get updated exports
...use module.attributes...
```

The typical usage pattern is that you import a module, then change its source code in a text editor, and then reload it. When you call `reload`, Python rereads the module file's source code and reruns its top-level statements. Perhaps the most important thing to know about `reload` is that it changes a module object *in-place*; it does not delete and re-create the module object. Because of that, every reference to a module object anywhere in your program is automatically affected by a reload. Here are the details:

- **reload runs a module file's new code in the module's current namespace.** Rerunning a module file's code overwrites its existing namespace, rather than deleting and re-creating it.

- **Top-level assignments in the file replace names with new values.** For instance, rerunning a `def` statement replaces the prior version of the function in the module's namespace by reassigning the function name.

- **Reloads impact all clients that use `import` to fetch modules.** Because clients that use `import` qualify to fetch attributes, they'll find new values in the module object after a reload.

- **Reloads impact future `from` clients only.** Clients that used `from` to fetch attributes in the past won't be affected by a reload; they'll still have references to the old objects fetched before the reload.

reload Example

To demonstrate, here's a more concrete example of `reload` in action. In the following, we'll change and reload a module file without stopping the interactive Python session. Reloads are used in many other scenarios, too (see the sidebar "Why You Will Care: Module Reloads" on page 559), but we'll keep things simple for illustration here. First, in the text editor of your choice, write a module file named *changer.py* with the following contents:

```
message = "First version"
def printer():
    print(message)
```

This module creates and exports two names—one bound to a string, and another to a function. Now, start the Python interpreter, import the module, and call the function it exports. The function will print the value of the global `message` variable:

```
% python
>>> import changer
>>> changer.printer()
First version
```

Keeping the interpreter active, now edit the module file in another window:

```
...modify changer.py without stopping Python...
% vi changer.py
```

Change the global `message` variable, as well as the `printer` function body:

```
message = "After editing"
def printer():
    print('reloaded:', message)
```

Then, return to the Python window and reload the module to fetch the new code. Notice in the following interaction that importing the module again has no effect; we get the original message, even though the file's been changed. We have to call `reload` in order to get the new version:

```
...back to the Python interpreter/program...

>>> import changer
>>> changer.printer()                    # No effect: uses loaded module
First version
>>> from imp import reload
>>> reload(changer)                      # Forces new code to load/run
<module 'changer' from 'changer.py'>
>>> changer.printer()                    # Runs the new version now
reloaded: After editing
```

Notice that `reload` actually *returns* the module object for us—its result is usually ignored, but because expression results are printed at the interactive prompt, Python shows a default <module 'name'...> representation.

Why You Will Care: Module Reloads

Besides allowing you to reload (and hence rerun) modules at the interactive prompt, module reloads are also useful in larger systems, especially when the cost of restarting the entire application is prohibitive. For instance, systems that must connect to servers over a network on startup are prime candidates for dynamic reloads.

They're also useful in GUI work (a widget's callback action can be changed while the GUI remains active), and when Python is used as an embedded language in a C or C++ program (the enclosing program can request a reload of the Python code it runs, without having to stop). See *Programming Python* for more on reloading GUI callbacks and embedded Python code.

More generally, reloads allow programs to provide highly dynamic interfaces. For instance, Python is often used as a *customization* language for larger systems—users can customize products by coding bits of Python code onsite, without having to recompile the entire product (or even having its source code at all). In such worlds, the Python code already adds a dynamic flavor by itself.

To be even more dynamic, though, such systems can automatically reload the Python customization code periodically at runtime. That way, users' changes are picked up while the system is running; there is no need to stop and restart each time the Python code is modified. Not all systems require such a dynamic approach, but for those that do, module reloads provide an easy-to-use dynamic customization tool.

Chapter Summary

This chapter delved into the basics of module coding tools—the `import` and `from` statements, and the `reload` call. We learned how the `from` statement simply adds an extra step that copies names out of a file after it has been imported, and how `reload` forces a file to be imported again without stopping and restarting Python. We also surveyed namespace concepts, saw what happens when imports are nested, explored the way files become module namespaces, and learned about some potential pitfalls of the `from` statement.

Although we've already seen enough to handle module files in our programs, the next chapter extends our coverage of the import model by presenting *package imports*—a way for our `import` statements to specify part of the directory path leading to the desired module. As we'll see, package imports give us a hierarchy that is useful in larger systems and allow us to break conflicts between same-named modules. Before we move on, though, here's a quick quiz on the concepts presented here.

Test Your Knowledge: Quiz

1. How do you make a module?
2. How is the `from` statement related to the `import` statement?
3. How is the `reload` function related to imports?
4. When must you use `import` instead of `from`?
5. Name three potential pitfalls of the `from` statement.
6. What...is the airspeed velocity of an unladen swallow?

Test Your Knowledge: Answers

1. To create a module, you just write a text file containing Python statements; every source code file is automatically a module, and there is no syntax for declaring one. Import operations load module files into module objects in memory. You can also make a module by writing code in an external language like C or Java, but such extension modules are beyond the scope of this book.

2. The `from` statement imports an entire module, like the `import` statement, but as an extra step it also copies one or more variables from the imported module into the scope where the `from` appears. This enables you to use the imported names directly (`name`) instead of having to go through the module (`module.name`).

3. By default, a module is imported only once per process. The `reload` function forces a module to be imported again. It is mostly used to pick up new versions of a module's source code during development, and in dynamic customization scenarios.

4. You must use `import` instead of `from` only when you need to access the same name in two different modules; because you'll have to specify the names of the enclosing modules, the two names will be unique.

5. The `from` statement can obscure the meaning of a variable (which module it is defined in), can have problems with the `reload` call (names may reference prior versions of objects), and can corrupt namespaces (it might silently overwrite names you are using in your scope). The `from *` form is worse in most regards—it can seriously corrupt namespaces and obscure the meaning of variables, so it is probably best used sparingly.

6. What do you mean? An African or European swallow?

CHAPTER 23

Module Packages

So far, when we've imported modules, we've been loading files. This represents typical module usage, and it's probably the technique you'll use for most imports you'll code early on in your Python career. However, the module import story is a bit richer than I have thus far implied.

In addition to a module name, an import can name a directory path. A directory of Python code is said to be a *package*, so such imports are known as *package imports*. In effect, a package import turns a directory on your computer into another Python name-space, with attributes corresponding to the subdirectories and module files that the directory contains.

This is a somewhat advanced feature, but the hierarchy it provides turns out to be handy for organizing the files in a large system and tends to simplify module search path settings. As we'll see, package imports are also sometimes required to resolve import ambiguities when multiple program files of the same name are installed on a single machine.

Because it is relevant to code in packages only, we'll also introduce Python's recent *relative imports* model and syntax here. As we'll see, this model modifies search paths and extends the from statement for imports within packages.

Package Import Basics

So, how do package imports work? In the place where you have been naming a simple file in your import statements, you can instead list a path of names separated by periods:

```
import dir1.dir2.mod
```

The same goes for from statements:

```
from dir1.dir2.mod import x
```

The "dotted" path in these statements is assumed to correspond to a path through the directory hierarchy on your machine, leading to the file *mod.py* (or similar; the extension may vary). That is, the preceding statements indicate that on your machine there is a directory *dir1*, which has a subdirectory *dir2*, which contains a module file *mod.py* (or similar).

Furthermore, these imports imply that *dir1* resides within some container directory *dir0*, which is a component of the Python module search path. In other words, the two `import` statements imply a directory structure that looks something like this (shown with DOS backslash separators):

```
dir0\dir1\dir2\mod.py          # Or mod.pyc, mod.so, etc.
```

The container directory *dir0* needs to be added to your module search path (unless it's the home directory of the top-level file), exactly as if *dir1* were a simple module file.

More generally, the leftmost component in a package import path is still relative to a directory included in the `sys.path` module search path list we met in Chapter 21. From there down, though, the `import` statements in your script give the directory paths leading to the modules explicitly.

Packages and Search Path Settings

If you use this feature, keep in mind that the directory paths in your `import` statements can only be variables separated by periods. You cannot use any platform-specific path syntax in your `import` statements, such as `C:\dir1`, `My Documents.dir2` or `../dir1`—these do not work syntactically. Instead, use platform-specific syntax in your module search path settings to name the container directories.

For instance, in the prior example, *dir0*—the directory name you add to your module search path—can be an arbitrarily long and platform-specific directory path leading up to *dir1*. Instead of using an invalid statement like this:

```
import C:\mycode\dir1\dir2\mod      # Error: illegal syntax
```

add *C:\mycode* to your PYTHONPATH variable or a *.pth* file (assuming it is not the program's home directory, in which case this step is not necessary), and say this in your script:

```
import dir1.dir2.mod
```

In effect, entries on the module search path provide platform-specific directory path prefixes, which lead to the leftmost names in `import` statements. `import` statements provide directory path tails in a platform-neutral fashion.*

---

* The dot path syntax was chosen partly for platform neutrality, but also because paths in `import` statements become real nested object paths. This syntax also means that you get odd error messages if you forget to omit the *.py* in your `import` statements. For example, `import mod.py` is assumed to be a directory path import—it loads *mod.py*, then tries to load a *mod\py.py*, and ultimately issues a potentially confusing "No module named py" error message.

Package __init__.py Files

If you choose to use package imports, there is one more constraint you must follow: each directory named within the path of a package import statement must contain a file named *__init__.py*, or your package imports will fail. That is, in the example we've been using, both *dir1* and *dir2* must contain a file called *__init__.py*; the container directory *dir0* does not require such a file because it's not listed in the import statement itself. More formally, for a directory structure such as this:

```
dir0\dir1\dir2\mod.py
```

and an import statement of the form:

```
import dir1.dir2.mod
```

the following rules apply:

- *dir1* and *dir2* both must contain an *__init__.py* file.
- *dir0*, the container, does not require an *__init__.py* file; this file will simply be ignored if present.
- *dir0*, not *dir0\dir1*, must be listed on the module search path (i.e., it must be the home directory, or be listed in your PYTHONPATH, etc.).

The net effect is that this example's directory structure should be as follows, with indentation designating directory nesting:

```
dir0\                          # Container on module search path
    dir1\
        __init__.py
        dir2\
            __init__.py
            mod.py
```

The *__init__.py* files can contain Python code, just like normal module files. They are partly present as a declaration to Python, however, and can be completely empty. As declarations, these files serve to prevent directories with common names from unintentionally hiding true modules that appear later on the module search path. Without this safeguard, Python might pick a directory that has nothing to do with your code, just because it appears in an earlier directory on the search path.

More generally, the *__init__.py* file serves as a hook for package-initialization-time actions, generates a module namespace for a directory, and implements the behavior of from * (i.e., from .. import *) statements when used with directory imports:

Package initialization
> The first time Python imports through a directory, it automatically runs all the code in the directory's *__init__.py* file. Because of that, these files are a natural place to put code to initialize the state required by files in a package. For instance, a package might use its initialization file to create required data files, open connections to

databases, and so on. Typically, _*init*_.py files are not meant to be useful if executed directly; they are run automatically when a package is first accessed.

Module namespace initialization

In the package import model, the directory paths in your script become real nested object paths after an import. For instance, in the preceding example, after the import the expression `dir1.dir2` works and returns a module object whose namespace contains all the names assigned by *dir2*'s _*init*_.py file. Such files provide a namespace for module objects created for directories, which have no real associated module files.

`from` * *statement behavior*

As an advanced feature, you can use _*all*_ lists in _*init*_.py files to define what is exported when a directory is imported with the `from` * statement form. In an _*init*_.py file, the _*all*_ list is taken to be the list of submodule names that should be imported when `from` * is used on the package (directory) name. If _*all*_ is not set, the `from` * statement does not automatically load submodules nested in the directory; instead, it loads just names defined by assignments in the directory's _*init*_.py file, including any submodules explicitly imported by code in this file. For instance, the statement `from submodule import X` in a directory's _*init*_.py makes the name X available in that directory's namespace. (We'll see additional roles for _*all*_ in Chapter 24.)

You can also simply leave these files empty, if their roles are beyond your needs (and frankly, they are often empty in practice). They must exist, though, for your directory imports to work at all.

> Don't confuse package _*init*_.py files with the class _init_ constructor methods we'll meet in the next part of the book. The former are files of code run when `imports` first step through a package directory, while the latter are called when an instance is created. Both have initialization roles, but they are otherwise very different.

Package Import Example

Let's actually code the example we've been talking about to show how initialization files and paths come into play. The following three files are coded in a directory *dir1* and its subdirectory *dir2*—comments give the path names of these files:

```
# dir1\__init__.py
print('dir1 init')
x = 1

# dir1\dir2\__init__.py
print('dir2 init')
y = 2
```

```
# dir1\dir2\mod.py
print('in mod.py')
z = 3
```

Here, *dir1* will be either a subdirectory of the one we're working in (i.e., the home directory), or a subdirectory of a directory that is listed on the module search path (technically, on `sys.path`). Either way, *dir1*'s container does not need an *__init__.py* file.

`import` statements run each directory's initialization file the first time that directory is traversed, as Python descends the path; `print` statements are included here to trace their execution. As with module files, an already imported directory may be passed to `reload` to force reexecution of that single item. As shown here, `reload` accepts a dotted pathname to reload nested directories and files:

```
% python
>>> import dir1.dir2.mod        # First imports run init files
dir1 init
dir2 init
in mod.py
>>>
>>> import dir1.dir2.mod        # Later imports do not
>>>
>>> from imp import reload      # Needed in 3.0
>>> reload(dir1)
dir1 init
<module 'dir1' from 'dir1\__init__.pyc'>
>>>
>>> reload(dir1.dir2)
dir2 init
<module 'dir1.dir2' from 'dir1\dir2\__init__.pyc'>
```

Once imported, the path in your `import` statement becomes a *nested object path* in your script. Here, `mod` is an object nested in the object `dir2`, which in turn is nested in the object `dir1`:

```
>>> dir1
<module 'dir1' from 'dir1\__init__.pyc'>
>>> dir1.dir2
<module 'dir1.dir2' from 'dir1\dir2\__init__.pyc'>
>>> dir1.dir2.mod
<module 'dir1.dir2.mod' from 'dir1\dir2\mod.pyc'>
```

In fact, each directory name in the path becomes a variable assigned to a module object whose namespace is initialized by all the assignments in that directory's *__init__.py* file. `dir1.x` refers to the variable `x` assigned in *dir1__init__.py*, much as `mod.z` refers to the variable `z` assigned in *mod.py*:

```
>>> dir1.x
1
>>> dir1.dir2.y
2
>>> dir1.dir2.mod.z
3
```

from Versus import with Packages

`import` statements can be somewhat inconvenient to use with packages, because you may have to retype the paths frequently in your program. In the prior section's example, for instance, you must retype and rerun the full path from `dir1` each time you want to reach `z`. If you try to access `dir2` or `mod` directly, you'll get an error:

```
>>> dir2.mod
NameError: name 'dir2' is not defined
>>> mod.z
NameError: name 'mod' is not defined
```

It's often more convenient, therefore, to use the `from` statement with packages to avoid retyping the paths at each access. Perhaps more importantly, if you ever restructure your directory tree, the `from` statement requires just one path update in your code, whereas `import`s may require many. The `import as` extension, discussed formally in the next chapter, can also help here by providing a shorter synonym for the full path:

```
% python
>>> from dir1.dir2 import mod        # Code path here only
dir1 init
dir2 init
in mod.py
>>> mod.z                            # Don't repeat path
3
>>> from dir1.dir2.mod import z
>>> z
3
>>> import dir1.dir2.mod as mod      # Use shorter name (see Chapter 24)
>>> mod.z
3
```

Why Use Package Imports?

If you're new to Python, make sure that you've mastered simple modules before stepping up to packages, as they are a somewhat advanced feature. They do serve useful roles, though, especially in larger programs: they make imports more informative, serve as an organizational tool, simplify your module search path, and can resolve ambiguities.

First of all, because package imports give some directory information in program files, they both make it easier to locate your files and serve as an organizational tool. Without package paths, you must often resort to consulting the module search path to find files. Moreover, if you organize your files into subdirectories for functional areas, package imports make it more obvious what role a module plays, and so make your code more readable. For example, a normal import of a file in a directory somewhere on the module search path, like this:

```
import utilities
```

offers much less information than an import that includes the path:

```
import database.client.utilities
```

Package imports can also greatly simplify your PYTHONPATH and *.pth* file search path settings. In fact, if you use explicit package imports for all your cross-directory imports, and you make those package imports relative to a common root directory where all your Python code is stored, you really only need a single entry on your search path: the common root. Finally, package imports serve to resolve ambiguities by making explicit exactly which files you want to import. The next section explores this role in more detail.

A Tale of Three Systems

The only time package imports are actually required is to resolve ambiguities that may arise when multiple programs with same-named files are installed on a single machine. This is something of an install issue, but it can also become a concern in general practice. Let's turn to a hypothetical scenario to illustrate.

Suppose that a programmer develops a Python program that contains a file called *utilities.py* for common utility code and a top-level file named *main.py* that users launch to start the program. All over this program, its files say import utilities to load and use the common code. When the program is shipped, it arrives as a single *.tar* or *.zip* file containing all the program's files, and when it is installed, it unpacks all its files into a single directory named *system1* on the target machine:

```
system1\
    utilities.py      # Common utility functions, classes
    main.py           # Launch this to start the program
    other.py          # Import utilities to load my tools
```

Now, suppose that a second programmer develops a different program with files also called *utilities.py* and *main.py*, and again uses import utilities throughout the program to load the common code file. When this second system is fetched and installed on the same computer as the first system, its files will unpack into a new directory called *system2* somewhere on the receiving machine (ensuring that they do not overwrite same-named files from the first system):

```
system2\
    utilities.py      # Common utilities
    main.py           # Launch this to run
    other.py          # Imports utilities
```

So far, there's no problem: both systems can coexist and run on the same machine. In fact, you won't even need to configure the module search path to use these programs on your computer—because Python always searches the home directory first (that is, the directory containing the top-level file), imports in either system's files will automatically see all the files in that system's directory. For instance, if you click on *system1\main.py*, all imports will search *system1* first. Similarly, if you launch *system2\main.py*, *system2* will be searched first instead. Remember, module search path settings are only needed to import across directory boundaries.

However, suppose that after you've installed these two programs on your machine, you decide that you'd like to use some of the code in each of the *utilities.py* files in a system of your own. It's common utility code, after all, and Python code by nature wants to be reused. In this case, you want to be able to say the following from code that you're writing in a third directory to load one of the two files:

```
import utilities
utilities.func('spam')
```

Now the problem starts to materialize. To make this work at all, you'll have to set the module search path to include the directories containing the *utilities.py* files. But which directory do you put first in the path—*system1* or *system2*?

The problem is the *linear* nature of the search path. It is always scanned from left to right, so no matter how long you ponder this dilemma, you will always get *utilities.py* from the directory listed first (leftmost) on the search path. As is, you'll never be able to import it from the other directory at all. You could try changing `sys.path` within your script before each import operation, but that's both extra work and highly error prone. By default, you're stuck.

This is the issue that packages actually fix. Rather than installing programs as flat lists of files in standalone directories, you can package and install them as *subdirectories* under a common root. For instance, you might organize all the code in this example as an install hierarchy that looks like this:

```
root\
    system1\
        __init__.py
        utilities.py
        main.py
        other.py
    system2\
        __init__.py
        utilities.py
        main.py
        other.py
    system3\                    # Here or elsewhere
        __init__.py             # Your new code here
        myfile.py
```

Now, add just the common root directory to your search path. If your code's imports are all relative to this common root, you can import *either* system's utility file with a package import—the enclosing directory name makes the path (and hence, the module reference) unique. In fact, you can import *both* utility files in the same module, as long as you use an `import` statement and repeat the full path each time you reference the utility modules:

```
import system1.utilities
import system2.utilities
system1.utilities.function('spam')
system2.utilities.function('eggs')
```

The names of the enclosing directories here make the module references unique.

Note that you have to use `import` instead of `from` with packages only if you need to access the same attribute in two or more paths. If the name of the called function here was different in each path, `from` statements could be used to avoid repeating the full package path whenever you call one of the functions, as described earlier.

Also, notice in the install hierarchy shown earlier that __init__.py files were added to the *system1* and *system2* directories to make this work, but not to the *root* directory. Only directories listed within `import` statements in your code require these files; as you'll recall, they are run automatically the first time the Python process imports through a package directory.

Technically, in this case the *system3* directory doesn't have to be under *root*—just the packages of code from which you will import. However, because you never know when your own modules might be useful in other programs, you might as well place them under the common *root* directory as well to avoid similar name-collision problems in the future.

Finally, notice that both of the two original systems' imports will keep working unchanged. Because their *home* directories are searched first, the addition of the common root on the search path is irrelevant to code in *system1* and *system2*; they can keep saying just `import utilities` and expect to find their own files. Moreover, if you're careful to unpack all your Python systems under a common root like this, path configuration becomes simple: you'll only need to add the common root directory, once.

Package Relative Imports

The coverage of package imports so far has focused mostly on importing package files from *outside* the package. Within the package itself, imports of package files can use the same path syntax as outside imports, but they can also make use of special intra-package search rules to simplify `import` statements. That is, rather than listing package import paths, imports within the package can be relative to the package.

The way this works is version-dependent today: Python 2.6 implicitly searches package directories first on imports, while 3.0 requires explicit relative import syntax. This 3.0 change can enhance code readability, by making same-package imports more obvious. If you're starting out in Python with version 3.0, your focus in this section will likely be on its new import syntax. If you've used other Python packages in the past, though, you'll probably also be interested in how the 3.0 model differs.

Changes in Python 3.0

The way import operations in packages work has changed slightly in Python 3.0. This change applies only to imports within files located in the package directories we've been studying in this chapter; imports in other files work as before. For imports in packages, though, Python 3.0 introduces two changes:

- It modifies the module import search path semantics to skip the package's own directory by default. Imports check only other components of the search path. These are known as "absolute" imports.

- It extends the syntax of `from` statements to allow them to explicitly request that imports search the package's directory only. This is known as "relative" import syntax.

These changes are fully present in Python 3.0. The new `from` statement relative syntax is also available in Python 2.6, but the default search path change must be enabled as an option. It's currently scheduled to be added in the 2.7 release[†]—this change is being phased in this way because the search path portion is not backward compatible with earlier Pythons.

The impact of this change is that in 3.0 (and optionally in 2.6), you must generally use special `from` syntax to import modules located in the same package as the importer, unless you spell out a complete path from a package root. Without this syntax, your package is not automatically searched.

Relative Import Basics

In Python 3.0 and 2.6, `from` statements can now use leading dots (".") to specify that they require modules located within the same package (known as *package relative imports*), instead of modules located elsewhere on the module import search path (called *absolute imports*). That is:

- In both Python 3.0 and 2.6, you can use leading dots in `from` statements to indicate that imports should be *relative* to the containing package—such imports will search for modules inside the package only and will not look for same-named modules located elsewhere on the import search path (`sys.path`). The net effect is that package modules override outside modules.

- In Python 2.6, normal imports in a package's code (without leading dots) currently default to a relative-then-absolute search path order—that is, they search the package's own directory first. However, in Python 3.0, imports within a package are absolute by default—in the absence of any special dot syntax, imports skip the containing package itself and look elsewhere on the `sys.path` search path.

[†] Yes, there will be a 2.7 release, and possibly 2.8 and later releases, in parallel with new releases in the 3.X line. As described in the Preface, both the Python 2 and Python 3 lines are expected to be fully supported for years to come, to accommodate the large existing Python 2 user and code bases.

For example, in both Python 3.0 and 2.6, a statement of the form:

```
from . import spam              # Relative to this package
```

instructs Python to import a module named spam located in the same package directory as the file in which this statement appears. Similarly, this statement:

```
from .spam import name
```

means "from a module named spam located in the same package as the file that contains this statement, import the variable name."

The behavior of a statement *without* the leading dot depends on which version of Python you use. In 2.6, such an import will still default to the current relative-then-absolute search path order (i.e., searching the package's directory first), unless a statement of the following form is included in the importing file:

```
from __future__ import absolute_import    # Required until 2.7?
```

If present, this statement enables the Python 3.0 absolute-by-default default search path change, described in the next paragraph.

In 3.0, an import without a leading dot always causes Python to skip the relative components of the module import search path and look instead in the absolute directories that sys.path contains. For instance, in 3.0's model, a statement of the following form will always find a string module somewhere on sys.path, instead of a module of the same name in the package:

```
import string                   # Skip this package's version
```

Without the from __future__ statement in 2.6, if there's a string module in the package, it will be imported instead. To get the same behavior in 3.0 and in 2.6 when the absolute import change is enabled, run a statement of the following form to force a relative import:

```
from . import string            # Searches this package only
```

This works in both Python 2.6 and 3.0 today. The only difference in the 3.0 model is that it is *required* in order to load a module that is located in the same package directory as the file in which this appears, when the module is given with a simple name.

Note that leading dots can be used to force relative imports only with the from statement, not with the import statement. In Python 3.0, the import modname statement is always absolute, skipping the containing package's directory. In 2.6, this statement form still performs relative imports today (i.e., the package's directory is searched first), but these will become absolute in Python 2.7, too. from statements without leading dots behave the same as import statements—absolute in 3.0 (skipping the package directory), and relative-then-absolute in 2.6 (searching the package directory first).

Other dot-based relative reference patterns are possible, too. Within a module file located in a package directory named *mypkg*, the following alternative import forms work as described:

```
from .string import name1, name2      # Imports names from mypkg.string
from . import string                  # Imports mypkg.string
from .. import string                 # Imports string sibling of mypkg
```

To understand these latter forms better, we need to understand the rationale behind this change.

Why Relative Imports?

This feature is designed to allow scripts to resolve ambiguities that can arise when a same-named file appears in multiple places on the module search path. Consider the following package directory:

```
mypkg\
    __init__.py
    main.py
    string.py
```

This defines a package named `mypkg` containing modules named `mypkg.main` and `mypkg.string`. Now, suppose that the `main` module tries to import a module named `string`. In Python 2.6 and earlier, Python will first look in the *mypkg* directory to perform a *relative* import. It will find and import the *string.py* file located there, assigning it to the name `string` in the `mypkg.main` module's namespace.

It could be, though, that the intent of this import was to load the Python standard library's `string` module instead. Unfortunately, in these versions of Python, there's no straightforward way to ignore `mypkg.string` and look for the standard library's `string` module located on the module search path. Moreover, we cannot resolve this with package import paths, because we cannot depend on any extra package directory structure above the standard library being present on every machine.

In other words, imports in packages can be ambiguous—within a package, it's not clear whether an `import spam` statement refers to a module within or outside the package. More accurately, a local module or package can hide another hanging directly off of `sys.path`, whether intentionally or not.

In practice, Python users can avoid reusing the names of standard library modules they need for modules of their own (if you need the standard `string`, don't name a new module `string`!). But this doesn't help if a package accidentally hides a standard module; moreover, Python might add a new standard library module in the future that has the same name as a module of your own. Code that relies on relative imports is also less easy to understand, because the reader may be confused about which module is intended to be used. It's better if the resolution can be made explicit in code.

The relative imports solution in 3.0

To address this dilemma, imports run within packages have changed in Python 3.0 (and as an option in 2.6) to be absolute. Under this model, an `import` statement of the following form in our example file *mypkg/main.py* will always find a `string` outside the package, via an absolute import search of `sys.path`:

```
import string                    # Imports string outside package
```

A `from` import without leading-dot syntax is considered absolute as well:

```
from string import name          # Imports name from string outside package
```

If you really want to import a module from your package without giving its full path from the package root, though, relative imports are still possible by using the dot syntax in the `from` statement:

```
from . import string             # Imports mypkg.string (relative)
```

This form imports the `string` module relative to the current package only and is the relative equivalent to the prior `import` example's absolute form; when this special relative syntax is used, the package's directory is the only directory searched.

We can also copy specific names from a module with relative syntax:

```
from .string import name1, name2     # Imports names from mypkg.string
```

This statement again refers to the `string` module relative to the current package. If this code appears in our `mypkg.main` module, for example, it will import `name1` and `name2` from `mypkg.string`.

In effect, the "." in a relative import is taken to stand for the package directory *containing* the file in which the import appears. An additional leading dot performs the relative import starting from the *parent* of the current package. For example, this statement:

```
from .. import spam              # Imports a sibling of mypkg
```

will load a sibling of `mypkg`—i.e., the `spam` module located in the package's own container directory, next to `mypkg`. More generally, code located in some module `A.B.C` can do any of these:

```
from . import D                  # Imports A.B.D    (. means A.B)
from .. import E                 # Imports A.E      (.. means A)

from .D import X                 # Imports A.B.D.X  (. means A.B)
from ..E import X                # Imports A.E.X    (.. means A)
```

Relative imports versus absolute package paths

Alternatively, a file can sometimes name its own package explicitly in an absolute import statement. For example, in the following, `mypkg` will be found in an absolute directory on `sys.path`:

```
from mypkg import string         # Imports mypkg.string (absolute)
```

However, this relies on both the configuration and the order of the module search path settings, while relative import dot syntax does not. In fact, this form requires that the directory immediately containing `mypkg` be included in the module search path. In general, absolute import statements must list all the directories below the package's root entry in `sys.path` when naming packages explicitly like this:

```
from system.section.mypkg import string    # system container on sys.path only
```

In large or deep packages, that could be much more work than a dot:

```
from . import string                       # Relative import syntax
```

With this latter form, the containing package is searched automatically, regardless of the search path settings.

The Scope of Relative Imports

Relative imports can seem a bit perplexing on first encounter, but it helps if you remember a few key points about them:

- **Relative imports apply to imports within packages only**. Keep in mind that this feature's module search path change applies only to `import` statements within module files located in a package. Normal imports coded outside package files still work exactly as described earlier, automatically searching the directory containing the top-level script first.

- **Relative imports apply to the from statement only**. Also remember that this feature's new syntax applies only to `from` statements, not `import` statements. It's detected by the fact that the module name in a `from` begins with one or more dots (periods). Module names that contain dots but don't have a leading dot are package imports, not relative imports.

- **The terminology is ambiguous**. Frankly, the terminology used to describe this feature is probably more confusing than it needs to be. Really, all imports are relative to something. Outside a package, imports are still relative to directories listed on the `sys.path` module search path. As we learned in Chapter 21, this path includes the program's container directory, `PYTHONPATH` settings, path file settings, and standard libraries. When working interactively, the program container directory is simply the current working directory.

  For imports made inside packages, 2.6 augments this behavior by searching the package itself first. In the 3.0 model, all that really changes is that normal "absolute" import syntax skips the package directory, but special "relative" import syntax causes it to be searched first and only. When we talk about 3.0 imports as being "absolute," what we really mean is that they are relative to the directories on `sys.path`, but not the package itself. Conversely, when we speak of "relative" imports, we mean they are relative to the package directory only. Some `sys.path` entries could, of course, be absolute or relative paths too. (And I could probably make up something more confusing, but it would be a stretch!)

In other words, "package relative imports" in 3.0 really just boil down to a removal of 2.6's special search path behavior for packages, along with the addition of special `from` syntax to explicitly request relative behavior. If you wrote your package imports in the past to not depend on 2.6's special implicit relative lookup (e.g., by always spelling out full paths from a package root), this change is largely a moot point. If you didn't, you'll need to update your package files to use the new `from` syntax for local package files.

Module Lookup Rules Summary

With packages and relative imports, the module search story in Python 3.0 in its entirety can be summarized as follows:

- Simple module names (e.g., A) are looked up by searching each directory on the `sys.path` list, from left to right. This list is constructed from both system defaults and user-configurable settings.

- Packages are simply directories of Python modules with a special *__init__.py* file, which enables A.B.C directory path syntax in imports. In an import of A.B.C, for example, the directory named A is located relative to the normal module import search of `sys.path`, B is another package subdirectory within A, and C is a module or other importable item within B.

- Within a package's files, normal `import` statements use the same `sys.path` search rule as imports elsewhere. Imports in packages using `from` statements and leading dots, however, are relative to the package; that is, only the package directory is checked, and the normal `sys.path` lookup is not used. In `from . import A`, for example, the module search is restricted to the directory containing the file in which this statement appears.

Relative Imports in Action

But enough theory: let's run some quick tests to demonstrate the concepts behind relative imports.

Imports outside packages

First of all, as mentioned previously, this feature does not impact imports outside a package. Thus, the following finds the standard library `string` module as expected:

```
C:\test> c:\Python30\python
>>> import string
>>> string
<module 'string' from 'c:\Python30\lib\string.py'>
```

But if we add a module of the same name in the directory we're working in, it is selected instead, because the first entry on the module search path is the current working directory (CWD):

```
# test\string.py
print('string' * 8)
```

```
C:\test> c:\Python30\python
>>> import string
stringstringstringstringstringstringstringstring
>>> string
<module 'string' from 'string.py'>
```

In other words, normal imports are still relative to the "home" directory (the top-level script's container, or the directory you're working in). In fact, relative import syntax is not even allowed in code that is not in a file being used as part of a package:

```
>>> from . import string
Traceback (most recent call last):
  File "<stdin>", line 1, in <module>
ValueError: Attempted relative import in non-package
```

In this and all examples in this section, code entered at the interactive prompt behaves the same as it would if run in a top-level script, because the first entry on `sys.path` is either the interactive working directory or the directory containing the top-level file. The only difference is that the start of `sys.path` is an absolute directory, not an empty string:

```
# test\main.py
import string
print(string)
```

```
C:\test> C:\python30\python main.py                    # Same results in 2.6
stringstringstringstringstringstringstringstring
<module 'string' from 'C:\test\string.py'>
```

Imports within packages

Now, let's get rid of the local `string` module we coded in the CWD and build a package directory there with two modules, including the required but empty *test\pkg __init__.py* file (which I'll omit here):

```
C:\test> del string*
C:\test> mkdir pkg
```

```
# test\pkg\spam.py
import eggs                          # <== Works in 2.6 but not 3.0!
print(eggs.X)
```

```
# test\pkg\eggs.py
X = 99999
import string
print(string)
```

The first file in this package tries to import the second with a normal `import` statement. Because this is taken to be relative in 2.6 but absolute in 3.0, it fails in the latter. That is, 2.6 searches the containing package first, but 3.0 does not. This is the noncompatible behavior you have to be aware of in 3.0:

```
C:\test> c:\Python26\python
>>> import pkg.spam
<module 'string' from 'c:\Python26\lib\string.pyc'>
99999

C:\test> c:\Python30\python
>>> import pkg.spam
Traceback (most recent call last):
  File "<stdin>", line 1, in <module>
  File "pkg\spam.py", line 1, in <module>
    import eggs
ImportError: No module named eggs
```

To make this work in both 2.6 and 3.0, change the first file to use the special relative import syntax, so that its import searches the package directory in 3.0, too:

```
# test\pkg\spam.py
from . import eggs                   # <== Use package relative import in 2.6 or 3.0
print(eggs.X)

# test\pkg\eggs.py
X = 99999
import string
print(string)

C:\test> c:\Python26\python
>>> import pkg.spam
<module 'string' from 'c:\Python26\lib\string.pyc'>
99999

C:\test> c:\Python30\python
>>> import pkg.spam
<module 'string' from 'c:\Python30\lib\string.py'>
99999
```

Imports are still relative to the CWD

Notice in the preceding example that the package modules still have access to standard library modules like `string`. Really, their imports are still relative to the entries on the module search path, even if those entries are relative themselves. If you add a `string` module to the CWD again, imports in a package will find it there instead of in the standard library. Although you can skip the package directory with an absolute import in 3.0, you still can't skip the home directory of the program that imports the package:

```
# test\string.py
print('string' * 8)

# test\pkg\spam.py
from . import eggs
```

```
print(eggs.X)
```

```
# test\pkg\eggs.py
X = 99999
import string                    # <== Gets string in CWD, not Python lib!
print(string)
```

```
C:\test> c:\Python30\python      # Same result in 2.6
>>> import pkg.spam
stringstringstringstringstringstringstringstring
<module 'string' from 'string.py'>
99999
```

Selecting modules with relative and absolute imports

To show how this applies to imports of standard library modules, reset the package one more time. Get rid of the local `string` module, and define a new one inside the package itself:

```
C:\test> del string*
```

```
# test\pkg\spam.py
import string                    # <== Relative in 2.6, absolute in 3.0
print(string)
```

```
# test\pkg\string.py
print('Ni' * 8)
```

Now, which version of the `string` module you get depends on which Python you use. As before, 3.0 interprets the import in the first file as absolute and skips the package, but 2.6 does not:

```
C:\test> c:\Python30\python
>>> import pkg.spam
<module 'string' from 'c:\Python30\lib\string.py'>
```

```
C:\test> c:\Python26\python
>>> import pkg.spam
NiNiNiNiNiNiNiNi
<module 'pkg.string' from 'pkg\string.py'>
```

Using relative import syntax in 3.0 forces the package to be searched again, as it is in 2.6—by using absolute or relative import syntax in 3.0, you can either skip or select the package directory explicitly. In fact, this is the use case that the 3.0 model addresses:

```
# test\pkg\spam.py
from . import string             # <== Relative in both 2.6 and 3.0
print(string)
```

```
# test\pkg\string.py
print('Ni' * 8)
```

```
C:\test> c:\Python30\python
>>> import pkg.spam
NiNiNiNiNiNiNiNi
```

```
<module 'pkg.string' from 'pkg\string.py'>

C:\test> c:\Python26\python
>>> import pkg.spam
NiNiNiNiNiNiNiNi
<module 'pkg.string' from 'pkg\string.py'>
```

It's important to note that relative import syntax is really a binding declaration, not just a preference. If we delete the *string.py* file in this example, the relative import in *spam.py fails* in both 3.0 and 2.6, instead of falling back on the standard library's version of this module (or any other):

```
# test\pkg\spam.py
from . import string          # <== Fails if no string.py here!

C:\test> C:\python30\python
>>> import pkg.spam
...text omitted...
ImportError: cannot import name string
```

Modules referenced by relative imports must exist in the package directory.

Imports are still relative to the CWD (again)

Although absolute imports let you skip package modules, they still rely on other components of sys.path. For one last test, let's define two string modules of our own. In the following, there is one module by that name in the CWD, one in the package, and another in the standard library:

```
# test\string.py
print('string' * 8)

# test\pkg\spam.py
from . import string          # <== Relative in both 2.6 and 3.0
print(string)

# test\pkg\string.py
print('Ni' * 8)
```

When we import the string module with relative import syntax, we get the version in the package, as desired:

```
C:\test> c:\Python30\python     # Same result in 2.6
>>> import pkg.spam
NiNiNiNiNiNiNiNi
<module 'pkg.string' from 'pkg\string.py'>
```

When absolute syntax is used, though, the module we get varies per version again. 2.6 interprets this as relative to the package, but 3.0 makes it "absolute," which in this case really just means it skips the package and loads the version relative to the CWD (*not* the version the standard library):

```
# test\string.py
print('string' * 8)
```

```
# test\pkg\spam.py
import string                          # <== Relative in 2.6, "absolute" in 3.0: CWD!
print(string)

# test\pkg\string.py
print('Ni' * 8)

C:\test> c:\Python30\python
>>> import pkg.spam
stringstringstringstringstringstringstringstring
<module 'string' from 'string.py'>

C:\test> c:\Python26\python
>>> import pkg.spam
NiNiNiNiNiNiNiNi
<module 'pkg.string' from 'pkg\string.pyc'>
```

As you can see, although packages can explicitly request modules within their own directories, their imports are otherwise still relative to the rest of the normal module search path. In this case, a file in the program using the package hides the standard library module the package may want. All that the change in 3.0 really accomplishes is allowing package code to select files either inside or outside the package (i.e., relatively or absolutely). Because import resolution can depend on an enclosing context that may not be foreseen, absolute imports in 3.0 are not a guarantee of finding a module in the standard library.

Experiment with these examples on your own for more insight. In practice, this is not usually as ad-hoc as it might seem: you can generally structure your imports, search paths, and module names to work the way you wish during development. You should keep in mind, though, that imports in larger systems may depend upon context of use, and the module import protocol is part of a successful library's design.

Now that you've learned about package-relative imports, also keep in mind that they may not always be your best option. Absolute package imports, relative to a directory on sys.path, are still sometimes preferred over both implicit package-relative imports in Python 2, and explicit package-relative import syntax in both Python 2 and 3.

Package-relative import syntax and Python 3.0's new absolute import search rules at least require relative imports from a package to be made explicit, and thus easier to understand and maintain. Files that use imports with dots, though, are implicitly bound to a package directory and cannot be used elsewhere without code changes.

Naturally, the extent to which this may impact your modules can vary per package; absolute imports may also require changes when directories are reorganized.

Chapter Summary

This chapter introduced Python's package import model—an optional but useful way to explicitly list part of the directory path leading up to your modules. Package imports are still relative to a directory on your module import search path, but rather than relying on Python to traverse the search path manually, your script gives the rest of the path to the module explicitly.

As we've seen, packages not only make imports more meaningful in larger systems, but also simplify import search path settings (if all cross-directory imports are relative to a common root directory) and resolve ambiguities when there is more than one module of the same name (including the name of the enclosing directory in a package import helps distinguish between them).

Because it's relevant only to code in packages, we also explored the newer relative import model here—a way for imports in package files to select modules in the same package using leading dots in a `from`, instead of relying on an older implicit package search rule.

In the next chapter, we will survey a handful of more advanced module-related topics, such as relative import syntax and the __name__ usage mode variable. As usual, though, we'll close out this chapter with a short quiz to test what you've learned here.

Test Your Knowledge: Quiz

1. What is the purpose of an *__init__.py* file in a module package directory?

2. How can you avoid repeating the full package path every time you reference a package's content?

3. Which directories require *__init__.py* files?

4. When must you use `import` instead of `from` with packages?

5. What is the difference between `from mypkg import spam` and `from . import spam`?

Test Your Knowledge: Answers

1. The *__init__.py* file serves to declare and initialize a module package; Python automatically runs its code the first time you import through a directory in a process. Its assigned variables become the attributes of the module object created in memory to correspond to that directory. It is also not optional—you can't import through a directory with package syntax unless it contains this file.

2. Use the `from` statement with a package to copy names out of the package directly, or use the `as` extension with the `import` statement to rename the path to a shorter synonym. In both cases, the path is listed in only one place, in the `from` or `import` statement.

3. Each directory listed in an `import` or `from` statement must contain an *__init__.py* file. Other directories, including the directory containing the leftmost component of a package path, do not need to include this file.

4. You must use `import` instead of `from` with packages only if you need to access the same name defined in more than one path. With `import`, the path makes the references unique, but `from` allows only one version of any given name.

5. `from mypkg import spam` is an *absolute* import—the search for `mypkg` skips the package directory and the module is located in an absolute directory in `sys.path`. A statement `from . import spam`, on the other hand, is a *relative* import—`spam` is looked up relative to the package in which this statement is contained before `sys.path` is searched.

## CHAPTER 24

Advanced Module Topics

This chapter concludes this part of the book with a collection of more advanced module-related topics—data hiding, the `__future__` module, the `__name__` variable, `sys.path` changes, listing tools, running modules by name string, transitive reloads, and so on—along with the standard set of gotchas and exercises related to what we've covered in this part of the book.

Along the way, we'll build some larger and more useful tools than we have so far, that combine functions and modules. Like functions, modules are more effective when their interfaces are well defined, so this chapter also briefly reviews module design concepts, some of which we have explored in prior chapters.

Despite the word "advanced" in this chapter's title, this is also something of a grab bag of additional module topics. Because some of the topics discussed here are widely used (especially the `__name__` trick), be sure to take a look before moving on to classes in the next part of the book.

Data Hiding in Modules

As we've seen, a Python module exports all the names assigned at the top level of its file. There is no notion of declaring which names should and shouldn't be visible outside the module. In fact, there's no way to prevent a client from changing names inside a module if it wants to.

In Python, data hiding in modules is a convention, not a syntactical constraint. If you want to break a module by trashing its names, you can, but fortunately, I've yet to meet a programmer who would. Some purists object to this liberal attitude toward data hiding, claiming that it means Python can't implement encapsulation. However, encapsulation in Python is more about packaging than about restricting.

Minimizing from * Damage: _X and __all__

As a special case, you can prefix names with a single underscore (e.g., _X) to prevent them from being copied out when a client imports a module's names with a from * statement. This really is intended only to minimize namespace pollution; because from * copies out all names, the importer may get more than it's bargained for (including names that overwrite names in the importer). Underscores aren't "private" declarations: you can still see and change such names with other import forms, such as the import statement.

Alternatively, you can achieve a hiding effect similar to the _X naming convention by assigning a list of variable name strings to the variable __all__ at the top level of the module. For example:

```
__all__ = ["Error", "encode", "decode"]     # Export these only
```

When this feature is used, the from * statement will copy out only those names listed in the __all__ list. In effect, this is the converse of the _X convention: __all__ identifies names to be copied, while _X identifies names not to be copied. Python looks for an __all__ list in the module first; if one is not defined, from * copies all names without a single leading underscore.

Like the _X convention, the __all__ list has meaning only to the from * statement form and does not amount to a privacy declaration. Module writers can use either trick to implement modules that are well behaved when used with from *. (See also the discussion of __all__ lists in package __init__.py files in Chapter 23; there, these lists declare submodules to be loaded for a from *.)

Enabling Future Language Features

Changes to the language that may potentially break existing code are introduced gradually. Initially, they appear as optional extensions, which are disabled by default. To turn on such extensions, use a special import statement of this form:

```
from __future__ import featurename
```

This statement should generally appear at the top of a module file (possibly after a docstring), because it enables special compilation of code on a per-module basis. It's also possible to submit this statement at the interactive prompt to experiment with upcoming language changes; the feature will then be available for the rest of the interactive session.

For example, in prior editions of this book, we had to use this statement form to demonstrate generator functions, which required a keyword that was not yet enabled by default (they use a *featurename* of generators). We also used this statement to activate 3.0 true division in Chapter 5, 3.0 print calls in Chapter 11, and 3.0 absolute imports for packages in Chapter 23.

All of these changes have the potential to break existing code in Python 2.6, so they are being phased in gradually as optional features enabled with this special import.

Mixed Usage Modes: __name__ and __main__

Here's another module-related trick that lets you both import a file as a module and run it as a standalone program. Each module has a built-in attribute called __name__, which Python sets automatically as follows:

- If the file is being run as a top-level program file, __name__ is set to the string "__main__" when it starts.
- If the file is being imported instead, __name__ is set to the module's name as known by its clients.

The upshot is that a module can test its own __name__ to determine whether it's being run or imported. For example, suppose we create the following module file, named *runme.py*, to export a single function called `tester`:

```
def tester():
    print("It's Christmas in Heaven...")

if __name__ == '__main__':          # Only when run
    tester()                        # Not when imported
```

This module defines a function for clients to import and use as usual:

```
% python
>>> import runme
>>> runme.tester()
It's Christmas in Heaven...
```

But, the module also includes code at the bottom that is set up to call the function when this file is run as a program:

```
% python runme.py
It's Christmas in Heaven...
```

In effect, a module's __name__ variable serves as a *usage mode flag*, allowing its code to be leveraged as both an importable library and a top-level script. Though simple, you'll see this hook used in nearly every realistic Python program file you are likely to encounter.

Perhaps the most common way you'll see the __name__ test applied is for *self-test* code. In short, you can package code that tests a module's exports in the module itself by wrapping it in a __name__ test at the bottom of the file. This way, you can use the file in clients by importing it, but also test its logic by running it from the system shell or via another launching scheme. In practice, self-test code at the bottom of a file under the __name__ test is probably the most common and simplest unit-testing protocol in Python. (Chapter 35 will discuss other commonly used options for testing Python code—as you'll see, the `unittest` and `doctest` standard library modules provide more advanced testing tools.)

The __name__ trick is also commonly used when writing files that can be used both as command-line utilities and as tool libraries. For instance, suppose you write a file-finder script in Python. You can get more mileage out of your code if you package it in functions and add a __name__ test in the file to automatically call those functions when the file is run standalone. That way, the script's code becomes reusable in other programs.

Unit Tests with __name__

In fact, we've already seen a prime example in this book of an instance where the __name__ check could be useful. In the section on arguments in Chapter 18, we coded a script that computed the minimum value from the set of arguments sent in:

```python
def minmax(test, *args):
    res = args[0]
    for arg in args[1:]:
        if test(arg, res):
            res = arg
    return res

def lessthan(x, y): return x < y
def grtrthan(x, y): return x > y

print(minmax(lessthan, 4, 2, 1, 5, 6, 3))      # Self-test code
print(minmax(grtrthan, 4, 2, 1, 5, 6, 3))
```

This script includes self-test code at the bottom, so we can test it without having to retype everything at the interactive command line each time we run it. The problem with the way it is currently coded, however, is that the output of the self-test call will appear every time this file is imported from another file to be used as a tool—not exactly a user-friendly feature! To improve it, we can wrap up the self-test call in a __name__ check, so that it will be launched only when the file is run as a top-level script, not when it is imported (this new version of the module file is renamed *min.py* here):

```python
print('I am:', __name__)

def minmax(test, *args):
    res = args[0]
    for arg in args[1:]:
        if test(arg, res):
            res = arg
    return res

def lessthan(x, y): return x < y
def grtrthan(x, y): return x > y

if __name__ == '__main__':
    print(minmax(lessthan, 4, 2, 1, 5, 6, 3))      # Self-test code
    print(minmax(grtrthan, 4, 2, 1, 5, 6, 3))
```

We're also printing the value of __name__ at the top here to trace its value. Python creates and assigns this usage-mode variable as soon as it starts loading a file. When we run this file as a top-level script, its name is set to __main__, so its self-test code kicks in automatically:

```
% python min.py
I am: __main__
1
6
```

But, if we import the file, its name is not __main__, so we must explicitly call the function to make it run:

```
>>> import min
I am: min
>>> min.minmax(min.lessthan, 's', 'p', 'a', 'm')
'a'
```

Again, regardless of whether this is used for testing, the net effect is that we get to use our code in two different roles—as a library module of tools, or as an executable program.

Using Command-Line Arguments with __name__

Here's a more substantial module example that demonstrates another way that the __name__ trick is commonly employed. The following module, *formats.py*, defines string formatting utilities for importers, but also checks its name to see if it is being run as a top-level script; if so, it tests and uses arguments listed on the system command line to run a canned or passed-in test. In Python, the sys.argv list contains *command-line arguments*—it is a list of strings reflecting words typed on the command line, where the first item is always the name of the script being run:

```
"""
Various specialized string display formatting utilities.
Test me with canned self-test or command-line arguments.
"""

def commas(N):
    """
    format positive integer-like N for display with
    commas between digit groupings: xxx,yyy,zzz
    """
    digits = str(N)
    assert(digits.isdigit())
    result = ''
    while digits:
        digits, last3 = digits[:-3], digits[-3:]
        result = (last3 + ',' + result) if result else last3
    return result

def money(N, width=0):
    """
```

```
        format number N for display with commas, 2 decimal digits,
        leading $ and sign, and optional padding: $ -xxx,yyy.zz
        """
    sign   = '-' if N < 0 else ''
    N      = abs(N)
    whole  = commas(int(N))
    fract  = ('%.2f' % N)[-2:]
    format = '%s%s.%s' % (sign, whole, fract)
    return '$%*s' % (width, format)

if __name__ == '__main__':
    def selftest():
        tests  = 0, 1          # fails: -1, 1.23
        tests += 12, 123, 1234, 12345, 123456, 1234567
        tests += 2 ** 32, 2 ** 100
        for test in tests:
            print(commas(test))

        print('')
        tests  = 0, 1, -1, 1.23, 1., 1.2, 3.14159
        tests += 12.34, 12.344, 12.345, 12.346
        tests += 2 ** 32, (2 ** 32 + .2345)
        tests += 1.2345, 1.2, 0.2345
        tests += -1.2345, -1.2, -0.2345
        tests += -(2 ** 32), -(2**32 + .2345)
        tests += (2 ** 100), -(2 ** 100)
        for test in tests:
            print('%s [%s]' % (money(test, 17), test))

    import sys
    if len(sys.argv) == 1:
        selftest()
    else:
        print(money(float(sys.argv[1]), int(sys.argv[2])))
```

This file works the same in Python 2.6 and 3.0. When run directly, it tests itself as before, but it uses options on the command line to control the test behavior. Run this file directly with no command-line arguments on your own to see what its self-test code prints. To test specific strings, pass them in on the command line along with a minimum field width:

```
C:\misc> python formats.py 999999999 0
$999,999,999.00

C:\misc> python formats.py -999999999 0
$-999,999,999.00

C:\misc> python formats.py 123456789012345 0
$123,456,789,012,345.00

C:\misc> python formats.py -123456789012345 25
$   -123,456,789,012,345.00

C:\misc> python formats.py 123.456 0
$123.46
```

```
C:\misc> python formats.py -123.454 0
$-123.45

C:\misc> python formats.py
...canned tests: try this yourself...
```

As before, because this code is instrumented for dual-mode usage, we can also import its tools normally in other contexts as library components:

```
>>> from formats import money, commas
>>> money(123.456)
'$123.46'
>>> money(-9999999.99, 15)
'$  -9,999,999.99'
>>> X = 99999999999999999999
>>> '%s (%s)' % (commas(X), X)
'99,999,999,999,999,999,999 (99999999999999999999)'
```

Because this file uses the *docstring* feature introduced in Chapter 15, we can use the help function to explore its tools as well—it serves as a general-purpose tool:

```
>>> import formats
>>> help(formats)
Help on module formats:

NAME
    formats

FILE
    c:\misc\formats.py

DESCRIPTION
    Various specialized string display formatting utilities.
    Test me with canned self-test or command-line arguments.

FUNCTIONS
    commas(N)
        format positive integer-like N for display with
        commas between digit groupings: xxx,yyy,zzz

    money(N, width=0)
        format number N for display with commas, 2 decimal digits,
        leading $ and sign, and optional padding: $  -xxx,yyy.zz
```

You can use command-line arguments in similar ways to provide general inputs to scripts that may also package their code as functions and classes for reuse by importers. For more advanced command-line processing, be sure to see the getopt and optparse modules in Python's standard library and manuals. In some scenarios, you might also use the built-in input function introduced in Chapter 3 and used in Chapter 10 to prompt the shell user for test inputs instead of pulling them from the command line.

Also see Chapter 7's discussion of the new {,d} string format method syntax that will be available in Python 3.1 and later; this formatting extension separates thousands groups with commas much like the code here. The module listed here, though, adds money formatting and serves as a manual alternative for comma insertion for Python versions before 3.1.

Changing the Module Search Path

In Chapter 21, we learned that the module search path is a list of directories that can be customized via the environment variable PYTHONPATH, and possibly via *.pth* files. What I haven't shown you until now is how a Python program itself can actually change the search path by changing a built-in list called sys.path (the path attribute in the built-in sys module). sys.path is initialized on startup, but thereafter you can delete, append, and reset its components however you like:

```
>>> import sys
>>> sys.path
['', 'C:\\users', 'C:\\Windows\\system32\\python30.zip', ...more deleted...]

>>> sys.path.append('C:\\sourcedir')     # Extend module search path
>>> import string                         # All imports search the new dir last
```

Once you've made such a change, it will impact future imports anywhere in the Python program, as all imports and all files share the single sys.path list. In fact, this list may be changed arbitrarily:

```
>>> sys.path = [r'd:\temp']               # Change module search path
>>> sys.path.append('c:\\lp4e\\examples') # For this process only
>>> sys.path
['d:\\temp', 'c:\\lp4e\\examples']

>>> import string
Traceback (most recent call last):
  File "<stdin>", line 1, in <module>
ImportError: No module named string
```

Thus, you can use this technique to dynamically configure a search path inside a Python program. Be careful, though: if you delete a critical directory from the path, you may lose access to critical utilities. In the prior example, for instance, we no longer have access to the string module because we deleted the Python source library's directory from the path.

Also, remember that such sys.path settings endure for only as long as the Python session or program (technically, process) that made them runs; they are not retained after Python exits. PYTHONPATH and *.pth* file path configurations live in the operating system instead of a running Python program, and so are more global: they are picked up by every program on your machine and live on after a program completes.

The as Extension for import and from

Both the `import` and `from` statements have been extended to allow an imported name to be given a different name in your script. The following `import` statement:

```
import modulename as name
```

is equivalent to:

```
import modulename
name = modulename
del modulename                          # Don't keep original name
```

After such an `import`, you can (and in fact must) use the name listed after the `as` to refer to the module. This works in a `from` statement, too, to assign a name imported from a file to a different name in your script:

```
from modulename import attrname as name
```

This extension is commonly used to provide short synonyms for longer names, and to avoid name clashes when you are already using a name in your script that would otherwise be overwritten by a normal `import` statement:

```
import reallylongmodulename as name     # Use shorter nickname
name.func()

from module1 import utility as util1    # Can have only 1 "utility"
from module2 import utility as util2
util1(); util2()
```

It also comes in handy for providing a short, simple name for an entire directory path when using the package import feature described in Chapter 23:

```
import dir1.dir2.mod as mod             # Only list full path once
mod.func()
```

Modules Are Objects: Metaprograms

Because modules expose most of their interesting properties as built-in attributes, it's easy to write programs that manage other programs. We usually call such manager programs *metaprograms* because they work on top of other systems. This is also referred to as *introspection*, because programs can see and process object internals. Introspection is an advanced feature, but it can be useful for building programming tools.

For instance, to get to an attribute called `name` in a module called `M`, we can use qualification or index the module's attribute dictionary, exposed in the built-in `__dict__` attribute we met briefly in Chapter 22. Python also exports the list of all loaded modules as the `sys.modules` dictionary (that is, the `modules` attribute of the `sys` module) and provides a built-in called `getattr` that lets us fetch attributes from their string names (it's like saying `object.attr`, but `attr` is an expression that yields a string at runtime). Because of that, all the following expressions reach the same attribute and object:

```
M.name                               # Qualify object
M.__dict__['name']                   # Index namespace dictionary manually
sys.modules['M'].name                # Index loaded-modules table manually
getattr(M, 'name')                   # Call built-in fetch function
```

By exposing module internals like this, Python helps you build programs about programs.[*] For example, here is a module named *mydir.py* that puts these ideas to work to implement a customized version of the built-in dir function. It defines and exports a function called listing, which takes a module object as an argument and prints a formatted listing of the module's namespace:

```
"""
mydir.py: a module that lists the namespaces of other modules
"""

seplen = 60
sepchr = '-'

def listing(module, verbose=True):
    sepline = sepchr * seplen
    if verbose:
        print(sepline)
        print('name:', module.__name__, 'file:', module.__file__)
        print(sepline)

    count = 0
    for attr in module.__dict__:                    # Scan namespace keys
        print('%02d) %s' % (count, attr), end = ' ')
        if attr.startswith('__'):
            print('<built-in name>')                # Skip __file__, etc.
        else:
            print(getattr(module, attr))             # Same as .__dict__[attr]
        count += 1

    if verbose:
        print(sepline)
        print(module.__name__, 'has %d names' % count)
        print(sepline)

if __name__ == '__main__':
    import mydir
    listing(mydir)                                   # Self-test code: list myself
```

Notice the docstring at the top; as in the prior *formats.py* example, because we may want to use this as a general tool, a docstring is coded to provide functional information accessible via __doc__ attributes or the help function (see Chapter 15 for details):

---

[*] As we saw in Chapter 17, because a function can access its enclosing module by going through the sys.modules table like this, it's possible to emulate the effect of the global statement. For instance, the effect of global X; X=0 can be simulated (albeit with much more typing!) by saying this inside a function: import sys; glob=sys.modules[__name__]; glob.X=0. Remember, each module gets a __name__ attribute for free; it's visible as a global name inside the functions within the module. This trick provides another way to change both local and global variables of the same name inside a function.

```
>>> import mydir
>>> help(mydir)
Help on module mydir:

NAME
    mydir - mydir.py: a module that lists the namespaces of other modules

FILE
    c:\users\veramark\mark\mydir.py

FUNCTIONS
    listing(module, verbose=True)

DATA
    sepchr = '-'
    seplen = 60
```

I've also provided *self-test* logic at the bottom of this module, which narcissistically imports and lists itself. Here's the sort of output produced in Python 3.0 (to use this in 2.6, enable 3.0 print calls with the __future__ import described in Chapter 11—the end keyword is 3.0-only):

```
C:\Users\veramark\Mark> c:\Python30\python mydir.py
------------------------------------------------------------
name: mydir file: C:\Users\veramark\Mark\mydir.py
------------------------------------------------------------
00) seplen 60
01) __builtins__ <built-in name>
02) __file__ <built-in name>
03) __package__ <built-in name>
04) listing <function listing at 0x026D3B70>
05) __name__ <built-in name>
06) sepchr -
07) __doc__ <built-in name>
------------------------------------------------------------
mydir has 8 names
------------------------------------------------------------
```

To use this as a tool for listing other modules, simply pass the modules in as objects to this file's function. Here it is listing attributes in the tkinter GUI module in the standard library (a.k.a. Tkinter in Python 2.6):

```
>>> import mydir
>>> import tkinter
>>> mydir.listing(tkinter)
------------------------------------------------------------
name: tkinter file: c:\PYTHON30\lib\tkinter\__init__.py
------------------------------------------------------------
00) getdouble <class 'float'>
01) MULTIPLE multiple
02) mainloop <function mainloop at 0x02913B70>
03) Canvas <class 'tkinter.Canvas'>
04) AtSelLast <function AtSelLast at 0x028FA7C8>
...many more name omitted...
151) StringVar <class 'tkinter.StringVar'>
```

```
152) ARC arc
153) At <function At at 0x028FA738>
154) NSEW nsew
155) SCROLL scroll
-----------------------------------------------------------------
tkinter has 156 names
-----------------------------------------------------------------
```

We'll meet getattr and its relatives again later. The point to notice here is that mydir is a program that lets you browse other programs. Because Python exposes its internals, you can process objects generically.[†]

Importing Modules by Name String

The module name in an import or from statement is a hardcoded variable name. Sometimes, though, your program will get the name of a module to be imported as a string at runtime (e.g., if a user selects a module name from within a GUI). Unfortunately, you can't use import statements directly to load a module given its name as a string—Python expects a variable name, not a string. For instance:

```
>>> import "string"
  File "<stdin>", line 1
    import "string"
                  ^
SyntaxError: invalid syntax
```

It also won't work to simply assign the string to a variable name:

```
x = "string"
import x
```

Here, Python will try to import a file *x.py*, not the string module—the name in an import statement both becomes a variable assigned to the loaded module and identifies the external file literally.

To get around this, you need to use special tools to load a module dynamically from a string that is generated at runtime. The most general approach is to construct an import statement as a string of Python code and pass it to the exec built-in function to run (exec is a statement in Python 2.6, but it can be used exactly as shown here—the parentheses are simply ignored):

```
>>> modname = "string"
>>> exec("import " + modname)        # Run a string of code
>>> string                           # Imported in this namespace
<module 'string' from 'c:\Python30\lib\string.py'>
```

---

† Tools such as mydir.listing can be preloaded into the interactive namespace by importing them in the file referenced by the PYTHONSTARTUP environment variable. Because code in the startup file runs in the interactive namespace (module _main_), importing common tools in the startup file can save you some typing. See Appendix A for more details.

The exec function (and its cousin for expressions, eval) compiles a string of code and passes it to the Python interpreter to be executed. In Python, the byte code compiler is available at runtime, so you can write programs that construct and run other programs like this. By default, exec runs the code in the current scope, but you can get more specific by passing in optional namespace dictionaries.

The only real drawback to exec is that it must compile the import statement each time it runs; if it runs many times, your code may run quicker if it uses the built-in __import__ function to load from a name string instead. The effect is similar, but __import__ returns the module object, so assign it to a name here to keep it:

```
>>> modname = "string"
>>> string = __import__(modname)
>>> string
<module 'string' from 'c:\Python30\lib\string.py'>
```

Transitive Module Reloads

We studied module reloads in Chapter 22, as a way to pick up changes in code without stopping and restarting a program. When you reload a module, though, Python only reloads that particular module's file; it doesn't automatically reload modules that the file being reloaded happens to import.

For example, if you reload some module A, and A imports modules B and C, the reload applies only to A, not to B and C. The statements inside A that import B and C are rerun during the reload, but they just fetch the already loaded B and C module objects (assuming they've been imported before). In actual code, here's the file *A.py*:

```
import B         # Not reloaded when A is
import C         # Just an import of an already loaded module

% python
>>> . . .
>>> from imp import reload
>>> reload(A)
```

By default, this means that you cannot depend on reloads picking up changes in all the modules in your program transitively—instead, you must use multiple reload calls to update the subcomponents independently. This can require substantial work for large systems you're testing interactively. You can design your systems to reload their subcomponents automatically by adding reload calls in parent modules like A, but this complicates the modules' code.

A better approach is to write a general tool to do transitive reloads automatically by scanning modules' __dict__ attributes and checking each item's type to find nested modules to reload. Such a utility function could call itself *recursively* to navigate arbitrarily shaped import dependency chains. Module __dict__ attributes were introduced earlier in, the section "Modules Are Objects: Metaprograms" on page 593, and the type call was presented in Chapter 9; we just need to combine the two tools.

For example, the module *reloadall.py* listed next has a `reload_all` function that auto-matically reloads a module, every module that the module imports, and so on, all the way to the bottom of each import chain. It uses a dictionary to keep track of already reloaded modules, recursion to walk the import chains, and the standard library's `types` module, which simply predefines `type` results for built-in types. The `visited` dictionary technique works to avoid cycles here when imports are recursive or redundant, because module objects can be dictionary keys (as we learned in Chapter 5, a set would offer similar functionality if we use `visited.add(module)` to insert):

```
"""
reloadall.py: transitively reload nested modules
"""

import types
from imp import reload                              # from required in 3.0

def status(module):
    print('reloading ' + module.__name__)

def transitive_reload(module, visited):
    if not module in visited:                       # Trap cycles, duplicates
        status(module)                              # Reload this module
        reload(module)                              # And visit children
        visited[module] = None
        for attrobj in module.__dict__.values():    # For all attrs
            if type(attrobj) == types.ModuleType:   # Recur if module
                transitive_reload(attrobj, visited)

def reload_all(*args):
    visited = {}
    for arg in args:
        if type(arg) == types.ModuleType:
            transitive_reload(arg, visited)

if __name__ == '__main__':
    import reloadall                                # Test code: reload myself
    reload_all(reloadall)                           # Should reload this, types
```

To use this utility, import its `reload_all` function and pass it the name of an already loaded module (like you would the built-in `reload` function). When the file runs stand-alone, its self-test code will test itself—it has to import itself because its own name is not defined in the file without an import (this code works in both 3.0 and 2.6 and prints identical output, because we've used + instead of a comma in the `print`):

```
C:\misc> c:\Python30\python reloadall.py
reloading reloadall
reloading types
```

Here is this module at work in 3.0 on some standard library modules. Notice how `os` is imported by `tkinter`, but `tkinter` reaches `sys` before `os` can (if you want to test this on Python 2.6, substitute `Tkinter` for `tkinter`):

```
>>> from reloadall import reload_all
>>> import os, tkinter

>>> reload_all(os)
reloading os
reloading copyreg
reloading ntpath
reloading genericpath
reloading stat
reloading sys
reloading errno

>>> reload_all(tkinter)
reloading tkinter
reloading _tkinter
reloading tkinter._fix
reloading sys
reloading ctypes
reloading os
reloading copyreg
reloading ntpath
reloading genericpath
reloading stat
reloading errno
reloading ctypes._endian
reloading tkinter.constants
```

And here is a session that shows the effect of normal versus transitive reloads—changes made to the two nested files are not picked up by reloads, unless the transitive utility is used:

```
import b                        # a.py
X = 1

import c                        # b.py
Y = 2

Z = 3                           # c.py

C:\misc> C:\Python30\python
>>> import a
>>> a.X, a.b.Y, a.b.c.Z
(1, 2, 3)
```

 # Change all three files' assignment values and save

```
>>> from imp import reload
>>> reload(a)                   # Normal reload is top level only
<module 'a' from 'a.py'>
>>> a.X, a.b.Y, a.b.c.Z
(111, 2, 3)

>>> from reloadall import reload_all
>>> reload_all(a)
reloading a
```

```
reloading b
reloading c
>>> a.X, a.b.Y, a.b.c.Z          # Reloads all nested modules too
(111, 222, 333)
```

For more insight, study and experiment with this example on your own; it's another importable tool you might want to add to your own source code library.

Module Design Concepts

Like functions, modules present design tradeoffs: you have to think about which functions go in which modules, module communication mechanisms, and so on. All of this will become clearer when you start writing bigger Python systems, but here are a few general ideas to keep in mind:

- **You're always in a module in Python**. There's no way to write code that doesn't live in some module. In fact, code typed at the interactive prompt really goes in a built-in module called __main__; the only unique things about the interactive prompt are that code runs and is discarded immediately, and expression results are printed automatically.

- **Minimize module coupling: global variables**. Like functions, modules work best if they're written to be closed boxes. As a rule of thumb, they should be as independent of global variables used within other modules as possible, except for functions and classes imported from them.

- **Maximize module cohesion: unified purpose**. You can minimize a module's couplings by maximizing its cohesion; if all the components of a module share a general purpose, you're less likely to depend on external names.

- **Modules should rarely change other modules' variables**. We illustrated this with code in Chapter 17, but it's worth repeating here: it's perfectly OK to use globals defined in another module (that's how clients import services, after all), but changing globals in another module is often a symptom of a design problem. There are exceptions, of course, but you should try to communicate results through devices such as function arguments and return values, not cross-module changes. Otherwise, your globals' values become dependent on the order of arbitrarily remote assignments in other files, and your modules become harder to understand and reuse.

As a summary, Figure 24-1 sketches the environment in which modules operate. Modules contain variables, functions, classes, and other modules (if imported). Functions have local variables of their own, as do classes—i.e., objects that live within modules, which we'll meet next in Chapter 25.

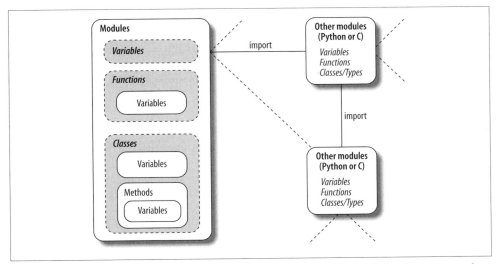

Figure 24-1. Module execution environment. Modules are imported, but modules also import and use other modules, which may be coded in Python or another language such as C. Modules in turn contain variables, functions, and classes to do their work, and their functions and classes may contain variables and other items of their own. At the top, though, programs are just sets of modules.

Module Gotchas

In this section, we'll take a look at the usual collection of boundary cases that make life interesting for Python beginners. Some are so obscure that it was hard to come up with examples, but most illustrate something important about the language.

Statement Order Matters in Top-Level Code

When a module is first imported (or reloaded), Python executes its statements one by one, from the top of the file to the bottom. This has a few subtle implications regarding forward references that are worth underscoring here:

- Code at the top level of a module file (not nested in a function) runs as soon as Python reaches it during an import; because of that, it can't reference names assigned lower in the file.
- Code inside a function body doesn't run until the function is called; because names in a function aren't resolved until the function actually runs, they can usually reference names anywhere in the file.

Generally, forward references are only a concern in top-level module code that executes immediately; functions can reference names arbitrarily. Here's an example that illustrates forward reference:

```
    func1()                             # Error: "func1" not yet assigned

    def func1():
        print(func2())                  # Okay: "func2" looked up later

    func1()                             # Error: "func2" not yet assigned

    def func2():
        return "Hello"

    func1()                             # Okay: "func1" and "func2" assigned
```

When this file is imported (or run as a standalone program), Python executes its statements from top to bottom. The first call to func1 fails because the func1 def hasn't run yet. The call to func2 inside func1 works as long as func2's def has been reached by the time func1 is called (it hasn't when the second top-level func1 call is run). The last call to func1 at the bottom of the file works because func1 and func2 have both been assigned.

Mixing defs with top-level code is not only hard to read, it's dependent on statement ordering. As a rule of thumb, if you need to mix immediate code with defs, put your defs at the top of the file and your top-level code at the bottom. That way, your functions are guaranteed to be defined and assigned by the time code that uses them runs.

from Copies Names but Doesn't Link

Although it's commonly used, the from statement is the source of a variety of potential gotchas in Python. The from statement is really an assignment to names in the importer's scope—a name-copy operation, not a name aliasing. The implications of this are the same as for all assignments in Python, but they're subtle, especially given that the code that shares the objects lives in different files. For instance, suppose we define the following module, *nested1.py*:

```
# nested1.py
X = 99
def printer(): print(X)
```

If we import its two names using from in another module, *nested2.py*, we get copies of those names, not links to them. Changing a name in the importer resets only the binding of the local version of that name, not the name in *nested1.py*:

```
# nested2.py
from nested1 import X, printer       # Copy names out
X = 88                               # Changes my "X" only!
printer()                            # nested1's X is still 99

% python nested2.py
99
```

If we use `import` to get the whole module and then assign to a qualified name, however, we change the name in *nested1.py*. Qualification directs Python to a name in the module object, rather than a name in the importer, *nested3.py*:

```
# nested3.py
import nested1              # Get module as a whole
nested1.X = 88             # OK: change nested1's X
nested1.printer()

% python nested3.py
88
```

from * Can Obscure the Meaning of Variables

I mentioned this earlier but saved the details for here. Because you don't list the variables you want when using the `from module import *` statement form, it can accidentally overwrite names you're already using in your scope. Worse, it can make it difficult to determine where a variable comes from. This is especially true if the `from *` form is used on more than one imported file.

For example, if you use `from *` on three modules, you'll have no way of knowing what a raw function call really means, short of searching all three external module files (all of which may be in other directories):

```
>>> from module1 import *       # Bad: may overwrite my names silently
>>> from module2 import *       # Worse: no way to tell what we get!
>>> from module3 import *
>>> . . .

>>> func()                      # Huh???
```

The solution again is not to do this: try to explicitly list the attributes you want in your `from` statements, and restrict the `from *` form to at most one imported module per file. That way, any undefined names must by deduction be in the module named in the single `from *`. You can avoid the issue altogether if you always use `import` instead of `from`, but that advice is too harsh; like much else in programming, `from` is a convenient tool if used wisely. Even this example isn't an absolute evil—it's OK for a program to use this technique to collect names in a single space for convenience, as long as it's well known.

reload May Not Impact from Imports

Here's another `from`-related gotcha: as discussed previously, because `from` copies (assigns) names when run, there's no link back to the modules where the names came from. Names imported with `from` simply become references to objects, which happen to have been referenced by the same names in the importee when the `from` ran.

Because of this behavior, reloading the importee has no effect on clients that import its names using `from`. That is, the client's names will still reference the original objects fetched with `from`, even if the names in the original module are later reset:

```
from module import X        # X may not reflect any module reloads!
. . .
from imp import reload
reload(module)              # Changes module, but not my names
X                           # Still references old object
```

To make reloads more effective, use `import` and name qualification instead of `from`. Because qualifications always go back to the module, they will find the new bindings of module names after reloading:

```
import module               # Get module, not names
. . .
from imp import reload
reload(module)              # Changes module in-place
module.X                    # Get current X: reflects module reloads
```

reload, from, and Interactive Testing

In fact, the prior gotcha is even more subtle than it appears. Chapter 3 warned that it's usually better not to launch programs with imports and reloads because of the complexities involved. Things get even worse when `from` is brought into the mix. Python beginners often stumble onto its issues in scenarios like the one outlined next. Say that after opening a module file in a text edit window, you launch an interactive session to load and test your module with `from`:

```
from module import function
function(1, 2, 3)
```

Finding a bug, you jump back to the edit window, make a change, and try to reload the module this way:

```
from imp import reload
reload(module)
```

This doesn't work, because the `from` statement assigned the name `function`, not `module`. To refer to the module in a `reload`, you have to first load it with an `import` statement at least once:

```
from imp import reload
import module
reload(module)
function(1, 2, 3)
```

However, this doesn't quite work either—`reload` updates the module object, but as discussed in the preceding section, names like `function` that were copied out of the module in the past still refer to the *old objects* (in this instance, the original version of the function). To really get the new function, you must refer to it as `module.function` after the `reload`, or rerun the `from`:

```
from imp import reload
import module
reload(module)
from module import function          # Or give up and use module.function()
function(1, 2, 3)
```

Now, the new version of the function will finally run.

As you can see, there are problems inherent in using `reload` with `from`: not only do you have to remember to reload after imports, but you also have to remember to rerun your `from` statements after reloads. This is complex enough to trip up even an expert once in a while. (In fact, the situation has gotten even worse in Python 3.0, because you must also remember to import `reload` itself!)

The short story is that you should not expect `reload` and `from` to play together nicely. The best policy is not to combine them at all—use `reload` with `import`, or launch your programs other ways, as suggested in Chapter 3: using the Run→Run Module menu option in IDLE, file icon clicks, system command lines, or the `exec` built-in function.

Recursive from Imports May Not Work

I saved the most bizarre (and, thankfully, obscure) gotcha for last. Because imports execute a file's statements from top to bottom, you need to be careful when using modules that import each other (known as *recursive imports*). Because the statements in a module may not all have been run when it imports another module, some of its names may not yet exist.

If you use `import` to fetch the module as a whole, this may or may not matter; the module's names won't be accessed until you later use qualification to fetch their values. But if you use `from` to fetch specific names, you must bear in mind that you will only have access to names in that module that have already been assigned.

For instance, take the following modules, `recur1` and `recur2`. `recur1` assigns a name X, and then imports `recur2` before assigning the name Y. At this point, `recur2` can fetch `recur1` as a whole with an `import` (it already exists in Python's internal modules table), but if it uses `from`, it will be able to see only the name X; the name Y, which is assigned below the `import` in `recur1`, doesn't yet exist, so you get an error:

```
# recur1.py
X = 1
import recur2                        # Run recur2 now if it doesn't exist
Y = 2
```

```
# recur2.py
from recur1 import X                 # OK: "X" already assigned
from recur1 import Y                 # Error: "Y" not yet assigned
```

```
C:\misc> C:\Python30\python
>>> import recur1
Traceback (most recent call last):
  File "<stdin>", line 1, in <module>
```

```
    File "recur1.py", line 2, in <module>
        import recur2
    File "recur2.py", line 2, in <module>
        from recur1 import Y
ImportError: cannot import name Y
```

Python avoids rerunning recur1's statements when they are imported recursively from recur2 (otherwise the imports would send the script into an infinite loop), but recur1's namespace is incomplete when it's imported by recur2.

The solution? Don't use from in recursive imports (no, really!). Python won't get stuck in a cycle if you do, but your programs will once again be dependent on the order of the statements in the modules.

There are two ways out of this gotcha:

- You can usually eliminate import cycles like this by careful design—maximizing cohesion and minimizing coupling are good first steps.

- If you can't break the cycles completely, postpone module name accesses by using import and qualification (instead of from), or by running your froms either inside functions (instead of at the top level of the module), or near the bottom of your file to defer their execution.

Chapter Summary

This chapter surveyed some more advanced module-related concepts. We studied data hiding techniques, enabling new language features with the __future__ module, the __name__ usage mode variable, transitive reloads, importing by name strings, and more. We also explored and summarized module design issues and looked at common mistakes related to modules to help you avoid them in your code.

The next chapter begins our look at Python's object-oriented programming tool, the class. Much of what we've covered in the last few chapters will apply there, too—classes live in modules and are namespaces as well, but they add an extra component to attribute lookup called *inheritance search*. As this is the last chapter in this part of the book, however, before we dive into that topic, be sure to work through this part's set of lab exercises. And before that, here is this chapter's quiz to review the topics covered here.

Test Your Knowledge: Quiz

1. What is significant about variables at the top level of a module whose names begin with a single underscore?

2. What does it mean when a module's __name__ variable is the string "__main__"?

3. If the user interactively types the name of a module to test, how can you import it?

4. How is changing `sys.path` different from setting `PYTHONPATH` to modify the module search path?

5. If the module `__future__` allows us to import from the future, can we also import from the past?

Test Your Knowledge: Answers

1. Variables at the top level of a module whose names begin with a single underscore are not copied out to the importing scope when the `from *` statement form is used. They can still be accessed by an `import` or the normal `from` statement form, though.

2. If a module's `__name__` variable is the string `"__main__"`, it means that the file is being executed as a top-level script instead of being imported from another file in the program. That is, the file is being used as a program, not a library.

3. User input usually comes into a script as a string; to import the referenced module given its string name, you can build and run an `import` statement with `exec`, or pass the string name in a call to the `__import__` function.

4. Changing `sys.path` only affects one running program, and is temporary—the change goes away when the program ends. `PYTHONPATH` settings live in the operating system—they are picked up globally by all programs on a machine, and changes to these settings endure after programs exit.

5. No, we can't import from the past in Python. We can install (or stubbornly use) an older version of the language, but the latest Python is generally the best Python.

Test Your Knowledge: Part V Exercises

See "Part V, Modules" on page 1121 in Appendix B for the solutions.

1. *Import basics.* Write a program that counts the lines and characters in a file (similar in spirit to *wc* on Unix). With your text editor, code a Python module called *mymod.py* that exports three top-level names:

   - A `countLines(name)` function that reads an input file and counts the number of lines in it (hint: `file.readlines` does most of the work for you, and `len` does the rest).

   - A `countChars(name)` function that reads an input file and counts the number of characters in it (hint: `file.read` returns a single string).

   - A `test(name)` function that calls both counting functions with a given input filename. Such a filename generally might be passed in, hardcoded, input with the `input` built-in function, or pulled from a command line via the `sys.argv` list shown in this chapter's *formats.py* example; for now, you can assume it's a passed-in function argument.

All three `mymod` functions should expect a filename string to be passed in. If you type more than two or three lines per function, you're working much too hard—use the hints I just gave!

Next, test your module interactively, using `import` and attribute references to fetch your exports. Does your PYTHONPATH need to include the directory where you created *mymod.py*? Try running your module on itself: e.g., `test("mymod.py")`. Note that `test` opens the file twice; if you're feeling ambitious, you may be able to improve this by passing an open file object into the two count functions (hint: `file.seek(0)` is a file rewind).

2. **from/from ***. Test your `mymod` module from exercise 1 interactively by using `from` to load the exports directly, first by name, then using the `from *` variant to fetch everything.

3. **__main__**. Add a line in your `mymod` module that calls the `test` function automatically only when the module is run as a script, not when it is imported. The line you add will probably test the value of __name__ for the string "__main__", as shown in this chapter. Try running your module from the system command line; then, import the module and test its functions interactively. Does it still work in both modes?

4. *Nested imports*. Write a second module, *myclient.py*, that imports `mymod` and tests its functions; then run `myclient` from the system command line. If `myclient` uses `from` to fetch from `mymod`, will `mymod`'s functions be accessible from the top level of `myclient`? What if it imports with `import` instead? Try coding both variations in `myclient` and test interactively by importing `myclient` and inspecting its __dict__ attribute.

5. *Package imports*. Import your file from a package. Create a subdirectory called *mypkg* nested in a directory on your module import search path, move the *mymod.py* module file you created in exercise 1 or 3 into the new directory, and try to import it with a package import of the form `import mypkg.mymod`.

   You'll need to add an __init__.py file in the directory your module was moved to make this go, but it should work on all major Python platforms (that's part of the reason Python uses "." as a path separator). The package directory you create can be simply a subdirectory of the one you're working in; if it is, it will be found via the home directory component of the search path, and you won't have to configure your path. Add some code to your __init__.py, and see if it runs on each import.

6. *Reloads*. Experiment with module reloads: perform the tests in Chapter 22's *changer.py* example, changing the called function's message and/or behavior repeatedly, without stopping the Python interpreter. Depending on your system, you might be able to edit `changer` in another window, or suspend the Python interpreter and edit in the same window (on Unix, a Ctrl-Z key combination usually suspends the current process, and an `fg` command later resumes it).

7. *Circular imports.*[‡] In the section on recursive import gotchas, importing `recur1` raised an error. But if you restart Python and import `recur2` interactively, the error doesn't occur—test this and see for yourself. Why do you think it works to import `recur2`, but not `recur1`? (Hint: Python stores new modules in the built-in `sys.modules` table—a dictionary—before running their code; later imports fetch the module from this table first, whether the module is "complete" yet or not.) Now, try running `recur1` as a top-level script file: **python recur1.py**. Do you get the same error that occurs when `recur1` is imported interactively? Why? (Hint: when modules are run as programs, they aren't imported, so this case has the same effect as importing `recur2` interactively; `recur2` is the first module imported.) What happens when you run `recur2` as a script?

[‡] Note that circular imports are extremely rare in practice. On the other hand, if you can understand why they are a potential problem, you know a lot about Python's import semantics.

## PART VI

Classes and OOP

## CHAPTER 25

OOP: The Big Picture

So far in this book, we've been using the term "object" generically. Really, the code written up to this point has been *object-based*—we've passed objects around our scripts, used them in expressions, called their methods, and so on. For our code to qualify as being truly *object-oriented* (OO), though, our objects will generally need to also participate in something called an *inheritance hierarchy*.

This chapter begins our exploration of the Python *class*—a device used to implement new kinds of objects in Python that support inheritance. Classes are Python's main object-oriented programming (OOP) tool, so we'll also look at OOP basics along the way in this part of the book. OOP offers a different and often more effective way of looking at programming, in which we factor code to minimize redundancy, and write new programs by *customizing* existing code instead of changing it in-place.

In Python, classes are created with a new statement: the `class` statement. As you'll see, the objects defined with classes can look a lot like the built-in types we studied earlier in the book. In fact, classes really just apply and extend the ideas we've already covered; roughly, they are packages of functions that use and process built-in object types. Classes, though, are designed to create and manage new objects, and they also support *inheritance*—a mechanism of code customization and reuse above and beyond anything we've seen so far.

One note up front: in Python, OOP is entirely optional, and you don't need to use classes just to get started. In fact, you can get plenty of work done with simpler constructs such as functions, or even simple top-level script code. Because using classes well requires some up-front planning, they tend to be of more interest to people who work in *strategic* mode (doing long-term product development) than to people who work in *tactical* mode (where time is in very short supply).

Still, as you'll see in this part of the book, classes turn out to be one of the most useful tools Python provides. When used well, classes can actually cut development time radically. They're also employed in popular Python tools like the tkinter GUI API, so most Python programmers will usually find at least a working knowledge of class basics helpful.

Why Use Classes?

Remember when I told you that programs "do things with stuff"? In simple terms, classes are just a way to define new sorts of stuff, reflecting real objects in a program's domain. For instance, suppose we decide to implement that hypothetical pizza-making robot we used as an example in Chapter 16. If we implement it using classes, we can model more of its real-world structure and relationships. Two aspects of OOP prove useful here:

Inheritance

Pizza-making robots are kinds of robots, so they possess the usual robot-y properties. In OOP terms, we say they "inherit" properties from the general category of all robots. These common properties need to be implemented only once for the general case and can be reused by all types of robots we may build in the future.

Composition

Pizza-making robots are really collections of components that work together as a team. For instance, for our robot to be successful, it might need arms to roll dough, motors to maneuver to the oven, and so on. In OOP parlance, our robot is an example of composition; it contains other objects that it activates to do its bidding. Each component might be coded as a class, which defines its own behavior and relationships.

General OOP ideas like inheritance and composition apply to any application that can be decomposed into a set of objects. For example, in typical GUI systems, interfaces are written as collections of widgets—buttons, labels, and so on—which are all drawn when their container is drawn (*composition*). Moreover, we may be able to write our own custom widgets—buttons with unique fonts, labels with new color schemes, and the like—which are specialized versions of more general interface devices (*inheritance*).

From a more concrete programming perspective, classes are Python program units, just like functions and modules: they are another compartment for packaging logic and data. In fact, classes also define new namespaces, much like modules. But, compared to other program units we've already seen, classes have three critical distinctions that make them more useful when it comes to building new objects:

Multiple instances

Classes are essentially factories for generating one or more objects. Every time we call a class, we generate a new object with a distinct namespace. Each object generated from a class has access to the class's attributes *and* gets a namespace of its own for data that varies per object.

Customization via inheritance

Classes also support the OOP notion of inheritance; we can extend a class by redefining its attributes outside the class itself. More generally, classes can build up namespace hierarchies, which define names to be used by objects created from classes in the hierarchy.

Operator overloading

By providing special protocol methods, classes can define objects that respond to the sorts of operations we saw at work on built-in types. For instance, objects made with classes can be sliced, concatenated, indexed, and so on. Python provides hooks that classes can use to intercept and implement any built-in type operation.

OOP from 30,000 Feet

Before we see what this all means in terms of code, I'd like to say a few words about the general ideas behind OOP. If you've never done anything object-oriented in your life before now, some of the terminology in this chapter may seem a bit perplexing on the first pass. Moreover, the motivation for these terms may be elusive until you've had a chance to study the ways that programmers apply them in larger systems. OOP is as much an experience as a technology.

Attribute Inheritance Search

The good news is that OOP is much simpler to understand and use in Python than in other languages, such as C++ or Java. As a dynamically typed scripting language, Python removes much of the syntactic clutter and complexity that clouds OOP in other tools. In fact, most of the OOP story in Python boils down to this expression:

```
object.attribute
```

We've been using this expression throughout the book to access module attributes, call methods of objects, and so on. When we say this to an object that is derived from a `class` statement, however, the expression kicks off a *search* in Python—it searches a tree of linked objects, looking for the first appearance of *attribute* that it can find. When classes are involved, the preceding Python expression effectively translates to the following in natural language:

Find the first occurrence of *attribute* by looking in *object*, then in all classes above it, from bottom to top and left to right.

In other words, attribute fetches are simply tree searches. The term *inheritance* is applied because objects lower in a tree inherit attributes attached to objects higher in that tree. As the search proceeds from the bottom up, in a sense, the objects linked into a tree are the union of all the attributes defined in all their tree parents, all the way up the tree.

In Python, this is all very literal: we really do build up trees of linked objects with code, and Python really does climb this tree at runtime searching for attributes every time we use the *object.attribute* expression. To make this more concrete, Figure 25-1 sketches an example of one of these trees.

In this figure, there is a tree of five objects labeled with variables, all of which have attached attributes, ready to be searched. More specifically, this tree links together three

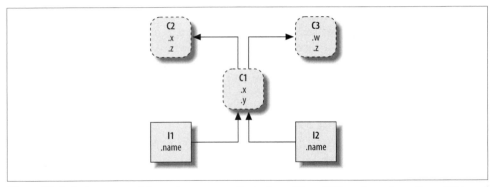

Figure 25-1. A class tree, with two instances at the bottom (I1 and I2), a class above them (C1), and two superclasses at the top (C2 and C3). All of these objects are namespaces (packages of variables), and the inheritance search is simply a search of the tree from bottom to top looking for the lowest occurrence of an attribute name. Code implies the shape of such trees.

class objects (the ovals C1, C2, and C3) and two *instance objects* (the rectangles I1 and I2) into an inheritance search tree. Notice that in the Python object model, classes and the instances you generate from them are two distinct object types:

Classes

> Serve as instance factories. Their attributes provide behavior—data and functions—that is inherited by all the instances generated from them (e.g., a function to compute an employee's salary from pay and hours).

Instances

> Represent the concrete items in a program's domain. Their attributes record data that varies per specific object (e.g., an employee's Social Security number).

In terms of search trees, an instance inherits attributes from its class, and a class inherits attributes from all classes above it in the tree.

In Figure 25-1, we can further categorize the ovals by their relative positions in the tree. We usually call classes higher in the tree (like C2 and C3) *superclasses*; classes lower in the tree (like C1) are known as *subclasses*.[*] These terms refer to relative tree positions and roles. Superclasses provide behavior shared by all their subclasses, but because the search proceeds from the bottom up, subclasses may override behavior defined in their superclasses by redefining superclass names lower in the tree.

As these last few words are really the crux of the matter of software customization in OOP, let's expand on this concept. Suppose we build up the tree in Figure 25-1, and then say this:

```
I2.w
```

---

[*] In other literature, you may also occasionally see the terms *base classes* and *derived classes* used to describe superclasses and subclasses, respectively.

Right away, this code invokes inheritance. Because this is an *object.attribute* expression, it triggers a search of the tree in Figure 25-1—Python will search for the attribute w by looking in I2 and above. Specifically, it will search the linked objects in this order:

    I2, C1, C2, C3

and stop at the first attached w it finds (or raise an error if w isn't found at all). In this case, w won't be found until C3 is searched because it appears only in that object. In other words, I2.w resolves to C3.w by virtue of the automatic search. In OOP terminology, I2 "inherits" the attribute w from C3.

Ultimately, the two instances inherit four attributes from their classes: w, x, y, and z. Other attribute references will wind up following different paths in the tree. For example:

- I1.x and I2.x both find x in C1 and stop because C1 is lower than C2.
- I1.y and I2.y both find y in C1 because that's the only place y appears.
- I1.z and I2.z both find z in C2 because C2 is further to the left than C3.
- I2.name finds name in I2 without climbing the tree at all.

Trace these searches through the tree in Figure 25-1 to get a feel for how inheritance searches work in Python.

The first item in the preceding list is perhaps the most important to notice—because C1 redefines the attribute x lower in the tree, it effectively *replaces* the version above it in C2. As you'll see in a moment, such redefinitions are at the heart of software customization in OOP—by redefining and replacing the attribute, C1 effectively customizes what it inherits from its superclasses.

Classes and Instances

Although they are technically two separate object types in the Python model, the classes and instances we put in these trees are almost identical—each type's main purpose is to serve as another kind of *namespace*—a package of variables, and a place where we can attach attributes. If classes and instances therefore sound like modules, they should; however, the objects in class trees also have automatically searched links to other namespace objects, and classes correspond to statements, not entire files.

The primary difference between classes and instances is that classes are a kind of *factory* for generating instances. For example, in a realistic application, we might have an Employee class that defines what it means to be an employee; from that class, we generate actual Employee instances. This is another difference between classes and modules: we only ever have one instance of a given module in memory (that's why we have to reload a module to get its new code), but with classes, we can make as many instances as we need.

Operationally, classes will usually have functions attached to them (e.g., `computeSalary`), and the instances will have more basic data items used by the class' functions (e.g., `hoursWorked`). In fact, the object-oriented model is not that different from the classic data-processing model of *programs* plus *records*; in OOP, instances are like records with "data," and classes are the "programs" for processing those records. In OOP, though, we also have the notion of an inheritance hierarchy, which supports software customization better than earlier models.

Class Method Calls

In the prior section, we saw how the attribute reference `I2.w` in our example class tree was translated to `C3.w` by the inheritance search procedure in Python. Perhaps just as important to understand as the inheritance of attributes, though, is what happens when we try to call methods (i.e., functions attached to classes as attributes).

If this `I2.w` reference is a *function* call, what it really means is "call the `C3.w` function to process `I2`." That is, Python will automatically map the call `I2.w()` into the call `C3.w(I2)`, passing in the instance as the first argument to the inherited function.

In fact, whenever we call a function attached to a class in this fashion, an instance of the class is always implied. This implied subject or context is part of the reason we refer to this as an *object-oriented* model—there is always a subject object when an operation is run. In a more realistic example, we might invoke a method called `giveRaise` attached as an attribute to an `Employee` class; such a call has no meaning unless qualified with the employee to whom the raise should be given.

As we'll see later, Python passes in the implied instance to a special first argument in the method, called `self` by convention. As we'll also learn, methods can be called through either an instance (e.g., `bob.giveRaise()`) or a class (e.g., `Employee.giveRaise(bob)`), and both forms serve purposes in our scripts. To see how methods receive their subjects, though, we need to move on to some code.

Coding Class Trees

Although we are speaking in the abstract here, there is tangible code behind all these ideas. We construct trees, and their objects with `class` statements and class calls, which we'll meet in more detail later. In short:

- Each `class` statement generates a new class object.
- Each time a class is called, it generates a new instance object.
- Instances are automatically linked to the classes from which they are created.
- Classes are linked to their superclasses by listing them in parentheses in a `class` header line; the left-to-right order there gives the order in the tree.

To build the tree in Figure 25-1, for example, we would run Python code of this form (I've omitted the guts of the `class` statements here):

```
class C2: ...                    # Make class objects (ovals)
class C3: ...
class C1(C2, C3): ...            # Linked to superclasses

I1 = C1()                        # Make instance objects (rectangles)
I2 = C1()                        # Linked to their classes
```

Here, we build the three class objects by running three `class` statements, and make the two instance objects by calling the class `C1` twice, as though it were a function. The instances remember the class they were made from, and the class `C1` remembers its listed superclasses.

Technically, this example is using something called *multiple inheritance*, which simply means that a class has more than one superclass above it in the class tree. In Python, if there is more than one superclass listed in parentheses in a `class` statement (like `C1`'s here), their left-to-right order gives the order in which those superclasses will be searched for attributes.

Because of the way inheritance searches proceed, the object to which you attach an attribute turns out to be crucial—it determines the name's scope. Attributes attached to instances pertain only to those single instances, but attributes attached to classes are shared by all their subclasses and instances. Later, we'll study the code that hangs attributes on these objects in depth. As we'll find:

- Attributes are usually attached to classes by assignments made within `class` statements, and not nested inside function `def` statements.

- Attributes are usually attached to instances by assignments to a special argument passed to functions inside classes, called `self`.

For example, classes provide behavior for their instances with functions created by coding `def` statements inside `class` statements. Because such nested `def`s assign names within the class, they wind up attaching attributes to the class object that will be inherited by all instances and subclasses:

```
class C1(C2, C3):                # Make and link class C1
    def setname(self, who):      # Assign name: C1.setname
        self.name = who          # Self is either I1 or I2

I1 = C1()                        # Make two instances
I2 = C1()
I1.setname('bob')                # Sets I1.name to 'bob'
I2.setname('mel')                # Sets I2.name to 'mel'
print(I1.name)                   # Prints 'bob'
```

There's nothing syntactically unique about def in this context. Operationally, when a def appears inside a class like this, it is usually known as a *method*, and it automatically receives a special first argument—called self by convention—that provides a handle back to the instance to be processed.†

Because classes are factories for multiple instances, their methods usually go through this automatically passed-in self argument whenever they need to fetch or set attributes of the particular instance being processed by a method call. In the preceding code, self is used to store a name in one of two instances.

Like simple variables, attributes of classes and instances are not declared ahead of time, but spring into existence the first time they are assigned values. When a method assigns to a self attribute, it creates or changes an attribute in an instance at the bottom of the class tree (i.e., one of the rectangles) because self automatically refers to the instance being processed.

In fact, because all the objects in class trees are just namespace objects, we can fetch or set any of their attributes by going through the appropriate names. Saying C1.setname is as valid as saying I1.setname, as long as the names C1 and I1 are in your code's scopes.

As currently coded, our C1 class doesn't attach a name attribute to an instance until the setname method is called. In fact, referencing I1.name before calling I1.setname would produce an undefined name error. If a class wants to guarantee that an attribute like name is always set in its instances, it more typically will fill out the attribute at construction time, like this:

```
class C1(C2, C3):
    def __init__(self, who):       # Set name when constructed
        self.name = who            # Self is either I1 or I2

I1 = C1('bob')                     # Sets I1.name to 'bob'
I2 = C1('mel')                     # Sets I2.name to 'mel'
print(I1.name)                     # Prints 'bob'
```

If it's coded and inherited, Python automatically calls a method named __init__ each time an instance is generated from a class. The new instance is passed in to the self argument of __init__ as usual, and any values listed in parentheses in the class call go to arguments two and beyond. The effect here is to initialize instances when they are made, without requiring extra method calls.

The __init__ method is known as the *constructor* because of when it is run. It's the most commonly used representative of a larger class of methods called *operator overloading methods*, which we'll discuss in more detail in the chapters that follow. Such methods are inherited in class trees as usual and have double underscores at the start and end of their names to make them distinct. Python runs them automatically when instances that support them appear in the corresponding operations, and they are

---

† If you've ever used C++ or Java, you'll recognize that Python's self is the same as the this pointer, but self is always explicit in Python to make attribute accesses more obvious.

mostly an alternative to using simple method calls. They're also optional: if omitted, the operations are not supported.

For example, to implement set intersection, a class might either provide a method named `intersect`, or overload the & expression operator to dispatch to the required logic by coding a method named `__and__`. Because the operator scheme makes instances look and feel more like built-in types, it allows some classes to provide a consistent and natural interface, and be compatible with code that expects a built-in type.

OOP Is About Code Reuse

And that, along with a few syntax details, is most of the OOP story in Python. Of course, there's a bit more to it than just inheritance. For example, operator overloading is much more general than I've described so far—classes may also provide their own implementations of operations such as indexing, fetching attributes, printing, and more. By and large, though, OOP is about looking up attributes in trees.

So why would we be interested in building and searching trees of objects? Although it takes some experience to see how, when used well, classes support code *reuse* in ways that other Python program components cannot. With classes, we code by customizing existing software, instead of either changing existing code in-place or starting from scratch for each new project.

At a fundamental level, classes are really just packages of functions and other names, much like modules. However, the automatic attribute inheritance search that we get with classes supports customization of software above and beyond what we can do with modules and functions. Moreover, classes provide a natural structure for code that localizes logic and names, and so aids in debugging.

For instance, because methods are simply functions with a special first argument, we can mimic some of their behavior by manually passing objects to be processed to simple functions. The participation of methods in class inheritance, though, allows us to naturally customize existing software by coding subclasses with new method definitions, rather than changing existing code in-place. There is really no such concept with modules and functions.

As an example, suppose you're assigned the task of implementing an employee database application. As a Python OOP programmer, you might begin by coding a general superclass that defines default behavior common to all the kinds of employees in your organization:

```
class Employee:                    # General superclass
    def computeSalary(self): ...   # Common or default behavior
    def giveRaise(self): ...
    def promote(self): ...
    def retire(self): ...
```

Once you've coded this general behavior, you can specialize it for each specific kind of employee to reflect how the various types differ from the norm. That is, you can code subclasses that customize just the bits of behavior that differ per employee type; the rest of the employee types' behavior will be inherited from the more general class. For example, if engineers have a unique salary computation rule (i.e., not hours times rate), you can replace just that one method in a subclass:

```
class Engineer(Employee):          # Specialized subclass
    def computeSalary(self): ...   # Something custom here
```

Because the `computeSalary` version here appears lower in the class tree, it will replace (override) the general version in `Employee`. You then create instances of the kinds of employee classes that the real employees belong to, to get the correct behavior:

```
bob = Employee()      # Default behavior
mel = Engineer()      # Custom salary calculator
```

Notice that you can make instances of any class in a tree, not just the ones at the bottom—the class you make an instance from determines the level at which the attribute search will begin. Ultimately, these two instance objects might wind up embedded in a larger container object (e.g., a list, or an instance of another class) that represents a department or company using the composition idea mentioned at the start of this chapter.

When you later ask for these employees' salaries, they will be computed according to the classes from which the objects were made, due to the principles of the inheritance search:‡

```
company = [bob, mel]              # A composite object
for emp in company:
    print(emp.computeSalary())    # Run this object's version
```

This is yet another instance of the idea of *polymorphism* introduced in Chapter 4 and revisited in Chapter 16. Recall that polymorphism means that the meaning of an operation depends on the object being operated on. Here, the method `computeSalary` is located by inheritance search in each object before it is called. In other applications, polymorphism might also be used to hide (i.e., *encapsulate*) interface differences. For example, a program that processes data streams might be coded to expect objects with input and output methods, without caring what those methods actually do:

```
def processor(reader, converter, writer):
    while 1:
        data = reader.read()
        if not data: break
```

---

‡ Note that the `company` list in this example could be stored in a file with Python object pickling, introduced in Chapter 9 when we met files, to yield a persistent employee database. Python also comes with a module named `shelve`, which would allow you to store the pickled representation of the class instances in an access-by-key filesystem; the third-party open source ZODB system does the same but has better support for production-quality object-oriented databases.

```
        data = converter(data)
        writer.write(data)
```

By passing in instances of subclasses that specialize the required `read` and `write` method interfaces for various data sources, we can reuse the `processor` function for any data source we need to use, both now and in the future:

```
class Reader:
    def read(self): ...           # Default behavior and tools
    def other(self): ...
class FileReader(Reader):
    def read(self): ...           # Read from a local file
class SocketReader(Reader):
    def read(self): ...           # Read from a network socket
...
processor(FileReader(...),   Converter,  FileWriter(...))
processor(SocketReader(...), Converter,  TapeWriter(...))
processor(FtpReader(...),    Converter,  XmlWriter(...))
```

Moreover, because the internal implementations of those `read` and `write` methods have been factored into single locations, they can be changed without impacting code such as this that uses them. In fact, the `processor` function might itself be a class to allow the conversion logic of `converter` to be filled in by inheritance, and to allow readers and writers to be embedded by composition (we'll see how this works later in this part of the book).

Once you get used to programming this way (by software customization), you'll find that when it's time to write a new program, much of your work may already be done—your task largely becomes one of mixing together existing superclasses that already implement the behavior required by your program. For example, someone else might have written the `Employee`, `Reader`, and `Writer` classes in this example for use in a completely different program. If so, you get all of that person's code "for free."

In fact, in many application domains, you can fetch or purchase collections of super-classes, known as *frameworks*, that implement common programming tasks as classes, ready to be mixed into your applications. These frameworks might provide database interfaces, testing protocols, GUI toolkits, and so on. With frameworks, you often simply code a subclass that fills in an expected method or two; the framework classes higher in the tree do most of the work for you. Programming in such an OOP world is just a matter of combining and specializing already debugged code by writing subclasses of your own.

Of course, it takes a while to learn how to leverage classes to achieve such OOP utopia. In practice, object-oriented work also entails substantial design work to fully realize the code reuse benefits of classes—to this end, programmers have begun cataloging common OOP structures, known as *design patterns*, to help with design issues. The actual code you write to do OOP in Python, though, is so simple that it will not in itself pose an additional obstacle to your OOP quest. To see why, you'll have to move on to Chapter 26.

Chapter Summary

We took an abstract look at classes and OOP in this chapter, taking in the big picture before we dive into syntax details. As we've seen, OOP is mostly about looking up attributes in trees of linked objects; we call this lookup an inheritance search. Objects at the bottom of the tree inherit attributes from objects higher up in the tree—a feature that enables us to program by customizing code, rather than changing it, or starting from scratch. When used well, this model of programming can cut development time radically.

The next chapter will begin to fill in the coding details behind the picture painted here. As we get deeper into Python classes, though, keep in mind that the OOP model in Python is very simple; as I've already stated, it's really just about looking up attributes in object trees. Before we move on, here's a quick quiz to review what we've covered here.

Test Your Knowledge: Quiz

1. What is the main point of OOP in Python?
2. Where does an inheritance search look for an attribute?
3. What is the difference between a class object and an instance object?
4. Why is the first argument in a class method function special?
5. What is the __init__ method used for?
6. How do you create a class instance?
7. How do you create a class?
8. How do you specify a class's superclasses?

Test Your Knowledge: Answers

1. OOP is about code reuse—you factor code to minimize redundancy and program by customizing what already exists instead of changing code in-place or starting from scratch.
2. An inheritance search looks for an attribute first in the instance object, then in the class the instance was created from, then in all higher superclasses, progressing from the bottom to the top of the object tree, and from left to right (by default). The search stops at the first place the attribute is found. Because the lowest version of a name found along the way wins, class hierarchies naturally support customization by extension.

3. Both class and instance objects are namespaces (packages of variables that appear as attributes). The main difference between them is that classes are a kind of factory for creating multiple instances. Classes also support operator overloading methods, which instances inherit, and treat any functions nested within them as special methods for processing instances.

4. The first argument in a class method function is special because it always receives the instance object that is the implied subject of the method call. It's usually called `self` by convention. Because method functions always have this implied subject object context by default, we say they are "object-oriented"—i.e., designed to process or change objects.

5. If the `__init__` method is coded or inherited in a class, Python calls it automatically each time an instance of that class is created. It's known as the constructor method; it is passed the new instance implicitly, as well as any arguments passed explicitly to the class name. It's also the most commonly used operator overloading method. If no `__init__` method is present, instances simply begin life as empty namespaces.

6. You create a class instance by calling the class name as though it were a function; any arguments passed into the class name show up as arguments two and beyond in the `__init__` constructor method. The new instance remembers the class it was created from for inheritance purposes.

7. You create a class by running a `class` statement; like function definitions, these statements normally run when the enclosing module file is imported (more on this in the next chapter).

8. You specify a class's superclasses by listing them in parentheses in the `class` statement, after the new class's name. The left-to-right order in which the classes are listed in the parentheses gives the left-to-right inheritance search order in the class tree.

## CHAPTER 26

Class Coding Basics

Now that we've talked about OOP in the abstract, it's time to see how this translates to actual code. This chapter begins to fill in the syntax details behind the class model in Python.

If you've never been exposed to OOP in the past, classes can seem somewhat complicated if taken in a single dose. To make class coding easier to absorb, we'll begin our detailed exploration of OOP by taking a first look at some basic classes in action in this chapter. We'll expand on the details introduced here in later chapters of this part of the book, but in their basic form, Python classes are easy to understand.

In fact, classes have just three primary distinctions. At a base level, they are mostly just namespaces, much like the modules we studied in Part V. Unlike modules, though, classes also have support for generating multiple objects, for namespace inheritance, and for operator overloading. Let's begin our `class` statement tour by exploring each of these three distinctions in turn.

Classes Generate Multiple Instance Objects

To understand how the multiple objects idea works, you have to first understand that there are two kinds of objects in Python's OOP model: *class* objects and *instance* objects. Class objects provide default behavior and serve as factories for instance objects. Instance objects are the real objects your programs process—each is a namespace in its own right, but inherits (i.e., has automatic access to) names in the class from which it was created. Class objects come from statements, and instances come from calls; each time you call a class, you get a new instance of that class.

This object-generation concept is very different from any of the other program constructs we've seen so far in this book. In effect, classes are essentially *factories* for generating multiple instances. By contrast, only one copy of each module is ever imported into a single program (in fact, one reason that we have to call `imp.reload` is to update the single module object so that changes are reflected once they've been made).

The following is a quick summary of the bare essentials of Python OOP. As you'll see, Python classes are in some ways similar to both `defs` and modules, but they may be quite different from what you're used to in other languages.

Class Objects Provide Default Behavior

When we run a `class` statement, we get a class object. Here's a rundown of the main properties of Python classes:

- **The class statement creates a class object and assigns it a name**. Just like the function `def` statement, the Python `class` statement is an *executable* statement. When reached and run, it generates a new class object and assigns it to the name in the `class` header. Also, like `defs`, `class` statements typically run when the files they are coded in are first imported.

- **Assignments inside class statements make class attributes**. Just like in module files, top-level assignments within a `class` statement (not nested in a `def`) generate attributes in a class object. Technically, the `class` statement scope *morphs* into the attribute namespace of the class object, just like a module's global scope. After running a `class` statement, class attributes are accessed by name qualification: *object.name*.

- **Class attributes provide object state and behavior**. Attributes of a class object record state information and behavior to be shared by all instances created from the class; function `def` statements nested inside a `class` generate *methods*, which process instances.

Instance Objects Are Concrete Items

When we call a class object, we get an instance object. Here's an overview of the key points behind class instances:

- **Calling a class object like a function makes a new instance object**. Each time a class is called, it creates and returns a new instance object. Instances represent concrete items in your program's domain.

- **Each instance object inherits class attributes and gets its own namespace**. Instance objects created from classes are new namespaces; they start out empty but inherit attributes that live in the class objects from which they were generated.

- **Assignments to attributes of self in methods make per-instance attributes.** Inside class method functions, the first argument (called self by convention) references the instance object being processed; assignments to attributes of self create or change data in the instance, not the class.

A First Example

Let's turn to a real example to show how these ideas work in practice. To begin, let's define a class named FirstClass by running a Python class statement interactively:

```
>>> class FirstClass:              # Define a class object
...     def setdata(self, value):  # Define class methods
...         self.data = value      # self is the instance
...     def display(self):
...         print(self.data)       # self.data: per instance
...
```

We're working interactively here, but typically, such a statement would be run when the module file it is coded in is imported. Like functions created with defs, this class won't even exist until Python reaches and runs this statement.

Like all compound statements, the class starts with a header line that lists the class name, followed by a body of one or more nested and (usually) indented statements. Here, the nested statements are defs; they define functions that implement the behavior the class means to export.

As we learned in Part IV, def is really an assignment. Here, it assigns function objects to the names setdata and display in the class statement's scope, and so generates attributes attached to the class: FirstClass.setdata and FirstClass.display. In fact, any name assigned at the top level of the class's nested block becomes an attribute of the class.

Functions inside a class are usually called *methods*. They're coded with normal defs, and they support everything we've learned about functions already (they can have defaults, return values, and so on). But in a method function, the first argument automatically receives an implied instance object when called—the subject of the call. We need to create a couple of instances to see how this works:

```
>>> x = FirstClass()    # Make two instances
>>> y = FirstClass()    # Each is a new namespace
```

By *calling* the class this way (notice the parentheses), we generate instance objects, which are just namespaces that have access to their classes' attributes. Properly speaking, at this point, we have three objects: two instances and a class. Really, we have three linked namespaces, as sketched in Figure 26-1. In OOP terms, we say that x "is a" FirstClass, as is y.

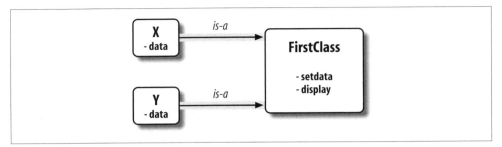

Figure 26-1. Classes and instances are linked namespace objects in a class tree that is searched by inheritance. Here, the "data" attribute is found in instances, but "setdata" and "display" are in the class above them.

The two instances start out empty but have links back to the class from which they were generated. If we qualify an instance with the name of an attribute that lives in the class object, Python fetches the name from the class by inheritance search (unless it also lives in the instance):

```
>>> x.setdata("King Arthur")    # Call methods: self is x
>>> y.setdata(3.14159)          # Runs: FirstClass.setdata(y, 3.14159)
```

Neither x nor y has a `setdata` attribute of its own, so to find it, Python follows the link from instance to class. And that's about all there is to inheritance in Python: it happens at attribute qualification time, and it just involves looking up names in linked objects (e.g., by following the is-a links in Figure 26-1).

In the `setdata` function inside `FirstClass`, the value passed in is assigned to `self.data`. Within a method, `self`—the name given to the leftmost argument by convention—automatically refers to the instance being processed (x or y), so the assignments store values in the instances' namespaces, not the class's (that's how the `data` names in Figure 26-1 are created).

Because classes can generate multiple instances, methods must go through the `self` argument to get to the instance to be processed. When we call the class's `display` method to print `self.data`, we see that it's different in each instance; on the other hand, the name `display` itself is the same in x and y, as it comes (is inherited) from the class:

```
>>> x.display()                 # self.data differs in each instance
King Arthur
>>> y.display()
3.14159
```

Notice that we stored different object types in the `data` member in each instance (a string, and a floating point). As with everything else in Python, there are no declarations for instance attributes (sometimes called *members*); they spring into existence the first time they are assigned values, just like simple variables. In fact, if we were to call `display` on one of our instances before calling `setdata`, we would trigger an undefined name error—the attribute named `data` doesn't even exist in memory until it is assigned within the `setdata` method.

As another way to appreciate how dynamic this model is, consider that we can change instance attributes in the class itself, by assigning to `self` in methods, or outside the class, by assigning to an explicit instance object:

```
>>> x.data = "New value"        # Can get/set attributes
>>> x.display()                 # Outside the class too
New value
```

Although less common, we could even generate a brand new attribute in the instance's namespace by assigning to its name outside the class's method functions:

```
>>> x.anothername = "spam"      # Can set new attributes here too!
```

This would attach a new attribute called `anothername`, which may or may not be used by any of the class's methods, to the instance object `x`. Classes usually create all of the instance's attributes by assignment to the `self` argument, but they don't have to; programs can fetch, change, or create attributes on any objects to which they have references.

Classes Are Customized by Inheritance

Besides serving as factories for generating multiple instance objects, classes also allow us to make changes by introducing new components (called *subclasses*), instead of changing existing components in-place. Instance objects generated from a class inherit the class's attributes. Python also allows classes to inherit from other classes, opening the door to coding *hierarchies* of classes that specialize behavior—by redefining attributes in subclasses that appear lower in the hierarchy, we override the more general definitions of those attributes higher in the tree. In effect, the further down the hierarchy we go, the more specific the software becomes. Here, too, there is no parallel with modules: their attributes live in a single, flat namespace that is not as amenable to customization.

In Python, instances inherit from classes, and classes inherit from superclasses. Here are the key ideas behind the machinery of attribute inheritance:

- **Superclasses are listed in parentheses in a `class` header**. To inherit attributes from another class, just list the class in parentheses in a `class` statement's header. The class that inherits is usually called a *subclass*, and the class that is inherited from is its *superclass*.

- **Classes inherit attributes from their superclasses**. Just as instances inherit the attribute names defined in their classes, classes inherit all the attribute names defined in their superclasses; Python finds them automatically when they're accessed, if they don't exist in the subclasses.

- **Instances inherit attributes from all accessible classes**. Each instance gets names from the class it's generated from, as well as all of that class's superclasses. When looking for a name, Python checks the instance, then its class, then all superclasses.

- **Each *object.attribute* reference invokes a new, independent search**. Python performs an independent search of the class tree for each attribute fetch expression. This includes references to instances and classes made outside `class` statements (e.g., `X.attr`), as well as references to attributes of the `self` instance argument in class method functions. Each `self.attr` expression in a method invokes a new search for `attr` in `self` and above.

- **Logic changes are made by subclassing, not by changing superclasses**. By redefining superclass names in subclasses lower in the hierarchy (class tree), subclasses replace and thus customize inherited behavior.

The net effect, and the main purpose of all this searching, is that classes support factoring and customization of code better than any other language tool we've seen so far. On the one hand, they allow us to minimize code redundancy (and so reduce maintenance costs) by factoring operations into a single, shared implementation; on the other, they allow us to program by customizing what already exists, rather than changing it in-place or starting from scratch.

A Second Example

To illustrate the role of inheritance, this next example builds on the previous one. First, we'll define a new class, `SecondClass`, that inherits all of `FirstClass`'s names and provides one of its own:

```
>>> class SecondClass(FirstClass):          # Inherits setdata
...     def display(self):                   # Changes display
...         print('Current value = "%s"' % self.data)
...
```

`SecondClass` defines the `display` method to print with a different format. By defining an attribute with the same name as an attribute in `FirstClass`, `SecondClass` effectively replaces the `display` attribute in its superclass.

Recall that inheritance searches proceed upward from instances, to subclasses, to superclasses, stopping at the first appearance of the attribute name that it finds. In this case, since the `display` name in `SecondClass` will be found before the one in `FirstClass`, we say that `SecondClass` *overrides* `FirstClass`'s `display`. Sometimes we call this act of replacing attributes by redefining them lower in the tree *overloading*.

The net effect here is that `SecondClass` specializes `FirstClass` by changing the behavior of the `display` method. On the other hand, `SecondClass` (and any instances created from it) still inherits the `setdata` method in `FirstClass` verbatim. Let's make an instance to demonstrate:

```
>>> z = SecondClass()
>>> z.setdata(42)          # Finds setdata in FirstClass
>>> z.display()            # Finds overridden method in SecondClass
Current value = "42"
```

As before, we make a `SecondClass` instance object by calling it. The `setdata` call still runs the version in `FirstClass`, but this time the `display` attribute comes from `Second Class` and prints a custom message. Figure 26-2 sketches the namespaces involved.

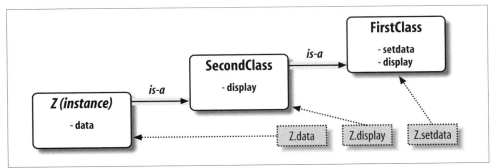

Figure 26-2. Specialization by overriding inherited names by redefining them in extensions lower in the class tree. Here, SecondClass redefines and so customizes the "display" method for its instances.

Now, here's a very important thing to notice about OOP: the specialization introduced in `SecondClass` is completely *external* to `FirstClass`. That is, it doesn't affect existing or future `FirstClass` objects, like the x from the prior example:

```
>>> x.display()            # x is still a FirstClass instance (old message)
New value
```

Rather than *changing* `FirstClass`, we *customized* it. Naturally, this is an artificial example, but as a rule, because inheritance allows us to make changes like this in external components (i.e., in subclasses), classes often support extension and reuse better than functions or modules can.

Classes Are Attributes in Modules

Before we move on, remember that there's nothing magic about a class name. It's just a variable assigned to an object when the `class` statement runs, and the object can be referenced with any normal expression. For instance, if our `FirstClass` was coded in a module file instead of being typed interactively, we could import it and use its name normally in a `class` header line:

```
from modulename import FirstClass      # Copy name into my scope
class SecondClass(FirstClass):          # Use class name directly
    def display(self): ...
```

Or, equivalently:

```
import modulename                                    # Access the whole module
class SecondClass(modulename.FirstClass):            # Qualify to reference
    def display(self): ...
```

Like everything else, class names always live within a module, so they must follow all the rules we studied in Part V. For example, more than one class can be coded in a single module file—like other statements in a module, `class` statements are run during imports to define names, and these names become distinct module attributes. More generally, each module may arbitrarily mix any number of variables, functions, and classes, and all names in a module behave the same way. The file *food.py* demonstrates:

```
# food.py
var = 1                              # food.var
def func():                          # food.func
    ...
class spam:                          # food.spam
    ...
class ham:                           # food.ham
    ...
class eggs:                          # food.eggs
    ...
```

This holds true even if the module and class happen to have the same name. For example, given the following file, *person.py*:

```
class person:
    ...
```

we need to go through the module to fetch the class as usual:

```
import person                        # Import module
x = person.person()                  # Class within module
```

Although this path may look redundant, it's required: `person.person` refers to the `person` class inside the `person` module. Saying just `person` gets the module, not the class, unless the `from` statement is used:

```
from person import person            # Get class from module
x = person()                         # Use class name
```

As with any other variable, we can never see a class in a file without first importing and somehow fetching it from its enclosing file. If this seems confusing, don't use the same name for a module and a class within it. In fact, common convention in Python dictates that class names should begin with an uppercase letter, to help make them more distinct:

```
import person                        # Lowercase for modules
x = person.Person()                  # Uppercase for classes
```

Also, keep in mind that although classes and modules are both namespaces for attaching attributes, they correspond to very different source code structures: a module reflects an entire *file*, but a class is a *statement* within a file. We'll say more about such distinctions later in this part of the book.

Classes Can Intercept Python Operators

Let's move on to the third major difference between classes and modules: operator overloading. In simple terms, *operator overloading* lets objects coded with classes intercept and respond to operations that work on built-in types: addition, slicing, printing, qualification, and so on. It's mostly just an automatic dispatch mechanism—expressions and other built-in operations route control to implementations in classes. Here, too, there is nothing similar in modules: modules can implement function calls, but not the behavior of expressions.

Although we could implement all class behavior as method functions, operator overloading lets objects be more tightly integrated with Python's object model. Moreover, because operator overloading makes our own objects act like built-ins, it tends to foster object interfaces that are more consistent and easier to learn, and it allows class-based objects to be processed by code written to expect a built-in type's interface. Here is a quick rundown of the main ideas behind overloading operators:

- **Methods named with double underscores (__X__) are special hooks**. Python operator overloading is implemented by providing specially named methods to intercept operations. The Python language defines a fixed and unchangeable mapping from each of these operations to a specially named method.

- **Such methods are called automatically when instances appear in built-in operations**. For instance, if an instance object inherits an __add__ method, that method is called whenever the object appears in a + expression. The method's return value becomes the result of the corresponding expression.

- **Classes may override most built-in type operations**. There are dozens of special operator overloading method names for intercepting and implementing nearly every operation available for built-in types. This includes expressions, but also basic operations like printing and object creation.

- **There are no defaults for operator overloading methods, and none are required**. If a class does not define or inherit an operator overloading method, it just means that the corresponding operation is not supported for the class's instances. If there is no __add__, for example, + expressions raise exceptions.

- **Operators allow classes to integrate with Python's object model**. By overloading type operations, user-defined objects implemented with classes can act just like built-ins, and so provide consistency as well as compatibility with expected interfaces.

Operator overloading is an optional feature; it's used primarily by people developing tools for other Python programmers, not by application developers. And, candidly, you probably shouldn't try to use it just because it seems "cool." Unless a class needs to mimic built-in type interfaces, it should usually stick to simpler named methods. Why would an employee database application support expressions like * and +, for example? Named methods like giveRaise and promote would usually make more sense.

Because of this, we won't go into details on every operator overloading method available in Python in this book. Still, there is one operator overloading method you are likely to see in almost every realistic Python class: the _init_ method, which is known as the *constructor* method and is used to initialize objects' state. You should pay special attention to this method, because _init_, along with the self argument, turns out to be a key requirement to understanding most OOP code in Python.

A Third Example

On to another example. This time, we'll define a subclass of SecondClass that implements three specially named attributes that Python will call automatically:

- _init_ is run when a new instance object is created (self is the new ThirdClass object).*

- _add_ is run when a ThirdClass instance appears in a + expression.

- _str_ is run when an object is printed (technically, when it's converted to its print string by the str built-in function or its Python internals equivalent).

Our new subclass also defines a normally named method named mul, which changes the instance object in-place. Here's the new subclass:

```
>>> class ThirdClass(SecondClass):          # Inherit from SecondClass
...     def __init__(self, value):          # On "ThirdClass(value)"
...         self.data = value
...     def __add__(self, other):           # On "self + other"
...         return ThirdClass(self.data + other)
...     def __str__(self):                  # On "print(self)", "str()"
...         return '[ThirdClass: %s]' % self.data
...     def mul(self, other):               # In-place change: named
...         self.data *= other
...
>>> a = ThirdClass('abc')                   # __init__ called
>>> a.display()                             # Inherited method called
Current value = "abc"
>>> print(a)                                # __str__: returns display string
[ThirdClass: abc]

>>> b = a + 'xyz'                           # __add__: makes a new instance
>>> b.display()                             # b has all ThirdClass methods
Current value = "abcxyz"
>>> print(b)                                # __str__: returns display string
[ThirdClass: abcxyz]

>>> a.mul(3)                                # mul: changes instance in-place
>>> print(a)
[ThirdClass: abcabcabc]
```

---

* Not to be confused with the _init_.py files in module packages! See Chapter 23 for more details.

ThirdClass "is a" SecondClass, so its instances inherit the customized display method from SecondClass. This time, though, ThirdClass creation calls pass an argument (e.g., "abc"). This argument is passed to the value argument in the __init__ constructor and assigned to self.data there. The net effect is that ThirdClass arranges to set the data attribute automatically at construction time, instead of requiring setdata calls after the fact.

Further, ThirdClass objects can now show up in + expressions and print calls. For +, Python passes the instance object on the left to the self argument in __add__ and the value on the right to other, as illustrated in Figure 26-3; whatever __add__ returns becomes the result of the + expression. For print, Python passes the object being printed to self in __str__; whatever string this method returns is taken to be the print string for the object. With __str__ we can use a normal print to display objects of this class, instead of calling the special display method.

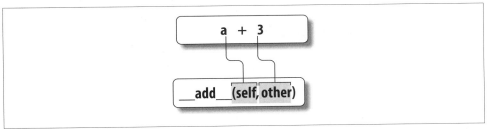

Figure 26-3. In operator overloading, expression operators and other built-in operations performed on class instances are mapped back to specially named methods in the class. These special methods are optional and may be inherited as usual. Here, a + expression triggers the __add__ method.

Specially named methods such as __init__, __add__, and __str__ are inherited by subclasses and instances, just like any other names assigned in a class. If they're not coded in a class, Python looks for such names in all its superclasses, as usual. Operator overloading method names are also not built-in or reserved words; they are just attributes that Python looks for when objects appear in various contexts. Python usually calls them automatically, but they may occasionally be called by your code as well; the __init__ method, for example, is often called manually to trigger superclass constructors (more on this later).

Notice that the __add__ method makes and returns a *new* instance object of its class, by calling ThirdClass with the result value. By contrast, mul *changes* the current instance object in-place, by reassigning the self attribute. We could overload the * expression to do the latter, but this would be too different from the behavior of * for built-in types such as numbers and strings, for which it always makes new objects. Common practice dictates that overloaded operators should work the same way that built-in operator implementations do. Because operator overloading is really just an expression-to-method dispatch mechanism, though, you can interpret operators any way you like in your own class objects.

Why Use Operator Overloading?

As a class designer, you can choose to use operator overloading or not. Your choice simply depends on how much you want your object to look and feel like built-in types. As mentioned earlier, if you omit an operator overloading method and do not inherit it from a superclass, the corresponding operation will not be supported for your instances; if it's attempted, an exception will be thrown (or a standard default will be used).

Frankly, many operator overloading methods tend to be used only when implementing objects that are mathematical in nature; a vector or matrix class may overload the addition operator, for example, but an employee class likely would not. For simpler classes, you might not use overloading at all, and would rely instead on explicit method calls to implement your objects' behavior.

On the other hand, you might decide to use operator overloading if you need to pass a user-defined object to a function that was coded to expect the operators available on a built-in type like a list or a dictionary. Implementing the same operator set in your class will ensure that your objects support the same expected object interface and so are compatible with the function. Although we won't cover every operator overloading method in this book, we'll see some additional operator overloading techniques in action in Chapter 29.

One overloading method we will explore here is the __init__ constructor method, which seems to show up in almost every realistic class. Because it allows classes to fill out the attributes in their newly created instances immediately, the constructor is useful for almost every kind of class you might code. In fact, even though instance attributes are not declared in Python, you can usually find out which attributes an instance will have by inspecting its class's __init__ method.

The World's Simplest Python Class

We've begun studying class statement syntax in detail in this chapter, but I'd again like to remind you that the basic inheritance model that classes produce is very simple—all it really involves is searching for attributes in trees of linked objects. In fact, we can create a class with nothing in it at all. The following statement makes a class with no attributes attached (an empty namespace object):

```
>>> class rec: pass          # Empty namespace object
```

We need the no-operation pass statement (discussed in Chapter 13) here because we don't have any methods to code. After we make the class by running this statement interactively, we can start attaching attributes to the class by assigning names to it completely outside of the original class statement:

```
>>> rec.name = 'Bob'          # Just objects with attributes
>>> rec.age  = 40
```

And, after we've created these attributes by assignment, we can fetch them with the usual syntax. When used this way, a class is roughly similar to a "struct" in C, or a "record" in Pascal. It's basically an object with field names attached to it (we can do similar work with dictionary keys, but it requires extra characters):

```
>>> print(rec.name)          # Like a C struct or a record
Bob
```

Notice that this works even though there are no instances of the class yet; classes are objects in their own right, even without instances. In fact, they are just self-contained namespaces, so as long as we have a reference to a class, we can set or change its attributes anytime we wish. Watch what happens when we do create two instances, though:

```
>>> x = rec()                # Instances inherit class names
>>> y = rec()
```

These instances begin their lives as completely empty namespace objects. Because they remember the class from which they were made, though, they will obtain the attributes we attached to the class by inheritance:

```
>>> x.name, y.name           # name is stored on the class only
('Bob', 'Bob')
```

Really, these instances have no attributes of their own; they simply fetch the name attribute from the class object where it is stored. If we do assign an attribute to an instance, though, it creates (or changes) the attribute in that object, and no other—attribute references kick off inheritance searches, but attribute assignments affect only the objects in which the assignments are made. Here, x gets its own name, but y still inherits the name attached to the class above it:

```
>>> x.name = 'Sue'           # But assignment changes x only
>>> rec.name, x.name, y.name
('Bob', 'Sue', 'Bob')
```

In fact, as we'll explore in more detail in Chapter 28, the attributes of a namespace object are usually implemented as dictionaries, and class inheritance trees are (generally speaking) just dictionaries with links to other dictionaries. If you know where to look, you can see this explicitly.

For example, the __dict__ attribute is the namespace dictionary for most class-based objects (some classes may also define attributes in __slots__, an advanced and seldom-used feature that we'll study in Chapters 30 and 31). The following was run in Python 3.0; the order of names and set of __X__ internal names present can vary from release to release, but the names we assigned are present in all:

```
>>> rec.__dict__.keys()
['__module__', 'name', 'age', '__dict__', '__weakref__', '__doc__']

>>> list(x.__dict__.keys())
['name']
```

```
>>> list(y.__dict__.keys())          # list() not required in Python 2.6
[]
```

Here, the class's namespace dictionary shows the name and age attributes we assigned to it, x has its own name, and y is still empty. Each instance has a link to its class for inheritance, though—it's called __class__, if you want to inspect it:

```
>>> x.__class__
<class '__main__.rec'>
```

Classes also have a __bases__ attribute, which is a tuple of their superclasses:

```
>>> rec.__bases__                     # () empty tuple in Python 2.6
(<class 'object'>,)
```

These two attributes are how class trees are literally represented in memory by Python.

The main point to take away from this look under the hood is that Python's class model is extremely dynamic. Classes and instances are just namespace objects, with attributes created on the fly by assignment. Those assignments usually happen within the class statements you code, but they can occur anywhere you have a reference to one of the objects in the tree.

Even methods, normally created by a def nested in a class, can be created completely independently of any class object. The following, for example, defines a simple function outside of any class that takes one argument:

```
>>> def upperName(self):
...     return self.name.upper()      # Still needs a self
```

There is nothing about a class here yet—it's a simple function, and it can be called as such at this point, provided we pass in an object with a name attribute (the name self does not make this special in any way):

```
>>> upperName(x)                      # Call as a simple function
'SUE'
```

If we assign this simple function to an attribute of our class, though, it becomes a method, callable through any instance (as well as through the class name itself, as long as we pass in an instance manually):[†]

```
>>> rec.method = upperName

>>> x.method()                        # Run method to process x
'SUE'

>>> y.method()                        # Same, but pass y to self
'BOB'
```

---

† In fact, this is one of the reasons the self argument must always be explicit in Python methods—because methods can be created as simple functions independent of a class, they need to make the implied instance argument explicit. They can be called as either functions or methods, and Python can neither guess nor assume that a simple function might eventually become a class method. The main reason for the explicit self argument, though, is to make the meanings of names more obvious: names not referenced through self are simple variables, while names referenced through self are obviously instance attributes.

```
>>> rec.method(x)                    # Can call through instance or class
'SUE'
```

Normally, classes are filled out by `class` statements, and instance attributes are created by assignments to `self` attributes in method functions. The point again, though, is that they don't have to be; OOP in Python really is mostly about looking up attributes in linked namespace objects.

Classes Versus Dictionaries

Although the simple classes of the prior section are meant to illustrate class model basics, the techniques they employ can also be used for real work. For example, Chapter 8 showed how to use dictionaries to record properties of entities in our programs. It turns out that classes can serve this role, too—they package information like dictionaries, but can also bundle processing logic in the form of methods. For reference, here is the example for dictionary-based records we used earlier in the book:

```
>>> rec = {}
>>> rec['name'] = 'mel'               # Dictionary-based record
>>> rec['age']  = 45
>>> rec['job']  = 'trainer/writer'
>>>
>>> print(rec['name'])
mel
```

This code emulates tools like records in other languages. As we just saw, though, there are also multiple ways to do the same with classes. Perhaps the simplest is this—trading keys for attributes:

```
>>> class rec: pass
...
>>> rec.name = 'mel'                  # Class-based record
>>> rec.age  = 45
>>> rec.job  = 'trainer/writer'
>>>
>>> print(rec.age)
45
```

This code has substantially less syntax than the dictionary equivalent. It uses an empty `class` statement to generate an empty namespace object. Once we make the empty class, we fill it out by assigning class attributes over time, as before.

This works, but a new `class` statement will be required for each distinct record we will need. Perhaps more typically, we can instead generate *instances* of an empty class to represent each distinct entity:

```
>>> class rec: pass
...
>>> pers1 = rec()                     # Instance-based records
>>> pers1.name = 'mel'
>>> pers1.job  = 'trainer'
```

```
>>> pers1.age   = 40
>>>
>>> pers2 = rec()
>>> pers2.name = 'vls'
>>> pers2.job  = 'developer'
>>>
>>> pers1.name, pers2.name
('mel', 'vls')
```

Here, we make two records from the same class. Instances start out life empty, just like classes. We then fill in the records by assigning to attributes. This time, though, there are two separate objects, and hence two separate name attributes. In fact, instances of the same class don't even have to have the same set of attribute names; in this example, one has a unique age name. Instances really are distinct namespaces, so each has a distinct attribute dictionary. Although they are normally filled out consistently by class methods, they are more flexible than you might expect.

Finally, we might instead code a more full-blown class to implement the record and its processing:

```
>>> class Person:
...     def __init__(self, name, job):      # Class = Data + Logic
...         self.name = name
...         self.job  = job
...     def info(self):
...         return (self.name, self.job)
...
>>> rec1 = Person('mel', 'trainer')
>>> rec2 = Person('vls', 'developer')
>>>
>>> rec1.job, rec2.info()
('trainer', ('vls', 'developer'))
```

This scheme also makes multiple instances, but the class is not empty this time: we've added *logic* (methods) to initialize instances at construction time and collect attributes into a tuple. The constructor imposes some consistency on instances here by always setting the name and job attributes. Together, the class's methods and instance attributes create a *package*, which combines both data and logic.

We could further extend this code by adding logic to compute salaries, parse names, and so on. Ultimately, we might link the class into a larger hierarchy to inherit an existing set of methods via the automatic attribute search of classes, or perhaps even store instances of the class in a file with Python object pickling to make them persistent. In fact, we will—in the next chapter, we'll expand on this analogy between classes and records with a more realistic running example that demonstrates class basics in action.

In the end, although types like dictionaries are flexible, classes allow us to add behavior to objects in ways that built-in types and simple functions do not directly support. Although we can store functions in dictionaries, too, using them to process implied instances is nowhere near as natural as it is in classes.

Chapter Summary

This chapter introduced the basics of coding classes in Python. We studied the syntax of the `class` statement, and we saw how to use it to build up a class inheritance tree. We also studied how Python automatically fills in the first argument in method functions, how attributes are attached to objects in a class tree by simple assignment, and how specially named operator overloading methods intercept and implement built-in operations for our instances (e.g., expressions and printing).

Now that we've learned all about the mechanics of coding classes in Python, the next chapter turns to a larger and more realistic example that ties together much of what we've learned about OOP so far. After that, we'll continue our look at class coding, taking a second pass over the model to fill in some of the details that were omitted here to keep things simple. First, though, let's work through a quiz to review the basics we've covered so far.

Test Your Knowledge: Quiz

1. How are classes related to modules?
2. How are instances and classes created?
3. Where and how are class attributes created?
4. Where and how are instance attributes created?
5. What does `self` mean in a Python class?
6. How is operator overloading coded in a Python class?
7. When might you want to support operator overloading in your classes?
8. Which operator overloading method is most commonly used?
9. What are the two key concepts required to understand Python OOP code?

Test Your Knowledge: Answers

1. Classes are always nested inside a module; they are attributes of a module object. Classes and modules are both namespaces, but classes correspond to statements (not entire files) and support the OOP notions of multiple instances, inheritance, and operator overloading. In a sense, a module is like a single-instance class, without inheritance, which corresponds to an entire file of code.
2. Classes are made by running `class` statements; instances are created by calling a class as though it were a function.

Step 1: Making Instances

OK, so much for the design phase—let's move on to implementation. Our first task is to start coding the main class, `Person`. In your favorite text editor, open a new file for the code we'll be writing. It's a fairly strong convention in Python to begin module names with a lowercase letter and class names with an uppercase letter; like the name of `self` arguments in methods, this is not required by the language, but it's so common that deviating might be confusing to people who later read your code. To conform, we'll call our new module file *person.py* and our class within it `Person`, like this:

```
# File person.py (start)

class Person:
```

All our work will be done in this file until later in this chapter. We can code any number of functions and classes in a single module file in Python, and this one's *person.py* name might not make much sense if we add unrelated components to it later. For now, we'll assume everything in it will be `Person`-related. It probably should be anyhow—as we've learned, modules tend to work best when they have a single, *cohesive* purpose.

Coding Constructors

Now, the first thing we want to do with our `Person` class is record basic information about people—to fill out record fields, if you will. Of course, these are known as instance object *attributes* in Python-speak, and they generally are created by assignment to `self` attributes in class method functions. The normal way to give instance attributes their first values is to assign them to `self` in the `__init__` *constructor method*, which contains code run automatically by Python each time an instance is created. Let's add one to our class:

```
# Add record field initialization

class Person:
    def __init__(self, name, job, pay):      # Constructor takes 3 arguments
        self.name = name                       # Fill out fields when created
        self.job  = job                        # self is the new instance object
        self.pay  = pay
```

This is a very common coding pattern: we pass in the data to be attached to an instance as arguments to the constructor method and assign them to `self` to retain them permanently. In OO terms, `self` is the newly created instance object, and `name`, `job`, and `pay` become *state information*—descriptive data saved on an object for later use. Although other techniques (such as enclosing scope references) can save details, too, instance attributes make this very explicit and easy to understand.

Notice that the argument names appear *twice* here. This code might seem a bit redundant at first, but it's not. The `job` argument, for example, is a local variable in the scope of the `__init__` function, but `self.job` is an attribute of the instance that's the implied subject of the method call. They are two different variables, which happen to have the same name. By assigning the `job` local to the `self.job` attribute with `self.job=job`, we save the passed-in `job` on the instance for later use. As usual in Python, where a name is assigned (or what object it is assigned to) determines what it means.

Speaking of arguments, there's really nothing magical about `__init__`, apart from the fact that it's called automatically when an instance is made and has a special first argument. Despite its weird name, it's a normal function and supports all the features of functions we've already covered. We can, for example, provide *defaults* for some of its arguments, so they need not be provided in cases where their values aren't available or useful.

To demonstrate, let's make the `job` argument optional—it will default to `None`, meaning the person being created is not (currently) employed. If `job` defaults to `None`, we'll probably want to default `pay` to `0`, too, for consistency (unless some of the people you know manage to get paid without having jobs!). In fact, we have to specify a default for `pay` because according to Python's syntax rules, any arguments in a function's header after the first default must all have defaults, too:

```python
# Add defaults for constructor arguments

class Person:
    def __init__(self, name, job=None, pay=0):      # Normal function args
        self.name = name
        self.job  = job
        self.pay  = pay
```

What this code means is that we'll need to pass in a name when making `Person`s, but `job` and `pay` are now optional; they'll default to `None` and `0` if omitted. The `self` argument, as usual, is filled in by Python automatically to refer to the instance object—assigning values to attributes of `self` attaches them to the new instance.

Testing As You Go

This class doesn't do much yet—it essentially just fills out the fields of a new record—but it's a real working class. At this point we could add more code to it for more features, but we won't do that yet. As you've probably begun to appreciate already, programming in Python is really a matter of *incremental prototyping*—you write some code, test it, write more code, test again, and so on. Because Python provides both an interactive session and nearly immediate turnaround after code changes, it's more natural to test as you go than to write a huge amount of code to test all at once.

Before adding more features, then, let's test what we've got so far by making a few instances of our class and displaying their attributes as created by the constructor. We could do this interactively, but as you've also probably surmised by now, interactive testing has its limits—it gets tedious to have to reimport modules and retype test cases each time you start a new testing session. More commonly, Python programmers use the interactive prompt for simple one-off tests but do more substantial testing by writing code at the bottom of the file that contains the objects to be tested, like this:

```
# Add incremental self-test code

class Person:
    def __init__(self, name, job=None, pay=0):
        self.name = name
        self.job  = job
        self.pay  = pay

bob = Person('Bob Smith')                          # Test the class
sue = Person('Sue Jones', job='dev', pay=100000)   # Runs __init__ automatically
print(bob.name, bob.pay)                           # Fetch attached attributes
print(sue.name, sue.pay)                           # sue's and bob's attrs differ
```

Notice here that the bob object accepts the defaults for job and pay, but sue provides values explicitly. Also note how we use *keyword arguments* when making sue; we could pass by position instead, but the keywords may help remind us later what the data is (and they allow us to pass the arguments in any left-to-right order we like). Again, despite its unusual name, __init__ is a normal function, supporting everything you already know about functions—including both defaults and pass-by-name keyword arguments.

When this file runs as a script, the test code at the bottom makes two instances of our class and prints two attributes of each (name and pay):

```
C:\misc> person.py
Bob Smith 0
Sue Jones 100000
```

You can also type this file's test code at Python's interactive prompt (assuming you import the Person class there first), but coding canned tests inside the module file like this makes it much easier to rerun them in the future.

Although this is fairly simple code, it's already demonstrating something important. Notice that bob's name is not sue's, and sue's pay is not bob's. Each is an independent record of information. Technically, bob and sue are both *namespace objects*—like all class instances, they each have their own independent copy of the state information created by the class. Because each instance of a class has its own set of self attributes, classes are a natural for recording information for multiple objects this way; just like built-in types, classes serve as a sort of *object factory*. Other Python program structures, such as functions and modules, have no such concept.

Using Code Two Ways

As is, the test code at the bottom of the file works, but there's a big catch—its top-level print statements run both when the file is run as a script and when it is imported as a module. This means if we ever decide to import the class in this file in order to use it somewhere else (and we will later in this chapter), we'll see the output of its test code every time the file is imported. That's not very good software citizenship, though: client programs probably don't care about our internal tests and won't want to see our output mixed in with their own.

Although we could split the test code off into a separate file, it's often more convenient to code tests in the same file as the items to be tested. It would be better to arrange to run the test statements at the bottom *only* when the file is run for testing, not when the file is imported. That's exactly what the module __name__ check is designed for, as you learned in the preceding part of this book. Here's what this addition looks like:

```
# Allow this file to be imported as well as run/tested

class Person:
    def __init__(self, name, job=None, pay=0):
        self.name = name
        self.job  = job
        self.pay  = pay

if __name__ == '__main__':              # When run for testing only
    # self-test code
    bob = Person('Bob Smith')
    sue = Person('Sue Jones', job='dev', pay=100000)
    print(bob.name, bob.pay)
    print(sue.name, sue.pay)
```

Now, we get exactly the behavior we're after—running the file as a top-level script tests it because its __name__ is __main__, but importing it as a library of classes later does not:

```
C:\misc> person.py
Bob Smith 0
Sue Jones 100000

c:\misc> python
Python 3.0.1 (r301:69561, Feb 13 2009, 20:04:18) ...
>>> import person
>>>
```

When imported, the file now defines the class, but does not use it. When run directly, this file creates two instances of our class as before, and prints two attributes of each; again, because each instance is an independent namespace object, the values of their attributes differ.

Version Portability Note

I'm running all the code in this chapter under Python 3.0, and using the 3.0 print function call syntax. If you run under 2.6 the code will work as-is, but you'll notice parentheses around some output lines because the extra parentheses in prints turn multiple items into a tuple:

```
c:\misc> c:\python26\python person.py
('Bob Smith', 0)
('Sue Jones', 100000)
```

If this difference is the sort of detail that might keep you awake at nights, simply remove the parentheses to use 2.6 print statements. You can also avoid the extra parentheses portably by using formatting to yield a single object to print. Either of the following works in both 2.6 and 3.0, though the method form is newer:

```
print('{0} {1}'.format(bob.name, bob.pay))    # New format method
print('%s %s' % (bob.name, bob.pay))          # Format expression
```

Step 2: Adding Behavior Methods

Everything looks good so far—at this point, our class is essentially a record *factory*; it creates and fills out fields of records (attributes of instances, in more Pythonic terms). Even as limited as it is, though, we can still run some operations on its objects. Although classes add an extra layer of structure, they ultimately do most of their work by embedding and processing basic *core data types* like lists and strings. In other words, if you already know how to use Python's simple core types, you already know much of the Python class story; classes are really just a minor structural extension.

For example, the name field of our objects is a simple string, so we can extract last names from our objects by splitting on spaces and indexing. These are all core data type operations, which work whether their subjects are embedded in class instances or not:

```
>>> name = 'Bob Smith'        # Simple string, outside class
>>> name.split()              # Extract last name
['Bob', 'Smith']
>>> name.split()[-1]          # Or [1], if always just two parts
'Smith'
```

Similarly, we can give an object a pay raise by updating its pay field—that is, by changing its state information in-place with an assignment. This task also involves basic operations that work on Python's core objects, regardless of whether they are standalone or embedded in a class structure:

```
>>> pay = 100000          # Simple variable, outside class
>>> pay *= 1.10           # Give a 10% raise
>>> print(pay)            # Or: pay = pay * 1.10, if you like to type
110000.0                  # Or: pay = pay + (pay * .10), if you _really_ do!
```

To apply these operations to the Person objects created by our script, simply do to bob.name and sue.pay what we just did to name and pay. The operations are the same, but the subject objects are attached to attributes in our class structure:

```
# Process embedded built-in types: strings, mutability

class Person:
    def __init__(self, name, job=None, pay=0):
        self.name = name
        self.job  = job
        self.pay  = pay

if __name__ == '__main__':
```

```
bob = Person('Bob Smith')
sue = Person('Sue Jones', job='dev', pay=100000)
print(bob.name, bob.pay)
print(sue.name, sue.pay)
print(bob.name.split()[-1])          # Extract object's last name
sue.pay *= 1.10                       # Give this object a raise
print(sue.pay)
```

We've added the last three lines here; when they're run, we extract bob's last name by using basic string and list operations and give sue a pay raise by modifying her pay attribute in-place with basic number operations. In a sense, sue is also a *mutable* object—her state changes in-place just like a list after an append call:

```
Bob Smith 0
Sue Jones 100000
Smith
110000.0
```

The preceding code works as planned, but if you show it to a veteran software developer he'll probably tell you that its general approach is not a great idea in practice. Hard-coding operations like these *outside* of the class can lead to maintenance problems in the future.

For example, what if you've hardcoded the last-name-extraction formula at many different places in your program? If you ever need to change the way it works (to support a new name structure, for instance), you'll need to hunt down and update *every* occurrence. Similarly, if the pay-raise code ever changes (e.g., to require approval or database updates), you may have multiple copies to modify. Just finding all the appearances of such code may be problematic in larger programs—they may be scattered across many files, split into individual steps, and so on.

Coding Methods

What we really want to do here is employ a software design concept known as *encapsulation*. The idea with encapsulation is to wrap up operation logic behind interfaces, such that each operation is coded only once in our program. That way, if our needs change in the future, there is just one copy to update. Moreover, we're free to change the single copy's internals almost arbitrarily, without breaking the code that uses it.

In Python terms, we want to code operations on objects in class *methods*, instead of littering them throughout our program. In fact, this is one of the things that classes are very good at—*factoring* code to remove redundancy and thus optimize maintainability. As an added bonus, turning operations into methods enables them to be applied to any instance of the class, not just those that they've been hardcoded to process.

This is all simpler in code than it may sound in theory. The following achieves encapsulation by moving the two operations from code outside the class into class methods. While we're at it, let's change our self-test code at the bottom to use the new methods we're creating, instead of hardcoding operations:

```
# Add methods to encapsulate operations for maintainability

class Person:
    def __init__(self, name, job=None, pay=0):
        self.name = name
        self.job  = job
        self.pay  = pay
    def lastName(self):                              # Behavior methods
        return self.name.split()[-1]                 # self is implied subject
    def giveRaise(self, percent):
        self.pay = int(self.pay * (1 + percent))     # Must change here only

if __name__ == '__main__':
    bob = Person('Bob Smith')
    sue = Person('Sue Jones', job='dev', pay=100000)
    print(bob.name, bob.pay)
    print(sue.name, sue.pay)
    print(bob.lastName(), sue.lastName())            # Use the new methods
    sue.giveRaise(.10)                               # instead of hardcoding
    print(sue.pay)
```

As we've learned, *methods* are simply normal functions that are attached to classes and designed to process instances of those classes. The instance is the subject of the method call and is passed to the method's `self` argument automatically.

The transformation to the methods in this version is straightforward. The new `lastName` method, for example, simply does to `self` what the previous version hardcoded for `bob`, because `self` is the implied subject when the method is called. `lastName` also returns the result, because this operation is a called function now; it computes a value for its caller to use, even if it is just to be printed. Similarly, the new `giveRaise` method just does to `self` what we did to `sue` before.

When run now, our file's output is similar to before—we've mostly just *refactored* the code to allow for easier changes in the future, not altered its behavior:

```
Bob Smith 0
Sue Jones 100000
Smith Jones
110000
```

A few coding details are worth pointing out here. First, notice that `sue`'s pay is now still an *integer* after a pay raise—we convert the math result back to an integer by calling the `int` built-in within the method. Changing the value to either `int` or `float` is probably not a significant concern for most purposes (integer and floating-point objects have the same interfaces and can be mixed within expressions), but we may need to address rounding issues in a real system (money probably matters to `Person`s!).

As we learned in Chapter 5, we might handle this by using the `round(N, 2)` built-in to round and retain cents, using the `decimal` type to fix precision, or storing monetary values as full floating-point numbers and displaying them with a `%.2f` or `{0:.2f}` formatting string to show cents. For this example, we'll simply truncate any cents with int. (For another idea, also see the money function in the *formats.py* module of Chapter 24; you can import this tool to show pay with commas, cents, and dollar signs.)

Second, notice that we're also printing sue's last name this time—because the last-name logic has been encapsulated in a method, we get to use it on *any instance* of the class. As we've seen, Python tells a method which instance to process by automatically passing it in to the first argument, usually called self. Specifically:

- In the first call, bob.lastName(), bob is the implied subject passed to self.
- In the second call, sue.lastName(), sue goes to self instead.

Trace through these calls to see how the instance winds up in self. The net effect is that the method fetches the name of the implied subject each time. The same happens for giveRaise. We could, for example, give bob a raise by calling giveRaise for both instances this way, too; but unfortunately, bob's zero pay will prevent him from getting a raise as the program is currently coded (something we may want to address in a future 2.0 release of our software).

Finally, notice that the giveRaise method assumes that percent is passed in as a floating-point number between zero and one. That may be too radical an assumption in the real world (a 1000% raise would probably be a bug for most of us!); we'll let it pass for this prototype, but we might want to test or at least document this in a future iteration of this code. Stay tuned for a rehash of this idea in a later chapter in this book, where we'll code something called *function decorators* and explore Python's assert statement—alternatives that can do the validity test for us automatically during development.

Step 3: Operator Overloading

At this point, we have a fairly full-featured class that generates and initializes instances, along with two new bits of behavior for processing instances (in the form of methods). So far, so good.

As it stands, though, testing is still a bit less convenient than it needs to be—to trace our objects, we have to manually fetch and print *individual attributes* (e.g., bob.name, sue.pay). It would be nice if displaying an instance all at once actually gave us some useful information. Unfortunately, the default display format for an instance object isn't very good—it displays the object's class name, and its address in memory (which is essentially useless in Python, except as a unique identifier).

To see this, change the last line in the script to print(sue) so it displays the object as a whole. Here's what you'll get (the output says that sue is an "object" in 3.0 and an "instance" in 2.6):

```
Bob Smith 0
Sue Jones 100000
Smith Jones
<__main__.Person object at 0x02614430>
```

Providing Print Displays

Fortunately, it's easy to do better by employing *operator overloading*—coding methods in a class that intercept and process built-in operations when run on the class's instances. Specifically, we can make use of what is probably the second most commonly used operator overloading method in Python, after __init__: the __str__ method introduced in the preceding chapter. __str__ is run automatically every time an instance is converted to its print string. Because that's what printing an object does, the net transitive effect is that printing an object displays whatever is returned by the object's __str__ method, if it either defines one itself or inherits one from a superclass (double-underscored names are inherited just like any other).

Technically speaking, the __init__ constructor method we've already coded is operator overloading too—it is run automatically at construction time to initialize a newly created instance. Constructors are so common, though, that they almost seem like a special case. More focused methods like __str__ allow us to tap into specific operations and provide *specialized behavior* when our objects are used in those contexts.

Let's put this into code. The following extends our class to give a custom display that lists attributes when our class's instances are displayed as a whole, instead of relying on the less useful default display:

```
# Add __str__ overload method for printing objects

class Person:
    def __init__(self, name, job=None, pay=0):
        self.name = name
        self.job  = job
        self.pay  = pay
    def lastName(self):
        return self.name.split()[-1]
    def giveRaise(self, percent):
        self.pay = int(self.pay * (1 + percent))
    def __str__(self):                                       # Added method
        return '[Person: %s, %s]' % (self.name, self.pay)    # String to print

if __name__ == '__main__':
    bob = Person('Bob Smith')
    sue = Person('Sue Jones', job='dev', pay=100000)
    print(bob)
    print(sue)
    print(bob.lastName(), sue.lastName())
    sue.giveRaise(.10)
    print(sue)
```

Notice that we're doing string % formatting to build the display string in __str__ here; at the bottom, classes use built-in type objects and operations like these to get their work done. Again, everything you've already learned about both built-in types and functions applies to class-based code. Classes largely just add an additional layer of *structure* that packages functions and data together and supports extensions.

We've also changed our self-test code to print objects directly, instead of printing individual attributes. When run, the output is more coherent and meaningful now; the "[...]" lines are returned by our new __str__, run automatically by print operations:

```
[Person: Bob Smith, 0]
[Person: Sue Jones, 100000]
Smith Jones
[Person: Sue Jones, 110000]
```

Here's a subtle point: as we'll learn in the next chapter, a related overloading method, __repr__, provides an as-code low-level display of an object when present. Sometimes classes provide both a __str__ for user-friendly displays and a __repr__ with extra details for developers to view. Because printing runs __str__ and the interactive prompt echoes results with __repr__, this can provide both target audiences with an appropriate display. Since we're not interested in displaying an as-code format, __str__ is sufficient for our class.

Step 4: Customizing Behavior by Subclassing

At this point, our class captures much of the OOP machinery in Python: it makes instances, provides behavior in methods, and even does a bit of operator overloading now to intercept print operations in __str__. It effectively packages our data and logic together into a single, self-contained *software component*, making it easy to locate code and straightforward to change it in the future. By allowing us to encapsulate behavior, it also allows us to factor that code to avoid redundancy and its associated maintenance headaches.

The only major OOP concept it does not yet capture is *customization by inheritance*. In some sense, we're already doing inheritance, because instances inherit methods from their classes. To demonstrate the real power of OOP, though, we need to define a superclass/subclass relationship that allows us to extend our software and replace bits of inherited behavior. That's the main idea behind OOP, after all; by fostering a coding model based upon customization of work already done, it can dramatically cut development time.

Coding Subclasses

As a next step, then, let's put OOP's methodology to use and customize our Person class by extending our software hierarchy. For the purpose of this tutorial, we'll define a subclass of Person called Manager that replaces the inherited giveRaise method with a more specialized version. Our new class begins as follows:

```
class Manager(Person):                      # Define a subclass of Person
```

This code means that we're defining a new class named Manager, which inherits from and may add customizations to the superclass Person. In plain terms, a Manager is almost like a `Person` (admittedly, a very long journey for a very small joke...), but `Manager` has a custom way to give raises.

For the sake of argument, let's assume that when a `Manager` gets a raise, it receives the passed-in percentage as usual, but also gets an extra bonus that defaults to 10%. For instance, if a `Manager`'s raise is specified as 10%, it will really get 20%. (Any relation to `Person`s living or dead is, of course, strictly coincidental.) Our new method begins as follows; because this redefinition of `giveRaise` will be closer in the class tree to `Manager` instances than the original version in `Person`, it effectively replaces, and thereby customizes, the operation. Recall that according to the inheritance search rules, the *lowest* version of the name wins:

```
class Manager(Person):                    # Inherit Person attrs
    def giveRaise(self, percent, bonus=.10):   # Redefine to customize
```

Augmenting Methods: The Bad Way

Now, there are two ways we might code this `Manager` customization: a good way and a bad way. Let's start with the *bad way*, since it might be a bit easier to understand. The bad way is to cut and paste the code of `giveRaise` in `Person` and modify it for `Manager`, like this:

```
class Manager(Person):
    def giveRaise(self, percent, bonus=.10):
        self.pay = int(self.pay * (1 + percent + bonus))    # Bad: cut-and-paste
```

This works as advertised—when we later call the `giveRaise` method of a `Manager` instance, it will run this custom version, which tacks on the extra bonus. So what's wrong with something that runs correctly?

The problem here is a very general one: any time you copy code with cut and paste, you essentially *double* your maintenance effort in the future. Think about it: because we copied the original version, if we ever have to change the way raises are given (and we probably will), we'll have to change the code in *two* places, not one. Although this is a small and artificial example, it's also representative of a universal issue—any time you're tempted to program by copying code this way, you probably want to look for a better approach.

Augmenting Methods: The Good Way

What we really want to do here is somehow *augment* the original `giveRaise`, instead of replacing it altogether. The *good way* to do that in Python is by calling to the original version directly, with augmented arguments, like this:

```
class Manager(Person):
    def giveRaise(self, percent, bonus=.10):
        Person.giveRaise(self, percent + bonus)    # Good: augment original
```

This code leverages the fact that a class method can always be called either through an *instance* (the usual way, where Python sends the instance to the `self` argument automatically) or through the *class* (the less common scheme, where you must pass the instance manually). In more symbolic terms, recall that a normal method call of this form:

```
instance.method(args...)
```

is automatically translated by Python into this equivalent form:

```
class.method(instance, args...)
```

where the class containing the method to be run is determined by the inheritance search rule applied to the method's name. You can code *either* form in your script, but there is a slight asymmetry between the two—you must remember to pass along the instance manually if you call through the class directly. The method always needs a subject instance one way or another, and Python provides it automatically only for calls made through an instance. For calls through the class name, you need to send an instance to `self` yourself; for code inside a method like `giveRaise`, `self` already *is* the subject of the call, and hence the instance to pass along.

Calling through the class directly effectively subverts inheritance and kicks the call higher up the class tree to run a specific version. In our case, we can use this technique to invoke the default `giveRaise` in `Person`, even though it's been redefined at the `Manager` level. In some sense, we *must* call through `Person` this way, because a `self.giveRaise()` inside `Manager`'s `giveRaise` code would loop—since `self` already is a `Manager`, `self.giveRaise()` would resolve again to `Manager.giveRaise`, and so on and so forth until available memory is exhausted.

This "good" version may seem like a small difference in code, but it can make a huge difference for future *code maintenance*—because the `giveRaise` logic lives in just one place now (`Person`'s method), we have only one version to change in the future as needs evolve. And really, this form captures our intent more directly anyhow—we want to perform the standard `giveRaise` operation, but simply tack on an extra bonus. Here's our entire module file with this step applied:

```
# Add customization of one behavior in a subclass

class Person:
    def __init__(self, name, job=None, pay=0):
        self.name = name
        self.job  = job
        self.pay  = pay
    def lastName(self):
        return self.name.split()[-1]
    def giveRaise(self, percent):
        self.pay = int(self.pay * (1 + percent))
    def __str__(self):
        return '[Person: %s, %s]' % (self.name, self.pay)

class Manager(Person):
```

```
            def giveRaise(self, percent, bonus=.10):        # Redefine at this level
                Person.giveRaise(self, percent + bonus)      # Call Person's version

    if __name__ == '__main__':
        bob = Person('Bob Smith')
        sue = Person('Sue Jones', job='dev', pay=100000)
        print(bob)
        print(sue)
        print(bob.lastName(), sue.lastName())
        sue.giveRaise(.10)
        print(sue)
        tom = Manager('Tom Jones', 'mgr', 50000)             # Make a Manager: __init__
        tom.giveRaise(.10)                                   # Runs custom version
        print(tom.lastName())                                # Runs inherited method
        print(tom)                                           # Runs inherited __str__
```

To test our Manager subclass customization, we've also added self-test code that makes a Manager, calls its methods, and prints it. Here's the new version's output:

```
[Person: Bob Smith, 0]
[Person: Sue Jones, 100000]
Smith Jones
[Person: Sue Jones, 110000]
Jones
[Person: Tom Jones, 60000]
```

Everything looks good here: bob and sue are as before, and when tom the Manager is given a 10% raise, he really gets 20% (his pay goes from $50K to $60K), because the customized giveRaise in Manager is run for him only. Also notice how printing tom as a whole at the end of the test code displays the nice format defined in Person's __str__: Manager objects get this, lastName, and the __init__ constructor method's code "for free" from Person, by inheritance.

Polymorphism in Action

To make this acquisition of inherited behavior even more striking, we can add the following code at the end of our file:

```
    if __name__ == '__main__':
        ...
        print('--All three--')
        for object in (bob, sue, tom):        # Process objects generically
            object.giveRaise(.10)             # Run this object's giveRaise
            print(object)                     # Run the common __str__
```

Here's the resulting output:

```
[Person: Bob Smith, 0]
[Person: Sue Jones, 100000]
Smith Jones
[Person: Sue Jones, 110000]
Jones
[Person: Tom Jones, 60000]
--All three--
```

```
[Person: Bob Smith, 0]
[Person: Sue Jones, 121000]
[Person: Tom Jones, 72000]
```

In the added code, object is *either* a Person or a Manager, and Python runs the appropriate giveRaise automatically—our original version in Person for bob and sue, and our customized version in Manager for tom. Trace the method calls yourself to see how Python selects the right giveRaise method for each object.

This is just Python's notion of *polymorphism*, which we met earlier in the book, at work again—what giveRaise does depends on what you do it to. Here, it's made all the more obvious when it selects from code we've written ourselves in classes. The practical effect in this code is that sue gets another 10% but tom gets another 20%, because giveRaise is dispatched based upon the object's type. As we've learned, polymorphism is at the heart of Python's flexibility. Passing any of our three objects to a function that calls a giveRaise method, for example, would have the same effect: the appropriate version would be run automatically, depending on which type of object was passed.

On the other hand, printing runs the *same* __str__ for all three objects, because it's coded just once in Person. Manager both specializes and applies the code we originally wrote in Person. Although this example is small, it's already leveraging OOP's talent for code customization and reuse; with classes, this almost seems automatic at times.

Inherit, Customize, and Extend

In fact, classes can be even more flexible than our example implies. In general, classes can *inherit*, *customize*, or *extend* existing code in superclasses. For example, although we're focused on customization here, we can also add unique methods to Manager that are not present in Person, if Managers require something completely different (Python namesake reference intended). The following snippet illustrates. Here, giveRaise redefines a superclass method to customize it, but someThingElse defines something new to extend:

```
class Person:
    def lastName(self): ...
    def giveRaise(self): ...
    def __str__(self): ...

class Manager(Person):                      # Inherit
    def giveRaise(self, ...): ...            # Customize
    def someThingElse(self, ...): ...        # Extend

tom = Manager()
tom.lastName()                               # Inherited verbatim
tom.giveRaise()                              # Customized version
tom.someThingElse()                          # Extension here
print(tom)                                   # Inherited overload method
```

Extra methods like this code's someThingElse *extend* the existing software and are available on Manager objects only, not on Persons. For the purposes of this tutorial, however, we'll limit our scope to customizing some of `Person`'s behavior by redefining it, not adding to it.

OOP: The Big Idea

As is, our code may be small, but it's fairly functional. And really, it already illustrates the main point behind OOP in general: in OOP, we program by *customizing* what has already been done, rather than copying or changing existing code. This isn't always an obvious win to newcomers at first glance, especially given the extra coding requirements of classes. But overall, the programming style implied by classes can cut development time radically compared to other approaches.

For instance, in our example we could theoretically have implemented a custom `giveRaise` operation without subclassing, but none of the other options yield code as optimal as ours:

- Although we could have simply coded `Manager` *from scratch* as new, independent code, we would have had to reimplement all the behaviors in `Person` that are the same for `Manager`s.

- Although we could have simply *changed* the existing `Person` class in-place for the requirements of `Manager`'s `giveRaise`, doing so would probably break the places where we still need the original `Person` behavior.

- Although we could have simply *copied* the `Person` class in its entirety, renamed the copy to `Manager`, and changed its `giveRaise`, doing so would introduce code redundancy that would double our work in the future—changes made to `Person` in the future would not be picked up automatically, but would have to be manually propagated to `Manager`'s code. As usual, the cut-and-paste approach may seem quick now, but it doubles your work in the future.

The *customizable hierarchies* we can build with classes provide a much better solution for software that will evolve over time. No other tools in Python support this development mode. Because we can tailor and extend our prior work by coding new subclasses, we can leverage what we've already done, rather than starting from scratch each time, breaking what already works, or introducing multiple copies of code that may all have to be updated in the future. When done right, OOP is a powerful programmer's ally.

Step 5: Customizing Constructors, Too

Our code works as it is, but if you study the current version closely, you may be struck by something a bit odd—it seems pointless to have to provide a `mgr` job name for `Manager` objects when we create them: this is already implied by the class itself. It would be better if we could somehow fill in this value automatically when a `Manager` is made.

The trick we need to improve on this turns out to be the *same* as the one we employed in the prior section: we want to customize the constructor logic for `Manager`s in such a way as to provide a job name automatically. In terms of code, we want to redefine an `__init__` method in `Manager` that provides the `mgr` string for us. And like with the `giveRaise` customization, we also want to run the original `__init__` in `Person` by calling through the class name, so it still initializes our objects' state information attributes.

The following extension will do the job—we've coded the new `Manager` constructor and changed the call that creates `tom` to not pass in the `mgr` job name:

```
# Add customization of constructor in a subclass

class Person:
    def __init__(self, name, job=None, pay=0):
        self.name = name
        self.job  = job
        self.pay  = pay
    def lastName(self):
        return self.name.split()[-1]
    def giveRaise(self, percent):
        self.pay = int(self.pay * (1 + percent))
    def __str__(self):
        return '[Person: %s, %s]' % (self.name, self.pay)

class Manager(Person):
    def __init__(self, name, pay):                      # Redefine constructor
        Person.__init__(self, name, 'mgr', pay)         # Run original with 'mgr'
    def giveRaise(self, percent, bonus=.10):
        Person.giveRaise(self, percent + bonus)

if __name__ == '__main__':
    bob = Person('Bob Smith')
    sue = Person('Sue Jones', job='dev', pay=100000)
    print(bob)
    print(sue)
    print(bob.lastName(), sue.lastName())
    sue.giveRaise(.10)
    print(sue)
    tom = Manager('Tom Jones', 50000)                   # Job name not needed:
    tom.giveRaise(.10)                                  # Implied/set by class
    print(tom.lastName())
    print(tom)
```

Again, we're using the same technique to augment the `__init__` constructor here that we used for `giveRaise` earlier—running the superclass version by calling through the class name directly and passing the `self` instance along explicitly. Although the constructor has a strange name, the effect is identical. Because we need `Person`'s construction logic to run too (to initialize instance attributes), we really have to call it this way; otherwise, instances would not have any attributes attached.

Calling superclass constructors from redefinitions this way turns out to be a very common coding pattern in Python. By itself, Python uses inheritance to look for and call only *one* `__init__` method at construction time—the *lowest* one in the class tree. If you need higher `__init__` methods to be run at construction time (and you usually do), you must call them manually through the superclass's name. The upside to this is that you can be explicit about which argument to pass up to the superclass's constructor and can choose to not call it at all: not calling the superclass constructor allows you to replace its logic altogether, rather than augmenting it.

The output of this file's self-test code is the same as before—we haven't changed what it does, we've simply restructured to get rid of some logical redundancy:

```
[Person: Bob Smith, 0]
[Person: Sue Jones, 100000]
Smith Jones
[Person: Sue Jones, 110000]
Jones
[Person: Tom Jones, 60000]
```

OOP Is Simpler Than You May Think

In this complete form, despite their sizes, our classes capture nearly all the important concepts in Python's OOP machinery:

- Instance creation—filling out instance attributes
- Behavior methods—encapsulating logic in class methods
- Operator overloading—providing behavior for built-in operations like printing
- Customizing behavior—redefining methods in subclasses to specialize them
- Customizing constructors—adding initialization logic to superclass steps

Most of these concepts are based upon just three simple ideas: the inheritance search for attributes in object trees, the special `self` argument in methods, and operator overloading's automatic dispatch to methods.

Along the way, we've also made our code easy to change in the future, by harnessing the class's propensity for factoring code to reduce *redundancy*. For example, we wrapped up logic in methods and called back to superclass methods from extensions to avoid having multiple copies of the same code. Most of these steps were a natural outgrowth of the structuring power of classes.

By and large, that's all there is to OOP in Python. Classes certainly can become larger than this, and there are some more advanced class concepts, such as decorators and metaclasses, which we will meet in later chapters. In terms of the basics, though, our classes already do it all. In fact, if you've grasped the workings of the classes we've written, most OOP Python code should now be within your reach.

Other Ways to Combine Classes

Having said that, I should also tell you that although the basic mechanics of OOP are simple in Python, some of the art in larger programs lies in the way that classes are put together. We're focusing on *inheritance* in this tutorial because that's the mechanism the Python language provides, but programmers sometimes combine classes in other ways, too. For example, a common coding pattern involves nesting objects inside each other to build up *composites*. We'll explore this pattern in more detail in Chapter 30, which is really more about design than about Python; as a quick example, though, we could use this composition idea to code our `Manager` extension by *embedding* a `Person`, instead of inheriting from it.

The following alternative does so by using the __getattr__ operator overloading method we will meet in Chapter 29 to intercept undefined attribute fetches and delegate them to the embedded object with the `getattr` built-in. The `giveRaise` method here still achieves customization, by changing the argument passed along to the embedded object. In effect, `Manager` becomes a controller layer that passes calls *down* to the embedded object, rather than *up* to superclass methods:

```
# Embedding-based Manager alternative

class Person:
    ...same...

class Manager:
    def __init__(self, name, pay):
        self.person = Person(name, 'mgr', pay)    # Embed a Person object
    def giveRaise(self, percent, bonus=.10):
        self.person.giveRaise(percent + bonus)    # Intercept and delegate
    def __getattr__(self, attr):
        return getattr(self.person, attr)         # Delegate all other attrs
    def __str__(self):
        return str(self.person)                   # Must overload again (in 3.0)

if __name__ == '__main__':
    ...same...
```

In fact, this `Manager` alternative is representative of a general coding pattern usually known as *delegation*—a composite-based structure that manages a wrapped object and propagates method calls to it. This pattern works in our example, but it requires about twice as much code and is less well suited than inheritance to the kinds of direct customizations we meant to express (in fact, no reasonable Python programmer would code this example this way in practice, except perhaps those writing general tutorials). `Manager` isn't really a `Person` here, so we need extra code to manually dispatch method calls to the embedded object; operator overloading methods like __str__ must be redefined (in 3.0, at least, as noted in the upcoming sidebar "Catching Built-in Attributes in 3.0" on page 664), and adding new `Manager` behavior is less straightforward since state information is one level removed.

Still, *object embedding*, and design patterns based upon it, can be a very good fit when embedded objects require more limited interaction with the container than direct customization implies. A controller layer like this alternative `Manager`, for example, might come in handy if we want to trace or validate calls to another object's methods (indeed, we will use a nearly identical coding pattern when we study *class decorators* later in the book). Moreover, a hypothetical `Department` class like the following could *aggregate* other objects in order to treat them as a set. Add this to the bottom of the *person.py* file to try this on your own:

```
# Aggregate embedded objects into a composite

...
bob = Person(...)
sue = Person(...)
tom = Manager(...)

class Department:
    def __init__(self, *args):
        self.members = list(args)
    def addMember(self, person):
        self.members.append(person)
    def giveRaises(self, percent):
        for person in self.members:
            person.giveRaise(percent)
    def showAll(self):
        for person in self.members:
            print(person)

development = Department(bob, sue)      # Embed objects in a composite
development.addMember(tom)
development.giveRaises(.10)             # Runs embedded objects' giveRaise
development.showAll()                   # Runs embedded objects' __str__s
```

Interestingly, this code uses both inheritance *and* composition—`Department` is a composite that embeds and controls other objects to aggregate, but the embedded `Person` and `Manager` objects themselves use inheritance to customize. As another example, a GUI might similarly use *inheritance* to customize the behavior or appearance of labels and buttons, but also *composition* to build up larger packages of embedded widgets, such as input forms, calculators, and text editors. The class structure to use depends on the objects you are trying to model.

Design issues like composition are explored in Chapter 30, so we'll postpone further investigations for now. But again, in terms of the basic mechanics of OOP in Python, our `Person` and `Manager` classes already tell the entire story. Having mastered the basics of OOP, though, developing general tools for applying it more easily in your scripts is often a natural next step—and the topic of the next section.

Catching Built-in Attributes in 3.0

In Python 3.0 (and 2.6 if new-style classes are used), the alternative delegation-based `Manager` class we just coded will not be able to intercept and delegate operator overloading method attributes like `__str__` without redefining them. Although we know that `__str__` is the only such name used in our specific example, this a general issue for delegation-based classes.

Recall that built-in operations like printing and indexing implicitly invoke operator overloading methods such as `__str__` and `__getitem__`. In 3.0, built-in operations like these do not route their implicit attribute fetches through generic attribute managers: neither __getattr__ (run for undefined attributes) nor its cousin __getattribute__ (run for all attributes) is invoked. This is why we have to redefine __str__ redundantly in the alternative Manager, in order to ensure that printing is routed to the embedded Person object when run in Python 3.0.

Technically, this happens because classic classes normally look up operator overloading names in instances at runtime, but new-style classes do not—they skip the instance entirely and look up such methods in classes. In 2.6 classic classes, built-ins *do* route attributes generically—printing, for example, routes __str__ through __getattr__. New-style classes also inherit a default for __str__ that would foil __getattr__, but __getattribute__ doesn't intercept the name in 3.0 either.

This is a change, but isn't a show-stopper—delegation-based classes can generally re-define operator overloading methods to delegate them to wrapped objects in 3.0, either manually or via tools or superclasses. This topic is too advanced to explore further in this tutorial, though, so don't sweat the details too much here. Watch for it to be revisited in the attribute management coverage of Chapter 37, and again in the context of Private class decorators in Chapter 38.

Step 6: Using Introspection Tools

Let's make one final tweak before we throw our objects onto a database. As they are, our classes are complete and demonstrate most of the basics of OOP in Python. They still have two remaining issues we probably should iron out, though, before we go live with them:

- First, if you look at the display of the objects as they are right now, you'll notice that when you print tom the Manager labels him as a Person. That's not technically incorrect, since Manager is a kind of customized and specialized Person. Still, it would be more accurate to display objects with the most specific (that is, *lowest*) classes possible.

- Second, and perhaps more importantly, the current display format shows *only* the attributes we include in our __str__, and that might not account for future goals. For example, we can't yet verify that tom's job name has been set to mgr correctly by Manager's constructor, because the __str__ we coded for Person does not print this field. Worse, if we ever expand or otherwise change the set of attributes as-signed to our objects in __init__, we'll have to remember to also update __str__ for new names to be displayed, or it will become out of sync over time.

The last point means that, yet again, we've made potential extra work for ourselves in the future by introducing *redundancy* in our code. Because any disparity in __str__ will be reflected in the program's output, this redundancy may be more obvious than the other forms we addressed earlier; still, avoiding extra work in the future is generally *a good thing*.

Special Class Attributes

We can address both issues with Python's *introspection tools*—special attributes and functions that give us access to some of the internals of objects' implementations. These tools are somewhat advanced and generally used more by people writing tools for other programmers to use than by programmers developing applications. Even so, a basic knowledge of some of these tools is useful because they allow us to write code that processes classes in generic ways. In our code, for example, there are two hooks that can help us out, both of which were introduced near the end of the preceding chapter:

- The built-in *instance.__class__* attribute provides a link from an instance to the class from which it was created. Classes in turn have a __name__, just like modules, and a __bases__ sequence that provides access to superclasses. We can use these here to print the name of the class from which an instance is made rather than one we've hardcoded.

- The built-in *object.__dict__* attribute provides a dictionary with one key/value pair for every attribute attached to a namespace object (including modules, classes, and instances). Because it is a dictionary, we can fetch its keys list, index by key, iterate over its keys, and so on, to process all attributes generically. We can use this here to print every attribute in any instance, not just those we hardcode in custom displays.

Here's what these tools look like in action at Python's interactive prompt. Notice how we load Person at the interactive prompt with a from statement here—class names live in and are imported from modules, exactly like function names and other variables:

```
>>> from person import Person
>>> bob = Person('Bob Smith')
>>> print(bob)                              # Show bob's __str__
[Person: Bob Smith, 0]

>>> bob.__class__                           # Show bob's class and its name
<class 'person.Person'>
>>> bob.__class__.__name__
'Person'

>>> list(bob.__dict__.keys())               # Attributes are really dict keys
['pay', 'job', 'name']                      # Use list to force list in 3.0

>>> for key in bob.__dict__:
...     print(key, '=>', bob.__dict__[key]) # Index manually

pay => 0
job => None
name => Bob Smith

>>> for key in bob.__dict__:
...     print(key, '=>', getattr(bob, key)) # obj.attr, but attr is a var

pay => 0
```

```
job => None
name => Bob Smith
```

As noted briefly in the prior chapter, some attributes accessible from an instance might not be stored in the __dict__ dictionary if the instance's class defines __slots__, an optional and relatively obscure feature of new-style classes (and all classes in Python 3.0) that stores attributes in an array and that we'll discuss in Chapters 30 and 31. Since slots really belong to classes instead of instances, and since they are very rarely used in any event, we can safely ignore them here and focus on the normal __dict__.

A Generic Display Tool

We can put these interfaces to work in a superclass that displays accurate class names and formats all attributes of an instance of any class. Open a new file in your text editor to code the following—it's a new, independent module named *classtools.py* that implements just such a class. Because its __str__ print overload uses generic introspection tools, it will work on *any instance*, regardless of its attributes set. And because this is a class, it automatically becomes a general formatting tool: thanks to inheritance, it can be mixed into *any class* that wishes to use its display format. As an added bonus, if we ever want to change how instances are displayed we need only change this class, as every class that inherits its __str__ will automatically pick up the new format when it's next run:

```
# File classtools.py (new)
"Assorted class utilities and tools"

class AttrDisplay:
    """
    Provides an inheritable print overload method that displays
    instances with their class names and a name=value pair for
    each attribute stored on the instance itself (but not attrs
    inherited from its classes). Can be mixed into any class,
    and will work on any instance.
    """
    def gatherAttrs(self):
        attrs = []
        for key in sorted(self.__dict__):
            attrs.append('%s=%s' % (key, getattr(self, key)))
        return ', '.join(attrs)
    def __str__(self):
        return '[%s: %s]' % (self.__class__.__name__, self.gatherAttrs())


if __name__ == '__main__':
    class TopTest(AttrDisplay):
        count = 0
        def __init__(self):
            self.attr1 = TopTest.count
            self.attr2 = TopTest.count+1
            TopTest.count += 2
```

```
class SubTest(TopTest):
    pass

X, Y = TopTest(), SubTest()
print(X)                              # Show all instance attrs
print(Y)                              # Show lowest class name
```

Notice the docstrings here—as a general-purpose tool, we want to add some functional documentation for potential users to read. As we saw in Chapter 15, docstrings can be placed at the top of simple functions and modules, and also at the start of classes and their methods; the help function and the PyDoc tool extracts and displays these automatically (we'll look at docstrings again in Chapter 28).

When run directly, this module's self-test makes two instances and prints them; the __str__ defined here shows the instance's class, and all its attributes names and values, in sorted attribute name order:

```
C:\misc> classtools.py
[TopTest: attr1=0, attr2=1]
[SubTest: attr1=2, attr2=3]
```

Instance Versus Class Attributes

If you study the classtools module's self-test code long enough, you'll notice that its class displays only *instance attributes*, attached to the self object at the bottom of the inheritance tree; that's what self's __dict__ contains. As an intended consequence, we don't see attributes inherited by the instance from classes above it in the tree (e.g., count in this file's self-test code). Inherited class attributes are attached to the class only, not copied down to instances.

If you ever do wish to include inherited attributes too, you can climb the __class__ link to the instance's class, use the __dict__ there to fetch class attributes, and then iterate through the class's __bases__ attribute to climb to even higher superclasses (repeating as necessary). If you're a fan of simple code, running a built-in dir call on the instance instead of using __dict__ and climbing would have much the same effect, since dir results include inherited names in the sorted results list:

```
>>> from person import Person
>>> bob = Person('Bob Smith')
```

 # In Python 2.6:

```
>>> bob.__dict__.keys()                     # Instance attrs only
['pay', 'job', 'name']
```

```
>>> dir(bob)                                # + inherited attrs in classes
['__doc__', '__init__', '__module__', '__str__', 'giveRaise', 'job',
'lastName', 'name', 'pay']
```

 # In Python 3.0:

```
>>> list(bob.__dict__.keys())          # 3.0 keys is a view, not a list
['pay', 'job', 'name']

>>> dir(bob)                            # 3.0 includes class type methods
['__class__', '__delattr__', '__dict__', '__doc__', '__eq__', '__format__',
'__ge__', '__getattribute__', '__gt__', '__hash__', '__init__', '__le__',
...more lines omitted...
'__setattr__', '__sizeof__', '__str__', '__subclasshook__', '__weakref__',
'giveRaise', 'job', 'lastName', 'name', 'pay']
```

The output here varies between Python 2.6 and 3.0, because 3.0's dict.keys is not a list, and 3.0's dir returns extra class-type implementation attributes. Technically, dir returns more in 3.0 because classes are all "new style" and inherit a large set of operator overloading names from the class type. In fact, you'll probably want to filter out most of the _X_ names in the 3.0 dir result, since they are internal implementation details and not something you'd normally want to display.

In the interest of space, we'll leave optional display of inherited class attributes with either tree climbs or dir as suggested experiments for now. For more hints on this front, though, watch for the *classtree.py* inheritance tree climber we will write in Chapter 28, and the *lister.py* attribute listers and climbers we'll code in Chapter 30.

Name Considerations in Tool Classes

One last subtlety here: because our AttrDisplay class in the classtools module is a general tool designed to be mixed into other arbitrary classes, we have to be aware of the potential for unintended *name collisions* with client classes. As is, I've assumed that client subclasses may want to use both its __str__ and gatherAttrs, but the latter of these may be more than a subclass expects—if a subclass innocently defines a gatherAttrs name of its own, it will likely break our class, because the lower version in the subclass will be used instead of ours.

To see this for yourself, add a gatherAttrs to TopTest in the file's self-test code; unless the new method is identical, or intentionally customizes the original, our tool class will no longer work as planned:

```
class TopTest(AttrDisplay):
    ....
    def gatherAttrs(self):          # Replaces method in AttrDisplay!
        return 'Spam'
```

This isn't necessarily bad—sometimes we want other methods to be available to subclasses, either for direct calls or for customization. If we really meant to provide a __str__ only, though, this is less than ideal.

To minimize the chances of name collisions like this, Python programmers often prefix methods not meant for external use with a *single underscore*: _gatherAttrs in our case. This isn't foolproof (what if another class defines _gatherAttrs, too?), but it's usually sufficient, and it's a common Python naming convention for methods internal to a class.

A better and less commonly used solution would be to use *two underscores* at the front of the method name only: __gatherAttrs for us. Python automatically expands such names to include the enclosing class's name, which makes them truly unique. This is a feature usually called *pseudoprivate class attributes*, which we'll expand on in Chapter 30. For now, we'll make both our methods available.

Our Classes' Final Form

Now, to use this generic tool in our classes, all we need to do is import it from its module, mix it in by inheritance in our top-level class, and get rid of the more specific __str__ we coded before. The new print overload method will be inherited by instances of Person, as well as Manager; Manager gets __str__ from Person, which now obtains it from the AttrDisplay coded in another module. Here is the final version of our *person.py* file with these changes applied:

```
# File person.py (final)

from classtools import AttrDisplay              # Use generic display tool

class Person(AttrDisplay):
    """
    Create and process person records
    """
    def __init__(self, name, job=None, pay=0):
        self.name = name
        self.job  = job
        self.pay  = pay
    def lastName(self):                          # Assumes last is last
        return self.name.split()[-1]
    def giveRaise(self, percent):                # Percent must be 0..1
        self.pay = int(self.pay * (1 + percent))

class Manager(Person):
    """
    A customized Person with special requirements
    """
    def __init__(self, name, pay):
        Person.__init__(self, name, 'mgr', pay)
    def giveRaise(self, percent, bonus=.10):
        Person.giveRaise(self, percent + bonus)

if __name__ == '__main__':
    bob = Person('Bob Smith')
    sue = Person('Sue Jones', job='dev', pay=100000)
    print(bob)
    print(sue)
    print(bob.lastName(), sue.lastName())
    sue.giveRaise(.10)
    print(sue)
    tom = Manager('Tom Jones', 50000)
    tom.giveRaise(.10)
```

```
    print(tom.lastName())
    print(tom)
```

As this is the final revision, we've added a few *comments* here to document our work—docstrings for functional descriptions and # for smaller notes, per best-practice conventions. When we run this code now, we see all the attributes of our objects, not just the ones we hardcoded in the original __str__. And our final issue is resolved: because `AttrDisplay` takes class names off the `self` instance directly, each object is shown with the name of its closest (lowest) class—`tom` displays as a `Manager` now, not a `Person`, and we can finally verify that his job name has been correctly filled in by the `Manager` constructor:

```
C:\misc> person.py
[Person: job=None, name=Bob Smith, pay=0]
[Person: job=dev, name=Sue Jones, pay=100000]
Smith Jones
[Person: job=dev, name=Sue Jones, pay=110000]
Jones
[Manager: job=mgr, name=Tom Jones, pay=60000]
```

This is the more useful display we were after. From a larger perspective, though, our attribute display class has become a *general tool*, which we can mix into any class by inheritance to leverage the display format it defines. Further, all its clients will automatically pick up future changes in our tool. Later in the book, we'll meet even more powerful class tool concepts, such as decorators and metaclasses; along with Python's introspection tools, they allow us to write code that augments and manages classes in structured and maintainable ways.

Step 7 (Final): Storing Objects in a Database

At this point, our work is almost complete. We now have a *two-module system* that not only implements our original design goals for representing people, but also provides a general attribute display tool we can use in other programs in the future. By coding functions and classes in module files, we've ensured that they naturally support reuse. And by coding our software as classes, we've ensured that it naturally supports extension.

Although our classes work as planned, though, the objects they create are not real database records. That is, if we kill Python, our instances will disappear—they're transient objects in memory and are not stored in a more permanent medium like a file, so they won't be available in future program runs. It turns out that it's easy to make instance objects more permanent, with a Python feature called *object persistence*—making objects live on after the program that creates them exits. As a final step in this tutorial, let's make our objects permanent.

Pickles and Shelves

Object persistence is implemented by three standard library modules, available in every Python:

`pickle`
> Serializes arbitrary Python objects to and from a string of bytes

`dbm` (named `anydbm` in Python 2.6)
> Implements an access-by-key filesystem for storing strings

`shelve`
> Uses the other two modules to store Python objects on a file by key

We met these modules very briefly in Chapter 9 when we studied file basics. They provide powerful data storage options. Although we can't do them complete justice in this tutorial or book, they are simple enough that a brief introduction is enough to get you started.

The `pickle` module is a sort of super-general object formatting and deformatting tool: given a nearly arbitrary Python object in memory, it's clever enough to convert the object to a string of bytes, which it can use later to reconstruct the original object in memory. The `pickle` module can handle almost any object you can create—lists, dictionaries, nested combinations thereof, and class instances. The latter are especially useful things to pickle, because they provide both data (attributes) and behavior (methods); in fact, the combination is roughly equivalent to "records" and "programs." Because `pickle` is so general, it can replace extra code you might otherwise write to create and parse custom text file representations for your objects. By storing an object's pickle string on a file, you effectively make it permanent and persistent: simply load and unpickle it later to re-create the original object.

Although it's easy to use `pickle` by itself to store objects in simple flat files and load them from there later, the `shelve` module provides an extra layer of structure that allows you to store pickled objects by *key*. `shelve` translates an object to its pickled string with `pickle` and stores that string under a key in a `dbm` file; when later loading, `shelve` fetches the pickled string by key and re-creates the original object in memory with `pickle`. This is all quite a trick, but to your script a shelve* of pickled objects looks just like a *dictionary*—you index by key to fetch, assign to keys to store, and use dictionary tools such as `len`, `in`, and `dict.keys` to get information. Shelves automatically map dictionary operations to objects stored in a file.

In fact, to your script the only coding difference between a shelve and a normal dictionary is that you must *open* shelves initially and must *close* them after making changes. The net effect is that a shelve provides a simple database for storing and fetching native Python objects by keys, and thus makes them persistent across program runs. It does

---

* Yes, we use "shelve" as a noun in Python, much to the chagrin of a variety of editors I've worked with over the years, both electronic and human.

not support query tools such as SQL, and it lacks some advanced features found in enterprise-level databases (such as true transaction processing), but native Python objects stored on a shelve may be processed with the full power of the Python language once they are fetched back by key.

Storing Objects on a Shelve Database

Pickling and shelves are somewhat advanced topics, and we won't go into all their details here; you can read more about them in the standard library manuals, as well as application-focused books such as *Programming Python*. This is all simpler in Python than in English, though, so let's jump into some code.

Let's write a new script that throws objects of our classes onto a shelve. In your text editor, open a new file we'll call *makedb.py*. Since this is a new file, we'll need to import our classes in order to create a few instances to store. We used `from` to load a class at the interactive prompt earlier, but really, as with functions and other variables, there are two ways to load a class from a file (class names are variables like any other, and not at all magic in this context):

```
import person                          # Load class with import
bob = person.Person(...)               # Go through module name

from person import Person              # Load class with from
bob = Person(...)                      # Use name directly
```

We'll use `from` to load in our script, just because it's a bit less to type. Copy or retype this code to make instances of our classes in the new script, so we have something to store (this is a simple demo, so we won't worry about the test-code redundancy here). Once we have some instances, it's almost trivial to store them on a shelve. We simply import the `shelve` module, open a new shelve with an external filename, assign the objects to keys in the shelve, and close the shelve when we're done because we've made changes:

```
# File makedb.py: store Person objects on a shelve database

from person import Person, Manager     # Load our classes
bob = Person('Bob Smith')              # Re-create objects to be stored
sue = Person('Sue Jones', job='dev', pay=100000)
tom = Manager('Tom Jones', 50000)

import shelve
db = shelve.open('persondb')           # Filename where objects are stored
for object in (bob, sue, tom):         # Use object's name attr as key
    db[object.name] = object           # Store object on shelve by key
db.close()                             # Close after making changes
```

Notice how we assign objects to the shelve using their own names as keys. This is just for convenience; in a shelve, the *key* can be any string, including one we might create to be unique using tools such as process IDs and timestamps (available in the `os` and `time` standard library modules). The only rule is that the keys must be strings and should be unique, since we can store just one object per key (though that object can be a list or dictionary containing many objects). The *values* we store under keys, though, can be Python objects of almost any sort: built-in types like strings, lists, and dictionaries, as well as user-defined class instances, and nested combinations of all of these.

That's all there is to it—if this script has no output when run, it means it probably worked; we're not printing anything, just creating and storing objects:

```
C:\misc> makedb.py
```

Exploring Shelves Interactively

At this point, there are one or more real files in the current directory whose names all start with "persondb". The actual files created can vary per platform, and just like in the built-in `open` function, the filename in `shelve.open()` is relative to the current working directory unless it includes a directory path. Wherever they are stored, these files implement a keyed-access file that contains the pickled representation of our three Python objects. Don't delete these files—they are your database, and are what you'll need to copy or transfer when you back up or move your storage.

You can look at the shelve's files if you want to, either from Windows Explorer or the Python shell, but they are binary hash files, and most of their content makes little sense outside the context of the `shelve` module. With Python 3.0 and no extra software installed, our database is stored in three files (in 2.6, it's just one file, *persondb*, because the `bsddb` extension module is preinstalled with Python for shelves; in 3.0, `bsddb` is a third-party open source add-on):

```
# Directory listing module: verify files are present

>>> import glob
>>> glob.glob('person*')
['person.py', 'person.pyc', 'persondb.bak', 'persondb.dat', 'persondb.dir']

# Type the file: text mode for string, binary mode for bytes

>>> print(open('persondb.dir').read())
'Tom Jones', (1024, 91)
...more omitted...

>>> print(open('persondb.dat', 'rb').read())
b'\x80\x03cperson\nPerson\nq\x00)\x81q\x01}q\x02(X\x03\x00\x00\x00payq\x03K...
...more omitted...
```

This content isn't impossible to decipher, but it can vary on different platforms and doesn't exactly qualify as a user-friendly database interface! To verify our work better, we can write another script, or poke around our shelve at the interactive prompt. Because shelves are Python objects containing Python objects, we can process them with normal Python syntax and development modes. Here, the interactive prompt effectively becomes a *database client*:

```
>>> import shelve
>>> db = shelve.open('persondb')            # Reopen the shelve

>>> len(db)                                 # Three 'records' stored
3
>>> list(db.keys())                         # keys is the index
['Tom Jones', 'Sue Jones', 'Bob Smith']     # list to make a list in 3.0

>>> bob = db['Bob Smith']                    # Fetch bob by key
>>> print(bob)                               # Runs __str__ from AttrDisplay
[Person: job=None, name=Bob Smith, pay=0]

>>> bob.lastName()                           # Runs lastName from Person
'Smith'

>>> for key in db:                           # Iterate, fetch, print
        print(key, '=>', db[key])

Tom Jones => [Manager: job=mgr, name=Tom Jones, pay=50000]
Sue Jones => [Person: job=dev, name=Sue Jones, pay=100000]
Bob Smith => [Person: job=None, name=Bob Smith, pay=0]

>>> for key in sorted(db):
        print(key, '=>', db[key])            # Iterate by sorted keys

Bob Smith => [Person: job=None, name=Bob Smith, pay=0]
Sue Jones => [Person: job=dev, name=Sue Jones, pay=100000]
Tom Jones => [Manager: job=mgr, name=Tom Jones, pay=50000]
```

Notice that we don't have to import our Person or Manager classes here in order to load or use our stored objects. For example, we can call bob's lastName method freely, and get his custom print display format automatically, even though we don't have his Person class in our scope here. This works because when Python pickles a class instance, it records its self instance attributes, along with the name of the class it was created from and the module where the class lives. When bob is later fetched from the shelve and unpickled, Python will automatically reimport the class and link bob to it.

The upshot of this scheme is that class instances automatically acquire all their class behavior when they are loaded in the future. We have to import our classes only to make new instances, not to process existing ones. Although a deliberate feature, this scheme has somewhat mixed consequences:

• The *downside* is that classes and their module's files must be importable when an instance is later loaded. More formally, pickleable classes must be coded at the top level of a module file accessible from a directory listed on the sys.path module search path (and shouldn't live in the most script files' module __main__ unless they're always in that module when used). Because of this external module file requirement, some applications choose to pickle simpler objects such as dictionaries or lists, especially if they are to be transferred across the Internet.

- The *upside* is that changes in a class's source code file are automatically picked up when instances of the class are loaded again; there is often no need to update stored objects themselves, since updating their class's code changes their behavior.

Shelves also have well-known limitations (the database suggestions at the end of this chapter mention a few of these). For simple object storage, though, shelves and pickles are remarkably easy-to-use tools.

Updating Objects on a Shelve

Now for one last script: let's write a program that updates an instance (record) each time it runs, to prove the point that our objects really are *persistent* (i.e., that their current values are available every time a Python program runs). The following file, *updatedb.py*, prints the database and gives a raise to one of our stored objects each time. If you trace through what's going on here, you'll notice that we're getting a lot of utility "for free"—printing our objects automatically employs the general __str__ overloading method, and we give raises by calling the giveRaise method we wrote earlier. This all "just works" for objects based on OOP's inheritance model, even when they live in a file:

```
# File updatedb.py: update Person object on database

import shelve
db = shelve.open('persondb')          # Reopen shelve with same filename

for key in sorted(db):                # Iterate to display database objects
    print(key, '\t=>', db[key])       # Prints with custom format

sue = db['Sue Jones']                 # Index by key to fetch
sue.giveRaise(.10)                    # Update in memory using class method
db['Sue Jones'] = sue                 # Assign to key to update in shelve
db.close()                            # Close after making changes
```

Because this script prints the database when it starts up, we have to run it a few times to see our objects change. Here it is in action, displaying all records and increasing sue's pay each time it's run (it's a pretty good script for sue...):

```
c:\misc> updatedb.py
Bob Smith       => [Person: job=None, name=Bob Smith, pay=0]
Sue Jones       => [Person: job=dev, name=Sue Jones, pay=100000]
Tom Jones       => [Manager: job=mgr, name=Tom Jones, pay=50000]

c:\misc> updatedb.py
Bob Smith       => [Person: job=None, name=Bob Smith, pay=0]
Sue Jones       => [Person: job=dev, name=Sue Jones, pay=110000]
Tom Jones       => [Manager: job=mgr, name=Tom Jones, pay=50000]

c:\misc> updatedb.py
Bob Smith       => [Person: job=None, name=Bob Smith, pay=0]
Sue Jones       => [Person: job=dev, name=Sue Jones, pay=121000]
Tom Jones       => [Manager: job=mgr, name=Tom Jones, pay=50000]

c:\misc> updatedb.py
```

```
Bob Smith      => [Person: job=None, name=Bob Smith, pay=0]
Sue Jones      => [Person: job=dev, name=Sue Jones, pay=133100]
Tom Jones      => [Manager: job=mgr, name=Tom Jones, pay=50000]
```

Again, what we see here is a product of the `shelve` and `pickle` tools we get from Python, and of the behavior we coded in our classes ourselves. And once again, we can verify our script's work at the interactive prompt (the shelve's equivalent of a database client):

```
c:\misc> python
>>> import shelve
>>> db = shelve.open('persondb')      # Reopen database
>>> rec = db['Sue Jones']             # Fetch object by key
>>> print(rec)
[Person: job=dev, name=Sue Jones, pay=146410]
>>> rec.lastName()
'Jones'
>>> rec.pay
146410
```

For another example of object persistence in this book, see the sidebar in Chapter 30 titled "Why You Will Care: Classes and Persistence" on page 746. It stores a somewhat larger composite object in a flat file with `pickle` instead of `shelve`, but the effect is similar. For more details on both pickles and shelves, see other books or Python's manuals.

Future Directions

And that's a wrap for this tutorial. At this point, you've seen all the basics of Python's OOP machinery in action, and you've learned ways to avoid redundancy and its associated maintenance issues in your code. You've built full-featured classes that do real work. As an added bonus, you've made them real database records by storing them in a Python shelve, so their information lives on persistently.

There is much more we could explore here, of course. For example, we could extend our classes to make them more realistic, add new kinds of behavior to them, and so on. Giving a raise, for instance, should in practice verify that pay increase rates are between zero and one—an extension we'll add when we meet decorators later in this book. You might also mutate this example into a personal contacts database, by changing the state information stored on objects, as well as the class methods used to process it. We'll leave this a suggested exercise open to your imagination.

We could also expand our scope to use tools that either come with Python or are freely available in the open source world:

GUIs

As is, we can only process our database with the interactive prompt's command-based interface, and scripts. We could also work on expanding our object database's usability by adding a graphical user interface for browsing and updating its records. GUIs can be built portably with either Python's `tkinter` (Tkinter in 2.6) standard library support, or third-party toolkits such as WxPython and PyQt. `tkinter` ships with Python, lets you build simple GUIs quickly, and is ideal for learning GUI programming techniques; WxPython and PyQt tend to be more complex to use but often produce higher-grade GUIs in the end.

Websites

Although GUIs are convenient and fast, the Web is hard to beat in terms of accessibility. We might also implement a website for browsing and updating records, instead of or in addition to GUIs and the interactive prompt. Websites can be constructed with either basic CGI scripting tools that come with Python, or full-featured third-party web frameworks such as Django, TurboGears, Pylons, web2Py, Zope, or Google's App Engine. On the Web, your data can still be stored in a shelve, pickle file, or other Python-based medium; the scripts that process it are simply run automatically on a server in response to requests from web browsers and other clients, and they produce HTML to interact with a user, either directly or by interfacing with Framework APIs.

Web services

Although web clients can often parse information in the replies from websites (a technique colorfully known as "screen scraping"), we might go further and provide a more direct way to fetch records on the Web via a web services interface such as SOAP or XML-RPC calls—APIs supported by either Python itself or the third-party open source domain. Such APIs return data in a more direct form, rather than embedded in the HTML of a reply page.

Databases

If our database becomes higher-volume or critical, we might eventually move it from shelves to a more full-featured storage mechanism such as the open source ZODB object-oriented database system (OODB), or a more traditional SQL-based relational database system such as MySQL, Oracle, PostgreSQL, or SQLite. Python itself comes with the in-process SQLite database system built-in, but other open source options are freely available on the Web. ZODB, for example, is similar to Python's `shelve` but addresses many of its limitations, supporting larger databases, concurrent updates, transaction processing, and automatic write-through on in-memory changes. SQL-based systems like MySQL offer enterprise-level tools for database storage and may be directly used from a within a Python script.

ORMs

If we do migrate to a relational database system for storage, we don't have to sacrifice Python's OOP tools. Object-relational mappers (ORMs) like SQLObject and SQLAlchemy can automatically map relational tables and rows to and from Python classes and instances, such that we can process the stored data using normal Python class syntax. This approach provides an alternative to OODBs like `shelve` and ZODB and leverages the power of both relational databases and Python's class model.

While I hope this introduction whets your appetite for future exploration, all of these topics are of course far beyond the scope of this tutorial and this book at large. If you want to explore any of them on your own, see the Web, Python's standard library manuals, and application-focused books such as *Programming Python*. In the latter I pick up this example where we've stopped here, showing how to add both a GUI and a website on top of the database to allow for browsing and updating instance records. I hope to see you there eventually, but first, let's return to class fundamentals and finish up the rest of the core Python language story.

Chapter Summary

In this chapter, we explored all the fundamentals of Python classes and OOP in action, by building upon a simple but real example, step by step. We added constructors, methods, operator overloading, customization with subclasses, and introspection tools, and we met other concepts (such as composition, delegation, and polymorphism) along the way.

In the end, we took objects created by our classes and made them persistent by storing them on a shelve object database—an easy-to-use system for saving and retrieving native Python objects by key. While exploring class basics, we also encountered multiple ways to factor our code to reduce redundancy and minimize future maintenance costs. Finally, we briefly previewed ways to extend our code with application-programming tools such as GUIs and databases, covered in follow-up books.

In the next chapters of this part of the book we'll return to our study of the details behind Python's class model and investigate its application to some of the design concepts used to combine classes in larger programs. Before we move ahead, though, let's work through this chapter's quiz to review what we covered here. Since we've already done a lot of hands-on work in this chapter, we'll close with a set of mostly theory-oriented questions designed to make you trace through some of the code and ponder some of the bigger ideas behind it.

Test Your Knowledge: Quiz

1. When we fetch a `Manager` object from the shelve and print it, where does the display format logic come from?

2. When we fetch a `Person` object from a shelve without importing its module, how does the object know that it has a `giveRaise` method that we can call?

3. Why is it so important to move processing into methods, instead of hardcoding it outside the class?

4. Why is it better to customize by subclassing rather than copying the original and modifying?

5. Why is it better to call back to a superclass method to run default actions, instead of copying and modifying its code in a subclass?

6. Why is it better to use tools like __dict__ that allow objects to be processed generically than to write more custom code for each type of class?

7. In general terms, when might you choose to use object embedding and composition instead of inheritance?

8. How might you modify the classes in this chapter to implement a personal contacts database in Python?

Test Your Knowledge: Answers

1. In the final version of our classes, Manager ultimately inherits its __str__ printing method from AttrDisplay in the separate classtools module. Manager doesn't have one itself, so the inheritance search climbs to its Person superclass; because there is no __str__ there either, the search climbs higher and finds it in AttrDisplay. The class names listed in parentheses in a class statement's header line provide the links to higher superclasses.

2. Shelves (really, the pickle module they use) automatically relink an instance to the class it was created from when that instance is later loaded back into memory. Python reimports the class from its module internally, creates an instance with its stored attributes, and sets the instance's __class__ link to point to its original class. This way, loaded instances automatically obtain all their original methods (like lastName, giveRaise, and __str__), even if we have not imported the instance's class into our scope.

3. It's important to move processing into methods so that there is only one copy to change in the future, and so that the methods can be run on any instance. This is Python's notion of *encapsulation*—wrapping up logic behind interfaces, to better support future code maintenance. If you don't do so, you create code redundancy that can multiply your work effort as the code evolves in the future.

4. Customizing with subclasses reduces development effort. In OOP, we code by *customizing* what has already been done, rather than copying or changing existing code. This is the real "big idea" in OOP—because we can easily extend our prior work by coding new subclasses, we can leverage what we've already done. This is much better than either starting from scratch each time, or introducing multiple redundant copies of code that may all have to be updated in the future.

5. Copying and modifying code *doubles* your potential work effort in the future, regardless of the context. If a subclass needs to perform default actions coded in a superclass method, it's much better to call back to the original through the superclass's name than to copy its code. This also holds true for superclass constructors. Again, copying code creates redundancy, which is a major issue as code evolves.

6. Generic tools can avoid hardcoded solutions that must be kept in sync with the rest of the class as it evolves over time. A generic `__str__` print method, for example, need not be updated each time a new attribute is added to instances in an `__init__` constructor. In addition, a generic `print` method inherited by all classes only appears, and need only be modified, in one place—changes in the generic version are picked up by all classes that inherit from the generic class. Again, eliminating code *redundancy* cuts future development effort; that's one of the primary assets classes bring to the table.

7. Inheritance is best at coding extensions based on direct customization (like our `Manager` specialization of `Person`). Composition is well suited to scenarios where multiple objects are aggregated into a whole and directed by a controller layer class. Inheritance passes calls up to reuse, and composition passes down to delegate. Inheritance and composition are not mutually exclusive; often, the objects embedded in a controller are themselves customizations based upon inheritance.

8. The classes in this chapter could be used as boilerplate "template" code to implement a variety of types of databases. Essentially, you can repurpose them by modifying the constructors to record different attributes and providing whatever methods are appropriate for the target application. For instance, you might use attributes such as `name`, `address`, `birthday`, `phone`, `email`, and so on for a contacts database, and methods appropriate for this purpose. A method named `sendmail`, for example, might use Python's standard library `smptlib` module to send an email to one of the contacts automatically when called (see Python's manuals or application-level books for more details on such tools). The `AttrDisplay` tool we wrote here could be used verbatim to print your objects, because it is intentionally generic. Most of the shelve database code here can be used to store your objects, too, with minor changes.

## CHAPTER 28

Class Coding Details

If you haven't quite gotten all of Python OOP yet, don't worry; now that we've had a quick tour, we're going to dig a bit deeper and study the concepts introduced earlier in further detail. In this and the following chapter, we'll take another look at class mechanics. Here, we're going to study classes, methods, and inheritance, formalizing and expanding on some of the coding ideas introduced in Chapter 26. Because the class is our last namespace tool, we'll summarize Python's namespace concepts here as well.

The next chapter continues this in-depth second pass over class mechanics by covering one specific aspect: operator overloading. Besides presenting the details, this chapter and the next also give us an opportunity to explore some larger classes than those we have studied so far.

The class Statement

Although the Python `class` statement may seem similar to tools in other OOP languages on the surface, on closer inspection, it is quite different from what some programmers are used to. For example, as in C++, the `class` statement is Python's main OOP tool, but unlike in C++, Python's `class` is not a declaration. Like a `def`, a `class` statement is an object builder, and an implicit assignment—when run, it generates a class object and stores a reference to it in the name used in the header. Also like a `def`, a `class` statement is true executable code—your class doesn't exist until Python reaches and runs the `class` statement that defines it (typically while importing the module it is coded in, but not before).

General Form

`class` is a compound statement, with a body of indented statements typically appearing under the header. In the header, superclasses are listed in parentheses after the class name, separated by commas. Listing more than one superclass leads to multiple inheritance (which we'll discuss more formally in Chapter 30). Here is the statement's general form:

```
class <name>(superclass,...):          # Assign to name
    data = value                       # Shared class data
    def method(self,...):              # Methods
        self.member = value            # Per-instance data
```

Within the `class` statement, any assignments generate class attributes, and specially named methods overload operators; for instance, a function called `__init__` is called at instance object construction time, if defined.

Example

As we've seen, classes are mostly just namespaces—that is, tools for defining names (i.e., attributes) that export data and logic to clients. So, how do you get from the `class` statement to a namespace?

Here's how. Just like in a module file, the statements nested in a `class` statement body create its attributes. When Python executes a `class` statement (not a call to a class), it runs all the statements in its body, from top to bottom. Assignments that happen during this process create names in the class's local scope, which become attributes in the associated class object. Because of this, classes resemble both modules and functions:

- Like functions, `class` statements are local scopes where names created by nested assignments live.
- Like names in a module, names assigned in a `class` statement become attributes in a class object.

The main distinction for classes is that their namespaces are also the basis of inheritance in Python; reference attributes that are not found in a class or instance object are fetched from other classes.

Because `class` is a compound statement, any sort of statement can be nested inside its body—`print`, `=`, `if`, `def`, and so on. All the statements inside the `class` statement run when the `class` statement itself runs (not when the class is later called to make an instance). Assigning names inside the `class` statement makes class attributes, and nested `def`s make class methods, but other assignments make attributes, too.

For example, assignments of simple nonfunction objects to class attributes produce *data attributes*, shared by all instances:

```
>>> class SharedData:
...     spam = 42          # Generates a class data attribute
...
>>> x = SharedData()       # Make two instances
>>> y = SharedData()
>>> x.spam, y.spam         # They inherit and share 'spam'
(42, 42)
```

Here, because the name `spam` is assigned at the top level of a `class` statement, it is attached to the class and so will be shared by all instances. We can change it by going through the class name, and we can refer to it through either instances or the class.[*]

```
>>> SharedData.spam = 99
>>> x.spam, y.spam, SharedData.spam
(99, 99, 99)
```

Such class attributes can be used to manage information that spans all the instances—a counter of the number of instances generated, for example (we'll expand on this idea by example in Chapter 31). Now, watch what happens if we assign the name `spam` through an instance instead of the class:

```
>>> x.spam = 88
>>> x.spam, y.spam, SharedData.spam
(88, 99, 99)
```

Assignments to instance attributes create or change the names in the instance, rather than in the shared class. More generally, inheritance searches occur only on attribute *references*, not on assignment: assigning to an object's attribute always changes that object, and no other.[†] For example, `y.spam` is looked up in the class by inheritance, but the assignment to `x.spam` attaches a name to `x` itself.

Here's a more comprehensive example of this behavior that stores the same name in two places. Suppose we run the following class:

```
class MixedNames:                            # Define class
    data = 'spam'                            # Assign class attr
    def __init__(self, value):               # Assign method name
        self.data = value                    # Assign instance attr
    def display(self):
        print(self.data, MixedNames.data)    # Instance attr, class attr
```

This class contains two `def`s, which bind class attributes to method functions. It also contains an = assignment statement; because this assignment assigns the name `data` inside the `class`, it lives in the class's local scope and becomes an attribute of the class object. Like all class attributes, this `data` is inherited and shared by all instances of the class that don't have `data` attributes of their own.

When we make instances of this class, the name `data` is attached to those instances by the assignment to `self.data` in the constructor method:

```
>>> x = MixedNames(1)     # Make two instance objects
>>> y = MixedNames(2)     # Each has its own data
```

---

[*] If you've used C++ you may recognize this as similar to the notion of C++'s "static" data members—members that are stored in the class, independent of instances. In Python, it's nothing special: all class attributes are just names assigned in the `class` statement, whether they happen to reference functions (C++'s "methods") or something else (C++'s "members"). In Chapter 31, we'll also meet Python static methods (akin to those in C++), which are just self-less functions that usually process class attributes.

[†] Unless the class has redefined the attribute assignment operation to do something unique with the `__setattr__` operator overloading method (discussed in Chapter 29).

```
>>> x.display(); y.display()      # self.data differs, MixedNames.data is the same
1 spam
2 spam
```

The net result is that `data` lives in two places: in the instance objects (created by the `self.data` assignment in `__init__`), and in the class from which they inherit names (created by the `data` assignment in the `class`). The class's `display` method prints both versions, by first qualifying the `self` instance, and then the class.

By using these techniques to store attributes in different objects, we determine their scope of visibility. When attached to classes, names are shared; in instances, names record per-instance data, not shared behavior or data. Although inheritance searches look up names for us, we can always get to an attribute anywhere in a tree by accessing the desired object directly.

In the preceding example, for instance, specifying `x.data` or `self.data` will return an instance name, which normally hides the same name in the class; however, `Mixed Names.data` grabs the class name explicitly. We'll see various roles for such coding patterns later; the next section describes one of the most common.

Methods

Because you already know about functions, you also know about methods in classes. Methods are just function objects created by `def` statements nested in a `class` statement's body. From an abstract perspective, methods provide behavior for instance objects to inherit. From a programming perspective, methods work in exactly the same way as simple functions, with one crucial exception: a method's first argument always receives the instance object that is the implied subject of the method call.

In other words, Python automatically maps instance method calls to class method functions as follows. Method calls made through an instance, like this:

```
instance.method(args...)
```

are automatically translated to class method function calls of this form:

```
class.method(instance, args...)
```

where the class is determined by locating the method name using Python's inheritance search procedure. In fact, both call forms are valid in Python.

Besides the normal inheritance of method attribute names, the special first argument is the only real magic behind method calls. In a class method, the first argument is usually called `self` by convention (technically, only its position is significant, not its name). This argument provides methods with a hook back to the instance that is the subject of the call—because classes generate many instance objects, they need to use this argument to manage data that varies per instance.

C++ programmers may recognize Python's `self` argument as being similar to C++'s `this` pointer. In Python, though, `self` is always explicit in your code: methods must always go through `self` to fetch or change attributes of the instance being processed by the current method call. This explicit nature of `self` is by design—the presence of this name makes it obvious that you are using instance attribute names in your script, not names in the local or global scope.

Method Example

To clarify these concepts, let's turn to an example. Suppose we define the following class:

```
class NextClass:                    # Define class
    def printer(self, text):        # Define method
        self.message = text         # Change instance
        print(self.message)         # Access instance
```

The name `printer` references a function object; because it's assigned in the `class` statement's scope, it becomes a class object attribute and is inherited by every instance made from the class. Normally, because methods like `printer` are designed to process instances, we call them through instances:

```
>>> x = NextClass()                 # Make instance

>>> x.printer('instance call')      # Call its method
instance call

>>> x.message                       # Instance changed
'instance call'
```

When we call the method by qualifying an instance like this, `printer` is first located by inheritance, and then its `self` argument is automatically assigned the instance object (x); the `text` argument gets the string passed at the call (`'instance call'`). Notice that because Python automatically passes the first argument to `self` for us, we only actually have to pass in one argument. Inside `printer`, the name `self` is used to access or set per-instance data because it refers back to the instance currently being processed.

Methods may be called in one of two ways—through an instance, or through the class itself. For example, we can also call `printer` by going through the class name, provided we pass an instance to the `self` argument explicitly:

```
>>> NextClass.printer(x, 'class call')    # Direct class call
class call

>>> x.message                             # Instance changed again
'class call'
```

Calls routed through the instance and the class have the exact same effect, as long as we pass the same instance object ourselves in the class form. By default, in fact, you get an error message if you try to call a method without any instance:

```
>>> NextClass.printer('bad call')
TypeError: unbound method printer() must be called with NextClass instance...
```

Calling Superclass Constructors

Methods are normally called through instances. Calls to methods through a class, though, do show up in a variety of special roles. One common scenario involves the constructor method. The __init__ method, like all attributes, is looked up by inheritance. This means that at construction time, Python locates and calls just one __init__. If subclass constructors need to guarantee that superclass construction-time logic runs, too, they generally must call the superclass's __init__ method explicitly through the class:

```
class Super:
    def __init__(self, x):
        ...default code...

class Sub(Super):
    def __init__(self, x, y):
        Super.__init__(self, x)      # Run superclass __init__
        ...custom code...            # Do my init actions

I = Sub(1, 2)
```

This is one of the few contexts in which your code is likely to call an operator over-loading method directly. Naturally, you should only call the superclass constructor this way if you really want it to run—without the call, the subclass replaces it completely. For a more realistic illustration of this technique in action, see the Manager class example in the prior chapter's tutorial.[‡]

Other Method Call Possibilities

This pattern of calling methods through a class is the general basis of extending (instead of completely replacing) inherited method behavior. In Chapter 31, we'll also meet a new option added in Python 2.2, *static methods*, that allow you to code methods that do not expect instance objects in their first arguments. Such methods can act like simple instanceless functions, with names that are local to the classes in which they are coded, and may be used to manage class data. A related concept, the *class method*, receives a class when called instead of an instance and can be used to manage per-class data. These are advanced and optional extensions, though; normally, you must always pass an instance to a method, whether it is called through an instance or a class.

[‡] On a somewhat related note, you can also code multiple __init__ methods within the same class, but only the last definition will be used; see Chapter 30 for more details on multiple method definitions.

Inheritance

The whole point of a namespace tool like the `class` statement is to support name inheritance. This section expands on some of the mechanisms and roles of attribute inheritance in Python.

In Python, inheritance happens when an object is qualified, and it involves searching an attribute definition tree (one or more namespaces). Every time you use an expression of the form *object.attr* (where *object* is an instance or class object), Python searches the namespace tree from bottom to top, beginning with *object*, looking for the first *attr* it can find. This includes references to `self` attributes in your methods. Because lower definitions in the tree override higher ones, inheritance forms the basis of specialization.

Attribute Tree Construction

Figure 28-1 summarizes the way namespace trees are constructed and populated with names. Generally:

- Instance attributes are generated by assignments to `self` attributes in methods.
- Class attributes are created by statements (assignments) in `class` statements.
- Superclass links are made by listing classes in parentheses in a `class` statement header.

The net result is a tree of attribute namespaces that leads from an instance, to the class it was generated from, to all the superclasses listed in the `class` header. Python searches upward in this tree, from instances to superclasses, each time you use qualification to fetch an attribute name from an instance object.§

Specializing Inherited Methods

The tree-searching model of inheritance just described turns out to be a great way to specialize systems. Because inheritance finds names in subclasses before it checks superclasses, subclasses can replace default behavior by redefining their superclasses' attributes. In fact, you can build entire systems as hierarchies of classes, which are extended by adding new external subclasses rather than changing existing logic in-place.

---

§ This description isn't 100% complete, because we can also create instance and class attributes by assigning to objects outside `class` statements—but that's a much less common and sometimes more error-prone approach (changes aren't isolated to `class` statements). In Python, all attributes are always accessible by default. We'll talk more about attribute name privacy in Chapter 29 when we study `__setattr__`, in Chapter 30 when we meet `__X` names, and again in Chapter 38, where we'll implement it with a class decorator.

The idea of redefining inherited names leads to a variety of specialization techniques. For instance, subclasses may *replace* inherited attributes completely, *provide* attributes that a superclass expects to find, and *extend* superclass methods by calling back to the superclass from an overridden method. We've already seen replacement in action. Here's an example that shows how extension works:

```
>>> class Super:
...     def method(self):
...         print('in Super.method')
...
>>> class Sub(Super):
...     def method(self):              # Override method
...         print('starting Sub.method')   # Add actions here
...         Super.method(self)          # Run default action
...         print('ending Sub.method')
...
```

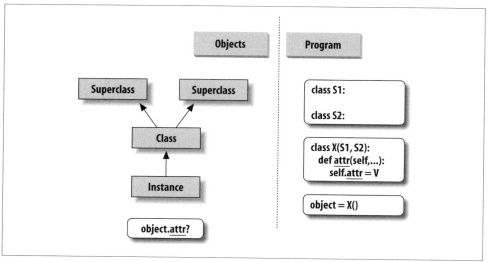

Figure 28-1. Program code creates a tree of objects in memory to be searched by attribute inheritance. Calling a class creates a new instance that remembers its class, running a class statement creates a new class, and superclasses are listed in parentheses in the class statement header. Each attribute reference triggers a new bottom-up tree search—even references to self attributes within a class's methods.

Direct superclass method calls are the crux of the matter here. The Sub class replaces Super's method function with its own specialized version, but within the replacement, Sub calls back to the version exported by Super to carry out the default behavior. In other words, Sub.method just extends Super.method's behavior, rather than replacing it completely:

```
>>> x = Super()                        # Make a Super instance
>>> x.method()                         # Runs Super.method
in Super.method

>>> x = Sub()                          # Make a Sub instance
>>> x.method()                         # Runs Sub.method, calls Super.method
starting Sub.method
in Super.method
ending Sub.method
```

This extension coding pattern is also commonly used with constructors; see the section "Methods" on page 686 for an example.

Class Interface Techniques

Extension is only one way to interface with a superclass. The file shown in this section, *specialize.py*, defines multiple classes that illustrate a variety of common techniques:

Super
 Defines a method function and a delegate that expects an action in a subclass.

Inheritor
 Doesn't provide any new names, so it gets everything defined in Super.

Replacer
 Overrides Super's method with a version of its own.

Extender
 Customizes Super's method by overriding and calling back to run the default.

Provider
 Implements the action method expected by Super's delegate method.

Study each of these subclasses to get a feel for the various ways they customize their common superclass. Here's the file:

```
class Super:
    def method(self):
        print('in Super.method')           # Default behavior
    def delegate(self):
        self.action()                       # Expected to be defined

class Inheritor(Super):                     # Inherit method verbatim
    pass

class Replacer(Super):                      # Replace method completely
    def method(self):
        print('in Replacer.method')

class Extender(Super):                      # Extend method behavior
    def method(self):
        print('starting Extender.method')
        Super.method(self)
        print('ending Extender.method')
```

```
class Provider(Super):                           # Fill in a required method
    def action(self):
        print('in Provider.action')

if __name__ == '__main__':
    for klass in (Inheritor, Replacer, Extender):
        print('\n' + klass.__name__ + '...')
        klass().method()
    print('\nProvider...')
    x = Provider()
    x.delegate()
```

A few things are worth pointing out here. First, the self-test code at the end of this example creates instances of three different classes in a `for` loop. Because classes are objects, you can put them in a tuple and create instances generically (more on this idea later). Classes also have the special __name__ attribute, like modules; it's preset to a string containing the name in the class header. Here's what happens when we run the file:

```
% python specialize.py

Inheritor...
in Super.method

Replacer...
in Replacer.method

Extender...
starting Extender.method
in Super.method
ending Extender.method

Provider...
in Provider.action
```

Abstract Superclasses

Notice how the `Provider` class in the prior example works. When we call the `delegate` method through a `Provider` instance, *two* independent inheritance searches occur:

1. On the initial `x.delegate` call, Python finds the `delegate` method in `Super` by searching the `Provider` instance and above. The instance `x` is passed into the method's `self` argument as usual.

2. Inside the `Super.delegate` method, `self.action` invokes a new, independent inheritance search of `self` and above. Because `self` references a `Provider` instance, the `action` method is located in the `Provider` subclass.

This "filling in the blanks" sort of coding structure is typical of OOP frameworks. At least in terms of the `delegate` method, the superclass in this example is what is sometimes called an *abstract superclass*—a class that expects parts of its behavior to be provided by its subclasses. If an expected method is not defined in a subclass, Python raises an undefined name exception when the inheritance search fails.

Class coders sometimes make such subclass requirements more obvious with `assert` statements, or by raising the built-in `NotImplementedError` exception with `raise` statements (we'll study statements that may trigger exceptions in depth in the next part of this book). As a quick preview, here's the `assert` scheme in action:

```
class Super:
    def delegate(self):
        self.action()
    def action(self):
        assert False, 'action must be defined!'     # If this version is called
```

```
>>> X = Super()
>>> X.delegate()
AssertionError: action must be defined!
```

We'll meet `assert` in Chapters 32 and 33; in short, if its first expression evaluates to false, it raises an exception with the provided error message. Here, the expression is always false so as to trigger an error message if a method is not redefined, and inheritance locates the version here. Alternatively, some classes simply raise a `NotImplementedError` exception directly in such method stubs to signal the mistake:

```
class Super:
    def delegate(self):
        self.action()
    def action(self):
        raise NotImplementedError('action must be defined!')
```

```
>>> X = Super()
>>> X.delegate()
NotImplementedError: action must be defined!
```

For instances of subclasses, we still get the exception unless the subclass provides the expected method to replace the default in the superclass:

```
>>> class Sub(Super): pass
...
>>> X = Sub()
>>> X.delegate()
NotImplementedError: action must be defined!
```

```
>>> class Sub(Super):
...         def action(self): print('spam')
...
>>> X = Sub()
>>> X.delegate()
spam
```

For a somewhat more realistic example of this section's concepts in action, see the "Zoo animal hierarchy" exercise (exercise 8) at the end of Chapter 31, and its solution in "Part VI, Classes and OOP" on page 1124 in Appendix B. Such taxonomies are a traditional way to introduce OOP, but they're a bit removed from most developers' job descriptions.

Python 2.6 and 3.0 Abstract Superclasses

As of Python 2.6 and 3.0, the prior section's abstract superclasses (a.k.a. "abstract base classes"), which require methods to be filled in by subclasses, may also be implemented with special class syntax. The way we code this varies slightly depending on the version. In Python 3.0, we use a keyword argument in a `class` header, along with special @ decorator syntax, both of which we'll study in detail later in this book:

```
from abc import ABCMeta, abstractmethod

class Super(metaclass=ABCMeta):
    @abstractmethod
    def method(self, ...):
        pass
```

But in Python 2.6, we use a class attribute instead:

```
class Super:
    __metaclass__ = ABCMeta
    @abstractmethod
    def method(self, ...):
        pass
```

Either way, the effect is the same—we can't make an instance unless the method is defined lower in the class tree. In 3.0, for example, here is the special syntax equivalent of the prior section's example:

```
>>> from abc import ABCMeta, abstractmethod
>>>
>>> class Super(metaclass=ABCMeta):
...     def delegate(self):
...         self.action()
...     @abstractmethod
...     def action(self):
...         pass
...
>>> X = Super()
TypeError: Can't instantiate abstract class Super with abstract methods action

>>> class Sub(Super): pass
...
>>> X = Sub()
TypeError: Can't instantiate abstract class Sub with abstract methods action

>>> class Sub(Super):
...     def action(self): print('spam')
...
>>> X = Sub()
>>> X.delegate()
spam
```

Coded this way, a class with an abstract method cannot be instantiated (that is, we cannot create an instance by calling it) unless all of its abstract methods have been defined in subclasses. Although this requires more code, the advantage of this approach is that errors for missing methods are issued when we attempt to make an instance of the class, not later when we try to call a missing method. This feature may also be used to define an expected interface, automatically verified in client classes.

Unfortunately, this scheme also relies on two advanced language tools we have not met yet—*function decorators*, introduced in Chapter 31 and covered in depth in Chapter 38, as well as *metaclass declarations*, mentioned in Chapter 31 and covered in Chapter 39—so we will finesse other facets of this option here. See Python's standard manuals for more on this, as well as precoded abstract superclasses Python provides.

Namespaces: The Whole Story

Now that we've examined class and instance objects, the Python namespace story is complete. For reference, I'll quickly summarize all the rules used to resolve names here. The first things you need to remember are that qualified and unqualified names are treated differently, and that some scopes serve to initialize object namespaces:

- Unqualified names (e.g., X) deal with scopes.
- Qualified attribute names (e.g., *object*.X) use object namespaces.
- Some scopes initialize object namespaces (for modules and classes).

Simple Names: Global Unless Assigned

Unqualified simple names follow the LEGB lexical scoping rule outlined for functions in Chapter 17:

Assignment (X = value)
> Makes names local: creates or changes the name X in the current local scope, unless declared global.

Reference (X)
> Looks for the name X in the current local scope, then any and all enclosing functions, then the current global scope, then the built-in scope.

Attribute Names: Object Namespaces

Qualified attribute names refer to attributes of specific objects and obey the rules for modules and classes. For class and instance objects, the reference rules are augmented to include the inheritance search procedure:

Assignment (object.X = value)

> Creates or alters the attribute name X in the namespace of the *object* being quali-fied, and none other. Inheritance-tree climbing happens only on attribute refer-ence, not on attribute assignment.

Reference (object.X)

> For class-based objects, searches for the attribute name X in *object*, then in all accessible classes above it, using the inheritance search procedure. For nonclass objects such as modules, fetches X from *object* directly.

The "Zen" of Python Namespaces: Assignments Classify Names

With distinct search procedures for qualified and unqualified names, and multiple lookup layers for both, it can sometimes be difficult to tell where a name will wind up going. In Python, the place where you *assign* a name is crucial—it fully determines the scope or object in which a name will reside. The file *manynames.py* illustrates how this principle translates to code and summarizes the namespace ideas we have seen through-out this book:

```
# manynames.py

X = 11                              # Global (module) name/attribute (X, or manynames.X)

def f():
    print(X)                        # Access global X (11)

def g():
    X = 22                          # Local (function) variable (X, hides module X)
    print(X)

class C:
    X = 33                          # Class attribute (C.X)
    def m(self):
        X = 44                      # Local variable in method (X)
        self.X = 55                 # Instance attribute (instance.X)
```

This file assigns the same name, X, five times. Because this name is assigned in five different locations, though, all five Xs in this program are completely different variables. From top to bottom, the assignments to X here generate: a module attribute (**11**), a local variable in a function (**22**), a class attribute (**33**), a local variable in a method (**44**), and an instance attribute (**55**). Although all five are named X, the fact that they are all as-signed at different places in the source code or to different objects makes all of these unique variables.

You should take the time to study this example carefully because it collects ideas we've been exploring throughout the last few parts of this book. When it makes sense to you, you will have achieved a sort of Python namespace nirvana. Of course, an alternative route to nirvana is to simply run the program and see what happens. Here's the re-mainder of this source file, which makes an instance and prints all the Xs that it can fetch:

```
# manynames.py, continued

if __name__ == '__main__':
    print(X)                    # 11: module (a.k.a. manynames.X outside file)
    f()                         # 11: global
    g()                         # 22: local
    print(X)                    # 11: module name unchanged

    obj = C()                   # Make instance
    print(obj.X)                # 33: class name inherited by instance

    obj.m()                     # Attach attribute name X to instance now
    print(obj.X)                # 55: instance
    print(C.X)                  # 33: class (a.k.a. obj.X if no X in instance)

    #print(C.m.X)               # FAILS: only visible in method
    #print(g.X)                 # FAILS: only visible in function
```

The outputs that are printed when the file is run are noted in the comments in the code; trace through them to see which variable named X is being accessed each time. Notice in particular that we can go through the class to fetch its attribute (C.X), but we can never fetch local variables in functions or methods from outside their def statements. Locals are visible only to other code within the def, and in fact only live in memory while a call to the function or method is executing.

Some of the names defined by this file are visible *outside the file* to other modules, but recall that we must always import before we can access names in another file—that is the main point of modules, after all:

```
# otherfile.py

import manynames

X = 66
print(X)                        # 66: the global here
print(manynames.X)              # 11: globals become attributes after imports

manynames.f()                   # 11: manynames's X, not the one here!
manynames.g()                   # 22: local in other file's function

print(manynames.C.X)            # 33: attribute of class in other module
I = manynames.C()
print(I.X)                      # 33: still from class here
I.m()
print(I.X)                      # 55: now from instance!
```

Notice here how manynames.f() prints the X in manynames, not the X assigned in this file—scopes are always determined by the position of assignments in your source code (i.e., lexically) and are never influenced by what imports what or who imports whom. Also, notice that the instance's own X is not created until we call I.m()—attributes, like all variables, spring into existence when assigned, and not before. Normally we create instance attributes by assigning them in class __init__ constructor methods, but this isn't the only option.

Finally, as we learned in Chapter 17, it's also possible for a function to *change* names outside itself, with `global` and (in Python 3.0) `nonlocal` statements—these statements provide write access, but also modify assignment's namespace binding rules:

```
X = 11                      # Global in module

def g1():
    print(X)                # Reference global in module

def g2():
    global X
    X = 22                  # Change global in module

def h1():
    X = 33                  # Local in function
    def nested():
        print(X)            # Reference local in enclosing scope

def h2():
    X = 33                  # Local in function
    def nested():
        nonlocal X          # Python 3.0 statement
        X = 44              # Change local in enclosing scope
```

Of course, you generally shouldn't use the same name for every variable in your script—but as this example demonstrates, even if you do, Python's namespaces will work to keep names used in one context from accidentally clashing with those used in another.

Namespace Dictionaries

In Chapter 22, we learned that module namespaces are actually implemented as dictionaries and exposed with the built-in __dict__ attribute. The same holds for class and instance objects: attribute qualification is really a dictionary indexing operation internally, and attribute inheritance is just a matter of searching linked dictionaries. In fact, instance and class objects are mostly just dictionaries with links inside Python. Python exposes these dictionaries, as well as the links between them, for use in advanced roles (e.g., for coding tools).

To help you understand how attributes work internally, let's work through an interactive session that traces the way namespace dictionaries grow when classes are involved. We saw a simpler version of this type of code in Chapter 26, but now that we know more about methods and superclasses, let's embellish it here. First, let's define a superclass and a subclass with methods that will store data in their instances:

```
>>> class super:
...     def hello(self):
...         self.data1 = 'spam'
...
>>> class sub(super):
...     def hola(self):
```

```
...        self.data2 = 'eggs'
...
```

When we make an instance of the subclass, the instance starts out with an empty
namespace dictionary, but it has links back to the class for the inheritance search to
follow. In fact, the inheritance tree is explicitly available in special attributes, which
you can inspect. Instances have a __class__ attribute that links to their class, and classes
have a __bases__ attribute that is a tuple containing links to higher superclasses (I'm
running this on Python 3.0; name formats and some internal attributes vary slightly in
2.6):

```
>>> X = sub()
>>> X.__dict__              # Instance namespace dict
{}

>>> X.__class__            # Class of instance
<class '__main__.sub'>

>>> sub.__bases__          # Superclasses of class
(<class '__main__.super'>,)

>>> super.__bases__        # () empty tuple in Python 2.6
(<class 'object'>,)
```

As classes assign to self attributes, they populate the instance objects—that is, attributes wind up in the instances' attribute namespace dictionaries, not in the classes'.
An instance object's namespace records data that can vary from instance to instance,
and self is a hook into that namespace:

```
>>> Y = sub()

>>> X.hello()
>>> X.__dict__
{'data1': 'spam'}

>>> X.hola()
>>> X.__dict__
{'data1': 'spam', 'data2': 'eggs'}

>>> sub.__dict__.keys()
['__module__', '__doc__', 'hola']

>>> super.__dict__.keys()
['__dict__', '__module__', '__weakref__', 'hello', '__doc__']

>>> Y.__dict__
{}
```

Notice the extra underscore names in the class dictionaries; Python sets these automatically. Most are not used in typical programs, but there are tools that use some of
them (e.g., __doc__ holds the docstrings discussed in Chapter 15).

Also, observe that Y, a second instance made at the start of this series, still has an empty namespace dictionary at the end, even though X's dictionary has been populated by assignments in methods. Again, each instance has an independent namespace dictionary, which starts out empty and can record completely different attributes than those recorded by the namespace dictionaries of other instances of the same class.

Because attributes are actually dictionary keys inside Python, there are really two ways to fetch and assign their values—by qualification, or by key indexing:

```
>>> X.data1, X.__dict__['data1']
('spam', 'spam')

>>> X.data3 = 'toast'
>>> X.__dict__
{'data1': 'spam', 'data3': 'toast', 'data2': 'eggs'}

>>> X.__dict__['data3'] = 'ham'
>>> X.data3
'ham'
```

This equivalence applies only to attributes actually attached to the instance, though. Because attribute fetch qualification also performs an inheritance search, it can access attributes that namespace dictionary indexing cannot. The inherited attribute X.hello, for instance, cannot be accessed by X.__dict__['hello'].

Finally, here is the built-in dir function we met in Chapters 4 and 15 at work on class and instance objects. This function works on anything with attributes: dir(*object*) is similar to an *object.*__dict__.keys() call. Notice, though, that dir sorts its list and includes some system attributes. As of Python 2.2, dir also collects inherited attributes automatically, and in 3.0 it includes names inherited from the object class that is an implied superclass of all classes:[||]

```
>>> X.__dict__, Y.__dict__
({'data1': 'spam', 'data3': 'ham', 'data2': 'eggs'}, {})
>>> list(X.__dict__.keys())                    # Need list in 3.0
['data1', 'data3', 'data2']

# In Python 2.6:

>>>> dir(X)
['__doc__', '__module__', 'data1', 'data2', 'data3', 'hello', 'hola']
>>> dir(sub)
['__doc__', '__module__', 'hello', 'hola']
>>> dir(super)
['__doc__', '__module__', 'hello']
```

[||] As you can see, the contents of attribute dictionaries and dir call results may change over time. For example, because Python now allows built-in types to be subclassed like classes, the contents of dir results for built-in types have expanded to include operator overloading methods, just like our dir results here for user-defined classes under Python 3.0. In general, attribute names with leading and trailing double underscores are interpreter-specific. Type subclasses will be discussed further in Chapter 31.

```
# In Python 3.0:

>>> dir(X)
['__class__', '__delattr__', '__dict__', '__doc__', '__eq__', '__format__',
...more omitted...
'data1', 'data2', 'data3', 'hello', 'hola']

>>> dir(sub)
['__class__', '__delattr__', '__dict__', '__doc__', '__eq__', '__format__',
...more omitted...
'hello', 'hola']

>>> dir(super)
['__class__', '__delattr__', '__dict__', '__doc__', '__eq__', '__format__',
...more omitted...
'hello'
]
```

Experiment with these special attributes on your own to get a better feel for how namespaces actually do their attribute business. Even if you will never use these in the kinds of programs you write, seeing that they are just normal dictionaries will help demystify the notion of namespaces in general.

Namespace Links

The prior section introduced the special __class__ and __bases__ instance and class attributes, without really explaining why you might care about them. In short, these attributes allow you to inspect inheritance hierarchies within your own code. For example, they can be used to display a class tree, as in the following example:

```
# classtree.py

"""
Climb inheritance trees using namespace links,
displaying higher superclasses with indentation
"""

def classtree(cls, indent):
    print('.' * indent + cls.__name__)       # Print class name here
    for supercls in cls.__bases__:           # Recur to all superclasses
        classtree(supercls, indent+3)        # May visit super > once

def instancetree(inst):
    print('Tree of %s' % inst)               # Show instance
    classtree(inst.__class__, 3)             # Climb to its class

def selftest():
    class A:        pass
    class B(A):     pass
    class C(A):     pass
    class D(B,C):   pass
    class E:        pass
    class F(D,E):   pass
```

```
    instancetree(B())
    instancetree(F())

if __name__ == '__main__': selftest()
```

The `classtree` function in this script is *recursive*—it prints a class's name using `__name__`, then climbs up to the superclasses by calling itself. This allows the function to traverse arbitrarily shaped class trees; the recursion climbs to the top, and stops at root superclasses that have empty `__bases__` attributes. When using recursion, each active level of a function gets its own copy of the local scope; here, this means that `cls` and `indent` are different at each `classtree` level.

Most of this file is self-test code. When run standalone in Python 3.0, it builds an empty class tree, makes two instances from it, and prints their class tree structures:

```
C:\misc> c:\python26\python classtree.py
Tree of <__main__.B instance at 0x02557328>
...B
......A
Tree of <__main__.F instance at 0x02557328>
...F
......D
.........B
............A
.........C
............A
......E
```

When run under Python 3.0, the tree includes the implied `object` superclasses that are automatically added above standalone classes, because all classes are "new style" in 3.0 (more on this change in Chapter 31):

```
C:\misc> c:\python30\python classtree.py
Tree of <__main__.B object at 0x02810650>
...B
......A
.........object
Tree of <__main__.F object at 0x02810650>
...F
......D
.........B
............A
...............object
.........C
............A
...............object
......E
.........object
```

Here, indentation marked by periods is used to denote class tree height. Of course, we could improve on this output format, and perhaps even sketch it in a GUI display. Even as is, though, we can import these functions anywhere we want a quick class tree display:

```
C:\misc> c:\python30\python
>>> class Emp: pass
...
>>> class Person(Emp): pass
>>> bob = Person()

>>> import classtree
>>> classtree.instancetree(bob)
Tree of <__main__.Person object at 0x028203B0>
...Person
......Emp
.........object
```

Regardless of whether you will ever code or use such tools, this example demonstrates one of the many ways that you can make use of special attributes that expose interpreter internals. You'll see another when we code the *lister.py* general-purpose class display tools in the section "Multiple Inheritance: "Mix-in" Classes" on page 758—there, we will extend this technique to also display attributes in each object in a class tree. And in the last part of this book, we'll revisit such tools in the context of Python tool building at large, to code tools that implement attribute privacy, argument validation, and more. While not for every Python programmer, access to internals enables powerful development tools.

Documentation Strings Revisited

The last section's example includes a docstring for its module, but remember that docstrings can be used for class components as well. Docstrings, which we covered in detail in Chapter 15, are string literals that show up at the top of various structures and are automatically saved by Python in the corresponding objects' __doc__ attributes. This works for module files, function defs, and classes and methods.

Now that we know more about classes and methods, the following file, *docstr.py*, provides a quick but comprehensive example that summarizes the places where docstrings can show up in your code. All of these can be triple-quoted blocks:

```
"I am: docstr.__doc__"

def func(args):
    "I am: docstr.func.__doc__"
    pass

class spam:
    "I am: spam.__doc__ or docstr.spam.__doc__"
    def method(self, arg):
        "I am: spam.method.__doc__ or self.method.__doc__"
        pass
```

The main advantage of documentation strings is that they stick around at runtime. Thus, if it's been coded as a docstring, you can qualify an object with its __doc__ attribute to fetch its documentation:

```
>>> import docstr
>>> docstr.__doc__
'I am: docstr.__doc__'

>>> docstr.func.__doc__
'I am: docstr.func.__doc__'

>>> docstr.spam.__doc__
'I am: spam.__doc__ or docstr.spam.__doc__'

>>> docstr.spam.method.__doc__
'I am: spam.method.__doc__ or self.method.__doc__'
```

A discussion of the *PyDoc* tool, which knows how to format all these strings in reports, appears in Chapter 15. Here it is running on our code under Python 2.6 (Python 3.0 shows additional attributes inherited from the implied object superclass in the new-style class model—run this on your own to see the 3.0 extras, and watch for more about this difference in Chapter 31):

```
>>> help(docstr)
Help on module docstr:

NAME
    docstr - I am: docstr.__doc__

FILE
    c:\misc\docstr.py

CLASSES
    spam

    class spam
     |  I am: spam.__doc__ or docstr.spam.__doc__
     |
     |  Methods defined here:
     |
     |  method(self, arg)
     |      I am: spam.method.__doc__ or self.method.__doc__

FUNCTIONS
    func(args)
        I am: docstr.func.__doc__
```

Documentation strings are available at runtime, but they are less flexible syntactically than # comments (which can appear anywhere in a program). Both forms are useful tools, and any program documentation is good (as long as it's accurate, of course!). As a best-practice rule of thumb, use docstrings for functional documentation (what your objects do) and hash-mark comments for more micro-level documentation (how arcane expressions work).

Classes Versus Modules

Let's wrap up this chapter by briefly comparing the topics of this book's last two parts: modules and classes. Because they're both about namespaces, the distinction can be confusing. In short:

- Modules
  - — Are data/logic packages
  - — Are created by writing Python files or C extensions
  - — Are used by being imported
- Classes
  - — Implement new objects
  - — Are created by `class` statements
  - — Are used by being called
  - — Always live within a module

Classes also support extra features that modules don't, such as operator overloading, multiple instance generation, and inheritance. Although both classes and modules are namespaces, you should be able to tell by now that they are very different things.

Chapter Summary

This chapter took us on a second, more in-depth tour of the OOP mechanisms of the Python language. We learned more about classes, methods, and inheritance, and we wrapped up the namespace story in Python by extending it to cover its application to classes. Along the way, we looked at some more advanced concepts, such as abstract superclasses, class data attributes, namespace dictionaries and links, and manual calls to superclass methods and constructors.

Now that we've learned all about the mechanics of coding classes in Python, Chapter 29 turns to a specific facet of those mechanics: operator overloading. After that we'll explore common design patterns, looking at some of the ways that classes are commonly used and combined to optimize code reuse. Before you read ahead, though, be sure to work though the usual chapter quiz to review what we've covered here.

Test Your Knowledge: Quiz

1. What is an abstract superclass?
2. What happens when a simple assignment statement appears at the top level of a `class` statement?

3. Why might a class need to manually call the __init__ method in a superclass?

4. How can you augment, instead of completely replacing, an inherited method?

5. What...was the capital of Assyria?

Test Your Knowledge: Answers

1. An abstract superclass is a class that calls a method, but does not inherit or define it—it expects the method to be filled in by a subclass. This is often used as a way to generalize classes when behavior cannot be predicted until a more specific subclass is coded. OOP frameworks also use this as a way to dispatch to client-defined, customizable operations.

2. When a simple assignment statement (X = Y) appears at the top level of a `class` statement, it attaches a data attribute to the class (*Class*.X). Like all class attributes, this will be shared by all instances; data attributes are not callable method functions, though.

3. A class must manually call the __init__ method in a superclass if it defines an __init__ constructor of its own and still wants the superclass's construction code to run. Python itself automatically runs just one constructor—the lowest one in the tree. Superclass constructors are called through the class name, passing in the `self` instance manually: *Superclass*.__init__(`self`, ...).

4. To augment instead of completely replacing an inherited method, redefine it in a subclass, but call back to the superclass's version of the method manually from the new version of the method in the subclass. That is, pass the `self` instance to the superclass's version of the method manually: *Superclass*.*method*(`self`, ...).

5. Ashur (or Qalat Sherqat), Calah (or Nimrud), the short-lived Dur Sharrukin (or Khorsabad), and finally Nineveh.

## CHAPTER 29

Operator Overloading

This chapter continues our in-depth survey of class mechanics by focusing on operator overloading. We looked briefly at operator overloading in prior chapters; here, we'll fill in more details and look at a handful of commonly used overloading methods. Although we won't demonstrate each of the many operator overloading methods available, those we will code here are a representative sample large enough to uncover the possibilities of this Python class feature.

The Basics

Really "operator overloading" simply means *intercepting* built-in operations in class methods—Python automatically invokes your methods when instances of the class appear in built-in operations, and your method's return value becomes the result of the corresponding operation. Here's a review of the key ideas behind overloading:

- Operator overloading lets classes intercept normal Python operations.
- Classes can overload all Python expression operators.
- Classes can also overload built-in operations such as printing, function calls, attribute access, etc.
- Overloading makes class instances act more like built-in types.
- Overloading is implemented by providing specially named class methods.

In other words, when certain specially named methods are provided in a class, Python automatically calls them when instances of the class appear in their associated expressions. As we've learned, operator overloading methods are never required and generally don't have defaults; if you don't code or inherit one, it just means that your class does not support the corresponding operation. When used, though, these methods allow classes to emulate the interfaces of built-in objects, and so appear more consistent.

Constructors and Expressions: __init__ and __sub__

Consider the following simple example: its Number class, coded in the file *number.py*, provides a method to intercept instance construction (__init__), as well as one for catching subtraction expressions (__sub__). Special methods such as these are the hooks that let you tie into built-in operations:

```
class Number:
    def __init__(self, start):        # On Number(start)
        self.data = start
    def __sub__(self, other):         # On instance - other
        return Number(self.data - other)    # Result is a new instance

>>> from number import Number         # Fetch class from module
>>> X = Number(5)                     # Number.__init__(X, 5)
>>> Y = X - 2                         # Number.__sub__(X, 2)
>>> Y.data                            # Y is new Number instance
3
```

As discussed previously, the __init__ constructor method seen in this code is the most commonly used operator overloading method in Python; it's present in most classes. In this chapter, we will tour some of the other tools available in this domain and look at example code that applies them in common use cases.

Common Operator Overloading Methods

Just about everything you can do to built-in objects such as integers and lists has a corresponding specially named method for overloading in classes. Table 29-1 lists a few of the most common; there are many more. In fact, many overloading methods come in multiple versions (e.g., __add__, __radd__, and __iadd__ for addition), which is one reason there are so many. See other Python books, or the Python language reference manual, for an exhaustive list of the special method names available.

Table 29-1. Common operator overloading methods

Method	Implements	Called for
__init__	Constructor	Object creation: X = Class(args)
__del__	Destructor	Object reclamation of X
__add__	Operator +	X + Y, X += Y if no __iadd__
__or__	Operator | (bitwise OR)	X | Y, X |= Y if no __ior__
__repr__, __str__	Printing, conversions	print(X), repr(X), str(X)
__call__	Function calls	X(*args, **kargs)
__getattr__	Attribute fetch	X.undefined
__setattr__	Attribute assignment	X.any = value
__delattr__	Attribute deletion	del X.any
__getattribute__	Attribute fetch	X.any

Method	Implements	Called for
__getitem__	Indexing, slicing, iteration	`X[key]`, `X[i:j]`, for loops and other iterations if no `__iter__`
__setitem__	Index and slice assignment	`X[key]` = value, `X[i:j]` = sequence
__delitem__	Index and slice deletion	`del X[key]`, `del X[i:j]`
__len__	Length	`len(X)`, truth tests if no `__bool__`
__bool__	Boolean tests	`bool(X)`, truth tests (named `__nonzero__` in 2.6)
__lt__, __gt__, __le__, __ge__, __eq__, __ne__	Comparisons	`X < Y, X > Y, X <= Y, X >= Y, X == Y, X != Y` (or else `__cmp__` in 2.6 only)
__radd__	Right-side operators	`Other + X`
__iadd__	In-place augmented operators	`X += Y` (or else `__add__`)
__iter__, __next__	Iteration contexts	`I=iter(X)`, `next(I)`; for loops, in if no `__contains__`, all comprehensions, `map(F,X)`, others (`__next__` is named next in 2.6)
__contains__	Membership test	`item in X` (any iterable)
__index__	Integer value	`hex(X)`, `bin(X)`, `oct(X)`, `O[X]`, `O[X:]` (replaces Python 2 `__oct__`, `__hex__`)
__enter__, __exit__	Context manager (Chapter 33)	`with obj as var:`
__get__, __set__, __delete__	Descriptor attributes (Chapter 37)	`X.attr`, `X.attr = value`, `del X.attr`
__new__	Creation (Chapter 39)	Object creation, before `__init__`

All overloading methods have names that start and end with two underscores to keep them distinct from other names you define in your classes. The mappings from special method names to expressions or operations are predefined by the Python language (and documented in the standard language manual). For example, the name __add__ always maps to + expressions by Python language definition, regardless of what an __add__ method's code actually does.

Operator overloading methods may be inherited from superclasses if not defined, just like any other methods. Operator overloading methods are also all optional—if you don't code or inherit one, that operation is simply unsupported by your class, and attempting it will raise an exception. Some built-in operations, like printing, have defaults (inherited for the implied object class in Python 3.0), but most built-ins fail for class instances if no corresponding operator overloading method is present.

Most overloading methods are used only in advanced programs that require objects to behave like built-ins; the __init__ constructor tends to appear in most classes, however, so pay special attention to it. We've already met the __init__ initialization-time constructor method, and a few of the others in Table 29-1. Let's explore some of the additional methods in the table by example.

Indexing and Slicing: __getitem__ and __setitem__

If defined in a class (or inherited by it), the __getitem__ method is called automatically for instance-indexing operations. When an instance X appears in an indexing expression like X[i], Python calls the __getitem__ method inherited by the instance, passing X to the first argument and the index in brackets to the second argument. For example, the following class returns the square of an index value:

```
>>> class Indexer:
...     def __getitem__(self, index):
...         return index ** 2
...
>>> X = Indexer()
>>> X[2]                              # X[i] calls X.__getitem__(i)
4

>>> for i in range(5):
...     print(X[i], end=' ')         # Runs __getitem__(X, i) each time
...
0 1 4 9 16
```

Intercepting Slices

Interestingly, in addition to indexing, __getitem__ is also called for *slice expressions*. Formally speaking, built-in types handle slicing the same way. Here, for example, is slicing at work on a built-in list, using upper and lower bounds and a stride (see Chapter 7 if you need a refresher on slicing):

```
>>> L = [5, 6, 7, 8, 9]
>>> L[2:4]                           # Slice with slice syntax
[7, 8]
>>> L[1:]
[6, 7, 8, 9]
>>> L[:-1]
[5, 6, 7, 8]
>>> L[::2]
[5, 7, 9]
```

Really, though, slicing bounds are bundled up into a *slice object* and passed to the list's implementation of indexing. In fact, you can always pass a slice object manually—slice syntax is mostly syntactic sugar for indexing with a slice object:

```
>>> L[slice(2, 4)]                   # Slice with slice objects
[7, 8]
>>> L[slice(1, None)]
[6, 7, 8, 9]
>>> L[slice(None, -1)]
[5, 6, 7, 8]
>>> L[slice(None, None, 2)]
[5, 7, 9]
```

This matters in classes with a __getitem__ method—the method will be called both for basic indexing (with an index) and for slicing (with a slice object). Our previous class won't handle slicing because its math assumes integer indexes are passed, but the following class will. When called for indexing, the argument is an integer as before:

```
>>> class Indexer:
...     data = [5, 6, 7, 8, 9]
...     def __getitem__(self, index):      # Called for index or slice
...         print('getitem:', index)
...         return self.data[index]         # Perform index or slice
...
>>> X = Indexer()
>>> X[0]                                     # Indexing sends __getitem__ an integer
getitem: 0
5
>>> X[1]
getitem: 1
6
>>> X[-1]
getitem: -1
9
```

When called for slicing, though, the method receives a slice object, which is simply passed along to the embedded list indexer in a new index expression:

```
>>> X[2:4]                                   # Slicing sends __getitem__ a slice object
getitem: slice(2, 4, None)
[7, 8]
>>> X[1:]
getitem: slice(1, None, None)
[6, 7, 8, 9]
>>> X[:-1]
getitem: slice(None, -1, None)
[5, 6, 7, 8]
>>> X[::2]
getitem: slice(None, None, 2)
[5, 7, 9]
```

If used, the __setitem__ index assignment method similarly intercepts both index and slice assignments—it receives a slice object for the latter, which may be passed along in another index assignment in the same way:

```
def __setitem__(self, index, value):        # Intercept index or slice assignment
    ...
    self.data[index] = value                 # Assign index or slice
```

In fact, __getitem__ may be called automatically in even more contexts than indexing and slicing, as the next section explains.

Slicing and Indexing in Python 2.6

Prior to Python 3.0, classes could also define __getslice__ and __setslice__ methods to intercept slice fetches and assignments specifically; they were passed the bounds of the slice expression and were preferred over __getitem__ and __setitem__ for slices.

These slice-specific methods have been removed in 3.0, so you should use __getitem__ and __setitem__ instead and allow for both indexes and slice objects as arguments. In most classes, this works without any special code, because indexing methods can manually pass along the slice object in the square brackets of another index expression (as in our example). See the section "Membership: __contains__, __iter__, and __getitem__" on page 718 for another example of slice interception at work.

Also, don't confuse the (arguably unfortunately named) __index__ method in Python 3.0 for index interception; this method returns an integer value for an instance when needed and is used by built-ins that convert to digit strings:

```
>>> class C:
...     def __index__(self):
...         return 255
...
>>> X = C()
>>> hex(X)              # Integer value
'0xff'
>>> bin(X)
'0b11111111'
>>> oct(X)
'0o377'
```

Although this method does not intercept instance indexing like __getitem__, it is also used in contexts that require an integer—including indexing:

```
>>> ('C' * 256)[255]
'C'
>>> ('C' * 256)[X]        # As index (not X[i])
'C'
>>> ('C' * 256)[X:]       # As index (not X[i:])
'C'
```

This method works the same way in Python 2.6, except that it is not called for the hex and oct built-in functions (use __hex__ and __oct__ in 2.6 instead to intercept these calls).

Index Iteration: __getitem__

Here's a trick that isn't always obvious to beginners, but turns out to be surprisingly useful. The for statement works by repeatedly indexing a sequence from zero to higher indexes, until an out-of-bounds exception is detected. Because of that, __getitem__ also turns out to be one way to overload iteration in Python—if this method is defined, for loops call the class's __getitem__ each time through, with successively higher offsets. It's a case of "buy one, get one free"—any built-in or user-defined object that responds to indexing also responds to iteration:

```
>>> class stepper:
...     def __getitem__(self, i):
...         return self.data[i]
...
```

```
>>> X = stepper()                   # X is a stepper object
>>> X.data = "Spam"
>>>
>>> X[1]                            # Indexing calls __getitem__
'p'
>>> for item in X:                  # for loops call __getitem__
...     print(item, end=' ')        # for indexes items 0..N
...
S p a m
```

In fact, it's really a case of "buy one, get a bunch free." Any class that supports for loops automatically supports all iteration contexts in Python, many of which we've seen in earlier chapters (iteration contexts were presented in Chapter 14). For example, the in membership test, list comprehensions, the map built-in, list and tuple assignments, and type constructors will also call __getitem__ automatically, if it's defined:

```
>>> 'p' in X                        # All call __getitem__ too
True

>>> [c for c in X]                  # List comprehension
['S', 'p', 'a', 'm']

>>> list(map(str.upper, X))         # map calls (use list() in 3.0)
['S', 'P', 'A', 'M']

>>> (a, b, c, d) = X                # Sequence assignments
>>> a, c, d
('S', 'a', 'm')

>>> list(X), tuple(X), ''.join(X)
(['S', 'p', 'a', 'm'], ('S', 'p', 'a', 'm'), 'Spam')

>>> X
<__main__.stepper object at 0x00A8D5D0>
```

In practice, this technique can be used to create objects that provide a sequence interface and to add logic to built-in sequence type operations; we'll revisit this idea when extending built-in types in Chapter 31.

Iterator Objects: __iter__ and __next__

Although the __getitem__ technique of the prior section works, it's really just a fallback for iteration. Today, all iteration contexts in Python will try the __iter__ method first, before trying __getitem__. That is, they prefer the iteration protocol we learned about in Chapter 14 to repeatedly indexing an object; only if the object does not support the iteration protocol is indexing attempted instead. Generally speaking, you should prefer __iter__ too—it supports general iteration contexts better than __getitem__ can.

Technically, iteration contexts work by calling the iter built-in function to try to find an __iter__ method, which is expected to return an iterator object. If it's provided, Python then repeatedly calls this iterator object's __next__ method to produce items until a `StopIteration` exception is raised. If no such `__iter__` method is found, Python falls back on the `__getitem__` scheme and repeatedly indexes by offsets as before, until an `IndexError` exception is raised. A `next` built-in function is also available as a convenience for manual iterations: `next(I)` is the same as `I.__next__()`.

 Version skew note: As described in Chapter 14, if you are using Python 2.6, the `I.__next__()` method just described is named `I.next()` in your Python, and the `next(I)` built-in is present for portability: it calls `I.next()` in 2.6 and `I.__next__()` in 3.0. Iteration works the same in 2.6 in all other respects.

User-Defined Iterators

In the `__iter__` scheme, classes implement user-defined iterators by simply implementing the iteration protocol introduced in Chapters 14 and 20 (refer back to those chapters for more background details on iterators). For example, the following file, *iters.py*, defines a user-defined iterator class that generates squares:

```python
class Squares:
    def __init__(self, start, stop):      # Save state when created
        self.value = start - 1
        self.stop  = stop
    def __iter__(self):                    # Get iterator object on iter
        return self
    def __next__(self):                    # Return a square on each iteration
        if self.value == self.stop:        # Also called by next built-in
            raise StopIteration
        self.value += 1
        return self.value ** 2

% python
>>> from iters import Squares
>>> for i in Squares(1, 5):               # for calls iter, which calls __iter__
...     print(i, end=' ')                 # Each iteration calls __next__
...
1 4 9 16 25
```

Here, the iterator object is simply the instance `self`, because the `__next__` method is part of this class. In more complex scenarios, the iterator object may be defined as a separate class and object with its own state information to support multiple active iterations over the same data (we'll see an example of this in a moment). The end of the iteration is signaled with a Python `raise` statement (more on raising exceptions in the next part of this book). Manual iterations work as for built-in types as well:

```python
>>> X = Squares(1, 5)                      # Iterate manually: what loops do
>>> I = iter(X)                            # iter calls __iter__
>>> next(I)                                # next calls __next__
1
>>> next(I)
4
```

```
...more omitted...
>>> next(I)
25
>>> next(I)                            # Can catch this in try statement
StopIteration
```

An equivalent coding of this iterator with __getitem__ might be less natural, because the for would then iterate through all offsets zero and higher; the offsets passed in would be only indirectly related to the range of values produced (0..N would need to map to start..stop). Because __iter__ objects retain explicitly managed state between next calls, they can be more general than __getitem__.

On the other hand, using iterators based on __iter__ can sometimes be more complex and less convenient than using __getitem__. They are really designed for iteration, not random indexing—in fact, they don't overload the indexing expression at all:

```
>>> X = Squares(1, 5)
>>> X[1]
AttributeError: Squares instance has no attribute '__getitem__'
```

The __iter__ scheme is also the implementation for all the other iteration contexts we saw in action for __getitem__ (membership tests, type constructors, sequence assignment, and so on). However, unlike our prior __getitem__ example, we also need to be aware that a class's __iter__ may be designed for a single traversal, not many. For example, the Squares class is a one-shot iteration; once you've iterated over an instance of that class, it's empty. You need to make a new iterator object for each new iteration:

```
>>> X = Squares(1, 5)
>>> [n for n in X]                     # Exhausts items
[1, 4, 9, 16, 25]
>>> [n for n in X]                     # Now it's empty
[]
>>> [n for n in Squares(1, 5)]         # Make a new iterator object
[1, 4, 9, 16, 25]
>>> list(Squares(1, 3))
[1, 4, 9]
```

Notice that this example would probably be simpler if it were coded with generator functions or expressions (topics introduced in Chapter 20 and related to iterators):

```
>>> def gsquares(start, stop):
...     for i in range(start, stop+1):
...         yield i ** 2
...
>>> for i in gsquares(1, 5):           # or: (x ** 2 for x in range(1, 5))
...     print(i, end=' ')
...
1 4 9 16 25
```

Unlike the class, the function automatically saves its state between iterations. Of course, for this artificial example, you could in fact skip both techniques and simply use a for loop, map, or a list comprehension to build the list all at once. The best and fastest way to accomplish a task in Python is often also the simplest:

```
>>> [x ** 2 for x in range(1, 6)]
[1, 4, 9, 16, 25]
```

However, classes may be better at modeling more complex iterations, especially when they can benefit from state information and inheritance hierarchies. The next section explores one such use case.

Multiple Iterators on One Object

Earlier, I mentioned that the iterator object may be defined as a separate class with its own state information to support multiple active iterations over the same data. Consider what happens when we step across a built-in type like a string:

```
>>> S = 'ace'
>>> for x in S:
...     for y in S:
...         print(x + y, end=' ')
...
aa ac ae ca cc ce ea ec ee
```

Here, the outer loop grabs an iterator from the string by calling iter, and each nested loop does the same to get an independent iterator. Because each active iterator has its own state information, each loop can maintain its own position in the string, regardless of any other active loops.

We saw related examples earlier, in Chapters 14 and 20. For instance, generator functions and expressions, as well as built-ins like map and zip, proved to be single-iterator objects; by contrast, the range built-in and other built-in types, like lists, support multiple active iterators with independent positions.

When we code user-defined iterators with classes, it's up to us to decide whether we will support a single active iteration or many. To achieve the multiple-iterator effect, __iter__ simply needs to define a new stateful object for the iterator, instead of returning self.

The following, for example, defines an iterator class that skips every other item on iterations. Because the iterator object is created anew for each iteration, it supports multiple active loops:

```
class SkipIterator:
    def __init__(self, wrapped):
        self.wrapped = wrapped          # Iterator state information
        self.offset  = 0
    def __next__(self):
        if self.offset >= len(self.wrapped):    # Terminate iterations
            raise StopIteration
        else:
            item = self.wrapped[self.offset]    # else return and skip
            self.offset += 2
            return item

class SkipObject:
```

```
          def __init__(self, wrapped):          # Save item to be used
              self.wrapped = wrapped
          def __iter__(self):
              return SkipIterator(self.wrapped)   # New iterator each time

  if __name__ == '__main__':
      alpha = 'abcdef'
      skipper = SkipObject(alpha)               # Make container object
      I = iter(skipper)                         # Make an iterator on it
      print(next(I), next(I), next(I))          # Visit offsets 0, 2, 4

      for x in skipper:             # for calls __iter__ automatically
          for y in skipper:         # Nested fors call __iter__ again each time
              print(x + y, end=' ') # Each iterator has its own state, offset
```

When run, this example works like the nested loops with built-in strings. Each active loop has its own position in the string because each obtains an independent iterator object that records its own state information:

```
% python skipper.py
a c e
aa ac ae ca cc ce ea ec ee
```

By contrast, our earlier `Squares` example supports just one active iteration, unless we call `Squares` again in nested loops to obtain new objects. Here, there is just one `SkipObject`, with multiple iterator objects created from it.

As before, we could achieve similar results with built-in tools—for example, slicing with a third bound to skip items:

```
>>> S = 'abcdef'
>>> for x in S[::2]:
...     for y in S[::2]:          # New objects on each iteration
...         print(x + y, end=' ')
...
aa ac ae ca cc ce ea ec ee
```

This isn't quite the same, though, for two reasons. First, each slice expression here will physically store the result list all at once in memory; iterators, on the other hand, produce just one value at a time, which can save substantial space for large result lists. Second, slices produce new objects, so we're not really iterating over the same object in multiple places here. To be closer to the class, we would need to make a single object to step across by slicing ahead of time:

```
>>> S = 'abcdef'
>>> S = S[::2]
>>> S
'ace'
>>> for x in S:
...     for y in S:              # Same object, new iterators
...         print(x + y, end=' ')
...
aa ac ae ca cc ce ea ec ee
```

This is more similar to our class-based solution, but it still stores the slice result in memory all at once (there is no generator form of built-in slicing today), and it's only equivalent for this particular case of skipping every other item.

Because iterators can do anything a class can do, they are much more general than this example may imply. Regardless of whether our applications require such generality, user-defined iterators are a powerful tool—they allow us to make arbitrary objects look and feel like the other sequences and iterables we have met in this book. We could use this technique with a database object, for example, to support iterations over database fetches, with multiple cursors into the same query result.

Membership: __contains__, __iter__, and __getitem__

The iteration story is even richer than we've seen thus far. Operator overloading is often *layered*: classes may provide specific methods, or more general alternatives used as fallback options. For example:

- Comparisons in Python 2.6 use specific methods such as __lt__ for less than if present, or else the general __cmp__. Python 3.0 uses only specific methods, not __cmp__, as discussed later in this chapter.

- Boolean tests similarly try a specific __bool__ first (to give an explicit True/False result), and if it's absent fall back on the more general __len__ (a nonzero length means True). As we'll also see later in this chapter, Python 2.6 works the same but uses the name __nonzero__ instead of __bool__.

In the iterations domain, classes normally implement the in membership operator as an iteration, using either the __iter__ method or the __getitem__ method. To support more specific membership, though, classes may code a __contains__ method—when present, this method is preferred over __iter__, which is preferred over __getitem__. The __contains__ method should define membership as applying to keys for a *mapping* (and can use quick lookups), and as a search for *sequences*.

Consider the following class, which codes all three methods and tests membership and various iteration contexts applied to an instance. Its methods print trace messages when called:

```
class Iters:
    def __init__(self, value):
        self.data = value
    def __getitem__(self, i):              # Fallback for iteration
        print('get[%s]:' % i, end='')       # Also for index, slice
        return self.data[i]
    def __iter__(self):                     # Preferred for iteration
        print('iter=> ', end='')            # Allows only 1 active iterator
        self.ix = 0
        return self
    def __next__(self):
        print('next:', end='')
```

```
            if self.ix == len(self.data): raise StopIteration
            item = self.data[self.ix]
            self.ix += 1
            return item
    def __contains__(self, x):                    # Preferred for 'in'
        print('contains: ', end='')
        return x in self.data


X = Iters([1, 2, 3, 4, 5])          # Make instance
print(3 in X)                       # Membership
for i in X:                         # For loops
    print(i, end=' | ')

print()
print([i ** 2 for i in X])          # Other iteration contexts
print( list(map(bin, X)) )

I = iter(X)                         # Manual iteration (what other contexts do)
while True:
    try:
        print(next(I), end=' @ ')
    except StopIteration:
        break
```

When run as it is, this script's output is as follows—the specific __contains__ intercepts membership, the general __iter__ catches other iteration contexts such that __next__ is called repeatedly, and __getitem__ is never called:

```
contains: True
iter=> next:1 | next:2 | next:3 | next:4 | next:5 | next:
iter=> next:next:next:next:next:next:[1, 4, 9, 16, 25]
iter=> next:next:next:next:next:next:['0b1', '0b10', '0b11', '0b100', '0b101']
iter=> next:1 @ next:2 @ next:3 @ next:4 @ next:5 @ next:
```

Watch what happens to this code's output if we comment out its __contains__ method, though—membership is now routed to the general __iter__ instead:

```
iter=> next:next:next:True
iter=> next:1 | next:2 | next:3 | next:4 | next:5 | next:
iter=> next:next:next:next:next:next:[1, 4, 9, 16, 25]
iter=> next:next:next:next:next:next:['0b1', '0b10', '0b11', '0b100', '0b101']
iter=> next:1 @ next:2 @ next:3 @ next:4 @ next:5 @ next:
```

And finally, here is the output if both __contains__ and __iter__ are commented out—the indexing __getitem__ fallback is called with successively higher indexes for membership and other iteration contexts:

```
get[0]:get[1]:get[2]:True
get[0]:1 | get[1]:2 | get[2]:3 | get[3]:4 | get[4]:5 | get[5]:
get[0]:get[1]:get[2]:get[3]:get[4]:get[5]:[1, 4, 9, 16, 25]
get[0]:get[1]:get[2]:get[3]:get[4]:get[5]:['0b1', '0b10', '0b11', '0b100','0b101']
get[0]:1 @ get[1]:2 @ get[2]:3 @ get[3]:4 @ get[4]:5 @ get[5]:
```

As we've seen, the __getitem__ method is even more general: besides iterations, it also intercepts explicit indexing as well as slicing. Slice expressions trigger __getitem__ with a slice object containing bounds, both for built-in types and user-defined classes, so slicing is automatic in our class:

```
>>> X = Iters('spam')                  # Indexing
>>> X[0]                               # __getitem__(0)
get[0]:'s'

>>> 'spam'[1:]                         # Slice syntax
'pam'
>>> 'spam'[slice(1, None)]             # Slice object
'pam'

>>> X[1:]                              # __getitem__(slice(..))
get[slice(1, None, None)]:'pam'
>>> X[:-1]
get[slice(None, -1, None)]:'spa'
```

In more realistic iteration use cases that are not sequence-oriented, though, the __iter__ method may be easier to write since it must not manage an integer index, and __contains__ allows for membership optimization as a special case.

Attribute Reference: __getattr__ and __setattr__

The __getattr__ method intercepts attribute qualifications. More specifically, it's called with the attribute name as a string whenever you try to qualify an instance with an *undefined* (nonexistent) attribute name. It is not called if Python can find the attribute using its inheritance tree search procedure. Because of its behavior, __getattr__ is useful as a hook for responding to attribute requests in a generic fashion. For example:

```
>>> class empty:
...     def __getattr__(self, attrname):
...         if attrname == "age":
...             return 40
...         else:
...             raise AttributeError(attrname)
...
>>> X = empty()
>>> X.age
40
>>> X.name
...error text omitted...
AttributeError: name
```

Here, the empty class and its instance X have no real attributes of their own, so the access to X.age gets routed to the __getattr__ method; self is assigned the instance (X), and attrname is assigned the undefined attribute name string ("age"). The class makes age look like a real attribute by returning a real value as the result of the X.age qualification expression (40). In effect, age becomes a *dynamically computed* attribute.

For attributes that the class doesn't know how to handle, __getattr__ raises the built-in AttributeError exception to tell Python that these are bona fide undefined names; asking for X.name triggers the error. You'll see __getattr__ again when we see delegation and properties at work in the next two chapters, and I'll say more about exceptions in Part VII.

A related overloading method, __setattr__, intercepts *all* attribute assignments. If this method is defined, self.attr = *value* becomes self.__setattr__('*attr*', *value*). This is a bit trickier to use because assigning to any self attributes within __setattr__ calls __setattr__ again, causing an infinite recursion loop (and eventually, a stack overflow exception!). If you want to use this method, be sure that it assigns any instance attributes by indexing the attribute dictionary, discussed in the next section. That is, use self.__dict__['name'] = x, not self.name = x:

```
>>> class accesscontrol:
...     def __setattr__(self, attr, value):
...         if attr == 'age':
...             self.__dict__[attr] = value
...         else:
...             raise AttributeError(attr + ' not allowed')
...
>>> X = accesscontrol()
>>> X.age = 40                          # Calls __setattr__
>>> X.age
40
>>> X.name = 'mel'
...text omitted...
AttributeError: name not allowed
```

These two attribute-access overloading methods allow you to control or specialize access to attributes in your objects. They tend to play highly specialized roles, some of which we'll explore later in this book.

Other Attribute Management Tools

For future reference, also note that there are other ways to manage attribute access in Python:

- The __getattribute__ method intercepts all attribute fetches, not just those that are undefined, but when using it you must be more cautious than with __getattr__ to avoid loops.
- The property built-in function allows us to associate methods with fetch and set operations on a specific class attribute.
- *Descriptors* provide a protocol for associating __get__ and __set__ methods of a class with accesses to a specific class attribute.

Because these are somewhat advanced tools not of interest to every Python programmer, we'll defer a look at properties until Chapter 31 and detailed coverage of all the attribute management techniques until Chapter 37.

Emulating Privacy for Instance Attributes: Part 1

The following code generalizes the previous example, to allow each subclass to have its own list of private names that cannot be assigned to its instances:

```
class PrivateExc(Exception): pass                  # More on exceptions later

class Privacy:
    def __setattr__(self, attrname, value):        # On self.attrname = value
        if attrname in self.privates:
            raise PrivateExc(attrname, self)
        else:
            self.__dict__[attrname] = value        # self.attrname = value loops!

class Test1(Privacy):
    privates = ['age']

class Test2(Privacy):
    privates = ['name', 'pay']
    def __init__(self):
        self.__dict__['name'] = 'Tom'

x = Test1()
y = Test2()

x.name = 'Bob'
y.name = 'Sue'                                      # Fails

y.age  = 30
x.age  = 40                                         # Fails
```

In fact, this is a first-cut solution for an implementation of *attribute privacy* in Python (i.e., disallowing changes to attribute names outside a class). Although Python doesn't support private declarations per se, techniques like this can emulate much of their purpose. This is a partial solution, though; to make it more effective, it must be augmented to allow subclasses to set private attributes more naturally, too, and to use __getattr__ and a wrapper (sometimes called a proxy) class to check for private attribute fetches.

We'll postpone a more complete solution to attribute privacy until Chapter 38, where we'll use *class decorators* to intercept and validate attributes more generally. Even though privacy can be emulated this way, though, it almost never is in practice. Python programmers are able to write large OOP frameworks and applications without private declarations—an interesting finding about access controls in general that is beyond the scope of our purposes here.

Catching attribute references and assignments is generally a useful technique; it supports *delegation*, a design technique that allows controller objects to wrap up embedded objects, add new behaviors, and route other operations back to the wrapped objects (more on delegation and wrapper classes in Chapter 30).

String Representation: __repr__ and __str__

The next example exercises the __init__ constructor and the __add__ overload method, both of which we've already seen, as well as defining a __repr__ method that returns a string representation for instances. String formatting is used to convert the managed self.data object to a string. If defined, __repr__ (or its sibling, __str__) is called automatically when class instances are printed or converted to strings. These methods allow you to define a better display format for your objects than the default instance display.

The default display of instance objects is neither useful nor pretty:

```
>>> class adder:
...     def __init__(self, value=0):
...         self.data = value          # Initialize data
...     def __add__(self, other):
...         self.data += other         # Add other in-place (bad!)
...
>>> x = adder()                        # Default displays
>>> print(x)
<__main__.adder object at 0x025D66B0>
>>> x
<__main__.adder object at 0x025D66B0>
```

But coding or inheriting string representation methods allows us to customize the display:

```
>>> class addrepr(adder):              # Inherit __init__, __add__
...     def __repr__(self):            # Add string representation
...         return 'addrepr(%s)' % self.data    # Convert to as-code string
...
>>> x = addrepr(2)                     # Runs __init__
>>> x + 1                              # Runs __add__
>>> x                                  # Runs __repr__
addrepr(3)
>>> print(x)                           # Runs __repr__
addrepr(3)
>>> str(x), repr(x)                    # Runs __repr__ for both
('addrepr(3)', 'addrepr(3)')
```

So why two display methods? Mostly, to support different audiences. In full detail:

- __str__ is tried first for the print operation and the str built-in function (the internal equivalent of which print runs). It generally should return a user-friendly display.

- __repr__ is used in all other contexts: for interactive echoes, the repr function, and nested appearances, as well as by print and str if no __str__ is present. It should generally return an as-code string that could be used to re-create the object, or a detailed display for developers.

In a nutshell, __repr__ is used everywhere, except by print and str when a __str__ is defined. Note, however, that while printing falls back on __repr__ if no __str__ is defined, the inverse is not true—other contexts, such as interactive echoes, use __repr__ only and don't try __str__ at all:

```
>>> class addstr(adder):
...     def __str__(self):              # __str__ but no __repr__
...         return '[Value: %s]' % self.data    # Convert to nice string
...
>>> x = addstr(3)
>>> x + 1
>>> x                                   # Default __repr__
<__main__.addstr object at 0x00B35EF0>
>>> print(x)                            # Runs __str__
[Value: 4]
>>> str(x), repr(x)
('[Value: 4]', '<__main__.addstr object at 0x00B35EF0>')
```

Because of this, __repr__ may be best if you want a *single* display for all contexts. By defining both methods, though, you can support different displays in different contexts—for example, an end-user display with __str__, and a low-level display for programmers to use during development with __repr__. In effect, __str__ simply overrides __repr__ for user-friendly display contexts:

```
>>> class addboth(adder):
...     def __str__(self):
...         return '[Value: %s]' % self.data    # User-friendly string
...     def __repr__(self):
...         return 'addboth(%s)' % self.data     # As-code string
...
>>> x = addboth(4)
>>> x + 1
>>> x                                   # Runs __repr__
addboth(5)
>>> print(x)                            # Runs __str__
[Value: 5]
>>> str(x), repr(x)
('[Value: 5]', 'addboth(5)')
```

I should mention two usage notes here. First, keep in mind that __str__ and __repr__ must both return strings; other result types are not converted and raise errors, so be sure to run them through a converter if needed. Second, depending on a container's string-conversion logic, the user-friendly display of __str__ might only apply when objects appear at the top level of a print operation; objects nested in larger objects might still print with their __repr__ or its default. The following illustrates both of these points:

```
>>> class Printer:
...     def __init__(self, val):
...         self.val = val
...     def __str__(self):              # Used for instance itself
...         return str(self.val)        # Convert to a string result
...
>>> objs = [Printer(2), Printer(3)]
>>> for x in objs: print(x)            # __str__ run when instance printed
...                                     # But not when instance in a list!
```

```
2
3
>>> print(objs)
[<__main__.Printer object at 0x025D06F0>, <__main__.Printer object at ...more...
>>> objs
[<__main__.Printer object at 0x025D06F0>, <__main__.Printer object at ...more...
```

To ensure that a custom display is run in all contexts regardless of the container, code
__repr__, not __str__; the former is run in all cases if the latter doesn't apply:

```
>>> class Printer:
...     def __init__(self, val):
...         self.val = val
...     def __repr__(self):          # __repr__ used by print if no __str__
...         return str(self.val)     # __repr__ used if echoed or nested
...
>>> objs = [Printer(2), Printer(3)]
>>> for x in objs: print(x)          # No __str__: runs __repr__
...
2
3
>>> print(objs)                      # Runs __repr__, not __str__
[2, 3]
>>> objs
[2, 3]
```

In practice, __str__ (or its low-level relative, __repr__) seems to be the second most
commonly used operator overloading method in Python scripts, behind __init__. Any
time you can print an object and see a custom display, one of these two tools is probably
in use.

Right-Side and In-Place Addition: __radd__ and __iadd__

Technically, the __add__ method that appeared in the prior example does not support
the use of instance objects on the right side of the + operator. To implement such
expressions, and hence support *commutative*-style operators, code the __radd__
method as well. Python calls __radd__ only when the object on the right side of the + is
your class instance, but the object on the left is not an instance of your class. The
__add__ method for the object on the left is called instead in all other cases:

```
>>> class Commuter:
...     def __init__(self, val):
...         self.val = val
...     def __add__(self, other):
...         print('add', self.val, other)
...         return self.val + other
...     def __radd__(self, other):
...         print('radd', self.val, other)
...         return other + self.val
...
>>> x = Commuter(88)
>>> y = Commuter(99)
```

```
>>> x + 1                      # __add__: instance + noninstance
add 88 1
89
>>> 1 + y                      # __radd__: noninstance + instance
radd 99 1
100
>>> x + y                      # __add__: instance + instance, triggers __radd__
add 88 <__main__.Commuter object at 0x02630910>
radd 99 88
187
```

Notice how the order is reversed in __radd__: self is really on the right of the +, and other is on the left. Also note that x and y are instances of the same class here; when instances of different classes appear mixed in an expression, Python prefers the class of the one on the left. When we add the two instances together, Python runs __add__, which in turn triggers __radd__ by simplifying the left operand.

In more realistic classes where the class type may need to be propagated in results, things can become trickier: type testing may be required to tell whether it's safe to convert and thus avoid nesting. For instance, without the isinstance test in the following, we could wind up with a Commuter whose val is another Commuter when two instances are added and __add__ triggers __radd__:

```
>>> class Commuter:                     # Propagate class type in results
...     def __init__(self, val):
...         self.val = val
...     def __add__(self, other):
...         if isinstance(other, Commuter): other = other.val
...         return Commuter(self.val + other)
...     def __radd__(self, other):
...         return Commuter(other + self.val)
...     def __str__(self):
...         return '<Commuter: %s>' % self.val
...
>>> x = Commuter(88)
>>> y = Commuter(99)
>>> print(x + 10)                       # Result is another Commuter instance
<Commuter: 98>
>>> print(10 + y)
<Commuter: 109>

>>> z = x + y                           # Not nested: doesn't recur to __radd__
>>> print(z)
<Commuter: 187>
>>> print(z + 10)
<Commuter: 197>
>>> print(z + z)
<Commuter: 374>
```

For truly commutative operations which do not require special-casing by position, it is also sometimes sufficient to alias the right-side __radd__ to the left-side __add__, by simply assigning the former name to the latter at the top-level of the class statement.

Right appearances will then trigger the single, shared __add__ method passing the right operand to self.

In-Place Addition

To also implement += in-place augmented addition, code either an __iadd__ or an __add__. The latter is used if the former is absent. In fact, the prior section's Commuter class supports += already for this reason, but __iadd__ allows for more efficient in-place changes:

```
>>> class Number:
...     def __init__(self, val):
...         self.val = val
...     def __iadd__(self, other):          # __iadd__ explicit: x += y
...         self.val += other               # Usually returns self
...         return self
...
>>> x = Number(5)
>>> x += 1
>>> x += 1
>>> x.val
7
>>> class Number:
...     def __init__(self, val):
...         self.val = val
...     def __add__(self, other):           # __add__ fallback: x = (x + y)
...         return Number(self.val + other) # Propagates class type
...
>>> x = Number(5)
>>> x += 1
>>> x += 1
>>> x.val
7
```

Every binary operator has similar right-side and in-place overloading methods that work the same (e.g., __mul__, __rmul__, and __imul__). Right-side methods are an advanced topic and tend to be fairly rarely used in practice; you only code them when you need operators to be commutative, and then only if you need to support such operators at all. For instance, a Vector class may use these tools, but an Employee or Button class probably would not.

Call Expressions: __call__

The __call__ method is called when your instance is called. No, this isn't a circular definition—if defined, Python runs a __call__ method for function call expressions applied to your instances, passing along whatever positional or keyword arguments were sent:

```
>>> class Callee:
...     def __call__(self, *pargs, **kargs):     # Intercept instance calls
```

```
...             print('Called:', pargs, kargs)          # Accept arbitrary arguments
...
>>> C = Callee()
>>> C(1, 2, 3)                                           # C is a callable object
Called: (1, 2, 3) {}
>>> C(1, 2, 3, x=4, y=5)
Called: (1, 2, 3) {'y': 5, 'x': 4}
```

More formally, all the argument-passing modes we explored in Chapter 18 are supported by the __call__ method—whatever is passed to the instance is passed to this method, along with the usual implied instance argument. For example, the method definitions:

```
class C:
    def __call__(self, a, b, c=5, d=6): ...          # Normals and defaults

class C:
    def __call__(self, *pargs, **kargs): ...          # Collect arbitrary arguments

class C:
    def __call__(self, *pargs, d=6, **kargs): ...     # 3.0 keyword-only argument
```

all match all the following instance calls:

```
X = C()
X(1, 2)                                    # Omit defaults
X(1, 2, 3, 4)                              # Positionals
X(a=1, b=2, d=4)                           # Keywords
X(*[1, 2], **dict(c=3, d=4))               # Unpack arbitrary arguments
X(1, *(2,), c=3, **dict(d=4))              # Mixed modes
```

The net effect is that classes and instances with a __call__ support the exact same argument syntax and semantics as normal functions and methods.

Intercepting call expression like this allows class instances to emulate the look and feel of things like functions, but also retain state information for use during calls (we saw a similar example while exploring scopes in Chapter 17, but you should be more familiar with operator overloading here):

```
>>> class Prod:
...     def __init__(self, value):             # Accept just one argument
...         self.value = value
...     def __call__(self, other):
...         return self.value * other
...
>>> x = Prod(2)                                # "Remembers" 2 in state
>>> x(3)                                       # 3 (passed) * 2 (state)
6
>>> x(4)
8
```

In this example, the __call__ may seem a bit gratuitous at first glance. A simple method can provide similar utility:

```
>>> class Prod:
...     def __init__(self, value):
```

```
...              self.value = value
...          def comp(self, other):
...              return self.value * other
...
>>> x = Prod(3)
>>> x.comp(3)
9
>>> x.comp(4)
12
```

However, __call__ can become more useful when interfacing with APIs that expect
functions—it allows us to code objects that conform to an expected function call interface, but also retain state information. In fact, it's probably the third most commonly
used operator overloading method, behind the __init__ constructor and the __str__
and __repr__ display-format alternatives.

Function Interfaces and Callback-Based Code

As an example, the tkinter GUI toolkit (named Tkinter in Python 2.6) allows you to
register functions as event handlers (a.k.a. callbacks); when events occur, tkinter calls
the registered objects. If you want an event handler to retain state between events, you
can register either a class's bound method or an instance that conforms to the expected
interface with __call__. In this section's code, both x.comp from the second example
and x from the first can pass as function-like objects this way.

I'll have more to say about bound methods in the next chapter, but for now, here's a
hypothetical example of __call__ applied to the GUI domain. The following class defines an object that supports a function-call interface, but also has state information
that remembers the color a button should change to when it is later pressed:

```
class Callback:
    def __init__(self, color):          # Function + state information
        self.color = color
    def __call__(self):                 # Support calls with no arguments
        print('turn', self.color)
```

Now, in the context of a GUI, we can register instances of this class as event handlers
for buttons, even though the GUI expects to be able to invoke event handlers as simple
functions with no arguments:

```
cb1 = Callback('blue')                  # Remember blue
cb2 = Callback('green')

B1 = Button(command=cb1)                # Register handlers
B2 = Button(command=cb2)                # Register handlers
```

When the button is later pressed, the instance object is called as a simple function,
exactly like in the following calls. Because it retains state as instance attributes, though,
it remembers what to do:

```
cb1()                                   # On events: prints 'blue'
cb2()                                   # Prints 'green'
```

In fact, this is probably the best way to retain state information in the Python language—better than the techniques discussed earlier for functions (global variables, enclosing function scope references, and default mutable arguments). With OOP, the state remembered is made explicit with attribute assignments; this makes its model generally the most Pythonic, though 3.X's `nonlocal` statement makes enclosing scopes a viable alternative in some roles.

Before we move on, there are two other ways that Python programmers sometimes tie information to a callback function like this. One option is to use default arguments in `lambda` functions:

```
cb3 = (lambda color='red': 'turn ' + color)   # Or: defaults
print(cb3())
```

The other is to use *bound methods* of a class. A bound method object is a kind of object that remembers the `self` instance and the referenced function. A bound method may therefore be called as a simple function without an instance later:

```
class Callback:
    def __init__(self, color):          # Class with state information
        self.color = color
    def changeColor(self):              # A normal named method
        print('turn', self.color)

cb1 = Callback('blue')
cb2 = Callback('yellow')

B1 = Button(command=cb1.changeColor)    # Reference, but don't call
B2 = Button(command=cb2.changeColor)    # Remembers function+self
```

In this case, when this button is later pressed it's as if the GUI does this, which invokes the `changeColor` method to process the object's state information:

```
object = Callback('blue')
cb = object.changeColor                 # Registered event handler
cb()                                    # On event prints 'blue'
```

Note that a lambda is not required here, because a bound method reference by itself already defers a call till later (again, more on bound methods in Chapter 30). This technique is simpler, but less general than overloading calls with `__call__`; again, watch for more about bound methods in the next chapter.

You'll also see another `__call__` example in Chapter 31, where we will use it to implement something known as a *function decorator*—a callable object often used to add a layer of logic on top of an embedded function. Because `__call__` allows us to attach state information to a callable object, it's a natural implementation technique for a function that must remember and call another function.

Comparisons: __lt__, __gt__, and Others

As suggested in Table 29-1, classes can define methods to catch all six comparison operators: <, >, <=, >=, ==, and !=. These methods are generally straightforward to use, but keep the following qualifications in mind:

- Unlike the __add__/__radd__ pairings discussed earlier, there are no right-side variants of comparison methods. Instead, reflective methods are used when only one operand supports comparison (e.g., __lt__ and __gt__ are each other's reflection).

- There are no implicit relationships among the comparison operators. The truth of == does not imply that != is false, for example, so both __eq__ and __ne__ should be defined to ensure that both operators behave correctly.

- In Python 2.6, a __cmp__ method is used by all comparisons if no more specific comparison methods are defined; it returns a number that is less than, equal to, or greater than zero, to signal less than, equal, and greater than results for the comparison of its two arguments (self and another operand). This method often uses the cmp(x, y) built-in to compute its result. Both the __cmp__ method and the cmp built-in function are removed in Python 3.0: use the more specific methods instead.

We don't have space for an in-depth exploration of comparison methods, but as a quick introduction, consider the following class and test code:

```
class C:
    data = 'spam'
    def __gt__(self, other):          # 3.0 and 2.6 version
        return self.data > other
    def __lt__(self, other):
        return self.data < other

X = C()
print(X > 'ham')                       # True  (runs __gt__)
print(X < 'ham')                       # False (runs __lt__)
```

When run under Python 3.0 or 2.6, the prints at the end display the expected results noted in their comments, because the class's methods intercept and implement comparison expressions.

The 2.6 __cmp__ Method (Removed in 3.0)

In Python 2.6, the __cmp__ method is used as a fallback if more specific methods are not defined: its integer result is used to evaluate the operator being run. The following produces the same result under 2.6, for example, but fails in 3.0 because __cmp__ is no longer used:

```
class C:
    data = 'spam'                      # 2.6 only
    def __cmp__(self, other):          # __cmp__ not used in 3.0
```

```
        return cmp(self.data, other)        # cmp not defined in 3.0

X = C()
print(X > 'ham')                            # True (runs __cmp__)
print(X < 'ham')                            # False (runs __cmp__)
```

Notice that this fails in 3.0 because __cmp__ is no longer special, not because the cmp built-in function is no longer present. If we change the prior class to the following to try to simulate the cmp call, the code still works in 2.6 but fails in 3.0:

```
class C:
    data = 'spam'
    def __cmp__(self, other):
        return (self.data > other) - (self.data < other)
```

 So why, you might be asking, did I just show you a comparison method that is no longer supported in 3.0? While it would be easier to erase history entirely, this book is designed to support both 2.6 and 3.0 readers. Because __cmp__ may appear in code 2.6 readers must reuse or maintain, it's fair game in this book. Moreover, __cmp__ was removed more abruptly than the __getslice__ method described earlier, and so may endure longer. If you use 3.0, though, or care about running your code under 3.0 in the future, don't use __cmp__ anymore: use the more specific comparison methods instead.

Boolean Tests: __bool__ and __len__

As mentioned earlier, classes may also define methods that give the Boolean nature of their instances—in Boolean contexts, Python first tries __bool__ to obtain a direct Boolean value and then, if that's missing, tries __len__ to determine a truth value from the object length. The first of these generally uses object state or other information to produce a Boolean result:

```
>>> class Truth:
...     def __bool__(self): return True
...
>>> X = Truth()
>>> if X: print('yes!')
...
yes!

>>> class Truth:
...     def __bool__(self): return False
...
>>> X = Truth()
>>> bool(X)
False
```

If this method is missing, Python falls back on length because a nonempty object is considered true (i.e., a nonzero length is taken to mean the object is true, and a zero length means it is false):

```
>>> class Truth:
...     def __len__(self): return 0
...
>>> X = Truth()
>>> if not X: print('no!')
...
no!
```

If both methods are present Python prefers __bool__ over __len__, because it is more specific:

```
>>> class Truth:
...     def __bool__(self): return True         # 3.0 tries __bool__ first
...     def __len__(self): return 0             # 2.6 tries __len__ first
...
>>> X = Truth()
>>> if X: print('yes!')
...
yes!
```

If neither truth method is defined, the object is vacuously considered true (which has potential implications for metaphysically inclined readers!):

```
>>> class Truth:
...     pass
...
>>> X = Truth()
>>> bool(X)
True
```

And now that we've managed to cross over into the realm of philosophy, let's move on to look at one last overloading context: object demise.

Booleans in Python 2.6

Python 2.6 users should use __nonzero__ instead of __bool__ in all of the code in the section "Boolean Tests: __bool__ and __len__" on page 732. Python 3.0 renamed the 2.6 __nonzero__ method to __bool__, but Boolean tests work the same otherwise (both 3.0 and 2.6 use __len__ as a fallback).

If you don't use the 2.6 name, the very first test in this section will work the same for you anyhow, but only because __bool__ is not recognized as a special method name in 2.6, and objects are considered true by default!

To witness this version difference live, you need to return False:

```
C:\misc> c:\python30\python
>>> class C:
...     def __bool__(self):
...         print('in bool')
...         return False
...
>>> X = C()
>>> bool(X)
in bool
False
```

```
>>> if X: print(99)
...
in bool
```

This works as advertised in 3.0. In 2.6, though, __bool__ is ignored and the object is always considered true:

```
C:\misc> c:\python26\python
>>> class C:
...     def __bool__(self):
...         print('in bool')
...         return False
...
>>> X = C()
>>> bool(X)
True
>>> if X: print(99)
...
99
```

In 2.6, use __nonzero__ for Boolean values (or return 0 from the __len__ fallback method to designate false):

```
C:\misc> c:\python26\python
>>> class C:
...     def __nonzero__(self):
...         print('in nonzero')
...         return False
...
>>> X = C()
>>> bool(X)
in nonzero
False
>>> if X: print(99)
...
in nonzero
```

But keep in mind that __nonzero__ works in 2.6 only; if used in 3.0 it will be silently ignored and the object will be classified as true by default—just like using __bool__ in 2.6!

Object Destruction: __del__

We've seen how the __init__ constructor is called whenever an instance is generated. Its counterpart, the destructor method __del__, is run automatically when an instance's space is being reclaimed (i.e., at "garbage collection" time):

```
>>> class Life:
...     def __init__(self, name='unknown'):
...         print('Hello', name)
...         self.name = name
...     def __del__(self):
...         print('Goodbye', self.name)
...
>>> brian = Life('Brian')
```

```
Hello Brian
>>> brian = 'loretta'
Goodbye Brian
```

Here, when brian is assigned a string, we lose the last reference to the Life instance and so trigger its destructor method. This works, and it may be useful for implementing some cleanup activities (such as terminating server connections). However, destructors are not as commonly used in Python as in some OOP languages, for a number of reasons.

For one thing, because Python automatically reclaims all space held by an instance when the instance is reclaimed, destructors are not necessary for space management.[*] For another, because you cannot always easily predict when an instance will be reclaimed, it's often better to code termination activities in an explicitly called method (or try/finally statement, described in the next part of the book); in some cases, there may be lingering references to your objects in system tables that prevent destructors from running.

 In fact, __del__ can be tricky to use for even more subtle reasons. Exceptions raised within it, for example, simply print a warning message to sys.stderr (the standard error stream) rather than triggering an exception event, because of the unpredictable context under which it is run by the garbage collector. In addition, cyclic (a.k.a. circular) references among objects may prevent garbage collection from happening when you expect it to; an optional cycle detector, enabled by default, can automatically collect such objects eventually, but only if they do not have __del__ methods. Since this is relatively obscure, we'll ignore further details here; see Python's standard manuals' coverage of both __del__ and the gc garbage collector module for more information.

Chapter Summary

That's as many overloading examples as we have space for here. Most of the other operator overloading methods work similarly to the ones we've explored, and all are just hooks for intercepting built-in type operations; some overloading methods, for example, have unique argument lists or return values. We'll see a few others in action later in the book:

- Chapter 33 uses the __enter__ and __exit__ with statement context manager methods.
- Chapter 37 uses the __get__ and __set__ class descriptor fetch/set methods.

---

[*] In the current C implementation of Python, you also don't need to close file objects held by the instance in destructors because they are automatically closed when reclaimed. However, as mentioned in Chapter 9, it's better to explicitly call file close methods because auto-close-on-reclaim is a feature of the implementation, not of the language itself (this behavior can vary under Jython, for instance).

- Chapter 39 uses the __new__ object creation method in the context of metaclasses.

In addition, some of the methods we've studied here, such as __call__ and __str__, will be employed by later examples in this book. For complete coverage, though, I'll defer to other documentation sources—see Python's standard language manual or reference books for details on additional overloading methods.

In the next chapter, we leave the realm of class mechanics behind to explore common design patterns—the ways that classes are commonly used and combined to optimize code reuse. Before you read on, though, take a moment to work though the chapter quiz below to review the concepts we've covered.

Test Your Knowledge: Quiz

1. What two operator overloading methods can you use to support iteration in your classes?
2. What two operator overloading methods handle printing, and in what contexts?
3. How can you intercept slice operations in a class?
4. How can you catch in-place addition in a class?
5. When should you provide operator overloading?

Test Your Knowledge: Answers

1. Classes can support iteration by defining (or inheriting) __getitem__ or __iter__. In all iteration contexts, Python tries to use __iter__ (which returns an object that supports the iteration protocol with a __next__ method) first: if no __iter__ is found by inheritance search, Python falls back on the __getitem__ indexing method (which is called repeatedly, with successively higher indexes).

2. The __str__ and __repr__ methods implement object print displays. The former is called by the print and str built-in functions; the latter is called by print and str if there is no __str__, and always by the repr built-in, interactive echoes, and nested appearances. That is, __repr__ is used everywhere, except by print and str when a __str__ is defined. A __str__ is usually used for user-friendly displays; __repr__ gives extra details or the object's as-code form.

3. Slicing is caught by the __getitem__ indexing method: it is called with a slice object, instead of a simple index. In Python 2.6, __getslice__ (defunct in 3.0) may be used as well.

4. In-place addition tries __iadd__ first, and __add__ with an assignment second. The same pattern holds true for all binary operators. The __radd__ method is also available for right-side addition.

5. When a class naturally matches, or needs to emulate, a built-in type's interfaces. For example, collections might imitate sequence or mapping interfaces. You generally shouldn't implement expression operators if they don't naturally map to your objects, though—use normally named methods instead.

## CHAPTER 30

Designing with Classes

So far in this part of the book, we've concentrated on using Python's OOP tool, the class. But OOP is also about *design issues*—i.e., how to use classes to model useful objects. This chapter will touch on a few core OOP ideas and present some additional examples that are more realistic than those shown so far.

Along the way, we'll code some common OOP design patterns in Python, such as inheritance, composition, delegation, and factories. We'll also investigate some design-focused class concepts, such as pseudoprivate attributes, multiple inheritance, and bound methods. Many of the design terms mentioned here require more explanation than I can provide in this book; if this material sparks your curiosity, I suggest exploring a text on OOP design or design patterns as a next step.

Python and OOP

Let's begin with a review—Python's implementation of OOP can be summarized by three ideas:

Inheritance
> Inheritance is based on attribute lookup in Python (in X.name expressions).

Polymorphism
> In X.method, the meaning of method depends on the type (class) of X.

Encapsulation
> Methods and operators implement behavior; data hiding is a convention by default.

By now, you should have a good feel for what inheritance is all about in Python. We've also talked about Python's polymorphism a few times already; it flows from Python's lack of type declarations. Because attributes are always resolved at runtime, objects that implement the same interfaces are interchangeable; clients don't need to know what sorts of objects are implementing the methods they call.

Encapsulation means packaging in Python—that is, hiding implementation details behind an object's interface. It does not mean enforced privacy, though that can be implemented with code, as we'll see in Chapter 38. Encapsulation allows the implementation of an object's interface to be changed without impacting the users of that object.

Overloading by Call Signatures (or Not)

Some OOP languages also define polymorphism to mean overloading functions based on the type signatures of their arguments. But because there are no type declarations in Python, this concept doesn't really apply; polymorphism in Python is based on object *interfaces*, not types.

You can try to overload methods by their argument lists, like this:

```
class C:
    def meth(self, x):
        ...
    def meth(self, x, y, z):
        ...
```

This code will run, but because the def simply assigns an object to a name in the class's scope, the last definition of the method function is the only one that will be retained (it's just as if you say X = 1 and then X = 2; X will be 2).

Type-based selections can always be coded using the type-testing ideas we met in Chapters 4 and 9, or the argument list tools introduced in Chapter 18:

```
class C:
    def meth(self, *args):
        if len(args) == 1:
            ...
        elif type(arg[0]) == int:
            ...
```

You normally shouldn't do this, though—as described in Chapter 16, you should write your code to expect an object interface, not a specific data type. That way, it will be useful for a broader category of types and applications, both now and in the future:

```
class C:
    def meth(self, x):
        x.operation()          # Assume x does the right thing
```

It's also generally considered better to use distinct method names for distinct operations, rather than relying on call signatures (no matter what language you code in).

Although Python's object model is straightforward, much of the art in OOP is in the way we combine classes to achieve a program's goals. The next section begins a tour of some of the ways larger programs use classes to their advantage.

OOP and Inheritance: "Is-a" Relationships

We've explored the mechanics of inheritance in depth already, but I'd like to show you an example of how it can be used to model real-world relationships. From a programmer's point of view, inheritance is kicked off by attribute qualifications, which trigger searches for names in instances, their classes, and then any superclasses. From a designer's point of view, inheritance is a way to specify set membership: a class defines a set of properties that may be inherited and customized by more specific sets (i.e., subclasses).

To illustrate, let's put that pizza-making robot we talked about at the start of this part of the book to work. Suppose we've decided to explore alternative career paths and open a pizza restaurant. One of the first things we'll need to do is hire employees to serve customers, prepare the food, and so on. Being engineers at heart, we've decided to build a robot to make the pizzas; but being politically and cybernetically correct, we've also decided to make our robot a full-fledged employee with a salary.

Our pizza shop team can be defined by the four classes in the example file, *employees.py*. The most general class, Employee, provides common behavior such as bumping up salaries (giveRaise) and printing (__repr__). There are two kinds of employees, and so two subclasses of Employee: Chef and Server. Both override the inherited work method to print more specific messages. Finally, our pizza robot is modeled by an even more specific class: PizzaRobot is a kind of Chef, which is a kind of Employee. In OOP terms, we call these relationships "is-a" links: a robot is a chef, which is a(n) employee. Here's the *employees.py* file:

```
class Employee:
    def __init__(self, name, salary=0):
        self.name   = name
        self.salary = salary
    def giveRaise(self, percent):
        self.salary = self.salary + (self.salary * percent)
    def work(self):
        print(self.name, "does stuff")
    def __repr__(self):
        return "<Employee: name=%s, salary=%s>" % (self.name, self.salary)

class Chef(Employee):
    def __init__(self, name):
        Employee.__init__(self, name, 50000)
    def work(self):
        print(self.name, "makes food")

class Server(Employee):
    def __init__(self, name):
        Employee.__init__(self, name, 40000)
    def work(self):
        print(self.name, "interfaces with customer")

class PizzaRobot(Chef):
```

```
        def __init__(self, name):
            Chef.__init__(self, name)
        def work(self):
            print(self.name, "makes pizza")

    if __name__ == "__main__":
        bob = PizzaRobot('bob')      # Make a robot named bob
        print(bob)                   # Run inherited __repr__
        bob.work()                   # Run type-specific action
        bob.giveRaise(0.20)          # Give bob a 20% raise
        print(bob); print()

        for klass in Employee, Chef, Server, PizzaRobot:
            obj = klass(klass.__name__)
            obj.work()
```

When we run the self-test code included in this module, we create a pizza-making robot named bob, which inherits names from three classes: PizzaRobot, Chef, and Employee. For instance, printing bob runs the Employee.__repr__ method, and giving bob a raise invokes Employee.giveRaise because that's where the inheritance search finds that method:

```
C:\python\examples> python employees.py
<Employee: name=bob, salary=50000>
bob makes pizza
<Employee: name=bob, salary=60000.0>

Employee does stuff
Chef makes food
Server interfaces with customer
PizzaRobot makes pizza
```

In a class hierarchy like this, you can usually make instances of any of the classes, not just the ones at the bottom. For instance, the for loop in this module's self-test code creates instances of all four classes; each responds differently when asked to work because the work method is different in each. Really, these classes just simulate real-world objects; work prints a message for the time being, but it could be expanded to do real work later.

OOP and Composition: "Has-a" Relationships

The notion of composition was introduced in Chapter 25. From a programmer's point of view, composition involves embedding other objects in a container object, and activating them to implement container methods. To a designer, composition is another way to represent relationships in a problem domain. But, rather than set membership, composition has to do with components—parts of a whole.

Composition also reflects the relationships between parts, called a "has-a" relationships. Some OOP design texts refer to composition as *aggregation* (or distinguish between the two terms by using aggregation to describe a weaker dependency between container and contained); in this text, a "composition" simply refers to a collection of embedded objects. The composite class generally provides an interface all its own and implements it by directing the embedded objects.

Now that we've implemented our employees, let's put them in the pizza shop and let them get busy. Our pizza shop is a composite object: it has an oven, and it has employees like servers and chefs. When a customer enters and places an order, the components of the shop spring into action—the server takes the order, the chef makes the pizza, and so on. The following example (the file *pizzashop.py*) simulates all the objects and relationships in this scenario:

```python
from employees import PizzaRobot, Server

class Customer:
    def __init__(self, name):
        self.name = name
    def order(self, server):
        print(self.name, "orders from", server)
    def pay(self, server):
        print(self.name, "pays for item to", server)

class Oven:
    def bake(self):
        print("oven bakes")

class PizzaShop:
    def __init__(self):
        self.server = Server('Pat')        # Embed other objects
        self.chef   = PizzaRobot('Bob')    # A robot named bob
        self.oven   = Oven()

    def order(self, name):
        customer = Customer(name)           # Activate other objects
        customer.order(self.server)         # Customer orders from server
        self.chef.work()
        self.oven.bake()
        customer.pay(self.server)

if __name__ == "__main__":
    scene = PizzaShop()                     # Make the composite
    scene.order('Homer')                    # Simulate Homer's order
    print('...')
    scene.order('Shaggy')                   # Simulate Shaggy's order
```

The PizzaShop class is a container and controller; its constructor makes and embeds instances of the employee classes we wrote in the last section, as well as an Oven class defined here. When this module's self-test code calls the PizzaShop order method, the embedded objects are asked to carry out their actions in turn. Notice that we make a new Customer object for each order, and we pass on the embedded Server object to Customer methods; customers come and go, but the server is part of the pizza shop composite. Also notice that employees are still involved in an inheritance relationship; composition and inheritance are complementary tools.

When we run this module, our pizza shop handles two orders—one from Homer, and then one from Shaggy:

```
C:\python\examples> python pizzashop.py
Homer orders from <Employee: name=Pat, salary=40000>
Bob makes pizza
oven bakes
Homer pays for item to <Employee: name=Pat, salary=40000>
...
Shaggy orders from <Employee: name=Pat, salary=40000>
Bob makes pizza
oven bakes
Shaggy pays for item to <Employee: name=Pat, salary=40000>
```

Again, this is mostly just a toy simulation, but the objects and interactions are representative of composites at work. As a rule of thumb, classes can represent just about any objects and relationships you can express in a sentence; just replace *nouns* with classes, and *verbs* with methods, and you'll have a first cut at a design.

Stream Processors Revisited

For a more realistic composition example, recall the generic data stream processor function we partially coded in the introduction to OOP in Chapter 25:

```
def processor(reader, converter, writer):
    while 1:
        data = reader.read()
        if not data: break
        data = converter(data)
        writer.write(data)
```

Rather than using a simple function here, we might code this as a class that uses composition to do its work to provide more structure and support inheritance. The following file, *streams.py*, demonstrates one way to code the class:

```
class Processor:
    def __init__(self, reader, writer):
        self.reader = reader
        self.writer = writer
    def process(self):
        while 1:
            data = self.reader.readline()
            if not data: break
            data = self.converter(data)
            self.writer.write(data)
    def converter(self, data):
        assert False, 'converter must be defined'     # Or raise exception
```

This class defines a `converter` method that it expects subclasses to fill in; it's an example of the *abstract superclass* model we outlined in Chapter 28 (more on `assert` in Part VII). Coded this way, `reader` and `writer` objects are embedded within the class instance (*composition*), and we supply the conversion logic in a subclass rather than passing in a converter function (*inheritance*). The file *converters.py* shows how:

```
from streams import Processor

class Uppercase(Processor):
    def converter(self, data):
        return data.upper()

if __name__ == '__main__':
    import sys
    obj = Uppercase(open('spam.txt'), sys.stdout)
    obj.process()
```

Here, the `Uppercase` class inherits the stream-processing loop logic (and anything else that may be coded in its superclasses). It needs to define only what is unique about it—the data conversion logic. When this file is run, it makes and runs an instance that reads from the file *spam.txt* and writes the uppercase equivalent of that file to the `stdout` stream:

```
C:\lp4e> type spam.txt
spam
Spam
SPAM!

C:\lp4e> python converters.py
SPAM
SPAM
SPAM!
```

To process different sorts of streams, pass in different sorts of objects to the class construction call. Here, we use an output file instead of a stream:

```
C:\lp4e> python
>>> import converters
>>> prog = converters.Uppercase(open('spam.txt'), open('spamup.txt', 'w'))
>>> prog.process()

C:\lp4e> type spamup.txt
SPAM
SPAM
SPAM!
```

But, as suggested earlier, we could also pass in arbitrary objects wrapped up in classes that define the required input and output method interfaces. Here's a simple example that passes in a writer class that wraps up the text inside HTML tags:

```
C:\lp4e> python
>>> from converters import Uppercase
>>>
>>> class HTMLize:
...         def write(self, line):
...             print('<PRE>%s</PRE>' % line.rstrip())
...
>>> Uppercase(open('spam.txt'), HTMLize()).process()
<PRE>SPAM</PRE>
<PRE>SPAM</PRE>
<PRE>SPAM!</PRE>
```

If you trace through this example's control flow, you'll see that we get both uppercase conversion (by inheritance) and HTML formatting (by composition), even though the core processing logic in the original `Processor` superclass knows nothing about either step. The processing code only cares that writers have a `write` method and that a method named `convert` is defined; it doesn't care what those methods do when they are called. Such polymorphism and encapsulation of logic is behind much of the power of classes.

As is, the `Processor` superclass only provides a file-scanning loop. In more realistic work, we might extend it to support additional programming tools for its subclasses, and, in the process, turn it into a full-blown framework. Coding such a tool once in a superclass enables you to reuse it in all of your programs. Even in this simple example, because so much is packaged and inherited with classes, all we had to code was the HTML formatting step; the rest was free.

For another example of composition at work, see exercise 9 at the end of Chapter 31 and its solution in Appendix B; it's similar to the pizza shop example. We've focused on inheritance in this book because that is the main tool that the Python language itself provides for OOP. But, in practice, composition is used as much as inheritance as a way to structure classes, especially in larger systems. As we've seen, inheritance and composition are often complementary (and sometimes alternative) techniques. Because composition is a design issue outside the scope of the Python language and this book, though, I'll defer to other resources for more on this topic.

Why You Will Care: Classes and Persistence

I've mentioned Python's `pickle` and `shelve` object persistence support a few times in this part of the book because it works especially well with class instances. In fact, these tools are often compelling enough to motivate the use of classes in general—by pickling or shelving a class instance, we get data storage that contains both data and logic combined.

For example, besides allowing us to simulate real-world interactions, the pizza shop classes developed in this chapter could also be used as the basis of a persistent restaurant database. Instances of classes can be stored away on disk in a single step using Python's `pickle` or `shelve` modules. We used shelves to store instances of classes in the OOP tutorial in Chapter 27, but the object pickling interface is remarkably easy to use as well:

```
import pickle
object = someClass()
file   = open(filename, 'wb')      # Create external file
pickle.dump(object, file)          # Save object in file

import pickle
file   = open(filename, 'rb')
object = pickle.load(file)         # Fetch it back later
```

Pickling converts in-memory objects to serialized byte streams (really, strings), which may be stored in files, sent across a network, and so on; unpickling converts back from byte streams to identical in-memory objects. Shelves are similar, but they automatically pickle objects to an access-by-key database, which exports a dictionary-like interface:

```
import shelve
object = someClass()
dbase  = shelve.open('filename')
dbase['key'] = object          # Save under key

import shelve
dbase  = shelve.open('filename')
object = dbase['key']          # Fetch it back later
```

In our pizza shop example, using classes to model employees means we can get a simple database of employees and shops with little extra work—pickling such instance objects to a file makes them persistent across Python program executions:

```
>>> from pizzashop import PizzaShop
>>> shop = PizzaShop()
>>> shop.server, shop.chef
(<Employee: name=Pat, salary=40000>, <Employee: name=Bob, salary=50000>)
>>> import pickle
>>> pickle.dump(shop, open('shopfile.dat', 'wb'))
```

This stores an entire composite shop object in a file all at once. To bring it back later in another session or program, a single step suffices as well. In fact, objects restored this way retain both state and behavior:

```
>>> import pickle
>>> obj = pickle.load(open('shopfile.dat', 'rb'))
>>> obj.server, obj.chef
(<Employee: name=Pat, salary=40000>, <Employee: name=Bob, salary=50000>)
>>> obj.order('Sue')
Sue orders from <Employee: name=Pat, salary=40000>
Bob makes pizza
oven bakes
Sue pays for item to <Employee: name=Pat, salary=40000>
```

See the standard library manual and later examples for more on pickles and shelves.

OOP and Delegation: "Wrapper" Objects

Beside inheritance and composition, object-oriented programmers often also talk about something called *delegation*, which usually implies controller objects that embed other objects to which they pass off operation requests. The controllers can take care of administrative activities, such as keeping track of accesses and so on. In Python, delegation is often implemented with the __getattr__ method hook; because it intercepts accesses to nonexistent attributes, a *wrapper* class (sometimes called a *proxy* class) can use __getattr__ to route arbitrary accesses to a wrapped object. The wrapper class retains the interface of the wrapped object and may add additional operations of its own.

Consider the file *trace.py*, for instance:

```
class wrapper:
    def __init__(self, object):
        self.wrapped = object                    # Save object
    def __getattr__(self, attrname):
        print('Trace:', attrname)                # Trace fetch
        return getattr(self.wrapped, attrname)   # Delegate fetch
```

Recall from Chapter 29 that __getattr__ gets the attribute name as a string. This code makes use of the getattr built-in function to fetch an attribute from the wrapped object by name string—getattr(X,N) is like X.N, except that N is an expression that evaluates to a string at runtime, not a variable. In fact, getattr(X,N) is similar to X.__dict__[N], but the former also performs an inheritance search, like X.N, while the latter does not (see "Namespace Dictionaries" on page 698 for more on the __dict__ attribute).

You can use the approach of this module's wrapper class to manage access to any object with attributes—lists, dictionaries, and even classes and instances. Here, the wrapper class simply prints a trace message on each attribute access and delegates the attribute request to the embedded wrapped object:

```
>>> from trace import wrapper
>>> x = wrapper([1,2,3])              # Wrap a list
>>> x.append(4)                       # Delegate to list method
Trace: append
>>> x.wrapped                         # Print my member
[1, 2, 3, 4]

>>> x = wrapper({"a": 1, "b": 2})     # Wrap a dictionary
>>> list(x.keys())                    # Delegate to dictionary method
Trace: keys
['a', 'b']
```

The net effect is to augment the entire interface of the wrapped object, with additional code in the wrapper class. We can use this to log our method calls, route method calls to extra or custom logic, and so on.

We'll revive the notions of wrapped objects and delegated operations as one way to extend built-in types in Chapter 31. If you are interested in the delegation design pattern, also watch for the discussions in Chapters 31 and 38 of *function decorators*, a strongly related concept designed to augment a specific function or method call rather than the entire interface of an object, and *class decorators*, which serve as a way to automatically add such delegation-based wrappers to all instances of a class.

Version skew note: In Python 2.6, operator overloading methods run by built-in operations are routed through generic attribute interception methods like __getattr__. Printing a wrapped object directly, for example, calls this method for __repr__ or __str__, which then passes the call on to the wrapped object. In Python 3.0, this no longer happens: printing does not trigger __getattr__, and a default display is used instead. In 3.0, new-style classes look up operator overloading methods in classes and skip the normal instance lookup entirely. We'll return to this issue in Chapter 37, in the context of managed attributes; for now, keep in mind that you may need to redefine operator overloading methods in wrapper classes (either by hand, by tools, or by superclasses) if you want them to be intercepted in 3.0.

Pseudoprivate Class Attributes

Besides larger structuring goals, class designs often must address name usage too. In Part V, we learned that every name assigned at the top level of a module file is exported. By default, the same holds for classes—data hiding is a convention, and clients may fetch or change any class or instance attribute they like. In fact, attributes are all "public" and "virtual," in C++ terms; they're all accessible everywhere and are looked up dynamically at runtime.[*]

That said, Python today does support the notion of name "mangling" (i.e., expansion) to localize some names in classes. Mangled names are sometimes misleadingly called "private attributes," but really this is just a way to *localize* a name to the class that created it—name mangling does not prevent access by code outside the class. This feature is mostly intended to avoid namespace collisions in instances, not to restrict access to names in general; mangled names are therefore better called "pseudoprivate" than "private."

Pseudoprivate names are an advanced and entirely optional feature, and you probably won't find them very useful until you start writing general tools or larger class hierarchies for use in multiprogrammer projects. In fact, they are not always used even when they probably should be—more commonly, Python programmers code internal names with a single underscore (e.g., _X), which is just an informal convention to let you know that a name shouldn't be changed (it means nothing to Python itself).

Because you may see this feature in other people's code, though, you need to be somewhat aware of it, even if you don't use it yourself.

---

[*] This tends to scare people with a C++ background unnecessarily. In Python, it's even possible to change or completely delete a class method at runtime. On the other hand, almost nobody ever does this in practical programs. As a scripting language, Python is more about enabling than restricting. Also, recall from our discussion of operator overloading in Chapter 29 that __getattr__ and __setattr__ can be used to emulate privacy, but are generally not used for this purpose in practice. More on this when we code a more realistic privacy decorator Chapter 38.

Name Mangling Overview

Here's how name mangling works: names inside a `class` statement that start with two underscores but don't end with two underscores are automatically expanded to include the name of the enclosing class. For instance, a name like `__X` within a class named `Spam` is changed to `_Spam__X` automatically: the original name is prefixed with a single underscore and the enclosing class's name. Because the modified name contains the name of the enclosing class, it's somewhat unique; it won't clash with similar names created by other classes in a hierarchy.

Name mangling happens only in `class` statements, and only for names that begin with two leading underscores. However, it happens for *every* name preceded with double underscores—both class attributes (like method names) and instance attribute names assigned to `self` attributes. For example, in a class named `Spam`, a method named `__meth` is mangled to `_Spam__meth`, and an instance attribute reference `self.__X` is transformed to `self._Spam__X`. Because more than one class may add attributes to an instance, this mangling helps avoid clashes—but we need to move on to an example to see how.

Why Use Pseudoprivate Attributes?

One of the main problems that the pseudoprivate attribute feature is meant to alleviate has to do with the way instance attributes are stored. In Python, all instance attributes wind up in the single instance object at the bottom of the class tree. This is different from the C++ model, where each class gets its own space for data members it defines.

Within a class method in Python, whenever a method assigns to a `self` attribute (e.g., `self.attr = value`), it changes or creates an attribute in the instance (inheritance searches happen only on reference, not on assignment). Because this is true even if multiple classes in a hierarchy assign to the same attribute, collisions are possible.

For example, suppose that when a programmer codes a class, she assumes that she owns the attribute name `X` in the instance. In this class's methods, the name is set, and later fetched:

```
class C1:
    def meth1(self): self.X = 88       # I assume X is mine
    def meth2(self): print(self.X)
```

Suppose further that another programmer, working in isolation, makes the same assumption in a class that he codes:

```
class C2:
    def metha(self): self.X = 99       # Me too
    def methb(self): print(self.X)
```

Both of these classes work by themselves. The problem arises if the two classes are ever mixed together in the same class tree:

```
class C3(C1, C2): ...
I = C3()                                    # Only 1 X in I!
```

Now, the value that each class gets back when it says self.X will depend on which class assigned it last. Because all assignments to self.X refer to the same single instance, there is only one X attribute—I.X—no matter how many classes use that attribute name.

To guarantee that an attribute belongs to the class that uses it, prefix the name with double underscores everywhere it is used in the class, as in this file, *private.py*:

```
class C1:
    def meth1(self): self.__X = 88          # Now X is mine
    def meth2(self): print(self.__X)        # Becomes _C1__X in I
class C2:
    def metha(self): self.__X = 99          # Me too
    def methb(self): print(self.__X)        # Becomes _C2__X in I

class C3(C1, C2): pass
I = C3()                                    # Two X names in I

I.meth1(); I.metha()
print(I.__dict__)
I.meth2(); I.methb()
```

When thus prefixed, the X attributes will be expanded to include the names of their classes before being added to the instance. If you run a dir call on I or inspect its namespace dictionary after the attributes have been assigned, you'll see the expanded names, _C1__X and _C2__X, but not X. Because the expansion makes the names unique within the instance, the class coders can safely assume that they truly own any names that they prefix with two underscores:

```
% python private.py
{'_C2__X': 99, '_C1__X': 88}
88
99
```

This trick can avoid potential name collisions in the instance, but note that it does not amount to true privacy. If you know the name of the enclosing class, you can still access either of these attributes anywhere you have a reference to the instance by using the fully expanded name (e.g., I._C1__X = 77). On the other hand, this feature makes it less likely that you will *accidentally* step on a class's names.

Pseudoprivate attributes are also useful in larger frameworks or tools, both to avoid introducing new method names that might accidentally hide definitions elsewhere in the class tree and to reduce the chance of internal methods being replaced by names defined lower in the tree. If a method is intended for use only within a class that may be mixed into other classes, the double underscore prefix ensures that the method won't interfere with other names in the tree, especially in multiple-inheritance scenarios:

```
class Super:
    def method(self): ...                   # A real application method

class Tool:
```

```
        def __method(self): ...              # Becomes _Tool__method
        def other(self): self.__method()     # Use my internal method

    class Sub1(Tool, Super): ...
        def actions(self): self.method()     # Runs Super.method as expected

    class Sub2(Tool):
        def __init__(self): self.method = 99  # Doesn't break Tool.__method
```

We met multiple inheritance briefly in Chapter 25 and will explore it in more detail later in this chapter. Recall that superclasses are searched according to their left-to-right order in class header lines. Here, this means Sub1 prefers Tool attributes to those in Super. Although in this example we could force Python to pick the application class's methods first by switching the order of the superclasses listed in the Sub1 class header, pseudoprivate attributes resolve the issue altogether. Pseudoprivate names also prevent subclasses from accidentally redefining the internal method's names, as in Sub2.

Again, I should note that this feature tends to be of use primarily for larger, multiprogrammer projects, and then only for selected names. Don't be tempted to clutter your code unnecessarily; only use this feature for names that truly need to be controlled by a single class. For simpler programs, it's probably overkill.

For more examples that make use of the __X naming feature, see the *lister.py* mix-in classes introduced later in this chapter, in the section on multiple inheritance, as well as the discussion of Private class decorators in Chapter 38. If you care about privacy in general, you might want to review the emulation of private instance attributes sketched in the section "Attribute Reference: __getattr__ and __setattr__" on page 720 in Chapter 29, and watch for the Private class decorator in Chapter 38 that we will base upon this special method. Although it's possible to emulate true access controls in Python classes, this is rarely done in practice, even for large systems.

Methods Are Objects: Bound or Unbound

Methods in general, and bound methods in particular, simplify the implementation of many design goals in Python. We met bound methods briefly while studying __call__ in Chapter 29. The full story, which we'll flesh out here, turns out to be more general and flexible than you might expect.

In Chapter 19, we learned how functions can be processed as normal objects. Methods are a kind of object too, and can be used generically in much the same way as other objects—they can be assigned, passed to functions, stored in data structures, and so on. Because class methods can be accessed from an instance or a class, though, they actually come in two flavors in Python:

Unbound class method objects: no `self`

Accessing a function attribute of a class by qualifying the class returns an unbound method object. To call the method, you must provide an instance object explicitly as the first argument. In Python 3.0, an unbound method is the same as a simple function and can be called though the class's name; in 2.6 it's a distinct type and cannot be called without providing an instance.

Bound instance method objects: `self` *+ function pairs*

Accessing a function attribute of a class by qualifying an instance returns a bound method object. Python automatically packages the instance with the function in the bound method object, so you don't need to pass an instance to call the method.

Both kinds of methods are full-fledged objects; they can be transferred around a program at will, just like strings and numbers. Both also require an instance in their first argument when run (i.e., a value for `self`). This is why we had to pass in an instance explicitly when calling superclass methods from subclass methods in the previous chapter; technically, such calls produce unbound method objects.

When calling a bound method object, Python provides an instance for you automatically—the instance used to create the bound method object. This means that bound method objects are usually interchangeable with simple function objects, and makes them especially useful for interfaces originally written for functions (see the sidebar "Why You Will Care: Bound Methods and Callbacks" on page 758 for a realistic example).

To illustrate, suppose we define the following class:

```
class Spam:
    def doit(self, message):
        print(message)
```

Now, in normal operation, we make an instance and call its method in a single step to print the passed-in argument:

```
object1 = Spam()
object1.doit('hello world')
```

Really, though, a *bound* method object is generated along the way, just before the method call's parentheses. In fact, we can fetch a bound method without actually calling it. An *object.name* qualification is an object expression. In the following, it returns a bound method object that packages the instance (`object1`) with the method function (`Spam.doit`). We can assign this bound method pair to another name and then call it as though it were a simple function:

```
object1 = Spam()
x = object1.doit          # Bound method object: instance+function
x('hello world')          # Same effect as object1.doit('...')
```

On the other hand, if we qualify the class to get to `doit`, we get back an *unbound* method object, which is simply a reference to the function object. To call this type of method, we must pass in an instance as the leftmost argument:

```
object1 = Spam()
t = Spam.doit            # Unbound method object (a function in 3.0: see ahead)
t(object1, 'howdy')      # Pass in instance (if the method expects one in 3.0)
```

By extension, the same rules apply within a class's method if we reference `self` attributes that refer to functions in the class. A `self.`*method* expression is a bound method object because `self` is an instance object:

```
class Eggs:
    def m1(self, n):
        print(n)
    def m2(self):
        x = self.m1          # Another bound method object
        x(42)                # Looks like a simple function

Eggs().m2()                  # Prints 42
```

Most of the time, you call methods immediately after fetching them with attribute qualification, so you don't always notice the method objects generated along the way. But if you start writing code that calls objects generically, you need to be careful to treat unbound methods specially—they normally require an explicit instance object to be passed in.[†]

Unbound Methods are Functions in 3.0

In Python 3.0, the language has dropped the notion of *unbound methods*. What we describe as an unbound method here is treated as a simple function in 3.0. For most purposes, this makes no difference to your code; either way, an instance will be passed to a method's first argument when it's called through an instance.

Programs that do explicit type testing might be impacted, though—if you print the type of an instance-less class method, it displays "unbound method" in 2.6, and "function" in 3.0.

Moreover, in 3.0 it is OK to call a method without an instance, as long as the method does not expect one and you call it only through the class and never through an instance. That is, Python 3.0 will pass along an instance to methods only for through-instance calls. When calling through a class, you must pass an instance manually only if the method expects one:

```
C:\misc> c:\python30\python
>>> class Selfless:
```

[†] See the discussion of static and class methods in Chapter 31 for an optional exception to this rule. Like bound methods, static methods can masquerade as basic functions because they do not expect instances when called. Python supports three kinds of class methods—instance, static, and class—and 3.0 allows simple functions in classes, too.

```
...       def __init__(self, data):
...           self.data = data
...       def selfless(arg1, arg2):        # A simple function in 3.0
...           return arg1 + arg2
...       def normal(self, arg1, arg2):    # Instance expected when called
...           return self.data + arg1 + arg2
...
>>> X = Selfless(2)
>>> X.normal(3, 4)                    # Instance passed to self automatically
9
>>> Selfless.normal(X, 3, 4)          # self expected by method: pass manually
9
>>> Selfless.selfless(3, 4)           # No instance: works in 3.0, fails in 2.6!
7
```

The last test in this fails in 2.6, because unbound methods require an instance to be passed by default; it works in 3.0 because such methods are treated as simple functions not requiring an instance. Although this removes some potential error trapping in 3.0 (what if a programmer accidentally forgets to pass an instance?), it allows class methods to be used as simple functions as long as they are not passed and do not expect a "self" instance argument.

The following two calls still fail in both 3.0 and 2.6, though—the first (calling through an instance) automatically passes an instance to a method that does not expect one, while the second (calling through a class) does not pass an instance to a method that does expect one:

```
>>> X.selfless(3, 4)
TypeError: selfless() takes exactly 2 positional arguments (3 given)

>>> Selfless.normal(3, 4)
TypeError: normal() takes exactly 3 positional arguments (2 given)
```

Because of this change, the `staticmethod` decorator described in the next chapter is not needed in 3.0 for methods without a `self` argument that are called only through the class name, and never through an instance—such methods are run as simple functions, without receiving an instance argument. In 2.6, such calls are errors unless an instance is passed manually (more on static methods in the next chapter).

It's important to be aware of the differences in behavior in 3.0, but bound methods are generally more important from a practical perspective anyway. Because they pair together the instance and function in a single object, they can be treated as callables generically. The next section demonstrates what this means in code.

 For a more visual illustration of unbound method treatment in Python 3.0 and 2.6, see also the *lister.py* example in the multiple inheritance section later in this chapter. Its classes print the value of methods fetched from both instances and classes, in both versions of Python.

Bound Methods and Other Callable Objects

As mentioned earlier, bound methods can be processed as generic objects, just like simple functions—they can be passed around a program arbitrarily. Moreover, because bound methods combine both a function and an instance in a single package, they can be treated like any other callable object and require no special syntax when invoked. The following, for example, stores four bound method objects in a list and calls them later with normal call expressions:

```
>>> class Number:
...     def __init__(self, base):
...         self.base = base
...     def double(self):
...         return self.base * 2
...     def triple(self):
...         return self.base * 3
...
>>> x = Number(2)                                 # Class instance objects
>>> y = Number(3)                                 # State + methods
>>> z = Number(4)
>>> x.double()                                    # Normal immediate calls
4

>>> acts = [x.double, y.double, y.triple, z.double]    # List of bound methods
>>> for act in acts:                              # Calls are deferred
...     print(act())                              # Call as though functions
...
4
6
9
8
```

Like simple functions, bound method objects have introspection information of their own, including attributes that give access to the instance object and method function they pair. Calling the bound method simply dispatches the pair:

```
>>> bound = x.double
>>> bound.__self__, bound.__func__
(<__main__.Number object at 0x0278F610>, <function double at 0x027A4ED0>)
>>> bound.__self__.base
2
>>> bound()                          # Calls bound.__func__(bound.__self__, ...)
4
```

In fact, bound methods are just one of a handful of callable object types in Python. As the following demonstrates, simple functions coded with a def or lambda, instances that inherit a __call__, and bound instance methods can all be treated and called the same way:

```
>>> def square(arg):
...     return arg ** 2                          # Simple functions (def or lambda)
...
>>> class Sum:
...     def __init__(self, val):                 # Callable instances
```

```
...          self.val = val
...      def __call__(self, arg):
...          return self.val + arg
...
>>> class Product:
...      def __init__(self, val):                    # Bound methods
...          self.val = val
...      def method(self, arg):
...          return self.val * arg
...
>>> sobject = Sum(2)
>>> pobject = Product(3)
>>> actions = [square, sobject, pobject.method]      # Function, instance, method

>>> for act in actions:                              # All 3 called same way
...      print(act(5))                                # Call any 1-arg callable
...
25
7
15
>>> actions[-1](5)                                   # Index, comprehensions, maps
15
>>> [act(5) for act in actions]
[25, 7, 15]
>>> list(map(lambda act: act(5), actions))
[25, 7, 15]
```

Technically speaking, classes belong in the callable objects category too, but we normally call them to generate instances rather than to do actual work, as shown here:

```
>>> class Negate:
...      def __init__(self, val):                    # Classes are callables too
...          self.val = -val                          # But called for object, not work
...      def __repr__(self):                          # Instance print format
...          return str(self.val)
...
>>> actions = [square, sobject, pobject.method, Negate]   # Call a class too
>>> for act in actions:
...      print(act(5))
...
25
7
15
-5
>>> [act(5) for act in actions]                      # Runs __repr__ not __str__!
[25, 7, 15, -5]

>>> table = {act(5): act for act in actions}         # 3.0 dict comprehension
>>> for (key, value) in table.items():
...      print('{0:2} => {1}'.format(key, value))     # 2.6/3.0 str.format
...
-5 => <class '__main__.Negate'>
25 => <function square at 0x025D4978>
15 => <bound method Product.method of <__main__.Product object at 0x025D0F90>>
 7 => <__main__.Sum object at 0x025D0F70>
```

As you can see, bound methods, and Python's callable objects model in general, are some of the many ways that Python's design makes for an incredibly flexible language.

You should now understand the method object model. For other examples of bound methods at work, see the upcoming sidebar "Why You Will Care: Bound Methods and Callbacks" as well as the prior chapter's discussion of callback handlers in the section on the method __call__.

Why You Will Care: Bound Methods and Callbacks

Because bound methods automatically pair an instance with a class method function, you can use them anywhere a simple function is expected. One of the most common places you'll see this idea put to work is in code that registers methods as event callback handlers in the tkinter GUI interface (named Tkinter in Python 2.6). Here's the simple case:

```
def handler():
    ...use globals for state...
...
widget = Button(text='spam', command=handler)
```

To register a handler for button click events, we usually pass a callable object that takes no arguments to the command keyword argument. Function names (and lambdas) work here, and so do class methods, as long as they are bound methods:

```
class MyWidget:
    def handler(self):
        ...use self.attr for state...
    def makewidgets(self):
        b = Button(text='spam', command=self.handler)
```

Here, the event handler is self.handler—a bound method object that remembers both self and MyGui.handler. Because self will refer to the original instance when handler is later invoked on events, the method will have access to instance attributes that can retain state between events. With simple functions, state normally must be retained in global variables or enclosing function scopes instead. See also the discussion of __call__ operator overloading in Chapter 29 for another way to make classes compatible with function-based APIs.

Multiple Inheritance: "Mix-in" Classes

Many class-based designs call for combining disparate sets of methods. In a class statement, more than one superclass can be listed in parentheses in the header line. When you do this, you use something called *multiple inheritance*—the class and its instances inherit names from *all* the listed superclasses.

When searching for an attribute, Python's inheritance search traverses all superclasses in the class header from left to right until a match is found. Technically, because any of the superclasses may have superclasses of its own, this search can be a bit more complex for larger class tress:

- In classic classes (the default until Python 3.0), the attribute search proceeds depth-first all the way to the top of the inheritance tree, and then from left to right.
- In new-style classes (and all classes in 3.0), the attribute search proceeds across by tree levels, in a more breadth-first fashion (see the new-style class discussion in the next chapter).

In either model, though, when a class has multiple superclasses, they are searched from left to right according to the order listed in the `class` statement header lines.

In general, multiple inheritance is good for modeling objects that belong to more than one set. For instance, a person may be an engineer, a writer, a musician, and so on, and inherit properties from all such sets. With multiple inheritance, objects obtain the union of the behavior in all their superclasses.

Perhaps the most common way multiple inheritance is used is to "mix in" general-purpose methods from superclasses. Such superclasses are usually called *mix-in classes*—they provide methods you add to application classes by inheritance. In a sense, mix-in classes are similar to modules: they provide packages of methods for use in their client subclasses. Unlike simple functions in modules, though, methods in mix-ins also have access to the `self` instance, for using state information and other methods. The next section demonstrates one common use case for such tools.

Coding Mix-in Display Classes

As we've seen, Python's default way to print a class instance object isn't incredibly useful:

```
>>> class Spam:
...     def __init__(self):          # No __repr__ or __str__
...         self.data1 = "food"
...
>>> X = Spam()
>>> print(X)                         # Default: class, address
<__main__.Spam object at 0x00864818>  # Displays "instance" in Python 2.6
```

As you saw in Chapter 29 when studying operator overloading, you can provide a `__str__` or `__repr__` method to implement a custom string representation of your own. But, rather than coding one of these in each and every class you wish to print, why not code it once in a general-purpose tool class and inherit it in all your classes?

That's what mix-ins are for. Defining a display method in a mix-in superclass once enables us to reuse it anywhere we want to see a custom display format. We've already seen tools that do related work:

- Chapter 27's `AttrDisplay` class formatted instance attributes in a generic `__str__` method, but it did not climb class trees and was used in single-inheritance mode only.

- Chapter 28's *classtree.py* module defined functions for climbing and sketching class trees, but it did not display object attributes along the way and was not architected as an inheritable class.

Here, we're going to revisit these examples' techniques and expand upon them to code a set of three mix-in classes that serve as generic display tools for listing instance attributes, inherited attributes, and attributes on all objects in a class tree. We'll also use our tools in multiple-inheritance mode and deploy coding techniques that make classes better suited to use as generic tools.

Listing instance attributes with __dict__

Let's get started with the simple case—listing attributes attached to an instance. The following class, coded in the file *lister.py*, defines a mix-in called `ListInstance` that overloads the `__str__` method for all classes that include it in their header lines. Because this is coded as a class, `ListInstance` is a generic tool whose formatting logic can be used for instances of any subclass:

```
# File lister.py

class ListInstance:
    """
    Mix-in class that provides a formatted print() or str() of
    instances via inheritance of __str__, coded here; displays
    instance attrs only; self is the instance of lowest class;
    uses __X names to avoid clashing with client's attrs
    """
    def __str__(self):
        return '<Instance of %s, address %s:\n%s>' % (
                          self.__class__.__name__,         # My class's name
                          id(self),                        # My address
                          self.__attrnames())             # name=value list
    def __attrnames(self):
        result = ''
        for attr in sorted(self.__dict__):                # Instance attr dict
            result += '\tname %s=%s\n' % (attr, self.__dict__[attr])
        return result
```

`ListInstance` uses some previously explored tricks to extract the instance's class name and attributes:

- Each instance has a built-in `__class__` attribute that references the class from which it was created, and each class has a `__name__` attribute that references the name in the header, so the expression `self.__class__.__name__` fetches the name of an instance's class.

- This class does most of its work by simply scanning the instance's attribute dictionary (remember, it's exported in __dict__) to build up a string showing the names and values of all instance attributes. The dictionary's keys are sorted to finesse any ordering differences across Python releases.

In these respects, ListInstance is similar to Chapter 27's attribute display; in fact, it's largely just a variation on a theme. Our class here uses two additional techniques, though:

- It displays the instance's memory address by calling the id built-function, which returns any object's address (by definition, a unique object identifier, which will be useful in later mutations of this code).
- It uses the *pseudoprivate* naming pattern for its worker method: __attrnames. As we learned earlier in his chapter, Python automatically localizes any such name to its enclosing class by expanding the attribute name to include the class name (in this case, it becomes _ListInstance__attrnames). This holds true for both class attributes (like methods) and instance attributes attached to self. This behavior is useful in a general tool like this, as it ensures that its names don't clash with any names used in its client subclasses.

Because ListInstance defines a __str__ operator overloading method, instances derived from this class display their attributes automatically when printed, giving a bit more information than a simple address. Here is the class in action, in single-inheritance mode (this code works the same in both Python 3.0 and 2.6):

```
>>> from lister import ListInstance
>>> class Spam(ListInstance):          # Inherit a __str__ method
...     def __init__(self):
...         self.data1 = 'food'
...
>>> x = Spam()
>>> print(x)                           # print() and str() run __str__
<Instance of Spam, address 40240880:
    name data1=food
>
```

You can also fetch the listing output as a string without printing it with str, and interactive echoes still use the default format:

```
>>> str(x)
'<Instance of Spam, address 40240880:\n\tname data1=food\n>'
>>> x                                  # The __repr__ still is a default
<__main__.Spam object at 0x026606F0>
```

The ListInstance class is useful for any classes you write—even classes that already have one or more superclasses. This is where *multiple inheritance* comes in handy: by adding ListInstance to the list of superclasses in a class header (i.e., mixing it in), you get its __str__ "for free" while still inheriting from the existing superclass(es). The file *testmixin.py* demonstrates:

```
# File testmixin.py

from lister import *                    # Get lister tool classes

class Super:
    def __init__(self):               # Superclass __init__
        self.data1 = 'spam'           # Create instance attrs
    def ham(self):
        pass

class Sub(Super, ListInstance):        # Mix in ham and a __str__
    def __init__(self):               # listers have access to self
        Super.__init__(self)
        self.data2 = 'eggs'           # More instance attrs
        self.data3 = 42
    def spam(self):                    # Define another method here
        pass

if __name__ == '__main__':
    X = Sub()
    print(X)                           # Run mixed-in __str__
```

Here, `Sub` inherits names from both `Super` and `ListInstance`; it's a composite of its own names and names in both its superclasses. When you make a `Sub` instance and print it, you automatically get the custom representation mixed in from `ListInstance` (in this case, this script's output is the same under both Python 3.0 and 2.6, except for object addresses):

```
C:\misc> C:\python30\python testmixin.py
<Instance of Sub, address 40962576:
        name data1=spam
        name data2=eggs
        name data3=42
>
```

`ListInstance` works in any class it's mixed into because `self` refers to an instance of the subclass that pulls this class in, whatever that may be. In a sense, mix-in classes are the class equivalent of modules—packages of methods useful in a variety of clients. For example, here is `Lister` working again in single-inheritance mode on a different class's instances, with `import` and attributes set outside the class:

```
>>> import lister
>>> class C(lister.ListInstance): pass
...
>>> x = C()
>>> x.a = 1; x.b = 2; x.c = 3
>>> print(x)
<Instance of C, address 40961776:
        name a=1
        name b=2
        name c=3
>
```

Besides the utility they provide, mix-ins optimize code maintenance, like all classes do. For example, if you later decide to extend `ListInstance`'s `__str__` to also print all the class attributes that an instance inherits, you're safe; because it's an inherited method, changing `__str__` automatically updates the display of each subclass that imports the class and mixes it in. Since it's now officially "later," let's move on to the next section to see what such an extension might look like.

Listing inherited attributes with dir

As it is, our `Lister` mix-in displays instance attributes only (i.e., names attached to the instance object itself). It's trivial to extend the class to display all the attributes accessible from an instance, though—both its own and those it inherits from its classes. The trick is to use the `dir` built-in function instead of scanning the instance's `__dict__` dictionary; the latter holds instance attributes only, but the former also collects all inherited attributes in Python 2.2 and later.

The following mutation codes this scheme; I've renamed it to facilitate simple testing, but if this were to *replace* the original version, all existing clients would pick up the new display automatically:

```python
# File lister.py, continued

class ListInherited:
    """
    Use dir() to collect both instance attrs and names
    inherited from its classes; Python 3.0 shows more
    names than 2.6 because of the implied object superclass
    in the new-style class model; getattr() fetches inherited
    names not in self.__dict__; use __str__, not __repr__,
    or else this loops when printing bound methods!
    """
    def __str__(self):
        return '<Instance of %s, address %s:\n%s>' % (
                    self.__class__.__name__,          # My class's name
                    id(self),                         # My address
                    self.__attrnames())               # name=value list
    def __attrnames(self):
        result = ''
        for attr in dir(self):                        # Instance dir()
            if attr[:2] == '__' and attr[-2:] == '__':  # Skip internals
                result += '\tname %s=<>\n' % attr
            else:
                result += '\tname %s=%s\n' % (attr, getattr(self, attr))
        return result
```

Notice that this code skips `__X__` names' values; most of these are internal names that we don't generally care about in a generic listing like this. This version also must use the `getattr` built-in function to fetch attributes by name string instead of using instance attribute dictionary indexing—`getattr` employs the inheritance search protocol, and some of the names we're listing here are not stored on the instance itself.

To test the new version, change the *testmixin.py* file to use this new class instead:

```
class Sub(Super, ListInherited):                        # Mix in a __str__
```

This file's output varies per release. In Python 2.6, we get the following; notice the name mangling at work in the lister's method name (I shortened its full value display to fit on this page):

```
C:\misc> c:\python26\python testmixin.py
<Instance of Sub, address 40073136:
        name _ListInherited__attrnames=<bound method Sub.__attrnames of <...more...>>
        name __doc__=<>
        name __init__=<>
        name __module__=<>
        name __str__=<>
        name data1=spam
        name data2=eggs
        name data3=42
        name ham=<bound method Sub.ham of <__main__.Sub instance at 0x026377B0>>
        name spam=<bound method Sub.spam of <__main__.Sub instance at 0x026377B0>>
>
```

In Python 3.0, more attributes are displayed because all classes are "new-style" and inherit names from the implied `object` superclass (more on this in Chapter 31). Because so many names are inherited from the default superclass, I've omitted many here; run this on your own for the full listing:

```
C:\misc> c:\python30\python testmixin.py
<Instance of Sub, address 40831792:
        name _ListInherited__attrnames=<bound method Sub.__attrnames of <...more...>>
        name __class__=<>
        name __delattr__=<>
        name __dict__=<>
        name __doc__=<>
        name __eq__=<>
        ...more names omitted...
        name __repr__=<>
        name __setattr__=<>
        name __sizeof__=<>
        name __str__=<>
        name __subclasshook__=<>
        name __weakref__=<>
        name data1=spam
        name data2=eggs
        name data3=42
        name ham=<bound method Sub.ham of <__main__.Sub object at 0x026F0B30>>
        name spam=<bound method Sub.spam of <__main__.Sub object at 0x026F0B30>>
>
```

One caution here—now that we're displaying inherited methods too, we have to use __str__ instead of __repr__ to overload printing. With __repr__, this code will *loop*—displaying the value of a method triggers the __repr__ of the method's class, in order to display the class. That is, if the lister's __repr__ tries to display a method, displaying the method's class will trigger the lister's __repr__ again. Subtle, but true! Change __str__ to __repr__ here to see this for yourself. If you must use __repr__ in such a context, you can avoid the loops by using isinstance to compare the type of attribute values against types.MethodType in the standard library, to know which items to skip.

Listing attributes per object in class trees

Let's code one last extension. As it is, our lister doesn't tell us which class an inherited name comes from. As we saw in the *classtree.py* example near the end of Chapter 28, though, it's straightforward to climb class inheritance trees in code. The following mix-in class makes use of this same technique to display attributes grouped by the classes they live in—it sketches the full class tree, displaying attributes attached to each object along the way. It does so by traversing the inheritance tree from an instance's __class__ to its class, and then from the class's __bases__ to all superclasses recursively, scanning object __dicts__s along the way:

```python
# File lister.py, continued

class ListTree:
    """
    Mix-in that returns an __str__ trace of the entire class
    tree and all its objects' attrs at and above self;
    run by print(), str() returns constructed string;
    uses __X attr names to avoid impacting clients;
    uses generator expr to recurse to superclasses;
    uses str.format() to make substitutions clearer
    """
    def __str__(self):
        self.__visited = {}
        return '<Instance of {0}, address {1}:\n{2}{3}>'.format(
                        self.__class__.__name__,
                        id(self),
                        self.__attrnames(self, 0),
                        self.__listclass(self.__class__, 4))

    def __listclass(self, aClass, indent):
        dots = '.' * indent
        if aClass in self.__visited:
            return '\n{0}<Class {1}:, address {2}: (see above)>\n'.format(
                        dots,
                        aClass.__name__,
                        id(aClass))
        else:
            self.__visited[aClass] = True
            genabove = (self.__listclass(c, indent+4) for c in aClass.__bases__)
            return '\n{0}<Class {1}, address {2}:\n{3}{4}{5}>\n'.format(
                        dots,
                        aClass.__name__,
                        id(aClass),
                        self.__attrnames(aClass, indent),
                        ''.join(genabove),
                        dots)

    def __attrnames(self, obj, indent):
```

```
        spaces = ' ' * (indent + 4)
        result = ''
        for attr in sorted(obj.__dict__):
            if attr.startswith('__') and attr.endswith('__'):
                result += spaces + '{0}=<>\n'.format(attr)
            else:
                result += spaces + '{0}={1}\n'.format(attr, getattr(obj, attr))
        return result
```

Note the use of a *generator expression* to direct the recursive calls for superclasses; it's activated by the nested string join method. Also see how this version uses the Python 3.0 and 2.6 string format method instead of % formatting expressions, to make substitutions clearer; when many substitutions are applied like this, explicit argument numbers may make the code easier to decipher. In short, in this version we exchange the first of the following lines for the second:

```
return '<Instance of %s, address %s:\n%s%s>' % (...)       # Expression
return '<Instance of {0}, address {1}:\n{2}{3}>'.format(...)   # Method
```

Now, change *testmixin.py* to inherit from this new class again to test:

```
class Sub(Super, ListTree):         # Mix in a __str__
```

The file's tree-sketcher output in Python 2.6 is then as follows:

```
C:\misc> c:\python26\python testmixin.py
<Instance of Sub, address 40728496:
    _ListTree__visited={}
    data1=spam
    data2=eggs
    data3=42

....<Class Sub, address 40701168:
        __doc__=<>
        __init__=<>
        __module__=<>
        spam=<unbound method Sub.spam>

........<Class Super, address 40701120:
            __doc__=<>
            __init__=<>
            __module__=<>
            ham=<unbound method Super.ham>
........>

........<Class ListTree, address 40700688:
            _ListTree__attrnames=<unbound method ListTree.__attrnames>
            _ListTree__listclass=<unbound method ListTree.__listclass>
            __doc__=<>
            __module__=<>
            __str__=<>
........>
....>
>
```

Notice in this output how methods are *unbound* now under 2.6, because we fetch them from classes directly, instead of from instances. Also observe how the lister's `__visited` table has its name mangled in the instance's attribute dictionary; unless we're very unlucky, this won't clash with other data there.

Under Python 3.0, we get extra attributes and superclasses again. Notice that unbound methods are simple *functions* in 3.0, as described in an earlier note in this chapter (and that again, I've deleted most built-in attributes in `object` to save space here; run this on your own for the complete listing):

```
C:\misc> c:\python30\python testmixin.py
<Instance of Sub, address 40635216:
    _ListTree__visited={}
    data1=spam
    data2=eggs
    data3=42

....<Class Sub, address 40914752:
        __doc__=<>
        __init__=<>
        __module__=<>
        spam=<function spam at 0x026D53D8>

........<Class Super, address 40829952:
            __dict__=<>
            __doc__=<>
            __init__=<>
            __module__=<>
            __weakref__=<>
            ham=<function ham at 0x026D5228>

............<Class object, address 505114624:
                __class__=<>
                __delattr__=<>
                __doc__=<>
                __eq__=<>
                ...more omitted...
                __repr__=<>
                __setattr__=<>
                __sizeof__=<>
                __str__=<>
                __subclasshook__=<>
............>
........>

........<Class ListTree, address 40829496:
            _ListTree__attrnames=<function __attrnames at 0x026D5660>
            _ListTree__listclass=<function __listclass at 0x026D56A8>
            __dict__=<>
            __doc__=<>
            __module__=<>
            __str__=<>
            __weakref__=<>
```

```
............<Class object:, address 505114624: (see above)>
........>
....>
>
```

This version avoids listing the same class object twice by keeping a table of classes *visited* so far (this is why an object's `id` is included—to serve as a key for a previously displayed item). Like the transitive module reloader of Chapter 24, a dictionary works to avoid repeats and cycles here because class objects may be dictionary keys; a set would provide similar functionality.

This version also takes care to avoid large internal objects by skipping __X__ names again. If you comment out the test for these names, their values will display normally. Here's an excerpt from the output in 2.6 with this temporary change made (it's much larger in its entirety, and it gets even worse in 3.0, which is why these names are probably better skipped!):

```
C:\misc> c:\python26\python testmixin.py
...more omitted...

........<Class ListTree, address 40700688:
          _ListTree__attrnames=<unbound method ListTree.__attrnames>
          _ListTree__listclass=<unbound method ListTree.__listclass>
          __doc__=
    Mix-in that returns the __str__ trace of the entire class
    tree and all its objects' attrs at and above self;
    run by print, str returns constructed string;
    uses __X attr names to avoid impacting clients;
    uses generator expr to recurse to superclasses;
    uses str.format() to make substitutions clearer

          __module__=lister
          __str__=<unbound method ListTree.__str__>
........>
```

For more fun, try mixing this class into something more substantial, like the `Button` class of Python's `tkinter` GUI toolkit module. In general, you'll want to name `List Tree` first (leftmost) in a `class` header, so its __str__ is picked up; `Button` has one, too, and the leftmost superclass is searched first in multiple inheritance. The output of the following is fairly massive (18K characters), so run this code on your own to see the full listing (and if you're using Python 2.6, recall that you should use `Tkinter` for the module name instead of `tkinter`):

```
>>> from lister import ListTree
>>> from tkinter import Button           # Both classes have a __str__
>>> class MyButton(ListTree, Button): pass  # ListTree first: use its __str__
...
>>> B = MyButton(text='spam')
>>> open('savetree.txt', 'w').write(str(B))  # Save to a file for later viewing
18247
>>> print(B)                             # Print the display here
<Instance of MyButton, address 44355632:
    _ListTree__visited={}
```

```
    _name=44355632
    _tclCommands=[]
    ...much more omitted...
>
```

Of course, there's much more we could do here (sketching the tree in a GUI might be a natural next step), but we'll leave further work as a suggested exercise. We'll also extend this code in the exercises at the end of this part of the book, to list superclass names in parentheses at the start of instance and class displays.

The main point here is that OOP is all about code reuse, and mix-in classes are a powerful example. Like almost everything else in programming, multiple inheritance can be a useful device when applied well. In practice, though, it is an advanced feature and can become complicated if used carelessly or excessively. We'll revisit this topic as a gotcha at the end of the next chapter. In that chapter, we'll also meet the new-style class model, which modifies the search order for one special multiple inheritance case. For more ideas, see also Python manuals for the `class.mro()` new-style class object method, which returns a list giving the class tree search order used by inheritance; this could be used by a class lister to show attribute sources.

 Supporting slots: Because they scan instance dictionaries, the `ListInstance` and `ListTree` classes presented here don't directly support attributes stored in *slots*—a newer and relatively rarely used option we'll meet in the next chapter, where instance attributes are declared in a `__slots__` class attribute. For example, if in *textmixin.py* we assign `__slots__=['data1']` in Super and `__slots__=['data3']` in Sub, only the `data2` attribute is displayed in the instance by these two lister classes; `ListTree` also displays `data1` and `data3`, but as attributes of the Super and Sub class objects and with a special format for their values (technically, they are class-level descriptors).

To better support slot attributes in these classes, change the `__dict__` scanning loops to also iterate through `__slots__` lists using code the next chapter will present, and use the `getattr` built-in function to fetch values instead of `__dict__` indexing (`ListTree` already does). Since instances inherit only the lowest class's `__slots__`, you may also need to come up with a policy when `__slots__` lists appear in multiple superclasses (`ListTree` already displays them as class attributes). `ListInherited` is immune to all this, because `dir` results combine both `__dict__` names and all classes' `__slots__` names.

Alternatively, as a policy we could simply let our code handle slot-based attributes as it currently does, rather than complicating it for a rare, advanced feature. Slots and normal instance attributes are different kinds of names. We'll investigate slots further in the next chapter; I omitted addressing them in these examples to avoid a forward dependency (not counting this note, of course!)—not exactly a valid design goal, but reasonable for a book.

Classes Are Objects: Generic Object Factories

Sometimes, class-based designs require objects to be created in response to conditions that can't be predicted when a program is written. The factory design pattern allows such a deferred approach. Due in large part to Python's flexibility, factories can take multiple forms, some of which don't seem special at all.

Because classes are objects, it's easy to pass them around a program, store them in data structures, and so on. You can also pass classes to functions that generate arbitrary kinds of objects; such functions are sometimes called *factories* in OOP design circles. Factories are a major undertaking in a strongly typed language such as C++ but are almost trivial to implement in Python. The call syntax we met in Chapter 18 can call any class with any number of constructor arguments in one step to generate any sort of instance:‡

```python
def factory(aClass, *args):              # Varargs tuple
    return aClass(*args)                 # Call aClass (or apply in 2.6 only)

class Spam:
    def doit(self, message):
        print(message)

class Person:
    def __init__(self, name, job):
        self.name = name
        self.job  = job

object1 = factory(Spam)                   # Make a Spam object
object2 = factory(Person, "Guido", "guru") # Make a Person object
```

In this code, we define an object generator function called `factory`. It expects to be passed a class object (any class will do) along with one or more arguments for the class's constructor. The function uses special "varargs" call syntax to call the function and return an instance.

The rest of the example simply defines two classes and generates instances of both by passing them to the `factory` function. And that's the only factory function you'll ever need to write in Python; it works for any class and any constructor arguments.

One possible improvement worth noting is that to support keyword arguments in constructor calls, the factory can collect them with a **args argument and pass them along in the class call, too:

```python
def factory(aClass, *args, **kwargs):    # +kwargs dict
    return aClass(*args, **kwargs)        # Call aClass
```

---

‡ Actually, this syntax can invoke any callable object, including functions, classes, and methods. Hence, the `factory` function here can also run any callable object, not just a class (despite the argument name). Also, as we learned in Chapter 18, Python 2.6 has an alternative to aClass(*args): the apply(aClass, args) built-in call, which has been removed in Python 3.0 because of its redundancy and limitations.

By now, you should know that everything is an "object" in Python, including things like classes, which are just compiler input in languages like C++. However, as mentioned at the start of this part of the book, only objects *derived* from classes are OOP objects in Python.

Why Factories?

So what good is the `factory` function (besides providing an excuse to illustrate class objects in this book)? Unfortunately, it's difficult to show applications of this design pattern without listing much more code than we have space for here. In general, though, such a factory might allow code to be insulated from the details of dynamically configured object construction.

For instance, recall the `processor` example presented in the abstract in Chapter 25, and then again as a composition example in this chapter. It accepts reader and writer objects for processing arbitrary data streams. The original version of this example manually passed in instances of specialized classes like `FileWriter` and `SocketReader` to customize the data streams being processed; later, we passed in hardcoded file, stream, and formatter objects. In a more dynamic scenario, external devices such as configuration files or GUIs might be used to configure the streams.

In such a dynamic world, we might not be able to hardcode the creation of stream interface objects in our scripts, but might instead create them at runtime according to the contents of a configuration file.

For example, the file might simply give the string name of a stream class to be imported from a module, plus an optional constructor call argument. Factory-style functions or code might come in handy here because they would allow us to fetch and pass in classes that are not hardcoded in our program ahead of time. Indeed, those classes might not even have existed at all when we wrote our code:

```
classname = ...parse from config file...
classarg  = ...parse from config file...

import streamtypes                            # Customizable code
aclass = getattr(streamtypes, classname)      # Fetch from module
reader = factory(aclass, classarg)            # Or aclass(classarg)
processor(reader, ...)
```

Here, the `getattr` built-in is again used to fetch a module attribute given a string name (it's like saying *obj.attr*, but *attr* is a string). Because this code snippet assumes a single constructor argument, it doesn't strictly need `factory` or `apply`—we could make an instance with just `aclass(classarg)`. They may prove more useful in the presence of unknown argument lists, however, and the general factory coding pattern can improve the code's flexibility.

Other Design-Related Topics

In this chapter, we've seen inheritance, composition, delegation, multiple inheritance, bound methods, and factories—all common patterns used to combine classes in Python programs. We've really only scratched the surface here in the design patterns domain, though. Elsewhere in this book you'll find coverage of other design-related topics, such as:

- *Abstract superclasses* (Chapter 28)
- *Decorators* (Chapters 31 and 38)
- *Type subclasses* (Chapter 31)
- *Static and class methods* (Chapter 31)
- *Managed attributes* (Chapter 37)
- *Metaclasses* (Chapters 31 and 39)

For more details on design patterns, though, we'll delegate to other resources on OOP at large. Although patterns are important in OOP work, and are often more natural in Python than other languages, they are not specific to Python itself.

Chapter Summary

In this chapter, we sampled common ways to use and combine classes to optimize their reusability and factoring benefits—what are usually considered design issues that are often independent of any particular programming language (though Python can make them easier to implement). We studied *delegation* (wrapping objects in proxy classes), *composition* (controlling embedded objects), and *inheritance* (acquiring behavior from other classes), as well as some more esoteric concepts such as pseudoprivate attributes, multiple inheritance, bound methods, and factories.

The next chapter ends our look at classes and OOP by surveying more advanced class-related topics; some of its material may be of more interest to tool writers than application programmers, but it still merits a review by most people who will do OOP in Python. First, though, another quick chapter quiz.

Test Your Knowledge: Quiz

1. What is multiple inheritance?
2. What is delegation?
3. What is composition?

4. What are bound methods?

5. What are pseudoprivate attributes used for?

Test Your Knowledge: Answers

1. Multiple inheritance occurs when a class inherits from more than one superclass; it's useful for mixing together multiple packages of class-based code. The left-to-right order in class statement headers determines the order of attribute searches.

2. Delegation involves wrapping an object in a proxy class, which adds extra behavior and passes other operations to the wrapped object. The proxy retains the interface of the wrapped object.

3. Composition is a technique whereby a controller class embeds and directs a number of objects, and provides an interface all its own; it's a way to build up larger structures with classes.

4. Bound methods combine an instance and a method function; you can call them without passing in an instance object explicitly because the original instance is still available.

5. Pseudoprivate attributes (whose names begin with two leading underscores: __X) are used to localize names to the enclosing class. This includes both class attributes like methods defined inside the class, and self instance attributes assigned inside the class. Such names are expanded to include the class name, which makes them unique.

## CHAPTER 31

Advanced Class Topics

This chapter concludes our look at OOP in Python by presenting a few more advanced class-related topics: we will survey subclassing built-in types, "new-style" class changes and extensions, static and class methods, function decorators, and more.

As we've seen, Python's OOP model is, at its core, very simple, and some of the topics presented in this chapter are so advanced and optional that you may not encounter them very often in your Python applications-programming career. In the interest of completeness, though, we'll round out our discussion of classes with a brief look at these advanced tools for OOP work.

As usual, because this is the last chapter in this part of the book, it ends with a section on class-related "gotchas," and the set of lab exercises for this part. I encourage you to work through the exercises to help cement the ideas we've studied here. I also suggest working on or studying larger OOP Python projects as a supplement to this book. As with much in computing, the benefits of OOP tend to become more apparent with practice.

 Content note: This chapter collects advanced class topics, but some are even too advanced for this chapter to cover well. Topics such as properties, descriptors, decorators, and metaclasses are only briefly mentioned here, and are covered more fully in the final part of this book. Be sure to look ahead for more complete examples and extended coverage of some of the subjects that fall into this chapter's category.

Extending Built-in Types

Besides implementing new kinds of objects, classes are sometimes used to extend the functionality of Python's built-in types to support more exotic data structures. For instance, to add queue insert and delete methods to lists, you can code classes that wrap (embed) a list object and export insert and delete methods that process the list specially, like the delegation technique we studied in Chapter 30. As of Python 2.2, you can also use inheritance to specialize built-in types. The next two sections show both techniques in action.

Extending Types by Embedding

Remember those set functions we wrote in Chapters 16 and 18? Here's what they look like brought back to life as a Python class. The following example (the file *setwrapper.py*) implements a new set object type by moving some of the set functions to methods and adding some basic operator overloading. For the most part, this class just wraps a Python list with extra set operations. But because it's a class, it also supports multiple instances and customization by inheritance in subclasses. Unlike our earlier functions, using classes here allows us to make multiple self-contained set objects with preset data and behavior, rather than passing lists into functions manually:

```
class Set:
    def __init__(self, value = []):       # Constructor
        self.data = []                    # Manages a list
        self.concat(value)

    def intersect(self, other):           # other is any sequence
        res = []                          # self is the subject
        for x in self.data:
            if x in other:                # Pick common items
                res.append(x)
        return Set(res)                   # Return a new Set

    def union(self, other):               # other is any sequence
        res = self.data[:]                # Copy of my list
        for x in other:                   # Add items in other
            if not x in res:
                res.append(x)
        return Set(res)

    def concat(self, value):              # value: list, Set...
        for x in value:                   # Removes duplicates
            if not x in self.data:
                self.data.append(x)

    def __len__(self):          return len(self.data)          # len(self)
    def __getitem__(self, key): return self.data[key]          # self[i]
    def __and__(self, other):   return self.intersect(other)   # self & other
    def __or__(self, other):    return self.union(other)       # self | other
    def __repr__(self):         return 'Set:' + repr(self.data) # print()
```

To use this class, we make instances, call methods, and run defined operators as usual:

```
x = Set([1, 3, 5, 7])
print(x.union(Set([1, 4, 7])))       # prints Set:[1, 3, 5, 7, 4]
print(x | Set([1, 4, 6]))            # prints Set:[1, 3, 5, 7, 4, 6]
```

Overloading operations such as indexing enables instances of our Set class to masquerade as real lists. Because you will interact with and extend this class in an exercise at the end of this chapter, I won't say much more about this code until Appendix B.

Extending Types by Subclassing

Beginning with Python 2.2, all the built-in types in the language can now be subclassed directly. Type-conversion functions such as list, str, dict, and tuple have become built-in type names—although transparent to your script, a type-conversion call (e.g., list('spam')) is now really an invocation of a type's object constructor.

This change allows you to customize or extend the behavior of built-in types with user-defined class statements: simply subclass the new type names to customize them. Instances of your type subclasses can be used anywhere that the original built-in type can appear. For example, suppose you have trouble getting used to the fact that Python list offsets begin at 0 instead of 1. Not to worry—you can always code your own subclass that customizes this core behavior of lists. The file *typesubclass.py* shows how:

```
# Subclass built-in list type/class
# Map 1..N to 0..N-1; call back to built-in version.

class MyList(list):
    def __getitem__(self, offset):
        print('(indexing %s at %s)' % (self, offset))
        return list.__getitem__(self, offset - 1)

if __name__ == '__main__':
    print(list('abc'))
    x = MyList('abc')               # __init__ inherited from list
    print(x)                        # __repr__ inherited from list

    print(x[1])                     # MyList.__getitem__
    print(x[3])                     # Customizes list superclass method

    x.append('spam'); print(x)      # Attributes from list superclass
    x.reverse();      print(x)
```

In this file, the MyList subclass extends the built-in list's __getitem__ indexing method only to map indexes 1 to N back to the required 0 to N–1. All it really does is decrement the submitted index and call back to the superclass's version of indexing, but it's enough to do the trick:

```
% python typesubclass.py
['a', 'b', 'c']
['a', 'b', 'c']
(indexing ['a', 'b', 'c'] at 1)
a
(indexing ['a', 'b', 'c'] at 3)
c
['a', 'b', 'c', 'spam']
['spam', 'c', 'b', 'a']
```

This output also includes tracing text the class prints on indexing. Of course, whether changing indexing this way is a good idea in general is another issue—users of your `MyList` class may very well be confused by such a core departure from Python sequence behavior. The ability to customize built-in types this way can be a powerful asset, though.

For instance, this coding pattern gives rise to an alternative way to code a set—as a subclass of the built-in list type, rather than a standalone class that manages an embedded list object, as shown earlier in this section. As we learned in Chapter 5, Python today comes with a powerful built-in set object, along with literal and comprehension syntax for making new sets. Coding one yourself, though, is still a great way to learn about type subclassing in general.

The following class, coded in the file *setsubclass.py*, customizes lists to add just methods and operators related to set processing. Because all other behavior is inherited from the built-in `list` superclass, this makes for a shorter and simpler alternative:

```
class Set(list):
    def __init__(self, value = []):          # Constructor
        list.__init__([])                     # Customizes list
        self.concat(value)                    # Copies mutable defaults

    def intersect(self, other):               # other is any sequence
        res = []                              # self is the subject
        for x in self:
            if x in other:                    # Pick common items
                res.append(x)
        return Set(res)                       # Return a new Set

    def union(self, other):                   # other is any sequence
        res = Set(self)                       # Copy me and my list
        res.concat(other)
        return res

    def concat(self, value):                  # value: list, Set . . .
        for x in value:                       # Removes duplicates
            if not x in self:
                self.append(x)

    def __and__(self, other): return self.intersect(other)
    def __or__(self, other):  return self.union(other)
    def __repr__(self):       return 'Set:' + list.__repr__(self)

if __name__ == '__main__':
    x = Set([1,3,5,7])
    y = Set([2,1,4,5,6])
    print(x, y, len(x))
    print(x.intersect(y), y.union(x))
    print(x & y, x | y)
    x.reverse(); print(x)
```

Here is the output of the self-test code at the end of this file. Because subclassing core types is an advanced feature, I'll omit further details here, but I invite you to trace through these results in the code to study its behavior:

```
% python setsubclass.py
Set:[1, 3, 5, 7] Set:[2, 1, 4, 5, 6] 4
Set:[1, 5] Set:[2, 1, 4, 5, 6, 3, 7]
Set:[1, 5] Set:[1, 3, 5, 7, 2, 4, 6]
Set:[7, 5, 3, 1]
```

There are more efficient ways to implement sets with dictionaries in Python, which replace the linear scans in the set implementations shown here with dictionary index operations (hashing) and so run much quicker. (For more details, see *Programming Python*.) If you're interested in sets, also take another look at the `set` object type we explored in Chapter 5; this type provides extensive set operations as built-in tools. Set implementations are fun to experiment with, but they are no longer strictly required in Python today.

For another type subclassing example, see the implementation of the `bool` type in Python 2.3 and later. As mentioned earlier in the book, `bool` is a subclass of `int` with two instances (`True` and `False`) that behave like the integers `1` and `0` but inherit custom string-representation methods that display their names.

The "New-Style" Class Model

In Release 2.2, Python introduced a new flavor of classes, known as "new-style" classes; classes following the original model became known as "classic classes" when compared to the new kind. In 3.0 the class story has merged, but it remains split for Python 2.X users:

- As of Python 3.0, all classes are automatically what we used to call "new-style," whether they explicitly inherit from `object` or not. All classes inherit from `object`, whether implicitly or explicitly, and all objects are instances of `object`.

- In Python 2.6 and earlier, classes must explicitly inherit from `object` (or another built-in type) to be considered "new-style" and obtain all new-style features.

Because all classes are automatically new-style in 3.0, the features of new-style classes are simply normal class features. I've opted to keep their descriptions in this section separate, however, in deference to users of Python 2.X code—classes in such code acquire new-style features only when they are derived from `object`.

In other words, when Python 3.0 users see descriptions of "new-style" features in this section, they should take them to be descriptions of existing features of their classes. For 2.6 readers, these are a set of optional extensions.

In Python 2.6 and earlier, the only syntactic difference for new-style classes is that they are derived from either a built-in type, such as `list`, or a special built-in class known as `object`. The built-in name `object` is provided to serve as a superclass for new-style classes if no other built-in type is appropriate to use:

```
class newstyle(object):
    ...normal code...
```

Any class derived from `object`, or any other built-in type, is automatically treated as a new-style class. As long as a built-in type is somewhere in the superclass tree, the new class is treated as a new-style class. Classes not derived from built-ins such as `object` are considered classic.

New-style classes are only slightly different from classic classes, and the ways in which they differ are irrelevant to the vast majority of Python users. Moreover, the classic class model still available in 2.6 works exactly as it has for almost two decades.

In fact, new-style classes are almost completely backward compatible with classic classes in syntax and behavior; they mostly just add a few advanced new features. However, because they modify a handful of class behaviors, they had to be introduced as a distinct tool so as to avoid impacting any existing code that depends on the prior behaviors. For example, some subtle differences, such as diamond pattern inheritance search and the behavior of built-in operations with managed attribute methods such as __getattr__, can cause some legacy code to fail if left unchanged.

The next two sections provide overviews of the ways the new-style classes differ and the new tools they provide. Again, because all classes are new-style today, these topics represent changes to Python 2.X readers but simply additional advanced class topics to Python 3.0 readers.

New-Style Class Changes

New-style classes differ from classic classes in a number of ways, some of which are subtle but can impact existing 2.X code and coding styles. Here are some of the most prominent ways they differ:

Classes and types merged
> Classes are now types, and types are now classes. In fact, the two are essentially synonyms. The `type(I)` built-in returns the class an instance is made from, instead of a generic instance type, and is normally the same as `I.__class__`. Moreover, classes are instances of the `type` class, `type` may be subclassed to customize class creation, and all classes (and hence types) inherit from `object`, which comes with a small set of default operator overloading methods.

Inheritance search order
> Diamond patterns of multiple inheritance have a slightly different search order— roughly, they are searched across before up, and more breadth-first than depth-first.

Attribute fetch for built-ins

The __getattr__ and __getattribute__ methods are no longer run for attributes implicitly fetched by built-in operations. This means that they are not called for __X__ operator overloading method names—the search for such names begins at classes, not instances.

New advanced tools

New-style classes have a set of new class tools, including slots, properties, descriptors, and the __getattribute__ method. Most of these have very specific tool-building purposes.

We discussed the third of these changes briefly in a sidebar in Chapter 27, and we'll revisit it in depth in the contexts of attribute management in Chapter 37 and privacy decorators in Chapter 38. Because the first and second of the changes just listed can break existing 2.X code, though, let's explore these in more detail before moving on to new-style additions.

Type Model Changes

In new-style classes, the distinction between type and class has vanished entirely. Classes themselves are types: the type object generates classes as its instances, and classes generate instances of their type. If fact, there is no real difference between built-in types like lists and strings and user-defined types coded as classes. This is why we can subclass built-in types, as shown earlier in this chapter—because subclassing a built-in type such as list qualifies a class as new-style, it becomes a user-defined type.

Besides allowing us to subclass built-in types, one of the contexts where this becomes most obvious is when we do explicit type testing. With Python 2.6's classic classes, the type of a class instance is a generic "instance," but the types of built-in objects are more specific:

```
C:\misc> c:\python26\python
>>> class C: pass                      # Classic classes in 2.6
...
>>> I = C()
>>> type(I)                            # Instances are made from classes
<type 'instance'>
>>> I.__class__
<class __main__.C at 0x025085A0>

>>> type(C)                            # But classes are not the same as types
<type 'classobj'>
>>> C.__class__
AttributeError: class C has no attribute '__class__'

>>> type([1, 2, 3])
<type 'list'>
>>> type(list)
<type 'type'>
```

```
>>> list.__class__
<type 'type'>
```

But with new-style classes in 2.6, the type of a class instance is the class it's created from, since classes are simply user-defined types—the type of an instance is its class, and the type of a user-defined class is the same as the type of a built-in object type. Classes have a __class__ attribute now, too, because they are instances of **type**:

```
C:\misc> c:\python26\python
>>> class C(object): pass                    # New-style classes in 2.6
...
>>> I = C()
>>> type(I)                                   # Type of instance is class it's made from
<class '__main__.C'>
>>> I.__class__
<class '__main__.C'>

>>> type(C)                                   # Classes are user-defined types
<type 'type'>
>>> C.__class__
<type 'type'>

>>> type([1, 2, 3])                           # Built-in types work the same way
<type 'list'>
>>> type(list)
<type 'type'>
>>> list.__class__
<type 'type'>
```

The same is true for all classes in Python 3.0, since all classes are automatically new-style, even if they have no explicit superclasses. In fact, the distinction between built-in types and user-defined class types melts away altogether in 3.0:

```
C:\misc> c:\python30\python
>>> class C: pass                             # All classes are new-style in 3.0
...
>>> I = C()
>>> type(I)                                   # Type of instance is class it's made from
<class '__main__.C'>
>>> I.__class__
<class '__main__.C'>

>>> type(C)                                   # Class is a type, and type is a class
<class 'type'>
>>> C.__class__
<class 'type'>

>>> type([1, 2, 3])                           # Classes and built-in types work the same
<class 'list'>
>>> type(list)
<class 'type'>
>>> list.__class__
<class 'type'>
```

As you can see, in 3.0 classes are types, but types are also classes. Technically, each class is generated by a *metaclass*—a class that is normally either type itself, or a subclass of it customized to augment or manage generated classes. Besides impacting code that does type testing, this turns out to be an important hook for tool developers. We'll talk more about metaclasses later in this chapter, and again in more detail in Chapter 39.

Implications for type testing

Besides providing for built-in type customization and metaclass hooks, the merging of classes and types in the new-style class model can impact code that does type testing. In Python 3.0, for example, the types of class instances compare directly and meaningfully, and in the same way as built-in type objects. This follows from the fact that classes are now types, and an instance's type is the instance's class:

```
C:\misc> c:\python30\python
>>> class C: pass
...
>>> class D: pass
...
>>> c = C()
>>> d = D()
>>> type(c) == type(d)          # 3.0: compares the instances' classes
False

>>> type(c), type(d)
(<class '__main__.C'>, <class '__main__.D'>)
>>> c.__class__, d.__class__
(<class '__main__.C'>, <class '__main__.D'>)

>>> c1, c2 = C(), C()
>>> type(c1) == type(c2)
True
```

With classic classes in 2.6 and earlier, though, comparing instance types is almost useless, because all instances have the same "instance" type. To truly compare types, the instance __class__ attributes must be compared (if you care about portability, this works in 3.0, too, but it's not required there):

```
C:\misc> c:\python26\python
>>> class C: pass
...
>>> class D: pass
...
>>> c = C()
>>> d = D()
>>> type(c) == type(d)          # 2.6: all instances are same type
True
>>> c.__class__ == d.__class__  # Must compare classes explicitly
False

>>> type(c), type(d)
(<type 'instance'>, <type 'instance'>)
```

```
>>> c.__class__, d.__class__
(<class __main__.C at 0x024585A0>, <class __main__.D at 0x024588D0>)
```

And as you should expect by now, new-style classes in 2.6 work the same as all classes in 3.0 in this regard—comparing instance types compares the instances' classes automatically:

```
C:\misc> c:\python26\python
>>> class C(object): pass
...
>>> class D(object): pass
...
>>> c = C()
>>> d = D()
>>> type(c) == type(d)                # 2.6 new-style: same as all in 3.0
False

>>> type(c), type(d)
(<class '__main__.C'>, <class '__main__.D'>)
>>> c.__class__, d.__class__
(<class '__main__.C'>, <class '__main__.D'>)
```

Of course, as I've pointed out numerous times in this book, type checking is usually the wrong thing to do in Python programs (we code to object interfaces, not object types), and the more general isinstance built-in is more likely what you'll want to use in the rare cases where instance class types must be queried. However, knowledge of Python's type model can help demystify the class model in general.

All objects derive from "object"

One other ramification of the type change in the new-style class model is that because all classes derive (inherit) from the class object either implicitly or explicitly, and because all types are now classes, every object derives from the object built-in class, whether directly or through a superclass. Consider the following interaction in Python 3.0 (code an explicit object superclass in 2.6 to make this work equivalently):

```
>>> class C: pass
...
>>> X = C()

>>> type(X)                # Type is now class instance was created from
<class '__main__.C'>
>>> type(C)
<class 'type'>
```

As before, the type of a class instance is the class it was made from, and the type of a class is the type class because classes and types have merged. It is also true, though, that the instance and class are both derived from the built-in object class, since this is an implicit or explicit superclass of every class:

```
>>> isinstance(X, object)
True
>>> isinstance(C, object)          # Classes always inherit from object
True
```

The same holds true for built-in types like lists and strings, because types are classes in the new-style model—built-in types are now classes, and their instances derive from `object`, too:

```
>>> type('spam')
<class 'str'>
>>> type(str)
<class 'type'>

>>> isinstance('spam', object)     # Same for built-in types (classes)
True
>>> isinstance(str, object)
True
```

In fact, `type` itself derives from `object`, and `object` derives from `type`, even though the two are different objects—a circular relationship that caps the object model and stems from the fact that types are classes that generate classes:

```
>>> type(type)                     # All classes are types, and vice versa
<class 'type'>
>>> type(object)
<class 'type'>

>>> isinstance(type, object)       # All classes derive from object, even type
True
>>> isinstance(object, type)       # Types make classes, and type is a class
True
>>> type is object
False
```

In practical terms, this model makes for fewer special cases than the prior type/class distinction of classic classes, and it allows us to write code that assumes and uses an `object` superclass. We'll see examples of the latter later in the book; for now, let's move on to explore other new-style changes.

Diamond Inheritance Change

One of the most visible changes in new-style classes is their slightly different inheritance search procedures for the so-called *diamond* pattern of multiple inheritance trees, where more than one superclass leads to the same higher superclass further above. The diamond pattern is an advanced design concept, is coded only rarely in Python practice, and has not been discussed in this book, so we won't dwell on this topic in depth.

In short, though, with *classic* classes, the inheritance search procedure is strictly depth first, and then left to right—Python climbs all the way to the top, hugging the left side of the tree, before it backs up and begins to look further to the right. In *new-style* classes, the search is more breadth-first in such cases—Python first looks in any superclasses to the right of the first one searched before ascending all the way to the common superclass at the top. In other words, the search proceeds across by levels before moving up. The search algorithm is a bit more complex than this, but this is as much as most programmers need to know.

Because of this change, lower superclasses can overload attributes of higher superclasses, regardless of the sort of multiple inheritance trees they are mixed into. Moreover, the new-style search rule avoids visiting the same superclass more than once when it is accessible from multiple subclasses.

Diamond inheritance example

To illustrate, consider this simplistic incarnation of the diamond multiple inheritance pattern for classic classes. Here, D's superclasses B and C both lead to the same common ancestor, A:

```
>>> class A:
        attr = 1          # Classic (Python 2.6)

>>> class B(A):           # B and C both lead to A
        pass

>>> class C(A):
        attr = 2

>>> class D(B, C):
        pass              # Tries A before C

>>> x = D()
>>> x.attr                # Searches x, D, B, A
1
```

The attribute here is found in superclass A, because with classic classes, the inheritance search climbs as high as it can before backing up and moving right—Python will search D, B, A, and then C, but will stop when attr is found in A, above B.

However, with new-style classes derived from a built-in like object, and all classes in 3.0, the search order is different: Python looks in C (to the right of B) before A (above B). That is, it searches D, B, C, and then A, and in this case, stops in C:

```
>>> class A(object):
        attr = 1          # New-style ("object" not required in 3.0)

>>> class B(A):
        pass

>>> class C(A):
        attr = 2

>>> class D(B, C):
        pass              # Tries C before A

>>> x = D()
```

```
>>> x.attr                    # Searches x, D, B, C
2
```

This change in the inheritance search procedure is based upon the assumption that if you mix in C lower in the tree, you probably intend to grab its attributes in preference to A's. It also assumes that C is always intended to override A's attributes in all contexts, which is probably true when it's used standalone but may not be when it's mixed into a diamond with classic classes—you might not even know that C may be mixed in like this when you code it.

Since it is most likely that the programmer meant that C should override A in this case, though, new-style classes visit C first. Otherwise, C could be essentially pointless in a diamond context: it could not customize A and would be used only for names unique to C.

Explicit conflict resolution

Of course, the problem with assumptions is that they assume things. If this search order deviation seems too subtle to remember, or if you want more control over the search process, you can always force the selection of an attribute from anywhere in the tree by assigning or otherwise naming the one you want at the place where the classes are mixed together:

```
>>> class A:
        attr = 1              # Classic

>>> class B(A):
        pass

>>> class C(A):
        attr = 2

>>> class D(B, C):
        attr = C.attr         # Choose C, to the right

>>> x = D()
>>> x.attr                    # Works like new-style (all 3.0)
2
```

Here, a tree of classic classes is emulating the search order of new-style classes: the assignment to the attribute in D picks the version in C, thereby subverting the normal inheritance search path (D.attr will be lowest in the tree). New-style classes can similarly emulate classic classes by choosing the attribute above at the place where the classes are mixed together:

```
>>> class A(object):
        attr = 1              # New-style

>>> class B(A):
        pass

>>> class C(A):
```

```
                      attr = 2
>>> class D(B, C):
            attr = B.attr          # Choose A.attr, above

>>> x = D()
>>> x.attr                        # Works like classic (default 2.6)
1
```

If you are willing to always resolve conflicts like this, you can largely ignore the search order difference and not rely on assumptions about what you meant when you coded your classes.

Naturally, attributes picked this way can also be method functions—methods are normal, assignable objects:

```
>>> class A:
            def meth(s): print('A.meth')

>>> class C(A):
            def meth(s): print('C.meth')

>>> class B(A):
            pass

>>> class D(B, C): pass            # Use default search order
>>> x = D()                        # Will vary per class type
>>> x.meth()                       # Defaults to classic order in 2.6
A.meth

>>> class D(B, C): meth = C.meth   # Pick C's method: new-style (and 3.0)
>>> x = D()
>>> x.meth()
C.meth

>>> class D(B, C): meth = B.meth   # Pick B's method: classic
>>> x = D()
>>> x.meth()
A.meth
```

Here, we select methods by explicitly assigning to names lower in the tree. We might also simply call the desired class explicitly; in practice, this pattern might be more common, especially for things like constructors:

```
class D(B, C):
    def meth(self):                # Redefine lower
        ...
        C.meth(self)               # Pick C's method by calling
```

Such selections by assignment or call at mix-in points can effectively insulate your code from this difference in class flavors. Explicitly resolving the conflicts this way ensures that your code won't vary per Python version in the future (apart from perhaps needing to derive classes from object or a built-in type for the new-style tools in 2.6). To trace how new-stye inheritance works by default, see also the `class.mro()` method mentioned in the preceding chapter's class lister examples.

 Even without the classic/new-style class divergence, the explicit method resolution technique shown here may come in handy in multiple inheritance scenarios in general. For instance, if you want part of a superclass on the left and part of a superclass on the right, you might need to tell Python which same-named attributes to choose by using explicit assignments in subclasses. We'll revisit this notion in a "gotcha" at the end of this chapter.

Also note that diamond inheritance patterns might be more problematic in some cases than I've implied here (e.g., what if B and C both have required constructors that call to the constructor in A?). Since such contexts are rare in real-world Python, we'll leave this topic outside this book's scope (but see the `super` built-in function for hints—besides providing generic access to superclasses in single inheritance trees, `super` supports a cooperative mode for resolving some conflicts in multiple inheritance trees).

Scope of search order change

In sum, by default, the diamond pattern is searched differently for classic and new-style classes, and this is a nonbackward-compatible change. Keep in mind, though, that this change primarily affects diamond pattern cases of multiple inheritance; new-style class inheritance works unchanged for most other inheritance tree structures. Further, it's not impossible that this entire issue may be of more theoretical than practical importance—because the new-style search wasn't significant enough to address until Python 2.2 and didn't become standard until 3.0, it seems unlikely to impact much Python code.

Having said that, I should also note that even though you might not code diamond patterns in classes you write yourself, because the implied `object` superclass is above every class in 3.0, *every* case of multiple inheritance exhibits the diamond pattern today. That is, in new-style classes, `object` automatically plays the role that the class A does in the example we just considered. Hence the new-style search rule not only modifies logical semantics, but also optimizes performance by avoiding visiting the same class more than once.

Just as important, the implied `object` superclass in the new-style model provides default methods for a variety of built-in operations, including the __str__ and __repr__ display format methods. Run a `dir(object)` to see which methods are provided. Without the new-style search order, in multiple inheritance cases the defaults in `object` would always override redefinitions in user-coded classes, unless they were always made in the leftmost superclass. In other words, the new-style class model itself makes using the new-style search order more critical!

For a more visual example of the implied `object` superclass in 3.0, and other examples of diamond patterns created by it, see the `ListTree` class's output in the *lister.py* example in the preceding chapter, as well as the *classtree.py* tree walker example in Chapter 28.

New-Style Class Extensions

Beyond the changes described in the prior section (which, frankly, may be too academic and obscure to matter to many readers of this book), new-style classes provide a handful of more advanced class tools that have more direct and practical application. The following sections provide an overview of each of these additional features, available for new-style class in Python 2.6 and all classes in Python 3.0.

Instance Slots

By assigning a sequence of string attribute names to a special `__slots__` class attribute, it is possible for a new-style class to both limit the set of legal attributes that instances of the class will have and optimize memory and speed performance.

This special attribute is typically set by assigning a sequence of string names to the variable `__slots__` at the top level of a `class` statement: only those names in the `__slots__` list can be assigned as instance attributes. However, like all names in Python, instance attribute names must still be assigned before they can be referenced, even if they're listed in `__slots__`. For example:

```
>>> class limiter(object):
...     __slots__ = ['age', 'name', 'job']
...
>>> x = limiter()
>>> x.age                            # Must assign before use
AttributeError: age

>>> x.age = 40
>>> x.age
40
>>> x.ape = 1000                     # Illegal: not in __slots__
AttributeError: 'limiter' object has no attribute 'ape'
```

Slots are something of a break with Python's dynamic nature, which dictates that any name may be created by assignment. However, this feature is envisioned as both a way to catch "typo" errors like this (assignments to illegal attribute names not in `__slots__` are detected), as well as an optimization mechanism. Allocating a namespace dictionary for every instance object can become expensive in terms of memory if many instances are created and only a few attributes are required. To save space and speed execution (to a degree that can vary per program), instead of allocating a dictionary for each instance, slot attributes are stored sequentially for quicker lookup.

Slots and generic code

In fact, some instances with slots may not have a __dict__ attribute dictionary at all, which can make some metaprograms more complex (including some coded in this book). Tools that generically list attributes or access attributes by string name, for example, must be careful to use more storage-neutral tools than __dict__, such as the getattr, setattr, and dir built-in functions, which apply to attributes based on either __dict__ or __slots__ storage. In some cases, both attribute sources may need to be queried for completeness.

For example, when slots are used, instances do not normally have an attribute dictionary—Python uses the class *descriptors* feature covered in Chapter 37 to allocate space for slot attributes in the instance instead. Only names in the slots list can be assigned to instances, but slot-based attributes can still be fetched and set by name using generic tools. In Python 3.0 (and in 2.6 for classes derived from object):

```
>>> class C:
...     __slots__ = ['a', 'b']          # __slots__ means no __dict__ by default
...
>>> X = C()
>>> X.a = 1
>>> X.a
1
>>> X.__dict__
AttributeError: 'C' object has no attribute '__dict__'
>>> getattr(X, 'a')
1
>>> setattr(X, 'b', 2)                  # But getattr() and setattr() still work
>>> X.b
2
>>> 'a' in dir(X)                       # And dir() finds slot attributes too
True
>>> 'b' in dir(X)
True
```

Without an attribute namespaces dictionary, it's not possible to assign new names to instances that are not names in the slots list:

```
>>> class D:
...     __slots__ = ['a', 'b']
...     def __init__(self): self.d = 4  # Cannot add new names if no __dict__
...
>>> X = D()
AttributeError: 'D' object has no attribute 'd'
```

However, extra attributes can still be accommodated by including __dict__ in __slots__, in order to allow for an attribute namespace dictionary. In this case, *both* storage mechanisms are used, but generic tools such as getattr allow us to treat them as a single set of attributes:

```
>>> class D:
...     __slots__ = ['a', 'b', '__dict__']   # List __dict__ to include one too
...     c = 3                                 # Class attrs work normally
```

```
...        def __init__(self): self.d = 4        # d put in __dict__, a in __slots__
...
>>> X = D()
>>> X.d
4
>>> X.__dict__                        # Some objects have both __dict__ and __slots__
{'d': 4}                              # getattr() can fetch either type of attr
>>> X.__slots__
['a', 'b', '__dict__']
>>> X.c
3
>>> X.a                               # All instance attrs undefined until assigned
AttributeError: a
>>> X.a = 1
>>> getattr(X, 'a',), getattr(X, 'c'), getattr(X, 'd')
(1, 3, 4)
```

Code that wishes to list just all instance attributes generically, though, may still need to allow for both storage forms, since `dir` also returns inherited attributes (this relies on dictionary iterators to collect keys):

```
>>> for attr in list(X.__dict__) + X.__slots__:
...     print(attr, '=>', getattr(X, attr))

d => 4
a => 1
b => 2
__dict__ => {'d': 4}
```

Since either can be omitted, this is more correctly coded as follows (`getattr` allows for defaults):

```
>>> for attr in list(getattr(X, '__dict__', [])) + getattr(X, '__slots__', []):
...     print(attr, '=>', getattr(X, attr))

d => 4
a => 1
b => 2
__dict__ => {'d': 4}
```

Multiple __slot__ lists in superclasses

Note, however, that this code addresses only slot names in the *lowest* __slots__ attribute inherited by an instance. If multiple classes in a class tree have their own __slots__ attributes, generic programs must develop other policies for listing attributes (e.g., classifying slot names as attributes of classes, not instances).

Slot declarations can appear in multiple classes in a class tree, but they are subject to a number of constraints that are somewhat difficult to rationalize unless you understand the implementation of slots as class-level descriptors (a tool we'll study in detail in the last part of this book):

- If a subclass inherits from a superclass without a __slots__, the __dict__ attribute of the superclass will always be accessible, making a __slots__ in the subclass meaningless.

- If a class defines the same slot name as a superclass, the version of the name defined by the superclass slot will be accessible only by fetching its descriptor directly from the superclass.

- Because the meaning of a __slots__ declaration is limited to the class in which it appears, subclasses will have a __dict__ unless they also define a __slots__.

In terms of listing instance attributes generically, slots in multiple classes might require manual class tree climbs, dir usage, or a policy that treats slot names as a different category of names altogether:

```
>>> class E:
...     __slots__ = ['c', 'd']          # Superclass has slots
...
>>> class D(E):
...     __slots__ = ['a', '__dict__']   # So does its subclass
...
>>> X = D()
>>> X.a = 1; X.b = 2; X.c = 3           # The instance is the union
>>> X.a, X.c
(1, 3)

>>> E.__slots__                         # But slots are not concatenated
['c', 'd']
>>> D.__slots__
['a', '__dict__']
>>> X.__slots__                         # Instance inherits "lowest" __slots__
['a', '__dict__']
>>> X.__dict__                          # And has its own an attr dict
{'b': 2}

>>> for attr in list(getattr(X, '__dict__', [])) + getattr(X, '__slots__', []):
...     print(attr, '=>', getattr(X, attr))
...
b => 2                                  # Superclass slots missed!
a => 1
__dict__ => {'b': 2}

>>> dir(X)                              # dir() includes all slot names
[...many names omitted... 'a', 'b', 'c', 'd']
```

When such generality is possible, slots are probably best treated as class attributes, rather than trying to mold them to appear the same as normal instance attributes. For more on slots in general, see the Python standard manual set. Also watch for an example that allows for attributes based on both __slots__ and __dict__ storage in the Private decorator discussion of Chapter 38.

For a prime example of why generic programs may need to care about slots, see the *lister.py* display mix-in classes example in the multiple inheritance section of the prior chapter; a note there describes the example's slot concerns. In such a tool that attempts to list attributes generically, slot usage requires either extra code or the implementation of policies regarding the handling of slot-based attributes in general.

Class Properties

A mechanism known as *properties* provides another way for new-style classes to define automatically called methods for access or assignment to instance attributes. At least for specific attributes, this feature is an alternative to many current uses of the __getattr__ and __setattr__ overloading methods we studied in Chapter 29. Properties have a similar effect to these two methods, but they incur an extra method call only for accesses to names that require dynamic computation. Properties (and slots) are based on a new notion of attribute descriptors, which is too advanced for us to cover here.

In short, a property is a type of object assigned to a class attribute name. A property is generated by calling the property built-in with three methods (handlers for get, set, and delete operations), as well as a docstring; if any argument is passed as None or omitted, that operation is not supported. Properties are typically assigned at the top level of a class statement [e.g., name = property(...)]. When thus assigned, accesses to the class attribute itself (e.g., obj.name) are automatically routed to one of the accessor methods passed into the property. For example, the __getattr__ method allows classes to intercept undefined attribute references:

```
>>> class classic:
...     def __getattr__(self, name):
...         if name == 'age':
...             return 40
...         else:
...             raise AttributeError
...
>>> x = classic()
>>> x.age                          # Runs __getattr__
40
>>> x.name                         # Runs __getattr__
AttributeError
```

Here is the same example, coded with properties instead (note that properties are available for all classes but require the new-style object derivation in 2.6 to work properly for intercepting attribute assignments):

```
>>> class newprops(object):
...     def getage(self):
...         return 40
...     age = property(getage, None, None, None)   # get, set, del, docs
...
>>> x = newprops()
>>> x.age                          # Runs getage
40
```

```
>>> x.name                                          # Normal fetch
AttributeError: newprops instance has no attribute 'name'
```

For some coding tasks, properties can be less complex and quicker to run than the traditional techniques. For example, when we add attribute *assignment* support, properties become more attractive—there's less code to type, and no extra method calls are incurred for assignments to attributes we don't wish to compute dynamically:

```
>>> class newprops(object):
...     def getage(self):
...         return 40
...     def setage(self, value):
...         print('set age:', value)
...         self._age = value
...     age = property(getage, setage, None, None)
...
>>> x = newprops()
>>> x.age                                           # Runs getage
40
>>> x.age = 42                                      # Runs setage
set age: 42
>>> x._age                                          # Normal fetch; no getage call
42
>>> x.job = 'trainer'                               # Normal assign; no setage call
>>> x.job                                           # Normal fetch; no getage call
'trainer'
```

The equivalent classic class incurs extra method calls for assignments to attributes not being managed and needs to route attribute assignments through the attribute dictionary (or, for new-style classes, to the object superclass's __setattr__) to avoid loops:

```
>>> class classic:
...     def __getattr__(self, name):               # On undefined reference
...         if name == 'age':
...             return 40
...         else:
...             raise AttributeError
...     def __setattr__(self, name, value):         # On all assignments
...         print('set:', name, value)
...         if name == 'age':
...             self.__dict__['_age'] = value
...         else:
...             self.__dict__[name] = value
...
>>> x = classic()
>>> x.age                                           # Runs __getattr__
40
>>> x.age = 41                                      # Runs __setattr__
set: age 41
>>> x._age                                          # Defined: no __getattr__ call
41
>>> x.job = 'trainer'                               # Runs __setattr__ again
set: job trainer
>>> x.job                                           # Defined: no __getattr__ call
'trainer'
```

Properties seem like a win for this simple example. However, some applications of __getattr__ and __setattr__ may still require more dynamic or generic interfaces than properties directly provide. For example, in many cases, the set of attributes to be supported cannot be determined when the class is coded, and may not even exist in any tangible form (e.g., when *delegating* arbitrary method references to a wrapped/ embedded object generically). In such cases, a generic __getattr__ or a __setattr__ attribute handler with a passed-in attribute name may be preferable. Because such generic handlers can also handle simpler cases, properties are often an optional extension.

For more details on both options, stay tuned for Chapter 37 in the final part of this book. As we'll see there, it's also possible to code properties using *function decorator syntax*, a topic introduced later in this chapter.

__getattribute__ and Descriptors

The __getattribute__ method, available for new-style classes only, allows a class to intercept *all* attribute references, not just undefined references, like __getattr__. It is also somewhat trickier to use than __getattr__: it is prone to loops, much like __setattr__, but in different ways.

In addition to properties and operator overloading methods, Python supports the notion of attribute *descriptors*—classes with __get__ and __set__ methods, assigned to class attributes and inherited by instances, that intercept read and write accesses to specific attributes. Descriptors are in a sense a more general form of properties; in fact, properties are a simplified way to define a specific type of descriptor, one that runs functions on access. Descriptors are also used to implement the slots feature we met earlier.

Because properties, __getattribute__, and descriptors are somewhat advanced topics, we'll defer the rest of their coverage, as well as more on properties, to Chapter 37 in the final part of this book.

Metaclasses

Most of the changes and feature additions of new-style classes integrate with the notion of subclassable types mentioned earlier in this chapter, because subclassable types and new-style classes were introduced in conjunction with a merging of the type/class dichotomy in Python 2.2 and beyond. As we've seen, in 3.0, this merging is complete: classes are now types, and types are classes.

Along with these changes, Python also grew a more coherent protocol for coding *metaclasses*, which are classes that subclass the **type** object and intercept class creation calls. As such, they provide a well-defined hook for management and augmentation of class objects. They are also an advanced topic that is optional for most Python programmers, so we'll postpone further details here. We'll meet metaclasses briefly later in this chapter in conjunction with class decorators, and we'll explore them in full detail in Chapter 39, in the final part of this book.

Static and Class Methods

As of Python 2.2, it is possible to define two kinds of methods within a class that can be called without an instance: *static* methods work roughly like simple instance-less functions inside a class, and *class* methods are passed a class instead of an instance. Although this feature was added in conjunction with the new-style classes discussed in the prior sections, static and class methods work for classic classes too.

To enable these method modes, special built-in functions called `staticmethod` and `classmethod` must be called within the class, or invoked with the decoration syntax we'll meet later in this chapter. In Python 3.0, instance-less methods called only through a class name do not require a `staticmethod` declaration, but such methods called through instances do.

Why the Special Methods?

As we've learned, a class method is normally passed an instance object in its first argument, to serve as the implied subject of the method call. Today, though, there are two ways to modify this model. Before I explain what they are, I should explain why this might matter to you.

Sometimes, programs need to process data associated with classes instead of instances. Consider keeping track of the number of instances created from a class, or maintaining a list of all of a class's instances that are currently in memory. This type of information and its processing are associated with the class rather than its instances. That is, the information is usually stored on the class itself and processed in the absence of any instance.

For such tasks, simple functions coded outside a class can often suffice—because they can access class attributes through the class name, they have access to class data and never require access to an instance. However, to better associate such code with a class, and to allow such processing to be customized with inheritance as usual, it would be better to code these types of functions inside the class itself. To make this work, we need methods in a class that are not passed, and do not expect, a `self` instance argument.

Python supports such goals with the notion of *static methods*—simple functions with no `self` argument that are nested in a class and are designed to work on class attributes instead of instance attributes. Static methods never receive an automatic `self` argument, whether called through a class or an instance. They usually keep track of information that spans all instances, rather than providing behavior for instances.

Although less commonly used, Python also supports the notion of *class methods*—methods of a class that are passed a class object in their first argument instead of an instance, regardless of whether they are called through an instance or a class. Such methods can access class data through their `self` class argument even if called through an instance. Normal methods (now known in formal circles as *instance methods*) still receive a subject instance when called; static and class methods do not.

Static Methods in 2.6 and 3.0

The concept of static methods is the same in both Python 2.6 and 3.0, but its implementation requirements have evolved somewhat in Python 3.0. Since this book covers both versions, I need to explain the differences in the two underlying models before we get to the code.

Really, we already began this story in the preceding chapter, when we explored the notion of unbound methods. Recall that both Python 2.6 and 3.0 always pass an instance to a method that is called through an instance. However, Python 3.0 treats methods fetched directly from a class differently than 2.6:

- In Python 2.6, fetching a method from a class produces an *unbound method*, which cannot be called without manually passing an instance.
- In Python 3.0, fetching a method from a class produces a *simple function*, which can be called normally with no instance present.

In other words, Python 2.6 class methods always require an instance to be passed in, whether they are called through an instance or a class. By contrast, in Python 3.0 we are required to pass an instance to a method only if the method expects one—methods without a `self` instance argument can be called through the class without passing an instance. That is, 3.0 allows simple functions in a class, as long as they do not expect and are not passed an instance argument. The net effect is that:

- In Python 2.6, we must always declare a method as static in order to call it without an instance, whether it is called through a class or an instance.
- In Python 3.0, we need not declare such methods as static if they will be called through a class only, but we must do so in order to call them through an instance.

To illustrate, suppose we want to use class attributes to count how many instances are generated from a class. The following file, *spam.py*, makes a first attempt—its class has a counter stored as a class attribute, a constructor that bumps up the counter by one each time a new instance is created, and a method that displays the counter's value. Remember, class attributes are shared by all instances. Therefore, storing the counter in the class object itself ensures that it effectively spans all instances:

```
class Spam:
    numInstances = 0
    def __init__(self):
        Spam.numInstances = Spam.numInstances + 1
```

```
    def printNumInstances():
        print("Number of instances created: ", Spam.numInstances)
```

The `printNumInstances` method is designed to process class data, not instance data—it's about *all* the instances, not any one in particular. Because of that, we want to be able to call it without having to pass an instance. Indeed, we don't want to make an instance to fetch the number of instances, because this would change the number of instances we're trying to fetch! In other words, we want a self-less "static" method.

Whether this code works or not, though, depends on which Python you use, and which way you call the method—through the class or through an instance. In 2.6 (and 2.X in general), calls to a self-less method function through both the class and instances fail (I've omitted some error text here for space):

```
C:\misc> c:\python26\python
>>> from spam import Spam
>>> a = Spam()                      # Cannot call unbound class methods in 2.6
>>> b = Spam()                      # Methods expect a self object by default
>>> c = Spam()

>>> Spam.printNumInstances()
TypeError: unbound method printNumInstances() must be called with Spam instance
as first argument (got nothing instead)
>>> a.printNumInstances()
TypeError: printNumInstances() takes no arguments (1 given)
```

The problem here is that unbound instance methods aren't exactly the same as simple functions in 2.6. Even though there are no arguments in the `def` header, the method still expects an instance to be passed in when it's called, because the function is associated with a class. In Python 3.0 (and later 3.X releases), calls to self-less methods made through classes work, but calls from instances fail:

```
C:\misc> c:\python30\python
>>> from spam import Spam
>>> a = Spam()                      # Can call functions in class in 3.0
>>> b = Spam()                      # Calls through instances still pass a self
>>> c = Spam()

>>> Spam.printNumInstances()        # Differs in 3.0
Number of instances created:   3
>>> a.printNumInstances()
TypeError: printNumInstances() takes no arguments (1 given)
```

That is, calls to instance-less methods like `printNumInstances` made through the *class* fail in Python 2.6 but work in Python 3.0. On the other hand, calls made through an *instance* fail in both Pythons, because an instance is automatically passed to a method that does not have an argument to receive it:

```
Spam.printNumInstances()            # Fails in 2.6, works in 3.0
instance.printNumInstances()        # Fails in both 2.6 and 3.0
```

If you're able to use 3.0 and stick with calling self-less methods through classes only, you already have a static method feature. However, to allow self-less methods to be called through classes in 2.6 and through instances in both 2.6 and 3.0, you need to either adopt other designs or be able to somehow mark such methods as special. Let's look at both options in turn.

Static Method Alternatives

Short of marking a self-less method as special, there are a few different coding structures that can be tried. If you want to call functions that access class members without an instance, perhaps the simplest idea is to just make them simple functions outside the class, not class methods. This way, an instance isn't expected in the call. For example, the following mutation of *spam.py* works the same in Python 3.0 and 2.6 (albeit displaying extra parentheses in 2.6 for its `print` statement):

```
def printNumInstances():
    print("Number of instances created: ", Spam.numInstances)

class Spam:
    numInstances = 0
    def __init__(self):
        Spam.numInstances = Spam.numInstances + 1

>>> import spam
>>> a = spam.Spam()
>>> b = spam.Spam()
>>> c = spam.Spam()
>>> spam.printNumInstances()          # But function may be too far removed
Number of instances created:  3       # And cannot be changed via inheritance
>>> spam.Spam.numInstances
3
```

Because the class name is accessible to the simple function as a global variable, this works fine. Also, note that the name of the function becomes global, but only to this single module; it will not clash with names in other files of the program.

Prior to static methods in Python, this structure was the general prescription. Because Python already provides modules as a namespace-partitioning tool, one could argue that there's not typically any need to package functions in classes unless they implement object behavior. Simple functions within modules like the one here do much of what instance-less class methods could, and are already associated with the class because they live in the same module.

Unfortunately, this approach is still less than ideal. For one thing, it adds to this file's scope an extra name that is used only for processing a single class. For another, the function is much less directly associated with the class; in fact, its definition could be hundreds of lines away. Perhaps worse, simple functions like this cannot be customized by inheritance, since they live outside a class's namespace: subclasses cannot directly replace or extend such a function by redefining it.

We might try to make this example work in a version-neutral way by using a normal method and always calling it through (or with) an instance, as usual:

```
class Spam:
    numInstances = 0
    def __init__(self):
        Spam.numInstances = Spam.numInstances + 1
    def printNumInstances(self):
        print("Number of instances created: ", Spam.numInstances)
```

```
>>> from spam import Spam
>>> a, b, c = Spam(), Spam(), Spam()
>>> a.printNumInstances()
Number of instances created:  3
>>> Spam.printNumInstances(a)
Number of instances created:  3
>>> Spam().printNumInstances()                # But fetching counter changes counter!
Number of instances created:  4
```

Unfortunately, as mentioned earlier, such an approach is completely unworkable if we don't have an instance available, and making an instance changes the class data, as illustrated in the last line here. A better solution would be to somehow mark a method inside a class as never requiring an instance. The next section shows how.

Using Static and Class Methods

Today, there is another option for coding simple functions associated with a class that may be called through either the class or its instances. As of Python 2.2, we can code classes with static and class methods, neither of which requires an instance argument to be passed in when invoked. To designate such methods, classes call the built-in functions `staticmethod` and `classmethod`, as hinted in the earlier discussion of new-style classes. Both mark a function object as special—i.e., as requiring no instance if static and requiring a class argument if a class method. For example:

```
class Methods:
    def imeth(self, x):            # Normal instance method: passed a self
        print(self, x)

    def smeth(x):                  # Static: no instance passed
        print(x)

    def cmeth(cls, x):             # Class: gets class, not instance
        print(cls, x)

    smeth = staticmethod(smeth)    # Make smeth a static method
    cmeth = classmethod(cmeth)     # Make cmeth a class method
```

Notice how the last two assignments in this code simply *reassign* the method names `smeth` and `cmeth`. Attributes are created and changed by any assignment in a `class` statement, so these final assignments simply overwrite the assignments made earlier by the `def`s.

Technically, Python now supports three kinds of class-related methods: *instance*, *static*, and *class*. Moreover, Python 3.0 extends this model by also allowing simple functions in a class to serve the role of static methods without extra protocol, when called through a class.

Instance methods are the normal (and default) case that we've seen in this book. An instance method must always be called with an instance object. When you call it through an instance, Python passes the instance to the first (leftmost) argument automatically; when you call it through a class, you must pass along the instance manually (for simplicity, I've omitted some class imports in interactive sessions like this one):

```
>>> obj = Methods()              # Make an instance

>>> obj.imeth(1)                 # Normal method, call through instance
<__main__.Methods object...> 1   # Becomes imeth(obj, 1)

>>> Methods.imeth(obj, 2)        # Normal method, call through class
<__main__.Methods object...> 2   # Instance passed explicitly
```

By contrast, *static methods* are called without an instance argument. Unlike simple functions outside a class, their names are local to the scopes of the classes in which they are defined, and they may be looked up by inheritance. Instance-less functions can be called through a class normally in Python 3.0, but never by default in 2.6. Using the staticmethod built-in allows such methods to also be called through an instance in 3.0 and through both a class and an instance in Python 2.6 (the first of these works in 3.0 without staticmethod, but the second does not):

```
>>> Methods.smeth(3)             # Static method, call through class
3                                # No instance passed or expected

>>> obj.smeth(4)                 # Static method, call through instance
4                                # Instance not passed
```

Class methods are similar, but Python automatically passes the class (not an instance) in to a class method's first (leftmost) argument, whether it is called through a class or an instance:

```
>>> Methods.cmeth(5)             # Class method, call through class
<class '__main__.Methods'> 5     # Becomes cmeth(Methods, 5)

>>> obj.cmeth(6)                 # Class method, call through instance
<class '__main__.Methods'> 6     # Becomes cmeth(Methods, 6)
```

Counting Instances with Static Methods

Now, given these built-ins, here is the static method equivalent of this section's instance-counting example—it marks the method as special, so it will never be passed an instance automatically:

```
class Spam:
    numInstances = 0                            # Use static method for class data
    def __init__(self):
        Spam.numInstances += 1
    def printNumInstances():
        print("Number of instances:", Spam.numInstances)
    printNumInstances = staticmethod(printNumInstances)
```

Using the static method built-in, our code now allows the self-less method to be called through the class or any instance of it, in both Python 2.6 and 3.0:

```
>>> a = Spam()
>>> b = Spam()
>>> c = Spam()
>>> Spam.printNumInstances()                    # Call as simple function
Number of instances: 3
>>> a.printNumInstances()                        # Instance argument not passed
Number of instances: 3
```

Compared to simply moving `printNumInstances` outside the class, as prescribed earlier, this version requires an extra `staticmethod` call; however, it localizes the function name in the class scope (so it won't clash with other names in the module), moves the function code closer to where it is used (inside the `class` statement), and allows subclasses to *customize* the static method with inheritance—a more convenient approach than importing functions from the files in which superclasses are coded. The following subclass and new testing session illustrate:

```
class Sub(Spam):
    def printNumInstances():                    # Override a static method
        print("Extra stuff...")                  # But call back to original
        Spam.printNumInstances()
    printNumInstances = staticmethod(printNumInstances)

>>> a = Sub()
>>> b = Sub()
>>> a.printNumInstances()                        # Call from subclass instance
Extra stuff...
Number of instances: 2
>>> Sub.printNumInstances()                      # Call from subclass itself
Extra stuff...
Number of instances: 2
>>> Spam.printNumInstances()
Number of instances: 2
```

Moreover, classes can inherit the static method without redefining it—it is run without an instance, regardless of where it is defined in a class tree:

```
>>> class Other(Spam): pass                      # Inherit static method verbatim

>>> c = Other()
>>> c.printNumInstances()
Number of instances: 3
```

Counting Instances with Class Methods

Interestingly, a *class method* can do similar work here—the following has the same behavior as the static method version listed earlier, but it uses a class method that receives the instance's class in its first argument. Rather than hardcoding the class name, the class method uses the automatically passed class object generically:

```
class Spam:
    numInstances = 0                          # Use class method instead of static
    def __init__(self):
        Spam.numInstances += 1
    def printNumInstances(cls):
        print("Number of instances:", cls.numInstances)
    printNumInstances = classmethod(printNumInstances)
```

This class is used in the same way as the prior versions, but its `printNumInstances` method receives the class, not the instance, when called from both the class and an instance:

```
>>> a, b = Spam(), Spam()
>>> a.printNumInstances()                     # Passes class to first argument
Number of instances: 2
>>> Spam.printNumInstances()                  # Also passes class to first argument
Number of instances: 2
```

When using class methods, though, keep in mind that they receive the most specific (i.e., *lowest*) class of the call's subject. This has some subtle implications when trying to update class data through the passed-in class. For example, if in module *test.py* we subclass to customize as before, augment `Spam.printNumInstances` to also display its `cls` argument, and start a new testing session:

```
class Spam:
    numInstances = 0                          # Trace class passed in
    def __init__(self):
        Spam.numInstances += 1
    def printNumInstances(cls):
        print("Number of instances:", cls.numInstances, cls)
    printNumInstances = classmethod(printNumInstances)

class Sub(Spam):
    def printNumInstances(cls):               # Override a class method
        print("Extra stuff...", cls)          # But call back to original
        Spam.printNumInstances()
    printNumInstances = classmethod(printNumInstances)

class Other(Spam): pass                       # Inherit class method verbatim
```

the lowest class is passed in whenever a class method is run, even for subclasses that have no class methods of their own:

```
>>> x, y = Sub(), Spam()
>>> x.printNumInstances()                     # Call from subclass instance
Extra stuff... <class 'test.Sub'>
Number of instances: 2 <class 'test.Spam'>
```

```
>>> Sub.printNumInstances()                    # Call from subclass itself
Extra stuff... <class 'test.Sub'>
Number of instances: 2 <class 'test.Spam'>
>>> y.printNumInstances()
Number of instances: 2 <class 'test.Spam'>
```

In the first call here, a class method call is made through an instance of the Sub subclass, and Python passes the lowest class, Sub, to the class method. All is well in this case—since Sub's redefinition of the method calls the Spam superclass's version explicitly, the superclass method in Spam receives itself in its first argument. But watch what happens for an object that simply inherits the class method:

```
>>> z = Other()
>>> z.printNumInstances()
Number of instances: 3 <class 'test.Other'>
```

This last call here passes Other to Spam's class method. This works in this example because *fetching* the counter finds it in Spam by inheritance. If this method tried to *assign* to the passed class's data, though, it would update Other, not Spam! In this specific case, Spam is probably better off hardcoding its own class name to update its data, rather than relying on the passed-in class argument.

Counting instances per class with class methods

In fact, because class methods always receive the lowest class in an instance's tree:

- *Static* methods and explicit class names may be a better solution for processing data local to a class.
- *Class* methods may be better suited to processing data that may differ for each class in a hierarchy.

Code that needs to manage *per-class* instance counters, for example, might be best off leveraging class methods. In the following, the top-level superclass uses a class method to manage state information that varies for and is stored on each class in the tree—similar in spirit to the way instance methods manage state information in class instances:

```
class Spam:
    numInstances = 0
    def count(cls):                         # Per-class instance counters
        cls.numInstances += 1               # cls is lowest class above instance
    def __init__(self):
        self.count()                        # Passes self.__class__ to count
    count = classmethod(count)

class Sub(Spam):
    numInstances = 0
    def __init__(self):                     # Redefines __init__
        Spam.__init__(self)

class Other(Spam):                          # Inherits __init__
    numInstances = 0
```

```
>>> x = Spam()
>>> y1, y2 = Sub(), Sub()
>>> z1, z2, z3 = Other(), Other(), Other()
>>> x.numInstances, y1.numInstances, z1.numInstances
(1, 2, 3)
>>> Spam.numInstances, Sub.numInstances, Other.numInstances
(1, 2, 3)
```

Static and class methods have additional advanced roles, which we will finesse here; see other resources for more use cases. In recent Python versions, though, the static and class method designations have become even simpler with the advent of function decoration syntax—a way to apply one function to another that has roles well beyond the static method use case that was its motivation. This syntax also allows us to augment classes in Python 2.6 and 3.0—to initialize data like the numInstances counter in the last example, for instance. The next section explains how.

Decorators and Metaclasses: Part 1

Because the staticmethod call technique described in the prior section initially seemed obscure to some users, a feature was eventually added to make the operation simpler. *Function decorators* provide a way to specify special operation modes for functions, by wrapping them in an extra layer of logic implemented as another function.

Function decorators turn out to be general tools: they are useful for adding many types of logic to functions besides the static method use case. For instance, they may be used to augment functions with code that logs calls made to them, checks the types of passed arguments during debugging, and so on. In some ways, function decorators are similar to the *delegation* design pattern we explored in Chapter 30, but they are designed to augment a specific function or method call, not an entire object interface.

Python provides some built-in function decorators for operations such as marking static methods, but programmers can also code arbitrary decorators of their own. Although they are not strictly tied to classes, user-defined function decorators often are coded as classes to save the original functions, along with other data, as state information. There's also a more recent related extension available in Python 2.6 and 3.0: *class decorators* are directly tied to the class model, and their roles overlap with *metaclasses*.

Function Decorator Basics

Syntactically, a function decorator is a sort of runtime declaration about the function that follows. A function decorator is coded on a line by itself just before the def statement that defines a function or method. It consists of the @ symbol, followed by what we call a *metafunction*—a function (or other callable object) that manages another function. Static methods today, for example, may be coded with decorator syntax like this:

```
class C:
    @staticmethod                              # Decoration syntax
    def meth():
        ...
```

Internally, this syntax has the same effect as the following (passing the function through the decorator and assigning the result back to the original name):

```
class C:
    def meth():
        ...
    meth = staticmethod(meth)                  # Rebind name
```

Decoration rebinds the method name to the decorator's result. The net effect is that calling the method function's name later actually triggers the result of its `staticmethod` decorator first. Because a decorator can return any sort of object, this allows the decorator to insert a layer of logic to be run on every call. The decorator function is free to return either the original function itself, or a new object that saves the original function passed to the decorator to be invoked indirectly after the extra logic layer runs.

With this addition, here's a better way to code our static method example from the prior section in either Python 2.6 or 3.0 (the `classmethod` decorator is used the same way):

```
class Spam:
    numInstances = 0
    def __init__(self):
        Spam.numInstances = Spam.numInstances + 1

    @staticmethod
    def printNumInstances():
        print("Number of instances created: ", Spam.numInstances)

a = Spam()
b = Spam()
c = Spam()
Spam.printNumInstances()      # Calls from both classes and instances work now!
a.printNumInstances()         # Both print "Number of instances created:  3"
```

Keep in mind that `staticmethod` is still a built-in function; it may be used in decoration syntax, just because it takes a function as argument and returns a callable. In fact, any such function can be used in this way—even user-defined functions we code ourselves, as the next section explains.

A First Function Decorator Example

Although Python provides a handful of built-in functions that can be used as decorators, we can also write custom decorators of our own. Because of their wide utility, we're going to devote an entire chapter to coding decorators in the final part of this book. As a quick example, though, let's look at a simple user-defined decorator at work.

Recall from Chapter 29 that the __call__ operator overloading method implements a function-call interface for class instances. The following code uses this to define a class that saves the decorated function in the instance and catches calls to the original name. Because this is a class, it also has state information (a counter of calls made):

```
class tracer:
    def __init__(self, func):
        self.calls = 0
        self.func  = func
    def __call__(self, *args):
        self.calls += 1
        print('call %s to %s' % (self.calls, self.func.__name__))
        self.func(*args)

@tracer                          # Same as spam = tracer(spam)
def spam(a, b, c):               # Wrap spam in a decorator object
    print(a, b, c)

spam(1, 2, 3)                    # Really calls the tracer wrapper object
spam('a', 'b', 'c')             # Invokes __call__ in class
spam(4, 5, 6)                    # __call__ adds logic and runs original object
```

Because the spam function is run through the tracer decorator, when the original spam name is called it actually triggers the __call__ method in the class. This method counts and logs the call, and then dispatches it to the original wrapped function. Note how the *name argument syntax is used to pack and unpack the passed-in arguments; because of this, this decorator can be used to wrap any function with any number of positional arguments.

The net effect, again, is to add a layer of logic to the original spam function. Here is the script's output—the first line comes from the tracer class, and the second comes from the spam function:

```
call 1 to spam
1 2 3
call 2 to spam
a b c
call 3 to spam
4 5 6
```

Trace through this example's code for more insight. As it is, this decorator works for any function that takes positional arguments, but it does not return the decorated function's *result*, doesn't handle *keyword* arguments, and cannot decorate class *method* functions (in short, for methods its __call__ would be passed a tracer instance only). As we'll see in Part VIII, there are a variety of ways to code function decorators, including nested def statements; some of the alternatives are better suited to methods than the version shown here.

Class Decorators and Metaclasses

Function decorators turned out to be so useful that Python 2.6 and 3.0 expanded the model, allowing decorators to be applied to classes as well as functions. In short, *class decorators* are similar to function decorators, but they are run at the end of a `class` statement to rebind a class name to a callable. As such, they can be used to either manage classes just after they are created, or insert a layer of wrapper logic to manage instances when they are later created. Symbolically, the code structure:

```
def decorator(aClass): ...

@decorator
class C: ...
```

is mapped to the following equivalent:

```
def decorator(aClass): ...

class C: ...
C = decorator(C)
```

The class decorator is free to augment the class itself, or return an object that intercepts later instance construction calls. For instance, in the example in the section "Counting instances per class with class methods" on page 805, we could use this hook to automatically augment the classes with instance counters and any other data required:

```
def count(aClass):
    aClass.numInstances = 0
    return aClass               # Return class itself, instead of a wrapper

@count
class Spam: ...                 # Same as Spam = count(Spam)

@count
class Sub(Spam): ...            # numInstances = 0 not needed here

@count
class Other(Spam): ...
```

Metaclasses are a similarly advanced class-based tool whose roles often intersect with those of class decorators. They provide an alternate model, which routes the creation of a class object to a subclass of the top-level **type** class, at the conclusion of a `class` statement:

```
class Meta(type):
    def __new__(meta, classname, supers, classdict): ...

class C(metaclass=Meta): ...
```

In Python 2.6, the effect is the same, but the coding differs—use a class attribute instead of a keyword argument in the `class` header:

```
class C:
    __metaclass__ = Meta
    ...
```

The metaclass generally redefines the `__new__` or `__init__` method of the `type` class, in order to assume control of the creation or initialization of a new class object. The net effect, as with class decorators, is to define code to be run automatically at class creation time. Both schemes are free to augment a class or return an arbitrary object to replace it—a protocol with almost limitless class-based possibilities.

For More Details

Naturally, there's much more to the decorator and metaclass stories than I've shown here. Although they are a general mechanism, decorators and metaclasses are advanced features of interest primarily to tool writers, not application programmers, so we'll defer additional coverage until the final part of this book:

- Chapter 37 shows how to code properties using function decorator syntax.
- Chapter 38 has much more on decorators, including more comprehensive examples.
- Chapter 39 covers metaclasses, and more on the class and instance management story.

Although these chapters cover advanced topics, they'll also provide us with a chance to see Python at work in more substantial examples than much of the rest of the book was able to provide.

Class Gotchas

Most class issues can be boiled down to namespace issues (which makes sense, given that classes are just namespaces with a few extra tricks). Some of the topics we'll cover in this section are more like case studies of advanced class usage than real problems, and one or two of these gotchas have been eased by recent Python releases.

Changing Class Attributes Can Have Side Effects

Theoretically speaking, classes (and class instances) are *mutable* objects. Like built-in lists and dictionaries, they can be changed in-place by assigning to their attributes— and as with lists and dictionaries, this means that changing a class or instance object may impact multiple references to it.

That's usually what we want (and is how objects change their state in general), but awareness of this issue becomes especially critical when changing class attributes. Because all instances generated from a class share the class's namespace, any changes at the class level are reflected in all instances, unless they have their own versions of the changed class attributes.

Because classes, modules, and instances are all just objects with attribute namespaces, you can normally change their attributes at runtime by assignments. Consider the following class. Inside the class body, the assignment to the name a generates an attribute X.a, which lives in the class object at runtime and will be inherited by all of X's instances:

```
>>> class X:
...     a = 1            # Class attribute
...
>>> I = X()
>>> I.a                  # Inherited by instance
1
>>> X.a
1
```

So far, so good—this is the normal case. But notice what happens when we change the class attribute dynamically outside the class statement: it also changes the attribute in every object that inherits from the class. Moreover, new instances created from the class during this session or program run also get the dynamically set value, regardless of what the class's source code says:

```
>>> X.a = 2            # May change more than X
>>> I.a                # I changes too
2
>>> J = X()            # J inherits from X's runtime values
>>> J.a                # (but assigning to J.a changes a in J, not X or I)
2
```

Is this a useful feature or a dangerous trap? You be the judge. As we learned in Chapter 26, you can actually get work done by changing class attributes without ever making a single instance; this technique can simulate the use of "records" or "structs" in other languages. As a refresher, consider the following unusual but legal Python program:

```
class X: pass            # Make a few attribute namespaces
class Y: pass

X.a = 1                  # Use class attributes as variables
X.b = 2                  # No instances anywhere to be found
X.c = 3
Y.a = X.a + X.b + X.c

for X.i in range(Y.a): print(X.i)    # Prints 0..5
```

Here, the classes X and Y work like "fileless" modules—namespaces for storing variables we don't want to clash. This is a perfectly legal Python programming trick, but it's less appropriate when applied to classes written by others; you can't always be sure that class attributes you change aren't critical to the class's internal behavior. If you're out to simulate a C struct, you may be better off changing instances than classes, as that way only one object is affected:

```
class Record: pass
X = Record()
X.name = 'bob'
X.job  = 'Pizza maker'
```

Changing Mutable Class Attributes Can Have Side Effects, Too

This gotcha is really an extension of the prior. Because class attributes are shared by all instances, if a class attribute references a mutable object, changing that object in-place from any instance impacts all instances at once:

```
>>> class C:
...     shared = []              # Class attribute
...     def __init__(self):
...         self.perobj = []     # Instance attribute
...
>>> x = C()                      # Two instances
>>> y = C()                      # Implicitly share class attrs
>>> y.shared, y.perobj
([], [])

>>> x.shared.append('spam')      # Impacts y's view too!
>>> x.perobj.append('spam')      # Impacts x's data only
>>> x.shared, x.perobj
(['spam'], ['spam'])

>>> y.shared, y.perobj           # y sees change made through x
(['spam'], [])
>>> C.shared                     # Stored on class and shared
['spam']
```

This effect is no different than many we've seen in this book already: mutable objects are shared by simple variables, globals are shared by functions, module-level objects are shared by multiple importers, and mutable function arguments are shared by the caller and the callee. All of these are cases of general behavior—multiple references to a mutable object—and all are impacted if the shared object is changed in-place from any reference. Here, this occurs in class attributes shared by all instances via inheritance, but it's the same phenomenon at work. It may be made more subtle by the different behavior of assignments to instance attributes themselves:

```
x.shared.append('spam')    # Changes shared object attached to class in-place
x.shared = 'spam'          # Changed or creates instance attribute attached to x
```

but again, this is not a problem, it's just something to be aware of; shared mutable class attributes can have many valid uses in Python programs.

Multiple Inheritance: Order Matters

This may be obvious by now, but it's worth underscoring: if you use multiple inheritance, the order in which superclasses are listed in the class statement header can be critical. Python always searches superclasses from left to right, according to their order in the header line.

For instance, in the multiple inheritance example we studied in Chapter 30, suppose that the Super class implemented a __str__ method, too:

```
class ListTree:
    def __str__(self): ...

class Super:
    def __str__(self): ...

class Sub(ListTree, Super):      # Get ListTree's __str__ by listing it first

x = Sub()                        # Inheritance searches ListTree before Super
```

Which class would we inherit it from—ListTree or Super? As inheritance searches proceed from left to right, we would get the method from whichever class is listed first (leftmost) in Sub's class header. Presumably, we would list ListTree first because its whole purpose is its custom __str__ (indeed, we had to do this in Chapter 30 when mixing this class with a tkinter.Button that had a __str__ of its own).

But now suppose Super and ListTree have their own versions of other same-named attributes, too. If we want one name from Super and another from ListTree, the order in which we list them in the class header won't help—we will have to override inheritance by manually assigning to the attribute name in the Sub class:

```
class ListTree:
    def __str__(self): ...
    def other(self): ...

class Super:
    def __str__(self): ...
    def other(self): ...

class Sub(ListTree, Super):      # Get ListTree's __str__ by listing it first
    other = Super.other          # But explicitly pick Super's version of other
    def __init__(self):
        ...

x = Sub()                        # Inheritance searches Sub before ListTree/Super
```

Here, the assignment to other within the Sub class creates Sub.other—a reference back to the Super.other object. Because it is lower in the tree, Sub.other effectively hides ListTree.other, the attribute that the inheritance search would normally find. Similarly, if we listed Super first in the class header to pick up its other, we would need to select ListTree's method explicitly:

```
class Sub(Super, ListTree):          # Get Super's other by order
    __str__ = Lister.__str__         # Explicitly pick Lister.__str__
```

Multiple inheritance is an advanced tool. Even if you understood the last paragraph, it's still a good idea to use it sparingly and carefully. Otherwise, the meaning of a name may come to depend on the order in which classes are mixed in an arbitrarily far-removed subclass. (For another example of the technique shown here in action, see the discussion of explicit conflict resolution in "The "New-Style" Class Model" on page 779.)

As a rule of thumb, multiple inheritance works best when your mix-in classes are as self-contained as possible—because they may be used in a variety of contexts, they should not make assumptions about names related to other classes in a tree. The pseudoprivate __X attributes feature we studied in Chapter 30 can help by localizing names that a class relies on owning and limiting the names that your mix-in classes add to the mix. In this example, for instance, if ListTree only means to export its custom __str__, it can name its other method __other to avoid clashing with like-named classes in the tree.

Methods, Classes, and Nested Scopes

This gotcha went away in Python 2.2 with the introduction of nested function scopes, but I've retained it here for historical perspective, for readers working with older Python releases, and because it demonstrates what happens to the new nested function scope rules when one layer of the nesting is a class.

Classes introduce local scopes, just as functions do, so the same sorts of scope behavior can happen in a class statement body. Moreover, methods are further nested functions, so the same issues apply. Confusion seems to be especially common when classes are nested.

In the following example (the file *nester.py*), the generate function returns an instance of the nested Spam class. Within its code, the class name Spam is assigned in the generate function's local scope. However, in versions of Python prior to 2.2, within the class's method function the class name Spam is not visible—method has access only to its own local scope, the module surrounding generate, and built-in names:

```
def generate():                      # Fails prior to Python 2.2, works later
    class Spam:
        count = 1
        def method(self):            # Name Spam not visible:
            print(Spam.count)        # not local (def), global (module), built-in
    return Spam()

generate().method()

C:\python\examples> python nester.py
...error text omitted...
```

```
    print(Spam.count)              # Not local (def), global (module), built-in
NameError: Spam
```

This example works in Python 2.2 and later because the local scopes of all enclosing function `def`s are automatically visible to nested `def`s (including nested method `def`s, as in this example). However, it doesn't work before 2.2 (we'll look at some possible solutions momentarily).

Note that even in 2.2 and later, method `def`s cannot see the local scope of the enclosing *class*; they can only see the local scopes of enclosing `def`s. That's why methods must go through the `self` instance or the class name to reference methods and other attributes defined in the enclosing `class` statement. For example, code in the method must use `self.count` or `Spam.count`, not just `count`.

If you're using a release prior to 2.2, there are a variety of ways to get the preceding example to work. One of the simplest is to move the name `Spam` out to the enclosing module's scope with a `global` declaration. Because `method` sees global names in the enclosing module, references to `Spam` will work:

```
def generate():
    global Spam                    # Force Spam to module scope
    class Spam:
        count = 1
        def method(self):
            print(Spam.count)      # Works: in global (enclosing module)
    return Spam()

generate().method()                # Prints 1
```

A better alternative would be to restructure the code such that the class `Spam` is defined at the top level of the module by virtue of its nesting level, rather than using `global` declarations. The nested `method` function and the top-level `generate` will then find `Spam` in their global scopes:

```
def generate():
    return Spam()

class Spam:                        # Define at top level of module
    count = 1
    def method(self):
        print(Spam.count)          # Works: in global (enclosing module)

generate().method()
```

In fact, this approach is recommended for all Python releases—code tends to be simpler in general if you avoid nesting classes and functions.

If you want to get complicated and tricky, you can also get rid of the `Spam` reference in `method` altogether by using the special `__class__` attribute, which returns an instance's class object:

```
def generate():
    class Spam:
```

```
            count = 1
        def method(self):
            print(self.__class__.count)        # Works: qualify to get class
    return Spam()

generate().method()
```

Delegation-Based Classes in 3.0: __getattr__ and built-ins

We met this issue briefly in our class tutorial in Chapter 27 and our delegation coverage in Chapter 30: classes that use the __getattr__ operator overloading method to delegate attribute fetches to wrapped objects will fail in Python 3.0 unless operator overloading methods are redefined in the wrapper class. In Python 3.0 (and 2.6, when new-style classes are used), the names of operator overloading methods implicitly fetched by built-in operations are not routed through generic attribute-interception methods. The __str__ method used by printing, for example, never invokes __getattr__. Instead, Python 3.0 looks up such names in classes and skips the normal runtime instance lookup mechanism entirely. To work around this, such methods must be redefined in wrapper classes, either by hand, with tools, or by definition in superclasses. We'll revisit this gotcha in Chapters 37 and 38.

"Overwrapping-itis"

When used well, the code reuse features of OOP make it excel at cutting development time. Sometimes, though, OOP's abstraction potential can be abused to the point of making code difficult to understand. If classes are layered too deeply, code can become obscure; you may have to search through many classes to discover what an operation does.

For example, I once worked in a C++ shop with thousands of classes (some machine-generated), and up to 15 levels of inheritance. Deciphering method calls in such a complex system was often a monumental task: multiple classes had to be consulted for even the most basic of operations. In fact, the logic of the system was so deeply wrapped that understanding a piece of code in some cases required days of wading through related files.

The most general rule of thumb of Python programming applies here, too: don't make things complicated unless they truly must be. Wrapping your code in multiple layers of classes to the point of incomprehensibility is always a bad idea. Abstraction is the basis of polymorphism and encapsulation, and it can be a very effective tool when used well. However, you'll simplify debugging and aid maintainability if you make your class interfaces intuitive, avoid making your code overly abstract, and keep your class hierarchies short and flat unless there is a good reason to do otherwise.

Chapter Summary

This chapter presented a handful of advanced class-related topics, including subclassing built-in types, new-style classes, static methods, and decorators. Most of these are optional extensions to the OOP model in Python, but they may become more useful as you start writing larger object-oriented programs. As mentioned earlier, our discussion of some of the more advanced class tools continues in the final part of this book; be sure to look ahead if you need more details on properties, descriptors, decorators, and metaclasses.

This is the end of the class part of this book, so you'll find the usual lab exercises at the end of the chapter—be sure to work through them to get some practice coding real classes. In the next chapter, we'll begin our look at our last core language topic, exceptions. Exceptions are Python's mechanism for communicating errors and other conditions to your code. This is a relatively lightweight topic, but I've saved it for last because exceptions are supposed to be coded as classes today. Before we tackle that final core subject, though, take a look at this chapter's quiz and the lab exercises.

Test Your Knowledge: Quiz

1. Name two ways to extend a built-in object type.
2. What are function decorators used for?
3. How do you code a new-style class?
4. How are new-style and classic classes different?
5. How are normal and static methods different?
6. How long should you wait before lobbing a "Holy Hand Grenade"?

Test Your Knowledge: Answers

1. You can embed a built-in object in a wrapper class, or subclass the built-in type directly. The latter approach tends to be simpler, as most original behavior is automatically inherited.
2. Function decorators are generally used to add to an existing function a layer of logic that is run each time the function is called. They can be used to log or count calls to a function, check its argument types, and so on. They are also used to "declare" static methods—simple functions in a class that are not passed an instance when called.

3. New-style classes are coded by inheriting from the `object` built-in class (or any other built-in type). In Python 3.0, all classes are new-style automatically, so this derivation is not required; in 2.6, classes with this derivation are new-style and those without it are "classic."

4. New-style classes search the diamond pattern of multiple inheritance trees differently—they essentially search breadth-first (across), instead of depth-first (up). New-style classes also change the result of the `type` built-in for instances and classes, do not run generic attribute fetch methods such as `__getattr__` for built-in operation methods, and support a set of advanced extra tools including properties, descriptors, and `__slots__` instance attribute lists.

5. Normal (instance) methods receive a `self` argument (the implied instance), but static methods do not. Static methods are simple functions nested in class objects. To make a method static, it must either be run through a special built-in function or be decorated with decorator syntax. Python 3.0 allows simple functions in a class to be called through the class without this step, but calls through instances still require static method declaration.

6. Three seconds. (Or, more accurately: "And the Lord spake, saying, 'First shalt thou take out the Holy Pin. Then, shalt thou count to three, no more, no less. Three shalt be the number thou shalt count, and the number of the counting shall be three. Four shalt thou not count, nor either count thou two, excepting that thou then proceed to three. Five is right out. Once the number three, being the third number, be reached, then lobbest thou thy Holy Hand Grenade of Antioch towards thy foe, who, being naughty in my sight, shall snuff it.'")*

Test Your Knowledge: Part VI Exercises

These exercises ask you to write a few classes and experiment with some existing code. Of course, the problem with existing code is that it must be existing. To work with the set class in exercise 5, either pull the class source code off this book's website (see the Preface for a pointer) or type it up by hand (it's fairly brief). These programs are starting to get more sophisticated, so be sure to check the solutions at the end of the book for pointers. You'll find them in Appendix B, under "Part VI, Classes and OOP" on page 1124.

1. *Inheritance*. Write a class called `Adder` that exports a method `add(self, x, y)` that prints a "Not Implemented" message. Then, define two subclasses of `Adder` that implement the `add` method:

   `ListAdder`

   With an `add` method that returns the concatenation of its two list arguments

---

* This quote is from *Monty Python and the Holy Grail*.

DictAdder

> With an **add** method that returns a new dictionary containing the items in both its two dictionary arguments (any definition of addition will do)

Experiment by making instances of all three of your classes interactively and calling their **add** methods.

Now, extend your **Adder** superclass to save an object in the instance with a constructor (e.g., assign **self.data** a list or a dictionary), and overload the + operator with an __add__ method to automatically dispatch to your **add** methods (e.g., X + Y triggers X.add(X.data,Y)). Where is the best place to put the constructors and operator overloading methods (i.e., in which classes)? What sorts of objects can you add to your class instances?

In practice, you might find it easier to code your **add** methods to accept just one real argument (e.g., add(self,y)), and add that one argument to the instance's current data (e.g., self.data + y). Does this make more sense than passing two arguments to **add**? Would you say this makes your classes more "object-oriented"?

2. *Operator overloading.* Write a class called **MyList** that shadows ("wraps") a Python list: it should overload most list operators and operations, including +, indexing, iteration, slicing, and list methods such as **append** and **sort**. See the Python reference manual for a list of all possible methods to support. Also, provide a constructor for your class that takes an existing list (or a **MyList** instance) and copies its components into an instance member. Experiment with your class interactively. Things to explore:

   a. Why is copying the initial value important here?

   b. Can you use an empty slice (e.g., start[:]) to copy the initial value if it's a **MyList** instance?

   c. Is there a general way to route list method calls to the wrapped list?

   d. Can you add a **MyList** and a regular list? How about a list and a **MyList** instance?

   e. What type of object should operations like + and slicing return? What about indexing operations?

   f. If you are working with a more recent Python release (version 2.2 or later), you may implement this sort of wrapper class by embedding a real list in a stand-alone class, or by extending the built-in list type with a subclass. Which is easier, and why?

3. *Subclassing.* Make a subclass of **MyList** from exercise 2 called **MyListSub**, which extends **MyList** to print a message to **stdout** before each overloaded operation is called and counts the number of calls. **MyListSub** should inherit basic method behavior from **MyList**. Adding a sequence to a **MyListSub** should print a message, increment the counter for + calls, and perform the superclass's method. Also, introduce a new method that prints the operation counters to **stdout**, and experiment with your class interactively. Do your counters count calls per instance, or per class (for all instances of the class)? How would you program the other option?

(Hint: it depends on which object the count members are assigned to: class members are shared by instances, but `self` members are per-instance data.)

4. *Attribute methods.* Write a class called `Meta` with methods that intercept every attribute qualification (both fetches and assignments), and print messages listing their arguments to `stdout`. Create a `Meta` instance, and experiment with qualifying it interactively. What happens when you try to use the instance in expressions? Try adding, indexing, and slicing the instance of your class. (Note: a fully generic approach based upon `__getattr__` will work in 2.6 but not 3.0, for reasons noted in Chapter 30 and restated in the solution to this exercise.)

5. *Set objects.* Experiment with the set class described in "Extending Types by Embedding" on page 776. Run commands to do the following sorts of operations:

   a. Create two sets of integers, and compute their intersection and union by using `&` and `|` operator expressions.

   b. Create a set from a string, and experiment with indexing your set. Which methods in the class are called?

   c. Try iterating through the items in your string set using a `for` loop. Which methods run this time?

   d. Try computing the intersection and union of your string set and a simple Python string. Does it work?

   e. Now, extend your set by subclassing to handle arbitrarily many operands using the `*args` argument form. (Hint: see the function versions of these algorithms in Chapter 18.) Compute intersections and unions of multiple operands with your set subclass. How can you intersect three or more sets, given that `&` has only two sides?

   f. How would you go about emulating other list operations in the set class? (Hint: `__add__` can catch concatenation, and `__getattr__` can pass most list method calls to the wrapped list.)

6. *Class tree links.* In "Namespaces: The Whole Story" on page 695 in Chapter 28 and in "Multiple Inheritance: "Mix-in" Classes" on page 758 in Chapter 30, I mentioned that classes have a `__bases__` attribute that returns a tuple of their superclass objects (the ones listed in parentheses in the class header). Use `__bases__` to extend the *lister.py* mix-in classes we wrote in Chapter 30 so that they print the names of the immediate superclasses of the instance's class. When you're done, the first line of the string representation should look like this (your address may vary):

   ```
   <Instance of Sub(Super, Lister), address 7841200:
   ```

7. *Composition.* Simulate a fast-food ordering scenario by defining four classes:

   Lunch
   > A container and controller class

Customer
    The actor who buys food

Employee
    The actor from whom a customer orders

Food
    What the customer buys

To get you started, here are the classes and methods you'll be defining:

```
class Lunch:
    def __init__(self)           # Make/embed Customer and Employee
    def order(self, foodName)    # Start a Customer order simulation
    def result(self)             # Ask the Customer what Food it has

class Customer:
    def __init__(self)                          # Initialize my food to None
    def placeOrder(self, foodName, employee)    # Place order with an Employee
    def printFood(self)                         # Print the name of my food

class Employee:
    def takeOrder(self, foodName)    # Return a Food, with requested name

class Food:
    def __init__(self, name)    # Store food name
```

The order simulation should work as follows:

a. The Lunch class's constructor should make and embed an instance of Customer and an instance of Employee, and it should export a method called order. When called, this order method should ask the Customer to place an order by calling its placeOrder method. The Customer's placeOrder method should in turn ask the Employee object for a new Food object by calling Employee's takeOrder method.

b. Food objects should store a food name string (e.g., "burritos"), passed down from Lunch.order, to Customer.placeOrder, to Employee.takeOrder, and finally to Food's constructor. The top-level Lunch class should also export a method called result, which asks the customer to print the name of the food it received from the Employee via the order (this can be used to test your simulation).

Note that Lunch needs to pass either the Employee or itself to the Customer to allow the Customer to call Employee methods.

Experiment with your classes interactively by importing the Lunch class, calling its order method to run an interaction, and then calling its result method to verify that the Customer got what he or she ordered. If you prefer, you can also simply code test cases as self-test code in the file where your classes are defined, using the module __name__ trick of Chapter 24. In this simulation, the Customer is the active agent; how would your classes change if Employee were the object that initiated customer/employee interaction instead?

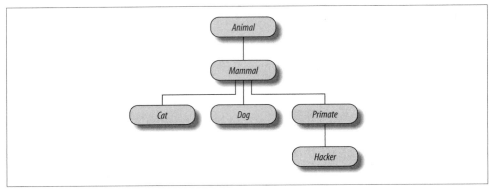

Figure 31-1. A zoo hierarchy composed of classes linked into a tree to be searched by attribute inheritance. Animal has a common "reply" method, but each class may have its own custom "speak" method called by "reply".

8. *Zoo animal hierarchy.* Consider the class tree shown in Figure 31-1.

   Code a set of six `class` statements to model this taxonomy with Python inheritance. Then, add a `speak` method to each of your classes that prints a unique message, and a `reply` method in your top-level `Animal` superclass that simply calls `self.speak` to invoke the category-specific message printer in a subclass below (this will kick off an independent inheritance search from `self`). Finally, remove the `speak` method from your `Hacker` class so that it picks up the default above it. When you're finished, your classes should work this way:

   ```
   % python
   >>> from zoo import Cat, Hacker
   >>> spot = Cat()
   >>> spot.reply()                    # Animal.reply; calls Cat.speak
   meow
   >>> data = Hacker()                 # Animal.reply; calls Primate.speak
   >>> data.reply()
   Hello world!
   ```

9. *The Dead Parrot Sketch.* Consider the object embedding structure captured in Figure 31-2.

   Code a set of Python classes to implement this structure with composition. Code your `Scene` object to define an `action` method, and embed instances of the `Customer`, `Clerk`, and `Parrot` classes (each of which should define a `line` method that prints a unique message). The embedded objects may either inherit from a common superclass that defines `line` and simply provide message text, or define `line` themselves. In the end, your classes should operate like this:

   ```
   % python
   >>> import parrot
   >>> parrot.Scene().action()         # Activate nested objects
   customer: "that's one ex-bird!"
   clerk: "no it isn't..."
   parrot: None
   ```

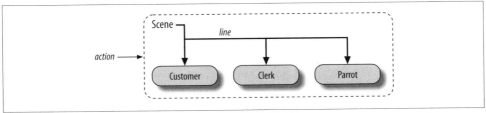

Figure 31-2. A scene composite with a controller class (Scene) that embeds and directs instances of three other classes (Customer, Clerk, Parrot). The embedded instance's classes may also participate in an inheritance hierarchy; composition and inheritance are often equally useful ways to structure classes for code reuse.

Why You Will Care: OOP by the Masters

When I teach Python classes, I invariably find that about halfway through the class, people who have used OOP in the past are following along intensely, while people who have not are beginning to glaze over (or nod off completely). The point behind the technology just isn't apparent.

In a book like this, I have the luxury of including material like the new Big Picture overview in Chapter 25, and the gradual tutorial of Chapter 27—in fact, you should probably review that section if you're starting to feel like OOP is just some computer science mumbo-jumbo.

In real classes, however, to help get the newcomers on board (and keep them awake), I have been known to stop and ask the experts in the audience why they use OOP. The answers they've given might help shed some light on the purpose of OOP, if you're new to the subject.

Here, then, with only a few embellishments, are the most common reasons to use OOP, as cited by my students over the years:

Code reuse
   This one's easy (and is the main reason for using OOP). By supporting inheritance, classes allow you to program by customization instead of starting each project from scratch.

Encapsulation
   Wrapping up implementation details behind object interfaces insulates users of a class from code changes.

Structure
   Classes provide new local scopes, which minimizes name clashes. They also provide a natural place to write and look for implementation code, and to manage object state.

Maintenance
   Classes naturally promote code factoring, which allows us to minimize redundancy. Thanks both to the structure and code reuse support of classes, usually only one copy of the code needs to be changed.

Consistency

> Classes and inheritance allow you to implement common interfaces, and hence create a common look and feel in your code; this eases debugging, comprehension, and maintenance.

Polymorphism

> This is more a property of OOP than a reason for using it, but by supporting code generality, polymorphism makes code more flexible and widely applicable, and hence more reusable.

Other

> And, of course, the number one reason students gave for using OOP: it looks good on a résumé! (OK, I threw this one in as a joke, but it is important to be familiar with OOP if you plan to work in the software field today.)

Finally, keep in mind what I said at the beginning of this part of the book: you won't fully appreciate OOP until you've used it for awhile. Pick a project, study larger examples, work through the exercises—do whatever it takes to get your feet wet with OO code; it's worth the effort.

## PART VII

Exceptions and Tools

## CHAPTER 32

Exception Basics

This part of the book deals with *exceptions*, which are events that can modify the flow of control through a program. In Python, exceptions are triggered automatically on errors, and they can be triggered and intercepted by your code. They are processed by four statements we'll study in this part, the first of which has two variations (listed separately here) and the last of which was an optional extension until Python 2.6 and 3.0:

try/except
    Catch and recover from exceptions raised by Python, or by you.

try/finally
    Perform cleanup actions, whether exceptions occur or not.

raise
    Trigger an exception manually in your code.

assert
    Conditionally trigger an exception in your code.

with/as
    Implement context managers in Python 2.6 and 3.0 (optional in 2.5).

This topic was saved until nearly the end of the book because you need to know about classes to code exceptions of your own. With a few exceptions (pun intended), though, you'll find that exception handling is simple in Python because it's integrated into the language itself as another high-level tool.

Why Use Exceptions?

In a nutshell, exceptions let us jump out of arbitrarily large chunks of a program. Consider the hypothetical pizza-making robot we discussed earlier in the book. Suppose we took the idea seriously and actually built such a machine. To make a pizza, our culinary automaton would need to execute a plan, which we would implement as a

Python program: it would take an order, prepare the dough, add toppings, bake the pie, and so on.

Now, suppose that something goes very wrong during the "bake the pie" step. Perhaps the oven is broken, or perhaps our robot miscalculates its reach and spontaneously combusts. Clearly, we want to be able to jump to code that handles such states quickly. As we have no hope of finishing the pizza task in such unusual cases, we might as well abandon the entire plan.

That's exactly what exceptions let you do: you can jump to an exception handler in a single step, abandoning all function calls begun since the exception handler was entered. Code in the exception handler can then respond to the raised exception as appropriate (by calling the fire department, for instance!).

One way to think of an exception is as a sort of structured "super go to." An *exception handler* (try statement) leaves a marker and executes some code. Somewhere further ahead in the program, an exception is raised that makes Python jump back to that marker, abandoning any active functions that were called after the marker was left. This protocol provides a coherent way to respond to unusual events. Moreover, because Python jumps to the handler statement immediately, your code is simpler—there is usually no need to check status codes after every call to a function that could possibly fail.

Exception Roles

In Python programs, exceptions are typically used for a variety of purposes. Here are some of their most common roles:

Error handling
> Python raises exceptions whenever it detects errors in programs at runtime. You can catch and respond to the errors in your code, or ignore the exceptions that are raised. If an error is ignored, Python's default exception-handling behavior kicks in: it stops the program and prints an error message. If you don't want this default behavior, code a try statement to catch and recover from the exception—Python will jump to your try handler when the error is detected, and your program will resume execution after the try.

Event notification
> Exceptions can also be used to signal valid conditions without you having to pass result flags around a program or test them explicitly. For instance, a search routine might raise an exception on failure, rather than returning an integer result code (and hoping that the code will never be a valid result).

Special-case handling
> Sometimes a condition may occur so rarely that it's hard to justify convoluting your code to handle it. You can often eliminate special-case code by handling unusual cases in exception handlers in higher levels of your program.

Termination actions

As you'll see, the `try/finally` statement allows you to guarantee that required closing-time operations will be performed, regardless of the presence or absence of exceptions in your programs.

Unusual control flows

Finally, because exceptions are a sort of high-level "go to," you can use them as the basis for implementing exotic control flows. For instance, although the language does not explicitly support backtracking, it can be implemented in Python by using exceptions and a bit of support logic to unwind assignments.* There is no "go to" statement in Python (thankfully!), but exceptions can sometimes serve similar roles.

We'll see such typical use cases in action later in this part of the book. For now, let's get started with a look at Python's exception-processing tools.

Exceptions: The Short Story

Compared to some other core language topics we've met in this book, exceptions are a fairly lightweight tool in Python. Because they are so simple, let's jump right into some code.

Default Exception Handler

Suppose we write the following function:

```
>>> def fetcher(obj, index):
...     return obj[index]
...
```

There's not much to this function—it simply indexes an object on a passed-in index. In normal operation, it returns the result of a legal index:

```
>>> x = 'spam'
>>> fetcher(x, 3)                    # Like x[3]
'm'
```

However, if we ask this function to index off the end of the string, an exception will be triggered when the function tries to run `obj[index]`. Python detects out-of-bounds indexing for sequences and reports it by *raising* (triggering) the built-in `IndexError` exception:

---

* True backtracking is an advanced topic that is not part of the Python language, so I won't say much more about it here (even the generator functions and expressions we met in Chapter 20 are not true backtracking—they simply respond to `next(G)` requests). Roughly, backtracking undoes all computations before it jumps; Python exceptions do not (i.e., variables assigned between the time a `try` statement is entered and the time an exception is raised are not reset to their prior values). See a book on artificial intelligence or the Prolog or Icon programming languages if you're curious.

```
>>> fetcher(x, 4)                          # Default handler - shell interface
Traceback (most recent call last):
  File "<stdin>", line 1, in <module>
  File "<stdin>", line 2, in fetcher
IndexError: string index out of range
```

Because our code does not explicitly catch this exception, it filters back up to the top level of the program and invokes the *default exception handler*, which simply prints the standard error message. By this point in the book, you've probably seen your share of standard error messages. They include the exception that was raised, along with a *stack trace*—a list of all the lines and functions that were active when the exception occurred.

The error message text here was printed by Python 3.0; it can vary slightly per release, and even per interactive shell. When coding interactively in the basic shell interface, the filename is just "<stdin>," meaning the standard input stream. When working in the IDLE GUI's interactive shell, the filename is "<pyshell>", and source lines are displayed, too. Either way, file line numbers are not very meaningful when there is no file (we'll see more interesting error messages later in this part of the book):

```
>>> fetcher(x, 4)                          # Default handler - IDLE GUI interface
Traceback (most recent call last):
  File "<pyshell#6>", line 1, in <module>
    fetcher(x, 4)
  File "<pyshell#3>", line 2, in fetcher
    return obj[index]
IndexError: string index out of range
```

In a more realistic program launched outside the interactive prompt, after printing an error message the default handler at the top also *terminates* the program immediately. That course of action makes sense for simple scripts; errors often should be fatal, and the best you can do when they occur is inspect the standard error message.

Catching Exceptions

Sometimes, this isn't what you want, though. Server programs, for instance, typically need to remain active even after internal errors. If you don't want the default exception behavior, wrap the call in a `try` statement to catch exceptions yourself:

```
>>> try:
...     fetcher(x, 4)
... except IndexError:                     # Catch and recover
...     print('got exception')
...
got exception
>>>
```

Now, Python jumps to your *handler* (the block under the `except` clause that names the exception raised) automatically when an exception is triggered while the `try` block is running. When working interactively like this, after the `except` clause runs, we wind up back at the Python prompt. In a more realistic program, `try` statements not only catch exceptions, but also *recover* from them:

```
>>> def catcher():
...     try:
...         fetcher(x, 4)
...     except IndexError:
...         print('got exception')
...     print('continuing')
...
>>> catcher()
got exception
continuing
>>>
```

This time, after the exception is caught and handled, the program resumes execution after the entire `try` statement that caught it—which is why we get the "continuing" message here. We don't see the standard error message, and the program continues on its way normally.

Raising Exceptions

So far, we've been letting Python raise exceptions for us by making mistakes (on purpose this time!), but our scripts can raise exceptions too—that is, exceptions can be raised by Python or by your program, and can be caught or not. To trigger an exception manually, simply run a `raise` statement. User-triggered exceptions are caught the same way as those Python raises. The following may not be the most useful Python code ever penned, but it makes the point:

```
>>> try:
...     raise IndexError            # Trigger exception manually
... except IndexError:
...     print('got exception')
...
got exception
```

As usual, if they're not caught, user-triggered exceptions are propagated up to the top-level default exception handler and terminate the program with a standard error message:

```
>>> raise IndexError
Traceback (most recent call last):
  File "<stdin>", line 1, in <module>
IndexError
```

As we'll see in the next chapter, the `assert` statement can be used to trigger exceptions, too—it's a conditional `raise`, used mostly for debugging purposes during development:

```
>>> assert False, 'Nobody expects the Spanish Inquisition!'
Traceback (most recent call last):
  File "<stdin>", line 1, in <module>
AssertionError: Nobody expects the Spanish Inquisition!
```

User-Defined Exceptions

The `raise` statement introduced in the prior section raises a built-in exception defined in Python's built-in scope. As you'll learn later in this part of the book, you can also define new exceptions of your own that are specific to your programs. User-defined exceptions are coded with *classes*, which inherit from a built-in exception class: usually the class named `Exception`. Class-based exceptions allow scripts to build exception categories, inherit behavior, and have attached state information:

```
>>> class Bad(Exception):              # User-defined exception
...     pass
...
>>> def doomed():
...     raise Bad()                    # Raise an instance
...
>>> try:
...     doomed()
... except Bad:                        # Catch class name
...     print('got Bad')
...
got Bad
>>>
```

Termination Actions

Finally, `try` statements can say "finally"—that is, they may include `finally` blocks. These look like `except` handlers for exceptions, but the `try/finally` combination specifies termination actions that always execute "on the way out," regardless of whether an exception occurs in the `try` block:

```
>>> try:
...     fetcher(x, 3)
... finally:                           # Termination actions
...     print('after fetch')
...
'm'
after fetch
>>>
```

Here, if the `try` block finishes without an exception, the `finally` block will run, and the program will resume after the entire `try`. In this case, this statement seems a bit silly—we might as well have simply typed the `print` right after a call to the function, and skipped the `try` altogether:

```
fetcher(x, 3)
print('after fetch')
```

There is a problem with coding this way, though: if the function call raises an exception, the `print` will never be reached. The `try/finally` combination avoids this pitfall—when an exception does occur in a `try` block, `finally` blocks are executed while the program is being unwound:

```
>>> def after():
...     try:
...         fetcher(x, 4)
...     finally:
...         print('after fetch')
...     print('after try?')
...
>>> after()
after fetch
Traceback (most recent call last):
  File "<stdin>", line 1, in <module>
  File "<stdin>", line 3, in after
  File "<stdin>", line 2, in fetcher
IndexError: string index out of range
>>>
```

Here, we don't get the "after try?" message because control does not resume after the try/finally block when an exception occurs. Instead, Python jumps back to run the finally action, and then propagates the exception up to a prior handler (in this case, to the default handler at the top). If we change the call inside this function so as not to trigger an exception, the finally code still runs, but the program continues after the try:

```
>>> def after():
...     try:
...         fetcher(x, 3)
...     finally:
...         print('after fetch')
...     print('after try?')
...
>>> after()
after fetch
after try?
>>>
```

In practice, try/except combinations are useful for catching and recovering from exceptions, and try/finally combinations come in handy to guarantee that termination actions will fire regardless of any exceptions that may occur in the try block's code. For instance, you might use try/except to catch errors raised by code that you import from a third-party library, and try/finally to ensure that calls to close files or terminate server connections are always run. We'll see some such practical examples later in this part of the book.

Although they serve conceptually distinct purposes, as of Python 2.5, we can now mix except and finally clauses in the same try statement—the finally is run on the way out regardless of whether an exception was raised, and regardless of whether the exception was caught by an except clause.

As we'll learn in the next chapter, Python 2.6 and 3.0 provide an alternative to try/finally when using some types of objects. The with/as statement runs an object's context management logic to guarantee that termination actions occur:

```
>>> with open('lumberjack.txt', 'w') as file:        # Always close file on exit
...     file.write('The larch!\n')
```

Although this option requires fewer lines of code, it's only applicable when processing certain object types, so try/finally is a more general termination structure. On the other hand, with/as may also run startup actions and supports user-defined context management code.

Why You Will Care: Error Checks

One way to see how exceptions are useful is to compare coding styles in Python and languages without exceptions. For instance, if you want to write robust programs in the C language, you generally have to test return values or status codes after every operation that could possibly go astray, and propagate the results of the tests as your programs run:

```
doStuff()
{                                    # C program
    if (doFirstThing() == ERROR)     # Detect errors everywhere
        return ERROR;                # even if not handled here
    if (doNextThing() == ERROR)
        return ERROR;
    ...
    return doLastThing();
}

main()
{
    if (doStuff() == ERROR)
        badEnding();
    else
        goodEnding();
}
```

In fact, realistic C programs often have as much code devoted to error detection as to doing actual work. But in Python, you don't have to be so methodical (and neurotic!). You can instead wrap arbitrarily vast pieces of a program in exception handlers and simply write the parts that do the actual work, assuming all is well:

```
def doStuff():          # Python code
    doFirstThing()      # We don't care about exceptions here,
    doNextThing()       # so we don't need to detect them
    ...
    doLastThing()

if __name__ == '__main__':
    try:
        doStuff()       # This is where we care about results,
    except:             # so it's the only place we must check
        badEnding()
    else:
        goodEnding()
```

Because control jumps immediately to a handler when an exception occurs, there's no need to instrument all your code to guard for errors. Moreover, because Python detects errors automatically, your code usually doesn't need to check for errors in the first place. The upshot is that exceptions let you largely ignore the unusual cases and avoid error-checking code.

Chapter Summary

And that is the majority of the exception story; exceptions really are a simple tool.

To summarize, Python exceptions are a high-level control flow device. They may be raised by Python, or by your own programs. In both cases, they may be ignored (to trigger the default error message), or caught by `try` statements (to be processed by your code). The `try` statement comes in two logical formats that, as of Python 2.5, can be combined—one that handles exceptions, and one that executes finalization code regardless of whether exceptions occur or not. Python's `raise` and `assert` statements trigger exceptions on demand (both built-ins and new exceptions we define with classes); the `with`/`as` statement is an alternative way to ensure that termination actions are carried out for objects that support it.

In the rest of this part of the book, we'll fill in some of the details about the statements involved, examine the other sorts of clauses that can appear under a `try`, and discuss class-based exception objects. The next chapter begins our tour by taking a closer look at the statements we introduced here. Before you turn the page, though, here are a few quiz questions to review.

Test Your Knowledge: Quiz

1. Name three things that exception processing is good for.
2. What happens to an exception if you don't do anything special to handle it?
3. How can your script recover from an exception?
4. Name two ways to trigger exceptions in your script.
5. Name two ways to specify actions to be run at termination time, whether an exception occurs or not.

Test Your Knowledge: Answers

1. Exception processing is useful for error handling, termination actions, and event notification. It can also simplify the handling of special cases and can be used to implement alternative control flows. In general, exception processing also cuts

down on the amount of error-checking code your program may require—because all errors filter up to handlers, you may not need to test the outcome of every operation.

2. Any uncaught exception eventually filters up to the default exception handler Python provides at the top of your program. This handler prints the familiar error message and shuts down your program.

3. If you don't want the default message and shutdown, you can code try/except statements to catch and recover from exceptions that are raised. Once an exception is caught, the exception is terminated and your program continues.

4. The raise and assert statements can be used to trigger an exception, exactly as if it had been raised by Python itself. In principle, you can also raise an exception by making a programming mistake, but that's not usually an explicit goal!

5. The try/finally statement can be used to ensure actions are run after a block of code exits, regardless of whether it raises an exception or not. The with/as statement can also be used to ensure termination actions are run, but only when processing object types that support it.

## CHAPTER 33

Exception Coding Details

In the prior chapter we took a quick look at exception-related statements in action. Here, we're going to dig a bit deeper—this chapter provides a more formal introduction to exception processing syntax in Python. Specifically, we'll explore the details behind the try, raise, assert, and with statements. As we'll see, although these statements are mostly straightforward, they offer powerful tools for dealing with exceptions in Python code.

 One procedural note up front: The exception story has changed in major ways in recent years. As of Python 2.5, the finally clause can appear in the same try statement as except and else clauses (previously, they could not be combined). Also, as of Python 3.0 and 2.6, the new with context manager statement has become official, and user-defined exceptions must now be coded as class instances, which should inherit from a built-in exception superclass. Moreover, 3.0 sports slightly modified syntax for the raise statement and except clauses. I will focus on the state of exceptions in Python 2.6 and 3.0 in this edition, but because you are still very likely to see the original techniques in code for some time to come, along the way I'll point out how things have evolved in this domain.

The try/except/else Statement

Now that we've seen the basics, it's time for the details. In the following discussion, I'll first present try/except/else and try/finally as separate statements, because in versions of Python prior to 2.5 they serve distinct roles and cannot be combined. As mentioned in the preceding note, in Python 2.5 and later except and finally can be mixed in a single try statement; I'll explain the implications of this change after we've explored the two original forms in isolation.

The try is a compound statement; its most complete form is sketched below. It starts with a try header line, followed by a block of (usually) indented statements, then one or more except clauses that identify exceptions to be caught, and an optional else clause at the end. The words try, except, and else are associated by indenting them to the same level (i.e., lining them up vertically). For reference, here's the general format in Python 3.0:

```
try:
    <statements>          # Run this main action first
except <name1>:
    <statements>          # Run if name1 is raised during try block
except (name2, name3):
    <statements>          # Run if any of these exceptions occur
except <name4> as <data>:
    <statements>          # Run if name4 is raised, and get instance raised
except:
    <statements>          # Run for all (other) exceptions raised
else:
    <statements>          # Run if no exception was raised during try block
```

In this statement, the block under the try header represents the *main action* of the statement—the code you're trying to run. The except clauses define *handlers* for exceptions raised during the try block, and the else clause (if coded) provides a handler to be run if *no* exceptions occur. The *<data>* entry here has to do with a feature of raise statements and exception classes, which we will discuss later in this chapter.

Here's how try statements work. When a try statement is entered, Python marks the current program context so it can return to it if an exception occurs. The statements nested under the try header are run first. What happens next depends on whether exceptions are raised while the try block's statements are running:

- If an exception *does* occur while the try block's statements are running, Python jumps back to the try and runs the statements under the first except clause that matches the raised exception. Control resumes below the entire try statement after the except block runs (unless the except block raises another exception).

- If an exception happens in the try block and *no* except clause matches, the exception is propagated up to the last matching try statement that was entered in the program or, if it's the first such statement, to the top level of the process (in which case Python kills the program and prints a default error message).

- If no exception occurs while the statements under the try header run, Python runs the statements under the else line (if present), and control then resumes below the entire try statement.

In other words, except clauses catch any exceptions that happen while the try block is running, and the else clause runs only if no exceptions happen while the try block runs.

except clauses are *focused* exception handlers—they catch exceptions that occur only within the statements in the associated try block. However, as the try block's statements can call functions coded elsewhere in a program, the source of an exception may be outside the try statement itself. I'll have more to say about this when we explore try nesting in Chapter 35.

try Statement Clauses

When you write a `try` statement, a variety of clauses can appear after the `try` header. Table 33-1 summarizes all the possible forms—you must use at least one. We've already met some of these: as you know, `except` clauses catch exceptions, `finally` clauses run on the way out, and `else` clauses run if no exceptions are encountered.

Syntactically, there may be any number of `except` clauses, but you can code `else` only if there is at least one `except`, and there can be only one `else` and one `finally`. Through Python 2.4, the `finally` clause must appear alone (without `else` or `except`); the `try/finally` is really a different statement. As of Python 2.5, however, a `finally` can appear in the same statement as `except` and `else` (more on the ordering rules later in this chapter when we meet the unified `try` statement).

Table 33-1. try statement clause forms

Clause form	Interpretation
`except:`	Catch all (or all other) exception types.
`except` *name*`:`	Catch a specific exception only.
`except` *name* `as` *value*`:`	Catch the listed exception and its instance.
`except` (*name1*, *name2*)`:`	Catch any of the listed exceptions.
`except` (*name1*, *name2*) `as` *value*`:`	Catch any listed exception and its instance.
`else:`	Run if no exceptions are raised.
`finally:`	Always perform this block.

We'll explore the entries with the extra `as` *value* part when we meet the `raise` statement. They provide access to the objects that are raised as exceptions.

The first and fourth entries in Table 33-1 are new here:

- `except` clauses that list no exception name (`except:`) catch *all* exceptions not previously listed in the `try` statement.
- `except` clauses that list a set of exceptions in parentheses (`except (e1, e2, e3):`) catch *any* of the listed exceptions.

Because Python looks for a match within a given `try` by inspecting the `except` clauses from top to bottom, the parenthesized version has the same effect as listing each exception in its own `except` clause, but you have to code the statement body only once. Here's an example of multiple `except` clauses at work, which demonstrates just how specific your handlers can be:

```
try:
    action()
except NameError:
    ...
except IndexError:
    ...
```

```
except KeyError:
    ...
except (AttributeError, TypeError, SyntaxError):
    ...
else:
    ...
```

In this example, if an exception is raised while the call to the `action` function is running, Python returns to the `try` and searches for the first `except` that names the exception raised. It inspects the `except` clauses from top to bottom and left to right, and runs the statements under the first one that matches. If none match, the exception is propagated past this `try`. Note that the `else` runs only when *no* exception occurs in `action`—it does not run when an exception without a matching `except` is raised.

If you really want a general "catch-all" clause, an empty `except` does the trick:

```
try:
    action()
except NameError:
    ...                     # Handle NameError
except IndexError:
    ...                     # Handle IndexError
except:
    ...                     # Handle all other exceptions
else:
    ...                     # Handle the no-exception case
```

The empty `except` clause is a sort of *wildcard* feature—because it catches everything, it allows your handlers to be as general or specific as you like. In some scenarios, this form may be more convenient than listing all possible exceptions in a `try`. For example, the following catches everything without listing anything:

```
try:
    action()
except:
    ...                     # Catch all possible exceptions
```

Empty `except`s also raise some design issues, though. Although convenient, they may catch unexpected system exceptions unrelated to your code, and they may inadvertently intercept exceptions meant for another handler. For example, even system exit calls in Python trigger exceptions, and you usually want these to pass. That said, this structure may also catch genuine programming mistakes for you which you probably want to see an error message. We'll revisit this as a gotcha at the end of this part of the book. For now, I'll just say "use with care."

Python 3.0 introduced an alternative that solves one of these problems—catching an exception named `Exception` has almost the same effect as an empty `except`, but ignores exceptions related to system exits:

```
try:
    action()
except Exception:
    ...                     # Catch all possible exceptions, except exits
```

This has most of the same convenience of the empty except, but also most of the same dangers. We'll explore how this form works its voodoo in the next chapter, when we study exception classes.

Version skew note: Python 3.0 requires the except E as V: handler clause form listed in Table 33-1 and used in this book, rather than the older except E, V: form. The latter form is still available (but not recommended) in Python 2.6: if used, it's converted to the former. The change was made to eliminate errors that occur when confusing the older form with two alternate exceptions, properly coded in 2.6 as except (E1, E2):. Because 3.0 supports the as form only, commas in a handler clause are always taken to mean a tuple, regardless of whether parentheses are used or not, and the values are interpreted as alternative exceptions to be caught. This change also modifies the scoping rules: with the new as syntax, the variable V is deleted at the end of the except block.

The try else Clause

The purpose of the else clause is not always immediately obvious to Python newcomers. Without it, though, there is no way to tell (without setting and checking Boolean flags) whether the flow of control has proceeded past a try statement because no exception was raised, or because an exception occurred and was handled:

```
try:
    ...run code...
except IndexError:
    ...handle exception...
# Did we get here because the try failed or not?
```

Much like the way else clauses in loops make the exit cause more apparent, the else clause provides syntax in a try that makes what has happened obvious and unambiguous:

```
try:
    ...run code...
except IndexError:
    ...handle exception...
else:
    ...no exception occurred...
```

You can *almost* emulate an else clause by moving its code into the try block:

```
try:
    ...run code...
    ...no exception occurred...
except IndexError:
    ...handle exception...
```

This can lead to incorrect exception classifications, though. If the "no exception occurred" action triggers an IndexError, it will register as a failure of the try block and erroneously trigger the exception handler below the try (subtle, but true!). By using an explicit else clause instead, you make the logic more obvious and guarantee that except handlers will run only for real failures in the code you're wrapping in a try, not for failures in the else case's action.

Example: Default Behavior

Because the control flow through a program is easier to capture in Python than in English, let's run some examples that further illustrate exception basics. I've mentioned that exceptions not caught by try statements percolate up to the top level of the Python process and run Python's default exception-handling logic (i.e., Python terminates the running program and prints a standard error message). Let's look at an example. Running the following module file, *bad.py*, generates a divide-by-zero exception:

```
def gobad(x, y):
    return x / y

def gosouth(x):
    print(gobad(x, 0))

gosouth(1)
```

Because the program ignores the exception it triggers, Python kills the program and prints a message:

```
% python bad.py
Traceback (most recent call last):
  File "bad.py", line 7, in <module>
    gosouth(1)
  File "bad.py", line 5, in gosouth
    print(gobad(x, 0))
  File "bad.py", line 2, in gobad
    return x / y
ZeroDivisionError: int division or modulo by zero
```

I ran this in a shell widow with Python 3.0. The message consists of a stack trace ("Traceback") and the name of and details about the exception that was raised. The stack trace lists all lines active when the exception occurred, from oldest to newest. Note that because we're not working at the interactive prompt, in this case the file and line number information is more useful. For example, here we can see that the bad divide happens at the last entry in the trace—line 2 of the file *bad.py*, a return statement.[*]

Because Python detects and reports all errors at runtime by raising exceptions, exceptions are intimately bound up with the ideas of error handling and debugging in general.

---

[*] As mentioned in the prior chapter, the text of error messages and stack traces tends to vary slightly over time and shells. Don't be alarmed if your error messages don't exactly match mine. When I ran this example in Python 3.0's IDLE GUI, for instance, its error message text showed filenames with full absolute directory paths.

If you've worked through this book's examples, you've undoubtedly seen an exception or two along the way—even typos usually generate a SyntaxError or other exception when a file is imported or executed (that's when the compiler is run). By default, you get a useful error display like the one just shown, which helps you track down the problem.

Often, this standard error message is all you need to resolve problems in your code. For more heavy-duty debugging jobs, you can catch exceptions with try statements, or use one of the debugging tools that I introduced in Chapter 3 and will summarize again in Chapter 35 (such as the pdb standard library module).

Example: Catching Built-in Exceptions

Python's default exception handling is often exactly what you want—especially for code in a top-level script file, an error generally should terminate your program immediately. For many programs, there is no need to be more specific about errors in your code.

Sometimes, though, you'll want to catch errors and recover from them instead. If you don't want your program terminated when Python raises an exception, simply catch it by wrapping the program logic in a try. This is an important capability for programs such as network servers, which must keep running persistently. For example, the following code catches and recovers from the TypeError Python raises immediately when you try to concatenate a list and a string (the + operator expects the same sequence type on both sides):

```
def kaboom(x, y):
    print(x + y)              # Trigger TypeError

try:
    kaboom([0,1,2], "spam")
except TypeError:             # Catch and recover here
    print('Hello world!')
print('resuming here')       # Continue here if exception or not
```

When the exception occurs in the function kaboom, control jumps to the try statement's except clause, which prints a message. Since an exception is "dead" after it's been caught like this, the program continues executing below the try rather than being terminated by Python. In effect, the code processes and clears the error, and your script recovers:

```
% python kaboom.py
Hello world!
resuming here
```

Notice that once you've caught an error, control resumes at the place where you caught it (i.e., after the try); there is no direct way to go back to the place where the exception occurred (here, in the function kaboom). In a sense, this makes exceptions more like simple jumps than function calls—there is no way to return to the code that triggered the error.

The try/finally Statement

The other flavor of the try statement is a specialization that has to do with finalization actions. If a finally clause is included in a try, Python will always run its block of statements "on the way out" of the try statement, whether an exception occurred while the try block was running or not. Its general form is:

```
try:
    <statements>            # Run this action first
finally:
    <statements>            # Always run this code on the way out
```

With this variant, Python begins by running the statement block associated with the try header line. What happens next depends on whether an exception occurs during the try block:

- If no exception occurs while the try block is running, Python jumps back to run the finally block and then continues execution past below the try statement.
- If an exception *does* occur during the try block's run, Python still comes back and runs the finally block, but it then propagates the exception up to a higher try or the top-level default handler; the program does not resume execution below the try statement. That is, the finally block is run even if an exception is raised, but unlike an except, the finally does not terminate the exception—it continues being raised after the finally block runs.

The try/finally form is useful when you want to be completely sure that an action will happen after some code runs, regardless of the exception behavior of the program. In practice, it allows you to specify cleanup actions that always must occur, such as file closes and server disconnects.

Note that the finally clause cannot be used in the same try statement as except and else in Python 2.4 and earlier, so the try/finally is best thought of as a distinct statement form if you are using an older release. In Python 2.5, and later, however, finally can appear in the same statement as except and else, so today there is really a single try statement with many optional clauses (more about this shortly). Whichever version you use, though, the finally clause still serves the same purpose—to specify "cleanup" actions that must always be run, regardless of any exceptions.

 As we'll also see later in this chapter, in Python 2.6 and 3.0, the new with statement and its context managers provide an object-based way to do similar work for exit actions. Unlike finally, this new statement also supports entry actions, but it is limited in scope to objects that implement the context manager protocol.

Example: Coding Termination Actions with try/finally

We saw some simple try/finally examples in the prior chapter. Here's a more realistic example that illustrates a typical role for this statement:

```
class MyError(Exception): pass

def stuff(file):
    raise MyError()

file = open('data', 'w')          # Open an output file
try:
    stuff(file)                   # Raises exception
finally:
    file.close()                  # Always close file to flush output buffers
print('not reached')              # Continue here only if no exception
```

In this code, we've wrapped a call to a file-processing function in a try with a finally clause to make sure that the file is always closed, and thus finalized, whether the function triggers an exception or not. This way, later code can be sure that the file's output buffer's content has been flushed from memory to disk. A similar code structure can guarantee that server connections are closed, and so on.

As we learned in Chapter 9, file objects are automatically closed on garbage collection; this is especially useful for temporary files that we don't assign to variables. However, it's not always easy to predict when garbage collection will occur, especially in larger programs. The try statement makes file closes more explicit and predictable and pertains to a specific block of code. It ensures that the file will be closed on block exit, regardless of whether an exception occurs or not.

This particular example's function isn't all that useful (it just raises an exception), but wrapping calls in try/finally statements is a good way to ensure that your closing-time (i.e., termination) activities always run. Again, Python always runs the code in your finally blocks, regardless of whether an exception happens in the try block.[†]

When the function here raises its exception, the control flow jumps back and runs the finally block to close the file. The exception is then propagated on to either another try or the default top-level handler, which prints the standard error message and shuts down the program; the statement after this try is never reached. If the function here did *not* raise an exception, the program would still execute the finally block to close the file, but it would then continue below the entire try statement.

Notice that the user-defined exception here is again defined with a class—as we'll see in the next chapter, exceptions today must all be class instances in both 2.6 and 3.0.

[†] Unless Python crashes completely, of course. It does a good job of avoiding this, though, by checking all possible errors as a program runs. When a program does crash hard, it is usually due to a bug in linked-in C extension code, outside of Python's scope.

Unified try/except/finally

In all versions of Python prior to Release 2.5 (for its first 15 years of life, more or less), the `try` statement came in two flavors and was really two separate statements—we could either use a `finally` to ensure that cleanup code was always run, or write `except` blocks to catch and recover from specific exceptions and optionally specify an `else` clause to be run if no exceptions occurred.

That is, the `finally` clause could not be mixed with `except` and `else`. This was partly because of implementation issues, and partly because the meaning of mixing the two seemed obscure—catching and recovering from exceptions seemed a disjoint concept from performing cleanup actions.

In Python 2.5 and later, though (including 2.6 and 3.0, the versions used in this book), the two statements have merged. Today, we can mix `finally`, `except`, and `else` clauses in the same statement. That is, we can now write a statement of this form:

```
try:                            # Merged form
    main-action
except Exception1:
    handler1
except Exception2:
    handler2
...
else:
    else-block
finally:
    finally-block
```

The code in this statement's *main-action* block is executed first, as usual. If that code raises an exception, all the `except` blocks are tested, one after another, looking for a match to the exception raised. If the exception raised is `Exception1`, the *handler1* block is executed; if it's `Exception2`, *handler2* is run, and so on. If no exception is raised, the *else-block* is executed.

No matter what's happened previously, the *finally-block* is executed once the main action block is complete and any raised exceptions have been handled. In fact, the code in the *finally-block* will be run even if there is an error in an exception handler or the *else-block* and a new exception is raised.

As always, the `finally` clause does not end the exception—if an exception is active when the *finally-block* is executed, it continues to be propagated after the *finally-block* runs, and control jumps somewhere else in the program (to another `try`, or to the default top-level handler). If no exception is active when the `finally` is run, control resumes after the entire `try` statement.

The net effect is that the `finally` is always run, regardless of whether:

- An exception occurred in the main action and was handled.
- An exception occurred in the main action and was not handled.

- No exceptions occurred in the main action.
- A new exception was triggered in one of the handlers.

Again, the `finally` serves to specify cleanup actions that must always occur on the way out of the `try`, regardless of what exceptions have been raised or handled.

Unified try Statement Syntax

When combined like this, the `try` statement must have either an `except` or a `finally`, and the order of its parts must be like this:

```
try -> except -> else -> finally
```

where the `else` and `finally` are optional, and there may be zero or more `except`, but there must be at least one `except` if an `else` appears. Really, the `try` statement consists of two parts: `except`s with an optional `else`, and/or the `finally`.

In fact, it's more accurate to describe the merged statement's syntactic form this way (square brackets mean optional and star means zero-or-more here):

```
try:                                # Format 1
    statements
except [type [as value]]:           # [type [, value]] in Python 2
    statements
[except [type [as value]]:
    statements]*
[else:
    statements]
[finally:
    statements]


try:                                # Format 2
    statements
finally:
    statements
```

Because of these rules, the `else` can appear only if there is at least one `except`, and it's always possible to mix `except` and `finally`, regardless of whether an `else` appears or not. It's also possible to mix `finally` and `else`, but only if an `except` appears too (though the `except` can omit an exception name to catch everything and run a `raise` statement, described later, to reraise the current exception). If you violate any of these ordering rules, Python will raise a syntax error exception before your code runs.

Combining finally and except by Nesting

Prior to Python 2.5, it is actually possible to combine `finally` and `except` clauses in a `try` by syntactically nesting a `try/except` in the `try` block of a `try/finally` statement (we'll explore this technique more fully in Chapter 35). In fact, the following has the same effect as the new merged form shown at the start of this section:

The raise Statement

To trigger exceptions explicitly, you can code **raise** statements. Their general form is simple—a **raise** statement consists of the word **raise**, optionally followed by the class to be raised or an instance of it:

```
raise <instance>        # Raise instance of class
raise <class>           # Make and raise instance of class
raise                   # Reraise the most recent exception
```

As mentioned earlier, exceptions are always instances of classes in Python 2.6 and 3.0. Hence, the first **raise** form here is the most common—we provide an *instance* directly, either created before the **raise** or within the **raise** statement itself. If we pass a *class* instead, Python calls the class with no constructor arguments, to create an instance to be raised; this form is equivalent to adding parentheses after the class reference. The last form reraises the most recently raised exception; it's commonly used in exception handlers to propagate exceptions that have been caught.

To make this clearer, let's look at some examples. With built-in exceptions, the following two forms are equivalent—both raise an instance of the exception class named, but the first creates the instance implicitly:

```
raise IndexError        # Class (instance created)
raise IndexError()      # Instance (created in statement)
```

We can also create the instance ahead of time—because the **raise** statement accepts any kind of object reference, the following two examples raise `IndexError` just like the prior two:

```
exc = IndexError()      # Create instance ahead of time
raise exc

excs = [IndexError, TypeError]
raise excs[0]
```

When an exception is raised, Python sends the raised instance along with the exception. If a **try** includes an `except name as X:` clause, the variable X will be assigned the instance provided in the **raise**:

```
try:
    ...
except IndexError as X:     # X assigned the raised instance object
    ...
```

The **as** is optional in a **try** handler (if it's omitted, the instance is simply not assigned to a name), but including it allows the handler to access both data in the instance and methods in the exception class.

This model works the same for user-defined exceptions we code with classes—the following, for example, passes to the exception class constructor arguments that become available in the handler through the assigned instance:

```
class MyExc(Exception): pass
...
raise MyExc('spam')              # Exception class with constructor args
...
try:
    ...
except MyExc as X:               # Instance attributes available in handler
    print(X.args)
```

Because this encroaches on the next chapter's topic, though, I'll defer further details until then.

Regardless of how you name them, exceptions are always identified by instance objects, and at most one is active at any given time. Once caught by an except clause anywhere in the program, an exception dies (i.e., won't propagate to another try), unless it's reraised by another raise statement or error.

Propagating Exceptions with raise

A raise statement that does not include an exception name or extra data value simply reraises the current exception. This form is typically used if you need to catch and handle an exception but don't want the exception to die in your code:

```
>>> try:
...     raise IndexError('spam')     # Exceptions remember arguments
... except IndexError:
...     print('propagating')
...     raise                        # Reraise most recent exception
...
propagating
Traceback (most recent call last):
  File "<stdin>", line 2, in <module>
IndexError: spam
```

Running a raise this way reraises the exception and propagates it to a higher handler (or the default handler at the top, which stops the program with a standard error message). Notice how the argument we passed to the exception class shows up in the error messages; you'll learn why this happens in the next chapter.

Python 3.0 Exception Chaining: raise from

Python 3.0 (but not 2.6) also allows raise statements to have an optional from clause:

```
raise exception from otherexception
```

When the from is used, the second expression specifies another exception class or instance to attach to the raised exception's __cause__ attribute. If the raised exception is not caught, Python prints both exceptions as part of the standard error message:

```
>>> try:
...     1 / 0
... except Exception as E:
```

```
...     raise TypeError('Bad!') from E
...
Traceback (most recent call last):
  File "<stdin>", line 2, in <module>
ZeroDivisionError: int division or modulo by zero

The above exception was the direct cause of the following exception:

Traceback (most recent call last):
  File "<stdin>", line 4, in <module>
TypeError: Bad!
```

When an exception is raised inside an exception handler, a similar procedure is followed implicitly: the previous exception is attached to the new exception's __context__ attribute and is again displayed in the standard error message if the exception goes uncaught. This is an advanced and still somewhat obscure extension, so see Python's manuals for more details.

 Version skew note: Python 3.0 no longer supports the raise *Exc, Args* form that is still available in Python 2.6. In 3.0, use the raise *Exc(Args)* instance-creation call form described in this book instead. The equivalent comma form in 2.6 is legacy syntax provided for compatibility with the now defunct string-based exceptions model, and it's deprecated in 2.6. If used, it is converted to the 3.0 call form. As in earlier releases, a raise *Exc* form is also allowed—it is converted to raise *Exc()* in both versions, calling the class constructor with no arguments.

The assert Statement

As a somewhat special case for debugging purposes, Python includes the assert statement. It is mostly just syntactic shorthand for a common raise usage pattern, and an assert can be thought of as a *conditional* raise statement. A statement of the form:

```
assert <test>, <data>          # The <data> part is optional
```

works like the following code:

```
if __debug__:
    if not <test>:
        raise AssertionError(<data>)
```

In other words, if the test evaluates to false, Python raises an exception: the data item (if it's provided) is used as the exception's constructor argument. Like all exceptions, the AssertionError exception will kill your program if it's not caught with a try, in which case the data item shows up as part of the error message.

As an added feature, assert statements may be removed from a compiled program's byte code if the -O Python command-line flag is used, thereby optimizing the program. AssertionError is a built-in exception, and the __debug__ flag is a built-in name that is automatically set to `True` unless the `-O` flag is used. Use a command line like `python -O main.py` to run in optimized mode and disable asserts.

Example: Trapping Constraints (but Not Errors!)

Assertions are typically used to verify program conditions during development. When displayed, their error message text automatically includes source code line information and the value listed in the `assert` statement. Consider the file *asserter.py*:

```
def f(x):
    assert x < 0, 'x must be negative'
    return x ** 2

% python
>>> import asserter
>>> asserter.f(1)
Traceback (most recent call last):
  File "<stdin>", line 1, in <module>
  File "asserter.py", line 2, in f
    assert x < 0, 'x must be negative'
AssertionError: x must be negative
```

It's important to keep in mind that `assert` is mostly intended for trapping user-defined constraints, not for catching genuine programming errors. Because Python traps programming errors itself, there is usually no need to code `assert`s to catch things like out-of-bounds indexes, type mismatches, and zero divides:

```
def reciprocal(x):
    assert x != 0            # A useless assert!
    return 1 / x             # Python checks for zero automatically
```

Such `assert`s are generally superfluous—because Python raises exceptions on errors automatically, you might as well let it do the job for you.‡ For another example of common `assert` usage, see the abstract superclass example in Chapter 28; there, we used `assert` to make calls to undefined methods fail with a message.

with/as Context Managers

Python 2.6 and 3.0 introduced a new exception-related statement—the `with`, and its optional `as` clause. This statement is designed to work with context manager objects, which support a new method-based protocol. This feature is also available as an option in 2.5, enabled with an `import` of this form:

```
from __future__ import with_statement
```

---

‡ In most cases, at least. As suggested earlier in the book, if a function has to perform long-running or unrecoverable actions before it reaches the place where an exception will be triggered, you still might want to test for errors. Even in this case, though, be careful not to make your tests overly specific or restrictive, or you will limit your code's utility.

In short, the with/as statement is designed to be an alternative to a common try/finally usage idiom; like that statement, it is intended for specifying termination-time or "cleanup" activities that must run regardless of whether an exception occurs in a processing step. Unlike try/finally, though, the with statement supports a richer object-based protocol for specifying both entry and exit actions around a block of code.

Python enhances some built-in tools with context managers, such as files that automatically close themselves and thread locks that automatically lock and unlock, but programmers can code context managers of their own with classes, too.

Basic Usage

The basic format of the with statement looks like this:

```
with expression [as variable]:
    with-block
```

The *expression* here is assumed to return an object that supports the context management protocol (more on this protocol in a moment). This object may also return a value that will be assigned to the name *variable* if the optional as clause is present.

Note that the *variable* is not necessarily assigned the *result* of the *expression*; the result of the *expression* is the object that supports the context protocol, and the *variable* may be assigned something else intended to be used inside the statement. The object returned by the *expression* may then run startup code before the *with-block* is started, as well as termination code after the block is done, regardless of whether the block raised an exception or not.

Some built-in Python objects have been augmented to support the context management protocol, and so can be used with the with statement. For example, file objects (covered in Chapter 9) have a context manager that automatically closes the file after the with block regardless of whether an exception is raised:

```
with open(r'C:\misc\data') as myfile:
    for line in myfile:
        print(line)
        ...more code here...
```

Here, the call to open returns a simple file object that is assigned to the name myfile. We can use myfile with the usual file tools—in this case, the file iterator reads line by line in the for loop.

However, this object also supports the context management protocol used by the with statement. After this with statement has run, the context management machinery guarantees that the file object referenced by myfile is automatically closed, even if the for loop raised an exception while processing the file.

Although file objects are automatically closed on garbage collection, it's not always straightforward to know when that will occur. The with statement in this role is an alternative that allows us to be sure that the close will occur after execution of a specific block of code. As we saw earlier, we can achieve a similar effect with the more general and explicit try/finally statement, but it requires four lines of administrative code instead of one in this case:

```
myfile = open(r'C:\misc\data')
try:
    for line in myfile:
        print(line)
        ...more code here...
finally:
    myfile.close()
```

We won't cover Python's multithreading modules in this book (for more on that topic, see follow-up application-level texts such as *Programming Python*), but the lock and condition synchronization objects they define may also be used with the with statement, because they support the context management protocol:

```
lock = threading.Lock()
with lock:
    # critical section of code
    ...access shared resources...
```

Here, the context management machinery guarantees that the lock is automatically acquired before the block is executed and released once the block is complete, regardless of exception outcomes.

As introduced in Chapter 5, the decimal module also uses context managers to simplify saving and restoring the current decimal context, which specifies the precision and rounding characteristics for calculations:

```
with decimal.localcontext() as ctx:
    ctx.prec = 2
    x = decimal.Decimal('1.00') / decimal.Decimal('3.00')
```

After this statement runs, the current thread's context manager state is automatically restored to what it was before the statement began. To do the same with a try/finally, we would need to save the context before and restore it manually.

The Context Management Protocol

Although some built-in types come with context managers, we can also write new ones of our own. To implement context managers, classes use special methods that fall into the operator overloading category to tap into the with statement. The interface expected of objects used in with statements is somewhat complex, and most programmers only need to know how to use existing context managers. For tool builders who might want to write new application-specific context managers, though, let's take a quick look at what's involved.

Here's how the with statement actually works:

1. The expression is evaluated, resulting in an object known as a *context manager* that must have __enter__ and __exit__ methods.

2. The context manager's __enter__ method is called. The value it returns is assigned to the variable in the **as** clause if present, or simply discarded otherwise.

3. The code in the nested **with** block is executed.

4. If the **with** block raises an exception, the __exit__(*type, value, traceback*) method is called with the exception details. Note that these are the same values returned by **sys.exc_info**, described in the Python manuals and later in this part of the book. If this method returns a false value, the exception is reraised; otherwise, the exception is terminated. The exception should normally be reraised so that it is propagated outside the **with** statement.

5. If the **with** block does not raise an exception, the __exit__ method is still called, but its *type*, *value*, and *traceback* arguments are all passed in as None.

Let's look at a quick demo of the protocol in action. The following defines a context manager object that traces the entry and exit of the **with** block in any **with** statement it is used for:

```
class TraceBlock:
    def message(self, arg):
        print('running', arg)
    def __enter__(self):
        print('starting with block')
        return self
    def __exit__(self, exc_type, exc_value, exc_tb):
        if exc_type is None:
            print('exited normally\n')
        else:
            print('raise an exception!', exc_type)
            return False                              # Propagate

with TraceBlock() as action:
    action.message('test 1')
    print('reached')

with TraceBlock() as action:
    action.message('test 2')
    raise TypeError
    print('not reached')
```

Notice that this class's __exit__ method returns False to propagate the exception; deleting the **return** statement would have the same effect, as the default None return value of functions is False by definition. Also notice that the __enter__ method returns self as the object to assign to the **as** variable; in other use cases, this might return a completely different object instead.

When run, the context manager traces the entry and exit of the **with** statement block with its __enter__ and __exit__ methods. Here's the script in action being run under Python 3.0 (it runs in 2.6, too, but prints some extra tuple parentheses):

```
% python withas.py
starting with block
running test 1
reached
exited normally

starting with block
running test 2
raise an exception! <class 'TypeError'>
Traceback (most recent call last):
  File "withas.py", line 20, in <module>
    raise TypeError
TypeError
```

Context managers are somewhat advanced devices for tool builders, so we'll skip additional details here (see Python's standard manuals for the full story—for example, there's a new `contextlib` standard module that provides additional tools for coding context managers). For simpler purposes, the `try`/`finally` statement provides sufficient support for termination-time activities.

 In the upcoming Python 3.1 release, the `with` statement may also specify multiple (sometimes referred to as "nested") context managers with new comma syntax. In the following, for example, both files' exit actions are automatically run when the statement block exits, regardless of exception outcomes:

```
with open('data') as fin, open('res', 'w') as fout:
    for line in fin:
        if 'some key' in line:
            fout.write(line)
```

Any number of context manager items may be listed, and multiple items work the same as nested `with` statements. In general, the 3.1 (and later) code:

```
with A() as a, B() as b:
    ...statements...
```

is equivalent to the following, which works in 3.1, 3.0, and 2.6:

```
with A() as a:
    with B() as b:
        ...statements...
```

See Python 3.1 release notes for additional details.

Chapter Summary

In this chapter, we took a more detailed look at exception processing by exploring the statements related to exceptions in Python: `try` to catch them, `raise` to trigger them, `assert` to raise them conditionally, and `with` to wrap code blocks in context managers that specify entry and exit actions.

So far, exceptions probably seem like a fairly lightweight tool, and in fact, they are; the only substantially complex thing about them is how they are identified. The next chapter continues our exploration by describing how to implement exception objects of your own; as you'll see, classes allow you to code new exceptions specific to your programs. Before we move ahead, though, let's work though the following short quiz on the basics covered here.

Test Your Knowledge: Quiz

1. What is the `try` statement for?
2. What are the two common variations of the `try` statement?
3. What is the `raise` statement for?
4. What is the `assert` statement designed to do, and what other statement is it like?
5. What is the `with/as` statement designed to do, and what other statement is it like?

Test Your Knowledge: Answers

1. The `try` statement catches and recovers from exceptions—it specifies a block of code to run, and one or more handlers for exceptions that may be raised during the block's execution.

2. The two common variations on the `try` statement are `try/except/else` (for catching exceptions) and `try/finally` (for specifying cleanup actions that must occur whether an exception is raised or not). In Python 2.4, these were separate statements that could be combined by syntactic nesting; in 2.5 and later, `except` and `finally` blocks may be mixed in the same statement, so the two statement forms are merged. In the merged form, the `finally` is still run on the way out of the `try`, regardless of what exceptions may have been raised or handled.

3. The `raise` statement raises (triggers) an exception. Python raises built-in exceptions on errors internally, but your scripts can trigger built-in or user-defined exceptions with `raise`, too.

4. The `assert` statement raises an `AssertionError` exception if a condition is false. It works like a conditional `raise` statement wrapped up in an `if` statement.

5. The `with/as` statement is designed to automate startup and termination activities that must occur around a block of code. It is roughly like a `try/finally` statement in that its exit actions run whether an exception occurred or not, but it allows a richer object-based protocol for specifying entry *and* exit actions.

## CHAPTER 34

Exception Objects

So far, I've been deliberately vague about what an exception actually *is*. As suggested in the prior chapter, in Python 2.6 and 3.0 both built-in and user-defined exceptions are identified by *class instance* objects. Although this means you must use object-oriented programming to define new exceptions in your programs, classes and OOP in general offer a number of benefits.

Here are some of the advantages of class-based exceptions:

- **They can be organized into categories**. Exception classes support future changes by providing categories—adding new exceptions in the future won't generally require changes in `try` statements.

- **They have attached state information**. Exception classes provide a natural place for us to store context information for use in the `try` handler—they may have both attached state information and callable methods, accessible through instances.

- **They support inheritance**. Class-based exceptions can participate in inheritance hierarchies to obtain and customize common behavior—inherited display methods, for example, can provide a common look and feel for error messages.

Because of these advantages, class-based exceptions support program evolution and larger systems well. In fact, all built-in exceptions are identified by classes and are organized into an inheritance tree, for the reasons just listed. You can do the same with user-defined exceptions of your own.

In Python 3.0, user-defined exceptions inherit from built-in exception superclasses. As we'll see here, because these superclasses provide useful defaults for printing and state retention, the task of coding user-defined exceptions also involves understanding the roles of these built-ins.

Version skew note: Python 2.6 and 3.0 both require exceptions to be defined by classes. In addition, 3.0 requires exception classes to be derived from the `BaseException` built-in exception superclass, either directly or indirectly. As we'll see, most programs inherit from this class's `Exception` subclass, to support catchall handlers for normal exception types—naming it in a handler will catch everything most programs should. Python 2.6 allows standalone classic classes to serve as exceptions, too, but it requires new-style classes to be derived from built-in exception classes, the same as 3.0.

Exceptions: Back to the Future

Once upon a time (well, prior to Python 2.6 and 3.0), it was possible to define exceptions in two different ways. This complicated `try` statements, `raise` statements, and Python in general. Today, there is only one way to do it. This is a good thing: it removes from the language substantial cruft accumulated for the sake of backward compatibility. Because the old way helps explain why exceptions are as they are today, though, and because it's not really possible to completely erase the history of something that has been used by a million people over the course of nearly two decades, let's begin our exploration of the present with a brief look at the past.

String Exceptions Are Right Out!

Prior to Python 2.6 and 3.0, it was possible to define exceptions with both class instances and string objects. String-based exceptions began issuing deprecation warnings in 2.5 and were removed in 2.6 and 3.0, so today you should use class-based exceptions, as shown in this book. If you work with legacy code, though, you might still come across string exceptions. They might also appear in tutorials and web resources written a few years ago (which qualifies as an eternity in Python years!).

String exceptions were straightforward to use—any string would do, and they matched by object identity, not value (that is, using `is`, not `==`):

```
C:\misc> C:\Python25\python
>>> myexc = "My exception string"          # Were we ever this young?
>>> try:
...     raise myexc
... except myexc:
...     print('caught')
...
caught
```

This form of exception was removed because it was not as good as classes for larger programs and code maintenance. Although you can't use string exceptions today, they actually provide a natural vehicle for introducing the class-based exceptions model.

Class-Based Exceptions

Strings were a simple way to define exceptions. As described earlier, however, classes have some added advantages that merit a quick look. Most prominently, they allow us to identify exception *categories* that are more flexible to use and maintain than simple strings. Moreover, classes naturally allow for attached exception details and support inheritance. Because they are the better approach, they are now required.

Coding details aside, the chief difference between string and class exceptions has to do with the way that exceptions raised are matched against except clauses in try statements:

- String exceptions were matched by simple *object identity*: the raised exception was matched to except clauses by Python's is test.
- Class exceptions are matched by *superclass relationships*: the raised exception matches an except clause if that except clause names the exception's class or any superclass of it.

That is, when a try statement's except clause lists a superclass, it catches instances of that superclass, as well as instances of all its subclasses lower in the class tree. The net effect is that class exceptions support the construction of exception *hierarchies*: superclasses become category names, and subclasses become specific kinds of exceptions within a category. By naming a general exception superclass, an except clause can catch an entire category of exceptions—any more specific subclass will match.

String exceptions had no such concept: because they were matched by simple object identity, there was no direct way to organize exceptions into more flexible categories or groups. The net result was that exception handlers were coupled with exception sets in a way that made changes difficult.

In addition to this category idea, class-based exceptions better support exception *state information* (attached to instances) and allow exceptions to participate in *inheritance hierarchies* (to obtain common behaviors). Because they offer all the benefits of classes and OOP in general, they provide a more powerful alternative to the now defunct string-based exceptions model in exchange for a small amount of additional code.

Coding Exceptions Classes

Let's look at an example to see how class exceptions translate to code. In the following file, *classexc.py*, we define a superclass called General and two subclasses called Specific1 and Specific2. This example illustrates the notion of exception categories— General is a category name, and its two subclasses are specific types of exceptions within the category. Handlers that catch General will also catch any subclasses of it, including Specific1 and Specific2:

```
class General(Exception): pass
class Specific1(General): pass
```

```
class Specific2(General): pass

def raiser0():
    X = General()          # Raise superclass instance
    raise X

def raiser1():
    X = Specific1()        # Raise subclass instance
    raise X

def raiser2():
    X = Specific2()        # Raise different subclass instance
    raise X

for func in (raiser0, raiser1, raiser2):
    try:
        func()
    except General:         # Match General or any subclass of it
        import sys
        print('caught:', sys.exc_info()[0])

C:\python30> python classexc.py
caught: <class '__main__.General'>
caught: <class '__main__.Specific1'>
caught: <class '__main__.Specific2'>
```

This code is mostly straightforward, but here are a few implementation notes:

Exception superclass

Classes used to build exception category trees have very few requirements—in fact, in this example they are mostly empty, with bodies that do nothing but pass. Notice, though, how the top-level class here inherits from the built-in Exception class. This is required in Python 3.0; Python 2.6 allows standalone classic classes to serve as exceptions too, but it requires new-style classes to be derived from built-in exception classes just like in 3.0. Although we don't employ it here, because Exception provides some useful behavior we'll meet later, it's a good idea to inherit from it in either Python.

Raising instances

In this code, we call classes to make *instances* for the raise statements. In the class exception model, we always raise and catch a class instance object. If we list a class name without parentheses in a raise, Python calls the class with no constructor argument to make an instance for us. Exception instances can be created before the raise, as done here, or within the raise statement itself.

Catching categories

This code includes functions that raise instances of all three of our classes as exceptions, as well as a top-level try that calls the functions and catches General exceptions. The same try also catches the two specific exceptions, because they are subclasses of General.

Exception details

The exception handler here uses the `sys.exc_info` call—as we'll see in more detail in the next chapter, it's how we can grab hold of the most recently raised exception in a generic fashion. Briefly, the first item in its result is the class of the exception raised, and the second is the actual instance raised. In a general `except` clause like the one here that catches all classes in a category, `sys.exc_info` is one way to determine exactly what's occurred. In this particular case, it's equivalent to fetching the instance's `__class__` attribute. As we'll see in the next chapter, the `sys.exc_info` scheme is also commonly used with empty `except` clauses that catch everything.

The last point merits further explanation. When an exception is caught, we can be sure that the instance raised is an instance of the class listed in the `except`, or one of its more specific subclasses. Because of this, the `__class__` attribute of the instance also gives the exception type. The following variant, for example, works the same as the prior example:

```
class General(Exception): pass
class Specific1(General): pass
class Specific2(General): pass

def raiser0(): raise General()
def raiser1(): raise Specific1()
def raiser2(): raise Specific2()

for func in (raiser0, raiser1, raiser2):
    try:
        func()
    except General as X:                # X is the raised instance
        print('caught:', X.__class__)   # Same as sys.exc_info()[0]
```

Because `__class__` can be used like this to determine the specific type of exception raised, `sys.exc_info` is more useful for empty `except` clauses that do not otherwise have a way to access the instance or its class. Furthermore, more realistic programs usually should *not have to care* about which specific exception was raised at all—by calling methods of the instance generically, we automatically dispatch to behavior tailored for the exception raised. More on this and `sys.exc_info` in the next chapter; also see Chapter 28 and Part VI at large if you've forgotten what `__class__` means in an instance.

Why Exception Hierarchies?

Because there are only three possible exceptions in the prior section's example, it doesn't really do justice to the utility of class exceptions. In fact, we could achieve the same effects by coding a list of exception names in parentheses within the `except` clause:

```
try:
    func()
except (General, Specific1, Specific2):     # Catch any of these
    ...
```

This approach worked for the defunct string exception model too. For large or high exception hierarchies, however, it may be easier to catch categories using class-based categories than to list every member of a category in a single except clause. Perhaps more importantly, you can extend exception hierarchies by adding new subclasses without breaking existing code.

Suppose, for example, you code a numeric programming library in Python, to be used by a large number of people. While you are writing your library, you identify two things that can go wrong with numbers in your code—division by zero, and numeric overflow. You document these as the two exceptions that your library may raise:

```
# mathlib.py

class Divzero(Exception): pass
class Oflow(Exception): pass

def func():
    ...
    raise Divzero()
```

Now, when people use your library, they typically wrap calls to your functions or classes in try statements that catch your two exceptions (if they do not catch your exceptions, exceptions from the library will kill their code):

```
# client.py

import mathlib

try:
    mathlib.func(...)
except (mathlib.Divzero, mathlib.Oflow):
    ...handle and recover...
```

This works fine, and lots of people start using your library. Six months down the road, though, you revise it (as programmers are prone to do). Along the way, you identify a new thing that can go wrong—underflow—and add that as a new exception:

```
# mathlib.py

class Divzero(Exception): pass
class Oflow(Exception): pass
class Uflow(Exception): pass
```

Unfortunately, when you re-release your code, you create a maintenance problem for your users. If they've listed your exceptions explicitly, they now have to go back and change every place they call your library to include the newly added exception name:

```
# client.py

try:
    mathlib.func(...)
except (mathlib.Divzero, mathlib.Oflow, mathlib.Uflow):
    ...handle and recover...
```

This may not be the end of the world. If your library is used only in-house, you can make the changes yourself. You might also ship a Python script that tries to fix such code automatically (it would probably be only a few dozen lines, and it would guess right at least some of the time). If many people have to change all their try statements each time you alter your exception set, though, this is not exactly the most polite of upgrade policies.

Your users might try to avoid this pitfall by coding empty except clauses to catch *all* possible exceptions:

```
# client.py

try:
    mathlib.func(...)
except:                          # Catch everything here
    ...handle and recover...
```

But this workaround might catch more than they bargained for—things like running out of memory, keyboard interrupts (Ctrl-C), system exits, and even typos in their own try block's code will all trigger exceptions, and such things should pass, not be caught and erroneously classified as library errors.

And really, in this scenario users want to catch and recover from *only* the specific exceptions the library is defined and documented to raise; if any other exception occurs during a library call, it's likely a genuine bug in the library (and probably time to contact the vendor!). As a rule of thumb, it's usually better to be specific than general in exception handlers—an idea we'll revisit as a "gotcha" in the next chapter.[*]

So what to do, then? Class exception hierarchies fix this dilemma completely. Rather than defining your library's exceptions as a set of autonomous classes, arrange them into a class tree with a common superclass to encompass the entire category:

```
# mathlib.py

class NumErr(Exception): pass
class Divzero(NumErr): pass
class Oflow(NumErr): pass
...
def func():
    ...
    raise DivZero()
```

This way, users of your library simply need to list the common superclass (i.e., category) to catch all of your library's exceptions, both now and in the future:

---

[*] As a clever student of mine suggested, the library module could also provide a tuple object that contains all the exceptions the library can possibly raise—the client could then import the tuple and name it in an except clause to catch all the library's exceptions (recall that including a tuple in an except means catch *any* of its exceptions). When new exceptions are added later, the library can just expand the exported tuple. This would work, but you'd still need to keep the tuple up-to-date with raised exceptions inside the library module. Also, class hierarchies offer more benefits than just categories—they also support inherited state and methods and a customization model that individual exceptions do not.

```
# client.py

import mathlib
...
try:
    mathlib.func(...)
except mathlib.NumErr:
    ...report and recover...
```

When you go back and hack your code again, you can add new exceptions as new subclasses of the common superclass:

```
# mathlib.py

...
class Uflow(NumErr): pass
```

The end result is that user code that catches your library's exceptions will keep working, *unchanged*. In fact, you are free to add, delete, and change exceptions arbitrarily in the future—as long as clients name the superclass, they are insulated from changes in your exceptions set. In other words, class exceptions provide a better answer to maintenance issues than strings do.

Class-based exception hierarchies also support state retention and inheritance in ways that make them ideal in larger programs. To understand these roles, though, we first need to see how user-defined exception classes relate to the built-in exceptions from which they inherit.

Built-in Exception Classes

I didn't really pull the prior section's examples out of thin air. All built-in exceptions that Python itself may raise are predefined class objects. Moreover, they are organized into a shallow hierarchy with general superclass categories and specific subclass types, much like the exceptions class tree we developed earlier.

In Python 3.0, all the familiar exceptions you've seen (e.g., SyntaxError) are really just predefined classes, available as built-in names in the module named builtins (in Python 2.6, they instead live in __builtin__ and are also attributes of the standard library module exceptions). In addition, Python organizes the built-in exceptions into a hierarchy, to support a variety of catching modes. For example:

BaseException
>   The top-level root superclass of exceptions. This class is not supposed to be directly inherited by user-defined classes (use Exception instead). It provides default printing and state retention behavior inherited by subclasses. If the str built-in is called on an instance of this class (e.g., by print), the class returns the display strings of the constructor arguments passed when the instance was created (or an empty string if there were no arguments). In addition, unless subclasses replace this class's

constructor, all of the arguments passed to this class at instance construction time are stored in its `args` attribute as a tuple.

Exception
> The top-level root superclass of application-related exceptions. This is an immediate subclass of `BaseException` and is superclass to every other built-in exception, except the system exit event classes (`SystemExit`, `KeyboardInterrupt`, and `GeneratorExit`). Almost all user-defined classes should inherit from this class, not `BaseException`. When this convention is followed, naming `Exception` in a `try` statement's handler ensures that your program will catch everything but system exit events, which should normally be allowed to pass. In effect, `Exception` becomes a catchall in `try` statements and is more accurate than an empty `except`.

ArithmeticError
> The superclass of all numeric errors (and a subclass of `Exception`).

OverflowError
> A subclass of `ArithmeticError` that identifies a specific numeric error.

And so on—you can read further about this structure in reference texts such as *Python Pocket Reference* or the Python library manual. Note that the exceptions class tree differs slightly between Python 3.0 and 2.6. Also note that you can see the class tree in the help text of the **exceptions** module in Python 2.6 only (this module is removed in 3.0). See Chapters 4 and 15 for help on `help`:

```
>>> import exceptions
>>> help(exceptions)
...lots of text omitted...
```

Built-in Exception Categories

The built-in class tree allows you to choose how specific or general your handlers will be. For example, the built-in exception `ArithmeticError` is a superclass for more specific exceptions such as `OverflowError` and `ZeroDivisionError`. By listing `ArithmeticError` in a `try`, you will catch any kind of numeric error raised; by listing just `OverflowError`, you will intercept just that specific type of error, and no others.

Similarly, because `Exception` is the superclass of all application-level exceptions in Python 3.0, you can generally use it as a *catchall*—the effect is much like an empty `except`, but it allows system exit exceptions to pass as they usually should:

```
try:
    action()
except Exception:
    ...handle all application exceptions...
else:
    ...handle no-exception case...
```

This doesn't quite work universally in Python 2.6, however, because standalone user-defined exceptions coded as classic classes are not required to be subclasses of the Exception root class. This technique is more reliable in Python 3.0, since it requires all classes to derive from built-in exceptions. Even in Python 3.0, though, this scheme suffers most of the same potential pitfalls as the empty except, as described in the prior chapter—it might intercept exceptions intended for elsewhere, and it might mask genuine programming errors. Since this is such a common issue, we'll revisit it as a "gotcha" in the next chapter.

Whether or not you will leverage the categories in the built-in class tree, it serves as a good example; by using similar techniques for class exceptions in your own code, you can provide exception sets that are flexible and easily modified.

Default Printing and State

Built-in exceptions also provide default print displays and state retention, which is often as much logic as user-defined classes require. Unless you redefine the constructors your classes inherit from them, any constructor arguments you pass to these classes are saved in the instance's args tuple attribute and are automatically displayed when the instance is printed (an empty tuple and display string are used if no constructor arguments are passed).

This explains why arguments passed to built-in exception classes show up in error messages—any constructor arguments are attached to the instance and displayed when the instance is printed:

```
>>> raise IndexError                       # Same as IndexError(): no arguments
Traceback (most recent call last):
  File "<stdin>", line 1, in <module>
IndexError

>>> raise IndexError('spam')               # Constructor argument attached, printed
Traceback (most recent call last):
  File "<stdin>", line 1, in <module>
IndexError: spam

>>> I = IndexError('spam')                 # Available in object attribute
>>> I.args
('spam',)
```

The same holds true for user-defined exceptions, because they inherit the constructor and display methods present in their built-in superclasses:

```
>>> class E(Exception): pass
...
>>> try:
...     raise E('spam')
... except E as X:
...     print(X, X.args)                   # Displays and saves constructor arguments
...
spam ('spam',)
```

```
>>> try:
...     raise E('spam', 'eggs', 'ham')
... except E as X:
...     print(X, X.args)
...
('spam', 'eggs', 'ham') ('spam', 'eggs', 'ham')
```

Note that exception instance objects are not strings themselves, but use the __str__ operator overloading protocol we studied in Chapter 29 to provide display strings when printed; to concatenate with real strings, perform manual conversions: str(X) + "string".

Although this automatic state and display support is useful by itself, for more specific display and state retention needs you can always redefine inherited methods such as __str__ and __init__ in Exception subclasses—the next section shows how.

Custom Print Displays

As we saw in the preceding section, by default, instances of class-based exceptions display whatever you passed to the class constructor when they are caught and printed:

```
>>> class MyBad(Exception): pass
...
>>> try:
...     raise MyBad('Sorry--my mistake!')
... except MyBad as X:
...     print(X)
...
Sorry--my mistake!
```

This inherited default display model is also used if the exception is displayed as part of an error message when the exception is not caught:

```
>>> raise MyBad('Sorry--my mistake!')
Traceback (most recent call last):
  File "<stdin>", line 1, in <module>
__main__.MyBad: Sorry--my mistake!
```

For many roles, this is sufficient. To provide a more custom display, though, you can define one of two string-representation overloading methods in your class (__repr__ or __str__) to return the string you want to display for your exception. The string the method returns will be displayed if the exception either is caught and printed or reaches the default handler:

```
>>> class MyBad(Exception):
...     def __str__(self):
...         return 'Always look on the bright side of life...'
...
>>> try:
...     raise MyBad()
... except MyBad as X:
...     print(X)
```

```
...
Always look on the bright side of life...

>>> raise MyBad()
Traceback (most recent call last):
  File "<stdin>", line 1, in <module>
__main__.MyBad: Always look on the bright side of life...
```

A subtle point to note here is that you generally must redefine __str__ for this purpose, because the built-in superclasses already have a __str__ method, and __str__ is preferred to __repr__ in most contexts (including printing). If you define a __repr__, printing will happily call the superclass's __str__ instead! See Chapter 29 for more details on these special methods.

Whatever your method returns is included in error messages for uncaught exceptions and used when exceptions are printed explicitly. The method returns a hardcoded string here to illustrate, but it can also perform arbitrary text processing, possibly using state information attached to the instance object. The next section looks at state information options.

Custom Data and Behavior

Besides supporting flexible hierarchies, exception classes also provide storage for extra state information as instance attributes. As we saw earlier, built-in exception superclasses provide a default constructor that automatically saves constructor arguments in an instance tuple attribute named args. Although the default constructor is adequate for many cases, for more custom needs we can provide a constructor of our own. In addition, classes may define methods for use in handlers that provide precoded exception processing logic.

Providing Exception Details

When an exception is raised, it may cross arbitrary file boundaries—the raise statement that triggers an exception and the try statement that catches it may be in completely different module files. It is not generally feasible to store extra details in global variables because the try statement might not know which file the globals reside in. Passing extra state information along in the exception itself allows the try statement to access it more reliably.

With classes, this is nearly automatic. As we've seen, when an exception is raised, Python passes the class instance object along with the exception. Code in try statements can access the raised instance by listing an extra variable after the as keyword in an except handler. This provides a natural hook for supplying data and behavior to the handler.

For example, a program that parses data files might signal a formatting error by raising an exception instance that is filled out with extra details about the error:

```
>>> class FormatError(Exception):
...     def __init__(self, line, file):
...         self.line = line
...         self.file = file
...
>>> def parser():
...     raise FormatError(42, file='spam.txt')      # When error found
...
>>> try:
...     parser()
... except FormatError as X:
...     print('Error at', X.file, X.line)
...
Error at spam.txt 42
```

In the except clause here, the variable X is assigned a reference to the instance that was generated when the exception was raised.[†] This gives access to the attributes attached to the instance by the custom constructor. Although we could rely on the default state retention of built-in superclasses, it's less relevant to our application:

```
>>> class FormatError(Exception): pass            # Inherited constructor
...
>>> def parser():
...     raise FormatError(42, 'spam.txt')         # No keywords allowed!
...
>>> try:
...     parser()
... except FormatError as X:
...     print('Error at:', X.args[0], X.args[1])  # Not specific to this app
...
Error at: 42 spam.txt
```

Providing Exception Methods

Besides enabling application-specific state information, custom constructors also better support extra behavior for exception objects. That is, the exception class can also define *methods* to be called in the handler. The following, for example, adds a method that uses exception state information to log errors to a file:

```
class FormatError(Exception):
    logfile = 'formaterror.txt'
    def __init__(self, line, file):
        self.line = line
        self.file = file
```

---

† As suggested earlier, the raised instance object is also available generically as the second item in the result tuple of the sys.exc_info() call—a tool that returns information about the most recently raised exception. This interface must be used if you do not list an exception name in an except clause but still need access to the exception that occurred, or to any of its attached state information or methods. More on sys.exc_info in the next chapter.

```
        def logerror(self):
            log = open(self.logfile, 'a')
            print('Error at', self.file, self.line, file=log)

    def parser():
        raise FormatError(40, 'spam.txt')

    try:
        parser()
    except FormatError as exc:
        exc.logerror()
```

When run, this script writes its error message to a file in response to method calls in the exception handler:

```
C:\misc> C:\Python30\python parse.py
C:\misc> type formaterror.txt
Error at spam.txt 40
```

In such a class, methods (like `logerror`) may also be inherited from superclasses, and instance attributes (like `line` and `file`) provide a place to save state information that provides extra context for use in later method calls. Moreover, exception classes are free to customize and extend inherited behavior. In other words, because they are defined with classes, all the benefits of OOP that we studied in Part VI are available for use with exceptions in Python.

Chapter Summary

In this chapter, we explored coding user-defined exceptions. As we learned, exceptions are implemented as class instance objects in Python 2.6 and 3.0 (an earlier string-based exception model alternative was available in earlier releases but has now been deprecated). Exception classes support the concept of exception hierarchies that ease maintenance, allow data and behavior to be attached to exceptions as instance attributes and methods, and allow exceptions to inherit data and behavior from superclasses.

We saw that in a `try` statement, catching a superclass catches that class as well as all subclasses below it in the class tree—superclasses become exception category names, and subclasses become more specific exception types within those categories. We also saw that the built-in exception superclasses we must inherit from provide usable defaults for printing and state retention, which we can override if desired.

The next chapter wraps up this part of the book by exploring some common use cases for exceptions and surveying tools commonly used by Python programmers. Before we get there, though, here's this chapter's quiz.

Test Your Knowledge: Quiz

1. What are the two new constraints on user-defined exceptions in Python 3.0?
2. How are raised class-based exceptions matched to handlers?
3. Name two ways that you can attach context information to exception objects.
4. Name two ways that you can specify the error message text for exception objects.
5. Why should you not use string-based exceptions anymore today?

Test Your Knowledge: Answers

1. In 3.0, exceptions must be defined by classes (that is, a class instance object is raised and caught). In addition, exception classes must be derived from the built-in class `BaseException` (most programs inherit from its `Exception` subclass, to support catchall handlers for normal kinds of exceptions).

2. Class-based exceptions match by superclass relationships: naming a superclass in an exception handler will catch instances of that class, as well as instances of any of its subclasses lower in the class tree. Because of this, you can think of superclasses as general exception categories and subclasses as more specific types of exceptions within those categories.

3. You can attach context information to class-based exceptions by filling out instance attributes in the instance object raised, usually in a custom class constructor. For simpler needs, built-in exception superclasses provide a constructor that stores its arguments on the instance automatically (in the attribute `args`). In exception handlers, you list a variable to be assigned to the raised instance, then go through this name to access attached state information and call any methods defined in the class.

4. The error message text in class-based exceptions can be specified with a custom `__str__` operator overloading method. For simpler needs, built-in exception superclasses automatically display anything you pass to the class constructor. Operations like `print` and `str` automatically fetch the display string of an exception object when is it printed either explicitly or as part of an error message.

5. Because Guido said so—they have been removed in both Python 2.6 and 3.0. Really, there are good reasons for this: string-based exceptions did not support categories, state information, or behavior inheritance in the way class-based exceptions do. In practice, this made string-based exceptions easier to use at first, when programs were small, but more complex to use as programs grew larger.

## CHAPTER 35

Designing with Exceptions

This chapter rounds out this part of the book with a collection of exception design topics and common use case examples, followed by this part's gotchas and exercises. Because this chapter also closes out the fundamentals portion of the book at large, it includes a brief overview of development tools as well to help you as you make the migration from Python beginner to Python application developer.

Nesting Exception Handlers

Our examples so far have used only a single **try** to catch exceptions, but what happens if one **try** is physically nested inside another? For that matter, what does it mean if a **try** calls a function that runs another **try**? Technically, **try** statements can nest, in terms of syntax and the runtime control flow through your code.

Both of these cases can be understood if you realize that Python *stacks* **try** statements at runtime. When an exception is raised, Python returns to the most recently entered **try** statement with a matching **except** clause. Because each **try** statement leaves a marker, Python can jump back to earlier **trys** by inspecting the stacked markers. This nesting of active handlers is what we mean when we talk about propagating exceptions up to "higher" handlers—such handlers are simply **try** statements entered earlier in the program's execution flow.

Figure 35-1 illustrates what occurs when **try** statements with **except** clauses nest at runtime. The amount of code that goes into a **try** block can be substantial, and it may contain function calls that invoke other code watching for the same exceptions. When an exception is eventually raised, Python jumps back to the most recently entered **try** statement that names that exception, runs that statement's **except** clause, and then resumes execution after that **try**.

Once the exception is caught, its life is over—control does not jump back to *all* matching **trys** that name the exception; only the first one is given the opportunity to handle it. In Figure 35-1, for instance, the **raise** statement in the function **func2** sends control back to the handler in **func1**, and then the program continues within **func1**.

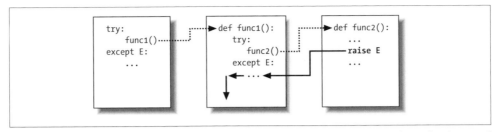

Figure 35-1. Nested try/except statements: when an exception is raised (by you or by Python), control jumps back to the most recently entered try statement with a matching except clause, and the program resumes after that try statement. except clauses intercept and stop the exception—they are where you process and recover from exceptions.

By contrast, when **try** statements that contain only **finally** clauses are nested, each **finally** block is run in turn when an exception occurs—Python continues propagating the exception up to other **trys**, and eventually perhaps to the top-level default handler (the standard error message printer). As Figure 35-2 illustrates, the **finally** clauses do not kill the exception—they just specify code to be run on the way out of each **try** during the exception propagation process. If there are many **try**/**finally** clauses active when an exception occurs, they will *all* be run, unless a **try**/**except** catches the exception somewhere along the way.

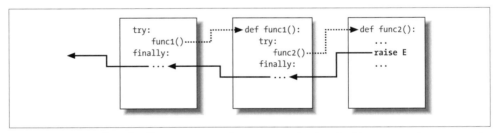

Figure 35-2. Nested try/finally statements: when an exception is raised here, control returns to the most recently entered try to run its finally statement, but then the exception keeps propagating to all finallys in all active try statements and eventually reaches the default top-level handler, where an error message is printed. finally clauses intercept (but do not stop) an exception—they are for actions to be performed "on the way out."

In other words, where the program goes when an exception is raised depends entirely upon *where it has been*—it's a function of the runtime flow of control through the script, not just its syntax. The propagation of an exception essentially proceeds backward through time to **try** statements that have been entered but not yet exited. This propagation stops as soon as control is unwound to a matching **except** clause, but not as it passes through **finally** clauses on the way.

Example: Control-Flow Nesting

Let's turn to an example to make this nesting concept more concrete. The following module file, *nestexc.py*, defines two functions. `action2` is coded to trigger an exception (you can't add numbers and sequences), and `action1` wraps a call to `action2` in a `try` handler, to catch the exception:

```
def action2():
    print(1 + [])                # Generate TypeError

def action1():
    try:
        action2()
    except TypeError:            # Most recent matching try
        print('inner try')

try:
    action1()
except TypeError:                # Here, only if action1 re-raises
    print('outer try')

% python nestexc.py
inner try
```

Notice, though, that the top-level module code at the bottom of the file wraps a call to `action1` in a `try` handler, too. When `action2` triggers the `TypeError` exception, there will be two active `try` statements—the one in `action1`, and the one at the top level of the module file. Python picks and runs just the most recent `try` with a matching `except`, which in this case is the `try` inside `action1`.

As I've mentioned, the place where an exception winds up jumping to depends on the control flow through the program at runtime. Because of this, to know where you will go, you need to know where you've been. In this case, where exceptions are handled is more a function of control flow than of statement syntax. However, we can also nest exception handlers syntactically—an equivalent case we'll look at next.

Example: Syntactic Nesting

As I mentioned when we looked at the new unified `try`/`except`/`finally` statement in Chapter 33, it is possible to nest `try` statements syntactically by their position in your source code:

```
try:
    try:
        action2()
    except TypeError:            # Most recent matching try
        print('inner try')
except TypeError:                # Here, only if nested handler re-raises
    print('outer try')
```

Really, this code just sets up the same handler-nesting structure as (and behaves identically to) the prior example. In fact, syntactic nesting works just like the cases sketched in Figures 35-1 and 35-2; the only difference is that the nested handlers are physically embedded in a **try** block, not coded in functions called elsewhere. For example, nested **finally** handlers all fire on an exception, whether they are nested syntactically or by means of the runtime flow through physically separated parts of your code:

```
>>> try:
...     try:
...         raise IndexError
...     finally:
...         print('spam')
... finally:
...     print('SPAM')
...
spam
SPAM
Traceback (most recent call last):
  File "<stdin>", line 3, in <module>
IndexError
```

See Figure 35-2 for a graphic illustration of this code's operation; the effect is the same, but the function logic has been inlined as nested statements here. For a more useful example of syntactic nesting at work, consider the following file, *except-finally.py*:

```
def raise1():  raise IndexError
def noraise(): return
def raise2():  raise SyntaxError

for func in (raise1, noraise, raise2):
    print('\n', func, sep='')
    try:
        try:
            func()
        except IndexError:
            print('caught IndexError')
    finally:
        print('finally run')
```

This code catches an exception if one is raised and performs a **finally** termination-time action regardless of whether an exception occurs. This may take a few moments to digest, but the effect is much like combining an **except** and a **finally** clause in a single **try** statement in Python 2.5 and later:

```
% python except-finally.py
<function raise1 at 0x026ECA98>
caught IndexError
finally run

<function noraise at 0x026ECA50>
finally run

<function raise2 at 0x026ECBB8>
finally run
```

```
Traceback (most recent call last):
  File "except-finally.py", line 9, in <module>
    func()
  File "except-finally.py", line 3, in raise2
    def raise2():  raise SyntaxError
SyntaxError: None
```

As we saw in Chapter 33, as of Python 2.5, `except` and `finally` clauses can be mixed in the same `try` statement. This makes some of the syntactic nesting described in this section unnecessary, though it still works, may appear in code written prior to Python 2.5 that you may encounter, and can be used as a technique for implementing alternative exception-handling behaviors.

Exception Idioms

We've seen the mechanics behind exceptions. Now let's take a look at some of the other ways they are typically used.

Exceptions Aren't Always Errors

In Python, all errors are exceptions, but not all exceptions are errors. For instance, we saw in Chapter 9 that file object read methods return an empty string at the end of a file. In contrast, the built-in `input` function (which we first met in Chapter 3 and deployed in an interactive loop in Chapter 10) reads a line of text from the standard input stream, `sys.stdin`, at each call and raises the built-in `EOFError` at end-of-file. (This function is known as `raw_input` in Python 2.6.)

Unlike file methods, this function does not return an empty string—an empty string from `input` means an empty line. Despite its name, the `EOFError` exception is just a signal in this context, not an error. Because of this behavior, unless the end-of-file should terminate a script, `input` often appears wrapped in a `try` handler and nested in a loop, as in the following code:

```
while True:
    try:
        line = input()          # Read line from stdin
    except EOFError:
        break                   # Exit loop at end-of-file
    else:
        ...process next line here...
```

Several other built-in exceptions are similarly signals, not errors—calling `sys.exit()` and pressing Ctrl-C on your keyboard, respectively, raise `SystemExit` and `KeyboardInterrupt`, for example. Python also has a set of built-in exceptions that represent *warnings* rather than errors; some of these are used to signal use of deprecated (phased out) language features. See the standard library manual's description of built-in exceptions for more information, and consult the `warnings` module's documentation for more on warnings.

Functions Can Signal Conditions with raise

User-defined exceptions can also signal nonerror conditions. For instance, a search routine can be coded to raise an exception when a match is found instead of returning a status flag for the caller to interpret. In the following, the try/except/else exception handler does the work of an if/else return-value tester:

```
class Found(Exception): pass

def searcher():
    if ...success...:
        raise Found()
    else:
        return

try:
    searcher()
except Found:                    # Exception if item was found
    ...success...
else:                            # else returned: not found
    ...failure...
```

More generally, such a coding structure may also be useful for any function that cannot return a sentinel value to designate success or failure. For instance, if all objects are potentially valid return values, it's impossible for any return value to signal unusual conditions. Exceptions provide a way to signal results without a return value:

```
class Failure(Exception): pass

def searcher():
    if ...success...:
        return ...founditem...
    else:
        raise Failure()

try:
    item = searcher()
except Failure:
    ...report...
else:
    ...use item here...
```

Because Python is dynamically typed and polymorphic to the core, exceptions, rather than sentinel return values, are the generally preferred way to signal such conditions.

Closing Files and Server Connections

We encountered examples in this category in Chapter 33. As a summary, though, exception processing tools are also commonly used to ensure that system resources are finalized, regardless of whether an error occurs during processing or not.

For example, some servers require connections to be closed in order to terminate a session. Similarly, output files may require close calls to flush their buffers to disk, and input files may consume file descriptors if not closed; although file objects are automatically closed when garbage collected if still open, it's sometimes difficult to be sure when that will occur.

The most general and explicit way to guarantee termination actions for a specific block of code is the try/finally statement:

```
myfile = open(r'C:\misc\script', 'w')
try:
    ...process myfile...
finally:
    myfile.close()
```

As we saw in Chapter 33, some objects make this easier in Python 2.6 and 3.0 by providing *context managers* run by the with/as statement that terminate or close the objects for us automatically:

```
with open(r'C:\misc\script', 'w') as myfile:
    ...process myfile...
```

So which option is better here? As usual, it depends on your programs. Compared to the try/finally, context managers are *more implicit*, which runs contrary to Python's general design philosophy. Context managers are also arguably *less general*—they are available only for select objects, and writing user-defined context managers to handle general termination requirements is more complex than coding a try/finally.

On the other hand, using existing context managers requires *less code* than using try/finally, as shown by the preceding examples. Moreover, the context manager protocol supports *entry* actions in addition to exit actions. Although the try/finally is perhaps the more widely applicable technique, context managers may be more appropriate where they are already available, or where their extra complexity is warranted.

Debugging with Outer try Statements

You can also make use of exception handlers to replace Python's default top-level exception-handling behavior. By wrapping an entire program (or a call to it) in an outer try in your top-level code, you can catch any exception that may occur while your program runs, thereby subverting the default program termination.

In the following, the empty except clause catches any uncaught exception raised while the program runs. To get hold of the actual exception that occurred, fetch the sys.exc_info function call result from the built-in sys module; it returns a tuple whose first two items contain the current exception's class and the instance object raised (more on sys.exc_info in a moment):

```
try:
    ...run program...
except:                          # All uncaught exceptions come here
    import sys
    print('uncaught!', sys.exc_info()[0], sys.exc_info()[1])
```

This structure is commonly used during development, to keep programs active even after errors occur—it allows you to run additional tests without having to restart. It's also used when testing other program code, as described in the next section.

Running In-Process Tests

You might combine some of the coding patterns we've just looked at in a test-driver application that tests other code within the same process:

```
import sys
log = open('testlog', 'a')
from testapi import moreTests, runNextTest, testName
def testdriver():
    while moreTests():
        try:
            runNextTest()
        except:
            print('FAILED', testName(), sys.exc_info()[:2], file=log)
        else:
            print('PASSED', testName(), file=log)
testdriver()
```

The `testdriver` function here cycles through a series of test calls (the module `testapi` is left abstract in this example). Because an uncaught exception in a test case would normally kill this test driver, you need to wrap test case calls in a `try` if you want to continue the testing process after a test fails. The empty `except` catches any uncaught exception generated by a test case as usual, and it uses `sys.exc_info` to log the exception to a file. The `else` clause is run when no exception occurs—the test success case.

Such boilerplate code is typical of systems that test functions, modules, and classes by running them in the same process as the test driver. In practice, however, testing can be much more sophisticated than this. For instance, to test external programs, you could instead check status codes or outputs generated by program-launching tools such as `os.system` and `os.popen`, covered in the standard library manual (such tools do not generally raise exceptions for errors in the external programs—in fact, the test cases may run in parallel with the test driver).

At the end of this chapter, we'll also meet some more complete testing frameworks provided by Python, such as `doctest` and PyUnit, which provide tools for comparing expected outputs with actual results.

More on sys.exc_info

The `sys.exc_info` result used in the last two sections allows an exception handler to gain access to the most recently raised exception generically. This is especially useful when using the empty `except` clause to catch everything blindly, to determine what was raised:

```
try:
    ...
except:
    # sys.exc_info()[0:2] are the exception class and instance
```

If no exception is being handled, this call it returns a tuple containing three None values. Otherwise, the values returned are (*type, value, traceback*), where:

- *type* is the exception class of the exception being handled.
- *value* is the exception class instance that was raised.
- *traceback* is a traceback object that represents the call stack at the point where the exception originally occurred (see the `traceback` module's documentation for tools that may be used in conjunction with this object to generate error messages manually).

As we saw in the prior chapter, `sys.exc_info` can also sometimes be useful to determine the specific exception type when catching exception category superclasses. As we saw, though, because in this case you can also get the exception type by fetching the __class__ attribute of the instance obtained with the `as` clause, `sys.exc_info` is mostly used by the empty `except` today:

```
try:
    ...
except General as instance:
    # instance.__class__ is the exception class
```

That said, using the instance object's interfaces and polymorphism is often a better approach than testing exception types—exception methods can be defined per class and run generically:

```
try:
    ...
except General as instance:
    # instance.method() does the right thing for this instance
```

As usual, being too specific in Python can limit your code's flexibility. A polymorphic approach like the last example here generally supports future evolution better.

Version skew note: In Python 2.6, the older tools `sys.exc_type` and `sys.exc_value` still work to fetch the most recent exception type and value, but they can manage only a single, global exception for the entire process. These two names have been removed in Python 3.0. The newer and preferred `sys.exc_info()` call available in both 2.6 and 3.0 instead keeps track of each thread's exception information, and so is thread-specific. Of course, this distinction matters only when using multiple threads in Python programs (a subject beyond this book's scope), but 3.0 forces the issue. See other resources for more details.

Exception Design Tips and Gotchas

I'm lumping design tips and gotchas together in this chapter, because it turns out that the most common gotchas largely stem from design issues. By and large, exceptions are easy to use in Python. The real art behind them is in deciding how specific or general your `except` clauses should be and how much code to wrap up in `try` statements. Let's address the second of these concerns first.

What Should Be Wrapped

In principle, you could wrap every statement in your script in its own `try`, but that would just be silly (the `try` statements would then need to be wrapped in `try` statements!). What to wrap is really a design issue that goes beyond the language itself, and it will become more apparent with use. But for now, here are a few rules of thumb:

- Operations that commonly fail should generally be wrapped in `try` statements. For example, operations that interface with system state (file opens, socket calls, and the like) are prime candidates for `trys`.

- However, there are exceptions to the prior rule—in a simple script, you may *want* failures of such operations to kill your program instead of being caught and ignored. This is especially true if the failure is a showstopper. Failures in Python typically result in useful error messages (not hard crashes), and this is often the best outcome you could hope for.

- You should implement termination actions in `try`/`finally` statements to guarantee their execution, unless a context manager is available as a `with`/`as` option. The `try`/`finally` statement form allows you to run code whether exceptions occur or not in arbitrary scenarios.

- It is sometimes more convenient to wrap the call to a large function in a single `try` statement, rather than littering the function itself with many `try` statements. That way, all exceptions in the function percolate up to the `try` around the call, and you reduce the amount of code within the function.

The types of programs you write will probably influence the amount of exception handling you code as well. Servers, for instance, must generally keep running persistently and so will likely require `try` statements to catch and recover from exceptions. In-process testing programs of the kind we saw in this chapter will probably handle exceptions as well. Simpler one-shot scripts, though, will often ignore exception handling completely because failure at any step requires script shutdown.

Catching Too Much: Avoid Empty except and Exception

On to the issue of handler generality. Python lets you pick and choose which exceptions to catch, but you sometimes have to be careful to not be too inclusive. For example, you've seen that an empty `except` clause catches *every* exception that might be raised while the code in the `try` block runs.

That's easy to code, and sometimes desirable, but you may also wind up intercepting an error that's expected by a `try` handler higher up in the exception nesting structure. For example, an exception handler such as the following catches and stops every exception that reaches it, regardless of whether another handler is waiting for it:

```
def func():
    try:
        ...                    # IndexError is raised in here
    except:
        ...                    # But everything comes here and dies!
try:
    func()
except IndexError:             # Exception should be processed here
    ...
```

Perhaps worse, such code might also catch unrelated system exceptions. Even things like memory errors, genuine programming mistakes, iteration stops, keyboard interrupts, and system exits raise exceptions in Python. Such exceptions should not usually be intercepted.

For example, scripts normally exit when control falls off the end of the top-level file. However, Python also provides a built-in `sys.exit(statuscode)` call to allow early terminations. This actually works by raising a built-in `SystemExit` exception to end the program, so that `try`/`finally` handlers run on the way out and special types of programs can intercept the event.[*] Because of this, a `try` with an empty `except` might unknowingly prevent a crucial exit, as in the following file (*exiter.py*):

```
import sys
def bye():
    sys.exit(40)               # Crucial error: abort now!
try:
    bye()
except:
    print('got it')            # Oops--we ignored the exit
```

---

[*] A related call, `os._exit`, also ends a program, but via an immediate termination—it skips cleanup actions and cannot be intercepted with `try`/`except` or `try`/`finally` blocks. It is usually only used in spawned child processes, a topic beyond this book's scope. See the library manual or follow-up texts for details.

```
    print('continuing...')

% python exiter.py
got it
continuing...
```

You simply might not expect all the kinds of exceptions that could occur during an operation. Using the built-in exception classes of the prior chapter can help in this particular case, because the Exception superclass is not a superclass of SystemExit:

```
try:
    bye()
except Exception:              # Won't catch exits, but _will_ catch many others
    ...
```

In other cases, though, this scheme is no better than an empty except clause—because Exception is a superclass above all built-in exceptions except system-exit events, it still has the potential to catch exceptions meant for elsewhere in the program.

Probably worst of all, both an empty except and catching the Exception class will also catch genuine programming errors, which should be allowed to pass most of the time. In fact, these two techniques can effectively *turn off* Python's error-reporting machinery, making it difficult to notice mistakes in your code. Consider this code, for example:

```
mydictionary = {...}
...
try:
    x = myditctionary['spam']    # Oops: misspelled
except:
    x = None                     # Assume we got KeyError
...continue here with x...
```

The coder here assumes that the only sort of error that can happen when indexing a dictionary is a missing key error. But because the name myditctionary is misspelled (it should say mydictionary), Python raises a NameError instead for the undefined name reference, which the handler will silently catch and ignore. The event handler will incorrectly fill in a default for the dictionary access, masking the program error. Moreover, catching Exception here would have the exact same effect as an empty except. If this happens in code that is far removed from the place where the fetched values are used, it might make for a very interesting debugging task!

As a rule of thumb, be as specific in your handlers as you can be—empty except clauses and Exception catchers are handy, but potentially error-prone. In the last example, for instance, you would be better off saying except KeyError: to make your intentions explicit and avoid intercepting unrelated events. In simpler scripts, the potential for problems might not be significant enough to outweigh the convenience of a catchall, but in general, general handlers are generally trouble.

Catching Too Little: Use Class-Based Categories

On the other hand, neither should handlers be too specific. When you list specific exceptions in a `try`, you catch only what you actually list. This isn't necessarily a bad thing, but if a system evolves to raise other exceptions in the future, you may need to go back and add them to exception lists elsewhere in your code.

We saw this phenomenon at work in the prior chapter. For instance, the following handler is written to treat `MyExcept1` and `MyExcept2` as normal cases and everything else as an error. Therefore, if you add a `MyExcept3` in the future, it will be processed as an error unless you update the exception list:

```
try:
    ...
except (MyExcept1, MyExcept2):     # Breaks if you add a MyExcept3
    ...                            # Non-errors
else:
    ...                            # Assumed to be an error
```

Luckily, careful use of the class-based exceptions we discussed in Chapter 33 can make this trap go away completely. As we saw, if you catch a general superclass, you can add and raise more specific subclasses in the future without having to extend `except` clause lists manually—the superclass becomes an extendible exceptions category:

```
try:
    ...
except SuccessCategoryName:        # OK if I add a myerror3 subclass
    ...                            # Non-errors
else:
    ...                            # Assumed to be an error
```

In other words, a little design goes a long way. The moral of the story is to be careful to be neither too general nor too specific in exception handlers, and to pick the granularity of your `try` statement wrappings wisely. Especially in larger systems, exception policies should be a part of the overall design.

Core Language Summary

Congratulations! This concludes your look at the core Python programming language. If you've gotten this far, you may consider yourself an Official Python Programmer (and should feel free to add Python to your résumé the next time you dig it out). You've already seen just about everything there is to see in the language itself, and all in much more depth than many practicing Python programmers initially do. You've studied built-in types, statements, and exceptions, as well as tools used to build up larger program units (functions, modules, and classes); you've even explored important design issues, OOP, program architecture, and more.

The Python Toolset

From this point forward, your future Python career will largely consist of becoming proficient with the *toolset* available for application-level Python programming. You'll find this to be an ongoing task. The standard library, for example, contains hundreds of modules, and the public domain offers still more tools. It's possible to spend a decade or more seeking proficiency with all these tools, especially as new ones are constantly appearing (trust me on this!).

Speaking generally, Python provides a hierarchy of toolsets:

Built-ins
> Built-in types like strings, lists, and dictionaries make it easy to write simple programs fast.

Python extensions
> For more demanding tasks, you can extend Python by writing your own functions, modules, and classes.

Compiled extensions
> Although we don't cover this topic in this book, Python can also be extended with modules written in an external language like C or C++.

Because Python layers its toolsets, you can decide how deeply your programs need to delve into this hierarchy for any given task—you can use built-ins for simple scripts, add Python-coded extensions for larger systems, and code compiled extensions for advanced work. We've only covered the first two of these categories in this book, and that's plenty to get you started doing substantial programming in Python.

Table 35-1 summarizes some of the sources of built-in or existing functionality available to Python programmers, and some topics you'll probably be busy exploring for the remainder of your Python career. Up until now, most of our examples have been very small and self-contained. They were written that way on purpose, to help you master the basics. But now that you know all about the core language, it's time to start learning how to use Python's built-in interfaces to do real work. You'll find that with a simple language like Python, common tasks are often much easier than you might expect.

Table 35-1. Python's toolbox categories

Category	Examples
Object types	Lists, dictionaries, files, strings
Functions	len, range, open
Exceptions	IndexError, KeyError
Modules	os, tkinter, pickle, re
Attributes	__dict__, __name__, __class__
Peripheral tools	NumPy, SWIG, Jython, IronPython, Django, etc.

Development Tools for Larger Projects

Once you've mastered the basics, you'll find your Python programs becoming sub-stantially larger than the examples you've experimented with so far. For developing larger systems, a set of development tools is available in Python and the public domain. You've seen some of these in action, and I've mentioned a few others. To help you on your way, here is a summary of some of the most commonly used tools in this domain:

PyDoc and docstrings

PyDoc's `help` function and HTML interfaces were introduced in Chapter 15. PyDoc provides a documentation system for your modules and objects and integrates with Python's docstrings feature. It is a standard part of the Python system—see the library manual for more details. Be sure to also refer back to the documentation source hints listed in Chapter 4 for information on other Python information resources.

PyChecker and PyLint

Because Python is such a dynamic language, some programming errors are not reported until your program runs (e.g., syntax errors are caught when a file is run or imported). This isn't a big drawback—as with most languages, it just means that you have to test your Python code before shipping it. At worst, with Python you essentially trade a compile phase for an initial testing phase. Furthermore, Python's dynamic nature, automatic error messages, and exception model make it easier and quicker to find and fix errors in Python than it is in some other languages (unlike C, for example, Python does not crash on errors).

The PyChecker and PyLint systems provide support for catching a large set of common errors ahead of time, before your script runs. They serve similar roles to the *lint* program in C development. Some Python groups run their code through PyChecker prior to testing or delivery, to catch any lurking potential problems. In fact, the Python standard library is regularly run through PyChecker before release. PyChecker and PyLint are third-party open source packages; you can find them at *http://www.python.org* or the PyPI website, or via your friendly neighborhood web search engine.

PyUnit (a.k.a. unittest*)*

In Chapter 24, we learned how to add self-test code to a Python file by using the `__name__ == '__main__'` trick at the bottom of the file. For more advanced testing purposes, Python comes with two testing support tools. The first, PyUnit (called `unittest` in the library manual), provides an object-oriented class framework for specifying and customizing test cases and expected results. It mimics the JUnit framework for Java. This is a sophisticated class-based unit testing system; see the Python library manual for details.

doctest

The `doctest` standard library module provides a second and simpler approach to regression testing, based upon Python's docstrings feature. Roughly, to use `doctest`, you cut and paste a log of an interactive testing session into the docstrings of your source files. `doctest` then extracts your docstrings, parses out the test cases and results, and reruns the tests to verify the expected results. `doctest`'s operation can be tailored in a variety of ways; see the library manual for more details.

IDEs

We discussed IDEs for Python in Chapter 3. IDEs such as IDLE provide a graphical environment for editing, running, debugging, and browsing your Python programs. Some advanced IDEs (such as Eclipse, Komodo, NetBeans, and Wing IDE) may support additional development tasks, including source control integration, code refactoring, project management tools, and more. See Chapter 3, the text editors page at *http://www.python.org*, and your favorite web search engine for more on available IDEs and GUI builders for Python.

Profilers

Because Python is so high-level and dynamic, intuitions about performance gleaned from experience with other languages usually don't apply to Python code. To truly isolate performance bottlenecks in your code, you need to add timing logic with clock tools in the `time` or `timeit` modules, or run your code under the `profile` module. We saw an example of the timing modules at work when comparing iteration tools' speeds in Chapter 20. Profiling is usually your first optimization step—profile to isolate bottlenecks, then time alternative codings of them.

`profile` is a standard library module that implements a source code profiler for Python; it runs a string of code you provide (e.g., a script file import, or a call to a function) and then, by default, prints a report to the standard output stream that gives performance statistics—number of calls to each function, time spent in each function, and more.

The `profile` module can be run as a script or imported, and it may be customized in various ways; for example, it can save run statistics to a file to be analyzed later with the `pstats` module. To profile interactively, import the `profile` module and call `profile.run('code')`, passing in the code you wish to profile as a string (e.g., a call to a function, or an import of an entire file). To profile from a system shell command line, use a command of the form `python -m profile main.py args...` (see Appendix A for more on this format). Also see Python's standard library manuals for other profiling options; the `cProfile` module, for example, has identical interfaces to `profile` but runs with less overhead, so it may be better suited to profiling long-running programs.

Debuggers

We also discussed debugging options in Chapter 3 (see its sidebar "Debugging Python Code" on page 69). As a review, most development IDEs for Python support GUI-based debugging, and the Python standard library also includes a source code debugger module called `pdb`. This module provides a command-line interface and works much like common C language debuggers (e.g., *dbx*, *gdb*).

Much like the profiler, the *pdb* debugger can be run either interactively or from a command line and can be imported and called from a Python program. To use it interactively, import the module, start running code by calling a `pdb` function (e.g., `pdb.run("main()")`), and then type debugging commands from *pdb*'s interactive prompt. To launch *pdb* from a system shell command line, use a command of the form `python -m pdb main.py args...` (see Appendix A for more on this format). *pdb* also includes a useful postmortem analysis call, `pdb.pm()`, which starts the debugger after an exception has been encountered.

Because IDEs such as IDLE also include point-and-click debugging interfaces, *pdb* isn't a critical a tool today, except when a GUI isn't available or when more control is desired. See Chapter 3 for tips on using IDLE's debugging GUI interfaces. Really, neither *pdb* nor IDEs seem to be used much in practice—as noted in Chapter 3, most programmers either insert `print` statements or simply read Python's error messages (not the most high-tech of approaches, but the practical tends to win the day in the Python world!).

Shipping options

In Chapter 2, we introduced common tools for packaging Python programs. *py2exe*, *PyInstaller*, and *freeze* can package byte code and the Python Virtual Machine into "frozen binary" standalone executables, which don't require that Python be installed on the target machine and fully hide your system's code. In addition, we learned in Chapter 2 that Python programs may be shipped in their source (*.py*) or byte code (*.pyc*) forms, and that import hooks support special packaging techniques such as automatic extraction of *.zip* files and byte code encryption.

We also briefly met the standard library's `distutils` modules, which provide packaging options for Python modules and packages, and C-coded extensions; see the Python manuals for more details. The emerging Python "eggs" third-party packaging system provides another alternative that also accounts for dependencies; search the Web for more details.

Optimization options

There are a couple of options for optimizing your programs. The Psyco system described in Chapter 2 provides a just-in-time compiler for translating Python byte code to binary machine code, and Shedskin offers a Python-to-C++ translator. You may also occasionally see *.pyo* optimized byte code files, generated and run with the `-O` Python command-line flag (discussed in Chapters 21 and 33); because this provides a very modest performance boost, however, it is not commonly used.

As a last resort, you can also move parts of your program to a compiled language such as C to boost performance; see the book *Programming Python* and the Python standard manuals for more on C extensions. In general, Python's speed also improves over time, so be sure to upgrade to the faster releases when possible.

Other hints for larger projects

    We've met a variety of language features in this text that will tend to become more useful once you start coding larger projects. These include module packages (Chapter 23), class-based exceptions (Chapter 33), class pseudoprivate attributes (Chapter 30), documentation strings (Chapter 15), module path configuration files (Chapter 21), hiding names from `from *` with `__all__` lists and `_X`-style names (Chapter 24), adding self-test code with the `__name__ == '__main__'` trick (Chapter 24), using common design rules for functions and modules (Chapters 17, 19, and 24), using object-oriented design patterns (Chapter 30 and others), and so on.

To learn about other large-scale Python development tools available in the public domain, be sure to browse the pages at the PyPI website at *http://www.python.org*, and the Web at large.

Chapter Summary

This chapter wrapped up the exceptions part of the book with a survey of related statements, a look at common exception use cases, and a brief summary of commonly used development tools.

This chapter also wrapped up the core material of this book. At this point, you've been exposed to the full subset of Python that most programmers use. In fact, if you have read this far, you should feel free to consider yourself an *official Python programmer*. Be sure to pick up a t-shirt the next time you're online.

The next and final part of this book is a collection of chapters dealing with topics that are advanced, but still in the core language category. These chapters are all *optional reading*, because not every Python programmer must delve into their subjects; indeed, most of you can stop here and begin exploring Python's roles in your application domains. Frankly, application libraries tend to be more important in practice than advanced (and to some, esoteric) language features.

On the other hand, if you do need to care about things like Unicode or binary data, have to deal with API-building tools such as descriptors, decorators, and metaclasses, or just want to dig a bit further in general, the next part of the book will help you get started. The larger examples in the final part will also give you a chance to see the concepts you've already learned being applied in more realistic ways.

As this is the end of the core material of this book, you get a break on the chapter quiz—just one question this time. As always, though, be sure to work through this part's closing exercises to cement what you've learned in the past few chapters; because the next part is optional reading, this is the final end-of-part exercises session. If you want to see some examples of how what you've learned comes together in real scripts drawn from common applications, check out the "solution" to exercise 4 in Appendix B.

Test Your Knowledge: Quiz

1. (This question is a repeat from the first quiz in Chapter 1—see, I told you it would be easy! :-) Why does "spam" show up in so many Python examples in books and on the Web?

Test Your Knowledge: Answers

1. Because Python is named after the British comedy group Monty Python (based on surveys I've conducted in classes, this is a much-too-well-kept secret in the Python world!). The spam reference comes from a Monty Python skit, where a couple who are trying to order food in a cafeteria keep getting drowned out by a chorus of Vikings singing a song about spam. No, really. And if I could insert an audio clip of that song here, I would....

Test Your Knowledge: Part VII Exercises

As we've reached the end of this part of the book, it's time for a few exception exercises to give you a chance to practice the basics. Exceptions really are simple tools; if you get these, you've probably mastered exceptions.

See "Part VII, Exceptions and Tools" on page 1132 in Appendix B for the solutions.

1. `try/except`. Write a function called `oops` that explicitly raises an `IndexError` exception when called. Then write another function that calls `oops` inside a `try/except` statement to catch the error. What happens if you change `oops` to raise a `KeyError` instead of an `IndexError`? Where do the names `KeyError` and `IndexError` come from? (Hint: recall that all unqualified names come from one of four scopes.)

2. *Exception objects and lists*. Change the `oops` function you just wrote to raise an exception you define yourself, called `MyError`. Identify your exception with a class. Then, extend the `try` statement in the catcher function to catch this exception and its instance in addition to `IndexError`, and print the instance you catch.

3. *Error handling*. Write a function called `safe(func, *args)` that runs any function with any number of arguments by using the `*name` arbitrary arguments call syntax, catches any exception raised while the function runs, and prints the exception using the `exc_info` call in the `sys` module. Then use your `safe` function to run your `oops` function from exercise 1 or 2. Put `safe` in a module file called *tools.py*, and pass it the `oops` function interactively. What kind of error messages do you get? Finally, expand `safe` to also print a Python stack trace when an error occurs by calling the built-in `print_exc` function in the standard `traceback` module (see the Python library reference manual for details).

4. *Self-study examples.* At the end of Appendix B, I've included a handful of example scripts developed as group exercises in live Python classes for you to study and run on your own in conjunction with Python's standard manual set. These are not described, and they use tools in the Python standard library that you'll have to research on your own. Still, for many readers, it helps to see how the concepts we've discussed in this book come together in real programs. If these whet your appetite for more, you can find a wealth of larger and more realistic application-level Python program examples in follow-up books like *Programming Python* and on the Web.

## PART VIII

Advanced Topics

String Changes in 3.0

One of the most noticeable changes in 3.0 is the mutation of string object types. In a nutshell, 2.X's `str` and `unicode` types have morphed into 3.0's `str` and `bytes` types, and a new mutable `bytearray` type has been added. The `bytearray` type is technically available in Python 2.6 too (though not earlier), but it's a back-port from 3.0 and does not as clearly distinguish between text and binary content in 2.6.

Especially if you process data that is either Unicode or binary in nature, these changes can have substantial impacts on your code. In fact, as a general rule of thumb, how much you need to care about this topic depends in large part upon which of the following categories you fall into:

- If you deal with non-ASCII *Unicode text*—for instance, in the context of internationalized applications and the results of some XML parsers—you will find support for text encodings to be different in 3.0, but also probably more direct, accessible, and seamless than in 2.6.

- If you deal with *binary data*—for example, in the form of image or audio files or packed data processed with the `struct` module—you will need to understand 3.0's new `bytes` object and 3.0's different and sharper distinction between text and binary data and files.

- If you fall into *neither* of the prior two categories, you can generally use strings in 3.0 much as you would in 2.6: with the general `str` string type, text files, and all the familiar string operations we studied earlier. Your strings will be encoded and decoded using your platform's default encoding (e.g., ASCII, or UTF-8 on Windows in the U.S.—`sys.getdefaultencoding()` gives your default if you care to check), but you probably won't notice.

In other words, if your text is always ASCII, you can get by with normal string objects and text files and can avoid most of the following story. As we'll see in a moment, ASCII is a simple kind of Unicode and a subset of other encodings, so string operations and files "just work" if your programs process ASCII text.

Even if you fall into the last of the three categories just mentioned, though, a basic understanding of 3.0's string model can help both to demystify some of the underlying behavior now, and to make mastering Unicode or binary data issues easier if they impact you in the future. Though applications are beyond our scope here, especially if you work with the Internet, files, directories, network interfaces, databases, pipes, and even GUIs, Unicode may no longer be an optional topic for you in Python 3.X.

Python 3.0's support for Unicode and binary data is also available in 2.6, albeit in different forms. Although our main focus in this chapter is on string types in 3.0, we'll explore some 2.6 differences along the way too. Regardless of which version you use, the tools we'll explore here can become important in many types of programs.

String Basics

Before we look at any code, let's begin with a general overview of Python's string model. To understand why 3.0 changed the way it did on this front, we have to start with a brief look at how characters are actually represented in computers.

Character Encoding Schemes

Most programmers think of strings as series of characters used to represent textual data. The way characters are stored in a computer's memory can vary, though, depending on what sort of character set must be recorded.

The *ASCII* standard was created in the U.S., and it defines many U.S. programmers' notion of text strings. ASCII defines character codes from 0 through 127 and allows each character to be stored in one 8-bit byte (only 7 bits of which are actually used). For example, the ASCII standard maps the character `'a'` to the integer value 97 (0x61 in hex), which is stored in a single byte in memory and files. If you wish to see how this works, Python's `ord` built-in function gives the binary value for a character, and `chr` returns the character for a given integer code value:

```
>>> ord('a')          # 'a' is a byte with binary value 97 in ASCII
97
>>> hex(97)
'0x61'
>>> chr(97)           # Binary value 97 stands for character 'a'
'a'
```

Sometimes one byte per character isn't enough, though. Various symbols and accented characters, for instance, do not fit into the range of possible characters defined by ASCII. To accommodate special characters, some standards allow all possible values in an 8-bit byte, 0 through 255, to represent characters, and assign the values 128 through 255 (outside ASCII's range) to special characters. One such standard, known as *Latin-1*, is widely used in Western Europe. In Latin-1, character codes above 127 are assigned to accented and otherwise special characters. The character assigned to byte value 196, for example, is a specially marked non-ASCII character:

```
>>> 0xC4
196
>>> chr(196)
'Ä'
```

This standard allows for a wide array of extra special characters. Still, some alphabets define so many characters that it is impossible to represent each of them as one byte. *Unicode* allows more flexibility. Unicode text is commonly referred to as "wide-character" strings, because each character may be represented with multiple bytes. Unicode is typically used in *internationalized* programs, to represent European and Asian character sets that have more characters than 8-bit bytes can represent.

To store such rich text in computer memory, we say that characters are translated to and from raw bytes using an *encoding*—the rules for translating a string of Unicode characters into a sequence of bytes, and extracting a string from a sequence of bytes. More procedurally, this translation back and forth between bytes and strings is defined by two terms:

- *Encoding* is the process of translating a string of characters into its raw bytes form, according to a desired encoding name.

- *Decoding* is the process of translating a raw string of bytes into its character string form, according to its encoding name.

That is, we *encode* from string to raw bytes, and *decode* from raw bytes to string. For some encodings, the translation process is trivial—ASCII and Latin-1, for instance, map each character to a single byte, so no translation work is required. For other encodings, the mapping can be more complex and yield multiple bytes per character.

The widely used *UTF-8* encoding, for example, allows a wide range of characters to be represented by employing a variable number of bytes scheme. Character codes less than 128 are represented as a single byte; codes between 128 and 0x7ff (2047) are turned into two bytes, where each byte has a value between 128 and 255; and codes above 0x7ff are turned into three- or four-byte sequences having values between 128 and 255. This keeps simple ASCII strings compact, sidesteps byte ordering issues, and avoids null (zero) bytes that can cause problems for C libraries and networking.

Because encodings' character maps assign characters to the same codes for compatibility, ASCII is a *subset* of both Latin-1 and UTF-8; that is, a valid ASCII character string is also a valid Latin-1- and UTF-8-encoded string. This is also true when the data is stored in files: every ASCII file is a valid UTF-8 file, because ASCII is a 7-bit subset of UTF-8.

Conversely, the UTF-8 encoding is binary compatible with ASCII for all character codes less than 128. Latin-1 and UTF-8 simply allow for additional characters: Latin-1 for characters mapped to values 128 through 255 within a byte, and UTF-8 for characters that may be represented with multiple bytes. Other encodings allow wider character sets in similar ways (e.g., UTF-16 and UTF-32 format strings with 2 and 4 bytes per each character, respectively), but all of these—ASCII, Latin-1, UTF-8, and many others—are considered to be Unicode.

To Python programmers, encodings are specified as strings containing the encoding's name. Python comes with roughly 100 different encodings; see the Python library reference for a complete list. Importing the module `encodings` and running `help(encodings)` shows you many encoding names as well; some are implemented in Python, and some in C. Some encodings have multiple names, too; for example, *latin-1*, *iso_8859_1*, and *8859* are all synonyms for the same encoding, Latin-1. We'll revisit encodings later in this chapter, when we study techniques for writing Unicode strings in a script.

For more on the Unicode story, see the Python standard manual set. It includes a "Unicode HOWTO" in its "Python HOWTOs" section, which provides additional background that we will skip here in the interest of space.

Python's String Types

At a more concrete level, the Python language provides string data types to represent character text in your scripts. The string types you will use in your scripts depend upon the version of Python you're using. *Python 2.X* has a general string type for representing binary data and simple 8-bit text like ASCII, along with a specific type for representing multibyte Unicode text:

- `str` for representing 8-bit text and binary data
- `unicode` for representing wide-character Unicode text

Python 2.X's two string types are different (`unicode` allows for the extra size of characters and has extra support for encoding and decoding), but their operation sets largely overlap. The `str` string type in 2.X is used for text that can be represented with 8-bit bytes, as well as binary data that represents absolute byte values.

By contrast, *Python 3.X* comes with three string object types—one for textual data and two for binary data:

- `str` for representing Unicode text (both 8-bit and wider)
- `bytes` for representing binary data (including encoded text)
- `bytearray`, a mutable flavor of the `bytes` type

As mentioned earlier, `bytearray` is also available in Python 2.6, but it's simply a back-port from 3.0 with less content-specific behavior and is generally considered a 3.0 type.

All three string types in 3.0 support similar operation sets, but they have different roles. The main goal behind this change in 3.X was to *merge* the normal and Unicode string types of 2.X into a single string type that supports both normal and Unicode text: developers wanted to remove the 2.X string dichotomy and make Unicode processing more natural. Given that ASCII and other 8-bit text is really a simple kind of Unicode, this convergence seems logically sound.

To achieve this, the 3.0 `str` type is defined as an *immutable sequence of characters* (not necessarily bytes), which may be either normal text such as ASCII with one byte per character, or richer character set text such as UTF-8 Unicode that may include multibyte characters. Strings processed by your script with this type are encoded per the platform default, but explicit encoding names may be provided to translate `str` objects to and from different schemes, both in memory and when transferring to and from files.

While 3.0's new `str` type does achieve the desired string/`unicode` merging, many programs still need to process raw binary data that is not encoded per any text format. Image and audio files, as well as packed data used to interface with devices or C programs you might process with Python's `struct` module, fall into this category. To support processing of truly binary data, therefore, a new type, `bytes`, also was introduced.

In 2.X, the general `str` type filled this binary data role, because strings were just sequences of bytes (the separate `unicode` type handles wide-character strings). In 3.0, the `bytes` type is defined as an *immutable sequence of 8-bit integers* representing absolute byte values. Moreover, the 3.0 `bytes` type supports almost all the same operations that the `str` type does; this includes string methods, sequence operations, and even `re` module pattern matching, but not string formatting.

A 3.0 `bytes` object really is a sequence of small integers, each of which is in the range 0 through 255; indexing a `bytes` returns an `int`, slicing one returns another `bytes`, and running the `list` built-in on one returns a list of integers, not characters. When processed with operations that assume characters, though, the contents of `bytes` objects are assumed to be ASCII-encoded bytes (e.g., the `isalpha` method assumes each byte is an ASCII character code). Further, `bytes` objects are printed as character strings instead of integers for convenience.

While they were at it, Python developers also added a `bytearray` type in 3.0. `bytearray` is a variant of `bytes` that is *mutable* and so supports in-place changes. It supports the usual string operations that `str` and `bytes` do, as well as many of the same in-place change operations as lists (e.g., the `append` and `extend` methods, and assignment to indexes). Assuming your strings can be treated as raw bytes, `bytearray` finally adds direct in-place mutability for string data—something not possible without conversion to a mutable type in Python 2, and not supported by Python 3.0's `str` or `bytes`.

Although Python 2.6 and 3.0 offer much the same functionality, they package it differently. In fact, the mapping from 2.6 to 3.0 string types is not direct—2.6's `str` equates to both `str` and `bytes` in 3.0, and 3.0's `str` equates to both `str` and `unicode` in 2.6. Moreover, the mutability of 3.0's `bytearray` is unique.

In practice, though, this asymmetry is not as daunting as it might sound. It boils down to the following: in 2.6, you will use `str` for simple text and binary data and `unicode` for more advanced forms of text; in 3.0, you'll use `str` for any kind of text (simple and Unicode) and `bytes` or `bytearray` for binary data. In practice, the choice is often made for you by the tools you use—especially in the case of file processing tools, the topic of the next section.[*]

---

[*] It may help to know that Python internally stores decoded strings in UTF-16 (roughly, UCS-2) format, with 2 bytes per character (a.k.a. Unicode "code pont"), unless compiled for 4 bytes/character. Encoded text is always translated to and from this internal form, in which text processing occurs.

Text and Binary Files

File I/O (input and output) has also been revamped in 3.0 to reflect the str/bytes distinction and automatically support encoding Unicode text. Python now makes a sharp platform-independent distinction between text files and binary files:

Text files

When a file is opened in *text mode*, reading its data automatically decodes its content and returns it as a str; writing takes a str and automatically encodes it before transferring it to the file. Both reads and writes translate per a platform default or a provided encoding name. Text-mode files also support universal end-of-line translation and additional encoding specification arguments. Depending on the encoding name, text files may also automatically process the byte order mark sequence at the start of a file (more on this momentarily).

Binary files

When a file is opened in *binary mode* by adding a b (lowercase only) to the mode string argument in the built-in open call, reading its data does not decode it in any way but simply returns its content raw and unchanged, as a bytes object; writing similarly takes a bytes object and transfers it to the file unchanged. Binary-mode files also accept a bytearray object for the content to be written to the file.

Because the language sharply differentiates between str and bytes, you must decide whether your data is text or binary in nature and use either str or bytes objects to represent its content in your script, as appropriate. Ultimately, the mode in which you open a file will dictate which type of object your script will use to represent its content:

- If you are processing image files, packed data created by other programs whose content you must extract, or some device data streams, chances are good that you will want to deal with it using bytes and *binary-mode* files. You might also opt for bytearray if you wish to update the data without making copies of it in memory.

- If instead you are processing something that is textual in nature, such as program output, HTML, internationalized text, or CSV or XML files, you'll probably want to use str and *text-mode* files.

Notice that the *mode string* argument to built-in function open (its second argument) becomes fairly crucial in Python 3.0—its content not only specifies a file *processing mode*, but also implies a Python *object type*. By adding a b to the mode string, you specify binary mode and will receive, or must provide, a bytes object to represent the file's content when reading or writing. Without the b, your file is processed in text mode, and you'll use str objects to represent its content in your script. For example, the modes rb, wb, and rb+ imply bytes; r, w+, and rt (the default) imply str.

Text-mode files also handle the *byte order marker* (BOM) sequence that may appear at the start of files under certain encoding schemes. In the UTF-16 and UTF-32 encodings, for example, the BOM specifies big- or little-endian format (essentially, which end of a bitstring is most significant). A UTF-8 text file may also include a BOM to declare that it is UTF-8 in general, but this isn't guaranteed. When reading and writing data using these encoding schemes, Python automatically skips or writes the BOM if it is implied by a general encoding name or if you provide a more specific encoding name to force the issue. For example, the BOM is always processed for "utf-16," the more specific encoding name "utf-16-le" species little-endian UTF-16 format, and the more specific encoding name "utf-8-sig" forces Python to both skip and write a BOM on input and output, respectively, for UTF-8 text (the general name "utf-8" does not).

We'll learn more about BOMs and files in general in the section "Handling the BOM in 3.0" on page 928. First, let's explore the implications of Python's new Unicode string model.

Python 3.0 Strings in Action

Let's step through a few examples that demonstrate how the 3.0 string types are used. One note up front: the code in this section was run with and applies to 3.0 only. Still, basic string operations are generally portable across Python versions. Simple ASCII strings represented with the `str` type work the same in 2.6 and 3.0 (and exactly as we saw in Chapter 7 of this book). Moreover, although there is no `bytes` type in Python 2.6 (it has just the general `str`), it can usually run code that thinks there is—in 2.6, the call `bytes(X)` is present as a synonym for `str(X)`, and the new literal form `b'...'` is taken to be the same as the normal string literal `'...'`. You may still run into version skew in some isolated cases, though; the 2.6 `bytes` call, for instance, does not allow the second argument (encoding name) required by 3.0's `bytes`.

Literals and Basic Properties

Python 3.0 string objects originate when you call a built-in function such as `str` or `bytes`, process a file created by calling `open` (described in the next section), or code literal syntax in your script. For the latter, a new literal form, `b'xxx'` (and equivalently, `B'xxx'`) is used to create `bytes` objects in 3.0, and `bytearray` objects may be created by calling the `bytearray` function, with a variety of possible arguments.

More formally, in 3.0 all the current string literal forms—`'xxx'`, `"xxx"`, and triple-quoted blocks—generate a `str`; adding a `b` or `B` just before any of them creates a `bytes` instead. This new `b'...'` bytes literal is similar in form to the `r'...'` raw string used to suppresses backslash escapes. Consider the following, run in 3.0:

```
C:\misc> c:\python30\python

>>> B = b'spam'          # Make a bytes object (8-bit bytes)
>>> S = 'eggs'           # Make a str object (Unicode characters, 8-bit or wider)

>>> type(B), type(S)
(<class 'bytes'>, <class 'str'>)

>>> B                    # Prints as a character string, really sequence of ints
```

```
       b'spam'
       >>> S
       'eggs'
```

The `bytes` object is actually a sequence of short integers, though it prints its content as characters whenever possible:

```
       >>> B[0], S[0]            # Indexing returns an int for bytes, str for str
       (115, 'e')

       >>> B[1:], S[1:]          # Slicing makes another bytes or str object
       (b'pam', 'ggs')

       >>> list(B), list(S)
       ([115, 112, 97, 109], ['e', 'g', 'g', 's'])    # bytes is really ints
```

The `bytes` object is immutable, just like `str` (though `bytearray`, described later, is not); you cannot assign a `str`, `bytes`, or integer to an offset of a `bytes` object. The `bytes` prefix also works for any string literal form:

```
       >>> B[0] = 'x'                           # Both are immutable
       TypeError: 'bytes' object does not support item assignment

       >>> S[0] = 'x'
       TypeError: 'str' object does not support item assignment

       >>> B = B"""                  # bytes prefix works on single, double, triple quotes
       ... xxxx
       ... yyyy
       ... """
       >>> B
       b'\nxxxx\nyyyy\n'
```

As mentioned earlier, in Python 2.6 the `b'xxx'` literal is present for compatibility but is the same as `'xxx'` and makes a `str`, and `bytes` is just a synonym for `str`; as you've seen, in 3.0 both of these address the distinct `bytes` type. Also note that the `u'xxx'` and `U'xxx'` Unicode string literal forms in 2.6 are *gone* in 3.0; use `'xxx'` instead, since all strings are Unicode, even if they contain all ASCII characters (more on writing non-ASCII Unicode text in the section "Coding Non-ASCII Text" on page 907).

Conversions

Although Python 2.X allowed `str` and `unicode` type objects to be mixed freely (if the strings contained only 7-bit ASCII text), 3.0 draws a much sharper distinction—`str` and `bytes` type objects *never* mix automatically in expressions and *never* are converted to one another automatically when passed to functions. A function that expects an argument to be a `str` object won't generally accept a `bytes`, and vice versa.

Because of this, Python 3.0 basically requires that you commit to one type or the other, or perform manual, explicit conversions:

- str.encode() and bytes(S, encoding) translate a string to its raw bytes form and create a bytes from a str in the process.

- bytes.decode() and str(B, encoding) translate raw bytes into its string form and create a str from a bytes in the process.

These encode and decode methods (as well as file objects, described in the next section) use either a default encoding for your platform or an explicitly passed-in encoding name. For example, in 3.0:

```
>>> S = 'eggs'
>>> S.encode()                        # str to bytes: encode text into raw bytes
b'eggs'

>>> bytes(S, encoding='ascii')        # str to bytes, alternative
b'eggs'

>>> B = b'spam'
>>> B.decode()                        # bytes to str: decode raw bytes into text
'spam'

>>> str(B, encoding='ascii')          # bytes to str, alternative
'spam'
```

Two cautions here. First of all, your platform's default encoding is available in the sys module, but the encoding argument to bytes is not optional, even though it is in str.encode (and bytes.decode).

Second, although calls to str do not require the encoding argument like bytes does, leaving it off in str calls does not mean it defaults—instead, a str call without an encoding returns the bytes object's print string, not its str converted form (this is usually not what you'll want!). Assuming B and S are still as in the prior listing:

```
>>> import sys
>>> sys.platform                      # Underlying platform
'win32'
>>> sys.getdefaultencoding()          # Default encoding for str here
'utf-8'

>>> bytes(S)
TypeError: string argument without an encoding

>>> str(B)                            # str without encoding
"b'spam'"                             # A print string, not conversion!
>>> len(str(B))
7
>>> len(str(B, encoding='ascii'))     # Use encoding to convert to str
4
```

Coding Unicode Strings

Encoding and decoding become more meaningful when you start dealing with actual non-ASCII Unicode text. To code arbitrary Unicode characters in your strings, some of which you might not even be able to type on your keyboard, Python string literals support both "\xNN" hex byte value escapes and "\uNNNN" and "\UNNNNNNNN" Unicode escapes in string literals. In Unicode escapes, the first form gives four hex digits to encode a 2-byte (16-bit) character code, and the second gives eight hex digits for a 4-byte (32-bit) code.

Coding ASCII Text

Let's step through some examples that demonstrate text coding basics. As we've seen, ASCII text is a simple type of Unicode, stored as a sequence of byte values that represent characters:

```
C:\misc> c:\python30\python

>>> ord('X')              # 'X' has binary value 88 in the default encoding
88
>>> chr(88)               # 88 stands for character 'X'
'X'

>>> S = 'XYZ'             # A Unicode string of ASCII text
>>> S
'XYZ'
>>> len(S)                # 3 characters long
3
>>> [ord(c) for c in S]   # 3 bytes with integer ordinal values
[88, 89, 90]
```

Normal 7-bit ASCII text like this is represented with one character per byte under each of the Unicode encoding schemes described earlier in this chapter:

```
>>> S.encode('ascii')     # Values 0..127 in 1 byte (7 bits) each
b'XYZ'
>>> S.encode('latin-1')   # Values 0..255 in 1 byte (8 bits) each
b'XYZ'
>>> S.encode('utf-8')     # Values 0..127 in 1 byte, 128..2047 in 2, others 3 or 4
b'XYZ'
```

In fact, the bytes objects returned by encoding ASCII text this way is really a sequence of short integers, which just happen to print as ASCII characters when possible:

```
>>> S.encode('latin-1')[0]
88
>>> list(S.encode('latin-1'))
[88, 89, 90]
```

Coding Non-ASCII Text

To code non-ASCII characters, you may use hex or Unicode escapes in your strings; hex escapes are limited to a single byte's value, but Unicode escapes can name characters with values two and four bytes wide. The hex values 0xCD and 0xE8, for instance, are codes for two special accented characters outside the 7-bit range of ASCII, but we can embed them in 3.0 `str` objects because `str` supports Unicode today:

```
>>> chr(0xc4)            # 0xC4, 0xE8: characters outside ASCII's range
'Ä'
>>> chr(0xe8)
'è'

>>> S = '\xc4\xe8'       # Single byte 8-bit hex escapes
>>> S
'Äè'

>>> S = '\u00c4\u00e8'   # 16-bit Unicode escapes
>>> S
'Äè'
>>> len(S)               # 2 characters long (not number of bytes!)
2
```

Encoding and Decoding Non-ASCII text

Now, if we try to *encode* a non-ASCII string into raw bytes using as ASCII, we'll get an error. Encoding as Latin-1 works, though, and allocates one byte per character; encoding as UTF-8 allocates 2 bytes per character instead. If you write this string to a file, the raw `bytes` shown here is what is actually stored on the file for the encoding types given:

```
>>> S = '\u00c4\u00e8'
>>> S
'Äè'
>>> len(S)
2

>>> S.encode('ascii')
UnicodeEncodeError: 'ascii' codec can't encode characters in position 0-1:
ordinal not in range(128)

>>> S.encode('latin-1')          # One byte per character
b'\xc4\xe8'

>>> S.encode('utf-8')            # Two bytes per character
b'\xc3\x84\xc3\xa8'

>>> len(S.encode('latin-1'))     # 2 bytes in latin-1, 4 in utf-8
2
>>> len(S.encode('utf-8'))
4
```

Note that you can also go the other way, reading raw bytes from a file and *decoding* them back to a Unicode string. However, as we'll see later, the encoding mode you give to the `open` call causes this decoding to be done for you automatically on input (and avoids issues that may arise from reading partial character sequences when reading by blocks of bytes):

```
>>> B = b'\xc4\xe8'
>>> B
b'\xc4\xe8'
>>> len(B)                      # 2 raw bytes, 2 characters
2
>>> B.decode('latin-1')         # Decode to latin-1 text
'Äè'

>>> B = b'\xc3\x84\xc3\xa8'
>>> len(B)                      # 4 raw bytes
4
>>> B.decode('utf-8')
'Äè'
>>> len(B.decode('utf-8'))      # 2 Unicode characters
2
```

Other Unicode Coding Techniques

Some encodings use even larger byte sequences to represent characters. When needed, you can specify both 16- and 32-bit Unicode values for characters in your strings—use "\u..." with four hex digits for the former, and "\U...." with eight hex digits for the latter:

```
>>> S = 'A\u00c4B\U000000e8C'
>>> S                           # A, B, C, and 2 non-ASCII characters
'AÄBèC'
>>> len(S)                      # 5 characters long
5

>>> S.encode('latin-1')
b'A\xc4B\xe8C'
>>> len(S.encode('latin-1'))    # 5 bytes in latin-1
5

>>> S.encode('utf-8')
b'A\xc3\x84B\xc3\xa8C'
>>> len(S.encode('utf-8'))      # 7 bytes in utf-8
7
```

Interestingly, some other encodings may use very different byte formats. The cp500 EBCDIC encoding, for example, doesn't even encode ASCII the same way as the encodings we've been using so far (since Python encodes and decodes for us, we only generally need to care about this when providing encoding names):

```
>>> S
'AÄBèC'
>>> S.encode('cp500')           # Two other Western European encodings
b'\xc1c\xc2T\xc3'
>>> S.encode('cp850')           # 5 bytes each
b'A\x8eB\x8aC'

>>> S = 'spam'                  # ASCII text is the same in most
>>> S.encode('latin-1')
b'spam'
```

```
>>> S.encode('utf-8')
b'spam'
>>> S.encode('cp500')                    # But not in cp500: IBM EBCDIC!
b'\xa2\x97\x81\x94'
>>> S.encode('cp850')
b'spam'
```

Technically speaking, you can also build Unicode strings piecemeal using chr instead
of Unicode or hex escapes, but this might become tedious for large strings:

```
>>> S = 'A' + chr(0xC4) + 'B' + chr(0xE8) + 'C'
>>> S
'AÄBèC'
```

Two cautions here. First, Python 3.0 allows special characters to be coded with both
hex and Unicode escapes in str strings, but only with hex escapes in bytes strings—
Unicode escape sequences are silently taken verbatim in bytes literals, not as escapes.
In fact, bytes must be decoded to str strings to print their non-ASCII characters
properly:

```
>>> S = 'A\xC4B\xE8C'                     # str recognizes hex and Unicode escapes
>>> S
'AÄBèC'

>>> S = 'A\u00C4B\U000000E8C'
>>> S
'AÄBèC'

>>> B = b'A\xC4B\xE8C'                     # bytes recognizes hex but not Unicode
>>> B
b'A\xc4B\xe8C'

>>> B = b'A\u00C4B\U000000E8C'             # Escape sequences taken literally!
>>> B
b'A\\u00C4B\\U000000E8C'

>>> B = b'A\xC4B\xE8C'                     # Use hex escapes for bytes
>>> B                                      # Prints non-ASCII as hex
b'A\xc4B\xe8C'
>>> print(B)
b'A\xc4B\xe8C'
>>> B.decode('latin-1')                    # Decode as latin-1 to interpret as text
'AÄBèC'
```

Second, bytes literals require characters either to be either ASCII characters or, if their
values are greater than 127, to be escaped; str stings, on the other hand, allow literals
containing any character in the source character set (which, as discussed later, defaults
to UTF-8 unless an encoding declaration is given in the source file):

```
>>> S = 'AÄBèC'                            # Chars from UTF-8 if no encoding declaration
>>> S
'AÄBèC'

>>> B = b'AÄBèC'
SyntaxError: bytes can only contain ASCII literal characters.
```

```
>>> B = b'A\xC4B\xE8C'                     # Chars must be ASCII, or escapes
>>> B
b'A\xc4B\xe8C'
>>> B.decode('latin-1')
'AÄBèC'

>>> S.encode()                             # Source code encoded per UTF-8 by default
b'A\xc3\x84B\xc3\xa8C'                     # Uses system default to encode, unless passed
>>> S.encode('utf-8')
b'A\xc3\x84B\xc3\xa8C'

>>> B.decode()                             # Raw bytes do not correspond to utf-8
UnicodeDecodeError: 'utf8' codec can't decode bytes in position 1-2: ...
```

Converting Encodings

So far, we've been encoding and decoding strings to inspect their structure. More generally, we can always *convert* a string to a different encoding than the source character set default, but we must provide an explicit encoding name to encode to and decode from:

```
>>> S = 'AÄBèC'
>>> S
'AÄBèC'
>>> S.encode()                             # Default utf-8 encoding
b'A\xc3\x84B\xc3\xa8C'

>>> T = S.encode('cp500')                  # Convert to EBCDIC
>>> T
b'\xc1c\xc2T\xc3'

>>> U = T.decode('cp500')                  # Convert back to Unicode
>>> U
'AÄBèC'

>>> U.encode()                             # Default utf-8 encoding again
b'A\xc3\x84B\xc3\xa8C'
```

Keep in mind that the special Unicode and hex character escapes are only necessary when you code non-ASCII Unicode strings manually. In practice, you'll often load such text from files instead. As we'll see later in this chapter, 3.0's file object (created with the open built-in function) automatically decodes text strings as they are read and encodes them when they are written; because of this, your script can often deal with strings generically, without having to code special characters directly.

Later in this chapter we'll also see that it's possible to convert between encodings when transferring strings to and from files, using a technique very similar to that in the last example; although you'll still need to provide explicit encoding names when opening a file, the file interface does most of the conversion work for you automatically. Either way, note that "conversion" here really just means encoding a text string to raw bytes per a different encoding scheme; decoded text has no encoding type, and is simply a string of Unicode code points (a.k.a. characters) in memory.

Coding Unicode Strings in Python 2.6

Now that I've shown you the basics of Unicode strings in 3.0, I need to explain that you can do much the same in 2.6, though the tools differ. `unicode` is available in Python 2.6, but it is a distinct data type from `str`, and it allows free mixing of normal and Unicode strings when they are compatible. In fact, you can essentially pretend 2.6's `str` is 3.0's `bytes` when it comes to decoding raw bytes into a Unicode string, as long as it's in the proper form. Here is 2.6 in action; unicode characters display in hex in 2.6 unless you explicitly print, and non-ASCII displays can vary per shell (most of this section ran in IDLE):

```
C:\misc> c:\python26\python
>>> import sys
>>> sys.version
'2.6 (r26:66721, Oct  2 2008, 11:35:03) [MSC v.1500 32 bit (Intel)]'

>>> S = 'A\xC4B\xE8C'            # String of 8-bit bytes
>>> print S                      # Some are non-ASCII
AÄBèC

>>> S.decode('latin-1')          # Decode byte to latin-1 Unicode
u'A\xc4B\xe8C'

>>> S.decode('utf-8')            # Not formatted as utf-8
UnicodeDecodeError: 'utf8' codec can't decode bytes in position 1-2: invalid data

>>> S.decode('ascii')            # Outside ASCII range
UnicodeDecodeError: 'ascii' codec can't decode byte 0xc4 in position 1: ordinal
not in range(128)
```

To store arbitrarily encoded Unicode text, make a `unicode` object with the `u'xxx'` literal form (this literal is no longer available in 3.0, since all strings support Unicode in 3.0):

```
>>> U = u'A\xC4B\xE8C'           # Make Unicode string, hex escapes
>>> U
u'A\xc4B\xe8C'
>>> print U
AÄBèC
```

Once you've created it, you can convert Unicode text to different raw byte encodings, similar to encoding `str` objects into `bytes` objects in 3.0:

```
>>> U.encode('latin-1')          # Encode per latin-1: 8-bit bytes
'A\xc4B\xe8C'
>>> U.encode('utf-8')            # Encode per utf-8: multibyte
'A\xc3\x84B\xc3\xa8C'
```

Non-ASCII characters can be coded with hex or Unicode escapes in string literals in 2.6, just as in 3.0. However, as with bytes in 3.0, the "\u..." and "\U..." escapes are recognized only for unicode strings in 2.6, not 8-bit str strings:

```
C:\misc> c:\python26\python
>>> U = u'A\xC4B\xE8C'                  # Hex escapes for non-ASCII
>>> U
u'A\xc4B\xe8C'
>>> print U
AÄBèC

>>> U = u'A\u00C4B\U000000E8C'          # Unicode escapes for non-ASCII
>>> U                                   # u" = 16 bits, U" = 32 bits
u'A\xc4B\xe8C'
>>> print U
AÄBèC

>>> S = 'A\xC4B\xE8C'                    # Hex escapes work
>>> S
'A\xc4B\xe8C'
>>> print S                              # But some print oddly, unless decoded
A-BFC
>>> print S.decode('latin-1')
AÄBèC

>>> S = 'A\u00C4B\U000000E8C'            # Not Unicode escapes: taken literally!
>>> S
'A\\u00C4B\\U000000E8C'
>>> print S
A\u00C4B\U000000E8C
>>> len(S)
19
```

Like 3.0's str and bytes, 2.6's unicode and str share nearly identical operation sets, so unless you need to convert to other encodings you can often treat unicode as though it were str. One of the primary differences between 2.6 and 3.0, though, is that unicode and non-Unicode str objects can be freely *mixed* in expressions, and as long as the str is compatible with the unicode's encoding Python will automatically convert it up to unicode (in 3.0, str and bytes never mix automatically and require manual conversions):

```
>>> u'ab' + 'cd'                         # Can mix if compatible in 2.6
u'abcd'                                  # 'ab' + b'cd' not allowed in 3.0
```

In fact, the difference in types is often trivial to your code in 2.6. Like normal strings, Unicode strings may be concatenated, indexed, sliced, matched with the re module, and so on, and they cannot be changed in-place. If you ever need to convert between the two types explicitly, you can use the built-in str and unicode functions:

```
>>> str(u'spam')                         # Unicode to normal
'spam'
>>> unicode('spam')                      # Normal to Unicode
u'spam'
```

However, this liberal approach to mixing string types in 2.6 only works if the string is compatible with the `unicode` object's encoding type:

```
>>> S = 'A\xC4B\xE8C'              # Can't mix if incompatible
>>> U = u'A\xC4B\xE8C'
>>> S + U
UnicodeDecodeError: 'ascii' codec can't decode byte 0xc4 in position 1: ordinal
not in range(128)

>>> S.decode('latin-1') + U        # Manual conversion still required
u'A\xc4B\xe8CA\xc4B\xe8C'

>>> print S.decode('latin-1') + U
AÄBèCAÄBèC
```

Finally, as we'll see in more detail later in this chapter, 2.6's `open` call supports only files of 8-bit bytes, returning their contents as `str` strings; it's up to you to interpret the contents as text or binary data and decode if needed. To read and write Unicode files and encode or decode their content automatically, use 2.6's `codecs.open` call, documented in the 2.6 library manual. This call provides much the same functionality as 3.0's `open` and uses 2.6 `unicode` objects to represent file content—reading a file translates encoded bytes into decoded Unicode characters, and writing translates strings to the desired encoding specified when the file is opened.

Source File Character Set Encoding Declarations

Unicode escape codes are fine for the occasional Unicode character in string literals, but they can become tedious if you need to embed non-ASCII text in your strings frequently. For strings you code within your script files, Python uses the UTF-8 encoding by default, but it allows you to change this to support arbitrary character sets by including a comment that names your desired encoding. The comment must be of this form and must appear as either the first or second line in your script in either Python 2.6 or 3.0:

```
# -*- coding: latin-1 -*-
```

When a comment of this form is present, Python will recognize strings represented natively in the given encoding. This means you can edit your script file in a text editor that accepts and displays accented and other non-ASCII characters correctly, and Python will decode them correctly in your string literals. For example, notice how the comment at the top of the following file, *text.py*, allows Latin-1 characters to be embedded in strings:

```
# -*- coding: latin-1 -*-

# Any of the following string literal forms work in latin-1.
# Changing the encoding above to either ascii or utf-8 fails,
# because the 0xc4 and 0xe8 in myStr1 are not valid in either.

myStr1 = 'aÄBèC'
```

```
myStr2 = 'A\u00c4B\U000000e8C'

myStr3 = 'A' + chr(0xC4) + 'B' + chr(0xE8) + 'C'

import sys
print('Default encoding:', sys.getdefaultencoding())

for aStr in myStr1, myStr2, myStr3:
    print('{0}, strlen={1}, '.format(aStr, len(aStr)), end='')

    bytes1 = aStr.encode()            # Per default utf-8: 2 bytes for non-ASCII
    bytes2 = aStr.encode('latin-1')   # One byte per char
    #bytes3 = aStr.encode('ascii')    # ASCII fails: outside 0..127 range

    print('byteslen1={0}, byteslen2={1}'.format(len(bytes1), len(bytes2)))
```

When run, this script produces the following output:

```
C:\misc> c:\python30\python text.py
Default encoding: utf-8
aÄBèC, strlen=5, byteslen1=7, byteslen2=5
AÄBèC, strlen=5, byteslen1=7, byteslen2=5
AÄBèC, strlen=5, byteslen1=7, byteslen2=5
```

Since most programmers are likely to fall back on the standard UTF-8 encoding, I'll defer to Python's standard manual set for more details on this option and other advanced Unicode support topics, such as properties and character name escapes in strings.

Using 3.0 Bytes Objects

We studied a wide variety of operations available for Python 3.0's general str string type in Chapter 7; the basic string type works identically in 2.6 and 3.0, so we won't rehash this topic. Instead, let's dig a bit deeper into the operation sets provided by the new bytes type in 3.0.

As mentioned previously, the 3.0 bytes object is a sequence of small integers, each of which is in the range 0 through 255, that happens to print as ASCII characters when displayed. It supports sequence operations and most of the same methods available on str objects (and present in 2.X's str type). However, bytes does not support the for mat method or the % formatting expression, and you cannot mix and match bytes and str type objects without explicit conversions—you generally will use all str type objects and text files for *text data*, and all bytes type objects and binary files for *binary data*.

Method Calls

If you really want to see what attributes str has that bytes doesn't, you can always check their dir built-in function results. The output can also tell you something about the expression operators they support (e.g., __mod__ and __rmod__ implement the % operator):

```
C:\misc> c:\python30\python
```

 # Attributes unique to str

```
>>> set(dir('abc')) - set(dir(b'abc'))
{'isprintable', 'format', '__mod__', 'encode', 'isidentifier',
'_formatter_field_name_split', 'isnumeric', '__rmod__', 'isdecimal',
'_formatter_parser', 'maketrans'}
```

 # Attributes unique to bytes

```
>>> set(dir(b'abc')) - set(dir('abc'))
{'decode', 'fromhex'}
```

As you can see, str and bytes have almost identical functionality. Their unique attributes are generally methods that don't apply to the other; for instance, decode translates a raw bytes into its str representation, and encode translates a string into its raw bytes representation. Most of the methods are the same, though bytes methods require bytes arguments (again, 3.0 string types don't mix). Also recall that bytes objects are immutable, just like str objects in both 2.6 and 3.0 (error messages here have been shortened for brevity):

```
>>> B = b'spam'                    # b'...' bytes literal
>>> B.find(b'pa')
1

>>> B.replace(b'pa', b'XY')        # bytes methods expect bytes arguments
b'sXYm'

>>> B.split(b'pa')
[b's', b'm']

>>> B
b'spam'

>>> B[0] = 'x'
TypeError: 'bytes' object does not support item assignment
```

One notable difference is that *string formatting* works only on str objects in 3.0, not on bytes objects (see Chapter 7 for more on string formatting expressions and methods):

```
>>> b'%s' % 99
TypeError: unsupported operand type(s) for %: 'bytes' and 'int'

>>> '%s' % 99
'99'

>>> b'{0}'.format(99)
AttributeError: 'bytes' object has no attribute 'format'
```

```
>>> '{0}'.format(99)
'99'
```

Sequence Operations

Besides method calls, all the usual generic sequence operations you know (and possibly love) from Python 2.X strings and lists work as expected on both `str` and `bytes` in 3.0; this includes indexing, slicing, concatenation, and so on. Notice in the following that indexing a `bytes` object returns an integer giving the byte's binary value; `bytes` really is a *sequence of 8-bit integers*, but it prints as a string of ASCII-coded characters when displayed as a whole for convenience. To check a given byte's value, use the `chr` built-in to convert it back to its character, as in the following:

```
>>> B = b'spam'                     # A sequence of small ints
>>> B                               # Prints as ASCII characters
b'spam'

>>> B[0]                            # Indexing yields an int
115
>>> B[-1]
109

>>> chr(B[0])                       # Show character for int
's'
>>> list(B)                         # Show all the byte's int values
[115, 112, 97, 109]

>>> B[1:], B[:-1]
(b'pam', b'spa')

>>> len(B)
4

>>> B + b'lmn'
b'spamlmn'
>>> B * 4
b'spamspamspamspam'
```

Other Ways to Make bytes Objects

So far, we've been mostly making `bytes` objects with the `b'...'` literal syntax; they can also be created by calling the `bytes` constructor with a `str` and an encoding name, calling the `bytes` constructor with an iterable of integers representing byte values, or encoding a `str` object per the default (or passed-in) encoding. As we've seen, encoding takes a `str` and returns the raw binary byte values of the string according to the encoding specification; conversely, decoding takes a raw `bytes` sequence and encodes it to its string representation—a series of possibly wide characters. Both operations create new string objects:

```
>>> B = b'abc'
>>> B
```

```
b'abc'

>>> B = bytes('abc', 'ascii')
>>> B
b'abc'

>>> ord('a')
97
>>> B = bytes([97, 98, 99])
>>> B
b'abc'

>>> B = 'spam'.encode()          # Or bytes()
>>> B
b'spam'
>>>
>>> S = B.decode()               # Or str()
>>> S
'spam'
```

From a larger perspective, the last two of these operations are really tools for *converting* between str and bytes, a topic introduced earlier and expanded upon in the next section.

Mixing String Types

In the replace call of the section "Method Calls" on page 915, we had to pass in two bytes objects—str types won't work there. Although Python 2.X automatically converts str to and from unicode when possible (i.e., when the str is 7-bit ASCII text), Python 3.0 requires specific string types in some contexts and expects manual conversions if needed:

```
# Must pass expected types to function and method calls

>>> B = b'spam'

>>> B.replace('pa', 'XY')
TypeError: expected an object with the buffer interface

>>> B.replace(b'pa', b'XY')
b'sXYm'

>>> B = B'spam'
>>> B.replace(bytes('pa'), bytes('xy'))
TypeError: string argument without an encoding

>>> B.replace(bytes('pa', 'ascii'), bytes('xy', 'utf-8'))
b'sxym'


# Must convert manually in mixed-type expressions

>>> b'ab' + 'cd'
```

```
TypeError: can't concat bytes to str

>>> b'ab'.decode() + 'cd'                    # bytes to str
'abcd'

>>> b'ab' + 'cd'.encode()                    # str to bytes
b'abcd'

>>> b'ab' + bytes('cd', 'ascii')             # str to bytes
b'abcd'
```

Although you can create `bytes` objects yourself to represent packed binary data, they can also be made automatically by reading files opened in binary mode, as we'll see in more detail later in this chapter. First, though, we should introduce `bytes`'s very close, and mutable, cousin.

Using 3.0 (and 2.6) bytearray Objects

So far we've focused on `str` and `bytes`, since they subsume Python 2's `unicode` and `str`. Python 3.0 has a third string type, though—`bytearray`, a mutable sequence of integers in the range 0 through 255, is essentially a mutable variant of `bytes`. As such, it supports the same string methods and sequence operations as `bytes`, as well as many of the mutable in-place-change operations supported by lists. The `bytearray` type is also available in Python 2.6 as a back-port from 3.0, but it does not enforce the strict text/binary distinction there that it does in 3.0.

Let's take a quick tour. `bytearray` objects may be created by calling the `bytearray` built-in. In Python 2.6, any string may be used to initialize:

```
# Creation in 2.6: a mutable sequence of small (0..255) ints

>>> S = 'spam'
>>> C = bytearray(S)                         # A back-port from 3.0 in 2.6
>>> C                                        # b'..' == '..' in 2.6 (str)
bytearray(b'spam')
```

In Python 3.0, an encoding name or byte string is required, because text and binary strings do not mix, though byte strings may reflect encoded Unicode text:

```
# Creation in 3.0: text/binary do not mix

>>> S = 'spam'
>>> C = bytearray(S)
TypeError: string argument without an encoding

>>> C = bytearray(S, 'latin1')               # A content-specific type in 3.0
>>> C
bytearray(b'spam')

>>> B = b'spam'                              # b'..' != '..' in 3.0 (bytes/str)
>>> C = bytearray(B)
```

```
>>> C
bytearray(b'spam')
```

Once created, bytearray objects are sequences of small integers like bytes and are mutable like lists, though they require an integer for index assignments, not a string (all of the following is a continuation of this session and is run under Python 3.0 unless otherwise noted—see comments for 2.6 usage notes):

```
# Mutable, but must assign ints, not strings

>>> C[0]
115

>>> C[0] = 'x'                          # This and the next work in 2.6
TypeError: an integer is required

>>> C[0] = b'x'
TypeError: an integer is required

>>> C[0] = ord('x')
>>> C
bytearray(b'xpam')

>>> C[1] = b'Y'[0]
>>> C
bytearray(b'xYam')
```

Processing bytearray objects borrows from both strings and lists, since they are mutable byte strings. Besides named methods, the __iadd__ and __setitem__ methods in bytearray implement += in-place concatenation and index assignment, respectively:

```
# Methods overlap with both str and bytes, but also has list's mutable methods

>>> set(dir(b'abc')) - set(dir(bytearray(b'abc')))
{'__getnewargs__'}

>>> set(dir(bytearray(b'abc'))) - set(dir(b'abc'))
{'insert', '__alloc__', 'reverse', 'extend', '__delitem__', 'pop', '__setitem__'
, '__iadd__', 'remove', 'append', '__imul__'}
```

You can change a bytearray in-place with both index assignment, as you've just seen, and list-like methods like those shown here (to change text in-place in 2.6, you would need to convert to and then from a list, with list(str) and ''.join(list)):

```
# Mutable method calls

>>> C
bytearray(b'xYam')

>>> C.append(b'LMN')                    # 2.6 requires string of size 1
TypeError: an integer is required

>>> C.append(ord('L'))
>>> C
bytearray(b'xYamL')
```

```
>>> C.extend(b'MNO')
>>> C
bytearray(b'xYamLMNO')
```

All the usual sequence operations and string methods work on bytearrays, as you would expect (notice that like bytes objects, their expressions and methods expect bytes arguments, not str arguments):

```
# Sequence operations and string methods

>>> C + b'!#'
bytearray(b'xYamLMNO!#')

>>> C[0]
120

>>> C[1:]
bytearray(b'YamLMNO')

>>> len(C)
8

>>> C
bytearray(b'xYamLMNO')

>>> C.replace('xY', 'sp')                    # This works in 2.6
TypeError: Type str doesn't support the buffer API

>>> C.replace(b'xY', b'sp')
bytearray(b'spamLMNO')

>>> C
bytearray(b'xYamLMNO')

>>> C * 4
bytearray(b'xYamLMNOxYamLMNOxYamLMNOxYamLMNO')
```

Finally, by way of summary, the following examples demonstrate how bytes and bytearray objects are sequences of ints, and str objects are sequences of characters:

```
# Binary versus text

>>> B                                        # B is same as S in 2.6
b'spam'
>>> list(B)
[115, 112, 97, 109]

>>> C
bytearray(b'xYamLMNO')
>>> list(C)
[120, 89, 97, 109, 76, 77, 78, 79]

>>> S
'spam'
```

```
>>> list(S)
['s', 'p', 'a', 'm']
```

Although all three Python 3.0 string types can contain character values and support many of the same operations, again, you should always:

- Use `str` for textual data.
- Use `bytes` for binary data.
- Use `bytearray` for binary data you wish to change in-place.

Related tools such as files, the next section's topic, often make the choice for you.

Using Text and Binary Files

This section expands on the impact of Python 3.0's string model on the file processing basics introduced earlier in the book. As mentioned earlier, the mode in which you open a file is crucial—it determines which object type you will use to represent the file's content in your script. Text mode implies `str` objects, and binary mode implies `bytes` objects:

- *Text-mode files* interpret file contents according to a Unicode *encoding*—either the default for your platform, or one whose name you pass in. By passing in an encoding name to `open`, you can force conversions for various types of Unicode files. Text-mode files also perform universal *line-end translations*: by default, all line-end forms map to the single `'\n'` character in your script, regardless of the platform on which you run it. As described earlier, text files also handle reading and writing the *byte order mark* (BOM) stored at the start-of-file in some Unicode encoding schemes.

- *Binary-mode files* instead return file content to you *raw*, as a sequence of integers representing byte values, with no encoding or decoding and no line-end translations.

The second argument to `open` determines whether you want text or binary processing, just as it does in 2.X Python—adding a "b" to this string implies binary mode (e.g., `"rb"` to read binary data files). The default mode is `"rt"`; this is the same as `"r"`, which means text input (just as in 2.X).

In 3.0, though, this mode argument to `open` also implies an *object type* for file content representation, regardless of the underlying platform—text files return a `str` for reads and expect one for writes, but binary files return a `bytes` for reads and expect one (or a `bytearray`) for writes.

Text File Basics

To demonstrate, let's begin with basic file I/O. As long as you're processing basic text files (e.g., ASCII) and don't care about circumventing the platform-default encoding of strings, files in 3.0 look and feel much as they do in 2.X (for that matter, so do strings in general). The following, for instance, writes one line of text to a file and reads it back in 3.0, exactly as it would in 2.6 (note that file is no longer a built-in name in 3.0, so it's perfectly OK to use it as a variable here):

```
C:\misc> c:\python30\python
```

 # Basic text files (and strings) work the same as in 2.X

```
>>> file = open('temp', 'w')
>>> size = file.write('abc\n')          # Returns number of bytes written
>>> file.close()                        # Manual close to flush output buffer

>>> file = open('temp')                 # Default mode is "r" (== "rt"): text input
>>> text = file.read()
>>> text
'abc\n'
>>> print(text)
abc
```

Text and Binary Modes in 3.0

In Python 2.6, there is no major distinction between text and binary files—both accept and return content as str strings. The only major difference is that text files automatically map \n end-of-line characters to and from \r\n on Windows, while binary files do not (I'm stringing operations together into one-liners here just for brevity):

```
C:\misc> c:\python26\python
>>> open('temp', 'w').write('abd\n')     # Write in text mode: adds \r
>>> open('temp', 'r').read()             # Read in text mode: drops \r
'abd\n'
>>> open('temp', 'rb').read()            # Read in binary mode: verbatim
'abd\r\n'

>>> open('temp', 'wb').write('abc\n')    # Write in binary mode
>>> open('temp', 'r').read()             # \n not expanded to \r\n
'abc\n'
>>> open('temp', 'rb').read()
'abc\n'
```

In Python 3.0, things are bit more complex because of the distinction between str for text data and bytes for binary data. To demonstrate, let's write a *text file* and read it back in both modes in 3.0. Notice that we are required to provide a str for writing, but reading gives us a str or a bytes, depending on the open mode:

```
C:\misc> c:\python30\python
```

 # Write and read a text file

```
>>> open('temp', 'w').write('abc\n')     # Text mode output, provide a str
4

>>> open('temp', 'r').read()             # Text mode input, returns a str
```

```
'abc\n'
>>> open('temp', 'rb').read()                 # Binary mode input, returns a bytes
b'abc\r\n'
```

Notice how on Windows text-mode files translate the \n *end-of-line* character to \r\n on output; on input, text mode translates the \r\n back to \n, but binary mode does not. This is the same in 2.6, and it's what we want for binary data (no translations should occur), although you can control this behavior with extra open arguments in 3.0 if desired.

Now let's do the same again, but with a *binary file*. We provide a bytes to write in this case, and we still get back a str or a bytes, depending on the input mode:

```
# Write and read a binary file
>>> open('temp', 'wb').write(b'abc\n')         # Binary mode output, provide a bytes
4
>>> open('temp', 'r').read()                   # Text mode input, returns a str
'abc\n'
>>> open('temp', 'rb').read()                  # Binary mode input, returns a bytes
b'abc\n'
```

Note that the \n end-of-line character is not expanded to \r\n in binary-mode output—again, a desired result for binary data. Type requirements and file behavior are the same even if the data we're writing to the binary file is truly binary in nature. In the following, for example, the "\x00" is a binary zero byte and not a printable character:

```
# Write and read truly binary data
>>> open('temp', 'wb').write(b'a\x00c')        # Provide a bytes
3
>>> open('temp', 'r').read()                   # Receive a str
'a\x00c'
>>> open('temp', 'rb').read()                  # Receive a bytes
b'a\x00c'
```

Binary-mode files always return contents as a bytes object, but accept either a bytes or bytearray object for writing; this naturally follows, given that bytearray is basically just a mutable variant of bytes. In fact, most APIs in Python 3.0 that accept a bytes also allow a bytearray:

```
# bytearrays work too
>>> BA = bytearray(b'\x01\x02\x03')
>>> open('temp', 'wb').write(BA)
3
>>> open('temp', 'r').read()
```

```
'\x01\x02\x03'

>>> open('temp', 'rb').read()
b'\x01\x02\x03'
```

Type and Content Mismatches

Notice that you cannot get away with violating Python's str/bytes type distinction when it comes to files. As the following examples illustrate, we get errors (shortened here) if we try to write a bytes to a text file or a str to a binary file:

```
# Types are not flexible for file content

>>> open('temp', 'w').write('abc\n')          # Text mode makes and requires str
4
>>> open('temp', 'w').write(b'abc\n')
TypeError: can't write bytes to text stream

>>> open('temp', 'wb').write(b'abc\n')         # Binary mode makes and requires bytes
4
>>> open('temp', 'wb').write('abc\n')
TypeError: can't write str to binary stream
```

This makes sense: text has no meaning in binary terms, before it is encoded. Although it is often possible to convert between the types by encoding str and decoding bytes, as described earlier in this chapter, you will usually want to stick to *either* str for text data or bytes for binary data. Because the str and bytes operation sets largely intersect, the choice won't be much of a dilemma for most programs (see the string tools coverage in the final section of this chapter for some prime examples of this).

In addition to type constraints, *file content* can matter in 3.0. Text-mode output files require a str instead of a bytes for content, so there is no way in 3.0 to write truly binary data to a text-mode file. Depending on the encoding rules, bytes outside the default character set can sometimes be embedded in a normal string, and they can always be written in binary mode. However, because text-mode input files in 3.0 must be able to decode content per a Unicode encoding, there is no way to read truly binary data in text mode:

```
# Can't read truly binary data in text mode

>>> chr(0xFF)                                  # FF is a valid char, FE is not
'ÿ'
>>> chr(0xFE)
UnicodeEncodeError: 'charmap' codec can't encode character '\xfe' in position 1...

>>> open('temp', 'w').write(b'\xFF\xFE\xFD')    # Can't use arbitrary bytes!
TypeError: can't write bytes to text stream

>>> open('temp', 'w').write('\xFF\xFE\xFD')     # Can write if embeddable in str
3
>>> open('temp', 'wb').write(b'\xFF\xFE\xFD')   # Can also write in binary mode
3
```

```
>>> open('temp', 'rb').read()                    # Can always read as binary bytes
b'\xff\xfe\xfd'

>>> open('temp', 'r').read()                      # Can't read text unless decodable!
UnicodeEncodeError: 'charmap' codec can't encode characters in position 2-3: ...
```

This last error stems from the fact that all text files in 3.0 are really Unicode text files, as the next section describes.

Using Unicode Files

So far, we've been reading and writing basic text and binary files, but what about processing Unicode files? It turns out to be easy to read and write Unicode text stored in files, because the 3.0 open call accepts an encoding for text files, which does the encoding and decoding for us automatically as data is transferred. This allows us to process Unicode text created with different encodings than the default for the platform, and store in different encodings to convert.

Reading and Writing Unicode in 3.0

In fact, we can *convert* a string to different encodings both manually with method calls and automatically on file input and output. We'll use the following Unicode string in this section to demonstrate:

```
C:\misc> c:\python30\python
>>> S = 'A\xc4B\xe8C'
>>> S                                              # 5-character string, non-ASCII
'AÄBèC'
>>> len(S)
5
```

Manual encoding

As we've already learned, we can always encode such a string to raw bytes according to the target encoding name:

```
# Encode manually with methods

>>> L = S.encode('latin-1')                        # 5 bytes when encoded as latin-1
>>> L
b'A\xc4B\xe8C'
>>> len(L)
5

>>> U = S.encode('utf-8')                          # 7 bytes when encoded as utf-8
>>> U
b'A\xc3\x84B\xc3\xa8C'
>>> len(U)
7
```

File output encoding

Now, to write our string to a text file in a particular encoding, we can simply pass the desired encoding name to open—although we could manually encode first and write in binary mode, there's no need to:

```
# Encoding automatically when written

>>> open('latindata', 'w', encoding='latin-1').write(S)     # Write as latin-1
5
>>> open('utf8data', 'w', encoding='utf-8').write(S)        # Write as utf-8
5

>>> open('latindata', 'rb').read()                          # Read raw bytes
b'A\xc4B\xe8C'

>>> open('utf8data', 'rb').read()                           # Different in files
b'A\xc3\x84B\xc3\xa8C'
```

File input decoding

Similarly, to read arbitrary Unicode data, we simply pass in the file's encoding type name to open, and it decodes from raw bytes to strings automatically; we could read raw bytes and decode manually too, but that can be tricky when reading in blocks (we might read an incomplete character), and it isn't necessary:

```
# Decoding automatically when read

>>> open('latindata', 'r', encoding='latin-1').read()       # Decoded on input
'AÄBèC'
>>> open('utf8data', 'r', encoding='utf-8').read()          # Per encoding type
'AÄBèC'

>>> X = open('latindata', 'rb').read()                      # Manual decoding:
>>> X.decode('latin-1')                                     # Not necessary
'AÄBèC'
>>> X = open('utf8data', 'rb').read()
>>> X.decode()                                              # UTF-8 is default
'AÄBèC'
```

Decoding mismatches

Finally, keep in mind that this behavior of files in 3.0 limits the kind of content you can load as text. As suggested in the prior section, Python 3.0 really must be able to decode the data in text files into a `str` string, according to either the default or a passed-in Unicode encoding name. Trying to open a truly binary data file in text mode, for example, is unlikely to work in 3.0 even if you use the correct object types:

```
>>> file = open('python.exe', 'r')
>>> text = file.read()
UnicodeDecodeError: 'charmap' codec can't decode byte 0x90 in position 2: ...

>>> file = open('python.exe', 'rb')
```

```
>>> data = file.read()
>>> data[:20]
b'MZ\x90\x00\x03\x00\x00\x00\x04\x00\x00\x00\xff\xff\x00\x00\xb8\x00\x00\x00'
```

The first of these examples might not fail in Python 2.X (normal files do not decode text), even though it probably should: reading the file may return corrupted data in the string, due to automatic end-of-line translations in text mode (any embedded \r\n bytes will be translated to \n on Windows when read). To treat file content as Unicode text in 2.6, we need to use special tools instead of the general **open** built-in function, as we'll see in a moment. First, though, let's turn to a more explosive topic....

Handling the BOM in 3.0

As described earlier in this chapter, some encoding schemes store a special *byte order marker* (BOM) sequence at the start of files, to specify data endianness or declare the encoding type. Python both skips this marker on input and writes it on output if the encoding name implies it, but we sometimes must use a specific encoding name to force BOM processing explicitly.

For example, when you save a text file in Windows Notepad, you can specify its encoding type in a drop-down list—simple ASCII text, UTF-8, or little- or big-endian UTF-16. If a one-line text file named *spam.txt* is saved in Notepad as the encoding type "ANSI," for instance, it's written as simple ASCII text without a BOM. When this file is read in binary mode in Python, we can see the actual bytes stored in the file. When it's read as text, Python performs end-of-line translation by default; we can decode it as explicit UTF-8 text since ASCII is a subset of this scheme (and UTF-8 is Python 3.0's default encoding):

```
c:\misc> C:\Python30\python                    # File saved in Notepad
>>> import sys
>>> sys.getdefaultencoding()
'utf-8'
>>> open('spam.txt', 'rb').read()              # ASCII (UTF-8) text file
b'spam\r\nSPAM\r\n'
>>> open('spam.txt', 'r').read()               # Text mode translates line-end
'spam\nSPAM\n'
>>> open('spam.txt', 'r', encoding='utf-8').read()
'spam\nSPAM\n'
```

If this file is instead saved as "UTF-8" in Notepad, it is prepended with a three-byte UTF-8 BOM sequence, and we need to give a more specific encoding name ("utf-8-sig") to force Python to skip the marker:

```
>>> open('spam.txt', 'rb').read()              # UTF-8 with 3-byte BOM
b'\xef\xbb\xbfspam\r\nSPAM\r\n'
>>> open('spam.txt', 'r').read()
'ï»¿spam\nSPAM\n'
>>> open('spam.txt', 'r', encoding='utf-8').read()
'\ufeffspam\nSPAM\n'
>>> open('spam.txt', 'r', encoding='utf-8-sig').read()
'spam\nSPAM\n'
```

If the file is stored as "Unicode big endian" in Notepad, we get UTF-16-format data in the file, prepended with a two-byte BOM sequence—the encoding name "utf-16" in Python skips the BOM because it is implied (since all UTF-16 files have a BOM), and "utf-16-be" handles the big-endian format but does not skip the BOM:

```
>>> open('spam.txt', 'rb').read()
b'\xfe\xff\x00s\x00p\x00a\x00m\x00\r\x00\n\x00S\x00P\x00A\x00M\x00\r\x00\n'
>>> open('spam.txt', 'r').read()
UnicodeEncodeError: 'charmap' codec can't encode character '\xfe' in position 1:...
>>> open('spam.txt', 'r', encoding='utf-16').read()
'spam\nSPAM\n'
>>> open('spam.txt', 'r', encoding='utf-16-be').read()
'\ufeffspam\nSPAM\n'
```

The same is generally true for *output*. When writing a Unicode file in Python code, we need a more explicit encoding name to force the BOM in UTF-8—"utf-8" does not write (or skip) the BOM, but "utf-8-sig" does:

```
>>> open('temp.txt', 'w', encoding='utf-8').write('spam\nSPAM\n')
10
>>> open('temp.txt', 'rb').read()                        # No BOM
b'spam\r\nSPAM\r\n'

>>> open('temp.txt', 'w', encoding='utf-8-sig').write('spam\nSPAM\n')
10
>>> open('temp.txt', 'rb').read()                        # Wrote BOM
b'\xef\xbb\xbfspam\r\nSPAM\r\n'

>>> open('temp.txt', 'r').read()
'ï»¿spam\nSPAM\n'
>>> open('temp.txt', 'r', encoding='utf-8').read()       # Keeps BOM
'\ufeffspam\nSPAM\n'
>>> open('temp.txt', 'r', encoding='utf-8-sig').read()   # Skips BOM
'spam\nSPAM\n'
```

Notice that although "utf-8" does not drop the BOM, data *without* a BOM can be read with both "utf-8" and "utf-8-sig"—use the latter for input if you're not sure whether a BOM is present in a file (and don't read this paragraph out loud in an airport security line!):

```
>>> open('temp.txt', 'w').write('spam\nSPAM\n')
10
>>> open('temp.txt', 'rb').read()                        # Data without BOM
b'spam\r\nSPAM\r\n'
>>> open('temp.txt', 'r').read()                         # Any utf-8 works
'spam\nSPAM\n'
>>> open('temp.txt', 'r', encoding='utf-8').read()
'spam\nSPAM\n'
>>> open('temp.txt', 'r', encoding='utf-8-sig').read()
'spam\nSPAM\n'
```

Finally, for the encoding name "utf-16," the BOM is handled automatically: on *output*, data is written in the platform's native endianness, and the BOM is always written; on *input*, data is decoded per the BOM, and the BOM is always stripped. More specific

UTF-16 encoding names can specify different endianness, though you may have to manually write and skip the BOM yourself in some scenarios if it is required or present:

```
>>> sys.byteorder
'little'
>>> open('temp.txt', 'w', encoding='utf-16').write('spam\nSPAM\n')
10
>>> open('temp.txt', 'rb').read()
b'\xff\xfes\x00p\x00a\x00m\x00\r\x00\n\x00S\x00P\x00A\x00M\x00\r\x00\n\x00'
>>> open('temp.txt', 'r', encoding='utf-16').read()
'spam\nSPAM\n'

>>> open('temp.txt', 'w', encoding='utf-16-be').write('\ufeffspam\nSPAM\n')
11
>>> open('spam.txt', 'rb').read()
b'\xfe\xff\x00s\x00p\x00a\x00m\x00\r\x00\n\x00S\x00P\x00A\x00M\x00\r\x00\n'
>>> open('temp.txt', 'r', encoding='utf-16').read()
'spam\nSPAM\n'
>>> open('temp.txt', 'r', encoding='utf-16-be').read()
'\ufeffspam\nSPAM\n'
```

The more specific UTF-16 encoding names work fine with BOM-less files, though "utf-16" requires one on input in order to determine byte order:

```
>>> open('temp.txt', 'w', encoding='utf-16-le').write('SPAM')
4
>>> open('temp.txt', 'rb').read()            # OK if BOM not present or expected
b'S\x00P\x00A\x00M\x00'
>>> open('temp.txt', 'r', encoding='utf-16-le').read()
'SPAM'
>>> open('temp.txt', 'r', encoding='utf-16').read()
UnicodeError: UTF-16 stream does not start with BOM
```

Experiment with these encodings yourself or see Python's library manuals for more details on the BOM.

Unicode Files in 2.6

The preceding discussion applies to Python 3.0's string types and files. You can achieve similar effects for Unicode files in 2.6, but the interface is different. If you replace str with unicode and open with codecs.open, the result is essentially the same in 2.6:

```
C:\misc> c:\python26\python
>>> S = u'A\xc4B\xe8C'
>>> print S
AÄBèC
>>> len(S)
5
>>> S.encode('latin-1')
'A\xc4B\xe8C'
>>> S.encode('utf-8')
'A\xc3\x84B\xc3\xa8C'

>>> import codecs
```

```
>>> codecs.open('latindata', 'w', encoding='latin-1').write(S)
>>> codecs.open('utfdata', 'w', encoding='utf-8').write(S)

>>> open('latindata', 'rb').read()
'A\xc4B\xe8C'
>>> open('utfdata', 'rb').read()
'A\xc3\x84B\xc3\xa8C'

>>> codecs.open('latindata', 'r', encoding='latin-1').read()
u'A\xc4B\xe8C'
>>> codecs.open('utfdata', 'r', encoding='utf-8').read()
u'A\xc4B\xe8C'
```

Other String Tool Changes in 3.0

Some of the other popular string-processing tools in Python's standard library have been revamped for the new str/bytes type dichotomy too. We won't cover any of these application-focused tools in much detail in this core language book, but to wrap up this chapter, here's a quick look at four of the major tools impacted: the re pattern-matching module, the struct binary data module, the pickle object serialization module, and the xml package for parsing XML text.

The re Pattern Matching Module

Python's re pattern-matching module supports text processing that is more general than that afforded by simple string method calls such as find, split, and replace. With re, strings that designate searching and splitting targets can be described by general patterns, instead of absolute text. This module has been generalized to work on objects of any string type in 3.0—str, bytes, and bytearray—and returns result substrings of the same type as the subject string.

Here it is at work in 3.0, extracting substrings from a line of text. Within pattern strings, (.*) means any character (.), zero or more times (*), saved away as a matched substring (()). Parts of the string matched by the parts of a pattern enclosed in parentheses are available after a successful match, via the group or groups method:

```
C:\misc> c:\python30\python
>>> import re
>>> S = 'Bugger all down here on earth!'      # Line of text
>>> B = b'Bugger all down here on earth!'     # Usually from a file

>>> re.match('(.*) down (.*) on (.*)', S).groups()    # Match line to pattern
('Bugger all', 'here', 'earth!')                       # Matched substrings

>>> re.match(b'(.*) down (.*) on (.*)', B).groups()   # bytes substrings
(b'Bugger all', b'here', b'earth!')
```

In Python 2.6 results are similar, but the unicode type is used for non-ASCII text, and str handles both 8-bit and binary text:

```
C:\misc> c:\python26\python
>>> import re
>>> S = 'Bugger all down here on earth!'          # Simple text and binary
>>> U = u'Bugger all down here on earth!'          # Unicode text

>>> re.match('(.*) down (.*) on (.*)', S).groups()
('Bugger all', 'here', 'earth!')

>>> re.match('(.*) down (.*) on (.*)', U).groups()
(u'Bugger all', u'here', u'earth!')
```

Since bytes and str support essentially the same operation sets, this type distinction is largely transparent. But note that, like in other APIs, you can't mix str and bytes types in its calls' arguments in 3.0 (although if you don't plan to do pattern matching on binary data, you probably don't need to care):

```
C:\misc> c:\python30\python
>>> import re
>>> S = 'Bugger all down here on earth!'
>>> B = b'Bugger all down here on earth!'

>>> re.match('(.*) down (.*) on (.*)', B).groups()
TypeError: can't use a string pattern on a bytes-like object

>>> re.match(b'(.*) down (.*) on (.*)', S).groups()
TypeError: can't use a bytes pattern on a string-like object

>>> re.match(b'(.*) down (.*) on (.*)', bytearray(B)).groups()
(bytearray(b'Bugger all'), bytearray(b'here'), bytearray(b'earth!'))

>>> re.match('(.*) down (.*) on (.*)', bytearray(B)).groups()
TypeError: can't use a string pattern on a bytes-like object
```

The struct Binary Data Module

The Python struct module, used to create and extract packed binary data from strings, also works the same in 3.0 as it does in 2.X, but packed data is represented as bytes and bytearray objects only, not str objects (which makes sense, given that it's intended for processing binary data, not arbitrarily encoded text).

Here are both Pythons in action, packing three objects into a string according to a binary type specification (they create a four-byte integer, a four-byte string, and a two-byte integer):

```
C:\misc> c:\python30\python
>>> from struct import pack
>>> pack('>i4sh', 7, 'spam', 8)          # bytes in 3.0 (8-bit string)
b'\x00\x00\x00\x07spam\x00\x08'

C:\misc> c:\python26\python
>>> from struct import pack
>>> pack('>i4sh', 7, 'spam', 8)          # str in 2.6 (8-bit string)
'\x00\x00\x00\x07spam\x00\x08'
```

Since **bytes** has an almost identical interface to that of **str** in 3.0 and 2.6, though, most programmers probably won't need to care—the change is irrelevant to most existing code, especially since reading from a binary file creates a **bytes** automatically. Although the last test in the following example fails on a type mismatch, most scripts will read binary data from a file, not create it as a string:

```
C:\misc> c:\python30\python
>>> import struct
>>> B = struct.pack('>i4sh', 7, 'spam', 8)
>>> B
b'\x00\x00\x00\x07spam\x00\x08'

>>> vals = struct.unpack('>i4sh', B)
>>> vals
(7, b'spam', 8)

>>> vals = struct.unpack('>i4sh', B.decode())
TypeError: 'str' does not have the buffer interface
```

Apart from the new syntax for bytes, creating and reading binary files works almost the same in 3.0 as it does in 2.X. Code like this is one of the main places where programmers will notice the **bytes** object type:

```
C:\misc> c:\python30\python

# Write values to a packed binary file

>>> F = open('data.bin', 'wb')                    # Open binary output file
>>> import struct
>>> data = struct.pack('>i4sh', 7, 'spam', 8)     # Create packed binary data
>>> data                                          # bytes in 3.0, not str
b'\x00\x00\x00\x07spam\x00\x08'
>>> F.write(data)                                 # Write to the file
10
>>> F.close()

# Read values from a packed binary file

>>> F = open('data.bin', 'rb')                    # Open binary input file
>>> data = F.read()                               # Read bytes
>>> data
b'\x00\x00\x00\x07spam\x00\x08'
>>> values = struct.unpack('>i4sh', data)         # Extract packed binary data
>>> values                                        # Back to Python objects
(7, b'spam', 8)
```

Once you've extracted packed binary data into Python objects like this, you can dig even further into the binary world if you have to—strings can be indexed and sliced to get individual bytes' values, individual bits can be extracted from integers with bitwise operators, and so on (see earlier in this book for more on the operations applied here):

```
>>> values                                        # Result of struct.unpack
(7, b'spam', 8)
```

```
# Accesssing bits of parsed integers

>>> bin(values[0])                          # Can get to bits in ints
'0b111'
>>> values[0] & 0x01                        # Test first (lowest) bit in int
1
>>> values[0] | 0b1010                      # Bitwise or: turn bits on
15
>>> bin(values[0] | 0b1010)                 # 15 decimal is 1111 binary
'0b1111'
>>> bin(values[0] ^ 0b1010)                 # Bitwise xor: off if both true
'0b1101'
>>> bool(values[0] & 0b100)                 # Test if bit 3 is on
True
>>> bool(values[0] & 0b1000)                # Test if bit 4 is set
False
```

Since parsed **bytes** strings are sequences of small integers, we can do similar processing with their individual bytes:

```
# Accessing bytes of parsed strings and bits within them

>>> values[1]
b'spam'
>>> values[1][0]                            # bytes string: sequence of ints
115
>>> values[1][1:]                           # Prints as ASCII characters
b'pam'
>>> bin(values[1][0])                       # Can get to bits of bytes in strings
'0b1110011'
>>> bin(values[1][0] | 0b1100)              # Turn bits on
'0b1111111'
>>> values[1][0] | 0b1100
127
```

Of course, most Python programmers don't deal with binary bits; Python has higher-level object types, like lists and dictionaries, that are generally a better choice for representing information in Python scripts. However, if you must use or produce lower-level data used by C programs, networking libraries, or other interfaces, Python has tools to assist.

The pickle Object Serialization Module

We met the `pickle` module briefly in Chapters 9 and 30. In Chapter 27, we also used the `shelve` module, which uses `pickle` internally. For completeness here, keep in mind that the Python 3.0 version of the `pickle` module always creates a **bytes** object, regardless of the default or passed-in "protocol" (data format level). You can see this by using the module's `dumps` call to return an object's pickle string:

```
C:\misc> C:\Python30\python
>>> import pickle                           # dumps() returns pickle string
```

```
>>> pickle.dumps([1, 2, 3])                          # Python 3.0 default protocol=3=binary
b'\x80\x03]q\x00(K\x01K\x02K\x03e.'

>>> pickle.dumps([1, 2, 3], protocol=0)              # ASCII protocol 0, but still bytes!
b'(lp0\nL1L\naL2L\naL3L\na.'
```

This implies that files used to store pickled objects must always be opened in *binary mode* in Python 3.0, since text files use str strings to represent data, not bytes—the dump call simply attempts to write the pickle string to an open output file:

```
>>> pickle.dump([1, 2, 3], open('temp', 'w'))        # Text files fail on bytes!
TypeError: can't write bytes to text stream          # Despite protocol value

>>> pickle.dump([1, 2, 3], open('temp', 'w'), protocol=0)
TypeError: can't write bytes to text stream

>>> pickle.dump([1, 2, 3], open('temp', 'wb'))       # Always use binary in 3.0

>>> open('temp', 'r').read()
UnicodeEncodeError: 'charmap' codec can't encode character '\u20ac' in ...
```

Because pickle data is not decodable Unicode text, the same is true on input—correct usage in 3.0 requires always writing and reading pickle data in binary modes:

```
>>> pickle.dump([1, 2, 3], open('temp', 'wb'))
>>> pickle.load(open('temp', 'rb'))
[1, 2, 3]
>>> open('temp', 'rb').read()
b'\x80\x03]q\x00(K\x01K\x02K\x03e.'
```

In Python 2.6 (and earlier), we can get by with text-mode files for pickled data, as long as the protocol is level 0 (the default in 2.6) and we use text mode consistently to convert line-ends:

```
C:\misc> c:\python26\python
>>> import pickle
>>> pickle.dumps([1, 2, 3])                          # Python 2.6 default=0=ASCII
'(lp0\nI1\naI2\naI3\na.'

>>> pickle.dumps([1, 2, 3], protocol=1)
']q\x00(K\x01K\x02K\x03e.'

>>> pickle.dump([1, 2, 3], open('temp', 'w'))        # Text mode works in 2.6
>>> pickle.load(open('temp'))
[1, 2, 3]
>>> open('temp').read()
'(lp0\nI1\naI2\naI3\na.'
```

If you care about version neutrality, though, or don't want to care about protocols or their version-specific defaults, always use binary-mode files for pickled data—the following works the same in Python 3.0 and 2.6:

```
>>> import pickle
>>> pickle.dump([1, 2, 3], open('temp', 'wb'))       # Version neutral
>>> pickle.load(open('temp', 'rb'))                  # And required in 3.0
[1, 2, 3]
```

Because almost all programs let Python pickle and unpickle objects automatically and do not deal with the content of pickled data itself, the requirement to always use binary file modes is the only significant incompatibility in Python 3's new pickling model. See reference books or Python's manuals for more details on object pickling.

XML Parsing Tools

XML is a tag-based language for defining structured information, commonly used to define documents and data shipped over the Web. Although some information can be extracted from XML text with basic string methods or the re pattern module, XML's nesting of constructs and arbitrary attribute text tend to make full parsing more accurate.

Because XML is such a pervasive format, Python itself comes with an entire package of XML parsing tools that support the SAX and DOM parsing models, as well as a package known as *ElementTree*—a Python-specific API for parsing and constructing XML. Beyond basic parsing, the open source domain provides support for additional XML tools, such as XPath, Xquery, XSLT, and more.

XML by definition represents text in Unicode form, to support internationalization. Although most of Python's XML parsing tools have always returned Unicode strings, in Python 3.0 their results have mutated from the 2.X unicode type to the 3.0 general str string type—which makes sense, given that 3.0's str string *is* Unicode, whether the encoding is ASCII or other.

We can't go into many details here, but to sample the flavor of this domain, suppose we have a simple XML text file, *mybooks.xml*:

```
<books>
    <date>2009</date>
    <title>Learning Python</title>
    <title>Programming Python</title>
    <title>Python Pocket Reference</title>
    <publisher>O'Reilly Media</publisher>
</books>
```

and we want to run a script to extract and display the content of all the nested title tags, as follows:

```
Learning Python
Programming Python
Python Pocket Reference
```

There are at least four basic ways to accomplish this (not counting more advanced tools like XPath). First, we could run basic *pattern matching* on the file's text, though this tends to be inaccurate if the text is unpredictable. Where applicable, the re module we met earlier does the job—its match method looks for a match at the start of a string, search scans ahead for a match, and the findall method used here locates all places where the pattern matches in the string (the result comes back as a list of matched substrings corresponding to parenthesized pattern groups, or tuples of such for multiple groups):

```
# File patternparse.py

import re
text  = open('mybooks.xml').read()
found = re.findall('<title>(.*)</title>', text)
for title in found: print(title)
```

Second, to be more robust, we could perform complete XML parsing with the standard library's *DOM parsing* support. DOM parses XML text into a tree of objects and provides an interface for navigating the tree to extract tag attributes and values; the interface is a formal specification, independent of Python:

```
# File domparse.py

from xml.dom.minidom import parse, Node
xmltree = parse('mybooks.xml')
for node1 in xmltree.getElementsByTagName('title'):
    for node2 in node1.childNodes:
        if node2.nodeType == Node.TEXT_NODE:
            print(node2.data)
```

As a third option, Python's standard library supports *SAX parsing* for XML. Under the SAX model, a class's methods receive callbacks as a parse progresses and use state information to keep track of where they are in the document and collect its data:

```
# File saxparse.py

import xml.sax.handler
class BookHandler(xml.sax.handler.ContentHandler):
    def __init__(self):
        self.inTitle = False
    def startElement(self, name, attributes):
        if name == 'title':
            self.inTitle = True
    def characters(self, data):
        if self.inTitle:
            print(data)
    def endElement(self, name):
        if name == 'title':
            self.inTitle = False

import xml.sax
parser = xml.sax.make_parser()
handler = BookHandler()
parser.setContentHandler(handler)
parser.parse('mybooks.xml')
```

Finally, the *ElementTree* system available in the **etree** package of the standard library can often achieve the same effects as XML DOM parsers, but with less code. It's a Python-specific way to both parse and generate XML text; after a parse, its API gives access to components of the document:

```
# File etreeparse.py

from xml.etree.ElementTree import parse
tree = parse('mybooks.xml')
for E in tree.findall('title'):
    print(E.text)
```

When run in either 2.6 or 3.0, all four of these scripts display the same printed result:

```
C:\misc> c:\python26\python domparse.py
Learning Python
Programming Python
Python Pocket Reference

C:\misc> c:\python30\python domparse.py
Learning Python
Programming Python
Python Pocket Reference
```

Technically, though, in 2.6 some of these scripts produce `unicode` string objects, while in 3.0 all produce `str` strings, since that type includes Unicode text (whether ASCII or other):

```
C:\misc> c:\python30\python
>>> from xml.dom.minidom import parse, Node
>>> xmltree = parse('mybooks.xml')
>>> for node in xmltree.getElementsByTagName('title'):
...     for node2 in node.childNodes:
...         if node2.nodeType == Node.TEXT_NODE:
...             node2.data
...
'Learning Python'
'Programming Python'
'Python Pocket Reference'

C:\misc> c:\python26\python
>>> ...same code...
...
u'Learning Python'
u'Programming Python'
u'Python Pocket Reference'
```

Programs that must deal with XML parsing results in nontrivial ways will need to account for the different object type in 3.0. Again, though, because all strings have nearly identical interfaces in both 2.6 and 3.0, most scripts won't be affected by the change; tools available on `unicode` in 2.6 are generally available on `str` in 3.0.

Regrettably, going into further XML parsing details is beyond this book's scope. If you are interested in text or XML parsing, it is covered in more detail in the applications-focused follow-up book *Programming Python*. For more details on `re`, `struct`, `pickle`, and XML, as well as the impacts of Unicode on other library tools such as filename expansion and directory walkers, consult the Web, the aforementioned book and others, and Python's standard library manual.

Chapter Summary

This chapter explored advanced string types available in Python 3.0 and 2.6 for processing Unicode text and binary data. As we saw, many programmers use ASCII text and can get by with the basic string type and its operations. For more advanced applications, Python's string models fully support both wide-character Unicode text (via the normal string type in 3.0 and a special type in 2.6) and byte-oriented data (represented with a **bytes** type in 3.0 and normal strings in 2.6).

In addition, we learned how Python's file object has mutated in 3.0 to automatically encode and decode Unicode text and deal with byte strings for binary-mode files. Finally, we briefly met some text and binary data tools in Python's library, and sampled their behavior in 3.0.

In the next chapter, we'll shift our focus to tool-builder topics, with a look at ways to manage access to object attributes by inserting automatically run code. Before we move on, though, here's a set of questions to review what we've learned here.

Test Your Knowledge: Quiz

1. What are the names and roles of string object types in Python 3.0?
2. What are the names and roles of string object types in Python 2.6?
3. What is the mapping between 2.6 and 3.0 string types?
4. How do Python 3.0's string types differ in terms of operations?
5. How can you code non-ASCII Unicode characters in a string in 3.0?
6. What are the main differences between text- and binary-mode files in Python 3.0?
7. How would you read a Unicode text file that contains text in a different encoding than the default for your platform?
8. How can you create a Unicode text file in a specific encoding format?
9. Why is ASCII text considered to be a kind of Unicode text?
10. How large an impact does Python 3.0's string types change have on your code?

Test Your Knowledge: Answers

1. Python 3.0 has three string types: **str** (for Unicode text, including ASCII), **bytes** (for binary data with absolute byte values), and **bytearray** (a mutable flavor of **bytes**). The **str** type usually represents content stored on a text file, and the other two types generally represent content stored on binary files.

2. Python 2.6 has two main string types: str (for 8-bit text and binary data) and unicode (for wide-character text). The str type is used for both text and binary file content; unicode is used for text file content that is generally more complex than 8 bits. Python 2.6 (but not earlier) also has 3.0's bytearray type, but it's mostly a back-port and doesn't exhibit the sharp text/binary distinction that it does in 3.0.

3. The mapping from 2.6 to 3.0 string types is not direct, because 2.6's str equates to both str and bytes in 3.0, and 3.0's str equates to both str and unicode in 2.6. The mutability of bytearray in 3.0 is also unique.

4. Python 3.0's string types share almost all the same operations: method calls, sequence operations, and even larger tools like pattern matching work the same way. On the other hand, only str supports string formatting operations, and bytearray has an additional set of operations that perform in-place changes. The str and bytes types also have methods for encoding and decoding text, respectively.

5. Non-ASCII Unicode characters can be coded in a string with both hex (\xNN) and Unicode (\uNNNN, \UNNNNNNNN) escapes. On some keyboards, some non-ASCII characters—certain Latin-1 characters, for example—can also be typed directly.

6. In 3.0, text-mode files assume their file content is Unicode text (even if it's ASCII) and automatically decode when reading and encode when writing. With binary-mode files, bytes are transferred to and from the file unchanged. The contents of text-mode files are usually represented as str objects in your script, and the contents of binary files are represented as bytes (or bytearray) objects. Text-mode files also handle the BOM for certain encoding types and automatically translate end-of-line sequences to and from the single \n character on input and output unless this is explicitly disabled; binary-mode files do not perform either of these steps.

7. To read files encoded in a different encoding than the default for your platform, simply pass the name of the file's encoding to the open built-in in 3.0 (codecs.open() in 2.6); data will be decoded per the specified encoding when it is read from the file. You can also read in binary mode and manually decode the bytes to a string by giving an encoding name, but this involves extra work and is somewhat error-prone for multibyte characters (you may accidentally read a partial character sequence).

8. To create a Unicode text file in a specific encoding format, pass the desired encoding name to open in 3.0 (codecs.open() in 2.6); strings will be encoded per the desired encoding when they are written to the file. You can also manually encode a string to bytes and write it in binary mode, but this is usually extra work.

9. ASCII text is considered to be a kind of Unicode text, because its 7-bit range of values is a subset of most Unicode encodings. For example, valid ASCII text is also valid Latin-1 text (Latin-1 simply assigns the remaining possible values in an 8-bit byte to additional characters) and valid UTF-8 text (UTF-8 defines a variable-byte scheme for representing more characters, but ASCII characters are still represented with the same codes, in a single byte).

10. The impact of Python 3.0's string types change depends upon the types of strings you use. For scripts that use simple ASCII text, there is probably no impact at all: the `str` string type works the same in 2.6 and 3.0 in this case. Moreover, although string-related tools in the standard library such as `re`, `struct`, `pickle`, and `xml` may technically use different types in 3.0 than in 2.6, the changes are largely irrelevant to most programs because 3.0's `str` and `bytes` and 2.6's `str` support almost identical interfaces. If you process Unicode data, the toolset you need has simply moved from 2.6's `unicode` and `codecs.open()` to 3.0's `str` and `open`. If you deal with binary data files, you'll need to deal with content as `bytes` objects; since they have a similar interface to 2.6 strings, though, the impact should again be minimal.

CHAPTER 37

Managed Attributes

This chapter expands on the *attribute interception* techniques introduced earlier, introduces another, and employs them in a handful of larger examples. Like everything in this part of the book, this chapter is classified as an advanced topic and optional reading, because most applications programmers don't need to care about the material discussed here—they can fetch and set attributes on objects without concern for attribute implementations. Especially for tools builders, though, managing attribute access can be an important part of flexible APIs.

Why Manage Attributes?

Object attributes are central to most Python programs—they are where we often store information about the entities our scripts process. Normally, attributes are simply names for objects; a person's `name` attribute, for example, might be a simple string, fetched and set with basic attribute syntax:

```
person.name              # Fetch attribute value
person.name = value      # Change attribute value
```

In most cases, the attribute lives in the object itself, or is inherited from a class from which it derives. That basic model suffices for most programs you will write in your Python career.

Sometimes, though, more flexibility is required. Suppose you've written a program to use a `name` attribute directly, but then your requirements change—for example, you decide that names should be validated with logic when set or mutated in some way when fetched. It's straightforward to code methods to manage access to the attribute's value (`valid` and `transform` are abstract here):

```
class Person:
    def getName(self):
        if not valid():
            raise TypeError('cannot fetch name')
        else:
            return self.name.transform()
```

```
        def setName(self, value):
            if not valid(value):
                raise TypeError('cannot change name')
            else:
                self.name = transform(value)

    person = Person()
    person.getName()
    person.setName('value')
```

However, this also requires changing all the places where names are used in the entire program—a possibly nontrivial task. Moreover, this approach requires the program to be aware of how values are exported: as simple names or called methods. If you begin with a method-based interface to data, clients are immune to changes; if you do not, they can become problematic.

This issue can crop up more often than you might expect. The value of a cell in a spreadsheet-like program, for instance, might begin its life as a simple discrete value, but later mutate into an arbitrary calculation. Since an object's interface should be flexible enough to support such future changes without breaking existing code, switching to methods later is less than ideal.

Inserting Code to Run on Attribute Access

A better solution would allow you to run code automatically on attribute access, if needed. At various points in this book, we've met Python tools that allow our scripts to dynamically compute attribute values when fetching them and validate or change attribute values when storing them. In this chapter, were going to expand on the tools already introduced, explore other available tools, and study some larger use-case examples in this domain. Specifically, this chapter presents:

- The __getattr__ and __setattr__ methods, for routing undefined attribute fetches and all attribute assignments to generic handler methods.
- The __getattribute__ method, for routing all attribute fetches to a generic handler method in new-style classes in 2.6 and all classes in 3.0.
- The property built-in, for routing specific attribute access to get and set handler functions, known as *properties*.
- The *descriptor protocol*, for routing specific attribute accesses to instances of classes with arbitrary get and set handler methods.

The first and third of these were briefly introduced in Part VI; the others are new topics introduced and covered here.

As we'll see, all four techniques share goals to some degree, and it's usually possible to code a given problem using any one of them. They do differ in some important ways, though. For example, the last two techniques listed here apply to specific attributes, whereas the first two are generic enough to be used by delegation-based classes that must route arbitrary attributes to wrapped objects. As we'll see, all four schemes also differ in both complexity and aesthetics, in ways you must see in action to judge for yourself.

Besides studying the specifics behind the four attribute interception techniques listed in this section, this chapter also presents an opportunity to explore larger programs than we've seen elsewhere in this book. The CardHolder case study at the end, for example, should serve as a self-study example of larger classes in action. We'll also be using some of the techniques outlined here in the next chapter to code decorators, so be sure you have at least a general understanding of these topics before you move on.

Properties

The property protocol allows us to route a specific attribute's get and set operations to functions or methods we provide, enabling us to insert code to be run automatically on attribute access, intercept attribute deletions, and provide documentation for the attributes if desired.

Properties are created with the property built-in and are assigned to class attributes, just like method functions. As such, they are inherited by subclasses and instances, like any other class attributes. Their access-interception functions are provided with the self instance argument, which grants access to state information and class attributes available on the subject instance.

A property manages a single, specific attribute; although it can't catch all attribute accesses generically, it allows us to control both fetch and assignment accesses and enables us to change an attribute from simple data to a computation freely, without breaking existing code. As we'll see, properties are strongly related to descriptors; they are essentially a restricted form of them.

The Basics

A property is created by assigning the result of a built-in function to a class attribute:

```
attribute = property(fget, fset, fdel, doc)
```

None of this built-in's arguments are required, and all default to None if not passed; such operations are not supported, and attempting them will raise an exception. When using them, we pass fget a function for intercepting attribute fetches, fset a function for assignments, and fdel a function for attribute deletions; the doc argument receives a documentation string for the attribute, if desired (otherwise the property copies the docstring of fget, if provided, which defaults to None). fget returns the computed attribute value, and fset and fdel return nothing (really, None).

This built-in call returns a property object, which we assign to the name of the attribute to be managed in the class scope, where it will be inherited by every instance.

A First Example

To demonstrate how this translates to working code, the following class uses a property to trace access to an attribute named name; the actual stored data is named _name so it does not clash with the property:

```
class Person:                               # Use (object) in 2.6
    def __init__(self, name):
        self._name = name
    def getName(self):
        print('fetch...')
        return self._name
    def setName(self, value):
        print('change...')
        self._name = value
    def delName(self):
        print('remove...')
        del self._name
    name = property(getName, setName, delName, "name property docs")

bob = Person('Bob Smith')                   # bob has a managed attribute
print(bob.name)                             # Runs getName
bob.name = 'Robert Smith'                   # Runs setName
print(bob.name)
del bob.name                                # Runs delName

print('-'*20)
sue = Person('Sue Jones')                   # sue inherits property too
print(sue.name)
print(Person.name.__doc__)                  # Or help(Person.name)
```

Properties are available in both 2.6 and 3.0, but they require new-style object derivation in 2.6 to work correctly for assignments—add object as a superclass here to run this in 2.6 (you can list the superclass in 3.0 too, but it's implied and not required).

This particular property doesn't do much—it simply intercepts and traces an attribute—but it serves to demonstrate the protocol. When this code is run, two instances inherit the property, just as they would any other attribute attached to their class. However, their attribute accesses are caught:

```
fetch...
Bob Smith
change...
fetch...
Robert Smith
remove...
--------------------
fetch...
Sue Jones
name property docs
```

Like all class attributes, properties are *inherited* by both instances and lower subclasses. If we change our example as follows, for example:

```
class Super:
    ...the original Person class code...
    name = property(getName, setName, delName, 'name property docs')

class Person(Super):
    pass                          # Properties are inherited

bob = Person('Bob Smith')
...rest unchanged...
```

the output is the same—the Person subclass inherits the name property from Super, and the bob instance gets it from Person. In terms of inheritance, properties work the same as normal methods; because they have access to the self instance argument, they can access instance state information like methods, as the next section demonstrates.

Computed Attributes

The example in the prior section simply traces attribute accesses. Usually, though, properties do much more—computing the value of an attribute dynamically when fetched, for example. The following example illustrates:

```
class PropSquare:
    def __init__(self, start):
        self.value = start
    def getX(self):                   # On attr fetch
        return self.value ** 2
    def setX(self, value):            # On attr assign
        self.value = value
    X = property(getX, setX)          # No delete or docs

P = PropSquare(3)        # 2 instances of class with property
Q = PropSquare(32)       # Each has different state information

print(P.X)               # 3 ** 2
P.X = 4
print(P.X)               # 4 ** 2
print(Q.X)               # 32 ** 2
```

This class defines an attribute X that is accessed as though it were static data, but really runs code to compute its value when fetched. The effect is much like an implicit method call. When the code is run, the value is stored in the instance as state information, but each time we fetch it via the managed attribute, its value is automatically squared:

```
9
16
1024
```

Notice that we've made two different instances—because property methods automatically receive a self argument, they have access to the state information stored in instances. In our case, this mean the fetch computes the square of the subject instance's data.

Coding Properties with Decorators

Although we're saving additional details until the next chapter, we introduced function decorator basics earlier, in Chapter 31. Recall that the function decorator syntax:

```
@decorator
def func(args): ...
```

is automatically translated to this equivalent by Python, to rebind the function name to the result of the **decorator** callable:

```
def func(args): ...
func = decorator(func)
```

Because of this mapping, it turns out that the **property** built-in can serve as a decorator, to define a function that will run automatically when an attribute is fetched:

```
class Person:
    @property
    def name(self): ...          # Rebinds: name = property(name)
```

When run, the decorated method is automatically passed to the first argument of the **property** built-in. This is really just alternative syntax for creating a property and rebinding the attribute name manually:

```
class Person:
    def name(self): ...
    name = property(name)
```

As of Python 2.6, property objects also have **getter**, **setter**, and **deleter** methods that assign the corresponding property accessor methods and return a copy of the property itself. We can use these to specify components of properties by decorating normal methods too, though the **getter** component is usually filled in automatically by the act of creating the property itself:

```
class Person:
    def __init__(self, name):
        self._name = name

    @property
    def name(self):              # name = property(name)
        "name property docs"
        print('fetch...')
        return self._name

    @name.setter
    def name(self, value):       # name = name.setter(name)
        print('change...')
        self._name = value

    @name.deleter
    def name(self):              # name = name.deleter(name)
        print('remove...')
        del self._name
```

```
bob = Person('Bob Smith')          # bob has a managed attribute
print(bob.name)                    # Runs name getter (name 1)
bob.name = 'Robert Smith'          # Runs name setter (name 2)
print(bob.name)
del bob.name                       # Runs name deleter (name 3)

print('-'*20)
sue = Person('Sue Jones')          # sue inherits property too
print(sue.name)
print(Person.name.__doc__)         # Or help(Person.name)
```

In fact, this code is equivalent to the first example in this section—decoration is just an alternative way to code properties in this case. When it's run, the results are the same:

```
fetch...
Bob Smith
change...
fetch...
Robert Smith
remove...
--------------------
fetch...
Sue Jones
name property docs
```

Compared to manual assignment of `property` results, in this case using decorators to code properties requires just three extra lines of code (a negligible difference). As is so often the case with alternative tools, the choice between the two techniques is largely subjective.

Descriptors

Descriptors provide an alternative way to intercept attribute access; they are strongly related to the properties discussed in the prior section. In fact, a property is a kind of descriptor—technically speaking, the `property` built-in is just a simplified way to create a specific type of descriptor that runs method functions on attribute accesses.

Functionally speaking, the descriptor protocol allows us to route a specific attribute's get and set operations to methods of a separate class object that we provide: they provide a way to insert code to be run automatically on attribute access, and they allow us to intercept attribute deletions and provide documentation for the attributes if desired.

Descriptors are created as independent *classes*, and they are assigned to class attributes just like method functions. Like any other class attribute, they are inherited by subclasses and instances. Their access-interception methods are provided with both a `self` for the descriptor itself, and the instance of the client class. Because of this, they can retain and use state information of their own, as well as state information of the subject instance. For example, a descriptor may call methods available in the client class, as well as descriptor-specific methods it defines.

Like a property, a descriptor manages a single, specific attribute; although it can't catch all attribute accesses generically, it provides control over both fetch and assignment accesses and allows us to change an attribute freely from simple data to a computation without breaking existing code. Properties really are just a convenient way to create a specific kind of descriptor, and as we shall see, they can be coded as descriptors directly.

Whereas properties are fairly narrow in scope, descriptors provide a more general solution. For instance, because they are coded as normal classes, descriptors have their own state, may participate in descriptor inheritance hierarchies, can use composition to aggregate objects, and provide a natural structure for coding internal methods and attribute documentation strings.

The Basics

As mentioned previously, descriptors are coded as separate classes and provide specially named accessor methods for the attribute access operations they wish to intercept—get, set, and deletion methods in the descriptor class are automatically run when the attribute assigned to the descriptor class instance is accessed in the corresponding way:

```
class Descriptor:
    "docstring goes here"
    def __get__(self, instance, owner): ...        # Return attr value
    def __set__(self, instance, value): ...        # Return nothing (None)
    def __delete__(self, instance): ...            # Return nothing (None)
```

Classes with any of these methods are considered descriptors, and their methods are special when one of their instances is assigned to another class's attribute—when the attribute is accessed, they are automatically invoked. If any of these methods are absent, it generally means that the corresponding type of access is not supported. Unlike with properties, however, omitting a __set__ allows the name to be redefined in an instance, thereby hiding the descriptor—to make an attribute *read-only*, you must define __set__ to catch assignments and raise an exception.

Descriptor method arguments

Before we code anything realistic, let's take a brief look at some fundamentals. All three descriptor methods outlined in the prior section are passed both the descriptor class instance (self) and the instance of the client class to which the descriptor instance is attached (instance).

The __get__ access method additionally receives an owner argument, specifying the class to which the descriptor instance is attached. Its instance argument is either the instance through which the attribute was accessed (for *instance*.attr), or None when the attribute is accessed through the owner class directly (for *class*.attr). The former of these generally computes a value for instance access, and the latter usually returns self if descriptor object access is supported.

For example, in the following, when X.attr is fetched, Python automatically runs the __get__ method of the Descriptor class to which the Subject.attr class attribute is assigned (as with properties, in Python 2.6 we must derive from object to use descriptors here; in 3.0 this is implied, but doesn't hurt):

```
>>> class Descriptor(object):
...     def __get__(self, instance, owner):
...         print(self, instance, owner, sep='\n')
...
>>> class Subject:
...     attr = Descriptor()          # Descriptor instance is class attr
...
>>> X = Subject()

>>> X.attr
<__main__.Descriptor object at 0x0281E690>
<__main__.Subject object at 0x028289B0>
<class '__main__.Subject'>

>>> Subject.attr
<__main__.Descriptor object at 0x0281E690>
None
<class '__main__.Subject'>
```

Notice the arguments automatically passed in to the __get__ method in the first attribute fetch—when X.attr is fetched, it's as though the following translation occurs (though the Subject.attr here doesn't invoke __get__ again):

```
X.attr  ->  Descriptor.__get__(Subject.attr, X, Subject)
```

The descriptor knows it is being accessed directly when its instance argument is None.

Read-only descriptors

As mentioned earlier, unlike with properties, with descriptors simply omitting the __set__ method isn't enough to make an attribute read-only, because the descriptor name can be assigned to an instance. In the following, the attribute assignment to X.a stores a in the instance object X, thereby hiding the descriptor stored in class C:

```
>>> class D:
...     def __get__(*args): print('get')
...
>>> class C:
...     a = D()
...
>>> X = C()
>>> X.a                              # Runs inherited descriptor __get__
get
>>> C.a
get
>>> X.a = 99                         # Stored on X, hiding C.a
>>> X.a
99
>>> list(X.__dict__.keys())
```

```
['a']
>>> Y = C()
>>> Y.a                              # Y still inherits descriptor
get
>>> C.a
get
```

This is the way all instance attribute assignments work in Python, and it allows classes to selectively override class-level defaults in their instances. To make a descriptor-based attribute read-only, catch the assignment in the descriptor class and raise an exception to prevent attribute assignment—when assigning an attribute that is a descriptor, Python effectively bypasses the normal instance-level assignment behavior and routes the operation to the descriptor object:

```
>>> class D:
...     def __get__(*args): print('get')
...     def __set__(*args): raise AttributeError('cannot set')
...
>>> class C:
...     a = D()
...
>>> X = C()
>>> X.a                              # Routed to C.a.__get__
get
>>> X.a = 99                         # Routed to C.a.__set__
AttributeError: cannot set
```

 Also be careful not to confuse the descriptor __delete__ method with the general __del__ method. The former is called on attempts to delete the managed attribute name on an instance of the owner class; the latter is the general instance destructor method, run when an instance of any kind of class is about to be garbage collected. __delete__ is more closely related to the __delattr__ generic attribute deletion method we'll meet later in this chapter. See Chapter 29 for more on operator overloading methods.

A First Example

To see how this all comes together in more realistic code, let's get started with the same first example we wrote for properties. The following defines a descriptor that intercepts access to an attribute named name in its clients. Its methods use their instance argument to access state information in the subject instance, where the name string is actually stored. Like properties, descriptors work properly only for new-style classes, so be sure to derive both classes in the following from object if you're using 2.6:

```
class Name:                          # Use (object) in 2.6
    "name descriptor docs"
    def __get__(self, instance, owner):
        print('fetch...')
        return instance._name
```

```
        def __set__(self, instance, value):
            print('change...')
            instance._name = value
        def __delete__(self, instance):
            print('remove...')
            del instance._name

    class Person:                          # Use (object) in 2.6
        def __init__(self, name):
            self._name = name
        name = Name()                      # Assign descriptor to attr

    bob = Person('Bob Smith')              # bob has a managed attribute
    print(bob.name)                        # Runs Name.__get__
    bob.name = 'Robert Smith'              # Runs Name.__set__
    print(bob.name)
    del bob.name                           # Runs Name.__delete__

    print('-'*20)
    sue = Person('Sue Jones')              # sue inherits descriptor too
    print(sue.name)
    print(Name.__doc__)                    # Or help(Name)
```

Notice in this code how we assign an instance of our descriptor class to a *class attribute* in the client class; because of this, it is inherited by all instances of the class, just like a class's methods. Really, we *must* assign the descriptor to a class attribute like this—it won't work if assigned to a self instance attribute instead. When the descriptor's __get__ method is run, it is passed three objects to define its context:

- self is the Name class instance.
- instance is the Person class instance.
- owner is the Person class.

When this code is run the descriptor's methods intercept accesses to the attribute, much like the property version. In fact, the output is the same again:

```
fetch...
Bob Smith
change...
fetch...
Robert Smith
remove...
--------------------
fetch...
Sue Jones
name descriptor docs
```

Also like in the property example, our descriptor class instance is a class attribute and thus is *inherited* by all instances of the client class and any subclasses. If we change the Person class in our example to the following, for instance, the output of our script is the same:

```
class CalcAttrs:
    X = DescState(2)                    # Descriptor class attr
    Y = 3                               # Class attr
    def __init__(self):
        self.Z = 4                      # Instance attr

obj = CalcAttrs()
print(obj.X, obj.Y, obj.Z)             # X is computed, others are not
obj.X = 5                              # X assignment is intercepted
obj.Y = 6
obj.Z = 7
print(obj.X, obj.Y, obj.Z)
```

This code's value information lives only in the *descriptor*, so there won't be a collision if the same name is used in the client's instance. Notice that only the descriptor attribute is managed here—get and set accesses to X are intercepted, but accesses to Y and Z are not (Y is attached to the client class and Z to the instance). When this code is run, X is computed when fetched:

```
DescState get
20 3 4
DescState set
DescState get
50 6 7
```

It's also feasible for a descriptor to store or use an attribute attached to the client class's instance, instead of itself. Unlike data stored in the descriptor itself, this allows for data that can vary per client class instance. The descriptor in the following example assumes the instance has an attribute _Y attached by the client class, and uses it to compute the value of the attribute it represents:

```
class InstState:                        # Using instance state
    def __get__(self, instance, owner):
        print('InstState get')          # Assume set by client class
        return instance._Y * 100
    def __set__(self, instance, value):
        print('InstState set')
        instance._Y = value

# Client class

class CalcAttrs:
    X = DescState(2)                    # Descriptor class attr
    Y = InstState()                     # Descriptor class attr
    def __init__(self):
        self._Y = 3                     # Instance attr
        self.Z  = 4                     # Instance attr

obj = CalcAttrs()
print(obj.X, obj.Y, obj.Z)             # X and Y are computed, Z is not
obj.X = 5                              # X and Y assignments intercepted
obj.Y = 6
```

```
    obj.Z = 7
    print(obj.X, obj.Y, obj.Z)
```

This time, X and Y are both assigned to descriptors and computed when fetched (X is assigned the descriptor of the prior example). The new descriptor here has no information itself, but it uses an attribute assumed to exist in the instance—that attribute is named _Y, to avoid collisions with the name of the descriptor itself. When this version is run the results are similar, but a second attribute is managed, using state that lives in the instance instead of the descriptor:

```
    DescState get
    InstState get
    20 300 4
    DescState set
    InstState set
    DescState get
    InstState get
    50 600 7
```

Both descriptor and instance state have roles. In fact, this is a general advantage that descriptors have over properties—because they have state of their own, they can easily retain data internally, without adding it to the namespace of the client instance object.

How Properties and Descriptors Relate

As mentioned earlier, properties and descriptors are strongly related—the property built-in is just a convenient way to create a descriptor. Now that you know how both work, you should also be able to see that it's possible to simulate the property built-in with a descriptor class like the following:

```
    class Property:
        def __init__(self, fget=None, fset=None, fdel=None, doc=None):
            self.fget = fget
            self.fset = fset
            self.fdel = fdel                    # Save unbound methods
            self.__doc__ = doc                  # or other callables

        def __get__(self, instance, instancetype=None):
            if instance is None:
                return self
            if self.fget is None:
                raise AttributeError("can't get attribute")
            return self.fget(instance)          # Pass instance to self
                                                # in property accessors
        def __set__(self, instance, value):
            if self.fset is None:
                raise AttributeError("can't set attribute")
            self.fset(instance, value)

        def __delete__(self, instance):
            if self.fdel is None:
                raise AttributeError("can't delete attribute")
            self.fdel(instance)
```

```
class Person:
    def getName(self): ...
    def setName(self, value): ...
    name = Property(getName, setName)          # Use like property()
```

This `Property` class catches attribute accesses with the descriptor protocol and routes requests to functions or methods passed in and saved in descriptor state when the class is created. Attribute fetches, for example, are routed from the `Person` class, to the `Property` class's `__get__` method, and back to the `Person` class's `getName`. With descriptors, this "just works."

Note that this descriptor class equivalent only handles basic property usage, though; to use @ *decorator syntax* to also specify set and delete operations, our `Property` class would also have to be extended with `setter` and `deleter` methods, which would save the decorated accessor function and return the property object (`self` should suffice). Since the `property` built-in already does this, we'll omit a formal coding of this extension here.

Also note that descriptors are used to implement Python's `__slots__`; instance attribute dictionaries are avoided by intercepting slot names with descriptors stored at the class level. See Chapter 31 for more on slots.

 In Chapter 38, we'll also make use of descriptors to implement function decorators that apply to both functions and methods. As you'll see there, because descriptors receive both descriptor and subject class instances they work well in this role, though nested functions are usually a simpler solution.

__getattr__ and __getattribute__

So far, we've studied properties and descriptors—tools for managing specific attributes. The `__getattr__` and `__getattribute__` operator overloading methods provide still other ways to intercept attribute fetches for class instances. Like properties and descriptors, they allow us to insert code to be run automatically when attributes are accessed; as we'll see, though, these two methods can be used in more general ways.

Attribute fetch interception comes in two flavors, coded with two different methods:

- `__getattr__` is run for *undefined* attributes—that is, attributes not stored on an instance or inherited from one of its classes.

- `__getattribute__` is run for *every* attribute, so when using it you must be cautious to avoid recursive loops by passing attribute accesses to a superclass.

We met the former of these in Chapter 29; it's available for all Python versions. The latter of these is available for new-style classes in 2.6, and for all (implicitly new-style) classes in 3.0. These two methods are representatives of a set of attribute interception

---

methods that also includes `__setattr__` and `__delattr__`. Because these methods have similar roles, we will generally treat them as a single topic here.

Unlike properties and descriptors, these methods are part of Python's *operator overloading* protocol—specially named methods of a class, inherited by subclasses, and run automatically when instances are used in the implied built-in operation. Like all methods of a class, they each receive a first `self` argument when called, giving access to any required instance state information or other methods of the class.

The `__getattr__` and `__getattribute__` methods are also more *generic* than properties and descriptors—they can be used to intercept access to any (or even all) instance attribute fetches, not just the specific name to which they are assigned. Because of this, these two methods are well suited to general *delegation*-based coding patterns—they can be used to implement wrapper objects that manage all attribute accesses for an embedded object. By contrast, we must define one property or descriptor for every attribute we wish to intercept.

Finally, these two methods are more *narrowly focused* than the alternatives we considered earlier: they intercept attribute fetches only, not assignments. To also catch attribute changes by assignment, we must code a `__setattr__` method—an operator overloading method run for every attribute fetch, which must take care to avoid recursive loops by routing attribute assignments through the instance namespace dictionary.

Although much less common, we can also code a `__delattr__` overloading method (which must avoid looping in the same way) to intercept attribute deletions. By contrast, properties and descriptors catch get, set, *and* delete operations by design.

Most of these operator overloading methods were introduced earlier in the book; here, we'll expand on their usage and study their roles in larger contexts.

The Basics

`__getattr__` and `__setattr__` were introduced in Chapters 29 and 31, and `__getattribute__` was mentioned briefly in Chapter 31. In short, if a class defines or inherits the following methods, they will be run automatically when an instance is used in the context described by the comments to the right:

```
def __getattr__(self, name):          # On undefined attribute fetch [obj.name]
def __getattribute__(self, name):      # On all attribute fetch [obj.name]
def __setattr__(self, name, value):    # On all attribute assignment [obj.name=value]
def __delattr__(self, name):           # On all attribute deletion [del obj.name]
```

In all of these, `self` is the subject instance object as usual, `name` is the string name of the attribute being accessed, and `value` is the object being assigned to the attribute. The two get methods normally return an attribute's value, and the other two return nothing (`None`). For example, to catch every attribute fetch, we can use either of the first two methods above, and to catch every attribute assignment we can use the third:

```
class Catcher:
    def __getattr__(self, name):
        print('Get:', name)
    def __setattr__(self, name, value):
        print('Set:', name, value)

X = Catcher()
X.job                          # Prints "Get: job"
X.pay                          # Prints "Get: pay"
X.pay = 99                     # Prints "Set: pay 99"
```

Such a coding structure can be used to implement the *delegation* design pattern we met earlier, in Chapter 30. Because all attribute are routed to our interception methods generically, we can validate and pass them along to embedded, managed objects. The following class (borrowed from Chapter 30), for example, traces *every* attribute fetch made to another object passed to the wrapper class:

```
class Wrapper:
    def __init__(self, object):
        self.wrapped = object          # Save object
    def __getattr__(self, attrname):
        print('Trace:', attrname)      # Trace fetch
        return getattr(self.wrapped, attrname)   # Delegate fetch
```

There is no such analog for properties and descriptors, short of coding accessors for every possible attribute in every possibly wrapped object.

Avoiding loops in attribute interception methods

These methods are generally straightforward to use; their only complex part is the potential for *looping* (a.k.a. recursing). Because __getattr__ is called for undefined attributes only, it can freely fetch other attributes within its own code. However, because __getattribute__ and __setattr__ are run for all attributes, their code needs to be careful when accessing other attributes to avoid calling themselves again and triggering a recursive loop.

For example, another attribute fetch run inside a __getattribute__ method's code will trigger __getattribute__ again, and the code will loop until memory is exhausted:

```
    def __getattribute__(self, name):
        x = self.other                     # LOOPS!
```

To work around this, route the fetch through a higher superclass instead to skip this level's version—the object class is always a superclass, and it serves well in this role:

```
    def __getattribute__(self, name):
        x = object.__getattribute__(self, 'other')   # Force higher to avoid me
```

For __setattr__, the situation is similar; assigning any attribute inside this method triggers __setattr__ again and creates a similar loop:

```
    def __setattr__(self, name, value):
        self.other = value                 # LOOPS!
```

To work around this problem, assign the attribute as a key in the instance's __dict__ namespace dictionary instead. This avoids direct attribute assignment:

```
def __setattr__(self, name, value):
    self.__dict__['other'] = value        # Use attr dict to avoid me
```

Although it's a less common approach, __setattr__ can also pass its own attribute assignments to a higher superclass to avoid looping, just like __getattribute__:

```
def __setattr__(self, name, value):
    object.__setattr__(self, 'other', value)   # Force higher to avoid me
```

By contrast, though, we *cannot* use the __dict__ trick to avoid loops in __getattribute__:

```
def __getattribute__(self, name):
    x = self.__dict__['other']            # LOOPS!
```

Fetching the __dict__ attribute itself triggers __getattribute__ again, causing a recursive loop. Strange but true!

The __delattr__ method is rarely used in practice, but when it is, it is called for every attribute deletion (just as __setattr__ is called for every attribute assignment). Therefore, you must take care to avoid loops when deleting attributes, by using the same techniques: namespace dictionaries or superclass method calls.

A First Example

All this is not nearly as complicated as the prior section may have implied. To see how to put these ideas to work, here is the same first example we used for properties and descriptors in action again, this time implemented with attribute operator overloading methods. Because these methods are so generic, we test attribute names here to know when a managed attribute is being accessed; others are allowed to pass normally:

```
class Person:
    def __init__(self, name):            # On [Person()]
        self._name = name                # Triggers __setattr__!

    def __getattr__(self, attr):         # On [obj.undefined]
        if attr == 'name':               # Intercept name: not stored
            print('fetch...')
            return self._name            # Does not loop: real attr
        else:                            # Others are errors
            raise AttributeError(attr)

    def __setattr__(self, attr, value):  # On [obj.any = value]
        if attr == 'name':
            print('change...')
            attr = '_name'               # Set internal name
        self.__dict__[attr] = value      # Avoid looping here

    def __delattr__(self, attr):         # On [del obj.any]
        if attr == 'name':
```

```
                  print('remove...')
                  attr = '_name'                    # Avoid looping here too
             del self.__dict__[attr]                 # but much less common

    bob = Person('Bob Smith')                 # bob has a managed attribute
    print(bob.name)                           # Runs __getattr__
    bob.name = 'Robert Smith'                 # Runs __setattr__
    print(bob.name)
    del bob.name                              # Runs __delattr__

    print('-'*20)
    sue = Person('Sue Jones')                 # sue inherits property too
    print(sue.name)
    #print(Person.name.__doc__)               # No equivalent here
```

Notice that the attribute assignment in the __init__ constructor triggers __setattr__ too—this method catches every attribute assignment, even those within the class itself. When this code is run, the same output is produced, but this time it's the result of Python's normal operator overloading mechanism and our attribute interception methods:

```
fetch...
Bob Smith
change...
fetch...
Robert Smith
remove...
--------------------
fetch...
Sue Jones
```

Also note that, unlike with properties and descriptors, there's no direct notion of specifying *documentation* for our attribute here; managed attributes exist within the code of our interception methods, not as distinct objects.

To achieve exactly the same results with __getattribute__, replace __getattr__ in the example with the following; because it catches all attribute fetches, this version must be careful to avoid looping by passing new fetches to a superclass, and it can't generally assume unknown names are errors:

```
    # Replace __getattr__ with this

    def __getattribute__(self, attr):                 # On [obj.any]
        if attr == 'name':                            # Intercept all names
            print('fetch...')
            attr = '_name'                            # Map to internal name
        return object.__getattribute__(self, attr)    # Avoid looping here
```

This example is equivalent to that coded for properties and descriptors, but it's a bit artificial, and it doesn't really highlight these tools in practice. Because they are generic, __getattr__ and __getattribute__ are probably more commonly used in delegation-base code (as sketched earlier), where attribute access is validated and routed to an embedded object. Where just a *single* attribute must be managed, properties and descriptors might do as well or better.

Computed Attributes

As before, our prior example doesn't really do anything but trace attribute fetches; it's not much more work to compute an attribute's value when fetched. As for properties and descriptors, the following creates a virtual attribute X that runs a calculation when fetched:

```
class AttrSquare:
    def __init__(self, start):
        self.value = start                      # Triggers __setattr__!

    def __getattr__(self, attr):                # On undefined attr fetch
        if attr == 'X':
            return self.value ** 2              # value is not undefined
        else:
            raise AttributeError(attr)

    def __setattr__(self, attr, value):         # On all attr assignments
        if attr == 'X':
            attr = 'value'
        self.__dict__[attr] = value

A = AttrSquare(3)        # 2 instances of class with overloading
B = AttrSquare(32)       # Each has different state information

print(A.X)               # 3 ** 2
A.X = 4
print(A.X)               # 4 ** 2
print(B.X)               # 32 ** 2
```

Running this code results in the same output that we got earlier when using properties and descriptors, but this script's mechanics are based on generic attribute interception methods:

```
9
16
1024
```

As before, we can achieve the same effect with __getattribute__ instead of __getattr__; the following replaces the fetch method with a __getattribute__ and changes the __setattr__ assignment method to avoid looping by using direct superclass method calls instead of __dict__ keys:

```
class AttrSquare:
    def __init__(self, start):
        self.value = start                      # Triggers __setattr__!

    def __getattribute__(self, attr):           # On all attr fetches
        if attr == 'X':
            return self.value ** 2              # Triggers __getattribute__ again!
```

```
        else:
            return object.__getattribute__(self, attr)

    def __setattr__(self, attr, value):        # On all attr assignments
        if attr == 'X':
            attr = 'value'
        object.__setattr__(self, attr, value)
```

When this version is run, the results are the same again. Notice the implicit routing going on in inside this class's methods:

- self.value=start inside the constructor triggers __setattr__
- self.value inside __getattribute__ triggers __getattribute__ again

In fact, __getattribute__ is run *twice* each time we fetch attribute X. This doesn't happen in the __getattr__ version, because the value attribute is not undefined. If you care about speed and want to avoid this, change __getattribute__ to use the superclass to fetch value as well:

```
    def __getattribute__(self, attr):
        if attr == 'X':
            return object.__getattribute__(self, 'value') ** 2
```

Of course, this still incurs a call to the superclass method, but not an additional recursive call before we get there. Add print calls to these methods to trace how and when they run.

__getattr__ and __getattribute__ Compared

To summarize the coding differences between __getattr__ and __getattribute__, the following example uses both to implement three attributes—attr1 is a class attribute, attr2 is an instance attribute, and attr3 is a virtual managed attribute computed when fetched:

```
class GetAttr:
    attr1 = 1
    def __init__(self):
        self.attr2 = 2
    def __getattr__(self, attr):        # On undefined attrs only
        print('get: ' + attr)          # Not attr1: inherited from class
        return 3                        # Not attr2: stored on instance

X = GetAttr()
print(X.attr1)
print(X.attr2)
print(X.attr3)

print('-'*40)

class GetAttribute(object):             # (object) needed in 2.6 only
    attr1 = 1
    def __init__(self):
        self.attr2 = 2
```

```
        def __getattribute__(self, attr):           # On all attr fetches
            print('get: ' + attr)                    # Use superclass to avoid looping here
            if attr == 'attr3':
                return 3
            else:
                return object.__getattribute__(self, attr)

    X = GetAttribute()
    print(X.attr1)
    print(X.attr2)
    print(X.attr3)
```

When run, the __getattr__ version intercepts only attr3 accesses, because it is undefined. The __getattribute__ version, on the other hand, intercepts all attribute fetches
and must route those it does not manage to the superclass fetcher to avoid loops:

```
1
2
get: attr3
3
----------------------------------------
get: attr1
1
get: attr2
2
get: attr3
3
```

Although __getattribute__ can catch more attribute fetches than __getattr__, in practice they are often just variations on a theme—if attributes are not physically stored,
the two have the same effect.

Management Techniques Compared

To summarize the coding differences in all four attribute management schemes we've
seen in this chapter, let's quickly step through a more comprehensive
computed-attribute example using each technique. The following version uses properties to intercept and calculate attributes named square and cube. Notice how their
base values are stored in names that begin with an underscore, so they don't clash with
the names of the properties themselves:

```
# 2 dynamically computed attributes with properties

class Powers:
    def __init__(self, square, cube):
        self._square = square          # _square is the base value
        self._cube  = cube             # square is the property name

    def getSquare(self):
        return self._square ** 2
    def setSquare(self, value):
        self._square = value
    square = property(getSquare, setSquare)
```

```
        def getCube(self):
            return self._cube ** 3
        cube = property(getCube)

X = Powers(3, 4)
print(X.square)          # 3 ** 2 = 9
print(X.cube)            # 4 ** 3 = 64
X.square = 5
print(X.square)          # 5 ** 2 = 25
```

To do the same with descriptors, we define the attributes with complete classes. Note that these descriptors store base values as instance state, so they must use leading underscores again so as not to clash with the names of descriptors (as we'll see in the final example of this chapter, we could avoid this renaming requirement by storing base values as descriptor state instead):

```
# Same, but with descriptors

class DescSquare:
    def __get__(self, instance, owner):
        return instance._square ** 2
    def __set__(self, instance, value):
        instance._square = value

class DescCube:
    def __get__(self, instance, owner):
        return instance._cube ** 3

class Powers:                                    # Use (object) in 2.6
    square = DescSquare()
    cube   = DescCube()
    def __init__(self, square, cube):
        self._square = square                    # "self.square = square" works too,
        self._cube   = cube                      # because it triggers desc __set__!

X = Powers(3, 4)
print(X.square)          # 3 ** 2 = 9
print(X.cube)            # 4 ** 3 = 64
X.square = 5
print(X.square)          # 5 ** 2 = 25
```

To achieve the same result with __getattr__ fetch interception, we again store base values with underscore-prefixed names so that accesses to managed names are undefined and thus invoke our method; we also need to code a __setattr__ to intercept assignments, and take care to avoid its potential for looping:

```
# Same, but with generic __getattr__ undefined attribute interception

class Powers:
    def __init__(self, square, cube):
        self._square = square
        self._cube   = cube

    def __getattr__(self, name):
```

```
            if name == 'square':
                return self._square ** 2
            elif name == 'cube':
                return self._cube ** 3
            else:
                raise TypeError('unknown attr:' + name)

        def __setattr__(self, name, value):
            if name == 'square':
                self.__dict__['_square'] = value
            else:
                self.__dict__[name] = value

X = Powers(3, 4)
print(X.square)          # 3 ** 2 = 9
print(X.cube)            # 4 ** 3 = 64
X.square = 5
print(X.square)          # 5 ** 2 = 25
```

The final option, coding this with __getattribute__, is similar to the prior version. Because we catch every attribute now, though, we must route base value fetches to a superclass to avoid looping:

```
# Same, but with generic __getattribute__ all attribute interception

class Powers:
    def __init__(self, square, cube):
        self._square = square
        self._cube   = cube
    def __getattribute__(self, name):
        if name == 'square':
            return object.__getattribute__(self, '_square') ** 2
        elif name == 'cube':
            return object.__getattribute__(self, '_cube') ** 3
        else:
            return object.__getattribute__(self, name)
    def __setattr__(self, name, value):
        if name == 'square':
            self.__dict__['_square'] = value
        else:
            self.__dict__[name] = value

X = Powers(3, 4)
print(X.square)          # 3 ** 2 = 9
print(X.cube)            # 4 ** 3 = 64
X.square = 5
print(X.square)          # 5 ** 2 = 25
```

As you can see, each technique takes a different form in code, but all four produce the same result when run:

```
9
64
25
```

For more on how these alternatives compare, and other coding options, stay tuned for a more realistic application of them in the attribute validation example in the section "Example: Attribute Validations" on page 975. First, though, we need to study a pitfall associated with two of these tools.

Intercepting Built-in Operation Attributes

When I introduced __getattr__ and __getattribute__, I stated that they intercept undefined and all attribute fetches, respectively, which makes them ideal for delegation-based coding patterns. While this is true for normally named attributes, their behavior needs some additional clarification: for method-name attributes implicitly fetched by built-in operations, these methods may *not be run at all*. This means that operator overloading method calls cannot be delegated to wrapped objects unless wrapper classes somehow redefine these methods themselves.

For example, attribute fetches for the __str__, __add__, and __getitem__ methods run implicitly by printing, + expressions, and indexing, respectively, are not routed to the generic attribute interception methods in 3.0. Specifically:

- In Python 3.0, *neither* __getattr__ nor __getattribute__ is run for such attributes.
- In Python 2.6, __getattr__ *is* run for such attributes if they are undefined in the class.
- In Python 2.6, __getattribute__ is available for new-style classes only and works as it does in 3.0.

In other words, in Python 3.0 classes (and 2.6 new-style classes), there is no direct way to generically intercept built-in operations like printing and addition. In Python 2.X, the methods such operations invoke are looked up at runtime in instances, like all other attributes; in Python 3.0 such methods are looked up in *classes* instead.

This change makes delegation-based coding patterns more complex in 3.0, since they cannot generically intercept operator overloading method calls and route them to an embedded object. This is not a showstopper—wrapper classes can work around this constraint by redefining all relevant operator overloading methods in the wrapper itself, in order to delegate calls. These extra methods can be added either manually, with tools, or by definition in and inheritance from common superclasses. This does, however, make wrappers more work than they used to be when operator overloading methods are a part of a wrapped object's interface.

Keep in mind that this issue applies only to __getattr__ and __getattribute__. Because properties and descriptors are defined for specific attributes only, they don't really apply to delegation-based classes at all—a single property or descriptor cannot be used to intercept arbitrary attributes. Moreover, a class that defines *both* operator overloading methods and attribute interception will work correctly, regardless of the type of attribute interception defined. Our concern here is only with classes that do not have operator overloading methods defined, but try to intercept them generically.

Consider the following example, the file *getattr.py*, which tests various attribute types and built-in operations on instances of classes containing __getattr__ and __getattribute__ methods:

```
class GetAttr:
    eggs = 88                    # eggs stored on class, spam on instance
    def __init__(self):
        self.spam = 77
    def __len__(self):           # len here, else __getattr__ called with __len__
        print('__len__: 42')
        return 42
    def __getattr__(self, attr):           # Provide __str__ if asked, else dummy func
        print('getattr: ' + attr)
        if attr == '__str__':
            return lambda *args: '[Getattr str]'
        else:
            return lambda *args: None

class GetAttribute(object):      # object required in 2.6, implied in 3.0
    eggs = 88                    # In 2.6 all are isinstance(object) auto
    def __init__(self):          # But must derive to get new-style tools,
        self.spam = 77           # incl __getattribute__, some __X__ defaults
    def __len__(self):
        print('__len__: 42')
        return 42
    def __getattribute__(self, attr):
        print('getattribute: ' + attr)
        if attr == '__str__':
            return lambda *args: '[GetAttribute str]'
        else:
            return lambda *args: None

for Class in GetAttr, GetAttribute:
    print('\n' + Class.__name__.ljust(50, '='))

    X = Class()
    X.eggs                       # Class attr
    X.spam                       # Instance attr
    X.other                      # Missing attr
    len(X)                       # __len__ defined explicitly

    try:                         # New-styles must support [], +, call directly: redefine
        X[0]                     # __getitem__?
    except:
        print('fail []')

    try:
        X + 99                   # __add__?
    except:
        print('fail +')

    try:
        X()                      # __call__? (implicit via built-in)
    except:
        print('fail ()')
```

```
X.__call__()              # __call__? (explicit, not inherited)

print(X.__str__())        # __str__? (explicit, inherited from type)
print(X)                  # __str__? (implicit via built-in)
```

When run under Python 2.6, __getattr__ *does* receive a variety of implicit attribute fetches for built-in operations, because Python looks up such attributes in instances normally. Conversely, __getattribute__ is *not* run for any of the operator overloading names, because such names are looked up in classes only:

```
C:\misc> c:\python26\python getattr.py

GetAttr=============================================
getattr: other
__len__: 42
getattr: __getitem__
getattr: __coerce__
getattr: __add__
getattr: __call__
getattr: __call__
getattr: __str__
[Getattr str]
getattr: __str__
[Getattr str]

GetAttribute========================================
getattribute: eggs
getattribute: spam
getattribute: other
__len__: 42
fail []
fail +
fail ()
getattribute: __call__
getattribute: __str__
[GetAttribute str]
<__main__.GetAttribute object at 0x025EA1D0>
```

Note how __getattr__ intercepts both implicit and explicit fetches of __call__ and __str__ in 2.6 here. By contrast, __getattribute__ fails to catch implicit fetches of either attribute name for built-in operations.

Really, the __getattribute__ case is the same in 2.6 as it is in 3.0, because in 2.6 classes must be made new-style by deriving from object to use this method. This code's object derivation is optional in 3.0 because all classes are new-style.

When run under Python 3.0, though, results for __getattr__ differ—*none* of the implicitly run operator overloading methods trigger *either* attribute interception method when their attributes are fetched by built-in operations. Python 3.0 skips the normal instance lookup mechanism when resolving such names:

```
C:\misc> c:\python30\python getattr.py

GetAttr=============================================
```

```
getattr: other
__len__: 42
fail []
fail +
fail ()
getattr: __call__
<__main__.GetAttr object at 0x025D17F0>
<__main__.GetAttr object at 0x025D17F0>

GetAttribute=====================================
getattribute: eggs
getattribute: spam
getattribute: other
__len__: 42
fail []
fail +
fail ()
getattribute: __call__
getattribute: __str__
[GetAttribute str]
<__main__.GetAttribute object at 0x025D1870>
```

We can trace these outputs back to prints in the script to see how this works:

- __str__ access fails to be caught twice by __getattr__ in 3.0: once for the built-in print, and once for explicit fetches because a default is inherited from the class (really, from the built-in object, which is a superclass to every class).

- __str__ fails to be caught only once by the __getattribute__ catchall, during the built-in print operation; explicit fetches bypass the inherited version.

- __call__ fails to be caught in both schemes in 3.0 for built-in call expressions, but it is intercepted by both when fetched explicitly; unlike with __str__, there is no inherited __call__ default to defeat __getattr__.

- __len__ is caught by both classes, simply because it is an explicitly defined method in the classes themselves—its name it is not routed to either __getattr__ or __get attribute__ in 3.0 if we delete the class's __len__ methods.

- All other built-in operations fail to be intercepted by both schemes in 3.0.

Again, the net effect is that operator overloading methods implicitly run by built-in operations are never routed through either attribute interception method in 3.0: Python 3.0 searches for such attributes in *classes* and skips instance lookup entirely.

This makes delegation-based wrapper classes more difficult to code in 3.0—if wrapped classes may contain operator overloading methods, those methods must be redefined redundantly in the wrapper class in order to delegate to the wrapped object. In general delegation tools, this can add many extra methods.

Of course, the addition of such methods can be partly automated by tools that augment classes with new methods (the class decorators and metaclasses of the next two chapters might help here). Moreover, a superclass might be able to define all these extra methods once, for inheritance in delegation-based classes. Still, delegation coding patterns require extra work in 3.0.

For a more realistic illustration of this phenomenon as well as its workaround, see the Private decorator example in the following chapter. There, we'll see that it's also possible to insert a __getattribute__ in the client class to retain its original type, although this method still won't be called for operator overloading methods; printing still runs a __str__ defined in such a class directly, for example, instead of routing the request through __getattribute__.

As another example, the next section resurrects our class tutorial example. Now that you understand how attribute interception works, I'll be able to explain one of its stranger bits.

 For an example of this 3.0 change at work in Python itself, see the discussion of the 3.0 os.popen object in Chapter 14. Because it is implemented with a wrapper that uses __getattr__ to delegate attribute fetches to an embedded object, it does not intercept the next(X) built-in iterator function in Python 3.0, which is defined to run __next__. It does, however, intercept and delegate explicit X.__next__() calls, because these are not routed through the built-in and are not inherited from a superclass like __str__ is.

This is equivalent to __call__ in our example—implicit calls for built-ins do not trigger __getattr__, but explicit calls to names not inherited from the class type do. In other words, this change impacts not only our delegators, but also those in the Python standard library! Given the scope of this change, it's possible that this behavior may evolve in the future, so be sure to verify this issue in later releases.

Delegation-Based Managers Revisited

The object-oriented tutorial of Chapter 27 presented a Manager class that used object embedding and method delegation to customize its superclass, rather than inheritance. Here is the code again for reference, with some irrelevant testing removed:

```
class Person:
    def __init__(self, name, job=None, pay=0):
        self.name = name
        self.job  = job
        self.pay  = pay
    def lastName(self):
        return self.name.split()[-1]
    def giveRaise(self, percent):
        self.pay = int(self.pay * (1 + percent))
    def __str__(self):
        return '[Person: %s, %s]' % (self.name, self.pay)

class Manager:
    def __init__(self, name, pay):
```

```
            self.person = Person(name, 'mgr', pay)        # Embed a Person object
        def giveRaise(self, percent, bonus=.10):
            self.person.giveRaise(percent + bonus)         # Intercept and delegate
        def __getattr__(self, attr):
            return getattr(self.person, attr)              # Delegate all other attrs
        def __str__(self):
            return str(self.person)                        # Must overload again (in 3.0)

    if __name__ == '__main__':
        sue = Person('Sue Jones', job='dev', pay=100000)
        print(sue.lastName())
        sue.giveRaise(.10)
        print(sue)
        tom = Manager('Tom Jones', 50000)         # Manager.__init__
        print(tom.lastName())                     # Manager.__getattr__ -> Person.lastName
        tom.giveRaise(.10)                        # Manager.giveRaise -> Person.giveRaise
        print(tom)                               # Manager.__str__ -> Person.__str__
```

Comments at the end of this file show which methods are invoked for a line's operation. In particular, notice how lastName calls are undefined in Manager, and thus are routed into the generic __getattr__ and from there on to the embedded Person object. Here is the script's output—Sue receives a 10% raise from Person, but Tom gets 20% because giveRaise is customized in Manager:

```
C:\misc> c:\python30\python person.py
Jones
[Person: Sue Jones, 110000]
Jones
[Person: Tom Jones, 60000]
```

By contrast, though, notice what occurs when we *print* a Manager at the end of the script: the wrapper class's __str__ is invoked, and it delegates to the embedded Person object's __str__. With that in mind, watch what happens if we *delete* the Manager.__str__ method in this code:

```
# Delete the Manager __str__ method

class Manager:
    def __init__(self, name, pay):
        self.person = Person(name, 'mgr', pay)        # Embed a Person object
    def giveRaise(self, percent, bonus=.10):
        self.person.giveRaise(percent + bonus)         # Intercept and delegate
    def __getattr__(self, attr):
        return getattr(self.person, attr)              # Delegate all other attrs
```

Now printing does *not* route its attribute fetch through the generic __getattr__ interceptor under Python 3.0 for Manager objects. Instead, a default __str__ display method inherited from the class's implicit object superclass is looked up and run (sue still prints correctly, because Person has an explicit __str__):

```
C:\misc> c:\python30\python person.py
Jones
[Person: Sue Jones, 110000]
```

```
Jones
<__main__.Manager object at 0x02A5AE30>
```

Curiously, running without a __str__ like this *does* trigger __getattr__ in Python 2.6, because operator overloading attributes are routed through this method, and classes do not inherit a default for __str__:

```
C:\misc> c:\python26\python person.py
Jones
[Person: Sue Jones, 110000]
Jones
[Person: Tom Jones, 60000]
```

Switching to __getattribute__ won't help 3.0 here either—like __getattr__, it is *not* run for operator overloading attributes implied by built-in operations in either Python 2.6 or 3.0:

```
# Replace __getattr_ with __getattribute__

class Manager:                                      # Use (object) in 2.6
    def __init__(self, name, pay):
        self.person = Person(name, 'mgr', pay)      # Embed a Person object
    def giveRaise(self, percent, bonus=.10):
        self.person.giveRaise(percent + bonus)      # Intercept and delegate
    def __getattribute__(self, attr):
        print('**', attr)
        if attr in ['person', 'giveRaise']:
            return object.__getattribute__(self, attr)   # Fetch my attrs
        else:
            return getattr(self.person, attr)            # Delegate all others
```

Regardless of which attribute interception method is used in 3.0, we still must include a redefined __str__ in Manager (as shown above) in order to intercept printing operations and route them to the embedded Person object:

```
C:\misc> c:\python30\python person.py
Jones
[Person: Sue Jones, 110000]
** lastName
** person
Jones
** giveRaise
** person
<__main__.Manager object at 0x028E0590>
```

Notice that __getattribute__ gets called *twice* here for methods—once for the method name, and again for the self.person embedded object fetch. We could avoid that with a different coding, but we would still have to redefine __str__ to catch printing, albeit differently here (self.person would cause this __getattribute__ to fail):

```
# Code __getattribute__ differently to minimize extra calls

class Manager:
    def __init__(self, name, pay):
        self.person = Person(name, 'mgr', pay)
```

```
    def __getattribute__(self, attr):
        print('**', attr)
        person = object.__getattribute__(self, 'person')
        if attr == 'giveRaise':
            return lambda percent: person.giveRaise(percent+.10)
        else:
            return getattr(person, attr)
    def __str__(self):
        person = object.__getattribute__(self, 'person')
        return str(person)
```

When this alternative runs, our object prints properly, but only because we've added an explicit __str__ in the wrapper—this attribute is still not routed to our generic attribute interception method:

```
Jones
[Person: Sue Jones, 110000]
** lastName
Jones
** giveRaise
[Person: Tom Jones, 60000]
```

That short story here is that delegation-based classes like Manager must redefine some operator overloading methods (like __str__) to route them to embedded objects in Python 3.0, but not in Python 2.6 unless new-style classes are used. Our only direct options seem to be using __getattr__ and Python 2.6, or redefining operator overloading methods in wrapper classes redundantly in 3.0.

Again, this isn't an impossible task; many wrappers can predict the set of operator overloading methods required, and tools and superclasses can automate part of this task. Moreover, not all classes use operator overloading methods (indeed, most application classes usually should not). It is, however, something to keep in mind for delegation coding models used in Python 3.0; when operator overloading methods are part of an object's interface, wrappers must accommodate them portably by redefining them locally.

Example: Attribute Validations

To close out this chapter, let's turn to a more realistic example, coded in all four of our attribute management schemes. The example we will use defines a CardHolder object with four attributes, three of which are managed. The managed attributes validate or transform values when fetched or stored. All four versions produce the same results for the same test code, but they implement their attributes in very different ways. The examples are included largely for self-study; although I won't go through their code in detail, they all use concepts we've already explored in this chapter.

Using Properties to Validate

Our first coding uses properties to manage three attributes. As usual, we could use simple methods instead of managed attributes, but properties help if we have been using attributes in existing code already. Properties run code automatically on attribute access, but are focused on a specific set of attributes; they cannot be used to intercept all attributes generically.

To understand this code, it's crucial to notice that the attribute assignments inside the __init__ constructor method trigger property setter methods too. When this method assigns to self.name, for example, it automatically invokes the setName method, which transforms the value and assigns it to an instance attribute called __name so it won't clash with the property's name.

This renaming (sometimes called *name mangling*) is necessary because properties use common instance state and have none of their own. Data is stored in an attribute called __name, and the attribute called name is always a property, not data.

In the end, this class manages attributes called name, age, and acct; allows the attribute addr to be accessed directly; and provides a read-only attribute called remain that is entirely virtual and computed on demand. For comparison purposes, this property-based coding weighs in at 39 lines of code:

```
class CardHolder:
    acctlen = 8                                    # Class data
    retireage = 59.5

    def __init__(self, acct, name, age, addr):
        self.acct = acct                           # Instance data
        self.name = name                           # These trigger prop setters too
        self.age  = age                            # __X mangled to have class name
        self.addr = addr                           # addr is not managed
                                                   # remain has no data
    def getName(self):
        return self.__name
    def setName(self, value):
        value = value.lower().replace(' ', '_')
        self.__name = value
    name = property(getName, setName)

    def getAge(self):
        return self.__age
    def setAge(self, value):
        if value < 0 or value > 150:
            raise ValueError('invalid age')
        else:
            self.__age = value
    age = property(getAge, setAge)

    def getAcct(self):
        return self.__acct[:-3] + '***'
    def setAcct(self, value):
```

```
            value = value.replace('-', '')
            if len(value) != self.acctlen:
                raise TypeError('invald acct number')
            else:
                self.__acct = value
    acct = property(getAcct, setAcct)

    def remainGet(self):                    # Could be a method, not attr
        return self.retireage - self.age    # Unless already using as attr
    remain = property(remainGet)
```

Self-test code

The following code tests our class; add this to the bottom of your file, or place the class in a module and import it first. We'll use this same testing code for all four versions of this example. When it runs, we make two instances of our managed-attribute class and fetch and change its various attributes. Operations expected to fail are wrapped in try statements:

```
bob = CardHolder('1234-5678', 'Bob Smith', 40, '123 main st')
print(bob.acct, bob.name, bob.age, bob.remain, bob.addr, sep=' / ')
bob.name = 'Bob Q. Smith'
bob.age  = 50
bob.acct = '23-45-67-89'
print(bob.acct, bob.name, bob.age, bob.remain, bob.addr, sep=' / ')

sue = CardHolder('5678-12-34', 'Sue Jones', 35, '124 main st')
print(sue.acct, sue.name, sue.age, sue.remain, sue.addr, sep=' / ')
try:
    sue.age = 200
except:
    print('Bad age for Sue')

try:
    sue.remain = 5
except:
    print("Can't set sue.remain")

try:
    sue.acct = '1234567'
except:
    print('Bad acct for Sue')
```

Here is the output of our self-test code; again, this is the same for all versions of this example. Trace through this code to see how the class's methods are invoked; accounts are displayed with some digits hidden, names are converted to a standard format, and time remaining until retirement is computed when fetched using a class attribute cutoff:

```
12345*** / bob_smith / 40 / 19.5 / 123 main st
23456*** / bob_q._smith / 50 / 9.5 / 123 main st
56781*** / sue_jones / 35 / 24.5 / 124 main st
Bad age for Sue
Can't set sue.remain
Bad acct for Sue
```

Using Descriptors to Validate

Now, let's recode our example using descriptors instead of properties. As we've seen, descriptors are very similar to properties in terms of functionality and roles; in fact, properties are basically a restricted form of descriptor. Like properties, descriptors are designed to handle specific attributes, not generic attribute access. Unlike properties, descriptors have their own state, and they're a more general scheme.

To understand this code, it's again important to notice that the attribute assignments inside the __init__ constructor method trigger descriptor __set__ methods. When the constructor method assigns to self.name, for example, it automatically invokes the Name.__set__() method, which transforms the value and assigns it to a descriptor attribute called name.

Unlike in the prior property-based variant, though, in this case the actual name value is attached to the *descriptor* object, not the client class instance. Although we could store this value in either instance or descriptor state, the latter avoids the need to mangle names with underscores to avoid collisions. In the CardHolder client class, the attribute called name is always a descriptor object, not data. The downside of this scheme is that state stored inside a descriptor itself is class-level data which is effectively shared by all client class instances, and so cannot vary between them.

In the end, this class implements the same attributes as the prior version: it manages attributes called name, age, and acct; allows the attribute addr to be accessed directly; and provides a read-only attribute called remain that is entirely virtual and computed on demand. Notice how we must catch assignments to the remain name in its descriptor and raise an exception; as we learned earlier, if we did not do this, assigning to this attribute of an instance would silently create an instance attribute that hides the class attribute descriptor. For comparison purposes, this descriptor-based coding takes 45 lines of code:

```
class CardHolder:
    acctlen = 8                              # Class data
    retireage = 59.5

    def __init__(self, acct, name, age, addr):
        self.acct = acct                     # Instance data
        self.name = name                     # These trigger __set__ calls too
        self.age  = age                      # __X not needed: in descriptor
        self.addr = addr                     # addr is not managed
                                             # remain has no data
    class Name:
        def __get__(self, instance, owner):  # Class names: CardHolder locals
            return self.name
        def __set__(self, instance, value):
            value = value.lower().replace(' ', '_')
            self.name = value
    name = Name()

    class Age:
```

```
        def __get__(self, instance, owner):
            return self.age                            # Use descriptor data
        def __set__(self, instance, value):
            if value < 0 or value > 150:
                raise ValueError('invalid age')
            else:
                self.age = value
    age = Age()

class Acct:
    def __get__(self, instance, owner):
        return self.acct[:-3] + '***'
    def __set__(self, instance, value):
        value = value.replace('-', '')
        if len(value) != instance.acctlen:            # Use instance class data
            raise TypeError('invald acct number')
        else:
            self.acct = value
    acct = Acct()

class Remain:
    def __get__(self, instance, owner):
        return instance.retireage - instance.age      # Triggers Age.__get__
    def __set__(self, instance, value):
        raise TypeError('cannot set remain')          # Else set allowed here
    remain = Remain()
```

Using __getattr__ to Validate

As we've seen, the __getattr__ method intercepts all undefined attributes, so it can be more generic than using properties or descriptors. For our example, we simply test the attribute name to know when a managed attribute is being fetched; others are stored physically on the instance and so never reach __getattr__. Although this approach is more general than using properties or descriptors, extra work may be required to imitate the specific-attribute focus of other tools. We need to check names at runtime, and we must code a __setattr__ in order to intercept and validate attribute assignments.

As for the property and descriptor versions of this example, it's critical to notice that the attribute assignments inside the __init__ constructor method trigger the class's __setattr__ method too. When this method assigns to self.name, for example, it automatically invokes the __setattr__ method, which transforms the value and assigns it to an instance attribute called name. By storing name on the instance, it ensures that future accesses will not trigger __getattr__. In contrast, acct is stored as _acct, so that later accesses to acct do invoke __getattr__.

In the end, this class, like the prior two, manages attributes called name, age, and acct; allows the attribute addr to be accessed directly; and provides a read-only attribute called remain that is entirely virtual and is computed on demand.

For comparison purposes, this alternative comes in at 32 lines of code—7 fewer than the property-based version, and 13 fewer than the version using descriptors. Clarity matters more than code size, of course, but extra code can sometimes imply extra development and maintenance work. Probably more important here are *roles*: generic tools like __getattr__ may be better suited to generic delegation, while properties and descriptors are more directly designed to manage specific attributes.

Also note that the code here incurs *extra calls* when setting unmanaged attributes (e.g., addr), although no extra calls are incurred for fetching unmanaged attributes, since they are defined. Though this will likely result in negligible overhead for most programs, properties and descriptors incur an extra call only when managed attributes are accessed.

Here's the __getattr__ version of our code:

```
class CardHolder:
    acctlen = 8                                       # Class data
    retireage = 59.5

    def __init__(self, acct, name, age, addr):
        self.acct = acct                              # Instance data
        self.name = name                              # These trigger __setattr__ too
        self.age  = age                               # _acct not mangled: name tested
        self.addr = addr                              # addr is not managed
                                                      # remain has no data
    def __getattr__(self, name):
        if name == 'acct':                                 # On undefined attr fetches
            return self._acct[:-3] + '***'                 # name, age, addr are defined
        elif name == 'remain':
            return self.retireage - self.age               # Doesn't trigger __getattr__
        else:
            raise AttributeError(name)

    def __setattr__(self, name, value):
        if name == 'name':                                 # On all attr assignments
            value = value.lower().replace(' ', '_')        # addr stored directly
        elif name == 'age':                                # acct mangled to _acct
            if value < 0 or value > 150:
                raise ValueError('invalid age')
        elif name == 'acct':
            name  = '_acct'
            value = value.replace('-', '')
            if len(value) != self.acctlen:
                raise TypeError('invald acct number')
        elif name == 'remain':
            raise TypeError('cannot set remain')
        self.__dict__[name] = value                        # Avoid looping
```

Using __getattribute__ to Validate

Our final variant uses the __getattribute__ catchall to intercept attribute fetches and manage them as needed. Every attribute fetch is caught here, so we test the attribute names to detect managed attributes and route all others to the superclass for normal fetch processing. This version uses the same __setattr__ to catch assignments as the prior version.

The code works very much like the __getattr__ version, so I won't repeat the full description here. Note, though, that because *every* attribute fetch is routed to __getattribute__, we don't need to mangle names to intercept them here (acct is stored as acct). On the other hand, this code must take care to route nonmanaged attribute fetches to a superclass to avoid looping.

Also notice that this version incurs extra calls for both setting and fetching unmanaged attributes (e.g., addr); if speed is paramount, this alternative may be the slowest of the bunch. For comparison purposes, this version amounts to 32 lines of code, just like the prior version:

```
class CardHolder:
    acctlen = 8                                    # Class data
    retireage = 59.5

    def __init__(self, acct, name, age, addr):
        self.acct = acct                           # Instance data
        self.name = name                           # These trigger __setattr__ too
        self.age  = age                            # acct not mangled: name tested
        self.addr = addr                           # addr is not managed
                                                   # remain has no data

    def __getattribute__(self, name):
        superget = object.__getattribute__         # Don't loop: one level up
        if name == 'acct':                         # On all attr fetches
            return superget(self, 'acct')[:-3] + '***'
        elif name == 'remain':
            return superget(self, 'retireage') - superget(self, 'age')
        else:
            return superget(self, name)            # name, age, addr: stored

    def __setattr__(self, name, value):
        if name == 'name':                         # On all attr assignments
            value = value.lower().replace(' ', '_')  # addr stored directly
        elif name == 'age':
            if value < 0 or value > 150:
                raise ValueError('invalid age')
        elif name == 'acct':
            value = value.replace('-', '')
            if len(value) != self.acctlen:
                raise TypeError('invald acct number')
        elif name == 'remain':
            raise TypeError('cannot set remain')
        self.__dict__[name] = value                # Avoid loops, orig names
```

Be sure to study and run this section's code on your own for more pointers on managed attribute coding techniques.

Chapter Summary

This chapter covered the various techniques for managing access to attributes in Python, including the __getattr__ and __getattribute__ operator overloading methods, class properties, and attribute descriptors. Along the way, it compared and contrasted these tools and presented a handful of use cases to demonstrate their behavior.

Chapter 38 continues our tool-building survey with a look at *decorators*—code run automatically at function and class creation time, rather than on attribute access. Before we continue, though, let's work through a set of questions to review what we've covered here.

Test Your Knowledge: Quiz

1. How do __getattr__ and __getattribute__ differ?
2. How do properties and descriptors differ?
3. How are properties and decorators related?
4. What are the main functional differences between __getattr__ and __getattribute__ and properties and descriptors?
5. Isn't all this feature comparison just a kind of argument?

Test Your Knowledge: Answers

1. The __getattr__ method is run for fetches of *undefined* attributes only—i.e., those not present on an instance and not inherited from any of its classes. By contrast, the __getattribute__ method is called for *every* attribute fetch, whether the attribute is defined or not. Because of this, code inside a __getattr__ can freely fetch other attributes if they are defined, whereas __getattribute__ must use special code for all such attribute fetches to avoid looping (it must route fetches to a superclass to skip itself).

2. Properties serve a specific role, while descriptors are more general. Properties define get, set, and delete functions for a specific attribute; descriptors provide a class with methods for these actions, too, but they provide extra flexibility to support more arbitrary actions. In fact, properties are really a simple way to create a specific kind of descriptor—one that runs functions on attribute accesses. Coding differs too: a property is created with a built-in function, and a descriptor is coded with a class; as such, descriptors can leverage all the usual OOP features of classes, such as inheritance. Moreover, in addition to the instance's state information, descriptors have local state of their own, so they can avoid name collisions in the instance.

3. Properties can be coded with decorator syntax. Because the `property` built-in accepts a single function argument, it can be used directly as a function decorator to define a fetch access property. Due to the name rebinding behavior of decorators, the name of the decorated function is assigned to a property whose get accessor is set to the original function decorated (`name = property(name)`). Property `setter` and `deleter` attributes allow us to further add set and delete accessors with decoration syntax—they set the accessor to the decorated function and return the augmented property.

4. The `__getattr__` and `__getattribute__` methods are more generic: they can be used to catch arbitrarily many attributes. In contrast, each property or descriptor provides access interception for only one *specific* attribute—we can't catch every attribute fetch with a single property or descriptor. On the other hand, properties and descriptors handle both attribute fetch and *assignment* by design: `__getattr__` and `__getattribute__` handle fetches only; to intercept assignments as well, `__setattr__` must also be coded. The implementation is also different: `__getattr__` and `__getattribute__` are operator overloading methods, whereas properties and descriptors are objects manually assigned to class attributes.

5. No it isn't. To quote from Python namesake *Monty Python's Flying Circus*:

```
An argument is a connected series of statements intended to establish a
proposition.
No it isn't.
Yes it is! It's not just contradiction.
Look, if I argue with you, I must take up a contrary position.
Yes, but that's not just saying "No it isn't."
Yes it is!
No it isn't!
Yes it is!
No it isn't. Argument is an intellectual process. Contradiction is just
the automatic gainsaying of any statement the other person makes.
(short pause)
No it isn't.
It is.
Not at all.
Now look...
```

Decorators

In the advanced class topics chapter of this book (Chapter 31), we met static and class methods and took a quick look at the @ decorator syntax Python offers for declaring them. We also met function decorators briefly in the prior chapter (Chapter 37), while exploring the `property` built-in's ability to serve as a decorator, and in Chapter 28 while studying the notion of abstract superclasses.

This chapter picks up where the previous decorator coverage left off. Here, we'll dig deeper into the inner workings of decorators and study more advanced ways to code new decorators ourselves. As we'll see, many of the concepts we studied in earlier chapters, such as state retention, show up regularly in decorators.

This is a somewhat advanced topic, and decorator construction tends to be of more interest to tool builders than to application programmers. Still, given that decorators are becoming increasingly common in popular Python frameworks, a basic understanding can help demystify their role, even if you're just a decorator user.

Besides covering decorator construction details, this chapter serves as a more realistic *case study* of Python in action. Because its examples are somewhat larger than most of the others we've seen in this book, they better illustrate how code comes together into more complete systems and tools. As an extra perk, much of the code we'll write here may be used as general-purpose tools in your day-to-day programs.

What's a Decorator?

Decoration is a way to specify management code for functions and classes. Decorators themselves take the form of callable objects (e.g., functions) that process other callable objects. As we saw earlier in this book, Python decorators come in two related flavors:

- *Function decorators* do name rebinding at function definition time, providing a layer of logic that can manage functions and methods, or later calls to them.
- *Class decorators* do name rebinding at class definition time, providing a layer of logic that can manage classes, or the instances created by calling them later.

Decorators do have some potential *drawbacks*, too—when they insert wrapper logic, they can alter the types of the decorated objects, and they may incur extra calls. On the other hand, the same considerations apply to any technique that adds wrapping logic to objects.

We'll explore these tradeoffs in the context of real code later in this chapter. Although the choice to use decorators is still somewhat subjective, their advantages are compelling enough that they are quickly becoming best practice in the Python world. To help you decide for yourself, let's turn to the details.

The Basics

Let's get started with a first-pass look at decoration behavior from a symbolic perspective. We'll write real code soon, but since most of the magic of decorators boils down to an automatic rebinding operation, it's important to understand this mapping first.

Function Decorators

Function decorators have been available in Python since version 2.5. As we saw earlier in this book, they are largely just syntactic sugar that runs one function through another at the end of a def statement, and rebinds the original function name to the result.

Usage

A function decorator is a kind of *runtime declaration* about the function whose definition follows. The decorator is coded on a line just before the def statement that defines a function or method, and it consists of the @ symbol followed by a reference to a *metafunction*—a function (or other callable object) that manages another function.

In terms of code, function decorators automatically map the following syntax:

```
@decorator              # Decorate function
def F(arg):
    ...

F(99)                   # Call function
```

into this equivalent form, where decorator is a one-argument callable object that returns a callable object with the same number of arguments as F:

```
def F(arg):
    ...
F = decorator(F)        # Rebind function name to decorator result

F(99)                   # Essentially calls decorator(F)(99)
```

This automatic name rebinding works on any `def` statement, whether it's for a simple function or a method within a class. When the function F is later called, it's actually calling the object *returned* by the decorator, which may be either another object that implements required wrapping logic, or the original function itself.

In other words, decoration essentially maps the first of the following into the second (though the decorator is really run only once, at decoration time):

```
func(6, 7)
decorator(func)(6, 7)
```

This automatic name rebinding accounts for the static method and property decoration syntax we met earlier in the book:

```
class C:
    @staticmethod
    def meth(...): ...          # meth = staticmethod(meth)

class C:
    @property
    def name(self): ...         # name = property(name)
```

In both cases, the method name is rebound to the result of a built-in function decorator, at the end of the `def` statement. Calling the original name later invokes whatever object the decorator returns.

Implementation

A decorator itself is a *callable that returns a callable*. That is, it returns the object to be called later when the decorated function is invoked through its original name—either a wrapper object to intercept later calls, or the original function augmented in some way. In fact, decorators can *be* any type of callable and *return* any type of callable: any combination of functions and classes may be used, though some are better suited to certain contexts.

For example, to tap into the decoration protocol in order to manage a function just after it is created, we might code a decorator of this form:

```
def decorator(F):
    # Process function F
    return F

@decorator
def func(): ...                 # func = decorator(func)
```

Because the original decorated function is assigned back to its name, this simply adds a post-creation step to function definition. Such a structure might be used to register a function to an API, assign function attributes, and so on.

In more typical use, to insert logic that intercepts later calls to a function, we might code a decorator to return a different object than the original function:

```
def decorator(F):
    # Save or use function F
    # Return a different callable: nested def, class with __call__, etc.

@decorator
def func(): ...                    # func = decorator(func)
```

This decorator is invoked at decoration time, and the callable it returns is invoked when the original function name is later called. The decorator itself receives the decorated function; the callable returned receives whatever arguments are later passed to the decorated function's name. This works the same for class *methods*: the implied instance object simply shows up in the first argument of the returned callable.

In skeleton terms, here's one common coding pattern that captures this idea—the decorator returns a wrapper that retains the original function in an enclosing scope:

```
def decorator(F):                  # On @ decoration
    def wrapper(*args):            # On wrapped function call
        # Use F and args
        # F(*args) calls original function
    return wrapper

@decorator                         # func = decorator(func)
def func(x, y):                    # func is passed to decorator's F
    ...

func(6, 7)                         # 6, 7 are passed to wrapper's *args
```

When the name func is later called, it really invokes the wrapper function returned by decorator; the wrapper function can then run the original func because it is still available in an *enclosing scope*. When coded this way, each decorated function produces a new scope to retain state.

To do the same with *classes*, we can overload the call operation and use instance attributes instead of enclosing scopes:

```
class decorator:
    def __init__(self, func):      # On @ decoration
        self.func = func
    def __call__(self, *args):     # On wrapped function call
        # Use self.func and args
        # self.func(*args) calls original function

@decorator                         # func = decorator(func)
def func(x, y):                    # func is passed to __init__
    ...

func(6, 7)                         # 6, 7 are passed to __call__'s *args
```

When the name func is later called now, it really invokes the __call__ operator overloading method of the instance created by decorator; the __call__ method can then run the original `func` because it is still available in an *instance attribute*. When coded this way, each decorated function produces a new instance to retain state.

Supporting method decoration

One subtle point about the prior class-based coding is that while it works to intercept simple function calls, it does not quite work when applied to class *method* functions:

```
class decorator:
    def __init__(self, func):          # func is method without instance
        self.func = func
    def __call__(self, *args):         # self is decorator instance
        # self.func(*args) fails!  # C instance not in args!

class C:
    @decorator
    def method(self, x, y):            # method = decorator(method)
        ...                            # Rebound to decorator instance
```

When coded this way, the decorated method is rebound to an instance of the decorator class, instead of a simple function.

The problem with this is that the `self` in the decorator's `__call__` receives the `decorator` class instance when the method is later run, and the instance of class `C` is never included in `*args`. This makes it impossible to dispatch the call to the original method—the decorator object retains the original method function, but it has no instance to pass to it.

To support *both* functions and methods, the nested function alternative works better:

```
def decorator(F):                      # F is func or method without instance
    def wrapper(*args):                # class instance in args[0] for method
        # F(*args) runs func or method
    return wrapper

@decorator
def func(x, y):                        # func = decorator(func)
    ...
func(6, 7)                             # Really calls wrapper(6, 7)

class C:
    @decorator
    def method(self, x, y):            # method = decorator(method)
        ...                            # Rebound to simple function

X = C()
X.method(6, 7)                         # Really calls wrapper(X, 6, 7)
```

When coded this way `wrapper` receives the `C` class instance in its first argument, so it can dispatch to the original method and access state information.

Technically, this nested-function version works because Python creates a bound method object and thus passes the subject class instance to the `self` argument only when a method attribute references a simple function; when it references an instance

Like function decorators, class decorators are commonly coded as either "factory" functions that create and return callables, classes that use __init__ or __call__ methods to intercept call operations, or some combination thereof. Factory functions typically retain state in enclosing scope references, and classes in attributes.

Supporting multiple instances

As with function decorators, with class decorators some callable type combinations work better than others. Consider the following invalid alternative to the class decorator of the prior example:

```
class Decorator:
    def __init__(self, C):              # On @ decoration
        self.C = C
    def __call__(self, *args):          # On instance creation
        self.wrapped = self.C(*args)
        return self
    def __getattr__(self, attrname):    # On atrribute fetch
        return getattr(self.wrapped, attrname)

@Decorator
class C: ...                            # C = Decorator(C)

x = C()
y = C()                                 # Overwrites x!
```

This code handles multiple decorated classes (each makes a new `Decorator` instance) and will intercept instance creation calls (each runs __call__). Unlike the prior version, however, this version fails to handle *multiple instances* of a given class—each instance creation call overwrites the prior saved instance. The original version does support multiple instances, because each instance creation call makes a new independent wrapper object. More generally, either of the following patterns supports multiple wrapped instances:

```
def decorator(C):                       # On @ decoration
    class Wrapper:
        def __init__(self, *args):      # On instance creation
            self.wrapped = C(*args)
    return Wrapper

class Wrapper: ...
def decorator(C):                       # On @ decoration
    def onCall(*args):                  # On instance creation
        return Wrapper(C(*args))        # Embed instance in instance
    return onCall
```

We'll study this phenomenon in a more realistic context later in the chapter; in practice, though, we must be careful to combine callable types properly to support our intent.

Decorator Nesting

Sometimes one decorator isn't enough. To support multiple steps of augmentation, decorator syntax allows you to add multiple layers of wrapper logic to a decorated function or method. When this feature is used, each decorator must appear on a line of its own. Decorator syntax of this form:

```
@A
@B
@C
def f(...):
    ...
```

runs the same as the following:

```
def f(...):
    ...
f = A(B(C(f)))
```

Here, the original function is passed through three different decorators, and the resulting callable object is assigned back to the original name. Each decorator processes the result of the prior, which may be the original function or an inserted wrapper.

If all the decorators insert wrappers, the net effect is that when the original function name is called, three different layers of wrapping object logic will be invoked, to augment the original function in three different ways. The last decorator listed is the first applied, and the most deeply nested (insert joke about "interior decorators" here...).

Just as for functions, multiple class decorators result in multiple nested function calls, and possibly multiple levels of wrapper logic around instance creation calls. For example, the following code:

```
@spam
@eggs
class C:
    ...

X = C()
```

is equivalent to the following:

```
class C:
    ...
C = spam(eggs(C))

X = C()
```

Again, each decorator is free to return either the original class or an inserted wrapper object. With wrappers, when an instance of the original C class is finally requested, the call is redirected to the wrapping layer objects provided by both the spam and eggs decorators, which may have arbitrarily different roles.

For example, the following do-nothing decorators simply return the decorated function:

```
def d1(F): return F
def d2(F): return F
def d3(F): return F

@d1
@d2
@d3
def func():                    # func = d1(d2(d3(func)))
    print('spam')

func()                         # Prints "spam"
```

The same syntax works on classes, as do these same do-nothing decorators.

When decorators insert wrapper function objects, though, they may augment the original function when called—the following concatenates to its result in the decorator layers, as it runs the layers from inner to outer:

```
def d1(F): return lambda: 'X' + F()
def d2(F): return lambda: 'Y' + F()
def d3(F): return lambda: 'Z' + F()

@d1
@d2
@d3
def func():                    # func = d1(d2(d3(func)))
    return 'spam'

print(func())                  # Prints "XYZspam"
```

We use `lambda` functions to implement wrapper layers here (each retains the wrapped function in an enclosing scope); in practice, wrappers can take the form of functions, callable classes, and more. When designed well, decorator nesting allows us to combine augmentation steps in a wide variety of ways.

Decorator Arguments

Both function and class decorators can also seem to take *arguments*, although really these arguments are passed to a callable that in effect *returns* the decorator, which in turn returns a callable. The following, for instance:

```
@decorator(A, B)
def F(arg):
    ...

F(99)
```

is automatically mapped into this equivalent form, where `decorator` is a callable that returns the actual decorator. The returned decorator in turn returns the callable run later for calls to the original function name:

```
def F(arg):
    ...
F = decorator(A, B)(F)        # Rebind F to result of decorator's return value

F(99)                         # Essentially calls decorator(A, B)(F)(99)
```

Decorator arguments are resolved before decoration ever occurs, and they are usually used to retain state information for use in later calls. The decorator function in this example, for instance, might take a form like the following:

```
def decorator(A, B):
    # Save or use A, B
    def actualDecorator(F):
        # Save or use function F
        # Return a callable: nested def, class with __call__, etc.
        return callable
    return actualDecorator
```

The outer function in this structure generally saves the decorator arguments away as state information, for use in the actual decorator, the callable it returns, or both. This code snippet retains the state information argument in enclosing function scope references, but class attributes are commonly used as well.

In other words, decorator arguments often imply *three levels of callables*: a callable to accept decorator arguments, which returns a callable to serve as decorator, which returns a callable to handle calls to the original function or class. Each of the three levels may be a function or class and may retain state in the form of scopes or class attributes. We'll see concrete examples of decorator arguments employed later in this chapter.

Decorators Manage Functions and Classes, Too

Although much of the rest of this chapter focuses on wrapping later calls to functions and classes, I should underscore that the decorator mechanism is more general than this—it is a protocol for passing functions and classes through a callable immediately after they are created. As such, it can also be used to invoke arbitrary post-creation processing:

```
def decorator(O):
    # Save or augment function or class O
    return O

@decorator
def F(): ...               # F = decorator(F)

@decorator
class C: ...               # C = decorator(C)
```

As long as we return the original decorated object this way instead of a wrapper, we can manage functions and classes themselves, not just later calls to them. We'll see more realistic examples later in this chapter that use this idea to register callable objects to an API with decoration and assign attributes to functions when they are created.

Coding Function Decorators

On to the code—in the rest of this chapter, we are going to study working examples that demonstrate the decorator concepts we just explored. This section presents a handful of function decorators at work, and the next shows class decorators in action. Following that, we'll close out with some larger case studies of class and function decorator usage.

Tracing Calls

To get started, let's revive the call tracer example we met in Chapter 31. The following defines and applies a function decorator that counts the number of calls made to the decorated function and prints a trace message for each call:

```
class tracer:
    def __init__(self, func):                # On @ decoration: save original func
        self.calls = 0
        self.func = func
    def __call__(self, *args):               # On later calls: run original func
        self.calls += 1
        print('call %s to %s' % (self.calls, self.func.__name__))
        self.func(*args)

@tracer
def spam(a, b, c):             # spam = tracer(spam)
    print(a + b + c)           # Wraps spam in a decorator object
```

Notice how each function decorated with this class will create a new instance, with its own saved function object and calls counter. Also observe how the *args argument syntax is used to pack and unpack arbitrarily many passed-in arguments. This generality enables this decorator to be used to wrap any function with any number of arguments (this version doesn't yet work on class methods, but we'll fix that later in this section).

Now, if we import this module's function and test it interactively, we get the following sort of behavior—each call generates a trace message initially, because the decorator class intercepts it. This code runs under both Python 2.6 and 3.0, as does all code in this chapter unless otherwise noted:

```
>>> from decorator1 import spam

>>> spam(1, 2, 3)             # Really calls the tracer wrapper object
call 1 to spam
6

>>> spam('a', 'b', 'c')       # Invokes __call__ in class
call 2 to spam
abc

>>> spam.calls                # Number calls in wrapper state information
2
```

```
>>> spam
<decorator1.tracer object at 0x02D9A730>
```

When run, the tracer class saves away the decorated function, and intercepts later calls to it, in order to add a layer of logic that counts and prints each call. Notice how the total number of calls shows up as an attribute of the decorated function—spam is really an instance of the tracer class when decorated (a finding that may have ramifications for programs that do type checking, but is generally benign).

For function calls, the @ decoration syntax can be more convenient than modifying each call to account for the extra logic level, and it avoids accidentally calling the original function directly. Consider a nondecorator equivalent such as the following:

```
calls = 0
def tracer(func, *args):
    global calls
    calls += 1
    print('call %s to %s' % (calls, func.__name__))
    func(*args)

def spam(a, b, c):
    print(a, b, c)

>>> spam(1, 2, 3)          # Normal non-traced call: accidental?
1 2 3

>>> tracer(spam, 1, 2, 3)    # Special traced call without decorators
call 1 to spam
1 2 3
```

This alternative can be used on any function without the special @ syntax, but unlike the decorator version, it requires extra syntax at every place where the function is called in your code; furthermore, its intent may not be as obvious, and it does not ensure that the extra layer will be invoked for normal calls. Although decorators are never *required* (we can always rebind names manually), they are often the most convenient option.

State Information Retention Options

The last example of the prior section raises an important issue. Function decorators have a variety of options for retaining state information provided at decoration time, for use during the actual function call. They generally need to support multiple decorated objects and multiple calls, but there are a number of ways to implement these goals: instance attributes, global variables, nonlocal variables, and function attributes can all be used for retaining state.

Class instance attributes

For example, here is an augmented version of the prior example, which adds support for *keyword* arguments and *returns* the wrapped function's result to support more use cases:

```
class tracer:                              # State via instance attributes
    def __init__(self, func):              # On @ decorator
        self.calls = 0                     # Save func for later call
        self.func  = func
    def __call__(self, *args, **kwargs):   # On call to original function
        self.calls += 1
        print('call %s to %s' % (self.calls, self.func.__name__))
        return self.func(*args, **kwargs)

@tracer
def spam(a, b, c):          # Same as: spam = tracer(spam)
    print(a + b + c)        # Triggers tracer.__init__

@tracer
def eggs(x, y):             # Same as: eggs = tracer(eggs)
    print(x ** y)           # Wraps eggs in a tracer object

spam(1, 2, 3)               # Really calls tracer instance: runs tracer.__call__
spam(a=4, b=5, c=6)         # spam is an instance attribute

eggs(2, 16)                 # Really calls tracer instance, self.func is eggs
eggs(4, y=4)                # self.calls is per-function here (need 3.0 nonlocal)
```

Like the original, this uses *class instance attributes* to save state explicitly. Both the wrapped function and the calls counter are *per-instance* information—each decoration gets its own copy. When run as a script under either 2.6 or 3.0, the output of this version is as follows; notice how the spam and eggs functions each have their own calls counter, because each decoration creates a new class instance:

```
call 1 to spam
6
call 2 to spam
15
call 1 to eggs
65536
call 2 to eggs
256
```

While useful for decorating functions, this coding scheme has issues when applied to methods (more on this later).

Enclosing scopes and globals

Enclosing def scope references and nested defs can often achieve the same effect, especially for static data like the decorated original function. In this example, though, we would also need a counter in the enclosing scope that changes on each call, and that's not possible in Python 2.6. In 2.6, we can either use classes and attributes, as we did earlier, or move the state variable out to the *global scope*, with global declarations:

```
calls = 0
def tracer(func):                          # State via enclosing scope and global
    def wrapper(*args, **kwargs):          # Instead of class attributes
        global calls                       # calls is global, not per-function
        calls += 1
        print('call %s to %s' % (calls, func.__name__))
        return func(*args, **kwargs)
    return wrapper

@tracer
def spam(a, b, c):           # Same as: spam = tracer(spam)
    print(a + b + c)

@tracer
def eggs(x, y):              # Same as: eggs = tracer(eggs)
    print(x ** y)

spam(1, 2, 3)                    # Really calls wrapper, bound to func
spam(a=4, b=5, c=6)              # wrapper calls spam

eggs(2, 16)                      # Really calls wrapper, bound to eggs
eggs(4, y=4)                     # Global calls is not per-function here!
```

Unfortunately, moving the counter out to the common global scope to allow it to be changed like this also means that it will be *shared* by every wrapped function. Unlike class instance attributes, global counters are cross-program, not per-function—the counter is incremented for *any* traced function call. You can tell the difference if you compare this version's output with the prior version's—the single, shared global call counter is incorrectly updated by calls to every decorated function:

```
call 1 to spam
6
call 2 to spam
15
call 3 to eggs
65536
call 4 to eggs
256
```

Enclosing scopes and nonlocals

Shared global state may be what we want in some cases. If we really want a *per-function* counter, though, we can either use classes as before, or make use of the new `nonlocal` statement in Python 3.0, described in Chapter 17. Because this new statement allows enclosing function scope variables to be changed, they can serve as per-decoration and changeable data:

```
def tracer(func):                         # State via enclosing scope and nonlocal
    calls = 0                             # Instead of class attrs or global
    def wrapper(*args, **kwargs):         # calls is per-function, not global
```

```
        nonlocal calls
        calls += 1
        print('call %s to %s' % (calls, func.__name__))
        return func(*args, **kwargs)
    return wrapper

@tracer
def spam(a, b, c):              # Same as: spam = tracer(spam)
    print(a + b + c)

@tracer
def eggs(x, y):                 # Same as: eggs = tracer(eggs)
    print(x ** y)

spam(1, 2, 3)                   # Really calls wrapper, bound to func
spam(a=4, b=5, c=6)             # wrapper calls spam

eggs(2, 16)                     # Really calls wrapper, bound to eggs
eggs(4, y=4)                    # Nonlocal calls _is_ not per-function here
```

Now, because enclosing scope variables are not cross-program globals, each wrapped function gets its own counter again, just as for classes and attributes. Here's the new output when run under 3.0:

```
call 1 to spam
6
call 2 to spam
15
call 1 to eggs
65536
call 2 to eggs
256
```

Function attributes

Finally, if you are not using Python 3.X and don't have a nonlocal statement, you may still be able to avoid globals and classes by making use of *function attributes* for some changeable state instead. In recent Pythons, we can assign arbitrary attributes to functions to attach them, with func.*attr=value*. In our example, we can simply use wrapper.calls for state. The following works the same as the preceding nonlocal version because the counter is again per-decorated-function, but it also runs in Python 2.6:

```
def tracer(func):                       # State via enclosing scope and func attr
    def wrapper(*args, **kwargs):       # calls is per-function, not global
        wrapper.calls += 1
        print('call %s to %s' % (wrapper.calls, func.__name__))
        return func(*args, **kwargs)
    wrapper.calls = 0
    return wrapper
```

Notice that this only works because the name wrapper is retained in the enclosing tracer function's scope. When we later increment wrapper.calls, we are not changing the name wrapper itself, so no nonlocal declaration is required.

This scheme was almost relegated to a footnote, because it is more obscure than `nonlocal` in 3.0 and is probably better saved for cases where other schemes don't help. However, we will employ it in an answer to one of the end-of-chapter questions, where we'll need to access the saved state from *outside* the decorator's code; nonlocals can only be seen inside the nested function itself, but function attributes have wider visibility.

Because decorators often imply multiple levels of callables, you can combine functions with enclosing scopes and classes with attributes to achieve a variety of coding structures. As we'll see later, though, this sometimes may be subtler than you expect—each decorated function should have its own state, and each decorated class may require state both for itself and for each generated instance.

In fact, as the next section will explain, if we want to apply function decorators to class methods, too, we also have to be careful about the distinction Python makes between decorators coded as callable class instance objects and decorators coded as functions.

Class Blunders I: Decorating Class Methods

When I wrote the first `tracer` function decorator above, I naively assumed that it could also be applied to any *method*—decorated methods should work the same, but the automatic `self` instance argument would simply be included at the front of *args. Unfortunately, I was wrong: when applied to a class's method, the first version of the `tracer` fails, because `self` is the instance of the decorator class and the instance of the decorated subject class is not included in *args. This is true in both Python 3.0 and 2.6.

I introduced this phenomenon earlier in this chapter, but now we can see it in the context of realistic working code. Given the class-based tracing decorator:

```
class tracer:
    def __init__(self, func):              # On @ decorator
        self.calls = 0                     # Save func for later call
        self.func  = func
    def __call__(self, *args, **kwargs):   # On call to original function
        self.calls += 1
        print('call %s to %s' % (self.calls, self.func.__name__))
        return self.func(*args, **kwargs)
```

decoration of simple functions works as advertised earlier:

```
@tracer
def spam(a, b, c):                         # spam = tracer(spam)
    print(a + b + c)                       # Triggers tracer.__init__

spam(1, 2, 3)                              # Runs tracer.__call__
spam(a=4, b=5, c=6)                        # spam is an instance attribute
```

However, decoration of class methods fails (more lucid readers might recognize this as our `Person` class resurrected from the object-oriented tutorial in Chapter 27):

```
class Person:
    def __init__(self, name, pay):
        self.name = name
        self.pay  = pay

    @tracer
    def giveRaise(self, percent):          # giveRaise = tracer(giverRaise)
        self.pay *= (1.0 + percent)

    @tracer
    def lastName(self):                     # lastName = tracer(lastName)
        return self.name.split()[-1]

bob = Person('Bob Smith', 50000)           # tracer remembers method funcs
bob.giveRaise(.25)                          # Runs tracer.__call__(???, .25)
print(bob.lastName())                       # Runs tracer.__call__(???)
```

The root of the problem here is in the `self` argument of the tracer class's `__call__` method—is it a `tracer` instance or a `Person` instance? We really need *both* as it's coded: the `tracer` for decorator state, and the `Person` for routing on to the original method. Really, `self` *must* be the `tracer` object, to provide access to `tracer`'s state information; this is true whether decorating a simple function or a method.

Unfortunately, when our decorated method name is rebound to a class instance object with a `__call__`, Python passes only the `tracer` *instance* to `self`; it doesn't pass along the `Person` subject in the arguments list at all. Moreover, because the `tracer` knows nothing about the `Person` instance we are trying to process with method calls, there's no way to create a bound method with an instance, and thus no way to correctly dispatch the call.

In fact, the prior listing winds up passing too few arguments to the decorated method, and results in an error. Add a line to the decorator's `__call__` to print all its arguments to verify this; as you can see, `self` is the `tracer`, and the `Person` instance is entirely absent:

```
<__main__.tracer object at 0x02D6AD90> (0.25,) {}
call 1 to giveRaise
Traceback (most recent call last):
  File "C:/misc/tracer.py", line 56, in <module>
    bob.giveRaise(.25)
  File "C:/misc/tracer.py", line 9, in __call__
    return self.func(*args, **kwargs)
TypeError: giveRaise() takes exactly 2 positional arguments (1 given)
```

As mentioned earlier, this happens because Python passes the implied subject instance to `self` when a method name is bound to a simple function only; when it is an instance of a callable class, that class's instance is passed instead. Technically, Python only makes a bound method object containing the subject instance when the method is a simple function.

Using nested functions to decorate methods

If you want your function decorators to work on *both* simple functions and class methods, the most straightforward solution lies in using one of the other state retention solutions described earlier—code your function decorator as nested `def`s, so that you don't depend on a single `self` instance argument to be both the wrapper class instance and the subject class instance.

The following alternative applies this fix using Python 3.0 nonlocals. Because decorated methods are rebound to simple functions instead of instance objects, Python correctly passes the `Person` object as the first argument, and the decorator propagates it on in the first item of `*args` to the `self` argument of the real, decorated methods:

```
# A decorator for both functions and methods

def tracer(func):                         # Use function, not class with __call__
    calls = 0                             # Else "self" is decorator instance only!
    def onCall(*args, **kwargs):
        nonlocal calls
        calls += 1
        print('call %s to %s' % (calls, func.__name__))
        return func(*args, **kwargs)
    return onCall


# Applies to simple functions

@tracer
def spam(a, b, c):                        # spam = tracer(spam)
    print(a + b + c)                      # onCall remembers spam

spam(1, 2, 3)                             # Runs onCall(1, 2, 3)
spam(a=4, b=5, c=6)


# Applies to class method functions too!

class Person:
    def __init__(self, name, pay):
        self.name = name
        self.pay  = pay

    @tracer
    def giveRaise(self, percent):         # giveRaise = tracer(giveRaise)
        self.pay *= (1.0 + percent)       # onCall remembers giveRaise

    @tracer
    def lastName(self):                   # lastName = tracer(lastName)
        return self.name.split()[-1]

print('methods...')
bob = Person('Bob Smith', 50000)
sue = Person('Sue Jones', 100000)
print(bob.name, sue.name)
```

```
sue.giveRaise(.10)                          # Runs onCall(sue, .10)
print(sue.pay)
print(bob.lastName(), sue.lastName())       # Runs onCall(bob), lastName in scopes
```

This version works the same on both functions and methods:

```
call 1 to spam
6
call 2 to spam
15
methods...
Bob Smith Sue Jones
call 1 to giveRaise
110000.0
call 1 to lastName
call 2 to lastName
Smith Jones
```

Using descriptors to decorate methods

Although the nested function solution illustrated in the prior section is the most straightforward way to support decorators that apply to both functions and class methods, other schemes are possible. The descriptor feature we explored in the prior chapter, for example, can help here as well.

Recall from our discussion in that chapter that a descriptor may be a class attribute assigned to objects with a __get__ method run automatically when that attribute is referenced and fetched (object derivation is required in Python 2.6, but not 3.0):

```
class Descriptor(object):
    def __get__(self, instance, owner): ...

class Subject:
    attr = Descriptor()

X = Subject()
X.attr          # Roughly runs Descriptor.__get__(Subject.attr, X, Subject)
```

Descriptors may also have __set__ and __del__ access methods, but we don't need them here. Now, because the descriptor's __get__ method receives *both* the descriptor class and subject class instances when invoked, it's well suited to decorating methods when we need both the decorator's state and the original class instance for dispatching calls. Consider the following alternative tracing decorator, which is also a descriptor:

```
class tracer(object):
    def __init__(self, func):               # On @ decorator
        self.calls = 0                      # Save func for later call
        self.func  = func
    def __call__(self, *args, **kwargs):    # On call to original func
        self.calls += 1
        print('call %s to %s' % (self.calls, self.func.__name__))
        return self.func(*args, **kwargs)
    def __get__(self, instance, owner):     # On method attribute fetch
        return wrapper(self, instance)
```

```
class wrapper:
    def __init__(self, desc, subj):            # Save both instances
        self.desc = desc                        # Route calls back to decr
        self.subj = subj
    def __call__(self, *args, **kwargs):
        return self.desc(self.subj, *args, **kwargs)   # Runs tracer.__call__

@tracer
def spam(a, b, c):                             # spam = tracer(spam)
    ...same as prior...                         # Uses __call__ only

class Person:
    @tracer
    def giveRaise(self, percent):              # giveRaise = tracer(giveRaise)
        ...same as prior...                     # Makes giveRaise a descriptor
```

This works the same as the preceding nested function coding. Decorated functions
invoke only its __call__, while decorated methods invoke its __get__ first to resolve
the method name fetch (on *instance.method*); the object returned by __get__ retains
the subject class instance and is then invoked to complete the call expression, thereby
triggering __call__ (on (*args...*)). For example, the test code's call to:

```
    sue.giveRaise(.10)                         # Runs __get__ then __call__
```

run's tracer.__get__ first, because the giveRaise attribute in the Person class has been
rebound to a descriptor by the function decorator. The call expression then triggers the
__call__ method of the returned wrapper object, which in turn invokes
tracer.__call__.

The wrapper object retains both descriptor and subject instances, so it can route control
back to the original decorator/descriptor class instance. In effect, the wrapper object
saves the subject class instance available during method attribute fetch and adds it to
the later call's arguments list, which is passed to __call__. Routing the call back to the
descriptor class instance this way is required in this application so that all calls to a
wrapped method use the same calls counter state information in the descriptor instance object.

Alternatively, we could use a nested function and enclosing scope references to achieve
the same effect—the following version works the same as the preceding one, by swap-
ping a class and object attributes for a nested function and scope references, but it
requires noticeably less code:

```
class tracer(object):
    def __init__(self, func):                  # On @ decorator
        self.calls = 0                          # Save func for later call
        self.func  = func
    def __call__(self, *args, **kwargs):       # On call to original func
        self.calls += 1
        print('call %s to %s' % (self.calls, self.func.__name__))
        return self.func(*args, **kwargs)
    def __get__(self, instance, owner):                # On method fetch
        def wrapper(*args, **kwargs):                   # Retain both inst
```

```
            return self(instance, *args, **kwargs)      # Runs __call__
        return wrapper
```

Add `print` statements to these alternatives' methods to trace the two-step get/call process on your own, and run them with the same test code as in the nested function alternative shown earlier. In either coding, this descriptor-based scheme is also substantially subtler than the nested function option, and so is probably a second choice here; it may be a useful coding pattern in other contexts, though.

In the rest of this chapter we're going to be fairly casual about using classes or functions to code our function decorators, as long as they are applied only to functions. Some decorators may not require the instance of the original class, and will still work on both functions and methods if coded as a class—something like Python's own `staticmethod` decorator, for example, wouldn't require an instance of the subject class (indeed, its whole point is to remove the instance from the call).

The moral of this story, though, is that if you want your decorators to work on both simple functions and class methods, you're better off using the nested-function-based coding pattern outlined here instead of a class with call interception.

Timing Calls

To sample the fuller flavor of what function decorators are capable of, let's turn to a different use case. Our next decorator times calls made to a decorated function—both the time for one call, and the total time among all calls. The decorator is applied to two functions, in order to compare the time requirements of list comprehensions and the `map` built-in call (for comparison, also see Chapter 20 for another nondecorator example that times iteration alternatives like these):

```
import time

class timer:
    def __init__(self, func):
        self.func     = func
        self.alltime = 0
    def __call__(self, *args, **kargs):
        start    = time.clock()
        result = self.func(*args, **kargs)
        elapsed = time.clock() - start
        self.alltime += elapsed
        print('%s: %.5f, %.5f' % (self.func.__name__, elapsed, self.alltime))
        return result

@timer
def listcomp(N):
    return [x * 2 for x in range(N)]

@timer
def mapcall(N):
    return map((lambda x: x * 2), range(N))
```

```
result = listcomp(5)                              # Time for this call, all calls, return value
listcomp(50000)
listcomp(500000)
listcomp(1000000)
print(result)
print('allTime = %s' % listcomp.alltime)         # Total time for all listcomp calls

print('')
result = mapcall(5)
mapcall(50000)
mapcall(500000)
mapcall(1000000)
print(result)
print('allTime = %s' % mapcall.alltime)          # Total time for all mapcall calls

print('map/comp = %s' % round(mapcall.alltime / listcomp.alltime, 3))
```

In this case, a nondecorator approach would allow the subject functions to be used with or without timing, but it would also complicate the call signature when timing is desired (we'd need to add code at every call instead of once at the def), and there would be no direct way to guarantee that all list builder calls in a program are routed through timer logic, short of finding and potentially changing them all.

When run in Python 2.6, the output of this file's self-test code is as follows:

```
listcomp: 0.00002, 0.00002
listcomp: 0.00910, 0.00912
listcomp: 0.09105, 0.10017
listcomp: 0.17605, 0.27622
[0, 2, 4, 6, 8]
allTime = 0.276223304917

mapcall: 0.00003, 0.00003
mapcall: 0.01363, 0.01366
mapcall: 0.13579, 0.14945
mapcall: 0.27648, 0.42593
[0, 2, 4, 6, 8]
allTime = 0.425933533452
map/comp = 1.542
```

Testing subtlety: I didn't run this under Python 3.0 because, as described in Chapter 14, the map built-in returns an *iterator* in 3.0, instead of an actual list as in 2.6. Hence, 3.0's map doesn't quite compare directly to a list comprehension's work (as is, the map test takes virtually no time at all in 3.0!).

If you wish to run this under 3.0, too, use list(map()) to force it to build a list like the list comprehension does, or else you're not really comparing apples to apples. Don't do so in 2.6, though—if you do, the map test will be charged for building two lists, not one.

The following sort of code would pick fairly for 2.6 and 3.0; note, though, that while this makes the comparison between list comprehensions and map more fair in either 2.6

or 3.0, because `range` is also an iterator in 3.0, the results for 2.6 and 3.0 won't compare directly:

```
...
import sys

@timer
def listcomp(N):
    return [x * 2 for x in range(N)]

if sys.version_info[0] == 2:
    @timer
    def mapcall(N):
        return map((lambda x: x * 2), range(N))
else:
    @timer
    def mapcall(N):
        return list(map((lambda x: x * 2), range(N)))
...
```

Finally, as we learned in the modules part of this book if you want to be able to reuse this decorator in other modules, you should indent the self-test code at the bottom of the file under a `__name__` == `'__main__'` test so it runs only when the file is run, not when it's imported. We won't do this, though, because we're about to add another feature to our code.

Adding Decorator Arguments

The timer decorator of the prior section works, but it would be nice if it was more configurable—providing an output label and turning trace messages on and off, for instance, might be useful in a general-purpose tool like this. Decorator arguments come in handy here: when they're coded properly, we can use them to specify configuration options that can vary for each decorated function. A label, for instance, might be added as follows:

```
def timer(label=''):
    def decorator(func):
        def onCall(*args):              # args passed to function
            ...                          # func retained in enclosing scope
            print(label, ...)            # label retained in enclosing scope
        return onCall
    return decorator                    # Returns that actual decorator

@timer('==>')                           # Like listcomp = timer('==>')(listcomp)
def listcomp(N): ...                    # listcomp is rebound to decorator

listcomp(...)                           # Really calls decorator
```

This code adds an enclosing scope to retain a decorator argument for use on a later actual call. When the `listcomp` function is defined, it really invokes `decorator` (the result of `timer`, run before decoration actually occurs), with the `label` value available in its enclosing scope. That is, `timer` *returns* the decorator, which remembers both the decorator argument and the original function and returns a callable which invokes the original function on later calls.

We can put this structure to use in our timer to allow a label and a trace control flag to be passed in at decoration time. Here's an example that does just that, coded in a module file named *mytools.py* so it can be imported as a general tool:

```
import time

def timer(label='', trace=True):           # On decorator args: retain args
    class Timer:
        def __init__(self, func):           # On @: retain decorated func
            self.func    = func
            self.alltime = 0
        def __call__(self, *args, **kargs):  # On calls: call original
            start   = time.clock()
            result  = self.func(*args, **kargs)
            elapsed = time.clock() - start
            self.alltime += elapsed
            if trace:
                format = '%s %s: %.5f, %.5f'
                values = (label, self.func.__name__, elapsed, self.alltime)
                print(format % values)
            return result
    return Timer
```

Mostly all we've done here is embed the original `Timer` class in an enclosing function, in order to create a scope that retains the decorator arguments. The outer `timer` function is called before decoration occurs, and it simply returns the `Timer` class to serve as the actual decorator. On decoration, an instance of `Timer` is made that remembers the decorated function itself, but also has access to the decorator arguments in the enclosing function scope.

This time, rather than embedding self-test code in this file, we'll run the decorator in a different file. Here's a client of our timer decorator, the module file *testseqs.py*, applying it to sequence iteration alternatives again:

```
from mytools import timer

@timer(label='[CCC]==>')
def listcomp(N):                       # Like listcomp = timer(...)(listcomp)
    return [x * 2 for x in range(N)]   # listcomp(...) triggers Timer.__call__

@timer(trace=True, label='[MMM]==>')
def mapcall(N):
    return map((lambda x: x * 2), range(N))

for func in (listcomp, mapcall):
    print('')
    result = func(5)            # Time for this call, all calls, return value
    func(50000)
    func(500000)
    func(1000000)
    print(result)
```

```
        self.rate = rate
    def pay(self):
        return self.hours * self.rate

@singleton                              # Spam = singleton(Spam)
class Spam:                             # Rebinds Spam to onCall
    def __init__(self, val):            # onCall remembers Spam
        self.attr = val

bob = Person('Bob', 40, 10)             # Really calls onCall
print(bob.name, bob.pay())

sue = Person('Sue', 50, 20)             # Same, single object
print(sue.name, sue.pay())

X = Spam(42)                            # One Person, one Spam
Y = Spam(99)
print(X.attr, Y.attr)
```

Now, when the `Person` or `Spam` class is later used to create an instance, the wrapping logic layer provided by the decorator routes instance construction calls to `onCall`, which in turn calls `getInstance` to manage and share a single instance per class, regardless of how many construction calls are made. Here's this code's output:

```
Bob 400
Bob 400
42 42
```

Interestingly, you can code a more self-contained solution here if you're able to use the `nonlocal` statement (available in Python 3.0 and later) to change enclosing scope names, as described earlier—the following alternative achieves an identical effect, by using one *enclosing scope* per class, instead of one global table entry per class:

```
def singleton(aClass):                  # On @ decoration
    instance = None
    def onCall(*args):                  # On instance creation
        nonlocal instance               # 3.0 and later nonlocal
        if instance == None:
            instance = aClass(*args)    # One scope per class
        return instance
    return onCall
```

This version works the same, but it does not depend on names in the global scope outside the decorator. In either Python 2.6 or 3.0, you can also code a self-contained solution with a class instead—the following uses one *instance* per class, rather than an enclosing scope or global table, and works the same as the other two versions (in fact, it relies on the same coding pattern that we will later see is a common decorator class blunder; here we *want* just one instance, but that's not always the case):

```
class singleton:
    def __init__(self, aClass):         # On @ decoration
        self.aClass = aClass
        self.instance = None
    def __call__(self, *args):          # On instance creation
```

```
    if self.instance == None:
        self.instance = self.aClass(*args)       # One instance per class
    return self.instance
```

To make this decorator a fully general-purpose tool, store it in an importable module file, indent the self-test code under a __name__ check, and add support for keyword arguments in construction calls with **kargs syntax (I'll leave this as a suggested exercise).

Tracing Object Interfaces

The singleton example of the prior section illustrated using class decorators to manage *all* the instances of a class. Another common use case for class decorators augments the interface of *each* generated instance. Class decorators can essentially install on instances a wrapper logic layer that manages access to their interfaces in some way.

For example, in Chapter 30, the __getattr__ operator overloading method is shown as a way to wrap up entire object interfaces of embedded instances, in order to implement the *delegation* coding pattern. We saw similar examples in the managed attribute coverage of the prior chapter. Recall that __getattr__ is run when an undefined attribute name is fetched; we can use this hook to intercept method calls in a controller class and propagate them to an embedded object.

For reference, here's the original nondecorator delegation example, working on two built-in type objects:

```
class Wrapper:
    def __init__(self, object):
        self.wrapped = object                     # Save object
    def __getattr__(self, attrname):
        print('Trace:', attrname)                 # Trace fetch
        return getattr(self.wrapped, attrname)    # Delegate fetch

>>> x = Wrapper([1,2,3])                           # Wrap a list
>>> x.append(4)                                    # Delegate to list method
Trace: append
>>> x.wrapped                                      # Print my member
[1, 2, 3, 4]

>>> x = Wrapper({"a": 1, "b": 2})                  # Wrap a dictionary
>>> list(x.keys())                                 # Delegate to dictionary method
Trace: keys                                        # Use list() in 3.0
['a', 'b']
```

In this code, the Wrapper class intercepts access to any of the wrapped object's attributes, prints a trace message, and uses the getattr built-in to pass off the request to the wrapped object. Specifically, it traces attribute accesses made *outside* the wrapped object's class; accesses inside the wrapped object's methods are not caught and run normally by design. This whole-interface model differs from the behavior of function decorators, which wrap up just one specific method.

Class decorators provide an alternative and convenient way to code this __getattr__ technique to wrap an entire interface. In 2.6 and 3.0, for example, the prior class example can be coded as a class decorator that triggers wrapped instance creation, instead of passing a pre-made instance into the wrapper's constructor (also augmented here to support keyword arguments with **kargs and to count the number of accesses made):

```
def Tracer(aClass):                             # On @ decorator
    class Wrapper:
        def __init__(self, *args, **kargs):     # On instance creation
            self.fetches = 0
            self.wrapped = aClass(*args, **kargs)   # Use enclosing scope name
        def __getattr__(self, attrname):
            print('Trace: ' + attrname)         # Catches all but own attrs
            self.fetches += 1
            return getattr(self.wrapped, attrname)  # Delegate to wrapped obj
    return Wrapper

@Tracer
class Spam:                                     # Spam = Tracer(Spam)
    def display(self):                          # Spam is rebound to Wrapper
        print('Spam!' * 8)

@Tracer
class Person:                                   # Person = Tracer(Person)
    def __init__(self, name, hours, rate):      # Wrapper remembers Person
        self.name = name
        self.hours = hours
        self.rate = rate
    def pay(self):                              # Accesses outside class traced
        return self.hours * self.rate           # In-method accesses not traced

food = Spam()                                   # Triggers Wrapper()
food.display()                                  # Triggers __getattr__
print([food.fetches])

bob = Person('Bob', 40, 50)                     # bob is really a Wrapper
print(bob.name)                                 # Wrapper embeds a Person
print(bob.pay())

print('')
sue = Person('Sue', rate=100, hours=60)         # sue is a different Wrapper
print(sue.name)                                 # with a different Person
print(sue.pay())

print(bob.name)                                 # bob has different state
print(bob.pay())
print([bob.fetches, sue.fetches])               # Wrapper attrs not traced
```

It's important to note that this is very different from the tracer decorator we met earlier. In "Coding Function Decorators" on page 998, we looked at decorators that enabled us to trace and time calls to a given function or method. In contrast, by intercepting instance creation calls, the class decorator here allows us to trace an entire object interface—i.e., accesses to any of its attributes.

The following is the output produced by this code under both 2.6 and 3.0: attribute fetches on instances of both the Spam and Person classes invoke the __getattr__ logic in the Wrapper class, because food and bob are really instances of Wrapper, thanks to the decorator's redirection of instance creation calls:

```
Trace: display
Spam! Spam! Spam! Spam! Spam! Spam! Spam! Spam!
[1]
Trace: name
Bob
Trace: pay
2000

Trace: name
Sue
Trace: pay
6000
Trace: name
Bob
Trace: pay
2000
[4, 2]
```

Notice that the preceding code decorates a user-defined class. Just like in the original example in Chapter 30, we can also use the decorator to wrap up a built-in type such as a list, as long as we either subclass to allow decoration syntax or perform the decoration manually—decorator syntax requires a class statement for the @ line.

In the following, x is really a Wrapper again due to the indirection of decoration (I moved the decorator class to module file *tracer.py* in order to reuse it this way):

```
>>> from tracer import Tracer          # Decorator moved to a module file

>>> @Tracer
... class MyList(list): pass           # MyList = Tracer(MyList)

>>> x = MyList([1, 2, 3])              # Triggers Wrapper()
>>> x.append(4)                        # Triggers __getattr__, append
Trace: append
>>> x.wrapped
[1, 2, 3, 4]

>>> WrapList = Tracer(list)            # Or perform decoration manually
>>> x = WrapList([4, 5, 6])           # Else subclass statement required
>>> x.append(7)
Trace: append
>>> x.wrapped
[4, 5, 6, 7]
```

The decorator approach allows us to move instance creation into the decorator itself, instead of requiring a premade object to be passed in. Although this seems like a minor difference, it lets us retain normal instance creation syntax and realize all the benefits of decorators in general. Rather than requiring all instance creation calls to route objects through a wrapper manually, we need only augment classes with decorator syntax:

```
@Tracer                                          # Decorator approach
class Person: ...
bob = Person('Bob', 40, 50)
sue = Person('Sue', rate=100, hours=60)

class Person: ...                                # Non-decorator approach
bob = Wrapper(Person('Bob', 40, 50))
sue = Wrapper(Person('Sue', rate=100, hours=60))
```

Assuming you will make more than one instance of a class, decorators will generally be a net win in terms of both code size and code maintenance.

 Attribute version skew note: As we learned in Chapter 37, __getattr__ will intercept accesses to operator overloading methods like __str__ and __repr__ in Python 2.6, but not in 3.0.

In Python 3.0, class instances inherit defaults for some (but not all) of these names from the class (really, from the automatic object super-class), because all classes are "new-style." Moreover, in 3.0 implicitly invoked attributes for built-in operations like printing and + are *not* routed through __getattr__ (or its cousin, __getattribute__). New-style classes look up such methods in *classes* and skip the normal instance lookup entirely.

Here, this means that the __getattr__-based tracing wrapper will auto-matically trace and propagate operator overloading calls in 2.6, but not in 3.0. To see this, display "x" directly at the end of the preceding in-teractive session—in 2.6 the attribute __repr__ is traced and the list prints as expected, but in 3.0 no trace occurs and the list prints using a default display for the Wrapper class:

```
>>> x                                # 2.6
Trace: __repr__
[4, 5, 6, 7]
>>> x                                # 3.0
<tracer.Wrapper object at 0x026C07D0>
```

To work the same in 3.0, operator overloading methods generally need to be redefined redundantly in the wrapper class, either by hand, by tools, or by definition in superclasses. Only simple named attributes will work the same in both versions. We'll see this version skew at work again in a Private decorator later in this chapter.

Class Blunders II: Retaining Multiple Instances

Curiously, the decorator function in this example can *almost* be coded as a class instead of a function, with the proper operator overloading protocol. The following slightly simplified alternative works similarly because its __init__ is triggered when the @ dec-orator is applied to the class, and its __call__ is triggered when a subject class instance is created. Our objects are really instances of Tracer this time, and we essentially just trade an enclosing scope reference for an instance attribute here:

```
class Tracer:
    def __init__(self, aClass):          # On @decorator
        self.aClass = aClass             # Use instance attribute
    def __call__(self, *args):           # On instance creation
        self.wrapped = self.aClass(*args) # ONE (LAST) INSTANCE PER CLASS!
        return self
    def __getattr__(self, attrname):
        print('Trace: ' + attrname)
        return getattr(self.wrapped, attrname)

@Tracer                                  # Triggers __init__
class Spam:                              # Like: Spam = Tracer(Spam)
    def display(self):
        print('Spam!' * 8)

...
food = Spam()                            # Triggers __call__
food.display()                           # Triggers __getattr__
```

As we saw in the abstract earlier, though, this class-only alternative handles multiple classes as before, but it won't quite work for *multiple instances* of a given class: each instance construction call triggers __call__, which overwrites the prior instance. The net effect is that Tracer saves just one instance—the last one created. Experiment with this yourself to see how, but here's an example of the problem:

```
@Tracer                                  # Person = Tracer(Person)
class Person:                            # Wrapper bound to Person
    def __init__(self, name):
        self.name = name

bob = Person('Bob')                      # bob is really a Wrapper
print(bob.name)                          # Wrapper embeds a Person
Sue = Person('Sue')
print(sue.name)                          # sue overwrites bob
print(bob.name)                          # OOPS: now bob's name is 'Sue'!
```

This code's output follows—because this tracer only has a single shared instance, the second overwrites the first:

```
Trace: name
Bob
Trace: name
Sue
Trace: name
Sue
```

The problem here is bad *state retention*—we make one decorator instance per class, but not per class instance, such that only the last instance is retained. The solution, as in our prior class blunder for decorating methods, lies in abandoning class-based decorators.

The earlier function-based `Tracer` version *does* work for multiple instances, because each instance construction call makes a new `Wrapper` instance, instead of overwriting the state of a single shared `Tracer` instance; the original nondecorator version handles multiple instances correctly for the same reason. Decorators are not only arguably magical, they can also be incredibly subtle!

Decorators Versus Manager Functions

Regardless of such subtleties, the `Tracer` class decorator example ultimately still relies on `__getattr__` to intercept fetches on a wrapped and embedded instance object. As we saw earlier, all we've really accomplished is moving the instance creation call inside a class, instead of passing the instance into a manager function. With the original non-decorator tracing example, we would simply code instance creation differently:

```
class Spam:                          # Non-decorator version
    ...                              # Any class will do
food = Wrapper(Spam())               # Special creation syntax

@Tracer
class Spam:                          # Decorator version
    ...                              # Requires @ syntax at class
food = Spam()                        # Normal creation syntax
```

Essentially, *class decorators* shift special syntax requirements from the instance creation call to the class statement itself. This is also true for the singleton example earlier in this section—rather than decorating a class and using normal instance creation calls, we could simply pass the class and its construction arguments into a manager function:

```
instances = {}
def getInstance(aClass, *args):
    if aClass not in instances:
        instances[aClass] = aClass(*args)
    return instances[aClass]

bob = getInstance(Person, 'Bob', 40, 10)     # Versus: bob = Person('Bob', 40, 10)
```

Alternatively, we could use Python's introspection facilities to fetch the class from an already-created instance (assuming creating an initial instance is acceptable):

```
instances = {}
def getInstance(object):
    aClass = object.__class__
    if aClass not in instances:
        instances[aClass] = object
    return instances[aClass]

bob = getInstance(Person('Bob', 40, 10))     # Versus: bob = Person('Bob', 40, 10)
```

The same holds true for *function decorators* like the tracer we wrote earlier: rather than decorating a function with logic that intercepts later calls, we could simply pass the function and its arguments into a manager that dispatches the call:

```
def func(x, y):                        # Nondecorator version
    ...                                # def tracer(func, args): ... func(*args)
result = tracer(func, (1, 2))          # Special call syntax

@tracer
def func(x, y):                        # Decorator version
    ...                                # Rebinds name: func = tracer(func)
result = func(1, 2)                    # Normal call syntax
```

Manager function approaches like this place the burden of using special syntax on *calls*, instead of expecting decoration syntax at function and class definitions.

Why Decorators? (Revisited)

So why did I just show you ways to *not* use decorators to implement singletons? As I mentioned at the start of this chapter, decorators present us with tradeoffs. Although syntax matters, we all too often forget to ask the "why" questions when confronted with new tools. Now that we've seen how decorators actually work, let's step back for a minute to glimpse the big picture here.

Like most language features, decorators have both pros and cons. For example, in the negatives column, *class decorators* suffer from two potential drawbacks:

Type changes
> As we've seen, when wrappers are inserted, a decorated function or class does not retain its *original type*—its name is rebound to a wrapper object, which might matter in programs that use object names or test object types. In the singleton example, both the decorator and manager function approaches retain the original class type for instances; in the tracer code, neither approach does, because wrappers are required.

Extra calls
> A wrapping layer added by decoration incurs the additional performance cost of an *extra call* each time the decorated object is invoked—calls are relatively time-expensive operations, so decoration wrappers can make a program slower. In the tracer code, both approaches require each attribute to be routed through a wrapper layer; the singleton example avoids extra calls by retaining the original class type.

Similar concerns apply with *function decorators*: both decoration and manager functions incur extra calls, and type changes generally occur when decorating (but not otherwise).

That said, neither of these is a very serious issue. For most programs, the type difference issue is unlikely to matter and the speed hit of the extra calls will be insignificant; furthermore, the latter occurs only when wrappers are used, can often be negated by simply removing the decorator when optimal performance is required, and is also incurred by nondecorator solutions that add wrapping logic (including *metaclasses*, as we'll see in Chapter 39).

Conversely, as we saw at the start of this chapter, decorators have three main advantages. Compared to the manager (a.k.a. "helper") function solutions of the prior section, decorators offer:

Explicit syntax

Decorators make augmentation explicit and obvious. Their @ syntax is easier to recognize than special code in calls that may appear anywhere in a source file—in our singleton and tracer examples, for instance, the decorator lines seem more likely to be noticed than extra code at calls would be. Moreover, decorators allow function and instance creation calls to use normal syntax familiar to all Python programmers.

Code maintenance

Decorators avoid repeated augmentation code at each function or class call. Because they appear just once, at the definition of the class or function itself, they obviate redundancy and simplify future code maintenance. For our singleton and tracer cases, we need to use special code at each call to use a manager function approach—extra work is required both initially and for any modifications that must be made in the future.

Consistency

Decorators make it less likely that a programmer will forget to use required wrapping logic. This derives mostly from the two prior advantages—because decoration is explicit and appears only once, at the decorated objects themselves, decorators promote more consistent and uniform API usage than special code that must be included at each call. In the singleton example, for instance, it would be easy to forget to route all class creation calls through special code, which would subvert the singleton management altogether.

Decorators also promote code *encapsulation* to reduce redundancy and minimize future maintenance effort; although other code structuring tools do too, decorators make this natural for augmentation tasks.

None of these benefits completely requires decorator syntax to be achieved, though, and decorator usage is ultimately a stylistic choice. That said, most programmers find them to be a net win, especially as a tool for using libraries and APIs correctly.

I can recall similar arguments being made both for and against constructor functions in classes—prior to the introduction of __init__ methods, the same effect was often achieved by running an instance through a method manually when creating it (e.g., X=Class().init()). Over time, though, despite being fundamentally a stylistic choice, the __init__ syntax came to be universally preferred because it was more explicit, consistent, and maintainable. Although you should be the judge, decorators seem to bring many of the same assets to the table.

Managing Functions and Classes Directly

Most of our examples in this chapter have been designed to intercept function and instance creation calls. Although this is typical for decorators, they are not limited to this role. Because decorators work by running new functions and classes through decorator code, they can also be used to manage function and class objects themselves, not just later calls made to them.

Imagine, for example, that you require methods or classes used by an application to be registered to an API for later processing (perhaps that API will call the objects later, in response to events). Although you could provide a registration function to be called manually after the objects are defined, decorators make your intent more explicit.

The following simple implementation of this idea defines a decorator that can be applied to both functions and classes, to add the object to a dictionary-based registry. Because it returns the object itself instead of a wrapper, it does not intercept later calls:

```
# Registering decorated objects to an API

registry = {}
def register(obj):                       # Both class and func decorator
    registry[obj.__name__] = obj         # Add to registry
    return obj                           # Return obj itself, not a wrapper

@register
def spam(x):
    return(x ** 2)                       # spam = register(spam)

@register
def ham(x):
    return(x ** 3)

@register
class Eggs:                              # Eggs = register(Eggs)
    def __init__(self, x):
        self.data = x ** 4
    def __str__(self):
        return str(self.data)

print('Registry:')
for name in registry:
    print(name, '=>', registry[name], type(registry[name]))

print('\nManual calls:')
print(spam(2))                          # Invoke objects manually
print(ham(2))                           # Later calls not intercepted
X = Eggs(2)
print(X)

print('\nRegistry calls:')
for name in registry:
    print(name, '=>', registry[name](3))    # Invoke from registry
```

When this code is run the decorated objects are added to the registry by name, but they still work as originally coded when they're called later, without being routed through a wrapper layer. In fact, our objects can be run both manually and from inside the registry table:

```
Registry:
Eggs => <class '__main__.Eggs'> <class 'type'>
ham => <function ham at 0x02CFB738> <class 'function'>
spam => <function spam at 0x02CFB6F0> <class 'function'>

Manual calls:
4
8
16

Registry calls:
Eggs => 81
ham => 27
spam => 9
```

A user interface might use this technique, for example, to register callback handlers for user actions. Handlers might be registered by function or class name, as done here, or decorator arguments could be used to specify the subject event; an extra def statement enclosing our decorator could be used to retain such arguments for use on decoration.

This example is artificial, but its technique is very general. For example, function decorators might also be used to process function attributes, and class decorators might insert new class attributes, or even new methods, dynamically. Consider the following function decorators—they assign function attributes to record information for later use by an API, but they do not insert a wrapper layer to intercept later calls:

```
# Augmenting decorated objects directly

>>> def decorate(func):
...     func.marked = True           # Assign function attribute for later use
...     return func
...
>>> @decorate
... def spam(a, b):
...     return a + b
...
>>> spam.marked
True

>>> def annotate(text):             # Same, but value is decorator argument
...     def decorate(func):
...         func.label = text
...         return func
...     return decorate
...
>>> @annotate('spam data')
... def spam(a, b):                  # spam = annotate(...)(spam)
...     return a + b
...
```

```
>>> spam(1, 2), spam.label
(3, 'spam data')
```

Such decorators augment functions and classes directly, without catching later calls to them. We'll see more examples of class decorations managing classes directly in the next chapter, because this turns out to encroach on the domain of *metaclasses*; for the remainder of this chapter, let's turn to two larger case studies of decorators at work.

Example: "Private" and "Public" Attributes

The final two sections of this chapter present larger examples of decorator use. Both are presented with minimal description, partly because this chapter has exceeded its size limits, but mostly because you should already understand decorator basics well enough to study these on your own. Being general-purpose tools, these examples give us a chance to see how decorator concepts come together in more useful code.

Implementing Private Attributes

The following *class decorator* implements a `Private` declaration for class instance attributes—that is, attributes stored on an instance, or inherited from one of its classes. It disallows fetch and change access to such attributes from *outside* the decorated class, but still allows the class itself to access those names freely within its methods. It's not exactly C++ or Java, but it provides similar access control as an option in Python.

We saw an incomplete first-cut implementation of instance attribute privacy for changes only in Chapter 29. The version here extends this concept to validate attribute fetches too, and it uses delegation instead of inheritance to implement the model. In fact, in a sense this is just an extension to the attribute tracer class decorator we met earlier.

Although this example utilizes the new syntactic sugar of class decorators to code attribute privacy, its attribute interception is ultimately still based upon the __getattr__ and __setattr__ operator overloading methods we met in prior chapters. When a private attribute access is detected, this version uses the `raise` statement to raise an exception, along with an error message; the exception may be caught in a `try` or allowed to terminate the script.

Here is the code, along with a self test at the bottom of the file. It will work under both Python 2.6 and 3.0 because it employs 3.0 `print` and `raise` syntax, though it catches operator overloading method attributes in 2.6 only (more on this in a moment):

```
"""
Privacy for attributes fetched from class instances.
See self-test code at end of file for a usage example.
Decorator same as: Doubler = Private('data', 'size')(Doubler).
Private returns onDecorator, onDecorator returns onInstance,
and each onInstance instance embeds a Doubler instance.
"""
```

```
traceMe = False
def trace(*args):
    if traceMe: print('[' + ' '.join(map(str, args)) + ']')

def Private(*privates):                             # privates in enclosing scope
    def onDecorator(aClass):                        # aClass in enclosing scope
        class onInstance:                           # wrapped in instance attribute
            def __init__(self, *args, **kargs):
                self.wrapped = aClass(*args, **kargs)
            def __getattr__(self, attr):            # My attrs don't call getattr
                trace('get:', attr)                 # Others assumed in wrapped
                if attr in privates:
                    raise TypeError('private attribute fetch: ' + attr)
                else:
                    return getattr(self.wrapped, attr)
            def __setattr__(self, attr, value):     # Outside accesses
                trace('set:', attr, value)          # Others run normally
                if attr == 'wrapped':               # Allow my attrs
                    self.__dict__[attr] = value     # Avoid looping
                elif attr in privates:
                    raise TypeError('private attribute change: ' + attr)
                else:
                    setattr(self.wrapped, attr, value)   # Wrapped obj attrs
        return onInstance                           # Or use __dict__
    return onDecorator


if __name__ == '__main__':
    traceMe = True

    @Private('data', 'size')                        # Doubler = Private(...)(Doubler)
    class Doubler:
        def __init__(self, label, start):
            self.label = label                      # Accesses inside the subject class
            self.data  = start                      # Not intercepted: run normally
        def size(self):
            return len(self.data)                   # Methods run with no checking
        def double(self):                           # Because privacy not inherited
            for i in range(self.size()):
                self.data[i] = self.data[i] * 2
        def display(self):
            print('%s => %s' % (self.label, self.data))

    X = Doubler('X is', [1, 2, 3])
    Y = Doubler('Y is', [-10, -20, -30])

    # The followng all succeed
    print(X.label)                                  # Accesses outside subject class
    X.display(); X.double(); X.display()            # Intercepted: validated, delegated
    print(Y.label)
    Y.display(); Y.double()
    Y.label = 'Spam'
    Y.display()
```

```
                # The following all fail properly
                """
                print(X.size())                # prints "TypeError: private attribute fetch: size"
                print(X.data)
                X.data = [1, 1, 1]
                X.size = lambda S: 0
                print(Y.data)
                print(Y.size())
                """
```

When `traceMe` is True, the module file's self-test code produces the following output. Notice how the decorator catches and validates both attribute fetches and assignments run outside of the wrapped class, but does not catch attribute accesses inside the class itself:

```
[set: wrapped <__main__.Doubler object at 0x02B2AAF0>]
[set: wrapped <__main__.Doubler object at 0x02B2AE70>]
[get: label]
X is
[get: display]
X is => [1, 2, 3]
[get: double]
[get: display]
X is => [2, 4, 6]
[get: label]
Y is
[get: display]
Y is => [-10, -20, -30]
[get: double]
[set: label Spam]
[get: display]
Spam => [-20, -40, -60]
```

Implementation Details I

This code is a bit complex, and you're probably best off tracing through it on your own to see how it works. To help you study, though, here are a few highlights worth mentioning.

Inheritance versus delegation

The first-cut privacy example shown in Chapter 29 used *inheritance* to mix in a `__setattr__` to catch accesses. Inheritance makes this difficult, however, because differentiating between accesses from inside or outside the class is not straightforward (inside access should be allowed to run normally, and outside access should be restricted). To work around this, the Chapter 29 example requires inheriting classes to use `__dict__` assignments to set attributes—an incomplete solution at best.

The version here uses *delegation* (embedding one object inside another) instead of inheritance; this pattern is better suited to our task, as it makes it much easier to distinguish between accesses inside and outside of the subject class. Attribute accesses from outside the subject class are intercepted by the wrapper layer's overloading methods and delegated to the class if valid; accesses inside the class itself (i.e., through `self` inside its methods' code) are not intercepted and are allowed to run normally without checks, because privacy is not inherited here.

Decorator arguments

The class decorator used here accepts any number of arguments, to name private attributes. What really happens, though, is that the arguments are passed to the `Private` function, and `Private` returns the decorator function to be applied to the subject class. So, the arguments are used before decoration ever occurs; `Private` returns the decorator, which in turn "remembers" the privates list as an enclosing scope reference.

State retention and enclosing scopes

Speaking of enclosing scopes, there are actually three levels of state retention at work in this code:

- The arguments to `Private` are used before decoration occurs and are retained as an enclosing scope reference for use in both `onDecorator` and `onInstance`.
- The class argument to `onDecorator` is used at decoration time and is retained as an enclosing scope reference for use at instance construction time.
- The wrapped instance object is retained as an instance attribute in `onInstance`, for use when attributes are later accessed from outside the class.

This all works fairly naturally, given Python's scope and namespace rules.

Using __dict__ and __slots__

The `__setattr__` in this code relies on an instance object's `__dict__` attribute namespace dictionary in order to set `onInstance`'s own `wrapped` attribute. As we learned in the prior chapter, it cannot assign an attribute directly without looping. However, it uses the `setattr` built-in instead of `__dict__` to set attributes in the wrapped object itself. Moreover, `getattr` is used to fetch attributes in the wrapped object, since they may be stored in the object itself or inherited by it.

Because of that, this code will work for most classes. You may recall from Chapter 31 that new-style classes with `__slots__` may not store attributes in a `__dict__`. However, because we only rely on a `__dict__` at the `onInstance` level here, not in the wrapped instance, and because `setattr` and `getattr` apply to attributes based on both `__dict__` and `__slots__`, our decorator applies to classes using either storage scheme.

Generalizing for Public Declarations, Too

Now that we have a `Private` implementation, it's straightforward to generalize the code to allow for `Public` declarations too—they are essentially the inverse of `Private` declarations, so we need only negate the inner test. The example listed in this section allows a class to use decorators to define a set of either `Private` or `Public` instance attributes (attributes stored on an instance or inherited from its classes), with the following semantics:

- `Private` declares attributes of a class's instances that cannot be fetched or assigned, except from within the code of the class's methods. That is, any name declared `Private` cannot be accessed from outside the class, while any name not declared `Private` can be freely fetched or assigned from outside the class.

- `Public` declares attributes of a class's instances that can be fetched or assigned from both outside the class and within the class's methods. That is, any name declared `Public` can be freely accessed anywhere, while any name not declared `Public` cannot be accessed from outside the class.

`Private` and `Public` declarations are intended to be mutually exclusive: when using `Private`, all undeclared names are considered `Public`, and when using `Public`, all undeclared names are considered `Private`. They are essentially inverses, though undeclared names not created by class methods behave slightly differently—they can be assigned and thus created outside the class under `Private` (all undeclared names are accessible), but not under `Public` (all undeclared names are inaccessible).

Again, study this code on your own to get a feel for how this works. Notice that this scheme adds an additional *fourth level of state retention* at the top, beyond that described in the preceding section: the test functions used by the `lambda`s are saved in an extra enclosing scope. This example is coded to run under either Python 2.6 or 3.0, though it comes with a caveat when run under 3.0 (explained briefly in the file's docstring and expanded on after the code):

```
"""
Class decorator with Private and Public attribute declarations.
Controls access to attributes stored on an instance, or inherited
by it from its classes. Private declares attribute names that
cannot be fetched or assigned outside the decorated class, and
Public declares all the names that can. Caveat: this works in
3.0 for normally named attributes only: __X__ operator overloading
methods implicitly run for built-in operations do not trigger
either __getattr__ or __getattribute__ in new-style classes.
Add __X__ methods here to intercept and delegate built-ins.
"""

traceMe = False
def trace(*args):
    if traceMe: print('[' + ' '.join(map(str, args)) + ']')

def accessControl(failIf):
    def onDecorator(aClass):
        class onInstance:
            def __init__(self, *args, **kargs):
                self.__wrapped = aClass(*args, **kargs)
            def __getattr__(self, attr):
```

```
                    trace('get:', attr)
                    if failIf(attr):
                        raise TypeError('private attribute fetch: ' + attr)
                    else:
                        return getattr(self.__wrapped, attr)
                def __setattr__(self, attr, value):
                    trace('set:', attr, value)
                    if attr == '_onInstance__wrapped':
                        self.__dict__[attr] = value
                    elif failIf(attr):
                        raise TypeError('private attribute change: ' + attr)
                    else:
                        setattr(self.__wrapped, attr, value)
            return onInstance
        return onDecorator

    def Private(*attributes):
        return accessControl(failIf=(lambda attr: attr in attributes))

    def Public(*attributes):
        return accessControl(failIf=(lambda attr: attr not in attributes))
```

See the prior example's self-test code for a usage example. Here's a quick look at these class decorators in action at the interactive prompt (they work the same in 2.6 and 3.0); as advertised, non-`Private` or `Public` names can be fetched and changed from outside the subject class, but `Private` or non-`Public` names cannot:

```
>>> from access import Private, Public

>>> @Private('age')                  # Person = Private('age')(Person)
... class Person:                    # Person = onInstance with state
...     def __init__(self, name, age):
...         self.name = name
...         self.age  = age          # Inside accesses run normally
...
>>> X = Person('Bob', 40)
>>> X.name                           # Outside accesses validated
'Bob'
>>> X.name = 'Sue'
>>> X.name
'Sue'
>>> X.age
TypeError: private attribute fetch: age
>>> X.age = 'Tom'
TypeError: private attribute change: age

>>> @Public('name')
... class Person:
...     def __init__(self, name, age):
...         self.name = name
...         self.age  = age
...
>>> X = Person('bob', 40)            # X is an onInstance
>>> X.name                           # onInstance embeds Person
'bob'
```

```
>>> X.name = 'Sue'
>>> X.name
'Sue'
>>> X.age
TypeError: private attribute fetch: age
>>> X.age = 'Tom'
TypeError: private attribute change: age
```

Implementation Details II

To help you analyze the code, here are a few final notes on this version. Since this is just a generalization of the preceding section's example, most of the notes there apply here as well.

Using __X pseudoprivate names

Besides generalizing, this version also makes use of Python's __X pseudoprivate name mangling feature (which we met in Chapter 30) to localize the wrapped attribute to the control class, by automatically prefixing it with the class name. This avoids the prior version's risk for collisions with a wrapped attribute that may be used by the real, wrapped class, and it's useful in a general tool like this. It's not quite "privacy," though, because the mangled name can be used freely outside the class. Notice that we also have to use the fully expanded name string ('_onInstance__wrapped') in __setattr__, because that's what Python changes it to.

Breaking privacy

Although this example does implement access controls for attributes of an instance and its classes, it is possible to subvert these controls in various ways—for instance, by going through the expanded version of the wrapped attribute explicitly (bob.pay might not work, but the fully mangled bob._onInstance__wrapped.pay could!). If you have to explicitly try to do so, though, these controls are probably sufficient for normal intended use. Of course, privacy controls can generally be subverted in any language if you try hard enough (#define private public may work in some C++ implementations, too). Although access controls can reduce accidental changes, much of this is up to programmers in any language; whenever source code may be changed, access control will always be a bit of a pipe dream.

Decorator tradeoffs

We could again achieve the same results without decorators, by using manager functions or coding the name rebinding of decorators manually; the decorator syntax, however, makes this consistent and a bit more obvious in the code. The chief potential downsides of this and any other wrapper-based approach are that attribute access incurs an extra call, and instances of decorated classes are not really instances of the original decorated class—if you test their type with X.__class__ or isinstance(X, C), for example, you'll find that they are instances of the *wrapper* class. Unless you plan to do introspection on objects' types, though, the type issue is probably irrelevant.

Open Issues

As is, this example works as planned under Python 2.6 and 3.0 (provided operator overloading methods to be delegated are redefined in the wrapper). As with most software, though, there is always room for improvement.

Caveat: operator overloading methods fail to delegate under 3.0

Like all delegation-based classes that use __getattr__, this decorator works cross-version for normally named attributes only; operator overloading methods like __str__ and __add__ work differently for new-style classes and so fail to reach the embedded object if defined there when this runs under 3.0.

As we learned in the prior chapter, classic classes look up operator overloading names in instances at runtime normally, but new-style classes do not—they skip the instance entirely and look up such methods in classes. Hence, the __X__ operator overloading methods implicitly run for built-in operations do *not* trigger either __getattr__ or __getattribute__ in new-style classes in 2.6 and all classes in 3.0; such attribute fetches skip our onInstance.__getattr__ altogether, so they cannot be validated or delegated.

Our decorator's class is not coded as new-style (by deriving from object), so it will catch operator overloading methods if run under 2.6. Since all classes are new-style automatically in 3.0, though, such methods will *fail* if they are coded on the embedded object. The simplest workaround in 3.0 is to redefine redundantly in onInstance all the operator overloading methods that can possibly be used in wrapped objects. Such extra methods can be added by hand, by tools that partly automate the task (e.g., with class decorators or the metaclasses discussed in the next chapter), or by definition in superclasses.

To see the difference yourself, try applying the decorator to a class that uses operator overloading methods under 2.6; validations work as before, and both the __str__ method used by printing and the __add__ method run for + invoke the decorator's __getattr__ and hence wind up being validated and delegated to the subject Person object correctly:

```
C:\misc> c:\python26\python
>>> from access import Private
>>> @Private('age')
... class Person:
...     def __init__(self):
...         self.age = 42
...     def __str__(self):
...         return 'Person: ' + str(self.age)
...     def __add__(self, yrs):
...         self.age += yrs
...
```

```
>>> X = Person()
>>> X.age                               # Name validations fail correctly
TypeError: private attribute fetch: age
>>> print(X)                            # __getattr__ => runs Person.__str__
Person: 42
>>> X + 10                              # __getattr__ => runs Person.__add__
>>> print(X)                            # __getattr__ => runs Person.__str__
Person: 52
```

When the same code is run under Python 3.0, though, the implicitly invoked __str__
and __add__ skip the decorator's __getattr__ and look for definitions in or above the
decorator class itself; print winds up finding the default display inherited from the class
type (technically, from the implied object superclass in 3.0), and + generates an error
because no default is inherited:

```
C:\misc> c:\python30\python
>>> from access import Private
>>> @Private('age')
... class Person:
...     def __init__(self):
...         self.age = 42
...     def __str__(self):
...         return 'Person: ' + str(self.age)
...     def __add__(self, yrs):
...         self.age += yrs
...
>>> X = Person()                        # Name validations still work
>>> X.age                               # But 3.0 fails to delegate built-ins!
TypeError: private attribute fetch: age
>>> print(X)
<access.onInstance object at 0x025E0790>
>>> X + 10
TypeError: unsupported operand type(s) for +: 'onInstance' and 'int'
>>> print(X)
<access.onInstance object at 0x025E0790>
```

Using the alternative __getattribute__ method won't help here—although it is defined
to catch every attribute reference (not just undefined names), it is also not run by built-
in operations. Python's property feature, which we met in Chapter 37, won't help here
either; recall that properties are automatically run code associated with *specific*
attributes defined when a class is written, and are not designed to handle arbitrary
attributes in wrapped objects.

As mentioned earlier, the most straightforward solution under 3.0 is to redundantly
redefine operator overloading names that may appear in embedded objects in
delegation-based classes like our decorator. This isn't ideal because it creates some code
redundancy, especially compared to 2.6 solutions. However, it isn't too major a coding
effort, can be automated to some extent with tools or superclasses, suffices to make
our decorator work in 3.0, and allows operator overloading names to be declared
Private or Public too (assuming each overloading method runs the failIf test
internally):

```
def accessControl(failIf):
    def onDecorator(aClass):
        class onInstance:
            def __init__(self, *args, **kargs):
                self.__wrapped = aClass(*args, **kargs)

            # Intercept and delegate operator overloading methods
            def __str__(self):
                return str(self.__wrapped)
            def __add__(self, other):
                return self.__wrapped + other
            def __getitem__(self, index):
                return self.__wrapped[index]         # If needed
            def __call__(self, *args, **kargs):
                return self.__wrapped(*arg, *kargs)  # If needed
            ...plus any others needed...

            # Intercept and delegate named attributes
            def __getattr__(self, attr):
                ...
            def __setattr__(self, attr, value):
                ...
        return onInstance
    return onDecorator
```

With such operator overloading methods added, the prior example with __str__ and __add__ works the same under 2.6 and 3.0, although a substantial amount of extra code may be required to accommodate 3.0—in principle, *every* operator overloading method that is not run automatically will need to be defined redundantly for 3.0 in a general tool class like this (which is why this extension is omitted in our code). Since every class is new-style in 3.0, delegation-based code is more difficult (though not impossible) in this release.

On the other hand, delegation wrappers could simply inherit from a common superclass that redefines operator overloading methods once, with standard delegation code. Moreover, tools such as additional class decorators or metaclasses might automate some of the work of adding such methods to delegation classes (see the class augmentation examples in Chapter 39 for details). Though still not as simple as the 2.6 solution, such techniques might help make 3.0 delegation classes more general.

Implementation alternatives: __getattribute__ inserts, call stack inspection

Although redundantly defining operator overloading methods in wrappers is probably the most straightforward workaround to Python 3.0 dilemma outlined in the prior section, it's not necessarily the only one. We don't have space to explore this issue much further here, so investigating other potential solutions is relegated to a suggested exercise. Because one dead-end alternative underscores class concepts well, though, it merits a brief mention.

One downside of this example is that instance objects are not truly instances of the original class—they are instances of the wrapper instead. In some programs that rely

---

on type testing, this might matter. To support such cases, we might try to achieve similar effects by *inserting* a __getattribute__ method into the original class, to catch *every* attribute reference made on its instances. This inserted method would pass valid requests up to its superclass to avoid loops, using the techniques we studied in the prior chapter. Here is the potential change to our class decorator's code:

```
# trace support as before

def accessControl(failIf):
    def onDecorator(aClass):
        def getattributes(self, attr):
            trace('get:', attr)
            if failIf(attr):
                raise TypeError('private attribute fetch: ' + attr)
            else:
                return object.__getattribute__(self, attr)
        aClass.__getattribute__ = getattributes
        return aClass
    return onDecorator

def Private(*attributes):
    return accessControl(failIf=(lambda attr: attr in attributes))

def Public(*attributes):
    return accessControl(failIf=(lambda attr: attr not in attributes))
```

This alternative addresses the type-testing issue but suffers from others. For example, it handles only attribute *fetches*—as is, this version allows private names to be *assigned* freely. Intercepting assignments would still have to use __setattr__, and either an instance wrapper object or another class method insertion. Adding an instance wrapper to catch assignments would change the type again, and inserting methods fails if the original class is using a __setattr__ of its own (or a __getattribute__, for that matter!). An inserted __setattr__ would also have to allow for a __slots__ in the client class.

In addition, this scheme does not address the *built-in* operation attributes issue described in the prior section, since __getattribute__ is not run in these contexts, either. In our case, if Person had a __str__ it would be run by print operations, but only because it was actually present in that class. As before, the __str__ attribute would *not* be routed to the inserted __getattribute__ method generically—printing would bypass this method altogether and call the class's __str__ directly.

Although this is probably better than not supporting operator overloading methods in a wrapped object at all (barring redefinition, at least), this scheme still cannot intercept and validate __X__ methods, making it impossible for any of them to be Private. Although most operator overloading methods are meant to be public, some might not be.

Much worse, because this nonwrapper approach works by adding a __getattribute__ to the decorated class, it also intercepts attribute accesses made *by the class itself* and validates them the same as accesses made from outside—this means the class's method won't be able to use `Private` names, either!

In fact, inserting methods this way is functionally equivalent to *inheriting* them, and implies the same constraints as our original Chapter 29 privacy code. To know whether an attribute access originated inside or outside the class, our method might need to inspect frame objects on the Python *call stack*. This might ultimately yield a solution (replace private attributes with properties or descriptors that check the stack, for example), but it would slow access further and is far too dark a magic for us to explore here.

While interesting, and possibly relevant for some other use cases, this method insertion technique doesn't meet our goals. We won't explore this option's coding pattern further here because we will study class augmentation techniques in the next chapter, in conjunction with metaclasses. As we'll see there, metaclasses are not strictly required for changing classes this way, because class decorators can often serve the same role.

Python Isn't About Control

Now that I've gone to such great lengths to add `Private` and `Public` attribute declarations for Python code, I must again remind you that it is not entirely *Pythonic* to add access controls to your classes like this. In fact, most Python programmers will probably find this example to be largely or totally irrelevant, apart from serving as a demonstration of decorators in action. Most large Python programs get by successfully without any such controls at all. If you do wish to regulate attribute access in order to eliminate coding mistakes, though, or happen to be a soon-to-be-ex-C++-or-Java programmer, most things are possible with Python's operator overloading and introspection tools.

Example: Validating Function Arguments

As a final example of the utility of decorators, this section develops a *function decorator* that automatically tests whether arguments passed to a function or method are within a valid numeric range. It's designed to be used during either development or production, and it can be used as a template for similar tasks (e.g., argument type testing, if you must). Because this chapter's size limits has been broached, this example's code is largely self-study material, with limited narrative; as usual, browse the code for more details.

The Goal

In the object-oriented tutorial of Chapter 27, we wrote a class that gave a raise to objects representing people based upon a passed-in percentage:

```
class Person:
    ...
```

```
def giveRaise(self, percent):
    self.pay = int(self.pay * (1 + percent))
```

There, we noted that if we wanted the code to be robust it would be a good idea to check the percentage to make sure it's not too large or too small. We could implement such a check with either if or assert statements in the method itself, using *inline tests*:

```
class Person:
    def giveRaise(self, percent):           # Validate with inline code
        if percent < 0.0 or percent > 1.0:
            raise TypeError, 'percent invalid'
        self.pay = int(self.pay * (1 + percent))

class Person:                                # Validate with asserts
    def giveRaise(self, percent):
        assert percent >= 0.0 and percent <= 1.0, 'percent invalid'
        self.pay = int(self.pay * (1 + percent))
```

However, this approach clutters up the method with inline tests that will probably be useful only during development. For more complex cases, this can become tedious (imagine trying to inline the code needed to implement the attribute privacy provided by the last section's decorator). Perhaps worse, if the validation logic ever needs to change, there may be arbitrarily many inline copies to find and update.

A more useful and interesting alternative would be to develop a general tool that can perform range tests for us automatically, for the arguments of any function or method we might code now or in the future. A *decorator* approach makes this explicit and convenient:

```
class Person:
    @rangetest(percent=(0.0, 1.0))          # Use decorator to validate
    def giveRaise(self, percent):
        self.pay = int(self.pay * (1 + percent))
```

Isolating validation logic in a decorator simplifies both clients and future maintenance.

Notice that our goal here is different than the attribute validations coded in the prior chapter's final example. Here, we mean to validate the values of *function arguments* when passed, rather than *attribute values* when set. Python's decorator and introspection tools allow us to code this new task just as easily.

A Basic Range-Testing Decorator for Positional Arguments

Let's start with a basic range test implementation. To keep things simple, we'll begin by coding a decorator that works only for positional arguments and assumes they always appear at the same position in every call; they cannot be passed by keyword name, and we don't support additional **args keywords in calls because this can invalidate the positions declared in the decorator. Code the following in a file called *devtools.py*:

```
def rangetest(*argchecks):                   # Validate positional arg ranges
    def onDecorator(func):
        if not __debug__:                    # True if "python -O main.py args..."
```

```
            return func                          # No-op: call original directly
        else:                                    # Else wrapper while debugging
            def onCall(*args):
                for (ix, low, high) in argchecks:
                    if args[ix] < low or args[ix] > high:
                        errmsg = 'Argument %s not in %s..%s' % (ix, low, high)
                        raise TypeError(errmsg)
                return func(*args)
            return onCall
    return onDecorator
```

As is, this code is mostly a rehash of the coding patterns we explored earlier: we use decorator arguments, nested scopes for state retention, and so on.

We also use nested `def` statements to ensure that this works for both simple functions and methods, as we learned earlier. When used for a class method, `onCall` receives the subject class's instance in the first item in `*args` and passes this along to `self` in the original method function; argument numbers in range tests start at 1 in this case, not 0.

Also notice this code's use of the `__debug__` built-in variable, though—Python sets this to `True`, unless it's being run with the `-O` optimize command-line flag (e.g., `python -O main.py`). When `__debug__` is `False`, the decorator returns the origin function unchanged, to avoid extra calls and their associated performance penalty.

This first iteration solution is used as follows:

```
# File devtools_test.py

from devtools import rangetest
print(__debug__)                            # False if "python –O main.py"

@rangetest((1, 0, 120))                     # persinfo = rangetest(...)(persinfo)
def persinfo(name, age):                    # age must be in 0..120
    print('%s is %s years old' % (name, age))

@rangetest([0, 1, 12], [1, 1, 31], [2, 0, 2009])
def birthday(M, D, Y):
    print('birthday = {0}/{1}/{2}'.format(M, D, Y))

class Person:
    def __init__(self, name, job, pay):
        self.job  = job
        self.pay  = pay

    @rangetest([1, 0.0, 1.0])               # giveRaise = rangetest(...)(giveRaise)
    def giveRaise(self, percent):           # Arg 0 is the self instance here
        self.pay = int(self.pay * (1 + percent))

# Comment lines raise TypeError unless "python -O" used on shell command line

persinfo('Bob Smith', 45)                   # Really runs onCall(...) with state
#persinfo('Bob Smith', 200)                 # Or person if –O cmd line argument

birthday(5, 31, 1963)
#birthday(5, 32, 1963)
```

```
sue = Person('Sue Jones', 'dev', 100000)
sue.giveRaise(.10)                        # Really runs onCall(self, .10)
print(sue.pay)                            # Or giveRaise(self, .10) if –O
#sue.giveRaise(1.10)
#print(sue.pay)
```

When run, valid calls in this code produce the following output (all the code in this section works the same under Python 2.6 and 3.0, because function decorators are supported in both, we're not using attribute delegation, and we use 3.0-style `print` calls and exception construction syntax):

```
C:\misc> C:\python30\python devtools_test.py
True
Bob Smith is 45 years old
birthday = 5/31/1963
110000
```

Uncommenting any of the invalid calls causes a `TypeError` to be raised by the decorator. Here's the result when the last two lines are allowed to run (as usual, I've omitted some of the error message text here to save space):

```
C:\misc> C:\python30\python devtools_test.py
True
Bob Smith is 45 years old
birthday = 5/31/1963
110000
TypeError: Argument 1 not in 0.0..1.0
```

Running Python with its –O flag at a system command line will disable range testing, but also avoid the performance overhead of the wrapping layer—we wind up calling the original undecorated function directly. Assuming this is a debugging tool only, you can use this flag to optimize your program for production use:

```
C:\misc> C:\python30\python -O devtools_test.py
False
Bob Smith is 45 years old
birthday = 5/31/1963
110000
231000
```

Generalizing for Keywords and Defaults, Too

The prior version illustrates the basics we need to employ, but it's fairly limited—it supports validating arguments passed by position only, and it does not validate keyword arguments (in fact, it assumes that no keywords are passed in a way that makes argument position numbers incorrect). Additionally, it does nothing about arguments with defaults that may be omitted in a given call. That's fine if all your arguments are passed by position and never defaulted, but less than ideal in a general tool. Python supports much more flexible argument-passing modes, which we're not yet addressing.

The mutation of our example shown next does better. By matching the wrapped function's expected arguments against the actual arguments passed in a call, it supports range validations for arguments passed by either position or keyword name, and it skips testing for default arguments omitted in the call. In short, arguments to be validated are specified by keyword arguments to the decorator, which later steps through both the *pargs positionals tuple and the **kargs keywords dictionary to validate.

```
"""
File devtools.py: function decorator that performs range-test
validation for passed arguments. Arguments are specified by
keyword to the decorator. In the actual call, arguments may
be passed by position or keyword, and defaults may be omitted.
See devtools_test.py for example use cases.
"""

trace = True

def rangetest(**argchecks):             # Validate ranges for both+defaults
    def onDecorator(func):              # onCall remembers func and argchecks
        if not __debug__:               # True if "python –O main.py args..."
            return func                 # Wrap if debugging; else use original
        else:
            import sys
            code     = func.__code__
            allargs  = code.co_varnames[:code.co_argcount]
            funcname = func.__name__

            def onCall(*pargs, **kargs):
                # All pargs match first N expected args by position
                # The rest must be in kargs or be omitted defaults
                positionals = list(allargs)
                positionals = positionals[:len(pargs)]

                for (argname, (low, high)) in argchecks.items():
                    # For all args to be checked
                    if argname in kargs:
                        # Was passed by name
                        if kargs[argname] < low or kargs[argname] > high:
                            errmsg = '{0} argument "{1}" not in {2}..{3}'
                            errmsg = errmsg.format(funcname, argname, low, high)
                            raise TypeError(errmsg)

                    elif argname in positionals:
                        # Was passed by position
                        position = positionals.index(argname)
                        if pargs[position] < low or pargs[position] > high:
                            errmsg = '{0} argument "{1}" not in {2}..{3}'
                            errmsg = errmsg.format(funcname, argname, low, high)
                            raise TypeError(errmsg)
                    else:
                        # Assume not passed: default
                        if trace:
                            print('Argument "{0}" defaulted'.format(argname))
```

```
            return func(*pargs, **kargs)        # OK: run original call
        return onCall
    return onDecorator
```

The following test script shows how the decorator is used—arguments to be validated are given by keyword decorator arguments, and at actual calls we can pass by name or position and omit arguments with defaults even if they are to be validated otherwise:

```
# File devtools_test.py
# Comment lines raise TypeError unless "python –O" used on shell command line
from devtools import rangetest


# Test functions, positional and keyword

@rangetest(age=(0, 120))                          # persinfo = rangetest(...)(persinfo)
def persinfo(name, age):
    print('%s is %s years old' % (name, age))

@rangetest(M=(1, 12), D=(1, 31), Y=(0, 2009))
def birthday(M, D, Y):
    print('birthday = {0}/{1}/{2}'.format(M, D, Y))

persinfo('Bob', 40)
persinfo(age=40, name='Bob')
birthday(5, D=1, Y=1963)
#persinfo('Bob', 150)
#persinfo(age=150, name='Bob')
#birthday(5, D=40, Y=1963)


# Test methods, positional and keyword

class Person:
    def __init__(self, name, job, pay):
        self.job = job
        self.pay = pay
                                                  # giveRaise = rangetest(...)(giveRaise)
    @rangetest(percent=(0.0, 1.0))                # percent passed by name or position
    def giveRaise(self, percent):
        self.pay = int(self.pay * (1 + percent))

bob = Person('Bob Smith', 'dev', 100000)
sue = Person('Sue Jones', 'dev', 100000)
bob.giveRaise(.10)
sue.giveRaise(percent=.20)
print(bob.pay, sue.pay)
#bob.giveRaise(1.10)
#bob.giveRaise(percent=1.20)


# Test omitted defaults: skipped

@rangetest(a=(1, 10), b=(1, 10), c=(1, 10), d=(1, 10))
def omitargs(a, b=7, c=8, d=9):
```

```
        print(a, b, c, d)

    omitargs(1, 2, 3, 4)
    omitargs(1, 2, 3)
    omitargs(1, 2, 3, d=4)
    omitargs(1, d=4)
    omitargs(d=4, a=1)
    omitargs(1, b=2, d=4)
    omitargs(d=8, c=7, a=1)
```

#omitargs(1, 2, 3, 11)	*# Bad d*
#omitargs(1, 2, 11)	*# Bad c*
#omitargs(1, 2, 3, d=11)	*# Bad d*
#omitargs(11, d=4)	*# Bad a*
#omitargs(d=4, a=11)	*# Bad a*
#omitargs(1, b=11, d=4)	*# Bad b*
#omitargs(d=8, c=7, a=11)	*# Bad a*

When this script is run, out-of-range arguments raise an exception as before, but arguments may be passed by either name or position, and omitted defaults are not validated. This code runs on both 2.6 and 3.0, but extra tuple parentheses print in 2.6. Trace its output and test this further on your own to experiment; it works as before, but its scope has been broadened:

```
C:\misc> C:\python30\python devtools_test.py
Bob is 40 years old
Bob is 40 years old
birthday = 5/1/1963
110000 120000
1 2 3 4
Argument "d" defaulted
1 2 3 9
1 2 3 4
Argument "c" defaulted
Argument "b" defaulted
1 7 8 4
Argument "c" defaulted
Argument "b" defaulted
1 7 8 4
Argument "c" defaulted
1 2 8 4
Argument "b" defaulted
1 7 7 8
```

On validation errors, we get an exception as before (unless the –O command-line argument is passed to Python) when one of the method test lines is uncommented:

```
TypeError: giveRaise argument "percent" not in 0.0..1.0
```

Implementation Details

This decorator's code relies on both introspection APIs and subtle constraints of argument passing. To be fully general we could in principle try to mimic Python's argument matching logic in its entirety to see which names have been passed in which modes, but that's far too much complexity for our tool. It would be better if we could somehow match arguments passed by name against the set of all expected arguments' names, in order to determine which position arguments actually appear in during a given call.

Function introspection

It turns out that the introspection API available on function objects and their associated code objects has exactly the tool we need. This API was briefly introduced in Chapter 19, but we'll actually put it to use here. The set of expected argument names is simply the first *N* variable names attached to a function's code object:

```python
# In Python 3.0 (and 2.6 for compatibility):
>>> def func(a, b, c, d):
...     x = 1
...     y = 2
...
>>> code = func.__code__                       # Code object of function object
>>> code.co_nlocals
6
>>> code.co_varnames                           # All local var names
('a', 'b', 'c', 'd', 'x', 'y')
>>> code.co_varnames[:code.co_argcount]        # First N locals are expected args
('a', 'b', 'c', 'd')

>>> import sys                                  # For backward compatibility
>>> sys.version_info                            # [0] is major release number
(3, 0, 0, 'final', 0)
>>> code = func.__code__ if sys.version_info[0] == 3 else func.func_code
```

The same API is available in older Pythons, but the func.__code__ attribute is spelled as func.func_code in 2.5 and earlier (the newer __code__ attribute is also redundantly available in 2.6 for portability). Run a `dir` call on function and code objects for more details.

Argument assumptions

Given this set of expected argument names, the solution relies on two constraints on argument passing order imposed by Python (these still hold true in both 2.6 and 3.0):

- At the call, all positional arguments appear before all keyword arguments.
- In the def, all nondefault arguments appear before all default arguments.

That is, a nonkeyword argument cannot generally follow a keyword argument at a call, and a nondefault argument cannot follow a default argument at a definition. All "name=value" syntax must appear after any simple "name" in both places.

To simplify our work, we can also make the assumption that a call is valid in general—i.e., that all arguments either will receive values (by name or position), or will be omitted intentionally to pick up defaults. This assumption won't necessarily hold, because the function has not yet actually been called when the wrapper logic tests validity—the call may still fail later when invoked by the wrapper layer, due to incorrect argument passing. As long as that doesn't cause the wrapper to fail any more badly, though, we can finesse the validity of the call. This helps, because validating calls before they are actually made would require us to emulate Python's argument-matching algorithm in full—again, too complex a procedure for our tool.

Matching algorithm

Now, given these constraints and assumptions, we can allow for both keywords and omitted default arguments in the call with this algorithm. When a call is intercepted, we can make the following assumptions:

- All *N* passed positional arguments in *pargs must match the first *N* expected arguments obtained from the function's code object. This is true per Python's call ordering rules, outlined earlier, since all positionals precede all keywords.

- To obtain the names of arguments actually passed by position, we can slice the list of all expected arguments up to the length *N* of the *pargs positionals tuple.

- Any arguments after the first *N* expected arguments either were passed by keyword or were defaulted by omission at the call.

- For each argument name to be validated, if it is in **kargs it was passed by name, and if it is in the first *N* expected arguments it was passed by position (in which case its relative position in the expected list gives its relative position in *pargs); otherwise, we can assume it was omitted in the call and defaulted and need not be checked.

In other words, we can skip tests for arguments that were omitted in a call by assuming that the first *N* actually passed positional arguments in *pargs must match the first *N* argument names in the list of all expected arguments, and that any others must either have been passed by keyword and thus be in **kargs, or have been defaulted. Under this scheme, the decorator will simply skip any argument to be checked that was omitted between the rightmost positional argument and the leftmost keyword argument, between keyword arguments, or after the rightmost positional in general. Trace through the decorator and its test script to see how this is realized in code.

Open Issues

Although our range-testing tool works as planned, two caveats remain. First, as mentioned earlier, calls to the original function that are not valid still fail in our final decorator. The following both trigger exceptions, for example:

```
omitargs()
omitargs(d=8, c=7, b=6)
```

These only fail, though, where we try to invoke the original function, at the end of the wrapper. While we could try to imitate Python's argument matching to avoid this, there's not much reason to do so—since the call would fail at this point anyhow, we might as well let Python's own argument-matching logic detect the problem for us.

Lastly, although our final version handles positional arguments, keyword arguments, and omitted defaults, it still doesn't do anything explicit about *args and **args that may be used in a decorated function that accepts arbitrarily many arguments. We probably don't need to care for our purposes, though:

- If an extra *keyword* argument is passed, its name will show up in **kargs and can be tested normally if mentioned to the decorator.

- If an extra keyword argument is *not* passed, its name won't be in either **kargs or the sliced expected positionals list, and it will thus not be checked—it is treated as though it were defaulted, even though it is really an optional extra argument.

- If an extra *positional* argument is passed, there's no way to reference it in the decorator anyhow—its name won't be in either **kargs or the sliced expected arguments list, so it will simply be skipped. Because such arguments are not listed in the function's definition, there's no way to map a name given to the decorator back to an expected relative position.

In other words, as it is the code supports testing arbitrary keyword arguments by name, but not arbitrary positionals that are unnamed and hence have no set position in the function's argument signature.

In principle, we could extend the decorator's interface to support *args in the decorated function, too, for the rare cases where this might be useful (e.g., a special argument name with a test to apply to all arguments in the wrapper's *pargs beyond the length of the expected arguments list). Since we've already exhausted the space allocation for this example, though, if you care about such improvements you've officially crossed over into the realm of suggested exercises.

Decorator Arguments Versus Function Annotations

Interestingly, the function annotation feature introduced in Python 3.0 could provide an alternative to the decorator arguments used by our example to specify range tests. As we learned in Chapter 19, annotations allow us to associate expressions with arguments and return values, by coding them in the def header line itself; Python collects annotations in a dictionary and attaches it to the annotated function.

We could use this in our example to code range limits in the header line, instead of in decorator arguments. We would still need a function decorator to wrap the function in order to intercept later calls, but we would essentially trade decorator argument syntax:

```
@rangetest(a=(1, 5), c=(0.0, 1.0))
def func(a, b, c):                      # func = rangetest(...)(func)
    print(a + b + c)
```

for annotation syntax like this:

```
@rangetest
def func(a:(1, 5), b, c:(0.0, 1.0)):
    print(a + b + c)
```

That is, the range constraints would be moved into the function itself, instead of being coded externally. The following script illustrates the structure of the resulting decorators under both schemes, in incomplete skeleton code. The decorator arguments code pattern is that of our complete solution shown earlier; the annotation alternative requires one less level of nesting, because it doesn't need to retain decorator arguments:

```
# Using decorator arguments

def rangetest(**argchecks):
    def onDecorator(func):
        def onCall(*pargs, **kargs):
            print(argchecks)
            for check in argchecks: pass        # Add validation code here
            return func(*pargs, **kargs)
        return onCall
    return onDecorator

@rangetest(a=(1, 5), c=(0.0, 1.0))
def func(a, b, c):                               # func = rangetest(...)(func)
    print(a + b + c)

func(1, 2, c=3)                                  # Runs onCall, argchecks in scope


# Using function annotations

def rangetest(func):
    def onCall(*pargs, **kargs):
        argchecks = func.__annotations__
        print(argchecks)
        for check in argchecks: pass             # Add validation code here
        return func(*pargs, **kargs)
    return onCall

@rangetest
def func(a:(1, 5), b, c:(0.0, 1.0)):             # func = rangetest(func)
    print(a + b + c)

func(1, 2, c=3)                                  # Runs onCall, annotations on func
```

When run, both schemes have access to the same validation test information, but in different forms—the decorator argument version's information is retained in an argument in an enclosing scope, and the annotation version's information is retained in an attribute of the function itself:

```
{'a': (1, 5), 'c': (0.0, 1.0)}
6
{'a': (1, 5), 'c': (0.0, 1.0)}
6
```

I'll leave fleshing out the rest of the annotation-based version as a suggested exercise; its code would be identical to that of our complete solution shown earlier, because range-test information is simply on the function instead of in an enclosing scope. Really, all this buys us is a different user interface for our tool—it will still need to match argument names against expected argument names to obtain relative positions as before.

In fact, using annotation instead of decorator arguments in this example actually *limits its utility*. For one thing, annotation only works under Python 3.0, so 2.6 is no longer supported; function decorators with arguments, on the other hand, work in both versions.

More importantly, by moving the validation specifications into the `def` header, we essentially commit the function to a *single role*—since annotation allows us to code only one expression per argument, it can have only one purpose. For instance, we cannot use range-test annotations for any other role.

By contrast, because decorator arguments are coded outside the function itself, they are both easier to remove and *more general*—the code of the function itself does not imply a single decoration purpose. In fact, by *nesting* decorators with arguments, we can apply multiple augmentation steps to the same function; annotation directly supports only one. With decorator arguments, the function itself also retains a simpler, normal appearance.

Still, if you have a single purpose in mind, and you can commit to supporting 3.X only, the choice between annotation and decorator arguments is largely stylistic and subjective. As is so often true in life, one person's annotation may well be another's syntactic clutter....

Other Applications: Type Testing (If You Insist!)

The coding pattern we've arrived at for processing arguments in decorators could be applied in other contexts. Checking argument data types at development time, for example, is a straightforward extension:

```python
def typetest(**argchecks):
    def onDecorator(func):
        ....
        def onCall(*pargs, **kargs):
            positionals = list(allargs)[:len(pargs)]
            for (argname, type) in argchecks.items():
                if argname in kargs:
                    if not isinstance(kargs[argname], type):
                        ...
                        raise TypeError(errmsg)
                elif argname in positionals:
                    position = positionals.index(argname)
                    if not isinstance(pargs[position], type):
                        ...
                        raise TypeError(errmsg)
```

```
                    else:
                               # Assume not passed: default
                    return func(*pargs, **kargs)
            return onCall
    return onDecorator

@typetest(a=int, c=float)
def func(a, b, c, d):                   # func = typetest(...)(func)
    ...

func(1, 2, 3.0, 4)                      # Okay
func('spam', 2, 99, 4)                  # Triggers exception correctly
```

In fact, we might even generalize further by passing in a test function, much as we did to add Public decorations earlier; a single copy of this sort of code would suffice for both range and type testing. Using function annotations instead of decorator arguments for such a decorator, as described in the prior section, would make this look even more like type declarations in other languages:

```
@typetest
def func(a: int, b, c: float, d):       # func = typetest(func)
    ...                                  # Gasp!...
```

As you should have learned in this book, though, this particular role is generally a bad idea in working code, and not at all Pythonic (in fact, it's often a symptom of an ex-C++ programmer's first attempts to use Python).

Type testing restricts your function to work on specific types only, instead of allowing it to operate on any types with compatible interfaces. In effect, it limits your code and breaks its flexibility. On the other hand, every rule has exceptions; type checking may come in handy in isolated cases while debugging and when interfacing with code written in more restrictive languages, such as C++. This general pattern of argument processing might also be applicable in a variety of less controversial roles.

Chapter Summary

In this chapter, we explored decorators—both the function and class varieties. As we learned, decorators are a way to insert code to be run automatically when a function or class is defined. When a decorator is used, Python rebinds a function or class name to the callable object it returns. This hook allows us to add a layer of wrapper logic to function calls and class instance creation calls, in order to manage functions and instances. As we also saw, manager functions and manual name rebinding can achieve the same effect, but decorators provide a more explicit and uniform solution.

As we'll see in the next chapter, class decorators can also be used to manage classes themselves, rather than just their instances. Because this functionality overlaps with metaclasses, the topic of the next chapter, you'll have to read ahead for the rest of this story. First, though, work through the following quiz. Because this chapter was mostly focused on its larger examples, its quiz will ask you to modify some of its code in order to review.

Test Your Knowledge: Quiz

1. As mentioned in one of this chapter's Notes, the timer function decorator with decorator arguments that we wrote in the section "Adding Decorator Arguments" on page 1010 can be applied only to simple *functions*, because it uses a nested class with a `__call__` operator overloading method to catch calls. This structure does not work for class *methods* because the decorator instance is passed to `self`, not the subject class instance. Rewrite this decorator so that it can be applied to both simple functions and class methods, and test it on both functions and methods. (Hint: see the section "Class Blunders I: Decorating Class Methods" on page 1003 for pointers.) Note that you may make use of assigning function object attributes to keep track of total time, since you won't have a nested class for state retention and can't access nonlocals from outside the decorator code.

2. The `Public`/`Private` class decorators we wrote in this chapter will add overhead to every attribute fetch in a decorated class. Although we could simply delete the `@` decoration line to gain speed, we could also augment the decorator itself to check the `__debug__` switch and perform no wrapping at all when the `-O` Python flag is passed on the command line (just as we did for the argument range-test decorators). That way, we can speed our program without changing its source, via command-line arguments (`python -O main.py...`). Code and test this extension.

Test Your Knowledge: Answers

1. Here's one way to code the first question's solution, and its output (albeit with class methods that run too fast to time). The trick lies in replacing nested classes with *nested functions*, so the `self` argument is not the decorator's instance, and assigning the total time to the decorator function itself so it can be fetched later through the original rebound name (see the section "State Information Retention Options" on page 999 of this chapter for details—functions support arbitrary attribute attachment, and the function name is an enclosing scope reference in this context).

```
import time

def timer(label='', trace=True):          # On decorator args: retain args
    def onDecorator(func):                # On @: retain decorated func
        def onCall(*args, **kargs):       # On calls: call original
            start   = time.clock()        # State is scopes + func attr
            result  = func(*args, **kargs)
            elapsed = time.clock() - start
```

```
            onCall.alltime += elapsed
            if trace:
                format = '%s%s: %.5f, %.5f'
                values = (label, func.__name__, elapsed, onCall.alltime)
                print(format % values)
            return result
        onCall.alltime = 0
        return onCall
    return onDecorator
```

Test on functions

```
@timer(trace=True, label='[CCC]==>')
def listcomp(N):                              # Like listcomp = timer(...)(listcomp)
    return [x * 2 for x in range(N)]          # listcomp(...) triggers onCall

@timer(trace=True, label='[MMM]==>')
def mapcall(N):
    return list(map((lambda x: x * 2), range(N)))   # list() for 3.0 views

for func in (listcomp, mapcall):
    result = func(5)                          # Time for this call, all calls, return value
    func(5000000)
    print(result)
    print('allTime = %s\n' % func.alltime)    # Total time for all calls
```

Test on methods

```
class Person:
    def __init__(self, name, pay):
        self.name = name
        self.pay  = pay

    @timer()
    def giveRaise(self, percent):             # giveRaise = timer()(giveRaise)
        self.pay *= (1.0 + percent)           # tracer remembers giveRaise

    @timer(label='**')
    def lastName(self):                       # lastName = timer(...)(lastName)
        return self.name.split()[-1]          # alltime per class, not instance

bob = Person('Bob Smith', 50000)
sue = Person('Sue Jones', 100000)
bob.giveRaise(.10)
sue.giveRaise(.20)                            # runs onCall(sue, .10)
print(bob.pay, sue.pay)
print(bob.lastName(), sue.lastName())         # runs onCall(bob), remembers lastName
print('%.5f %.5f' % (Person.giveRaise.alltime, Person.lastName.alltime))
```

Expected output

```
[CCC]==>listcomp: 0.00002, 0.00002
[CCC]==>listcomp: 1.19636, 1.19638
[0, 2, 4, 6, 8]
allTime = 1.19637775192
```

```
[MMM]==>mapcall: 0.00002, 0.00002
[MMM]==>mapcall: 2.29260, 2.29262
[0, 2, 4, 6, 8]
allTime = 2.2926232943

giveRaise: 0.00001, 0.00001
giveRaise: 0.00001, 0.00002
55000.0 120000.0
**lastName: 0.00001, 0.00001
**lastName: 0.00001, 0.00002
Smith Jones
0.00002 0.00002
```

2. The following satisfies the second question—it's been augmented to return the original class in optimized mode (-O), so attribute accesses don't incur a speed hit. Really, all I did was add the debug mode test statements and indent the class further to the right. Add operator overloading method redefinitions to the wrapper class if you want to support delegation of these to the subject class in 3.0, too (2.6 routes these through __getattr__, but 3.0 and new-style classes in 2.6 do not).

```python
traceMe = False
def trace(*args):
    if traceMe: print('[' + ' '.join(map(str, args)) + ']')

def accessControl(failIf):
    def onDecorator(aClass):
        if not __debug__:
            return aClass
        else:
            class onInstance:
                def __init__(self, *args, **kargs):
                    self.__wrapped = aClass(*args, **kargs)
                def __getattr__(self, attr):
                    trace('get:', attr)
                    if failIf(attr):
                        raise TypeError('private attribute fetch: ' + attr)
                    else:
                        return getattr(self.__wrapped, attr)
                def __setattr__(self, attr, value):
                    trace('set:', attr, value)
                    if attr == '_onInstance__wrapped':
                        self.__dict__[attr] = value
                    elif failIf(attr):
                        raise TypeError('private attribute change: ' + attr)
                    else:
                        setattr(self.__wrapped, attr, value)
            return onInstance
    return onDecorator

def Private(*attributes):
    return accessControl(failIf=(lambda attr: attr in attributes))

def Public(*attributes):
    return accessControl(failIf=(lambda attr: attr not in attributes))
```

```
# Test code: split me off to another file to reuse decorator

@Private('age')                         # Person = Private('age')(Person)
class Person:                           # Person = onInstance with state
    def __init__(self, name, age):
        self.name = name
        self.age  = age                 # Inside accesses run normally

X = Person('Bob', 40)
print(X.name)                           # Outside accesses validated
X.name = 'Sue'
print(X.name)
#print(X.age)      # FAILS unles "python -O"
#X.age = 999       # ditto
#print(X.age)      # ditto

@Public('name')
class Person:
    def __init__(self, name, age):
        self.name = name
        self.age  = age

X = Person('bob', 40)                   # X is an onInstance
print(X.name)                           # onInstance embeds Person
X.name = 'Sue'
print(X.name)
#print(X.age)      # FAILS unless "python -O main.py"
#X.age = 999       # ditto
#print(X.age)      # ditto
```

## CHAPTER 39

Metaclasses

In the prior chapter, we explored decorators and studied various examples of their use. In this final chapter of the book, we're going continue our tool-builders focus and investigate another advanced topic: *metaclasses*.

In a sense, metaclasses simply extend the code-insertion model of decorators. As we learned in the prior chapter, function and class decorators allow us to intercept and augment function calls and class instance creation calls. In a similar sprit, metaclasses allow us to intercept and augment *class creation*—they provide an API for inserting extra logic to be run at the conclusion of a `class` statement, albeit in different ways than decorators. As such, they provide a general protocol for managing class objects in a program.

Like all the subjects dealt with in this part of the book, this is an *advanced topic* that can be investigated on an as-needed basis. In practice, metaclasses allow us to gain a high level of control over how a set of classes work. This is a powerful concept, and metaclasses are not intended for most application programmers (nor, frankly, the faint of heart!).

On the other hand, metaclasses open the door to a variety of coding patterns that may be difficult or impossible to achieve otherwise, and they are especially of interest to programmers seeking to write flexible APIs or programming tools for others to use. Even if you don't fall into that category, metaclasses can teach you much about Python's class model in general.

As in the prior chapter, part of our goal here is also to show more realistic code examples than we did earlier in this book. Although metaclasses are a core language topic and not themselves an application domain, part of this chapter's goal is to spark your interest in exploring larger application-programming examples after you finish this book.

To Metaclass or Not to Metaclass

Metaclasses are perhaps the most advanced topic in this book, if not the Python language as a whole. To borrow a quote from the *comp.lang.python* newsgroup by veteran Python core developer Tim Peters (who is also the author of the famous "import this" Python motto):

> [Metaclasses] are deeper magic than 99% of users should ever worry about. If you wonder whether you need them, you don't (the people who actually need them know with certainty that they need them, and don't need an explanation about why).

In other words, metaclasses are primarily intended for programmers building APIs and tools for others to use. In many (if not most) cases, they are probably not the best choice in applications work. This is especially true if you're developing code that other people will use in the future. Coding something "because it seems cool" is not generally a reasonable justification, unless you are experimenting or learning.

Still, metaclasses have a wide variety of potential roles, and it's important to know when they can be useful. For example, they can be used to enhance classes with features like tracing, object persistence, exception logging, and more. They can also be used to construct portions of a class at runtime based upon configuration files, apply function decorators to every method of a class generically, verify conformance to expected interfaces, and so on.

In their more grandiose incarnations, metaclasses can even be used to implement alternative coding patterns such as aspect-oriented programming, object/relational mappers (ORMs) for databases, and more. Although there are often alternative ways to achieve such results (as we'll see, the roles of class decorators and metaclasses often intersect), metaclasses provide a formal model tailored to those tasks. We don't have space to explore all such applications first-hand in this chapter but you should feel free to search the Web for additional use cases after studying the basics here.

Probably the reason for studying metaclasses most relevant to this book is that this topic can help demystify Python's class mechanics in general. Although you may or may not code or reuse them in your work, a cursory understanding of metaclasses can impart a deeper understanding of Python at large.

Increasing Levels of Magic

Most of this book has focused on straightforward application-coding techniques, as most programmers spend their time writing modules, functions, and classes to achieve real-world goals. They may use classes and make instances, and might even do a bit of operator overloading, but they probably won't get too deep into the details of how their classes actually work.

However, in this book we've also seen a variety of tools that allow us to control Python's behavior in generic ways, and that often have more to do with Python internals or tool building than with application-programming domains:

Introspection attributes
> Special attributes like `__class__` and `__dict__` allow us to inspect internal implementation aspects of Python objects, in order to process them generically—to list all attributes of an object, display a class's name, and so on.

Operator overloading methods
> Specially named methods such as `__str__` and `__add__` coded in classes intercept and provide behavior for built-in operations applied to class instances, such as printing, expression operators, and so on. They are run automatically in response to built-in operations and allow classes to conform to expected interfaces.

Attribute interception methods
> A special category of operator overloading methods provide a way to intercept attribute accesses on instances generically: `__getattr__`, `__setattr__`, and `__getattribute__` allow wrapper classes to insert automatically run code that may validate attribute requests and delegate them to embedded objects. They allow any number of attributes of an object—either selected attributes, or all of them—to be computed when accessed.

Class properties
> The `property` built-in allows us to associate code with a specific class attribute that is automatically run when the attribute is fetched, assigned, or deleted. Though not as generic as the prior paragraph's tools, properties allow for automatic code invocation on access to specific attributes.

Class attribute descriptors
> Really, `property` is a succinct way to define an attribute descriptor that runs functions on access automatically. Descriptors allow us to code in a separate class `__get__`, `__set__`, and `__delete__` handler methods that are run automatically when an attribute assigned to an instance of that class is accessed. They provide a general way to insert automatically run code when a specific attribute is accessed, and they are triggered after an attribute is looked up normally.

Function and class decorators
> As we saw in Chapter 38, the special `@callable` syntax for decorators allows us to add logic to be automatically run when a function is called or a class instance is created. This wrapper logic can trace or time calls, validate arguments, manage all instances of a class, augment instances with extra behavior such as attribute fetch validation, and more. Decorator syntax inserts name-rebinding logic to be run at the end of function and class definition statements—decorated function and class names are rebound to callable objects that intercept later calls.

As mentioned in this chapter's introduction, *metaclasses* are a continuation of this story—they allow us to insert logic to be run automatically when a class object is created, at the end of a `class` statement. This logic doesn't rebind the class name to a decorator callable, but rather routes creation of the class itself to specialized logic.

In other words, metaclasses are ultimately just another way to define *automatically run code*. Via metaclasses and the other tools just listed, Python provides ways for us to interject logic in a variety of contexts—at operator evaluation, attribute access, function calls, class instance creation, and now class object creation.

Unlike class decorators, which usually add logic to be run at *instance* creation time, metaclasses run at *class* creation time; as such, they are hooks generally used for managing or augmenting classes, instead of their instances.

For example, metaclasses can be used to add decoration to all methods of classes automatically, register all classes in use to an API, add user-interface logic to classes automatically, create or extend classes from simplified specifications in text files, and so on. Because we can control how classes are made (and by proxy the behavior their instances acquire), their applicability is potentially very wide.

As we've also seen, many of these advanced Python tools have *intersecting roles*. For example, attributes can often be managed with properties, descriptors, or attribute interception methods. As we'll see in this chapter, class decorators and metaclasses can often be used interchangeably as well. Although class decorators are often used to manage instances, they can be used to manage classes instead; similarly, while metaclasses are designed to augment class construction, they can often insert code to manage instances, too. Since the choice of which technique to use is sometimes purely subjective, knowledge of the alternatives can help you pick the right tool for a given task.

The Downside of "Helper" Functions

Also like the decorators of the prior chapter, metaclasses are often optional, from a theoretical perspective. We can usually achieve the same effect by passing class objects through *manager functions* (sometimes known as "helper" functions), much as we can achieve the goals of decorators by passing functions and instances through manager code. Just like decorators, though, metaclasses:

- Provide a more formal and explicit structure
- Help ensure that application programmers won't forget to augment their classes according to an API's requirements
- Avoid code redundancy and its associated maintenance costs by factoring class customization logic into a single location, the metaclass

To illustrate, suppose we want to automatically insert a method into a set of classes. Of course, we could do this with simple *inheritance*, if the subject method is known when we code the classes. In that case, we can simply code the method in a superclass and have all the classes in question inherit from it:

```
class Extras:
    def extra(self, args):        # Normal inheritance: too static
        ...

class Client1(Extras): ...        # Clients inherit extra methods
class Client2(Extras): ...
class Client3(Extras): ...

X = Client1()                     # Make an instance
X.extra()                         # Run the extra methods
```

Sometimes, though, it's impossible to predict such augmentation when classes are coded. Consider the case where classes are augmented in response to choices made in a user interface at runtime, or to specifications typed in a configuration file. Although we could code every class in our imaginary set to *manually* check these, too, it's a lot to ask of clients (`required` is abstract here—it's something to be filled in):

```
def extra(self, arg): ...

class Client1: ...                # Client augments: too distributed
if required():
    Client1.extra = extra

class Client2: ...
if required():
    Client2.extra = extra

class Client3: ...
if required():
    Client3.extra = extra

X = Client1()
X.extra()
```

We can add methods to a class after the `class` statement like this because a class method is just a function that is associated with a class and has a first argument to receive the `self` instance. Although this works, it puts all the burden of augmentation on client classes (and assumes they'll remember to do this at all!).

It would be better from a maintenance perspective to isolate the choice logic in a single place. We might encapsulate some of this extra work by routing classes though a *manager function*—such a manager function would extend the class as required and handle all the work of runtime testing and configuration:

```
def extra(self, arg): ...

def extras(Class):                # Manager function: too manual
    if required():
        Class.extra = extra

class Client1: ...
```

```
extras(Client1)

class Client2: ...
extras(Client2)

class Client3: ...
extras(Client3)

X = Client1()
X.extra()
```

This code runs the class through a manager function immediately after it is created. Although manager functions like this one can achieve our goal here, they still put a fairly heavy burden on class coders, who must understand the requirements and adhere to them in their code. It would be better if there were a simple way to enforce the augmentation in the subject classes, so that they don't need to deal with and can't forget to use the augmentation. In other words, we'd like to be able to insert some code to run *automatically* at the end of a `class` statement, to augment the class.

This is exactly what *metaclasses* do—by declaring a metaclass, we tell Python to route the creation of the class object to another class we provide:

```
def extra(self, arg): ...

class Extras(type):
    def __init__(Class, classname, superclasses, attributedict):
        if required():
            Class.extra = extra

class Client1(metaclass=Extras): ...    # Metaclass declaration only
class Client2(metaclass=Extras): ...    # Client class is instance of meta
class Client3(metaclass=Extras): ...

X = Client1()                           # X is instance of Client1
X.extra()
```

Because Python invokes the metaclass automatically at the end of the `class` statement when the new class is created, it can augment, register, or otherwise manage the class as needed. Moreover, the only requirement for the client classes is that they declare the metaclass; every class that does so will automatically acquire whatever augmentation the metaclass provides, both now and in the future if the metaclass changes. Although it may be difficult to see in this small example, metaclasses generally handle such tasks better than other approaches.

Metaclasses Versus Class Decorators: Round 1

Having said that, it's also interesting to note that the *class decorators* described in the preceding chapter sometimes overlap with metaclasses in terms of functionality. Although they are typically used for managing or augmenting instances, class decorators can also augment classes, independent of any created instances.

For example, suppose we coded our manager function to return the augmented class, instead of simply modifying it in-place. This would allow a greater degree of flexibility, because the manager would be free to return any type of object that implements the class's expected interface:

```
def extra(self, arg): ...

def extras(Class):
    if required():
        Class.extra = extra
    return Class

class Client1: ...
Client1 = extras(Client1)

class Client2: ...
Client2 = extras(Client2)

class Client3: ...
Client3 = extras(Client3)

X = Client1()
X.extra()
```

If you think this is starting to look reminiscent of class decorators, you're right. In the prior chapter we presented class decorators as a tool for augmenting *instance* creation calls. Because they work by automatically rebinding a class name to the result of a function, though, there's no reason that we can't use them to augment the class before any instances are ever created. That is, class decorators can apply extra logic to *classes*, not just *instances*, at creation time:

```
def extra(self, arg): ...

def extras(Class):
    if required():
        Class.extra = extra
    return Class

@extras
class Client1: ...          # Client1 = extras(Client1)

@extras
class Client2: ...          # Rebinds class independent of instances

@extras
class Client3: ...

X = Client1()               # Makes instance of augmented class
X.extra()                   # X is instance of original Client1
```

Decorators essentially automate the prior example's manual name rebinding here. Just like with metaclasses, because the decorator returns the original class, instances are made from it, not from a wrapper object. In fact, instance creation is not intercepted at all.

In this specific case—adding methods to a class when it's created—the choice between metaclasses and decorators is somewhat arbitrary. Decorators can be used to manage *both* instances and classes, and they intersect with metaclasses in the second of these roles.

However, this really addresses only one operational mode of metaclasses. As we'll see, decorators correspond to metaclass __init__ methods in this role, but metaclasses have additional customization hooks. As we'll also see, in addition to class initialization, metaclasses can perform arbitrary construction tasks that might be more difficult with decorators.

Moreover, although decorators can manage both instances and classes, the converse is not as direct—metaclasses are designed to manage classes, and applying them to managing *instances* is less straightforward. We'll explore this difference in code later in this chapter.

Much of this section's code has been abstract, but we'll flesh it out into a real working example later in this chapter. To fully understand how metaclasses work, though, we first need to get a clearer picture of their underlying model.

The Metaclass Model

To really understand how metaclasses do their work, you need to understand a bit more about Python's type model and what happens at the end of a class statement.

Classes Are Instances of type

So far in this book, we've done most of our work by making instances of built-in types like lists and strings, as well as instances of classes we code ourselves. As we've seen, instances of classes have some state information attributes of their own, but they also inherit behavioral attributes from the classes from which they are made. The same holds true for built-in types; list instances, for example, have values of their own, but they inherit methods from the list type.

While we can get a lot done with such instance objects, Python's type model turns out to be a bit richer than I've formally described. Really, there's a hole in the model we've seen thus far: if instances are created from classes, what is it that creates our classes? It turns out that classes are instances of something, too:

- In *Python 3.0*, user-defined class objects are instances of the object named type, which is itself a class.
- In *Python 2.6*, new-style classes inherit from object, which is a subclass of type; classic classes are instances of type and are not created from a class.

We explored the notion of types in Chapter 9 and the relationship of classes to types in Chapter 31, but let's review the basics here so we can see how they apply to metaclasses.

Recall that the type built-in returns the type of any object (which is itself an object). For built-in types like lists, the type of the instance is the built-in list type, but the type of the list type is the type type itself—the type object at the top of the hierarchy creates specific types, and specific types create instances. You can see this for yourself at the interactive prompt. In Python 3.0, for example:

```
C:\misc> c:\python30\python
>>> type([])                    # In 3.0 list is instance of list type
<class 'list'>
>>> type(type([]))              # Type of list is type class
<class 'type'>

>>> type(list)                  # Same, but with type names
<class 'type'>
>>> type(type)                  # Type of type is type: top of hierarchy
<class 'type'>
```

As we learned when studying new-style class changes in Chapter 31, the same is generally true in Python 2.6 (and older), but types are not quite the same as classes—type is a unique kind of built-in object that caps the type hierarchy and is used to construct types:

```
C:\misc> c:\python26\python
>>> type([])                    # In 2.6, type is a bit different
<type 'list'>
>>> type(type([]))
<type 'type'>

>>> type(list)
<type 'type'>
>>> type(type)
<type 'type'>
```

It turns out that the type/instance relationship holds true for classes as well: instances are created from classes, and classes are created from type. In Python 3.0, though, the notion of a "type" is merged with the notion of a "class." In fact, the two are essentially synonyms—*classes are types, and types are classes*. That is:

- Types are defined by classes that derive from type.
- User-defined classes are instances of type classes.
- User-defined classes are types that generate instances of their own.

As we saw earlier, this equivalence effects code that tests the type of instances: the type of an instance is the class from which it was generated. It also has implications for the way that classes are created that turn out to be the key to this chapter's subject. Because classes are normally created from a root type class by default, most programmers don't need to think about this type/class equivalence. However, it opens up new possibilities for customizing both classes and their instances.

For example, classes in 3.0 (and new-style classes in 2.6) are instances of the **type** class, and instance objects are instances of their classes; in fact, classes now have a __class__ that links to **type**, just as an instance has a __class__ that links to the class from which it was made:

```
C:\misc> c:\python30\python
>>> class C: pass                        # 3.0 class object (new-style)
...
>>> X = C()                              # Class instance object

>>> type(X)                              # Instance is instance of class
<class '__main__.C'>
>>> X.__class__                          # Instance's class
<class '__main__.C'>

>>> type(C)                              # Class is instance of type
<class 'type'>
>>> C.__class__                          # Class's class is type
<class 'type'>
```

Notice especially the last two lines here—classes are instances of the **type** class, just as normal instances are instances of a class. This works the same for both built-ins and user-defined class types in 3.0. In fact, classes are not really a separate concept at all: they are simply user-defined types, and **type** itself is defined by a class.

In Python 2.6, things work similarly for new-style classes derived from **object**, because this enables 3.0 class behavior:

```
C:\misc> c:\python26\python
>>> class C(object): pass                # In 2.6 new-style classes,
...                                      # classes have a class too
>>> X = C()

>>> type(X)
<class '__main__.C'>
>>> type(C)
<type 'type'>

>>> X.__class__
<class '__main__.C'>
>>> C.__class__
<type 'type'>
```

Classic classes in 2.6 are a bit different, though—because they reflect the class model in older Python releases, they do not have a __class__ link, and like built-in types in 2.6 they are instances of **type**, not a type class:

```
C:\misc> c:\python26\python
>>> class C: pass                        # In 2.6 classic classes,
...                                      # classes have no class themselves
>>> X = C()
```

```
>>> type(X)
<type 'instance'>
>>> type(C)
<type 'classobj'>

>>> X.__class__
<class __main__.C at 0x005F85A0>
>>> C.__class__
AttributeError: class C has no attribute '__class__'
```

Metaclasses Are Subclasses of Type

So why do we care that classes are instances of a **type** class in 3.0? It turns out that this is the hook that allows us to code metaclasses. Because the notion of *type* is the same as *class* today, we can subclass **type** with normal object-oriented techniques and class syntax to customize it. And because classes are really instances of the **type** class, creating classes from customized subclasses of **type** allows us to implement custom kinds of classes. In full detail, this all works out quite naturally—in 3.0, and in 2.6 new-style classes:

- **type** is a class that generates user-defined classes.
- Metaclasses are subclasses of the **type** class.
- Class objects are instances of the **type** class, or a subclass thereof.
- Instance objects are generated from a class.

In other words, to control the way classes are created and augment their behavior, all we need to do is specify that a user-defined class be created from a user-defined meta-class instead of the normal **type** class.

Notice that this *type instance* relationship is not quite the same as *inheritance*: user-defined classes may also have superclasses from which they and their instances inherit attributes (inheritance superclasses are listed in parentheses in the **class** statement and show up in a class's __bases__ tuple). The type from which a class is created, and of which it is an instance, is a different relationship. The next section describes the procedure Python follows to implement this instance-of type relationship.

Class Statement Protocol

Subclassing the **type** class to customize it is really only half of the magic behind meta-classes. We still need to somehow route a class's creation to the metaclass, instead of the default **type**. To fully understand how this is arranged, we also need to know how class statements do their business.

We've already learned that when Python reaches a **class** statement, it runs its nested block of code to create its attributes—all the names assigned at the top level of the nested code block generate attributes in the resulting class object. These names are usually method functions created by nested `def`s, but they can also be arbitrary attributes assigned to create class data shared by all instances.

Technically speaking, Python follows a standard protocol to make this happen: at the *end of a class statement*, and after running all its nested code in a namespace dictionary, it calls the `type` object to create the `class` object:

```
class = type(classname, superclasses, attributedict)
```

The `type` object in turn defines a `__call__` operator overloading method that runs two other methods when the `type` object is called:

```
type.__new__(typeclass, classname, superclasses, attributedict)
type.__init__(class, classname, superclasses, attributedict)
```

The `__new__` method creates and returns the new `class` object, and then the `__init__` method initializes the newly created object. As we'll see in a moment, these are the hooks that metaclass subclasses of `type` generally use to customize classes.

For example, given a class definition like the following:

```
class Spam(Eggs):          # Inherits from Eggs
    data = 1               # Class data attribute
    def meth(self, arg):   # Class method attribute
        pass
```

Python will internally run the nested code block to create two attributes of the class (`data` and `meth`), and then call the `type` object to generate the `class` object at the end of the `class` statement:

```
Spam = type('Spam', (Eggs,), {'data': 1, 'meth': meth, '__module__': '__main__'})
```

Because this call is made at the end of the `class` statement, it's an ideal hook for augmenting or otherwise processing a class. The trick lies in replacing `type` with a custom subclass that will intercept this call. The next section shows how.

Declaring Metaclasses

As we've just seen, classes are created by the `type` class by default. To tell Python to create a class with a custom metaclass instead, you simply need to declare a metaclass to intercept the normal class creation call. How you do so depends on which Python version you are using. In Python 3.0, list the desired metaclass as a keyword argument in the `class` header:

```
class Spam(metaclass=Meta):          # 3.0 and later
```

Inheritance superclasses can be listed in the header as well, before the metaclass. In the following, for example, the new class `Spam` inherits from `Eggs` but is also an instance of and is created by `Meta`:

```
class Spam(Eggs, metaclass=Meta):          # Other supers okay
```

We can get the same effect in Python 2.6, but we must specify the metaclass differently—using a class attribute instead of a keyword argument. The `object` derivation is required to make this a new-style class, and this form no longer works in 3.0 as the attribute is simply ignored:

```
class spam(object):                          # 2.6 version (only)
    __metaclass__ = Meta
```

In 2.6, a module-global `__metaclass__` variable is also available to link all classes in the module to a metaclass. This is no longer supported in 3.0, as it was intended as a temporary measure to make it easier to default to new-style classes without deriving every class from `object`.

When declared in these ways, the call to create the `class` object run at the end of the `class` statement is modified to invoke the metaclass instead of the `type` default:

```
class = Meta(classname, superclasses, attributedict)
```

And because the metaclass is a subclass of `type`, the `type` class's `__call__` delegates the calls to create and initialize the new `class` object to the metaclass, if it defines custom versions of these methods:

```
Meta.__new__(Meta, classname, superclasses, attributedict)
Meta.__init__(class, classname, superclasses, attributedict)
```

To demonstrate, here's the prior section's example again, augmented with a 3.0 metaclass specification:

```
class Spam(Eggs, metaclass=Meta):      # Inherits from Eggs, instance of Meta
    data = 1                           # Class data attribute
    def meth(self, arg):               # Class method attribute
        pass
```

At the end of this `class` statement, Python internally runs the following to create the `class` object:

```
Spam = Meta('Spam', (Eggs,), {'data': 1, 'meth': meth, '__module__': '__main__'})
```

If the metaclass defines its own versions of `__new__` or `__init__`, they will be invoked in turn during this call by the inherited `type` class's `__call__` method, to create and initialize the new class. The next section shows how we might go about coding this final piece of the metaclass puzzle.

Coding Metaclasses

So far, we've seen how Python routes class creation calls to a metaclass, if one is provided. How, though, do we actually code a metaclass that customizes `type`?

It turns out that you already know most of the story—metaclasses are coded with normal Python `class` statements and semantics. Their only substantial distinctions are that Python calls them automatically at the end of a `class` statement, and that they must adhere to the interface expected by the `type` superclass.

A Basic Metaclass

Perhaps the simplest metaclass you can code is simply a subclass of `type` with a `__new__` method that creates the class object by running the default version in `type`. A metaclass `__new__` like this is run by the `__call__` method inherited from `type`; it typically performs whatever customization is required and calls the `type` superclass's `__new__` method to create and return the new class object:

```
class Meta(type):
    def __new__(meta, classname, supers, classdict):
        # Run by inherited type.__call__
        return type.__new__(meta, classname, supers, classdict)
```

This metaclass doesn't really do anything (we might as well let the default `type` class create the class), but it demonstrates the way a metaclass taps into the metaclass hook to customize—because the metaclass is called at the end of a `class` statement, and because the `type` object's `__call__` dispatches to the `__new__` and `__init__` methods, code we provide in these methods can manage all the classes created from the metaclass.

Here's our example in action again, with prints added to the metaclass and the file at large to trace:

```
class MetaOne(type):
    def __new__(meta, classname, supers, classdict):
        print('In MetaOne.new:', classname, supers, classdict, sep='\n...')
        return type.__new__(meta, classname, supers, classdict)

class Eggs:
    pass

print('making class')
class Spam(Eggs, metaclass=MetaOne):    # Inherits from Eggs, instance of Meta
    data = 1                            # Class data attribute
    def meth(self, arg):                # Class method attribute
        pass

print('making instance')
X = Spam()
print('data:', X.data)
```

Here, `Spam` inherits from `Eggs` and is an instance of `MetaOne`, but `X` is an instance of and inherits from `Spam`. When this code is run with Python 3.0, notice how the metaclass is invoked at the *end* of the `class` statement, before we ever make an instance—metaclasses are for processing classes, and classes are for processing instances:

```
making class
In MetaOne.new:
...Spam
...(<class '__main__.Eggs'>,)
...{'__module__': '__main__', 'data': 1, 'meth': <function meth at 0x02AEBA08>}
making instance
data: 1
```

Customizing Construction and Initialization

Metaclasses can also tap into the __init__ protocol invoked by the type object's __call__: in general, __new__ creates and returns the class object, and __init__ initializes the already created class. Metaclasses can use both hooks to manage the class at creation time:

```
class MetaOne(type):
    def __new__(meta, classname, supers, classdict):
        print('In MetaOne.new: ', classname, supers, classdict, sep='\n...')
        return type.__new__(meta, classname, supers, classdict)

    def __init__(Class, classname, supers, classdict):
        print('In MetaOne init:', classname, supers, classdict, sep='\n...')
        print('...init class object:', list(Class.__dict__.keys()))

class Eggs:
    pass

print('making class')
class Spam(Eggs, metaclass=MetaOne):     # Inherits from Eggs, instance of Meta
    data = 1                             # Class data attribute
    def meth(self, arg):                 # Class method attribute
        pass

print('making instance')
X = Spam()
print('data:', X.data)
```

In this case, the class initialization method is run after the class construction method, but both run at the end of the class statement before any instances are made (conversely, an __init__ in Spam would run at instance creation time, and is not affected or run by the metaclass's __init__):

```
making class
In MetaOne.new:
...Spam
...(<class '__main__.Eggs'>,)
...{'__module__': '__main__', 'data': 1, 'meth': <function meth at 0x02AAB810>}
In MetaOne init:
...Spam
...(<class '__main__.Eggs'>,)
...{'__module__': '__main__', 'data': 1, 'meth': <function meth at 0x02AAB810>}
...init class object: ['__module__', 'data', 'meth', '__doc__']
making instance
data: 1
```

Other Metaclass Coding Techniques

Although redefining the type superclass's __new__ and __init__ methods is the most common way metaclasses insert logic into the class object creation process, other schemes are possible, too.

Using simple factory functions

For example, metaclasses need not really be classes at all. As we've learned, the class statement issues a simple call to create a class at the conclusion of its processing. Because of this, *any callable object* can in principle be used as a metaclass, provided it accepts the arguments passed and returns an object compatible with the intended class. In fact, a simple object factory function will serve just as well as a class:

```
# A simple function can serve as a metaclass too

def MetaFunc(classname, supers, classdict):
    print('In MetaFunc: ', classname, supers, classdict, sep='\n...')
    return type(classname, supers, classdict)

class Eggs:
    pass

print('making class')
class Spam(Eggs, metaclass=MetaFunc):        # Run simple function at end
    data = 1                                 # Function returns class
    def meth(self, args):
        pass

print('making instance')
X = Spam()
print('data:', X.data)
```

When run, the function is called at the end of the declaring class statement, and it returns the expected new class object. The function is simply catching the call that the type object's __call__ normally intercepts by default:

```
making class
In MetaFunc:
...Spam
...(<class '__main__.Eggs'>,)
...{'__module__': '__main__', 'data': 1, 'meth': <function meth at 0x02B8B6A8>}
making instance
data: 1
```

Overloading class creation calls with metaclasses

Since they participate in normal OOP mechanics, it's also possible for metaclasses to catch the *creation call* at the end of a class statement directly, by redefining the type object's __call__. The required protocol is a bit involved, though:

```
# __call__ can be redefined, metas can have metas

class SuperMeta(type):
    def __call__(meta, classname, supers, classdict):
        print('In SuperMeta.call: ', classname, supers, classdict, sep='\n...')
        return type.__call__(meta, classname, supers, classdict)

class SubMeta(type, metaclass=SuperMeta):
    def __new__(meta, classname, supers, classdict):
```

```
            print('In SubMeta.new: ', classname, supers, classdict, sep='\n...')
            return type.__new__(meta, classname, supers, classdict)

        def __init__(Class, classname, supers, classdict):
            print('In SubMeta init:', classname, supers, classdict, sep='\n...')
            print('...init class object:', list(Class.__dict__.keys()))

class Eggs:
    pass

print('making class')
class Spam(Eggs, metaclass=SubMeta):
    data = 1
    def meth(self, arg):
        pass

print('making instance')
X = Spam()
print('data:', X.data)
```

When this code is run, all three redefined methods run in turn. This is essentially what the **type** object does by default:

```
making class
In SuperMeta.call:
...Spam
...(<class '__main__.Eggs'>,)
...{'__module__': '__main__', 'data': 1, 'meth': <function meth at 0x02B7BA98>}
In SubMeta.new:
...Spam
...(<class '__main__.Eggs'>,)
...{'__module__': '__main__', 'data': 1, 'meth': <function meth at 0x02B7BA98>}
In SubMeta init:
...Spam
...(<class '__main__.Eggs'>,)
...{'__module__': '__main__', 'data': 1, 'meth': <function meth at 0x02B7BA98>}
...init class object: ['__module__', 'data', 'meth', '__doc__']
making instance
data: 1
```

Overloading class creation calls with normal classes

The preceding example is complicated by the fact that metaclasses are used to create class objects, but don't generate instances of themselves. Because of this, with metaclasses name lookup rules are somewhat different than what we are accustomed to. The __call__ method, for example, is looked up in the class of an object; for metaclasses, this means the metaclass of a metaclass.

To use normal inheritance-based name lookup, we can achieve the same effect with normal classes and instances. The output of the following is the same as the preceding version, but note that __new__ and __init__ must have different names here, or else they will run when the SubMeta instance is created, not when it is later called as a metaclass:

```
class SuperMeta:
    def __call__(self, classname, supers, classdict):
        print('In SuperMeta.call: ', classname, supers, classdict, sep='\n...')
        Class = self.__New__(classname, supers, classdict)
        self.__Init__(Class, classname, supers, classdict)
        return Class

class SubMeta(SuperMeta):
    def __New__(self, classname, supers, classdict):
        print('In SubMeta.new: ', classname, supers, classdict, sep='\n...')
        return type(classname, supers, classdict)

    def __Init__(self, Class, classname, supers, classdict):
        print('In SubMeta init:', classname, supers, classdict, sep='\n...')
        print('...init class object:', list(Class.__dict__.keys()))

class Eggs:
    pass

print('making class')
class Spam(Eggs, metaclass=SubMeta()):        # Meta is normal class instance
    data = 1                                   # Called at end of statement
    def meth(self, arg):
        pass

print('making instance')
X = Spam()
print('data:', X.data)
```

Although these alternative forms work, most metaclasses get their work done by redefining the type superclass's __new__ and __init__; in practice, this is usually as much
control as is required, and it's often simpler than other schemes. However, we'll see
later that a simple function-based metaclass can often work much like a class decorator,
which allows the metaclasses to manage instances as well as classes.

Instances Versus Inheritance

Because metaclasses are specified in similar ways to inheritance superclasses, they can
be a bit confusing at first glance. A few key points should help summarize and clarify
the model:

- **Metaclasses inherit from the type class**. Although they have a special role,
  metaclasses are coded with class statements and follow the usual OOP model in
  Python. For example, as subclasses of type, they can redefine the type object's
  methods, overriding and customizing them as needed. Metaclasses typically redefine the type class's __new__ and __init__ to customize class creation and initialization, but they can also redefine __call__ if they wish to catch the end-of-class
  creation call directly. Although it's unusual, they can even be simple functions that
  return arbitrary objects, instead of type subclasses.

- **Metaclass declarations are inherited by subclasses**. The `metaclass=M` declaration in a user-defined class is *inherited* by the class's subclasses, too, so the metaclass will run for the construction of each class that inherits this specification in a superclass chain.

- **Metaclass attributes are not inherited by class instances**. Metaclass declarations specify an *instance* relationship, which is not the same as inheritance. Because classes are instances of metaclasses, the behavior defined in a metaclass applies to the class, but not the class's later instances. Instances obtain behavior from their classes and superclasses, but not from any metaclasses. Technically, instance attribute lookups usually search only the `__dict__` dictionaries of the instance and all its classes; the metaclass is not included in inheritance lookup.

To illustrate the last two points, consider the following example:

```
class MetaOne(type):
    def __new__(meta, classname, supers, classdict):    # Redefine type method
        print('In MetaOne.new:', classname)
        return type.__new__(meta, classname, supers, classdict)
    def toast(self):
        print('toast')

class Super(metaclass=MetaOne):         # Metaclass inherited by subs too
    def spam(self):                     # MetaOne run twice for two classes
        print('spam')

class C(Super):                         # Superclass: inheritance versus instance
    def eggs(self):                     # Classes inherit from superclasses
        print('eggs')                   # But not from metclasses

X = C()
X.eggs()            # Inherited from C
X.spam()            # Inherited from Super
X.toast()           # Not inherited from metaclass
```

When this code is run, the metaclass handles construction of *both* client classes, and instances inherit class attributes but *not* metaclass attributes:

```
In MetaOne.new: Super
In MetaOne.new: C
eggs
spam
AttributeError: 'C' object has no attribute 'toast'
```

Although detail matters, it's important to keep the big picture in mind when dealing with metaclasses. Metaclasses like those we've seen here will be run automatically for every class that declares them. Unlike the helper function approaches we saw earlier, such classes will automatically acquire whatever augmentation the metaclass provides. Moreover, changes in such augmentation only need to be coded in one place—the metaclass—which simplifies making modifications as our needs evolve. Like so many tools in Python, metaclasses ease maintenance work by eliminating redundancy. To fully sample their power, though, we need to move on to some larger use-case examples.

Example: Adding Methods to Classes

In this and the following section, we're going to study examples of two common use cases for metaclasses: adding methods to a class, and decorating all methods automatically. These are just two of the many metaclass roles, which unfortunately consume the space we have left for this chapter; again, you should consult the Web for more advanced applications. These examples are representative of metaclasses in action, though, and they suffice to illustrate the basics.

Moreover, both give us an opportunity to contrast class decorators and metaclasses—our first example compares metaclass- and decorator-based implementations of class augmentation and instance wrapping, and the second applies a decorator with a metaclass first and then with another decorator. As you'll see, the two tools are often interchangeable, and even complementary.

Manual Augmentation

Earlier in this chapter, we looked at skeleton code that augmented classes by adding methods to them in various ways. As we saw, simple class-based inheritance suffices if the extra methods are statically known when the class is coded. Composition via object embedding can often achieve the same effect too. For more dynamic scenarios, though, other techniques are sometimes required—helper functions can usually suffice, but metaclasses provide an explicit structure and minimize the maintenance costs of changes in the future.

Let's put these ideas in action here with working code. Consider the following example of manual class augmentation—it adds two methods to two classes, after they have been created:

```
# Extend manually - adding new methods to classes

class Client1:
    def __init__(self, value):
        self.value = value
    def spam(self):
        return self.value * 2

class Client2:
    value = 'ni?'

def eggsfunc(obj):
    return obj.value * 4

def hamfunc(obj, value):
    return value + 'ham'

Client1.eggs = eggsfunc
Client1.ham  = hamfunc

Client2.eggs = eggsfunc
```

```
Client2.ham    = hamfunc

X = Client1('Ni!')
print(X.spam())
print(X.eggs())
print(X.ham('bacon'))

Y = Client2()
print(Y.eggs())
print(Y.ham('bacon'))
```

This works because methods can always be assigned to a class after it's been created, as long as the methods assigned are functions with an extra first argument to receive the subject `self` instance—this argument can be used to access state information accessible from the class instance, even though the function is defined independently of the class.

When this code runs, we receive the output of a method coded inside the first class, as well as the two methods added to the classes after the fact:

```
Ni!Ni!
Ni!Ni!Ni!Ni!
baconham
ni?ni?ni?ni?
baconham
```

This scheme works well in isolated cases and can be used to fill out a class arbitrarily at runtime. It suffers from a potentially major downside, though: we have to repeat the augmentation code for every class that needs these methods. In our case, it wasn't too onerous to add the two methods to both classes, but in more complex scenarios this approach can be time-consuming and error-prone. If we ever forget to do this consistently, or we ever need to change the augmentation, we can run into problems.

Metaclass-Based Augmentation

Although manual augmentation works, in larger programs it would be better if we could apply such changes to an entire set of classes automatically. That way, we'd avoid the chance of the augmentation being botched for any given class. Moreover, coding the augmentation in a single location better supports future changes—all classes in the set will pick up changes automatically.

One way to meet this goal is to use metaclasses. If we code the augmentation in a metaclass, every class that declares that metaclass will be augmented uniformly and correctly and will automatically pick up any changes made in the future. The following code demonstrates:

```
# Extend with a metaclass - supports future changes better

def eggsfunc(obj):
    return obj.value * 4
```

```
    def hamfunc(obj, value):
        return value + 'ham'

class Extender(type):
    def __new__(meta, classname, supers, classdict):
        classdict['eggs'] = eggsfunc
        classdict['ham']  = hamfunc
        return type.__new__(meta, classname, supers, classdict)

class Client1(metaclass=Extender):
    def __init__(self, value):
        self.value = value
    def spam(self):
        return self.value * 2

class Client2(metaclass=Extender):
    value = 'ni?'

X = Client1('Ni!')
print(X.spam())
print(X.eggs())
print(X.ham('bacon'))

Y = Client2()
print(Y.eggs())
print(Y.ham('bacon'))
```

This time, both of the client classes are extended with the new methods because they are instances of a metaclass that performs the augmentation. When run, this version's output is the same as before—we haven't changed what the code does, we've just refactored it to encapsulate the augmentation more cleanly:

```
Ni!Ni!
Ni!Ni!Ni!Ni!
baconham
ni?ni?ni?ni?
baconham
```

Notice that the metaclass in this example still performs a fairly static task: adding two known methods to every class that declares it. In fact, if all we need to do is always add the same two methods to a set of classes, we might as well code them in a normal superclass and inherit in subclasses. In practice, though, the metaclass structure supports much more dynamic behavior. For instance, the subject class might also be configured based upon arbitrary logic at runtime:

```
# Can also configure class based on runtime tests

class MetaExtend(type):
    def __new__(meta, classname, supers, classdict):
        if sometest():
            classdict['eggs'] = eggsfunc1
        else:
            classdict['eggs'] = eggsfunc2
        if someothertest():
```

```
        classdict['ham']  = hamfunc
    else:
        classdict['ham']  = lambda *args: 'Not supported'
    return type.__new__(meta, classname, supers, classdict)
```

Metaclasses Versus Class Decorators: Round 2

Just in case this chapter has not yet managed to make your head explode, keep in mind again that the prior chapter's class decorators often overlap with this chapter's meta-classes in terms of functionality. This derives from the fact that:

- Class decorators rebind class names to the result of a function at the end of a **class** statement.
- Metaclasses work by routing class object creation through an object at the end of a **class** statement.

Although these are slightly different models, in practice they can usually achieve the same goals, albeit in different ways. In fact, class decorators can be used to manage both instances of a class and the class itself. While decorators can manage classes naturally, though, it's somewhat less straightforward for metaclasses to manage instances. Metaclasses are probably best used for class object management.

Decorator-based augmentation

For example, the prior section's metaclass example, which adds methods to a class on creation, can also be coded as a class decorator; in this mode, decorators roughly correspond to the __init__ method of metaclasses, since the class object has already been created by the time the decorator is invoked. Also like with metaclasses, the original class type is retained, since no wrapper object layer is inserted. The output of the following is the same as that of the prior metaclass code:

```
# Extend with a decorator: same as providing __init__ in a metaclass

def eggsfunc(obj):
    return obj.value * 4

def hamfunc(obj, value):
    return value + 'ham'

def Extender(aClass):
    aClass.eggs = eggsfunc          # Manages class, not instance
    aClass.ham  = hamfunc           # Equiv to metaclass __init__
    return aClass

@Extender
class Client1:                      # Client1 = Extender(Client1)
    def __init__(self, value):      # Rebound at end of class stmt
        self.value = value
    def spam(self):
        return self.value * 2
```

```
@Extender
class Client2:
    value = 'ni?'

X = Client1('Ni!')                                         # X is a Client1 instance
print(X.spam())
print(X.eggs())
print(X.ham('bacon'))

Y = Client2()
print(Y.eggs())
print(Y.ham('bacon'))
```

In other words, at least in certain cases, decorators can manage classes as easily as
metaclasses. The converse isn't quite so straightforward, though; metaclasses can be
used to manage instances, but only with a certain amount of magic. The next section
demonstrates.

Managing instances instead of classes

As we've just seen, class decorators can often serve the same *class-management* role as
metaclasses. Metaclasses can often serve the same *instance-management* role as decorators, too, but this is a bit more complex. That is:

- *Class decorators* can manage both classes and instances.
- *Metaclasses* can manage both classes and instances, but instances take extra work.

That said, certain applications may be better coded in one or the other. For example,
consider the following class decorator example from the prior chapter; it's used to print
a trace message whenever any normally named attribute of a class instance is fetched:

```
# Class decorator to trace external instance attribute fetches

def Tracer(aClass):                                         # On @ decorator
    class Wrapper:
        def __init__(self, *args, **kargs):                 # On instance creation
            self.wrapped = aClass(*args, **kargs)           # Use enclosing scope name
        def __getattr__(self, attrname):
            print('Trace:', attrname)                       # Catches all but .wrapped
            return getattr(self.wrapped, attrname)          # Delegate to wrapped object
    return Wrapper

@Tracer
class Person:                                               # Person = Tracer(Person)
    def __init__(self, name, hours, rate):                  # Wrapper remembers Person
        self.name = name
        self.hours = hours
        self.rate = rate                                    # In-method fetch not traced
    def pay(self):
        return self.hours * self.rate

bob = Person('Bob', 40, 50)                                 # bob is really a Wrapper
```

1076 | Chapter 39: Metaclasses

```
print(bob.name)                                    # Wrapper embeds a Person
print(bob.pay())                                   # Triggers __getattr__
```

When this code is run, the decorator uses class name rebinding to wrap instance objects in an object that produces the trace lines in the following output:

```
Trace: name
Bob
Trace: pay
2000
```

Although it's possible for a metaclass to achieve the same effect, it seems less straight-forward conceptually. Metaclasses are designed explicitly to manage class object creation, and they have an interface tailored for this purpose. To use a metaclass to manage instances, we have to rely on a bit more magic. The following metaclass has the same effect and output as the prior decorator:

```
# Manage instances like the prior example, but with a metaclass

def Tracer(classname, supers, classdict):          # On class creation call
    aClass = type(classname, supers, classdict)    # Make client class
    class Wrapper:
        def __init__(self, *args, **kargs):        # On instance creation
            self.wrapped = aClass(*args, **kargs)
        def __getattr__(self, attrname):
            print('Trace:', attrname)              # Catches all but .wrapped
            return getattr(self.wrapped, attrname) # Delegate to wrapped object
    return Wrapper

class Person(metaclass=Tracer):                    # Make Person with Tracer
    def __init__(self, name, hours, rate):         # Wrapper remembers Person
        self.name = name
        self.hours = hours
        self.rate = rate                           # In-method fetch not traced
    def pay(self):
        return self.hours * self.rate

bob = Person('Bob', 40, 50)                        # bob is really a Wrapper
print(bob.name)                                    # Wrapper embeds a Person
print(bob.pay())                                   # Triggers __getattr__
```

This works, but it relies on two tricks. First, it must use a simple function instead of a class, because **type** subclasses must adhere to object creation protocols. Second, it must manually create the subject class by calling **type** manually; it needs to return an instance wrapper, but metaclasses are also responsible for creating and returning the subject class. Really, we're using the metaclass protocol to imitate decorators in this example, rather than vice versa; because both run at the conclusion of a **class** statement, in many roles they are just variations on a theme. This metaclass version produces the same output as the decorator when run live:

```
Trace: name
Bob
Trace: pay
2000
```

You should study both versions of these examples for yourself to weigh their tradeoffs. In general, though, metaclasses are probably best suited to class management, due to their design; class decorators can manage either instances or classes, though they may not be the best option for more advanced metaclass roles that we don't have space to cover in this book (if you want to learn more about decorators and metaclasses after reading this chapter, search the Web or Python's standard manuals). The next section concludes this chapter with one more common use case—applying operations to a class's methods automatically.

Example: Applying Decorators to Methods

As we saw in the prior section, because they are both run at the end of a `class` statement, metaclasses and decorators can often be used *interchangeably*, albeit with different syntax. The choice between the two is arbitrary in many contexts. It's also possible to use them in *combination*, as complementary tools. In this section, we'll explore an example of just such a combination—applying a function decorator to all the methods of a class.

Tracing with Decoration Manually

In the prior chapter we coded two function decorators, one that traced and counted all calls made to a decorated function and another that timed such calls. They took various forms there, some of which were applicable to both functions and methods and some of which were not. The following collects both decorators' final forms into a module file for reuse and reference here:

```
# File mytools.py: assorted decorator tools

def tracer(func):                          # Use function, not class with __call__
    calls = 0                              # Else self is decorator instance only
    def onCall(*args, **kwargs):
        nonlocal calls
        calls += 1
        print('call %s to %s' % (calls, func.__name__))
        return func(*args, **kwargs)
    return onCall

import time
def timer(label='', trace=True):           # On decorator args: retain args
    def onDecorator(func):                 # On @: retain decorated func
        def onCall(*args, **kargs):        # On calls: call original
            start   = time.clock()         # State is scopes + func attr
            result  = func(*args, **kargs)
            elapsed = time.clock() - start
            onCall.alltime += elapsed
            if trace:
                format = '%s%s: %.5f, %.5f'
                values = (label, func.__name__, elapsed, onCall.alltime)
                print(format % values)
```

```
        return result
    onCall.alltime = 0
    return onCall
return onDecorator
```

As we learned in the prior chapter, to use these decorators manually, we simply import them from the module and code the decoration @ syntax before each method we wish to trace or time:

```
from mytools import tracer

class Person:
    @tracer
    def __init__(self, name, pay):
        self.name = name
        self.pay  = pay

    @tracer
    def giveRaise(self, percent):         # giveRaise = tracer(giverRaise)
        self.pay *= (1.0 + percent)       # onCall remembers giveRaise

    @tracer
    def lastName(self):                   # lastName = tracer(lastName)
        return self.name.split()[-1]

bob = Person('Bob Smith', 50000)
sue = Person('Sue Jones', 100000)
print(bob.name, sue.name)
sue.giveRaise(.10)                        # Runs onCall(sue, .10)
print(sue.pay)
print(bob.lastName(), sue.lastName())     # Runs onCall(bob), remembers lastName
```

When this code is run, we get the following output—calls to decorated methods are routed to logic that intercepts and then delegates the call, because the original method names have been bound to the decorator:

```
call 1 to __init__
call 2 to __init__
Bob Smith Sue Jones
call 1 to giveRaise
110000.0
call 1 to lastName
call 2 to lastName
Smith Jones
```

Tracing with Metaclasses and Decorators

The manual decoration scheme of the prior section works, but it requires us to add decoration syntax before *each* method we wish to trace and to later remove that syntax when we no longer desire tracing. If we want to trace every method of a class, this can become tedious in larger programs. It would be better if we could somehow apply the tracer decorator to all of a class's methods automatically.

With metaclasses, we can do exactly that—because they are run when a class is constructed, they are a natural place to add decoration wrappers to a class's methods. By scanning the class's attribute dictionary and testing for function objects there, we can automatically run methods through the decorator and rebind the original names to the results. The effect is the same as the automatic method name rebinding of decorators, but we can apply it more globally:

```
# Metaclass that adds tracing decorator to every method of a client class

from types import FunctionType
from mytools import tracer

class MetaTrace(type):
    def __new__(meta, classname, supers, classdict):
        for attr, attrval in classdict.items():
            if type(attrval) is FunctionType:                  # Method?
                classdict[attr] = tracer(attrval)              # Decorate it
        return type.__new__(meta, classname, supers, classdict)   # Make class

class Person(metaclass=MetaTrace):
    def __init__(self, name, pay):
        self.name = name
        self.pay  = pay
    def giveRaise(self, percent):
        self.pay *= (1.0 + percent)
    def lastName(self):
        return self.name.split()[-1]

bob = Person('Bob Smith', 50000)
sue = Person('Sue Jones', 100000)
print(bob.name, sue.name)
sue.giveRaise(.10)
print(sue.pay)
print(bob.lastName(), sue.lastName())
```

When this code is run, the results are the same as before—calls to methods are routed to the tracing decorator first for tracing, and then propagated on to the original method:

```
call 1 to __init__
call 2 to __init__
Bob Smith Sue Jones
call 1 to giveRaise
110000.0
call 1 to lastName
call 2 to lastName
Smith Jones
```

The result you see here is a combination of decorator and metaclass work—the metaclass automatically applies the function decorator to every method at class creation time, and the function decorator automatically intercepts method calls in order to print the trace messages in this output. The combination "just works," thanks to the generality of both tools.

Applying Any Decorator to Methods

The prior metaclass example works for just one specific function decorator—tracing. However, it's trivial to generalize this to apply *any* decorator to all the methods of a class. All we have to do is add an outer scope layer to retain the desired decorator, much like we did for decorators in the prior chapter. The following, for example, codes such a generalization and then uses it to apply the tracer decorator again:

```
# Metaclass factory: apply any decorator to all methods of a class

from types import FunctionType
from mytools import tracer, timer

def decorateAll(decorator):
    class MetaDecorate(type):
        def __new__(meta, classname, supers, classdict):
            for attr, attrval in classdict.items():
                if type(attrval) is FunctionType:
                    classdict[attr] = decorator(attrval)
            return type.__new__(meta, classname, supers, classdict)
    return MetaDecorate

class Person(metaclass=decorateAll(tracer)):      # Apply a decorator to all
    def __init__(self, name, pay):
        self.name = name
        self.pay  = pay
    def giveRaise(self, percent):
        self.pay *= (1.0 + percent)
    def lastName(self):
        return self.name.split()[-1]

bob = Person('Bob Smith', 50000)
sue = Person('Sue Jones', 100000)
print(bob.name, sue.name)
sue.giveRaise(.10)
print(sue.pay)
print(bob.lastName(), sue.lastName())
```

When this code is run as it is, the output is again the same as that of the previous examples—we're still ultimately decorating every method in a client class with the tracer function decorator, but we're doing so in a more generic fashion:

```
call 1 to __init__
call 2 to __init__
Bob Smith Sue Jones
call 1 to giveRaise
110000.0
call 1 to lastName
call 2 to lastName
Smith Jones
```

Now, to apply a different decorator to the methods, we can simply replace the decorator name in the class header line. To use the timer function decorator shown earlier, for example, we could use either of the last two header lines in the following when defining our class—the first accepts the timer's default arguments, and the second specifies label text:

```
class Person(metaclass=decorateAll(tracer)):              # Apply tracer

class Person(metaclass=decorateAll(timer())):             # Apply timer, defaults

class Person(metaclass=decorateAll(timer(label='**'))):   # Decorator arguments
```

Notice that this scheme cannot support nondefault decorator arguments differing per method, but it can pass in decorator arguments that apply to all methods, as done here. To test, use the last of these metaclass declarations to apply the timer, and add the following lines at the end of the script:

```
# If using timer: total time per method

print('-'*40)
print('%.5f' % Person.__init__.alltime)
print('%.5f' % Person.giveRaise.alltime)
print('%.5f' % Person.lastName.alltime)
```

The new output is as follows—the metaclass wraps methods in timer decorators now, so we can tell how long each and every call takes, for every method of the class:

```
**__init__: 0.00001, 0.00001
**__init__: 0.00001, 0.00002
Bob Smith Sue Jones
**giveRaise: 0.00001, 0.00001
110000.0
**lastName: 0.00001, 0.00001
**lastName: 0.00001, 0.00002
Smith Jones
----------------------------------------
0.00002
0.00001
0.00002
```

Metaclasses Versus Class Decorators: Round 3

Class decorators intersect with metaclasses here, too. The following version replaces the preceding example's metaclass with a class decorator. It defines and uses a *class decorator that applies a function decorator* to all methods of a class. Although the prior sentence may sound more like a Zen statement than a technical description, this all works quite naturally—Python's decorators support arbitrary nesting and combinations:

```
# Class decorator factory: apply any decorator to all methods of a class

from types import FunctionType
from mytools import tracer, timer

def decorateAll(decorator):
    def DecoDecorate(aClass):
```

```
            for attr, attrval in aClass.__dict__.items():
                if type(attrval) is FunctionType:
                    setattr(aClass, attr, decorator(attrval))      # Not __dict__
            return aClass
        return DecoDecorate

    @decorateAll(tracer)                          # Use a class decorator
    class Person:                                 # Applies func decorator to methods
        def __init__(self, name, pay):            # Person = decorateAll(..)(Person)
            self.name = name                      # Person = DecoDecorate(Person)
            self.pay  = pay
        def giveRaise(self, percent):
            self.pay *= (1.0 + percent)
        def lastName(self):
            return self.name.split()[-1]

    bob = Person('Bob Smith', 50000)
    sue = Person('Sue Jones', 100000)
    print(bob.name, sue.name)
    sue.giveRaise(.10)
    print(sue.pay)
    print(bob.lastName(), sue.lastName())
```

When this code is run as it is, the class decorator applies the tracer function decorator to every method and produces a trace message on calls (the output is the same as that of the preceding metaclass version of this example):

```
    call 1 to __init__
    call 2 to __init__
    Bob Smith Sue Jones
    call 1 to giveRaise
    110000.0
    call 1 to lastName
    call 2 to lastName
    Smith Jones
```

Notice that the class decorator returns the original, augmented class, not a wrapper layer for it (as is common when wrapping instance objects instead). As for the metaclass version, we retain the type of the original class—an instance of Person is an instance of Person, not of some wrapper class. In fact, this class decorator deals with class creation only; instance creation calls are not intercepted at all.

This distinction can matter in programs that require type testing for instances to yield the original class, not a wrapper. When augmenting a class instead of an instance, class decorators can retain the original class type. The class's methods are not their original functions because they are rebound to decorators, but this is less important in practice, and it's true in the metaclass alternative as well.

Also note that, like the metaclass version, this structure cannot support function decorator arguments that differ per method, but it can handle such arguments if they apply to all methods. To use this scheme to apply the timer decorator, for example, either of the last two decoration lines in the following will suffice if coded just before our class definition—the first uses decorator argument defaults, and the second provides one explicitly:

```
@decorateAll(tracer)              # Decorate all with tracer

@decorateAll(timer())             # Decorate all with timer, defaults

@decorateAll(timer(label='@@'))   # Same but pass a decorator argument
```

As before, let's use the last of these decorator lines and add the following at the end of the script to test our example with a different decorator:

```
# If using timer: total time per method

print('-'*40)
print('%.5f' % Person.__init__.alltime)
print('%.5f' % Person.giveRaise.alltime)
print('%.5f' % Person.lastName.alltime)
```

The same sort of output appears—for every method we get timing data for each and all calls, but we've passed a different label argument to the timer decorator:

```
@@__init__: 0.00001, 0.00001
@@__init__: 0.00001, 0.00002
Bob Smith Sue Jones
@@giveRaise: 0.00001, 0.00001
110000.0
@@lastName: 0.00001, 0.00001
@@lastName: 0.00001, 0.00002
Smith Jones
----------------------------------------
0.00002
0.00001
0.00002
```

As you can see, metaclasses and class decorators are not only often interchangeable, but also commonly complementary. Both provide advanced but powerful ways to customize and manage both class and instance objects, because both ultimately allow you to insert code into the class creation process. Although some more advanced applications may be better coded with one or the other, the way you choose or combine these two tools in many cases is largely up to you.

"Optional" Language Features

I included a quote near the start of this chapter about metaclasses not being of interest to 99% of Python programmers, to underscore their relative obscurity. That statement is not quite accurate, though, and not just numerically so.

The quote's author is a friend of mine from the early days of Python, and I don't mean to pick on anyone unfairly. Moreover, I've often made such statements about language feature obscurity myself—in this very book, in fact.

The problem, though, is that such statements really only apply to people who work alone and only ever use code that they've written themselves. As soon as an "optional" advanced language feature is used by *anyone* in an organization, it is no longer optional—it is effectively imposed on *everyone* in the organization. The same holds true for externally developed software you use in your systems—if the software's author uses an advanced language feature, it's no longer entirely optional for you, because you have to understand the feature to use or change the code.

This observation applies to all the advanced tools listed near the beginning of this chapter—decorators, properties, descriptors, metaclasses, and so on. If any person or program you need to work with uses them, they automatically become part of your required knowledge base too. That is, *nothing is truly "optional" if nothing is truly optional*. Most of us don't get to pick and choose.

This is why some Python old-timers (myself included) sometimes lament that Python seems to have grown larger and more complex over time. New features added by veterans seem to have raised the intellectual bar for newcomers. Although Python's core ideas, like dynamic typing and built-in types, have remained essentially the same, its advanced additions can become required reading for any Python programmer. I chose to cover these topics here for this reason, despite the omission of most in prior editions. It's not possible to skip the advanced stuff if it's in code you have to understand.

On the other hand, Python is still much simpler than most of its contemporaries and perhaps only as complex as its many roles require, and many new learners can pick up advanced topics as needed. And frankly, application programmers tend to spend most of their time dealing with *libraries and extensions*, not advanced and sometimes arcane language features. For instance, the book *Programming Python*, a follow-up to this one, deals mostly with the marriage of Python to application libraries for tasks such as GUIs, databases, and the Web, not with esoteric language tools.

The flipside of this growth is that Python has become more *powerful*. When used well, tools like decorators and metaclasses are not only arguably "cool," but allow creative programmers to build more flexible and useful APIs for other programmers to use. As we've seen, they can also provide good solutions to problems of encapsulation and maintenance.

Whether this justifies the potential expansion of required Python knowledge is up to you to decide. Unfortunately, a person's skill level often decides this issue by default—more advanced programmers like more advanced tools and tend to forget about their impact on other camps. Fortunately, though, this isn't an absolute; good programmers also understand that *simplicity is good engineering*, and advanced tools should be used only when warranted. This is true in any programming language, but especially in a language like Python that is frequently exposed to new or novice programmers as an extension tool.

If you're still not buying this, keep in mind that there are very many Python users who are not comfortable with even basic OOP and classes. Trust me on this; I've met thousands of them. Python-based systems that require their users to master the nuances of metaclasses, decorators, and the like should probably scale their market expectations accordingly.

Chapter Summary

In this chapter, we studied metaclasses and explored examples of them in action. Metaclasses allow us to tap into the class creation protocol of Python, in order to manage or augment user-defined classes. Because they automate this process, they can provide better solutions for API writers then manual code or helper functions; because they encapsulate such code, they can minimize maintenance costs better than some other approaches.

Along the way, we also saw how the roles of class decorators and metaclasses often intersect: because both run at the conclusion of a `class` statement, they can sometimes be used interchangeably. Class decorators can be used to manage both class and instance objects; metaclasses can, too, although they are more directly targeted toward classes.

Since this chapter covered an advanced topic, we'll work through just a few quiz questions to review the basics (if you've made it this far in a chapter on metaclasses, you probably already deserve extra credit!). Because this is the last part of the book, we'll forego the end-of-part exercises. Be sure to see the appendixes that follow for pointers on installation steps, and the solutions to the prior parts' exercises.

Once you finish the quiz, you've officially reached the end of this book. Now that you know Python inside and out, your next step, should you choose to take it, is to explore the libraries, techniques, and tools available in the application domains in which you work. Because Python is so widely used, you'll find ample resources for using it in almost any application you can think of—from GUIs, the Web, and databases to numeric programming, robotics, and system administration.

This is where Python starts to become truly fun, but this is also where this book's story ends, and others' begin. For pointers on where to turn after this book, see the list of recommended follow-up texts in the Preface. Good luck with your journey. And of course, "Always look on the bright side of Life!"

Test Your Knowledge: Quiz

1. What is a metaclass?
2. How do you declare the metaclass of a class?
3. How do class decorators overlap with metaclasses for managing classes?
4. How do class decorators overlap with metaclasses for managing instances?
5. Would you rather count decorators or metaclasses amongst your weaponry? (And please phrase your answer in terms of a popular Monty Python skit.)

Test Your Knowledge: Answers

1. A metaclass is a class used to create a class. Normal classes are instances of the type class by default. Metaclasses are usually subclasses of the type class, which redefines class creation protocol methods in order to customize the class creation call issued at the end of a class statement; they typically redefine the methods __new__ and __init__ to tap into the class creation protocol. Metaclasses can also be coded other ways—as simple functions, for example—but they are responsible for making and returning an object for the new class.

2. In Python 3.0 and later, use a keyword argument in the class header line: class C(metaclass=M). In Python 2.X, use a class attribute instead: __metaclass__ = M. In 3.0, the class header line can also name normal superclasses (a.k.a. base classes) before the metaclass keyword argument.

3. Because both are automatically triggered at the end of a class statement, class decorators and metaclasses can both be used to manage classes. Decorators rebind a class name to a callable's result and metaclasses route class creation through a callable, but both hooks can be used for similar purposes. To manage classes, decorators simply augment and return the original class objects. Metaclasses augment a class after they create it.

4. Because both are automatically triggered at the end of a class statement, class decorators and metaclasses can both be used to manage class instances, by inserting a wrapper object to catch instance creation calls. Decorators may rebind the class name to a callable run on instance creation that retains the original class object. Metaclasses can do the same, but they must also create the class object, so their usage is somewhat more complex in this role.

5. Our chief weapon is decorators...decorators and metaclasses...metaclasses and decorators.... Our two weapons are metaclasses and decorators...and ruthless efficiency.... Our *three* weapons are metaclasses, decorators, and ruthless efficiency...and an almost fanatical devotion to Guido.... Our *four*...no....*Amongst* our weapons.... Amongst our weaponry...are such elements as metaclasses, decorators.... I'll come in again....

## PART IX

Appendixes

Installation and Configuration

This appendix provides additional installation and configuration details as a resource for people new to such topics.

Installing the Python Interpreter

Because you need the Python interpreter to run Python scripts, the first step in using Python is usually installing Python. Unless one is already available on your machine, you'll need to fetch, install, and possibly configure a recent version of Python on your computer. You'll only need to do this once per machine, and if you will be running a frozen binary (described in Chapter 2) or self-installing system, you may not need to do much more.

Is Python Already Present?

Before you do anything else, check whether you already have a recent Python on your machine. If you are working on Linux, Mac OS X, or some Unix systems, Python is probably already installed on your computer, though it may be one or two releases behind the cutting edge. Here's how to check:

- On Windows, check whether there is a Python entry in the Start button's All Programs menu (at the bottom left of the screen).
- On Mac OS X, open a Terminal window (Applications→Utilities→Terminal) and type **python** at the prompt.
- On Linux and Unix, type **python** at a shell prompt (a.k.a. terminal window), and see what happens. Alternatively, try searching for "python" in the usual places—*/usr/bin*, */usr/local/bin*, etc.

If you find a Python, make sure it's a recent version. Although any recent Python will do for most of this text, this edition focuses on Python 3.0 and 2.6 specifically, so you may want to install one of these to run some of the examples in this book.

Speaking of versions, I recommend starting out with Python 3.0 or later if you're learning Python anew and don't need to deal with existing 2.X code; otherwise, you should generally use Python 2.6. Some popular Python-based systems still use older releases, though (2.5 is still widespread), so if you're working with existing systems be sure to use a version relevant to your needs; the next section describes locations where you can fetch a variety of Python versions.

Where to Get Python

If there is no Python on your machine, you will need to install one yourself. The good news is that Python is an open source system that is freely available on the Web and very easy to install on most platforms.

You can always fetch the latest and greatest standard Python release from *http://www .python.org*, Python's official website. Look for the Downloads link on that page, and choose a release for the platform on which you will be working. You'll find prebuilt self-installer files for Windows (run to install), Installer Disk Images for Mac OS X (installed per Mac conventions), the full source code distribution (typically compiled on Linux, Unix, or OS X machines to generate an interpreter), and more.

Although Python is standard on Linux these days, you can also find RPMs for Linux on the Web (unpack them with *rpm*). Python's website also has links to pages where versions for other platforms are maintained, either at Python.org itself or offsite. A Google web search is another great way to find Python packages. Among other platforms, you can find Python pre-built for iPods, Palm handhelds, Nokia cell phones, PlayStation and PSP, Solaris, AS/400, and Windows Mobile.

If you find yourself pining for a Unix environment on a Windows machine, you might also be interested in installing *Cygwin* and its version of Python (see *http://www.cygwin .com*). Cygwin is a GPL-licensed library and toolset that provides full Unix functionality on Windows machines, and it includes a prebuilt Python that makes use of the all the Unix tools provided.

You can also find Python on CD-ROMs supplied with Linux distributions, included with some products and computer systems, and enclosed with some other Python books. These tend to lag behind the current release somewhat, but usually not seriously so.

In addition, you can find Python in some free and commercial development bundles. For example, ActiveState distributes Python as part of its *ActivePython*, a package that combines standard Python with extensions for Windows development such as PyWin32, an IDE called PythonWin (described in Chapter 3), and other commonly used extensions. Python can also be had today in the *Enthought* Python Distribution— a package aimed at scientific computing needs—as well as in *Portable Python*, preconfigured to run directly from a portable device. Search the Web for details.

Finally, if you are interested in alternative Python implementations, run a web search to check out *Jython* (the Python port to the Java environment) and *IronPython* (Python for the C#/.NET world), both of which are described in Chapter 2. Installation of these systems is beyond the scope of this book.

Installation Steps

Once you've downloaded Python, you need to install it. Installation steps are very platform-specific, but here are a few pointers for the major Python platforms:

Windows

On Windows, Python comes as a self-installer MSI program file—simply double-click on its file icon, and answer Yes or Next at every prompt to perform a default install. The default install includes Python's documentation set and support for `tkinter` (`Tkinter` in Python 2.6) GUIs, shelve databases, and the IDLE development GUI. Python 3.0 and 2.6 are normally installed in the directories *C:\Python30* and *C:\Python26*, though this can be changed at install time.

For convenience, after the install Python shows up in the Start button's All Programs menu. Python's menu there has five entries that give quick access to common tasks: starting the IDLE user interface, reading module documentation, starting an interactive session, reading Python's standard manuals in a web browser, and uninstalling. Most of these options involve concepts explored in detail elsewhere in this text.

When installed on Windows, Python also by default automatically registers itself to be the program that opens Python files when their icons are clicked (a program launch technique described in Chapter 3). It is also possible to build Python from its source code on Windows, but this is not commonly done.

One note for Windows Vista users: security features of the some versions of Vista change some of the rules for using MSI installer files. Although this may be a nonissue by the time you read these words, see the sidebar "The Python MSI Installer on Windows Vista" on page 1094 in this appendix for assistance if the current Python installer does not work, or does not place Python in the correct place on your machine.

Linux

On Linux, Python is available as one or more RPM files, which you unpack in the usual way (consult the RPM manpage for details). Depending on which RPMs you download, there may be one for Python itself, and another that adds support for `tkinter` GUIs and the IDLE environment. Because Linux is a Unix-like system, the next paragraph applies as well.

Unix

On Unix systems, Python is usually compiled from its full C source code distribution. This usually only requires you to unpack the file and run simple `config` and `make` commands; Python configures its own build procedure automatically, according to the system on which it is being compiled. However, be sure to see the package's *README* file for more details on this process. Because Python is open source, its source code may be used and distributed free of charge.

On other platforms the installation details can differ widely, but they generally follow the platform's normal conventions. Installing the "Pippy" port of Python for PalmOS, for example, requires a hotsync operation with your PDA, and Python for the Sharp Zaurus Linux-based PDA comes as one or more *.ipk* files, which you simply run to install it. Because additional install procedures for both executable and source forms are well documented, though, we'll skip further details here.

The Python MSI Installer on Windows Vista

As I write this, the Python self-installer for Windows is an *.msi* installation file. This format works fine on Windows XP (simply double-click on the file, and it runs), but it can have issues on some versions of Windows Vista. In particular, running the MSI installer by clicking on it may cause Python to be installed at the root of the *C:* drive, instead of in the correct *C:\PythonXX* directory. Python still works in the root directory, but this is not the correct place to install it.

This is a Vista security-related issue; in short, MSI files are not true executables, so they do not correctly inherit administrator permissions, even if run by the administrator user. Instead, MSI files are run via the Windows Registry—their filenames are associated with the MSI installer program.

This problem seems to be either Python- or Vista-version specific. On a recent laptop, for example, Python 2.6 and 3.0 installed without issue. To install Python 2.5.2 on my Vista-based OQO handheld, though, I had to use a command-line approach to force the required administrator permissions.

If Python doesn't install in the right place for you, here's the workaround: go to your Start button, select the All Programs entry, choose Accessories, right-click on the Command Prompt entry there, choose "Run as administrator," and select Continue in the access control dialog. Now, within the Command Prompt window, issue a *cd* command to change to the directory where your Python MSI installer file resides (e.g., `cd C:\user\downloads`), and then run the MSI installer manually by typing a command line of the form `msiexec /i python-2.5.1.msi`. Finally, follow the usual GUI interactions to complete the install.

Naturally, this behavior may change over time. This procedure may not be required in every version of Vista, and additional workarounds may be possible (such as disabling Vista security, if you dare). It's also possible that the Python self-installer may eventually be provided in a different format that obviates this problem—as a true executable, for instance. Be sure to try your installer by simply clicking its icon to see if it works properly before attempting any workarounds.

Configuring Python

After you've installed Python, you may want to configure some system settings that impact the way Python runs your code. (If you are just getting started with the language, you can probably skip this section completely; there is usually no need to specify any system settings for basic programs.)

Generally speaking, parts of the Python interpreter's behavior can be configured with environment variable settings and command-line options. In this section, we'll take a brief look at both, but be sure to see other documentation sources for more details on the topics we introduce here.

Python Environment Variables

Environment variables—known to some as shell variables, or DOS variables—are system-wide settings that live outside Python and thus can be used to customize the interpreter's behavior each time it is run on a given computer. Python recognizes a handful of environment variable settings, but only a few are used often enough to warrant explanation here. Table A-1 summarizes the main Python-related environment variable settings.

Table A-1. Important environment variables

Variable	Role
PATH (or path)	System shell search path (for finding "python")
PYTHONPATH	Python module search path (for imports)
PYTHONSTARTUP	Path to Python interactive startup file
TCL_LIBRARY, TK_LIBRARY	GUI extension variables (tkinter)

These variables are straightforward to use, but here are a few pointers:

PATH
> The PATH setting lists a set of directories that the operating system searches for executable programs. It should normally include the directory where your Python interpreter lives (the *python* program on Unix, or the *python.exe* file on Windows).
>
> You don't need to set this variable at all if you are willing to work in the directory where Python resides, or type the full path to Python in command lines. On Windows, for instance, the PATH is irrelevant if you run a **cd C:\Python30** before running any code (to change to the directory where Python lives), or always type **C:\Python30\python** instead of just **python** (giving a full path). Also, note that PATH settings are mostly for launching programs from command lines; they are usually irrelevant when launching via icon clicks and IDEs.

PYTHONPATH

The PYTHONPATH setting serves a role similar to PATH: the Python interpreter consults the PYTHONPATH variable to locate module files when you import them in a program. If used, this variable is set to a platform-dependent list of directory names, separated by colons on Unix and semicolons on Windows. This list normally includes just your own source code directories. Its content is merged into the sys.path module import search path, along with the script's directory, any path file settings, and standard library directories.

You don't need to set this variable unless you will be performing cross-directory imports—because Python always searches the home directory of the program's top-level file automatically, this setting is required only if a module needs to import another module that lives in a different directory. See also the discussion of *.pth* path files later in this appendix for an alternative to PYTHONPATH. For more on the module search path, refer to Chapter 21.

PYTHONSTARTUP

If PYTHONSTARTUP is set to the pathname of a file of Python code, Python executes the file's code automatically whenever you start the interactive interpreter, as though you had typed it at the interactive command line. This is a rarely used but handy way to make sure you always load certain utilities when working interactively; it saves an import.

tkinter *settings*

If you wish to use the tkinter GUI toolkit (named Tkinter in 2.6), you might have to set the two GUI variables in the last line of Table A-1 to the names of the source library directories of the Tcl and Tk systems (much like PYTHONPATH). However, these settings are not required on Windows systems (where tkinter support is installed alongside Python), and they're usually not required elsewhere if Tcl and Tk reside in standard directories.

Note that because these environment settings are external to Python itself, *when* you set them is usually irrelevant: this can be done before or after Python is installed, as long as they are set the way you require before Python is actually *run*.

Getting tkinter (and IDLE) GUI Support on Linux

The IDLE interface described in Chapter 2 is a Python tkinter GUI program. The tkinter module (named Tkinter in 2.6) is a GUI toolkit, and it's a complete, standard component of Python on Windows and some other platforms. On some Linux systems, though, the underlying GUI library may not be a standard installed component. To add GUI support to your Python on Linux if needed, try running a command line of the form **yum tkinter** to automatically install tkinter's underlying libraries. This should work on Linux distributions (and some other systems) on which the *yum* installation program is available.

How to Set Configuration Options

The way to set Python-related environment variables, and what to set them to, depends on the type of computer you're working on. And again, remember that you won't necessarily have to set these at all right away; especially if you're working in IDLE (described in Chapter 3), configuration is not required up front.

But suppose, for illustration, that you have generally useful module files in directories called *utilities* and *package1* somewhere on your machine, and you want to be able to import these modules from files located in other directories. That is, to load a file called *spam.py* from the *utilities* directory, you want to be able to say:

```
import spam
```

from another file located anywhere on your computer. To make this work, you'll have to configure your module search path one way or another to include the directory containing *spam.py*. Here are a few tips on this process.

Unix/Linux shell variables

On Unix systems, the way to set environment variables depends on the shell you use. Under the *csh* shell, you might add a line like the following in your *.cshrc* or *.login* file to set the Python module search path:

```
setenv PYTHONPATH /usr/home/pycode/utilities:/usr/lib/pycode/package1
```

This tells Python to look for imported modules in two user-defined directories. Alternatively, if you're using the *ksh* shell, the setting might instead appear in your *.kshrc* file and look like this:

```
export PYTHONPATH="/usr/home/pycode/utilities:/usr/lib/pycode/package1"
```

Other shells may use different (but analogous) syntax.

DOS variables (Windows)

If you are using MS-DOS, or some older flavors of Windows, you may need to add an environment variable configuration command to your *C:\autoexec.bat* file, and reboot your machine for the changes to take effect. The configuration command on such machines has a syntax unique to DOS:

```
set PYTHONPATH=c:\pycode\utilities;d:\pycode\package1
```

You can type such a command in a DOS console window, too, but the setting will then be active only for that one console window. Changing your *.bat* file makes the change permanent and global to all programs.

Windows environment variable GUI

On more recent versions of Windows, including XP and Vista, you can instead set PYTHONPATH and other variables via the system environment variable GUI without having to edit files or reboot. On XP, select the Control Panel, choose the System icon, pick the Advanced tab, and click the Environment Variables button to edit or add new variables (PYTHONPATH is usually a user variable). Use the same variable name and values syntax shown in the DOS set command earlier. The procedure is similar on Vista, but you may have to verify operations along the way.

You do not need to reboot your machine, but be sure to restart Python if it's open so that it picks up your changes—it configures its path at startup time only. If you're working in a Windows Command Prompt window, you'll probably need to restart that to pick up your changes as well.

Windows registry

If you are an experienced Windows user, you may also be able to configure the module search path by using the Windows Registry Editor. Go to Start→Run... and type **regedit**. Assuming the typical registry tool is on your machine, you can then navigate to Python's entries and make your changes. This is a delicate and error-prone procedure, though, so unless you're familiar with the registry, I suggest using other options (indeed, this is akin to performing brain surgery on your computer, so be careful!).

Path files

Finally, if you choose to extend the module search path with a *.pth* file instead of the PYTHONPATH variable, you might instead code a text file that looks like the following on Windows (e.g., file *C:\Python30\mypath.pth*):

```
c:\pycode\utilities
d:\pycode\package1
```

Its contents will differ per platform, and its container directory may differ per both platform and Python release. Python locates this file automatically when it starts up.

Directory names in path files may be absolute, or relative to the directory containing the path file; multiple *.pth* files can be used (all their directories are added), and *.pth* files may appear in various automatically checked directories that are platform- and version-specific. In general, a Python release numbered Python *N.M* typically looks for path files in *C:\PythonNM* and *C:\PythonNM\Lib\site-packages* on Windows, and in */usr/local/lib/pythonN.M/site-packages* and */usr/local/lib/site-python* on Unix and Linux. See Chapter 21 for more on using path files to configure the sys.path import search path.

Because environment settings are often optional, and because this isn't a book on operating system shells, I'll defer to other sources for further details. Consult your system shell's manpages or other documentation for more information, and if you have trouble figuring out what your settings should be, ask your system administrator or another local expert for help.

Python Command-Line Options

When you start Python from a system command line (a.k.a. a shell prompt), you can pass in a variety of option flags to control how Python runs. Unlike system-wide environment variables, command-line options can be different each time you run a script. The complete form of a Python command-line invocation in 3.0 looks like this (2.6 is roughly the same, with a few option differences):

```
python [-bBdEhiOsSuvVWx?] [-c command | -m module-name | script | - ] [args]
```

Most command lines only make use of the *script* and *args* parts of this format, to run a program's source file with arguments to be used by the program itself. To illustrate, consider the following script file, *main,py*, which prints the command-line arguments list made available to the script as `sys.argv`:

```
# File main.py
import sys
print(sys.argv)
```

In the following command line, both `python` and `main.py` can also be complete directory paths, and the three arguments (`a b -c`) meant for the script show up in the `sys.argv` list. The first item in `sys.argv` is always the script file's name, when it is known:

```
c:\Python30> python main.py a b -c          # Most common: run a script file
['main.py', 'a', 'b', '-c']
```

Other code format specification options allow you to specify Python code to be run on the command line itself (`-c`), to accept code to run from the standard input stream (a `-` means read from a pipe or redirected input stream file), and so on:

```
c:\Python30> python -c "print(2 ** 100)"    # Read code from command argument
1267650600228229401496703205376

c:\Python30> python -c "import main"        # Import a file to run its code
['-c']

c:\Python30> python - < main.py a b -c      # Read code from standard input
['-', 'a', 'b', '-c']

c:\Python30> python - a b -c < main.py      # Same effect as prior line
['-', 'a', 'b', '-c']
```

The `-m` code specification locates a module on Python's module search path (`sys.path`) and runs it as a top-level script (as module `__main__`). Leave off the ".py" suffix here, since the filename is a module:

```
c:\Python30> python -m main a b -c          # Locate/run module as script
['c:\\Python30\\main.py', 'a', 'b', '-c']
```

The `-m` option also supports running modules in packages with relative import syntax, as well as modules located in *.zip* archives. This switch is commonly used to run the `pdb` debugger and `profile` profiler modules from a command line for a script invocation rather than interactively, though this usage mode seems to have changed somewhat in

3.0 (profile appears to have been affected by the removal of execfile in 3.0, and pdb steps into superfluous input/output code in the new 3.0 io module):

```
c:\Python30> python -m pdb main.py a b -c          # Debug a script
--Return--
> c:\python30\lib\io.py(762)closed()->False
-> return self.raw.closed
(Pdb) c

c:\Python30> C:\python26\python -m pdb main.py a b -c   # Better in 2.6?
> c:\python30\main.py(1)<module>()
-> import sys
(Pdb) c

c:\Python30> python -m profile main.py a b -c      # Profile a script

c:\Python30> python -m cProfile main.py a b -c     # Low-overhead profiler
```

Immediately after the "python" and before the designation of code to be run, Python accepts additional arguments that control its own behavior. These arguments are consumed by Python itself and are not meant for the script being run. For example, -O runs Python in optimized mode, -u forces standard streams to be unbuffered, and –i enters interactive mode after running a script:

```
c:\Python30> python –u main.py a b -c         # Unbuffered output streams
```

Python 2.6 supports additional options that promote 3.0 compatibility (-3, -Q) and detecting inconsistent tab indentation usage, which is always detected and reported in 3.0 (-t; see Chapter 12). See the Python manuals or reference texts for more details on available command-line options. Or better yet, ask Python itself—run a command-line form like this:

```
c:\Python30> python -?
```

to request Python's help display, which documents available command-line options. If you deal with complex command lines, be sure to also check out the standard library modules getopt and optparse, which support more sophisticated command-line processing.

For More Help

Python's standard manual set today includes valuable pointers for usage on various platforms. The standard manual set is available in your Start button on Windows after Python is installed (option "Python Manuals"), and online at *http://www.python.org*. Look for the manual set's top-level section titled "Using Python" for more platform-specific pointers and hints, as well as up-to-date cross-platform environment and command-line details.

As always, the Web is your friend, too, especially in a field that often evolves faster than books like this can be updated. Given Python's widespread adoption, chances are good that answers to any usage questions you may have can be found with a web search.

Solutions to End-of-Part Exercises

Part I, Getting Started

See "Test Your Knowledge: Part I Exercises" on page 72 in Chapter 3 for the exercises.

1. *Interaction*. Assuming Python is configured properly, the interaction should look something like the following (you can run this any way you like (in IDLE, from a shell prompt, and so on):

```
% python
...copyright information lines...
>>> "Hello World!"
'Hello World!'
>>>                     # Use Ctrl-D or Ctrl-Z to exit, or close window
```

2. *Programs*. Your code (i.e., module) file *module1.py* and the operating system shell interactions should look like this:

```
print('Hello module world!')

% python module1.py
Hello module world!
```

Again, feel free to run this other ways—by clicking the file's icon, by using IDLE's Run→Run Module menu option, and so on.

3. *Modules*. The following interaction listing illustrates running a module file by importing it:

```
% python
>>> import module1
Hello module world!
>>>
```

Remember that you will need to reload the module to run it again without stopping and restarting the interpreter. The question about moving the file to a different directory and importing it again is a trick question: if Python generates a *module1.pyc* file in the original directory, it uses that when you import the module, even if the source code (.py) file has been moved to a directory not in Python's search path. The *.pyc* file is written automatically if Python has access to the source file's directory; it contains the compiled byte code version of a module. See Chapter 3 for more on modules.

4. *Scripts.* Assuming your platform supports the #! trick, your solution will look like the following (although your #! line may need to list another path on your machine):

```
#!/usr/local/bin/python          (or #!/usr/bin/env python)
print('Hello module world!')
% chmod +x module1.py

% module1.py
Hello module world!
```

5. *Errors.* The following interaction (run in Python 3.0) demonstrates the sorts of error messages you'll get when you complete this exercise. Really, you're triggering Python exceptions; the default exception-handling behavior terminates the running Python program and prints an error message and stack trace on the screen The stack trace shows where you were in a program when the exception occurred (if function calls are active when the error happens, the "Traceback" section displays all active call levels). In Part VII, you will learn that you can catch exceptions using **try** statements and process them arbitrarily; you'll also see there that Python includes a full-blown source code debugger for special error-detection requirements. For now, notice that Python gives meaningful messages when programming errors occur, instead of crashing silently:

```
% python
>>> 2 ** 500
327339060789614187001318969682759915221664204604306478948329136809613379640467455488327009232590415715088668412756007100921725654588539305332852758 9376
>>>
>>> 1 / 0
Traceback (most recent call last):
  File "<stdin>", line 1, in <module>
ZeroDivisionError: int division or modulo by zero
>>>
>>> spam
Traceback (most recent call last):
  File "<stdin>", line 1, in <module>
NameError: name 'spam' is not defined
```

6. *Breaks and cycles.* When you type this code:

```
L = [1, 2]
L.append(L)
```

you create a cyclic data structure in Python. In Python releases before 1.5.1, the Python printer wasn't smart enough to detect cycles in objects, and it would print an unending stream of [1, 2, [1, 2, [1, 2, [1, 2, and so on, until you hit the break-key combination on your machine (which, technically, raises a keyboard-interrupt exception that prints a default message). Beginning with Python 1.5.1,

---

the printer is clever enough to detect cycles and prints [[...]] instead to let you know that it has detected a loop in the object's structure and avoided getting stuck printing forever.

The reason for the cycle is subtle and requires information you will glean in Part II, so this is something of a preview. But in short, assignments in Python always generate *references* to objects, not copies of them. You can think of objects as chunks of memory and of references as implicitly followed pointers. When you run the first assignment above, the name L becomes a named reference to a two-item list object—a pointer to a piece of memory. Python lists are really arrays of object references, with an append method that changes the array in-place by tacking on another object reference at the end. Here, the append call adds a reference to the front of L at the end of L, which leads to the cycle illustrated in Figure B-1: a pointer at the end of the list that points back to the front of the list.

Besides being printed specially, as you'll learn in Chapter 6 cyclic objects must also be handled specially by Python's garbage collector, or their space will remain unreclaimed even when they are no longer in use. Though rare in practice, in some programs that traverse arbitrary objects or structures you might have to detect such cycles yourself by keeping track of where you've been to avoid looping. Believe it or not, cyclic data structures can sometimes be useful, despite their special-case printing.

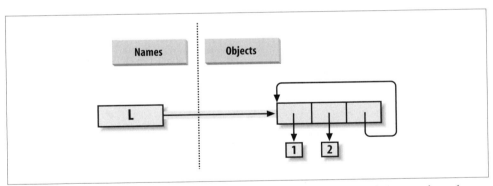

Figure B-1. A cyclic object, created by appending a list to itself. By default, Python appends a reference to the original list, not a copy of the list.

Part II, Types and Operations

See "Test Your Knowledge: Part II Exercises" on page 257 in Chapter 9 for the exercises.

1. *The basics.* Here are the sorts of results you should get, along with a few comments about their meaning. Again, note that ; is used in a few of these to squeeze more than one statement onto a single line (the ; is a statement separator), and commas

build up tuples displayed in parentheses. Also keep in mind that the / division result near the top differs in Python 2.6 and 3.0 (see Chapter 5 for details), and the `list` wrapper around dictionary method calls is needed to display results in 3.0, but not 2.6 (see Chapter 8):

```
# Numbers

>>> 2 ** 16                                    # 2 raised to the power 16
65536
>>> 2 / 5, 2 / 5.0                             # Integer / truncates in 2.6, but not 3.0
(0.40000000000000002, 0.40000000000000002)

# Strings

>>> "spam" + "eggs"                            # Concatenation
'spameggs'
>>> S = "ham"
>>> "eggs " + S
'eggs ham'
>>> S * 5                                      # Repetition
'hamhamhamhamham'
>>> S[:0]                                      # An empty slice at the front -- [0:0]
''                                             # Empty of same type as object sliced

>>> "green %s and %s" % ("eggs", S)            # Formatting
'green eggs and ham'
>>> 'green {0} and {1}'.format('eggs', S)
'green eggs and ham'

# Tuples

>>> ('x',)[0]                                  # Indexing a single-item tuple
'x'
>>> ('x', 'y')[1]                              # Indexing a 2-item tuple
'y'

# Lists

>>> L = [1,2,3] + [4,5,6]                      # List operations
>>> L, L[:], L[:0], L[-2], L[-2:]
([1, 2, 3, 4, 5, 6], [1, 2, 3, 4, 5, 6], [], 5, [5, 6])
>>> ([1,2,3]+[4,5,6])[2:4]
[3, 4]
>>> [L[2], L[3]]                               # Fetch from offsets; store in a list
[3, 4]
>>> L.reverse(); L                             # Method: reverse list in-place
[6, 5, 4, 3, 2, 1]
>>> L.sort(); L                                # Method: sort list in-place
[1, 2, 3, 4, 5, 6]
>>> L.index(4)                                 # Method: offset of first 4 (search)
3

# Dictionaries

>>> {'a':1, 'b':2}['b']                        # Index a dictionary by key
```

```
2
>>> D = {'x':1, 'y':2, 'z':3}
>>> D['w'] = 0                           # Create a new entry
>>> D['x'] + D['w']
1
>>> D[(1,2,3)] = 4                       # A tuple used as a key (immutable)

>>> D
{'w': 0, 'z': 3, 'y': 2, (1, 2, 3): 4, 'x': 1}

>>> list(D.keys()), list(D.values()), (1,2,3) in D    # Methods, key test
(['w', 'z', 'y', (1, 2, 3), 'x'], [0, 3, 2, 4, 1], True)

# Empties

>>> [[]], ["",[],(),{},None]             # Lots of nothings: empty objects
([[]], ['', [], (), {}, None])
```

2. *Indexing and slicing.* Indexing out of bounds (e.g., L[4]) raises an error; Python always checks to make sure that all offsets are within the bounds of a sequence.

On the other hand, slicing out of bounds (e.g., L[-1000:100]) works because Python scales out-of-bounds slices so that they always fit (the limits are set to zero and the sequence length, if required).

Extracting a sequence in reverse, with the lower bound greater than the higher bound (e.g., L[3:1]), doesn't really work. You get back an empty slice ([ ]) because Python scales the slice limits to make sure that the lower bound is always less than or equal to the upper bound (e.g., L[3:1] is scaled to L[3:3], the empty insertion point at offset 3). Python slices are always extracted from left to right, even if you use negative indexes (they are first converted to positive indexes by adding the sequence length). Note that Python 2.3's three-limit slices modify this behavior somewhat. For instance, L[3:1:-1] does extract from right to left:

```
>>> L = [1, 2, 3, 4]
>>> L[4]
Traceback (innermost last):
  File "<stdin>", line 1, in ?
IndexError: list index out of range
>>> L[-1000:100]
[1, 2, 3, 4]
>>> L[3:1]
[]
>>> L
[1, 2, 3, 4]
>>> L[3:1] = ['?']
>>> L
[1, 2, 3, '?', 4]
```

3. *Indexing, slicing, and del.* Your interaction with the interpreter should look something like the following code. Note that assigning an empty list to an offset stores an empty list object there, but assigning an empty list to a slice deletes the slice. Slice assignment expects another sequence, or you'll get a type error; it inserts items *inside* the sequence assigned, not the sequence itself:

```
>>> L = [1,2,3,4]
>>> L[2] = []
>>> L
[1, 2, [], 4]
>>> L[2:3] = []
>>> L
[1, 2, 4]
>>> del L[0]
>>> L
[2, 4]
>>> del L[1:]
>>> L
[2]
>>> L[1:2] = 1
Traceback (innermost last):
  File "<stdin>", line 1, in ?
TypeError: illegal argument type for built-in operation
```

4. *Tuple assignment.* The values of X and Y are swapped. When tuples appear on the left and right of an assignment symbol (=), Python assigns objects on the right to targets on the left according to their positions. This is probably easiest to understand by noting that the targets on the left aren't a real tuple, even though they look like one; they are simply a set of independent assignment targets. The items on the right are a tuple, which gets unpacked during the assignment (the tuple provides the temporary assignment needed to achieve the swap effect):

```
>>> X = 'spam'
>>> Y = 'eggs'
>>> X, Y = Y, X
>>> X
'eggs'
>>> Y
'spam'
```

5. *Dictionary keys.* Any immutable object can be used as a dictionary key, including integers, tuples, strings, and so on. This really is a dictionary, even though some of its keys look like integer offsets. Mixed-type keys work fine, too:

```
>>> D = {}
>>> D[1] = 'a'
>>> D[2] = 'b'
>>> D[(1, 2, 3)] = 'c'
>>> D
{1: 'a', 2: 'b', (1, 2, 3): 'c'}
```

6. *Dictionary indexing.* Indexing a nonexistent key (D['d']) raises an error; assigning to a nonexistent key (D['d']='spam') creates a new dictionary entry. On the other hand, out-of-bounds indexing for lists raises an error too, but so do out-of-bounds assignments. Variable names work like dictionary keys; they must have already been assigned when referenced, but they are created when first assigned. In fact, variable names can be processed as dictionary keys if you wish (they're made visible in module namespace or stack-frame dictionaries):

```
>>> D = {'a':1, 'b':2, 'c':3}
>>> D['a']
1
>>> D['d']
Traceback (innermost last):
  File "<stdin>", line 1, in ?
KeyError: d
>>> D['d'] = 4
>>> D
{'b': 2, 'd': 4, 'a': 1, 'c': 3}
>>>
>>> L = [0, 1]
>>> L[2]
Traceback (innermost last):
  File "<stdin>", line 1, in ?
IndexError: list index out of range
>>> L[2] = 3
Traceback (innermost last):
  File "<stdin>", line 1, in ?
IndexError: list assignment index out of range
```

7. *Generic operations.* Question answers:

- The + operator doesn't work on different/mixed types (e.g., string + list, list + tuple).

- + doesn't work for dictionaries, as they aren't sequences.

- The append method works only for lists, not strings, and keys works only on dictionaries. append assumes its target is mutable, since it's an in-place extension; strings are immutable.

- Slicing and concatenation always return a new object of the same type as the objects processed:

```
>>> "x" + 1
Traceback (innermost last):
  File "<stdin>", line 1, in ?
TypeError: illegal argument type for built-in operation
>>>
>>> {} + {}
Traceback (innermost last):
  File "<stdin>", line 1, in ?
TypeError: bad operand type(s) for +
>>>
>>> [].append(9)
>>> "".append('s')
Traceback (innermost last):
  File "<stdin>", line 1, in ?
AttributeError: attribute-less object
>>>
>>> list({}.keys())          # list needed in 3.0, not 2.6
[]
>>> [].keys()
Traceback (innermost last):
  File "<stdin>", line 1, in ?
AttributeError: keys
```

```
>>>
>>> [][:]
[]
>>> ""[:]
''
```

8. *String indexing.* This is a bit of a trick question—Because strings are collections of one-character strings, every time you index a string, you get back a string that can be indexed again. S[0][0][0][0][0] just keeps indexing the first character over and over. This generally doesn't work for lists (lists can hold arbitrary objects) unless the list contains strings:

```
>>> S = "spam"
>>> S[0][0][0][0][0]
's'
>>> L = ['s', 'p']
>>> L[0][0][0]
's'
```

9. *Immutable types.* Either of the following solutions works. Index assignment doesn't, because strings are immutable:

```
>>> S = "spam"
>>> S = S[0] + 'l' + S[2:]
>>> S
'slam'
>>> S = S[0] + 'l' + S[2] + S[3]
>>> S
'slam'
```

(See also the Python 3.0 bytearray string type in Chapter 36—it's a mutable sequence of small integers that is essentially processed the same as a string.)

10. *Nesting.* Here is a sample:

```
>>> me = {'name':('John', 'Q', 'Doe'), 'age':'?', 'job':'engineer'}
>>> me['job']
'engineer'
>>> me['name'][2]
'Doe'
```

11. *Files.* Here's one way to create and read back a text file in Python (ls is a Unix command; use dir on Windows):

```
# File: maker.py
file = open('myfile.txt', 'w')
file.write('Hello file world!\n')      # Or: open().write()
file.close()                            # close not always needed

# File: reader.py
file = open('myfile.txt')               # 'r' is default open mode
print(file.read())                      # Or print(open().read())

% python maker.py
% python reader.py
Hello file world!
```

```
% ls -l myfile.txt
-rwxrwxrwa  1 0        0           19 Apr 13 16:33 myfile.txt
```

Part III, Statements and Syntax

See "Test Your Knowledge: Part III Exercises" on page 392 in Chapter 15 for the exercises.

1. *Coding basic loops.* As you work through this exercise, you'll wind up with code that looks like the following:

   ```
   >>> S = 'spam'
   >>> for c in S:
   ...     print(ord(c))
   ...
   115
   112
   97
   109

   >>> x = 0
   >>> for c in S: x += ord(c)          # Or: x = x + ord(c)
   ...
   >>> x
   433

   >>> x = []
   >>> for c in S: x.append(ord(c))
   ...
   >>> x
   [115, 112, 97, 109]

   >>> list(map(ord, S))                # list() required in 3.0, not 2.6
   [115, 112, 97, 109]
   ```

2. *Backslash characters.* The example prints the bell character (\a) 50 times; assuming your machine can handle it, and when it's run outside of IDLE, you may get a series of beeps (or one sustained tone, if your machine is fast enough). Hey—I warned you.

3. *Sorting dictionaries.* Here's one way to work through this exercise (see Chapter 8 or Chapter 14 if this doesn't make sense). Remember, you really do have to split up the keys and sort calls like this because sort returns None. In Python 2.2 and later, you can iterate through dictionary keys directly without calling keys (e.g., for key in D:), but the keys list will not be sorted like it is by this code. In more recent Pythons, you can achieve the same effect with the sorted built-in, too:

   ```
   >>> D = {'a':1, 'b':2, 'c':3, 'd':4, 'e':5, 'f':6, 'g':7}
   >>> D
   {'f': 6, 'c': 3, 'a': 1, 'g': 7, 'e': 5, 'd': 4, 'b': 2}
   >>>
   >>> keys = list(D.keys())            # list() required in 3.0, not in 2.6
   ```

```
>>> keys.sort()
>>> for key in keys:
...     print(key, '=>', D[key])
...
a => 1
b => 2
c => 3
d => 4
e => 5
f => 6
g => 7

>>> for key in sorted(D):          # Better, in more recent Pythons
...     print(key, '=>', D[key])
```

4. *Program logic alternatives.* Here's some sample code for the solutions. For step e, assign the result of 2 ** X to a variable outside the loops of steps a and b, and use it inside the loop. Your results may vary a bit; this exercise is mostly designed to get you playing with code alternatives, so anything reasonable gets full credit:

```
# a

L = [1, 2, 4, 8, 16, 32, 64]
X = 5

i = 0
while i < len(L):
    if 2 ** X == L[i]:
        print('at index', i)
        break
    i += 1
else:
    print(X, 'not found')


# b

L = [1, 2, 4, 8, 16, 32, 64]
X = 5

for p in L:
    if (2 ** X) == p:
        print((2 ** X), 'was found at', L.index(p))
        break
else:
    print(X, 'not found')


# c

L = [1, 2, 4, 8, 16, 32, 64]
X = 5

if (2 ** X) in L:
    print((2 ** X), 'was found at', L.index(2 ** X))
```

```
    else:
        print(X, 'not found')


# d

X = 5
L = []
for i in range(7): L.append(2 ** i)
print(L)

if (2 ** X) in L:
    print((2 ** X), 'was found at', L.index(2 ** X))
else:
    print(X, 'not found')


# f

X = 5
L = list(map(lambda x: 2**x, range(7)))        # or [2**x for x in range(7)]
print(L)                                       # list() to print all in 3.0, not 2.6

if (2 ** X) in L:
    print((2 ** X), 'was found at', L.index(2 ** X))
else:
    print(X, 'not found')
```

Part IV, Functions

See "Test Your Knowledge: Part IV Exercises" on page 526 in Chapter 20 for the exercises.

1. *The basics.* There's not much to this one, but notice that using `print` (and hence your function) is technically a *polymorphic* operation, which does the right thing for each type of object:

```
% python
>>> def func(x): print(x)
...
>>> func("spam")
spam
>>> func(42)
42
>>> func([1, 2, 3])
[1, 2, 3]
>>> func({'food': 'spam'})
{'food': 'spam'}
```

2. *Arguments.* Here's a sample solution. Remember that you have to use `print` to see results in the test calls because a file isn't the same as code typed interactively; Python doesn't normally echo the results of expression statements in files:

```
def adder(x, y):
    return x + y

print(adder(2, 3))
print(adder('spam', 'eggs'))
print(adder(['a', 'b'], ['c', 'd']))
```

```
% python mod.py
5
spameggs
['a', 'b', 'c', 'd']
```

3. *varargs*. Two alternative `adder` functions are shown in the following file, *adders.py*. The hard part here is figuring out how to initialize an accumulator to an empty value of whatever type is passed in. The first solution uses manual type testing to look for an integer, and an empty slice of the first argument (assumed to be a sequence) if the argument is determined not to be an integer. The second solution uses the first argument to initialize and scan items 2 and beyond, much like one of the `min` function variants shown in Chapter 18.

The second solution is better. Both of these assume all arguments are of the same type, and neither works on dictionaries (as we saw in Part II, + doesn't work on mixed types or dictionaries). You could add a type test and special code to allow dictionaries, too, but that's extra credit.

```
def adder1(*args):
    print('adder1', end=' ')
    if type(args[0]) == type(0):     # Integer?
        sum = 0                       # Init to zero
    else:                             # else sequence:
        sum = args[0][:0]             # Use empty slice of arg1
    for arg in args:
        sum = sum + arg
    return sum

def adder2(*args):
    print('adder2', end=' ')
    sum = args[0]                     # Init to arg1
    for next in args[1:]:
        sum += next                   # Add items 2..N
    return sum

for func in (adder1, adder2):
    print(func(2, 3, 4))
    print(func('spam', 'eggs', 'toast'))
    print(func(['a', 'b'], ['c', 'd'], ['e', 'f']))
```

```
% python adders.py
adder1 9
adder1 spameggstoast
adder1 ['a', 'b', 'c', 'd', 'e', 'f']
adder2 9
adder2 spameggstoast
adder2 ['a', 'b', 'c', 'd', 'e', 'f']
```

4. *Keywords.* Here is my solution to the first and second parts of this exercise (coded in the file *mod.py*). To iterate over keyword arguments, use the **args form in the function header and use a loop (e.g., `for x in args.keys(): use args[x]`), or use `args.values()` to make this the same as summing *args positionals:

```
def adder(good=1, bad=2, ugly=3):
    return good + bad + ugly

print(adder())
print(adder(5))
print(adder(5, 6))
print(adder(5, 6, 7))
print(adder(ugly=7, good=6, bad=5))

% python mod.py
6
10
14
18
18
```

```
# Second part solutions

def adder1(*args):                      # Sum any number of positional args
    tot = args[0]
    for arg in args[1:]:
        tot += arg
    return tot

def adder2(**args):                     # Sum any number of keyword args
    argskeys = list(args.keys())        # list needed in 3.0!
    tot = args[argskeys[0]]
    for key in argskeys[1:]:
        tot += args[key]
    return tot

def adder3(**args):                     # Same, but convert to list of values
    args = list(args.values())          # list needed to index in 3.0!
    tot = args[0]
    for arg in args[1:]:
        tot += arg
    return tot

def adder4(**args):                     # Same, but reuse positional version
    return adder1(*args.values())

print(adder1(1, 2, 3),       adder1('aa', 'bb', 'cc'))
print(adder2(a=1, b=2, c=3), adder2(a='aa', b='bb', c='cc'))
print(adder3(a=1, b=2, c=3), adder3(a='aa', b='bb', c='cc'))
print(adder4(a=1, b=2, c=3), adder4(a='aa', b='bb', c='cc'))
```

5. (and 6.) Here are my solutions to exercises 5 and 6 (file *dicts.py*). These are just coding exercises, though, because Python 1.5 added the dictionary methods D.copy() and D1.update(D2) to handle things like copying and adding (merging) dictionaries. (See Python's library manual or O'Reilly's *Python Pocket Reference* for more details.) X[:] doesn't work for dictionaries, as they're not sequences (see Chapter 8 for details). Also, remember that if you assign (e = d) rather than copying, you generate a reference to a *shared* dictionary object; changing d changes e, too:

```
def copyDict(old):
    new = {}
    for key in old.keys():
        new[key] = old[key]
    return new

def addDict(d1, d2):
    new = {}
    for key in d1.keys():
        new[key] = d1[key]
    for key in d2.keys():
        new[key] = d2[key]
    return new
```

```
% python
>>> from dicts import *
>>> d = {1: 1, 2: 2}
>>> e = copyDict(d)
>>> d[2] = '?'
>>> d
{1: 1, 2: '?'}
>>> e
{1: 1, 2: 2}

>>> x = {1: 1}
>>> y = {2: 2}
>>> z = addDict(x, y)
>>> z
{1: 1, 2: 2}
```

6. See #5.

7. *More argument-matching examples.* Here is the sort of interaction you should get, along with comments that explain the matching that goes on:

```
def f1(a, b): print(a, b)              # Normal args

def f2(a, *b): print(a, b)             # Positional varargs

def f3(a, **b): print(a, b)            # Keyword varargs

def f4(a, *b, **c): print(a, b, c)     # Mixed modes

def f5(a, b=2, c=3): print(a, b, c)    # Defaults
```

```
    def f6(a, b=2, *c): print(a, b, c)        # Defaults and positional varargs


    % python
    >>> f1(1, 2)                               # Matched by position (order matters)
    1 2
    >>> f1(b=2, a=1)                           # Matched by name (order doesn't matter)
    1 2

    >>> f2(1, 2, 3)                            # Extra positionals collected in a tuple
    1 (2, 3)

    >>> f3(1, x=2, y=3)                        # Extra keywords collected in a dictionary
    1 {'x': 2, 'y': 3}

    >>> f4(1, 2, 3, x=2, y=3)                  # Extra of both kinds
    1 (2, 3) {'x': 2, 'y': 3}

    >>> f5(1)                                  # Both defaults kick in
    1 2 3
    >>> f5(1, 4)                               # Only one default used
    1 4 3

    >>> f6(1)                                  # One argument: matches "a"
    1 2 ()
    >>> f6(1, 3, 4)                            # Extra positional collected
    1 3 (4,)
```

8. *Primes revisited.* Here is the primes example, wrapped up in a function and a module (file *primes.py*) so it can be run multiple times. I added an `if` test to trap negatives, 0, and 1. I also changed / to // in this edition to make this solution immune to the Python 3.0 / true division changes we studied in Chapter 5, and to enable it to support floating-point numbers (uncomment the `from` statement and change // to / to see the differences in 2.6):

```
    #from __future__ import division

    def prime(y):
        if y <= 1:                             # For some y > 1
            print(y, 'not prime')
        else:
            x = y // 2                         # 3.0 / fails
            while x > 1:
                if y % x == 0:                 # No remainder?
                    print(y, 'has factor', x)
                    break                      # Skip else
                x -= 1
            else:
                print(y, 'is prime')

    prime(13); prime(13.0)
    prime(15); prime(15.0)
    prime(3);  prime(2)
    prime(1);  prime(-3)
```

Here is the module in action; the `//` operator allows it to work for floating-point numbers too, even though it perhaps should not:

```
% python primes.py
13 is prime
13.0 is prime
15 has factor 5
15.0 has factor 5.0
3 is prime
2 is prime
1 not prime
-3 not prime
```

This function still isn't very reusable—it could return values, instead of printing —but it's enough to run experiments. It's also not a strict mathematical prime (floating points work), and it's still inefficient. Improvements are left as exercises for more mathematically minded readers. (Hint: a `for` loop over `range(y, 1, -1)` may be a bit quicker than the `while`, but the algorithm is the real bottleneck here.) To time alternatives, use the built-in `time` module and coding patterns like those used in this general function-call timer (see the library manual for details):

```
def timer(reps, func, *args):
    import time
    start = time.clock()
    for i in range(reps):
        func(*args)
    return time.clock() - start
```

9. *List comprehensions*. Here is the sort of code you should write; I may have a preference, but I'm not telling:

```
>>> values = [2, 4, 9, 16, 25]
>>> import math

>>> res = []
>>> for x in values: res.append(math.sqrt(x))
...
>>> res
[1.4142135623730951, 2.0, 3.0, 4.0, 5.0]

>>> list(map(math.sqrt, values))
[1.4142135623730951, 2.0, 3.0, 4.0, 5.0]

>>> [math.sqrt(x) for x in values]
[1.4142135623730951, 2.0, 3.0, 4.0, 5.0]
```

10. *Timing tools*. Here is some code I wrote to time the three square root options, along with the results in 2.6 and 3.0. The last result of each function is printed to verify that all three do the same work:

```
# File mytimer.py (2.6 and 3.0)

...same as listed in Chapter 20...

# File timesqrt.py
```

```
import sys, mytimer
reps = 10000
repslist = range(reps)              # Pull out range list time for 2.6

from math import sqrt               # Not math.sqrt: adds attr fetch time
def mathMod():
    for i in repslist:
        res = sqrt(i)
    return res

def powCall():
    for i in repslist:
        res = pow(i, .5)
    return res

def powExpr():
    for i in repslist:
        res = i ** .5
    return res

print(sys.version)
for tester in (mytimer.timer, mytimer.best):
    print('<%s>' % tester.__name__)
    for test in (mathMod, powCall, powExpr):
        elapsed, result = tester(test)
        print ('-'*35)
        print ('%s: %.5f => %s' %
                (test.__name__, elapsed, result))
```

Following are the test results for Python 3.0 and 2.6. For both, it looks like the math module is quicker than the ** expression, which is quicker than the pow call; however, you should try this with your code and on your own machine and version of Python. Also, note that Python 3.0 is nearly twice as slow as 2.6 on this test; 3.1 or later might perform better (time this in the future to see for yourself):

```
c:\misc> c:\python30\python timesqrt.py
3.0.1 (r301:69561, Feb 13 2009, 20:04:18) [MSC v.1500 32 bit (Intel)]
<timer>
-----------------------------------
mathMod: 5.33906 => 99.994999875
-----------------------------------
powCall: 7.29689 => 99.994999875
-----------------------------------
powExpr: 5.95770 => 99.994999875
<best>
-----------------------------------
mathMod: 0.00497 => 99.994999875
-----------------------------------
powCall: 0.00671 => 99.994999875
-----------------------------------
powExpr: 0.00540 => 99.994999875


c:\misc> c:\python26\python timesqrt.py
```

```
2.6.1 (r261:67517, Dec  4 2008, 16:51:00) [MSC v.1500 32 bit (Intel)]
<timer>
-----------------------------------
mathMod: 2.61226 => 99.994999875
-----------------------------------
powCall: 4.33705 => 99.994999875
-----------------------------------
powExpr: 3.12502 => 99.994999875
<best>
-----------------------------------
mathMod: 0.00236 => 99.994999875
-----------------------------------
powCall: 0.00402 => 99.994999875
-----------------------------------
powExpr: 0.00287 => 99.994999875
```

To time the relative speeds of Python 3.0 *dictionary comprehensions* and equivalent for loops interactively, run a session like the following. It appears that the two are roughly the same in this regard under Python 3.0; unlike list comprehensions, though, manual loops are slightly faster than dictionary comprehensions today (though the difference isn't exactly earth-shattering—at the end we save half a second when making 50 dictionaries of 1,000,000 items each). Again, rather than taking these results as gospel you should investigate further on your own, on your computer and with your Python:

```
c:\misc> c:\python30\python
>>>
>>> def dictcomp(I):
...     return {i: i for i in range(I)}
...
>>> def dictloop(I):
...     new = {}
...     for i in range(I): new[i] = i
...     return new
...
>>> dictcomp(10)
{0: 0, 1: 1, 2: 2, 3: 3, 4: 4, 5: 5, 6: 6, 7: 7, 8: 8, 9: 9}
>>> dictloop(10)
{0: 0, 1: 1, 2: 2, 3: 3, 4: 4, 5: 5, 6: 6, 7: 7, 8: 8, 9: 9}
>>>
>>> from mytimer import best, timer
>>> best(dictcomp, 10000)[0]              # 10,000-item dict
0.0013519874732672577
>>> best(dictloop, 10000)[0]
0.001132965223233029
>>>
>>> best(dictcomp, 100000)[0]             # 100,000 items: 10 times slower
0.01816089754424155
>>> best(dictloop, 100000)[0]
0.01643484018219965
>>>
>>> best(dictcomp, 1000000)[0]            # 1,000,000 items: 10X time
0.18685105229855026
>>> best(dictloop, 1000000)[0]            # Time for making one dict
```

```
0.1769041177020938
>>>
>>> timer(dictcomp, 1000000, _reps=50)[0]          # 1,000,000-item dict
10.692516087938543
>>> timer(dictloop, 1000000, _reps=50)[0]          # Time for making 50
10.197276050447755
```

Part V, Modules

See "Test Your Knowledge: Part V Exercises" on page 607 in Chapter 24 for the exercises.

1. *Import basics.* When you're done, your file (*mymod.py*) and interaction should look similar to the following; remember that Python can read a whole file into a list of line strings, and the len built-in returns the lengths of strings and lists:

```
def countLines(name):
    file = open(name)
    return len(file.readlines())

def countChars(name):
    return len(open(name).read())

def test(name):                                    # Or pass file object
    return countLines(name), countChars(name)      # Or return a dictionary
```

```
% python
>>> import mymod
>>> mymod.test('mymod.py')
(10, 291)
```

Note that these functions load the entire file in memory all at once, so they won't work for pathologically large files too big for your machine's memory. To be more robust, you could read line by line with iterators instead and count as you go:

```
def countLines(name):
    tot = 0
    for line in open(name): tot += 1
    return tot

def countChars(name):
    tot = 0
    for line in open(name): tot += len(line)
    return tot
```

A generator expression can have the same effect: sum(len(line) for line in open(name)). On Unix, you can verify your output with a wc command; on Windows, right-click on your file to view its properties. Note that your script may report fewer characters than Windows does—for portability, Python converts Windows \r\n line-end markers to \n, thereby dropping one byte (character) per line. To match byte counts with Windows exactly, you must open in binary mode ('rb'), or add the number of bytes corresponding to the number of lines.

The "ambitious" part of this exercise (passing in a file object so you only open the file once), will require you to use the **seek** method of the built-in file object. It works like C's **fseek** call (and calls it behind the scenes): **seek** resets the current position in the file to a passed-in offset. After a **seek**, future input/output operations are relative to the new position. To rewind to the start of a file without closing and reopening it, call `file.seek(0)`; the file **read** methods all pick up at the current position in the file, so you need to rewind to reread. Here's what this tweak would look like:

```
def countLines(file):
    file.seek(0)                                # Rewind to start of file
    return len(file.readlines())

def countChars(file):
    file.seek(0)                                # Ditto (rewind if needed)
    return len(file.read())

def test(name):
    file = open(name)                           # Pass file object
    return countLines(file), countChars(file)   # Open file only once

>>> import mymod2
>>> mymod2.test("mymod2.py")
(11, 392)
```

2. from/from *. Here's the from * part; replace * with countChars to do the rest:

```
% python
>>> from mymod import *
>>> countChars("mymod.py")
291
```

3. __main__. If you code it properly, it works in either mode (program run or module import):

```
def countLines(name):
    file = open(name)
    return len(file.readlines())

def countChars(name):
    return len(open(name).read())

def test(name):                                      # Or pass file object
    return countLines(name), countChars(name)        # Or return a dictionary

if __name__ == '__main__':
    print(test('mymod.py'))

% python mymod.py
(13, 346)
```

This is where I would probably begin to consider using command-line arguments or user input to provide the filename to be counted, instead of hardcoding it in the script (see Chapter 24 for more on **sys.argv**, and Chapter 10 for more on **input**):

```
if __name__ == '__main__':
    print(test(input('Enter file name:')))

if __name__ == '__main__':
    import sys
    print(test(sys.argv[1]))
```

4. *Nested imports*. Here is my solution (file *myclient.py*):

```
from mymod import countLines, countChars
print(countLines('mymod.py'), countChars('mymod.py'))

% python myclient.py
13 346
```

As for the rest of this one, mymod's functions are accessible (that is, importable) from the top level of myclient, since from simply assigns to names in the importer (it works as if mymod's defs appeared in myclient). For example, another file can say:

```
import myclient
myclient.countLines(...)

from myclient import countChars
countChars(...)
```

If myclient used import instead of from, you'd need to use a path to get to the functions in mymod through myclient:

```
import myclient
myclient.mymod.countLines(...)

from myclient import mymod
mymod.countChars(...)
```

In general, you can define *collector* modules that import all the names from other modules so they're available in a single convenience module. Using the following code, you get three different copies of the name somename (mod1.somename, collec tor.somename, and __main__.somename); all three share the same integer object initially, and only the name somename exists at the interactive prompt as is:

```
# File mod1.py
somename = 42
```

```
# File collector.py
from mod1 import *        # Collect lots of names here
from mod2 import *        # from assigns to my names
from mod3 import *
```

```
>>> from collector import somename
```

5. *Package imports*. For this, I put the *mymod.py* solution file listed for exercise 3 into a directory package. The following is what I did to set up the directory and its required *__init__.py* file in a Windows console interface; you'll need to interpolate for other platforms (e.g., use mv and vi instead of move and edit). This works in any

directory (I just happened to run my commands in Python's install directory), and you can do some of this from a file explorer GUI, too.

When I was done, I had a *mypkg* subdirectory that contained the files *__init__.py* and *mymod.py*. You need an *__init__.py* in the *mypkg* directory, but not in its parent; *mypkg* is located in the home directory component of the module search path. Notice how a `print` statement coded in the directory's initialization file fires only the first time it is imported, not the second:

```
C:\python30> mkdir mypkg
C:\Python30> move mymod.py mypkg\mymod.py
C:\Python30> edit mypkg\__init__.py
...coded a print statement...
C:\Python30> python
>>> import mypkg.mymod
initializing mypkg
>>> mypkg.mymod.countLines('mypkg\mymod.py')
13
>>> from mypkg.mymod import countChars
>>> countChars('mypkg\mymod.py')
346
```

6. *Reloads*. This exercise just asks you to experiment with changing the *changer.py* example in the book, so there's nothing to show here.

7. *Circular imports*. The short story is that importing `recur2` first works because the recursive import then happens at the import in `recur1`, not at a `from` in `recur2`.

    The long story goes like this: importing `recur2` first works because the recursive import from `recur1` to `recur2` fetches `recur2` as a whole, instead of getting specific names. `recur2` is incomplete when it's imported from `recur1`, but because it uses `import` instead of `from`, you're safe: Python finds and returns the already created `recur2` module object and continues to run the rest of `recur1` without a glitch. When the `recur2` import resumes, the second `from` finds the name Y in `recur1` (it's been run completely), so no error is reported. Running a file as a script is not the same as importing it as a module; these cases are the same as running the first `import` or `from` in the script interactively. For instance, running `recur1` as a script is the same as importing `recur2` interactively, as `recur2` is the first module imported in `recur1`.

Part VI, Classes and OOP

See "Test Your Knowledge: Part VI Exercises" on page 818 in Chapter 31 for the exercises.

1. *Inheritance*. Here's the solution code for this exercise (file *adder.py*), along with some interactive tests. The `__add__` overload has to appear only once, in the superclass, as it invokes type-specific add methods in subclasses:

```
class Adder:
    def add(self, x, y):
```

```
              print('not implemented!')
        def __init__(self, start=[]):
            self.data = start
        def __add__(self, other):                    # Or in subclasses?
            return self.add(self.data, other)         # Or return type?

    class ListAdder(Adder):
        def add(self, x, y):
            return x + y

    class DictAdder(Adder):
        def add(self, x, y):
            new = {}
            for k in x.keys(): new[k] = x[k]
            for k in y.keys(): new[k] = y[k]
            return new

% python
>>> from adder import *
>>> x = Adder()
>>> x.add(1, 2)
not implemented!
>>> x = ListAdder()
>>> x.add([1], [2])
[1, 2]
>>> x = DictAdder()
>>> x.add({1:1}, {2:2})
{1: 1, 2: 2}

>>> x = Adder([1])
>>> x + [2]
not implemented!
>>>
>>> x = ListAdder([1])
>>> x + [2]
[1, 2]
>>> [2] + x
Traceback (innermost last):
  File "<stdin>", line 1, in ?
TypeError: __add__ nor __radd__ defined for these operands
```

Notice in the last test that you get an error for expressions where a class instance appears on the right of a +; if you want to fix this, use __radd__ methods, as described in "Operator Overloading" in Chapter 29.

If you are saving a value in the instance anyhow, you might as well rewrite the add method to take just one argument, in the spirit of other examples in this part of the book:

```
    class Adder:
        def __init__(self, start=[]):
            self.data = start
        def __add__(self, other):                    # Pass a single argument
            return self.add(other)                    # The left side is in self
        def add(self, y):
```

```
            print('not implemented!')

    class ListAdder(Adder):
        def add(self, y):
            return self.data + y

    class DictAdder(Adder):
        def add(self, y):
            pass                          # Change to use self.data instead of x

    x = ListAdder([1, 2, 3])
    y = x + [4, 5, 6]
    print(y)                              # Prints [1, 2, 3, 4, 5, 6]
```

Because values are attached to objects rather than passed around, this version is arguably more object-oriented. And, once you've gotten to this point, you'll probably find that you can get rid of add altogether and simply define type-specific __add__ methods in the two subclasses.

2. *Operator overloading.* The solution code (file *mylist.py*) uses a few operator overloading methods that the text didn't say much about, but they should be straightforward to understand. Copying the initial value in the constructor is important because it may be mutable; you don't want to change or have a reference to an object that's possibly shared somewhere outside the class. The __getattr__ method routes calls to the wrapped list. For hints on an easier way to code this in Python 2.2 and later, see "Extending Types by Subclassing" on page 777 in Chapter 31:

```
    class MyList:
        def __init__(self, start):
            #self.wrapped = start[:]      # Copy start: no side effects
            self.wrapped = []             # Make sure it's a list here
            for x in start: self.wrapped.append(x)
        def __add__(self, other):
            return MyList(self.wrapped + other)
        def __mul__(self, time):
            return MyList(self.wrapped * time)
        def __getitem__(self, offset):
            return self.wrapped[offset]
        def __len__(self):
            return len(self.wrapped)
        def __getslice__(self, low, high):
            return MyList(self.wrapped[low:high])
        def append(self, node):
            self.wrapped.append(node)
        def __getattr__(self, name):      # Other methods: sort/reverse/etc
            return getattr(self.wrapped, name)
        def __repr__(self):
            return repr(self.wrapped)

    if __name__ == '__main__':
        x = MyList('spam')
        print(x)
        print(x[2])
        print(x[1:])
```

```
print(x + ['eggs'])
print(x * 3)
x.append('a')
x.sort()
for c in x: print(c, end=' ')
```

```
% python mylist.py
['s', 'p', 'a', 'm']
a
['p', 'a', 'm']
['s', 'p', 'a', 'm', 'eggs']
['s', 'p', 'a', 'm', 's', 'p', 'a', 'm', 's', 'p', 'a', 'm']
a a m p s
```

Note that it's important to copy the start value by appending instead of slicing here, because otherwise the result may not be a true list and so will not respond to expected list methods, such as append (e.g., slicing a string returns another string, not a list). You would be able to copy a MyList start value by slicing because its class overloads the slicing operation and provides the expected list interface; however, you need to avoid slice-based copying for objects such as strings.

3. *Subclassing.* My solution (*mysub.py*) appears below. Your solution should be similar:

```
from mylist import MyList

class MyListSub(MyList):
    calls = 0                              # Shared by instances

    def __init__(self, start):
        self.adds = 0                      # Varies in each instance
        MyList.__init__(self, start)

    def __add__(self, other):
        MyListSub.calls += 1               # Class-wide counter
        self.adds += 1                     # Per-instance counts
        return MyList.__add__(self, other)

    def stats(self):
        return self.calls, self.adds       # All adds, my adds

if __name__ == '__main__':
    x = MyListSub('spam')
    y = MyListSub('foo')
    print(x[2])
    print(x[1:])
    print(x + ['eggs'])
    print(x + ['toast'])
    print(y + ['bar'])
    print(x.stats())
```

```
% python mysub.py
a
['p', 'a', 'm']
['s', 'p', 'a', 'm', 'eggs']
```

```
['s', 'p', 'a', 'm', 'toast']
['f', 'o', 'o', 'bar']
(3, 2)
```

4. *Attribute methods.* I worked through this exercise as follows. Notice that in Python 2.6, operators try to fetch attributes through __getattr__, too; you need to return a value to make them work. Caveat: as noted in Chapter 30, __getattr__ is *not* called for built-in operations in Python 3.0, so the following expression won't work as shown; in 3.0, a class like this must redefine __X__ operator overloading methods explicitly. More on this in Chapters 30, 37, and 38.

```
>>> class Meta:
...     def __getattr__(self, name):
...         print('get', name)
...     def __setattr__(self, name, value):
...         print('set', name, value)
...
>>> x = Meta()
>>> x.append
get append
>>> x.spam = "pork"
set spam pork
>>>
>>> x + 2
get __coerce__
Traceback (innermost last):
  File "<stdin>", line 1, in ?
TypeError: call of non-function
>>>
>>> x[1]
get __getitem__
Traceback (innermost last):
  File "<stdin>", line 1, in ?
TypeError: call of non-function

>>> x[1:5]
get __len__
Traceback (innermost last):
  File "<stdin>", line 1, in ?
TypeError: call of non-function
```

5. *Set objects.* Here's the sort of interaction you should get. Comments explain which methods are called. Also, note that sets are a built-in type in Python today, so this is largely just a coding exercise (see Chapter 5 for more on sets).

```
% python
>>> from setwrapper import Set
>>> x = Set([1, 2, 3, 4])          # Runs __init__
>>> y = Set([3, 4, 5])

>>> x & y                          # __and__, intersect, then __repr__
Set:[3, 4]
>>> x | y                          # __or__, union, then __repr__
Set:[1, 2, 3, 4, 5]
```

```
>>> z = Set("hello")                    # __init__ removes duplicates
>>> z[0], z[-1]                         # __getitem__
('h', 'o')

>>> for c in z: print(c, end=' ')       # __getitem__
...
h e l o
>>> len(z), z                           # __len__, __repr__
(4, Set:['h', 'e', 'l', 'o'])

>>> z & "mello", z | "mello"
(Set:['e', 'l', 'o'], Set:['h', 'e', 'l', 'o', 'm'])
```

My solution to the multiple-operand extension subclass looks like the following class (file *multiset.py*). It only needs to replace two methods in the original set. The class's documentation string explains how it works:

```python
from setwrapper import Set

class MultiSet(Set):
    """
    Inherits all Set names, but extends intersect
    and union to support multiple operands; note
    that "self" is still the first argument (stored
    in the *args argument now); also note that the
    inherited & and | operators call the new methods
    here with 2 arguments, but processing more than
    2 requires a method call, not an expression:
    """

    def intersect(self, *others):
        res = []
        for x in self:                  # Scan first sequence
            for other in others:        # For all other args
                if x not in other: break # Item in each one?
            else:                       # No: break out of loop
                res.append(x)           # Yes: add item to end
        return Set(res)

    def union(*args):                   # self is args[0]
        res = []
        for seq in args:                # For all args
            for x in seq:               # For all nodes
                if not x in res:
                    res.append(x)       # Add new items to result
        return Set(res)
```

Your interaction with the extension will look something like the following. Note that you can intersect by using & or calling intersect, but you must call intersect for three or more operands; & is a binary (two-sided) operator. Also, note that we could have called MultiSet simply Set to make this change more transparent if we used setwrapper.Set to refer to the original within multiset:

```
>>> from multiset import *
>>> x = MultiSet([1,2,3,4])
```

```
>>> y = MultiSet([3,4,5])
>>> z = MultiSet([0,1,2])

>>> x & y, x | y                                    # Two operands
(Set:[3, 4], Set:[1, 2, 3, 4, 5])

>>> x.intersect(y, z)                               # Three operands
Set:[]
>>> x.union(y, z)
Set:[1, 2, 3, 4, 5, 0]
>>> x.intersect([1,2,3], [2,3,4], [1,2,3])          # Four operands
Set:[2, 3]
>>> x.union(range(10))                              # Non-MultiSets work, too
Set:[1, 2, 3, 4, 0, 5, 6, 7, 8, 9]
```

6. *Class tree links*. Here is the way I changed the lister classes, and a rerun of the test to show its format. Do the same for the `dir`-based version, and also do this when formatting class objects in the tree climber variant:

```
class ListInstance:
    def __str__(self):
        return '<Instance of %s(%s), address %s:\n%s>' % (
                        self.__class__.__name__,         # My class's name
                        self.__supers(),                 # My class's own supers
                        id(self),                        # My address
                        self.__attrnames()) )            # name=value list
    def __attrnames(self):
        ...unchanged...
    def __supers(self):
        names = []
        for super in self.__class__.__bases__:           # One level up from class
            names.append(super.__name__)                 # name, not str(super)
        return ', '.join(names)
```

```
C:\misc> python testmixin.py
<Instance of Sub(Super, ListInstance), address 7841200:
        name data1=spam
        name data2=eggs
        name data3=42
>
```

7. *Composition*. My solution is below (file *lunch.py*), with comments from the description mixed in with the code. This is one case where it's probably easier to express a problem in Python than it is in English:

```
class Lunch:
    def __init__(self):                          # Make/embed Customer, Employee
        self.cust = Customer()
        self.empl = Employee()
    def order(self, foodName):                   # Start Customer order simulation
        self.cust.placeOrder(foodName, self.empl)
    def result(self):                            # Ask the Customer about its Food
        self.cust.printFood()

class Customer:
    def __init__(self):                          # Initialize my food to None
```

```
        self.food = None
    def placeOrder(self, foodName, employee):      # Place order with Employee
        self.food = employee.takeOrder(foodName)
    def printFood(self):                           # Print the name of my food
        print(self.food.name)

class Employee:
    def takeOrder(self, foodName):                 # Return Food, with desired name
        return Food(foodName)

class Food:
    def __init__(self, name):                      # Store food name
        self.name = name

if __name__ == '__main__':
    x = Lunch()                                    # Self-test code
    x.order('burritos')                            # If run, not imported
    x.result()
    x.order('pizza')
    x.result()
```

```
% python lunch.py
burritos
pizza
```

8. *Zoo animal hierarchy.* Here is the way I coded the taxonomy in Python (file *zoo.py*); it's artificial, but the general coding pattern applies to many real structures, from GUIs to employee databases. Notice that the self.speak reference in Animal triggers an independent inheritance search, which finds speak in a subclass. Test this interactively per the exercise description. Try extending this hierarchy with new classes, and making instances of various classes in the tree:

```
class Animal:
    def reply(self):   self.speak()              # Back to subclass
    def speak(self):   print('spam')             # Custom message

class Mammal(Animal):
    def speak(self):   print('huh?')

class Cat(Mammal):
    def speak(self):   print('meow')

class Dog(Mammal):
    def speak(self):   print('bark')

class Primate(Mammal):
    def speak(self):   print('Hello world!')

class Hacker(Primate): pass                       # Inherit from Primate
```

9. *The Dead Parrot Sketch.* Here's how I implemented this one (file *parrot.py*). Notice how the line method in the Actor superclass works: by accessing self attributes twice, it sends Python back to the instance twice, and hence invokes *two* inheritance searches—self.name and self.says() find information in the specific subclasses:

```
class Actor:
    def line(self): print(self.name + ':', repr(self.says()))

class Customer(Actor):
    name = 'customer'
    def says(self): return "that's one ex-bird!"

class Clerk(Actor):
    name = 'clerk'
    def says(self): return "no it isn't..."

class Parrot(Actor):
    name = 'parrot'
    def says(self): return None

class Scene:
    def __init__(self):
        self.clerk    = Clerk()          # Embed some instances
        self.customer = Customer()       # Scene is a composite
        self.subject  = Parrot()

    def action(self):
        self.customer.line()             # Delegate to embedded
        self.clerk.line()
        self.subject.line()
```

Part VII, Exceptions and Tools

See "Test Your Knowledge: Part VII Exercises" on page 893 in Chapter 35 for the exercises.

1. try/except. My version of the oops function (file *oops.py*) follows. As for the noncoding questions, changing oops to raise a KeyError instead of an IndexError means that the try handler won't catch the exception (it "percolates" to the top level and triggers Python's default error message). The names KeyError and Index Error come from the outermost built-in names scope. Import builtins (__builtin__ in Python 2.6) and pass it as an argument to the dir function to see for yourself:

```
def oops():
    raise IndexError()

def doomed():
    try:
        oops()
    except IndexError:
```

```
            print('caught an index error!')
        else:
            print('no error caught...')

    if __name__ == '__main__': doomed()
```

2. *Exception objects and lists.* Here's the way I extended this module for an exception of my own:

```
class MyError(Exception): pass

def oops():
    raise MyError('Spam!')

def doomed():
    try:
        oops()
    except IndexError:
        print('caught an index error!')
    except MyError as data:
        print('caught error:', MyError, data)
    else:
        print('no error caught...')

if __name__ == '__main__':
    doomed()
```

```
% python oops.py
caught error: <class '__main__.MyError'> Spam!
```

Like all class exceptions, the instance comes back as the extra data; the error message shows both the class (<...>) and its instance (Spam!). The instance must be inheriting both an __init__ and a __repr__ or __str__ from Python's Exception class, or it would print like the class does. See Chapter 34 for details on how this works in built-in exception classes.

3. *Error handling.* Here's one way to solve this one (file *safe2.py*). I did my tests in a file, rather than interactively, but the results are about the same.

```
import sys, traceback

def safe(entry, *args):
    try:
        entry(*args)                          # Catch everything else
    except:
        traceback.print_exc()
        print('Got', sys.exc_info()[0], sys.exc_info()[1])

import oops
safe(oops.oops)
```

```
% python safe2.py
```

```
Traceback (innermost last):
  File "safe2.py", line 5, in safe
    entry(*args)                              # Catch everything else
  File "oops.py", line 4, in oops
    raise MyError('Spam!')
oops.MyError: Spam!
Got Spam!
```

4. Here are a few examples for you to study as time allows; for more, see follow-up books and the Web:

```
# Find the largest Python source file in a single directory

import os, glob
dirname = r'C:\Python30\Lib'

allsizes = []
allpy = glob.glob(dirname + os.sep + '*.py')
for filename in allpy:
    filesize = os.path.getsize(filename)
    allsizes.append((filesize, filename))

allsizes.sort()
print(allsizes[:2])
print(allsizes[-2:])
```

```
# Find the largest Python source file in an entire directory tree

import sys, os, pprint
if sys.platform[:3] == 'win':
    dirname = r'C:\Python30\Lib'
else:
    dirname = '/usr/lib/python'

allsizes = []
for (thisDir, subsHere, filesHere) in os.walk(dirname):
    for filename in filesHere:
        if filename.endswith('.py'):
            fullname = os.path.join(thisDir, filename)
            fullsize = os.path.getsize(fullname)
            allsizes.append((fullsize, fullname))

allsizes.sort()
pprint.pprint(allsizes[:2])
pprint.pprint(allsizes[-2:])
```

```
# Find the largest Python source file on the module import search path

import sys, os, pprint
visited  = {}
allsizes = []
for srcdir in sys.path:
    for (thisDir, subsHere, filesHere) in os.walk(srcdir):
        thisDir = os.path.normpath(thisDir)
```

```
            if thisDir.upper() in visited:
                continue
            else:
                visited[thisDir.upper()] = True
            for filename in filesHere:
                if filename.endswith('.py'):
                    pypath  = os.path.join(thisDir, filename)
                    try:
                        pysize = os.path.getsize(pypath)
                    except:
                        print('skipping', pypath)
                    allsizes.append((pysize, pypath))

allsizes.sort()
pprint.pprint(allsizes[:3])
pprint.pprint(allsizes[-3:])
```

```
# Sum columns in a text file separated by commas

filename = 'data.txt'
sums = {}

for line in open(filename):
    cols = line.split(',')
    nums = [int(col) for col in cols]
    for (ix, num) in enumerate(nums):
        sums[ix] = sums.get(ix, 0) + num

for key in sorted(sums):
    print(key, '=', sums[key])
```

```
# Similar to prior, but using lists instead of dictionaries for sums

import sys
filename = sys.argv[1]
numcols  = int(sys.argv[2])
totals   = [0] * numcols

for line in open(filename):
    cols = line.split(',')
    nums = [int(x) for x in cols]
    totals = [(x + y) for (x, y) in zip(totals, nums)]

print(totals)
```

```
# Test for regressions in the output of a set of scripts

import os
testscripts = [dict(script='test1.py', args=''),       # Or glob script/args dir
               dict(script='test2.py', args='spam')]

for testcase in testscripts:
```

```
        commandline = '%(script)s %(args)s' % testcase
        output = os.popen(commandline).read()
        result = testcase['script'] + '.result'
        if not os.path.exists(result):
            open(result, 'w').write(output)
            print('Created:', result)
        else:
            priorresult = open(result).read()
            if output != priorresult:
                print('FAILED:', testcase['script'])
                print(output)
            else:
                print('Passed:', testcase['script'])


# Build GUI with tkinter (Tkinter in 2.6) with buttons that change color and grow

from tkinter import *                              # Use Tkinter in 2.6
import random
fontsize = 25
colors = ['red', 'green', 'blue', 'yellow', 'orange', 'white', 'cyan', 'purple']

def reply(text):
    print(text)
    popup = Toplevel()
    color = random.choice(colors)
    Label(popup, text='Popup', bg='black', fg=color).pack()
    L.config(fg=color)

def timer():
    L.config(fg=random.choice(colors))
    win.after(250, timer)

def grow():
    global fontsize
    fontsize += 5
    L.config(font=('arial', fontsize, 'italic'))
    win.after(100, grow)

win = Tk()
L = Label(win, text='Spam',
          font=('arial', fontsize, 'italic'), fg='yellow', bg='navy',
          relief=RAISED)
L.pack(side=TOP, expand=YES, fill=BOTH)
Button(win, text='press', command=(lambda: reply('red'))).pack(side=BOTTOM,fill=X)
Button(win, text='timer', command=timer).pack(side=BOTTOM, fill=X)
Button(win, text='grow', command=grow).pack(side=BOTTOM, fill=X)
win.mainloop()


# Similar to prior, but use classes so each window has own state information

from tkinter import *
import random
```

```
class MyGui:
    """
    A GUI with buttons that change color and make the label grow
    """
    colors = ['blue', 'green', 'orange', 'red', 'brown', 'yellow']

    def __init__(self, parent, title='popup'):
        parent.title(title)
        self.growing = False
        self.fontsize = 10
        self.lab = Label(parent, text='Gui1', fg='white', bg='navy')
        self.lab.pack(expand=YES, fill=BOTH)
        Button(parent, text='Spam', command=self.reply).pack(side=LEFT)
        Button(parent, text='Grow', command=self.grow).pack(side=LEFT)
        Button(parent, text='Stop', command=self.stop).pack(side=LEFT)

    def reply(self):
        "change the button's color at random on Spam presses"
        self.fontsize += 5
        color = random.choice(self.colors)
        self.lab.config(bg=color,
                font=('courier', self.fontsize, 'bold italic'))

    def grow(self):
        "start making the label grow on Grow presses"
        self.growing = True
        self.grower()

    def grower(self):
        if self.growing:
            self.fontsize += 5
            self.lab.config(font=('courier', self.fontsize, 'bold'))
            self.lab.after(500, self.grower)

    def stop(self):
        "stop the button growing on Stop presses"
        self.growing = False

class MySubGui(MyGui):
    colors = ['black', 'purple']            # Customize to change color choices

MyGui(Tk(), 'main')
MyGui(Toplevel())
MySubGui(Toplevel())
mainloop()


# Email inbox scanning and maintenance utility

"""
scan pop email box, fetching just headers, allowing
deletions without downloading the complete message
"""

import poplib, getpass, sys
```

```
mailserver = 'your pop email server name here'                          # pop.rmi.net
mailuser   = 'your pop email user name here'                            # brian
mailpasswd = getpass.getpass('Password for %s?' % mailserver)

print('Connecting...')
server = poplib.POP3(mailserver)
server.user(mailuser)
server.pass_(mailpasswd)

try:
    print(server.getwelcome())
    msgCount, mboxSize = server.stat()
    print('There are', msgCount, 'mail messages, size ', mboxSize)
    msginfo = server.list()
    print(msginfo)
    for i in range(msgCount):
        msgnum  = i+1
        msgsize = msginfo[1][i].split()[1]
        resp, hdrlines, octets = server.top(msgnum, 0)                  # Get hdrs only
        print('-'*80)
        print('[%d: octets=%d, size=%s]' % (msgnum, octets, msgsize))
        for line in hdrlines: print(line)

        if input('Print?') in ['y', 'Y']:
            for line in server.retr(msgnum)[1]: print(line)            # Get whole msg
        if input('Delete?') in ['y', 'Y']:
            print('deleting')
            server.dele(msgnum)                                        # Delete on srvr
        else:
            print('skipping')
finally:
    server.quit()                                                      # Make sure we unlock mbox
input('Bye.')                                                          # Keep window up on Windows


# CGI server-side script to interact with a web browser

#!/usr/bin/python
import cgi
form = cgi.FieldStorage()                                              # Parse form data
print("Content-type: text/html\n")                                     # hdr plus blank line
print("<HTML>")
print("<title>Reply Page</title>")                                     # HTML reply page
print("<BODY>")
if not 'user' in form:
    print("<h1>Who are you?</h1>")
else:
    print("<h1>Hello <i>%s</i>!</h1>" % cgi.escape(form['user'].value))
print("</BODY></HTML>")


# Database script to populate and query a MySql database

from MySQLdb import Connect
```

```
conn = Connect(host='localhost', user='root', passwd='darling')
curs = conn.cursor()
try:
    curs.execute('drop database testpeopledb')
except:
    pass                                               # Did not exist

curs.execute('create database testpeopledb')
curs.execute('use testpeopledb')
curs.execute('create table people (name char(30), job char(10), pay int(4))')

curs.execute('insert people values (%s, %s, %s)', ('Bob', 'dev', 50000))
curs.execute('insert people values (%s, %s, %s)', ('Sue', 'dev', 60000))
curs.execute('insert people values (%s, %s, %s)', ('Ann', 'mgr', 40000))

curs.execute('select * from people')
for row in curs.fetchall():
    print(row)

curs.execute('select * from people where name = %s', ('Bob',))
print(curs.description)
colnames = [desc[0] for desc in curs.description]
while True:
    print('-' * 30)
    row = curs.fetchone()
    if not row: break
    for (name, value) in zip(colnames, row):
        print('%s => %s' % (name, value))

conn.commit()                                          # Save inserted records


# Database script to populate a shelve with Python objects

# see also Chapter 27 shelve and Chapter 30 pickle examples

rec1 = {'name': {'first': 'Bob', 'last': 'Smith'},
        'job':  ['dev', 'mgr'],
        'age':  40.5}

rec2 = {'name': {'first': 'Sue', 'last': 'Jones'},
        'job':  ['mgr'],
        'age':  35.0}

import shelve
db = shelve.open('dbfile')
db['bob'] = rec1
db['sue'] = rec2
db.close()


# Database script to print and update shelve created in prior script

import shelve
db = shelve.open('dbfile')
```

```
for key in db:
    print(key, '=>', db[key])

bob = db['bob']
bob['age'] += 1
db['bob'] = bob
db.close()
```

Index

Symbols

% (formatting operator), 181, 189
= and == (equality operators), 246
* (repetition) operator, 202
@ symbol, 806
\ (backslash), 272, 320
\ (backslash) escape sequences, 87
& (bitwise AND operator), 110
| (bitwise or operator), 110
^ (bitwise XOR operator), 110
: (colon), 266, 389
{ } (curly braces), 80, 110, 271
    dictionaries and, 92, 210
    set comprehensions and, 139
    sets and, 137, 223
/ and // (division operators), 110, 112
    (see also division)
" (double quotes) and strings, 160
... (ellipses), 332
= and == (equality operators), 110, 153
#! (hash bang), 48
(hash character), 45, 378
>, >=, <, <= (magnitude comparison
    operators), 110
– (minus operator), 110
* (multiplication operator), 110
( ) (parentheses), 267, 271, 320
    functions and, 391
    generator expressions and, 499
    tuples and, 98
+ (plus operator), 110, 202
"\u..." and "\U..." escapes, 913
% (remainder operator), 110
; (semicolon), 267, 271

>> and << (shift operators), 110
' (single quotes) and strings, 160
[ ] (square brackets), 80, 110, 271
    dictionaries and, 211
    list comprehensions and, 361, 488, 506
    lists and, 91, 201
_ (underscore), 586
__add__ method, 636
__all__ variable, 586
__bases__ attribute, 699, 701
__bool__ method, 732
__call__ method, 727
    function interfaces and, 729
__class__ attribute, 699, 701
__cmp__ method (Python 2.6), 731
__contains__ method, 718
__del__ method, 734
__delattr__ method, 959
__delete__ method, 952
__dict__ attribute, 552
__doc__ attribute, 379, 703
__enter__ method, 856
__eq__ method, 731
__exit__ method, 856
__get__ method, 708, 950
__getattr__ method, 720, 816, 944, 958–975
    computed attributes, 963
    delegation using, 747
    delegation-based managers, 972
    example, 961
    interception of built-in attributes, 968
    loops, avoiding in interception methods,
        960
    __getattribute__, compared to, 964
__getattribute__ method, 796, 944, 958–975

We'd like to hear your suggestions for improving our indexes. Send email to *index@oreilly.com*.